The Life of John Milton

BLACKWELL CRITICAL BIOGRAPHIES

General Editor: Claude Rawson

This acclaimed series offers informative and durable biographies of important authors, British, European, and North American, which will include substantial critical discussion of their works. An underlying objective is to re-establish the notion that books are written by people who lived in particular times and places. This objective is pursued not by programmatic assertions or strenuous point-making, but through practical persuasion of volumes which offer intelligent criticism within well-researched biographical text.

1	Derek Pearsall	*The Life of Geoffrey Chaucer*
2	Robert DeMaria, Jr	*The Life of Samuel Johnson*
3	Clyde de L. Ryals	*The Life of Robert Browning*
4	John Batchelor	*The Life of Joseph Conrad*
5	Richard Gray	*The Life of William Faulkner*
6	John Sutherland	*The Life of Walter Scott*
7	Rosemary Ashton	*The Life of Samuel Taylor Coleridge*
8	Douglas Lane Patey	*The Life of Evelyn Waugh*
9	Paul Turner	*The Life of Thomas Hardy*
10	John Williams	*The Life of Goethe*
11	Nicholas Hewitt	*The Life of Céline*

The Life of John Milton

A Critical Biography

Barbara K. Lewalski

First published 2000
Reprinted 2002

Blackwell Publishers Ltd
108 Cowley Road
Oxford OX4 1JF
UK

Blackwell Publishers Inc.
350 Main Street
Malden, Massachusetts 02148
USA

British Library Cataloguing in Publication Data

A CIP catalogue record for this book is available from the British Library.

Library of Congress Cataloging-in-Publication Data

Lewalski, Barbara Kiefer, 1931–
The life of John Milton : a critical biography / by Barbara Kiefer Lewalski.
p. cm. — (Blackwell critical biographies)
Includes bibliographical references and index.
ISBN 0–631–17665–9 (alk. paper)
1. Milton, John, 1608 – 1674. 2. Poets, English—Early modern, 1500–1700—Biography I. Title. II. Series

PR3581.L45 2001
821'.4—dc21
[B] 00–034320

Typeset in 10 on 12 pt Bembo
by Ace Filmsetting Ltd, Frome, Somerset
Printed in Great Britain by T. J. International Ltd, Padstow, Cornwall

This book is printed on acid-free paper.

For Ken, David, and Laurence

Contents

Plates

[Plate section located between pp. 334–5 of text]

Preface

More than two centuries ago Samuel Johnson pronounced categorically, as was his wont, that "Nobody can write the life of a man but those who have eat and drunk and lived in social intercourse with him." Social intercourse with Milton being now impossible, I have to hope that living in intellectual and aesthetic intercourse with his works for most of my professional life will do. A literary biography should, I believe, focus on what is of primary importance in a writer: his or her works. Milton more than most demands to be seen as an author of many kinds of works: magnificent poems in all the major genres – lyric, dramatic, epic – but also polemics, history, theology, and treatises on political, ecclesiastical, educational, and social issues. No writer before Milton fashioned himself quite so self-consciously as an author. He often signs his title pages "The Author John Milton" or "The Author J. M." He incorporates passages of autobiography that make something like a *bildungsroman* of his early life. He claims poetry and also his polemic service to church and country as a vocation. And he often presents himself as prophet–teacher and as inspired Bard. In text after text he calls attention to his authorial self engaging with the problems of the work in hand: justifying the use of invective and satire in his antiprelatical tracts; making occasion in *The Reason of Church Government* to comment on the kinds of poems he might write; and registering in the divorce tracts and elsewhere the conflict he feels between citing authorities and claiming originality. In *Paradise Lost,* Milton constructs his Bardic self in collaboration with his "heavenly Muse" in four extended Proems whose length and personal reference are without precedent in earlier epics. While all these autobiographical passages are designed to serve poetic or polemical purposes, they also allow us to glimpse the emergence of the modern idea of authorship.

Postmodern literary theory, with its emphasis on the instability and undecidability of both texts and history, challenges the fundamental assumptions of biography, which has to ground itself on empiricism, probability, and narrative. To focus on the endlessly proliferating meanings that can be found in Milton's texts and on the uncertain dating of many of his works would not produce a biography of Milton but an essay about the problematics of such an enterprise. For most readers and writers of literary biography the interest lies in what we can know or probably conclude about the life, character, thought, and works of the person treated, what we can reasonably suppose about the order of composition of his or her works, what story makes best sense of all the evidence in hand. In constructing my narrative about this complex man I try to take account of the messiness and contingencies of life and history and to avoid some obvious pitfalls: assuming a teleology of growth and development, or offering a single interpretative key, or presenting an always integrated and self-consistent Milton. There will be and should be as many versions of Milton as there are Milton biographers, and readers will have to judge this one by its plausibility and its insight.

Because Milton was a public figure and because he was so self-conscious about his role as polemicist and poet, we have more extensive materials relating to him than we have for any other important writer to his date. J. Milton French has published five volumes of Milton's *Life Records:* birth, baptism, and marriage records, property deeds, wills and other legal documents, together with many contemporary references to him. A new *Chronology* compiled by Gordon Campbell adds several items to this record and corrects some errors. We have some sketches of Milton's life by persons who knew him well or knew those who did: his nephew Edward Phillips, his pupil Cyriack Skinner, and those seventeenth-century compilers of brief lives of contemporary worthies, John Aubrey and Anthony à Wood. Several early eighteenth-century editors and biographers of Milton collected facts and anecdotes (some of them dubious) from many sources; in the late nineteenth century David Masson's six-volume *Life* gathered a treasure-trove of historical as well as biographical information; and in 1968 William Riley Parker published the two-volume standard biography, to which Gordon Campbell has recently supplied a very useful appendix of updated notes. Since Parker's *Life*, however, many additional aids to biographical research and interpretation have become available: the last four volumes of the Yale Milton's *Prose,* John Shawcross's invaluable *Milton Bibliography for the years 1624–1700*, several shorter biographies and investigations of particular aspects of Milton's life, and some extended analyses of little-studied works, including Milton's State Papers, Latin poems, and *History of Britain.* A new Milton biography at the new millennium has the challenge and the opportunity to rethink the course of Milton's life, thought, and writing with the benefit of all the new scholarship. Still, some significant problems remain, and my investigations have not solved them definitively. I can only offer plausible inferences about, among other things, the date of *L'Allegro* and *Il Penseroso* or *Ad Patrem* or the "Blindness" sonnet, or what Milton was doing from 1646 to 1649, or which wife Milton addressed as his "late espoused saint," or exactly when *Paradise Lost* and *Samson Agonistes* were begun and finished, or when Milton's daughters left home.

A new Milton biography has especially the challenge and the opportunity to rethink his life in a new interpretative milieu. I hope to bring into focus a Milton rather different from the figure portrayed in some earlier biographical accounts: the transcendent poet who mostly soared above contemporary struggles; or the Christian humanist whose poetry and prose gives eloquent voice to mainstream Christian theology and philosophy; or the "Grand Whig" whose dedication to advancing individual liberty was straightforward and uncompromised; or the polemicist and poet who sharply segregated the products of his right and his left hand; or the leftist Milton whose poems are often thinly veiled political allegory; or the deconstructed Milton who serves as a sounding board for multiple and contradictory cultural voices. Recent historiography on the English Civil War and Interregnum – both revisionist and counter-revisionist – has extended and complicated our knowledge of that period and Milton's place in it. Also, some of the best recent Milton criticism has explored the complex ways his poems and prose works respond to their historical moment and material circumstances, while attending as well to how they engage with literary models and intellectual traditions, and how they address issues of enduring interest to modern readers. We now have richly contextualized studies of Milton's treatment of women, gender, companionate marriage, love and sex; of Milton's republicanism, animist materialism, and radical Christian humanism; and of the relation of his poems to an emerging literary marketplace and to Restoration politics and cultural norms. As well, we have many illuminating analyses of genre, texture, and style in Milton's poems and prose works, sometimes probing the interrelationships between those two modes. This biography is indebted on every page to the community of Miltonists, past and present, on whose work it gratefully builds.

I undertake here to describe the quotidian John Milton at the various stages of his life and also to treat all his prose and poetry, to tell two stories that intersect continually but are in some important ways different stories. To that end, the second part of each chapter is an in-depth discussion of a particular work or works from the relevant years, focusing on the development of Milton's ideas and his art. I also endeavor to attend to the many contexts in which Milton's works demand to be seen. Because he was a public figure – Latin Secretary to the Republic and to Cromwell's Protectorate and an official polemicist for both – he was responsible for a large body of state papers and polemic tracts that have to be examined in their immediate historical circumstances. More broadly, because his life and writings as political thinker, theologian, and poet were so intimately connected with the political and religious conflicts and the culture wars of his times, those connections must be examined at every stage. More broadly still, because the context for Milton's poetry and prose is virtually the entire Western literary and intellectual tradition, I have tried to recognize that in a very real sense Milton saw Homer and Virgil and Cicero and Ovid and several other great poets and thinkers as his contemporaries, as much as Cromwell or Bradshaw or Marvell or Vane.

The Milton I present in these pages is a man who began even as a young poet to construct himself as a new kind of author, one who commands all the resources of learning and art but links them to radical politics, reformist poetics, and the inherently revolutionary power of prophecy. He was deeply involved with the major intellectual and political issues of his time, developing, arguing passionately for, and in some cases changing his views about, the central issues fought about in the revolution and after: monarchy, tyranny, idolatry, rebellion, liberty, republicanism, popular sovereignty, religious toleration, separation of church and state. He also took up issues on the periphery of the contemporary discourses: divorce, unlicensed publication, intellectual freedom, reformed education. And in his unpublished theological treatise *De Doctrina Christiana* he set out most fully a number of extreme positions and attitudes also present in his other works: Arianism, Arminianism, monism, mortalism, a qualified antinomianism, creation *ex Deo*, the absolute authority of the individual conscience illumined by the Spirit, the priority of the inward Spirit's testimony over scripture itself, and the need to interpret scripture according to the dictates of reason, charity, and the good of humankind. The Milton in these pages did not, as is sometimes supposed, retreat from political concerns after the Restoration: his major poems – *Paradise Lost, Paradise Regained,* and *Samson Agonistes* – are profoundly and daringly political as well as being superlative aesthetic achievements. They dramatize in terms relevant to the Restoration milieu subjects Milton had addressed earlier – monarchy, tyranny, rebellion, idolatry, inner liberty, love and marriage – but with new emphasis on the nature of Christ's kingdom and on the difficulties of interpreting God's word and his action in history. In these last poems Milton employs the educative power and imaginative reach of poetry to help readers better understand themselves, the human condition, and the ways of Providence, so they might learn to live as free moral agents and as virtuous citizens who value and deserve personal and political liberty.

A biographer cannot, I expect, get very close to a subject she does not like. I like and admire Milton for many things: for his readiness to judge received doctrine by the standards of reason, charity, human experience, and human good; for his far-reaching – even though not total – commitment to intellectual freedom and toleration; for his republican ideals, albeit compromised in times of crisis; for his insistence on free will as the ground of human dignity; for his delight in natural beauty and exuberant creativity; for his efforts to imagine marriage and its sexual pleasure as founded on companionship of the mind and spirit, albeit partly undermined by his assumptions about gender hierarchy; for the courage it took to write *The Readie & Easie Way to Establish a Free Commonwealth* on the eve of the Restoration; and for the largeness of spirit that enabled him to write his three greatest poems when totally blind and disillusioned by the defeat of the political cause he had served for twenty years. Milton the man had his share of faults and flaws and limitations, as I trust this biography recognizes. But they do not diminish the achievement of the poet, "soaring in the high region of his fancies with his garland and singing robes about him."

Acknowledgments

I cannot begin to indicate, let alone properly thank, all the scholars, past and present, whose writings or comments have contributed to this book. To mention them here by name would be to replicate the notes and bibliography, which are themselves only a partial and inadequate record of debts accumulated over a scholarly lifetime of reading and thinking about Milton and his milieu. I have profited especially from stimulating and helpful responses to portions of this work in progress by colleagues in the Northeast Milton Seminar, the Milton Society of America, the International Milton Symposia at Bangor and at York, the Literature and History Conference at Reading, England, the Renaissance Society of America Conference in Florence, and the Renaissance Doctoral Conference at Harvard. Several libraries and their research librarians made needed resources available: the British Library, the Bodleian Library, Trinity College and Christ's College Libraries in Cambridge University, the Public Record Office, the Guildhall (London), the Widener and Houghton Libraries at Harvard University, the Folger Shakespeare Library, the New York Public Library, the J. Pierpont Morgan Library, and the Newberry Library.

Special thanks are due to Gordon Campbell, who kindly sent me a typescript of his *Milton Chronology* before publication, to Cedric Brown who did the same with his *John Milton: A Literary Life*, to Susanne Woods, who read the entire manuscript and pushed me to think harder about several issues, to Violet Halpert who read proof with the expertise of a Miltonist and an editor, to colleagues at Harvard who supplied answers to particular questions, and to several generations of graduate students in Milton seminars at Harvard and Brown who were a continuing source of valuable ideas and insights. David Lewalski used his graphic skills to make my photograph of Milton's gravestone useable.

This book was especially fortunate in its editors: the series editor Claude Rawson who invited the biography and gave the manuscript a meticulous and helpful reading, Andrew McNeillie of Blackwell Publishers, who offered encouragement, suggestions, and enthusiastic response at several stages, and the copy-editor Jack Messenger who tidied up many loose ends. Several former and present graduate students provided research assistance at various stages: Susan Thornberg, Douglas Trevor, Wendy Hyman, and Sarah Wall. Any remaining errors are my own.

Parts of some chapters have appeared, in substantially different form, in journals and collections. I thank their editors as well as the Cambridge University Press and the Duquesne University Press for permission to use material from these essays: "How radical was the Young Milton," in *Heretical Milton*, eds. John Rumrich and Stephen Dobranski, reprinted with the permission of Cambridge University Press, 1998; "Milton's *Comus* and the Politics of Masquing," in *The Politics of the Stuart Court Masque*, eds. David Bevington and Peter Holbrook, Cambridge University Press, 1998; and "Educational Projects and Epic Paedeia: Milton and the Hartlib Circle," in *Literary Milton: Text, Pretext, Context*, eds. Diana Benet and Michael Lieb, Duquesne University Press, 1994. I also thank the editors and the Pittsburgh University Press for permission to use materials from the following essays: "Milton's *Samson* and the 'New Acquist of True [political] Experience," is from *Milton Studies* 24, James D. Simmonds, Ed., © 1989 by University of Pittsburgh Press. Material from this article is used by permission of the University of Pittsburgh Press; "Milton: Divine Revelation and the Poetics of Experience," *Milton Studies* 28: *Riven Unities: Authority and Experience, Self and Other in Milton's Poetry*, Wendy Furman, Christopher Grose, William Shullenberger, Guest Eds., © 1992 by University of Pittsburgh Press. Material from this article is used by permission of the University of Pittsburgh Press; "Milton and *De Doctrina Christiana*: Evidences of Authorship," is from *Milton Studies* 36, Albert C. Labriola, Ed., © 1998 by University of Pittsburgh Press. Material from this article is used by permission of the University of Pittsburgh Press; and "*Paradise Lost* and Milton's Politics," is from *Milton Studies* 38: *John Milton: The Writer in his Works*, Albert C. Labriola and Michael Lieb, Eds., © 2000 by University of Pittsburgh Press. Material from this article is used by permission of the University of Pittsburgh Press.

Abbreviations

AV	The Holy Bible, 1611 (Authorized Version)
BL	The British Library
Carey	John Carey, ed., *John Milton: Complete Shorter Poems*
CSPD	Calendar of State Papers, Domestic Series
Chronology	Gordon Campbell, *A Milton Chronology*
CM	*The Works of John Milton*, ed. Frank A. Patterson, et al.
CPW	*Complete Prose Works of John Milton,* ed. Don M. Wolfe, et al.
DNB	*Dictionary of National Biography*
EL	*The Early Lives of Milton,* ed. Helen Darbishire
Fletcher	Harris Francis Fletcher, *The Intellectual Development of John Milton*
Fowler	Alastair Fowler, ed., *John Milton: Paradise Lost*
Hughes	Merritt Y. Hughes, ed., *John Milton: Complete Poems and Major Prose*
Hill	Christopher Hill, *Milton and the English Revolution*
LR	J. Milton French, ed., *The Life Records of John Milton*
Masson	David Masson, *The Life of John Milton: Narrated in Connexion with the Political, Ecclesiastical and Literary History of His Time*
ME	*A Milton Encyclopedia,* ed. William B. Hunter, et al.
MQ	*Milton Quarterly*, ed. Roy C. Flannagan, et al.
MS	*Milton Studies*, ed. James D. Simmonds and Albert C. Labriola
Parker	William Riley Parker, *Milton: A Biography*
PMLA	*Publications of the Modern Language Association*
Poems, 1645	*Poems of Mr. John Milton*, 1645
Poems, 1673	*Poems, etc. Upon Several Occasions. By Mr. John Milton,* 1673
PRO	Public Record Office
SP	State Papers, Domestic Series

Sprott	*John Milton: A Maske. The Earlier Versions*, ed. S. E. Sprott
SR 1554–1640	*Stationers Registers, 1554–1640,* ed. Edward Arber
SR 1640–1708	*Stationers Registers, 1640–1708,* ed. George E. B. Eyre, et al.
TM	The Trinity manuscript
Variorum	*A Variorum Commentary on the Poems of John Milton*, ed. Douglas Bush, et. al.
Wood	Anthony á Wood, *Athenae Oxonienses*, 1500–1690, ed. Philip Bliss

1

"The Childhood Shews the Man" 1608–1625

Milton's childhood and schooldays turned out to be a fortunate seedplot for a budding poet. Though his father expected him to take orders in the church, he encouraged and nurtured his poetic talents, his sheer delight in learning, and his wide-ranging scholarship. His schoolmasters taught him languages, literature, and verse writing (in Latin and Greek), and two of them became his friends. He also began a friendship with a schoolmate that was to be the most intense emotional attachment of his youth. He was reared in a bourgeois Puritan milieu that fostered in him qualities of self-discipline, diligent preparation for one's intended vocation, and responsibility before God for the development and use of one's talents, as well as a commitment to reformist, militant Protestantism. He grew up amid the sights and sounds and stimuli a great city like London can provide, and was conscious from early childhood of growing religious and political conflict in English society. These factors interacted with the gifts of nature: poetic genius, a prodigious intelligence, a serious and introspective temperament, a slender body, delicate features, and weak eyes.

In early youth Milton developed character traits and attitudes that lasted a lifetime: lofty aspirations and a driving compulsion to emulate and surpass the best and noblest; very exacting standards of personal morality and accomplishment; high expectations for human institutions (schools, marriage, government, the church); a disposition to challenge and resist institutional authorities who fell short of such standards; and a strong need for and high idealism about friendship and love. He gave evidence as a schoolboy of his intellectual and poetic gifts but may have begun to worry even then, as he certainly did later, about his comparatively slow maturation.

Milton's own retrospective comments supply much of what we know about his early years. Most often he resorts to autobiography for the rhetorical purpose of defending his qualifications and his character from polemic attack, but even so, his remarks offer a fascinating insight into how he wished to remember his boyhood and represent it to others.

"Destined . . . in Early Childhood for the Study of Literature," and for the Church

Milton was born into a prosperous middle-class family of Puritan leanings and considerable culture, on "the 9th of December 1608 die Veneris [Friday] half an howr after 6 in the morning," as he himself noted in a family Bible.[1] On December 20 he was baptized in his parish church of All Hallows, Bread Street.[2] The Miltons subleased spacious apartments on five floors of a building known as the Spread Eagle and also as the White Bear, on the east side of Bread Street, close to Cheapside – a street that was, according to Stow's *Survey of London,* "wholly inhabited by rich merchants," many of them in the cloth trade.[3] Milton's childhood home was a big house in the busy center of London, then a city of some 220,000. At the poet's birth his father was about 46 and his mother about 36, and he had one older sibling, a sister, Anne (birthdate unknown). His maternal grandmother Ellen Jeffrey, then widowed, lived with the family until her death in 1611, and a younger brother Christopher was baptized December 3, 1615, at All Hallows.[4] Two sisters died in infancy: Sara, christened for her mother on July 15, 1612 and buried on August 6; Tabitha, baptized on January 30, 1614 and buried on August 3, 1615.[5] Besides the immediate family the household contained several apprentices and household servants.

The poet's father, John Milton senior (1562?–1647), came from a yeoman family settled around the village of Stanton St John near Oxford. John Aubrey's notes toward a life of Milton, gathered from family members and contemporaries, state that his father was "brought-up" in Oxford university, "at Christchurch": his later musical interests and achievements suggest that he was trained there as a boy chorister.[6] His father, Richard Milton, held fast to the Roman Catholic religion and paid fines for recusancy; John senior embraced Protestantism and (according to an often-repeated family story) was cast out and disinherited when Richard found him reading an English Bible.[7] He came to London about 1583, was apprenticed to a scrivener, and in 1600 was admitted to the Company of Scriveners. His profession combined some functions of a notary, financial adviser, money-lender, and contract lawyer: records show that he drew bonds between borrowers and lenders, invested money for others, bought and sold property, loaned money at high interest, and gave depositions in legal cases. His shop on the ground floor bore the sign of the Spread Eagle, the scriveners' emblem. The poet's nephew and biographer Edward Phillips states that by "Industry and prudent conduct of his Affairs" Milton's father (Phillips' grandfather) obtained a "Competent Estate, whereby he was enabled to make a handsom Provision both for the Education and Maintenance of his

Children."[8] In 1615, 1622, and 1625 he held minor offices in the Scriveners' Company. Later, in a rhetorical defense of himself, Milton claimed descent from an "honorable family" and described his father as a man of "supreme integrity"(*CPW* IV.1, 612) – a quality not often associated with scriveners. But he nowhere refers to more distant ancestors or seeks to trace a family tree, preferring to begin his story with the self-made bourgeois scrivener.

Milton senior's considerable ability and reputation as a composer of madrigals and psalm settings contributed greatly to his son's enduring passion for music and to his development as a poet. Aubrey called attention to the "delicate, tuneable voice" of young John, noting that "his father instructed him" and that he played often on a small organ in the family home; he was also said to have played the bass-viol.[9] Edward Phillips calls up the image of Milton taking part in small domestic consorts, either singing or playing: "Hee had an excellent Ear, and could bear a part both in Vocal & Instrumental Music" (*EL* 32). Through his father, Milton came into social contact with music publishers and composers such as Thomas Myriell, John Tomkins, Thomas Morley, and Henry Lawes. Edward Phillips describes the prosperous scrivener attending to business and music in happy combination: "he did not so far quit his own Generous and Ingenious Inclinations, as to make himself wholly a Slave to the World; for he sometimes found vacant hours to the Study (which he made his recreation) of the Noble Science of Musick" (*EL* 1). His skill was such, noted Aubrey, that he once composed an I*n Nomine* of 40 parts, and for his songs "gained the Reputation of a considerable Master in this most charming of all the Liberal Sciences."[10] He contributed a song, "Fair Orian," to a volume in tribute to Queen Elizabeth, *The Triumphs of Oriana* (1601), and four religious anthems to William Leighton's collection, *The Teares, or Lamentations of a Sorrowfull Soule* (1614),[11] joining such distinguished composers as Thomas Morley, John Wilbye, Thomas Weelkes, and William Byrd. He also provided four-part settings for six psalms in Thomas Ravenscroft's popular collection, *The Whole Book of Psalmes*.[12] That he had some interest in theater is indicated by his appointment in 1620 as one of the four trustees of the Blackfriars Playhouse.[13] But his gifts did not extend to poetry, as is evident from his pedestrian commendatory sonnet for John Lane, who wrote an equally pedestrian poetic tribute to Milton senior's musical gifts.[14] The scrivener's experience as amateur composer probably disposed him to assume that his son might pursue his literary interests along with his intended profession, the ministry. Milton later claimed that "My father destined me in early childhood for the study of literature" (*CPW* IV.1, 612), but also stated, in different rhetorical circumstances, that "by the intentions of my parents and friends I was destin'd of a child, and in mine own resolutions" to serve the church (*CPW* I, 822).

Almost nothing is known about Milton's mother, Sara Jeffrey (1572?–1637), the elder daughter of a merchant tailor, Paul Jeffrey, and his wife Ellen, of St Swithin's parish, London. There is no record of Sara's marriage to John senior, but it probably occurred in 1599 or 1600; on May 12, 1601 they buried at All Hallows an unnamed infant who died soon after birth.[15] Milton's pupil and friend Cyriack Skinner attributes some of the scrivener's success to "the Consortship of a prudent virtuous Wife," and Edward Phillips termed her "a Woman of Incomparable Vertue and Goodness."[16] Milton described her as "a woman of purest reputation, celebrated throughout the neighborhood for her acts of charity" (*CPW* IV.1, 612). These laconic phrases are not entirely formulaic: they praise a woman who fulfilled the duties prescribed for the bourgeois Protestant wife – helpmeet to her husband and dispenser of a prosperous family's charity. Aubrey supplies another detail, that she "had very weake eies, & used spectacles p[re]sently after she was thirty yeares old," whereas the scrivener "read with out spectacles at 84" (*EL* 4–5). Aubrey, the family, and Milton himself apparently believed that he inherited his weak eyes from his mother.[17] Milton's rather impersonal description of her might suggest some lack of warmth in their relationship, or it may simply indicate that he took pride in, and found rhetorical force in, the public recognition of her goodness. His only other mention of her links her death with his decision to travel abroad. Milton often refers to his father as a major beneficent influence on his development, but if he felt some important debt to his mother he did not say so.

As a boy John Milton went to church and catechism at All Hallows, where the respected Puritan minister Richard Stock (1559?–1626) had been rector since 1611. Stock preached twice on Sunday, demanded strict observance of the Sabbath, inveighed against Roman Catholics and Jesuits, urged continuous reading of the Bible and the English commentaries, and catechized the parish children daily for an hour before school, boys and girls on alternate days. Milton later repudiated Stock's sabbatarianism, defense of tithes, and conservative views of marriage and divorce, but his antipapist diatribes and his readiness to censure the sins of the powerful – usurers, oppressors of the poor, morally lax aristocrats – likely had an enduring influence.[18] And of course Milton began reading the Bible early.

Sitting under a Puritan minister and growing up among hard-working tradesmen proud of their steadily expanding wealth, power, and status as citizens of London, Milton would have become conscious early on of political, religious, and cultural strains in the national fabric. While the divisions were not yet unbridgeable, they were manifestly widening during the Jacobean era (1603–25). A king who vigorously defended royal absolutism was opposed by a parliament increasingly jealous of its rights and privileges. A pacifist king disposed to mediate between Catholic and Protestant powers in Europe and a queen openly supportive of Spanish interests were opposed by a militant war party eager to fight for international Protestantism – especially after the loss of Bohemia and the Palatinate by the Protestant Elector Palatine touched off the Thirty Years War.[19] A court perceived as extravagant, morally decadent, infiltrated by Papists, rife with scandal, and increasingly controlled by the king's homosexual favorites was opposed by a London citizenry self-styled as hard-working, wealth-producing, and morally upright, and a county-based aristocracy sensible of its diminished honor and power. An established church perceived to be clinging to the idolatrous remnants of Roman Catholic liturgy, ceremony, and church government, and to be promoting an Arminian theology that made some place for free will and personal merit, was opposed by an energetic Puritan clergy bent on preaching the Word of God, reforming morals, holding fast to Calvinist predestinarian theology, and bringing the government of the English church into closer harmony with the Presbyterian model in Geneva and Scotland. A bright child had to be aware, at least subconsciously, that his life would be affected by such controversies and tensions.

The 1612 family Bible (Authorized Version) into which Milton later entered records of family births and deaths contains what seem to be a coherent set of underlinings and marginal annotations with the initials KJ marking verses from 2 Chronicles, Ezra, Nehemiah, and Psalms. Cedric Brown argues plausibly that the initials invite comparison of various biblical kings with King James and that they were most likely made in 1620–5, reflecting concerns among militant Protestants about the danger from Catholic enemies, the defection of kings, foreign and idolatrous queens, and purity of religion.[20] While the annotator cannot be identified – the handwriting does not seem to match that of Milton's father, nor the scant samples we have of Milton's youthful hand – the likely presence of the Bible in the Milton family reinforces the evidence that he grew up in a reformist political milieu.

Much of Milton's childhood was given over to study, arranged by a father who was eager to give his extraordinary son the best education possible. Between the ages of five and seven, most likely from a private tutor, Milton learned to read and write in English and to do arithmetic; seven was the usual age for beginning Latin with a tutor or at a grammar school. Milton mentions having "sundry masters and teachers both at home and at the schools" (*CPW* I, 809) but we know the name of only one, Thomas Young (1587?–1655), a Scots Presbyterian who may have been recommended by Stock. Richard Baxter commended his great learning, judgment, piety, and humility, and especially his knowledge of the church Fathers.[21] Thomas Young seems to have been Milton's tutor between the ages of nine and twelve and was apparently the schoolmaster Aubrey heard about from Milton's widow: "Anno Dom. 1619 he was ten yeares old, as by his picture, & was then a Poet. his schoolmaster was a puritan in Essex, who cutt his haire short"(*EL* 2). Young's benefice, Ware, is in Hertfordshire, not Essex, but it is very close to the Essex border and about 20 miles from London.[22] Aubrey's note points to the striking portrait, said to be by Cornelius Janssen, depicting an elegantly garbed, rather wistful child with close-cropped auburn hair – almost certainly Milton (plate 1).[23] His parents had him painted as a young gentleman and the haircut (ascribed to the tutor) marks him also as a young Puritan.

In a Latin letter written at college Milton addressed Young as "best of Teachers" and as another Father who merits his "unparalled gratitude"; in a Latin Elegy to Young he recalls that "Under his guidance I first visited the Aonian retreats . . . I drank the Pierian waters and by the favor of Clio I thrice wet my blessed lips with Castalian wine."[24] This could mean that Young was Milton's first teacher in classics, beginning around 1615 when he was seven, but the terms probably suggest that Young introduced Milton to the reading and writing of Latin (and perhaps Greek) poetry at some later stage. If the "thrice" ("ter ora") refers to three years under Young's tutelege, their association probably began about 1618, since Young went to Hamburg in 1620 as chaplain to the Merchant Adventurers. Young was clearly an important influence in nurturing Milton's classicism and his Puritanism.

While continuing the home tutorials Milton's father also sent him to one of the finest grammar schools in the country, St Paul's, founded in 1512 by the humanist John Colet and managed by the Mercers Company of London.[25] He may have entered at age seven (1615), but probably did so at Young's departure in 1620.[26] He was then twelve, the age Milton proposed for entry into his model academy in *Of Education*, and he would then have joined the Upper School (forms five to eight). In the *Defensio Secunda* (1654), Milton designated his twelfth year as marking a new intensity of application to his books: "For the study of literature . . . I had so keen an appetite that from my twelfth year scarcely ever did I leave my studies for my bed before the hour of midnight." Answering taunts that his blindness was a divine punishment for wickedness, he claimed rather that these youthful nocturnal studies were "the first cause of injury to my eyes, whose natural weakness was augmented by frequent headaches." But, he continued, "since none of these defects slackened my assault upon knowledge, my father took care that I should be instructed daily both in school and under other masters at home" (*CPW* IV.1, 612). He represented these arrangements as the admirable manifestation of his father's care and affection in nurturing his natural talents for languages, literature, and philosophy. From Milton's brother Christopher, Aubrey was led to associate his nocturnal study with going to school and making poetry: "When he went to Schoole, when he was very young he studied very hard and sate-up very late, commonly till 12 or one aclock at night, & his father ordered ye mayde to sitt-up for him, and in those yeares composed many Copies of verses, which might well become a riper age."[27] Breaking through this language of industry and paternal encouragement is the image of a delighted child enthralled by learning and literature.

Whenever he became a "pigeon of Pauls" – the epithet bestowed on the schoolboys in allusion to the many pigeons in Paul's courtyard – Milton then entered into a stimulating environment for a poet-in-the-making. The school was located in a stone building at the northeast corner of the courtyard only a few blocks from the Milton home in Bread Street. Walking back and forth, Milton daily passed by the thronging booksellers' stalls in the courtyard, which he was later to frequent. Also, he daily saw the massive (then gothic) cathedral with its clustered pillars, pointed arches, and famous rose window; and often heard the music of organ and choir; on occasion he may have heard sermons by John Donne, who was Dean of St Paul's from 1621 to 1631. The Milton family likely knew John Tomkins the cathedral organist, given Milton senior's musical connections and the fact that both men contributed settings for Ravenscroft's *Psalmes*. These early sights and sounds contribute to a memorable passage in *Il Penseroso*:

> But let my due feet never fail,
> To walk the studious Cloysters pale,
> And love the high embowed Roof,
> With antick Pillars massy proof,
> And storied Windows richly dight,
> Casting a dimm religious light.
> There let the pealing Organ blow,
> To the full voic'd Quire below
> In Service high, and Anthems cleer,
> As may with sweetnes, through mine ear,
> Dissolve me into extasies,
> And bring all Heav'n before mine eyes. (ll. 155–66)

John Strype, a student of Paul's from 1657 to 1661, describes the physical appearance and operation of the school at that period. It was much the same as when Milton was there:

> The Schoole House is large and spacious, fronting the Street on the *East* of St. *Paul's* Cathedral. It consisteth of Eight *Classes* or Forms: in the first whereof Children learn their Rudiments; and so according to their Proficiency are advanced unto the other Forms till they rise to the Eighth. Whence, being commonly made perfect Grammarians, good orators and Poets, well instructed in *Latin, Greek,* and *Hebrew*, and sometime in other *Oriental* Languages, they remove to the Universities. . . . The School is governed and taught by two Masters, *viz*. an High Master, and a Surmaster, and a Chaplain: Whose customary Office was to read the *Latin* Prayers in the *School* . . . and to instruct the Children of the two first Forms in the Elements of the *Latin* Tongue, and also in the Catechism and Christian Manners; for which there is a Room called the *Vestibulum*, being the Anti-room to the School, where the Youth are to be initiated into the Grounds and Principles of Christian Knowledge, as a good and proper Introduction into other Human Learning.[28]

The high master taught and dictated from a chair on a raised platform at the front of the schoolroom. A curtain that could be drawn aside separated the first four forms taught by the surmaster from the last four taught by the high master; an under-usher helped teach the younger boys. The pupils sat on benches arranged in three tiers along each side of the long hall; the best scholar in each of the forms (Milton, often?) had a small desk of his own. There was also a chapel for divine services.

The school was charged by its statutes to admit 153 students. A prospective student must already know how to "rede & wryte latyn & englisshe sufficiently, soo that he be able to rede & wryte his owne lessons."[29] The school was free, save for a fee of fourpence at entrance which was to be paid to a poor scholar or poor man for keeping the school clean. Students attended classes for eight hours – from seven to eleven in the morning and one to five in the afternoon – for about 242 days, with half-holidays on Thursdays. The rules required the boys to speak only in Latin, to sit in the places assigned, to write neatly, to have books and writing implements always ready, to ask questions when in doubt, and to serve, if asked, as pupil teachers for the younger children. Milton's angry denunciation in *Areopagitica*, "I hate a pupil teacher, I endure not an instructer that comes to me under the wardship of an overseeing fist" (*CPW* II, 533) may register his antipathy to this practice at Paul's.

Milton's teachers at Paul's were Alexander Gil (1564–1635), the high master, William Sound the surmaster, and Oliver Smythe the under-usher. Gil was a Greek and Latin scholar and theologian of considerable repute, and his theological writings – *A Treatise Concerning the Trinitie* (1601) and *The Sacred Philosophie of the Holy Scripture* (1635) – defended the uses of reason in religion. If Young helped form Milton as a Puritan, Gil pointed him toward the tradition of Protestant rationalism from Hooker to the Cambridge Platonists. Gil was also an avid proponent of English spelling reform and the preservation of native Anglo-Saxon elements in the English language – views urged in his *Logonomia Anglica* (1619), an English grammar for foreign students. That book's practice of illustrating rhetorical schemes and tropes from the English poets – Spenser ("our Homer"), George Wither ("our Juvenal"), Samuel Daniel ("our Lucan"), Philip Sidney ("our Anacreon"), John Harington ("our Martial") – suggests that Gil may have encouraged that early love of English and of the English poets that Milton attests to in his poem "At a Vacation Exercise." In his masque *Time Vindicated* (1623), Ben Jonson ridiculed Gil's practice of having his pupils turn George Wither's satires into Latin, but such a practice indicates that Gil was remarkably progressive in attempting to bring contemporary English poetry into relation with the Latin canon. Gil also had a reputation for flogging that exceeded the norm in an age when the practice was common. Aubrey calls him "a very ingeniose person" but given to "moodes and humours, particularly his whipping fits."[30]

In describing his schoolboy self later, Milton emphasized his warm relationships with various teachers and friends who valued and nurtured his talents. In curiously involuted terms, as if afraid to offend good taste in recording such comments, he points to his teachers' early praise of him as prose writer and poet: "it was found that whether ought was impos'd me by them . . . or betak'n to of mine own choise in English, or other tongue, prosing or versing, but chiefly this latter, the stile by certain vital signes it had, was likely to live" (*CPW* I, 809). He found a good friend and early literary mentor in the high master's son, Alexander Gil, Jr. (c. 1597–1642), who became under-usher at Paul's in 1621. Milton was then in the higher forms, so Gil Jr. was not formally his teacher. Milton's later letters to him (in Latin) refer to their "almost constant conversations" at school, from which he never departed "without a visible increase and growth of Knowledge, quite as if I had been to some Market of Learning" (*CPW* I, 314). He exchanged poems and literary critiques with Gil over several years, and expressed his admiration for Gil's Latin and Greek poetry, for his judgment as a critic, and for his politics. On the basis of his collected Latin verse (1632) Anthony à Wood termed the younger Gil "one of the best Latin poets in the nation."[31] While Milton was still at Paul's Gil wrote Latin and Greek occasional poems and contributed several of them to miscellanies; he also wrote a virulent poem (1623) celebrating the death of over 90 Roman Catholics when their chapel in Blackfriars collapsed. That poem afforded Milton an example close to hand of militant Protestant politics and poetics.[32]

Some 30 of Milton's schoolmates at Paul's have been identified, among them Nathaniel Gil, another son of the headmaster, and Henry Myriell, son of the music publisher Thomas Myriell.[33] But Milton seems to have formed only one close friendship, with Charles Diodati (1609–38). The headnote to his funeral elegy for Diodati in 1639 emphasizes their special amity based on shared interests: they "had pursued the same studies" and were "most intimate friends from childhood on."[34] The Diodatis were a distinguished Protestant family who became voluntary exiles from Catholic Italy. Charles's father, Theodore, was a prominent London physician with patients at court and in aristocratic families. His uncle was Giovanni Diodati of Geneva, a well-known Calvinist theologian, Hebraeist, promoter of international Protestant collaboration, and distinguished biblical scholar, known especially for his translation of the Bible into Italian (1603) and for his *Pious Annotations upon the Bible*, published in English translation in 1645. Milton visited him in Geneva in 1639 and may have met him when he visited England in 1619 and 1627.[35]

Charles Diodati entered St Paul's School in 1617 or 1618; if Milton entered in 1620 they were schoolfellows for three years. Charles, though a few months younger than Milton, was conspicuously on a faster track: he went to Paul's earlier and left earlier, matriculating at Trinity College, Oxford at age 13 (February 7, 1623). Less than three years later (1625) he graduated AB when Milton was in his first year of college; and nine months before Milton took his Baccalaureate Diodati received his Master's degree (1628). He was an accomplished Latinist and poet who published an artful Latin poetic tribute to William Camden in 1624, while Milton was still at school.[36] He seems to have been one of those bright students to whom everything in the realm of conventional academic expectation comes very easily. Milton admired and loved Diodati for his virtue, his liveliness, his conversation, his learning, and his poetry. But Diodati's precocious accomplishment probably contributed to Milton's anxieties about his tardiness in fulfilling his obvious promise.

Milton completed the regular curriculum of studies at Paul's, which retained John Colet's humanist emphasis on pure classical Latin and Greek models for reading, writing, and speaking.[37] He probably covered with his tutor(s) at home the matter of the first four forms, which would have included the Latin grammar text by William Lily, first master of Paul's (mandated by royal authority),[38] Cato's *Disticha Moralia*, Aesop's Fables, Erasmus's *Colloquies*, Caesar for history, Terence's Comedies, Ovid's *De Tristibus, Heroides* and *Metamorphoses*, and several elegiac poets, especially Ovid. He memorized grammar rules and model passages, paraphrased Latin texts and analyzed in minute detail their language and rhetorical figures, translated passages from Latin to English and back again, and wrote short themes and poems on various topics drawn from or imitating Aesop, Cato, Cicero, Ovid, and Terence. He read a good deal of Latin literature, and started Greek. And of course he studied the Bible and the principles of Protestant Christianity.

In the Upper School (the last four forms) when he was certainly at Paul's, he studied Greek grammar and continued with Latin. He would have been assigned selections from Sallust, Virgil's *Eclogues*, *Georgics*, and *Aeneid*, Cicero's *Epistles* and *Offices*, Horace, Martial, Persius, and Juvenal. In Greek, in addition to the Greek New Testament, he read poetry from Hesiod, Pindar, Theocritus, Homer, and Euripides, Isocrates or Democritus for oratory, Plutarch's Moral Essays, and perhaps Dionysius for history. He became adept at keeping commonplace books of notable passages from his reading, arranged by topic; at double translation of Greek into Latin and back again; at freely imitating the best models – Cicero for letters and orations, Ovid and Propertius for elegiac verse, verse letters and brief narratives, and Virgil for other poetic styles and genres. In his last year he began Hebrew grammar and read the Hebrew Psalter. However, the school offered only meager instruction in the mathematical sciences of the quadrivium: Arithmetic, Geometry, Music, and (Ptolemaic) Astronomy.[39] Students' extra-curricular activities included viewing an occasional play (probably Terence) at the Mercer's Hall, and disputing – traditionally on St Bartholomew's Eve – about principles of grammar with students from other schools.[40]

Milton was also taught to compose and declaim more or less original Latin and Greek themes and orations on set topics, and to write poems of various kinds in several meters. A few of his school exercises survive in manuscript: a Latin essay and Latin verses on the theme of "Early Rising" probably date from his final two years at Paul's.[41] The essay is based on and takes its title from a proverb in Lily's *Grammar*, "Betimes in the Morning Leave Thy Bed"; its structure follows closely a model theme in Reinhard Lorich's widely used rhetorical exercise book based on Aphthonius' *Progymnasmata*; and it is filled with echoes of Cicero, Virgil, Quintilian, Homer, Lily, Erasmus, and more, in a typical display of schoolboy learning.[42] His "Carmen Elegiaca," twenty lines in elegiac verse, offers a stock catalogue of the delights of dawn and spring filled with echoes of Ovid, Catullus, Virgil, Propertius, and Horace, among others.[43] Also, an eight-line poem in lesser Aesclepiad meter, "Ignavus satrapam," is based on *Aeneid* 9.176–449, the slaughter wreaked on the sleeping Rutulians by Nilus and Euryalus. Milton may have preserved these set exercises because their theme – anxiety about time and the need to make proper use of it – was important to him early and late. In his 1673 *Poems* Milton chose to publish some elegiac verses on Aesop's fable of the Peasant and the Landlord, "Apologus De Rustico Et Hero," that probably originated as a school assignment of the sort William Bullokar proposed in his *Aesop's Fables in True Orthography* (1585). Milton's closest model and the source of some verbal parallels was Mantuan's Latin metrical version of the fable.[44] He published in the 1645 *Poems* another early exercise, the Greek epigram "Philosophus ad regem," written to a King as from a Philosopher wrongfully condemned to death because captured along with some criminals. It may have been a school assignment, but its sharp warning to the king that the philosopher's death will silence a wise man the city badly needs shows schoolboy Milton voicing an early critique of kings.

Milton credited his father with giving him early access to languages and sciences outside the usual school curriculum, by tutorial instruction: "I had from my first yeeres by the ceaseless diligence and care of my father, whom God recompence, bin exercis'd to the tongues, and some sciences, as my age would suffer, by sundry masters and teachers both at home and at the schooles" (*CPW* I, 808–9). In "Ad Patrem" (1637?) he specifies French, Italian and Hebrew (possibly including Aramaic and Syriac)[45] as the languages he then learned in addition to his schoolboy Latin and Greek:

> I will not mention a father's usual generosities, for greater things have a claim on me. It was at your expense, dear father, after I had got the mastery of the language of Romulus and the graces of Latin, and acquired the lofty speech of the magniloquent Greeks which is fit for the lips of Jove himself, that you persuaded me to add the flowers which France boasts and the eloquence which the modern Italian pours from his degenerate mouth – testifying by his accent to the barbarian wars – and the mysteries uttered by the Palestinian prophet. (Hughes, ll. 77–85)

Milton's *Apology Against a Pamphlet* (1642) includes a fascinating retrospective account of his literary interests and private reading from schooldays through the university and after (*CPW* I, 889–90). Though designed to demonstrate how his early reading led him to develop a lofty ideal of premarital chastity as an answer to scurrilous charges that he was licentious and frequented brothels, the narrative rings true enough. It tells the story of a sensitive, bookish schoolboy and aspiring poet who found in literature a means of sublimation and a support for the sexual abstinence urged upon him by his strong sense of religious duty, his adolescent anxieties, and his high idealism in matters of love and sex. Some of this reading (and certainly his reflections upon it) pertain to his Cambridge years and after, but we can preview the passage here since he claims to have begun working through this reading program while yet at Paul's. The climactic organization of the several kinds – elegies, Italian sonnets, romances, philosophy, the Bible – is only partly chronological: it recognizes their relative nobility and importance in forming his standard of sexual morality. He offers the review as "the summe of my thoughts in this matter through the course of my yeares and studies" (*CPW* I, 888).

Again pointing with pride to the "good learning" bestowed upon him at "those

places, where the opinion was it might be soonest attain'd," he notes that at school he studied the authors "most commended," and that he was at first most attracted to, and best able to imitate, the elegiac poets, Ovid, Propertius, and others:

> Some were grave Orators & Historians; whose matter me thought I lov'd indeed, but as my age then was, so I understood them; others were smooth Elegiack Poets, whereof the Schooles are not scarce. Whom both for the pleasing sound of their numerous writing, which in imitation I found most easie; and most agreeable to natures part in me, and for their matter which what it is, there be few who know not, I was so allur'd to read, that no recreation came to me better welcome. (*CPW* I, 889)

He insists that he found moral value in those often erotic poets by supposing that they meant to celebrate "high perfections" under various women's names: clearly, he was disposed early on to redeem recalcitrant texts by forcing them to conform to a nobler interpretation. Also, he claims that these poets sparked his resolve to choose his own objects of praise "much more wisely, and with more love of vertue" than they sometimes did. They taught him, as well, to distinguish between biography and art: "if I found those authors any where speaking unworthy things of themselves; or unchaste of those names which before they had extoll'd . . . from that time forward their art I still applauded, but the men I deplor'd" (*CPW* I, 889–90).

He then turned to Dante and Petrarch, in whom he found a more elevated concept of love: "the two famous renowners of *Beatrice* and *Laura* who never write but honour of them to whom they devote their verse, displaying sublime and pure thoughts, without transgression" (*CPW* I, 890). Romances – Spenser, Chaucer, perhaps Malory, and no doubt others – he identifies as recreational reading, "whether my younger feet wander'd" (*CPW* I, 890–1). Romances were notorious for inciting to wantonness, but Milton insists that they strengthened his idealism and commitment to premarital celibacy and chaste marital love:

> Next . . . I betook me among those lofty Fables and Romances, which recount in solemne canto's the deeds of Knighthood founded by our victorious Kings; & from hence had in renowne over all Christendome. There I read it in the oath of every Knight, that he should defend to the expence of his best blood, or of his life, if it so befell him, the honour and chastity of Virgin or Matron. From whence even then I learnt what a noble vertue chastity sure must be. . . . Only this my minde gave me that every free and gentle spirit without that oath ought to be borne a Knight . . . to secure and protect the weaknesse of any attempted chastity. So that even those books which to many others have bin the fuell of wantonnesse and loose living, I cannot thinke how unlesse by divine indulgence prov'd to me so many incitements as you have heard, to the love and stedfast observation of [chastity]. (*CPW* I, 890–1)

Though he claims to have "tasted by no means superficially the sweetness of philosophy" as a schoolboy (*CPW* IV.1, 613) he assigns to his "riper yeares" readings from Plato and Xenophon that further refined his concept of virtuous love (*CPW* I, 891–2). But he points to his continued reading and instruction in the Bible from early childhood as providing the firmest basis for his developing views about chastity, gender hierarchy, and virtuous marriage:

> Last of all not in time, but as perfection is last, that care was ever had of me, with my earliest capacity not to be negligently train'd in the precepts of Christian Religion. . . . Having had the doctrine of holy Scripture unfolding those chaste and high mysteries with timeliest care infus'd, that *the body is for the Lord and the Lord for the body*, thus also I argu'd to my selfe; that if unchastity in a woman whom Saint *Paul* termes the glory of man, be such a scandall and dishonour, then certainly in a man who is both the image and glory of God, it must, though commonly not so thought, be much more deflouring and dishonourable. (*CPW* I, 892)

While Milton was still at school his sister Anne married Edward Phillips, a government official, at St Stephen's Walbrook on November 22, 1623; the minister who officiated, Thomas Myriell, was the music collector who published Milton senior's songs.[46] The scrivener bestowed a considerable dowry upon Anne: £800 as well as property rights secured to her interest and that of her future children. Milton and his mother Sara witnessed the settlement; this is Milton's first recorded signature.[47] Their first child, John, was baptized on January 16, 1625. Milton entered Cambridge that year, at age 16, later than several of his schoolmates but better prepared than most by his rigorous program of preparatory studies.

"The Stile by Certain Vital Signes it Had, Was Likely to Live"

The story of Milton's writing also begins during these early years. According to John Aubrey he wrote poetry from the age of ten (*EL* 2, 10), though he preserved very few examples. But he chose to publish two free psalm paraphrases written in 1623–4 that sound some continuing themes: Psalm 114 in English decasyllabic couplets and Psalm 136 in iambic tetrameter. He dated them carefully in 1645 as "done by the Author at fifteen years old," and placed them just after the Nativity Ode. These may have been school exercises, or they may have been proposed by Milton senior, who had composed several psalm settings. Alternatively, the choice of psalms may have been Milton's own. Psalm 114, "When Israel went out of Egypt, and the house of Jacob from the barbarous people," had political resonance in late 1623: that Exodus Psalm was sung in thanksgiving at St Paul's Cathedral when Prince Charles delighted the nation by returning from Spain in October without the Catholic Infanta he had hoped to wed.[48] The 136th Psalm, "O give thanks unto the Lord: for he is good: for his mercy endureth for ever," had a similar resonance, since its chief example of God's goodness is the Exodus story of Israel's deliverance from Pharoah and establishment in the Promised Land.

These psalms, Milton's earliest extant English poems, were influenced by George Buchanan's Latin metrical psalter (1566) and Joshua Sylvester's enormously popular translation of Du Bartas under the title, *Divine Weekes and Workes*.[49] Milton imitates Du Bartas's vowel elisions, use of simple meters and simple rhymes, ornate language, and picturesque epithets. He calls on Sylvester for some linguistic embellishments – "glassy floods," "crystal fountains," "Erythraean main" (for the Red Sea), and "walls of glass" (for the Red Sea divided). In devising compound epithets he looks to both Homer and Sylvester: for example, the sea's "froth-becurled head," God's "thunder-clasping hand," the "golden-tressed sun."[50] Also, these earliest English poems display Milton's characteristic fascination with unusual geographical names and verbal sonorities.

Milton elaborates the eight verses of Psalm 114 into 18 pentameter lines, and makes each of the 26 verses of Psalm 136 into a four-line stanza with a couplet refrain. At times his lines have no biblical equivalent. In the *Book of Common Prayer* the first two lines of Psalm 114 simply record the Exodus event: "When Israel came out of Egypt, and the house of Jacob from among the strange people, / Judah was his sanctuary, and Israel his dominion." But Milton's six-line paraphrase underscores the Israelites' hard-won liberty and God's protective power:

> When the blest seed of *Terah's* faithfull Son,
> After long toil their liberty had won,
> And past from Pharian fields to *Canaan* Land,
> Led by the strength of the Almighties hand,
> *Jehovah's* wonders were in *Israel* shown,
> His praise and glory was in Israel known.

Also, his paraphrase of Psalm 136 echoes Buchanan's "Cui domini rerum submittunt sceptra tyranni" in offering a politically charged interpretation of "Lord of Lords":

> O let us his praises tell,
> That doth the wrathful tyrants quell.
> For his mercies ay endure,
> Ever faithfull, ever sure.

It is remarkable but hardly surprising that the original passages in the 15-year-old Milton's psalm paraphrases reveal attitudes prevalent in his cultural milieu and announce themes that he reiterated throughout his life and in many forms: the people's hard struggle for liberty and God's power to destroy tyrants.

2

"To Cambridge . . . For Seven Years" 1625–1632

Milton wrote appreciatively about his childhood and schooldays, with some patina of nostalgia, but he was disappointed by and sharply critical of the education he received at Cambridge University. He completed, while constantly complaining about, the required studies and exercises in disputation for the Baccalaureate and Master of Arts degrees. But he felt alienated from the curriculum and from his fellow students, finding, he lamented, "almost no intellectual companions here" (*CPW* I, 314). He came to Cambridge intending to prepare for ordination and, as his commitment to poetry intensified, probably hoped to combine poetry and the ministry as had John Donne, George Herbert, Giles and Phineas Fletcher, and others. Yet in his collegiate writings he never speaks of himself as a prospective minister but always as a poet and scholar; clearly those were the roles engaging his mind and heart. While Milton portrayed his relations with his Cambridge associates as uneasy and sometimes hostile, he continued to express warm regard for three friends whose learning, poetry, and reformist politics he had long admired: Thomas Young, his former tutor, Alexander Gil, the mentor–friend from St Paul's School, with whom he continued to exchange poems, and his dearest comrade, Charles Diodati.

Milton's early works return often to concerns common among late adolescents – awakening sexuality, relations with peers, the mix of work and leisure, the worth of academic studies, choice of vocation, politics – providing the basis for what may be the most complete self-portrait of the author as a young man before the nineteenth century. His works show us something of how he saw his student self and how he represented that self to others: as an early rebel against authority, as a young man much affected by feminine beauty yet defiantly chaste, as an ardent but very discriminating friend, as a lover of London pleasures but also of nature and the English countryside, as a zealous reformist Protestant, as a severe critic of his college education and his student peers, and above all, as an aspiring poet.

His writings in these years trace his early development as poet and rhetorician, cultivating his technical skills and deepening his religious and political engagement. His undergraduate *Prolusions* foreshadow and prepare for his later polemics, affording him practice in conventional modes of argumentation and rhetorical suasion as well as in challenging authority. As poet, he recurred often to some common poetic subjects: springtime, love, death, friendship, religion, the poet's life. He also looked to many models and tried out a great variety of genres and poetic styles, in Latin and English, but in most of them he soon discovered his own voice. When he discussed his early reading program and literary models in 1642,[1] he recorded his recognition – probably while still a student at Cambridge – that life and poetry are closely interconnected:

> And long it was not after, when I was confirm'd in this opinion, that he who would not be frustrate of his hope to write well hereafter in laudable things, ought him selfe to bee a true Poem, that is, a composition, and patterne of the best and honorablest things; not presuming to sing high praises of heroick men, or famous Cities, unlesse he have in himselfe the experience and the practice of all that which is praise-worthy. (*Apology*, *CPW* I, 890)

Within and among several of his early works he staged a debate about alternative kinds of life and poetry, setting up choices or at least some assessment of relative value. Those alternatives include: sensuous delight and asceticism, eroticism and chastity, retired leisure and arduous labor, academic oratory and poetry, classical and Christian myth, Latin and English language, elegy and the higher poetic forms, mirth and melancholy.

Some of Milton's early writings can be dated precisely but several others cannot; we have to weigh probabilities when attempting to place them in Milton's development as an author. Of his surviving university exercises known as *Prolusions*, first published in 1674, we can only date Prolusion VI with confidence. Also, some of the dates Milton assigned to his early poems in his 1645 and 1673 collections are demonstrably too early – due, perhaps, to his own forgetfulness long after the fact, or to printers' errors, or to his subconscious effort to compensate for a sense of belated development. His usual dating formula, *anno aetatis*, means in his usage, "written at the age of."

All but two of Milton's undergraduate poems are in Latin, replete with classical allusions and adapted phrases; since Latin was still the international language, collegiate poets regularly practiced their skills in Latin verse. But most of Milton's Latin poems rise well above the flood of imitative Latin verse the age produced: Dr Johnson observed that Milton was "the first Englishman who, after the revival of letters, wrote Latin verse with classick elegance."[2] The chief influence on Milton's early poems was Ovid, but there are many others: Virgil, Horace, Propertius, Tibullus, Catullus, Callimachus, Seneca, Lucan, Statius, and such neo-Latin poets as George

Buchanan, Joannes Secundus, and Marullo.[3] Rather than imitating specific poems, Milton absorbs, plays with, and freely transforms Ovid and the others, turning them to his own purposes.[4] He began with Elegy, "which in imitation I found most easie; and most agreeable to natures part in me" (*CPW* I, 889), and he used that meter – paired lines of alternating dactyllic hexameter and pentameter – for several traditional purposes: three verse letters (Elegies I, IV, VI), two funeral elegies (Elegies II and III), a love elegy (Elegy VII), and an erotic celebration of spring (Elegy V). He also wrote in other Latin meters and kinds: epigrams, a satiric mini-epic, funeral poems. His graduate years saw a decisive turn to the vernacular: Petrarchan sonnets in Italian, and in English some epitaphs and lovely lyrics as well as three English masterpieces: the hymn *On the Morning of Christ's Nativity*, and the companion poems *L'Allegro* and *Il Penseroso*.

Significantly, throughout his university career Milton's muse entirely ignored the various royal and courtly occasions celebrated by other university poets – the death and funeral of James I, the coronation and wedding of Charles I, the visits of Charles and Buckingham to the university, the births and deaths of royal children. Unlike Donne and Herbert, this serious-minded young bourgeois poet seems never to have thought about courtiership; though not yet an antiroyalist, he showed no inclination whatever to look to the court for patronage or imaginative stimulus. Some of his collegiate writing bears an overt or covert political charge – vehemently anti-Catholic, anti-Laudian, critical of Stuart religious repression, supportive of Protestant militancy in Europe, prophetic – a politics that aligns him with reformist and oppositional views. We can sometimes glimpse in the student Milton the Puritan revolutionary in the making.

"I Devoted Myself to the Traditional Disciplines and Liberal Arts"

Milton the avid student no doubt came to the university expecting to find an exciting intellectual community: challenging studies, learned teachers, stimulating companions. He registered at Christ's College, Cambridge, on February 12, 1625; he may have remained in college or returned to London for some weeks before taking the matriculation oath in the university on April 9.[5] On those trips he may or may not have traveled with old Hobson the Carrier, but he surely did so sometimes. Once a week Thomas Hobson (1544–1630) ferried students between Cambridge and London and also rented horses and carriages to them, making them accept whatever horse or equipage stood nearest the stable door – hence the phrase, "Hobson's Choice." Easter term, which began April 28 that year, was the usual entry period; graduation came four years later, at the Bachelors' commencement at the end of March. Milton began college at 16, the most common age of entry to Cambridge colleges in the 1620s.[6] Many students came at age 12 or 13, though

Henry Peacham declared that the college program was much beyond the "childish capacities" of such "tender plants," and that "scarce one among twentie" succeeded.[7] Such a student population contributed to Milton's sense of alienation at college.

Most students came from moderately well-to-do families, and, like Milton, paid fees of about £50 a year as "lesser pensioners." Above them in rank were the "fellow-commoners" or "greater pensioners" – the sons of nobles and wealthy gentry who paid most, had the best accommodation, and dined at high table. Below them were the sizars who paid least, performed various menial duties and had inferior accommodation. Very able poor students might receive exhibitions from their schools or college scholarships. A fellow Pauline, Richard Pory, registered at Christ's along with Milton; other student contemporaries whom he may have known but never mentions include, at Christ's, the poet John Cleveland and the Cambridge Platonist Henry More, and in other colleges, the poet Richard Crashaw and the playwright Thomas Randolph.[8]

When Milton came up to Cambridge in 1625 he found a town of around five thousand and a university with sixteen colleges, inhabited by more than three thousand men and boys. The Arts faculty was then educating unprecedented numbers of young gentlemen to fill various positions in English society, but a primary role was still the preparation of ministers. Many students left before taking the Baccalaureate degree, some to read law at the Inns of Court, some to take up appointments in the court or county bureaucracy, some to live on their estates or enter into commerce. Prospective ministers proceeded to the Master of Arts degree and ordination; some other bachelors entered graduate faculties of law and medicine. An occasional graduate might be elected as a fellow of his college and stay on to tutor students and proceed (usually) to an advanced degree in divinity.

At both Cambridge and Oxford the colleges were the principal sites of the students' education. Milton and his father probably chose Christ's – founded in 1505 and in 1625 the third largest college with some 265 members – because of its strong reformist traditions. During Elizabeth's reign many residents of Christ's were in trouble for non-conformity or for Puritanism. Recent fellows and students included the famous reformist and Puritan theologians William Ames, William Perkins, Lawrence Chaderton, Hugh Broughton, Thomas Goodwin, Edward Dering, Andrew Willett, and John Smyth the Se-Baptist.[9] But shortly before and during Milton's years Christ's, like Sidney Sussex and Emmanuel, were marked by heightened conflict between their Calvinist/Puritan traditions and the growing power of the Laudian faction throughout the university. The Master of Christ's, Thomas Bainbridge (1622–46), was not strongly partisan, but the 13 fellows were sharply divided in their opinions and allegiances.[10]

Christ's College in 1625 was attractive, with open fields (Christ's Piece) to the east and the river Cam about half a mile beyond them. Surrounding the spacious court were two-story buildings of sandstone and red brick, comprising living quarters, master's lodge, dining hall, and chapel (plate 2). Beyond were extensive gardens for master and fellows, an orchard, and an enclosed tennis court. Throughout the university student living quarters were crowded. At Christ's, the fellows occupied first-floor rooms in the courtyard buildings, perhaps sharing with their sizars. Sleeping chambers held two, three, or even four students, usually with separate beds; some rooms had studies attached. In violation of university statutes, overflow students were lodged in a nearby inn, the Brazen George. Tradition, unsupported by any evidence, has assigned Milton a choice first-floor room at the left side of the courtyard; he might possibly have shared this room with another student toward the end of his college career, but for much of it he probably lodged with one or two roommates in less desirable quarters, such as the small wooden "New Building" known as "Rat's Hall."

At college the tutor stood *in loco parentis* to his students, had major responsibility for their instruction, and often took charge of the money for their fees, books, and living expenses. One of the two most respected tutors at Christ's during Milton's years was his own first tutor, William Chappell, famed for his erudition, his strictness with his pupils, his Arminian (anti-predestinarian) theology, and his formidable disputations in the university assemblies – including one with King James.[11] During the 1620s he had more than twice as many students as any other tutor – which may testify to his reputation, his popularity, or simply his readiness to take on paying work. Joseph Mede was still more renowned. He was a student of divinity and mathematics, an authority on Homer, a Socratic teacher noted for tailoring instruction to his students' needs and interests, and a distinguished biblical exegete best known for his *Clavis Apocalyptica* (1627), a scholarly analysis and application of biblical apocalyptic prophecy to contemporary history which went far to legitimate millenarianism among mainstream Puritans before, during, and after the revolution.[12] Mede was also part of a network of correspondence relaying news of the court, the government, and especially of European affairs and the Thirty Years War.[13] Milton may, or may not, have had much contact with Mede, but his millenarianism and his attention to the fortunes of European Protestants formed part of the intellectual milieu of Christ's.

The academic year had three regular terms: Michaelmas (October 10 to December 16); Lent (January 13 to the second Friday before Easter); and Easter (from the second Wednesday after Easter to the Friday after the first Tuesday in July – the day commencement exercises were held for graduate degrees). Then came the "long vacation" or Midsummer term. Students assembled in chapel at 5 a.m. for morning service and perhaps a brief talk, called a "commonplace," by one of the fellows. After breakfast small groups met for tutorials in their tutors' rooms, and for sessions at which lectors read Aristotle and other texts with them. They might also attend or participate in disputations to prepare for or fulfill degree requirements. After lunch they attended other disputations in college or in the "Public Schools" (assemblies) of the university, or spent time in private study. Though not required to do so they could and Milton probably did attend lectures by the distinguished Regius Professors of the university: Robert Creighton (Greek), Robert Metcalfe (Hebrew), and Samuel Collins (Divinity). Milton may also have heard the eloquent Puritan preacher Richard Sibbes of Catherine Hall and the poet George Herbert, though the latter's duties as the university's Public Orator (until 1627) were then chiefly performed by a deputy. After Vespers and dinner students were free. Statutes, not rigorously enforced in Milton's day, forbade them to be out of college after nine (or ten) at night, to go into town without special permission, or to visit taverns. Except during hours of relaxation they were to speak only Latin, Greek, or Hebrew. Misbehavior, defiance of the rules, or absence from required sessions were penalized according to seriousness, by fines, rustication for a limited period, corporal punishment, and expulsion.

We do not know exactly what Milton studied at Cambridge.[14] During Milton's years the curricular emphasis was on logic, rhetoric, ethics, metaphysics, and theology. The amount of time given to Greek, Hebrew, politics, geography, classical history, and (ancient) science – physics, astronomy, biology, geology, etc. – depended largely on the tutor's interests and capacities and to some degree on the student's.[15] Joseph Mede's records of student book purchases indicate that his students chiefly read Aristotle and compendiums based on Aristotle, though also Ramist logics and rhetorics.[16] The university had a mathematics professor, and Bacon had won some converts in his *Alma Mater* to the new science and philosophy, but there was no formal study of modern science, modern history or vernacular literature. Milton evidently went well beyond the norm in mathematics, Hebrew, and Greek, his mastery of which is evident from his carefully annotated copy of Aratus purchased in 1631.[17] As time permitted he no doubt followed his own recommendation in Prolusion III for wide reading in history, science, and the modern literatures. Mede's accounts indicate that some students paid for special tutors in French, music, fencing, and horsemanship. Milton may have done so: he later takes pride in the mastery of his weapon (*CPW* IV.1, 583) and in his good Italian.

Rhetoric was pervasive, mastered chiefly by practice. Tutors assigned handbooks based on Cicero, Quintilian, Aristotle, Aphthonius, the Ramist Omer Talon, Bartholomaeus Keckermann, and others, and from the first term on practiced their students in disputation to prepare them for the required public orations and disputations on logic, ethics, physics, metaphysics, and theology. Third- and fourth-year students, called sophisters, disputed regularly in college or in university assemblies called the Public Schools. They defended or attacked propositions (as assigned), both in extempore speeches and in carefully organized and memorized Latin orations that were supposed to make effective use of logical argument, rhetorical proofs, and stylistic flourishes. In the final year, as part of the exercises for the Baccalaureate, they were required by statute (not always strictly enforced) to maintain two Latin theses on selected moral or metaphysical topics ("Responsions" or "Acts"), against three opponents belonging to other colleges; and to serve as opponent on two such occasions.[18]

Shortly before Milton began his first official term (Easter term, 1625) he would have heard of the death of King James (March 27); the university held solemn ceremonies marking the king's funeral (May 7). His pastor at All Hallows, Richard Stock, died April 20, and Milton just possibly encountered his successor, the noted collector of travel narratives, Samuel Purchas, whose work he later used extensively in his *History of Moscovia*.[19] During Milton's second term the university was virtually closed down by plague. It hit London in April, 1625, soon claiming some 35,000 victims – one-sixth of the population. By August Cambridge was so badly stricken that all public occasions at the university ceased, to resume only in December. Milton may have spent these months in London or at some rural retreat with his family.[20]

Lent and Easter terms, 1626, were eventful for Milton. In March he evidently had a serious altercation with his tutor Chappell which resulted in a brief rustication at home. While the time of this conflict is uncertain, I suspect it happened at this early stage in Milton's university career, before he learned how to cope with a milieu he found frustrating.[21] We can only speculate as to the offense given to or perceived by Chappell. Insubordination, perhaps – arising from Milton's impatience with scholastic logic-chopping, staged debates, and the repetitious review of materials he had already mastered, and with a tutor too busy and important to give him much personal attention? Theology, perhaps – Milton was still a Calvinist predestinarian and Chappell was said to have "Arminianized" many of his students. A personality conflict, perhaps – with Chapell (unlike Young and Gil) failing to recognize that he had to do with a prodigious talent and Milton bristling to find his gifts undervalued? Politics, perhaps – with Milton offering unguarded expressions of anti-Laudian or anti-court sentiments? John Aubrey alludes ambiguously to the Chapell incident, citing as authority Milton's younger brother Christopher:

> [Milton] was a very hard student in the University, & p[er]formed all his exercises there wth very good Applause. His lst Tutor there was Mr. Chappell, from whom receiving some unkindnesse, ⋆whip't him⋆ he was afterwards (though it seemed / [symbol for "contrary to"] ye Rules of ye College) transferred to the Tuition of one Mr. Tovell [Nathanial Tovey], who dyed Parson of Lutterworth. (*EL* 10)

The words ⋆whip't him⋆ are inserted above the line, perhaps indicating information Aubrey picked up later and it may be from a less reliable source: whipping was common enough for younger boys though not for 17-year-olds, and not by tutors.[22] But Milton changed tutors at his return, an unusual procedure indicating that something serious had happened. And a later letter from Bishop John Bramhall claims (evidently on Chappell's authority) that Milton was "turned away by him as he well deserved to have been both out of the University and out of the society of men."[23]

From London Milton wrote a Latin verse letter (Elegy I) to his dearest friend

Charles Diodati, portraying him as a Platonic soulmate who shares his love of learning and poetry, a "charming companion" with a "heart that loves me and a head so true." Milton describes himself as having a very good time in London, and waxes eloquent about the joys of girl-watching and the beauty of English women. Sounding the notes of youthful rebellion and protesting a little too much, he declares himself happily freed from a harsh tutor and a university atmosphere inimical to poetry: "I am not pining away for my rooms, recently forbidden to me. . . . How badly that place suits the worshippers of Phoebus! I do not like having always to stomach the threats of a stern tutor and other things which my spirit will not tolerate (ll. 12–16).[24]

Elegy I echoes but rings changes on Ovid's *Tristia* and *Epistulae ex Ponto*,[25] constructing a narrative of erotic awakening and chaste resistance against the model of Ovid, in terms that suggest an experience more literary than passionate. It fashions a witty cross-comparison between Ovid's unhappy exile from Rome at Tomis where he lacked books, pleasures, and poetic stimuli, and Milton's delightful exile from Cambridge to London, where he enjoys "welcome leisure" devoted to the "mild Muses," as well as "books, which are my life," walks in the nearby countryside, the theater, and other pleasures that nourish the poet. Milton's references to plays, however, smack of the study rather than the stage – tragic plots from Aeschylus and Sophocles and stock characters from Latin comedy.[26] The poem is a witty putdown of the university, whose "reedy fens" recall the swamps of Ovid's Tomis, and whose clamorous disputations and harsh tutors are as destructive as Tomis was to a poet's soul. The cross-comparison makes Milton's place of exile idyllic and his university "home" the true exile. Elegy I develops the classic elegiac motifs of springtime, attraction to female beauty, and danger from Cupid, but in a playful and strikingly un-Ovidian reversal, this speaker does not surrender to a lady or to Cupid but preserves his chastity.[27] At poem's end, London is reconceived as the haunt of Circe from which, "with the help of divine moly," Milton will soon escape back to Cambridge, to "the hum of the noisy Schools" (l. 90).

The exile was over by Easter term. Milton's new tutor, Nathanial Tovey, then about 27 years old, was a Calvinist and a Ramist; his friendship with Chappell and his family connections with the Diodatis may have eased the reassignment.[28] During Easter term the university was much exercised over two issues that heightened the conflict between Laudian Arminians and Calvinists. A book by Richard Montagu, a former fellow of King's, provocatively linked Cambridge and the church as a whole with Arminianism, depicting recent Calvinist predestinarianism as an aberration in both institutions.[29] Also, elections for a new university chancellor, an honorific but politically symbolic post, were being hotly contested: the king backed his favorite, Buckingham, then under indictment by the House of Commons, while the Commons itself and those Cambridge Masters of Arts with Calvinist sympathies supported Thomas Howard, Earl of Berkshire.[30] At Christ's the master, Thomas Bainbridge, supported Buckingham, and the fellows split about evenly. With many abstentions and amid charges of undue pressure and a rigged election, the university votes went for Buckingham by a slight majority[31] and he was duly installed on July 13.

Milton's second academic year (1626–7) gave large scope to his Latin muse. Beginning in Michaelmas term, the 17-year-old poet engaged issues of mortality for the first time. In the aftermath of his trouble with Chappell, he seems to have been eager to make his mark on the local scene as an accomplished Latin poet, so he joined other university poets in penning verse tributes to several former and present Cantabridgians who died that autumn. These four funeral poems – two in elegiacs, two calling upon other resources of meter and tone – are conventional exercises, somewhat uneven in quality but nicely suited to their subjects. All of them mix mythological allusions with Christian motifs.

The most likely order of composition does not exactly correspond to the order of the deaths. Milton probably wrote Elegy II, "In Obitum Praeconis Academici Cantabrigiensis," a 24-line poem for the university beadle Richard Ridding, almost immediately after his death on September 26, 1626.[32] It is based on a witty conceit, that the Beadle Death has now summoned one of his own, the university mace-bearer and cryer. There is no consolation, only the wish that "wailing Elegy" might fill all the schools with her dirge. The obsequy "In Obitum Procancellarii Medicii" for the vice-chancellor, Dr John Gostlin, master of Caius College and Regius Professor of Medicine (d. October 21, 1626) was probably completed next; it is written in Horatian alcaic stanzas and has a somewhat Horatian tone. Milton placed it first in the *Sylvarum Liber* section of his 1645 *Poems*, with a claim that it was written at age 16 – impossible, since that was the year before Gostlin died. Leo Miller suggests, plausibly, that the first twenty lines and the last four have no necessary relation to Gostlin and may well have been written earlier, to compete with Charles Diodati's published funeral poem for Camden, also twenty-four lines and also in alcaic stanzas, which Milton's poem seems at times to echo.[33] If some part of this poem was written at age 16, Milton would want to emphasize that fact; he often exaggerates his own youthfulness, or his poems' early dates, as a subconscious defense against his sense of belated achievement. Lines 21–44 make the poem appropriate to Gostlin, developing the irony that the physician Gostlin could not save himself, that Death and the Fates have jealously killed one who was all too successful in helping others elude death. The consolation asks an eternal dwelling in Elysium for this "glorious shepherd of Pallas' flock," but does not answer the harsh question posed: why does Death take the exceptional and noble with the same stroke as the ignorant and useless?

The other funeral poems celebrate bishops who had Cambridge connections as alumni and former fellows and masters. But Milton praises them simply as good men and is pointedly silent about their episcopal office. Elegy III, for the eminent prelate Lancelot Andrewes, Bishop of Winchester (d. September 25, 1626), must have been written, or at least completed, in early December if the allusions to "clarus dux" and "frater verendus," refer, as most critics suppose, to the deaths, respectively, of Christian of Brunswick (June 6, 1626) and Count Ernest of Mansfeld (November 29, 1626). It was followed shortly by an obsequy for Nicholas Felton, Bishop of Ely (d. October 6, 1626) whose death Milton claims to have heard about while his cheeks were "still wet and stained with tears" from paying his "sad respects" to the bier of Andrewes (his funeral was November 11). Both poems register Milton's reformist concerns. Felton had spoken at Cambridge a few months earlier in support of Berkshire over Buckingham. And into the Andrewes elegy Milton introduced what seems an extraneous lament for the lost Protestant heroes in the Thirty Years War: "Then I remembered that glorious duke and his brother, whose bones were burned on untimely pyres; and I remembered the Heroes whom Belgia saw rapt into the skies – the lost leaders whom the whole nation mourned."[34] The lines pass oblique judgment on those unheroic English leaders – James I and Charles I – who have kept England from joining the continental Protestants in arms against Rome.

Elegy III, "In Obitum Praesulis Wintoniensis" (68 lines), the most accomplished of Milton's early funeral poems, opens with a generalized but personal lament for the senseless, indiscriminate ravages of Libitina, goddess of corpses, linking the plague in London with the untimely loss of the Protestant heroes. "Pitiless Death" destroys all nature and also exceptional spirits like Andrewes and the heroes. The consolation is an ecstatic dream-vision in which the speaker sees angels welcoming Andrewes to a sensuous garden filled with light, flowers, silver streams, and gentle winds – a fusion of Elysium with the Christian heaven. But upon waking the speaker somewhat disconcertingly quotes Ovid (*Amores* I.v), referring to a dream of blissful love-making with Corinna: "May dreams like these often befall me." "In obitum Praesulis Eliensis" for Bishop Felton employs iambics (68 lines, alternating trimeter and dimeter) – an appropriate choice for this poem's long and fierce invective against Death. The consolation here is provided by Felton's voice from beyond the grave – a forecast of St Peter's interpolation in *Lycidas* – redefining Death as God's appointed guide to the afterlife and describing his own journey through the heavens to the "gleaming gate of Olympus." The poem concludes abruptly with Felton's refusal to describe the blissful place – "For me it is enough to enjoy it eternally." Here the speaker has no dream vision, and makes no response.

Milton also assigned to 1626 his longest and most ambitious Latin poem to date, "In quintum Novembris," a miniature epic on the thwarting of the Guy Fawkes Gunpowder Plot (1605), the design by a cabal of Roman Catholics to blow up king and parliament.[35] The poem registers Milton's sympathy with reformist Protestantism; it exudes Protestant zeal and Virgilian aspiration. The immediate occasion may have been a university celebration of Guy Fawkes Day, November 5, 1626; but the near collapse of Protestant military hopes in Europe after the loss of many Protestant leaders and the defeat at Breda (June, 1625) may have prompted Milton to treat at this time that earlier miraculous rescue of English Protestantism, as an incitement to greater English militancy in the Thirty Years War. The poem's 226 hexameter lines mix the heroic and the grotesque, florid expressions of awe and horror with irony and mockery. There are four parts: Satan surveys the earth and determines to subvert peaceful, religious England where alone he is thwarted; in Rome, disguised as a Franciscan friar, he incites the pope to destroy the English parliament; the pope summons "fierce-eyed Murder" and "double-tongued Treachery" from their allegorical cave and dispatches them to the task; but God, betimes, stirs up many-tongued Fame to reveal the plot. Seventeen-year-old Milton may have thought to emulate sixteen-year-old Virgil in writing a brief epic, but he looked past Virgil's *Gnat* to *The Aeneid* for heroic conception and many motifs: aereal surveys, dream visitations, the epithet "pius" for King James, a cave with allegorical inhabitants, and Fame. Milton's Tower of Fame owes something to Ovid and perhaps also to Chaucer; the allegorical portraits of Murder and Treason evoke Spenser; and the plotting in Hell recalls Tasso's *Gerusalemme Liberata*.[36] In this Satan we at times glimpse anticipations of his magnificent namesake in *Paradise Lost*, but most elements of this poem are stock features of anti-papist satire: the devil personating a Franciscan friar, the foolish ceremonies of Roman liturgy, the pope as hypocrite and whoremonger. The capture of the plotters and the Guy Fawkes celebrations are crowded into the last seven lines, keeping the emphasis on the danger and threat from diabolic Catholic powers – which continue in the Thirty Years War.

Milton wrote four undated Latin epigrams on the Gunpowder Plot titled "In Proditionem Bombardicam," perhaps for this or another Guy Fawkes Day; the second must postdate November 1625 since it mentions the death of James I. They ring satiric changes on the theme of the papists' vicious attempt to dispatch James to the other world. A related epigram on the inventor of gunpowder, "In inventorem Bombardae," is probably but not certainly a Guy Fawkes poem based on ironic praise. All are in elegiacs, with striking images of sulphurous fire, smoke, and powerful explosions.

In March, 1627, the new Chancellor Buckingham visited Cambridge, feted by ceremonies, banquets, and tributes. Milton, typically, wrote no verses for this royal favorite, but that same March he composed Elegy IV, a graceful Latin verse letter to his admired former tutor Thomas Young, now a pastor at Hamburg and a voluntary exile for his Puritan views. Associating himself with Young's Puritanism, Milton constructs Young as the victim of a harsh regime, exposed by Stuart policies to the dangers of the continental religious wars:

> You are living among strangers, in poverty and loneliness, while all around you echoes the horrifying noise of war. In your need you seek in a foreign land the sustenance which your ancestral home denied you. O native country, hard-hearted parent . . . is it fitting that you should expose your innocent children in this way?[37]

Expressing concern for Young's safety and anger over his exile, Milton invites him to compare himself with Elijah and Paul, persecuted by rulers but protected by

God. Provocatively, the comparison with the prophet Elijah forced to flee from King Ahab and Queen Jezebel seems to invite application to Charles and his Roman Catholic Queen Henrietta Maria. Elegy IV acknowledges Milton's debt to his former tutor for leading him to the classical muses, and displays it with allusions to Aeolus, Media, Jason, Alcibiades, Socrates, Alexander, Achilles, Phoinix and more. He also invokes the topics of friendship – "This man is more to me than one half of my soul" – and ends by taking on the role of moral counsellor, a stance sanctioned by the genre but yet a remarkable reversal of roles *vis-à-vis* his teacher: "Remember to hope: . . . Triumph over your misfortunes with sheer greatness of spirit. Do not doubt that some day you will enjoy happier times and be able to see your home again" (ll. 123–6).[38] In an accompanying prose letter dated March 26, Milton thanked Young belatedly for the gift of a Hebrew Bible, and professed to "rejoice and almost exult" that this "Father" and "best of Teachers" has now become an equal friend.[39]

That spring Milton was in London on two occasions (May 25 and June 11, and perhaps for the interval between those dates) to sign legal documents along with his father. One was for the purchase of property in St Martin in the Fields, the other for a loan to Richard Powell earning annual interest of £24 which Milton senior made payable to his son, to give him some long-term financial security.[40] Elegy VII was probably written that spring; the subject is an amorous springtime adventure in London.[41] This Latin poem rings comic changes on that very common Ovidian topic, Cupid's vengeance on one who claims to be impervious to his arrows. Reprising Elegy I, the speaker again delights in watching bevies of beautiful girls, but this time Cupid makes him fall painfully in love with one of them at first sight, using a characteristic Ovidian strategy:

> Losing no time he swung on the girl's eyelashes, then on her mouth, then jumped between her lips, then perched on her cheek – and wherever the nimble archer landed (alas for me) he hit my defenceless breast in a thousand pieces. In an instant passions I had never felt before entered my heart – I burned inwardly with love: my whole being was aflame. (ll. 69–74)[42]

Then the lady vanishes, leaving the grieving but still chaste speaker unsure whether to seek relief or bask in his delightful misery. This very literary story may or may not have a basis in life experience, but it casts some light on the young Milton's imagination of erotic feeling. Throughout, the speaker directs lighthearted irony against himself: he loses the girl because he is too love-struck to make contact with her, and at the end he both wants and does not want release from his delicious pain.[43] The elegy adopts Ovid's anti-sentimentality, but avoids his frank sensuality.

While Milton was writing these Latin poems he may also have produced (or revised) his very skillful English translation of Horace's "Ad Pyrrham" (I.5), spoken by an experienced man who has foresworn love and who predicts sorrow for a naive young lover he sees courting the beautiful but faithless Pyrrha. The date is, however, very uncertain.[44] The poem itself is a *tour de force:* it often succeeds in capturing the Horatian tone; it achieves the verbal exactness the headnote claims, "Rendered almost word for word without rhyme according to the Latin measure, as near as the language will permit"; and it is Milton's only attempt to render Latin quantitative measures into English verse.

The reformist sympathies Milton expressed to Young were probably reinforced a few months later by the brouhaha over a lectureship in history founded by Fulke Greville, Lord Brooke. By order of Laud and by royal injunction the lectureship was cancelled after the incumbent, Dr Isacc Dorislaus of Leyden, delivered in December, 1627, his first two lectures on Tacitus, the classical historian often seen as a rallying point for republicanism and resistance to tyranny. Reportedly, Dorislaus also defended the Dutch for upholding their liberties against Spain. According to Matthew Wren the lectures contained "dangerous passages . . . appliable to the exasperations of these villanous times."[45]

During his third academic year, 1627–8, Milton claimed an English poetic voice for the first time in an original poem. "On the Death of a Fair Infant Dying of a Cough" was written about his sister Anne's daughter, according to her son, Edward Phillips (*EL* 62). When he first published the poem in 1673 Milton dated it at age 17 (two years earlier), but the subject is almost certainly his 2-year-old niece, also named Anne, who was buried January 22, 1628.[46] The error may have been a simple fault of memory so many years later, or prompted (like the Gostlin error) by Milton's subconscious wish to compensate for his sense of belated accomplishment, or else a scribal error, reading 17 for 19. The poem's details fit Anne: her death in winter, her birth in the throes of a plague epidemic (late December, 1625 or early January, 1626), and her mother's pregnancy with another child, Elizabeth, baptized on April 9, 1628 (*LR* I, 152–3). English is an appropriate language choice for the child subject and the immediate audience, Milton's sister. The eleven-stanza funeral ode finds its chief models in Spenserian poets like the Fletchers, in neo-Latin funeral epigrams on the death of children for the use of the flower motif, and in Pindaric odes for the myths and mythic transformations.[47] The seven-line stanzas meld Chaucerian rime royal with the Spenserian stanza, retaining the Spenserian final alexandrine as well as Spenserian archaisms and schemes of alliteration and assonance. This early poem already displays Milton's characteristic use of classical motifs and myths to carry Christian meaning, and his habit of moving from a particular scene or event to cosmic perspectives and significances. Milton apostrophizes the infant as a blasted primrose, and develops a myth of her as a 'maiden' unwittingly destroyed by the bumbling caresses of Winter, personified as an elderly Deity enamoured of her beauty. She is made to embody the power of innocence to slake God's wrath for sin and drive off "black perdition" and "slaughtering pestilence." One consolation – that the child's redemptive "office" continues in heaven – is perhaps too hasty and elliptic (l. 70). But Milton also urges his sister to find grounds for patience and hope in her new pregnancy: "This if thou do he [God] will an offspring give, / That till the world's last end shall make thy name to live." With Virgil's Fourth "Messianic" Eclogue as a reference point, the expected child is made to figure Christ who brings redemption and immortal life to faithful Christians.

Milton again visited London that spring but did not stay long, intending, as he wrote to Alexander Gil on July 2, to spend most of the long summer vacation in Cambridge, enjoying "a deeply Literary leisure . . . in the Cloisters of the Muses."[48] That sentiment recurs often. Milton sometimes accepts and sometimes explicitly rejects the role of ascetic, presenting himself as one who enjoys, in rhythmic balance to arduous study, the refreshment of leisure and refined pleasures.

During his Cambridge years Milton quickly developed what was to be a lifelong antipathy to the university curriculum, which he blamed for producing ignorant statesmen, ministers and citizens.[49] The university is the first of many institutions Milton would castigate, and in some ways the most fundamental, since he consistently identifies sound education as the basis of all lasting reform. In *The Likeliest Means* (1659) he voices a profound disdain, evidently acquired during his college years, for untalented scholarship students who are turned by the university into ignorant ministers. The elitism underlying that disdain is clear, but Milton's standard is merit and dedication rather than social class as such:

> It is well known that the better half of them, and oft times poor and pittiful boyes of no merit or promising hopes that might intitle them to publick provision but thir povertie and the unjust favor of friends, have had the most of thir breeding both at schoole and universitie by schollarships, exhibitions and fellowships at the publick cost. . . . [They] seldom continue there till they have well got through Logic, thir first rudiments; . . . And those theological disputations there held . . . rather perplex and leaven pure doctrin with scholastical trash then enable any minister to the better preaching of the gospel. (*CPW* VII, 314–17)

He began to criticize, satirize, or denounce the university in his Latin academic orations known as the *Prolusions*: the seven that he preserved and published much later (1674) show him challenging the educational establishment on the very occasions of his assigned college exercises. The *Prolusions* are of several types: declamations or exercises in rhetorical persuasion (nos. 1, 2, 3, and 7) usually upholding one side of a topic in debate; disputations or exercises in logical argumentation (4 and 5); and a parody of these kinds (6). In them he often inveighs against the vapid scholasticism of the curriculum, especially the set disputations on Aristotelian topics, commenting, sometimes with pity, often with scorn, on the ill-educated students it produced.

Prolusions I, II, and VI were probably written during Milton's third year, the usual time for sophisters (second- and third-year students) to begin public disputations. In Prolusion VI (July or August, 1628) Milton refers to an earlier oration which he thought would elicit "hostility and dislike" from his fellow students due to "disagreements concerning our studies," but which instead met with "quite unusual applause on every hand" (*CPW* I, 267). That was probably Prolusion I, delivered in college, in which Milton was assigned to defend the affirmative to the question "Whether Day or Night is the Most Excellent," and in which he anticipates audience hostility. He meets it by witty abuse of his opponents – a rhetorical ploy which also reveals his scorn for those fellow students who engage in disputations with only a few shards of learning,

> who lack all intelligence, reasoning power, and sound judgment, and who pride themselves on the ridiculous effervescing froth of their verbiage . . . once they have come to the end of their stock of phrases and platitudes you will find them unable to utter so much as a syllable, as dumb as the frogs of Seriphus. (*CPW* I, 220)

Heaping insults upon those ignorant enough to oppose him might seem an unlikely strategy, but apparently it was successful: the students perhaps enjoyed Milton's flagrant challenge to the first rule of rhetoric drummed into all of them, to seek the good will of the audience.

For his unpromising subject Milton employs the traditional six-part structure – exordium, narration, division, confirmation, refutation, peroration – but relies chiefly on a rhetoric of association, linking Day with classical myths and images that have joyful and heavenly connotations, and Night with those evoking misery, darkness, death, and Hell. This may have been Milton's first major public disputation; the references to midwinter point to delivery in December or January, 1627–8. Milton describes Prolusion II, "On the Harmony of the Spheres," as a brief rhetorical prelude to a disputation on that topic in the Public Schools (the general university assembly), and as part of a day-long "festal train of eloquence" (*CPW* I, 234) – possibly some students' commencement acts for 1628. Milton's speech challenges the hegemony of Aristotle at the university by defending the truth of poetry, specifically the poetic and allegorical truth of the Pythagorean music of the spheres, against Aristotle's literal-minded, "scientific" disparagement of that myth. The tone hovers between seriousness and banter.

By the end of his third undergraduate year Milton had won recognition and respect. On July 2, 1628 he wrote to Gil that he had been invited by one of the fellows of Christ's to supply the comic or parodic verses in Latin customarily printed and distributed at a philosophical disputation for the graduate commencement on July 1. He implies that such an invitation carried some cachet and was not often extended to undergraduates. His verses may have been "Naturam non pati senium" (That Nature does not suffer from Old Age) – perhaps the topic of the day's exercise. In this 19-line poem in dactyllic hexameter, with allusions to Lucretius' *De rerum natura,* Ovid's *Metamorphosis*, and Du Bartas's *Semaine*, Milton aligns himself with Bacon and other modernists committed to science and progress. Emphatically denying the common notion that the world is growing old and decaying, he argues rather that the processes of the universe are as powerful and the earth as fertile as ever.[50] Alternatively, his poem may have been "De Idea Platonica quemadmodum Aristoteles intellexit" (Of the Platonic Ideal Form as understood by Aristotle), a good-natured burlesque in iambic trimeter that he described as "light-minded nonsense." The tone is ironic throughout as Milton assumes the role of a literal-minded Aristotelian challenging the notion of Platonic ideal forms by looking everywhere in vain for the Platonic archetype of man – in the stars, in the moon, in the brain of Jove. Both poems are marked by a sophisticated use of meter, flamboyant rhetoric, and a profusion of mythological allusions.

Milton sent the poem, one of these or some other,[51] to Gil with the letter of July 2, describing him as "the keenest judge of Poetry in general and the most honest judge of mine," and lamenting with some bitterness that he has found no such friend at Cambridge – "almost no intellectual companions here" (*CPW* I, 314). The letter also underscores the danger his ignorant fellow students, most of them prospective ministers, pose to the church that Milton still, presumably, expected to serve in that role:

> There is really hardly any one among us, as far as I know, who, almost completely unskilled and unlearned in Philology and Philosophy alike, does not flutter off to Theology unfledged, quite content to touch that also most lightly, learning barely enough for sticking together a short harangue by any method whatever and patching it with worn-out pieces from various sources – a practice carried far enough to make one fear that the priestly Ignorance of a former age may gradually attack our Clergy. (*CPW* I, 314)

Milton nowhere mentions any Cambridge friend save for Edward King, who is described in the headnote to *Lycidas* as "a learned friend." Though clearly idealized, that poem's description of their life as fellow-poets at Cambridge may suggest some amicable associations,[52] but King's strong royalist and Laudian sympathies make intimacy unlikely, and there are no other signs of it – no exchanges of letters, no other references to King. As the letter to Gil indicates, in his first undergraduate years Milton seems to have been so disenchanted with Cambridge that he did not seek or make close friends. And his often-expressed contempt for his fellow students and the education in which they had a considerable career stake can hardly have endeared him to them.

Nevertheless, in July or August, 1628 Milton was chosen by his fellow students to be "Father" (writer and presenter) of the annual vacation festival at Christ's, replacing the student leader who had suddenly "departed" after a prank that involved cutting off the water supply to the town. The selection of Milton indicates that his peers recognized his ability to produce on demand, in Latin, what that occasion called for: pungent satire, scurrilous puns, and boistrous humor targeted upon college personages and situations. Milton registers surprise and some ironic pleasure in his role and in the "new-found friendliness" of his fellows, but there is irony in his inordinate praise of them as "men eminent for their learning, the very flower as it were of the University" (*CPW* I, 267–8). Also, despite his defense of such recreation as essential "relaxation or breathing space" (I, 271) amid the rigors of study, he shows some ambivalence about this playacting, as he distinguishes sharply between his present role and his true nature: "I have put off and for the moment laid aside my usual habit, and if anything I may say is loose or licentious, put it down to the suggestion, not of my real mind and character, but of the needs of the moment and the genius of the place" (I, 277).

His oration for the festival, Prolusion VI, "Sportive Exercises on Occasion are not inconsistent with philosophical Studies," is an inventive parody and satire of university scholastic exercises.[53] It is in two parts. First a mock oration argues the good uses of play against nay-saying, "crabbed and surly" masters; it mixes jocularity and irony, marshaling a phalanx of witty ancients – Homer, Socrates, Cicero, Pericles, Erasmus's *Praise of Folly*, and even Jove. Then the Prolusion proper deflates that argument with a pastiche of undergraduate humor: vulgar jokes about decaying teeth, burping, farting, foul-smelling breath; jibes at particular students and college officials by name, punning on elements of the festival banquet (Sparkes, Bird, Goose, Furnise); and jests about the collegians' frustrated sexual urges to play the "father" in town. Issues of identity fraught with some anxiety surface in Milton's witty jokes about the irony of his change of title from "Lady" to "Father," a title assuming sexual experience; it is not hard to imagine the taunts that fastened the nickname "The Lady of Christ's" on a slender, refined, defiantly chaste, highly intellectual and artistically inclined adolescent. But he responds here with a bold, passionate, class-inflected but remarkably advanced gender critique. Rejecting what he takes to be his fellow-students' false criteria of masculinity emanating from their low, and lower-class, experience (rough physical labor, brothel-going, denigration of the arts), he constructs himself by contrast as one whose culture and taste in no way undermine his masculinity:

> But, I ask, how does it happen that I have so quickly become a Father? . . . Some of late called me "the Lady." But why do I seem to them too little of a man? . . . It is, I suppose, because I have never brought myself to toss off great bumpers like a prize-fighter, or because my hand has never grown horny with driving a plough, or because I was never a farm hand at seven or laid myself down full length in the midday sun; or last perhaps because I never showed my virility in the way these brothellers do. But I wish they could leave playing the ass as readily as I the woman . . . Hortensius also, the most eminent orator after Cicero, was called by Torquatus Dionysia the lyre-player. His reply was, "I would rather be Dionysia indeed than a man without taste, culture, or urbanity, like you, Torquatus." (*CPW* I, 283–4)

This defensive but trenchant analysis probably reveals more about Milton than do speculations about his possible disabling repressions, unresolved Oedipal complex, or latent homosexuality. He concludes this address with a scoffing reference to the Isle of Ré, recalling the ignominious failure of the English naval expedition under Buckingham to aid the French Huguenots of La Rochelle (July–October, 1627). He thereby extends his ridicule to the king's favorite, who was also the newly elected chancellor of the university.

Then he ends the exercise on his own terms, shifting suddenly from comic Latin prose to serious English verse. In that poem, "At a Vacation Exercise in the Colledge,"[54] he associates himself with Renaissance efforts to promote the vernacular languages. Invoking the English language itself as his Muse, he proclaims an abiding devotion and debt to it that reaches back to infancy and forward to those poems on "graver subjects" that he hopes soon to write: hymns of the heavenly gods, sacred poems of creation and of nature's marvels, and especially epic and romance in the vein of Homer and Spenser – "Kings and Queens and *Hero's* old, / Such as the wise *Demodocus* once told / In solemn Songs at King *Alcinous* feast" (ll. 47–9). His turn to English was hardly exclusive: in the next decade he would write his most accomplished Latin poems. But this is the first of many statements celebrating his native tongue and the English nation, as well as the first statement of his poetics. Rejecting the "new fangled toys" and "triming slight" that delight our "late fantasticks" (the metaphysical style?), Milton proposes to clothe his "naked thoughts" with the "richest Robes, and gay'st attire" the English language can provide (ll. 19–23). The poem embodies this poetics with its graceful Jonsonian couplets and Spenserian imagery and sonorities; at moments it also foreshadows the Miltonic sublimity to come.

Milton preserved only about forty lines in English heroic couplets from the allegorical entertainment he devised for this festival occasion; "the rest was Prose," his 1673 text explains. He himself took the part of the Aristotelian Absolute Being, or Ens, presenting his "sons," the ten Predicaments of Being: Substance, Quantity, Quality, Relation, Place, Time, Position, Possession, Action, and Passion.[55] The poem incorporates a sonorous catalogue of English rivers recalling Spenser's wedding of Thames and Medway and Drayton's *Polyolbion.* This entertainment, suited aptly to its occasion, was useful apprentice work for *Arcades* and *Comus.*

On July 21 Milton accepted an invitation to visit his former tutor Thomas Young, recently returned to England and settled into a living at Stowmarket: "I shall come with pleasure, to enjoy the delights of the season and, no less, the delights of your conversation" (*CPW* I, 315). Their conversations and Milton's reflections that summer no doubt turned often to national events: the king's signing (after long resistance) of the Petition of Right (June 7); the appointment of the Arminian Anglo-Catholic William Laud as Bishop of London (July, 1628) with all that portended for the Romanizing direction of the English church; and the assassination of the king's favorite, Buckingham (August 23). Milton's friend, Alexander Gil, promptly got himself into deep trouble for toasting the assassination and writing brazenly injudicious verses that termed Buckingham a Ganymede to King James and King Charles, "the old fool and the young one." In November the Court of Star Chamber degraded Gil from his ministry and his Oxford degrees, fined him £2,000, and sentenced him to lose both his ears. At the petition of his father and powerful friends the physical mutilation was remitted, but Gil remained in prison for over two years.[56] This episode brought home to Milton the costs of antimonarchical satire, and surely reinforced his growing antipathy for the Stuart court.

Prolusion III, "An Attack on the Scholastic Philosophy," was most likely delivered in the Public Schools of the university sometime during Milton's final academic year, 1628–9. The topic may have been set and Milton assigned the negative, but the vehemence with which he attacked the chief business of Cambridge undergraduate education may point to the basis of his earlier trouble with Chappell, that renowned controversialist. Now, in the wake of his role in the recent vacation festivities, he presented himself as spokesman for a (no longer hostile) student audience. Directly challenging the sterile scholasticism of the academic establishment with its enthronement of Aristotle as primary authority in all areas, he describes his own intense boredom with it as an index of common student experience:

> If I can at all judge your feelings by my own, what pleasure can there possibly be in the petty disputations of sour old men. . . . Many a time, when the duty of tracing out these petty subtleties for a while has been laid upon me, when my mind has been dulled and my sight blurred by continued reading . . . how often have I wished that instead of having these fooleries forced upon me, I had been set to clean out the stable of Augeas again. (*CPW* I, 241–2)

Emphasizing his own case, he underscores the antipathy between these arid studies and those fostered by the Muses:

> Believe me, my learned friends, when I go through these empty quibbles as I often must, against my will, it seems to me as if I were forcing my way through rough and rocky wastes, desolate wildernesses, and precipitous mountain gorges. And so it is not likely that the dainty and elegant Muses preside over these ragged and tattered studies, or consent to be the patrons of their maudlin partisans. (*CPW* I, 243)

His scorn breaks through as he challenges his fellow students to recognize how they are being duped and blighted by this curriculum:

> The supreme result of all this earnest labour is to make you a more finished fool and cleverer contriver of conceits, and to endow you with a more expert ignorance: and no wonder, since all these problems at which you have been working in such torment and anxiety have no existence in reality at all, but like unreal ghosts and phantoms without substance obsess minds already disordered and empty of all true wisdom. (*CPW* I, 245)

Invoking the Ciceronean triad – to delight, instruct, and persuade – he argues that Scholastic philosophy cannot delight because its "dry and lifeless" style is tedious and boring; it cannot instruct because its topics are empty quibbles with "no existence in reality at all" and its arguments merely "shed deep darkness over the whole question"; and it has no power to "incite to noble acts" (*CPW* I, 241–6). Then, turning from invective to praise, he exalts and passionately urges study of the humanistic subjects that do fulfill those criteria: "divine poetry" which raises the soul aloft to heaven, rhetoric, which "captivates the minds of men," and history, which evokes tears and mournful joy – that last surely evoking in the audience memories of the Dorislaus affair. He also commends geography, natural science of all sorts, astronomy, and moral philosophy. His parting ironic advice to his hearers – to follow Aristotle "who is already your delight" (*CPW* I, 247) – taunts them for making him their only authority, but also points them to all the subjects in his corpus that are ignored in a curriculum focused on the *Organon*.

Some part of that final academic year was given over to meeting degree requirements. Prolusions IV and V, which defend highly technical theses based on Scholastic physics and metaphysics, may have been the two Responsions required for Milton's Baccalaureate degree. These are logical disputations on topics of the kind Milton denounced in Prolusion III and burlesqued in "De Idea Platonica"; and they are remarkable for the brio and skill with which Milton makes these exercises display their own sterility even as he performs them. Milton's polemic bent and resistance to authority are by now well honed. Prolusion IV, "In the Destruction of any Substance there can be no Resolution into First Matter," was delivered in the college.[57] In it, Milton cites numerous authorities, lists contradictory opinions, and makes subtle distinctions, intermixing them with complaints about the confusion and boredom all this is causing him and his audience. He also places the argument proper within an ironic frame allegorizing the combat of Truth and Error; Truth at length flies to Heaven leaving Error to control the schools, and Milton wittily aligns himself with the flight of Truth as he offers to "beat a retreat" so as "to spare you boredom" (*CPW* I, 256). Prolusion V, "There are no Partial Forms in an Animal in Addition to the Whole," was delivered in the Public Schools. In it Milton offers ironically to cite "weightiest authorities; for it is not to be expected that I should add anything of my own" (*CPW* I, 259). But he soon breaks off his list of authorities and his argument, surely surprising his audience by devoting half his speech to Roman history (with Dorislaus fresh in memory) and to another allegory of the struggle of Truth and Error, casting himself as a warrior for Truth.

During Lent term Milton supplicated for his degree and was awarded it on March 26, 1629, after signing the three required Articles of Religion: that the king is the only head of the church in England, that the *Book of Common Prayer* is lawful to use, and that the Thirty-nine Articles contain nothing contrary to the Word of God.[58] Evidently he had no serious objection to that gesture. His was the fourth name on the university honors list of twenty-four undergraduates in a graduating class of 259, and the first from his college. The Oslow portrait (plate 3), generally assumed to be of Milton at about this time, emphasizes the subject's large serious eyes and delicate features. He looks years younger than the age inscribed, "21."[59]

While working toward his Master of Arts degree (1629–32) Milton was not obliged to maintain strict residency requirements, and we cannot be sure where he was for much of that time. His academic responsibilities were simply to continue his studies, perhaps dispute on occasion with sophisters, and prepare for the Master's degree "Acts." He probably held open the option of preparing for the ministry, but he did not take orders as a deacon when he became eligible at age 23, nor yet when he took his degree a year later.

In April, 1629, he wrote Elegy V, "In Adventum Veris" (On the Approach of Spring), his most creative appropriation of Ovid and the most sensual of his elegies.[60] It is one of his finest Latin poems and, along with Elegy VI, brings his experiments with Ovidian elegy to a fitting climax. Elegy V distills classical myths and Latin and neo-Latin poetry about springtime and love into a veritable hymn to fertility.[61] It combines elegiac couplets and an elegiac poet's welcome to spring with a hymnic structure invoking and responding to Apollo as god of nature, of lovemaking, and of poets, modeled on Callimachus's "Hymn to Apollo" and its imitators.[62] Milton celebrates in lush, exuberant language the vibrant erotic desire pulsating through all nature with the coming of spring, and the potent sexual energies unleashed in the earth itself, in the creatures, in all the pagan deities, and in young men and women stirred to love. A central image is the passion of the earth for the sun:

> The reviving earth throws off her hated old age and craves thy embraces, O Phoebus. She craves them and she is worthy of them; for what is lovelier than she as she voluptuously bares her fertile breast and breathes the perfume of Arabian harvests and pours sweet spices and scent of Paphian roses from her lovely lips? . . . the wanton earth breathes out her passion, and her thronging children follow hard after her example.[63]

The poem is all exuberant celebration: there is no moralizing, no *carpe diem* advice. It alludes approvingly to the erotic myths of various pagan gods – Jove, Pan, Venus, the satyrs – and prays for their continued presence: "Long may every grove possess its deities!" (l. 133). Milton's Muse is awakened by all this to new ecstasy of song, the renewal of his own creative powers – "this madness and this sacred ecstasy" – such that he joins his voice with the nightingale to welcome spring and invoke Apollo. But he does not imagine himself sharing in the general sexual frenzy.

He may have attended Commencement exercises on July 7, 1629 to see Charles Diodati incorporated Master of Arts[64] and to enjoy a visit with his friend. Two undated Greek letters from Diodati to Milton may have been written that summer or autumn; the use of Greek ostentatiously displays the learning of both.[65] One urges Milton to follow through with a projected outing, which is to be filled with the delights of nature – "the air and the sun and the river, and trees and little birds and earth and men will laugh and dance with us" – and especially with the joys of "philosophical and learned conversation" (*CPW* I, 336). The other, written from someplace in the country, reports Diodati's pleasure in nature and in holiday festivities, but also his regrettable lack of "some noble soul skilled in conversation . . . a good companion, learned and initiate" – by implication, Milton. He ends with jesting advice to Milton to relax his unremitting studies:

> But you, extraordinary man, why do you despise the gifts of nature? Why such inexcusable perseverance, bending over books and studies day and night? Live, laugh, enjoy your youth and the hours, and stop reading the serious, the light, and the indolent works of ancient wise men, wearing yourself out the while. I, who in all other things am your inferior, in this one thing, in knowing the proper limit of labor, both seem to myself, and am, your better. Farewell, and be merry, but not in the manner of Sardanapalus in Soli. (*CPW* I, 337)

The alllusion pointedly separates the merry pleasures he urges from the debauchery and sodomy associated with the Assyrian king. Here, typically, these friends make their differences in temperament and lifestyle a matter of good-natured jest. Each regards himself and his friend as poet and scholar, but Diodati is cast by both as a merry, carefree, pleasure-loving extrovert (like l'Allegro), and Milton as a sober, bookish recluse (like il Penseroso). Their exchanges are filled with warm affection, intimacy of spirit, and eager anticipations of reunions, with some overtones of homoeroticism – most likely unacknowledged as such by either one.[66] We have no letters in prose from Milton to Diodati, but Milton's verse letters to him contrast their lifestyles and their poetry in similar terms; these friends no doubt exchanged several such letters, now lost, and met as occasion offered.

Milton may have been at Cambridge the following September for the visit of the new chancellor, Henry Rich, Earl of Holland (elected after Buckingham's assassination), at which time an honorary Master of Arts was awarded to Peter Paul Rubens and several Latin comedies were performed, among them Philip Stubbes's *Fraus Honesta* (The Honest Fraud). In December, 1629 Milton was in London, where he purchased a copy of Giovanni della Casa's sonnets.[67] He also received a letter and poems (now lost) from Diodati, who was evidently celebrating Christmas in Cheshire. The heading of Milton's verse letter, Elegy VI, sent as a response, explains these circumstances:

> To Charles Diodati, staying in the country. Who, when he wrote on the thirteenth of December, begging that his verses might be excused if they were not so good as usual, pled that in the midst of the festivities with which he had been received by his friends, he was not able to cultivate the Muses very prosperously. He had this answer.[68]

Milton's poem wittily sets his own holiday asceticism against Diodati's indulgence:

> On an empty stomach I send you a wish for the good health of which you, with a full one, may perhaps feel the lack. . . . You would like to be informed by a song how I return your love and how fond I am of you. Believe me, you can hardly learn it from this song, for my love is not confined by narrow meters and it is too sound to use the lame feet of elegy. (ll. 1–8)[69]

The tone is urbane and playful as Milton analyzes their different modes of life and poetry, associating Diodati's festive life with the light elegy, and his own present abstemious life with epic or sacred subjects.

Elegy VI is a counterstatement to Elegy V, replaying some of its motifs in another key: here the festivities, banquets, wine, dance, love, and song of "hilarious December" counter nature's erotic pleasures in springtime, and the denizens of the springtime groves are replaced by patrons of winter festivals. Elegy VI also contrasts two kinds of poetry and the lifestyles appropriate to each – staging, it might seem, a young poet's "Hercules choice." Milton identifies Diodati with the festive life and elegiac verse, and locates himself with epic and hymnic poets – Homer, Tiresias, Linus, Orpheus – whose high subjects require an ascetic and chaste life. The gay elegy and the epic (or the lofty literary hymn) he identifies as countergenres, arising from and expressive of contrary modes of life:

> For many of the gods patronize the gay elegy and she calls whom she will to her measures. . . . For such poets, then, grand banquets are allowable and frequent potations of old wine. But he whose theme is wars and heaven under Jupiter in his prime, and pious heroes and chieftains half-divine, and he who sings now of the sacred counsels of the gods on high, and now of the infernal realms where the fierce dog howls, let him live sparingly, like the Samian teacher, and let herbs furnish his innocent diet. . . . Beyond this, his youth must be innocent of crimes and chaste, his conduct irreproachable and his hands stainless. His character should be like yours, O Priest, when, glorious with sacred vestments and lustral water, you arise to go into the presence of the angry deities. . . . For truly, the bard is sacred to the gods and is their priest. His hidden heart and his lips alike breathe out Jove. (ll. 49–78)[70]

He ends by describing his Nativity Ode as an example of the latter kind, mixing epic, hymnic, and pastoral topics:

> If you will know what I am doing (if only you think it of any importance to know whether I am doing anything) – I am singing the heaven-descended King, the bringer of peace, and the blessed times promised in the sacred books – the infant cries of our God and his stabling under a mean roof who, with his Father, governs the realms above. I am singing the starry sky and the hosts that sang high in air, and the gods that were suddenly destroyed in their own shrines. (ll. 81–6)[71]

Milton is serious about reporting his high poetic aspirations and his ode *On the Morning of Christ's Nativity* as the first major realization of them. Terming it his gift "for the birthday of Christ" written at daybreak on Christmas morning, he no doubt saw special significance in this poem's composition just after his own important twenty-first birthday (December 9, 1629). Despite their differences in temperament, again underscored in the parenthetical comment alluding to Diodati's more frivolous occupations, Milton expects his soulmate to understand him very well – his jests, his indirections, his reach toward bardic, prophetic poetry, and the remarkable achievement his Nativity poem is. Elegy VI finds place for the lower as well as the higher poetic kinds, and the playful tone precludes reading it as Milton's decisive rejection of lighter subjects. But Milton here reaffirms in stronger terms than in the "Vacation Exercise" his desire to attempt the highest subjects, and to take on the role of bardic Poet–Priest. The Nativity Ode, Milton's first major poem, is discussed later in this chapter: its conception and technique, its reach toward prophetic poetry, and its reformist politics, adumbrated especially in the long catalogue of pagan gods expelled from their shrines, registering Puritan anxiety in 1629 about the "papist idolatry" fostered by Laud.

Milton's promise in Elegy VI to recite his strains to Diodati suggests that they met sometime that winter, before Diodati left for Geneva where he studied theology from April 16, 1630 to (at least) September 15, 1631.[72] Buoyed by his impressive achievement in the Nativity Ode, Milton undertook a companion poem, "The Passion," probably during the Lenten season of 1630: Good Friday that year fell on March 26. He used the same stanza as in the "Proem" to the Nativity Ode, and explicitly invited comparison and contrast: "Erewhile" his Muse joined with angels to celebrate Christ's birth with "Ethereal mirth"; now he will tune his song "to sorrow" to treat his Passion (ll. 1–8). Rejecting the epic mode of Vida's *Christiad,* he chose the "softer" strings of funeral elegy. His earlier poems in this genre did well enough for a bishop and a university official, but an elegy on Christ's passion and death demands convincing expressions of profound emotion which Milton could not produce. His Protestant imagination was not stirred by the Passion, and he found no way in elegy, as he had in the Nativity ode, to move from the personal and local to the universal. So his conceits become ever more extravagant and the text becomes painfully self-referential – a poem about Milton trying to work up the proper emotions to write a Passion poem: "I tune my song," "my Harpe," "my *Phoebus,*" "my roving vers," "Me softer airs befit," "Befriend me night," "my flatter'd fancy," "my sorrows," "my tears," "My spirit," "my soul in holy vision," "Mine eye," "my feeble hands," "My plaining vers," and again, "my tears," "my sorrows." After eight stanzas he broke off, but published the fragment both in 1645 and 1673, with an explanation staging his own failure: "This Subject the Author finding to be above the yeers he had, when he wrote it, and nothing satisfi'd with what was begun, left it unfinisht."[73] This experience – perhaps the first time Milton fell so far short of meeting the demands of his poetic subject – evidently led him to a crucial insight that he wished to mark formally, for himself and others. This failure is probably the "frustration" he alludes to later in the *Apology*, as confirming his belief that maturity and experience of life are needed to treat the highest subjects. He turns next to secular subjects, but not, I think, from acute distress over this failure or disabling doubts about the role of prophet–poet he claimed in the Nativity ode.[74] He could, after all, reasonably hope to achieve the requisite maturity in due course.

On May 20, 1630 Milton answered a letter from Alexander Gil inviting criticism of an accompanying Latin poem, apparently *In Silvam-Ducis*, a long celebration of Protestant Henry of Nassau's capture of Hertogenbosch (September, 1629).[75] Milton ends his high praise of that poem – "really great Verses, everywhere redolent both of truly Poetical Majesty and Virgilian genius" – with the hope that Gil might soon have cause to celebrate "our own affairs, at last more fortunate" (*CPW* I, 315–17). With that wish, Milton associates himself explicitly with reformists urging greater English militancy in the international Protestant cause. It responds to a spate of recent discouraging events: parliament had been dismissed on March 4, 1629, beginning what was to become Charles's 11-year personal rule. Laud was clearly in control of the nation's ecclesiastical policy, directing it toward Arminianism and Catholic ceremony. The king continued lukewarm in supporting the embattled European Protestants in the Thirty Years War, and his ongoing negotiations with Spain for the return of the Palatinate were an exercise in futility.

That spring brought another terrible visitation of plague to London and Cambridge. By the end of April most of the colleges were formally closed and all university exercises adjourned.[76] While the university was closed Milton probably lived in the London suburb of Hammersmith, where his father had recently taken up residence.[77] Spending spring and summer in a rural retreat prompted Milton's return to familiar poetic topics – springtime, love, death – but now in other genres and styles. The lighthearted English song "On May Morning" is an aubade with close affinities to Elizabethan lyricists and the lyric Jonson. May, personified as a girl in a Mayday processional dance led by Venus, embodies "Mirth and youth and warm desire," and the poet, as spokesman for all nature, welcomes her with an elegant, carefully crafted song: two quatrains of five-stress and four-stress lines respectively, and a final couplet. Also, Milton's first English sonnet, "O Nightingale," has affinities with Nightingale sonnets in Italian, with medieval debates between the nightingale as harbinger of love and the cuckoo as emblem of infidelity, and also with the celebration of spring in Elegy V.[78] Begging to hear the nightingale's song, the speaker defines himself in Petrarchan terms as both lover and poet: "Whether the Muse, or Love call thee his mate, / Both them I serve, and of their train am I." As he did in Elegy V and will often do again, Milton makes the nightingale a multivalent symbol for the poet.

A Petrarchan mini-sonnet sequence in Italian – two sonnets, a one-stanza canzone or song, then three more sonnets may also date from this time.[79] In it Milton stages another love experience which may be wholly literary, although the sonnet lady's name (Emilia) and the specific characteristics ascribed to her – black eyes, multilingualism, a ravishing singing voice – suggest an actual person, possibly a kinswoman or family friend of Diodati's to whom Milton was attracted, or to whom he wished to pay a graceful compliment. The fact that the fourth sonnet is addressed to Diodati strengthens that assumption.[80] Whether or not such a lady urged him to write love sonnets in Italian as he claims in the "Canzone," the more important reason for that language was surely literary: having mastered the Ovidian love elegy in Latin, he evidently decided to try out the other major mode of love poetry in the European tradition in *its* original language, which he can now use accurately and flexibly, though with occasional archaisms. Sonnet IV stages a formal opposition in genre and attitude to the Elegies, as the speaker repudiates his former praises of English beauties and his former defiance of love, acknowledging that he is now captivated by this foreign dark beauty. The sequence is indebted to Petrarch, Tasso, and Bembo, but especially to Giovanni della Casa (whose sonnets Milton purchased the previous December) for the pervasive use of parallelism, balance, and antithesis and for a structure in which the rhetorical argument plays off against the sonnet form.[81] The rhyme scheme follows the Italian sonnet paradigm, though with a concluding couplet (abba abba cdcdee).

The sequence employs familiar Petrarchan topics: the lady's name, Emilia, is revealed cryptically by reference to that region of Italy; her beauty and "high virtue" are "the arrows and bows of love"; potent fire flashes from her eyes which are like suns; and the humble, devoted lover sighs painful sighs and suffers from love's incurable dart. But this speaker resists and redefines conventional Petrarchan roles, revising Petrarch as he did Ovid. His sonnet lady is not coy or reserved or forbidding, but "gentle" and gracious; her eyes and hair are alien black, not blue and gold; and she is no silent object of adoration but charms her lover with bilingual speech and enthralling songs. Also, this lover–poet carefully avoids Petrarchan subjection to the bonds of Cupid and the lady's power. His is no all-encompassing Petrarchan passion: only at a single point is his heart found "less unyielding" to love's dart. Moreover, Emilia is not his Muse, like Petrarch's Laura and other sonnet-ladies; to the contrary, the Italian love poetry she inspires diverts him from the greater poetic achievements in English which promise, his friends remind him, an "immortal guerdon" of fame (the Canzone). More surprising still, the last sonnet (VI) is a curious self-blason, praising the speaker's own moral virtues and poetic aspirations – "the mind's gifts, high courage, and the sounding lyre and the Muses"[82] – rather than the physical beauties of the lady. In this Petrarchan staging of desire, the Miltonic speaker retains his autonomy and insists on his own virtue and worth.

In August 1630 Milton's sister Anne Phillips gave birth to the son, Edward, who was to become his uncle's pupil, amanuensis, and biographer (*LR* I, 221). The plague had abated in Cambridge by October, but when Joseph Mede returned to Christ's shortly before October 20 he found "neither scholar nor fellow returned but Mr. Tovey only." Formal exercises were deferred to December 16.[83] If Milton returned in late autumn he would have found Edward King, a new A.B. just 18 years old, appointed by royal mandate to a vacated fellowship. King's father and elder brother were important administrators in Ireland and his godfather was an Irish bishop. Milton had no such court patronage or family influence, and statutes mandating geographical distribution of the fellows made him technically ineligible for this fellowship. He probably had few if any regrets, given his disenchantment with university education and his growing disinclination to the usual fellowship requirements of ordination and celibacy. But, as with Charles Diodati, he again had to witness the very visible success of another bright young man some years his junior. Late that year he would have received the good news of Alexander Gil's full pardon (November 30).

Milton affixed the date 1630 to his first published poem, the 16-line "Epitaph on the admirable Dramatick Poet, W. Shakespeare," for the 1632 Second Folio of Shakespeare's plays.[84] We do not know the intermediary who brought the as yet unknown Milton to the attention of the publishers: possibly it came about through his father's associations in musical or theatrical circles (he was a trustee of Blackfriars Theatre). Milton's poem, along with one other added in the new edition, is unsigned; the rest carry authors' names or initials. The anonymity may testify to Milton's continuing sense of unreadiness, to an unease shared with many English gentlemen about writing for the print marketplace, or to a desire to make his formal public debut with some more impressive poem or volume of poetry.[85] In style and form – iambic pentameter couplets that combine formality with restrained feeling – this epitaph shows some debt to Jonson, especially to Jonson's own tribute to Shakespeare, reprinted in this edition. Both poems apostrophize Shakespeare and deliver critical judgments. Also, several elements of conception and diction – the "piled Stones" as opposed to living works, and especially the Spenserian archaism, "Starypointing *Pyramid*" – echo an epitaph, circulating in manuscript, that was attributed to Shakespeare himself in the seventeenth century.[86] Milton's tribute to Shakespeare involved, it seems, his deft imitation of a supposed Shakespeare poem. But Milton's poem reworks the conventional conceit that a poet's best monument is his works, making Shakespeare's readers his true "live-long Monument": their wonder and astonishment turn them to "Marble with too much conceiving."[87] Building on his supposed imitation of Shakespeare in this poem, Milton explicitly claims the Bard as his model, describing him as "my Shakespeare" and his poetry as "Delphic," inspired. But he also calls anxious attention to Shakespeare's "easy numbers," which put to shame the "slow-endeavoring art" Milton associates with himself.

For much of Lent and Easter terms, 1631, Milton was almost certainly in Cambridge. His brother Christopher was admitted to Christ's on February 15 (*LR* I, 227); Milton probably helped him settle in and influenced his choice of Tovey as tutor. Milton's poems of these months are Cambridge poems. Two lighthearted, whimsical English epitaphs "On the University Carrier" are his anonymous contributions to the spate of collegiate versifying prompted by the death of Hobson the carrier on January 1, 1631, at almost 86 years of age.[88] Milton used the same meter as the Shakespeare tribute for both epitaphs, which turn on the conceit that Hobson died from inactivity forced on him by the plague. In the first poem Death, unable to catch Hobson while he drove his cart, finds him at home and, like a kindly chamberlain, settles him down for the night. The second is more outrageously witty, filled with puns, paradoxes, and wordplay: "Too long vacation hastned on his term" (l. 14); "One Carrier put down to make six bearers" (l. 20); "Ease was his chief disease" (l. 21); "his wain was his increase" (l. 32). The facetious and irreverent tone of these poems – modified by some warmth of feeling for the old man – is geared to a student audience, but the poems found a much wider audience in manuscript and print anthologies.[89]

Another English poem of that year, Milton's 75-line "Epitaph on the Marchioness of *Winchester*" honors Jane Paulet, eldest daughter of Thomas, Viscount Savage of Cheshire, wife of the fifth marquess, and kinswoman of the university chancellor. She died on April 15, 1631 at age 23, following a stillbirth but from an infection caused by lancing an abcess in her cheek. Ben Jonson, William Davanant, and several other poets produced elegies for her, and Milton's reference to "som Flowers, and som Bays / . . . Sent thee from the banks of *Came*" (ll. 57–9) suggests that a university miscellany was projected. Milton probably intended this poem to call his gifts to the attention of likely aristocratic patrons. If he had qualms about celebrating the wife of a prominent Roman Catholic, they may have been quieted by rumors that "she was inclining to become a Protestant."[90] This poem tries on another Jonsonian style: octo- and heptasyllabic couplets, but with complex shifts between iambic and trochaic rhythms.[91] Though longer than most epitaphs, it begins conventionally by seeming to voice the inscription on the tombstone: "This rich Marble doth enterr / The honor'd Wife of *Winchester,* / A Viscount's daughter, an Earls heir." The speaker then describes the Marchioness, emphasizing the pathos of her early death and that of her stillborn infant: Atropos came instead of Lucina, "And with remorseles cruelty, / Spoil'd at once both fruit and tree" (ll. 29–30). Then he addresses her in heaven, placed with Rachel who also died in childbed; this is apparently Milton's first allusion to Dante, who (for the same reason) located Beatrice with Rachel in the third rank of the celestial rose.[92]

In Prolusion VII Milton indicates that he spent the summer of 1631 in some delightful village that greatly stimulated his intellectual and poetic growth – probably Hammersmith, the "country place" that his father moved to permanently at about this time.[93] The brilliantly inventive companion poems *L'Allegro* and *Il Penseroso* were most likely the poetic fruits of that summer.[94] These delightful poems (discussed in the second section of this chapter) appear to turn aside from the lofty purposes of the Nativity ode, but in fact they stage a choice of life and literary kinds, and also seek to reclaim some kinds of art and poetry from what Milton saw as their degraded uses as court poetry and in Laudian worship. These months also brought family changes. February, 1631, saw the death of the niece Elizabeth whose prospective birth Milton had heralded in the "Fair Infant." In August Milton's brother-in-law (Anne's husband Edward Phillips) died and about two months later John Phillips, the other nephew who was to be Milton's pupil, was born. On January 5, 1632, Anne married Thomas Agar, a friend of her first husband and his successor as deputy clerk of the crown in the Court of Chancery.[95] Milton may have attended the wedding.

In the final year of his academic career (1631–2) Milton spent some time at Cambridge meeting the formal requirements for his Master of Arts degree, which had been reduced in practice to one or two Responsions and a single College Oration. That year he again passed up an opportunity to celebrate a royal birth (Princess Mary) and a royal visit. If he was in Cambridge in March, he may have seen King Charles and Queen Henrietta Maria and viewed the two English comedies presented for their entertainment, *The Rival Friends* by Peter Hausted of Queen's (a crashing failure), and *The Jealous Lovers* by Thomas Randolph of Trinity (a great success). And he was surely shocked by the news of Vice-Chancellor Butts's suicide on Easter Sunday, 1632; Butts was said to be despondent over the king's criticism of his use of funds, and over the court's dislike of Hausted's comedy which he had sponsored.[96] In 1642 Milton spoke harshly of collegiate playacting, countering charges that he attended theaters in London by denouncing the authorized but demeaning plays performed at the university by ordained or prospective ministers. He admits attending those, sometimes, but only as a scoffing critic:

> In the Colleges [they] . . . have bin seene so oft upon the Stage writhing and unboning their Clergie limmes to all the antick and dishonest gestures of Trinculo's, Buffons, and Bawds; . . . they thought themselves gallant men, and I thought them fools, they made sport, and I laught, they mispronounc't, and I mislik't, and to make up the *atticisme*, they were out, and I hist. . . . If it be unlawfull to sit and behold a mercenary Comedian personating that which is least unseemely for a hireling to doe, how much more blamefull is it to indure the sight of as vile things acted by persons either enter'd, or presently to enter into the ministery. (*Apology, CPW* I, 887–8)

Whether or not this passage represents Milton's attitude toward dramatic productions while at Cambridge, clearly he came to regard much playacting as degraded and unworthy recreation. Yet even in the year Puritans closed the theaters, Milton distanced himself with a subjunctive – "if" – from the ordinance making stage plays unlawful.

Milton's seventh and most elaborate prolusion (1632?), "Learning brings more Blessings to Men than Ignorance," was presumably his Masters' oration; he defended the title proposition in the college chapel for perhaps an hour. Summing up his Cambridge experiences and looking forward, he presented himself before the audience of students and fellows as scholar and poet, not prospective clergyman.

The oration reprises many Miltonic themes – denunciation of the university and its curriculum, ardor for learning, praise of history and natural history – elaborating them in Platonic and Baconian terms "at much greater length than is customary in this place" (*CPW* I, 306).

Combining critique and counsel with extraordinary personal testimony, he builds his case for learning on its necessity to happiness, eternal and temporal: without it we cannot contemplate rightly the creation or the Creator, nor establish states on a firm foundation, nor preserve religion and piety which the Dark Ages almost extinguished. Expressing a desire to gain a "thorough knowledge of all the arts and sciences . . . by long and concentrated study," he identifies the university itself as the chief hindrance to that goal because of "the loss of time caused by these constant interruptions," i.e. the required disputations. In sweeping terms he denounces the folly and the barbarous language scholastic disputation has introduced into all branches of study, grammar, rhetoric, logic, mathematics, and especially jurisprudence, which suffers especially from "a jargon which one might well take for some Red Indian dialect, or even no human speech at all" (*CPW* I, 288–301). With implicit reference to himself as model, he urges his hearers "from our childhood onward" to allot to every day "its lesson and diligent study" and to tame the "first impulses of headstrong youth" by reason and temperance, assuring them that such practices, together with a reformed education directed to what is useful, would make learning easy. His eloquent paean to learning of all kinds as affording the keenest of pleasures is both rhetorically persuasive and profoundly self-revelatory:

> What a thing it is to grasp the nature of the whole firmament and of its stars. . . . Besides this, what delight it affords to the mind to take its flight through the history and geography of every nation and to observe the changes in the conditions of kingdoms, races, cities, and peoples, to the increase of wisdom and righteousness. This, my hearers, is to live in every period of the world's history, and to be as it were coeval with time itself. . . . I pass over a pleasure with which none can compare – to be the oracle of many nations, to find one's home regarded as a kind of temple, to be a man whom kings and states invite to come to them. . . . These are the rewards of study. (*CPW* I, 295–7)

Revealingly, Milton here associates youthful sexual activity with contamination, insisting on the need to keep "the divine vigour of our minds unstained and uncontaminated by any impurity or pollution" (*CPW* I, 300). He uses Petrarchan language to describe, not a mistress, but his "deepest desire," learning:

> Now I may at any rate be permitted to sing the praises of Learning, from whose embrace I have been torn, and as it were assuage my longing for the absent beloved by speaking of her . . . for who would regard it as an interruption when he is called upon to praise or defend the object of his affection, his admiration, and his deepest desire. (*CPW* I, 290)

Milton took some pride in having preserved his virginity at Cambridge, motivated by religious duty and the high idealism he voiced in the *Apology*.[97] Some of his poems (Elegies I and VII, and the Italian sonnets) had staged an awareness and imagination of erotic impulses not acted upon, and Prolusions VI and VII defend such deferral. In this valediction to Cambridge, Milton puts on hold the problem of the place of love and sex in his life as scholar and poet. He does, however, envisage other special pleasures for the scholar, notably friendship – with reference, it seems, to his own experience with a few but choice friends:

> The chief part of human happiness is derived from the society of one's fellows and the formation of friendships. . . . I admit that the man who is almost entirely absorbed and immersed in study . . . is less expert in the nicer formalities of social life. But if such a man once forms a worthy and congenial friendship, there is none who cultivates it more assiduously. For what can we imagine more delightful and happy than those conversations of learned and wise men. (*CPW* I, 295)

If Milton could not yet attain to the "experience and practice" – and inspiration – he thought needful for high poetry, he could at least gain the necessary learning. Prolusion VII makes clear that he expected to do so, imagining for himself a delightful life of "cultured and liberal leisure" chiefly devoted to study. Drawing a sharp contrast with the futile university regimen, he insists on the importance of leisure, self-directed study, solitude, and pleasure for the "development and well-being of the mind" and the growth of a poet, citing his own recent experience as evidence:

> I can myself call to witness the woods and rivers and the beloved village elms, under whose shade I enjoyed in the summer just passed (if I may tell the secrets of goddesses) such sweet intercourse with the Muses, as I still remember with delight. There I too, amid rural scenes and woodland solitudes, felt that I had enjoyed a season of growth in a life of seclusion. (*CPW* I, 289)

He means to enjoy again the solitude he had come increasingly to value as the proper milieu for both scholarship and poetry.[98] In that retirement he will immerse himself in all the areas of learning Cambridge ignored, and court the Muses.

During Lent term Milton supplicated for his Masters' degree. To receive it he had again to subscribe to the three Articles of Religion, and he was still willing to do so.[99] He graduated Master of Arts *cum laude* at the commencement of July 3, 1632, one of 207 Bachelors from the several colleges, and the first of the 27 students from Christ's to sign the graduation book – probably a recognition of his standing. In the *Second Defence* (1654) he insists (answering a libellous accusation and eliding his earlier problems) that he left Cambridge with the general respect of the college and the regret of the fellows:

> There, untouched by any reproach, in the good graces of all upright men, for seven years I devoted myself to the traditional disciplines and liberal arts, until I had attained the degree of Master, as it is called, *cum laude*. Then . . . of my own free will I returned home, to the regret of most of the fellows of the college, who bestowed on me no little honor. (*CPW* IV.1, 613)

The new masters had to swear to continue their "regency" or active studies in the university for five additional years, though normally only those holding fellowships did so. Milton instead began a five-year "regency" of private studies at home.

"Early Song"

On the Morning of Christ's Nativity (December, 1629) is Milton's first major poem, but already it displays elements that remain constants in Milton's poetry: allusiveness, revisionism, mixture of genres, stunning originality, cosmic scope, prophetic voice. Its theme is the Incarnation and its meaning to humankind, nature, and the entire cosmos. There are two parts. A four stanza Proem (six lines of iambic pentameter and a concluding alexandrine) imitates verse forms in Chaucer, Spenser, and Milton's own "Fair Infant." The speaker is both humble and audacious. Placing himself with the shepherds who came first to the manger, he offers the hymn that follows as his gift to the infant Christ, terming it a "humble ode," a pastoral.[100] But he also titles it a hymn, associating it with the angelic hymns at the Nativity and also with the messianic prophecies of Isaiah: "And joyn thy voice unto the Angel Quire, / From out his secret Altar toucht with hallow'd fire" (ll. 27–8).[101] With these lines Milton formally assumes the role of prophet–poet.

In the "Hymn" proper he invents, with striking success, a strophe for the English ode: eight-line stanzas with lines of varying lengths (6 6 10 6 6 10 8 12), culminating in a stately alexandrine; and an intricate, interlaced rhyme scheme (aabccbdd).[102] It looks back to various exemplars of the high lyric: Homeric hymns and Pindaric odes to Apollo; their neo-Latin imitators Marullo and Pontano; and their Christian counterparts, the literary hymns of Prudentius, Minturno, Mantuan, and Spenser.[103] There are many Spenserian elements: allegorical personifications, the masque-like descent of the "meek-eyd Peace," and onomatopoeia – descriptions of the old serpent who "Swindges the scaly Horrour of his foulded tail" (l. 172) and of the Last Judgment at which "The wakefull trump of doom must thunder through the deep" (l. 156). As a pastoral the poem revises Virgil's Fourth Eclogue, which celebrated (probably) the birth of the Roman consul Pollio's son as the beginning of a new Golden Age.[104] Milton celebrates the birth of the Messiah who will restore the true Golden Age at the Millennium.

The Nativity Ode also offers a counterstatement, an alternative vision, to Milton's own Elegy V: a winter poem set against that spring poem; a celebration of the incarnate Christian God against that celebration of Apollo and the pagan deities; an anticipated but deferred restoration of the Golden Age against that celebration of the annual springtime renewal of Nature. Some topics are directly contrasted. In Elegy V the earth delights in the embraces of the Sun-God; in the Nativity Ode she can no longer "wanton with the Sun her lusty Paramour" (l. 36). In Elegy V the poet urges the classical gods to remain in their forest homes; in the Nativity ode he celebrates the expulsion of all the pagan gods from all their shrines. The effect is not to repudiate the earlier poem but to re-view its classical ethos from a "higher" Christian perspective. This poem also sets up a contrast to the "Fair Infant" funeral ode, underscored by the use of the same stanzaic form in the Proem. That poem treats the death, this one the birth, of a fair infant in winter; that infant in figure, this one in truth, is able to slake God's wrath for sin; there a remarkable birth was predicted, here one is celebrated; there, Astraea and Mercy (or Truth) returned to Heaven, here, they descend to earth again.

The "Hymn" section centers on the uneasy encounter of the natural order with this supernatural event.[105] In conception and structure it develops strategies which come to be characteristic of Milton's poems. For one, the particular subject is made to encompass all time and space as Milton continually shifts the focus from the morning of Christ's nativity back to Creation and forward to Doomsday, and, in cinematographic fashion, from the Bethlehem scenes to the widest cosmic perspective. The poem moves quickly from the manger scene to Nature herself, first personified as a wanton harlot camouflaging her guilt with a "Saintly Vail" of snow, and then as the awestruck natural order responding as if to the Second Coming, not the first: the stars will not take flight and the sun supposes himself made superfluous by the greater Sun/Son. Another homely scene follows – the Shepherds chatting and tending their sheep – and at once opens out to the hymns of the angelic choir and the music of the spheres, described in wonderfully evocative lines:

Ring out ye Crystall sphears,
Once bless our human ears,
    (If ye have power to touch our senses so)
And let your silver chime
Move in melodious time,
    And let the Base of Heav'ns deep Organ blow,
And with your ninefold harmony
Make up full consort to th'Angelike symphony.

For if such holy Song
Enwrap our fancy long,
    Time will run back, and fetch the age of gold (ll.125–35)

This music leads the poet's imagination from Creation to the Millennium and from the Nativity to Doomsday, as he joins nature in supposing that the Golden Age is indeed imminent.[106] Then he is abruptly recalled to the Nativity moment: "But wisest Fate sayes no" (l. 154). Another strategy that Milton uses to impressive effect here, and that becomes characteristic of him, is the complex interplay of classical myth and Christian story. The pagan gods, understood literally, are conquered by Christ, but Christ is himself figured as the "mighty *Pan*" come to live among the shepherds and as an infant Hercules strangling in his cradle the giant serpent Satan and all his monster crew.

The final section of the poem focuses on the immediate effects of the Nativity, beginning with the "old Dragon" bound and opening out to the prospect of all the Pagan Gods fleeing from all their shrines, described in terms of their relative degrees of darkness and disorder – from the utter blackness of Moloch to the shadowy "Moon-lov'd maze" of the "yellow-skirted *Fayes*" (ll. 235–6). In this section especially, the poem's reformist political meanings are emphasized. Milton reproves easy speculation that the Millennium is imminent. The length of the catalogue of idols suggests, by a kind of formal mimesis, the long and difficult process that must precede it: completing the reformation of the church by ridding humankind of all its idols, lovely as well as hideous. The "old Dragon" whose sway is now retrenched and the Typhon strangled by the infant Herculean Christ point not only to Satan but also, for contemporary Protestants, to the Roman church and its power. By opposing Christ, the new Sun/Son, to the old Sun God Apollo and dramatizing the silencing of Apollo's oracles at Christ's birth, Milton sets Christ's power against what Apollo the Sun-God had come to symbolize as a prominent iconographical symbol of Renaissance popes and aggressive Vatican power and as the self-chosen emblem of the Stuart kings, James I and Charles I.[107] Many images in Milton's descriptions of the several pagan gods – "consecrated Earth," "service quaint," "sable-stoled Sorcerers," "Heav'ns Queen and Mother both" (suggesting the cult of the Virgin) – register the heightened concern in 1629 over the "popish idolatry" which Laud's steadily increasing power was seen to promote.[108] Also, by December, 1629 Henrietta Maria was known to be pregnant, and the expected royal birth was being heralded by references to Virgil's Fourth Eclogue, projecting a Stuart Golden Age.[109] Milton's Nativity poem insists that the true Golden Age must be foreshadowed by the divine child, and will come only at the Millennium, when idols old and new have been cast out. The final stanza shifts the perspective back to the Bethlehem scene and the "Courtly stable" – an oxymoron emblematic of the poem's paradoxical mode, but also one that transfers kingly power and state from earthly monarchs to their only proper locus, Christ. The poem is a remarkable achievement in conception and poetic craft for the 21-year-old poet.

The graceful, urbane companion poems, *L'Allegro* and *Il Penseroso,* climax Milton's university years and his early poetic development. They explore the ideal pleasures appropriate to contrasting lifestyles – "heart-easing Mirth," "divinest Melancholy" – that a poet might choose, or might choose at different times, or in sequence.[110] As celebrations of their respective deities – the Grace Euphrosyne (Youthful Mirth) and the allegorical figure imagined as a deity, Melancholy – both poems are modeled on the classical hymn. But they also incorporate elements of several other kinds: the academic prolusion or debate, the Theocritan pastoral idyl of the ideal day and its festivals, the Theophrastian prose "character" with such titles as "The Happy Man" or "The Melancholy Man," the encomium, and the demonstrative or eulogistic oration with its traditional categories of praise: the goods of nature (ancestry and birth), the goods of fortune (friends and circumstances of life), and the goods of character (actions and virtues). *L'Allegro* especially shows the continuing influence of Jonson's lyric manner, his clarity, delicacy, and grace. It also evokes the Shakespeare of *A Midsummer Night's Dream* and *Romeo and Juliet*. The final couplet of each poem echoes and answers the question posed in Marlowe's "Come live with me and be my love" and its Elizabethan analogues. But despite the familiarity of these elements, Milton's paired poems have no close antecedents.[111]

Metrically and rhythmically also these poems are a *tour de force*. Both begin with a ten-line prelude, with alternating lines of six and ten (or eleven) syllables and an intricate rhyme pattern. For the rest, both use the verse form of the Winchester epitaph – octosyllabic couplets with seven-syllable lines freely intermingled, and with complex shifts between rising and falling rhythms, iambic and trochaic feet and lines. Milton is now so skillful with metrics that from the same verse form he can produce utterly different tonal effects. In *L'Allegro* the quick short vowels, the monosyllables, the liquid consonants, and the frequent trochaic rhythms trip over the tongue in a mimesis of youthful frolic – an English version of Anacreontic verse:

> Haste thee nymph, and bring with thee
> Jest and youthful jollity,
> Quips and Cranks, and wanton Wiles,
> Nods, and Becks, and Wreathed Smiles (ll. 25–8)

In *Il Penseroso* polysyllables, clusters of consonants, and a liberal use of spondaic feet produce a deliberate and somber tone:

> Com pensive Nun, devout and pure,
> Sober, stedfast, and demure,
> All in a robe of darkest grain,
> Flowing with majestick train (ll. 31–4)

Structurally, both follow closely the model of the classical hymn: first, an exorcism or banishment of the opposing deity; then an invocation to the deity celebrated (Mirth, Melancholy); then a celebration of her qualities and activities; and finally a prayer to be admitted to her company. The first five sections of the two poems are closely paralleled, save that those in *Il Penseroso* are a little longer. The chief structural difference comes in the sixth section and in *Il Penseroso's* eight-line coda, which has no parallel in *L'Allegro*.

L'Allegro is a praise of youthful mirth, innocent joy, lighthearted pleasure, freedom from care. The Prologue banishes this speaker's conception of melancholy, "loathed Melancholy," the disease caused by an imbalance of black bile and associated with depression and madness. Then the speaker invites and praises Mirth, personified as the youthful Grace Euphrosyne and associated with Neoplatonic interpretations of the three Graces as exfoliations of Venus, as in Botticelli's *Primavera.* Milton reworks the myth of her origin, setting aside her more usual derivation from Bacchus and Venus (intimating wanton sensuality and excess) for the "sager" myth deriving her from purer sources evocative of Springtime: Zephyr, the West Wind, and Aurora, the Dawn.[112] Her associates are Jests, Sports, and Laughter; her special companion and defining quality is "The Mountain Nymph, sweet Liberty" (l. 36). The sociable daytime pleasures of Mirth's devotee are portrayed at length, in a series of delightful pastoral scenes that mix classical shepherds and shepherdesses – Corydon, Thyrsis, Phillis – with the sights and sounds, the sunshine holidays, and the folk-tales of rural England. Then the speaker details in briefer compass the nocturnal but still sociable pleasures L'Allegro seeks in "Towred Cities": festivals, knighly jousts, court masques, stage comedies.

Il Penseroso celebrates Melancholy, seen by him as the saturnine temperament which seeks solitude, the scholarly life, and religious contemplation.[113] Again, a ten-line prologue banishes this speaker's conception of Mirth – "vain deluding joyes." The speaker then invites and praises Melancholy: she is sage and holy with a majestic stateliness and a rapt soul; her visage is saintly and black, "staid Wisdoms hue" – something like the figure in Albrecht Dürer's famous engraving *Melancholia* – and her parents are Saturn and Saturn's daughter, Vesta. Her companions are calm Peace and Quiet, Spare Fast, and Silence; and her chief associate and defining characteristic is "The Cherub Contemplation" (l. 54). Reversing *L'Allegro,* this poem describes at greatest length the nocturnal pleasures of Melancholy's man – philosophical studies, and "Gorgeous Tragedy" in the theater. During the day il Penseroso hides himself from the Sun, enjoying "twilight groves," "shadows brown," and sleep filled with mysterious dreams.

Milton contrasts and evaluates these modes of life as imagined ideals, adumbrated through literary kinds. There might seem to be surprising affinities with the Cavalier poets in l'Allegro's pastoralism, his apparent elitist denial of rural labor, and his attendance at masques and stage plays. And even more surprising affinities with Roman Catholic or Laudian ritual might seem to be registered in Il Penseroso's fondness for the architecture, art, and organ music of cathedrals and his final retreat to a monastic hermitage.[114] But Milton's project uses these images to quite another purpose: to define and evaluate lifestyles in terms of literary modes, and to reclaim genres and art forms from debased to valid uses. Milton does not, here or elsewhere, repudiate pastoral, stage plays, or masques because he thinks Cavaliers have debased them, or church music and art because he thinks Laudians use them in the service of idolatry. Rather, these poems reclaim such art for innocent delight by excising any hint of licentiousness, or courtly Neoplatonism, or idolatry.

L'Allegro's essence, youthful mirth, is displayed in the activities and values of the pastoral mode and the literary genres harmonious with it: rural folk- and faery-tales of Queen Mab and Goblin; court masques and pageants; Jonson's "learned" comedy; romantic comedies in which "sweetest *Shakespear* fancies child / Warble[s] his native Wood-notes wilde" (ll. 133–4); and love songs in the Greek Lydian mode. Those soothing (or as Plato thought, enervating) songs are described in wonderfully mimetic lines:

> And ever against eating Cares,
> Lap me in soft *Lydian* Aires,
> Married to immortal verse
> Such as the meeting soul may pierce
> In notes, with many a winding bout
> Of lincked sweetnes long drawn out,
> With wanton heed, and giddy cunning,
> The melting voice through mazes running:
> Untwisting all the chains that ty
> The hidden soul of harmony.
> That *Orpheus* self may heave his head
> From golden slumber on a bed
> Of heapt *Elysian* flowres, and hear
> Such streins as would have won the ear
> Of *Pluto*, to have quite set free
> His half regain'd *Eurydice* (ll. 135–50)

This music wakens Orpheus, the figure of the poet, though it seems rather to charm than rouse him to any activity; and it promises, but only in the subjunctive mood, power over Pluto. Lydian music and the life of Mirth are not in any way tainted, only limited, as the conditional terms of the final couplet also indicate: "These delights, if thou canst give, / Mirth with thee, I mean to live."

In *Il Penseroso* the Romance mode presents the activities, pleasures, and values of a solitary scholar-errant. He wanders through a mysterious gothic landscape with a melancholy nightingale, a "high lonely Towr," a drowsy bellman, a cathedral cloister with "high embowed Roof," storied stained-glass windows, "dimm religious light," a "pealing Organ" and a "full voic'd Quire" engaged in "Service high," and a hermitage with mossy cells. These images are appropriate to the medievalism and romance decorum of the poem. Melancholy's devotee enjoys the esoteric philosophy of Plato and Hermes Trismegistus, romances like Chaucer's unfinished *Squire's Tale* for their marvels and their allegory, Greek tragedies about Thebes and Troy by Aeschylus and Euripides, and bardic hymns like that of Orpheus, whose power here, more decisively than in *L'Allegro,* "made Hell grant what Love did seek" (l. 108). Finally, il Penseroso turns to Christian music that produces ecstasy and vision:

> There let the pealing Organ blow
> To the full voic'd Quire below,
> In Service high, and Anthems clear,
> As may with sweetnes, through mine ear,
> Dissolve me into extasies,
> And bring all Heav'n before mine eyes (ll. 161–6)

The title personages of both poems are drawn with some playfulness, as ideal but exaggerated types. Yet through them Milton again contrasts kinds of art and life and sets them in some hierarchical relation. A progression is implied from the genres l'Allegro enjoys to the higher kinds il Penseroso delights in – from folk-tales to allegorical romance, from comedy to tragedy, from Lydian airs to bardic and Christian hymns. More important, the eight-line coda of *Il Penseroso* disrupts the poems' parallelism by opening to the future:

> And may at last my weary age
> Find out the peaceful hermitage,
> The Hairy Gown and Mossy Cell,
> Where I may sit and rightly spell,
> Of every Star that Heav'n doth shew,
> And every Herb that sips the dew;
> Till old experience do attain
> To somthing like Prophetic strain (ll. 167–74)

The coda makes Milton's poetic strategy clear. He does not, obviously, plan a monastic retreat for himself nor hold it forth as an ideal, but he makes those images, appropriate to the medievalizing, romance mode of the poem, figure his aspiration to prophetic poetry. In *Il Penseroso*, age has its place, bringing true knowledge of nature and the ripening of "old experience" into "somthing like Prophetic strain." *L'Allegro* portrays the lifestyle of youth as a cyclic round, beginning with Mirth's man awakening from sleep and ending with the drowsing Orpheus. Melancholy's man begins with the evening and ends in waking ecstasy, the vision of heaven, all embracing scientific learning, and prophecy. In these poems Milton stages an ideal solution to his youthful anxieties about slow development, lifestyles, and poetry – a natural progression from *L'Allegro* to the higher life and art of *Il Penseroso,* which offers to lead, after "long experience," beyond ecstatic vision to prophetic poetry that can convey that vision to others.

3

"Studious Retirement:" Hammersmith and Horton 1632–1638

When Milton graduated from Cambridge in July, 1632, he went to live with his parents in the London suburb of Hammersmith. About three years later he moved with them further into the country, to the village of Horton in Buckinghamshire. We have few records of his quotidian activities in these years, nor do we know the dates and sequence of much that he wrote. But he began two remarkable notebooks that provide an invaluable record of his poetic development and his self-directed studies: the Trinity manuscript, chiefly poems and largely autograph; and a Commonplace Book that excerpts and organizes some of his reading. Several questions remain unresolved: When did Milton decide against the ministry and for poetry?[1] Why did he take so long to prepare himself? And why was there a three-year hiatus in which (so far as we know) he wrote no poetry (1635–7)? In these years the issue of vocation appears to impinge on all Milton's other concerns: his relationships with friends and with his father, the demands of chastity, the threat of death.

In the Hammersmith and Horton years Milton committed himself more and more earnestly to poetry and to learning without resolving the nagging question, what work was he called to do in the world? No seventeenth-century gentleman could imagine making a career, much less a living, as a poet. Milton rejoiced in his escape from business and the law, and the ministry seemed less and less viable to him as the Laudian takeover of the church accelerated. If he did not overtly reject a clerical role, neither did he imagine himself undertaking it. In accepting commissions for two aristocratic entertainments – *Arcades* and *A Maske*, popularly known as *Comus* – he may have hoped to attract some settled patronage, perhaps as tutor or secretary in a noble, soundly Protestant household like that of Bridgewater or the Countess of Derby. These were years of considerable anxiety and self-doubt. Milton was painfully conscious that by comparison with his peers and by outside measures of success he had been slow to mature: he had no profession, no independent household, and no public recognition as a poet. Yet he refused to present himself in the public arena: his epitaph for Shakespeare (1632) and his masque (1637) were published anonymously, and *Lycidas* (1638) bore only his initials. For *Lycidas* such anonymity might have seemed prudent, given the poem's vehement attack on the Laudian church. Also, he was perhaps restrained by the expectation that a gentleman (the class he could now claim as a university graduate) should circulate his poems privately to patrons and friends, not expose them to the masses. But the pattern of deferral and anonymity suggests that he felt himself unprepared for the great work he hoped to produce, and unwilling to stake his claim on these occasional pieces. Yet the strong religious and reformist impulse in all his works – and most emphatically in *Lycidas* – distinguishes them clearly from the *jeux* of gentlemen poets and indicates that he sought, even in anonymity, to find and address a "fit audience."

Despite his anxieties, the few poems Milton did produce in these years reach new heights of achievement. He continued the practice of setting poem against poem as alternative or progressive explorations of the same theme or problem, but he now looked to new models: the Italian madrigal and canzone, the English entertainment and masque, and the pastoral funeral elegy. He developed some features of his mature style: the verse paragraph and the long sonorous sentence extending over several lines of verse. Also, he used English verse for the first time to probe his own emotional crises and anxieties, achieving a new intensity of feeling. This increasing mastery of his poetic craft helped him find the confidence in late 1637 to claim poetry as his true vocation and to prepare to publish his most impressive works to date, *A Maske* and *Lycidas*. At that time or in early 1638 he most likely wrote *Ad Patrem,* urging his father to support his further preparation as a poet.

"I Do Not Know What . . . God May Have Decreed for Me"

Some time after September, 1631, Milton's father the scrivener (then about 70 years old) left the business in Bread Street to his partner Thomas Bower and retired to Hammersmith in the county of Middlesex; he was there by September, 1632 and still there in January, 1635.[2] By May, 1636 and perhaps earlier, the family had removed to Horton (about 17 miles from London); the outbreak of plague that summer may have been a factor.[3] Milton's account of his studies during these years seems to pertain chiefly to Hammersmith, though his life probably kept much the same contour in both places:

> At my father's country place, whither he had retired to spend his declining years, I devoted myself entirely to the study of Greek and Latin writers, completely at leisure, not, however, without sometimes exchanging the country for the city, either to purchase books or to become acquainted with some new discovery in mathematics or music, in which I then took the keenest pleasure. (*CPW* IV.1, 613–14)

Hammersmith was a hamlet on the north bank of the Thames in the parish of Fulham, about seven miles west of St Paul's Cathedral.[4] Milton's earlier references to country walks and sojourns may suggest that this or another rural residence served the family for some years as a refuge from the plague and the heat of summer.[5] The London excursions he refers to would have been comparatively easy from Hammersmith. His efforts to keep up with new developments in music were no doubt facilitated by his father's connections with the London music world.[6] His mathematical interests he may have pursued at Gresham College, the only center in London for lectures and studies in that subject.[7]

Living once again with his family, Milton had reason to reaffirm his conviction that the commercial and legal professions were not for him. Edward Phillips supposed, wrongly, that the scrivener, "having got an Estate to his content," left off the cares of business when he retired (*EL* 55). In fact, he was involved for several years with suits and countersuits pertaining to two complex Chancery cases, in which plaintiffs Rose Downer and John Cotton and their heirs charged Milton senior and Thomas Bower with mismanagement of funds entrusted to them for lending out. There seems to have been some sharp practice and bad faith in the first case and perhaps in the second, though most witnesses and the court judgments ascribed the fault to Bower. As a partner, however, Milton senior retained some liability.[8] By 1637 the poet's younger brother Christopher was a practicing lawyer; after spending only five terms at Cambridge, he left when Milton did and at age 17 began studying law at the Inner Temple. He drafted some legal papers in the Cotton affair, including a petition on April 1 that his father be allowed, by reason of age and infirmity, to give his depositions at Horton rather than Westminster.[9]

During the 1630s also, changes in the English church reinforced Milton's doubts about taking orders. Before Laud, many Puritans and other reform-minded Protestants were able to swear, as Milton himself did when he took his degrees, to the lawfulness of the *Book of Common Prayer* and the truth of the Thirty-nine Articles. Like most of Queen Elizabeth's bishops, they could understand the Articles in a Calvinist sense and (like Thomas Young at Stowmarket) they could often avoid compliance with such ritual and ceremony as offended their consciences. But after Laud became Archbishop of Canterbury on August 6, 1633 he accelerated the process of recasting the church in a high church mold, leading it, many feared, ever closer to Rome. He appointed his own men – Arminian bishops, university officers, and parish clergy – who rigorously repressed Calvinist predestinarian doctrine and Puritan efforts to reform church ritual and government. New ordinances required fixed altars rather than communion tables, the full panoply of vestments and sacramental rituals, strict adherence to the *Book of Common Prayer*, and diligent supervision by bishops to enforce all this. Bishops were also to eject Puritan-leaning ministers and to control lectureships and private chaplaincies – common resorts for Puritan preachers outside the parish structure. Orders designed to silence Puritans forbade any dispute in sermons or tracts about the meaning of any of the Thirty-nine Articles. Laud enforced these ordinances by a regime of censorship and repression that he termed, all too aptly, "Thorough." Offences were tried in ecclesiastical or Star Chamber courts – outside the protections of Common Law – and punishments were often brutal, as in the case of the Puritan pamphleteers John Bastwick, Henry Burton, and William Prynne, who had their ears hacked off in June, 1637. Charles and Laud also undertook to impose ecclesiastical canons and the *Book of Common Prayer* on Presbyterian Scotland. The rural retreat of Hammersmith could afford Milton no escape from these issues, nor from continuing dismaying reports of Protestant losses in the continental wars.

Milton's self-prescribed program of reading at Hammersmith seems to have been largely in classical literature and philosophy. He states in the *Second Defense* that he devoted himself "entirely" to the Greek and Latin writers, and in the *Apology* he points especially to "*Plato* and his equall *Xenophon*" as one focus of his "ceaseless round of study and reading" in his "riper yeares" after childhood and youth (*CPW* I, 891). This classical program is reflected in books purchased by Milton at this time, some bearing his annotations: Euripides' *Tragedies* and Lycophron's *Alexandra* in 1634 and Terence's *Comedies* in 1635.[10] Very likely he also obtained his friend Alexander Gil's Latin poems, *Epinikion* (1631), celebrating the victories of the Protestant military hero and Swedish king, Gustavus Adolphus, and *Parerga* (1632), his collected poems.[11] Perhaps he also purchased the Shakespeare Second Folio (1632) containing his own epitaph to Shakespeare.

As an aspiring poet, whatever else he might do, Milton had to determine how to situate himself in the culture wars that intensified during the 1630s. That issue was forced soon after he left Cambridge for Hammersmith, when he was invited to contribute a poetic entertainment as part of the festivities in honor of Alice Spencer, Dowager Countess of Derby. The court was then promoting a fashionable cult of Platonic Love as a benign representation and vindication of royal absolutism and the personal rule (1629–40), when Charles ruled without parliament. In the court masques of the 1630s the royal pair displayed themselves under various mythological and pastoral guises as enacting the union of Heroic Virtue (Charles) and Divine Beauty or Love (Henrietta Maria, often personating Venus or Juno).[12] Many of them contain some representation of contemporary problems and some covert critique of the personal rule, but their primary effect is to mystify and reinforce it. By comparison with Jacobean masques, Caroline masques were even more exotic and prodigiously expensive, sets and machinery were more elaborate, antimasques much more numerous, and dramatic speech more prominent. The ideality of Charles's reign was often imaged in pastoral terms: the queen is Chloris/Flora in *Chloridia* (1631); the court is imaged as the Valley of Tempe in *Tempe Restored* (1632); and in *Coelum Britannicum* (1634) the reformed heaven (modeled on the court of Charles) is represented as a garden with parterres, fountains and grottoes.[13] The king and queen danced in many masques, symbolizing their personal and active control of all the discordant elements represented in the antimasques – unruly passions, discontented and mutinous elements in the populace, and threats from abroad. At the end the royal and noble masquers unmasked and participated with other members of the court in elaborate dances (the Revels), figuring the continual intermixing of the ideal world and the Stuart court. Also, Cavalier poets associated with the court wrote lyrics imbued with the fashionable Platonism and pastoralism, or with a playful licentiousness.

During the 1630s King Charles sought to extend the cultural control of the court and the Laudian church throughout the country. He reissued Jacobean proclamations commanding gentry and nobility back to their country estates to keep hospitality in the traditional fashion, especially at festival times of Christmas and Easter. On October 18, 1633 he reissued James I's highly controversial *Book of Sports*. Citing the common people's need for exercise and recreation, the document urges the continuance of traditional rural sports and festivities in every parish after divine service on Sunday:

> For our good people's lawful recreation, our pleasure likewise is, that after the end of divine service our good people be not disturbed, letted or discouraged from any lawful recreation, such as dancing, either men or women; archery for men, leaping, vaulting, or any other such harmless recreation, nor from having of May-games, whitsunales, and Morris-dances; and the setting up of May-poles and other sports therewith used.[14]

In the same proclamation he called upon bishops to constrain "all the Puritans and precisians" either to conform or leave the country, and so strike down "the contemners of our authority and adversaries of our Church." This ordinance links Laudian church ritual with traditional rural festivities, making them instruments of royal authority and control under the careful supervision of parish clergy.

Puritans denounced both court and country sports on religious grounds: they saw masques, maypoles and morrises as palpable occasions of sin and the royally prescribed recreations as prophanations of the Sabbath. Nor were they unaware of the politics of the king's festivals. The contemporary Puritan historian Lucy Hutchinson saw masques and sports as a vehicle for spreading the court's immorality and idolatry throughout the kingdom, distracting people from true religion and from the political crisis:

> The generality of the gentry of the land soone learnt the Court fashion, and every greate house in the country became a sty of uncleannesse. To keepe the people in their deplorable security till vengeance overtooke them, they were entertain'd with masks, stage playes, and various sorts of ruder sports. Then began Murther, incest, Adultery, drunkennesse, swearing, fornication and all sorts of ribaldry to be no conceal'd but countenanced vices, favour'd wherever they were privately practis'd because they held such conformity with the Court example.[15]

William Prynne staked out the most extreme Puritan position in *Histrio-Mastix: or, The Players Scourge and Actors Tragedy* (1633 [1632]),[16] a passionate tirade of over 1,000 pages against stage-plays, masques, masque dancing, maypoles and rural festivals, country sports on the Sabbath, Laudian ritual, stained-glass windows, and much more. This blanket denunciation of Caroline culture was probably a factor in Charles's decision to reissue the *Book of Sports* a few months later. Prynne strikes directly at the king and queen with stories of kings and magistrates who met untimely ends after encouraging or participating in theatrical productions. One reference to "Women actors, notorious whores" and another to "scurrilous amorous pastorals" were taken to refer to the queen, who was then rehearsing her ladies for a presentation of Walter Montague's *Shepheard's Paradise*, in which the women took men's as well as women's roles.[17] Both Charles and Henrietta Maria were implicated in Prynne's attacks on Christmastide masques as "amorous, mixt, voluptuous, unchristian, that I say not, Pagan dancing, to Gods, to Christs dishonour, Religion's scandall, Chastities shipwracke, sinnes advantage, and the eternall ruine of many pretious soules."[18] In February, 1633, Prynne was imprisoned by the Star Chamber, and a year later was stripped of his academic degrees, ejected from the legal profession, and pilloried at Westminster and Cheapside; he saw his books burned before him, had his ears cropped, and was remanded to life imprisonment. The severity of the sentence indicates the high stakes in these culture wars; according to one judge, "This booke is to effect disobedyence to the state, and a generall dislyke unto all governments."[19]

Milton's "Entertainment"[20] for the Countess of Derby allowed him to place himself in the long line of staunch Protestant writers she patronized, most notably Spenser. The widow of Lord Strange, Earl of Derby, as well as of Lord Keeper Egerton, she was the matriarch of a large family and her estate, Harefield in Middlesex, was only a few miles from Hammersmith. Milton probably obtained the invitation through some musician friend – probably Henry Lawes, a member of the royal music and also music master to the Countess's Egerton grandchildren who later performed in *A Maske*.[21] There is considerable dispute as to when these festivities took place and, as a related issue, when Milton began his Trinity manuscript, in which *Arcades* (The Arcadians) is the first item.[22] As Cedric Brown argues, August–October, 1632 seems most likely.[23] The manuscript text is not a first draft, but Milton continued to work on it, entering several pre- and post-performance changes.[24]

In 1632 the dowager countess, then 73 years old, was supporting and educating several grandchildren at Harefield: two daughters of her youngest daughter Elizabeth, Countess of Hastings, whose family was in dire financial straits; and three children of her eldest daughter Anne, Countess of Castlehaven, from her first marriage to Baron Chandos.[25] In a separate household she helped support Anne and Anne's eldest daughter Elizabeth after Anne's second husband Castlehaven was executed in May, 1631, for outrageous sexual abuse of them both. On numerous occasions Castlehaven had his servants rape his wife and stepdaughter (who was married to his own son); he was also accused of sodomy with his servants, and of popery.[26] The more prosperous family of the dowager countess's second daughter Frances, wife of Sir John Egerton, Earl of Bridgewater, lived at Ashridge, only 16 miles away. Milton's entertainment makes tactful use of the dowager countess's role as a bulwark of strength to her family, without referring directly to the notorious Castlehaven scandal.

Arcades was performed in the great hall by some of the countess's resident and visiting grandchildren and some others. It proposes to reclaim pastoral from the court, intimating the superiority of these Harefield festivities and the virtues of this noble Protestant lady and her household over the queen and her suspect pastoral entertainments. The term "Entertainment" relates *Arcades* to the genre usually employed to welcome visiting royalty or their surrogates to a noble house; most often its topics praise the visitor who brings the benefits and virtues of the court ethos to the hosts. But in Milton's reformed entertainment it is the visitors, coming in pastoral guise from the "Arcadian" court, who pay homage to a far superior rural queen of a better Arcadia, directed by Genius, its guardian spirit. The countess replaces the king in the chair of state, and displays royal and divine accoutrements. A "sudden blaze of majesty" flames from her "radiant state" and "shining throne," which is also a "princely shrine" for an "unparalel'd" maternal deity: "Such a rural Queen / All *Arcadia* hath not seen."[27] The critique of the court is sharpened in a pair of lines added in the Trinity manuscript to the two last songs by Genius: "Though *Syrinx* your *Pans* Mistres were / Yet *Syrinx* well might wait on her."[28] The Arcadia/ Pan myth had been taken over by the Stuarts, so these lines exalt the countess above Henrietta Maria and the Caroline court. That comparative valuation would not be lost on this audience: the countess herself had danced in Queen Anne's masques; one Egerton grandchild, Penelope, had danced in *Chloridia* (1631), and three more – Alice (the Lady of *Comus*) and her elder sisters Katherine and Elizabeth – had danced in Queen Henrietta's *Tempe Restored* (1632).[29]

Milton also began to explore here what his *Maske* would develop fully: a stance toward art and recreation that repudiates both the court aesthetics and Prynne's wholesale prohibitions. Genius – probably acted by a servant–musician attached to the countess's household – is the gardener/guardian of the place, embodying the curative and harmony-producing powers of music and poetry. The virtues of Harefield are said to be nurtured by good art as well as by the ruling Lady. Genius cures conditions that symbolize the evils of the fallen world – noisome winds, blasting vapors, evil dew, worms with cankered venom – and he nourishes all nature by his "puissant words." Also, he hears the music of the spheres (inaudible to mortals) and recognizes music's capacity, "To lull the daughters of *Necessity*, / And keep unsteddy Nature to her law" (69–70). His songs attempt some imitation of that music as they both celebrate and nurture the countess's virtue. Genius's last song calls on the visitors to leave off their Arcadian dances to serve this more excellent queen,[30] a gesture that associates the better aesthetics he is promoting with the virtues of a soundly Protestant aristocracy. Milton's Entertainment seeks both to confirm and to educate these aristocrats in these virtues. There is no evidence, however, that he had any personal contact with them, nor is it at all likely that he saw *Arcades* presented at Harefield.

On or shortly after his twenty-fourth birthday (December 9, 1632) Milton wrote an anxious sonnet that begins "How soon hath Time the suttle theef of youth, / Stoln on his wing my three and twentieth yeer!"[31] Though its date has been contested (1631 or 1632) Milton's usual way of referring to his age in dating his poems makes 1632 probable.[32] The poem marks a breakthrough in Milton's use of the Petrarchan sonnet. While Sonnets I–VI treat conventional love themes in somewhat novel terms, Sonnet VII explores a psychological and spiritual crisis occasioned by Milton's birthday. He laments his tardy development in relation to more "timely-happy spirits" – Diodati perhaps, or Edward King – in terms broad enough to refer to personal, career, and poetic development. This sonnet characterizes Time as a thief stealing away his youth: his "late spring" has brought no "bud or blossom" of accomplishment. At age 24 he sees himself as not yet a man: his external semblance belies his lack of "inward ripenes" – intellectual and spiritual maturity – as well as his lack of the achievements that should attend maturity. The sestet proposes a resolution in God's predestinating will: his lot is fixed, "however mean, or high," his own "ripenes," fast or slow, must accord with it, and Time is thereby refigured as a guide leading inexorably to it. Some consolation for late bloomers is provided by allusion in the sestet to the parable of the vineyard (Matthew 20:1–16), in which a Master sent latecomers as well as early arrivals to work in his vineyard, rewarding them according to his will, not their labors. But the sonnet's final lines introduce new anxieties: the Miltonic speaker must have "grace" to use his Time and God's gifts well, under the ever-watchful eye of a strict and exacting God, "my great task Master."[33] The perfectly regular Petrarchan metrical pattern of this sonnet – a sharp turn between octave and sestet and strong end-stops at lines 2, 4, 8, 12, and 14 – departs from the enjambments more usual with Milton, so that by formal mimesis the theme of exact fulfillment of a divinely predestined lot is imaged in a sonnet form that is itself "in strictest measure eev'n."

Milton included this sonnet in a 1633 letter to an unidentified older friend, almost certainly a clergyman, whom Milton met from time to time, probably in London.[34] In an encounter just past, Milton states, this man criticized his delay in taking orders (he became eligible on his twenty-fourth birthday), ascribing it to self-indulgent and excessive study, and an inclination to seek obscure retirement (*CPW* I, 319–21). Milton's letter is in English, not Latin, suggesting that the friend was not Thomas Young and not a Cambridge academic acquaintance. It is composed directly into the Trinity manuscript as the third item, in two much-corrected versions that register Milton's difficulty in explaining himself. He offers excuses for his present way of life in terms that range from earnest to jocular, but he is curiously unforthcoming about his vocational plans. Clearly, this friend was not an intimate with whom Milton could share his innermost doubts and aspirations. He frankly admits to "tardie moving" and "a certaine belatednesse," and he reveals his anxieties in surprisingly harsh descriptions of his retired life. It is "as yet obscure, & unserviceable to mankind"; its conditions are like those caused by the "sin of curiosity . . . wherby a man cutts himselfe off from all action & becomes the most helplesse, pusilanimous & unweapon'd creature in the [world]." It is also an "affected solitarinesse" that denies the most powerful inclinations of a man and a scholar – family and fame:

> There is against yt [his supposed inclination to the retired life] a much more potent inclination imbred which about this tyme of a mans life sollicits most, the desire of house & family of his owne to which nothing is esteemed more helpefull then the early entring into credible employment . . . and though this were anough yet there is to this another act if not of pure, yet of refined nature no lesse available to dissuade prolonged obscurity, a desire of honour & repute, & immortall fame seated in the brest of every true scholar which all make hast to by the readiest ways of publishing & divulging conceived merits as well those that shall as those that never shall obtaine it. (*CPW* I, 319–20)

I think we need not doubt the strength of both desires, and their expression here may shed some light on Milton's preoccupation with chastity during these years. He recognizes that he is in no position to marry until he is settled in a career, and he considers himself bound on religious grounds to live a celibate life until he marries. So, typically, he makes a great virtue of his necessity. Also, the curious mix of diffidence and high aspiration he admits to suggests one reason he published his first poems hesitantly and anonymously: he wanted the work for which he first became known to win the fame he craved – unlike those unworthy others who foolishly rush into print. As for the ministry, he does not commit to it, nor yet quite reject it, but explains (awkwardly) that his delay stems from much reflection on the import of the parable of the talents,

> from due & tymely obedience to that command in the gospell set out by the terrible seasing of him that hid the talent. it is more probable therfore that not the endlesse delight of speculation but this very consideration of that great commandment does not presse forward as soone as may be to underg[o] but keeps off with a sacred reverence & religious advisement how best to undergoe[,] not taking thought of beeing late so it give advantage to be more fit. (*CPW* I, 320)

He can jest about himself as a minister – since he has tired this auditor by preaching he would surely tire a congregation – but he cannot seriously project himself into that role. To this friend he says nothing about poetry.

Perhaps prompted by these anxieties, Milton wrote at about this time three short odes on religious themes in complex metrical patterns, perfecting in them the long, elaborate verse sentence which is a hallmark of his later poetry. "Upon the Circumcision" – a competent but uninspired poem – may be first, written about the time of the feast, January 1, 1633. Milton explicitly pairs it with the Nativity Ode, as his speaker invites the angels who joyfully sang of the nativity to mourn now the first blood shed by Christ. The poem is meant to substitute for the failed "Passion," treating the "wounding smart" of Christ's circumcision as type and augury of that event. The metrics of the two 14-line stanzas and their complex, interwoven rhyme pattern derive from the Italian canzone, specifically Petrarch's canzone (number 366) to the Virgin.[35] This poem and "On Time" were copied into, not composed in, the Trinity manuscript, as items four and five.

"On Time" reprises the topic of Sonnet VII, but in very different terms. Those two poems comprise another of Milton's contrastive pairs, in which the second makes some advance upon the first in thematic and formal terms. In the sonnet the Miltonic speaker probes his personal anxieties and his own exacting faith; in "On Time" he voices the transcendent faith of the Christian community in the promise of eternal life. The latter poem, an ode with affinities to the Italian madrigal, is conceived as a joyous celebration of the victory of Eternity over Time. The first long sentence (lines 1–8) is an execration against Time, portraying it in slow, ponderous rhythms as an envious, leaden-stepping glutton with power only over "mortal dross." The second long sentence (lines 9–22) swells and soars with religious fervor as it describes Eternity, where "Joy shall overtake us as a flood" and where "we shall for ever sit, / Triumphing over Death, and Chance, and thee O Time." The meter is chiefly iambic, with line lengths varying from six to twelve syllables and a sonorous concluding alexandrine; the rhyme scheme includes alternating rhymes, enclosed rhymes, and couplets. The (crossed out) heading in the Trinity manuscript, "To be set on a clock case," indicates that the poem was initially conceived as an inscription.

"At a solemn Musick," the finest of these small religious odes, is an ectastic celebration of the conjunction of sacred vocal music and poetry. These arts are apostrophized as Sirens – "Sphear-born harmonious Sisters, Voice, and Verse[36] – who can transport the hearer from earth to heaven. This ode was composed directly in the Trinity manuscript as the second item: two rough drafts (crossed out) and a fair copy follow immediately after *Arcades*. The title points to a specific musical event, perhaps a memorable vocal concert Milton attended in London. This poem also reprises elements of the Nativity ode: the angelic choir and the music of the spheres at Christ's birth that almost restore the Platonic/Pythagorean/biblical vision of universal harmony in the Golden Age and at the Millennium. Here, a festive concert of vocal music evokes that same "undisturbed Song of pure concent."[37] In a 24-line sentence imitating the sonorities and modulations of song, the speaker first apostrophizes Voice and Verse as inspiring a vision of the trumpet-blowing Seraphim, the harping Cherubim, and the hymning Saints before God's throne, then imagines that we might answer their song "with undiscording voice" as we did before sin distroyed that harmony. The poem concludes with a prayer that we might sing in tune with Heaven until God joins us to his celestial consort. The form again recalls the Italian madrigal with irregular line lengths – chiefly pentameter, though with some seven-syllable lines and a concluding alexandrine – and a rhyme scheme that moves from alternating rhymes to couplets, breaking that pattern with the rhyming lines 9 and 15. This brief ode shows Milton in full command of the sublimities of the high lyric.

Sometime in 1634 Milton received a commission for a masque in honor of the Earl of Bridgewater, to celebrate his first visit to the regions he was charged to administer by his appointment in 1631 as Lord President of the Council of Wales and Lord Lieutenant of the Welsh and border counties. The invitation may have come directly from the Egerton family who knew Milton from *Arcades*, but it was more likely tendered by Lawes who, as servant to Bridgewater and music master to his children, had charge of planning the entertainment. Milton's *Maske* was performed on Michaelmas night (September 29, 1634) in the great hall at Ludlow; Henry Lawes contributed most and perhaps all of the music.[38] Bridgewater's character and Ludlow's distance from the court gave Milton space to create for this occasion a masque that radically challenges the cultural politics of that court genre. Though a royalist and a friend of the king and Buckingham, Bridgewater was a Calvinist, a conscientious judge, and a governor who resisted Laud's efforts to impose rigid religious conformity in his region.[39] Milton's reformed masque builds brilliantly upon the specific occasion, presenting the earl's three unmarried children – Lady Alice, age 15, the young heir John, Lord Brackley, age 11, and Thomas, age 9 – on a journey to their father's house for a celebration, aided by a Guardian Spirit who is Alice's own music master, Lawes. But their journey takes on overtones of the journey of life and of contemporary life, with the children lost in the dark woods and the Lady confronting the temptations of Comus. With his bestial rout Comus is made to figure on one level Cavalier licentiousness, Laudian ritual, the depravities of court masques and feasts, as well as the unruly holiday pastimes – maypoles, morris dances, Whitsunales – promoted by the *Book of Sports* Charles I had reissued the previous year. Comus embodies as well the seductive power of false rhetoric and the threat of rape.

Milton titled his work simply *A Maske* and dated it 1634 in the Trinity manuscript: it is discussed on pages 76–81. The *TM* text shows several kinds and stages of revision, all in Milton's hand.[40] Pre-performance changes involve shifting or adding to some passages and altering stage directions as Milton gained, probably from Lawes, a better sense of the resources available – singers, dancers, machinery. Given the length of the masque, Milton probably began writing in the spring and turned a fair copy (now lost) over to Lawes before Lawes left London in early July to accompany the Egertons on their "Progress" in the region.[41] Subsequently, performance requirements and social decorum led someone, probably again Lawes, to make extensive revisions that do some violence to Milton's conception and with which he had little or nothing to do; the Bridgewater manuscript is substantially a record of the acting version.[42] Part of the Epilogue is transferred to the beginning to make a catchy opening song for the Attendant Spirit. Lady Alice's long part is much shortened, in part perhaps to make fewer performance demands on the young girl, but chiefly to blunt the sexual threat to her. Her expressions of fear and vulnerability are cut, as are Comus's explicit sexual advances and his arguments against virginity.[43] Not surprisingly, the parts of the brothers are expanded: in the acting version though not in Milton's text the Elder Brother helps to summon Sabrina and direct the return home. Clearly, the young heir had to be given a more active and more successful role than Milton had allowed for.

On December 4, 1634 Milton answered a Latin letter and poem from Alexander Gil with a Latin letter and a Greek version of Psalm 114 which, he states, was composed on impulse a week before, "according to the rules of Greek Heroic song" (*CPW* I, 321). He excuses his possibly rusty Greek by explaining that he has not written poetry in that language since leaving school, because in this age a Greek poet "sings mostly to the deaf." His poem's heroic matter and manner contrast as sharply as possible with the witty, titillating epithalamium Gil sent him.[44] He turned back to the psalm he had rendered into English as a schoolboy, still finding contemporary relevance in that celebration of Israel's deliverance from Egyptian tyranny, and indeed sharpening the political point by a translation terming God the only rightful king of his people: "Only surely then were the Children of Juda a holy race, / And among the people God was king ruling strongly."[45] Milton may have hoped his psalm would prompt his friend to return to his earlier poetic vein, celebrating Protestant militancy.[46] He ends his letter with a proposal to meet Gil in London the following Monday "among the booksellers," i.e. in St Paul's Churchyard; the casual arrangement suggests they may often have met there. He also urges Gil cryptically "to promote our business with that Doctor, this year's President of the College," and to "go to him immediately on my behalf" (*CPW* I, 322). Milton may have been seeking access to the library at Sion College, the corporate body of ministers in London, to further his historical studies,[47] or perhaps to Gresham College to pursue his mathematical and musical interests.

For nearly three years after this, Milton wrote no poetry, or none that he preserved. On July 28, 1635 he may have attended the wedding of John Diodati (Charles's brother) at St Margaret's, Westminster, and enjoyed a reunion with his friend.[48] On November 17, 1635, Alexander Gil senior died at age 71; and Milton would have learned soon that his friend succeeded to his father's post as High Master of St Paul's School.[49]

Sometime in 1636 the Miltons moved to Horton, a peaceful village close to Windsor, nestled among the trees and brooks and meadows of Berkshire.[50] As Christopher Hill notes, it was not quite a pastoral retreat: the Horton papermill was a trouble site, and nearby Colnbrook had some history of radical activity.[51] But it had and has a village green and a fine church, Saint Michael's, with a magnificent Norman doorway and other parts dating from 1160. Henry Bulstrode owned the manor house and leased to Milton senior a property called Berkin Manor, which stood in its own small wooded park at the east of the village.[52] Sometime in 1635 Milton was incorporated Master of Arts at Oxford, a pro forma courtesy to Cambridge degree holders which allowed him access to the Bodleian Library, about 35 miles from Horton.[53]

Horton provided a peaceful setting for Milton's rigorous program of reading and study in these years, much of which was in early church history and the history of the Western Empire through the thirteenth century. Milton's *Apology* (1642) states that after spending "some years" on the stories of the Greeks and Romans (at Hammersmith) he came "in the method of time to that age wherein the Church had obtain'd a Christian Emperor," i.e. to the history of the church before and in the reign of Constantine. Looking back on that cycle of studies, he reports that he expected to find in the Fathers and the early church examples of "wisdom and goodnesse" but instead found "nothing but ambition, corruption, contention, combustion." The reports of the Councils he found "so tedious and unprofitable" that to do more than sample them would be "losse of time irrecoverable" (*CPW* I, 943–4). In *Of Reformation* (1641) he complains that the crabbed, abstruse style of the Fathers undermines both doctrinal clarity and good language: "the knotty Africanisms, the pamper'd metafors; the intricat, and involv'd sentences . . . besides the fantastick, and declamatory flashes; the crosse-jingling periods" (*CPW* I, 568). Milton may not have drawn all these conclusions at Horton, but he dates his moral and aesthetic distaste for the patristic texts to that period. If he undertook such studies in part to prepare for the ministry he had not yet consciously rejected, his distaste for such reading would make that office less and less attractive.

His reading in secular history he summarized in a letter to Diodati (November 23, 1637):

> By continued reading I have brought the affairs of the Greeks to the time when they ceased to be Greeks. I have been occupied for a long time by the obscure history of the Italians under the Longobards, Franks, and Germans, to the time when liberty was granted them by Rudolph, King of Germany [*c.* 1273]. From there it will be better to read separately about what each State did by its own Effort. . . . If you conveniently can, please send me Giustiniani, Historian of the Veneti. On my word I shall see either that he is well cared for until your arrival, or, if you prefer, that he is returned to you shortly. (*CPW* I, 327)[54]

He also bought books: William Ames's important book of Protestant casuistry, *Conscientia* (1635), perhaps shortly after its publication; John Chrysostom's *Orationes LXXX* in 1636*;* and *Allegoriae in Homeri fabulas de diis* of Heraclides of Pontus in 1637.[55]

Milton probably began his Commonplace Book in 1635 or 1636,[56] organizing it into three broad categories, Ethical, Economic, and Political; entries are chiefly in

Latin, Greek, and Italian, with some later entries in English and French. Shawcross speculates that he began it only in the autumn of 1637, after he had virtually completed the reading program described in the letter to Diodati, on the assumption that this book relates to his preparation as a poet, a vocation he could only affirm after working through debilitating strains in his homoerotic relationship with Diodati and after his mother's death.[57] But this date rests on a highly speculative psychological profile for Milton, and a questionable view of his purposes in the Commonplace Book. It is surely more likely that Milton began taking notes as he read, as part of his preparation as a scholar. What we can say, on the evidence of handwriting, the form of "e" used, the Diodati letter, and other considerations, is that during the Horton period – from 1635 or 1636 to May, 1638 when he left for the Continent – Milton took notes in this Commonplace Book from about 28 books.[58] There are no entries from the classics or the Bible, but a now lost *Index Theologicus* may have been started about this time or a little later.[59] Milton's first entries in the "Ethical" category were to the following topics: moral evil, avarice, gluttony, suicide, the knowledge of literature, curiosity, music, sloth, lying. In the "Economic" (Domestic) category he gathered texts on these subjects: food, conduct, matrimony, the education of children, poverty, alms, and usury. And in the "Political" section he collected texts under these heads: state, kings (two pages) subjects, nobility, property and taxes, plague, athletic games, and public shows. Milton seems to have begun his studies on early church history and theology with Eusebius's *Ecclesiastical History* and *Life of Constantine*.[60] He then proceeded to other historians and church Fathers, among them Tertullian, Ignatius, Clement of Alexandria, Sulpicius Severus, Cyprian, Justin Martyr, Procopius, Sigonius, and Nicophoras Gregoras.[61] He also took notes on literary texts: Prudentius's *Peristephanon;* Dante's *Convivio* and *Commedia*,[62] Boccaccio's *Vita di Dante* and Ariosto's *Orlando Furioso*.

Some entries cast light on Milton's concerns and attitudes at this juncture. Excerpts from Tertullian and Cyprian against public shows (and a later note refuting those arguments) relate to the recreation controversy and the issues around masking and plays. Caroline censorship likely prompted his approving citation of patristic arguments allowing Christians to read profane writers. Several entries defend marriage for bishops and clergy, as well as polygamy among the Jews and bigamy in Christian times, indicating Milton's disposition to question orthodox views of marriage well before his own marriage and divorce tracts. His uncertainties about a career choice probably prompted this comment on a passage in Dante: "The nature of each person should be especially observed and not bent in another direction; for God does not intend all people for one thing, but for each one his own work" (*CPW* I, 405). Among the several entries under "King" are instances of censure and the deposition of rulers, as well as an extract from Sulpicius Severus which Milton often used in later polemic argument: "the name of kings has always been hateful to free peoples, and he [God] condemns the action of the Hebrews in choosing to exchange their freedom for servitude" (*CPW* I, 440). Milton's antiroyalist sentiments were already in evidence.

In 1637 there were several plague deaths in Horton, and in that year also Milton had to confront the harsh facts of human mortality in more personal terms. His mother Sara died in April and was buried three days later at the top of the center aisle in the chancel of Horton church, under a plain blue stone inscribed, "Heare Lyeth the Body of Sara Milton the Wife of John Milton Who Died the 3rd of April, 1637."[63] The placement testifies to the family's prominence. On August 9 Ben Jonson was buried in Westminster Abbey, marking what must have seemed to Milton the end of a literary era. Soon after, Milton would have heard about the death on August 10 of his college associate Edward King, whose ship hit a rock and foundered off the coast of Cornwall as he was en route to Ireland to visit his family. A memorial volume was planned at Cambridge and Milton was asked, or volunteered, to contribute to it.

Late in 1637 or early in 1638 Lawes published the text of *A Maske*.[64] In his dedication to Lord Brackley, who had played the Elder Brother, Lawes explains that he decided to publish the work because, "Although not openly acknowledg'd by the Author, yet it is a legitimate off-spring, so lovely, and so much desired, that the often copying of it hath tir'd my pen to give my severall friends satisfaction."[65] This suggests that Lawes had already presented fair copies of the acting version to Bridgewater and several others.[66] But Milton evidently did not want to have the acting version published, with its cuts, its changed opening, and its redistribution of parts; he used instead the version in the Trinity manuscript, but with several additions and changes. His reason for remaining anonymous is hinted at in the epigraph on the title page from Virgil's Second Eclogue: "Eheu quid volui misero mihi! floribus austrum Perditus" (Alas what wish, poor wretch, has been mine? I have let in the south wind to my flowers). This may be the stance of a gentleman fastidious about avoiding public display, but it more obviously points to a young artist anxious about his first foray into the public arena, and perhaps uneasy about readers' responses to a work that defies expectations, generic and cultural.[67] Protected by anonymity, Milton revised and augmented his text for publication, assuming a public poet's responsibility to teach and please a larger audience.

Probably in late autumn, 1637, he added two substantial passages to the Trinity manuscript text: an expanded epilogue, and a long speech by the Lady extolling Chastity and Virginity, followed by Comus's awestruck testimony to that power in her. The terms glorify the doctrine and mystery of virginity:

> to him that dares
> Arme his profane tongue with reproachfull words
> Against the Sun-clad power of Chastitie
> Faine would I something say, yet to what end?
> Thou hast nor Eare, nor Soule to apprehend
> The sublime notion, and high mysterie
> That must be utter'd to unfold the sage
> And serious doctrine of Virginitie.[68]

Whatever else might contribute to Milton's new emphasis on chastity and virginity at this juncture, some explanation is provided by his reading. He later states in the *Apology* (1642) that he reaffirmed and refined his boyhood ideal of spiritual love and chastity during these years of study, as he read and reflected on Plato, Paul, and the Book of Revelation:

> Thus from the Laureat fraternity of Poets, riper years and the ceaselesse round of study and reading led me to the shady spaces of philosophy, but chiefly to the divine volumes of *Plato,* and his equal *Xenophon.* Where if I should tell ye what I learnt, of chastity and love, I meane that which is truly so, whose charming cup is only vertue which she bears in her hand to those who are worthy. The rest are cheated with a thick intoxicating potion which a certaine Sorceresse the abuser of loves name carries about; and how the first and chiefest office of love, begins and ends in the soule, producing those happy twins of her divine generation knowledge and vertue. . . . But having had the doctrine of holy Scripture unfolding those chaste and high mysteries with timeliest care infus'd, that *the body is for the Lord and the Lord for the body,* thus also I argu'd to my selfe, that if unchastity in a woman whom Saint *Paul* termes the glory of man, be such a scandall and dishonour, then certainly in a man who is both the image and glory of God, it must, though commonly not so thought, be much more deflouring and dishonourable. . . . Nor did I slumber over that place expressing such high rewards of ever accompanying the Lambe, with those celestiall songs to others inapprehensible, but not to those who were not defil'd with women, which doubtlesse meanes fornication: For mariage must not be call'd a defilement. (*CPW* I, 891–3)

The imagery of this passage – the exaltation of chastity, the Circean sorceress's cup, the twin birth produced by spiritual love – draws on the same nexus of concepts, attitudes, and images that informs *Comus.* While it is surely simplistic to identify "the Lady of Christ's" with the Lady of *Comus*, the *Apology* indicates that Milton held himself bound to the ideal of chastity, which for the unmarried means virginity. A healthy young man striving over several years to sublimate his sex drive in the service of that ideal might naturally enough extol its value. Milton's additions to *A Maske* do not mystify virginity as an ideal permanent condition or as inherently superior to the chastity which includes faithful marital love – a point Milton insists on in the *Apology*. Rather, as in the passage quoted, they emphasize the virgin's honor and power as a subset of "The Sun-clad power of Chastitie," the subset appropriate to the 15-year-old Lady – and to himself – in their present condition of life.

During the autumn of 1637 Milton evidently felt restive and isolated at Horton and made several trips to London. In a Latin letter of November 2,[69] from London, he sought to reclaim an intimacy with Charles Diodati after some period of time when the two were out of touch. Chiding his friend for failing to write or visit, Milton refers to recent visits to London when he sought news of Charles from his brother and looked for him in his old haunts without success. He chides Diodati for failing to keep his promise to visit Horton, and urges him to settle someplace where they might "visit each other, at least sometimes." The letter's tone does not suggest a falling out, only the problems of distance and the call of other worries and duties.[70] In excusing his own remissness Milton refers, as he had so often, to their differences in temperament and habits, and offers an illuminating insight into his own method of study:

> I am naturally slow and lazy to write, as you well know; whereas you on the other hand, whether by nature or by habit, can usually be drawn into this sort of Correspondence with ease. At the same time it is in my favor that your habit of studying permits you to pause frequently, visit friends, write much, and sometimes make a journey. But my temperament allows no delay, no rest, no anxiety – or at least thought – about scarcely anything to distract me, until I attain my object and complete some great period, as it were, of my studies. And wholly for this reason, not another please, has it happened that I undertake even courtesies more tardily than you. (*CPW* I, 323–4)

This statement may also go far to explain his poetic silence in these years, and at some later periods: if he could not interrupt a cycle of studies to write letters, he could hardly allow the far greater distraction of writing poetry.

Diodati's answer (now lost) evidently reported that he had completed his apprenticeship and was practicing medicine somewhere in the North. Milton's reply of November 23, also in Latin and posted from London, plays wittily with Diodati's new conquest of the "citadel of Medicine," and predicts fame for him in that endeavor. Chiding him for involvement with domestic matters[71] to the exclusion of "urban companionships," Milton urges him to "at least make your winter quarters with us" – presumably in London, where Milton is thinking of moving to escape from his country isolation:

> I shall now tell you seriously what I am planning: to move into one of the Inns of Court, wherever there is a pleasant and shady walk; for that dwelling will be more satisfactory, both for companionship, if I wish to remain at home, and as a more suitable headquarters, if I choose to venture forth. Where I am now, as you know, I live in obscurity and cramped quarters. (*CPW* I, 327)

Milton is not thinking of law as a profession, but of following the course taken by many young gentlemen: residing at the Inns of Court to make contacts and improve chances of preferment.

In this letter Milton seeks to explain himself to his dearest friend in language suffused with his readings of Plato. He virtually conflates his love for Diodati's beauty of spirit with his own desire to create poetry worthy of fame, and grounds both in his very nature as a lover of the Platonic Idea of the Beautiful:

> Know that I cannot help loving people like you. For though I do not know what else God may have decreed for me, this certainly is true: He has instilled into me, if into anyone, a vehement love of the beautiful. Not so diligently is Ceres, according to the Fables, said to have sought her daughter Proserpina, as I seek for this idea of the beautiful, as if for some glorious image, throughout all the shapes and forms of things. . . . Whence it happens that if I find anywhere one who, despising the warped judgment of the public, dares to feel and speak and be that which the greatest wisdom throughout all ages has taught to be best, I shall cling to him immediately from a kind of necessity. But if I, whether by nature or by my fate, am so equipped that I can by no effort and labor of mine rise to such glory and height of fame, still, I think that neither men nor Gods forbid me to reverence and honor those who have attained that glory or who are successfully aspiring to it. (*CPW* I, 326–7)

He praises Diodati here as one of a choice band of noble spirits. And Diodati's example, as one who gave over ministerial studies for medicine, may have prompted Milton to declare for the first time unambiguously – albeit diffidently and with self-deprecating humor – that he is first and foremost a poet seeking the Idea of Beauty and immortal fame:

> Listen, Diodati, but in secret, lest I blush; and let me talk to you grandiloquently for a while. You ask what I am thinking of? So help me God, an immortality of fame. What am I doing? Growing my wings and practising flight. But my Pegasus still raises himself on very tender wings. (*CPW* I, 327)

The new flight he was practicing in November, 1637 was the pastoral elegy *Lycidas*. Confronting a world in which Edward King could be cut off at age 25 with his aspirations, talents, and promise unfulfilled, the Miltonic speaker calls into agonizing question the value of undertaking the arduous vocations of poet and minister. The poem is dated "Novemb: 1637" in the Trinity manuscript, and is heavily revised.[72] The Cambridge memorial volume, *Justa Edouardo King Naufrago*, probably appeared early in 1638.[73] The first part, twenty Latin and three Greek poems, includes contributions by Edward's younger brother Henry King and by the future Cambridge Platonist Henry More; the second part, thirteen English poems with separate title page, includes verses by Joseph Beaumont, John Cleveland and (again) Henry King. *Lycidas* came last, the longest poem in Part II and the crown and climax of the volume. As did some others, Milton signed his poem with his initials only, J. M. It was not carefully printed, and two extant copies bear corrections in Milton's hand.[74] *Lycidas* is discussed on pages 81–6.

Milton's readiness to contribute to this Cambridge volume might seem surprising, given that King was not a close friend and that by 1637 King's royalist and Laudian sentiments were evident in his court poems.[75] Milton deals with King's politics by entirely eliding them, constructing him instead as the last best hope of reform, now lost. The other contributors to *Justa Edouardo King Naufrago* – chiefly clerics and other college fellows like King himself – associate King closely with the church and the university he served;[76] Milton sharply dissociates him from the corrupt church, making St Peter praise him as a single good minister among the unnumbered "Blind mouthes" who feed only their own bellies, and whose wretched sermons leave their flocks famished and prey to the Roman Catholic wolf. Milton's contribution is also differentiated from the others in genre and mode as well as, of course, aesthetic quality: it is the only true pastoral elegy,[77] and the only poem rising to apocalyptic diatribe and prophecy. Christopher Hill suggests that Milton employed pastoral to disguise his furious attack on the Laudian church, but that seems dubious;[78] censors and readers could hardly miss the point in 1638 – the reason, perhaps, that Milton signed with his initials only. The volume's compilers, the clerical contributers, and Milton's Cambridge audience might have been uneasy with this passage, but they could hardly protest without seeming to identify themselves as likely objects of Peter's denunciation.

Unlike the other elegists, Milton's focus is not on King but on his own anxieties about vocation, poetic and religious. King's death affected Milton so strongly because King's situation so nearly resembles Milton's own: they had shared youthful pleasures and poetic beginnings at Cambridge and had had common vocational goals. Three years Milton's junior, King was also a poet of sorts; he served the church as an ordained minister, and he had continued a scholarly life as a fellow of Christ's. The fact that he (like Milton) had not yet fulfilled his youthful promise and now would never do so forced Milton to confront the terror of mortality in relation to the issue of vocation. St Peter's vehement denunciation consigning the English church to destruction from "That two-handed engine at the door" indicates that Milton had by this time quite abandoned the idea of taking orders, though he might not consider that decision irrevocable should a major reformation occur. That Milton was reaching toward a role of service to God outside the church, as a poet, is intimated in the proposition that Lycidas's ministerial role will also be preserved in another form. As the "Genius of the shore" he will aid wanderers in the "perilous flood of life" – perhaps through his exemplary story retold in Milton's poem.

At some point during his "studious retirement" Milton wrote "Ad Patrem," a sophisticated Latin verse epistle which is in part a praise of his father for fostering his education and self-education, in part a defense of poetry against his father's supposed disparagement of it, and in part an implicit persuasion to his father to accept his vocation as a poet and continue to support him in it. The various dates assigned by scholars – as early as 1632 and as late as 1645 – are closely related to their various speculative scenarios about Milton's personal development during these years.[79] I think it likely that "Ad Patrem" was written in the final weeks of 1637 or early 1638, just after publication of *A Maske* and *Lycidas,* or in immediate expectation of their appearance. Hearing such declarations as Milton had made to Diodati in November – that he saw himself as, above all else, a poet – might well have given Milton senior some pause, coupled as they evidently were with requests that, after supporting his son's protracted studies for five years, he now finance a stay at the Inns of Court and/or send him on the Grand Tour. Even if Milton senior sympathized with his son's inability to resolve on ordination in the Laudian church and took pride in his poetry, he was surely voicing concern as to what his son would finally do to support himself, and when. Though the attitudes Milton ascribes to his father are probably exaggerated – "You should not despise the poet's task"; "Do not persist . . . in your contempt for the sacred Muses"; "You may pretend to hate the delicate Muses, but I do not believe in your hatred" – these lines likely register the scrivener's expressed doubts as to where his son's desire to devote his life to poetry would lead, absent a patron who is nowhere on the horizon.[80]

With "Ad Patrem" Milton turned to dactyllic hexameters that flow into longer units, akin to the English verse paragraphs he used in *Lycidas* at about the same time. As a defense of poetry, the poem sounds some familiar Renaissance themes: poetry's divine origins, the poet's fellowship with the gods, the bard's heroic and divine subjects, and Orpheus as a figure for the poet in that his song could move stones and trees and Hell itself. As he does also in *Lycidas*, Milton emphasizes the poet's priestly and prophetic roles and his part in heavenly song:

> By song Apollo's priestesses and the trembling Sibyl, with blanched features, lay bare the mysteries of the far-away future. Songs are composed by the sacrificing priest at the altar. . . . When we return to our native Olympus and the everlasting ages of immutable eternity are established, we shall walk, crowned with gold, through the temples of the skies and with the harp's soft accompaniment we shall sing sweet songs to which the stars shall echo and the vault of heaven from pole to pole.[81]

Though deeply felt, this defense is also part of Milton's rhetorical strategy to persuade his father to accept and support him as a poet.

By means of a skillful construction of personae, Milton was able to handle with tact and poetic decorum the clash between the young poet's lofty concept of poetry and the father's deprecation of it.[82] He creates his father's portrait by repeated praises of his paternal generosity, his skill in music, and his appreciation for learning, which led him to foster Milton's education and self-education; such a father is simply mistaken in thinking that he hates the Muses. Milton's self-portrait is a complement to his father's: he is filled with gratitude, deferential to his father but firm in upholding the good cause of poetry, modest about his own past accomplishments but confident of the future. The choice of Latin for this poem also honors Milton senior as a man of education and culture who is able to appreciate learned poetry and the son who can produce it. This is a graceful poetic tribute, but also strikingly effective as rhetoric.

The young man who wondered, in Sonnet VII, what his lot might prove to be is now, after more than five years' study and soul-searching, ready to proclaim unhesitatingly that "it is my lot to have been born a poet" ("Nunc tibi quid mirum, si me genuisse poëtam," l. 61). This is bold and new. No previous English poet had made anything like Milton's forthright claim to the role of poet as the essence of his self-definition. He implies, with rhetorical finesse, that he came by his poetic gift partly as a matter of inheritance from his amateur musician father, emphasizing their mutual interests and talents: "why does it seem strange to you that we, who are so closely united by blood, should pursue sister arts and kindred interests?"[83] He ascribes it also, gratefully, to the education his father provided, which exactly suited the needs of a poet: not only Latin and Greek at school but also private tuition in Hebrew, French and Italian, and the opportunity after university to study any and all areas of knowledge he wishes to pursue. Finally, he ascribes it to the generosity of a father who did not force him to business ("the field of lucre") or to "the law and the evil administration of the national statutes," but allowed him leisure to develop as a poet:

> Because you wish to enrich the mind which you have carefully cultivated, you lead me far away from the uproar of cities into these high retreats of delightful leisure beside the Aonian stream, and you permit me to walk there by Phoebus' side, his blessed companion.[84]

He then pledges to come forth from his obscurity – a gesture toward *A Maske* and *Lycidas*. He virtually promises his father that he will attain fame, but also registers considerable anxiety that his poems might not be well received:

> Therefore, however humble my present place in the company of learned men, I shall sit with the ivy and laurel of a victor. I shall no longer mingle unknown with the dull rabble and my walk shall be far from the sight of profane eyes. Begone, sleepless cares and complaints, and the twisted glances of envy with goatish leer. Malevolent Calumny, open not your dragon gorge. You have no power to harm me, O detestable band; and I am not under your jurisdiction.[85]

He concludes this poem with an apostrophe to his "juvenile verses," urging them "if only you dare hope for immortality" to preserve this eulogy of his father "as an example to remote ages." Though he couched this statement in the conditional, Milton could now believe that the poems he has thus far written might win enduring fame.

From his several works – and what he did not write – critics have inferred different developmental narratives to explain Milton's inner life during these years. In Parker's account, Milton senior was determined that his son should enter the ministry and saw *A Maske* as a distressing diversion from that course; Milton, to pacify him, wrote "Ad Patrem" in 1634, left off writing poetry for three years, immersed himself in ecclesiastical history and patristics (studies pertinent to the ministry), and in 1637 let *A Maske* be published without his name. Those gestures, and the example of *Lycidas* as a kind of poetic ministry, reconciled Milton senior to his son's poetry and persuaded him to finance his Grand Tour.[86] Ernest Sirluck, pointing to Milton's new emphasis on virginity in the 1637 *Maske*, argues that Milton resolved his career anxieties and a three-year writer's block by making a covenant of sacrificial celibacy in 1637, confirming his dedication as God's poet–priest – a gesture that empowered him to claim his poetic vocation.[87] Kerrigan finds in the paralyzed virgin of *A Maske* a version of Milton's own poetic and sexual paralysis due to oedipal pressures, from which he was largely released by the death of his mother in 1637; he was then able to leave home and move closer to a mature sexuality, as evidenced in the images of (heavenly) erotic fulfillment in the expanded epilogue of the 1637 *Maske*.[88] In Shawcross's scenario, Milton's 1637 letters to Diodati indicate that he has at last come to terms with a debilitating disruption some years earlier in their repressed or perhaps overt homosexual relationship. His new emphasis on virginity is a means of sublimating that attraction, and the Trinity manuscript and Commonplace Book (both begun, Shawcross thinks, in 1637) are evidence of his restored creativity.[89]

Whatever validity there may be to one or another of these narratives, they rest on scant evidence and unsubstantiated assumptions. Milton's two brief references to his mother hardly afford evidence of an oedipal struggle resolved by her death. His cryptic comment in the *Defensio Secunda* linking his trip abroad to his mother's death – "I became desirous, my mother having died, of seeing foreign parts, especially Italy, and with my father's consent I set forth" (*CPW* IV.1, 614) – seems intended simply to underscore Milton's filial piety: he had the consent of his father and no longer needed to seek that of his mother. Or, the phrase may imply that she had been seriously ill for some time and he felt he could not leave under those circumstances. Milton's statement that his father initially intended him for the ministry does not mean that he stubbornly insisted on that career for his son and disapproved of *A Maske*. Milton's exaltation of virginity in 1637 does not imply that this staunch Protestant made a temporary vow of celibacy – a gesture he would surely see as popish. Nor do Milton's 1637 letters to Diodati point to Milton's new acceptance of homosexual feelings or activities he had earlier denied; the sexual *double entendres* in Latin that Shawcross points to in those letters are not convincing, as virtually any text could be made to yield such meanings if pressed. And the assimilation of Diodati to the class of Neoplatonic beautiful and noble souls suggests, if anything along these lines, the continued sublimation of homoerotic feeling.

The narrative Milton constructs about himself in the letters and poems of these years is rather different and I think more illuminating. At the center of his conscious mind was the problem of vocation, which he saw not only in terms of his own talents, inclinations, and opportunities, but also with reference to public duties – the needs of church and nation. He defined himself as poet and scholar, but neither role could provide a livelihood in itself, except for playwrights or commercial hacks. A gentleman needed a patron, another career, or financial independence, but Milton made no effort to invite court patronage, he was not offered a college fellowship, he hated law and business, he found no patron or post in a great family, and his resistance to the ministry steadily increased, thanks both to Laud and his own deepest inclinations. All this sufficiently accounts for his anxieties, his sense of belatedness by comparison with his contemporaries, and his insistance on more and more preparation as he sought to account to himself, to others, and to God for his delay in taking up a life's work. He justified delaying the moment of decision on the humanist ground that his inadequate formal education must be supplemented by further study, as well as on the Puritan principle that the all-important choice of vocation must follow God's as yet unclear directive. By late 1637 he had received some clarifications, and his father soon agreed to continue his support, apparently reassured by "Ad Patrem" and by the publication, in hand or imminent, of *A Maske* and *Lycidas*.

In the early months of 1638 Milton's plans for a European tour took shape. His brother Christopher had recently married Thomasine Webber, who probably began to live at Horton by November, 1637, freeing Milton from whatever contraints the needs of his recently widowed father, now 77 years old, might have imposed.[90] His projected travels (with the manservant a gentleman would need) could be expected to cost Milton senior the considerable sum of £250 or £300 a year.[91] Milton applied to Henry Lawes for help with a passport that would allow him to visit Rome – normally forbidden to English travellers – and in April Lawes secured the requisite documents.[92]

In March or early April Milton, through a mutual friend,[93] sought acquaintance with Sir Henry Wotton, Provost of Eton and erstwhile ambassador to various countries, including Venice. After an initial meeting Milton wrote Wotton on April 6 asking advice in planning his journey and enclosing a copy of the recently printed *Comus*. On April 13, answering this (now lost) letter, Wotton lamented that he did not meet Milton before, proclaimed his delight in Milton's conversation, and praised *Comus* enthusiastically, especially the "Dorique delicacy in your Songs and Odes, whereunto I must confess plainly to have seen yet nothing parallel in our Language" (*CPW* I, 341). He first read it, he states, "som good while before, with singular delight" and he thanks Milton "for intimating unto me (how modestly soever) the true Artificer." He recommends a route for the journey, provides Milton with letters of introduction for Paris, and tenders some prudent advice (once offered to him) for an ardent Protestant travelling in Rome: "*I pensieri stretti, & il viso sciolto* [your thoughts close, and your countenance open] will go safely over the whole World" (*CPW* I, 342). Milton surely found this learned man's praise of his work and gestures of friendship a powerful confirmation of his commitment to poetry, as well as a happy augury of forthcoming encounters with European literati.

"Since it is My Lot to Have Been Born a Poet"

In all its stages but most emphatically in its final forms (1637/1645), Milton's *Maske Presented at Ludlow Castle* is a reformed masque. It makes large claims for the poet's educative role as it locates virtue in, and teaches virtue to, a worthy noble family while delivering a trenchant critique of the Caroline ethos embodied in court masques. It is in some ways a complement to *Arcades,* elaborating issues and motifs briefly treated in that 109-line Entertainment. Both works undertake to reform their genres and the values associated with them; both have at their center a journey to a virtuous household; both exalt aristocratic virtue and criticize the court; and both emphasize the curative powers of local pastoral figures and of good art: poetry, song, dance. The themes of *A Maske* explore the nature of temptation, the problem of deception and illusion in the fallen world, and the danger of taking false pleasures for true ones. Making the Egerton children's journey to their father's Ludlow Castle a figure for the journey of life to a divine Father's house, the masque puts on display their sound education and virtue, intimating that the moral health of the nation depends upon the formation of such young aristocrats.

There is no close source, but Milton draws eclectically on his wide reading. The realm from which the Attendant Spirit, first named Daemon, is sent to guard the children owes something to Plato's *Phaedo* and to Spenser's Garden of Adonis. The sensualist magician Comus, son of Circe and leader of a beast-headed rout, draws upon the Circe myth in the *Odyssey* and in Ovid, on Acrasia's Bower of Bliss, and on Jonson's masque *Pleasure Reconciled to Virtue.*[94] The central plot situation of two brothers searching for a sister lost in the dark wood and captured by Comus recalls Peele's *Old Wives Tale.* The trial of the Lady recalls but contrasts with Spenser's Amoret enslaved by Busirane (*FQ* III, 12): Comus paralyzes the Lady by magic and tries to seduce her with powerful rhetoric, but unlike Amoret she produces a powerful verbal defense. Her release by the chaste Sabrina, nymph of the River Severn, recalls the curative role of the virgin healer Clorin in Fletcher's *Faithful Shepherdess.* The Elder Brother's glorification of chastity owes much to Plato, to Renaissance Neoplatonism, and to Spenser's Britomart. The entire masque tradition supplies the terms for the main masque scene at Ludlow Castle where the children dance their victory over temptation; and contemporary Caroline masques such as *Tempe Restored* (1632) and *Coelum Britannicum* (1634) embody the norms Milton writes against.[95] There are verbal and metrical echoes from *A Midsummer Night's Dream, The Tempest,* and other Shakespeare plays, and the Book of Revelation stands behind some of the imagery of the Spirit's Epilogue. Also, Milton uses a mix of verse forms: iambic pentameter for most of the dialogue, octosyllabic couplets (echoing and perverting *L'Allegro*) for Comus's address to his rout, and songs in a variety of intricate stanzas.

Despite the extensive dialogue and some dramatic tension in the Lady's encounter with Comus, this is not a drama but a masque, as its title indicates. Dances are at the heart of masques, though we cannot now recover their visual impact: here, the antic dances of Comus's rout, the rustic dances of the shepherds, the masque dances of the children at Ludlow (probably followed by Revels).[96] Songs, composed by Henry Lawes, also have special prominence: the Lady's haunting song invoking Echo, the Attendant Spirit's song invoking Sabrina, Sabrina's lovely lyrics, the Attendant Spirit's song presenting the children to their parents at Ludlow Castle. The dialogue often resembles formal debate – a presentation of opposed positions – first by the two brothers, then by the Lady and Comus. The masque transformations are produced through Sabrina's songs and rituals; and the children's virtue is exhibited and celebrated in their masque dances at Ludlow.

In form, theme, and spirit, however, this is a reformed *Masque*, projecting reformist religious and political values. It requires no expensive and elaborate machinery – no cloud machines for the Attendant Spirit, no elaborate sets. The principal characters, the three children, are not masqued allegorical or mythic figures as an audience would expect; only Comus, Sabrina, and the Attendant Spirit (Lawes, disguised as the Shepherd Thrysis) are true masquers. And while the lost Lady sees "visibly" the forms of those virtues especially necessary to her in her plight – faith, hope, and chastity – they are not masque personifications but the inhabitants of her own mind. Bridgewater is described as a representative of the ancient British nation holding power directly from Neptune and Jove, the gods of sea and sky; his connection with the Stuart court is elided.[97] The ideal masque world is Ludlow Castle not the Stuart court, and it is attained through pilgrimage; it does not, as is usual in masques, simply appear and dispel all dangers. Nor are the monarchs the agents of cure and renewal: that role belongs to Sabrina as an instrument of divine grace from the region, the Welsh countryside, and as an embodiment of the transformative power of song and poetry. Also, the Platonism in this masque is a far cry from that of the Caroline court: external form does not reflect internal worth, and evil is conceived in Protestant, not Platonic terms. At the end of this masque evil remains: the dark wood is still dangerous to pass through and Comus is neither conquered, nor transformed, nor reconciled.

Comus himself is a species of court masquer, enacting "dazzling Spells" and marvelous spectacles, but they only "cheate the eye with bleare illusion" (154–5).[98] He deceptively claims the world of pastoral by his shepherd disguise and his offer to guide the Lady to a "low / But loyall cottage"(319–20), alluding to the pastoralism so prevalent in court masques. But instead he leads her to a decadent court with an elaborate banquet and a beast-headed entourage – a none-too-subtle allusion to the licentious Cavaliers. In formal terms, this is a surprise: a masque audience would expect the court scene to be the main masque after the antimasque in the dark wood with the antic dances of Comus's rout. Instead, Milton's court is another antimasque – not the locus of virtue and grace but Comus's own residence.

As do several of his early poems, Milton's masque also contrasts alternative styles of life and art, but now in starker terms of good and evil. Comus's perversion of natural sensuality is opposed to the "Sun-clad power of Chastitie" (782) in the Lady – with both concepts receiving nuanced and complex definition over the course of the work. Milton's Comus is not the traditional belly god of drunkenness and gluttony but has the power and attractiveness of a natural force and a contemporary cultural ideal. As Cedric Brown notes, he is the right tempter for the occasion, presenting these young aristocrats with the refined, dissolute, licentious Cavalier lifestyle they must learn to resist.[99] His beast-headed rout images the deformation of human nature when passions supplant reason, and their antimasque dances display the art associated with this manner of life: "Tipsie dance, and Jollitie" (104), producing what the Lady recognizes as the sound "Of Riot, and ill-manag'd Merriment" (172). Poised against the Comus-ideal is the Lady's chastity and the better art embodied in the songs of the Lady, the Attendant Spirit, and Sabrina, and especially the masque dances at Ludlow Castle.

That better art points to the overarching concept of chastity as the principle that orders sensuality, pleasure, and love, holding nature, human nature, and art to their right uses. Those uses include the dynastic marriage Lady Alice surely expects; virginity is the proper, though only temporary, condition for her. Milton's masque seeks to detach the larger virtue of chastity from the "idolatrous" Catholic queen and the court's mystifications of her chaste marital love by vesting it in a learned Protestant virgin. But Milton undermines any notion of magical powers attaching to chastity or virginity. The haunting music and poetry of the Lady's Echo Song leave Comus awestruck, but do not deflect him from his licentious purposes, as Fletcher's Satyr was transformed by simply viewing the virgin Clorin. In the debate between the Lady's brothers, the younger, a pessimistic realist, expects his sister to suffer rape or worse violence, given her exposed condition in an evil world, while the elder, a Platonic idealist, believes that chastity alone will protect her from savages, bandits, or any other evil – as if she were a Diana or a Clorin or a militant Britomart "clad in compleat steele" (421). But in the Lady's sounder view, chastity is a principle of spiritual integrity, not a physical state or a magic charm. In the dark wood and when paralyzed in Comus's chair she confronts the reality of deception, physical danger, and sexual violence, yet insists upon her power of spiritual resistance:

> Thou canst not touch the freedome of my mind
> With all thy charms, although this corporall rind
> Thou hast immanacl'd, while heav'n sees good (ll. 663–5).

At Comus's castle Comus and the Lady display their opposed values and rhetorical styles in a formal debate on the questions, what kind of pleasure accords with Nature, and what is the nature of nature? In an initial exchange Comus offers the Lady his Circean cup of sensual pleasure, ease, refreshment, balm, and joy as the true principle of nature. But she, pointing to his earlier lies and to the beast-headed creatures, retorts that "none / But such as are good men can give good things" (703). In richly sensuous language, mesmerizing in its very sounds and rhythms, Comus then proposes a vision of nature so prolific in its abundance and vitality that its bounty bids fair to strangle the world unless humans consume, consume, consume, with riotous abandon:

> Wherefore did Nature powre her bounties forth
> With such a full and unwithdrawing hand,
> Covering the earth with odours, fruits, and flocks
> Thronging the seas with spawn inumerable
> But all to please, and sate the curious tast?
> . . .
>   If all the world
> Should in a pet of temperance feed on Pulse
> . . .
> [Nature] would be quite surcharg'd with her own weight,
> And strangl'd with her wast fertilitie;
> Th'earth cumber'd, and the wing'd aire dark't with plumes. (ll. 710–30)

Drawing the issue to the folly of virginity in such a nature, Comus echoes countless Cavalier seduction poems on the theme of *Carpe Diem* and *Carpe Floream*:

> List Ladie, be not coy, and be not cozen'd
> With that same vaunted name Virginitie;
> Beautie is natures coine, must not be hoorded,
> But must be currant, and the good thereof
> Consists in mutuall and partaken blisse,
> Unsavorie in th'injoyment of it selfe.
> If you let slip time, like a neglected rose
> It withers on the stalke with languish't head.
> Beautie is nature's brag, and must be showne
> In courts, at feasts, and high solemnities
> Where most may wonder at the workmanship;
> It is for homely features to keepe home. (ll. 737–48)

The Lady's rejoinder, couched in trenchant language with a satiric edge, denounces the profligate and wasteful consumption Comus promotes, and the court masques so notoriously exhibit. Challenging his vision of an excessively prolific nature and the rhetorical excess he uses to describe it – the "dazling fence" of his "deere Wit, and gay Rhetorick"(790–1) – she offers a description of nature that squares with the fallen world of common experience and ends with a remarkably egalitarian argument, for its time, for the right of the worthy poor to share equitably in the earth's bounty:

> If every just man that now pines with want
> Had but a moderate, and beseeming share
> Of that which lewdly-pamper'd Luxurie
> Now heaps upon some few with vast excesse,
> Natures full blessings would be well dispenc't
> In unsuperfluous even proportion,
> And she no whit encomber'd with her store. (ll. 768–74)

In Caroline court masques the evils of social disorder and disruption are commonly associated with the lower classes, not, as here, with the waste and extravagance of the court and the wealthy elites. The Lady refuses to answer Comus's challenge to chastity and virginity on the ground that he is utterly unable to understand those concepts, but her few words opening that topic leave him awestruck, as her song did earlier.[100] Finding his rhetorical art countered by her logic and "sacred vehemence" (795), he turns to force.

The rescue scene demystifies the divine interventions and the male heroics common in masques. Set against Comus's role as magician and illusionist is the Attendant Spirit's role as teacher, dispensing heaven's aid through human means, not miracles. He advises the brothers how to rescue their sister, and provides them with haemony (sound education in temperance or in scripture), like the moly that protected Ulysses from Circe. But surprisingly, the brothers' brave but impetuous swordplay achieves only a partial rescue: they chase Comus away but cannot release the Lady – perhaps because as males they cannot reverse the phallic power of Comus's wand. The Spirit then has recourse to female power tendered through poetry, a story by his teacher Meliboeus (Spenser, in *FQ*, II.x.19) about an innocent virgin murdered because she was the product of an adulterous union and then transformed into the nymph of the Severn river which flows near Ludlow into Wales. Sabrina's tainted origin points to original sin as the source of the Lady's plight, paralyzed in a chair "Smear'd with gummes of glutenous heate"(916) – subject, that is, despite her own virtue to unruly sensuality and unable to free herself, to attain salvation by her own merits.

When the Spirit's song invokes Sabrina the masque transformations begin, and issues only partly settled by debate are resolved in song and dance. Sabrina's transformation from victim to deity, and her existence in the world of poetry and myth, make her an appropriate emblem and agent for the divine grace necessary to free the Lady. As agent of grace, she sprinkles water drops in a ceremony suggestive of baptism. As a classical female deity, she is invoked from among a company of female water deities and protectors of humans – Leucothea, Thetis, Parthenope, Ligea, and other nymphs – whose nurturing care can aid their mortal sister.[101] As daughter of Locrine, she calls up heroic myths of Aeneas, Anchises, Brute, and Trojan Britain as an impetus for national reformation, connecting the Egertons with that heroic past rather than the present Stuarts. As a personage in Spenser's poem and as a singer herself she figures the power of true poetry to counter unruly sensuality and debased rhetoric. She is the good poet whose elegant songs and rituals free the Lady from the spells of the bad poet, Comus, and confirm her in her own arts of song. And as nymph of the local river she brings the Lady into the region her Father governs, and to a virtuous household that can partly control fallen nature and nurture good pleasures.

The masque festivities at Ludlow Castle include the rustic dances of shepherds in a recuperation of pastoral from Comus's (and the court's) deformation of it. The presentation song by the Attendant Spirit and the children's masque dances figure and display their triumph: as the Spirit declares, they "triumph in victorious dance / Ore sensuall Folly, and Intemperance" (974–5). The scene images the virtuous pleasure, beauty, and art that accord with the life of chastity, intimating that they can be best nurtured in the households of the country aristocracy. If we compare *Coelum Britannicum*, Thomas Carew's sumptuous court masque of 1634 in which the Caroline court is a model for the reformation of Olympus itself, it will be evident how completely Milton has reversed the usual politics of masquing.

The Spirit's epilogue, in quick octosyllabic couplets, provides another perspective on virtue and pleasure. In the much expanded 1637 version, the Venus/Adonis and Cupid/Psyche myths are presented as commentary on the masque action.[102] The Spirit flies to his own region, the Garden of the Hesperides, filled with sensuous delights but still, like Ludlow, a place where fallen nature is mending but not wholly cured. In explicit contrast to the joyous and free lovemaking of Venus and Adonis in Spenser's Garden of Adonis, and especially to the fusion of the Caroline court with the court of heaven in *Coelum Britannicum*, Milton underscores the distance between earthly virtue and heavenly perfection. Adonis here is only "waxing well of his deepe wound" inflicted by the boar, commonly allegorized as sensuality, and Venus sits "sadly" beside him (1,000–1). The Spirit then refers to a higher realm where the cures and pleasures are perfect, where the Celestial Cupid (Christ) will at length welcome Psyche (a figure for the Soul, the Lady, and the Bride of Revelation) after her long journey and trials, and where the twins Youth and Joy will be born from their union. Later, in Milton's *Apology for Smectymnuus* (1642), the twin progeny of Platonic love are said to be Knowledge and Virtue. The rewards in both cases are for spiritual lovers, not virgins as such. Milton's *Maske* is clearly a generic *tour de force* that conjoins and explores, as one subtle and complex ideal, chastity, true pleasure, and good art, setting them against what he saw as their debased counterparts, nurtured by the pastoralism and Neoplatonism of the Caroline court masques.

Lycidas is the *chef-d'oeuvre* of Milton's early poetry, and one of the greatest lyrics in the language. In it Milton confronts and works through his most profound personal concerns: about vocation, about early death, about belatedness and unfulfillment, about the worth of poetry. He also sounds the leitmotifs of reformist politics: the dangers posed by a corrupt clergy and church, the menace of Rome, the adumbrations of apocalypse, the call to prophecy. The opening phrase, "Yet once more," prepares for such inclusiveness.[103] It places this poem in the series of funeral poems Milton has hitherto written for deceased Cantabridgians and others, in the long series of pastoral funeral elegies stretching back to Theocritus, and in a series of biblical warnings and apocalyptic prophecies beginning with those words, especially Hebrews 12:26–8.[104] Also, the opening lines establish Lycidas/King and the Miltonic speaker as virtual alter egos: since Lycidas was cut off before his time, the Miltonic "uncouth swain" must sing an elegy before his poetic gifts are ripe, plucking with "forc'd fingers rude" (4) the unripe laurel and myrtle leaves. The death of Lycidas seems to demonstrate the uselessness of exceptional talent, lofty ambition, and noble ideals, to show human life and nature alike given over to meaningless chaos. The poem achieves a stunning fusion of intense feeling and consummate art.

The headnote identifies this poem as a monody, a funeral song by a single singer,[105] though in fact other speakers are quoted in the poem and the coda introduces another poetic voice. The song also has affinities with the Pindaric ode, especially in its uses of mythic transformations.[106] The generic topics of funeral elegy – praise, lament, consolation – are present, though not as distinct parts of the poem.[107] This is Milton's first extended use in English of verse paragraphs of irregular length. The verse is chiefly iambic pentameter with occasional short lines and a very irregular rhyme scheme that owes something to the Italian canzone: the poem's metrical form intensifies tensions, denies surface smoothness, and prevents facile resolutions. Virtually every line echoes other pastoral elegies by classical, neo-Latin, and vernacular Renaissance poets: Theocritus, Moschus, Bion, Virgil, Petrarch, Castiglione, Mantuan, Joannes Secundus, Sannazaro, Spenser, and many more.[108] Yet no previous, or I think subsequent, funeral poem has the scope, dimension, poignancy and power of *Lycidas*; it is, paradoxically, at once the most derivative and most original of elegies.

Milton's choice of the pastoral mode – by then out of fashion for funeral elegies – might have surprised contemporaries, but that choice enabled him to call upon the rich symbolic resonances Renaissance pastoral had come to embody. Imaging the harmony of nature and humankind in the Golden Age, pastoral traditionally portrays the rhythms of human life and death in harmony with the rhythms of the seasons. In classical tradition the shepherd is the poet, and pastoral is a way of exploring the relation of art and nature. In biblical tradition the shepherd is pastor of his flock, like Christ the Good Shepherd. He may also be a prophet like Moses, Isaiah, or David, all of them called to that role from tending sheep. Pastoral also allows for political comment, as in Spenser's *Shepheards Calender*.[109]

As Milton develops the usual topics of pastoral elegy, he evokes the pastoral vision again and again, then dramatizes its collapse. The dead poet and the living mourner are presented as companion shepherds singing and tending sheep in a *locus amoenus* – an idealized Cambridge University characterized by pastoral *otium*. The swain then questions the nymphs, the muses, and the classical gods as to why they did not prevent the death. There is a procession of mourners, associated appropriately with water: Triton who excuses the sea deities from responsibility for the shipwreck; Camus, God of the River Cam; St Peter as "Pilot of the *Galilean* Lake." There is also an extended flower passage in which nature is urged to pay the tribute of its beauty to the dead shepherd's bier. The first collapse of pastoral obliterates the poignantly nostalgic pastoral scene enjoyed by the youthful companion shepherds, in which nature, humankind, and poetic ambitions seem to be in harmony, unthreatened by the fact or even the thought of mortality. Lycidas's death shatters this idyl, revealing in nature not the ordered seasonal processes of mellowing and fruition that pastoral assumes, but rather the wanton destruction of youth and beauty: the blighted rosebud, the taintworm destroying the weanling sheep, and the frost-bitten flowers in early spring. Elsewhere, Milton signals the collapses of pastoral by genre shifts, as when the oaten flute is interrupted by notes in a "higher mood" – the epic speech of divine Apollo and the "dread voice" of St Peter.

In the poem's first central panel the swain identifies passionately with the plight of the lost poet: the Nymphs do not protect their Bards who may be subject to the savagery and mindless violence symbolized in the myth of Orpheus. So often invoked as the type of poets, Orpheus here figures their extreme peril: even the Muse Calliope could not save her son from horrific death and dismemberment by the Maenads, who embody the dark forces of nature and savagery that so easily overcome the fragile civilizing arts.[110] If poetic talent, labor, and the noble desire for fame can be so early and so easily snuffed out, why not live a life of ease and pleasure and pastoral love: why not "sport with *Amaryllis* in the shade, / Or with the tangles of Neaera's hair?" instead of devoting "laborious dayes" to "the thankles Muse?" (66–7). The swain's anger and frustration are rendered in graphic, appalling metaphors of the "blind *Fury*" and the "thin-spun life":

> *Fame* is the spur that the clear spirit doth raise
> (That last infirmity of Noble mind)
> To scorn delights, and live laborious dayes;
> But the fair Guerdon when we hope to find,
> And think to burst out into sudden blaze,
> Comes the blind *Fury* with th'abhorred shears,
> And slits the thin-spun life (ll. 70–6)

The swain finds some typically Miltonic consolation as he relives (with a difference) the experience of another great poet, Virgil, and feels his "trembling ears" touched by Apollo.[111] Figuring God in the aspect of true critic, Apollo assures the living swain and the dead Lycidas of fame in the Platonic sense – not praise of the masses but of the best, the "perfet witnes of all judging *Jove*" (82) that promises enduring fame in Heaven.

That answer, however incomplete, encourages the swain to recall pastoral – "O Fountain *Arethuse*" – and evoke a pastoral myth of fulfilled love in Arethusa's union with the river Alphaeus. But then, as he questions the water deities, their denial of any responsibility for this death again places it outside the order of nature and pastoral. It suits Milton's purpose to ignore the rock that caused the shipwreck, so as to portray this death as inexplicable: "It was that fatall and perfidious Bark / Built in th'eclipse, and rigg'd with curses dark, / That sunk so low that sacred head of thine" (100–2). Those lines reverberate with dark connotations, but the primary metaphor is that of sailing on the seas of life in the frail bark of the human body, subject to the "curse" of mortality because of the Fall. That, the metaphor suggests, is why Lycidas died, and why pastoral assumptions cannot deal with it.

The poem's second central panel mourns the lost pastor whose death has removed a sorely needed, worthy exception to the general greed and ignorance of the clergy – a last chance at reformation. The River Cam offers a brief pastoral lament for the loss of the university's "dearest pledge," but St Peter wholly quells the pastoral music with his fierce jeremiad against the Laudian church and clergy. His scornful paradox, "Blind mouthes," brilliantly exposes the ignorance, ambition, and greediness of those bad shepherds who seek only to feed their own bellies, leaving the hungry sheep "swoln with wind" produced by Laudian ceremony and conformity, and subject to the ravages of the Roman Catholic "grim Woolf" raging freely in the Caroline court, especially among the queen's ladies:[112]

> Blind mouthes! that scarce themselves know how to hold
> A Sheep-hook, or have learn'd ought els the least
> That to the faithfull Herdmans art belongs!
> What recks it them? What need they? They are sped;
> And when they list, their lean and flashy songs
> Grate on their scrannel Pipes of wretched straw,
> The hungry Sheep look up, and are not fed,
> But swoln with wind, and the rank mist they draw,
> Rot inwardly, and foul contagion spread:
> Besides what the grim Woolf with privy paw
> Daily devours apace, and nothing sed. (ll. 119–29)

Peter's tirade and King's death resonate with the passage in Isaiah 56:10–57:1 that warns of blind watchmen, greedy and drunken shepherds, and the righteous man "taken away from the evil to come" – often cited as auguries of impending national disaster.[113] The passage holds no promise of reformation, but the very fierceness of Peter's invective voicing God's wrath and promising imminent divine retribution supplies a kind of consolation – an apocalyptic prophecy that some formidable if ambiguous "two-handed engine" stands ready "at the door" to smite the guilty and cleanse the church.[114]

After this terrible diatribe the swain again recalls pastoral, the frightened river

Alphaeus and the Sicilian muse, producing a flower passage exquisite in its delicacy and beauty. He imagines Lycidas's funeral bier heaped with the various flowers into which heroes of classical myth were transformed, providing for them a kind of immortality in nature. But this consolation soon collapses, based as it is on a "false surmise" of harmony between humankind and nature. Lycidas's body is not here to be honored but is subject to the horrors of the monstrous deep:

> Ay me! Whilst thee the shores, and sounding Seas
> Wash far away, where ere thy bones are hurld,
> Whether beyond the stormy *Hebrides*,
> Where thou perhaps under the whelming tide
> Visit'st the bottom of the monstrous world. (ll. 154–8)

From this spiritual nadir the movement from inadequate or false to true consolation begins, catching up earlier intimations of resurrection in the myths of Orpheus, Hyacinth, Amaranthus, and Peter. The tone modulates from horror to hope, from the violence of "bones hurld" to the peace of "Sleep'st by the fable of Bellerus old" (160). The swain now sees St Michael's Mount off the Cornish coast where Lycidas drowned as an image of heavenly protection (warding against Spain), and finds similar import in the myth of the poet Orion saved by dolphins (a type of Jonah). The line, "Weep no more, woful Shepherds weep no more" (165) – an echo of the poem's first line – marks the turn to true consolation. The swain reads nature's symbol of resurrection from the sea – the sun sinks into the ocean at night and rises from it at dawn – as a type of the divine Son who walked the waves and through whose power St Peter, and now Lycidas, were "sunk low, but mounted high" (172). At length he calls up an ecstatic vision of a heavenly pastoral scene in which Lycidas enjoys true *otium* beside heavenly streams (from the Book of Revelation), with both his vocational roles preserved. As poet he is now a participant in the "unexpressive nuptiall song" (177) of the Lamb and the harmonies of heaven. As pastor he is now the "Genius of the shore" (183), a guide (by means of his exemplary story immortalized in the poem) to all who wander in the "perilous flood" of human life. Also, mythologized as a classical Genius or place deity, he can be imagined as a protector of English Protestants crossing the Irish sea (like King's family) to conquer and colonize the rebellious Catholic Irish.[115] Pastoral has collapsed again, but now into the higher mode of prophetic vision, which reclaims it. Though painfully inadequate to the fallen human condition, pastoral is seen to have its true locus in heaven.

The new voice introduced in the eight-line coda may be the most surprising feature of this always surprising poem. A more mature poetic self has been voicing the "uncouth" swain's monody; and he now places in wider perspective the swain's hard-won movement from despair to affirmation of life, which the poet's readers have been led to share:

Thus sang the uncouth Swain to th'Okes and rills,
While the still morn went out with Sandals gray;
He touch'd the tender stops of various Quills,
With eager thought warbling his *Dorick* lay:
And now the Sun had stretch'd out all the hills,
And now was dropt into the Western bay;
At last he rose, and twitch'd his Mantle blew:
To morrow to fresh Woods, and Pastures new. (ll. 186–93)

Having had his vision of the perfected pastoral in heaven, the swain is restored to hope and direction through the example of Lycidas–King, and can now take up his several pastoral roles in the world. He retains his shepherd's blue mantle and turns boldly to pastoral poetry – "With eager thought warbling his *Dorick* lay." Blue is also the color of Aaron's priestly robes (Exodus 28:31), intimating that, like Lycidas, the swain will continue some kind of ministry in the church. And as he twitches his mantle, he assumes poetry's prophetic/teaching role – like an Elisha receiving the mantle of prophecy from an Elijah taken up to heaven.[116] The Coda presents the story of Lycidas inside the story of the swain, both of them exempla for the Miltonic speaker of the coda, and the reader. As it reprises the daily cycle of pastoral – forth at dawn, home at evening – it opens up to the promise of new adventures, personal and literary. In it Milton can represent himself as ready to move on to the next stage of life and poetry and national reformation – most immediately to the "fresh Woods, and Pastures new" of his projected European trip.

4

"I Became Desirous . . . of Seeing Foreign Parts, Especially Italy" 1638–1639

Milton traveled on the Continent, by his own imprecise reckoning, for "a year and three months, more or less" – that is, from late April or early May, 1638 to late July or early August, 1639.[1] He was taking the grand tour some years later than was usual for privileged young gentlemen, and not simply to acquire a veneer of culture. By his years of study he was prepared for the experience as few others can have been. He had the classical tradition in his bones. He could speak French and Italian well. He had read Dante, Petrarch, Ariosto, Tasso and other texts in the vernacular. And he was already a neo-Latin poet of great distinction, if as yet little reputation.

These travels provided an important catalyst for Milton's personal growth. He left home permanently. He left rural Horton for cosmopolitan Europe. He left the isolation of solitary study for the attractive social and intellectual life of the Italian academies. He met first-hand the diverse faces of Roman Catholicism in France and in several parts of Italy. He left a culture deeply marked by iconoclasm to encounter the full glory of Renaissance and Baroque painting and sculpture and architecture. He had opportunities to hear the new music of Monteverdi and others. He met and had cordial conversation with some of the great men of the era: Hugo Grotius, Galileo, Cardinal Francesco Barberini. Perhaps most important, thanks to his letters of introduction but even more to his own evident intellectual distinction and poetic talent, he was welcomed by the literati throughout Italy as one of their own. One consequence of all this was a great boost of self-confidence in the rightness of his chosen vocation as poet. Another, despite his deep love for Italy and his Italian friends, was a reaffirmation of his own Englishness and of English Protestant culture.

Milton's account in the *Defensio Secunda* is the only source for the general outline of his travels,[2] with some additions from his other prose tracts, a few Italian records, and some letters and poems exchanged with Italian friends. That account, however, was not intended as autobiography but as rhetoric, designed to emphasize his sterling reputation with the learned of Europe. It is nonetheless revealing, as it registers Milton's obvious delight in many new friendships founded upon mutual admiration of learning and talent. He reveled in the attentions paid him by both great men and young prodigies, and in their gratifying praises of his poetry. The academies, especially those in Florence, he saw as an ideal environment to nurture poetic creativity and scholarly achievement; these private associations of scholars and literati combined during their frequent meetings social warmth, intellectual exchange, poetic performance, and literary criticism. But his remarks are general and often imprecise. It is usually not possible to trace the details of Milton's travels – when he arrived and left each place, what he saw and did, when he met the persons he mentions. It is even more difficult to determine his reactions to much that he saw – for example, Italian art, which he nowhere mentions. His polemic purposes did not invite such commentary, and there are no travel diaries or intimate personal letters to family or friends. Writing this phase of Milton's life involves treading a fine line between judicious speculation and unwarranted guesses.

Milton's poems of this period are the product of his Latin muse, and they exhibit his mastery of several genres of conventional coterie compliment and tribute. Their dense classical echoes and allusiveness display his learning and poetic skill to his Italian friends, who were evidently impressed. But they are much more than conventional exercises: often they address themes developed in earlier poems and continue Milton's practice of setting up within and between his poems alternative versions of life and art. Also, they often challenge genre and convention as they probe topics of profound personal significance to Milton – music, death, friendship, poetry. And the most impressive of them – *Mansus* and the *Epitaphium Damonis* – explore issues of Milton's poetics and his self-construction as a poet.

"I Have Sat Among their Lerned Men, For that Honor I Had"

Milton's projected route through France, Italy, and Switzerland closely parallels the itinerary of most other touring Englishmen of the era (plate 4). With his gentleman servant, he set off from London soon after the middle of April to (probably) Dover, crossed the Channel by boat to Calais, then proceeded as rapidly as possible to Paris, his first major stop. Milton says nothing of travel conditions in France and Italy, but they were often difficult: overland travel was chiefly on horseback; decent accommodation was hard to find; travelers had to comply with different police regulations in the several states; money had to be exchanged; certificates of health had to be obtained for the Italian cities; highwaymen and gypsies posed real dangers. Milton carried a letter of introduction from Henry Wotton, "a most distinguished gentleman" whose letters "gave signal proof of his esteem for me," to the British embassy in Paris, and he obtained others from the English ambassador to France, Sir John

Scudamore, to English merchants along his route, requesting their assistance to him.[3]

Milton probably arrived in Paris in early May but remained only "some days" (*CPW* IV.1, 615). Cyriack Skinner explains his rapid transit through France by the fact that he had "no admiration" for this kingdom's "manners & Genius."[4] In *Of Education* (1644) Milton projects as one benefit of English educational reform that we will not then need "the *Mounsieurs* of *Paris* to take our hopefull youth into thir slight and prodigall custodies and send them over back again transform'd into mimics, apes & Kicshoes" (*CPW* II, 414). The France Milton encountered was the absolutist France of Louis XIII and Cardinal Richelieu. Richelieu had allied France with the Protestant powers in the Thirty Years War to counter the threatened hegemony of Spain and the Holy Roman Emperor, but at home he relentlessly suppressed Huguenot political power. His destruction of La Rochelle (1628), which the Huguenots had defended long and courageously, had gone into the annals of Protestant martyrology. Still, even a few days would allow Milton to vist some Parisian sights – the Louvre, Notre Dame, the newly built palace of the Luxembourg, the Palais Royal, the Jardin des Plantes. While in Paris he might have heard about the recently founded Académie Française (1635) and the recent production of Corneille's *The Cid* at the Théâtre Française.

He mentions only two contacts in Paris, neither of them French: the first, Lord Scudamore, introduced him "of his own initiative" to the second, Hugo Grotius, "a most learned man . . . whom I ardently desired to meet" (*CPW* IV.1, 615). Grotius, the famed Dutch international jurist, was then in exile from his native Holland as an Arminian opponent to that state's Calvinist orthodoxy and a strong supporter of religious toleration; from 1635 he had served as ambassador to the French king from Queen Christiana of Sweden. Milton would have had several reasons for his "ardent" interest in Grotius. He was perhaps already thinking his way toward positions that he would later hold and that Grotius had already defended in various writings: natural law theory, the basis of government in social contract, broad religious toleration for Protestants, an Arminian concept of free will, and aristocratic republicanism.[5] Already something of an anti-monarchist, Milton would find a good deal to discuss with Grotius, who had written in *De Jure belli ac pacis* that monarchy and liberty are as incompatible as slavery and freedom: "As then personal Liberty excludes the Dominion of a Master, so does civil Liberty exclude Royalty, and all manner of Sovereignty properly so called [i.e. arbitrary rule]" – though people might freely choose these unfree conditions of life.[6] Milton may already have read, or then learned about, Grotius's important dramatic works – *Adamus Exul* (1601) and *Christus Patiens* (1617) – on subjects he himself would later treat.[7] Upon leaving Paris Milton made for Nice (rather than Marseilles as Wotton had suggested), probably traveling to Orléans, then along the Loire to Lyons and through Provence. That journey took perhaps two weeks.

Much of the Italy Milton visited was directly or indirectly controlled by Spain.

His entry point, Nice, was part of the Duchy of Savoy, then embroiled in almost constant power struggles for territory, and in alliance by turns with Spain and France. From Nice he proceeded by boat to Genoa, then an independent republic ruled by Councils, a Senate, and a Doge, but strongly Spanish in sympathy and fashion; its bankers and brokers served as financial agents for Spain throughout Italy. From the sea he could take in the splendid cityscape with its two hundred palaces, of which the Villa Doria was the most spectacular. He had a few days there to observe some of them more closely – their marble and painted exteriors and their spectacular gardens and waterworks. Then he sailed on to the trading port of Livorno (Leghorn), a free port where all nations and religions – Jews, Turks, Protestants – enjoyed liberty and traded freely in goods and in galley slaves. From this entry to the Grand Duchy of Tuscany he traveled by land some 14 miles to Pisa, stopping briefly and no doubt visiting the most obvious landmarks: the ancient Duomo and Baptistery, the famous university, the Leaning Tower. He perhaps wondered, as did John Evelyn who covered much the same route six years later, "how it is supported from immediately falling."[8]

He proceeded to Florence for two months or so, perhaps arriving in early July and he was certainly still there in mid-September, 1638.[9] En route home he returned to Florence for another such period (*c.* March 15–May 15, 1639). Though the glory days of Florence were over, the ghosts of the past were everywhere: in the monuments, the art, the literature, the institutions, and the historical memory of Milton's friends. Milton already knew most of the great names and soon learned of others, understanding their contributions better in their Florentine context: Cosimo and Lorenzo di Medici, Ficino, Alberti, Leonardo, Dante, Petrarch, Machiavelli, Guicciardini, Savonarola, Giotto, Donatello, Masaccio, Fra Angelico, Michelangelo. The reigning Medici Grand Duke, Ferdinand II, was a great patron of the arts and of Galileo, though his inability to protect the scientist from the Inquisition testifies to that family's and Tuscany's declining power, political and economic. According to Edward Phillips Milton was much taken with the ambiance of the city and its noble structures – including, we may suppose, the Duomo with its Campanile and Baptistery, the Signoria, the Palazzo Vecchio, the Pitti Palace and its gardens, Santa Croce, San Lorenzo with the crypts of all the Medici, the bridges over the Arno, the Boboli Gardens, and Fiesole, the ancient seat of the Etruscan people, with its breathtaking prospect over the city (plate 5). We do not know what art Milton saw in Florence or if he spent much time with it – he says nothing about that. But in addition to what was in churches and other public places his friends could have given him access to several great private collections.[10]

The intellectual and social life of the academies was Milton's chief delight in Florence. Several academic friendships evidently began during his first visit to Florence and continued during the second. Though he also attended academies in Rome, he thought of that institution as distinctively Florentine, and of his Florentine academic friends as valued comrades in the service of the Muses:

> There I at once became the friend of many gentlemen eminent in rank and learning, whose private academies I frequented – a Florentine institution which deserves great praise not only for promoting humane studies but also for encouraging friendly intercourse. Time will never destroy my recollection – ever welcome and delightful – of you, Jacopo Gaddi, Carlo Dati, Frescobaldi, Coltellini, Buonmattei, Chimentelli, Francini, and many others. (*CPW* IV.1, 615–17)

This summary in Milton's *Defensio Secunda* – and no doubt some of his verbal descriptions – are echoed in Edward Phillips's account of his uncle's stay in Florence:

> In this City he met with many charming Objects, which Invited him to stay a longer time than he intended; the pleasant Scituation of the Place, the Nobleness of the Structures, the exact Humanity and Civility of the Inhabitants, the more Polite and Refined sort of Language there, than elsewhere. During the time of his stay here, which was about Two Months, he Visited all the private Academies of the City, which are Places establish'd for the improvement of Wit and Learning, and maintained a Correspondence and perpetual Friendship among Gentlemen fitly qualified for such an Institution: and such sort of Academies there are in all or most of the most noted Cities in *Italy*. Visiting these Places, he was soon taken notice of by the most Learned and Ingenious of the Nobility, and the Grand Wits of *Florence*, who caress'd him with all the Honours and Civilities imaginable; particularly *Jacobo Gaddi, Carolo Dati, Antonio Francini, Frescobaldo, Cultellino, Bonmatthei, and Clementillo*: Whereof *Gaddi* [Francini] hath a large Elegant *Italian Canzonet* in his Praise: *Dati*, a Latin Epistle; both Printed before his Latin Poems. (*EL* 56–7)

The tradition of the Florentine academies originated with the famous Neoplatonic Academy of Cosimo di Medici and Ficino, which looked back to Plato's Academy for its inspiration, and which had helped to renew the intellectual life of Europe.[11] If its Seicento descendants – constrained by Tridentine orthodoxy, weighed down by pedantry, and often distracted by frivolities – fell off from that ideal, they nonetheless had it in memory. The academies met frequently, sometimes weekly, under the aegis of a princely or noble patron; often they took ironic names and their members adopted cryptic nicknames. Their activities, carefully recorded by a secretary, involved literary readings or recitations of new works (followed by critique and defense), translations of Greek and Latin into Italian, analyses of ancient and modern texts (Petrarch was especially popular), and debates on linguistic and other topics. Many, especially in Naples, proscribed and scrupulously avoided any form of theological debate or analysis of scripture.[12] Consciously modeled after the Platonic symposium, they were also convivial meeting places for friends, and often held sumptuous banquets. Many were notable for welcoming visiting scholars from abroad.

During the years 1635–9 the celebrated Florentine Academy had presentations and discussions on such topics as Torricelli's experiments, distributative justice, the qualities of a saintly prince, paraphrases of the Psalms, a new treatise on music, and recent scholarship on Galileo, Tacitus, and Guicciardini.[13] Milton may have attended some sessions of that academy and of the Academia della Crusca, whose major concern was the purity of the Tuscan language and whose major work was a great dictionary, the *Vocabulario*, first published in 1612. But his most intimate associations were with smaller, private academies, especially the Svogliati (the Will-less), and the Apatisti (the Passionless).[14] These groups had a strongly literary cast, though the latter had a scientific branch as well. They met frequently, the Svogliati weekly, on Thursdays, to listen to presentations and original works by members and visitors: poems, plays, theological essays, moral "characters," and lives of the saints.[15] The Svogliati books record Milton's attendance and performance on September 6/16: "To the members of the Academy gathered in considerable numbers some compositions were read, and particularly John Milton, an Englishman, read a very learned Latin poem [multo erudita] in hexameters" (*LR* I, 389). Most likely, he read "Naturam non pati senium" – certainly an erudite philosophical work with which to impress academicians.[16] Later, he describes reciting "some trifles which I had in memory, compos'd at under twenty or thereabout (for the manner is that every one must give some proof of his wit and reading there)" – a description which would best fit "Naturam" (*CPW* I, 809–10). It is very likely that he attended other meetings of the Svogliati during his first stay in Florence – several meetings are recorded but not a list of attendees – as he did on at least three occasions during his second visit. He may have been admitted to membership, as foreign scholars sometimes were. On June 28/July 8 the Svogliati minutes make tantalizing reference (without name attached) to "an English man of letters who wanted to enter the academy," and on July 5/15 to the acceptance of one Mr. . . . (name omitted, perhaps to be added later) into the society.[17] The first date seems rather early for Milton's arrival in Florence, but it is possible, since he stayed only "some days" in Paris. Though the minutes are not extant, a later manuscript list of Apatisti members in 1638 includes "Giovanni Milton inglese."[18] The secretary of the Apatisti was Milton's friend Carlo Dati, and that academy was known for attracting foreign members and encouraging multilingual presentations.

Jacopo Gaddi was a prime mover on the Florentine intellectual scene: himself a noted poet and scholar, he founded the Svogliati, which reportedly included the best wits of Florence.[19] A generous patron of learning and the arts, he was also famous for his hospitality to foreign men of letters. His academy met in his new palazzo (now the Hotel Astoria) in Via del Giglio, with its extensive collection of antiquities, paintings and books, and at the Villa Camerata near Fiesole, whose botannical gardens held plants from all Europe and Egypt.[20] Benedetto Buonmattei, priest, scholar, and professor at Pisa, was a chief pillar in all the Florentine academies. Author of a commentary on Dante and several other works, his *chef-d'ouevre* was a two-volume account of Tuscan grammar, *Della Lingua Toscana* (1643).[21] Milton took great interest in this work-in-progress and seems to have discussed it with him on several occasions. On August 31/September 10, 1638 he wrote a long Latin letter to Buonmattei, offering both praise and advice. He extols the grammar as a work second only to that of the founder of a wise government, since it will prevent the decline that accompanies linguistic carelessness and will make the state "truly noble, and splendid, and brilliant" (*CPW* I, 329). He advises Buonmattei to include, for the benefit of foreigners, "a little something on right pronunciation" and some suggestions as to which Florentine authors to read after the best-known names, citing himself as one of those Buonmattei should address: "Certainly I, who have not merely wet my lips in these [classical] Languages but have drunk deeper drafts – as much as anyone of my years, am nevertheless glad to go for a feast to Dante and Petrarch, and to a good many of your other authors" (*CPW* I, 330). He wrote the letter in Latin rather than Tuscan as a further argument, "that you may understand that I wish that Tongue clarified for me by your precepts, and to confess my awkwardness and ignorance plainly in Latin" (*CPW* I, 332). Buonmattei did not incorporate these suggestions.

Carlo Dati seems to have been Milton's closest friend in Italy. He was only 19 in 1638 – another of those bright prodigies who crossed Milton's path – and was already astonishing his elders by his scientific learning and his eloquence. He also enjoyed entertaining foreign scholars and literati. His many interests are evident from his later publications: a respected study of the four principal Greek painters of antiquity, panegyric poetry, and several mathematical, antiquarian, and philological tracts.[22] Dati is the only Italian friend with whom Milton exchanged letters (in 1647–8), in one of which Dati reports his appointment to the chair and lectureship of humane letters at the Florentine Academy (*CPW* II, 762–75). Other Florentine friends identified by Milton are Agostino Coltellini, founder of the Apatisti, Benedetto Fioretti, president of that academy, Valerio Chimentelli, Pietro Frescobaldi, and the poet Antonio Francini.[23] Milton did not name the poet Antonio Malatesti in the *Defensio Secunda*, but greeted him in the 1647 letter to Dati as one of those "especially fond of me."[24] During the Florence visit Malastesti presented to Milton a fifty-sonnet sequence he had written the previous summer, entitled *La Tina: Equivoci Rusticali;* he dedicated it to "the most illustrious Gentleman and Most Worthy Master Signor John Milton, Noble Englishman." The sonnets were an elaborate linguistic joke, each one carrying a risqué double entendre.[25] This gift suggests that Milton's Florentine friends credited him with an earthy sense of humor.

One highlight of Milton's stay in Florence was his visit to "the famous *Galileo*, grown old, a prisner to the Inquisition, for thinking in Astronomy otherwise then the Franciscan and Dominican licencers thought" (*CPW* II, 538). Galileo was condemned in 1633, and thereafter confined under a kind of house arrest, his activities limited. Seventy-five years old in 1638 and almost totally blind, Galileo lived in a pleasant villa at Arcetri, a short distance from Florence. Milton might have visited him there, or at the home of his illegitimate son Vincenzo on the Costa San Giorgio, where he stayed at times for medical treatment.[26] The visit may have been arranged through Vincenzo, whom Milton knew, or through Dati, who had been Galileo's pupil.[27] What they talked about, and whether Milton might have looked through a telescope, must remain matters of speculation. Conceivably, Milton purchased or was given a copy of Galileo's *Dialogo . . . sopra i due massimi sistemi del mondo, tolemaico, e copernicano,* published in Florence in 1632, but if so it was a clandestine copy, since the work had been banned since 1633.[28] It is possible though not very likely that Milton visited the Abbey of Vallombrosa, a beauty spot about 18 miles from Florence and the site of the famous "Autumnal leaves" simile in *Paradise Lost* (I, 300–4); the valley was noted for its many varieties of trees.[29]

Sometime in late September Milton left Florence for Rome, taking the usual route through the medieval city of Siena, with its walls, its striking Gothic cathedral of black and white marble, and its ancient baptistery and university. Passing through Viterbo, he probably entered Rome by the Porta del Populo and along the Via Flaminia, where there were many lodging places.[30] He was in Rome for "nearly two months" (October and much of November, 1638), and for as long again on his return trip (January and February, 1639). Milton made a point of his attention to "the antiquities," though much that the modern tourist sees was then covered over. Like Evelyn and most other tourists, he might have engaged the services of a "sightsman," the seventeenth-century version of a tour guide who made his living by showing strangers around the city. As he made the rounds of the Coliseum, the Capitol, the Tarpeian Rock, the Pantheon, the temples, the arches, the aqueducts, the Via Appia, and the ancient gates, Milton laid in a sense of ancient Latium, the Roman Republic, and the Empire that would enliven his readings of Virgil, Ovid, Horace and Livy, and that he would reimagine in several passages of his great epics. Walking about, he could also take the measure of the present city, the center of Catholic Christendom: around 110,000 priests and nuns bustling everywhere, magnificent Baroque churches, the Vatican, the overwhelming spaces of St Peter's.

While the papacy was not the power in Europe that it had been in the previous century, the reigning Pope Urban VIII (Maffeo Barberini) was a forceful secular prince who enlarged the territories of the Papal States, involved himself in the power plays of the Thirty Years War and among the various Italian states, encouraged the Jesuits in their Counter-Reformation activities, and completed several grand Baroque building projects (the Bernini baldacchino at St Peter's, Borromini's church of San Carlino, the Barberini Palace at the Quattro Fontane). In the Renaissance manner, he also wrote poems in Latin, Greek, and Italian,[31] and patronized artists, musicians, and dramatists. And in the Renaissance tradition of papal nepotism, he packed the College of Cardinals with members of his family and made his nephew, Cardinal Francesco Barberini, his chief counsellor and *Praefectus Urbis* (something like a mayor of Rome). As Masson observes, "Rome all but belonged to the Barberini, whose family symbol of the bees met the eyes on all the public buildings, and on their carriages in the public drives."[32]

Milton would have had letters of introduction from his Florentine friends to some of the Roman literati, whom he characterizes as "men endowed with both learning and wit" (*CPW* IV.1, 618), and through them he could have had entrée to Roman academies devoted to literature, eloquence, and poetry. It is quite likely that he attended meetings of the Fantastici, since he received an astonishingly laudatory epigram from one of its members, Giovanni Salzilli, a lyric poet of some repute whose poems had appeared the previous year in a volume of verse by that academy's members.[33] I think it somewhat more likely that Salzilli's tribute was presented on Milton's first visit to Rome rather than on his return visit, since he is likely to have sought connections with Roman academies at once, having so enjoyed the academies in Florence. Salzilli's tribute suggests that Milton had made some display of his poetry in Latin, Greek, and Italian and that he had spoken about his intentions to write epic. Milton published it among the several commendations prefacing the Latin section of his 1645 *Poems*:

> To John Milton, Englishman, who deserves to be Crowned with the Triple Laurel wreath of Poetry, Greek certainly, Latin, and Tuscan, an Epigram by Joannes Salsillus, Roman.
>
> Yield Meles, let Mincius yield with lowered urn;
> Let Sebetus cease to speak constantly of Tasso.
> But let the victorious Thames carry his waves higher than all the rest
> For through you, Milton, he alone will be equal to all three.[34]

Milton responded to Salzilli's florid epigram with a 41-line Latin verse epistle *Ad Salzillum,* "Scazons addressed to Salzilli, a Roman poet, when he was ill."[35] He acknowledges with a polite disclaimer (l. 8) Salzilli's hyperbolic praises that "quite undeservedly . . . ranks me above great and divine poets" – Homer, Virgil, and Tasso – but his deft allusions to Greek, Latin, and contemporary Italian poems intimate that he might indeed merit such praise. Chiefly, however, the poem laments Salzilli's desperate illness and expresses Milton's hopes for his recovery.[36] His metrical choice is a witty gesture to Salzilli's illness – scazons, a halting or "limping" meter created by substituting a spondee or trochee for the final foot, departing from the iambic norm.[37] The poem alludes to many myths associated with Rome – Faunus, Evander, Numa, Portumnus, and especially the river Tiber – and those allusions forge complex links with Salzilli's own poems, after the manner of learned civility honored in the academies. It also exhibits the etymological word-play the academicians so much enjoyed.[38]

The poem revisits some themes of *Lycidas*, posing alternatives. Both poems are concerned with the danger to poets from nature, set over against the power of their art to control nature. Here the problem is posed through Salzilli, whose wasted body may indicate a mortal illness, even though he writes elegant Greek lyrics in the vein of the Lesbian poets Sappho and Alcaeus. The speaker asks the goddess Health and especially Apollo, the god both of poetry and of healing, to cure Salzilli, and points to his own case as a hopeful example of heavenly aid to poets. Like Aeneas and unlike Lycidas/King, Milton had endured on the seas the fiercest of raging winds, but he avoided shipwreck and made his way to the "fertile soil of Italy" as to his cultural home. So he can hope that Salzilli, "restored once more to his dear Muses," will again take up the poet's mission to delight and to civilize. Then he will again "soothe the neighboring meadows with his sweet song,"[39] and, like another Orpheus, his song will calm the flood-swollen Tiber which would otherwise threaten both the harvests of farmers and the monuments of ancient kings.

On October 20/30 Milton accepted a dinner invitation from the English Jesuit College in Rome. The Travellers' Book of the college records that "On the 30 of October [1638] dined in our College, the illustrious Mr. N. Cary brother of the Baron Falkland, Dr. Holding of Lancaster, Mr. N. Fortescue, and Mr. Milton, with his servant, English nobles, and they were magnificently received" *(LR* I, 393). Cary was Patrick Cary, the 14-year-old son of Viscount Falkland and brother of Lucius; Holding was the secular priest Henry Holden; Fortescue was either Sir John or Sir Nicholas.[40] Such invitations were customarily extended to Englishmen of rank and education, Catholic or Protestant, who were passing through Rome. Milton was clearly willing to rise to this occasion and take his own measure of the hated Jesuits. When Evelyn later dined in that college he was much impressed by its facade of rich marble, its "noble Portico and Court," and "two noble Libraries."[41]

Milton also met and received from one Selvaggi a poetic tribute that he also published in the 1645 *Poems,* evidently taking him for a native Roman on the basis of his associations and his splendid Italian. In fact he was an English Benedictine, David Codner, who used the alias Matthew Savage or Matteo Selvaggio.[42] His epigrammatic tribute also likens Milton to the great epic poets:

> Greece may exult in her Homer, Roman may exult in her Virgil;
> England exults in one equalling either of these.
> Selvaggi[43]

Anthony á Wood reports (on dubious evidence) that Milton sometimes met another traveling Englishman, one Thomas Gawen (1610?–84), a fellow of New College, Oxford.[44] With his passionate interest in music, Milton found occasions during both visits to sample the richness of Roman musical life. Much was available: oratorios, street ballads, vocal concerts, new musical dramas called *melodramma,* and early operas by Monteverdi, based on recitative and arias.[45]

Late in November, 1638 (probably), Milton set out for Naples, a journey of over a hundred miles. He stayed about a month. Naples was the center of Spanish rule and influence in Italy and the headquarters of the Spanish army. A Spanish province since 1502, it was ruled by a resident Spanish viceroy; the upper classes aped Spanish fashion and spoke a language that was more than half Spanish. But the power of the nobility had declined, the lower classes and the general economy suffered under heavy taxation, and intellectual life was rigorously controlled by strict censorship of books and by suppressing dissident native sons like Telesio and Bruno.[46] Naples had made some attempts to overturn Spanish rule: the philosopher Tommaso Campanella served a 30-year prison term for his part in an abortive uprising in 1598,[47] and other revolts occurred in 1622 and 1636.

Milton traveled by coach to Naples, in a large caravan so as to deter the notorious brigands that plagued travelers on that route. Evelyn's party a few years later laid on 30 armed guards to convoy them through the cork woods along the Appian Way south.[48] Milton had the company of a "certain Eremite Friar" (*CPW* IV.1, 618) who promised to, and did, introduce him to Giovanni Battista Manso, Marquis of Villa – statesman, soldier, author, and notable exemplar of generous and intelligent literary patronage. After the Italian epic poet Tasso was released from a distressing period of incarceration as a lunatic, he was Manso's guest at his villa near Naples, where he revised his great epic, *Gerusalemme Liberata* (1581) into *Gerusalemme Conquistata* (1593) and wrote a poem on the Creation, *Le Sette Giornate del Mondo Creato* (1592) as well as a dialogue on friendship titled *Il Manso* (1596), in tribute to his host.[49] Manso was also patron and sometimes host to the most famous narrative poet of the next generation, Giovanni Battista Marino, author of the sensuous, langorous, and elaborately ornamented *L'Adone* (1623) on the subject of Venus and Adonis, and of *La Strage degl'Innocenti* (1632) on the Massacre of the Innocents.[50] Manso erected a splendid tomb and monument for Marino and wrote a *Life of Tasso*.[51] He was also founder, director, and patron of the most famous Neapolitan academy, the Otiosi (the Idlers), and of the College Dei Nobili, a school to educate young Neapolitan nobles in intellectual culture, the arts, and martial practices.[52] Milton may have attended meetings of the Otiosi, held in Manso's beautiful Puteoli villa on the sea coast, and enjoyed Manso's hospitality there on other occasions.

When Milton met him, Manso was 78 years old. Milton states that "he personally conducted me through the various quarters of the city and the Viceregal Court, and more than once came to my lodgings to call" (*CPW* IV.1, 618). Besides the viceroy's splendid palace on the great central avenue, flanked by many other palaces, churches, and public buildings, the sightseeing tour(s) likely included the magnificent bay, the tombs of Virgil and Sannazaro, the villa of Cicero, the spacious squares with their fountains, and perhaps Vesuvius, Lake Avernus, Cuma and the Cumaean Sibyl's cave, and the beautiful Isle of Capri. All about Milton swirled the noisy and flamboyant life of this crowded city, with at least 200,000 people, eight times the population of Rome. There were more than four hundred churches, thousands of clergy, hundreds of beggars, fashionable courtesans, and a steady stream of street musicians, wandering players, *Commedia dell'Arte* masquers, and fervent religious processions.

Before Milton left Naples, Manso presented him with gifts – probably two of his own books[53] – and also a distich to which Milton gave pride of place among the commendations in his 1645 *Poems*. It wittily applies to Milton the pun attributed by Bede to Gregory the Great:

> Joannes Baptista Mansus, Marquis of Villa, Neapolitan, to John Milton, Englishman
>
> If your mind, form, grace, features, and manners were equalled by your religion,
> Then, by Hercules, you would be no "Angle" but a very angel.[54]

Not only does Manso's little distich voice a reservation about Milton's religion, it also says nothing about him as a poet. So Milton put his powers on show in *Mansus* (discussed on pages 112–14), an elegant Latin verse epistle in which he gratefully acknowledges gestures of friendship from Manso, and, modestly but confidently, places himself in the line of poets who celebrated Manso as patron. The headnote addresses him as "a man particularly famous among Italians for the glory of his genius and his literary studies," who has honored him during his stay at Naples "with the greatest kindness and conferred on him many humane services."[55] He states that he sent the poem to Manso before leaving Naples, "in order that he might not appear ungrateful."

Milton states in the *Defensio Secunda* that he had intended to travel on to Sicily and Greece, but changed his plans when the English merchants in Naples passed along "sad tidings of civil war from England" (*CPW* IV.1, 618–19). That tour extension may have been rather nebulous, since such a trip was off the course of the usual "Grand Tour," but Milton's strong interest in things Greek probably led him to make at least tentative plans and then revise them. The First Bishops' War with the Scots was not proclaimed officially until February 27, 1639, but Milton might have heard about levies of money, the mustering of troops, and the deposition of the Scottish bishops in November, all signs of trouble ahead.[56] In Naples also he might have received the sad news of Charles Diodati's death late in August, 1638.[57] If so, the loss of this oldest and dearest friend likely prompted him to plan a considerable stay again with those amiable new friends in Florence, and arrange to spend some time in Geneva with Diodati's uncle. Milton intimates that he hastened home after hearing news of war, but in fact the return journey to England took more than seven months. The reasons for urgency were much less obvious in late 1638 than they seemed in retrospect in 1654, when Milton summarized his travels as part of an *apologia* for himself. He also reports receiving a warning from those same English merchants in Naples about a plot against him should he return to Rome: "As I was on the point of returning to Rome, I was warned by merchants that they had learned through letters of plots laid against me by the English Jesuits, should I return to Rome, because of the freedom with which I had spoken about religion" (*CPW* IV.1, 619). He probably exaggerated the danger in 1654, to present himself as an embattled Protestant threatened by the hated Jesuits rather than as a traveler reveling in the delights of the place.

But there may have been something in it, given that other English Protestants in this period reported concerns for their personal safety in Rome,[58] and that Milton was often less than prudent in airing his religious views. Milton himself had experienced some uneasiness and restriction in Naples because of his overt religious testimony: Manso reportedly told him regretfully that he "wished to show me many more attentions, [but] he could not do so in that city, since I was unwilling to be circumspect in regard to religion" (*CPW* IV.1, 618). Some years later the Dutch philologist and poet Nicolaas Heinsius, who traveled extensively in Italy, commented on the enemies Milton made there:

> That Englishman [Milton] was hated by the Italians, among whom he lived a long time, on account of his over-strict morals, because he both disputed freely about religion, and on any occasion whatever prated very bitterly against the Roman Pontiff.[59]

If Milton exaggerated the threat to him from the English Jesuits so as to present himself as a defender of the faith in the very bastions of the enemy, he took obvious pride in returning and facing down hostility, and perhaps danger, with appropriate courage:

> I nevertheless returned to Rome. What I was, if any man inquired, I concealed from no one. For almost two more months, in the very stronghold of the Pope, if anyone attacked the orthodox religion, I openly, as before, defended it. Thus, by the will of God, I returned again in safety to Florence. (*CPW* IV.1, 619)[60]

Milton evidently did not believe his danger to be very great, since he remained in Rome for another two months (January–February, 1639). He was there during Carnival (eleven days before the beginning of Lent), when entertainments of all sorts were staged: *Commedia dell'Arte* masks, comedies, *melodrammas*, musical performances, and street theater. A high point of this visit was his meeting with Lukas Holste, arranged by Alessandro Cherubini, another erudite young scholar (especially of Plato), but already suffering from the illness that would cause his death at age 28.[61] Holste, a native of Hamburg who had studied at Oxford, was a distinguished scholar and editor of Greek manuscripts, secretary and librarian to Cardinal Francesco Barberini, and librarian of the Vatican collections. In a letter to Holste from Florence (March 19/29, 1639) Milton expresses profound gratitude for the extraordinary favors Holste had extended to him, instancing expecially a tour through the Vatican library, the opportunity to examine Holste's own notes on some Greek manuscripts, and the access to Cardinal Barberini arranged by him:

> Although I can remember (and often do) many courteous and cordial favors which I have received in my hasty journey through Italy, still, I do not know whether I can rightly say that I have had greater tokens of kindness from anyone on such short acquaintance than from you. (*CPW* I, 333)

The Vatican library, with its magnificent collections of European and Oriental books and of precious, ancient manuscripts, would have impressed Milton as it did Evelyn and numerous later visitors, as "the most nobly built, furnish'd, and beautified in the world."[62] Holste had also honored Milton with a commission to copy for him portions of a Medici manuscript at the Laurentian library in Florence, and gave him as a gift his recently published edition of the *Sententiae* of several ancient philosophers.[63] Acknowledging that Holste may treat all Englishmen well because he himself studied in England, Milton nevertheless hopes and thinks that he has been specially favored: "if you have distinguished me from the rest and esteemed me enough to want my friendship, I both congratulate myself on your opinion and at the same time consider it due more to your generosity than to my merit" (*CPW* I, 334).

A few days after this meeting Milton attended a public musical entertainment put on by Cardinal Francesco Barberini in the newly completed Palazzo Barberini at the Quattro Fontane – apparently the comic opera *Chi soffre speri* by Cardinal Giulio Rospigliosi (later to be Pope Clement IX), with music by Virgilio Mazzocchi and Marco Marazzuoli and stage design by Bernini. It was performed there on February 17/27, 1639 to an audience of around 3,500, including Cardinal Mazarin.[64] Milton was surprised and gratified by the attention Cardinal Barberini paid him at that event and the next day at a private audience, attributing these gestures to the good offices of Holste:

> When . . . he gave that public Musical entertainment with truly Roman magnificence, he himself, waiting at the door, singled me out in so great a throng and, almost seizing me by the hand, welcomed me in an exceedingly honorable manner. When on this account I paid my respects to him the following day . . . no one of highest rank could be more kindly nor more courteous. (*CPW* I, 334)

In fact, other traveling Englishmen reported comparable hospitality from Cardinal Francesco, who acted as "Protector" of the traveling nationals of England, Portugal, Scotland, Aragon, and Switzerland.[65] Milton was clearly impressed by Berberini's graciousness of manner, intelligence, and culture, praising him to Holste in terms that might seem surprising from the militantly Protestant Milton. Partly this is courtesy and decorum: to such exalted and gracious personages Milton can offer appropriate gratitude and deference. Yet he constructs his praises carefully, eliding the cardinal's ecclesiastical role and portraying him rather as welcoming host and true heir to the great Italian Renaissance patrons of learning and the arts:

> Extend my most respectful greetings to his Eminence the Cardinal, whose great virtues and zeal for what is right, so ready to further all the Liberal Arts, are always before my eyes – also that gentle and, may I say, humble loftiness of spirit, which alone has taught him to distinguish himself by effacing himself. . . . Such humility can prove to most other Princes how alien to and how far different from true magnanimity are their surly arrogance and courtly haughtiness. Nor do I think that while he lives anyone will any longer miss the Estensi, Farnesi, or Medici, formerly the patrons of learned men. (*CPW* I, 335)

Milton heard at least one concert of solo song by Leonora Baroni, and paid hyperbolic tribute to her in three Latin epigrams. Since the second poem refers to Tasso's madness as a result of his love for another Leonora, it is likely Milton wrote these tributes on this second visit to Rome, after his visit to Manso, who had dealt with this incident in his *Vita di Tasso*. Baroni was the only female member of the Umoristi (Humorists) Academy, was showered with gifts by nobles, cardinals, and popes, and was rumored to be the mistress of Cardinal Rospighiosi and Cardinal Mazarin.[66] She was the rage of Rome, and ecstatically praised: a few months after Milton's visit, a volume of tributes to her in several languages, *Applausi poetici*, was published, containing poems by several of Milton's acquaintances (among them Holste).[67] Milton was no doubt shown some of these and was prompted to offer his own praises; his epigrams, *Ad Leonoram Romae Canentem* (To Leonora Singing in Rome), contain hyperbolic compliments not unlike those in other poems praising her. But his response to her art of solo song was quite genuine: he seems to have found a certain sublimity in the female singing voice, a quality emphasized in his descriptions of the Lady and Sabrina in *A Maske* and Emilia in his Italian sonnets. Still, Leonora's remarkable musical talent and professionalism would be a new experience for him. She was sometimes accompanied on the lyre by her mother Adriana (also a famous singer and musician), or by her sister on the harp; at other times she accompanied herself on theorbo, harp, or viol. She was also the composer of over thirty arias.[68] The French musician, André Maugars, praised her musicianship and especially the powerful effect her expressive style had on audiences:

> She understands [music] perfectly well, and even composes. All of this means that she has absolute control over what she sings, and that she pronounces and expresses the sense of the words perfectly. . . . She sings with . . . gentle seriousness. Her voice is of high range, accurate, sonorous, harmonious. . . . [Her song] threw me into such raptures that I forgot my mortality and believed myself to be already among the angels, enjoying the delights of the blessed.[69]

Milton's epigrams for Leonora rework a familiar motif in Prolusion II, the Nativity ode, and *At a Solemn Music*: the mystic harmony between heaven and earth that music alone can recreate. He gives that mystic power an earthly embodiment in Leonora, representing her, under various figures, as its conduit. The first Leonora epigram (10 lines) invites pairing in some respects with Milton's little ode, *At a Solemn Music*, which celebrates voice and verse as "Sphear-born" Neoplatonic sirens that elevate the soul to heaven. This epigram makes Leonora's song a vehicle for God's voice which, either directly or through some Neoplatonic "Third Mind" ("mens tertia") teaches "mortal hearers how they may gradually become accustomed to immortal tones." Milton goes well beyond conventional hyperbole in associating Leonora's voice with that of God himself: "the music of your voice itself bespeaks the presence of God / . . . In you alone he speaks and possesses all His other creatures in silence."[70] The second epigram (12 lines) recalls Leonora d'Este for whose love Tasso ran mad, opposing her to this Leonora, whose harmonious song would have cured Tasso's rages, brought "peace into his diseased breast," and restored him to himself. The third epigram (8 lines) also looks back to *At a Solemn Music*, constructing Leonora as another kind of siren – Parthenope – whose haunting voice casts spells on mariners. The Neapolitans, foolishly supposing her dead, honored Parthenope with a splendid monument, but that siren is in fact Leonora, who has left Naples for Rome and now "lays the spell of her song upon both men and gods."

Probably in early March Milton returned to Florence, where he remained another two months, meeting his friends again and attending meetings of the academies – more frequently than before, it seems. On March 7/17, records of the Svogliati list him among those who "brought and read some noble Latin verses."[71] At another meeting of that academy on March 14/24 Buonmattei expounded a chapter of the *Ethics*, then "an elegy and a sonnet were recited by Signor Cavalcanti, various Tuscan poems [were recited] by Signors Bartolommei, Buonmattei, and Doni, who read a scene from his tragedy, and various Latin poems [were read] by Signor Milton, and an epigram by Signor Girolami" (*LR* I, 409). Milton may have read his recently composed epigrams to Leonora or the tribute to Manso. On March 21/31 he again attended a Svogliati meeting, though not as a contributor (*LR* I, 414). He attempted to carry out Holste's commission to copy a manuscript in the Laurentian library, but learned that library rules would not allow it, and in his letter of March 19/29 to Holste he suggested another expedient.[72]

Returning to Florence after three months' travel was like coming home: he found "friends who were as anxious to see me as if it were my native land to which I had returned" (*CPW* IV.1, 619). It was during this second visit that he probably received the tributes of Dati and Francini[73] that he later included among the commendations to the Latin/Greek section of his 1645 *Poems;* in the *Epitaphium Damonis* (line 137) he mentions them as the two friends who made his name known in Italy. While hyperbole is common in such encomia, the specific terms suggest what the Italian academicians, especially the youthful ones, found attractive in Milton: his wide learning, his skill in several languages (especially the Tuscan dialect), his highminded virtue, and his lofty poetic aspirations. The warmth of their praise indicates that they liked him and found him amiable, sociable, and eager for new cultural experiences; an austere or defensive mien would not elicit such comment. Dati offered his "tribute of admiration, reverence and love" in Latin prose:

> To John Milton of London
>
> A young man distinguished by the land of his birth and by his personal merits.
>
> To a man who, through his journeys to foreign lands, has viewed with care many places, by his studies has viewed every place the wild world over, to the end that, like a modern Ulysses, he might learn all things from every people everywhere.
>
> To a polyglot, on whose lips languages already wholly dead live again with such vigor and might that all idioms, when employed to praise him, lose power of utterance. Yet so justly does he know them all, that he understands the expressions of admiration and applause called forth from the people by his own wisdom.
>
> To a man whose gifts of mind and body move the senses to admiration, and yet through that very admiration rob them of their own motion, whose works exhort applause, yet by their beauty stifle the voice of the praisers.
>
> To one in whose memory the whole world is lodged, in whose intellect is wisdom, in whose will is a passion for glory, in whose mouth is eloquence; who, with astronomy as his guide, hears the harmonious strains of the heavenly spheres; who, with philosophy as his teacher, reads and interprets those marks of nature's marvels by which the greatness of God is portrayed; who, with assiduous reading of these authors as his companion, probes the secrets of antiquity, the ruins of ages, the labyrinths of learning . . .[74]

Dati signed himself a lover of Milton's great virtues.

Francini's tribute is a long, hyperbolic Italian ode which begins by praising England as a refuge of virtue, and then extols Milton as scholar, poet, and linguist. This poem asserts (for the first time) that Milton knew Spanish:

> So, enamoured of beautiful fame
> Milton quitting your native skies as a pilgrim
> You passed through various places
> Seeking after Sciences and Arts;
> You beheld the realms ruled by France
> And now the most worthy heroes of Italy.
> . . .
> All those born in Florence
> Or who have learned there the art of speaking Tuscan,
> Whose eternal deeds
> The world honors the memory in learned pages
> You have desired to seek after as your treasure,
> And have conversed with them in their works.
>
> In vain for you in proud Babel
> Did Jove confuse the tongues
> When through different languages

By her own self the tower fell onto the plain.
Whose song offers not only to England her noblest speech
But also to Spain, France, Tuscany, and Greece and Rome.

The most profound secrets
Which Nature conceals in heaven or in earth
Even to superhuman geniuses
Too often covetously has hidden them and locked them up
You have clearly understood, and arrived at the end
To the great frontier of moral virtue.
. . .
Give me your own sweet lyre,
If you wish that I sing of your own sweet song
That exalts you to the skies
Making you a celestial man of the highest honor.
Thames will state that this is conceded
Through thee as her swan she equals Parnassus.[75]

Over the months, and in various places, Milton's responses to Italy altered as he took on various roles: at times the enthusiastic visitor, at times the polite guest, at other times the polemicist framing an argument. Like many northern Europeans he delighted in the climate, describing to Salzilli his escape from the frozen North to sunny Italy, a region which nurtures wit and talent:

> [I am] that London-bred Milton who recently left his nest and his own quarter of the sky – where the worst of the winds in its headlong flight, with its lungs uncontrollably raging, rolls its panting gusts beneath the heavens – and came to the genial soil of Italy to see its cities, which their proud fame has made familiar, and its men and its talented and cultured youth.[76]

To Manso he portrayed himself in similar terms, as an "alien muse . . . poorly nourished under the frozen Bear," whose countrymen "in the long nights endure the wintry Boötes" (*Mansus,* ll. 27–37). The balmy Italian days evidently brought to the fore Milton's lifelong belief that England's cold northern climate might pose a serious obstacle to poetic creation. Often he declared his great love for Italy. To Buonmattei he pronounced himself "such a lover of your Nation that no other, I think, is a greater" (*CPW* I, 330). In the *Defensio Secunda* he insists that he went to Italy, not to escape an evil reputation at home but to find a long-admired cultural home: "I knew beforehand that Italy was not, as you think, a refuge or asylum for criminals, but rather the lodging place of *humanitas* and of all the arts of civilization, and so I found it" (*CPW* IV.1, 609). Chiefly he loved Florence, "that city, which I have always admired above all others because of the elegance, not just of its tongue, but also of its wit" (*CPW* IV.1, 615), and it is usually Florence he thinks of when he praises Italy for the arts of civilization.

However, he sometimes had difficulty treading the fine line between the politeness required of a guest in a Catholic country and the testimony to truth required of a committed Protestant, and those strains sharpened for him the contrasts between England and Italy, Protestant and Catholic cultures. Wotton's recommendation of discreet silence about religion and related political issues (*CPW* I, 342) was not a course calculated to appeal to the fiercely intellectual and argumentative Milton. He worked out, he says, a different policy: "I would not indeed begin a conversation about religion, but if questioned about my faith would hide nothing, whatever the consequences" (*CPW* IV.1, 619). That policy worked well enough in Florence where his friends were tolerant of his views on religious matters (*CPW* II, 764). In *Areopagitica* he refers to learned Italians who themselves denounced the Inquisition and pointed to its restraints on intellectual activity as the cause of Italy's decline from her former greatness. His immediate segue to Galileo associates those sentiments with the Florentine intellectuals:

> I could recount what I have seen and heard in other Countries, where this kind of inquisition tyrannizes; when I have sat among their lerned men, for that honor I had, and bin counted happy to be born in such a place of *Philosophic* freedom, as they suppos'd England was, while themselvs did nothing but bemoan the servil condition into which lerning amongst them was brought; that this was it which had dampt the glory of Italian wits; that nothing had bin there writt'n now these many years but flattery and fustian. There it was that I found and visited the famous *Galileo* grown old, a prisner to the Inquisition, for thinking in Astronomy otherwise then the Franciscan and Dominican liscensers thought. And though I knew that England then was groaning loudest under the Prelaticall yoak, neverthelesse I took it as a pledge of future happines, that other Nations were so perswaded of her liberty (*CPW* II, 537–8)

He also reports that he heard the Jesuits denounced as "the onely corrupters of youth and good learning" by "many wise, and learned men in *Italy*." But in Rome he was awash in ambiguities. There was the attraction of the antiquities. There was glorious music. There was the "truly Roman magnificence" (*CPW* I, 334) of the elaborate opera he attended in the Barberini palace, and the exquisite courtesy and culture of his Cardinal host. But there were also the "treacherous" Jesuits, the display of idolatrous worship, and the seductions of the flesh. Later, Milton often sorted out his impressions of Italy by the formula, "good humanist Florence, bad popish Rome."[77]

Before leaving Florence Milton took a few days for an excursion to Lucca, a tiny republic which had managed to remain independent, peaceful, and prosperous,[78] and which was reputedly the site where the purest Italian was spoken. If Milton had recently heard of Charles Diodati's death, that pilgrimage to the family's native region would have had a special poignancy. He then crossed the Apennines and "hastened" to Venice by way of Bologna and Ferrara, both of them part of the Papal States. From Bologna on, travelers often went by boat along the network of canals and the Po.[79] Though Milton passed quickly through those two cities, they would have had rich associations for him: Bologna the seat of the oldest university in Italy (and already famous for sausages); Ferrara the former principality of the d'Este family, home of Ariosto and (for a time) Tasso.

In Venice Milton spent about a month (probably May, 1639) "exploring that city" and shipping off, Phillips reports, all the "curious and rare Books which he had pick'd up in his Travels" (*EL* 59) and probably adding some Venetian purchases.[80] His explorations surely included the obvious attractions: San Marco with its mosaics, the Square, the Doge's Palace, the Grand Canal and the Rialto, the new Church of Santa Maria della Salute constructed in thanksgiving for the ending of the terrible plague of 1630 which had killed some 700,000 people throughout the province, 50,000 in the city itself.[81] As he explored, Milton would have observed the fascinating, exuberant, cosmopolitan life of the city: gondolas ferrying passengers up and down the network of canals, flamboyant courtesans decked out in red and yellow, mountebanks attracting crowds in the Square, prostitutes plying their trade, men and women of rank resplendant in silks, satins, and velvets, fine ladies teetering on extremely high heeled shoes (*choppines*), artisans displaying their famous lace and Murano glass. Contemporary travelers reported that one could "heare all the languages of Christendom" in this pleasure center of Europe, and also take in the sights and sounds of the exotic East. Thomas Coryat describes such a scene:

> The strange variety of the severall Nations . . . we every day met with in the Streets & Piazza of Jewes, Turks, Armenians, Persians, Moores, Greekes, Sclavonians, some with their Targets and boucklers, & all in their native fashions, negotiating in this famous *Emporium*, which is allways crouded with strangers.[82]

There was also music, especially opera and organ concerts. Monteverdi was Maestro di Capella of San Marco when Milton was in Venice; his opera *L'Arianna* was produced there in 1639 and he was publishing much new music. Edward Phillips states that books Milton shipped home from Venice included "a Chest or two of choice Musick-books of the best Masters flourishing about that time in *Italy*" (*EL* 59). He specifies Luca Marenzio, Claudio Monteverdi, Orazio Vecchi, Antonio Cifra, Don Carlo Gesualdo the Prince of Venosa, and "several others" – some of the most distinguished music of the time. They were known for madrigals, motets, theater music, sacred songs and instrumental music; and in the case of Monteverdi, operas that combine monody with madrigal choruses.[83] From Venice Milton may have taken a side trip to Padua and even, like Evelyn, attended an anatomy lecture and demonstration at that famous university.[84]

In the Venetian state Milton could observe at first hand a long-lived aristocratic republic, the form of government he came to regard as best suited to promote human dignity and freedom. It was the only truly independent and powerful republic in Italy, and the only Italian state that consistently opposed the presence of

Spain. Milton's later tracts suggest that he paid close attention to the structure called for by its ancient constitution: an elected Doge and Senate, a Grand Council composed of all the noble families, and assorted executive councils.[85] Venice was famous for its stable government and commercial prosperity, and was seen as the modern embodiment of the Greek and Roman republican ideal: Evelyn observes that the Venetian republic had endured longer than any of the four ancient monarchies, and that it ruled vast regions around the Adriatic, in Italy, Greece, Crete, Rhodes, and Slavonia.[86] Like most travelers, Milton probably did not recognize that the republic's institutions were in some decline: the state had become an oligarchy, the list of noble families with political privileges shrank greatly, inscription had to be purchased, major offices remained in the hands of a few families, non-noble classes had no political privileges, and the Council of Ten wielded enormous power as they dealt in secret with all matters pertaining to the security of the state.[87]

The Venice Milton visited was the most tolerant state in Italy, and saw itself as defender of liberty against Turk, Spaniard, and pope. Peace with the Turks had held since the Battle of Lepanto (1573), allowing Venetian trade with the East to flourish. Venice set itself in constant, if often disguised, opposition to Spain's military and diplomatic ventures in surrounding states; it supported the sovereignty of the Protestant Grisons in nearby Valtellina, excluded Spanish ships from the Adriatic Sea, and had recently thwarted an attempted *coup d'etat* (1618) mounted by the Spanish ambassador to take over Venice for Spain. Venice also took considerable pride in maintaining lay jurisdiction over the Inquisition, the censors, and any clergy charged with crimes; in 1606 the pope issued a bull of excommunication over the issue of ecclesiastical courts, but the state held firm and took the occasion to expel the Jesuits, keeping them out till 1657. Milton later cited with great respect the eminent Venetian scholar Fra Paolo Sarpi, whose *History of the Council of Trent* (1619) launched a powerful attack on the secular power of the papacy.[88]

After his month in Venice Milton proceeded to Geneva "by way of Verona, Milan, and the Pennine Alps, and then along Lake Leman" (Lake Geneva) (*CPW* IV.1, 619–20). With his interest in antiquities, Milton likely viewed the great ampitheater at Verona (the Arena), reported by Evelyn to be the "most intire now extant in the world of ancient remaines."[89] Passing through Brescia to the Venetian frontier, he entered the Spanish Milanese territories and crossed the fertile Lombard plains, whose abundant olive trees, vineyards and streams led Evelyn to call it "the Paradise of all Lombardy."[90] But all was not paradisal. Lombardy was the site of frequent battles in the 1630s between Savoy, Spain, the Hapsburgs, and France. In no part of Italy was the power of the church more extensive, repression of thought more complete, the Inquisition more severe and dangerous, and the power of the Spanish governor more absolute. The great plague of 1630 had devastated the small region of the Milanese more severely than other parts of Italy, causing some 180,000 deaths. Milton's stay in Milan itself was brief, but the city would have held many points of interest for him: the splendid Duomo; the library of the Ambrosiana with its 15,000 manuscripts and precious editions of Virgil, Boccaccio, and Bembo; Petrarch's house; and many sites associated with Saint Ambrose and Saint Augustine.[91] Evelyn termed it "one of the princliest citties in *Europe*" with 100 churches, 71 monasteries, 40,000 inhabitants, "sumptuous Palaces," circular walls, and a strong citadel.[92]

Milton crossed the Pennine Alps into Switzerland either by the Great Saint Bernard pass or by the Simplon. Though the vistas were spectacular, contemporary travelers like Evelyn registered their wonder only from below and at a distance. The passage itself was so arduous (on foot or muleback) that Evelyn's impressions are taken up with the freezing snow, the "strange, horrid & fierfull craggs," the "terrible roaring" of the cataracts, the extreme cold, and the fierceness of the mountain dwellers.[93] Whichever route Milton took he experienced those conditions; then he passed through part of the Valais (Valasia) and Savoy, to Lake Geneva.

Arriving in sober Calvinist Geneva, after being for so long both attracted and repelled by Catholic Italy, must have afforded Milton some psychic relief. He could again speak openly about religion and politics, though he may have chafed under some of the restraints in this Calvinist theocracy. Also, Switzerland offered him experience of another republic, of a unique kind, with loosely federated cantons, some Catholic, some Protestant, which variously contained French, German, and Italian populations. Milton's chief associate in Geneva was Charles Diodati's uncle, Giovanni Diodati, biblical scholar and translator, theologian, and educator of Protestant princes, among them Charles Gustavus of Sweden and the scions of several German houses.[94] Milton states that he was "daily" in his society so he may have stayed with him; here he surely learned the specifics (whatever they were) about his friend's death, and could grieve for him with the family.[95] Through Diodati he probably met some of the distinguished scholars and theologians at Geneva: Theodore Tronchin, Frederick Spanheim, and perhaps even Alexander More, professor of Greek in the university, whom he was later to denounce vehemently in the *Defensio Secunda*. One known acquaintance was Camillo Cerdogni, a Neapolitan Protestant nobleman who was a refugee and teacher in Geneva; he kept an album of visitors' autographs which Milton inscribed on June 10, 1639 with two wholly characteristic epigraphs: the conclusion of his own *Maske*, "if Vertue feeble were / Heaven it selfe would stoope to her"; and a quotation from Horace: "I change my sky but not my mind when I cross the sea."[96] Writing later of his arrival in Geneva, Milton insisted that he had remained faithful to sound religion and morals in all those perilous papist places he had now passed through: "[I] call God to witness that in all these places, where so much licence exists, I lived free and untouched by the slightest sin or reproach, reflecting constantly that although I might hide from the gaze of men, I could not elude the sight of God" (*CPW* IV.1, 620). Probably he again bought books.[97]

He returned home through France "by the same route as before," that is by Lyons, along the Loire, Orléans, Paris, Calais, and the Channel.[98] He evidently arrived home in late July or early August, 1639.[99] Amidst all the challenges of setting up a new household and taking up life in London, Milton had one piece of unfinished business intimately connected with his Italian voyage: a poetic tribute to Charles Diodati. His Latin funeral poem, *Epitaphium Damonis* (discussed on pages 114–19), was evidently written late in 1639 or early in 1640. It is his most autobiographical poem, filled with anguish for the loss of his oldest, and perhaps only, truly intimate friend. The headnote states that "from childhood [they] had pursued the same interests and were most affectionate friends," and describes Diodati as "a youth who, while he lived, was outstanding for genius, learning, and every other splendid virtue."[100] The poem itself says little about Diodati, save for a few lines underscoring the irony that this physician could not be saved by his own medicines and arts (ll. 150–4). In *Lycidas* and *Mansus* Milton was led by the contemplation of other deaths to imagine his own death under various circumstances; but here he confronts the immense void left in the survivor's life when his best-loved companion dies. The pain, grief, and sense of loss erupt from passionate love, transposed into the Neoplatonic register of the union of souls. That is underscored in the poem's conclusion, in which Damon/Diodati, as a chaste youth and unmarried, is seen to enjoy the rewards designed for virgins in the all-encompassing ecstasies of heaven:

> Because the blush of modesty and a youth without stain were your choice, and because you never tasted the delight of the marriage bed, see – virginal honors are reserved for you! Your radiant head circled with a gleaming crown, the joyful, shady branches of leafy palm in your hands, you will take part for ever in the immortal marriage-rite, where singing is heard and the lyre rages in the midst of the ecstatic dances, and where the festal orgies rave in Bacchic frenzy under the thyrsus of Zion. (ll. 212–19)[101]

In this passage, classical evocations of bliss are fused with several allusions to the heavenly marriage feast in Revelation, but the fact that only one of them pertains specifically to virgins tells against the view that Milton idealizes virginity as the most perfect state.[102] Virginity is singled out for praise here because it is presumably Diodati's state (and, as yet, Milton's). The poem was printed anonymously and privately, probably in 1640.[103]

Milton no doubt sent copies to Diodati's family and to friends in Italy, especially Dati and Francini who are affectionately mentioned by name in the poem, in recognition of and response to the encomia they presented to him in Florence. Apparently, however, Milton had no further contact with his academy friends until 1647, when Dati wrote him a (now lost) letter. Milton's answer, dated April 20, 1647,[104] refers to those lines in the *Epitaphium* as proof of his love for Dati, and describes his acute sense of loss in being separated from his Florentine friends:

> That separation [from Florence], I may not conceal from you, was also very painful for me; and it fixed those stings in my heart which even now rankle whenever I think that, reluctant and actually torn away, I left so many companions and at the same time such good friends, and such congenial ones in a single city – a city distant indeed but to me most dear. . . . I could think of nothing pleasanter than to recall my dearest memory of you all, of you, Dati, especially. (*CPW* II, 763)

He promises to send Dati the Latin portion of his 1645 *Poems,* bespeaking for "those words spoken rather sharply on some pages against the Roman Pope" the same tolerance his friends accorded him in Florence when he expressed his religious views among them:

> Now I beg you to obtain from my other friends (for of you I am certain) that same indulgence to freedom of speech which, as you know, you have been used to granting in the past with singular kindness – I do not mean to your Dante and Petrarch in this case but to me; I crave it now whenever mention be made of your religion according to our custom. (*CPW* II, 764)

Fond as he was of them, keeping up with friends through correspondence was not one of Milton's strong points. He offers Dati a strained excuse for failing to write sooner – that if he had written first he would have had to write to all his Florentine friends – an excuse somewhat reminiscent of his explanation to Diodati in 1637 for a similar procrastination.[105] But he sends warm greetings to them all: "Give my best greeting to Coltellini, Francini, Frescobaldi, Malatesta, Chimentelli the younger, and any other of our group whom you know to be especially fond of me – in short to the whole Gaddian Academy" (*CPW* II, 765).[106]

The most important and enduring effect of Milton's "Grand Tour" may well have been his associations in the Florentine academies. In *The Reason of Church Government* (1642) he describes the recognition his poetry received in the academies – both the collegiate "trifles" he repeated from memory and the new poems he composed in less than ideal conditions – as a formative experience reconfirming his vocation as a poet:

> In the privat Academies of *Italy*, whither I was favor'd to resort, perceiving that some trifles which I had in memory, compos'd at under twenty or thereabout (for the manner is that every one must give some proof of his wit and reading there) met with acceptance above what was lookt for, and other things which I had shifted in scarsity of books and conveniences to patch up amongst them, were receiv'd with written Encomiums, which the Italian is not forward to bestow on men of this side the *Alps*, I began thus farre to assent both to them and divers of my friends here at home, and not lesse to an inward prompting which now grew daily upon me, that by labour and intent study (which I take to be my portion in this life), joyn'd with the strong propensity of nature, I might perhaps leave something so written to aftertimes, as they should not willingly let it die. (*CPW* I, 809–10)

He indicates further that the experience of exchanging Latin poems with his Italian friends helped him decide not to join the fraternity of worthy neo-Latin poets but to become instead an epic poet in English. Italy also supplied a model for this determination in Ariosto's decision to write in the vernacular Italian:

> Not only for that I knew it would be hard to arrive at the second rank among the Latines, I apply'd my selfe to that resolution which *Ariosto* follow'd against the perswasions of *Bembo,* to fix all the industry and art I could unite to the adorning of my native tongue . . . to be an interpreter & relater of the best and sagest things among mine own Citizens throughout this Iland in the mother dialect . . . not caring to be once nam'd abroad, though perhaps I could attaine to that, but content with these British Ilands as my world. (*CPW* I, 810–12)

In 1642 also he thought back to the Florentine academy as a model for a similar English institution that might provide cultural support for a reformed community:

> [We might] civilize, adorn and make discreet our minds by the learned and affable meeting of frequent Acadamies, and the procurement of wise and artfull recitations sweetned with eloquent and graceful inticements to the love and practice of justice, temperance and fortitude. (*CPW* I, 819)

In his later prose and poetry, Milton drew upon his travel experiences constantly but in subtle and often indirect ways. They contribute something to the sharp oppositions in his polemic tracts, setting English Protestant culture against the Rome of popes, prelates, and the Inquisition. Galileo is a reference point for the case against censorship in *Areopagitica* and an emblem of scientific exploration and speculation in *Paradise Lost.* Venice offers something to Milton's ideas about republican government and Spanish Italy to his hatred of Spain. Baroque Rome, and especially St Peter's, contributes to the portrait of Pandemonium in *Paradise Lost* (I. 710–30), and the whole experience of Rome (and perhaps Capri) informs the Temptation of Rome in *Paradise Regained* (IV. 44–97). Other influences are less tangible: how do the various remembered landscapes contribute to Milton's portrayal of Eden and of Hell? How does the art he saw help shape his imaginative vision? How does the music he heard help define the place of music in his verse, as symbol and as form? Milton's travels provided a fund of impressions that mesh with the imaginative stimulus of his wide reading, ready to be used and transformed for his various polemic and literary purposes.

"Love of the Sweet Muse Detained that Shepherd"

Both *Mansus* and *Epitaphium Damonis* develop more fully the poetic role that Milton claimed and defended not long before, in "Ad Patrem." There is a pleasant irony in the fact that he announced his intention to become a major *English* poet in *Latin* poems which are exquisite achievements in that linguistic medium. If Milton was preparing to bid his Latin muse farewell, he did so in fine style.

Mansus, a 100-line verse letter in hexameters, has, as Anthony Low points out, several purposes: "to repay a kindness, to immortalize a patron, to claim a similar immortality for poets, to continue a conversation, to answer a backhanded compliment [Manso's distich], to bridge as well as to acknowledge the gap between poet and recipient."[107] It probes issues also central to *Ad Salzillum* but more profoundly: the power of poets and of poetry, the aid poets may receive (here, from an earthly patron), and the inevitability of death. As a praise of Manso, the poem reverses many generic norms for panegyric: instead of the expected emphasis on the duty of poets to honor their patrons, Milton insists on the duty and high privilege of patrons to befriend and assist poets. Manso's epigram for Milton did not honor him as a poet, so (reprising "Ad Patrem") Milton takes on the role of a worthy son respectfully asserting his worth to another father ("Manse pater," l. 25), who might not accept him as a poet or value his poetry. As in "Ad Patrem," the son hopes the brilliance and elegance of his poem and his skillful rhetorical address will make his case to a man who demonstrably did and does value poetry.

Milton's poem shares some elements with many Italian encomia that had recently been presented to Manso from contemporary litterati and that he had appended to his own collection of verse, *Poesie Nomiche* (1635), but it is more remarkable for the differences.[108] For one thing, Milton's poem makes no reference to Manso as a poet, praising him solely in the role of patron and friend to poets: his greatness and claim to fame inheres in promoting their fame. For another, for all its graciousness and urbanity, Milton's poem centers on himself as poet, not Manso and his achievements. Milton represents his encounter with Manso as a significant moment in his growing consciousness of himself as an aspiring English epic poet: the poem's controlling conceit is Milton's insertion of himself into the line of epic poets Manso had fostered. Manso was "once bound to the great Tasso by a happy friendship"; then Marino "took pleasure in being called your foster-child"; now he has honored "a young foreigner," the present author, with supreme kindness.[109]

Milton also sets himself in the English poetic line of Chaucer, Spenser, and the Druids, and in doing so he voices and dispels his often-expressed anxiety that poetry might not thrive in England's cold climate:

> Therefore, father Manso, in the name of Clio and of great Phoebus, I, a young pilgrim sent from Hyperborean skies, wish you health and long life. You, who are so good, will not despise an alien Muse, which, though poorly nourished under the frozen Bear, has recently presumed to make her rash flight through the cities of Italy. I believe that in the dim shadows of night I too have heard the swans singing on our river, where the silvery Thames with pure urns spreads her green locks wide in the swell of the ocean. And Tityrus [Chaucer] also long ago made his way to these shores. . . . We also worship Phoebus.[110]

The reference to England as the land of the Hyperboreans associates it with the mythic northern land in Pindar's *Olympian 3* and *Pythian 10,* where the arts thrive and where Apollo and the Muses are especially honored. That allusion solves the problem of the frozen North by making Britain a land of poets, and making Milton a British poet–messenger of Apollo.[111] Milton also names as his muse Clio, the muse of history and so of historical epic (l. 24). The praises of his academy friends comparing him to Homer, Virgil, and Tasso indicate that he had been talking about plans for a historical epic. But the direct link with Tasso through his friend and patron Manso prompts Milton's clearest statement yet about the subject of his projected epic – King Arthur and the Round Table, the early British kings battling the Saxons, and the legends surrounding Arthur's miraculous preservation in the other world and promised return to rule over Britain:

> O, if my lot might but bestow such a friend upon me, a friend who understands how to honor the devotees of Phoebus – if ever I shall summon back our native kings into our songs, and Arthur, waging his wars beneath the earth, or if ever I shall proclaim the magnanimous heroes of the table which their mutual fidelity made invincible, and (if only the spirit be with me) shall shatter the Saxon phalanxes under the British Mars![112]

With deft and gracious compliments, Milton praises Manso for his hospitality to Tasso and Marino, but underscores the greater benefit the patron has gained from these relationships. Echoing Virgil's famous line from the Georgics, "Fortunate senex," Milton derives Manso's claim to immortality from his association with these poets, who will preserve his fame much more than he will theirs by monuments or biographies:

> Fortunate old man. For wherever the glory and the mighty name of Torquato shall be celebrated through all the world, and wherever the glorious reputation of the immortal Marino shall spread, your name and fame also shall constantly be in men's mouths, and with flight no less swift than theirs you shall mount the way of immortality.[113]

Only one dear to the gods could befriend a great poet, and the evidence of their favor is Manso's continued vigor: "Therefore your old age is green with lingering bloom and . . . your spirit strong and the power of your mind at its height" (ll. 74–7). By implication, those mental faculties are still able to discern merit in his new poet–guest, who (by further implication) honors Manso more by accepting his hospitality than Manso honors him by offering it. This very poem will add to Manso's honors: "If my Muse has breath sufficient, you too shall sit among the victorious ivy and laurels" (5–6).

Manso's place of honor is with the patrons: Gallus, the friend of Ovid and Virgil, and Maecenas, the patron of Horace and Propertius. Milton emphasizes the hierarchy of honors by creating and applying to the poet–patron relationship a myth of

Apollo visiting the cave of Chiron, the centaur who was tutor to Achilles and Aesculapius. In Milton's myth Apollo, exiled from Olympus for a year, visits Chiron and sings in his cave, producing effects like those caused by that other figure for the poet, Orpheus: trees are uprooted, rivers overflow, wild animals are gentled. Tasso, Marino, and Milton are the (divine) guests, like Apollo, and Manso the humble host, like Chiron.[114] The poet-figures are always primary: Apollo, Virgil, Horace, Tasso, Marino, Milton. In the next rank are the patrons who help them: Chiron, Gallus, Maecenas, Manso.

Milton fantasizes about finding a worthy patron like Manso whose aid would enable him to write an English epic in Tasso's vein and would thereby resolve the still-open question of career and livelihood. As Manso cared for Tasso during his last years and provided a tomb and monument for Marino, Milton imagines that on his deathbed he might be honored and cared for by a patron–friend who would erect a fitting monument for him and spread his fame. In *Lycidas* Milton imagined himself as a young and unfulfilled poet threatened by early death; here he evokes a happier portrait of himself full of years and achievements, and receiving due honors on earth as well as in heaven. But, in a final reversal, the imagined patron does not proclaim the poet Milton's fame. Since Manso's epigram with its angle/angel pun had classed Protestant Milton with barbarians in need of conversion and had ignored his poetry, Milton has to assert his own claim to the heavenly rewards due to faith and righteousness, and pronounce his own praises in a classical apotheosis on Olympus:

> Then, if there be such a thing as faith and assured rewards of the righteous, I my self, far remote in the ethereal homes of the gods who dwell in heaven, whither labor and a pure mind and ardent virtue lead, shall look down upon these events – as much as the fates permit – from some part of that mysterious world, and with a serene spirit and a face suffused with smiles and rosy light, I shall congratulate myself [plaudam mihi] on ethereal Olympus.[115]

Milton is serious in this riposte to Manso and in pressing the claims of poets over patrons, but he diffuses any offense by wit and playfulness. The final line echoes a Horatian satire in which a miser applauds himself on his riches, an allusion that tempers with ironic self-mockery what might otherwise seem pompous self-righteousness.[116] Nonetheless, this eliding of the patron intimates that the patronage relationship will not do for an independent-minded and free-speaking Protestant poet, even as the apostrophe to Manso as an old man, however fortunate and vigorous, intimates that such patronage belongs to another era. The poem achieves its multiple purposes with a delicately balanced mix of tones that allow for a poet's boldly revisionary claims without violating the decorum of panegyric and gracious civility.

Epitaphium Damonis (219 lines) is Milton's most impressive achievement as a

Latin poet. The choice of Latin is appropriate, since Milton's poetic and epistolary exchanges with Diodati were always in the classical languages. Yet this choice must also have been prompted by Milton's realization that he could not hope in English to surpass *Lycidas,* though he wanted to produce a superlative funeral poem for his dearest friend. So he set himself a different poetic challenge, not only in language and meter but also in the conception and treatment of the pastoral mode. As the final poem in the Latin–Greek section of Milton's 1645 *Poems, Epitaphium Damonis* stands as a counterpart to *Lycidas*, the final poem in the vernacular section; and it explores a different problem posed by death. In *Lycidas* the issue for the speaker is, how can he and why should he devote himself to poetry and God's service when Lycidas's death seems to indicate that the world is chaotic and life is meaningless. In *Epitaphium Damonis* the speaker's problem is, how can he bear to go on with his life, his duty to God and country, and his new plans for heroic verse, given his terrible loneliness with Damon gone.

The meter is dactyllic hexameter, not the elegiacs Milton chose twice before for Latin funeral poems. The title aligns Milton's poem with the Greek *epitaphios*, a generic label that often designates laments expressing a strong sense of personal loss.[117] Even more than *Lycidas* this poem reverberates with echoes from the entire pastoral tradition – most insistently Virgil's Eclogues and Georgics, but also Theocritus and his Greek successors, Castiglione's *Alcon*, and many more.[118] Like *Lycidas* also, this poem is energized by striking departures from and challenges to pastoral norms, culminating here in a renunciation of pastoral.

One major departure, in line with the poem's intense focus on the grief of Thyrsis/ Milton, is the absence of the expected pathetic fallacy. Nature does not mourn for Damon/Diodati. The crops and the sheep do not suffer because of their own sorrow for Damon but because Thyrsis neglects them. The several shepherds and shepherdesses do not form a procession of mourners to lament for Damon, but seek vainly to console Thyrsis. Nor do any figures from the classical or Christian supernatural answer questions or offer any consolation. In this regard, *Epitaphium Damonis* is the antithesis of *Lycidas*. There the swain cries out, "Who would not sing for *Lycidas*?" and many do; but this poem is truly the lament of a single singer.[119] Structurally, however, both poems use a framing device introducing the voice of a different speaker. *Lycidas* ends with a coda in which the Miltonic speaker records what has happened to the swain who sang for Lycidas; *Epitaphium Damonis* begins with a proem in which the Miltonic speaker introduces the swain Thyrsis and sets the stage for his song. That proem explains that this poem is belated because Thyrsis was detained by the poetic delights of Florence, but when he returned home, familiar places intensified his sense of loss:

> Love of the sweet Muse detained that shepherd in the Tuscan city. But when he had filled his mind full and the care of the flock that he had left behind him recalled him to his home, and when he sat down under the accustomed elm, then truly, then at

last, he felt the loss of his friend, and he began to pour out his tremendous sorrow in words like these.[120]

The content of the refrain marks perhaps the most striking departure from the pastoral norm, ringing changes on the final line in Virgil's Eclogue 10 in which the poet bids farewell to the pastoral world by sending his young goats home fully fed.[121] Thyrsis, however, reiterates over and over again his shocking refusal to fulfill his pastoral duties in the wake of Damon's loss: "Go home unfed, for your master has no time for you, my lambs" (Ite domum impasti, domino jam non vacat, agni) (l. 18). Though his reasons are very different, Thyrsis places himself by this refrain with the bad shepherds in *Lycidas* whom St Peter excoriated for neglecting their sheep. Thyrsis is so devastated by Damon's death that he turns his back on the commitment to shepherding figured both in the songs of poet–shepherds and the labors of pastor–shepherds tending church and nation.[122] As he refuses again and again to feed his hungry sheep he repudiates the poetic and prophetic responsibility the Miltonic swain accepted at the conclusion of *Lycidas*, and that Thyrsis intended to take up when "the care of the flock that he had left behind him recalled him" from singing in that quintessential pastoral land, Italy (ll. 14–15).

Milton makes this refrain, repeated 17 times without verbal variation, the structural pivot of the poem and the means by which it moves from lament to consolation. In an artistic *tour de force*, he invests it with ever-changing meaning as Thyrsis/Milton comes to terms, by degrees, with his loss and signals his progress.[123] In its first uses, the refrain indicates that Thyrsis finds his sheep, and the responsibilities they figure, to be an annoying distraction that he cannot cope with in his profound grief. He promises to secure Damon's fame by his poem, but his attention is fixed on the loss of the only friend who could truly share his thoughts and his emotional life:

> But what at last is to become of me? What faithful companion will stay by my side as you always did when the cold was cruel and the frost thick on the ground . . . Who now is to beguile my days with conversation and song? Go home unfed, for your master has no time for you, my lambs. To whom shall I confide my heart? Who will teach me to alleviate my mordant cares and shorten the long night with delightful conversation . . . Who then will bring back to me your mirth and Attic salt, your culture and humor? . . . Alone now I stray through the fields, alone through the pastures. . . . A man can hardly find a comrade for himself in a thousand; or, if one is granted to us by a fate at last not unkind to our prayers, a day and hour when we apprehend nothing snatches him away, leaving an eternal loss to all the years.[124]

Thyrsis walks undelighted through pastures and groves, and turns away the efforts of other shepherds to call him back to pastoral activities and pleasures. At line 93 the refrain conveys his rejection of the Virgilian pastoral world which holds no solace for him.

Then Thyrsis recalls Italy, finding some consolation in linking Damon closely with his experiences there. He first questions the value of the journey that caused his absence from the deathbed of Damon: "Alas! what wandering fancy carried me across the skyey cliffs of the snow-bound Alps to unknown shores? Was it of such importance to have seen buried Rome, even though it were what it was when, long ago Tityrus [from Virgil's First Eclogue] left his fields to see it?" (ll. 113–16). The Alps reference recalls the spectacular scenery of Milton's return trip and the allusion to "buried Rome" may register his disappointment that so many of the antiquities were covered over. But he cannot really regret the journey or even the delay, as he delightedly describes his participation in the Florentine academies under the figure of a pastoral singing contest, catching up Damon/Diodati into that fellowship:

> I shall never weary of your memory, Tuscan shepherds, youths in the service of the Muses, yet here was grace and here was gentleness; you also, Damon, were a Tuscan, tracing your lineage from the ancient city of Lucca. Ah, what a man was I when I lay beside cool, murmuring Arno, where the soft grass grows by the poplar grove, and I could pluck the violets and the myrtle shoots and listen to Menalcas competing with Lycidas. And I myself even dared to compete, and I think that I did not much displease, for your gifts are still in my possession, the baskets of reeds and osiers and the pipes with fastenings of wax. Even their beech trees learned my name from Dati and Francini, men who were both famous for their song and their learning, and both were of Lydian blood.[125]

That revealing exclamation – "what a man was I" – comments with wry self-awareness on the pleasure Milton took in these poetic exchanges, which bolstered his self-confidence and stoked his ambition.

The refrain at line 161 brushes aside "*silvae*" in anticipation of the epic to come, though with considerable anxiety. Thyrsis/Milton tells of attempting a new song on new pipes: some nights ago he started work on it but the new pipes broke. Yet he is ready to reenact Virgil's course – to take leave of the forests and move beyond pastoral verse and such small kinds.[126] He bids a fond farewell to the Latin poetry he exchanged with Diodati and his Italian friends, citing with some regret a maxim recognizing inevitable human limitation: one man cannot do everything. He has now determined to write a British historical epic for his countrymen, and he sketches out in more elaborate detail than ever before his intent to begin with the most ancient records and the Arthurian legends:

> And myself – for I do not know what grand song my pipe was sounding – it is now eleven nights and a day – perhaps I was setting my lips to new pipes, but their fastenings snapped and they fell asunder and could carry the grave notes no further. I am afraid that I am vain, yet I will relate it. Give way, then, O forest.
>
> Go home unfed, for your master has no time for you, my lambs. I, for my part, am resolved to tell the story of the Trojan ships in the Rutupian sea, and of the ancient kingdom of Inogene, the daughter of Pandrasus, and of the chiefs, Brennus and

> Arviragus, and of old Belinus, and of the Armorican settlers who came at last under British law. Then I shall tell of Igraine pregnant with Arthur by fatal deception, the counterfeiting of Gorlois features and arms by Merlin's treachery. And then, O my pipe, if life is granted me, you shall be left dangling on some old pine tree far away and quite forgotten by me, or else, quite changed, you shall shrill forth a British theme to your native Muses. What then? One man cannot do everything nor so much as hope to do everything.[127]

After this extended account of plans for an Arthuriad, at the last occurrence of the refrain at line 179 he dismisses his lambs, now less in annoyance or grief than in the confidence of a new poetic direction.

But a sense of painful irony returns as Thyrsis recalls his eager anticipation of sharing with Damon all that the Italian journey meant to him, symbolized by Manso's gift of elaborately decorated cups:

> These things I was keeping for you in the tough-barked laurel. These and more also – and in addition the two cups which Manso gave me – Manso, who is not the least glory of the Chalcidian shore. They are a marvellous work of art, and he is a marvellous man.[128]

The two cups have as their most prominent carved figures the phoenix and the Neoplatonic Amor, an allusion to two of Manso's books.[129] These and the other carved figures occasion new sorrow as they point to the things Milton so wanted to share: his rededication to epic and the epic line of Tasso; the "perfumed springtime" of those balmy days; the art he saw; and the philosophical discussions in the academies. Yet the ecphrasis also offers consolation, since many of the engraved figures are classical and biblical symbols of renewal and resurrection – the Red Sea, Arabia, the Phoenix, Aurora, Olympus. The definitive turn to consolation comes as the Neoplatonic Amor provides the terms for transforming earthly love to heavenly. Extolling Damon's heroic unsullied virtue, Thyrsis locates him now "among the souls of heroes and the immortal gods," and associates that ascent with his own advance from pastoral to heroic poetic themes. In a faint echo of the refrain he bids farewell again, not to his lambs but to his tears (l. 202). Also, in a parallel to Lycidas's role as "genius of the shore," Thyrsis imagines Damon as still able, from heaven, to "assist and gently favor me" (ll. 207–8). Thyrsis now addresses his friend both by his celestial name Diodatus (the gift of God), and by his pastoral name, "Damon," the name by which he will still be known in earthly forests – a gesture that leaves some place for pastoral. Yet in contrast to the pastoral imagery in the apotheosis and coda of *Lycidas*, the ecstatic vision with which this poem concludes shows Damon/Diodati enjoying, not pastoral delights but a transcendant version of the Christmastide festivities Milton imagined for him in Elegy VI: he participates in sanctified bacchic revelries and festal orgies at the immortal marriage feast.

With the *Epitaphium Damonis* Milton bids poignant farewell to the dearest friend of his youth, to Italy, to neo-Latin poetry, and to pastoral. He distills the meaning of past experiences and defines his future poetic course in the most precise terms yet. He ends this meditation on vocation, loss, and the experience of Italy with a firm resolution to take on the great responsibility of writing an English heroic poem addressed to his entire nation. This, he now believes, must be the major work God intends for him.

5

"All Mouths Were Opened Against . . . the Bishops" 1639–1642

When Milton returned to England in July or August, 1639, the nation was in a state of precarious peace. The First Bishops' War with Scotland began and ended while he was away. The Scots responded to the king's efforts to impose Laudian ecclesiastical directives upon them by repudiating bishops and the *Book of Common Prayer* and establishing a national Presbyterian church.[1] Taking this as a direct challenge to his authority, the king launched a military action against Scotland in January, 1639, but suffered a disastrous embarrassment as his outnumbered, demoralized, and disordered forces retreated without engaging the enemy in a formal battle. A peace accord was signed on June 19, 1639, but Charles left little doubt that he meant to return to subdue his rebellious Scots subjects.

In England as well the first major clash was over bishops and liturgy. The classic historiography of the English Revolution, associated with Samuel Gardiner, Max Weber, R. W. Tawney, Lawrence Stone, and Christopher Hill, interprets that event in terms of social and ideological conflicts: of Anglicanism with Puritanism, of royal with parliamentary supremacy, of a patriarchal economy with emergent individualism, of a rising middle class with a declining aristocracy, and of theories of absolute monarchy with social contract theories of the state.[2] Some revisionist historians – Conrad Russell, John Morrill, Kevin Sharpe, and Mark Kishlansky – deny the importance of such factors, arguing that traditional belief systems and hierarchies remained stable in local communities and attributing the outbreak of war to accidents, mistakes, and functional breakdowns in government exacerbated by irrational fears of popery.[3] But whatever the larger force of the revisionist argument (itself under revision),[4] Milton clearly thought the revolution was about profound religious and political differences, and intended his polemical tracts to participate in the fierce parliamentary debates and pamphlet wars prompted by those conflicts.

Writing of these years later in the *Defensio Secunda* (1654), Milton portrays himself as a scholar who made a reasoned and conscientious decision to interrupt the studies he was "blissfully" pursuing to write several tracts, led by a strong sense of duty to God, truth, the common good, and his Smectymnuan friends. He was aware, he says, of a crisis moment. Parliament was acting "with vigor," freedom of speech was restored, "all mouths were opened" against the bishops, and men were taking the first steps on "the true path to liberty." He claims for his tracts a large and effective role in the polemical Bishops' Wars:

> Since, moreover, I had so practiced myself from youth that I was above all things unable to disregard the laws of God and man, and since I had asked myself whether I should be of any future use if I now failed my country (or rather the church and so many of my brothers who were exposing themselves to danger for the sake of the Gospel) I decided, although at the time occupied with certain other matters, to devote to this conflict all my talents and all my active powers.
>
> First, therefore, I addressed to a certain friend two books on the reformation of the English church. Then, since two bishops of particularly high repute were asserting their prerogatives against certain eminent ministers, and I concluded that on those subjects which I had mastered solely for love of truth and out of regard for Christian duty, I could express myself at least as well as those who were wrangling for their own profit and unjust authority, I replied to one of the bishops [Ussher] in two books, of which the first was entitled, *Of Prelatical Episcopacy* and the second *The Reason of Church-Government*, while to the other bishop [Hall] I made reply in certain *Animadversions* and later in an *Apology*. I brought succor to the ministers who were, as it was said, scarcely able to withstand the eloquence of this bishop, and from that time onward, if the bishops made any response, I took a hand. (*CPW* IV.1, 622–3)

In 1640–2 Milton's self-construction was more complex. In all the antiprelatical tracts he is concerned with how he sees himself and how he will show himself to others. He claims several roles, varying the mix as genre and rhetorical purpose dictate: scholar, humanist critic, rhetorician, teacher, patriot, satirist, reformist poet, prophet, and bard. In his polemic he uses the various resources of learning, reason, passion, ardor, delight, invective, metaphor, and sublimity available to those several roles. At times he represents himself driven to fury over the tyranny, the lavish lifestyle, and the popish idolatry of the bishops, justifying his vituperation and his impassioned cries for reformation and apocalypse as the zeal of a prophet, an English Elijah. Like many reformers in 1641–2 he is touched by millenarian expectation and eager to help prepare for the apocalypse, whose glories he celebrates in occasional bursts of prophetic and poetic fervor. In his last two tracts, *The Reason of Church-Government* and the *Apology*, he draws extended and revealing self-portraits that conjoin these several roles.

Milton's five antiprelatical tracts undertake to defame the bishops by every rhetorical means, so as to eradicate them "root and branch" from both civil and ecclesiastical offices, along with their "popish" liturgy, canons, courts, privileges, property, and wealth. Though Milton sometimes addresses his episcopal antagonists and their treatises, his rhetoric is mainly directed to moderate Puritans and especially members of parliament, to persuade them that the "Root and Branch" legislation must pass. His basic argument is the fundamental Protestant principle that scripture alone must determine all matters of religion, including liturgical practice and church government or "discipline." He associates himself at this juncture with the Presbyterian version of church government, arguing that it alone has scriptural warrant, but his emphasis is much more on eradicating the bishops than on defending the Presbyterian model; at least subconsciously he seems already less than comfortable with Presbyterianism. He does not load his texts with biblical citations like most Presbyterian controversialists, nor does he comment much on the biblical proof texts commonly invoked to support the Presbyterian system, but instead appeals continually and often explicitly to the "spirit" of the gospel. By the standard of the wholly spiritual, humble, and egalitarian ministry instituted by Christ he finds the episcopal institution an abomination, meriting his almost visceral disgust. But his concept of a ministry without coercive power or tithes or any function not open to the laity, and his emphasis on all God's people as prophets, distance him from Presbyterianism, with its clerical authority, tithes, and repression of dissent. Milton is moving, even at this stage, toward Independency.

Theologically Milton is still an orthodox Trinitarian and – at least nominally – a predestinarian Calvinist: he prays to the Trinity and refers to Arius, Socinus, and Arminius as heretics.[5] But his emphasis on the power of nations and individuals to help realize providential history departs from the usual Calvinist insistence on God's control of individual lives, history, and the millennial moment.[6] Also, while Milton still recognizes the king and still accepts the traditional concept of England as a mixed commonwealth sharing power between king, lords, and commons, he insists that parliament alone can reform church and state, thereby according it the preponderance of power in the state and placing himself in the vangard of an emerging English republicanism.

In these first tracts Milton confronted polemical challenges for which he was only partly prepared by classical rhetorical theory and his university debates. Broadsides, newsletters, and especially the Marprelate papers of the 1588–9 afforded some precedents, but England had as yet seen nothing like the outpouring of tracts in the 1640s, addressed to contemporary controversies.[7] Milton's tracts participate in common polemical modes, looking especially to the example of Luther, Wyclif, and Martin Marprelate,[8] but they are strikingly original in their imagistic exuberance, their experimentation with genre and rhetorical style, and their sheer verbal energy. He also diverges far from contemporary norms of controversy in refusing to marshal authorities and indicate them by marginal citation; Milton's margins are defiantly bare.[9] Milton sees and presents himself in these tracts as a learned scholar, but one whose essential characteristic is an intellectual independence neither constrained by nor needing support from human authorities. That self-construction will receive increasing emphasis over time. He also works out in these tracts a poetics of satire that justifies vehement invective as a "sanctifi'd bitternesse" having precedent in the biblical prophets. That poetics also sanctions his uncommonly severe *ad hominem* attacks on grounds of an assumed equation between author and text: barbarous prose and slavish ideas emanate from and are indicators of a depraved life.[10] By the same token, Milton's lengthy autobiographical passages serve not only to answer personal attacks, but also as ethical proof, presenting his texts as the arguments and rhetoric of a good man. Prophetic testimony is also prominent in these tracts, as Milton relates his polemic to his vocation as bard and identifies his own destiny with that of the nation. His greatest poetic achievement, he now supposes, may be to celebrate the perfecting of the English nation as the Millennium approaches.

"I Decided . . . to Devote to this Conflict All My Talents"

After visiting his father and various friends – perhaps Thomas Young and Alexander Gil – Milton set up for himself in London. His lodging, Edward Phillips reports, was in "St. *Brides* Church-yard, at the House of one *Russel*, a Taylor" (*EL* 60). That was near Fleet Street, not far from St Paul's and his childhood home in Bread Street. Milton now had some financial independence from loans his father had placed in his name.[11] He supplemented his income by tutoring a few private pupils, beginning with his nephews: John Phillips boarded with him and John's elder brother Edward was at first a day pupil. Milton's flat was somewhat cramped and noisy, but he probably stayed there until autumn, 1640: it was hard, he later observed, to find a suitable house "in such upset and tumultuous times" (*CPW* IV.1, 621). At St Bride's he wrote the *Epitaphium Damonis*, made an abortive start on an epic,[12] undertook a course of reading in English and European history, started to note down ideas for literary projects, and began to develop and implement his ideas about educating the young.

From late 1639 to mid-1641 or thereabouts he made seven pages of notes in the Trinity manuscript,[13] listing nearly one hundred titles for possible literary projects drawn from the Bible and British history, several with one or two sentences of elaboration and a few with more extended plot summaries. He chiefly considered topics for dramas, perhaps drawn to the shorter kind by Aristotle's preference for tragedy, but more likely by his failure to get on with an epic. His serious reading in the English chronicles led him to recognize that the Arthurian epic he had been proposing for several years did not meet Tasso's, and his own, requirement that an epic subject be based on history. The Trinity list includes only one epic subject, clearly historical: "A Heroicall Poem may be founded somwhere in Alfreds reigne, especially at his issuing out of Edelingsey on the Danes. whose actions are wel like those of Ulysses" (*TM* 38). Two topics are conceived as pastoral dramas and the rest as tragedy.

Filled with additions and interlineations, these pages offer a revealing insight into Milton's way of identifying and imagining possible subjects at this stage; some topics anticipate elements of his major poems written nearly thirty years later. The first page contains two lists of characters – crossed out – under the title *Paradise Lost*, and a longer sketch developing that topic. Other Old Testament subjects from Genesis through Daniel fill out that page and the next, and several on Samson reveal Milton's early attraction to that subject.[14] Titles are listed in two columns, usually with citation of biblical chapter and verse and occasionally a summary sentence or two.[15] Under the heading "British Trag[edies]," the third and fourth pages list, in order and by number, thirty-three topics from the Roman Conquest to the Norman Conquest, often with cross reference to a chronicle source[16] and sometimes with a very brief plot summary. The fifth and sixth pages contain expanded summaries (a half-page or so each) of four topics Milton evidently thought most promising: "Baptistes," on John the Baptist; "Abram from Morea, or Isaak redeemd"; "Sodom," renamed as he worked on it "Cupids funeral pile. Sodom Burning";[17] and a fourth version of the Fall story, titled "Adam unparadiz'd." The last page contains five brief sketches of early Scottish history under the heading "Scotch stories or rather brittish of the north parts." Crowded in on the last two pages are seven topics from Christ's life, with a brief sketch of the last, "Christus patiens."

The two longer versions of the Fall tragedy are conceived as some fusion of classical tragedy, miracle play, and masque: five acts, a Euripidean prologue, the Fall occurring offstage, a mix of biblical and allegorical characters, and a "mask of all the evills of this life & world."[18] Edward Phillips saw several verses for the beginning of a "Fall" tragedy, including ten lines that Milton later used in Satan's speech on Mount Niphates (*PL* IV, 32–41).[19] The other extended drafts of tragedies are more strictly classical, with historical events and characters, choruses, messengers, and pathetic speeches.[20] The longest of them, "Sodom Burning," explicitly invites a parallel to contemporary affairs: "Then, calling to the thunders, lightning, and fires, he [the Angel] bids them hear the call of God to come and destroy a godless nation . . . with some short warning to other nations to take heed."[21]

During his first year home Milton watched the political crisis worsen. Both the king and his chief adviser, the Earl of Strafford, attracted fierce animosity for seeking heavy subscriptions and extra-legal taxes to renew war with the Scots. On April 13, 1640 the king convened the Short Parliament, so named because he suspended it three weeks later for attending to the redress of grievances rather than funds for the war. Some days later the Convocation of Clergy, at Laud's behest, issued new and soon notorious canons requiring conformity in liturgy and preaching and requiring that all clergymen take the infamous "et cetera" oath: to refuse any change in "the government of this Church by Archbishops, Bishops, Deans and Archdeacons, etc. as it now stands established and by right ought to stand." All this led to riots in the City for several days in May. Charles launched the Second Bishops' War that summer, but when the king's troops faced off against the Scots army near

Newcastle on August 28, 1640 the royal forces were soon routed. The Scots occupied Newcastle, Durham, Tynemouth, and all Northumberland, and a preliminary treaty on October 27 required the king to maintain them there until final terms were agreed. Under pressure from the Scots and his dissaffected English subjects, Charles also agreed to call a new parliament.

Milton probably moved house about the time that new parliament assembled on November 3, 1640. He needed, Edward Phillips explains,

> a place to dispose his Books in, and other Goods fit for the furnishing of a good handsome House . . . a pretty Garden-House he took in *Aldersgate*-Street, at the end of an Entry, and therefore the fitter for his turn, by the reason of the Privacy, besides that there are few Streets in *London* more free from Noise then that.[22]

This rented house was situated just beyond the city walls outside Aldersgate, in the second precinct of St Botolph's parish. A servant, Jane Yates, managed the household tasks and Edward Phillips joined his brother John as a boarding pupil. Phillips explains that Milton set himself and his pupils a program of "hard Study, and spare Diet," but that he also enjoyed a young man's pleasures about town, permitting himself every three or four weeks a "Gawdy-day" with two Gray's Inn friends – "Young Sparks of his Acquaintance . . . the *Beau's* of those times."[23] This occasional conviviality is in line with Milton's belief that he and all men need some recreation as a balance to arduous labor.[24]

Milton taught his nephews for about six years (1640–6). Edward Phillips's report of their studies corresponds in essence to the more elaborate and detailed model Milton set forth in *Of Education* (1644).[25] "Through his excellent judgment and way of Teaching," Phillips explains, the students read "many Authors, both of the Latin and Greek . . . far above the Pedantry of common publick Schooles (where such Authors are scarce ever heard of)." He specifies the "four Grand authors" in Latin (presumably Virgil, Horace, Ovid, and Cicero) and also several other Latin and Greek texts in literature, moral philosophy, mathematics, natural science, astronomy, and warfare.[26] In Italian they read Giovanni Villani's history of Florence and in French, Pierre d'Avity's world geography.[27] They learned enough Hebrew, Chaldean [Aramaic], and Syriac "to go through the *Pentateuch,*" some part of the Chaldee Paraphrase, and several chapters of Matthew's gospel. On Sundays they read a chapter of the Greek Testament and heard Milton expound it; they also wrote from his dictation "some part . . . of a Tractate which he though fit to collect from the ablest of Divines . . . *Amesius, Wollebius,* &. *viz.* A perfect System of Divinity" (*EL* 61). This was apparently the starting point for Milton's *De Doctrina Christiana,* written many years later but following the general organization of topics in Wolleb and Ames.

Taking heart from the convening of parliament, Milton felt free to concern himself with his own affairs in his new house, "willingly leaving the outcome of these events, first of all to God, and then to those to whom the people had entrusted with this office" (*CPW* IV.1, 621). Among those leading the reform movement in the Lords were Bedford, Essex, Warwick, and Saye and Sele; and in the Commons, John Pym, John Hampden, John Selden, Francis Rous, Oliver Cromwell, Henry Martin, and Henry Vane, Jr. There were two overarching issues: securing and expanding the rights of parliament against the king's perceived absolutist tendencies; and either restricting the power of, or wholly abolishing, the bishops. Parliament acted quickly to release and compensate Laud's Puritan victims (Prynne, Burton, Bastwick, and Lilburne), to declare the Laudian canons void, to abolish ship-money, to abrogate the hated Star Chamber and other special courts, and to enact a law for triennial parliaments. On November 25 parliament impeached Strafford for plotting to use the Irish army to subdue Scotland and England, and for advising the king that he was not bound by "rules of government" in raising money for his Scots wars.[28] In December they began impeachment proceedings against Laud for "subversion of the laws . . . and of religion" and on March 1, 1641 sent him to the Tower. Strafford's long treason trial ended abruptly with a Bill of Attainder passed by parliament and signed, with great reluctance, by the king; he was executed on May 12, 1641. On May 10 parliament passed an act prohibiting its dissolution except by its own consent, the legal ground which allowed it to become the Long Parliament. The presence of the Scots army in the North and of the Scots Commissioners in London negotiating a treaty – not signed until August, 1641 – kept up continual pressure for reform, civil and ecclesiastical.

While Milton observed these events from the sidelines, his private studies helped him place the developing conflict in historical perspective and prepared him to speak to the issues. In 1639–42 he chiefly read English and British history, taking notes in his Commonplace Book on Bede, William of Malmesbury, Stow, Hardyng, Holinshed, Speed, Sir Thomas Smith, William Camden, John Hayward, William Lambard, André du Chesne, George Buchanan, Edmund Campion, Edmund Spenser's *View of the Present State of Ireland,* and others.[29] For European history he read Sleiden, Paulus Jovius, Machiavelli, Savonarola, Sarpi, Thuanus (du Thou), and others.[30] He also took a few notes from literary works (Chaucer's *Canterbury Tales* and *Romaunt of the Rose*, and Gower's *Confessio Amantis*), classical and patristic texts (Aristotle, Caesar's *Commentaries,* Lactantius, Cyprian), Cuspinian's history of the Roman emperors, Sozomon's ecclesiastical history, Sinibaldus on the generation of man, and Ascham.[31] His few additions to the Moral and Economic Indices in his Commonplace Book include some that speak to his immediate concerns, among them a summary of Bede's little story "about an Englishman who was suddenly made a poet by divine Providence."[32] Most entries are to the Political Index, and many have contemporary relevance. Citing Stow on King Alfred turning the old laws into English, Milton suggests application to the king's prerogative courts: "I would he liv'd now to rid us of this norman gibbrish."[33] Several entries under the topic "Property and Taxes" and "Official Robbery or Extortion" vent Milton's bourgeois anger over Charles's hated levies. Harold Harefoot "exacting ship monie" is one among many examples he cites of kings who were "pollers" (plunderers) and lost their subjects' love or provoked rebellion by exorbitant levies for unwise wars or private corruption (*CPW* I, 480). Camden's counterexample of Queen Elizabeth's moderation in taxing and spending leads Milton to generalize that a king should not tax excessively, since "need, if anything, plunges the English into revolt" (484). Under the topic "Of Allies" he cites Roger Ascham to the effect that "Our league and union with the Scots [is] a thing most profitable, & naturall."[34] The topic "Of Civil War" elicits examples of "the danger of calling in forraine aids" that relate to Charles's rumored plans to call in Irish or French armies (499).

Entries under such heads as "King," "The Tyrant," "Subject," "The State," "Of War," "Laws," and "Courtiers," collect examples of limitations on royal power: coronation oaths, Magna Carta, and the judgments of historians, e.g. Sir Thomas Smith's dictum that the act of a king not approved by the people or established by parliament is "taken for nothing, either to bind the k., his successors, or his subjects."[35] Other citations point to kings rightfully resisted in arms or deposed for tyranny: Richard II, Edward II, King John, and the Holy Roman Emperor attacked by the German Protestant Princes. Holinshed's account of Richard II leads to an observation about tyranny with clear contemporary relevance: "to say that the lives and goods of the subject are in the hands of the K. and at his disposition is . . . most tyrannous and unprincely" (446).[36] Several entries indicate a heightening of Milton's antimonarchist and republican sentiments, notably his summary of Machiavelli's views as to why a commonwealth is preferable to a monarchy: "because more excellent men come from a commonwealth than from a kingdom; because in the former virtue is honored most of the time and is not feared as in a kingdom" (421).[37]

Throughout these months pulpits and presses resounded with denunciations of or support for the bishops and the *Book of Common Prayer.* Royalist Laudians defended the established liturgy and episcopacy as divine ordinances, and bishops' secular offices and power as essential supports to the monarchy: "No Bishop, no King." More moderate Anglicans argued that liturgical practices and bishops' powers developed over time but have biblical and apostolic precedent and sanction; some were willing to relax liturgical mandates and also, if that became necessary, to remove bishops from the House of Lords and strip them of most political functions. Reformist Puritans sought to replace the "popish" liturgy of the *Book of Common Prayer* and to abolish bishops. Presbyterians claimed a biblical mandate for Presbyterian church government, in which ministers (presbyters), deacons, and lay elders govern individual parishes, and parish councils are linked together through regional synods and a national assembly. The separatist sects (chiefly Congregationalists, Brownists, Independents, and Anabaptists) wanted no national church, only individual gathered communities of the elect. Many went into exile in Holland or New England during previous decades, but were now gaining strength in England and pressing their demands for toleration. The anti-episcopal agitation which united many disparate groups was fueled by fears and passions associating the bishops with popery, idolatry, tyranny over conscience, evil counsel to the king, and pompous excesses in lifestyle and ceremony that affronted the sober bourgeois. On December 11, 1640 a petition signed by some 15,000 from the City of London (probably including Milton)[38] called for abolition of episcopal government "with all its dependencies, roots, and branches." On January 23, 1641 a compromise petition signed by more than 700 clergy – including Edward Calamy and Stephen Marshall, two of the Presbyterian controversialists Milton supported in his first tracts – called for the bishops' removal from parliament and all secular offices and from some ecclesiastical functions.[39] Moderates on both sides were promoting some such compromise. On May 1 the Commons passed an Exclusion Bill and gave preliminary approval on May 27 to a "Root and Branch" bill abolishing Episcopacy altogether. But on June 8 the Lords rejected Exclusion.

Milton, following the controversy intently from his study, may have been invited by his tutor and friend Thomas Young to serve God's cause with his pen, or he may have volunteered to do so. At Laud's instigation Bishop Joseph Hall of Exeter had published in February, 1640, under his initials, a 260-page treatise, *Episcopacie by Divine Right Asserted*, which argued from scripture texts, patristic testimony, and ancient church practice that episcopacy was ordained by God.[40] In January, 1641, as the clamor over bishops and liturgy intensified, Hall published under the same initials *An Humble Remonstrance to the High Court of Parliament*; it retreats from *jure divino* claims but finds apostolic warrant for bishops and bewails the "furious and malignant spirits" venting libels against them.[41] The most substantial of the several answers to Hall appeared around March 20, 1641 under the name "Smectymnuus" – an acronymn formed from the initials of the Presbyterian ministers Stephen Marshall, Edmund Calamy, Thomas Young, Matthew Newcomen, and William Sperstow. Young was the primary author of this 93-page tract, also addressed to parliament, *An Answer to a booke entituled, An Humble Remonstrance. In Which, the Original of Liturgy and Episcopacy is Discussed.* It denounces the "Popish" liturgy of the *Book of Common Prayer* and argues scripture warrant for Presbyterian church government from the fact that in scripture and in the primitive church bishop and presbyter are synonymous terms, both referring to ministers of individual churches.[42] Milton almost certainly wrote or contributed largely to the tract's nine-page postscript, a historical review of English prelacy as a danger to church and state in all ages, producing "those bitter fruits *Pride, Rebellion, Treason, Unthankefulnes*."[43]

By April 12, 1641 Hall published, anonymously, a 188-page response, *A Defence of the Humble Remonstrance, against the Frivolous and false Exceptions of Smectymnuus*; it was addressed to the king and was much sharper in tone than his previous tracts.[44] Conceding that bishop and presbyter were at first synonymous terms, he nonetheless insists that the office of bishop derives from the apostles and that hierarchy was always present in the church, warranting the evolution of the present episcopal structure. He ridicules the "free prayer" by unlettered artisans that Puritans would substitute for the beauty and decorum of a liturgy sanctioned by scripture and antiquity, and denounces the rebellion of so many "ill-bred sons" against their mother church. He scoffs especially at Milton's historical "Postscript" as a plagiarized patchwork – a charge which Milton sharply denied.[45] Hall also solicited a treatise from the respected moderate Archbishop of Armagh, James Ussher.[46] Ussher's proposal to amalgamate the episcopal and presbyterian systems, with bishops and archbishops presiding over diocesan and provincial synods, was in private circulation in May and June, 1641; it influenced discussions in the parliament and attracted considerable support from moderates on both sides.[47] Toward the end of May Ussher responded to Hall's request with a 16-page tract, *The Judgment of Doctor Rainoldes touching the Originall of Episcopacy. More largely confirmed out of Antiquity.*[48] Ussher does not claim the divine institution of bishops but rather their appointment by the apostles, citing the usual scripture passages and a flurry of ancient texts.

In late May, 1641, shortly after Strafford's execution, Milton's *Of Reformation Touching Church-Discipline in England: And the Causes that hitherto have hindred it* was published anonymously. He does not respond to particular tracts, but supports Root and Branch with a hard-hitting blast against bishops and the Anglican liturgy, employing a fiery, scornful rhetoric closer to William Prynne than to Smectymnuus. Milton employs a familiar genre of political commentary, the Letter to a Friend, which allows him to address an implied sympathetic auditor but one who is perhaps hesitant about Root and Branch reform and who might be attracted to a compromise. This tract is unlike anything that had yet appeared in the polemic wars. Milton's often-criticized scanting of logical argument in favor of the arts of rhetoric and the rich resources of poetic language[49] – especially, graphic body imagery – is designed to scuttle compromise by rendering episcopacy disgusting. He does, however, present himself as a historian reviewing the record of bishops in the early church. Drawing evidence from his recent readings in English history and his earlier readings in the Fathers and the Councils,[50] he charges bishops with continually frustrating the cause of Reformation, weakening monarchs, and abusing the people's liberties. He briefly restates Presbyterian scripture-based arguments about church order, but he is already moving beyond that system and the Smectymnuans as he emphasizes the laity's right to exercise all church functions and points to signs of an "extraordinary effusion of *Gods* Spirit upon every age, and sexe" (*CPW* I, 566). He also begins to conceive England in proto-republican terms.[51] As well, he begins in this tract to develop and defend a poetics of satire. He excuses his vehement invective by the need "to vindicate the spotlesse *Truth* from an ignominious bondage," and justifies his daring iconoclastic critique of the Fathers and even the martyred Marian bishops on the ground that their "faults and blemishes" must be exposed, lest "mens fond opinion should thus idolize them" (535).[52] He also imagines himself as prophetic bard, singing in the Millennium. The argument and art of this treatise are discussed on pages 141–5.

Of Reformation came in for a passing rebuke in a pseudonymous treatise, *A Compendious Discourse, Proving Episcopacy to be of Apostolicall and Consequently of Divine Institution*, published on May 31, 1641 under the pseudonym Peloni Almoni.[53] Almost immediately Milton took up his pen again, to answer Ussher's tract directly and incidentally Almoni's and Hall's. In June or July, 1641 his brief anonymous treatise appeared: *Of Prelatical Episcopacy, and Whether it may be deduc't from the Apostolical times by vertue of those Testimonies which are alledg'd to that purpose in some late Treatises: One whereof goes under the name of James, Arch-bishop of Armagh.* The ground of Milton's argument is, again, *sola scriptura*, that only scripture has divine authority, its "brightnesse, and perfection" furnishing an "all sufficiency" of spiritual knowledge that needs no "supplement" from tradition or patristic testimony to determine church government.[54] Since Hall and Ussher have conceded that the terms "bishop" and "presbyter" are used interchangeably in the New Testament, Milton need not argue that point here,[55] so he simply declares victory on the first page. In strict logic, then, the rest of the tract is irrelevant.[56] But since Milton hopes to persuade those confused or undecided about eliminating bishops, he continues the argument. He presents himself as a learned historical and textual scholar who has uncovered manifold problems with the ancient authorities, and so has decided "that I could do Religion, and my Country no better service for the time then doing my utmost endeavour to recall the people of God from this vaine forraging after straw, and to reduce them to their firme stations under the standard of the Gospell" (*CPW* I, 627). Thomas Corns observes that by refusing to engage on its own terms the historical evidence for bishops presented by Hall and Ussher, Milton fails to live up to the scholarly claims he makes for himself.[57] But Milton undertakes here to discredit all such evidence *en masse,* catching up individual items in that sweeping dismissal.

Milton's strategy is to denigrate all the patristic authorities and texts cited by Ussher – Ignatius, Leontius, Polycarp, Eusebius, Photius, Polycrates, Irenaeus, Papias, and others – by showing their insufficiency, inconvenience, and impiety, so as to leave scripture standing alone as the only authority on church government. Giving most attention to the topic of "insufficiency," he heaps up historical circumstances and textual problems that, he insists, reveal the patristic texts to be unreliable, obscure, contradictory, mistaken, absurd, heretical, corrupt, or spurious. They are also "inconvenient" for Protestants in that many who testify for bishops also support the office of pope. Their "impiety" lies in defying Christ's injunction that "no tittle of his word shall fall to the ground" by creating an unscriptural ecclesiastical structure (652). Poetic language is less prominent here than in *Of Reformation*, but Milton again wields degrading images and adjectives as a polemic weapon. Tradition is a "broken reed" (624); antiquity is "an indigested heap, and frie of Authors" (626), a "petty-fog of witnesses" (648), "offalls and sweepings" (651). And the contrast between the true and perfect gospel and corrupt ancient authorities is again rendered in striking metaphors of the body and family relationships:

> We doe injuriously in thinking to tast better the pure Evangelick Manna by seasoning our mouths with the tainted scraps, and fragments of an unknown table; and searching among the verminous and polluted rags dropt overworn from the toyling shoulders of Time, with these deformedly to quilt, and interlace the intire, the spotlesse, and undecaying robe of Truth, the daughter not of Time, but of Heaven, only bred up heer below in Christian hearts, between two grave & holy nurses the Doctrine, and Discipline of the Gospel (639).

At about the same time (June 26, 1641) the Smectymnuans published their 219-page answer to Hall, addressed to the two houses of parliament and entitled *A Vindication of the Answer to the Humble Remonstrance, from the Unjust Imputations of Frivolousnesse and Falsehood: Wherein the Cause of Liturgy and Episcopacy is further debated*. Complaining vigorously about the Remonstrant's scoffs and taunts, they answer his charges point for point, reviewing the biblical evidence against episcopacy and a required liturgy and for Presbyterian church government.[58] During these weeks Milton was also working on his answer to Hall, a sharply satiric and sometimes scurrilous anonymous tract, *Animadversions upon the Remonstrants Defence, Against Smectymnuus*, probably published in July. Now thoroughly out of patience with arguments about ancient sources, he promises to spare the reader an immersion in the "labyrinth of controversall antiquity" (such as his last tract demanded), and instead to show "truth vindicated, and Sophistry taken short at the first false bound."[59] He engages Hall's tract section by section, using the common polemic strategy of extracting passages from Hall and appending to each, dialogue-wise, a sharp rejoinder or argument.[60] He proudly claims association with the Smectymnuans and other reformers – "these free-spoken, and plaine harted men that are the eyes of their Country, and the prospective glasses of their Prince" (*CPW* I, 670) – but he eschews their moderate tone. Instead, his preface works out more fully a poetics of satire, and a justification for vehement invective as an appropriate use of "those two most rationall faculties of humane intellect anger and laughter." "Grim laughter," he insists, "hath oft-times a strong and sinewy force in teaching and confuting" (663–4). He finds precedent for such satire in Solomonic precept and Christian example, and he also places himself in the line of iconoclastic prophets who were "Transported with the zeale of truth to a well heated fervencie" (663): Daniel destroying the image of Nebuchadnezzar or Elijah destroying Baal (699–700).

Milton's strategy here is to discredit Hall and the bishops by a steady onslaught of scurrilous gibes, invective, scornful epithets, sarcasm, hyperbolic parody, puns, and (again) degrading images of the body. Targeting Hall's literary reputation as verse satirist and the polemic persona he has fashioned for himself as a tolerant, moderate, scholarly Senecan moralist, Milton scoffs at his terse, antithetical, satiric sententiae, heaps scorn on his "blabbing Bookes" and "toothlesse Satyrs,"[61] and constructs Hall as the false prophet personified, the antithesis of himself as true prophet. He makes Hall's stylistic defects a mirror of his and the prelates' moral defects: they are concerned only with "superiority, pride, ease, and the belly" (665), and they have "poyson'd and choak'd" the universities, producing a hireling clergy of "mercenary stripplings" with "Simoniacall fathers" (718). He taunts them with insults – "Wipe your fat corpulencies out of our light" (732) – and with derisive laughter: "Ha, ha, ha" (726). Also, defending the Root and Branch petitioners against Hall's elitist dismissal of them as "Libellous Separatist" tradesmen, Milton offers a derisive summary of the bishops' entire course of life:

> Our great Clarks think that these men, because they have a Trade (as *Christ himselfe,* and Saint *Paul* had) cannot therefore attaine to some good measure of knowledge, and to a reason of their actions, as well as they that spend their youth in loitering, bezzling, and harlotting, their studies in unprofitable questions, and barbarous sophistry, their middle age in ambition, and idlenesse, their old age in avarice, dotage, and diseases.[62]

Responding to Hall's charge that the Smectymnuans spit in the face of their Mother Church, Milton offers a scathing revision of that family metaphor:

> Marke Readers, the crafty scope of these Prelates, they endeavour to impresse deeply into weak, and superstitious fancies the awfull notion of a mother, that hereby they might cheat them into a blind and implicite obedience to whatsoever they shall decree, or think fit . . . whatsoever they say she sayes, must be a deadly sin of disobedience not to beleeve. So that we who by Gods speciall grace have shak'n off the servitude of a great male Tyrant, our pretended Father the Pope, should now, if we be not betimes aware of these wily teachers, sink under the slavery of a Female notion . . . [and] make ourselves rather the Bastards, or the Centaurs of their spirituall fornications.[63]

His literary strategies include allegory – an extended representation of antiquity as a giant idol, an "unactive, and liveless *Colossus*" that the iconoclastic weapon of scripture will easily throw down and crumble "like the chaffe of the Summer threshing floores" (700). He also encapsulates his argument in a parable, presented as a law case. A painstaking gardener (the minister of a congregation) carefully plants, weeds, and maintains his garden, but is overborn by a strange gardener (the bishop) "that never knew the soyle, never handl'd a Dibble or Spade to set the least potherbe that grew there, much lesse had edur'd an houres sweat or chilnesse, and yet challenges as his right the binding or unbinding of every flower, the clipping of every bush, the weeding and worming of every bed" (the bishops' power of discipline, jurisdiction, and regulation of parishes). The native gardener refuses, but the stranger insists that the Lord of the soil has given him this office and "ten fold your wages." The conclusion remains unwritten since the fate of Root and Branch is still in doubt: "what was determin'd I cannot tell you till the end of this Parliament" (716–17).

Animadversions has no overarching argument, though Milton often reiterates his central point that scripture alone must decide religious controversies (681, 699–700). He also begins to formulate some characteristic ideas. Anticipating *Areopagitica,* he rejoices that removal of the prelates' "proud *Imprimaturs*" allows Englishmen "liberty of speaking, then which nothing is more sweet to man" (669). Anticipating the divorce tracts, he points to the essential humanistic spirit of the Bible: "every rule, and instrument of necessary knowledge that God hath given us, ought to be . . . weilded and manag'd by the life of man without penning him up from the duties of humane society, and such . . . is the holy Bible" (699). Anticipating the *Likeliest Means* (1659), he denies ministers any special status by ordination or learning and hints at church disestablishment.[64] Even without tithes and wealthy livings, he argues, God can stir up "rich Fathers [like Milton senior] to bestow exquisite education upon their Children, and so dedicate them to the service of the Gospell" – as ministers and presumably also as lay-prophets like Milton (721).

As he did in *Of Reformation,* Milton imagines himself participating in the great apocalyptic motion of the "renovating and re-ingendring Spirit of God" (703) and celebrating the new outpouring of God's spirit in England: God has ever had the English nation "under the speciall indulgent eye of his providence" and now again is "manifestly come down among us, to doe some remarkable good to our Church or state" (703–4). Rising to the high style and assuming a prophetic voice, he offers a long, passionate, poetic prayer couched in imagery from Revelation – the very opposite of Hall's aphoristic Senecan style – for the full perfection of the church in the Millennial kingdom at hand:

> Who is there that cannot trace thee now in thy beamy walke through the midst of thy Sanctuary, amidst those golden *candlesticks*. . . . Come therefore O thou that hast the seven starres in thy right hand [Revelation 1:16], appoint thy chosen *Preists* according to their Orders, and courses of old, to minister before thee . . . O perfect, and accomplish thy glorious acts; . . . When thou hast settl'd peace in the Church, and righteous judgement in the Kingdome, then shall all thy Saints addresse their voyces of joy, and triumph to thee, standing on the shoare of that red Sea into which our enemies had almost driven us. (705–6)

And he again imagines himself as a prophet–poet singing of and in that Millennial kingdom:

> And he that now for haste snatches up a plain ungarnish't present as a thanke-offering to thee . . . may then perhaps take up a Harp, and sing thee an elaborate Song to Generations . . . thy Kingdome is now at hand, and thou standing at the dore. Come forth out of thy Royall Chambers, O Prince of all the Kings of the earth, put on the visible roabes of thy imperiall Majesty, take up that unlimited Scepter which thy

> Almighty Father hath bequeath'd thee; for now the voice of thy Bride calls thee, and all creatures sigh to bee renew'd. (706–7)

Later, in the *Apology,* he defends this prayer against the charge that it is "big-mouth'd" and "theatricall," terming it rather prophetic poetry: it is not "a prayer so much as a hymne in prose frequent both in the Prophets, and in humane authors" (*CPW* I, 930).

Throughout the summer and autumn of 1641 the pamphlet warfare escalated, with some tracts denouncing the bishops and demanding reforms and others decrying the threat of civil and religious anarchy and the proliferation of sects. In August the Commons impeached and sent to the Tower 13 bishops who had most vigorously suppported Laud's canons, including Joseph Hall. On September 1 they removed altar rails, relics, crucifixes, images, and sabbath sports. Plague and smallpox, as well as the king's decision to visit Scotland, forced parliament to recess in early September, but when it reconvened on October 23 the Commons again passed an Exclusion Bill to remove bishops from the House of Lords, prompted in part by the king's appointment of four new bishops at a time when the status of bishops was under debate. At about the same time came horrific news of an uprising in Ireland, with perhaps 30,000 English and Scottish Protestants massacred and mutilated by the enraged Catholic populace they had degraded and dispossessed. But parliament refused to support an invasion of Ireland unless it could wrest away the king's traditional control of the army, fearing that after putting down the Irish revolt he would turn the army on the obstreperous English parliament and people.

Through November and December debates in parliament and petitions to it revolved around the *Grand Remonstrance,* 206 articles summarizing the grievances of the past 16 years, detailing the parliament's notable accomplishments, calling for a general synod to settle church government, and urging removal of obstacles to further reform, notably the bishops in the House of Lords and the king's "papist" privy counsellors. Though addressed to the king, publication of that document was intended to whip up popular agitation for the reforms, to the dismay of some supporters in parliament.[65] Sir Edward Dering demanded, "Wherefore is this Descension from a Parliament to a People? . . . And why are we told that the People are expectant for a Declaration? . . . I neither look for cure of our complaints from the common People, nor do desire to be cured by them."[66] Demonstrations and threats by mobs of London apprentices throughout the Christmas season prompted twelve bishops to sign a protest on December 27 declaring that they could not attend the House of Lords without protection, and that anything done in their absence must be considered void. This was construed as a treasonous effort to subvert parliament and the petitioning bishops were sent to the Tower, an act that virtually eliminated bishops from the House of Lords in fact if not by law. On January 4, 1642, the king committed a major gaffe when he sent armed troops to the Commons' chamber to arrest for treason five redoutable parliamentary leaders: Denzil Hollis, Sir Arthur Haselrig, John Pym, John Hampden, and William Strode. They escaped into the City and many thousands rose in arms to protect them. Unwilling to deal directly with parliament after this fiasco, the king left Whitehall on January 10 with the queen and Prince of Wales, moving first to Hampton Court and then to Windsor. On January 11 parliament reassembled, carrying the five members back to the chamber in triumph.

Milton evidently wrote his fourth tract, *The Reason of Church-Government Urg'd against Prelaty*, during the anxious weeks of November and December, 1641, completed it by January 1, and saw it published in January or February, 1642.[67] This was the first treatise to which Milton affixed his full name, "By Mr. John Milton." While most of the treatise deals broadly with the issue of church government, in three chapters Milton answers a recent collection of nine tracts and extracts, *Certain Briefe Treatises Written by Diverse Learned Men, Concerning the Ancient and Moderne Government of the Church*,[68] specifically addressing those of Ussher and Lancelot Andrewes. For the most part, the several authors present the episcopal system as an appropriate development from Old Testament, apostolic, and early church practice but not as *jure divino*, and therefore open to some reform and compromise. Engaging these episcopal moderates allowed Milton to argue that exclusion and reform – which seem to be on the horizon – are not enough, and to align himself again with the vociferous populist petitions for uprooting the bishops root and branch. But in contrast to his last two explicitly confrontational treatises, in this one Milton does not even name the collection he is answering. Most of the treatise is devoted to exposing the bishops as "malignant, hostile, [and] destructive" (861) to religion, civil government, king, parliament, people, law, liberty, wealth, and learning, and to describing an alternative New Testament church government – nominally Presbyterianism but in fact close to Independency. In this signed tract Milton also introduces himself formally to his audience in a lengthy "Preface" to Book II that functions both as *apologia* and as ethical proof of his argument: it is a remarkable personal statement about his education and arduous study, his life choices, his poetics, and his sense of vocation as prophet and bard. This tract is discussed on pages 145–53.

During the first weeks of 1642 a torrent of pamphlets for and against bishops poured from the presses. Reform leaders also promoted street demonstrations and petitions to the Commons from Londoners of all sorts: poor people, poor laboring men, porters, tradesmen's wives, widows, gentlewomen.[69] On February 5 the Lords finally passed the Bishops' Exclusion Bill and to the surprise of many the king signed it, probably expecting that a military victory over parliament would soon enable him to reverse it. On February 23 Queen Henrietta Maria and Princess Mary left for Holland with the crown jewels, and Charles moved north, arriving at York around March 19. On February 23 also, the Smectymnuan Stephen Marshall preached a fast-day sermon to the Commons, *Meroz Cursed*, on a text that soon became a clarion call to arouse the Puritan faithful to support God's cause against his enemies.[70] On March 5 Parliament passed without the king's assent a Militia

Ordinance giving parliament control of the armed forces, but Charles continued with plans to lead an army to Ireland, claiming sole control of the army as his prerogative.

Sometime after the first of the year, probably in March, an anonymous 40-page answer to Milton's *Animadversions* appeared, *A Modest Confutation of a Slanderous and Scurrilous Libell, Entituled, Animadversions upon the Remonstrants Defense Against Smectymnuus*.[71] Hall (then in prison) may have collaborated with one of his sons in writing it, as Milton claims to have heard (*CPW* I, 897). The Confuter identifies himself as a "young scholar" seeking to answer in kind the bitter and scornful attacks on Hall's life and books by an adversary he describes as a "Scurrilous Mime," and a "grim, lowring, bitter fool."[72] Alluding to a particularly scurrilous attack on the bishops (*CPW* I, 677), the Confuter offers to infer the unknown writer's immoral character and lifestyle from

> some scattered passages in his own writings. . . . It is like he spent his youth, in loytering, bezelling, and harlotting [after which] grown to an Impostume in the brest of the University, he was at length vomitted out thence into a Suburbe sinke about London. . . . He that would finde him after dinner, must search the *Play-Houses*, or the *Bordelli*, for there I have traced him. . . . [Now he] blasphemes God and the King as ordinarily as erewhile he drank Sack and swore.[73]

Milton's 55-page answer, entitled *An Apology against a Pamphlet Call'd A Modest Confutation of the Animadversions upon the Remonstrant against Smectymnuus*, probably appeared shortly after the first week in April.[74] Though this treatise is anonymous, Milton seems to expect readers of *Reason of Church-Government* to recognize him as he restates his qualifications for writing about ecclesiastical issues: "gifts of Gods imparting" and "the wearisome labours and studious watchings, wherein I have spent and tir'd out almost a whole youth" (*CPW* I, 869). And indeed, any discerning reader of the two tracts would know that there could hardly be two such figures on the contemporary scene.[75] Milton engages the *Confutation* section by section, with jibes, sarcasm, fierce banter, vituperation, and *ad hominem* arguments, heaping scorn on Hall as prose stylist, satirist, and theologian, and on the supposed young speaker – "thou lozel Bachelour of Art" (*CPW* I, 920). Straining to explain his apparent disregard of the biblical injunction to forgive enemies, he argues his need to deflect scandal from the cause of truth and from his Smectymnuan associates, since he now writes "not as mine own person, but as a member incorporate into that truth whereof I was perswaded, and whereof I had declar'd openly to be a partaker" (871). But the fiercely individualistic Milton cannot long contain himself within the corporate identity, nor can he maintain the distance he asserts between himself and his satiric persona: "The author is ever distinguisht from the person he introduces" (880). To the contrary, in this tract he constructs another self-portrait and further develops and defends his poetics of satire, in part to justify and explain the authorial self he presented in *Reason of Church-Government*. The *Apology* continues fierce attacks on the bishops and the liturgy, setting against them the spirit of the gospel and its meritocratic implications for the church. If men were children under the law, "the Gospell is our manhood" (950), so the laity – "divers plaine and solid men, that have learnt by the experience of a good conscience, what it is to be well taught" (935) – can be trusted to judge ministers.

Stylistically, the *Apology* ranges from fierce invective to lofty praise. The satire is trenchant, and often based (again) on graphic body imagery: "This tormenter of semicolons is as good at dismembring and slitting sentences, as his grave Fathers the Prelates have bin at stigmatizing & slitting noses" (894). "A more seditious and Butcherly Speech no Cell of *Loyola* could have belch't" (896). "Ye have started back from the purity of Scripture which is the only rule of reformation, to the old vomit of your Traditions" (912). Quoting Horace and Gower, Milton makes stylistic vigor and satiric vehemence a touchstone for moral force and devotion to truth. His opponents' dullness and faults of style are themselves evidence of their vacuity and lukewarmness in God's service. Hall's seductive rhetoric and fashionable curt Senecan aphorisms and sententiae are disparaged as a "coy flurting stile" and "frumps and curtall jibes" (872–3).[76] His *Mundus alter & idem* is "the idlest and the paltriest Mime that ever mounted upon banke" (880). The Confuter "comes so lazily on in a Similie . . . and demeanes himselfe in the dull expression so like a dough kneaded thing, that he hath not spirit anough left him . . . as to avoide nonsense" (910). A comparable failure of energy and spirit convicts the required Anglican liturgy, which is "in conception leane and dry, of affections empty and unmoving, of passion, or any heigth whereto the soule might soar upon the wings of zeale, destitute and barren."[77] Similarly, the Anglican pulpits display "the lofty nakednesse of your *Latinizing* Barbarian, and the finicall goosery of your neat Sermon-actor" (935). By contrast, Milton claims to be a rhetorician in Augustine's terms, according to which rhetoric and style flow naturally from devotion to truth:

> Although I cannot say that I am utterly untrain'd in those rules which best Rhetoricians have giv'n, or unacquainted with those examples which the prime authors of eloquence have written in any learned tongu, yet true eloquence I find to be none, but the serious and hearty love of truth: And that whose mind so ever is fully possest with a fervent desire to know good things, and with the dearest charity to infuse the knowledge of them into others, when such a man would speak, his words . . . like so many nimble and airy servitors trip about him at command, and in well order'd files, as he would wish, fall aptly into their own places.[78]

Building upon this conception of rhetoric, Milton gives the most complete account yet of his poetics of satire, now equated with Godly zeal. He contrasts such satire with Hall's *Tooth-lesse Satyrs*, a title he ridicules as an oxymoronic absurdity. Deriving satire from tragedy, Milton insists that it must "strike high, and adventure dangerously at the most eminent vices among the greatest persons," citing Langland's *Piers Plowman* as example (916). He justifies "throwing out indignation, or scorn upon an object that deserves it" (899) by the precepts of Aristotle, Cicero, and Quintilian, by Luther's use of tart rhetoric in the church's cause, and by biblical and classical examples (Elijah, Solomon, Horace, Cicero, Seneca). His chief authority is Christ, who used all styles of teaching: "sometimes by a milde and familiar converse, sometimes with plaine and impartiall home-speaking . . . otherwhiles with bitter and irefull rebukes if not teaching yet leaving excuselesse those his wilfull impugners" (899–900). Some of Christ's followers "were indu'd with a staid moderation, and soundnesse of argument to teach and convince the rationall and soberminded" (900), but others employed a "sanctifi'd bitternesse" (901) against the corrupt and carnal. Even the Spirit of God in scripture uses and thereby licenses obscenities and immodest terms for such purposes. Such zeal convicts the prelates' calls for moderation as reprehensible lukewarmness (868–9) and welcomes fierce polemic battle. At the highest pitch Milton links satire of that sort to the role of poet–prophet:

> ([If] I may have leave to soare a while as the Poets use) then Zeale whose substance is ethereal, arming in compleat diamond ascends his fiery Chariot drawn with two blazing Meteors figur'd like beasts, but of a higher breed then any the Zodiack yeilds, resembling two of those four which *Ezechiel* and *S. John* saw, the one visag'd like a Lion to express power, high autority and indignation, the other of count'nance like a man to cast derision and scorne upon perverse and fraudulent seducers; with these the invincible warriour Zeale shaking loosely the slack reins drives over the heads of Scarlet Prelats, and such as are insolent to maintaine traditions, bruising their stiffe necks under his flaming wheels. Thus did the true Prophets of old combat with the false. (900)

Alternatively, he lavishes praises on parliament – termed "the high and *sovran* Court of Parliament" – to encourage it to enact the Root and Branch legislation.[79] He describes members of parliament as the founders and leaders of an aristocratic republic: some are nobles, most are of a "knowne and well-reputed ancestry, which is a great advantage toward virtue," and they have happily overcome the empty and superstitious education they received at the universities (923). They are "publick benefactors" who act from "mature wisdome, deliberat vertue, and deere affection to the publick good" (922); they were chosen by "God and man" to be "both the great reformers of the Church, and the restorers of the Common-wealth"; and so they merit recognition as "Fathers of their countrey."[80] He praises them especially for their openness to all petitioners: "the meanest artizans and labourers, at other times also women, and often the younger sort of servants" (926) – all those who recently agitated for Root and Branch. Though no democrat, Milton identifies with the agitators fanning the flames of reform, noting proudly that he himself joined "in petition with good men" (878). This was probably the Root and Branch

Petition of December 11, 1640, which was offered, Milton claimed in *Animadversions,* by "great numbers of sober, and considerable men" as well as honest tradesmen (676). At length, with a fine rhetorical flourish, he intimates that parliament dare not fail to achieve church reform, since God himself has become their agent:

> At other times we count it ample honour when God voutsafes to make man the instrument and subordinate worker of his gracious will . . . [but] to them he hath bin pleas'd to make himselfe the agent, and immediat performer of their desires; dissolving their difficulties when they are thought inexplicable . . . what is it when God himselfe condescends, and workes with his own hands to fulfill the requests of men . . . I see who is their assistant, who their confederat, who hath ingag'd his omnipotent arme, to support and crown with successe . . . the full and perfet reformation of his Church. (927–8)

With this notion of God seconding human agency, Milton has given over, whether he fully realizes it or not, Calvinist predestinarian orthodoxy.

Milton also provides an autobiographical narrative to counter the Confuter's false and formulaic "character" of him as licentious, riotous, and penurious.[81] He did not spend an "inordinat and riotous youth" at the university. He was not "vomited out thence" but left after taking two degrees. The fellows of Christ's showed him "favour and respect . . . above any of my equals," desiring him to stay on after graduation and testifying in several letters to "their singular good affection" and friendship.[82] Nor does he now live wantonly in a "Suburb sinke": he rises early with the birds, he reads "good Authors" or has them read to him "till the attention bee weary, or memory have his full fraught," and he exercises for health, mental alertness, and in preparation for military service, when "the cause of religion, and our Countries liberty . . . shall require firme hearts in sound bodies to stand and cover their stations, rather then to see the ruine of our Protestation, and the inforcement of a slavish life."[83] This suggests that Milton now expects an armed struggle, and that he may have been drilling with the trained bands;[84] in any event, he imagines himself as a martial as well as a polemic Christian warrior. He does not deny that he goes to playhouses in London, but counters that he saw much worse at approved university theatricals, where clergymen and ministers-to-be made of themselves a "foule and ignominious" spectacle.[85]

He flatly denies that he spends his evenings in bordellos, offering as evidence an account of the moral formation produced by his studies and private reading. He learned lessons of idealistic chastity and love, honor to women, and due self-regard from the classical Orators, Historians, and Elegiack Poets, from Dante's and Petrarch's sonnets, from "lofty Fables and Romances," from Plato and Xenophon, from the Pauline epistles, and from the descriptions in the Book of Revelation of the glory awaiting those "not defil'd with women" – which means fornication, he insists, since "marriage must not be call'd a defilement."[86] As other safeguards against licentiousness he points proudly to his temperament and explains (as he did in Prolusion VI to his college mates) his admittedly uncommon ideal of masculine chastity:

> A certaine nicenesse of nature, an honest haughtinesse, and self-esteem either of what I was, or what I might be, (which let envie call pride) and lastly that modesty, [which] . . . kept me still above those low descents of minde, beneath which he must deject and plunge himself, that can agree to salable and unlawfull prostitutions. . . . Thus also I argu'd to my selfe; that if unchastity in a woman whom Saint *Paul* termes the glory of man, be such a scandall and dishonour, then certainly in a man who is both the image and glory of God, it must, though commonly not so thought, be much more deflouring and dishonourable.[87]

The bourgeois Milton is quick to insist that his comfortable economic situation allows him the freedom and privileges of a gentleman:

> This I cannot omit without ingratitude to that providence above, who hath ever bred me up in plenty, although my life hath not bin unexpensive in learning, and voyaging about, so long as it shall please him to lend mee what he hath hitherto thought good, which is anough to serve me in all honest and liberall occasions, and something over besides. (929)

So he need not seek a lectureship (a post often held by Puritan ministers), which the Confuter assumes he wants, and can scornfully reject the ordination that post would demand: "I am . . . as farre distant from a Lecturer, as the meerest Laick, for any consecrating hand of a Prelat that shall ever touch me" (931). Nor need he make his fortune by marrying a rich widow as the Confuter alledges, but instead aligns himself with those "who both in prudence and elegance of spirit would choose a virgin of mean fortunes honestly bred, before the wealthiest widow" (929). Now settled in his own house, Milton was perhaps giving some thought to marriage, and thinking where to find a likely virgin.

Milton reaffirms in this self-portrait his primary identification as poet, and affirms a direct connection between that poetic role and his present service to God, church, and country. The high poet must write out of wide experience, and can only make his poem out of the values and virtues he has cultivated within himself:

> He who would not be frustrate of his hope to write well hereafter in laudable things, ought him selfe to bee a true Poem, that is, a composition, and patterne of the best and honourablest things; not presuming to sing high praises of heroick men, or famous Cities, unlesse he have in himselfe the experience and the practice of all that which is praise-worthy. (890)

Over the next months England drifted toward war, despite a flurry of messages between the king at York and the parliament at Westminster seeking to resolve differences. The army remained the chief sticking point. Many peers and several members of Commons gravitated to the king. Most disconcerting was the flight on May 21 of Lord Keeper Littleton with the Great Seal, which removed that symbol of legitimacy from Westminster and vacated the woolsack (the chair) of the House of Lords. The king was purchasing arms from the sale of the crown jewels and sending out requisitions for money; parliament was also raising contributions from sympathetic noblemen and from the City; both sides were casting about for troops and wooing the Scots. On July 12 parliament voted to raise an army, naming the Earl of Essex commander-in-chief. On August 22, 1642 the king, along with Charles, Prince of Wales, stood before a force of some 2,000 horse and foot gathered in Nottingham, unfurled his royal standard, and summoned all leigemen to his aid. That act officially launched the Civil War.

"Transported with the Zeale of Truth to a Well Heated Fervencie"

Three of Milton's antiprelatical tracts answer specific treatises and satirize their authors, but *Of Reformation* and *The Reason of Church-Government* treat the issues of ecclesiastical reform in broader terms and with more conscious art. They share certain stylistic qualities: long, elaborate sentences with multiple clauses, sometimes ordered in balanced Ciceronean periods and more often in a loosely associative, interwoven structure projecting energy, vitality, and zealous fervor.[88] But they are couched in two distinct polemic modes and are quite different in stance and tone. *Of Reformation* employs a brilliantly inventive, luxuriant, eloquent, vividly imagistic prose, rich in lexical variety, elaborate metaphor, epithets, descriptive terms, allegory, and graphic imagery. By contrast, *The Reason of Church-Government* claims to be, and for the most part is, a "well-temper'd discourse" (*CPW* I, 746) of reasoned argument, though enlivened with biblical allusion, metaphor, allegory, and some invective. The dense poetic texture and complex syntax of these treatises have seemed to some critics to limit their effectiveness,[89] but that language, here and elsewhere, makes its own extra-rational appeal to the senses and the emotions. When he turned to polemic, Milton brought with him the linguistic sensibilities and the self-image of a poet.

Of Reformation, conceived as a Letter to a Friend, develops its argument in two loosely organized books. A long exordium introduces the pervasive body imagery as well as a historical narrative tracing the corruption of the church under Constantine and the popes and the glorious Reformation begun under Wyclif, but now partly frustrated by the bishops' continued "popish" practices. Milton portrays England as an elect but backsliding nation, now poised to respond to an apocalyptic moment. The proposition offers to "declare those Causes that hinder the forwarding of *true Discipline*" (*CPW* I, 528), and then personalizes those causes as Antiquarians, Libertines, and Politicians. Book I develops an argument against the Antiquarians, those who justify episcopacy from the testimony of the church Fathers. It asserts, first, that scripture identifies bishops with presbyters "elected by the popular voyce, undiocest, unrevenu'd, unlorded" (549); second, that the patristic texts are often contradictory and even heretical; and finally, that the Fathers themselves made scripture (not their own writings) the only guide for Christians. Invoking an ancient axiom, Milton contrasts his appeal to scripture with the bishops' appeal to custom: "Custome without Truth is but agedness of Error."[90] Casting himself as a humanist critic of rhetoric, he sets the "sober, plain, and unaffected stile of the Scriptures" against the stylistic fustian of the Fathers: the "knotty Africanisms, the pamper'd metafors; the intricat, and involv'd sentences," the "crosse-jingling periods" (568), taking that stylistic depravity to be a sign of vacuity and deceit. The Libertines he dismisses in a single paragraph, claiming that they fear Presbyterianism because it would discipline their lust, licentiousness, and drunkenness.

Book II deals with the Politicians, those who argue that bishops are necessary to the English monarchy – "No bishop, no king." A new, long exordium contrasts debased modern politics which promotes the subjection and rape of the people, with the true art of politics – "to train up a Nation in true wisdom and vertue" (571). To the argument that episcopacy is best suited to the English monarchy, Milton counters with his major proposition in Book II, that it has rather tended to the destruction of monarchy. From Constantine's time onward bishops have challenged kings and usurped secular power. Laudian policy forced thousands of English people into exile abroad, depopulating and weakening the nation. The "*Spanioliz'd Bishops*" (587) fostered alliances with hated Spain, turned Charles against the Dutch and other natural Protestant allies, and promoted a fraternal war with the Scots. Also, by their "idolatrous erection of Temples beautified exquisitely to outvie the Papists" the prelates have wasted the public treasury and deprived schools, ministers, and the poor of proper support (590). Moreover, by assaulting the people's liberties and property, they provoke popular commotions that undermine the king. Denying the structural analogy royalists drew between bishop and king in their respective spheres, Milton argues that the reformed church government is in fact closest to the English "mixed" monarchy, and he formulates that governmental ideal in proto-republican terms:

> There is no Civill *Goverment* that hath beene known . . . more divinely and harmoniously tun'd, more equally ballanc'd as it were by the hand and scale of Justice, then is the Common-wealth of *England*: where under a free, and untutor'd *Monarch*, the noblest, worthiest, and most prudent men, with full approbation, and suffrage of the People have in their power the supreame, and finall determination of highest Affaires. Now if Conformity of Church *Discipline* to the Civill be so desir'd, there can be nothing more parallel, more uniform, then when under the Soveraigne prince *Christs* Vicegerent . . . the *godliest*, the *wisest*, the *learnedest* Ministers in their severall charges

> have the instructing and disciplining of *Gods people* by whose full and free Election they are consecrated to that holy and equall *Aristocracy*. And why should not the Piety, and Conscience of *Englishmen* as members of the Church be trusted in the election of Pastors . . . as well as their worldly wisedomes are priviledg'd as *members* of the *State* in suffraging their Knights, and Burgesses.[91]

According to this Miltonic ideal, a "free, and untutor'd *Monarch*" – presumably one not under the thumb of Strafford or Laud or a privy council – is head of both church and state; the people freely elect both parliamentary representatives and ministers; and the "supreme" civil and spiritual power is explicitly located in the "Aristocratic" element – the elected parliament of "noblest, worthiest, and most prudent men," and the proposed elected ministry.

But Milton's most telling arguments are conveyed in poetic and rhetorical terms, through pervasive imagery of the body and of monstrous generation. He unleashes a torrent of repulsive images calculated to elicit readers' revulsion, even as they reveal his own, passionate disgust for prelates who, he declares, have for centuries served their own bellies and wielded power over the people's consciences and bodies (579), making the people's relation to God one of "thral-like feare" and "Servile crouching" (522). Ministers raised to a bishopric soon "exhale and reake out" most of their zeale and gifts, producing a "queazy temper of luke-warmnesse that gives a Vomit to God himselfe" (536–7). The institution of episcopacy is "an universall rottennes, and gangrene" in the church; and the Laudian liturgy, instead of being "purg'd, and Physick't," was given into the control of prelates "belching the soure Crudities of yesterdayes *Poperie*" (540). Far from descending legitimately from the church Fathers, prelacy and the Laudian liturgy are monsters and breeders of monsters:

> The soure levin of humane Traditions mixt in one putrifi'd Masse with the poisonous dregs of hypocrisie in the hearts of *Prelates* that lye basking in the Sunny warmth of Wealth, and Promotion, is the Serpents Egge that will hatch an *Antichrist* wheresoever, and ingender the same Monster as big, or little as the Lump is which breeds him.[92]

Also, Milton develops a striking body–state analogy directly opposed to that conveyed by the frontispiece in Hobbes's Le*viathan* (1651). The commonwealth, Milton declares, ought to be "as one huge Christian personage, one mighty growth, and stature of an honest man, as big, and compact in vertue as in body," but modern politicans seek only "how to keep up the floting carcas of a crazie, and diseased Monarchy" (572). Elaborating this analogy, Milton constructs a fable that revises the familiar story of the body politic in Livy, and recasts the usual allegorical equivalences in quasi-republican terms.[93] In Milton's version, "the Body summon'd all the Members to meet in the Guild for the common good:" that is, the state as a whole, not the king as head, summons its representatives to parliament. In most versions of this fable the people and their representatives are divided into societal estates (soldiers, clergy, artisans, etc.) or political estates: lords (temporal and spiritual) and commons (knights, gentry, and burgesses), but in Milton's version the MPs are taken collectively. When they assemble they are alarmed to find next to the Head (the king) "a huge and monstrous Wen little lesse then the Head it selfe, growing to it by a narrower excrescency" (583). The Wen claims to merit its place because it is an ornament and strength to Head and Body, but a wise philosopher who knew all the Body's "Charters, Lawes, and Tenures" denounces this "swolne Tumor":

> Wilt thou (quoth he) that art but a bottle of vitious and harden'd excrements, contend with the lawfull and free-borne [parliament] members, whose certaine number is set by ancient, and unrepealable Statute? head thou art none, though thou receive this huge substance from it, what office bearst thou? What good canst thou shew by thee done to the Common-weale? . . . thou containst no good thing in thee, but a heape of hard, and loathsome uncleannes, and art to the head a foul disfigurment and burden, when I have cut thee off, and open'd thee, as by the help of these implements I will doe, all men shall see. (584)

The root and branch allegory is obvious: the lords spiritual are no estate of the realm but a cancer: "We must . . . cut away from the publick body the noysom, and diseased tumor of Prelacie" (598).

Body imagery also supplies the terms for reform. The church order mandated in scripture is evident if we but "purge with sovrain eyesalve that intellectual ray" implanted in us by God (566). Preaching exposes sin, but Presbyterian discipline will lay "the *salve* to the very *Orifice* of the wound" (526). Milton says little about the specifics of Presbyterianism but instead describes an ideal church government whose ministers are elected by the laity, who are associated together in "brotherly equality" (549), who are honored as fathers and physicians of the soul, and who are therefore willingly given a "free and plentifull provision of outward necessaries" without, it is implied, enforced tithes (600). Church discipline should involve only "sage and Christianly *Admonition*, brotherly *Love*, flaming *Charity*, and *Zeale* . . . paternall *Sorrow*, or Paternall *Joy*, milde *Severity*, melting *Compassion*," and it should relinquish all power over the body and the purse such as the prelates wielded, "the truccage of perishing Coine, and Butcherly execution of Tormentors, Rooks, and Rakeshames" (591). Milton may not have realized how firmly the Presbyterians were committed to clerical authority, tithes, and the suppression of dissent, but he probably hoped to challenge them to adhere more closely to the spirit of the gospel.

In *Of Reformation* Milton presents himself as conjoining the roles of polemicist, prophet, and poet. He not only argues by metaphor but also relates reformation to the highest poetic inspiration, challenging his countrymen to merit the national epic he might someday sing: "Be the *Praise* and *Heroick Song* of all POSTERITY;

. . . joyn your invisible might to doe worthy, and Godlike deeds" (597). For the present, he imagines himself as an elegiac poet voicing the sorrows of contemporary England, who, like the weeping Jerusalem in Lamentations, mourns as a mother for her exiled Puritan children:

> O Sir, if we could but see the shape of our deare Mother *England*, as Poets are wont to give a personal form to what they please, how would she appeare, think ye, but in a mourning weed, with ashes on her head, and teares abundantly flowing from her eyes, to behold so many of her children expos'd at once, and thrust from things of dearest necessity, because their conscience could not assent to things which the Bishops thought *indifferent*. (585)

The tract ends with a Millenarian prophecy that constructs the king, in his role as head of church and state, as simply a placeholder for Christ, the "Eternall and shortly-expected" Messiah King, who will put an end to all earthly tyrannies and proclaim his own "universal and milde *Monarchy* through Heaven and Earth" (616). In that Millennium he imagines a fierce vengeance for the vaunting prelates and their supporters: they will be debased below the other damned, who will exercise a "*Raving* and *Bestiall Tyranny* over them as their *Slaves* and *Negro's*" (616–17). He cries out in prophetic lamentation and prayer as he considers the immense obstacles to the church's reformation: "*Tri-personall* GODHEAD! looke upon this thy poore and almost spent, and expiring *Church*, leave her not thus a prey to these importunate *Wolves*."[94] But then he imagines himself as bard celebrating and helping to perfect the reformed society that will herald Christ's millennial kingdom, where there will be no earthly kings and yet all who have labored for the "*Common good* of *Religion* and their *Countrey*" will exercise kingly rule, and a Miltonic bard will find his highest poetic subject:

> Then amidst the *Hymns*, and *Halleluiahs* of *Saints* some one may perhaps bee heard offering at high *strains* to new and lofty *Measures* to sing and celebrate thy *divine Mercies, and marvelous Judgements* in this Land throughout all AGES; whereby this great and Warlike Nation instructed and inur'd to the fervant and continuall practice of *Truth* and *Righteousnesse*, and casting farre from her the *rags* of her old *vices* may presse on hard to that *high* and *happy* emulation to be found the *soberest, wisest*, and most *Christian People* at that day when thou the Eternall and shortly-expected King shalt open the Clouds to judge the severall Kingdomes of the World, and distributing *Nationall Honours* and *Rewards* to Religious and just *Common-wealths*, shalt put an end to all Earthly *Tyrannies*, proclaiming thy universal and milde *Monarchy* through Heaven and Earth. (616)

In *The Reason of Church-Government* Milton again presents himself as polemicist–prophet–poet, but his emphasis here is on inspired testimony and teaching rather than zealous denunciation or anticipated bardic celebration. He devotes only three chapters to engaging the tracts of Bishops Hall and Ussher,[95] and otherwise makes a broad argument against episcopacy and (ostensibly) for the Presbyterian model as the church government mandated by scripture. But what he describes is a more nearly ideal church order based on the spirit of the gospel, the concept of reason, the nature of discipline, and the equality of clergy and laity. The "Reason" of the title has seemed to some a misnomer, since Milton does not build a closely reasoned argument from the usual scripture proof-texts, and also seems to set the authority of scripture against human reason:

> Let them chaunt while they will of prerogatives, we shall tell them of Scripture; of custom, we of Scripture; of Acts and Statutes, stil of Scripture, til the quick and pearcing word enter to the dividing of their soules, & the mighty weaknes of the Gospel throw down the weak mightines of mans reasoning.[96]

But in Milton's terms the title is apt, since his project is to make manifest God's reasons for the church government laid down in scripture, reasons not there stated "because to him that heeds attentively the drift and scope of Christian profession, they easily imply themselves" (*CPW* I, 750). This is an appeal to the entire scope or spirit of the gospel to clarify the divine rationale left implicit in particular texts.

Book I focuses on what Milton sees as the essence of church government, the right ordering or "discipline" of individual members. Pointing to the universal need for discipline – "there is not that thing in the world of more grave and urgent importance throughout the whole life of man, then is discipline" (751) – he concludes that God as father of his family the church must have provided a discipline for "training it up under his owne all-wise and dear Oeconomy."[97] He cites several texts from Titus and Timothy and the precedent of the Old Testament Temple worship to argue this conclusion, but he flatly denies that the Old Testament can offer any kind of model for New Testament church government. The reason, again, is the spirit of the gospel:

> That the Gospell is the end and fulfilling of the Law, our liberty also from the bondage of the Law I plainly reade. How then the ripe age of the Gospell should be put to schoole againe, and learn to governe her selfe from the infancy of the Law, the stronger to imitate the weaker, the freeman to follow the captive, the learned to be lesson'd by the rude, will be a hard undertaking to evince. (763)

To counter the bishops' claim that episcopacy developed over time as a sanctioned means to counter schism, Milton castigates prelacy as itself the chief promoter of schism. It divides English Protestants from reformed churches abroad, it has forced many into separation and exile, and it has affixed sectarian labels on good Christians, first terming them "Lollards and Hussites" and now "Puritans, and Brownists . . . Familists and Adamites, or worse" (788). But Presbyterians as well as prelates would reject Milton's argument – anticipating *Areopagitica* – that religious controversy itself is a positive good:

> The reforming of a Church . . . is never brought to effect without the fierce encounter of truth and falshood together, if, as it were the splinters and shares of so violent a jousting, there fall from between the shock many fond errors and fanatick opinions, which when truth has the upper hand, and the reformation shall be perfeted, will easily be rid out of the way, or kept so low, as that they shall be only the exercise of our knowledge, not the disturbance, or interruption of our faith. (796)

In Book II the term "reason" is virtually synonymous with spirit or purpose, as Milton offers to demonstrate how prelacy opposes "the reason and end of the Gospel." Prelacy is a "church-tyranny," whereas Christ took the form of a servant and teacher. Its ceremonies are fleshly and polluted, "gaudy glisterings," whereas Christ established a spiritual ministry. Also, the prelates' exercise of civil power – legal jurisdiction, tithes, penalties, and torture – confounds the "economicall and paternall" government prescribed in the gospel:

> How can the Prelates justifie to have turn'd the fatherly orders of Christs household, the blessed meaknesse of his lowly roof, those ever open and inviting dores of his dwelling house . . . into the barre of a proud judiciall court where fees and clamours keep shop . . . [using] begg'd and borrow'd force from worldly autority. (848–9)

The civil magistrate under the gospel has power to punish only external evils – "injustice, rapine, lust, cruelty or the like" – so as to maintain "the outward peace and wel-fare of the Commonwealth" (835–6). The church has only spiritual power over the inner man, which may involve pleadings, counsels, reproofs, and if necessary excommunication, but touches "neither life, nor limme, nor any worldly possession" (847). Milton's own sense of vocation led him to understand the gospel precept that all God's people are "a royal Priesthood" as mandating an ecclesiastical meritocracy whereby all ministerial functions (teaching, expounding scripture, discipline) "ought to be free and open to any Christian man though never so laick, if his capacity, his faith, and prudent demeanour commend him" (844).

The tract concludes with the damage prelacy does to the state, and its redress. Instead of the "perfect freedom" of the gospel (854), prelacy produces "perfect slavery," giving over "your bodies, your wives, your children, your liberties, your Parlaments, all these things . . . to the arbitrary and illegall dispose of . . . a King" (851). The solution, Root and Branch, Milton urges in two long literary passages. The first is a romance allegory of prelacy as the dragon which must be slain by a new St George – the worthies in parliament:

> Our Princes and Knights . . . should make it their Knightly adventure to pursue & vanquish this mighty sailewing'd monster that menaces to swallow up the Land, unlesse

> her bottomlesse gorge may be satisfi'd with the blood of the Kings daughter the Church; and may, as she was wont, fill her dark and infamous den with the bones of the Saints. (857)

The second is a biblical allegory of the king as Samson, the laws as his strength-giving hair, and the prelates as the Delilah that shaved his locks and delivered him to his enemies. It ends with some hope that the king will return to the laws and destroy the prelates, at whatever painful cost to himself:

> I cannot better liken the state and person of a King then to that mighty Nazarite *Samson*; who . . . grows up to a noble strength and perfection with those his illustrious and sunny locks the laws waving and curling about his god like shoulders. And while he keeps them about him undimisht and unshorn, he may with the jaw-bone of an Asse, that is, with the word of his meanest officer suppresse and put to confusion thousands of those that rise against his just power. But laying down his head among the strumpet flatteries of Prelats, while he sleeps and thinks no harme, they wickedly shaving off all those bright and waighty tresses of his laws and . . . deliver him over to indirect and violent councels, which as those Philistims put out the fair, and farre-sighted eyes of his natural discerning, and make him grinde in the prison house of their sinister ends and practices upon him. Till he knowing his prelatical rasor to have bereft him of his wonted might, nourish again his puissant hair, the golden beames of Law and Right; and they sternly shook, thunder with ruin upon the heads of those his evil cousellors, but not without great affliction to himselfe. (858–9)

Then Milton adapts the story of Sodom and Gomorrah to the choice the Lords must make about Root and Branch. Let them spare prelacy if it contains even one good thing but if, "as nothing can be surer," it is found wholly "maglignant, hostile, [and] destructive,"

> Then let your severe and impartial doom imitate the divine vengeance [on Sodom]: rain down your punishing force upon this godlesse and oppressing government: and bring such a dead Sea of subversion upon her, that she may never in this Land rise more to afflict the holy reformed Church, and the elect people of God. (861)

In this, the first work to bear his full name, Milton used the "Preface" to the second book to draw an elaborate and multifaceted self-portrait to introduce himself to the "intelligent and equal [impartial] auditor."[98] He did not place his long autobiographical statement where we might expect it, at the beginning of his tract, choosing to focus attention first on his argument, not himself. Placed as it is, it can serve Milton's personal agenda and also act as a forceful "ethical proof," displaying the author's knowledge, virtue, and authority to speak to the question at issue. Though he was 33 years old in 1642, Milton presents himself as a youth, open to criticism for contesting "with men of high estimation" while his years were green (806); that conventional modesty topos has some validity in that Milton was unknown and Hall and Ussher were older, established figures. But it is more than convention. As he did in *Lycidas,* he again frets about having to write "out of mine own season, when I have [not] . . . yet compleated to my mind the full circle of my private studies" (807). Now he admits that he has a tendency to make such excuses, being "too inquisitive or suspitious of my self and mine own doings" (804).

In drawing his self-portrait Milton emphasizes the burdens laid on him by his several roles. Emphasizing the sound education and opportunities for study and travel that have made him a learned scholar, he bears the heavy charge imposed by the parable of the talents:

> Remembring also that God even to a strictnesse requires the improvement of these his entrusted gifts, [he] cannot but sustain a sorer burden of mind, and more pressing then any supportable toil, or waight, which the body can labour under; how and in what manner he shall dispose and employ those summes of knowledge and illumination, which God hath sent him into this world to trade with. (801)

Now, however, the immediate use for his talents is much clearer than it was in "How soon hath Time" or the accompanying "Letter" to his clerical friend: he must help to overthrow the prelates and thereby advance reform.[99] He renders in graphic dialogue the plagues of conscience he will forever suffer if he fails in this crisis to give God some return for the unusual and unearned privilege of learning granted to him:

> I foresee what stories I should heare within my selfe, all my life after, of discourage and reproach. Timorous and ingratefull, the Church of God is now again at the foot of her insulting enemies: and thou bewailst, what matters it for thee or thy bewailing? when time was, thou couldst not find a syllable of all that thou hadst read, or studied, to utter in her behalfe. Yet ease and leasure was given thee for thy retired thoughts out of the sweat of other men. Thou hadst the diligence, the parts, the language of a man, if a vain subject were to be adorn'd or beautifi'd, but when the cause of God and his Church was to be pleaded, for which purpose that tongue was given thee which thou hast, God listen'd if he could heare thy voice among his zealous servants, but thou wert domb as a beast; from hence forward be that which thine own brutish silence hath made thee. (804–5)

As a prophet called to testify and teach, he bears a special burden. Like Jeremiah lamenting that he was born a man of strife and contention (Jeremiah 15:10), or John of Patmos finding the Book of Revelation bitter in his belly (Revelation 10:9), or Isaiah required against his will to blow the trumpet of God's denunciation (Isaiah 58:1), he struggles against God's call but finds his word "a torment to keep back:"

> And although divine inspiration must certainly have been sweet to those ancient profets, yet the irksomnesse of that truth which they brought was so unpleasant to

> them, that every where they call it a burden. . . . But when God commands to take the trumpet and blow a dolorous or a jarring blast, it lies not in mans will what he shall say, or what he shall conceal.[100]

Yet as a scholar and an accomplished rhetorician he finds polemic distasteful. It does not allow for anything "elaborately compos'd," or for the "full circle" of learning to be completed, or for overlaying the text with "the curious touches of art" (807). Nevertheless, he willingly undertakes this "unlearned drudgery," since "God by his Secretary conscience" enjoins it (822).

Finally, claiming his primary identity as poet he finds prose itself somewhat onorous, "wherin knowing my self inferior to my self, led by the genial power of nature to another task, I have the use . . . but of my left hand" (808). This may not pertain to the passionate, poetic, prophetic prose he sometimes produces, but to the cool discourse of this tract and to the difficulties of prose autobiography, mirrored in his sometimes involuted syntax. Whereas "a Poet soaring in the high region of his fancies with his garland and singing robes about him" can write easily of his expansive Bardic self, "for me sitting here below in the cool element of prose, a mortall thing among many readers of no Empyreall conceit, to venture and divulge unusual things of my selfe, I shall petition to the gentler sort, it may not be envy to me" (808). He then reviews the stages by which he came to recognize his vocation as poet. His father had him exercised in "the tongues, and some sciences." His teachers praised his style "prosing or versing, but chiefly the latter" as "likely to live." The Italian academics offered him "written Encomiums" (810), and several "friends here at home" offered encouragement. But the final confirmation came from within: "An inward prompting . . . now grew daily upon me, that by labour and intent study (which I take to be my portion in this life) joyn'd with the strong propensity of nature, I might perhaps leave something so written to aftertimes, as they should not willingly let it die" (810). He proceeds to reaffirm his great project of writing a national epic that will advance "Gods glory by the honour and instruction of my country." Turning all his industry and art "to the adorning of my native tongue," he intends to become "an interpreter & relater of the best and sagest things among mine own Citizens throughout this Iland," emulating what "the greatest and choycest wits of *Athens, Rome*, or modern *Italy*, and those Hebrews of old" did for their countries. He expects to have one advantage over all of them, the true subject matter available to a Protestant Christian (811–12).

After another contorted and somewhat embarrassed excuse for continuing his self-revelation,[101] Milton describes his poetics – the most complete statement he ever made about the kinds, subjects, nature, and uses of poetry. Of the three major kinds – epic, drama, and lyric – he gives most attention to epic, distinguishing two varieties: "diffuse," modeled on Homer, Virgil, and Tasso, and "brief," modeled on the Book of Job. As to structure, he considers whether to follow Aristotle's prescription for a tightly unified plot beginning *in medias res*, or to follow "nature," i.e. to create an episodic plot like Ariosto's, beginning *ab ovo*. He is still committed to a national subject, but having abandoned unhistorical Arthur, he now wonders "what K[ing] or Knight before the [Norman] conquest might be chosen in whom to lay the pattern of a Christian Heroe" and, following Tasso, he invites suggestions from some potential learned patron. "The instinct of nature" leads him to epic, but he fears that such high achievement might be frustrated by the cold English climate or, he now worries, by "the fate of this age." He also thinks of writing drama (as the lists in the Trinity manuscript reaffirm), and speculates whether that kind might be "more doctrinal and exemplary to a Nation" than epic. The models he points to are classical tragedy, "wherein *Sophocles* and *Euripides* raigne," the Song of Solomon as a "divine pastoral drama," and the Apocalypse of St John as "the majestick image of a high and stately Tragedy."[102] And he is still attracted to the high lyric like his own "Nativity ode," finding models in "those magnifick Odes and Hymns" of Pindar and Callimachus, worthy for art though faulty in matter, and especially in the Psalms and other biblical songs which he ranks far above all other lyric poetry, "not in their divine argument alone, but in the very critical art of composition" (815–16). Such linkage of biblical with classical models – a constant in Milton's poetic practice – indicates his sense of the Bible as a compendium of literary genres and poetic art. Next he turns to the subjects and the effects of the various kinds of poetry. It serves to "allay the perturbations of the mind, and set the affections in right tune" (tragedy); to celebrate God and his works ("Hymns"); to "sing the victorious agonies of Martyrs and Saints" (odes); to treat "the deeds and triumphs of just and pious Nations doing valiantly through faith against the enemies of Christ" (epic); and to "deplore the general relapses of Kingdoms and States from justice and Gods true worship" (jeremiad).[103] The jeremiad is an unusual addition to the list of genres, but one that Milton evidently thought relevant to the times.

He also emphasizes the moral and civic uses of poetry. Invoking the Horatian formula that poetry should teach by delighting, he expounds that formula as Sidney did, to mean dressing Truth elegantly and making the rugged paths of virtue seem easy. He supposes that poetry, so conceived, might supplant "the writings and interludes of libidinous and ignorant Poetasters" that now corrupt the English youth and gentry (818), and help reform English culture. He also proposes a national cultural program to reform "our publick sports, and festival pastimes" – the Sunday games, dancing, maypoles, and other festivities promoted by the king's *Book of Sports* and vehemently denounced by Prynne and other Puritans.[104] Milton would reform, not abolish, public recreation, in keeping with his long-held belief that leisure is a necessary respite from arduous labor. One element in his projected cultural program involves "wise and artfull recitations" of poetry in various public assemblies as a means to entice the citizenry to the "love and practice of justice, temperance and fortitude, instructing and bettering the Nation at all opportunities, that the call of wisdom and vertu may be heard every where" (819). Another element involves academies on the Florentine model to "civilize, adorn, and make discreet our minds." He also calls for martial exercises to "inure and harden our bodies . . . to all warlike skil and performance," a proposal no doubt prompted by the growing likelihood of war, and with it the need for a citizen militia.

Then, Milton formally covenants with his countrymen to become a national epic poet, though he supposes that will be possible only after the yoke of prelaty is removed, "under whose inquisitorius and tyrannical duncery no free and splendid wit can flourish" (820). He believes he has, or will then have, the requisite qualifications:

> These [poetic] abilities, wheresoever they be found, are the inspired guift of God rarely bestow'd, but yet to some (though most abuse) in every Nation; . . . Neither do I think it shame to covnant with any knowing reader, that for some few yeers yet I may go on trust with him toward the payment of what I am now indebted, as being a work not to be rays'd by the heat of youth, or the vapours of wine . . . nor to be obtain'd by the invocation of Dame Memory and her siren daughters, but by devout prayer to that eternall Spirit who can enrich with all utterance and knowledge, and sends out his Seraphim with the hallow'd fire of his Altar to touch and purify the lips of whom he pleases: to this must be added industrious and select reading, steddy observation, insight into all seemly and generous arts and affaires. (816, 820–1)

This statement asserts that high poetry is not the product of youth, or stimulants, or slavish imitation of the classics – Dame Memory and the Muses – but flows from an inborn gift, arduous study, wide experience of life (which Milton's present engagement with political issues will help to supply), and, most important, divine inspiration. Significantly, he insists on a close relation between learning and inspiration: Milton as prophet is not a vessel for extempore enthusiastic testimony like some radical sectaries; and Milton as bard is not a vehicle for the Platonic divine afflatus. In *Of Reformation* and *Animadversions* he took on at times the prophetic voice of zealous denunciation, apocalyptic prayer, and millennial vision, but not so here. Perhaps for that voice he needed anonymity. Here he claims and seeks to exercise the role of prophet–teacher, with a power akin to and perhaps surpassing that of the pulpit, "to imbreed and cherish in a great people the seeds of vertu, and public civility" (816). Returning to immediate polemic issues, he ends this preface by constructing himself in yet another role, a prospective minister forced by Laud and the prelates from the vocation to which "I was destin'd as a child" and so with a rightful claim to speak on church matters. While he had probably decided against the ministry by 1637, he suggests here, partly for rhetorical effect, that the final sticking point was the notorious "et cetera" oath of 1640[105] – still a burning issue:

> Comming to some maturity of yeers and perceaving what tyranny had invaded the Church, that he who would take Orders must subscribe slave, and take an oath withall, which unlesse he took with a conscience that would retch, he must either strait purjure, or split his faith, I though it better to preferre a blameless silence before the sacred

> office of speaking bought, and begun with servitude and foreswearing. Howsoever thus Church-outed by the Prelats, hence may appear the right I have to meddle in these matters, as before, the necessity and constraint appear'd. (822–3)

The mix and multiplicity of roles that Milton adopts in his five antiprelatical tracts as a matter of rhetorical self-presentation also show him working through issues of identity for himself. He has to confront several issues: How should he account to himself and others for the fact that he is not moving ahead with the poetic career he had committed himself to in his Italian travels? As a polemicist, can he realize a prophetic calling outside the ministry? What weapons should he wield as satirist and controversialist? And how does the polemicist's role sort with that of scholar and poet? He presents himself in these tracts as a learned scholar, a cosmopolitan man of letters, an engaged patriot, a Christian warrior for truth, a satirist, a poet, and a teacher of his countrymen in the mold of the good orator as defined by Cicero and Quintilian,[106] and especially of Christ, who "came downe amongst us to bee a teacher" (*CPW* I, 722). Milton links polemics and poetry closely and constantly, joining the role of satirist to those of prophet and poet and all three with the destiny of England as elect nation. That mix of roles indicates that he did not suppose he was making a momentous choice between left hand and right, polemic and poetry, but rather, that he was devoting his talents to an immediate goal: the removal of the bishops, as the major obstacle to reform in church, state, and English culture.

In these first tracts Milton sets himelf in the line of satiric and prophetic poets who promoted reform. In *Of Reformation* he quotes Dante, Petrarch, and Ariosto on the evils Constantine brought to the church and affirms from his own experience how much Italy glories in those "famousest men for wit and learning" (*CPW* I, 558–60). He also cites approvingly the satires of "our Chaucer" against the "popish" ecclesiastics.[107] In other antiprelatical tracts as well, he places himself in the tradition of English patriot–poets who were teachers and reformers: in *Animadversions* he points to the pastoral satire of "our admired Spencer" against the prelates as having "some presage of these reforming times" (*CPW* I, 722–3); and in the *Apology* he cites "our old Poet *Gower*" against the bishops and the Donation of Constantine (946–7). He develops in these pamphlets a poetics of satire, grounded in "lively zeale," that looks beyond the secular precedent of Juvenal's angry man and Martin Marprelate's scornful insults[108] to the zealous Old Testament prophets (Elijah, Jeremiah, Isaiah) who denounced God's enemies and called for reformation. In all these tracts he claims a poet's license to use a panoply of poetic resources: metaphor, imagery, allegory, fable, apostrophe, and a rich mix of figures and genres. He envisions himself achieving his highest poetic flights in some millennial future, but at this juncture he readily takes on the role of prophet–teacher, whose zealous, poetic testimony to truth can advance reformation and so prepare for that future.

6

"Domestic or Personal Liberty" 1642–1645

In the *Second Defense* Milton claims that his treatises on domestic liberty were part of an overarching, preconceived plan. But that account, written a decade later, elides the stimulus of occasion, though it retains some hint of Milton's intensely personal investment in the issues of divorce and censorship:

> I observed that there are, in all, three varieties of liberty without which civilized life is scarcely possible, namely ecclesiastical liberty, domestic or personal liberty, and civil liberty, and since I had already written about the first, while I saw that the magistrates were vigorously attending to the third, I took as my province the remaining one, the second or domestic kind. This too seemed to be concerned with three problems: the nature of marriage itself, the education of the children, and finally the existence of freedom to express oneself. Hence I set forth my views of marriage, not only its proper contraction, but also, if need be, its dissolution. . . . Concerning this matter then I published several books, at the very time when man and wife were often bitter foes, he dwelling at home with their children, she, the mother of the family, in the camp of the enemy, threatening her husband with death and disaster. Next, in one small volume, I discussed the education of children, a brief treatment to be sure, but sufficient, as I thought, for those who devote to the subject the attention it deserves. For nothing can be more efficacious than education in moulding the minds of men to virtue (whence arises true and internal liberty), in governing the state effectively, and preserving it for the longest possible space of time. Lastly I wrote, on the model of a genuine speech, the *Areopagitica*, concerning freedom of the press, that the judgment of truth and falsehood, what should be printed and what suppressed, ought not to be in the hands of a few men (and these mostly ignorant and of vulgar discernment) charged with the inspection of books, at whose will or whim virtually everyone is prevented from publishing aught that surpasses the understanding of the mob. (*CPW* IV.1, 624–6)

In 1643–5 Milton faced a new polemic challenge: how to make effective use of painful personal experience. The divorce tracts register something of how he perceived his sexual and marital experiences. He wrote nothing so charged with unconscious self-revelation as his passionate descriptions of loneliness, courtship, and incompatible wives, and of the wife he wanted but did not get. He wrote almost no poetry in these years: only three sonnets, so far as we know. Nor did he, as before, construct himself as a poet turned polemicist, promising himself and his readers that he would soon write poetry again. That may be, as Ernest Sirluck argues, because his painful marital mistake led him to question his God-given vocation,[1] or he may simply have found himself distracted from high creativity by emotional angst. He describes the pain of loneliness, disappointment, and despair so feelingly that he must have experienced it acutely.

As he did in the antiprelatical tracts, Milton again sees and presents himself as a scholarly author, but he now defines that role more complexly. He is less willing than before to cite authorities in support of his arguments, lest he undermine his own autonomy, authority, and originality. He had, it seems, a visceral distate for seeming to peddle others' ideas like a pedant or a second-rate thinker. He put his name to most of his tracts of this period, proudly proclaiming his "willingness to avouch what might be question'd";[2] he also approved the law requiring identification of author and printer as a means of securing authors' rights (*CPW* II, 491). As mechanisms of control fell into disuse with the war, he embraced the new openness of the print marketplace and celebrated, in *Areopagitica,* the free circulation of ideas it was promoting. He portrays his authorial role as involving many others: courageous romance hero uncovering lost truth, public benefactor, citizen–adviser to the parliament in the mold of Cicero and other classical orators, and prophet – though not now, as in *Of Reformation* and *Animadversions,* in the apocalyptic or bardic mode. If he does not now write about becoming a poet, he does write – especially in *Areopagitica* – dense, figurative, sometimes sublimely poetic prose.

This period was a radicalizing stage in the evolution of Milton's political and theological ideas. In the antiprelatical tracts he distanced himself from his Presbyterian associates, but in these tracts he wholly severs his bond with them by his views on divorce and toleration and by his attacks on literalistic biblical exegesis.[3] Also, he now conceives the Mosaic Law in very different terms. In the antiprelatical tracts he emphasized its servility: as a law of bondage abrogated for Christians by the gospel covenant of grace it could afford no ground for prelates to look to the Jewish high priests as a precedent for their office. Here, he emphasizes the perfection of the Law and the enduring validity for Christians of all those parts of it that incorporate the moral laws of nature – including the divorce law of Deuteronomy 24:1. At this period Milton still accepts predestination, but his insistence that God binds himself "like a just lawgiver to his own prescriptions" (*CPW* II, 292–3), and his emphasis on responsible human choice as the essence of virtue and as a force for historical change, show him well on his way to an Arminian position on free will.[4] He is also, as Stephen Fallon notes, well on his way to his later monism when he insists, as no other contemporary marriage theorists did, that a union of minds is *essential* to a couple's becoming one flesh.[5] In addition, his poignant appeal to human experience as a basis for understanding God's intentions and explicating his Word is potentially very radical, though he offers it as a ground for reasoned argument and not (like some sectaries) for enthusiastic personal testimony. More directly than any of his contemporaries Milton linked together educational reform, abolition of censorship, and religious toleration as essential elements in creating a republican political ethos and a liberty-loving citizenry.

"Sitting By . . . Studious Lamps"

Around May 29, 1642, just before the formal outbreak of war, Milton paid a visit to Richard Powell, landed squire and justice of the peace in Forest Hill near Oxford, perhaps to arrange payment of overdue interest on an investment loan.[6] En route, he probably visited his father and brother Christopher in Reading. He returned after a month with a bride, Powell's 17-year-old daughter, Mary.[7] Milton's nephew and pupil Edward Phillips, then 12 years old and living with Milton, describes the suddenness of the event, the surprise it elicited, and the immediate aftermath:

> About *Whitsuntide* it was, or a little after, that he took a Journey into the Country; no body about him certainly knowing the Reason, or that it was any more than a Journey of Recreation: after a Month's stay, home he returns a Married-man, that went out a Batchelor; his Wife being *Mary*, the Eldest Daughter of Mr. *Richard Powell*, then a Justice of Peace, of *Forrest-hil*, near *Shotover* in *Oxfordshire*; some few of her nearest Relations accompanying the Bride to her new Habitation; which by reason the Father nor any body else were yet come, was able to receive them; where the Feasting held for some days in Celebration of the Nuptials, and for entertainment of the Bride's Friends. At length they took their leave, and returning to *Forresthill*, left the Sister behind; probably not much to her satisfaction, as appeared by the Sequel; by that time she had for a Month or thereabout led a Philosophical Life (after having been used to a great House, and much Company and Joviality). Her Friends, possibly incited by her own desire, made earnest suit by Letter, to have her Company the remaining part of the Summer, which was granted, on condition of her return at the time appointed, *Michaelmas* [September 29], or thereabout. (*EL* 63–4)

Why did Milton marry in haste and why Mary Powell? As a 34-year-old schoolmaster and householder he was ready to settle down and was probably looking around for a likely young virgin of good family, as he had hinted in the *Apology*.[8] But how account for his failure to recognize signs of incompatibility? What we know of him supplies some explanation: he was responsive to female beauty and had a lofty view of marriage as a rare companionship of mind as well as body, but he had little direct experience of women. Also, his as yet unexamined cultural assumptions about a virgin's modest demeanor and a young bride's malleability and subjection to her husband probably led him to suppose that, once married, Mary would be eager to share his interests and conform herself to his ways. Richard Powell, whose numerous family included five daughters to find marriage portions for, was no doubt eager to encourage a prospective son-in-law who might afford him some needed forbearance in financial matters. Their political differences – the Powells were royalists and Milton a staunch parliamentarian – would not have seemed insurmountable in mid-summer, 1642. Negotiations were in hand between the king and parliament and most Englishmen thought that if war broke out it would be soon over. Powell paid the interest he owed Milton and promised him a dowry of £1,000 with Mary, which was never paid.

Why did Mary return home for a visit so soon after the marriage? Phillips's explanation, 52 years later, suggests that, after the excitement of the wedding festivities wore off, the young bride was lonely in Milton's sober household, missing her large family and accustomed social activities.[9] If there were other problems – temperamental, sexual, political – the young Phillips missed them or refrained from discussing them. But his rather circumstantial narrative is the only first-hand account we have:

> *Michaelmas* being come, and no news of his Wife's return, he sent for her by Letter; and receiving no answer, sent several other Letters, which were also unanswered; so that at last he dispatch'd down a Foot-Messenger with a Letter, desiring her return; but that Messenger came back not only without an answer, at least a satisfactory one, but to the best of my remembrance, reported that he was dismissed with some sort of Contempt. This proceeding, in all probability, was grounded upon no other Cause but this, namely, that the Family being generally addicted to the Cavalier Party, as they called it, and some of them possibly ingaged in the King's Service, who by this time had his Head Quarters at *Oxford*, and was in some Prospect of Success, they began to repent them of having Matched the Eldest Daughter of the Family to a Person so contrary to them in Opinion; and thought it would be a blot in their Escutcheon, when ever that Court should come to Flourish again. (*EL* 64–5)

The Powells would likely have sent Mary home to her husband soon had not political circumstances dictated otherwise, once war had begun and the king's party at first had the better of it. Mary was evidently quite willing to stay, especially after the king's army and court (with its attendant society) took up quarters in Oxford in late October. On January 16, 1643, traffic with Oxford was prohibited and Milton could no longer write or send messengers. Deeply disappointed by his brief experience with an incompatible wife, he had now to deal with the disgrace and sexual frustration of being a deserted husband.

One of parliament's first acts after hostilities began on August 22, 1642 was to abolish public sports and stage plays, as unsuited to the calamitous times, "being Spectacles of Pleasure, too commonly expressing lascivious Mirth and levity."[10] In the early skirmishes the king's forces, led by Prince Rupert and other commanders of some experience, had the advantage over parliament's troops – militia and volunteers – led by Robert Devereaux, Earl of Essex, as commander-in-chief. Parliament's strength was chiefly in the eastern and midland counties, the king's in the north and west, including Wales. Soon after the indecisive Battle of Edgehill (Warwickshire) on October 23, 1642, the king's forces took Reading and Horton, Milton's old residence. Londoners feared an attack on the City with the attendant horrors of sacking, pillage, and devastation, but on November 13, in the suburb of Turnham Green, Essex's army and the London trained bands turned back the king's army with no shots fired. Milton later explained, somewhat defensively, that he did not join the trained bands or army because he thought he could better serve his country with his mind and pen.[11]

The threatened attack on the City prompted Milton's Sonnet VIII, "On his dore when ye Citty expected an assault." It was first conceived as a paper so placed, urging the royalist soldiers to spare the poet's house.[12] Apparently, Milton wrote only three poems in these years, but in taking up the sonnet genre after a ten-year hiatus he marked out new territory for it. Sonnet VIII inaugurates the political sonnet in the English tradition.[13] Fusing personal experience and historical event, it treats a public military crisis in lyric terms. Joining the epigram-inscription with the Petrarchan sonnet, this tonally complex poem addresses a potentially threatening royalist officer, some "Captain or Colonel, or Knight in Arms." The Miltonic speaker is a propertied London poet who offers to strike a bargain: poetic fame for the officer if he spares the poet and his house, the "Muses Bowre." Milton reads this situation through two famous classical stories: Alexander the Great spared Pindar's house in the sack of Thebes; and the Spartan Lysander spared Athens from destruction, moved by verses from Euripides's *Electra*. Milton's allusion presents London as a new Athens, cradle of democratic culture, which royalists are invited to recognize as superior to their Oxford/Sparta.[14] But Milton's hope is tempered by anxiety and self-irony: he is no Pindar or Euripides – at least not yet; and the royalist officer is no Alexander. Unspoken, troubling questions abide: How vulnerable are poetry and the poet in wartime? Can an unknown Milton be a spokesman for poetry's power? Could poetry, in modern times, save the poet, his house, and his city?

Milton wrote two other sonnets in the years 1642–5. Sonnets IX and X are praises of women in terms wholly outside the Petrarchan ethos and conventions that governed Milton's Sonnets II–VI as they did most sonnets to women.[15] They present two very different female ideals, both embodying qualities apparently lacking in Mary Powell. Sonnet IX, "Lady that in the prime of earliest youth," is untitled and its subject unknown: she may be someone known to Milton, or entirely fictional.[16] The sonnet describes her in quasi-allegorical terms as a young virgin who has given herself to religious study and who is seen to embody biblical metaphors and reprise biblical roles. She has shunned the "broad way and the green" (Matthew 7:13–14) to labor with the few "up the Hill of heav'nly Truth," and, in her devotion to spiritual truth, she has chosen "The better part with *Mary*, and with

Ruth."[17] She endures with "pity and ruth," though at some emotional cost, those friends who contemn her choices. The resolution describes her heavenly reward in terms of erotic pleasure: this "Virgin wise and pure," whose lamp is filled with oil to greet the Bridegroom (Matthew 25:1–13), will join him as he "Passes to bliss" with his "feastful friends."

Sonnet X, titled "To ye Lady Margaret Ley," is addressed to a neighbor in Aldersgate Street to whom Milton turned for friendship and companionship during the years of his wife's absence.[18] Margaret's political sympathies are unknown: her own family were royalists but her husband John Hobson fought for parliament as a lieutenant-colonel in the trained bands (the Westminster Regiment), and Milton's poem locates her with the lovers of liberty.[19] Edward Phillips describes Margaret's wit and intellect, and her admiration for Milton, in terms that hint at a mutual attraction reaching beyond social friendship, though almost certainly not, given Milton's strict principles, to an affair:

> Our Author, now as it were a single man again, made it his chief diversion now and then in an Evening to visit the Lady *Margaret Lee*, daughter to the —— [James] *Lee*, Earl of *Marlborough*, Lord High Treasurer of *England*, and President of the Privy Councel to King *James* the First. This Lady, being a Woman of great Wit and Ingenuity, had a particular Honour for him, and took much delight in his Company, as likewise her Husband Captain *Hobson*, a very Accomplish'd Gentleman; and with what Esteem he at the same time had for Her, appears by a Sonnet he made in praise of her. (*EL* 64)

Phillips's account and Milton's sonnet suggest that Milton saw in the witty and virtuous Margaret some version of what he wanted in a wife and did not obtain.

But the sonnet does not focus on her personal qualities. Milton praises Margaret Ley by investing her with the nobility and virtues of her father: "by you, / Madam, me thinks I see him living yet." This praise by praising family is a common rhetorical gesture, but it is complicated here by Milton's emphasis on the insecurity of historical knowledge, recent or ancient, domestic or political. The sonnet describes Sir James Ley, erstwhile Chief Justice, Lord High Treasurer, and Lord President of the Council, as "unstain'd with gold or fee," and as brought to his death by the dissolution of parliament (March 4, 1629) that began Charles I's eleven-year arbitrary rule: "Till the sad breaking of that Parlament / Broke him." But Ley probably succumbed on March 10 to simple physical decrepitude, there is no evidence that he had parliamentarian sympathies, and some had questioned his fiscal integrity and administrative competence.[20] The octave of the sonnet reads Ley's story through a legend about Isocrates, dubious but widely accepted by classical and Renaissance authors: "that Old man eloquent" was thought to have starved himself to death after Phillip of Macedon conquered Athens and Thebes in 338 BC.[21] Milton probably believed both stories, but in the sestet he underscores the fragility of the historical record, emphasizing rather its present uses: Milton, "later born," did not know "the dayes / Wherin your Father flourisht," save through Margaret's praise of his virtues; and she (also "later born") necessarily relied on her father's account. The resolution is found in Margaret's own embodiment of Ley's virtues and attitudes toward liberty – so evident "That all both judge you to relate them true, / And to possess them, Honour'd Margaret." And on that authority Milton's sonnet can read this history in terms useful to the cause of virtue and liberty.

Reading, the home of Milton's father and brother Christopher, again became a war zone in April, 1643 and surrendered to Essex on April 27. Milton's father (then about eighty) came to him in Aldersgate Street. He lived there, Phillips reports, "wholly retired to his Rest and Devotion, without the least trouble imaginable" (*EL* 64). Christopher cast his lot with the royalists at Oxford, at one point serving as a Royal Commisioner of Excise for Wells.[22] About this time Milton took on at least one additional student, Cyriack Skinner.[23] Phillips comments that "the Studies went on with so much the more Vigour as there were more Hands and Heads employ'd" (*EL* 64).

Some of Milton's own studies, beyond the specialized reading required by his divorce tracts and the literature he no doubt read continuously, can be tracked in the Commonplace Book, which was largely complete by 1646.[24] During the years before and just after his Italian journey, he chiefly took notes from classical history, early church history, and English and European history.[25] In the years 1643–6 he continued reading histories of the Roman Empire and of particular nations, and histories of the church, notably Sarpi's history of the Council of Trent from which he made numerous extracts.[26] He also returned to some histories he had used before: de Thou's *Historia sui Temporis*, and Girard's history of France.[27] He read as well selected biblical commentaries and Judaica, especially John Selden's *De Jure Naturali et Gentium* and *Uxor Hebraica*.[28] For civil and ecclesiastical law and politics he read Justinian's *Institutes*, Joannes Leunclavius [Johann Löwenklau], Henry Spelman, and Bodin's *De Republica*, as well as treatises on military strategy and noble titles.[29] Books of or about literature include Francesco Berni's version of the *Orlando Innamorato*; Sidney, *Arcadia*; Boccalini, *De' Ragguagli di Parnasso*; Tasso, *Gerusalemme Liberata*; Thomasini, *Petrarcha Redivivus*; and Tassoni, *Pensieri*.[30] Other extracts are taken from Raleigh's *History of the World* and Purchas's *Pilgrimes*.[31]

Milton added extracts under each major category: Moral, Economic (Domestic), and Political.[32] Several "Economic" topics are pertinent to his immediate concerns. Under Marriage (two headings), Concubinage, and Divorce (two headings), he notes examples of unorthodox views and practices, including divorce.[33] Citing claims by physicians that copulation "without love is cold, unpleasant, unfruitful, harmful, bestial, abominable,"[34] he concludes "Therefore it is intolerable that either one or at least the innocent one should be bound unwillingly by so monstrous a fetter." To the Political Index he adds extracts under several topics – King (three headings), The Tyrant (two headings), The King of England, Subject, Liberty, Of Laws, and Of Civil War – many of which address issues brought to the fore by the outbreak of war: tyranny, the rights of citizens and parliaments, limitations on the monarch's power by conditions or parliaments or elections, and legitimate resistance to monarchs by arms or deposition.[35] From Gildas he determines that British kings were anointed "as kings, but not by God . . . Contrary to what the people now think, namely, that all kings are the anointed of God" (*CPW* I, 474). He also collected extracts on toleration and the censorship of books, citing Sarpi on the Roman *Index* and de Thou on the benefits of reading books by opponents (451–2).

Intense negotiations with the king continued between February and April, 1643,[36] and many complained that the parliamentary generals were fighting less than vigorously, expecting a negotiated settlement. In May and June the king's efforts to bring over an Irish army to provoke uprisings in London and Scotland became known, provoking general outrage. Prompted by threats of plots and conspiracies, parliament on June 14, 1643 enacted a strict Licensing Order to control the proliferation of presses and pamphlets that had been largely unregulated since the abolition of Star Chamber on July 5, 1641.[37] The Stationers Company – wealthy booksellers who were the legal owners of copyright in printed matter and who held monopoly control over printing – were also complaining of the threat to their rights and purses from the deluge of pirated and unlicensed works from illegal presses. Substantially replicating Charles I's repressive Star Chamber Decree of 1637,[38] the new ordinance required licensing and registration of all publications, signatures of author and printer, copyright guarantees, control of imported publications, search and seizure of unlicensed presses and printed matter, and the arrest and imprisonment of offenders. The Stationers Company was charged with enforcing these measures.

On July 1 the long awaited Westminster Assembly convened, with a charge to advise parliament on religious matters. Its overwhelmingly Presbyterian and clerical membership continually pressured parliament to establish a national Presbyterian church and to suppress heresy, sects, and schisms.[39] During its five-year tenure, the Westminster Assembly revised the Thirty-nine Articles along Calvinistic lines, abolished the *Book of Common Prayer* and recommended a new Directory of Worship, ejected many Laudian, Arminian, and "malignant" (royalist) clergy, and supervised the appointment of Puritan ministers in their places. Their most difficult challenge was church government. Commissioners from Scotland insisted on the Scots Presbyterian model, Erastians in parliament sought to secure parliament's powers against clerical domination, and the five Congregationalist divines in the assembly tried to obtain some accommodation for those who, like themselves, differed from the Presbyterians only on some matters of church government.[40] The Independents and the more radical sectaries vigorously opposed any national or synodal organization, recognizing only independent "gathered" congregations of the elect; they agitated for a broad-based toleration of most or all Protestant sects and very occasionally for universal toleration.

As the summer of 1643 wore on parliament's forces lost several battles, and a "peace" party gained strength, but they were bitterly opposed by fiery preachers and mobs of London petitioners. In late September parliament adopted the *Solemn League and Covenant*, which had already been passed by the Scots Assembly: it was subscribed by parliament members, office-holders, ministers, and men of all ranks, including Milton.[41] The signatories pledged to preserve the reformed religion in Scotland, to reform religion in England and Ireland "according to the Word of God, and the example of the best Reformed Churches," to bring the three kingdoms "to the nearest Conjunction and Uniformity in Religion, Confession of Faith, Forme of Church Government, [and] directory for Worship," and to extirpate "Popery, Prelacy . . . Superstition, Heresie, Schisme, Profanenesse, and whatsoever shall be found to be contrary to sound Doctrine, and the power of Godlinesse." But the covenant also included a formula that was to prove deeply divisive when its several political purposes could no longer be reconciled:

> We shall . . . endeavour with our Estates, and Lives, mutually to preserve the Rights and Priviledges of Parliaments, and the Liberties of the Kingdomes: and to preserve, and defend the Kings Majesties Person, and Authority, in the preservation and defence of the true Religion and Liberties of the Kingdome . . . And that we have no thoughts, or intentions to diminish his Majesties just Power and Greatnesse.[42]

During that winter the Scottish armies failed to win the victories hoped for and in consequence the Scots lost some clout in the Westminster Assembly. On December 8, 1643, the great parliament leader John Pym died. On January 22, 1644 parliament met with 22 Peers and 280 Commoners, and on the same day the king opened an anti-parliament at Oxford of 49 Peers and 121 Commoners faithful to his cause; he prorogued it on April 16. Through all this, Milton continued his quotidian life of study, teaching, and visiting friends: Lady Margaret Ley and her husband Colonel Hobson, the bookseller George Thomason and his wife Catherine, and William Blackborough, a relative living nearby.[43]

During these anxious months Milton turned aside from the ecclesiastical and political issues foregrounded in the national debate, and published several tracts relating to marriage and divorce: two editions of *The Doctrine and Discipline of Divorce* (*DDD* 1 and *DDD* 2); *The Judgement of Martin Bucer, Concerning Divorce*; *Tetrachordon*; and *Colasterion*. He was led to this topic by his personal experience of marital incompatibility; as he later observed, we are mostly moved to protest wrongs by the "spurre of self-concernment" (*CPW* II, 226). However, he generalizes that experience, envisioning multitudes of Englishmen suffering in broken marriages but held back by mind-forged manacles of misunderstood scripture from seeking legitimate release in divorce: "Lamented experience daily teaches" the painful folly of holding men to a bondage beyond their strength to endure (*DDD* 1, 171). Civil divorce with right to remarry was permitted for adultery and desertion in Protestant countries on the Continent, but English law (still adjudicated in ecclesiastical courts) allowed in such cases only separation from bed and board, though grounds were sometimes found – or stretched – to grant annulments with right of remarriage. In strict terms, an annulment required demonstration that there had been no marriage because physical defects prevented consummation, or because the parties were too closely related (violating the incest taboo), or because there was forced consent or a prior betrothal. Milton's proposal of divorce for incompatibility moves far beyond the continental Protestant norm: it has precedent in Jewish law and in a few Protestant treatises, but was virtually unheard of in England.

In his divorce tracts Milton's experience with Mary Powell is refracted through two seemingly contradictory portraits of an unfit wife. The primary one is of a wife unfit for conversation and companionship because of mental dullness and "deadnes of spirit" (*DDD* 1, 178): "an uncomplying discord of nature," "an image of earth and fleam (*DDD* 1, 153), "mute and spiritles" (*DDD* 1, 151), "a helplesse, unaffectionate and sullen masse whose very company represents the visible and exactest figure of lonlines it selfe" (*CPW* II, 670). Such images do not seem to fit the social young woman Phillips describes, but they register Milton's baffled resentment over Mary's lack of interest in and unwillingness or inability to share the intellectual pleasures at the center of his life. Another portrait, in *DDD* 2 and especially *Tetrachordon,* is of a wife who slights her husband and contends "in point of house-rule who shall be the head, not for any parity of wisdome, for that were somthing reasonable, but out of a female pride" (*CPW* II, 324): "a desertrice" (605), "an intolerable adversary," and a bitter political foe (591). Annabel Patterson suggests that these portraits may parallel the course of Mary's relationship with Milton: from the passive aggression of the early weeks when she simply resisted any participation in Milton's activities, to the active defiance signaled by her desertion and refusal to return.[44] Milton directs his rage outward, so as not to have to admit what he probably sensed at some level: that he himself – inexperienced with women, set in his ways – shares responsibility for Mary's unresponsiveness.

Milton's divorce tracts demand root and branch reform in the most fundamental institution of society, the family. And since the Protestant family was seen to be the foundation of the Protestant state, Milton could and did present these tracts as a vital contribution to the national struggle, while many of his contemporaries thought they threatened the very basis of society. Central to Milton's position is his definition of the primary end of marriage as a fellowship of the mind and spirit, whereas most Early Modern marriage manuals and sermons give priority to the other two usually cited purposes, procreation and the relief of lust. Milton's ordering is not unique, but his passion in defending it is. His bold, even foolhardy, campaign testifies to his confidence in the momentum of reform at this juncture, in the power of his own rhetoric to affect its course, and in the progressive unfolding of truth through study and prophetic revelation. All of his divorce tracts address parliament as the only locus of political power, again registering Milton's incipient if not yet formal republicanism.

On August 1, 1643 Milton published *The Doctrine and Discipline of Divorce: Restor'd to the Good of Both Sexes, From the bondage of Canon Law, and other mistakes, to Christian freedom, guided by the Rule of Charity. Wherein also many places of Scripture, have recover'd their long-lost meaning. Seasonable to be now thought on in the Reformation intended.* The tract carried no signature, no preface, and only the initials of two printers and a place of purchase;[45] in defiance of the recent law, it was neither licensed nor registered with the Stationers. In his *Judgement of Martin Bucer* a year later, Milton claims that he had wanted his argument to be taken on its own merits rather than that his name "should sway the reader either for me or against me" (*CPW* II, 434). No doubt there were other reasons for anonymity and illicit publication: the certainty that a license would be refused, and Milton's worry that his treatise might be discounted as the railings of a deserted husband. His argument is based almost wholly on scripture and on the painful experience of incompatible wedlock, with a few supporting citations from Hugo Grotius and some rabbinical commentary. Milton seems to have expected, naively, that his argument would be welcomed or at least respectfully heard: he proffers it to the "candid view both of Church and Magistrate" (*DDD* 1, 145–6) – that is, to parliament and the staunchly Presbyterian Westminster Assembly. The work proved popular. The entire first edition, a printing of perhaps twelve hundred or more copies, was exhausted within five or six months.

This tract contains Milton's core argument for divorce and his most passionate and emotionally charged language. The subtitle previews the tract's scope, purpose, and loose structure. In both editions Milton presents himself as a laborious and learned scholar, a courageous hero, and a public benefactor,[46] who has "with much labour and faithfull diligence first found out, or at least with a fearlesse and communicative candor first publisht to the manifest good of Christendome," the true meaning of the relevant biblical texts (*CPW* II, 226). Moreover,

> In this generall labour of reformation . . . he that can but lend us the clue that windes out this labyrinth of servitude to such a reasonable and expedient liberty as this, deserves to be reck'n'd among the publick benefactors of civill and humane life; above the inventors of wine and oyle. (*DDD* 1, 145–6)

In the formal proposition, Milton offers to prove, "either from Scripture or light of reason,"

> That indisposition, unfitnes, or contrariety of mind, arising from a cause in nature unchangable, hindring and ever likely to hinder the main benefits of conjugall society, which are solace and peace, is a greater reason of divorce than naturall frigidity, especially if there be no children, and that there be mutuall consent. (147)

He marshals his reasons and rhetorical strategies against two projected opponents: those who place the essence of marriage in the physical union, and those who hold strictly by the letter of scripture. The fundamental ground for his argument is that God's institution of marriage in Eden – "It is not good that man should be alone; I will make him a help meet for him" (Genesis 2:18) – locates the essence of marriage in the "apt and cheerfull conversation" of man and woman; God, he insists, did not mention "the purpose of generation till afterwards, as being but a secondary end in dignity" (144). He also appeals to the Protestant definition of marriage as a covenant between the parties, not a sacrament. From the corollary, that a covenant is null if its primary end cannot be met, he concludes that, since the evils of solitariness are only intensified if spouses are incompatible, they can and should divorce.

As powerful support for this argument he constructs throughout the tract a scenario of disappointment in marriage, reframing his own story in the language of reason, myth,[47] and the common experience of Englishmen. An especially revealing passage about how an inexperienced, chaste young man can easily be deluded in choosing a wife encodes Milton's own narrative of his chaste youth, delayed sexual awakening, courtship under the usual social restraints, misapprehensions reinforced by cultural assumptions about the proper behavior of virgins, too hasty marriage, and finally, profound disappointment in the mate's mind and temperament:

> The soberest and best govern'd men are le[a]st practiz'd in these affairs; and who knows not that the bashfull mutenes of a virgin may oft-times hide all the unlivelines and naturall sloth which is really unfit for conversation; nor is there that freedom of accesse granted or presum'd, as may suffice to a perfect discerning till too late: and where any indisposition is suspected, what more usuall than the perswasion of friends, that acquaintance, as it encreases, will amend all. And lastly, it is not strange though many who have spent their youth chastly, are in some things not so quicksighted, while they hast too eagerly to light the nuptiall torch. . . . Since they who have liv'd most loosely by reason of their bold accustoming, prove most successfull in their matches, because their wild affections unsetling at will, have been as so many divorces to teach them experience. When as the sober man honouring the appearance of modestie, and hoping well of every sociall virtue under that veile, may easily chance to meet, if not with a body impenetrable, yet often with a minde to all other due conversation inaccessible, and to all the more estimable and superior purposes of matrimony uselesse and almost liveles; and what a solace, what a fit help such a consort would be through the whole life of a man, is lesse paine to conjecture than to have experience. (150)

Milton is the one who spent his youth "chastly" expecting to find in marriage his "chiefest earthly comforts" and especially relief from "unkindly solitarines" – that "rationall burning" which, he insists revealingly, cannot be subdued as the body's sexual impulses easily can be by spare diet and hard work (146–53). Complaints about the loneliness and melancholy of single life, or worse, the loneliness of a life with an incompatible spouse, sound like a leitmotif through this tract, poignantly revealing the intensity of Milton's felt need for a soulmate, a female companion who would, in some ways at least, take Diodati's place. His idealistic expectations are evident in his descriptions of the desired soulmate and companion: "a fit conversing soul," "an intimate and speaking help" against all the sorrows and casualties of life, "a ready and reviving associate," the "copartner of a sweet and gladsome society" (151–3), who is lively, intelligent, and eager to share his ideas and interests. With such hopes dashed, a disappointed man of melancholy temperament – a scholarly *penseroso* like Milton – is condemned, the tract asserts, to a wedded loneliness threatening health, faith, and even life itself (149). He suffers "a daily trouble and paine of losse in some degree like that which Reprobates feel" (148); he may "mutin against divine providence" and give way to that "melancholy despair which we see in many wedded persons" (153), and so be disabled for public or private employment (161). Milton did not give way to despair, or give over teaching and writing, but he could not, it seems, write much poetry.

Milton allows that such unhappiness may afflict either party (260), but his scenario takes the form of a parodic romance in which the earthbound, unfit wife threatens to subvert the male protagonist's spiritual quest and search for transcendence.[48] This scenario finds biblical warrant in Paul's advice to leave a seducing idolatress (155–8) – and Milton probably intends some allusion to the "seducing idolatress" on the throne, the Roman Catholic Queen Henrietta Maria.[49]

Milton castigates as carnal and brutish those who support the present divorce laws, which take account only of physical conditions: impotence, frigidity, consanguinity, adultery, desertion. Married persons who are found "suitably weapon'd to the least possibilitie of sensuall enjoyment" are made "spight of *antipathy* to fadge together" (144), though "instead of beeing one flesh, they will be rather two carkasses chain'd unnaturally together; or as it may happ'n, a living soule bound to a dead corps" (177). Paul's dictum, "It is better to marry than to burn" (1 Corinthians 7:9) refers, Milton insists, vehemently if implausibly, to that longing for companionship which Adam felt even in Eden; it cannot be "the meer motion of carnall lust, not the meer goad of a sensitive desire; God does not principally take care for such cattell" (151). This language goads the reader to repudiate such baseness and to identify rather with gentle and generous persons like Milton, who recognize that mental and social deficiencies are far more serious grounds for divorce than are the accepted physical defects.

At length Milton has to confront directly the biblical text (Matthew 19:3–9) in which Christ seems to prohibit divorce except for adultery, and to rescind the Mosaic law (Deuteronomy 24:1–2) allowing divorce if a man finds "some uncleanness" in his wife:

> The Pharasees also came unto him, tempting him, and saying unto him, is it lawful for a man to put away his wife for every cause?
>
> And he answered and said unto them. Have ye not read, that he which made them at the beginning made them male and female.

> And said, For this cause shall a man leave father and mother, and shall cleave to his wife: and they twain shall be one flesh?
>
> Wherefore they are no more twain but one flesh. What therefore God hath joined together, let not man put asunder.
>
> They say unto him, Why did Moses then command to give a writing of divorcement, and to put her away?
>
> He saith unto them. Moses because of the hardness of your hearts suffered you to put away your wives: but from the beginning it was not so.
>
> And I say unto you. Whosoever shall put away his wife, except it be for fornication, and shall marry another, committeth adultery: and whoso marrieth her which is put away doth commit adultery. (AV)

Milton's strategy is to overwhelm the literal terms of this text, which he does not quote in full, by reading it in terms of his governing exegetical principle, that every text must be interpreted with reference to its specific context and circumstances, and its consonance with the gospel's overriding purpose and spirit, charity:

> There is scarse any one saying in the Gospel, but must be read with limitations and distinctions, to be rightly understood; for Christ gives no full comments or continu'd discourses, but scatters the heavnly grain of his doctrin like pearle heer and there, which requires a skilfull and laborious gatherer; who must compare the words he finds, with other precepts, with the end of every ordinance, and with the general *analogy* of Evangelick doctrine: otherwise many particular sayings would be but strange repugnant riddles. (182)

The explicit context for Christ's statements is Deuteronomy 24:1, the Mosaic permission to divorce and remarry. Milton argues that Christ cannot have meant to label that permission adultery and to rescind it, for this would mean that God allowed sinful adultery to his chosen people for two millennia (168–72). It is "absurd to imagine that the covnant of grace should reform the exact and perfect law of works, eternal and immutable" (173), since Christ himself promised not to abrogate "the least jot or tittle" of it. The Mosaic permission is "a grave and prudent Law, full of moral equity, full of due consideration toward nature," and it therefore remains applicable to Christians (168). Also, Milton establishes a philological context for defining "fornication" in Matthew 19.9 and "some uncleanness" in Deuteronomy 24:1 to mean not simply unchastity but any obstinancy, headstrong behavior, or stubbornness leading to irreconcilable dislike.[50] Citing Josephus, the Septuagint and Chaldaean texts of the Bible, and the rabbinical commentary of Kimchi, Levi ben Gerson, and Rashi (180–1), Milton here begins a reliance on the Hebrew Bible and Hebraic scholarship that will greatly increase in the later divorce tracts.[51] He also quotes from Grotius, but, characteristically, calls attention to "what mine own thoughts gave me, before I had seen his annotations" (178).[52] In addition, he analyzes the immediate circumstances of Christ's prohibition and concludes that it was intended, not as a directive for Christians, but as a deliberately misleading statement to baffle the Pharisees who had abused the Mosaic permission by divorcing for light causes (168–70).

His primary interpretative touchstone is the essential spirit of the gospel, charity, which must be "the interpreter and guide of our faith" (145): he states flatly that "wee cannot safely assent to any precept writt'n in the Bible, but as charity commends it to us" (183).[53] Milton heaps scorn on those who rest "in the meere element of the Text" (145) with an "obstinate literality" and an "alphabeticall servility" (164). That stance is at odds with the core Protestant belief in a single sense of scripture easily understood by the elect, which was Milton's basic assumption in the antiprelatical tracts, though even there he described the qualities that should mark a gospel church, rather than explicating the usual scripture proof texts for a Presbyterian form of government.[54] Now he argues explicitly that "the supreme dictate of charitie" demands reinterpretation of the Matthew text in the light of reason and human experience, since its literal terms endanger human good, religious faith, and even life itself (151).[55] The tract concludes with a reference to Matthew 22:40, which subsumes "all the law and the Profets" in two commandments, to love God and neighbor.[56]

As for the "discipline" or ordering of divorce, Milton removes jurisdiction over it from the ecclesiastical courts and vests the power to divorce entirely in the husband. Ministers and elders may question him as to whether the incompatibility is grave and irreconcilable (188), and the civil courts may rule on "dowries, jointures, and the like," to set just conditions (186–8), but neither church nor state may forbid the parties to divorce and remarry if they choose. Dismissing objections stemming from the danger of social dislocation or injustice to the wife, he insists that the wife would be harmed more by living with an unjust man, or in a loveless marriage, or permanently separated like a married widow. He resorts to gender stereotypes in assuming that the wife would be glad to avoid a trial, "It being also an unseemly affront to the sequestr'd and vail'd modesty of that sex, to have her unpleasingnes and other concealements bandied up and down, and aggravated in open Court by those hir'd maisters of tongue-fence" (186–7). But the determining consideration for him is the man's hierarchical right:

> For ev'n the freedom and eminence of mans creation gives him to be a Law in this matter to himself, beeing the head of the other sex which was made for him: whom therfore though he ought not to injure, yet neither should he be forc't to retain in society to his own overthrow, nor to hear any judge therin above himself. (186)

The logic of Milton's arguments from contract and incompatibility would allow the woman as well as the man to institute divorce procedures, but in this first tract his concept of gender hierarchy, and his still intense hurt and anger, prevent him from raising that issue.

On February 2, 1644, the second edition of *Doctrine and Discipline* appeared, "revis'd and much augmented," indeed, almost doubled in size.[57] The subtitle offers to restore "the true meaning of Scripture in the Law and Gospel compar'd," pointing to the tract's new emphasis on the harmony of Law and Gospel and especially on the meaning of Deuteronomy 24:1.[58] Milton's initials appear on the title page and the preface is signed in full, "John Milton." Anonymity, he explains in *Bucer*, did not serve his intended purpose: his style gave him away and "some of the Clergie began to inveigh and exclaim on what I was credibly inform'd they had not read," so he determined to show his detractors "a name that could easily contemn such an indiscreet kind of censure" (*CPW*, II, 434). He evidently attempted to get *DDD* 2 licensed and was denied;[59] also, neither printer nor bookseller cared to affix his name or even his initials to this unlicensed, scandalous tract. This edition is presented in a more orderly form than the first: two books divided into chapters, each headed by a brief summary of topics. It also comes across as a more temperate tract: it retains the appeals to common experience, the rhetoric of disgust and denigration, and the barely concealed personal testimony, but here their impact is diffused by the more elaborate apparatus. While it makes substantially the same case, it adds some new arguments, more exegesis of scripture, and new authorities.

The title page and a new epistle direct this revision "To the parliament of England, with the Assembly," but Milton focuses entirely on parliament, to whose wisdom and piety he appeals from "the clamor of so much envie and impertinence" (224), and whose protection he gratefully acknowledges (233).[60] Now writing under his own name, he presents himself as citizen–adviser to the parliamentary "Worthies" (*CPW* II, 232), locating himself with other reformers attacked "by the ruder sort, but not by discreet and well nurtur'd men" (224) such as, he presumes, the MPs are. He also casts himself as a new Josiah who has recovered a "most necessary, most charitable, and yet most injur'd Statute of *Moses*" buried "under the rubbish of Canonicall ignorance: as once the whole law was . . . in *Josiahs* time."[61] As well, he portrays himself again as a courageous solitary hero who, with the aid of the "illuminating Spirit," has undertaken a romance quest, "a high enterprise and a hard, and such as every seventh Son of a seventh Son does not venture on" (224). Primarily, he is a learned scholar and teacher, "gifted with abilities of mind that may raise him to so high an undertaking" (224). He explains his decision to write in English rather than Latin, because of "the esteem I have of my Countries judgement, and the love I beare to my native language," but despite this appeal to a wider audience (which he came to regret)[62] he especially addresses "the choisest and the learnedest" (233). And, as he did in the antiprelatical tracts, he insists that as "an instructed Christian" (224) he has as much right to address religious matters as any cleric: "I want neither pall nor mitre, I stay neither for ordination nor induction, but in the firm faith of a knowing Christian, which is the best and truest endowment of the keyes" (281–2).

In a skillful and bold rhetorical move Milton identifies his own case with parliament's. They too have suffered from "the experience of your owne uprightnesse mis-interpreted" (225). Their political and ecclesiastical reforms cannot succeed without reforming marriage and divorce, on which depends "not only the spiritfull and orderly life of our grown men, but the willing and carefull education of our children" (229–30). And their justifications for dissolving the people's covenant of allegiance when a ruler's tyranny subverts its fundamental purposes apply equally to his argument about dissolving a marriage covenant whose ends are not met:

> He who marries, intends as little to conspire his own ruine, as he that swears Allegiance: and as a whole people is in proportion to an ill Government, so is one man to an ill mariage. If they against any authority, Covnant, or Statute, may by the soveraign edict of charity, save not only their lives, but honest liberties from unworthy bondage, as well may he against any private Covnant, which hee never enter'd to his mischief, redeem himself from unsupportable disturbances to honest peace, and just contentment. . . . For no effect of tyranny can sit more heavy on the Common-wealth, then this houshold unhappines on the family. (229)

This epistle also challenges the Westminster Assembly to support his divorce reforms and so become the true Defenders of the Faith they claim to be, by becoming Defenders of Charity: "Who so preferrs either Matrimony, or other Ordinance before the good of man and the plain exigence of Charity, let him professe Papist, or Protestant, or what he will, he is no better than a Pharise, and understands not the Gospel" (233).

The most important change foregrounds the Mosaic law of divorce (Deuteronomy 24:1), that "pure and solid Law of God," as the linchpin of the entire argument (351). A new, long passage in chapter 1 insists on its enduring applicability to Christians, and begins to define the term "uncleanness" as "*any reall nakednes:* which by all the learned interpreters is refer'd to the mind, as well as to the body" (243–4). Christ's prohibition, he concludes, pertained only to lesser matters than the "uncleanness" for which Moses permitted divorce, "those natural and perpetual hindrances of society [which] . . . annihilate the bands of mariage more then adultery."[63] The authorities he cites indicate that between the first and second editions of this tract, Milton studied much more intensively the Hebrew Bible and its Hebraist commentators: "the Rabbins," Maimonides ("famous above the rest"), Grotius, and Paulus Fagius.[64] He singles out especially the most famous English Hebraist, the "learned *Selden*" whose *Law of Nature & of Nations* he recommends as a supplement to his own tract, for the evidence it marshals that to refuse divorce is against the Law of Nature and of "God himself, lawgiving in person to his sanctified people."[65]

Some added passages indicate developments in Milton's thought. One such is his remarkable portrait of a rational God, so very different from the Calvinist arbitrary deity whose reasons and will are unfathomable:

> God hath not two wills but one will, much lesse two contrary. . . . The hidden wayes of his providence we adore & search not; but the law is his reveled wil, his complete, his evident, and certain will; herein he appears to us as it were in human shape, enters into cov'nant with us, swears to keep it, binds himself like a just lawgiver to his own prescriptions, gives himself to be understood by men, judges and is judg'd, measures and is commensurat to right reason.[66]

Other added passages stridently reaffirm gender hierarchy. Beza's supposition that Moses permitted divorce chiefly to afford relief for afflicted wives is "Palpably uxorious! Who can be ignorant that woman was created for man, and not man for woman; and that a husband may be injur'd as insufferably in mariage as a wife . . . is it not most likely that God in his Law had more pitty towards the man thus wedlockt, then towards the woman that was created for another" (324–5). Also, he greatly expands the section marshaling biblical evidence for divorcing an idolatrous wife, lest she "seduce us from the true worship of God, or defile and daily scandalize our conscience" (263).

Among the additions to *DDD* 2 are several small but revealing allegories. In one, (female) Custom who is a "meer face," a "swollen visage of counterfeit knowledge and literature," aggressively joins herself with (male) Error, "a blind and Serpentine body," but Milton – as romance hero – undertakes the "high enterprise" of engaging this monster (222–4). In another, Milton is both father and mother to (female) Truth, producing her from his head as Jupiter did Minerva, but also giving birth to her, relegating Time, usually the mother of Truth, to the role of midwife:

> Shee [Truth] never comes into the world, but like a Bastard, to the ignominy of him that brought her forth: till Time the Midwife rather then the mother of Truth, have washt and salted the Infant, declar'd her legitimat, and Churcht the father of his young *Minerva*, from the needlesse causes of his purgation.[67]

These curious gender shifts are dictated by Milton's need to accommodate the myth of Truth to himself as male teacher, but they also reveal Milton's subconscious disposition to elide or subsume to himself the female sphere of experience.[68]

James Turner states that in *Doctrine and Discipline* Milton's images for woman and for physical sex are "authentically ugly,"[69] linking the sex act to animality or disease or servile labor. It is the "promiscuous draining of a carnal rage (*DDD* 1, 189), which releases the waste products of the distempered and overheated body – "the quintessence of an excrement" (*DDD* 1, 149). Such language cannot be explained simply as rhetoric: like the degrading body imagery in antiprelatical tracts it also registers Milton's disgust – here, apparently, his repugnance – for some of his sexual experiences. But Milton does not disparage the female body and physical sex as such; what he finds repellent is loveless sex. Absent a loving union of mind and spirit, he experiences the sexual act as slavery – grinding "in the mill of an undelighted and servil copulation" (*CPW* II, 258) – and as a crime against nature: "the most injurious and unnaturall tribute that can be extorted from a person endew'd with reason, [is] to be made to pay out the best substance of his body, and of his soul too, as some think, when either for just and powerfull causes he cannot like, or from unequall causes finds not recompence" (*CPW* II, 271). Here, semen is the quintessence, not of an excrement but of both soul and body.

Milton insists that "not to be belov'd, and yet retain'd, is the greatest injury to a gentle spirit" (*DDD* 1, 152), which none can rightly estimate "unlesse he have a soul gentle anough, and spacious anough to contemplate what is true love" (*CPW* II, 333). Behind all this is a rather remarkable critique of contemporary gender norms that recalls the protest of the Cambridge student who so scornfully objected in Prolusion VI to a definition of masculinity based on frequenting taverns and brothels.[70] He also challenges the near-universal designation of adultery as the gravest affront to marriage and to masculine honor:

> For that fault committed [adultery] argues not alwaies a hatred either natural or incidental against whom it is committed; neither does it inferre a disability of all future helpfulnes, or loyalty, or loving agreement, being once past, and pardon'd, where it can be pardon'd. . . . a grave and prudent Law of *Moses* . . . contains a cause of divorce greater beyond compare then that for adultery . . . this being but a transient injury, and soon amended, I mean as to the party against whom the trespasse is. (331–3)

Milton's ideal of a wife as a "fit conversing soul" challenges conventional belief that her value resides essentially in her physical beauty, chastity, and fertility. And he flatly denies the assumption that a man can easily separate sexual pleasure from the realm of emotion and intellect: "where the minde and person pleases aptly, there some unaccomplishment of the bodies delight may be better born with, than when the minde hangs off in an unclosing disproportion, though the body be as it ought; for there all corporall delight will soon become unsavoury and contemptible" (*DDD* 1, 148).

On or before June 5, 1644 Milton published an eight-page tractate, simply headed *Of Education, To Master Samuel Hartlib,* couched as a letter to that emigré scholar from Elbing, who had become a one-man institution for scholarly and scientific exchange among scholars in England and abroad. Hartlib was involved with projects for educational reform at all levels, as well as libraries, foundations for the poor, scientific discoveries and inventions, and schemes for promoting Protestant unity; his circle of associates forms a link between Bacon and the post-Restoration Royal Society.[71] This time Milton's tract was registered and officially licensed, but its brevity and its format – without title page, author's name, or publication data – suggests that it was privately printed for limited circulation to the Hartlib circle and perhaps a few others. Milton evidently decided not to interrupt his focus on divorce to work out his educational ideas in the detail necessary for public presentation.

He probably came to know Hartlib sometime between April and September,

1643; a note by Hartlib within that period states that "Mr. Milton of Aldersgate Street has written many good books a great traveller and full of projects and inventions."[72] Also, there is evidence in Hartlib's papers that Milton contributed three shillings to the development of an engine of war for use against royalist cavalry, the invention of one Edmund Felton for which Hartlib was seeking subscriptions.[73] In *Of Education* Milton praised Hartlib as "a person sent hither by some good providence from a farre country to be the occasion and incitement of great good to this Iland" – an opinion shared, he states, by "men of most approved wisdom and some of highest authority among us" (*CPW* II, 363). Hartlib circulated the tract but did not supply, nor did Milton probably seek, a prefatory commendation such as was common in works Hartlib formally sponsored: Milton probably did not want that appearance of patronage.[74] But several members showed interest in this treatise and in other works of Milton's: Hartlib took note of the publication of his *Doctrine and Discipline of Divorce;* John Dury termed Milton's education tractate "brief and general," but took over some elements of it into his own model; John Hall thought it excellent and "desired Milton's acquaintance"; and Sir Cheney Culpepper criticized the lack of "particulars" though he thought it contained "good sprinklings," and was sufficiently impressed to inquire about Milton's charges for taking on a pupil.[75] Milton may have acquired a pupil or two through these channels.

Milton described his treatise as a response to Hartlib's "earnest entreaties" to set forth the ideas he had expressed during their several "incidentall discourses" (363) about education. Hartlib was much influenced by the Moravian scholar Jan Amos Comenius and promoted his ideas about education and about preparing a compendium of all knowledge.[76] Milton shared with Hartlib and Comenius the belief that a reformed commonwealth requires educational reform – "for the want whereof this nation perishes" (363) – and also a desire to reform the teaching of languages and the school curriculum. But Milton rather curtly dismisses the seminal Comenian texts: "To search what many modern *Janua's* and *Didactics* more then ever I shall read, have projected, my inclination leads me not" (364–6). That statement is probably disingenuous: as a practising schoolmaster Milton almost certainly knew Comenius's *Janua linguarum reserata*, a much discussed and widely used manual for teaching Latin, and he had probably encountered summaries of Comenius's *Didactica Magna*, containing schemes for an articulated school system from the cradle to the university for both sexes and all ranks and levels of ability.[77] Milton's dismissive statement allows him to distance himself from the Hartlib–Comenian educational project without, in courtesy to Hartlib, spelling out his disagreements. Also, this statement and this stance is a version of Milton's thoroughly characteristic claim to originality. He declines to work out his debts to "old renowned Authors," and insists he has not even read the most famous modern educational reformer. Out of benevolence to others and at the specific behest of Hartlib he simply offers a "few observations," the offshoots "of many studious and contemplative yeers altogether spent in search of religious and civil knowledge" (364–6). Nor does he identify himself as a schoolmaster drawing upon his own experience, probably because his status as gentleman–scholar might be compromised by that comparatively lowly role.[78] Yet he imagines the teacher his program requires in the familiar, heroic terms: "this is not a bow for every man to shoot in that counts himselfe a teacher; but will require sinews almost equall to those which Homer gave Ulysses" (415).

Though there are important points of connection, *Of Education* is not a Comenian tract.[79] Like Hartlib and Comenius, Milton proposes the use of public funds to establish schools "in every City throughout this land, which would tend much to the encrease of learning and civility every where" (380–1),[80] but unlike them he explicitly declines to work out a comprehensive articulated system of schools for all classes and both sexes (414). Milton's are private academies, each designed for about 150 of "our noble and gentle youth" (406) between the ages of 12 and 21; they require at entrance literacy in English and some prior preparation, and promise a complete education to the level of Master of Arts, replacing the university education Milton so scorned. Milton agrees with Comenius and Hartlib that the logic chopping, metaphysical subtleties, and rhetoric currently taught in schools and universities should be replaced by a Baconian emphasis on "useful" knowledge; that education should proceed from "sensible things" to subjects more abstract; that the process, while rigorous, should also be delightful; that languages should be studied, not for the "words or lexicons" (369) but to make available the "experience and . . . wisdom" of others; and that present methods of learning Latin and Greek are prodigiously wasteful of time and ineffective. Instead of Comenius's famous *Janua*, however, Milton would begin with the grammar now used (Lily) "or any better,"[81] and proceed quickly to pronunciation and the reading of good authors. Also, he eschews the epitomes and encyclopedias that form the core of Comenian education, outlining instead an elaborate program of reading major texts (classical and some modern) in all subjects, linking together literary, scientific, and philosophical texts in a remarkable and unusual interdisciplinary program. He has no Baconian–Comenian belief in perfect methods or systems, nor in the Comenian dream of *Pansophia* – a grand cooperative compendium of all knowledge that will resolve dissent into unity. Rather, he will soon insist in *Areopagitica* that truth is best advanced by a constant clash of opinions that promotes arduous intellectual struggle and individual choice.

Milton's core educational ideas were formed by his own education at St Paul's School, by his own highly disciplined five-year reading program after university, and by his experience in working out a similar reading program in his little private school for his nephews and a few other boys. He proclaims both a religious and civic humanist purpose for education: "The end then of learning is to repair the ruins of our first parents by regaining to know God aright . . . as we may the neerest by possessing our souls of true vertue" (366–7); "I call therefore a compleate and generous Education that which fits a man to perform justly, skilfully and magnanimously all the offices both private and publike of peace and war" (377–9). In his proposed curriculum, after the basics of Latin grammar, arithmetic, and geometry, the boys would turn first to subjects founded on the senses: agriculture and geography; then Greek; then Greek and Latin texts on natural science, astronomy, meteorology, architecture, and physics; then the "instrumental" sciences of trigonometry, fortification, architecture, military engineering, meteors, zoology, anatomy, and medicine.[82] Along with their natural science Milton's students would read the poetry of nature: pastoral, georgic, Lucretius, and other "scientific" poems. After these sense-based studies, they are ready for subjects grounded in reason. Their moral philosophy – Plato, Xenophon, Cicero, Plutarch, and the like – is to be "reduc't in their nightward studies" by the "determinat sentence" of scripture (396–7). Their studies in economics (household management) are to be leavened with choice Greek, Latin, and Italian domestic comedies and tragedies, the boys having by now learned "at any odde hour the *Italian* tongue" (397). Their studies of politics, law, and history are to be matched with the great classical epics and tragedies and the orations of Cicero and Demosthenes. Milton's course, like that of Comenius, ends with logic and rhetoric, but Milton, not surprisingly, adds poetics. Formal compositions employing these skills are also reserved to this late stage: they are not for the "empty wits" of children, but should arise from independent reflection based on "long reading, and observing" (372). Sundays are for theology and church history; by their final years the students – some of them prospective ministers – will have learned "the Hebrew Tongue at a set hour," along with the Chaldean (Aramaic) and Syriac dialects, so they can read the scriptures in the original (400).

After meals and exercise they hear or perform music for voice, organ, or lute, to compose their spirits and passions. With the nation embroiled in civil war, Milton also mandates military training – not only gentleman's swordplay and wrestling but also "embattailing, marching, encamping, fortifying, beseiging, battering" and tactics, to make the students "perfect Commanders in the service of their country" (411–12). They are also to learn something of the practical and experiential knowledge Hartlib and Dury located in their Vulgar or Mechanical schools, gaining "a reall tincture of natural knowledge" from presentations and demonstrations by "Hunters, fowlers, Fishermen, Shepherds, Gardeners, *Apothecaries* . . . Architects, Engineers, Mariners, *Anatomists*" (393–4), as well as by springtime travels to observe agriculture, trade, military encampments, ships and seafights. At age 24 or so – but not earlier, lest they be corrupted – they might travel to foreign lands "to enlarge experience and make wise observation" (414).

Milton's brief excursus into matters of education did not deflect his attention from the divorce issue. According to his own credible account, three months after publishing the revised *Doctrine and Discipline,* that is, in late April or early May, 1644, he discovered a welcome ally in Martin Bucer, a leader of the Reformation with special ties to England. Edward VI had appointed him Professor of Divinity at Cambridge, and Bucer dedicated his treatise, *De Regno Christi,* to Edward.[83] On August 6 Milton addressed to the "Supreme Court of parliament" a tract entitled

The Judgement of Martin Bucer, concerning Divorce, which sometimes translates and sometimes epitomizes the chapters of Bucer's work dealing with marriage and divorce.[84] The preface, signed "John Milton," offers the work as from Bucer and himself. This time he pointedly ignores the Westminster Assembly, complaining bitterly about the response of his former Presbyterian colleagues, "of whose profession and supposed knowledge I had better hope," and dismayed by the fact that those who praised him for the antiprelatical tracts have now "lavishly traduc'd" him but refused him the courtesy of a formal response:

> They have stood now almost this whole year clamouring a farre off, while the book hath bin twice printed, twice bought up, & never once vouchsaft a friendly conference with the author, who would be glad and thankfull to be shewn an error, either by privat dispute, or public answer, and could retract, as well as wise men before him; might also be worth the gaining, as one who heertofore, hath done good service to the church. (*CPW* II, 435–7)

Bucer was licensed by John Downham, registered by the Stationers on July 15, and the title page bears the imprimatur, "Publisht by Authoritie." The epigraph – "Art thou a teacher of Israel, and know'st not these things?" (John 3:10) – ridicules his clerical detractors who, in denouncing Milton's views on divorce as "licentious, new, and dangerous" (436), have unwittingly defamed the venerable Bucer. Anticipating *Areopagitica,* Milton underscores the irony and the danger in the fact that he, as an English patriot, had only tried in his divorce tracts to do "for mine own Country" what those "admired strangers," Bucer and Erasmus, did for it, but Bucer on divorce could be licensed while Milton on divorce could not:

> If these thir books . . . be publisht and republisht . . . and mine containing but the same thing, shall in a time of reformation, a time of free speaking, free writing, not find a permission to the Presse, I referre me to wisest men, whether truth be suffer'd to be truth, or liberty to be liberty now among us, and be not again in danger of new fetters and captivity after all our hopes and labours lost: and whether learning be not (which our enemies too profetically fear'd) in the way to be trodd'n down again by ignorance.[85]

He begins with thirteen testimonials to Bucer as biblical scholar and reformer – and five to Bucer's associate Paulus Fagius – from Calvin, Beza, John Foxe, Peter Martyr, and others. Then, taking up the role of adviser to parliament, he charges them in a lengthy epistle to fulfill their "inestimable trust, the asserting of our just liberties" (438). Terming Bucer "the Apostle of our Church," he argues his special claim to their attention since, in a book written for England, he proposed divorce "as a most necessary and prime part of discipline in every Christian government" (432).

But while Milton here enlists the "the autority, the lerning, godlines" of Bucer

(439) to overcome opposition to his *Doctrine and Discipline*, he registers a keen sense of conflict between such appeals to authority and his insistent claims to scholarly autonomy and independence. He uses much of his preface to construct an elaborate narrative about writing his divorce tracts first and then discovering various confirming authorities: "I ow no light, or leading receav'd from any man in the discovery of this truth, what time I first undertook it in *the doctrine and discipline of divorce*, and had only the infallible grounds of Scripture to be my guide" (433). He insists that he found Grotius's supporting argument only after he finished writing *DDD* 1 and then added a few citations – a sequence of events indicating that God "intended to prove me, whether I durst alone take up a rightful cause against a world of disesteem, & found I durst" (434). He added further references to Grotius in *DDD* 2, characterizing him as an "able assistant," who broached "at much distance" somewhat parallel concepts of "the law of charity and the true end of wedlock" (434). He also found Paulus Fagius's "somewhat brief" comments on the divorce question, which he used chiefly to silence his critics, "thinking sure they would respect so grave an author, at lest to the moderating of their odious inferences" (435). Bucer he heard about when *DDD 2* had been out for three months, and he was amazed to find "the same opinion, confirm'd with the same reasons which in that publisht book without the help or imitation of any precedent Writer, I had labour'd out, and laid together" (435–6). He insists on the status of a "collateral teacher" with Bucer and Fagius (436), whom he casts simply as character-witnesses:

> Not that I have now more confidence by the addition of these great Authors to my party; for what I wrote was not my opinion, but my knowledge; evn then when I could trace no footstep in the way I went: nor that I think to win upon your apprehensions with numbers and with names, rather then with reasons, yet certainly the worst of my detracters will not except against so good a baile of my integritie and judgement, as now appeares for me. (439–40)

His method as translator also asserts his independence, and reveals his distaste for that exercise. He explains that he translated only "so much of this Treatise as runs parallel" to his own *Doctrine and Discipline of Divorce,* i.e. that marriage is a civil, not an ecclesiastical, matter; that there can be no true marriage without love and consent; that Christ could not have branded as adultery a practice God allowed to his own people; that the passage in Matthew 19 reproved the Pharisees for divorcing for light causes; that the institution of marriage in Eden defined as its primary purpose the communication of all duties with affection and benevolence; and that the commonwealth cannot be reformed until the family is.[86] He summarizes some chapters, epitomizes some passages, and freely condenses Bucer's prolix Latin, skipping clauses, sentences, and even paragraphs, but he generally renders Bucer's meaning fairly. Occasionally, he adds a few words or phrases (usually italicized) to clarify a point for his English audience. In a postscript he somewhat truculently defends this freedom, insisting that he has exercised an author's prerogatives even as a translator: "[I] never could delight in long citations, much lesse in whole traductions; Whether it be natural disposition or education in me, or that my mother bore me a speaker of what God made mine own, and not a translator" (478). He portrays himself, however, as God's agent in the divorce controversy, "a passive instrument under some power and counsel higher and better then can be human" (433). Milton the translator can demand equal status with his author since he is a teacher and prophet instructed not by Bucer but by God. He vows to continue publishing what "may render me best serviceable, either to this age, or if it so happ'n, to posteritie" (440), apparently recognizing that his ideas about companionate marriage and divorce for incompatibility may have to await a more enlightened age.

On July 2, 1644 the bloody Battle of Marston Moor was fought just outside York, and proved a turning point for the parliamentary forces. More than 4,000 men were lost, most on the king's side. York surrendered on July 5, placing the entire north of England in parliament's hands, save for a few towns. Chief credit for the victory went to Lieutenant-General Oliver Cromwell, greatly enhancing his military and political reputation and influence. During these months also the Toleration Controversy intensified, as Presbyterians continued to insist on the duty of the Christian magistrate to establish the Presbyterian church and enforce conformity to it, in doctrine, worship, and church order. Alternatively, Erastian and other secular-minded parliamentarians thought that toleration, as broad as could be obtained, was the key to civic harmony.[87] Independents and Sectaries in the army and the gathered churches sounded a call for broad toleration, grounding it on their rightful Christian liberty to follow their consciences. Most tolerationists allowed the magistrate some role in the church's defense and stopped short of tolerating open religious practice far outside the mainstream, e.g. Anabaptists, Antinomians, Familists, Jews, Turks, and especially Roman Catholics.[88] Roger Williams, recently returned from New England, set forth the most radical sectarian tolerationist position: that to protect the elect from the sinful civil order and to allow for ongoing revelations of the Spirit, Christ has completely separated church and state, so the magistrate must tolerate any and all religious opinion and practice – even Roman Catholics, Jews, and Muslims – since he has power only in civil matters.[89]

Milton's divorce tracts became something of a *cause célèbre* in this Toleration Controversy. In calls for the suppression of notoriously wicked opinions, Milton is often linked with the tolerationist Williams and the mortalist Richard Overton, who argued in *Mans Mortalitie* that the soul dies with the body and both rise together at the Last Day.[90] In July, 1644 the Westminster Assembly urged parliament to rein in the burgeoning sects and scandalous publications. On August 9 the Commons ordered Williams's *Bloudy Tenant to* be burned for promoting "the Toleration of all sorts of Religion." On August 13 Herbert Palmer's sermon to the two houses of parliament raged against "ungodly Toleration pleaded for under pretence of

Liberty of Conscience," and cited, as audacious examples of the threat it posed to religion and civil order, blasphemers, idolators, heretics, those who refuse to take oaths, bear arms, or pay taxes, and Milton on divorce:

> If any plead Conscience for the Lawfulness of Polygamy; (or for divorce for other causes then Christ and His Apostles mention; of which a *wicked booke* is abroad and *uncensured,* though *deserving to be burnt,* whose *Author* hath been *so impudent* as to *set his Name* to it and *dedicate it to yourselves*); or for Liberty to *marry incestuously* – will you grant a *Toleration* for all *this*?[91]

In late August the Stationers petitioned parliament to enforce the laws against unlicensed, blasphemous pamphlets and protect the Stationers' franchise, and the Commons charged its Committee on Printing to seek out "the Authors, Printers, and Publishers, of the Pamphlets against the Immortality of the Soul [Overton] and Concerning Divorce."[92] On September 13 Cromwell, whose stock as a successful military leader was rising steadily, drafted a motion in parliament for a limited toleration of Independency.[93] A few days later the formidable William Prynne denounced Independency and the tolerationist pamphlets of Williams and others, that have contributed to "the late dangerous increase of many *Anabaptistical, Antinomian, Heresicall, Atheisticall opinions, as of the soules mortalitie, divorce at pleasure, &c.* . . . which I hope our Grand Council will speedily and carefully suppress."[94] In early November Palmer's sermon with its attack on Milton was published.

On or before November 14, 1644 an anonymous reply to Milton's *DDD* 1 appeared, *An Answer to a Book, Intituled, The Doctrine and Discipline of Divorce.*[95] A specific reference to Milton's residence at Aldersgate, and perhaps to the hastiness of his marriage,[96] indicates that the author had some knowledge of Milton, but he either did not know, or chose to ignore, the expanded *DDD* 2 and the *Bucer* treatise. This 44-page pamphlet was hardly the serious scholarly answer Milton so often called for, though its legalistic arguments support the hearsay that the chief author was a lawyer. With some elitist scorn, Milton reports hearing rumors that the tract was written by "an actual Serving-man . . . turn'd Sollicitor" (*CPW* II, 726–7), with help from one or two fledgling divines and from the noted Presbyterian divine Joseph Caryl who licensed the tract and added a gratuitous commendation.[97] The anonymous answerer disposes briskly of Milton's enumerated reasons for divorce, repeating the literal interpretations of the scripture texts that Milton sought to reinterpret, and appealing often to Canon law and English law. He ridicules Milton's comments on wives, wryly observing that most are not, in Milton's nastiest phrase, "images of earth and fleame," but have spirit enough for other men of good qualities, whether or not they can "speak Hebrew, Greek, Latine, & French, and dispute canon law" as Milton seems to expect.[98] Adopting the tone of a man of the world answering a woolly headed fanatic whose descriptions of love and of marriage he found simply incomprehensible, he declares himself baffled by Milton's notion of incompatibility and emphasis on "fit conversation,"[99] and likens Milton's paean to marriage as a "Mystery of Love" to the "wilde, mad, and franticke divinitie" of the Antinomian women preachers of Aldgate. His strongest arguments call attention to practical issues Milton ignores: the plight of the children of divorced couples, the wife's legal rights and how to enforce them, and the social disgrace a divorced wife would suffer.[100]

When this reply appeared, Milton's *Areopagitica*, published about November 23, 1644, was already in press. That tract was also prompted by personal experience – the fact that Milton's divorce tracts fell foul of the new licensing ordinance – but he also claimed to voice the "generall murmur" of many learned authors who "loaded me with entreaties and perswasions" to serve as their spokesman (*CPW* II, 539). Constructed as an oration to parliament, *Areopagitica* came forth without printer's or bookseller's names – too dangerous for them – but with Milton's name boldly inscribed on the title page: *Areopagitica; a Speech of Mr. John Milton for the Liberty of Unlicenc'd Printing, To the Parlament of England.*[101] As everyone knows, Milton's argument, couched in poetic imagery and high rhetoric, has become a cornerstone in the liberal defense of freedom of speech, press, and thought. Its argument and art are discussed on pages 190–7.

Areopagitica calls for the free circulation and conflict of ideas and for broad though not absolute religious toleration, representing these as essential preconditions for the development of free citizens. Specifically, he calls for parliament to replace its new order for prior censorship of books with that of January 29, 1642, which simply required registration of authors' or printers' names (and thereby helped secure their rights).[102] Milton has only scorn for his former Presbyterian colleagues who have forgotten their own experience of persecution and now seek to be inquisitors themselves (*CPW* II, 568–9). He castigates the Stationers Company, as idle "*patentees* and *monopolizers*" seeking to retain their monopoly in the book trade and to make vassels of authors and printers who "labour in an honest profession to which learning is indetted."[103] Intellectually he associates himself with the parliamentary Erastians and their leader John Selden, as well as with Independents and Sectaries whose watchword was toleration. During these months he probably came to know personally some of the radicals linked with him as proper targets for censorship: John Goodwin, Roger Williams, and Richard Overton.

Areopagitica, like *Of Education,* is concerned with preparing citizens for the reformed commonwealth in the making, envisioned as an aristocratic republic, not a monarchy. In the education tractate, Milton sketched out the humanist principles and plan of studies that would best prepare upper-class youth for future leadership roles. In *Areopagitica* he proposed continuous unrestricted reading, writing, and disputation to exercise mature citizens in making the free choices through which they will grow in knowledge and virtue, learn to value liberty, and act to secure it in the state. Milton's highly structured course of study in *Of Education* might seem at odds with the intellectual freedom *Areopagitica* celebrates. But Milton clearly believed that a carefully designed program of reading and study is precisely the means to help youths acquire the learning, experience, and values that free citizens will need to make sound choices.

About this time Milton began experiencing vision problems that went well beyond the severe headaches he suffered as a child. He associated his symptoms with digestive problems and found some relief in physical exercise:

> I noticed my sight becoming weak and growing dim, and at the same time my spleen and all my viscera burdened and shaken with flatulence. And even in the morning, if I began as usual to read, I noticed that my eyes felt immediate pain deep within and turned from reading, though later refreshed after moderate bodily exercise; as often as I looked at a lamp, a sort of rainbow seemed to obscure it. Soon a mist appearing in the left part of the left eye (for that eye became clouded some years before the other) removed from my sight everything on that side.[104]

Edward Phillips states that he was "perpetually tampering with Physick" to preserve his sight (*EL* 72). His disease may have been glaucoma exacerbated by nervous tension, retinal detachment, optic neuropathy, or a pituitary tumor compressing the optic chiasm.[105] In 1644 he did not necessarily expect to become totally blind, but he surely feared that possibility as only a person whose life is centered on books could do.

The next few months brought important structural changes to the army and the church. In early December Cromwell, long dissatisfied with the conduct of the war under Essex, Manchester, and Waller, orchestrated parliament's passage of a Self-Denying Ordinance,[106] which paved the way for their honorable retirement and prepared for the "New Modeling" of the army under Sir Thomas Fairfax, ordered on February 15, 1645. The Westminster Assembly completed much of its business, recommending to parliament a national Presbyterian Church Government with classes, synods, and provincial and national assemblies. Parliament passed the requisite laws in January, 1645, but made some accommodation to Independent churches by refusing to define local congregations strictly by parish lines. The treason trial of Archbishop Laud, which began on March 12, 1644, concluded at last with his conviction and execution on January 10, 1645. But a new round of negotiations with the king which began in November, 1644 broke off in February, 1645, accomplishing nothing.[107]

Milton's *Doctrine and Discipline* continued to attract censure. The Stationers, no doubt piqued by Milton's insults in *Areopagitica*, complained to the Lords on December 28, 1644 of the "frequent printing of scandalous Books by divers, as Hesekiah Woodward and Jo. Milton," and order was taken for their examination.[108] Woodward was examined, confessed to writing "some papers" and was released on bond on December 31.[109] Milton either was not examined (there is no official record of it) or, as Cyriack Skinner claims, the judges, "whether approving the Doctrine, or not favoring his Accusers, soon dismiss'd him" (*EL* 24). A few weeks later, Daniel Featley urged the Lords and Commons to strike the "smartest strokes" against the "most damnable doctrines" of Williams and Overton as well as "a Tractate of Divorce, in which the bonds of marriage are let loose to inordinate lust."[110]

Milton probably worked on his last two divorce tracts at the same time and both were published on or before March 4, 1645. Both are unlicensed, unregistered, and without publication data, though the author is clearly identified.[111] *Tetrachordon,* named for a four-stringed Greek lyre, refers to four passages in scripture dealing with marriage and divorce which must be made to harmonize. Addressing a scholarly audience, this long, thoughtful argument of some 110 quarto pages develops a detailed exegesis of the four passages and appends testimonies that concur in some part with Milton's views. It was written, he explains, because "some friends" who were persuaded by the reasonings in his *Doctrine and Discipline* urged a more extensive discussion of the scripture proofs, while others wanted "more autorities and citations" (*CPW* II, 582). This tract is Milton's most fully developed argument on the divorce issue and related gender issues, as well as his most extensive foray into biblical exegesis before *De Doctrina Christiana.* Its argument and method are discussed on pages 185–90.

A six-page preface addresses the tract to parliament, thanking them profusely for doing nothing, despite "furious incitements," that would "give the least interruption or disrepute either to the Author, or to the Book" (579). Now, attacked publically in parliament by Palmer, Milton claims the right to clear his own "honest name" and that of his friends (581). He charges Palmer with ignorance, wickedness, and impudence. By attacking Milton he also attacks the revered Bucer, as he should have known since Milton's translation was published a week before he preached his sermon and months before it was published (580–1). Also, Palmer himself elsewhere used against the king the same natural law argument about revoking covenants that Milton used to legitimize divorce.[112] Featley's "late equivocating treatise" he condemns as a piece of "deep prelatical malignance against the present state."

Daringly, he intimates that if the marriage law is not reformed men such as himself will be justified in arranging their own divorces, if they have the "manlinesse to expostulate the right of their due ransom, and to second their own occasions" (585). He ends the preface with an indication that he is tiring of the seemingly fruitless effort – "Henceforth, except new cause be giv'n, I shall say lesse and lesse" – and a gesture to the future: "perhaps in time to come, others will know how to esteem" his argument better. Yet given parliament's "glorious changes and renovations," he hopes that England need wait "for no other Deliverers" (585).

Colasterion[113] (the name means "punishment") was published at the same time as *Tetrachordon*; it is a furious diatribe against the unlucky "cock-braind solliciter" who dared to answer *DDD* 1 (anonymously), and the "drones nest" of clergy assisting him, with a few thrusts at the licenser-cum-collaborator Caryl. Milton claims to have heard rumors for months that some group of writers was preparing a confutation of his *Doctrine and Discipline*, "but it lay . . . half a year after unfinisht in the press"; betimes he met with the occasional "by-blow" from the Presbyterian pulpit, and with the "jolly slander" (*CPW* II, 727, 722) of Prynne. The Answerer's summary argument and condescending tone obviously infuriated Milton, and he responds in kind, with a barrage of insults and rhetorical abuse justified by the title page epigraph from Proverbs 26.5: "Answer a Fool according to his folly, lest hee bee wise in his own conceit." In passing, Milton also challenges Prynne, who misrepresented him as sanctioning "Divorce at pleasure" (722), to answer him without recourse to "old and stale suppositions" and his usual "gout and dropsy of a big margent, litter'd and overlaid with crude and huddl'd quotations" (724). He also reproves the licenser, Joseph Caryl, for his gratuitous commendation and his reputed help to the ignorant Answerer, extending that reproof to his former Presbyterian colleagues who have forgotten his aid to Smectymnuus:

> When you suffer'd this nameles hangman to cast into public such a despightfull contumely upon a name and person deserving of the Church and State equally to your self, and one who hath don more to the present advancement of your own Tribe, then you or many of them have don for themselvs, you forgot to bee either honest, Religious, or discreet. (753)

Milton's rhetoric of abuse serves here, as other strategies do elsewhere, to divide the audience into those of gentle spirit who can comprehend his view of marriage, and those of servile mind who cannot. By designating the answerer as a "Servingman . . . turned Sollicitor" (726–7), Milton turns class prejudice into an effective rhetorical weapon to force that division. However, its basis is not class as such, but the qualities of mind that should accompany birth and station. When the servingman rose to be a solicitor he did not elevate his mind, whereas Milton's "gentle" readers should identify with his "gentle" sentiments:

> For how should hee, a Servingman both by nature and by function, an Idiot by breeding, and a Solliciter by presumption, ever come to know, or feel within himself, what the meaning is of gentle? . . . The Servitor would know what I mean by conversation, declaring his capacity nothing refin'd since his Law-puddering, but still the same it was in the Pantry, and at the Dresser. . . . To men of quality I have said anough, and experience confirms by daily example, that wisest, sobrest, justest men are somtimes miserably mistak'n in their chois. (741–2)

Milton's scathing tirades reveal that he takes the man's "illiterat and arrogant" treatise as a personal affront to his own status as learned scholar and gentleman. The answerer is a "Pork" unfit for disputations of Philosophy (737), an "illiterat" who mispells his Greek, Latin, and Hebrew quotations (II, 724–5), a "fleamy clodd"

(740), a "Brain-worm" and "Country Hinde," "a meer and arrant petti-fogger" (743), "a snout" for whom no language is "low and degenerat anough" (747). Milton thinks he deserves a learned opponent, and promises to answer in a very different vein "any man equal to the matter" who will dispute with "civility and faire Argument" (757–8). In *Tetrachordon* he managed an argument in that civil mode, and seemed to suggest that he was ready to give over this fight for now. But this unworthy answer evidently infuriated him and caused him to change his mind, provoking him to promise in *Colasterion* to "refuse no occasion, and avoid no adversary, either to maintane what I have begun, or to give it up for better reason" (727).

Spring and summer of 1645 brought striking changes in the nation and in Milton's household. With Cromwell as lieutenant-general under Fairfax, the New Model Army won notable victories. The Battle of Naseby (June 14) was a major turning point of the war. The king, who commanded in person, suffered a major rout with some 5,000 of his men captured, including major officers and much artillery. Also, his secret cabinet was seized, containing incriminating revelations of covert dealings with the Irish and the continental Catholic powers. Edward Phillips states – though there is no confirming evidence – that about this time there was talk of making Milton an adjutant-general in Waller's army – a post that would involve giving counsel and advice to the general.[114] But Milton took a different path. He leased a large house in the Barbican opening off Aldergate Street, with a view to expanding his school. According to Phillips he also hoped to marry again – ready, perhaps, to proclaim his own divorce as *Tetrachordon* had hinted. Nothing is known of the young woman in question beyond Phillips's report that she is "one of Dr. *Davis's* Daughters, a very Handsome and Witty Gentlewoman, but averse, it is said, to this Motion" (*EL* 66). This time, it seems, Milton sought a woman of wit.

The plan, whatever it amounted to, was circumvented by the reconciliation of Milton and Mary Powell, probably in early summer, 1645.[115] That was stage-managed, Phillips suggests, by the royalist Powells – suddenly vulnerable in the wake of the king's declining fortunes and needing the protection of a well-connected Puritan – in collaboration with Milton's relatives, the Blackboroughs. Just possibly the scheme was triggered by Milton sending Mary a bill of divorce. Phillips describes the reconciliation in terms that clearly owe a good deal to imagination and conjecture, and his evaluation of Milton's feelings and motives may be over-generous: he was then 15 years old and certainly not an eyewitness to the scene. But his is the only version we have from someone close to the event:

> The Intelligence hereof [of the proposed marriage with Miss Davis], and the then declining State of the king's Cause, and consequently of the Circumstances of Justice *Powell's* family, caused them to set all Engines on Work, to restore the late Married Woman to the Station wherein they a little before had planted her; at last this device was pitch'd upon . . . the Friends on both sides concentring in the same action though

> on different behalfs. One time above the rest, he [Milton] making the usual visit [to his relative Blackborough], the Wife was ready in another Room, and on a sudden he was surprised to see one whom he thought to have never seen more, making Submission and begging Pardon on her Knees before him; he might probably at first make some shew of aversion and rejection; but partly his own generous nature, more inclinable to Reconciliation than to perseverance in Anger and Revenge; and partly the strong intercession of Friends on both sides, soon brought him to an Act of Oblivion, and a firm League of Peace for the future. (*EL* 66–7)

However it happened, there was a reconciliation. With his big new house and expanding school, Milton needed a wife and Miss Davis was "averse" to whatever irregular proposal he may have made. The attraction Milton initially felt toward Mary was perhaps rekindled, and he no doubt hoped that she, now three years older, would prove more conformable to his ways and more conversable. Mary stayed with Isabel Webber, the mother-in-law of Milton's brother Christopher, until the new house in the Barbican was ready. There the couple would make a fresh start.

"To Know, to Utter, to Argue Freely According to Conscience"

The name Milton gave to his most considered statement on marriage, divorce, and gender, *Tetrachordon*, signifies the four strings of a Greek lyre that, sounded together properly, make a harmonious chord. This tract largely avoids the heated rhetoric and the personal animus of the other divorce tracts: by his manner and tone Milton presents himself here as a learned scholar addressing other scholars. The untranslated Greek epigraph from Euripides's *Medea* on the title page specifically invites such an audience: "For if thou bring strange wisdom unto dullards / Useless thou shalt be counted as not wise / And if thy fame outshine those heretofore / Held wise, thou shalt be odious in men's eyes."[116] In the preface Milton presents himself as citizen–adviser to the parliament and casts its members as part of his learned audience, reminding them that "in the right reformation of a Common-wealth" domestic suffering should be addressed first (*CPW* II, 585). He retells yet once more the story of his engagement with the topic of divorce, thanking parliament profusely for protecting him from the "rash vulgar" and from his vociferous clerical critics, Palmer, Featley, and others. He excoriates those critics for meeting his pleas for a reasoned answer to his argument with "undervaluing silence," or "a rayling word or two" (583), noting that such treatment threatens all learning: if "his diligence, his learning, his elocution . . . shall be turn'd now to a disadvantage and suspicion against him . . . why are men bred up with such care and expence to a life of perpetual studies" (584)

The title page indicates the work's scope, and its intended support to the argument of *The Doctrine and Discipline of Divorce.*[117] The genre is biblical exegesis: "Expositions upon the foure chief places in Scripture." Offered as a "plain and Christian *Talmud*" (635), the tract quotes and analyzes the relevant Bible passages dealing with marriage and divorce, drawing extensively on the Hebraic exegetical tradition without citing specific names, and on a few Christian exegetes. It restates and clarifies Milton's basic arguments for divorce, strengthens his interpretations of the biblical texts, and advances some new positions. But his most persuasive argument is conveyed by the expanded explanation of his ideal of marriage as a union of minds and spirits, and by his insistence that every ordinance, and most especially marriage law, must be interpreted by the overarching principle of charity and human good: "it is not the stubborn letter must govern us, but the divine and softning breath of charity which turns and windes the dictat of every positive command, and shapes it to the good of mankind" (604–5).

He treats the Genesis texts first (Genesis 1:27–8; 2:18–24), to define "what was Mariage in the beginning . . . and what from hence to judge of nullity, or divorce" (614). From them he concludes that man created in the image of God is invested with liberty, so that "no ordinance human or from heav'n can binde against the good of man" (588); that God sought by marriage to remedy loneliness, "the first thing which Gods eye nam'd not good"; that he instituted marriage "like to a man deliberating," and thereby "according to naturall reason, not impulsive command" (595); and that, in consequence, spouses unfitted for that "civil and religious concord, which is the inward essence of wedlock" (605) either were never married or else their marriages automatically dissolve. A new argument reinterprets the phrase "one flesh," referring it not to sexual consummation but rather, in monist terms, to the union of minds that is necessary to produce physical union: "Wee know that flesh can neither joyn, nor keep together two bodies of it self; what is it then must make them one flesh, but likenes, but fitness of mind and disposition, which may breed the Spirit of concord, and union between them?"[118]

Commenting on Deuteronomy 24:1–2, the Mosaic permission to divorce, Milton elaborates two issues he treated earlier. First, "the current of all antiquity both Jewish and Christian" defines this as "a just and pure Law," not simply a custom or a dispensation. Second, "uncleanness" does not mean adultery but, rather, according to expositors who "began to understand the Hebrew Text," as any "nakedness" (II, 621) of mind or body preventing participation in the loving society which marriage should be. This law of God, he argues, agrees with the institution of marriage in Genesis and is consonant with that law of nature that teaches us to avoid self-destruction; it frees the afflicted from sexual slavery and injury (626), it offers mercy when the marriage is "really brokn, or else was really never joyn'd" (632), and it rescues children from a marriage marked by wrath and perturbation. He also denies that it will breed license or much confusion. There will be inevitable abuses, but God would rather have the law look "with pitty upon the difficulties of his own, then with rigor upon the boundlesse riots of them who serv another Maister" (634).

Turning to Matthew 5:31–2 and 19:2–11, he now accounts more adequately for the difficulties those texts pose. He clarifies the status of the Mosaic Law for Christians: the ceremonial and that part of the judicial law which is "meerely *judaicall*" (i.e. pertaining to the Jews alone) are abrogated for them, but the part that pertains to morality (as divorce law surely does) is part of the enduring natural law and cannot be abrogated (II, 642–3). That Mosaic law of divorce also accords with the gospel rule of charity, defined in humanistic terms: "the great and almost only commandment of the Gospel, is to command nothing against the good of man" (638–9). As well, Milton now finds a more useful interpretation for Christ's term, "hardness of heart." He repeats his former explanation, that Christ used that phrase to rebuke the Pharisee questioners who had abused the Mosiac law by divorcing for frivolous reasons; to them he offered "nott so much a teaching, as an intangling" (642). But now Milton also applies that phrase to all postlapsarian humanity, whose fallenness gave rise to the "*secondary law of nature and of nations*" that is the sanction for many necessary but imperfect human institutions:

> Partly for this hardnesse of heart, the imperfection and decay of man from original righteousnesse, it was that God suffer'd not divorce onely, but all that which by Civilians is term'd the *secondary law of nature and of nations*. He suffer'd his own people to wast and spoyle and slay by warre, to lead captives, to be som maisters, som servants, some to be princes, others to be subjects, hee suffer'd propriety to divide all things . . . some to bee undeservedly rich, others to bee undeservingly poore. All which till hardnesse of heart came in, was most unjust; whenas prime nature made us all equall. . . . If therefore we abolish divorce as only suffer'd for hardnes of heart, we may as well abolish the whole law of nations, as only sufferd for the same cause.[119]

Because of this universal hardness of heart, marriage cannot now be the perfect and therefore indissoluble union Christ pointed to when he declared, "in the beginning it was not so":

> While man and woman were both perfet each to other, there needed no divorce; but when they both degenerated to imperfection, & oft times grew to be an intolerable evil each to other, then law more justly did permitt the alienating of that evil which mistake made proper. . . . [Now] the rule of perfection is not so much that which was don in the beginning, as that which now is nearest to the rule of charity. (665, 667)

In *Tetrachordon* Milton also gives a more comprehensive exposition than before of the term "fornication," accommodating it to his argument according to two understandings of the term. If it means adultery, as most think, then Christ here forbids divorce for offenses *less* than adultery and does not even address the "natural unmeetnes" – much more serious than adultery – which always dissolves marriage. But a sounder meaning is provided in the Hebrew Bible and its commentaries, where fornication means sometimes whoredom, often idolatry, and at times Miltonic incompatibility: "a constant alienation and disaffection of mind . . . when to be a tolerable wife is either naturally not in their power, or obstinatly not in their will" (673). He explains that in the use of this word and often elsewhere the evangelist "Hebraizes" – perhaps because God intended that expositors to "acknowledge Gods ancient people their betters" (671) and recognize that without the oriental dialects they were liable to err. He admits, however, that he cannot explain why Christ calls those who marry after divorce adulterers, but he is so persuaded every biblical prescription must be measured in terms of human good, that he is prepared in hard cases to give over the letter entirely: Christ may have meant to challenge good men "to expound him in this place, as in all other his precepts, not by the written letter, but by that unerring paraphrase of Christian love and Charity, which is the summe of all commands, and the perfection" (677–8).

The last text, Paul's dictum that a Christian may divorce a departing infidel (1 Corinthians 7:10–16), Milton reads as a blanket permission to Christians to divorce a heretical or idolatrous or grossly profane spouse. Then, noting that expositors often stretch this text to cover cases of marital desertion, he redefines it in his own terms, to include "any hainous default against the main ends of matrimony . . . not only a local absence but an intolerable society" (691).

Tetrachordon also clarifies the wife's status in marriage and divorce. With the aid of Paul, Milton interprets Genesis 1:27, "In the image of God created he him," as decisive evidence of gender hierarchy in the creation:

> Had the Image of God bin equally common to them both, it had no doubt bin said, in the image of God created he them. But *St Paul* ends the controversie by explaining that the woman is not primarily and immediatly the image of God, but in reference to the man. . . . Neverthelesse man is not to hold her as a servant, but receives her into a part of that empire which God proclaims him to, though not equally, yet largely, as his own image and glory: for it is no small glory to him, that a creature so like him should be made subject to him. (589)

Now, however, he explicitly recognizes, as he did not before, the wife's right to divorce an unfit husband, locating it in her "proportional" share in the image of God and her Christian liberty as one of Christ's redeemed. She can claim that right also by the Pauline permission to divorce an infidel, and so by extension any wicked mate: "the wife also . . . being her self the redeem'd of Christ, is not still bound to be the vassall of him, who is the bondslave of Satan . . . but hath recours to the wing of charity and protection of the Church" (591). Then, by a radical redefinition of the term "deserting infidel," Milton extends to the wife the right to divorce any unfit spouse:

> That man or wife who hates in wedloc, is perpetually unsociable, unpeacefull, or unduteous, either not being able, or not willing to performe what the maine ends of mariage demand in helpe and solace . . . is worse then an infidel. . . . The blamelesse person therefore hath as good a plea to sue out his delivery from this bondage, as from the desertion of an infidel. (691)

Yet how such divorce is to be managed remains ambiguous. Milton does not, as before, place all decisions categorically in the male head of household, but leaves them to the private consciences of the man and the woman. Though they should abide by Christ's caveat against divorce for light causes, they could in practice divorce for any cause by mutual consent. But Milton does not suggest any mechanism by which a wife, against her husband's wishes, could act on the rights he now accords her.

The tract concludes with a historical survey that reviews the status of divorce in law and theory from early Christian times to the present. Characteristically, Milton offers this parade of theologians and legal theorists only to satisfy "the weaker sort" who rely on authority. He claims that these authorities have "tended toward" his position, but asserts, characteristically, that he is yet "something first" in producing a full-scale treatment of this topic (693). And again he flatly denies that these authorities have influenced him: "God, I solemnly attest him, withheld from my knowledge the consenting judgement of these men so late, untill they could not bee my instructers, but only my unexpected witnesses to partial men" (716).

Milton's emphasis in *Tetrachordon* on the fallenness of all human institutions may be a first step toward forgiving both himself and Mary. Though he expounds the Genesis creation story as grounding man's right to divorce securely on "that indeleble character of priority which God crown'd him with" (589–90), yet the Genesis terms for what a wife ought to be – "*another self, a second self, a very self it self*" (600) – prompt Milton to complicate his view of female nature and gender norms. One description of a wife seems to relegate her to the domestic sphere: "in the Scriptures, and in the gravest Poets and Philosophers I finde the properties and excellencies of a wife set out only from domestic virtues" (613). Yet, significantly, he does not call up the usual list of womanly virtues: silence, chastity, obedience and good housewifery. Instead, responding to the "crabbed opinion" of Augustine that for all purposes other than procreation God might better have created a male companion for Adam (597), and perhaps to the quip of the "rank serving man" that Milton expects a wife to speak Hebrew, Greek, Latin, and French and be able to dispute Canon law, he constructs the image of a joyous, lighthearted, intelligent companion who will share and give delight to the leisure all men need after arduous labor:

> No mortall nature can endure either in the actions of Religion, or study of wisdome, without somtime slackning the cords of intense thought and labour. . . . We cannot therefore alwayes be contemplative, or pragmaticall abroad, but have need of som delightfull intermissions, wherin the enlarg'd soul may leav off a while her severe

> schooling; and like a glad youth in wandring vacancy, may keep her hollidaies to joy and harmles pastime: which as she cannot well doe without company, so in no company so well as where the different sexe in most resembling unlikenes, and most unlike resemblance cannot but please best and be pleas'd in the aptitude of that variety. (596–7)

This formulation seems an unfortunate restriction of the ideal of "fit conversation," but it is worth noting that Milton's examples are Wisdom playing before the Almighty (Proverbs 8), and the "ravishment and erring fondness" in wedded leisures described in the Song of Songs (597).[120]

Milton knew some women capable of more than intelligent playfulness. Sonnet IX praised a studious, religious young woman, actual or ideal, who devoted herself to the things of the mind and the spirit. Sonnet X praised his married friend Lady Margaret Ley as the remarkable embodiment of her father's noble virtues. He comes close to rethinking gender roles in *Tetrachordon* when, probably thinking of such cases, he allows for "particular exceptions" to the norms of marital hierarchy: "if she exceed her husband in prudence and dexterity, and he contentedly yeeld . . . a superior and more naturall law comes in, that the wiser should govern the lesse wise, whether male or female" (589). As early as Prolusion VI he was ready to challenge stereotypes of masculinity in defence of his own values and lifestyle; and in the divorce tracts he is led by common experience, and his own experience, to challenge conventional assumptions about love, sex, marriage, and adultery, and to recognize how social customs and constraints militate against choosing a mate wisely. Experience also led him to formulate this exception to gender hierarchy for superior women but, as the terms of his formulation indicate, he cannot break free of the ideology of hierarchy, which must sabotage his companionate ideal, to embrace the gender equality which alone could realize it. That concept had to await another century.

Milton's most literary and most enduring tract, *Areopagitica*, transforms the Renaissance genre of "Advice to Princes" into a republican advice to a council or senate. He links the concept of civic humanism rooted in classical republicanism to the Puritan prophetic vision of England as a New Israel, challenging parliament and the English people to realize that ideal at this propitious historical moment. Specifically, they should replace their new licensing ordinance for the pre-publication censorship of books with one simply requiring the name of the publisher and/or author and guaranteeing copyright. The liberty he proposes is far-reaching but not absolute: his metaphor of the censor as a cross-legged Juno preventing a birth offers to protect manuscripts at delivery but assumes that after they emerge they can and should fend for themselves in the marketplace of ideas.[121] Like humans they may be prosecuted for libel and "mischief" (apparently scandal and sedition), after publication and by due legal process (*CPW* II, 491, 569).

Milton's anti-licensing position also involves tolerating religious dissent, so Milton's tract draws upon and contributes to the lively controversy about religious toleration in 1644. Unlike Roger Williams who proposed complete religious toleration, for Milton the sticking point was Roman Catholicism: "I mean not tolerated Popery, and open superstition, which as it extirpats all religions and civil supremacies, so it self should be extirpat" (565). In the divided Europe of the Thirty Years War, he cannot imagine Catholics who are not a political threat to England; also, by placing papal authority above the individual conscience, Catholicism denies the free exercise of choice that Milton sees as the cornerstone of all religion and ethics. His tolerationist argument would protect everyone's liberty of conscience and most Protestant religious practice, but not the open practice of "popish" idolatry or "that which is impious or evil absolutely either against faith or maners" (565) – a phrase that retains some role for the magistrate in religious matters. It might refer to Ranter doctrine and sexual practices, and perhaps to the Antinomian Familists' supposed promotion of sexual promiscuity. Behind this reservation of power to the magistrates might lie the rabbinic concept of natural law as embodied in the so-called Noachide laws imposed by God on all humankind and thought to include prohibitions on blasphemy and idolatry.[122]

The title, alluding to the written oration presented by Isocrates to the Ecclesia or popular assembly of Athens on the subject of the powers exercised by the Areopagus, the Court of the Wise,[123] identifies Milton's tract as a deliberative oration. He self-consciously takes on the role of the Greek orator Isocrates, "who from his private house wrote that discourse to the Parlament of *Athens*, that perswades them to change the forme of *Democraty* which was then establisht" (489). Addressing his tract to the "High Court of Parlament," Milton offers to advise them as to "what might be done better" to advance the public good and promote liberty (486–8), making here his most overt and artful claim to the role of citizen–adviser to the state. His terms import the ethos of Athenian democracy, hinting that London has become a new Athens, a center of vibrant political and cultural life; in Milton's "speech" we hear echoes of Pericles's funeral oration celebrating Athenian democracy. But Milton expects his literate reader to recognize that his proposals for reform stand in direct opposition to those of Isocrates and Plato because they are based on a different ethics and politics. Isocrates proposed that the Areopagus reform Athenian morals by reinstating censorship over citizens' activities, and Plato proposed in the *Republic* and the *Laws* to banish most literature lest it corrupt a virtuous citizenry. Milton insists that only reading of all kinds, forcing the continuous, free, and active choice between good and evil, will allow the good to advance in virtue and truth to vanquish error, thereby producing rational citizens with a developed Protestant conscience and a classical sense of civic duty. Milton may be the first to address directly the issue of how to construct a liberty-loving republican citizenry who will support radical reform. *Areopagitica* validates and defends the emerging public sphere, the marketplace of ideas open to ordinary citizens, that was being created in revolutionary England by the deluge of pamphlets and newsbooks.[124]

In this tract Milton does not speak of himself as a poet, but he embodies that role throughout, in a poetic style vibrant with striking images and figures, little allegories, small narratives. Often these derive from epic and romance. Milton constructs citizen–readers and writers who are engaged in "Wars of Truth," which involve combat and danger, heroic adventures and trials, constant struggles, difficult quests, and which stimulate intellectual energy and cultural vibrancy. Moreover, as David Norbrook observes, the allusive, literary character of this tract and its sublimity of style give the lie to royalist claims that the revolution's democratizing impulses will level and degrade culture.[125] On his title page Milton includes an epigraph taken from Euripides's *The Suppliant Women*, identifying his own "speech" to the English parliament with Theseus's speech defending Athenian democracy and its freedom of speech against Theban tyranny:

> This is true Liberty when free born men
> Having to advise the public may speak free,
> Which he who can, and will, deserv's high praise,
> Who neither can nor will, may hold his peace;
> What can be juster in a State then this?[126]

Milton saw his self-image as a virtuous and learned citizen–author compromised by prior censorship, which undermines the autonomy and authority that role demands. He describes the demeaning constraints of censorship in language charged with resentment and frustration founded on personal experience:

> What advantage is it to be a man over it is to be a boy at school . . . if serious and elaborat writings, as if they were no more then the theam of a Grammar lad under his Pedagogue must not be utter'd without the cursory eyes of a temporizing and extemporizing licencer. . . . When a man writes to the world, he summons up all his reason and deliberation to assist him; he searches, meditats, is industrious, and likely consults and confers with his judicious friends; after all which done he takes himself to be inform'd in what he writes, as well as any that writ before him; if in this most consummat act of his fidelity and ripenesse, no years, no industry, no former proof of his abilities can bring him to that state of maturity, as not to be still mistrusted and suspected, unlesse [he appear] . . . with . . . his censors hand on the back of his title to be his bayl and surety, that he is no idiot, or seducer, it cannot be but a dishonor and derogation to the author, to the book, to the priviledge and dignity of Learning. (531–2)

As a further insult, an author who wishes to make changes in press must "trudge again to his leav-giver," often many times, or else allow the book to come forth "wors then he had made it, which to a diligent writer is the greatest melancholy and vexation that can befall." He queries angrily,

> How can a man teach with autority, which is the life of teaching, how can he be a Doctor in his book as he ought to be, or else had better be silent, whenas all he

> teachers, all he delivers, is but under the tuition, under the correction of his patriarchal licencer to blot or alter . . . I hate a pupil teacher, I endure not an instructer that comes to me under the wardship of an overseeing fist. (532–3)

He invokes some authorities here, especially those calculated to impress parliament: Paolo Sarpi, Lord Brooke, Bacon, and especially Selden – "one of your own now sitting in Parlament, the chief of learned men reputed in this Land" (II, 513) – noting that Selden's *De Juri Naturali* defends the Talmudic method of collating all opinions, including errors.[127] Also, by emphasizing his exchanges with the Italian literati and Galileo he reinforces his own status as a respected scholar who can speak to the censorship issue from a cosmopolitan perspective (537–9).

The tract retains the parts of a deliberative oration: an exordium praising parliament for its reformations to date and its willingness to accept advice, a partition, four arguments, and a long peroration. The first argument – the evil origins of censorship – is historical and often satiric. Representing censorship as papist in origin and in essence because it suppresses liberty of conscience, he links to Roman Catholicism not only the "apishly Romanizing" Laud and Charles I, but also the Presbyterian supporters of the new censorship law. At one point he turns the censorship process into a satiric pantomime played out on the title pages of licensed treatises, in sharp contrast to his own title page and its Euripidean celebration of free speech: "Sometimes 5 *Imprimaturs* are seen together dialogue-wise in the Piatza of one Title page, complementing and ducking each to other with their shav'n reverences, whether the Author, who stands by in perplexity at the foot of his Epistle, shall to the Press or to the spunge" (504). But he begins this argument in the heroic register, personifying books as living author–heroes, the prodigiously active and admittedly sometimes dangerous essence of master-spirits:

> Books . . . are as lively, and as vigorously productive, as those fabulous Dragons teeth; and being sown up and down, may chance to spring up armed men. And yet, on the other hand unlesse warinesse be us'd, as good almost kill a Man as kill a good Book; who kills a Man kills a reasonable creature, Gods Image; but hee who destroyes a good Booke, kills reason it selfe, kills the Image of God, as it were in the eye . . . a good Booke is the pretious life-blood of a master-spirit, imbalm'd and treasur'd up on purpose to a life beyond life. (492–3)

He warns against subjecting such spirits to "persecution" or "martyrdom," or even – should the whole impression be distroyed – to "a kinde of massacre." Sharon Achinstein notes that by offering two versions of the trial of books – by censors or by the public – Milton builds choice into his very rhetoric, helping thereby to construct the readers and citizens he wants and the republic needs.[128]

The second argument, that the virtuous can only profit by reading all kinds of books, begins with a comparison of books to food, which is freed from all legal restrictions under the gospel and regulated only by reason and temperance. Milton extends that freedom to whatever enters into the mind, proposing an ethics based on continuous, reasoned choices between good and evil, "For reason is but choosing" (527). He portrays those choices in epic-romance imagery of difficult trials, athletic contests, and heroic warfare, with Spenser's Guyon as model:

> Good and evill we know in the field of this World grow up together almost inseparably; and the knowledge of good is so involv'd and interwoven with the knowledge of evill, and in so many cunning resemblances hardly to be discern'd, that those confused seeds which were impos'd on *Psyche* as an incessant labour to cull out, and sort asunder, were not more intermixt. . . . And perhaps this is that doom which *Adam* fell into of knowing good and evill, that is to say of knowing good by evill. As therefore the state of man now is; what wisdome can there be to choose, what continence to forbeare without the knowledge of evill? He that can apprehend and consider vice with all her baits and seeming pleasures, and yet abstain, and yet distinguish, and yet prefer that which is truly better, he is the true warfaring Christian. I cannot praise a fugitive and cloister'd vertue, unexercis'd & unbreath'd, that never sallies out and sees her adversary, but slinks out of the race, where that immortall garland is to be run for, not without dust and heat. Assuredly we bring not innocence into the world, we bring impurity much rather: that which purifies us is triall, and triall is by what is contrary. That vertue therefore which is but a youngling in the contemplation of evill, and knows not the utmost that vice promises to her followers, and rejects it, is but a blank vertue, not a pure; her whitenesse is but an excrementall whitenesse; Which was the reason why our sage and serious Poet *Spencer,* whom I dare be known to think a better teacher than *Scotus* or *Aquinas*, describing true temperance under the person of *Guion*, brings him in with his palmer through the cave of Mammon, and the bowr of earthly blisse that he might see and know, and yet abstain.[129]

Bad books allow a judicious reader precisely the vicarious experience of vice and error that he needs to live virtuously in this world: "how can we more safely, and with lesse danger scout into the regions of sin and falsity then by reading all manner of tractats, and hearing all manner of reason?" (516–17). As for the weak and ignorant, they may be exhorted to forbear reading dangerous books, but they cannot be compelled.

The third argument, that censorship cannot promote virtue and good manners, is developed partly by a *reductio ad absurdum* enumeration of all the other practices regulators would have to control – all recreation, pastimes, music, eating, dressing, and social activities – and partly by an insistence that men good enough to be licensers would not want the job. More important, Milton insists that choice must be the foundation of the political order as it is of ethics.[130] The fanciful utopias of Plato, Bacon, and More are, like sequestered virtue, useless: England cannot "sequester out of the world into *Atlantick* and *Eutopian* polities," but must perforce strive "to ordain wisely as in this world of evill, in the midd'st whereof God hath plac't us unavoidably" (526). Even in Eden, Milton supposed that virtue was dependent on continual trial and resistance to temptation:

> Many there be that complain of divin Providence for suffering *Adam* to transgresse, foolish tongues! when God gave him reason, he gave him freedom to choose, for reason is but choosing . . . God therefore left him free, set before him a provoking object, ever almost in his eyes; herein consisted his merit, herein the right of his reward, the praise of his abstinence. Wherefore did he creat passions within us, pleasures round about us, but that these rightly temper'd are the very ingredients of virtu? (527)

Confident that his core ethical principle is also God's, he gives short shrift to Puritan efforts to force outward conformity on the wicked: "God sure esteems the growth and compleating of one vertuous person, more then the restraint of ten vitious" (528).

The fourth argument describes how censorship harms church and state by its affront to learned men, to learning, and to truth itself. That affront extends to "every knowing person" alive or dead: to the common people who are supposed "giddy, vitious, and ungrounded," unable to be trusted with an English pamphlet (536); and to ministers whose flocks are thought to be so ill-taught that "the whiffe of every new pamphlet should stagger them out of thir catechism" (537). Their repressive mindset makes Presbyterians no better than the bishops, and augurs ill for the future: those who "startle thus betimes at a meer unlicens'd pamphlet will after a while be afraid of every conventicle, and a while after will make a conventicle of every Christian meeting" (541). Milton reminds those who decry heresy that faith thrives by exercise, not passive acceptance, and that by sound Protestant principles "A man may be a heretick in the truth" if he takes on implicit faith what his pastor tells him (543). He meets the outcry against sects and schisms with a striking poetic passage that produces an entire reversal of terms. Religious truth is not a unified body at risk from divisive forces, but is already a dismembered and scattered body – a female Osiris figure, evoking also the image of persecuted martyrs. The labors of all questing scholarly adventurers are required to bring the parts together, a process that cannot be finished until the Second Coming:

> Truth indeed came once into the world with her divine Master, and was a perfect shape . . . [but later] arose a wicked race of deceivers, who as that story goes of the *Ægyptian Typhon* with his conspirators, how they dealt with the good *Osiris*, took the virgin Truth, hewd her lovely form into a thousand peeces, and scatter'd them to the four winds. From that time ever since, the sad friends of Truth, such as durst appear, imitating the carefull search that *Isis* made for the mangl'd body of *Osiris*, went up and down gathering up limb by limb still as they could find them. We have not yet found them all, Lords and Commons, nor ever shall doe, till her Masters second comming. . . . Suffer not these licencing prohibitions to stand at every place of opportunity forbidding and disturbing them that continue seeking, that continue to do our obsequies to the torn body of our martyr'd Saint. We boast our light; but if we look not wisely on the Sun it self, it smites us into darkness . . . The light which we have gain'd, was giv'n us, not to be ever staring on, but by it to discover onward things more remote from our knowledge. (549–50)

The long poetic peroration appeals in rousing terms to the patriotism and reformist goals of the "Lords and Commons of England," who ought to recognize and nurture an English citizenry that is politically aware and active, not a slavish, conformist rabble as in the Catholic nations: "consider what Nation it is whereof ye are, and whereof ye are the governours: a Nation not slow and dull, but of a quick, ingenious, and piercing spirit, acute to invent, subtle and sinewy to discourse, not beneath the reach of any point the highest that human capacity can soar to" (551). Milton sketches a history in which God's calls to reformation have regularly come "first to his English-men" (553), and he claims that now, "by all concurrence of signs," England is at another such climactic moment, with parliament as the agency by which the elect nation can advance its hitherto "slow-moving" Reformation (565) and fulfill its destiny. They must recognize that conflict and seeming schism may have regenerative, not tragic, consequences: "Where there is much desire to learn, there of necessity will be much arguing, much writing, many opinions; for opinion in good men is but knowledge in the making" (554). In this hopeful peroration Truth is also refigured, with Spenser again providing some terms. Truth is not now a dismembered virgin but an unconquerable Amazon, a Britomart:

> Though all the windes of doctrin were let loose to play upon the earth, so Truth be in the field, we do injuriously by licensing and prohibiting to misdoubt her strength. Let her and Falshood grapple; who ever knew Truth put to the wors, in a free and open encounter. . . . Who knows not that Truth is strong next to the Almighty; she needs no policies, nor stratatems, nor licencings to make her victorious, those are the shifts and defences that error uses against her power. (561–3)

If bound by licensers she may, like Proteus, turn herself into false shapes, yet her own nature has something of Proteus in it, since "She may have more shapes then one".[131]

At this auspicious, reforming moment Milton again claims the role of prophet: "When God shakes a Kingdome with strong and healthfull commotions to a generall reforming," he calls "men of rare abilities," like Milton, to discover new truths (566). Now, however, Milton does not see himself as a solitary voice crying in the wilderness as in the divorce tracts, but as a participant in a lively, though widely dispersed, scholarly community. Even when London was under siege such men – including, he implies, himself – were "disputing, reasoning, reading, inventing, discoursing, ev'n to a rarity, and admiration, things not before discourst or writt'n of" (557). London is also a prophetic milieu: Milton portrays it as a City of Refuge (Numbers 35:11–24) in an England that is becoming a Nation of Prophets (Numbers 11:29), thereby fulfilling Moses' desire that "not only our sev'nty Elders, but all the Lords people are become Prophets" (555–6). These texts may carry millenarian overtones, but Milton no longer seems to think that Christ's Second Coming is imminent: his focus is on the transformations needed now. And, as always for Milton, the mode of prophecy is not sudden supernatural illumination but painstaking scholarship and authorship:

> Behold now this vast City; a City of refuge, the mansion-house of liberty . . . there be pens and heads there, sitting by their studious lamps, musing, searching, revolving new notions and ideas wherewith to present, as with their homage and their fealty the approaching Reformation: others as fast reading, trying all things, assenting to the force of reason and convincement. . . . What wants there . . . but wise and faithfull labourers, to make a knowing people, a Nation of Prophets, of Sages, and of Worthies.[132]

These resonant Hebraic images figure England as a New Israel that eschews uniformity for a higher unity. City and nation are made up of many men studying and writing in their private chambers but through their books actively engaging with one another – a sharp iconographic contrast to the royalist figure of the body politic as one man with body and limbs subservient to the monarchical head, or to the later Hobbesian figure of the sovereign containing all other bodies. Similarly, the church is figured in terms of building the Lord's Temple, a process requiring "many schisms and many dissections made in the quarry and in the timber," so that the stones are laid artfully together, "contiguous" but not cemented (555).

Then, taking on the voice of the poet–prophet as he did in *Of Reformation* and *Animadversions*, Milton envisions England under the metaphors of the awakening Samson or an eagle renewed to youth and power:

> Methinks I see in my mind a noble and puissant Nation rousing herself like a strong man after sleep, and shaking her invincible locks: Methinks I see her as an Eagle muing her mighty youth, and kindling her undazl'd eyes at the full midday beam; purging and unscaling her long abused sight at the fountain it self of heav'nly radiance. (557–8)

In ringing, vehement tones, Milton proclaims in this tract his own need and right to participate in the national and religious renewal: "Give me the liberty to know, to utter, and to argue freely according to conscience, above all liberties" (560).

7

"Service . . . Between Private Walls" 1645–1649

During 1645–9 Milton attended chiefly to his concerns as poet, schoolmaster, scholar, and head of a growing family. Reporting on this period in his *Defensio Secunda* (1654), he claims that, until the king's trial, he felt no need to address the issue of civil liberty as a complement to his treatises on ecclesiastical and domestic liberty, since "it was being adequately dealt with by the magistrates" (*CPW* IV.1, 626). That retrospective account elides his mounting disillusion with the course of reform and with the Long Parliament. He does, however, implicitly criticize that parliament's failure to honor and make use of his gifts and his counsel, observing that he gained nothing from his former services to church and state save the enjoyment of "a good conscience, good repute among good men, and this honorable freedom of speech" (627). He states also that his finances were strained by wartime taxes and withheld revenues:

> Other men gained for themselves advantages, other men secured offices at no cost to themselves. As for me, no man has ever seen me seeking office, no man has ever seen me soliciting aught through my friends, clinging with suppliant expression to the doors of Parliament, or loitering in the hallways of the lower assemblies. I kept myself at home for the most part, and from my own revenues, though often they were in large part withheld because of the civil disturbance [probably the continued legal controversies over the Powell properties], I endured the tax – by no means entirely just – that was laid on me and maintained my frugal way of life. (627)

During these years of withdrawal from the arena of polemic combat, Milton collected and published his early poems and brought several scholarly enterprises to partial or substantial completion: a manual on grammar and another on logic, a geographical and historical account of Russia, and a history of early Britain. When he published his early poems late in 1645, he evidently supposed, now that the fortunes of war had shifted to parliament's side and the end of armed conflict was in sight, that this was a likely moment to take up his poetic vocation again and, as he had recommended in the *Reason of Church-Government*,[1] to provide a reforming society with some of the good art needed to help form its culture. He had reason to expect a period of quiet for poetic activity, but anxieties over the state of reformation in the country and frustrations at home as his household was overrun by his Powell in-laws kept him from producing much new verse. He had time for the Muses in these years, but his circumstances did not allow for the leisurely play of ideas and the focused concentration he needed for writing poems of some scope. But he continued to experiment boldly with the sonnet genre, producing an epigram-sonnet of friendship to Henry Lawes, an epitaph-sonnet on Catherine Thomason, three political sonnets in the satiric mode – two on his divorce tracts, and a *sonetto caudato* or "tailed" sonnet of 20 lines on religious repression – and a political sonnet to Fairfax in the heroic register, mixing praise with advice.

As the king was brought to trial, condemned, and executed in December, 1648 and January, 1649, Milton was galvanized to polemic activity again. Drawing on his extensive studies of ancient and modern history and politics, he sought to challenge and educate his countrymen to seize this unprecedented opportunity to secure their liberties in a free commonwealth. Milton more than most illustrates Hobbes's comment ascribing the overthrow of the English monarchy to classically educated men whose studies of Tacitus, Livy, Sallust, Cicero, and others persuaded them that the best and noblest form of government is an aristocratic republic:

> There were an exceeding great number of Men of the better sort, that had been so educated, as that in their youth having read the Books written by famous men of the Antient *Grecian* and *Roman* Commonwealths, concerning their Polity and great Actions, in which Book[s] the Popular Government was extold by that glorious Name of Liberty, and Monarchy disgraced by the Name of Tyranny: they became thereby in love with their form of Government.[2]

"The Extremely Turbulent State of Our Britain"

During the summer of 1645 Milton prepared to move to his large new house at number 17, the Barbican, a short street off Aldersgate Street (plate 6).[3] It was only a few minutes' walk from the house he was leaving. He took up residence there in September or early October, along with his wife, his father, now 82, and the pupils already with him – John and Edward Phillips, Cyriack Skinner, and perhaps one or two more.[4] Two other students came soon: Thomas Gardiner of Essex (about 17) and Richard Barry, second Earl of Barrymore (about 15), who was sent to him by his aunt and Milton's friend, Katherine Jones, Viscountess Ranelagh.[5] There may have been a few others, but Edward Phillips comments that "the accession of scholars was not great."[6]

As Milton negotiated his move, the tide had turned against the king. The Battle of Naseby, June 14, 1645, was the beginning of the end. In Scotland the royalist troops under the Earl of Montrose and major general Alaster Macdonald MacColkittoch had taken much of the country, but on September 13 the Scots Presbyterian forces decisively defeated the royalists at Philiphaugh. Parliament's forces won a succession of victories in the North, and by the middle of October the New Model Army under Fairfax and Cromwell had forced what remained of the royalist troops in the West and Southwest into Devon and Cornwall. The king returned to Oxford on November 5 and during the winter could observe his enemies gradually closing in on him.

Even before moving house Milton probably began to arrange for the publication of his poems, and on October 6 the bookseller Humphrey Moseley registered the volume with the Stationers.[7] Moseley's preface to Milton's *Poems* declares his intention to publish *belles lettres* rather than the more popular and "more vendible" political pamphlets, in an effort to "renew the wonted honour and esteem of our English tongue." He states that he sought out these poems: "The Authors more peculiar excellency in these [poetic] studies, was too well known to conceal his Papers, or to keep me from attempting to sollicit them from him."[8] He may have done so, encouraged as he claimed to be by the "courteous" reception given to "Mr. Wallers late choice Peeces" which he had published a few months earlier. Milton was no doubt pleased to find a publisher committed to poetry, and he apparently saw the war's hopeful turn as a proper moment to publish. Moseley did not yet, but soon would, have a list dominated by royalist and Cavalier verse.[9] He underscores Waller's court connections but the title he supplied, *Poems, &c. Written by Mr. Ed. Waller . . . lately a Member of the Honourable House of Commons*, presents him as the parliament supporter he was before he was mixed up in a royalist plot.[10] Over the next two months Milton made corrections, read proof, and had his portrait engraved by William Marshall for the frontispiece. It was not flattering, and Milton registered his displeasure in a satiric epigram under it, as well as a comment in the *Pro Se Defensio* (1655) stating that he had bowed to "the suggestion and solicitation of a bookseller" and allowed himself "to be crudely engraved by an unskillful engraver because there was no other in the city at that time."[11] Moseley's preface, the portrait, and the title page with its emphasis on Milton's connection with Henry Lawes, "Gentleman of the Kings Chappel, and one of his Maiesties Private Musick," are at some odds with the reformed poetics and politics conveyed by Milton's organization and emphases in the volume. The complex gestures of self-representation in Milton's first formal presentation of himself to his countrymen as a poet are analyzed on pages 226–8.

It is likely that Milton sent Henry Lawes a presentation copy of the *Poems,* along with his sonnet to Lawes dated February 9, 1645 (1646) and titled in the Trinity manuscript "To my freind Mr. Hen. Laws."[12] By that title and style of address – "Harry," not Lawes or even Henry – Milton claimed the status of familiar friend.

He thereby removed this commendatory poem from the realm of politics and established personal terms for its inclusion in Lawes's 1648 volume, which he dedicated with heartfelt emotion to the then defeated and imprisoned king.[13] In praising Lawes as the "first" in England to set a poet's lyrics "with just note & accent," Milton's sonnet exaggerates somewhat, though many contemporaries agreed that his settings "best" honored the English tongue and Lawes later made the same claims for himself, somewhat more modestly.[14] Lawes along with some others in his generation produced settings that eschewed harmony and counterpoint in favor of recitative and declamatory song, accommodating musical stress and quantity to verbal values so as to set off the poet's words and sense.[15] Milton's sonnet has affinities with the Italian sonnet tradition of Della Casa in its blend of formality and intimacy. It also imports many features of the Jonsonian epigram: the judicious tone, the very precise terms of the compliment, the praises offered as from one worthy to another. Yet within the decorum of praise for Lawes, Milton's sonnet deftly enforces the priority of poet over composer, and of verse over music, that is implicit in Lawes's own method. Lawes is a "Preist of Phoebus quire" (the poets) and his role is to tune "thir happiest lines in hymn or story," implying that he serves poets, and that they belong to Apollo himself. In the final tercet Milton likens himself to Dante meeting his composer friend – affectionately addressed as "Casella mio" – at the threshold of Purgatory:

> Dante shall give Fame leav to set thee higher
>   Then his Casella, whom he woo'd to sing
>   Met in the milder shades of Purgatory.

The implied comparison is brilliantly apt: Casella, it was said, was especially gifted in the art of setting words to music, and he answered Dante by singing one of Dante's own canzoni which he had presumably set, even as Lawes had set Milton's songs in *A Maske*.[16]

Despite the optimism prompted by the New Model Army's successes, Milton had cause for alarm as threats to religious toleration increased. Presbyterianism was being settled by law. On August 19, 1645 an ordinance was passed providing for the election of elders and the organization of parishes "under the Government of Congregational, Classical, Provincial, and National Assemblies," beginning with London, and further details were worked out in a series of ordinances in March, 1646.[17] Independent and sectarian congregations sought some accommodation or toleration within this establishment and the army pressed for wider toleration. Cromwell took the occasion of his striking victory at Naseby to plead their cause before parliament: "He that ventures his life for the liberty of his country, I wish he [may] trust God for the liberty of his conscience, and you for the liberty he fights for."[18] But the Presbyterian leadership mounted an all-out campaign against toleration and the tolerationists as the Devil's progeny, responsible for unleashing a swarm of dastardly blasphemies and heresies.[19] Paul Best was imprisoned on June 10, 1645, to be tried for his life for "horrible" anti-Trinitarianism. John Goodman of Coleman Street and Henry Burton of Friday Street, strong voices for toleration, were expelled from their livings. The Leveller John Lilburne was remanded to prison in August for attacks on parliament and its speaker. There was a new barrage of antitolerationist pamphlets,[20] and protests against the sects were mounted in the strongly Presbyterian City of London. On January 1, 1646 the clergy associated with Sion College denounced the evils of toleration to the assembly: "wee detest and abhorre the much endeavoured Toleration."[21] This was followed on January 15–16 by antitolerationist petitions from the lord mayor and aldermen of London, pointing with horror to the "Superstition, Heresie, Schisme, and Profanenesse . . . and such Blasphemies as the Petitioners tremble to think on" which were vented in the City by women preachers.[22] On January 29 two Baptist preachers were arrested for distributing copies of their Confession of Faith.[23]

Milton was made part of this controversy as his views on divorce continued to be cited as a prime example of reprehensible heresy. In early May, 1645, Ephraim Pagitt listed Williams, Overton, and Milton as notorious "Atheists [who] . . . preach, print, and practise their hereticall opinions openly: for books, *vide* the bloudy Tenet, witnesse a Tractate of divorce, in which the bonds [of marriage] are let loose to inordinate lust: a pamphlet also in which the soul is laid asleep from the hour of death unto the hour of judgement."[24] Later editions carry an engraved frontispiece with emblematic figures of six notable heretics – Anabaptist, Jesuit, Familist, Antinomian, Divorcer, and Seeker; a similar engraving in a 1646 broadside shows the Divorcer driving his wife away with a rod (plate 7).[25] A special section in Pagitt's book is headed "Divorcers:"

> These I term Divorsers, that would be quit of their wives for slight occasions, and to maintaine this opinion, one hath published a Tractate of divorce, in which the bonds of marriage are let loose to inordinate lust, putting away wives for meny other causes, besides that which our Saviour only approveth; namely, in case of adulterie, who groundeth his Error upon the word of God, *Gen. 2.18. I will make him a helpe meet for him.* And therefore if she be not an helper, nor meet for him, he may put her away, saith this Author which opinion is flat contrary to the words of our Saviour.[26]

In November, 1645, the Scots Commissioner Robert Baillie charged that "Mr Milton permits any man to put away his wife upon his meere pleasure without any fault, and without the cognysance of any judge."[27] Baillie also associated Milton with notorious views ascribed to Samuel Gorton and Ann Hutchinson in New England, among them, allowing a woman to desert a husband "when he is not willing to follow her in her Church-way." Milton's doctrine of divorce is number 154 in Thomas Edward's voluminous catalogue of dangerous sects and heresies, *Gangraena*

(February, 1646), though he summarized Milton rather more fairly than did most of his detractors:

> That tis lawfull for a man to put away his wife upon indisposition, unfitnesse, or contrariety of minde arising from a cause in nature unchangeable; and for disproportion and deadnesse of spirit, or something distastefull and averse in the immutable bent of na[ture]; and man in regard of the freedome and eminency of his creation, is a law to himself in this matter, being head of the other sex, which was made for him, neither need he hear any judge therein above himself.[28]

In the second part (May, 1646), Edwards associated Milton with the female preacher and lace-woman, Mrs Attaway, who reportedly appealed to his doctrine of divorce as justification for leaving her unsanctified husband and running away with one William Jenny, who was also married.[29] Amidst all this, Milton must have rejoiced at the publication late in 1645 or early in 1646 of the *Uxor Ebraica* by the distinguished Hebraist and parliamentarian John Selden; later, he often cited Selden's learned and exhaustive discussion of the Jewish law of marriage and divorce as support for his own views.[30]

Milton responded to these personal attacks, and the larger threat to English liberties that they embody, with poems rather than pamphlets: three sonnets not then published but no doubt sent to friends and perhaps to sympathetic MPs. Like "Captain and Colonel," the first two, probably written in the early months of 1646, focus on an event in his own life that had widespread national ramifications. Their place in the Trinity manuscript suggests (but does not prove) that they were written after the sonnet to Lawes and that the sonnet beginning "I did but prompt the age to quit their clogs / By the known rules of ancient liberty" was written first.[31] Under the heading "On the detraction which follow'd upon my writing certain treatises," that sonnet castigates the "barbarous noise" of his attackers who "bawl for freedom" but have come woefully short of that mark, "For all this wast of wealth, & loss of blood." It is a savage counter-attack on the Presbyterian clergy and pamphleteers who vilified Milton as a licentious heretic. The imagery, reinforced by the hissing of sibilants, reduces those opponents to animals and their arguments to mindless animal noises: they comprise a whole menagerie of "Owls and buzzards, asses, apes and dogs." And they are like the "hindes that were transform'd to frogs" who railed at Latona and her twin progeny (Apollo and Diana) in Ovid, and the "hogs" who could not appreciate the "pearl" of the gospel preached to them (Matthew 7:6).[32] Against that characterization Milton presents himself as a classical republican orator recalling freeborn citizens to their "ancient liberty" of free speech and divorce, and also as a Christian prophet who recovered in his divorce tracts the gospel truth that makes men free (John 8:32). The sestet invites a right-minded audience to recognize that the Presbyterians' failure to understand true liberty in Milton's case spotlights vices in them that threaten the primary ends for which the revolution was mounted:

[They] bawl for freedom in their senseles mood,
And still revolt when Truth would set them free.
License they mean, when they cry liberty,
For who loves that, must first be wise, & good;
but from that mark how farr they roav, we see
for all this wast of wealth, & loss of blood. (ll. 9–14)

The audience has, however, to parse those lines, which point somewhat elliptically to concepts central to Milton's thinking.[33] The principle that only the wise and good can truly understand and value liberty looks back to those political theorists – Cicero, Livy, Machiavelli – who insisted that falling off from virtue opens the way to tyranny. Later, in the *Tenure* and the "Digression" to his *History of Britain* Milton charges the Presbyterian leadership with corruption, fraud, mismanagement, ambition, self-aggrandizement, hunger for power, theological ignorance, and a disposition to persecute; but here he assumes all that as common knowledge. The line "License they mean, when they cry liberty" echoes Livy's somewhat comparable charge against aristocratic youth corrupted by wealth who sought their own license (freedom and privileges) rather than the liberty of all. Milton implies here, as he often did later, that since only the good can love liberty, the goodness of people or leaders (for political purposes) can be measured by whether they love liberty and further its cause.

The second sonnet on the divorce tracts, "A Book was writ of late call'd *Tetrachordon*," complains of the opposite problem. This tract is being ignored by common stall-readers who are put off by its Greek title that promises serious scholarship. The tone is mostly light, social, at times self-deprecating, with some burlesque rhyme. The octave contains a scene of wry comedy as the personified book – "wov'n close, both matter, form, & stile" – is said to have "walk'd the Town a while" attracting "good intellects," but now is "seldom pour'd on." A dialogue develops in which stall-readers complain of the book's hard title and Milton protests that they seem able to put their tongues around the barbarous Scots names of the royalist General Montrose's officers.

Cries the stall-reader, bless us! what a word on
a title page is this! and som in file
stand spelling fals, while one might walk to Mile-
End Green. Why is it harder Sirs then Gordon,
Colkitto, or Macdonnell, or Galasp?[34]

The sonnet voices, however wittily, Milton's irritation and dismay that his most scholarly and densely argued tract has been all but ignored. Implicit in this retort is his challenge to English citizens to attend to something besides the latest war news, and to resist Scottish influence on English affairs. It also makes the stall-readers' resistance to Greek signify a hatred of learning that threatens the revolution as much as Presbyterian repression does. Milton constructs himself as a latter-day Sir John Cheke, the great Protestant humanist and founder of his own school, St Paul's, observing with heavy irony that Cheke's age, like his own, "hated not learning wors then toad or Asp" (not worse, but as much).[35] Yet Cheke taught Greek to King Edward and to students at Cambridge (and promoted the Reformation), whereas Milton's book with its Greek title has had no success teaching a deliberately ignorant populace. This sonnet offers no way to bridge the gulf opened up between the academy and the city street.

Sometime during the next several months of 1646 Milton probably wrote his *sonetto cauduto* or sonnet with a coda or tail, titled in the Trinity manuscript, "On the Forcers of Conscience."[36] In June a compromise was reached on the matter of parliamentary authority over church judiciaries, clearing the way for establishing presbyteries, classes, and provincial synods nationwide; they were settled first in London and Lancaster.[37] Throughout the autumn a committee of the Commons was occupied with an ordinance for the suppression of blasphemies and heresies, providing for fines, imprisonment, scourging, and hanging for various religious offenses. In this sonnet Milton takes on the role of spokesman for the nation and specifically for the Independent tolerationist cause, chastising the Presbyterians for venality, Pharisaical hypocrisy, ambition, corruption, and power-grabbing. In a trenchant figure, he portrays them as all too ready to "seize the widow'd whore Plurality" from the prelates whom they deposed but in fact envied. In powerful, prophetic terms, he challenges those calling so avidly for religious persecution: "Dare yee for this adjure the civill sword / To force our Consciences that Christ sett free / And ride us with a classic Hierarchy / Taught yee by mere A. S. & *Rotherford*."[38] He devises snide epithets for the antitolerationists: "shallow Edwards & Scotch What d'ye call" point to Thomas Edwards of *Gangraena* fame and Robert Baillie, the Scots commissioner and author of the *Dissuasive*.[39] These men label as heretics men (like Milton) of pure "life, learning, faith."

This sonnet form, developed in Italy for comic or satirical purposes, adds to the usual fourteen lines one or more "tails" of two and a half lines, meant to sting or lash the subject. Milton, in what may be the first use of the form in English,[40] adds two, using them to propose a political resolution:

That so the Parlament
May with their wholesome & preventive sheares
Clip your Phylacteries though bauke your eares
And succour our just feares
When they shall read this cleerly in your charge
New Presbyter is but old Preist writt large. (ll. 15–20)

He seems to call for a polemic campaign to expose the Presbyterian machinations, "worse then those of Trent."[41] The specific proposal, "Clip your Phylacteries," alludes to Matthew 23:1–8, where Christ warns his disciples against following the scribes and Pharisees who wear phylacteries to display their religion before men but bind "heavy burdens and grevious to be borne . . . on men's shoulders." Parliament, similarly warned, should cut off the Presbyterians' efforts to impose their ways on others, but (in a spirit very different from the persecuting Laudians or Presbyterians) should refrain from persecuting them. The specific allusion is to Prynne, now a would-be persecutor himself though his own ears had been forfeit to earlier persecutors.[42] The witty, epigrammatic final line makes the point that Laudian priest and Presbyterian presbyter are interchangeable even as the names for them are identical in meaning: "New Presbyter is but old Preist writt large."

During the first months of 1646 the king had been intriguing with the Irish and the French to land troops in England, and tried to engage the pope to promote an uprising of English Roman Catholics. But with defeat looming, on April 27 he escaped from Oxford disguised as a servant and sought protection from the Scots, who withdrew with him to Newcastle on May 13. On June 10 the king ordered his commanders to surrender, Oxford did so on June 24, and by August the first Civil War was over. For the rest of the year the king engaged in protracted negotiations with various factions – the Scots forces, the English parliament, and assorted Presbyterians and Independents – playing those entities and their interests off against each other. Parliament sent "Nineteen Propositions" to the king in July, demanding that he take the Covenant, consent to the abolition of episcopacy root and branch in England, Wales, and Ireland, approve the proceedings of the Westminster Assembly, and surrender control of the army to parliament for 20 years. In his counterproposals the king sought to avoid taking the Covenant, to preserve episcopacy in some fashion in England, and to regain power over the army more quickly.

The war's ending had immediate consequences for Milton. By late April his royalist brother Christopher was back in London with his wife and children. He took the Covenant as required and compounded for his sequestered property on August 25, aided, Edward Phillips claims, by "his brother's interest with the then prevailing party."[43] When the surrender of Oxford reclaimed that city from the royalists and opened it to travel, Milton was able to send a full set of his prose pamphlets and his recently published *Poems* to John Rouse, librarian of the Bodleian, who had requested them.[44] Rouse probably knew Milton when he lived at Horton and used the library's collections. Milton's respectful inscription – "To the most learned man, and excellent judge of books" – indicates mutual scholarly interests rather than a close friendship; thanks to Rouse, Milton rejoices, his books will live forever in this celebrated library where envy and calumny are driven far off.[45] He was clearly delighted that such immortality was now assured for the work of both his right and his left hands.

Much less happily, Oxford's surrender subjected Milton to an inundation of his Powell in-laws: by early July at least five Powell children under sixteen, their parents, and perhaps some older children came to take up residence with the Miltons in the Barbican house. They had been dispossessed of their Forest Hill property due to Richard Powell's debts and tangled finances, and the requirement that, as a delinquent royalist, he compound for the rest of his heavily mortgaged assets.[46] Milton rose to need and family responsibility, but must have felt considerable ambivalence about extending hospitality to the feckless father-in-law who had defaulted both on the interest he owed Milton from the 1627 bond and on Mary's dowry, and to the mother-in-law who, Mary reportedly claimed, had incited her to desert Milton.[47]

These chances of war meant that Mary had her own family with her when she gave birth to her first child, named Anne for Mary's mother and perhaps also for Milton's sister Anne. Milton's Bible records the event: "My daughter Anne was born July the 29 on the fast at eevning about half an houre after six 1646."[48] Edward Phillips describes the infant as "a brave girl," which suggests that she did not at first show signs of her lifelong lameness and defective speech.[49] His ambiguous comment – "whether by ill Constitution, or want of Care, she grew more and more decrepit" – may be simply a formula, or it may imply that her handicaps, if not congenital, were caused or aggravated by some unspecified neglect – from inept doctors? or Anne's wet-nurse? or lack of attention to her needs?

Milton carried on with his school for a time, though his much-expanded family brought profound changes to his quiet scholarly routine.[50] During his years of teaching, Milton may have made good progress on a projected, though now lost, Latin *Thesaurus*.[51] Also, he began and may have substantially completed two works of pedagogy that were published decades later, with various revisions and additions. As first conceived, the *Accidence Commenc't Grammar* is Milton's effort to produce a new school grammar for the reformed commonwealth he expected to emerge from the wars.[52] In *Of Education* (1644) Milton indicated that his system for teaching Latin quickly and efficiently involved beginning with Lily's grammar "or any better," referring perhaps to the text he was writing. It offers a replacement for the grammar by William Lily and John Colet, mandated from 1540 on for use in the schools in its usual two-part format: a *Shorte Introduction* in English, with a more elaborate *Brevissima Institutio* in Latin.[53] Milton does not dispense with formal grammar in favor of vocabulary and memorized phrases as in Comenius's system, but instead seeks to bring students through the grammatical preliminaries with dispatch so they may quickly begin reading classical works. He takes about 60 percent of his 500 or so examples from Lily, and many of his innovations were anticipated in other grammars, especially those that follow, as his does, the method of the French Calvinist philosopher and educational reformer Petrus Ramus.[54] But he could fairly claim that his grammar follows Ramus more closely than the others in his definitions, brevity, and organization by dichotomous pairs; and that he brought several innovations together in one text.[55] In place of Lily's two-part volume of almost 200 pages, Milton produced one English volume of 65 pages. He defines grammar as Ramus does, as the art of speaking or writing well; and he divides it as Ramus does, into two parts, Etymology and Syntax, omitting the other usual topics, orthography and prosody.[56] He also excluded exceptional cases, compressed rules and examples, and replaced formal definitions of terms with semantic definitions based on meaning. Moreover, he deleted from Lily examples which reinforce structures of royal and ecclesiastical authority: prayers, expressions of loyalty to the monarch, responses from the catechism, and virtually all examples using the word "rex." And he added some two hundred new examples, among them several quotations from Cicero dealing with the struggle for liberty and justice against oppressive power.[57] As Lily's grammar had helped form monarchical principles in generation after generation of schoolboys, Milton's grammar would subtly insinuate the values of a republican culture.

In all likelihood, Milton also drafted most of his Ramist logic, in Latin, while he was teaching the subject; it was published in 1672, with some later additions,[58] under the title *Artis Logicae Plenior Institutio ad Petri Rami Methodum Concinnata.* It coalesces and abridges in one continuous text (219 pages) the famous 95-page *Dialecticae libri duo* (1572) by Petrus Ramus and an 800-page commentary by George Downame, adding also an exercise in logical analysis taken from Downame.[59] Ramus's revisionist logic and "method," based on the dichotomized division of all subjects into axioms proceeding from the general to the particular, challenged Aristotle's *Organon,* still the foundation of the Scholastic trivium taught in schools and universities. Ramism was especially influential in the Protestant nations of northern Europe where Ramus was perceived as both scholar and martyr, having met his death in the notorious massacre of some 3,000 Protestants on St Bartholomew's day (August 24, 1572). Milton knew Ramist logic from Christ's College, which had a long tradition of distinguished Ramist fellows: Laurence Chaderton, William Perkins, and Downame himself, who had been University Professor of Logic from 1590 to 1616.

Like his *Grammar,* Milton's *Logic* is a relatively brief volume designed to be useful to students. As a teacher, Milton evidently found Ramist simplification and codification of Aristotelian logic helpful, though he insists on using the more inclusive term "logic" – defined as "the art of reasoning well" – instead of Ramus's preferred term "dialectic" with its connotations of question and answer or debate (*CPW* VIII, 217). He offers an approving, though much condensed, discussion of Ramus's method, using it in this treatise and in his *Grammar.* However, by restricting it to teaching knowledge already attained he implies that other methods may be useful for discovering new knowledge. As a poet, Milton no doubt approved of Ramus's use of poetic examples. But while Ramus made logic the basis for poetry as for all other knowledge,[60] Milton refused that simple equation, stating that poets and orators, when they seek to evoke pleasure or other emotions, use methods best known to themselves (391–5).

Late in 1646 Milton wrote an epigraph-sonnet titled in the Trinity manuscript "On ye religious memory of Mrs. Catharine Thomason, my christian freind deceas'd

16 Decem. 1646."[61] Catharine was the wife of the bookseller George Thomason and was herself a woman of bookish interests, as is evident from the extensive personal library she bequeathed to her children. Milton called George Thomason "a most familiar acquaintance," and four of his tracts in Thomason's vast collection are inscribed *Ex Dono Authoris*.[62] But this sonnet treats Catharine's virtues and qualities in allegorical rather than personal terms: it is conceived as a mini-allegory on the Coming of Death, recasting that medieval topic in Protestant terms.[63] Catharine Thomason is led to heavenly bliss by a series of allegorical personages. First, "Faith & Love," which never parted from her, "rip'n'd" her "just soul," and she resigned "this earthly load / of death, call'd life." Then her "Works & Almes" followed her but not, as in *Everyman,* as her sole companions and evidence of merit; rather, it is because they are led by Faith and Love and clothed by Faith that they can fly up and speak "the truth of thee in glorious theames / before the Judge." The sonnet closes with a conventional image of Catharine drinking, like *Lycidas,* at "pure immortal streames" – an indication that Milton is not yet a Mortalist.

On December 13, 1646 Milton witnessed the will of his father-in-Law, Richard Powell, who died shortly before January 1, 1647.[64] His will disposed of the Forest Hill property to his son and the Wheatley estate to his executor, an office his wife accepted so as to secure Wheatley to herself.[65] Both properties were heavily mortgaged. Ignoring his lack of funds, Powell also called for payment of his numerous debts, including his daughter's dowry to Milton. Anticipating Powell's impending death, Milton in mid-December began legal procedures which extended over several years to establish his claim against the Powell estate for his £300 bond, with overdue interest, dating from 1627. That bond took precedence over later debts,[66] giving Milton a claim on Wheatley. In the event, Milton's legal proceedings to secure his claim also helped his in-laws retain some rights in their property and allowed for their resettlement – a culmination devoutly desired from Milton's perspective, whatever he may have felt about the financial arrangements. The Oxfordshire court seized the Wheatley property on August 5, 1647 but allowed Anne Powell to claim her widow's thirds from its income for three years; on November 20 Milton was granted full possession of the property and its income until his debt was settled. Milton paid Anne her thirds "as he conceiveth rightfully" until a court disallowed that arrangement in 1651; he may have permitted her to live rent free in the manor house as the only way to get the Powells out of his own house.[67] On whatever terms, she was in residence there with her family on August 5, 1647.[68]

About the time his father-in-law died Milton learned that the 1645 *Poems* he had sent to the Bodleian had gone astray, though the volume of prose tracts had arrived. Rouse the librarian wrote to request another copy, and Milton complied, sending with it an elegant Latin ode, "Ad Joannem Rousiam," dated January 23, 1647.[69] Despite all the distractions Milton was able to produce a Latin poem of consummate art and originality, which is also an exercise in poetic self-representation. It is discussed along with the 1645 *Poems* on page 229. Rouse's request seems to have prompted Milton to offer his prose works to other repositories; he inscribed one such volume, "To the most learned man, Patrick Young [the Keeper of the King's Library], John Milton sends these works . . . content with a few such readers."[70] That winter John Hall, a member of the Hartlib circle, sought Hartlib's advice about corresponding with and gaining an introduction to Milton, "who is here said to be the author of that excellent discourse of Education you were pleased to impart"; but Milton apparently did not encourage this relationship.[71]

On March 15, 1647 Milton buried his own father in the church of St Giles, Cripplegate. He was at least 84 and still able to read without glasses,[72] though his son was already experiencing serious vision problems. Milton inherited a "moderate patrimony" from his father, including a house on Bread Street.[73] Soon after, on April 20, 1647, Milton answered a letter from his Florentine friend Carlo Dati (three previous letters from Dati had gone astray), and entrusted it to George Thomason or his apprentice as they left for Italy to buy books.[74] In, for him, unusually direct language though without naming names, Milton indicates the emotional strains caused by the ubiquitous Powell entourage, the several recent deaths (Diodati, his father, Alexander Gil, Catharine Thomason), the absence of congenial friends like the Italian academicians, and more generally, by the continuing danger to life, property, and literature in a nation torn by civil war. The letter is suffused with nostalgia for the literary leisure he enjoyed in Italy, now sadly lost:

> Soon an even heavier mood creeps over me, a mood in which I am accustomed often to bewail my lot, to lament that those whom perhaps proximity or some unprofitable tie has bound to me, whether by accident or by law, those, commendable in no other way, daily sit beside me, weary me – even exhaust me, in fact – as often as they please; whereas those whom character, temperament, interests had so finely united are now nearly all grudged me by death or most hostile distance and are for the most part so quickly torn from my sight that I am forced to live in almost perpetual solitude. . . . Since I returned home, there has been an additional reason for silence in the extremely turbulent state of our Britain, which quickly compelled me to turn my mind from my studies to protecting life and property in any way I could. Do you think there can be any safe retreat for literary leisure among so many civil battles, so much slaughter, flight, and pillaging of goods? (*CPW* II, 762–4)

This distress over domestic and civil tumults he offers as a tacit excuse for writing little poetry during these years; it seems a sufficient explanation. But he has published his *Poems,* he reports proudly to Dati, promising him the Latin section and begging his Florentine friends to indulge him for the anti-papal satire in some poems.[75]

The patrimony from his father and the prospect of the Powells' departure allowed Milton to close his little academy and seek a smaller house where he could again live the life of a scholar and poet. In early 1647 he may well have supposed that the conflicts would soon be settled on terms that would restore the king with limitations on his powers, and would establish Presbyterianism with some guarantees for liberty of conscience. In January, 1647 the Scots had surrendered the king to the English parliament, who settled him at Holmby House in Northamptonshire and continued to treat with him. The victorious army, largely composed of Independents and sectaries, could be expected to keep up the pressure for toleration. Milton evidently felt that he could do little in these matters, a conclusion likely reinforced by the continuing attacks on his divorce tracts.[76] But hope for a satisfactory settlement could not long be sustained as negotiations continued in stalemate and parliament moved to disband the New Model Army, which for their part refused to disband until they received their arrears of pay, full amnesty for their wartime actions, and some guarantee of religious toleration. The rank and file increasingly took part with the Levellers faction, who were calling for legal reforms, extension of suffrage, abolition of tithes and monopolies, and sometimes for a republican government vested in a single representative house.[77]

Summer saw the rift between the army and parliament growing wider and another developing between the senior officers and the rank and file, who came to consider themselves and were considered by some Levellers to be the legitimate voice of the common people, given the Commons' egregious failure to enact their desired reforms.[78] Several regiments appointed agitators to represent them, both offficers and agitators flooded parliament with their several petitions,[79] and at a great rendezvous at Newmarket the regiments joined together in a *Solemn Engagement* (June 5) not to disband until their concerns were addressed. On July 4 Colonel Joyce abducted the king from Holmby and placed him under the control of the army, after which the officers began treating with him on the basis of their own platform, calling for biennial parliaments, increased power to the Commons, reform of electorates, parliamentary control of the army for ten years, and freedom of Protestant religious practice. From its new position of strength, the army forced the removal of some parliament members it regarded as enemies and the restoration of some ousted Independents to the city militia, actions soon reversed when Presbyterian London unleashed a flood of inflammatory petitions and rioted in the streets. After the speakers of both houses, together with many moderates in parliament, fled to the army to escape the London mobs, the army marched into the City of London on August 4–6, quelled the riots, restored the moderate MPs, and again expelled the previously expelled "enemies." The king, then settled at Hampton Court, continued to play for time, entertaining emissaries from the parliament, the Scots, and the army, then headquartered six miles away at Putney.

According to Edward Phillips it was "not long after the March of *Fairfax* and *Cromwel* through the City of *London* with the whole Army, to quell the Insurrections" that Milton moved from the Barbican into a smaller house in High Holborn, opening at the back into Lincolns-Inn Fields. Here, Phillips reports, "he liv'd a private and quiet Life, still prosecuting his Studies and curious Search into Knowledge, the grand Affair perpetually of his Life" (*EL* 68). He may have continued to tutor his nephews, but did not continue his academy.[80] In November, 1647 Milton received another letter from Carlo Dati replying to his of April 20; it is filled with news and includes a lengthy literary commentary on figurative usages in several Latin and Italian poets.[81] Milton's reply may have been lost, but very likely there was none; as Milton earlier admitted to Diodati, he found it difficult to turn from his studies or writing to answer correspondence.[82] Over the next several months he was probably working on two books published much later: the *History of Britain* (1670) and *Brief History of Moscovia* (1682). Hartlib heard in July, 1648 that Milton was at work on those projects, though he exaggerates their scope: "Milton is not only writing a Univ. History of Engl. but also an Epitome of all Purcha's Volumes."[83] Milton's preface to the *Moscovia,* added later, claims that he undertook it "at a vacant time" and gave it over when diverted by "other occasions"; some periods during 1647–8 seem the most likely "vacant time."[84]

The *Moscovia* is an epitome or compilation of facts about Russian topography, regions, climate, curious manners and customs, government, and the fundamental character of the people, together with a brief political history and an account of the English ambassadors to that country. It is drawn almost exclusively from Hakluyt and Purchas, whose volumes include several English travelers' accounts of Russia.[85] Milton appends a list of 18 such accounts on which his compilation is based, terming them "Eyewitnesses, or immediate relaters of such as were." In his preface he describes his text as an experiment in writing a geography that is neither too brief nor too expansive, which might serve as an example to others; he may have begun it when teaching geography to his students. Some topics resonate with his immediate concerns: the history of Russian tyrants and tyranny; an extended report of Russia's salvation from the chaos of civil war by a "mean Man" who persuaded them to choose an able general, to eliminate corruption, and to pay the soldiers well; and a report (not in Hakluyt or Purchas) of the Russian husband's right to divorce "upon utter dislike."[86]

Throughout the autumn of 1647 distrust intensified between the more conservative army officers and the rank and file, many of whom held Leveller or Millenarian views. On October 15, an inflammatory manifesto signed by the agitators of five regiments, *The Case of the Armie Truly Stated*, denounced the army leadership for ignoring the grievances of both the troops and the common people and reaffirmed the army *Declaration* of June 14, which proclaimed that they took up arms "for the peoples just rights and liberties, and not as mercenary Souldiers . . . and that . . . they proceeded upon the principles of right and freedom, and upon the law of nature and Nations."[87] The *Case* urged the Leveller social and economic program – religious toleration, drastic simplification of the laws and courts, and abolition of tithes, excise taxes, and monopolies – and also the Leveller political program: supremacy of the Commons unconstrained by any negative vote by king or Lords, prompt dissolution of the Long Parliament, biennial parliaments, and manhood suffrage except for royalists during a set period and servants subject to others' wills. These provisions were codified into the first version of an *Agreement of the People*, the nucleus of a written republican constitution, which was to guarantee the fundamentals of government and the people's rights. Both documents proclaimed that "all power is originally and essentially in the whole body of the people"; that the Laws of Reason and of Nature take precedence over civil and common law; that the Civil War had returned the country to a state of nature where the truncated Commons, or the army, or others might act to secure the common interest; but that only a new constitution subscribed by the whole population could refound civil society and government.[88] The *Agreement* was debated at Putney from October 28 to November 1, but rifts widened as the high officers, especially Cromwell and Henry Ireton, held out for a property qualification for suffrage and sought to retain some role for the king and a House of Lords.[89] The king's escape to the Isle of Wight on November 11 forced an uneasy *rapprochement* between officers and troops, and between the army and parliament. In early January, 1648, parliament, infuriated by the king's continued stalling, passed a resolution of "No Further Addresses" to the king, but he had concluded a secret agreement with the Scots, trading the establishment of Presbyterianism in England for three years for a Scottish invasion to restore him to the throne. In April and May, royalist uprisings in Wales, Cornwall, Devonshire, and the North launched the Second Civil War.

That April Milton voiced his mounting anxiety over these events by translating Psalms 80–8.[90] He used the common meter (alternating lines of eight and six syllables) employed in most psalters, perhaps with a view to offering these psalms to the commission charged to revise the psalter, but in any case because that meter allowed for some approximation to Hebraic psalmic parallelism.[91] Their themes – God's displeasure with his chosen people and prayers for divine guidance for a nation racked with conspiracies and surrounded by enemies – resonate with the worrying turn of events. Fusing his voice with that of the psalmist, Milton cries out to God to save a new Israel and a new prophet beleagured by enemies on all sides and threatened by the treachery of friends – with allusion to the Scots (and some English) Presbyterians who now support the king.[92] Milton's additions to the Hebraic texts, usually italicized, show him applying the psalmist's laments and the divine denunciations to dangers from present foes, e.g. both "*Kings and lordly States*" (parliament leaders):

> God in the great assembly stands
> *Of Kings and lordly States,*
> Amongst the gods on both his hands
> He judges and debates.
> How long will ye pervert the right
> With judgment false and wrong
> Favoring the wicked *by your might,*
> *Who thence grow bold and strong?*[93]

Be not thou silent *now at length*
O God hold not thy peace,
Sit not thou still O god of *strength,*
We cry and do not cease.
For lo thy *furious* foes *now* swell
And storm outrageously,
And they that hate thee *proud and fell*
Exalt their heads full high.
(Psalm 83:1–8)

Lover and friend thou hast remov'd
And sever'd from me far.
They *fly me now whom I have lov'd,*
And as in darkness are.
(Psalm 88:69–72)

Yet these psalms also sound an affirmative theme, an assurance that at last deliverance will come and the Kingdom of God will be established in a repentant and reformed Israel (and England.) Milton expands on that theme (sometimes without italics), in language linking such reform to the – perhaps imminent – Millennial reign of Christ the King:

To his dear Saints he will speak peace,
But let them never more
Return to folly, *but surcease*
To trespass as before.
Surely to such as do him fear
Salvation is at hand,
And glory shall *ere long appear*
To dwell within Our land.
. . .
Before him Righteousness shall go
His Royal Harbinger,
Then will he come, and not be slow.
His footsteps cannot err.[94]

Milton's dismay and anger surely increased when parliament on May 2 completed passage of its long debated "Ordinance for the Suppression of Blasphemies and Heresies" – a red flag to the army Independents and sectaries who were at that very moment fighting in its name. That law provided the death penalty for atheism, anti-Trinitarianism, and other major errors (unless recanted), and imprisonment for lesser ones such as promoting Arminianism and Anabaptism, denouncing Presbyterian church government, and denying the necessity of Sabbath observance.[95] Milton himself held or would soon hold many of these views; he was already an Arminian. Making matters worse, on July 8 the Scots invaded as promised, and the fleet (which had defected to Prince Charles, in Holland) blockaded the mouth of the Thames, seizing trading vessels and their goods. And parliament, increasingly conservative, disclaimed any desire to change the fundamental constitution of Kings, Lords and Commons and rescinded its vote of No Addresses.

Sometime between July 8 and August 17, Milton addressed a sonnet to the army's commander-in-chief, titled in the Trinity manuscript "On ye Lord Gen. Fairfax at ye seige of Colchester," and probably sent it to him.[96] Fairfax was besieging some 3,000 royalist soldiers in that town. This is the first of Milton's sonnets to great men in the exalted encomiastic manner of Tasso's "Heroic Sonnets," but Milton mixes his high praise with urgent advice. The octave pays tribute to Fairfax's "firm, unshak'n vertue" – the term suggests both strength and goodness – as the basis for his striking military successes which are the envy of Europe's kings and an augury of continued success. He is cast as a Hercules figure lopping off the Hydra heads of "new rebellions" and Scottish perfidy. But the sestet urges him to take on the "nobler task" of reforming the civil order, where a psychomachia rages that requires the exercise of his proven "vertue":

> For what can Warr, but endless warr still breed,
> Till Truth, & Right from Violence be freed,
> And Public Faith cleard from the shamefull brand
> Of Public Fraud. In vain doth Valour bleed
> While Avarice, & Rapine share the land. (ll. 10–14)

The specific evils pointed to by these personifications – greed, corruption, fraudulent use of public monies, defaulting on debts guaranteed by the public faith, religious repression – are laid at the door of the Presbyterian parliament in the "Digression" to Milton's *History of Britain,* also probably written during these months. The profusion of evils suggests that Herculean Fairfax needs to cleanse the English Augean stables. Evidently Milton was now ready to look to the army and its noble commander-in-chief as the best hope to settle the government.

The Second Civil War was over by the end of August. Cromwell won a stunning victory at Preston over the Scottish and English armies (August 17–19) and Fairfax on August 28 accepted the famine-induced surrender of the royalist forces at Colchester. In September parliament began a "personal treaty" with the king in Wales,[97] but Charles, still hoping for an invasion from Ireland or Europe or for an opportunity to escape, continued his delaying tactics. As this crisis intensified, Milton would have heard news of the Treaty of Westphalia (October 14/24) bringing to an end the catastrophic Thirty Years Wars of religion. A few days later his second child was born, a daughter named Mary after her mother, and Milton recorded the event in his family Bible: "My daughter Mary was born on Wednesday Octob.

25th on the fast day in the morning about 6 a clock 1648."[98] She was baptized on November 7 at St Giles in the Fields.[99]

On November 20 the army presented its "Grand Remonstrance" to a fearful parliament. Penned chiefly by Ireton, it urged much of the familiar army–Leveller program, including an Agreement of the People and a demand that the king be brought to justice for the "treason, blood and mischief he is therein guilty of."[100] On November 28 the Treaty of Newport collapsed over Charles's insistence on preserving bishops. Out of patience, on December 1 the army seized the king and conveyed him to Hurst Castle in Hampshire. When parliament denounced that action and insisted on renewing negotiations with him, the army's response was Pride's Purge. On December 6 and during the next few days, soldiers under Colonel Pride excluded or arrested well over two hundred parliament members; others, staggered by the affront to parliamentary authority, withdrew voluntarily, leaving in place the so called Rump Parliament of about eighty Commons who were joined by five or six Lords.[101]

Milton probably began the *History of Britain* in tandem with or soon after he finished the draft of *Moscovia* (perhaps in late 1647), and was at work on it in the months of crisis during and after the Second Civil War. His comment in the *Defensio Secunda* is, I think, misleading in seeming to indicate that he wrote all of the first four books in the five or six weeks after completing his *Tenure of Kings and Magistrates* in early February, 1649 and before receiving an appointment from the Commonwealth government in mid-March.[102] Milton probably could have written that much that fast but this scenario is unlikely. In July, 1648 Hartlib knew Milton was at work on this project, and Milton's imprecision about dating is indicated by the fact that he could not have completed Book IV in 1649 since he relies for some part of it on a book published in 1652.[103] I suspect he wrote Book I just after completing *Moscovia;* it has the manner and tone of a rather detached scholarly endeavor. But Books II and III, and the "Digression" on the Long Parliament, resonate with the course of contemporary events and Milton's anxieties during and after the Second Civil War in 1648. Milton probably drafted them then, and after finishing T*enure* turned back to revise them and write the first part of Book IV, breaking off where Bede's account ends, in the year 731. If that is so, his statement in the *Defensio Secunda* would refer to the period when he revised and finished this part of his project.

When Milton decided to write the history of his nation from earliest times to the present, he rose to a call by Henry Saville, John Haywood, Samuel Daniel, and Francis Bacon, among others, for a history that would break free of the ponderous chronicle format. However, he chose not to follow some other models available – William Camden's "antiquitarian" chorography (he had termed such books "rakeing in the Foundations of old Abbies and Cathedrals"), or John Selden's elaborate scholarly analyses of particular institutions (e.g. tithes), or Thomas May's republican history of the English parliament which focused on the triumphs of liberty during the century past.[104] Instead he undertook to revive the humanist ideal of history as counsel, not now to princes but to parliament and the people, in a literary style appropriate to that purpose:

> I intend not with controversies and quotations to delay or interrupt the smooth course of History . . . but shall endevor that which hitherto hath bin needed most, with plain, and lightsom brevity, to relate well and orderly things worth the noting, so as may best instruct and benefit them that read . . . imploring divine assistance, that it may redound to his glory, and to the good of the *British* Nation. (*CPW* V.1, 4)

The overarching lesson Milton derives from his history is that the British people from earliest times have displayed a troubling, innate characteristic: though valorous in war, they sadly lack the civic virtues needed to sustain free governments and their own liberties. He means to help his countrymen recognize their present danger from this disposition, and to counter it by choosing men of "solid & elaborate breeding" as leaders, and also by gaining "ripe understanding and many civil vertues . . . from forren writings & examples of best ages."[105] That educative purpose suggests that he probably intended to publish all or some part of the *History* soon, but before he reached a suitable stopping point more urgent duties intervened.

Milton tried to adhere to certain historiographical principles. He does not undertake new primary research but follows and condenses what he takes to be the most reliable previous account(s), judging by plausibility and proximity to the events treated. For example: "*Suetonius* writes that *Claudius* found heer no resistance . . . but this seems not probable"; or again, "if *Beda* err not, living neer 500 years after, yet our antientest Author of this report" (*CPW* V.1, 67, 97). He avoids rhetorical speeches like those in Thucydides and Livy, "unless known for certain to have bin so spok'n in effect as they are writ'n, nor then, unless worth rehearsal" (80). Yet he narrates a few scenes dramatically, e.g. Caractacus before Claudian, and Leir and his daughters dividing the kingdom (drawing on Holinshed and perhaps Shakespeare). He assumes that the nobility or baseness of persons and deeds is mirrored in the style of the history written about them, taking the historian's style as an image of the culture: noble deeds in the service of liberty against tyrants call forth eloquent histories; degenerate civilizations produce foolish or trivial ones.

Throughout, Milton underscores those aspects of the historical record that have contemporary application. One recurrent motif, that women who exercise power in government or on the battlefield are almost always reprehensible and absurd, has an unidentified contemporary referent in Queen Henrietta Maria, often denounced by the Puritans for dictating policy to her husband and attempting to raise European armies in his support.[106] The Roman Empress Agrippina is said to have presented "a new and disdained sight to the manly Eyes of *Romans*, a Woeman sitting public in her Female pride among Ensignes and Armed Cohorts" (72). The Briton Queen Cartismandua was a traitor to her country and her husband and was opposed by her own subjects, "who detested . . . thir Subjection to the Monarchie of a Woeman, a peece of manhood not every day to be found among *Britans*" (74). Even Boadicea, normally portrayed as a British heroine, is in Milton's account barbarous and foolish in leading a military uprising against the Romans with "no rule, no foresight, no forecast, . . . such confusion, such impotence, as seem'd likest not to a Warr, but to the wild hurrey of a distracted Woeman, with as mad a Crew at her heeles."[107] Virtually the only exception in his role-call of wicked or foolish female rulers is Leir's daughter Cordelia, whose nephews rose against her, "not bearing that a Kingdom should be govern'd by a Woman," but they had no warrant to "raise that quarrel against a Woman so worthy" (25). Another recurrent motif finds lessons for religious liberty and separation of church and state. Britain was led to profess Christianity by King Lucius, but true faith appears "more sincere . . . without publick Authority or against it" (97). Early bishops came to a council at their own charge, "far above the Presbyters of our Age; who like well to sit in Assembly on the publick stipend" (116). King Ethelbert and multitudes of his people were converted by Augustine but that king compelled none, having learned "that Christian Religion ought to be voluntary, not compell'd" (189).

For his first book, the beginnings of the nation to the coming of Julius Caesar, Milton found no worthy history to follow, whether because literacy came long after, or records were lost or destroyed, or, as he seems rather to suspect, because the wise men of those times perceived "not only how unworthy, how pervers, how corrupt, but often how ignoble, how petty, how below all History the persons and thir actions were" (1–2). He protests the dubious or fabulous character of all the old stories from pre-Roman Britain – Albion, Brutus, Locrine, Dunwallo, Lud – but has decided to relate them anyway, as possibly containing "reliques of something true," and as repositories for poets who "by thir Art will know, how to use them judiciously" (3). For early Britain he perforce relies almost entirely on Geoffrey of Monmouth, promising to avoid what is "impossible and absurd" (9), but inviting a thoroughly skeptical reading of his reports. In Book III he rejects categorically the stories of King Arthur, based as they are on Geoffrey's "fabulous book" written 600 years after their supposed date and unconfirmed by any independent historian. His tone reveals his annoyance that he himself was misled into accepting "Legends for good story" when he earlier considered writing an Arthuriad (166).

With Book II he turns with relief to reliable Roman historians in whom "daylight and truth meet us with a cleer dawn" (37): Caesar, Sallust, Tacitus, Suetonius, Dio, Diodorus. He follows them closely, condensing, summarizing, and occasionally clarifying points through minor additions, deletions, and changes in organization. He explains the absence of British historians contemporary with the Romans by the principle that cultures get the historians they deserve:

> Worthy deeds are not often destitute of worthy relaters: as by a certain Fate great Acts and great Eloquence have most commonly gon hand in hand. . . . He whose just and

> true valour uses the necessity of Warr and Dominion . . . to bring in Liberty against Tyrants, Law and Civility among barbarous Nations . . . honours and hath recourse to the aid of Eloquence, his freindliest and best supply. . . . when the esteem of Science and liberal study waxes low in the Common-wealth, wee may presume that also there all civil Vertue, and worthy action is grown as low to a decline: and then Eloquence . . . corrupts also and fades; at least resignes her office of relating to illiterat and frivolous Historians. (39–40)

Milton tells a complex story of Rome in Britain, about an advanced nation that conquered courageous and fiercely resisting savage inhabitants and brought them civilization. The British equalled the Romans for "courage and warlike readiness" in sudden onsets, but were inferior in weapons, strategy, and fortifications, and were disadvantaged by fighting naked. They lacked skill in farming, wore skins of beasts, painted their bodies with woad (sometimes decoratively), had only rudimentary towns, constantly warred among themselves, permitted polyandry and incest, and were led by "factious and ambitious" Druid priests who practiced divination and human sacrifice. Rome "beate us into some civilitie; likely else to have continue'd longer in a barbarous and savage manner of life" (61). But the Roman story is complicated after Julius Caesar "tyrannously had made himself Emperor of the *Roman* Commonwealth" (61). Then the corruption and tyranny of the magistrates prompted various British tribes to uprisings and resistance, often provoked "by heaviest sufferings" and hatred of servitude (77). Milton treats some of these uprisings as noble though unsuccessful efforts to regain liberty (Caractacus, Venusius, Cassibelan), though he found Boadicea's similar attempt wholly despicable. He reports Titus's impressive achievements in Britain – building houses, temples, and seats of justice, and promoting education in the liberal arts and Latin eloquence – but noted that the British people became degenerate through imitating Roman "Vice, and voluptuous life . . . which the foolisher sort call'd civilitie, but was indeed a secret Art to prepare them for bondage."[108] He ends Book II with Honorius releasing the Britons from Roman jurisdiction just before Rome fell, so that "by all right" the government reverted to the Britons themselves, "to live after thir own Laws." Yet along with this opportunity came the decline of all those Roman benefits: "Learning, Valour, Eloquence, History, Civility, and eev'n Language" (127).

Book III and the Digression may have been drafted during the frantic weeks after the Second Civil War ended in late August, 1648, as Milton sought with some urgency to apply the lessons of British history to his own time. At the beginning of Book III he draws out parallels between the "confused Anarchy" following the departure of the Romans from Britain and the situation of England in "this intereign" after "the late civil broils:"

> The late civil broils had cast us into a condition not much unlike to what the *Britans* then were in, when the imperial jurisdiction departing hence left them to the sway of thir own Councils; which times by comparing seriously with these later, and that

> confused Anarchy with this intereign, we may be able from two such remarkable turns of State, producing like events among us, to raise a knowledg of our selves both great and weighty, by judging hence what kind of men the *Britans* generally are in matters of so high enterprise . . . [rather than] for want of self-knowledge, to enterprise rashly and come off miserably in great undertakings. (129–30)

That suggests recent final closure to the wars. The power struggles among the now twice-defeated and imprisoned king, the parliament, the army, and the Scots, extending into December after Pride's Purge, are better termed an anarchic "interreign" than are the weeks after the king's execution when a Commonwealth was being instituted. Most of the so called Digression seems also to date from this time.[109]

In Milton's reading, the ancient Britons could not take advantage of fair opportunities for self-government, having by long subjection been made "servile in mind, sloathful of body" (130). Also, they were badly served by their ambitious, tyrannous, dissolute, and corrupt leaders and clergy, so they lacked "the wisdom, the virtue, the labour, to use and maintain true libertie" and govern themselves well. Plagued by marauding Picts and Scots, they did not defend "what was to be dearer than life, thir liberty, against an Enemy not stronger than themselves" (131–2) and instead sought protection from foreign (Saxon) kings. For his perspective in Book III, Milton relies heavily on the sixth-century monk Gildas's *De Excidio et Conquestu Britanniae*, echoing his dark version of the post-Roman age in which the downfall of the Britons, by analogy with the ancient Israelites, is linked to their corruption and perversity.[110] In the long Digression intended for insertion at this point, Milton asserts that the English in the "late commotions" have been placed in a parallel situation and seem all too likely to display the same character flaw, giving over the opportunity for self-government and re-establishing monarchical rule:

> It may withal bee enquir'd . . . why they who had the chiefe management therin having attain'd, though not so easilie, to a condition which had set before them civil government in all her formes, and giv'n them to bee masters of thir own choise, were not found able after so many years doeing and undoeing to hitt so much as into any good and laudable way that might shew us hopes of a just and well amended common-wealth to come. (441)

The Digression explicitly compares the chaos and rampant vice in Britain after the departure of the Romans to the manifold evils and corruptions in England. In the prophetic mode of Gildas's jeremiad, Milton denounces the Presbyterian Long Parliament for misuse of power in the service of their own "profit and ambition," thereby sabotaging the great opportunity won on the battlefield to settle a free commonwealth:

> For a parlament being calld and as was thought many things to redress . . . [but] straite every one betooke himself, setting the common-wealth behinde and his private ends

> before, to doe as his owne profit or ambition led him. Then was justice delai'd & soone after deny'd, spite and favour determin'd all: hence faction, then treacherie both at home & in the field, ev'ry where wrong & oppression. . . . Some who had bin calld from shops & warehouses without other merit to sit in supreme councel[s] and committees, as thir breeding was, fell to hucster the common-wealth. . . . Thir votes and ordinances which men look'd should have contain'd the repealing of bad laws & the immediate constitution of better, resounded with nothing els but new impositions, taxes, excises, yearlie, monthlie, weeklie[,] not to reck'n the offices, gifts, and preferments bestowed and shar'd among themselves. (443–5)

Also, the Presbyterian divines of the Westminster Assembly devoted themselves to avarice, place-seeking, and religious oppression:

> And if the state were in this plight, religion was not in much better: to reforme which a certaine number of divines wer[e] called . . . [who] wanted not impudence . . . to seise into thir hands or not unwillinglie to accept (besides one sometimes two or more of the best Livings) collegiat masterships in the universitie, rich lectures in the cittie, setting saile to all windes that might blow gaine into thir covetous bosomes. . . . And yet the main doctrin for which they tooke such pay . . . was but to tell us in effect that thir doctrin was worth nothing and the spiritual power of thir ministrie less available then bodilie compulsion; . . . thir intents were cleere to be no other then to have set up a spir[i]tual tyrannie by a secular power to the advancing of thir owne authorit[ie] above the magist[r]ate. (447)

As well, economic grievances abound, to which the scrivener's son testifies indignantly, alluding to his difficulties in collecting debts from the Powells' sequestered estates, and to his loss of money and goods loaned voluntarily or taken up in assessments under the now discredited guarantee of the "public faith."[111]

> They in the meane while who were ever faithfullest to thir cause, and freely aided them in person, or with thir substance [were] . . . slighted soone after and quite bereav'd of thir just debts by greedy sequestration . . . yet were withall no less burden'd in all extraordinarie assessments and oppressions then whom they tooke to be disaffected. . . . That faith which ought to bee kept as sacred and inviolable as any thing holy, the public faith, after infinite summs receiv'd & all the wealth of the church, not better imploy'd, but swallow'd up into a private gulfe, was not ere long asham'd to confess bankrupt.[112]

All this has scandalized the people, now grown "worse & more disordinate, to receave or to digest any libertie at all" (449).[113]

After this digression, Milton took up his historical narrative again, treating in Books III and IV the continued attacks of the Picts and Scots, the Britons' reliance on and then subjugation by the Saxons, the conflicts between Christian and pagan and between Roman and Celtic Christianity, and the struggles for supremacy among the various Saxon tribes and kingdoms – all of which produced almost unremitting internal strife throughout the land. Milton laments that for this period he must rely on sources – Nennius, Bede, the Anglo-Saxon Chronicle, Monmouth, Malmesbury – that he finds barbarous in style, unreliable in reporting civil matters, and in most matters of religion "blind, astonish'd, and strook with superstition . . . in one word, Monks" (127–8). Again, he often invites his readers to skepticism. He pauses in his narrative at another fair but lost opportunity for the English to govern themselves: the notable military victory at Badon which gave them a 44-year peace untroubled by the Saxons. Following Gildas closely, Milton details their corruptions in terms that resonate with present conditions: kings who had degenerated to "all Tyranny and vitious life" and clergy who were "Unlerned, Unapprehensive, yet impudent; suttle Prowlers, Pastors in Name, but indeed Wolves . . . seising on the Ministry as a Trade, not as a Spiritual Charge, . . . bunglers at the Scripture" (174–5). Therefore, when war broke out again, the Saxons drove the Britons from most of the country. This is a story, Milton concludes, of "the many miseries and desolations, brought by divine hand on a perverse Nation"(183). He accurately describes Book IV of his history as a "scatterd story" of civil matters, and voices his frustration that his primary source for it, Bede, offers something closer to a Calendar than an interpretative history: "Thir actions we read of, were most commonly Wars, but for what cause wag'd or by what Councells carried on, no care was had to let us know: wherby thir strength and violence we understand, of thir wisedom, reason, or justice, little or nothing" (229–30).

In December, 1648 the army's seizure of power and its determination to bring the king to trial threw constitutional issues into clear relief. Appealing to a time-honored political principle invoked by all sides since the beginning of the Revolution, *Salus Populi Suprema Lex* (the preservation of the Commonwealth is the first law of nature), the officers held that their actions were warranted in the present extreme crisis, though they sought to preserve some shards of legality by claiming to act under the authority of the Commons.[114] Moderates who held tenaciously to the rule of law under the old constitution still hoped to restore the king with strict limitations on his power; even Cromwell still hoped for some such settlement. The Levellers saw the enactment of an Agreement of the People as the prime necessity so that the government might be settled under a new social compact and written constitution. Millenarians often discounted the importance of any civil settlement given their expectation of the imminent appearance of King Jesus. The Council of Officers met for five weeks in December and January to discuss a new version of the Agreement, but it foundered this time over the issue of religious toleration: some Levellers and sectaries would deny the magistrate any power in religious matters, while the officers held out for his power to protect and maintain Protestant religion and to restrain palpable wickedness: atheists, Roman Catholics, idolators, and some radicals.[115] Believing themselves "cozen'd and deceived" by the officers, the Levellers now opposed taking any action to bring the king to justice until the Agreement of the People could be settled.[116]

On January 4, 1649 the remnant of the Commons (the Rump) formally declared their own supremacy without king or house of peers, proclaiming a *de facto* republic. On January 6, a commission of some 135 men, headed by Fairfax, Cromwell, and Ireton, was appointed to try the king, but Fairfax and more than eighty others soon withdrew. About this time Milton received another letter from Carlo Dati announcing his receipt of two copies of Milton's "most learned" Latin *Poems,* reporting his own recent achievements, and passing along "affectionate greetings" from Frescobaldi, Cotellini, Francini, Vincenzio Galilei (Galileo's son), and others.[117] Milton was probably pleased, but apparently did not reply; just then his carefree life with his academy friends must have seemed very remote indeed.

Given his sense that the nation was poised at a defining moment, Milton may have been among the crowds in the galleries that witnessed the dramatic spectacle of the king's trial, which began on January 20, 1649 in the Great Hall at Westminster. John Bradshaw presided over a court attended by only sixty to seventy of the appointed commissioners, but packed with lawyers on both sides, as well as soldiers and spectators on the floor and in the galleries. Bradshaw read out the charge of "High Treason and other High Crimes," specifying that Charles broke his Coronation oath,

> out of a wicked design to erect and uphold in himself an unlimited and tyrannical power to rule according to his will, and to overthrow the rights and liberties of the people; yea, to take away and make void the foundations thereof . . . which by the fundamental constitution of this kingdom were reserved on the people's behalf in the right and power of frequent and successive Parliaments or national meetings in council; he . . . hath traitorously and maliciously levied War against the present parliament and the people therein represented.[118]

Every day, Charles kept his hat on in defiance of the court's authority, and refused to answer the charges against him on the ground that a sovereign king cannot be judged by any earthly power. The court pronounced him in contempt and heard several witnesses against him. On January 27 he was sentenced: "Charles Stuart, as a Tyrant, Traitor, Murderer, and public Enemy to the good people of this nation, shall be put to death by the severing his head from his body."[119] Fifty-nine of the commissioners signed the death warrant.

Throughout the trial, the Presbyterian pulpits and presses exploded with denunciations, and Milton entered the fray with *The Tenure of Kings and Magistrates.* In the *Second Defense* (1654) he offers a carefully reconstructed account of the purposes and timing of the *Tenure,* in which he portrays himself as a private citizen and scholar who took no part in the polemics or decisions concerning Charles himself, but who was moved by the furor and lies of the Presbyterians during the king's trial to offer a theoretical analysis of tyranny:

> Nor did I write anything about the right of kings, until the king, having been declared an enemy by parliament and vanquished in the field, was pleading his cause as a prisoner before the judges and was condemned to death. Then at last, when certain Presbyterian ministers, formerly bitter enemies of Charles . . . persisted in attacking the decree which parliament had passed concerning the king . . . and caused as much tumult as they could, even daring to assert that the doctrines of Protestants and all reformed churches shrank from such an outrageous sentence against kings, I concluded that I must openly oppose so open a lie. Not even then, however, did I write or advise anything concerning Charles, but demonstrated what was in general permissible against tyrants, adducing not a few testimonies from the foremost theologians. . . . This book did not appear until after the death of the king, having been written to reconcile men's minds, rather than to determine anything about Charles (which was not my affair, but that of the magistrates, and which had by then been effected). (*CPW* IV.1, 626–7)

He claims here that the *Tenure* was written "to reconcile men's minds" to the *fait accompli* of Charles's death by defending the general proposition that execution of a tyrant is lawful, rather than to judge the king's case. But Milton's various references to "the proceedings now in Parlament against the King" (*CPW* III, 222) indicate that the tract was largely written during the king's trial, and Milton did seek to intervene in the unfolding scenario. He defends the acts of the army, justifies the existing government of army officers and the Rump Parliament, seeks to inculcate republican beliefs in his countrymen, and undertakes to bolster the courage of a wavering populace subjected to a torrent of Presbyterian sermons and tracts. He ridicules recent tracts by William Prynne, John Gauden, and Henry Hammond, but reserves his special fury for the "dancing divines" of the Westminster Assembly and Sion College, notably the *Serious and Faithful Representation* signed by 47 London ministers on January 18, and *A Vindication of the Ministers* of January 27, "subscribed with the ostentation of great Characters and little moment."[120] Events, however, outran Milton's pen and the king's execution intervened before he finished it.

It is at least possible that Milton joined the large and tumultuous crowd on that wintry January 30 to witness the momentous event: the executioners in black masks; the spectators kept at a distance so that Charles's last words were inaudible to most; Charles kneeling on the scaffold with outstretched arms; the "dismal Universal Groan" that reportedly greeted the fallen axe.[121] Yet Milton's comments about that event never claim the authority of personal observation and could derive from the many published reports and descriptions of the scene, e.g. "Granted . . . that the common soldiers behaved rather insolently" (*CPW* IV.2, 644). If he were there, he more than most would have registered the irony as Charles I, with dignity and courage, enacted his last role on the black-draped scaffold stage erected outside Inigo Jones's Banquetting Room at Whitehall where he had danced so many masque roles. Andrew Marvell's famous lines memorably evoke the scene both men may (or may not) have witnessed:

That thence the *Royal Actor* born
The *Tragick Scaffold* might adorn,
  While round the armed Bands
  Did clap their bloody hands.
He nothing common did, or mean
Upon the memorable Scene:
  But with his keener Eye
  The Axes edge did try:
Nor call'd the *Gods* with vulger spight
To vindicate his helpless Right,
  But bow'd his comely Head
  Down, as upon a Bed.[122]

Milton was less conflicted. While he would not (I think) clap his hands, he surely believed that justice was served when the axe fell.

Steps were taken immediately to form and secure the new republic. During the first week of February the Commons passed resolutions to abolish the office of king and the House of Lords; on February 13 a 41-member Council of State was named to serve as executive; on February 22 an Engagement, to be subscribed by council members and later by other officials, called for "the settling of this nation for the future in way of a Republic, without king or House of Lords."[123] But the infant Commonwealth was threatened on all sides. Scotland and Ireland proclaimed the exiled Prince Charles king and armies were gathering in both countries. A book purportedly written by Charles I in prison, *Eikon Basilike: The True Portraicture of His Sacred Majesty in his Solitudes and Sufferings*, began circulating immediately after the execution, eliciting an onrush of sympathy for the monarch. The royalist news sheets vehemently denounced the new government and demanded the coronation of Charles II. In a flurry of tracts and petitions the disaffected Levellers and their supporters in the army denounced the Rump Parliament, the army grandees, and the other institutions of the new republic as having no sound claim to represent the sovereign people without the constitutional form of an Agreement of the People.[124] In these unsettled circumstances, proposals to dissolve the Rump Parliament and hold new elections came to seem foolhardy.

Milton's *Tenure* was published *c.* Febrary 13, 1649, the first declaration of support by a person of note outside parliament. At this crisis moment Milton chose, courageously, to cast his lot publically with the regicides. He may have hoped by this gesture to call his gifts to the attention of the new men in power in the Commons and Council of State. The full title indicates the tract's scope: *The Tenure of Kings and Magistrates: proving, That it is Lawfull, and hath been held so through all Ages, for any, who have the Power, to call to account a Tyrant, or wicked king, and after due conviction, to depose, and put him to death; if the ordinary magistate have neglected, or deny'd to doe it. And that they, who of late so much blame Deposing, are the Men that did it themselves.*[125] The tract makes what seems a calculated effort to draw parliamentarians, army officers, and Levellers together again in the common cause. Milton was some kind of republican at this juncture, but in his own terms. He was prepared to support, now as later, such government structures as seemed necessary to create and preserve the new state and those freedoms of religion and thought he cared most about. The tract's rhetoric and political theory are discussed on pages 229–35.

"My Labors . . . Have Hardly Been in Vain"

The publication of Milton's *Poems* late in 1645 and of the *Tenure* in February, 1649, were for Milton crucial gestures of self-presentation in the public arena. With the first, he introduced himself formally to a cultivated English readership as an notable English poet. With the second, he took on, unasked, quite another role, that of polemic defender of the revolution and theorist of the new republic. As he indicated in *The Reason of Church-Government,* he turned from one role to the other, in response to what he thought God and the times required of him in particular circumstances.

In the final months of 1645 Milton evidently decided – perhaps in response to Moseley's invitation – that it was time to fulfill the covenant he had made with his countrymen three years earlier, to produce poetry that might "imbreed and cherish in a great people the seeds of vertu, and publick civility."[126] If he could not yet produce the great national epic, he would offer something on account. The moment would have seemed auspicious to collect and publish most of the poems he had thus far written, and to resume the long-postponed work of his right hand: the leisure and peace needed for poetry might be hoped for now, as the fortunes of war shifted to parliament's side and his marriage was mended. The title of the small octavo calls attention to its scope, claims authorial sanction and supervision, and emphasizes Milton's association with Henry Lawes: *Poems of Mr. John Milton, Both English and Latin, Compos'd at several times. Printed by his true Copies. The Songs were set in Musick by Mr. Henry Lawes Gentleman of the Kings Chappel, and one of his Maiesties Private Musick* (1645).

But what kind of poet does this volume introduce? It has been seen by some as a bid for respectability, in which Milton sought to distance himself from his recent polemics and to associate his book with contemporary Cavalier collections.[127] The prefatory matter invites such a reading, but that is chiefly the work of the bookseller Herbert Moseley, whose publications sought to create a gallery of courtly poets, using much the same title page format and associating many of them with the court musician Henry Lawes.[128] Moseley's presentation of Milton is fraught with ambiguities. He allows that readers may prefer "more trivial Airs" than Milton's, whom he properly places in the tradition of "our famous Spencer."[129] He also commissioned, and to Milton's dismay used as frontispiece, William Marshall's notoriously distorted engraved portrait of Milton, which claims to represent him at age 21 but makes him look more like 51 (plate 8). Richard Johnson points out that the face divides in the middle: one side is that of a youthful poet, the other, that of a crabbed controversialist.[130] However, Milton had his revenge – incidentally showing himself not immune to a touch of vanity – by causing Marshall, who knew no Greek, to inscribe under the portrait a witty Greek epigram ridiculing it:

> That an unskilful hand had carved this print
> You'd say at once, seeing that living face;
> But, finding here no jot of me, my friends,
> Laugh at the botching artist's mis-attempt.[131]

Also, by his title-page epigraph from Virgil's Eclogue VII Milton presents himself as predestined Bard (*vati . . . futuro*),[132] explicitly refusing the 'Cavalier' construction laid upon him by the title page and some other features of Moseley's apparatus.

In the 1645 volume Milton presents himself as a new kind of reformist poet. He organizes his poetic production over more than twenty years so as to underscore his development toward that role. He probably approved and may have suggested the design for the frontispiece which contains the wretched portrait, since it previews the character of the volume appropriately. He sits before a drapery pulled back at one corner to reveal a pastoral landscape with a shepherd piping and figures dancing on the lawn, indicating the pastoral mode governing several of these poems. In the corner niches are four Muses suggestive of the poet's generic range: Erato (elegy and erotic poetry), Melpomene (tragedy), Clio (History), and Urania (Divine poetry). These poems display Milton's command of several languages and all the resources of high culture, sharply distinguishing him from a Puritan plain-style poet like George Wither.[133] But he separates himself as decisively from Cavalier lyricists, court masque writers, and Anglican devotional poets, with poems designed to reclaim and reform several genres dominated by them. He also claims a poetic mode shunned by the Cavaliers: prophecy.

The multiple languages, the poetic variety, and the several commendations from learned friends – the Italian Catholic literati and Sir Henry Wotton, as well as Lawes's laudatory preface to the 1637 *Maske* – allow Milton to present himself as a man of many parts: scholar, humanist, man of the world, highly accomplished Latin poet, new English Bard.[134] But he means those parts to cohere with his self-presentation as reformist poet, and in large part he makes them do so. The commendatory poems show him accurately as a man whose friendships transcend ideological barriers, but he does not identify with the politics or religion of those friends. Also, these commendations make a gesture of unusual poetic independence, suggesting that this as yet little-known poet need not depend on courtly or aristocratic patrons but can be introduced to the world by a distinguished coterie of scholars and artists at home and abroad. He includes in this volume almost all of his poems written to date, even the unfinished "Passion" which he describes as "above the years he had."

That inclusiveness is a self-fashioning gesture by which the new reformist poet constructs a record of his poetic growth, even of his failures. He makes frequent, though occasionally inaccurate, notations of the age at which particular poems were written, the errors tending to push back the dates of composition so as to underscore both his preciosity and the distance traveled. We might wonder about the inclusion of the funeral poems for Bishop Felton, Jane Paulet, and especially Bishop Lancelot Andrewes, who was recently a target of Milton's anti-episcopal tracts. But, as I have suggested earlier, he would not have considered these poems, at the time and in the circumstances of their writing, to be in any real conflict with his reformist agenda, so he would see no reason to exclude them now.[135] His Ovidian love elegies he now presents as youthful folly – "These empty monuments to my idleness" – adding after the last elegy (number 7) a recantation that stages his conversion from Ovid to Plato.[136]

By the organization of this volume Milton constructs himself as *vates*, not Cavalier lyricist. A contemporary reader who made the comparison that bookseller Moseley suggests would quickly see that Milton is no Waller. In his prefatory epistle Waller casts off poetry as a youthful toy, offering his *Poems* as "not onely all I have done, but all I ever mean to doe in this kind."[137] Milton offers his volume as an earnest of greater poems to come from the future bard. Waller's poems – all in English and haphazardly arranged – are mostly witty or elegant love songs, poems to or about patrons, and poems on royal personages or occasions. Milton's – in Latin and English, with a few in Italian and Greek – emphasize his learning, his intellectual and poetic growth, and his self-construction as a reformist prophet–poet. His classical poems, many of them juvenilia, are placed last: a book of elegies and epigrams, followed by a book of *Sylvae* (in several meters), ending with the Latin dirge for Diodati that bids farewell to Italy, to Latin poetry, and to pastoral, and also reports a first attempt at epic. This classical part is preceded by *A Maske,* again revised and expanded to underscore its critique of the court masque and the court ethos. The vernacular lyric "book" is placed first – mostly English poems but also the Italian sonnets. Waller's lyric collection begins as do many Cavalier collections with several poems on King Charles; Milton's begins with the Nativity ode, a poem celebrating the birth of the Divine King and proclaiming at the outset Milton's dedication of himself as prophet–poet. It is followed by his psalm paraphrases at age 15, indicating that his earliest poetic ventures had a religious and reformist cast. His last English lyric, *Lycidas*, is given a new headnote pointing to the poem's prophecy, now fulfilled, of "the ruine of our corrupted Clergy, then in their height." Far from eliding his polemics, this note formally links them to his poetry. Milton evidently saw his 1645 *Poems*, not as a volume of would-be Cavalier poetry, but as a worthy alternative – a volume of learned, delightful, reformed poems that would advance the project he began in several of his early poems and formally proposed in *The Reason of Church-government*: to help transform English culture through good art.

"Ad Joannem Rousium" continues this self-representation and directs a reading of the volume in such terms. It is a verse letter sent in January 1647 to John Rouse, librarian of the Bodleian Library in Oxford, along with the replacement copy of the *Poems* which had initially gone astray. But it is also conceived as an ode whose several addresses and apostrophes are directed to the book itself. As Stella Revard has noted,[138] it joins the elegiac and Pindaric modes, allowing Milton to represent his progress from the lower to the higher lyric kinds. Milton first presents himself as a carefree, witty, genial, and playful poet in the private elegiac mode of Ovid, Horace, or Catullus, one who "played, footloose" and "trifled with his native lute or . . . Daunian quill" (ll. 6–10).[139] But by degrees he takes on the role of an inspired Pindaric poet who is divinely appointed to purge the land of evils, to promote religious, political, and social order, to honor heroes, and to serve the Muses. Beginning in a mock-epic vein with a familiar address to his lost "Twin-membered book" (Latin and English poems within a single cover), he imagines its adventures: stolen or lost through a messenger's carelessness, it is perhaps imprisoned in some den or dive or subject to "the calloused hand of an illiterate dealer." But now, in a new copy, it will be welcomed by Rouse, "faithful warden of immortal works," into the delightful groves of the Muses at Oxford, to be preserved from the present "vulgar mob of readers" for a more receptive "sane posterity." This is the last poem Milton wrote in Latin, and it is by design experimental. In an appended note Milton explains that he sought to imitate in Latin the mixed formalism and freedom of Pindar or a Greek chorus, taking the liberty of changing meters and introducing free verse. He retains the strophe–antistrophe–epode structure but, as his note explains, rather for convenience in reading ("commode legendi") than in conformity to classical rules. The experiment has drawn the ire of purists and the high praise of critics sympathetic to Milton's achievement in producing a metrical scheme consonant with the poem's purposes and its complex mix of tones.[140]

The poem relates itself consciously to the new political circumstances. In January, 1647 the book will go to a liberated Oxford, from which the king and the degenerate Cavaliers have been expelled, and that happy sanctuary of the Muses – imagined as a Delphic temple with Rouse as its priest – will honor and preserve the book of a true poet, Milton. Milton alternates praises of Rouse with denunciations of the "degenerate idleness of our effeminate luxury" (vices associated with royalists), of the "accursed tumults among the citizens" that banished the Muses (ll. 26–32), and of the Harpies that fouled Pegasus's river (Oxford had long been a bastion of royalist soldiers and courtiers). But with peace restored, Milton can at length assume a high poetic role. No longer terming his poems "trifles" but rather "labors" – with intimations of Herculean labors – he expects them to find a place among the "glorous monuments of heroes" and the sublime Greek and Latin authors (ll. 49–50, 71–3).

The king's trial and execution led Milton to quite another self-definition as, with

The Tenure of Kings and Magistrates, he rejoined the public debate about public affairs. That treatise, designed rather like a deliberative oration meant to persuade, has as its overarching rhetorical purpose the rallying of as large a part of the populace as possible to support or at least accept the trial, the regicide, and the new commonwealth. Several elements are intertwined here, somewhat disjointedly: castigation of backsliding Presbyterians, rhetorical appeals to the fragmenting revolutionary parties, defenses of tyrannicide, and development of a republican political theory derived from classical and contemporary sources, and the Bible. Milton's *Tenure* is especially interesting as his own urgent exploration of republican ideas at a crisis moment, tailored to immediate circumstances and to the needs of polemic argument. It is at once an important document in the development of English republican thought and an illuminating register of Milton's political thought during the king's trial and just after his execution.

Milton claims in this tract to address issues of theory, leaving the magistrates to judge the special case of Charles I. But such judgment, he insists, pertains only to "the uprighter sort of them, and of the people, though in number less by many, in whom faction least hath prevaild above the Law of nature and right reason" (*CPW* III, 197). This principle provides a rationale for the actions of the army and the extraordinary commission that tried the king. And though Milton does not mention Charles, he makes clear his own judgment on the king's case by using language that echoes the indictment on which he was tried:[141]

> But this I dare owne as part of my faith, that if such a one there be, by whose Commission, whole massachers have been committed on his faithfull Subjects, his Provinces offerd to pawn or alienation, as the hire of those whom he had sollicited to come in and destroy whole Citties and Countries; be he King, or Tyrant, or Emperour, the Sword of Justice is above him; in whose hand soever is found sufficient power to avenge the effusion and so great a deluge of innocent blood. For if all human power to execute, not accidentally but intendedly, the wrath of God upon evil doers without exception, be of God; then that power, whether ordinary, or if that faile, extraordinary so executing that intent of God, is lawfull, and not to be resisted. (197–8)

As well, he often echoes emerging English theory during the past decade on popular sovereignty and government based on contract – especially Leveller formulations – but without naming names or aligning himself with any party. This is in part a rhetorical gesture, to make common cause among the various factions through the fiction that his treatise is a only a theoretical exposition of the issues. But it is also Milton's characteristic posture of working out his own positions without reliance on authorities or the formulations of others.

The tract begins with some equations. Milton associates the king's political tyranny with that slavery to custom and unruly passions that mark his supporters as bad men, and insists that only good men, free of such slavery, can properly love liberty:

> If men within themselves would be govern'd by reason, and not genereally give up thir understanding to a double tyrannie, of Custom from without, and blind affections within, they would discerne better, what it is to favour and uphold the Tyrant of a Nation. But being slaves within doors, no wonder that they strive so much to have the public State conformably govern'd to the inward vitious rule, by which they govern themselves. For indeed none can love freedom heartilie, but good men; the rest love not freedom but licence; which never hath more scope or more indulgence then under Tyrants. (190)

Such assertions, often reiterated, echo a core of classical and modern writers on politics whom Milton had studied assiduously over many years: Aristotle, Cicero, Lucan, Sallust, Suetonius, Tacitus, Livy, Machiavelli.[142] From that reading Milton has concluded that the virtues needed by both rulers and ruled to sustain liberty in a free commonwealth include reason, justice, magnanimity, temperance, fortitude, and strong commitment to the common good and the preservation of liberty. Classical theory regarding slavery and freedom also underpins Milton's redefinition of tyranny. According to Roman political thought as developed by Cicero, Livy, Tacitus, Sallust, and others, a slave is subject to someone else's power, a citizen is not.[143] So for Milton tyranny is not simply the illegal seizure of a throne or vicious deeds against the people, but any absolute monarchy or any claims to a sphere of royal prerogative outside the law, since such power, even if not abused, makes slaves of the people. On this point Milton also cites Aristotle: "Monarchy unaccountable, is the worst sort of Tyranny; and least of all to be endur'd by free born men" (204).

Throughout the tract Milton launches a ferocious attack on the Presbyterian ministers, whose pulpits were ringing with denunciations of the trial and the regicide as covenant-breaking and sacrilege. As he later describes it: "I attacked, almost as if I were haranguing an assembly, the pre-eminent ignorance or insolence of these ministers, who had given promise of better things" (*CPW* IV.1, 626). His caustic language has the rhetorical function of discrediting them, but it also displays his seething rage against these backsliders from the revolution: they are "Apostate Scarcrowes"(*CPW* III, 194), "dancing Divines" (195), "Mercenary noisemakers" (236), "pragmatical Sidesmen of every popular tumult and Sedition" (241), "Ministers of Mammon instead of Christ" (242). The moral charges against them are much the same as in the *History of Britain* – venality, ambition, place-seeking, money-grubbing, ignorance – and he again castigates their repressive efforts to "bind other mens consciences" (239). But here he especially emphasizes their political sins. They themselves were fiercest in stirring up the revolt against Charles, and in doing so they "devested him, disannointed him, nay curs'd him all over in thir Pulpits and thir Pamphlets" (191) and essentially unkinged him, kingship being a relation that involves subjects offering obedience to rulers. Indeed, in fighting against him they might well have killed him themselves, on the battlefield. But now they have ignominiously turned their coats, denouncing the consequences of the actions they began, only because (Milton unfairly charges) affairs are not being managed "to the intire advantages of thir own Faction" (191). He also attacks the host of "Vulgar and irrational men" (peers, lawyers), whose opposition derives from slavish adherence to the ancient constitution: "Some contesting for privileges, customs, forms, and that old entanglement of Iniquity, thir gibrish Lawes, though the badge of thir ancient slavery" (192–3). This is an allusion to the so called "Norman Yoke" of oppressive laws which, one resistance theory claimed, had been foisted on the English at the Norman Conquest. Others who plead for mercy for Charles do so out of "levitie and shallowness of minde," or a "seditious pity" that would endanger the entire nation (193).

Milton reaches out, however, to those who have heretofore dared to act or at least approve actions "above the form of Law and Custom" but who now "begin to swerve, and almost shiver at the Majesty and grandeur of som noble deed . . . disputing presidents, forms, and circumstances, while the Common-wealth nigh perishes" (194). That category could include Fairfax and the other commissioners who absented themselves from the trial, the MPs who voluntarily left the House, and Levellers who oppose action against the king until an Agreement of the People is in place. To these he wishes "better instruction, and vertue equal to thir calling," offering "as my dutie is" to bestow the former on them. In the last portion of the tract, he analyzes biblical texts and marshals a host of examples from biblical, classical, and modern European and English history as precedents and justification for deposing or executing tyrants.

But he first develops a much more sweeping republican argument that echoes Leveller theories of popular sovereignty in vesting the power to choose and change governments and governors in the people generally, not in inferior magistrates as Calvinist resistance theory had it. Also, Milton's title, *The Tenure of Kings and Magistrates*, extends the people's right to change their government at will not only to King Charles but also to those other magistrates, the Long Parliament. But unlike the Levellers, Milton adapts his republican theory to the exigencies of the time as well as to his underlying assumptions about slavishness and citizenship, arguing that good men who love liberty (e.g. the truncated Commons, the army, and the commissioners) may rightfully act as "the people" in these extraordinary circumstances.

Milton's argument for popular sovereignty builds on traditional political theory that derives legitimate government from the consent of the governed, tendered through an originary contract or covenant, mythic or actual. Elements of that theory – drawn from Aristotle, Augustine, Aquinas, Richard Hooker, and other classical, medieval, and early-modern sources – had been invoked by recent theorists of resistance to argue that kings are accountable to their people to abide by the terms of that contract, e.g. George Buchanan's *De Juri Regni apud Scotos* (1597), the *Vindiciae Contra Tyrannos*, Henry Parker's *Jus Populi* (1644), and Samuel Rutherford's *Lex, Rex: The Law and the Prince* (1644). During the previous decade such theory had become a starting point for Puritan political discourse, reinforced by theological analyses of biblical covenants between God and his people, by the legal concept that the ancient constitution of England and Magna Carta subject the king to the law, and by Leveller efforts to literalize the originary myth in a written constitution, an Agreement of the People. Most theorists assumed, however, that "the people" who have rights as citizens are an educated, propertied, male elite. The categorical terms with which Milton introduces his version of the contract theory – "No man who knows ought, can be so stupid to deny" (198) – evoke this common ground.

In Milton's version men were created free, "born to command and not to obey" until the Fall introduced sin and violence among them, leading them "by common league to bind each other" from injury and for common defense. This is a social compact constructing societies: "Citties, Townes, and Common-wealths." This pact proving insufficient to control wrongdoers, the people ordained "som authority" – a king if one man were most worthy, magistrates if several were of equal worth – "not to be thir Lords and Maiesters . . . but, to be thir Deputies and Commissioners" to execute the powers that reside inherently in each man (198–9). This establishes a political compact. When these rulers at length fell prey to the temptations of absolute power, the people invented laws to limit magistrates, "so man . . . might no more rule over them, but law and reason" (200). When laws were ignored or misapplied, the people formalized the governmental compact, requiring kings and magistrates to take oaths "to doe impartial justice by Law: who upon those termes and no other, receav'd Alleageance from the people . . . ofttimes with express warning, that if the King or Magistrate prov'd unfaithfull to his trust, the people would be disingag'd." Then they added counselors and parliaments to have care of the public safety, "with him or without him, at set times or at all times" (200). These last two stages of the originary myth Milton grounds in history, citing examples of coronation oaths.

His conclusion from this narrative is to insist (in contrast to Hooker and Hobbes) that the political compact can be abrogated since essential sovereignty always remains in the people: "The power of Kings and Magistrates is nothing else, but what is only derivative, transferr'd and commited to them in trust from the People, to the Common good of them all, in whom the power yet remains fundamentally, and cannot be tak'n from them, without a violation of thir natural birthright" (202). But for Milton, in contrast to Hobbes and the Levellers, repudiation of the political contract does not abrogate the social contract and return men to the state of nature. Milton also insists that royalist theories arguing the king's right to his throne by inheritance (in Filmer's view the king inherits by descent from Adam),[144] and divine-right theories based on Romans 13:1 and 1 Samuel 8, that the king is answerable to none but God, make the people slaves and overturn all law and government. Throughout the tract, Milton draws out the metaphorical implications of the term "tenure" to represent the king as a bondsman who holds his office or "tenure" from the people on condition he fulfill his covenant with them.[145] As for that explicit covenant "The Solemn League and Covenant," which the Presbyterians understood as a binding contract to protect the king's life and office, Milton repeats a principle often used by Puritans to justify taking up arms and affirmed by him earlier in the divorce tracts: covenants cannot bind against the laws of nature and reason always implicit in them.

He then applies this theory to the people's sovereign right to change any government at will:

> It follows lastly, that since the King or Magistrate holds his autoritie of the people . . . then may the people as oft as they shall judge it for the best, either choose him or reject him, retaine him or depose him though no Tyrant, meerly by the liberty and right of free born Men, to be govern'd as seems to them best. (206)

Indeed, any restraint of the citizens from choosing and changing governments is itself tyranny, since if they are citizens and not slaves they – not the king, as in the usual royalist analogy – have the power and rights of the master of a household:

> Surely they that shall boast, as we doe, to be a free Nation, and not have in themselves the power to remove, or abolish any governour supreme, or subordinat, with the goverment it self upon urgent causes, may please thir fancy with a ridiculous and painted freedom, fit to coz'n babies; but are indeed under tyranny and servitude; as wanting that power, which is the root and sourse of all liberty, to dispose and *oeconomize* in the Land which God hath giv'n them, as Maisters of Family in thir own house and free inheritance. (236–7)

Milton's readiness to argue that, at least temporarily, the patently unrepresentative Commons and the army might act as and for the people arises in part from his disgust with the Long Parliament, so vigorously expressed in the Digression to the *History of Britain*. He also assumes the principle of *Salus Populi* as justifying these extra-legal measures in times of emergency. But his explicit justification is the worthiness of those who have stayed the course amid many backsliders, thereby proving themselves to be a natural aristocracy of worthies who, on Aristotelian principles, ought to rule. The evidence of their goodness is not religious orthodoxy or signs of Calvinist election, but manifest love of liberty – "none can love freedom heartilie but good men" – and the battlefield victories that indicate God's favor to them (192). With Machiavelli in the background, Milton turns the royalist reading of Romans 13:1 against the royalists, arguing that the powers to be obeyed now are those who are presently in power: "If all human power to execute, not accidentally but intendedly, the wrath of God upon evil doers without exception, be of God; then that power, whether ordinary, or if that faile, extraordinary, so executing that intent of God, is lawfull, and not to be resisted" (198).

Characteristically, Milton offers to show that scripture and reason perfectly agree on principles of government, even as they do on divorce: "This, though it cannot but stand with plain reason, shall be made good also by Scripture" (206). A version of republican theory, based both on biblical and classical sources, is a constant in Milton's political argument over the next decade. One biblical proof text, often cited by royalists as validation for the king's absolute power to do good or evil without any right of resistance by the people, is 1 Samuel 8, which records the Israelites' desire for a king like other nations to replace the prophet–judge Samuel. God granted their request after warning them of the great evils the kings they want will inflict on them. Antiroyalists expounded the passage as validating a people's right to change even the government God had provided them, but also as rendering God's warning about the evils of monarchy, and his displeasure with the Israelites for rejecting his own kingship for that of an earthly king. Milton makes both points (202, 207), and also implies that God's ancient government under the Judges has some near conformity to the new English republic which recognizes only God as king:

> As God was heretofore angry with the Jews who rejected him and his forme of Goverment to choose a king, so that he will bless us, and be propitious to us who reject a king to make him onely our leader and supreme governour in the conformity as neer as may be of his own ancient goverment; if we have at least but so much worth in us to entertain the sense of our future happiness, and the courage to receave what God voutsafes us: wherein we have the honour to precede other Nations who are now labouring to be our followers. (236)

Milton also interprets a New Testament text he will soon elaborate more fully: Christ's charge to the sons of Zebedee (Luke 22:25) not to seek dominion over others as do the kings of the Gentiles, but rather to "esteem themselves Ministers and Servants to the public" (217).

In *Tenure*, Milton's republicanism has less to do with government structures than with ethos. He does not demand the elimination of monarchy as such, nor does he provide that the sovereign legislature be truly representative. Here, as later, he cared less about the institutions of government than about protecting religious and intellectual liberty and promoting what he and many others at this juncture regarded as the essence of a "free commonwealth:" government founded upon consent, the rule of law not of men, governors who remain the servants of the people, and government for the common good rather than in the interests of one or a few.[146] But he also goes very far indeed in discrediting kings, in arguing the right of the people to choose and change magistrates and governments at their pleasure, and even in suggesting that republican government has special divine sanction. In these terms he gives positive theoretical reinforcement to the English republic just then aborning.

8

"The So-called Council of State . . . Desired to Employ My Services" 1649–1652

Milton took great pride in his appointment to serve the Commonwealth as Secretary for Foreign Languages. He was gratified to be part of the daring experiment in republican government in a post that made use of his formidable linguistic and polemical skills. It was the kind of public service his whole life had prepared him for. Soon he was caught up in a whirl of activities and responsibilities largely set by others, a life very different indeed from his former retired life as scholar and poet. He saw the beleaguered new government ringed about by enemies in Ireland, Scotland, and much of Europe, threatened at home by royalist resistance, opposed by former supporters, and disliked by much of the populace. He was eager to help it establish credibility by writing its letters to foreign states in elegant Latin,[1] and by answering the most formidable polemic attacks upon it: King Charles's supposed testament from the grave, and an influential Latin treatise by the famous French scholar, Claude Saumaise (Salmasius). In the *Defensio Secunda* (1654) he provides his own account of the circumstances in which he was offered this appointment and these commissions:

> The so called Council of State, which was then for the first time established by the authority of Parliament, summoned me, though I was expecting no such event, and desired to employ my services, especially in connection with foreign affairs. Not long afterwards there appeared a book attributed to the king, and plainly written with great malice against Parliament. Bidden to reply to this, I opposed to the *Eikon* the *Eikonoklastes,* not, as I am falsely charged, "insulting the departed spirit of the king," but thinking that Queen Truth should be preferred to King Charles. . . . Then Salmasius appeared. So far were they from spending a long time (as More alleges) seeking one who would reply to him, that all, of their own accord, at once named me, then present in the Council. (IV.1, 627–8)

Some duties – licensing the weekly government news sheet, authorizing an occasional foreign book, examining the papers of some suspected enemies of the state

– the author of *Areopagitica* may have found distasteful though necessary; apparently he did not deny any licenses. As an officer in the new government he had to come to terms with the compromises attendant upon power and to accept some pragmatic modifications of his tolerationist and republican ideals. His chief responsibility was to put into good Latin official letters to foreign states, treaty negotiations, and various diplomatic exchanges. He also translated letters from foreign governments into English and attended the Council of State or one of its committees as required, usually to translate at meetings with foreign envoys. Though Milton was not in a policy-making position, he regularly encountered and surely hoped to influence the men who sat at the helm of state, among them Cromwell, Fairfax, John Bradshaw (the council president), Henry Vane, and Bulstrode Whitelocke. Bradshaw and Vane he counted as friends.

During these three years Milton was already blind in one eye, and the other was failing "slowly and gradually" (*CPW* IV.2, 869). The process was accelerated, he believed, by the demands of his long Latin answer to Salmasius. The government continued to need his services, but he had to cope with the restrictions imposed by his worsening vision, and with mounting fears of becoming totally blind. His writings of this period sound two major and related themes. One is a fierce attack on idolatry, which, in the very broad definition he develops, is not simply devotion paid to pagan deities or to the images and ritual of Roman Catholicism but, rather, the disposition to attach divinity or special sanctity to any person – pope or king or prelate, or any human institution or material form. So Miltonic iconoclasm is not smashing religious art or suppressing church music but, rather, a relentless effort to disabuse the populace of that disposition, which he sees as predisposing them to slavishness. The other theme is the defense of republicanism on classical and biblical grounds as the government best suited to free, mature, and self-reliant citizens. Invoking the classical idea that the best government is aristocracy, rule by the worthiest citizens, Milton can proclaim England a republic (despite its unrepresentative parliament) by defining its worthiest citizens as those who love and defend liberty. Baffled and dismayed that so many remain disaffected from the English republic, he is willing to make pragmatic compromises to preserve it while (he hopes) the populace can learn better republican values. Apparently he found no time to write poetry and must have wondered if he would ever again do so.

"I Take it on Me as a Work Assign'd"

The recommendation of Milton as Secretary for Foreign Languages may have come from the president of the council John Bradshaw, who had been Milton's attorney in 1647 in the Powell affair,[2] or from Luke Robinson, formerly his fellow student at Christ's College. Edward Phillips explains his alternative title, "Latin Secretary," by referring to a council resolution to use only Latin in diplomatic exchanges, as being

> most proper to maintain a Correspondence among the Learned of all Nations in this part of the World; scorning to carry on their Affairs in the Wheedling, Lisping Jargon of the Cringing *French*, especially having a Minister of State able to cope with the ablest any Prince or State could imploy for the Latin tongue. (*EL* 69)

Phillips's comment seems to reflect Milton's own attitude to the "servility" of Louis XIV's court,[3] and his humanist desire to display the new republic's ability to match any in the use of correct, elegant, Ciceronean Latin. Milton was 41 and already blind in his left eye when he was offered the post on March 13 or 14, 1649 by a delegation sent to his house in Holborn.[4] On March 15 he was formally appointed at the same salary paid to his predecessor, Georg Weckherlin, a little more than £288 a year.[5] He became part of the permanent Secretariat headed by Gualter Frost, general secretary to the Council of State with overall responsibility for its papers and correspondence; that bureau also included his son Gualter Frost, Jr. as assistant, Sir Oliver Fleming as master of ceremonies, and Edward Dendy as sergeant at arms. A "Shadow Secretariat" occasionally called upon for translation or correspondence included, among others, Samuel Hartlib, the addressee of *Of Education*, and others of his circle, Theodore Haak, John Dury, and John Hall.[6] Some of these men already were and the rest soon would be Milton's familiar acquaintances. On March 20 Milton took the required oath of secrecy pertaining to his office, at which time he probably met Cromwell for the first time.

The Council of State was forty-members strong, but seldom had half that number in attendance. Its function was executive but it also discussed and proposed legislation to the parliament, whose average attendance was fifty to sixty members and often much less.[7] Thirty-one of the council members were also in parliament, five were lawyers or judges, three were officers (Cromwell, Fairfax, Phillip Skippon), four were peers, thirteen had been regicides.[8] Like the Rump Parliament, the council represented a mix of interests: Independents, moderate Presbyterians, social conservatives, social reformers, army grandees, republicans, pragmatists. This unwieldy coalition held together during these first years to deal with enormous problems: the imminent threat of invasion from Ireland and Scotland to restore Charles II; fears of invasion from Europe; royalist plots and uprisings at home; Presbyterian demands that the government establish Presbyterianism nationwide and suppress the rapidly proliferating sects; a barrage of Leveller and republican polemic demanding a representative legislature, relief to debtors, law reform, abolition of titles, and religious toleration; agitation and sometimes mutiny by the rank and file soldiers demanding arrears of pay and Leveller social reforms; an onslaught of anti-government newsletters filled with biting royalist satire; damage to English trade from attacks at sea and dubiety about existing trade agreements; and widespread disaffection in the largely Presbyterian City of London and the largely royalist west country and Wales. Exacerbating these difficulties was the ever-increasing need for money to support the large army required to suppress rebellion in Ireland, Scotland, and at home, and also to strengthen the navy. Rising excise taxes, large assessments on property, loans guaranteed by the increasingly suspect "public faith," and the free quartering of unpaid soldiers strained the loyalty even of the regime's supporters.[9] Milton was sometimes in the council as it considered these problems; it met every day except Sunday and often in late evening sessions. From early 1651 onward, however, it seems that he did not attend council meetings unless specifically requested, but did meet often with its Committee on Foreign Affairs.[10]

At first Milton had little foreign correspondence. The initial efforts of the new republic to establish formal diplomatic relationships with European states were sabotaged by royalist exiles in the various European capitols, who undermined, threatened, attacked, and sometimes murdered England's envoys. During 1649 Milton wrote three letters and perhaps more to the Senate of the City of Hamburg, traditionally a close trading partner of England.[11] He turned into sometimes eloquent Latin the English drafts prepared by members of the council, and then made the changes required by the council and by parliament. This was the usual procedure, though Milton was sometimes instructed to compose letters himself with only general directives as to substance, and then submit them for approval.[12] On March 22, 1649 he was ordered to produce Latin versions of two letters protesting attacks by exiled royalists on members of the Merchant Adventurers Trading Company, which had a permanent colony in Hamburg.[13] The first letter eloquently justifies England's decision to "convert the haughty tyranny of royal power into the form of a free state," and formally requests that extant treaties for the protection of English merchants in Hamburg be respected.[14] The second complains more forcefully, and demands prompt punishment for an assault set on by Charles II's agent in Hamburg against the company's chaplain, who barely escaped with his life. The Hamburg Senate responded in a letter dated June 15/25 which Milton probably translated, professing friendship but complaining of shoddy wares and dishonesty from the English traders. Parliament sent out Milton's Latin reply on August 10, promising to correct such abuses but again insisting that Hamburg restrain and punish attacks on the merchants (*CPW* V.2, 489–95). Milton only had a few other incoming letters to translate, chiefly from the United Provinces expressing profound regret over the murder by royalist exiles of England's first envoy to the Hague, Isaac Dorislaus – the same man who had given the aborted history lectures in Cambridge during Milton's undergraduate days.[15] He was murdered by royalist exiles in May, soon after his arrival in the Hague.[16]

The council called soon on Milton's polemical skills. On March 26 he was asked to "make some observations upon a paper lately printed called old & new Chaines" (*LR* 2, 239), a tract by John Lilburne and other Levellers called *The Second Part of England's New Chains Discovered*. More inflammatory than its predecessor,[17] this tract denounced the regicide, opposed the projected invasion of Ireland, blasted the Council of State and the army grandees as ambitious, power-hungry usurpers, claimed that the new government had overturned the English constitution and laws and was oppressing the common soldiers and the people, and called for a new, representative parliament, liberty of conscience, a free press, and the revival of army agitators. On March 28, Milton attended the council to receive a commission relating to Ireland, and so may have heard the Leveller authors – Lilburne, Walwyn, Overton, and Thomas Prince – examined, charged with high treason, and sent to the Tower. Lilburne later claimed that from outside the council door he overheard Cromwell say, "I tell you Sir, you have no other way to deal with these men but to break them in pieces."[18] The council perceived Leveller opposition to the government and also their democratic ideology and reform agenda to be dangerously destabilizing in present circumstances. Leveller agitation promoted mutinies among the restive and still unpaid troops, which Fairfax and Cromwell suppressed with considerable violence and finally crushed at Burford on May 15.

Milton did not produce the requested "Observations" on the Leveller tract. No doubt the council gave precedence to the Ireland commission, but Milton may have demurred or at least waited the council out.[19] Though he nowhere mentions the Levellers and generally supported government policy, Milton agreed with Leveller demands for toleration, a free press, and abolition of tithes. Also, he probably felt considerable affinity with Overton and Walwyn, whose writings had so often been denounced in company with his own divorce tracts.[20] Lilburne and the other three Levellers were acquitted of treason and released from the Tower on November 8, 1649, touching off wild celebrations in the City.

The council's other charge to Milton was to "make some observations" on four documents pertaining to Ireland.[21] The Catholic Confederacy in Ireland, which in 1641 began an armed revolt against English domination, was wooed by Charles I to serve as a potential invasion force to put down the English rebellion. On January 17, 1649 the royalist lord lieutenant, James Butler, Earl of Ormond, signed a peace treaty with the Irish Confederacy in the king's name, offering them almost total political independence and religious freedom in return for such military aid. That offer was probably disingenuous and meant to be repudiated should Charles or his son regain the throne, but the confederacy credited it and joined Ormond's army to secure Ireland for Charles II. Royalist forces were also gathering in Scotland, but Ireland was thought to pose a more immediate threat. Milton was to comment on these four documents: the *Articles of Peace* signed by Ormond; a letter of March 9 from Ormond urging Colonel Michael Jones, governor of Dublin and commander of troops loyal to parliament, to defect to Charles II; Jones's reply of March 14 denouncing the treaty as illegal and proclaiming his loyalty to parliament; and a tract entitled *A Necessary Representation of the Present Evills* (February 15) by the Presbytery at Belfast which denounced the regicide and the new republic. Milton's twenty-page *Observations* appeared around May 16 without his name attached but with the notation, "Publisht by Autority"; he evidently regarded it as an official document.[22] Its polemic plays skillfully on common English attitudes: disdain for the "savage" Irish, revulsion over the bloody 1641 massacre of English residents in Ireland, and Protestant hatred of popish idolatry.

But Milton tailors this quasi-official treatise to his own concerns, which are less with the barbarous Irish than with Scottish influence on English politics. Repellent as Milton's comments about the Irish sometimes are, his tract does not, like much other polemic of early 1649, call for their eradication, or accuse them of cannibalism, or recount massacre horror stories to fuel the English appetite for revenge.[23] His emphases indicate his priorities. He gives only four-and-a-half pages of comment to the thirty-three pages of Ormond's Treaty of Peace with the Irish Rebels, evidently expecting English Protestants of all stripes to agree readily that its generous terms constitute a traitorous sellout of the interests of the English state and church in Ireland. He gives the same space to Ormond's two-page letter attempting to subvert Colonel Jones. But the four-and-a-half page *Representation* by the Ulster Presbyters elicits thirteen pages of refutation, since its fierce denunciation of the regicide and the English republic articulates views widely shared by English Presbyterians. Milton's tract contributes to his government's effort to discredit the defiant Presbyterian clergy at home while seeking the acquiescence of the people.[24] By linking the royalist Ormond and the Ulster Presbyterian clerics with the rebel Irish papists, he seeks to force a sharp division between that treasonous alliance and good English Protestants.

Milton's comments on the treaty redirect much of the English rage from the Irish and toward King Charles and Ormond. In granting an Act of Oblivion for "all the [Irish] Murders, Massacres, Treasons, Pyracies" from 1641 onward, the king has "sold away that justice . . . due for the bloud of more than 200000, of his Subjects, . . . assassinated and cut in pieces by those *Irish* Barbarians."[25] The first article of the treaty, which excuses the Irish from taking the Oath of Supremacy to the English monarch as head of the church and substitutes a simple oath of allegiance, grants the Irish "a Condition of freedome superior to what any *English* Protestant durst have demanded" (*CPW* III, 302). The second and twelfth articles, which negate laws requiring English approval of Irish parliaments and legislation, enable the Irish "to throw off all subjection to this Realme" (303). The ninth allows them a militia, and other articles grant them choice of magistrates and judges, repossession of lands, and control of their own "Schools, Abbeyes, and Revenues, Garrisons, Fortresses, Townes," thereby committing "the whole managing both of peace and warre . . . to Papists, and the chiefe Leaders of that Rebellion" (309, 305). The treaty traitorously gives "to mortall Enemies" part of the English patrimony, acting to "disalliege a whole Feudary Kingdome from the ancient Dominion of *England*" (307). In Milton's formulation, the feudal overlord is not the king but England itself, and Milton cites several cases (as he does also in his Commonplace Book) that deny the king's right to alienate the nation's patrimony for any cause.[26]

On many issues Milton was able to think his way beyond received opinion and prejudice, but not so in regard to England's colonization of Ireland: that nation, he thinks, belongs to England by conquest and in feudal vassalage. He sees no parallel between the Irish struggle for independence and religious liberty and his own commitment to political and religious liberty in England. One reason is that he does see a parallel between the Irish "barbarians" now and the English barbarians who, as he noted in his *History of Britain*, had to be civilized by the conquering Romans.[27] He concludes, however, citing their "absurd and savage Customes,"[28] that the Irish have not yet profited from English civilizing, but have showed themselves "not onely sottish but indocible and averse from all Civility and amendment, . . . rejecting the ingenuity of all other Nations to improve and waxe more civill by a civilizing Conquest, though all these many yeares better showne and taught" (304). A further reason is his conviction that the "poyson" of idolatry and "public Superstitions"(309) spread by the Roman church must be suppressed before Ireland can be civilized. By giving the Irish control of their institutions, the king and Ormond have given Rome, "this grand Enemy and persecutor of the true Church . . . root to grow up and spread his poyson" (309), thereby also endangering England. Milton judges the king's treaty with the Irish by the republican principle of human equality. He has no right to act arbitrarily, and he is not imitating the divine kingship in doing so, as royalists claim: "Why . . . should [the king] sit himselfe like a demigod in lawlesse and unbounded *anarchy*; refusing to be accountable for that autority over men naturally his equals, which God himself without a reason givn is not wont to exercise over his creatures?" (307–8).

In his comments on Ormond's letter to Jones and on the statement by the Ulster Presbyters, Milton emphasizes their folly and treachery in making common cause with the Irish. Appealing to English chauvinism, he inveighs against those "unhallow'd Priestlings" the Ulster Presbyters (mostly settlers from Scotland) who seek to dictate in church and state to the "sovran Magistracy of *England*, by whose autoritie and in whose right they inhabit there" (322, 333). To answer Ormond's charge that the regicide was an act of anarchy and murder, Milton points to victories in battle as some evidence of divine approval: "the hand of God appear'd . . . evidently on our side."[29] But he bases his case chiefly on English law and institutions. Reminding the Ulster Presbyters that their own John Knox "taught professedly the doctrine of deposing, and of killing Kings," he makes it a matter of glory to the English that they proceeded "by the deliberate and well-weighd Sentence of a legal Judicature"(329), not by military force or assassination. To answer the charge that killing the king broke the Solemn League and Covenant, Milton restates his principle that all covenants are conditional and this one explicitly conditional on the king's preservation "*of true Religion, and our liberties*" (331–2). To answer Ormond's charge that the English substituted for the traditional Three Estates the "*Dreggs and Scum of the House of Commons*," Milton defends the worthiness of those members and especially Cromwell, whose nobility is founded on "valour and high merit" as well as "eminent and remarkable Deeds." He locates the essence of parliament not in the Three Estates as such but in "the Supream and generall Councell of a Nation, consisting of whomsoever chos'n and assembld for the public good," claiming far greater antiquity for such councils than for the Estates model (312–15).

Milton answers the charges of Ormond and the Presbyters that the English have abandoned true religion and are promoting irreligion, blasphemy, paganism, and atheism by the countercharge that, by supporting the papist antichrist in Ireland, Charles and Ormond are themselves the most dangerous subverters of religion and upholders of blasphemy: "What more blasphemous not opinion but whole Religion then Popery, plung'd into Idolatrous and Ceremoniall Superstition, the very death of all true Religion" (316). By contrast, the English parliament "have every where brok'n their Temporall power, thrown down their public Superstitions, and confin'd them to the bare enjoyment of that which is not in our reach, their Consciences" (309). The republic also supports "all true Ministers of the Gospel" as they preach and exercise spiritual discipline – the only means of advancing true religion that Christ sanctions. He also intends such comments as advice to the new republic to hold out against Presbyterian pressures to enforce orthodoxy: the civil sword, Milton insists, must act only against "Civill offenses." He allows some exceptions to this formula, but hedges them about with qualifications. The magistrate may suppress the open practice of Roman Catholicism as the fountainhead of idolatry and therein subversive of all religion and liberty. As for "declar'd atheists" and "malicious enemies of God, and of Christ," he observes that "Parlament . . . professes not to tolerate such, but with all befitting endeavours to suppresse them" (311). However, he does not identity himself with that formula from the recent Blasphemy Act, nor does he indicate what, if any, punishment he envisages for them or for the idolatrous papists. Instead, he warns that such epithets are often dangerously misapplied, for example by royalists to the Presbyterians who began the rebellion and to the regicide members of the present government.[30] He brands as an "audacious calumny" the charge that the English embrace "*Paganism and Judaism in the arms of toleration*," but insists that "while we detest *Judaism*, we know our selves commanded by St. *Paul, Rom.* 11 [11:18] to respect the *Jews*, and by all means to endeavor thir conversion" (326) – perhaps suggesting agreement with the proposal of some Independents to invite the Jews back to England.[31] He also advises his government that the Covenant does not require settling Presbyterianism throughout England, but only where it is desired:

> As we perceave it [Presbyterianism] aspiring to be a compulsive power upon all without exception . . . or to require the fleshly arm of Magistracy in the execution of a spirituall Discipline, to punish and amerce by any corporall infliction those whose consciences cannot be edifi'd . . . we hold it no more to be *the hedg and bulwark of Religion*, then the Popish and Prelaticall Courts, or the *Spanish Inquisition.* (326)

Noting that the Commonwealth is continuing ministers' stipends, he refrains from stating his opposition to that arrangement, but he does observe, hopefully, that "they think not money or Stipend to be the best encouragement of a true Pastor," and he reminds them that the Donation of Constantine was the beginning of the church's decline (309–10). Milton used his first assignment for the new government to urge them a good deal further along the path to religious toleration than most were prepared to travel.

When he wrote his *Observations* Milton could not have foreseen what havoc Cromwell's army was soon to wreck in Ireland but, given his characterization of the Irish, he probably accepted it as necessary. Most Englishmen did. Over the next several months, in a series of fierce and bloody battles – Dublin, Drogheda, Wexford, Kilkenny – Cromwell's army slaughtered and butchered the native Irish without quarter in a frenzy of religious hatred and revenge.[32]

During 1649 Milton had little diplomatic correspondence and the council gave him other duties. He was asked to survey the papers of persons suspected of treasonous or illegal acts: on April 20, the letters of one Mr Watkins, to look for evidence "concerning the exportacion of any prohibited goods"; and later the papers of John Lee (May 30) and Mr Small (June 11).[33] On July 16 he was given some kind of supervision over materials in the State Paper Office.[34] On November 21 he was charged to complete an examination of Lady Killigrew's papers, seized in May on suspicion that she was plotting with the enemy; he evidently cleared her, since three days later she had the pass she needed to go abroad (*LR* II, 274). Soon, though, the council recognized that it needed Milton to answer the most important polemic challenge facing the new state, the enormously popular book attributed to the late king, *Eikon Basilike*.[35] It appointed John Hall to deal with less threatening polemic attacks.[36]

Milton soon moved from Holborn to lodgings more convenient to the council's meeting place at Whitehall. His new dwelling, Edward Phillips states, was "at one Thomson's next door to the Bull-head Tavern at Charing Cross, opening into the Spring Garden"[37] – near what would now be 49, Charing Cross Lane. Thomson is unknown, though the name may indicate some connection with Milton's friend, the bookseller George Thomason. Milton's activities now settled into a regular pattern: on some days, walking a few blocks to Whitehall to attend the council when summoned for correspondence, or to follow the course of some negotiations, or for other duties; otherwise, working at home on the treatise he was assigned to write, perhaps assisted by his younger nephew John Phillips, as scribe.

As Milton labored on his answer to the king's book, his divorce tracts continued to draw fire from, among others, his old antagonist Joseph Hall, who denounced his "licentious" encouragement to arbitrary divorces, exclaiming piously, "Wo is me; To what a passe is the world come that a Christian pretending to Reformation should dare to tender so loose a project to the publique."[38] But the *Tenure* was proving useful to other supporters of the republic. In a tract of May 30, the radical Independent minister of Coleman Street, John Goodwin, quoted extensively from Milton's biblical and historical precedents for tyrannicide and for armed defenses of Protestant religion, and also paraphrased some Miltonic generalizations, e.g. "Tyrants by a kind of naturall instinct both hate and fear none more than the true Church and Saints of God."[39]

On June 23 the council asked Milton to "examine the papers of Pragmaticus, and [report] what he finds in them to the Councell" (*LR* II, 256–7). Pragmaticus was Marchamont Nedham, the most prolific, inventive, witty, satiric, and ideologically flexible of the writers involved with the numerous weekly "Mercuries," or newsbooks. Besides reporting domestic and foreign news more or less accurately, these small pamphlets, often published without license and by underground presses, flourished throughout the 1640s as potent propaganda instruments for several political positions: parliamentarian, royalist, Leveller, army.[40] Nedham's several shifts of allegiance had made him notorious. During the First Civil War he employed his barbed and railing style to argue parliament's cause in *Mercurius Britanicus*.[41] He was briefly imprisoned in August, 1645 and again in May, 1646 for mocking and denouncing the king as a tyrant with bloody hands at a time when parliament was seeking accommodation with him. In September, 1647, moved perhaps by sheer opportunism or perhaps frustrated by the government stalemate, he turned his coat, made his peace with the king, and began to publish the witty, urbane, sexually slanderous and politically devastating royalist newsbook, *Mercurius Pragmaticus*. After publishing it for two years, sometimes sporadically, he was arrested on June 18 and imprisoned at Newgate. When Milton examined his papers (presumably issues of *Pragmaticus*) he would have appreciated the very witty satire though not the message: denunciation of the army, the Rump Parliament, and the regicide, and in the last issues an open call for the return of Charles II.[42] Nedham escaped in August but was soon recaptured. On November 14 he was set free – having agreed to change sides again and write for the republic.[43] The fact that Milton and Nedham became friends soon after this suggests that Milton may have helped in the effort to recall Nedham to his earlier republican allegiance.[44]

The crackdown on Nedham came while parliament was discussing and then implementing a new Press Act, passed on September 20, 1649 and intended to stem the flood of royalist and Leveller polemic.[45] The Act chiefly targeted the antigovernment newsbooks, with their potent mix of accurate news, rumor, hearsay, flagrant lies, scurrility, insult, and diatribe. It provided, under heavy penalties and sureties from publishers, printers, binders, and booksellers, that no newsbooks could be published without a license granted by designated officials.[46] Books *per se*, save for foreign imports, were tacitly exempted from pre-publication licensing, though serious penalties awaited writers, printers, and even possessors of books and pamphlets later judged to be seditious or scandalous. This tacit exemption for books – a significant change from the 1643 Ordinance Milton had denounced in *Areopagitica* – may be due to his influence.[47] Sometime in 1650 Hartlib quoted Milton's explanation of the new law to him, in terms that accord with *Areopagitica*'s position: "There are no Licensers appointed by the last Act so that everybody may enter in his booke without License, provided the Printers or authors name bee entered that they may be forth coming if required."[48] Of course Milton had to realize that the prescribed penalties for publications later found to be at fault would constrain printers and booksellers in their publication decisions. He probably wasted few tears on the ephemeral newsbooks swept away by the ordinance, but supposed the Act might later be modified when the republic was more secure.

Sometime before September 30, the second edition of Milton's *Tenure* was published. Its twelve added pages bolster Milton's argument against the Presbyterian clergy, who are still vehemently denouncing the regicide and the Commonwealth government in pulpits and pamphlets.[49] To discredit their claim that "the disposing or punishing of a King or Tyrant *is against the constant Judgement of all Protestant Divines*" (*CPW* III, 257), Milton marshals extracts from Luther, Zwingli, Calvin, Bucer, Paraeus, Knox, Cartwright, Christopher Goodman, and others, affirming the right to resist, depose, and sometimes kill a monarch who is a tyrant or enemy of God. His strategy is to distinguish that central tradition – "our fathers in the faith" – from the new Presbyterian divines who are now "gorging themselves like Harpy's on those simonious places and preferments of thir outed predecessors" and who, like those deposed prelates, seek to tyrannize over conscience (251–2). Also, quoting from a Presbyterian pamphlet of 1643, *Scripture and Reason Pleaded for Defensive Arms*, he shows that their own arguments for armed resistance to the king allow by logical extension for trying and executing him. At one point Milton's prophetic voice breaks through the polemic, interpreting the regicide and the founding of a republic as auguries of the Millennium. Then there will be no more earthly kings, only Christ,

> who is our only King, the root of *David*, and whose Kingdom is eternal righteousness, with all those that Warr under him, whose happiness and final hopes are laid up in that only just & rightful kingdom (which we pray incessantly may com soon, and in so praying wish hasty ruin and destruction to all Tyrants), eev'n he our immortal King, and all that love him, must of necessity have in abomination these blind and lame Defenders. (256)

But Milton invokes this millennial expectation chiefly as an argument pertaining to government in the interim. A republican commonwealth, Milton implies, is the only political structure that allows Christ his place now as the only rightful king, and by overturning tyrants begins properly to prepare for that millennial rule.

On October 24 the council charged Milton and/or the sergeant at arms to evaluate the writings of a notorious ex-parliament member, Clement Walker, who fell foul of the Act by publishing fierce denunciations of the regicide, the Independents, and the Rump Parliament, in support of Charles II.[50] If Milton performed this task he would have found his own *Tenure*, and himself, tarred with the pitch attaching to his divorce argument:

> There is lately come forth a book of John Melton's (a Libertine, that thinketh his Wife a Manacle, and his very Garters to be Shackles and Fetters to him; one that (after the Independent fashion) will be tied by no obligation to God or Man), wherein he

> undertaketh to prove, That it is lawfull for any that have power to call to account, Depose, and put to Death wicked Kings and Tyrants (after due conviction) if the ordinary Magistrate neglect it.[51]

On December 16, 1649 Milton licensed a French translation of various documents, speeches, and narratives pertaining to the trial and death of Charles I.[52] Milton was to ascertain that this documentary collection was what it purported to be (it was), and not disguised royalist propaganda.

During the summer and autumn of 1649 Milton concentrated on his answer to *Eikon Basilike: The Portraiture of his Sacred Majestie in his Solitudes and Sufferings,* which began to circulate immediately after the king's execution.[53] That prodigiously popular book, largely and perhaps entirely ghostwritten by a Presbyterian divine, John Gauden,[54] but purporting to be the reflections and meditations of Charles I while awaiting his trial and execution, was easily the most dangerous royalist polemic challenge to the new government. It presents the dead king as a second Christ, a second David, a martyr holding fast to his beliefs, and a well-meaning, gracious monarch. Its several chapters purport to offer Charles's version of the principal events of the 1640s, from the calling of the Long Parliament to just before his execution, each chapter ending with prayers; it concludes with a letter of "advice" to the future Charles II. New material was added after March 15 to sound a yet more personal tone: an account of the king's last conversation with his children and four "Divine Meditations," conceived as preparations for death, which he was said to have used in prison and then handed to Bishop Juxon on the scaffold.[55] The whole was calculated to evoke a rush of sympathy for Charles and outrage against his executioners. Within one year of its first appearance the king's book went through more than thirty-five editions in London and twenty-five more in Ireland and abroad;[56] extracts from the prayers and meditations were also often reprinted.

Royalists and defenders of the regicide promptly joined in polemic battle over the book and its authorship. Among the defenders, Clement Walker described it as "full fraught with Wisdom Divine and Humane" and the anonymous author of *The Princely Pellican* published segments from "his Majesties Divine Meditations," insisting vehemently on the king's authorship.[57] Late in August the first full-scale answer appeared: *Eikon Alethine. The Portraiture of Truths most sacred Majesty.*[58] It engages with *Eikon Basilike* chapter by chapter, but its primary strategy is to portray the book as a forgery whose style points to the author as "Some Prelaticall Levite gaping after a Bishoprick, Deanery, or the like."[59] The frontispiece engraving displays a curtain pulled back to reveal the true author in academic/clerical robes (plate 9), and the wordplay on Gauden's name – "gaudy phrase," "gaudy outside," "gaudily drest" – indicates that that author's identity was an open secret.[60] With considerable rhetorical force the author of *Eikon Alethine* urges his countrymen not to be mesmerized by this "Gorgon" because they think it to be the king's book, and not to betray mother England "now travailing with Liberty and ready to bring forth a man-child."[61] A few days later, *Eikon Episte or, the faithful Portraiture of a Loyall Subject* answered *Eikon Alethine*, following that text and *Eikon Basilike* chapter by chapter and offering "to handle all the controverted points relating to these times." Imploring Englishmen not to murder the issue of the king's brain as they did him, this author gives insistent personal testimony to the king's authorship: "I take it to be the Kings Book. I am sure of it; I know his hand; I have seen the manuscript; I have heard him own it; the world believes it."[62]

Though he knew better, Milton dealt with the book as the king's, believing that he had especially to deal with the "idolatrous" image of the king in that book, whoever constructed it. In October or possibly early November "The Author J. M." published *Eikonoklastes, in Answer to a Book Intitl'd Eikon Basilike. The Portrature of his Sacred Majesty in his Solitudes and Sufferings.*[63] Like *Eikon Alethine*, it also followed *Eikon Basilike* chapter by chapter, charging that the king's interpretations of his actions and intentions are in every case false and dishonest and that his carefully crafted self-portrait as sainted martyr and second Christ is sheer hypocrisy, especially in light of his appropriation of Pamela's prayer from Sidney's *Arcadia* as his own prayer. Milton was very proud of this treatise, later casting himself as the solitary hero who managed to slay the resurrected king for good: "I alone, when the king rose again as it were from the dead and in his posthumous volume commended himself to the people by new slyness and meretricious arguments, did recently overcome and do away with him" (*CPW* IV.1, 306). Milton's answer to the king's book with its powerful rhetorical challenge is analyzed on pages 264–71.

On November 19 the council recognized the value of Milton's services in practical terms, granting him lodgings in Whitehall, at the Scotland Yard end.[64] He probably moved soon; such quarters were in great demand and his daily life was surely eased by living so close to the council's meeting rooms.

On January 8, 1650, the council ordered Milton to "prepare something in answer to the Booke of Saltmasius, and when hee hath done itt bring itt to the Councell" (*LR* II, 286), a task he later described as that of "publicly defending . . . the cause of the English people and thus of Liberty herself."[65] Salmasius's *Defensio Regia pro Carolo I*, dedicated to Charles II, was in print in Europe by November, 1649, and said to be on its way to England.[66] Salmasius, a professor at the University of Leyden, had an impressive scholarly reputation on the Continent as a commentator on classical and patristic texts (Solinus, Epictetus, Tertullian, the *Tabula Cebetis*) and as the author of some thirty books, including studies of usury, of the Greek tongue, and of Greek and Roman law. Praised by Richelieu as one of the three consummate scholars of the age,[67] he was offered many inducements to honor France, Holland, and Sweden with his presence. When he wrote *Defensio Regia* and when Milton's reply appeared he was scholar-in-residence at the court of Queen Christina of Sweden. Since Salmasius was a Protestant who had written against the pope and episcopacy, his attack on the English rebels and regicides was all the more formidable. The *Defensio Regia* sounded a clarion call to the kings of Europe, and to royalists in England, to unite against the illegal new republic and place Charles II on his rightful throne.

As he rose to the defense of the new republic against Salmasius, Milton had to confront directly the questionable status of an unrepresentative government founded on revolution and military force, an issue sharply focused by the bitter and divisive Engagement Controversy. The government, in an effort to secure the loyalty of its public servants, required their subscription to this formula: "I do declare and promise that I will be true and faithful to the Commonwealth of England as the same is now established, without a King or House of Lords."[68] On October 11, 1649 all members of parliament were required to sign the Engagement, and soon after all officers and servicemen in the army and navy, all judges and officials of courts of law, all who held municipal posts, all graduates and officers of the universities, all masters and scholars of the colleges, all ministers admitted to a benefice, and all state pensioners. On January 2, 1650 it was required of citizens generally, with voting rights and access to the courts denied to those who refused.[69] Though the Engagement was not an oath and did not (as some had wanted) require approval of the regicide, it proved counterproductive. Many Presbyterians (including Fairfax, the commander-in-chief of the Commonwealth's army) refused to sign it on grounds of conscience, citing the oath they swore in the Solemn League and Covenant to uphold the government of king, lords, and commons. Levellers believed the present government unrepresentative and therefore illegal. Royalists did not want to be on record with such a pledge, should the political winds shift. Algernon Sidney was prescient in his protest to the council "that such a test would prove a snare to many an honest man, but every knave would slip through it."[70] Royalist polemics urged just such "knavish" behavior: sign, with the firm intention of breaking the illegal promise when circumstances allowed. John Dury and Marchamont Nedham produced Hobbesian arguments for signing: citizens have the duty and responsibility to secure civil peace by giving allegiance to whatever powers God has established over them.[71] Nedham, in *The Case of the Commonwealth of England, Stated*, cites Roman historians and Machiavelli on the benefits of a republic but offers an unvarnished Machiavellian account of the origins of government – not social compact but blatant force: "the Power of the Sword is, and ever hath been the foundation of all Titles to Government." And, as a corollary, "A Government erected by a Prevailing Part of the people, is as valid *De Jure*, as if it had the ratifying Consent of the whole."[72] Milton's tracts did not address the Engagement Controversy directly but, while he recognized victory on the battlefield as usually a sign of divine favor, he based the government's claim to allegiance not on force but on the right of good men who love liberty to represent the whole people. In a state letter to Hamburg (January 4, 1650) he defended the Engagement in terms that probably reflect his own as well as the council's position, as a legitimate demand of allegiance from those who hold office in the government or enjoy its benefits (*CPW* V.2, 496–8).

Another source of disunity and danger was the republic's increasingly obstreperous left flank, who were alarming Presbyterians and others intent on promoting religious orthodoxy and morality, as well as men of property, lawyers, and political leaders worried about government stability. Despite imprisonment and press controls, Levellers continued to publish pamphlets denouncing the government as illegitimate and demanding an Agreement of the People, a representative parliament, expansion of suffrage, toleration, and reform of the laws, courts, and taxes.[73] More threatening in principle, though not in fact, were the so called True Levellers or Diggers, at first only twenty or thirty poor men who set out on April 1, 1649 to cultivate the waste lands on St George's Hill and elsewhere in Surrey, as a symbolic claim to rights in the common lands, and in theory, to all property. Sporadic raids by landowners culminated a year later in the total destruction of their settlements, huts, and furniture, but their leader, Gerrard Winstanley, continued to press their claims in often eloquent manifestos argued from an allegorical exegesis of Genesis and other biblical texts. Beginning with *The True Levellers Standard Advanced* (*c.* April 26, 1649) and ending with *The Law of Freedom in a Platform* (*c.* February 20, 1652) presented to Oliver Cromwell, the Digger tracts projected a utopia based on Christian communism.[74] Still more alarming, out of all proportion to their scant numbers, were the Ranters, an antinomian sect whose members believed that God dwelt in them and by his grace rendered all their acts sinless; some acted out that belief in open sexual license and nakedness or in blasphemy and swearing – whence their name. Some Ranter tracts of 1649–50, wildly imagistic, experiential, and mystical, urged such behavior as evidence of their inner light.[75]

The government also feared invasion from Scotland. With the royalists in Ireland losing badly, Prince Charles came to terms with the Scottish parliament and kirk. He took the Covenant in May, 1650, promised to establish Presbyterianism in Scotland and England, accepted the Scottish throne, and prepared to lead an invading army which, it was supposed, would be supported by royalists and Presbyterians throughout England. Cromwell was recalled from Ireland where victory was now assured; he returned on June 1 to great acclaim. The most insightful tribute to him was Marvell's tonally complex "Horatian Ode upon Cromwel's Return from Ireland," which praises Cromwell as a force of nature and destiny who, like a Caesar back from Gaul, is still (but may not always be) the republic's good servant: "Nor yet grown stiffer with Command, / But still in the *Republick's* hand." Marvell's poem also recognizes, in Machiavellian terms, the republic's necessary reliance on Cromwell's armed might: "The same *Arts* that did *gain* / A *Pow'r* must it *maintain*."[76] When the government decided on a pre-emptive invasion of Scotland, Fairfax resigned as commander-in-chief, and Cromwell took command on June 26. His striking victory at Dunbar on September 3, 1650 turned the tide for England, though the war continued for another year; on September 3, 1651 he won a decisive victory at Worcester, forcing Scotland into submission and prompting Charles to escape in disguise to France.

Such external and internal dangers forced political compromises that Milton accepted as necessary. Early in 1650 there were proposals for elections to fill up parliament to the number of 400, but the sitting members determined that the infant Commonwealth, like the infant Moses, could best be nursed by its own mother – the Rump. That issue was often revisited but always reached the same impasse, given the very real danger that a more representative body would restore the king. In May and June parliament acceeded to Presbyterian demands for regulation of public morality, passing laws to make incest and adultery punishable by death, fornication by three months' imprisonment, and Sabbath-breaking and profane oaths by fines. On August 9 it enacted a Blasphemy Act, chiefly targeting the Ranters. It provided six months' imprisonment for a first offense and banishment on pain of death for a second, but effectively restricted blasphemy to two cases: claiming that any human person was God or a manifestation of God; and affirming that acts of gross immorality (e.g. swearing, promiscuous sexual behavior, group sex) are not sinful or are in fact religious practices. Milton saw this Act as a distinct improvement over the ordinance of 1648, which had specified the death penalty for a wide range of theological opinions.[77] This new Act, he later declared, defined blasphemy "so far as it is a crime belonging to civil judicature . . . in plane English more warily, more judiciously, more orthodoxally then twice thir number of divines have don in many a prolix volume."[78] He did not comment on the prescribed punishments.

Throughout 1650 Milton gave primary attention to his Latin answer to Salmasius, which was delayed, he explained in his preface, by "precarious health" that required him to "work at intervals and hardly for an hour at a time, though the task calls for continuous study and composition" (*CPW* IV.1, 307). Four years later, he portrayed his decision to answer Salmasius as a kind of Hercules' choice, in which he followed a heroic path of duty even though he believed it would hasten the onset of total blindness:

> When the business of replying to the royal defense had been officially assigned to me, and at the same time I was afflicted at once by ill health and the virtual loss of my remaining eye, and the doctors were making learned predictions that if I should undertake this task, I would shortly lose both eyes, I was not in the least deterred by the warning. I seemed to hear, not the voice of the doctor (even that of Aesculapius, issuing from the shrine at Epidaurus), but the sound of a certain more divine monitor within. And I thought that two lots had now been set before me by a certain command of fate: the one blindness, the other, duty. Either I must necessarily endure the loss of my eyes, or I must abandon my most solemn duty. . . . Then I reflected that many men have bought with greater evil smaller good; with death, glory. To me, on the contrary, was offered a greater good at the price of a smaller evil: that I could at the cost of blindness alone fulfill the most honorable requirement of my duty. As duty is of itself more substantial than glory, so it ought to be for every man more desirable and illustrious. I resolved therefore that I must employ this brief use of my eyes while yet I could for the greatest possible benefit to the state. (*CPW* IV.1, 587–8)

During these busy months Milton probably had little time for uninterrupted study, but some of the extracts entered around 1650 in his Commonplace Book bear directly on his development of republican theory in the *Defensio*. They include several passages summarized from Machiavelli's *Discorsi*, e.g. that "Machiavelli much prefers a republican form to monarchy" because it chooses better magistrates and councillors, and that rebellions were often the means by which people regained their liberty, as well as being "the principal means of keeping Rome free.[79] His *Defensio* was authorized by the council on December 23, 1650, and registered with the Stationers on December 31, for publication "both in Latin and English."[80] Perhaps delayed by Milton's difficulties in proofreading, it did not appear until February 24, 1651.

Milton was reappointed to the office of Secretary for Foreign Tongues in February 1650 and again took the oath of secrecy.[81] That June the council showed its appreciation by making provision for his greater comfort, allowing him a warrant from the sale of the king's goods for "such hangings as shall bee sufficient for the furnishing of his Lodgings in Whitehall" (*LR* II, 314). It would be fascinating to know what "hangings" or pictures Milton chose.

His diplomatic work increased during 1650, some of it prompted by continuing hostilities against the Merchant Adventurers in Hamburg. Milton may have drafted (not merely translated) parliament's letter of January 4, 1650 to the Hamburg Senate protesting that members of the company were being prevented from taking the Engagement: it defends the Engagement, insists tactfully that this is strictly England's business, and reminds the senate that the English Commonwealth is now "remarkably prosperous," having crushed its enemies everywhere.[82] A credentialling letter, dated April 2, introduced the new envoy to Hamburg, Richard Bradshaw, nephew to the council president.[83]

Another focus of Milton's work as Latin Secretary concerned Portugal and Spain, at war since 1640 over Portugal's declaration of independence from Spain.[84] Grateful for Stuart support of Portugal's independence, King John IV of Portugal allowed the royalist fleet to use the Tagus river to attack, plunder, and capture the republic's merchant ships and freighters. Phillip IV of Spain, battling the Netherlands and France as well as Portugal, gave somewhat ambivalent support to the republic: he was the first king to send an ambassador and he opened Spanish ports to parliament's fleets. Milton's letter from parliament to King John (January 25, 1650) vigorously protests that Portugal is protecting these "English pirates and renegades"; it also urges the king to deny recognition to Charles Stuart's "pseudo-ambassadors" and to accord it to "ourselves, on whom, with God's manifest favor, the control of England has devolved," threatening that otherwise the "sizeable and mutually profitable commerce of our merchants with the Portuguese" must end (*CPW* V.2, 500).[85] On February 4, 1650 parliament sent letters in Milton's formal Latin credentialling Anthony Ascham as diplomatic resident to Spain, and Charles Vane, brother of Sir Henry Vane, to Portugal,[86] but within three months Vane had to flee Lisbon in fear of his life. After Admiral Blake blockaded Prince Rupert's fleet in the port of Lisbon, Milton wrote for parliament (April 27) urging King John to drive out the "pirates" or else to permit the English fleet to attack them in Portuguese ports. Responding to further Portuguese provocations,[87] during the summer and autumn of 1650 Blake destroyed the Portuguese fleet and soundly defeated the royalist fleet in harbor; its remnants fled to the Spanish port of Cartagena, and England demanded the return of those ships and their merchandise. Milton translated for the council two letters from Phillip to the governor of Cartagena, along with his cover letter to Blake (January 7, 1651), directing that the goods though not the ships be released (*CPW* V.1, 532–8) – the first clear evidence that Milton knew Spanish.

Relations between England and Spain were complicated by the murder of the newly appointed resident Ascham by royalist exiles the day after his arrival in Madrid (June 6, 1650). The assassins escaped punishment for the next year or so by taking sanctuary in a church. Milton wrote for parliament a series of increasingly outraged letters to Phillip and probably translated his responses. On June 28, 1650, parliament appeals to Phillip's honor to deliver "suitable and speedy punishment" to the assassins; on January 21–2, 1651, they acknowledge his efforts but insist that "unless justice be satisfied without delay . . . *we see not on what ground sincere and lasting friendship can rest*" (*CPW* V.2, 523–4, 539–43). A year later the issue was still unresolved and protests continued.[88]

Besides preparing a few other letters and translations,[89] Milton was given other tasks. On February 2, 1650 he was directed to receive and store in the paper office any public papers still in the hands of former officials, on June 25, to summarize examinations taken by the army during an insurrection in Essex, and on August 14, to join a committee to inventory the records of the Westminster Assembly.[90] On June 25 also he was directed to examine the papers of his old nemesis William Prynne, and to seize any papers "by him written, or in his Custody of dangerous nature against the Commonwealth."[91] Apparently he was also asked to examine one foreign book that required authorization under the Press Act, and acted on it according to his own liberal standards. The *Journal of the House of Commons* refers to a "note under the Hand of John Milton" on August 10, 1650 that seems to have authorized William Dugard to publish the Socinian *Racovian Catechism*, with its "heretical" denial of Christ's divinity. Dugard entered this Latin work in the Stationers Register on November 13, 1651 and published it soon after.[92] It may be that attending to this licensing duty prompted Milton to begin to question Trinitarian doctrine, which he repudiates in *De Doctrina Christiana*.

As Milton prepared his *Defensio* for publication, his other polemics remained a focus of attention and controversy. On January 14, 1650 the council arranged to send some of his books – presumably *Tenure* and *Eikonoklastes* – to be distributed abroad.[93] Sometime after June 19 a second edition of *Eikonoklastes* appeared, with a few added passages.[94] An anonymous answer to that work, Joseph Jane's *Eikon Aklastos*, was written sometime before December 4, 1650 and published several months later. Either Jane did not recognize Milton from his initials or chose to term him simply "The Iconoclast" or "The Libeller," to emphasize his point that *Eikonoklastes* presents "the Rebells Image . . . the dissolution of all bonds morall, Civill, and Religious, of all orders and degrees among men." He denounces Milton's arguments chapter by chapter, insists on the king's authorship of *Eikon Basilike*, and makes a special point of defending Pamela's prayer as appropriate for the king's use.[95] On May 20, 1651 the council ordered John Dury to translate *Eikonoklastes* into French.[96]

In February, 1651 the Council of State reappointed its foreign secretary and he again took the oath of secrecy. He had already been given the task of licensing Marchamont Nedham's newsletter, *Mercurius Politicus*, which began to appear regularly on June 13, 1650 and quickly proved a much livelier and more successful enterprise than the official newsbooks.[97] During 1650 copies were published without formal registration or were registered in batches of two or three after publication, under the general rubric "by permission of authority."[98] But from the end of January, 1651 and continuing for a year, the issues are registered by the publisher Thomas Newcomb with the formula, "Entered for his Copy under the hand of Master Milton a pamphlet called, *Mercurius Politicus*." Until May 22 Milton continued licensing several issues at once, after publication; thereafter the entries are made weekly on the date of publication until January 22, 1652, when Milton (almost blind) was relieved of this duty.[99] Milton, however, was away from London at least from late August to October 15, as the diary of the diplomat Herman Mylius indicates.[100] He may have been gone longer: the council assigned him no duties between June 7 and October 26. During his absence someone else must have licensed *Mercurius Politicus* over Milton's name, further suggesting that the authorities expected, and Milton performed, only a perfunctory supervision of Nedham's journal. No doubt Milton met with Nedham sometimes, beginning a relation that ripened into friendship. We can imagine them discussing how best to defend the republic, Nedham seeking to appeal to the interests of the several groups and Milton arguing the role and rights of virtuous, liberty-loving citizens.[101] Portions of Nedham's *Case of the Commonwealth* (May 8, 1650) were being reprinted as lead editorials in *Mercurius Politicus* (numbers 16–69).

During the first half of 1651 Milton was involved in the lengthy negotiations between a committee of the council and the Portuguese envoy Joao de Guimarães, who was sent to England in December, 1650 to try to resolve the hostilities between the two countries. Milton wrote a letter for the council on December 19, 1650, insisting that Guimarães's title and powers be clarified; on February 10, 1651 he was ordered to attend the negotiating meetings between Guimarães and the Committee on Foreign Affairs, presumably to translate English draft documents into Latin for the Portuguese, and their responses into English.[102] He would also have been needed as an interpreter, since the meetings were conducted in Latin and in both vernaculars. When parliament found the problems intractable and broke off negotiations, Milton was ordered (May 16) to get a complete list of Guimarães's retinue to expedite their passports. On other fronts, he wrote a letter for parliament to the Senate of Danzig (February 6, 1650) urging that city not to enforce Poland's imposition of a tax on English trade goods to aid Charles II (*CPW* V.2, 544–5). On March 28 he was ordered to translate the "Intercursus Magna," a treaty signed in 1495 between England, Austria, and Holland that the Dutch were proposing as a basis for negotiations then in progress in the Hague.[103] During the spring and summer Milton wrote letters protesting various injuries – arrests, seizures of goods, and sometimes violence – offered to English merchants in areas controlled by Spain: Malaga, Flanders, and the Canary Islands.[104] The Canary Islands letter survives in the council's English and Milton's Latin versions, providing an indication of how Milton often improved upon the drafts he was given to work from.[105]

Milton's answer to Salmasius was published on February 24, 1651.[106] The title page showcases its author: *Joannis Miltoni Angli Pro Populo Anglicano Defensio Contra Claudii Anonymi, aliàs Salmasii, Defensionem Regiam*. In testimony of its status, many copies bore the official arms of the Commonwealth, a shield with English cross and Irish harp within. Milton's title, *Defense of the English People*, plays off Salmasius's title, *Defense of the King*, and he presents himself (again) as a solitary hero–scholar taking up an epic-like challenge. His tract follows Salmasius chapter by chapter, answering his charges, satirizing his Latinity and his scholarly practices, and jeering at him as a hen-pecked husband, slavish at home and in his politics. It also offers a forceful defense of the English republic and an elaboration of Milton's developing republican theory. The argument and rhetoric of this formidable Latin treatise are discussed on pages 271–7.

On March 5 the council arranged for reprints as needed, and in 1651 there were at least two reissues, several European editions, and a Dutch translation.[107] Soon a second English edition, "Emendatior," was published as an elegant folio, often on heavy paper with lined margins, and Milton gave several of these as presentation copies.[108] At about the same time Milton had another cause for elation and pride: the birth of his first son, carefully recorded in the family Bible: "My son, John, was born on Sunday March the 16th about half an hower past nine at night 1650 [1651]."[109] He was, happily, spared some vision to greet both these hopeful off-spring. On June 18 the council offered official thanks for the *Defensio* and an award of £100 which Milton refused, scorning to appear to write for reward as he claimed Salmasius had done.[110] Canceling that order, the council voted him more elaborate thanks in terms that must have gratified him:

> The Councel takeing notice of the manie good services performed by Mr. John Mylton their Secretarie for forreigne languages to this State and commonwealth particularlie of his booke in Vindication of the Parliament and people of England against the calumnies and invectives of Salmasius, have thought fitt to declare their resentment [appreciation] and good acceptance of the same and that the thankes of the Councel bee returned to Mr. Mylton, and their sense represented in that behalfe, (*LR* III, 43)

He was also gratified by reports of the sensation the book was causing in learned circles abroad, in anticipation and at publication.[111] Europeans appear to have delighted with the contest, watching with grudging admiration to see the great Salmasius equaled or bested by an unknown Englishman. They also appreciated Milton's Latin and his rhetoric, whatever they thought of his ideas. Milton was surely pleased to hear that by March 14/24 twenty-five copies had been ordered for members of the Dutch government.[112] On March 30 a correspondent from the Hague wrote that Salmasius's ill health might prevent his expected reply to "Milton's book, which here is very much applauded."[113] On July 1, a letter from Leyden reported that Milton's book had been burned in Toulouse and Paris, "for fear of making State-Heretiques," that its doctrine "begins to be studied and disputed more of late," and that it would be still more eagerly sought after the burning.[114] On July 9/19, a correspondent from Paris wrote:

> M. Milton's Book hath been burnt by the hands of the common Executioner. . . . It is so farr liked and approved by the ingenuous sort of men, that all the Copies, sent hither out of the Low-Countries were long since dispersed, and it was designed here for the Press, whereof notice being taken, it is made Treason for any to print, vend, or have it in posssession; so great a hatred is born to any piece that speaks liberty and Freedom to this miserable people.[115]

A largely erroneous but often repeated story had it that Milton's book led Queen Christina of Sweden to reverse her former high opinion of Salmasius, causing him to flee her court in disgrace and decline into an early death.[116] Salmasius's enemies and rivals, Isaac Vossius and Nicholaas Heinsius, were prime movers in circulating this tale, as well as other disparaging gossip about Salmasius as a henpecked husband and disgraced scholar.[117] Still, Vossius's report of his own, and the queen's, surprise to discover the unknown Milton's learning and stylistic excellence is credible: "I had expected nothing of such quality from an Englishman"; "In the presence of many, she [Christina] spoke highly of the genius of the man, and his manner of writing."[118] Not surprisingly, Milton believed the reports of Salmasius's disgrace at Christina's court. In 1654 he made that story part of his self-construction as an epic hero who, on the field of polemic battle, conquered and humiliated the scholar of giant reputation, Salmasius:

> When he with insults was attacking us and our battle array, and our leaders looked first of all to me, I met him in single combat and plunged into his reviling throat this pen, the weapon of his own choice. And (unless I wish to reject outright and disparage the views and opinions of so many intelligent readers everywhere, in no way bound or indebted to me) I bore off the spoils of honor. That this is actually the truth and no empty boast finds ready proof in the following event – which I believe did not occur without the will of God. . . . When Salmasius had been courteously summoned by Her Most Serene Majesty, the Queen of the Swedes (whose devotion to the liberal

> arts and to men of learning has never been surpassed) and had gone thither, there in the very place where he was living as a highly honored guest, he was overtaken by my *Defence*, while he was expecting nothing of the kind. Nearly everyone read it immediately, and the Queen hereself. . . [I]f I may report what is frequently mentioned and is no secret, so great a reversal of opinion suddenly took place that he who the day before had flourished in the highest favor now all but withered away. (*CPW* IV.1, 556–7)

Milton also took pride in receiving recognition, congratulations, and visits from distinguished Europeans:

> I can truthfully assert that from the time when my *Defence* was first published, and kindled the enthusiasm of its readers, no ambassador from any prince or state who was then in the city failed to congratulate me, if we chanced to meet, or omitted to seek an interview with me at his own house, or to visit me at mine.[119]

One of these was Christopher Arnold, a traveler from Germany, who described Milton as a "strenuous defender" of the republic, praised his *Areopagitica*, and observed that he "enters readily into talk; his style is pure and his writing most terse."[120] On November 19, 1651 Milton dictated an entry for Arnold's autograph book, which included a laudatory address in Latin to this "most learned man" and, as his own motto, a modified Greek quotation from 2 Corinthians 12:9: "I am perfected in weakness."[121] He signed it himself.

Yet Milton's new fame did not shield him from mundane problems. In April, 1651 a parliamentary committee, charged to give members of parliament priority in the assignment of rooms in Whitehall, tried to eject the Milton family, but the Council of State managed to stay the order, clearly valuing Milton's service and sensitive to his needs as his vision deteriorated (*LR* III, 20). In June, responding to another order for Milton's "speedie remove out of his lodgings," four council members met with the committee, "to acquaint them with the Case of Mr. Milton . . . and to endeavour with them that the said Mr. Milton may bee Continued where hee is in regard of the employment which he is in to the Councel, which necessitates him to reside neere the Councel" (*LR* III, 42). He was again reprieved, but the uncertainty was surely unsettling.

He had legal and financial concerns as well, arising chiefly from the Wheatley properties he held from the Powells, as a means to recover debts they owed him.[122] In 1649 Milton's mother-in-law Anne Powell began a long series of protests and petitions to obtain redress for the illegal seizure and sale of personal property and timber from the Forest Hill estate; she won judgments in her favor but could not get them enforced.[123] Her problems, and Milton's, were exacerbated by a law passed August 1, 1650, designed to keep royalists from evading composition by fictional transfers of property to parliamentarian friends: it required all who held royalist property to compound for it. Milton petitioned to compound for Wheatley but neglected to follow through; under threat of sequestration he completed the process on February 25, 1651, paying a fine of £130 and charges (*LR* III, 8). The problem for Anne Powell concerned her widow's thirds, which Milton had sent her regularly out of the rents for Wheatley, but which the Committee on Compositions now refused to allow, denying her any rights in this composition and referring her to the courts to sue for her thirds.[124] In July 1651 she petitioned again, in somewhat exaggerated terms, pleading extreme poverty and asking the committee to direct Milton to continue her thirds, "to preserve her & her [eight] children from starving." Milton, as a representative of the hated new government and as an unsatisfactory son-in-law, was made the scapegoat for her many difficulties: she claimed (wrongly) that he had "allowance given him for the petitioners thirds" and had stopped paying her voluntarily. A note attached to this petition a few days later reveals her deep animosity, as well as her readiness to rewrite the domestic history of Milton and Mary:

> By the law she might recover her thirds without doubt, but she is so extreame poor, she hath not wherewithall to prosecute, & besides Mr Milton is a harsh & Chollericke man, & married to Mrs. Powells daughter, who would be undone, if any such course were taken against him by Mrs. Powell, he having turned away his wife heretofore for a long space upon [a small occasion, cancelled] some other occasion.[125]

Just below this is a copy of a note from Milton indicating his willingness to continue paying the thirds, if that sum were excluded from calculation of the sum he must compound for:

> Although I have compounded for my extent & shalbe so much the longer in receiving my debt, yet at the request of Mrs. Powell in regard of her present necessitys I am contented as farre as belongs to my consent to allow her the 3ds of what I receive from the estate, if the Committee shall so order it, that what I allow her may not be reckoned upon my account.

Despite Milton's offer, the committee again refused to allow Anne Powell's thirds from the Wheatley revenues. Milton may have done something else to help her but that seems unlikely, given the antagonism between them.[126]

In late summer, 1651, the first substantial response to Milton's *Defensio* was published anonymously in Antwerp: *Pro Rege et Populo Anglicano Apologia, contra Johannis Polypragmatici (alias Miltoni Angli) Defensionem Destructivam Regis et Populi Anglicani*.[127] The author of this 220-page duodecimo was a royalist clergyman living abroad, John Rowland, who undertook to damp down the "sulphurous fire" of Milton's words until Salmasius could drown it with his own "full flood."[128] The twelve chapters of often defective Latin consist mainly of quotations from Milton followed by paragraphs of rebuttal denigrating him and praising Salmasius. Milton wanted to reserve his energies to meet the expected reply from Salmasius and so delegated the task of answering *Pro Rege* to his younger nephew John. According to Edward Phillips, Milton gave John's text careful "Examination and Polishment," supplying "such exact Emendations before it went to Press, that it might have very well passed for his" (*EL* 71). No doubt he did: he would want to be sure that this defense of him, addressed to Europe, would meet (as it does) rigorous standards of scholarship and Latinity. If Milton added the occasional paragraph or page – or more – there is no way to tell. In his preface, John elides any such help, gaining rhetorical points by representing his opponent as wholly unworthy of the great Milton's attention:

> Everyone agreed that it was much beneath the dignity and eloquence of that cultured and polished writer to stoop to digging up dunghills and to rebutting the wild prating of an unbridled, foolish babbler. But for my own part, swayed not only by devotion to country but by love of that liberty recently restored to us, and likewise bound by many ties of duty to that gentleman whom I have always honored and who is now attacked by this scurrilous fellow – I could not refrain from undertaking, even though unasked, to blunt the impudence of this utterly impertinent scoundrel.[129]

The writing was completed by mid-September.[130] Since Milton was out of town for some weeks before October 15, John probably gave him a draft upon his return. The treatise was published on December 24, 1651 or shortly before, with the title, *Joannis Philippi Angli Responsio Ad Apologiam Anonymi cujusdam tenebrionis pro Rege & Populo Anglicano infantissiman.*[131] As custom dictated, Phillips followed Rowland's – ultimately Salmasius's – organization, quoting brief snatches of Rowland's text and ridiculing his facts, logic, and style, often with witty wordplay.

Milton's absence may have involved a retreat to the nearby countryside – perhaps Hammersmith if he still had property there; Mylius was told that he was "vier meilen" from London.[132] He may have been trying some last desperate measures to stave off blindness, or he may have sought a salubrious place to recover his health, damaged by previous barbaric cures. A later letter (1654) to the Athenian scholar Leonard Philaras contains a poignant account of his symptoms and sensations at this time, "some months before my sight was completely destroyed":

> Everything which I distinguished when I myself was still seemed to swim, now to the right, now to the left. Certain permanent vapors seem to have settled upon my entire forehead and temples, which press and oppress my eyes with a sort of sleepy heaviness, especially from mealtime to evening. . . . While considerable sight still remained, when I would first go to bed and lie on one side or the other, abundant light would dart from my closed eyes; then, as sight daily diminished, colors proportionately darker would burst forth with violence and a sort of crash from within. (*CPW* IV.2, 869)

Skinner's biography refers to the "Issues and Seatons" used in an effort to save or retrieve the sight of Milton's blinded eye, concluding that the treatment may have hastened the loss of his other eye (*EL* 28). Seatoning, for treating chronic headache and inflammation of the eyes, involved piercing the skin just below the hairline, passing through the holes a hot cautery with a diamond point and then a needle with thread dipped in egg white and rose oil. Other standard remedies included cupping, bloodletting, caustics applied to the back of the head, and violent laxative purges.[133] Such "cures" surely heightened Milton's physical misery and also his mental anguish since they did not work. After he returned and resumed his duties, he soon had further cause for anxiety: when the new Council of State convened on December 1, 1651, it did not at once reappoint him, doubtful, perhaps, about his continued usefulness. It did so on December 29 (*LR* III, 115), but through those wintry days, and as he passed his forty-third birthday on December 9, he must have feared that his proud public service to the new republic would soon end. On December 17 he made what he described as "a necessary and sudden move" from the Whitehall lodgings "for the sake of my health"; other likely considerations were anxiety about reappointment and his growing family – a new baby was expected in about four months.[134] He may also have had a final eviction notice from the Parliament Committee. Edward Phillips describes the amenities of the new residence: "a pretty Garden-house in Petty-France (York Street) in Westminster, next door to the Lord Scudamore's, and opening into St. James Park" (plate 10).[135] Milton always enjoyed a garden and was no doubt pleased to renew contact with the diplomat who had entertained him some years ago in Paris. But he could no longer enjoy the vistas.

When Milton returned in mid-October, still in poor health, he found that diplomatic activities had accelerated after the Battle of Worcester (September 3, 1651), which convinced the European powers that the monarchy was not about to return and they must deal seriously with the new republic. Envoys were sent from Sweden, Denmark, and Tuscany. Also, a large mission from the United Provinces arrived in December, headed by the Dutch poet and diplomat Jacob Cats; it sought repeal or modification of the Navigation Act of October 9, 1651, which was designed to undercut the Dutch monopoly on shipping by requiring that all imports to England be carried in English ships or ships of the country of origin. Overshadowed by these envoys with more important business, Hermann Mylius, emissary from Count Anthon of Oldenburg, was attempting to secure a formal Latin *Salvaguardia* or Safeguard to protect merchants of that small German principality from seizure of their goods and vessels by English warships carrying on their undeclared naval war with Portugal and France. He also wanted a Rescript in English, to be shown to ships' captains, officers, or others as needed. Not surprisingly, the English government found little time for Oldenburg during the busy months when it was securing peace and union with the Scots, enforcing the Navigation Act, debating and ultimately deciding not to call a new parliament, and appointing new members to the Council of State. So Mylius's affair dragged on for seven months (he arrived in London on August 28, 1651 and left in March, 1652), during which time he persistently sought out, visited, and wrote to every influential person he could approach,[136] singling out Milton and John Dury as his special patrons. He kept a detailed diary or *Tagebuch*[137] of all his encounters and negotiations, which, together with several letters to and from Milton, provide the most detailed information we have about the state of Milton's health and vision during these months, about the quotidian duties and frustrations of his busy public life, and about the transformation of what began as a formal diplomatic association between Milton and Mylius into something like friendship.

Styling himself "an appraiser and admirer of your merits," Mylius wrote to Milton the day after Milton's return (October 16), indicating he had "long wished" to have a conference with him (*CPW* IV.2, 828). Milton arranged and then twice postponed such a meeting with the polite excuse of pressing business; probably, however, he recalled or was reminded that he was bound by his oath of secrecy not to have private conferences with diplomats without permission.[138] On October 20 Mylius had his first formal audience with the committee appointed to hear his request.[139] Milton stood at the right of Whitelocke, the chairman, translating Mylius's remarks into English for the committee and theirs into Latin for him, and making notes on the documents Mylius supplied; he could still see well enough to do that.[140] Mylius sent a draft copy of parts of the proposed Safeguard to Milton in a letter of October 25, and wrote a series of obsequious letters pressing for an interview. On October 26 and 27, and November 7, Milton again made and canceled arrangements for a meeting, claiming the pressure of work and "ill health" (*CPW* IV.2, 831–2). While true enough,[141] these excuses also show Milton coping diplomatically with the very persistent Mylius. He returned the drafts of the Safeguard with the reassuring comment that it was in good order and was being dealt with "by those to whom it has been entrusted" (Whitelocke's committee).[142] On November 24 Mylius was told by a messenger that Milton had delivered the draft copy and thought the affair "would now start to move,"[143] that Milton "would very much like to visit me but headache and pain in his eyes made it impossible," and that "I should rely on his diligent support and assistance in private." Mylius's December 1 diary entry records his perception that "Milton was almost blind, so the others were taking on all the business."[144] On December 17, frustrated by still more delays, he appealed to Milton again: "Unless you, Great pride and pillar of my interests, prompt and prod, my case will remain motionless" (*CPW* IV.2, 834).

On December 31 Milton, his reappointment now formalized, wrote to Mylius in more intimate terms, addressing him as "Hermannus" and explaining his failure to write sooner by a revealing comment on his recent difficulties (ill health, moving house). He also reports on his efforts to advance the Oldenburg business:

> First then, know that ill health, which is almost my perpetual enemy, caused delay; next, for the sake of my health, came a necessary and sudden move to another house, which I had chanced to begin on that very day on which your letter was brought to

> me; finally, without doubt, comes my shame at having nothing to tell you about your business which I thought would please you. For when, the day after, I chanced to meet Mr. Frost, and inquired carefully of him whether any answer to you was decided upon (for, being ill, I myself was often absent from the Council), he replied, rather disturbed, that nothing was yet decided. . . . [T]oday, I hope, I have accomplished [something]; for when in the Council I had twice reminded Lord President Whitelocke of your business, he brought it up at once: with the result that consideration of a prompt answer to you is set for tomorrow.[145]

On January 3, 1652 Mylius at last had a private conference with Milton, who was either given permission for that or else decided to bend a rule or two.[146] Mylius's diary records that Milton was again suffering greatly "from headache and suffusion in the eyes," that they discussed the constitutions of England and Rome and Milton's *Defensio*, and that Milton gave him a copy of John Phillips's *Responsio*, asking his opinion of it. Milton had to report, however, that other business had prevented the council from acting on the Safeguard.[147]

As the year turned, the council had more work for Milton. The Tuscan ambasssdor, in London since May, was carrying on protracted negotiations about the seizure of Tuscan goods on French and Portuguese ships captured by the English; on January 2 the council approved papers dealing with that matter and ordered Milton to draft "a Letter in Latine of the Substance of what was now here read in English" to Ferdinand II, Grand Duke of Tuscany, requesting and promising the continuation of cordial relations (*LR* III, 133). In that letter, dated January 20, Milton used the leeway given him in this directive to make a quasi-autobiographical allusion to the happy experience in Florence of "certain youths, the noblest and most honorable of our nation, who either journey through your cities or sojourn there to improve their studies."[148] On January 30, 1652 he had to write for the council to the Spanish ambassador to protest that an "argument drawn from religion" (the resort of Ascham's murderers to sanctuary) had thus far prevented revenge for that "abominable murder."[149] He was also busy with letters and translations pertaining to negotiations with the Dutch ambassadors over the Navigation Act and over seizures of Dutch ships carrying French cargo. The most important of those letters (dated January 30) declined the Dutch request to reopen negotiations for a closer alliance of the two republics (the previous year the Dutch had refused England's proposals to that end), refused to rescind or modify the Navigation Act, and asserted the justice of the seizures.[150] On March 12 he again wrote to Hamburg about the Merchant Adventurers' problems, demanding much-delayed justice for the kidnapping of some merchants and an assault on their preacher, as well as reparations for new vexations (*CPW* V.2, 584–7).

Along with all this Milton tried during January and February to help poor Mylius. On January 7 Mylius visited Milton, then busy with a Tuscan letter, and urged Milton to show him the version of the Safeguard that he was sending to the council.[151] The next day Milton stretched a point and did so, explaining, with irony probably lost on Mylius, that the document was substantially as Mylius wrote it though somewhat pared down: "Certain things I found it necessary to insert; others I condensed; I hardly believe the Council wishes it longer" (*CPW* IV.2, 838). That same day Mylius wrote back with fulsome thanks and also visited Milton to request a few changes, about which Milton "made notes in the margin" – he could still see well enough to do that. Milton also agreed to have his amanuensis make a fair copy of the English Rescript with Mylius's changes.[152] On January 9 Milton visited Mylius, apparently for the first time, showed the Rescript to him, and gave him a copy of Rowland's *Apologia* against his *Defensio;* in a letter of January 13 Mylius denounced its "shamelessness" and "worthless and infamous filth" (*CPW* IV.2, 840–1). On January 20 Milton wrote to report another snag: he was "present as usual in the Council" when some members questioned whether Oldenburg's quarrel with Bremen might disrupt England's amicable relations with that Protestant city,[153] and the vote was again delayed. On February 5, at last, the council dealt with the matter while Milton was absent, probably due to ill health. But it passed only the English Rescript, not the more important Safeguard – which was then somehow mislaid. Milton was hard pressed to explain this to Mylius, who visited him on February 9 to protest that this repulse dishonored him and his count. His diary entry records Milton's comment on this contretemps, laying it to the council members' occupations and lack of political or cosmopolitan experience: "These men were mechanics, soldiers, home grown, strong and bold enough, in public political matters mostly inexperienced." He urged Mylius not to "blame the Commonwealth, or the sounder men," noting that "among the forty persons who were in the Council, not more than three or four had ever been outside England; but among them there were Sons of Mercury [merchants] and of Mars [soldiers] enough."[154] That candid comment reveals something of Milton's embarrassment when the republic's leaders revealed their limitations to cultivated Europeans. The next day Milton wrote to Mylius that he brought up the matter again, and thought the council had simply failed to grasp the issue: "most of them seemed to me not to have paid enough attention, rather than to have been unwilling to concede what you ask, for they thought they had granted in that document [the Rescript] whatever you wished"(*CPW* IV.2, 844).

On February 11 the Safeguard was at last approved in an English version and Milton was ordered to translate it into Latin. The next day Mylius visited Milton to protest that it did not include his added language extending the Safeguard to the count's successors and heirs. Milton explained that he dared not add that language without express order of the council, since "he had already suffered rather harsh words and had to let himself be stepped on, because he had showed me the drafts, and had conducted private correspondence with me."[155] That Milton may have received some reprimand is suggested in his letter of February 12 to Whitelocke, explaining at some length why he thought it allowable to show the drafts to Mylius. But at the same time he made a last pitch for Mylius, commenting that he thought the language about successors seems "but just" in view of the count's advanced age.[156] The next day he wrote his "most esteemed Herman" that he did not know the result since rain kept him from the council meeting; he had now to walk in from Petty France. This letter and that to Whitelocke are in the hand of Edward Phillips, who was evidently serving as occasional scribe for his uncle.[157] On February 17 parliament passed the Latin Safeguard as prepared by Milton but without the language about successors. Milton's autograph signature guaranteed its exact conformity to the English original. At a casual meeting in the park Mylius heard from Milton that the succession language had been refused.[158] On March 2 the council, with Milton present, formally presented Mylius with the document, tendering their "friendship and service" to his Lord and himself (*LR* III, 204). His diary entry of March 6 records his farewell to Milton the previous day, "with thanks in deeds and in words" – the deed being a cash gift equal to £25. Milton reciprocated with an affirmation of friendship "in the most lavish terms," and with two copies of the Safeguard in English as well as the Latin original, all "signed by his own hand." As most of us can, Milton could sign his name without looking, but he was now totally blind. Mylius commented on this date, with some sense of pathos, that Milton is "wholly deprived of his sight in his forty-second year and so in the flower and prime of his age."[159]

"To Meet the Force of [their] Reason in Any Field Whatsoever"

With his major tracts of 1649–51, Milton saw himself meeting formidable polemic challenges – the king's book and Salmasius's *Defensio Regia* – and offering his most important service yet to God and country. For later readers these are not his most attractive prose works: their organization and style are governed by the works he is answering rather than, as in *Areopagitica,* by his own self-contained argument. Yet they show Milton developing impressive rhetorical strategies to challenge the republic's enemies, and also engaging issues long important to him and now at the center of his thought: liberty, toleration, republican government, the sway of idolatry over the populace, and the role and rights of good men who love liberty. He was persuaded by Aristotle, Machiavelli, and the classical republican theorists that governments endure or change according to the nature of their people, and that republics require a virtuous, liberty-loving citizenry. So he was distressed about what the widespread popular disaffection might portend for the new English republic. He also feared that the English would continue to exhibit the basic character he ascribed to them in the *History of Britain*: brave and noble in battle but unskilled in the political virtues needed to govern. These works struggle with urgent questions: How can a populace deformed by a servile, monarchical culture be transformed into the citizenry a republic needs? And how can it find worthy leaders who will preserve it? Milton's task, he supposes, is to influence those leaders and educate that populace.

In *Eikonoklastes* (*c.* October 6, 1649) Milton faced an almost impossible task: to dispel the rush of sympathy for the king so skillfully evoked by the book ascribed to him. Some forty-seven different frontispieces decorated the various editions of *Eikon Basilike,* mostly variations of the original design by William Marshall showing Charles kneeling in prayer and grasping a crown of thorns (inscribed *Gratia*), with his regal crown at his feet (inscribed *Vanitas*) and a crown of gold awaiting him above (inscribed *Gloria*); in the emblematic landscape, a palm tree hung with weights and a rock blasted by tempests represent the king's virtue strengthened by trial (plate 11).[160] Marshall's portrait of Charles contrasts sharply with his unflattering engraving of Milton in the 1645 *Poems*, reinforcing the suspicion that the Milton portrait was intended as satire.[161] The Marshall engraving prepares for the image or icon of the king conveyed in the text: a second David, deeply religious in his psalm-like prayers; a misunderstood monarch innocent of any deliberate wrongdoing, who always intended the best for the English people, a loving father to his children and his subjects; a defeated king negotiating honorably with his captors; a man of high culture, mildness, restraint, moderation, and peace persecuted by vulgar and bloodthirsty enemies; and now a martyr for conscience in refusing to compromise on bishops and liturgy and his ancient prerogatives. Like the frontispiece engraving, the text also identifies him as a second Christ in his sufferings and in his gestures of forgiving his enemies.[162] Charles regrets that he was sold by the Scots to parliament at a higher rate than Christ by Judas; he likens his negotiations with parliament to Christ tempted by Satan; and he begs God to forgive the English people in Christ's words, "they know not what they do." The pathos and sentiment, the simple, earnest language in which Charles defends his actions, the fiction that this text contains the king's private reflections and meditations rather than polemic argument, and the construction of this book as deathbed testimony – now heard from the grave – produced a nearly irresistible rhetorical effect.

Milton recognized the magnitude of his problem. He needed to counter the powerful appeal of that "idol" book to an irrational and misguided multitude, but his rigorous iconoclastic analysis could only persuade reasonable men. To undermine the myths promoted by the visual and theatrical modes used to create the king's "Portraiture" – as the subtitle of *Eikon Basilike* has it – he subjects that portrait to a penetrating verbal critique. And he develops that critique by posing insistent questions that require readers to weigh and judge, to give or withhold assent, in an effort to teach them how to engage with such duplicitous texts[163] (plate 12). But beyond the rhetoric, Milton's treatise derives a good deal of its energy and power from his fierce personal response to the king as a corrupt author and to his book as specious, deceptive court art.[164] His analysis implies, but does not state, what a good author and good art should be.

In the preface he carefully constructs his authorial stance. Acknowledging that it may seem meanspirited "To descant on the misfortunes of a person fall'n from so high a dignity" (*CPW* III, 337), he insists that this task was "assigned, rather than by me chos'n or affected," and was finished "leasurely" (339) amidst other duties. He has, he assures his readers, "better and more certaine" means to attain fame than engaging with kings, who are typically "weak at Arguments" (337). But this king cannot claim the respectful silence normally accorded the faults of the dead, since he has continued to argue his case to the world "as in his Book alive."[165] So Milton, like an epic hero or an Abdiel in prospect, takes on the role of designated champion of the republic, ready to meet "the force of his [the king's] reason in any field whatsoever, the force and equipage of whose Armes they [the republic's armies] have so oft'n met victoriously."[166] His book's title, he explains, refers to the chosen surname of many Greek emperors who "after long tradition of Idolatry in the Church, took courage, and broke all superstitious Images to peeces" (343). Milton Ikonoklastes undertakes a similar work: to destroy the idol many have made of the king within the book and of the king's book itself, "almost adoring it" and setting it "next the Bible" (339–40). He hints that he too has seen through the pretence about the king's authorship: he plays on Gauden's name, "the gaudy name of Majesty" (338); he alludes to some "secret *Coadjutor*" whom some "stick not to name" (346); and he speculates on stylistic grounds that the whole work shows the hand of "som other Author"(393). But since the book has become an idol to the "blockish vulgar" only because "a King is said to be the Author" (339), he engages it on those terms. And as the king's book presents him as the suffering hero of his own tragedy, Milton undertakes to reassign its genre from tragedy to providential comedy.

The construction of audience creates special difficulties since Milton, prophet-like, castigates the idolatrous populace as fiercely as the book-idol they worship. He addresses his work chiefly to those "staid and well-principl'd men" who can be led to see the falsehoods, pretence, and wicked principles writ large in the king's book and who will then extend their Puritan hatred of idolatry to that "civil kinde of Idolatry" being invited by and offered to the king's image.[167] He invites that regrettably small elite to separate itself sharply from the "mad multitude," the "ingratefull and pervers generation," the "miserable, credulous, deluded thing that creature is, which is call'd the Vulgar; who . . . will beleeve such vain-glories as these" (345–6, 426). As rhetoric, this language neatly reverses *Eikon Basilike*'s association of high culture and gentility with the king's supporters and vulgar barbarism with his opponents. But it also voices Milton's profound disappointment with many of his countrymen. Still, by locating the sources of their servility in courts and clerics, he holds out hope that they may in due course be reformed by a republican ethos:

> Now, with a besotted and degenerate baseness of spirit, except some few, who yet retain in them the old English fortitude and love of Freedom, and have testifi'd it by thir matchless deeds, the rest, imbastardiz'd from the ancient nobleness of thir Ancestors, are ready to fall flatt and give adoration to the Image and Memory of this Man, who hath offer'd at more cunning fetches to undermine our Liberties, and putt Tyranny into an Art, then any British King before him. Which low dejection and debase-

ment of mind in the people I must confess I cannot willingly ascribe to the natural disposition of an Englishman, but rather to two other causes. First, to the Prelats and thir fellow-teachers, though of another Name and Sect [the Presbyterians], whose Pulpit stuff, both first and last, hath bin the Doctrin and perpetual infusion of sevility and wretchedness to all thir hearers. (344)

More rigorously than he did in *Animadversions* and *Colasterion*, Milton follows his opponent's structure chapter by chapter, quoting and then refuting his propositions and his arguments. Against the king's royalist rewriting of recent history, Milton sets his republican versions, drawing largely on Thomas May's *History of Parliament*. Some examples: the king claims that he willingly convoked the Long Parliament, but in fact he always hated parliaments and called this one only to fund his Scots war, "condemn'd and abominated by the whole Kingdom" (354). The king denounces the Irish rebels, but from start to finish was "ever friendly to the Irish Papists" and in "secret intercours" with them to invade England.[168] The king rails against unlawful popular tumults, but those tumults hastened much needed reform:

If there were a man of iron, such as *Talus*, by our Poet *Spencer*, is fain'd to be the page of Justice, who with his iron flaile could doe all this, and expeditiously, without those deceitfull formes and circumstances of Law, worse then ceremonies in Religion; I say God send it don, whether by one *Talus*, or by a thousand. . . . This iron flaile the People . . . drove the Bishops out of thir Baronies, out of thir Cathedrals, out the Lords House . . . threw down the High Commission and Star-chamber, [and] gave us a Triennial Parlament. (390–1)

Moreover, the king's negotiations with parliament were duplicitous, his counsels of patience and forgiveness to his son are not to be trusted, and his claims of inviolability as the "Lords Anointed" are contradicted by justifications of tyrannicide from the Bible, history, and Natural Law.[169] By such analysis Milton sought to teach his audience how to read as free citizens of a republic: to weigh fine-sounding words against actions, and to recognize propaganda that plays with emotions and sentiment.[170]

Milton also requires his readers to choose between two versions of the state. Charles's model produces tyranny and servility: the king wields supreme power, controlling the army, governing the church, calling and dismissing parliament, and retaining a negative voice over legislation. In Milton's republican model parliament, as the people's representative, is supreme in all these areas, and it was the king's persistent refusal to recognize this fact that caused the civil war and the regicide. Milton's argument presumes, with classical notions of monarchy as slavery in the background, that a nascent republicanism was implied by England's very nature as a free people. If they have to depend on a king's assent for any needful thing, they are not free "but a multitude of Vassalls in the Possession and domaine of one absolute Lord" (458). The king had no right to govern except by law and

"Law in a Free Nation hath bin ever public reason, the enacted reason of a Parlament" (360). The king had no right to dismiss parliament or to exercise a negative vote over its acts, since it is absurd "that the judgement of one man, not as a wise or good man, but as a King, and oft times a wilfull, proud, and wicked King, should outweigh the prudence, and all the vertue of an elected Parlament" (409). Indeed, "Laws are in the hands of Parlament to change or abrogate, as they shall see best for the Common-wealth; eev'n to the taking away of King-ship it self" (458). The king's claim of conscience is specious for he has no right to impose his private conscience regarding bishops and liturgy on the entire nation represented in parliament or on Christian individuals assured of liberty by Christ. Also, power over the army belongs to parliament, not to the king: if the power of the sword is separated from the power of law as seated in parliament, "then would that power of the Sword be soon maister of the law, & being at one mans disposal, might, when he pleas'd, controule the Law" (454). Milton may, like Marvell in "An Horatian Ode," recognize that this principle might come to be applicable to Cromwell, but this is not the place to say so. At times Milton appeals explicitly to the principle of representation, to equate parliament with the Commons. The king and the Lords represent only themselves but the Commons are the "whole Parlament, assembl'd by election, and indu'd with the plenipotence of a free Nation, to make Laws" (410). In fact, "the Commons are the whole Kingdom" (415): they "sit in that body, not *as his* [the king's] *Subjects* but as his Superiors, call'd, not by him but by the Law . . . as oft as great affaires require, *to be his Counselers and Dictators*" (463). In affirming these republican principles, Milton elides any question of the Rump's legitimacy or representativeness after Pride's Purge, and also elides the role of the army.

Milton's principal rhetorical challenge is to destroy the idol the king has made of himself as martyr and saint, as a second David voicing psalmic prayers, and as a second Christ in his sufferings and death. He counters those identifications by associating Charles instead with an array of despots from biblical and ancient history: Ahab, Herod, Saul, Nimrod, Nebuchadnezzar, Uzziah, Pharoah, Reheboam, Ahaz, Cataline, Agrippa, Caligula, Nero, and even Lucifer.[171] He also associates Charles's tyranny with what he sees as its natural psychological concomitant: servile subjection to his wife. His letters at Naseby show him "govern'd by a Woman" (538) and his praises of her "almost to Sonnetting" place him with other "effeminate and Uxorious Magistrates" who have brought danger and dishonor to nations (420–1).

In his prophetic role as iconoclast, Milton castigates Charles as a deceptive idol and hypocritical actor. He is a masquer in his book as he was at court, devising fictions and using disguises, cosmetics, and costumes. The frontispiece of *Eikon Basilike* is "drawn out to the full measure of a Masking Scene," but those "quaint Emblems and devices begg'd from the old Pageantry of some Twelf-nights entertainment at *Whitehall*" will not make a saint or martyr (342–3). In his dealings with parliament Charles thrust out "on the Scene . . . an Antimasque of two bugbeares, *Noveltie* and *Perturbation*" to frighten those attempting reformation (533). His supposed sanctity is mere "Stage-work" (530): like many tyrants he wears a "Saints vizard," and his staged prayers resemble and sometimes echo those of Shakespeare's Richard III (361–3). And his book, in its theatrical "garb" and "dress," seems to be a work of poetry, not politics:

> The Simily wherwith he begins I was about to have found fault with, as in a garb somwhat more Poeticall then for a Statist: but meeting with many straines of like dress in other of his Essaies, and hearing him reported a more diligent reader of Poets, then of Politicians, I begun to think that the whole Book might perhaps be intended a peece of Poetrie. The words are good, the fiction smooth and cleanly; there wanted onely Rime, and that, they say is bestow'd upon it lately. (406)[172]

This sentiment seems strange coming from a poet, but it is glossed by Milton's earlier reference to the "easy literature of custom" (339). That category would include facile court genres that are the product of feigning and mere elegance, not the bardic poetry Milton aspired to, which is the the product of "industrie and judicious paines" and inspiration. Milton underscores the difference by subjecting the king's metaphors to a literary critic's analysis, to uncover what that bad poet unwittingly reveals of himself through them. Most telling is the absurd, indeed incestuous, sexual metaphor the king develops in claiming that his reason is as necessary to the "begetting, or bringing forth" of any act of parliament as the sun's influence is to any production in nature:

> So that the Parlament, it seems, is but a Female, and without his procreative reason, the Laws which they can produce are but windeggs. . . . [C]ertainly it was a Parlament that first created Kings. . . . He ought then to have so thought of a Parlament, if he count it not Male, as of his Mother, which, to civil being, created both him, and the Royalty he wore. And if it hath bin anciently interpreted the presaging signe of a future Tyrant, but to dream of copulation with his Mother, what can it be less then actual Tyranny to affirme waking, that the Parlament, which is his Mother, can neither conceive nor bring forth *any autoritative Act* without his Masculine coition. Nay that his reason is as Celestial and lifegiving to the Parlament, as the Suns influence is to the Earth: What other notions but these, or such like, could swell up *Caligula* to think himself a God. (467)

Milton would have readers see the king's "idle" book and his own strenuous treatise as exemplars of two kinds of poetry and two kinds of authors. The king's book, patched up of facile and unacknowledged borrowings, pretense, and foolish metaphors, promotes indolent, credulous reading: it is itself an idol and it promotes idolatry. Milton's, like worthy poetry, promotes diligent effort, rigorous judgment, and difficult interpretation as the only means to gather up some shards of *Areopagitica's* dismembered truth.

In line with this, and most damaging of all, Milton convicts the supposedly saintly king as a plagiarist of others' prayers, so deficient in piety that even when preparing for death he cannot pray to God in his own words. Charles presents his prayers throughout as "a kind of privat Psalter" (560), claiming as his own "many penitential verses out of *Davids* Psalmes" (553).[173] Much worse, he also plagiarized the pagan Pamela's prayer out of Sidney's *Arcadia*. That prayer is the first of four prayers at the end of *Eikon Basilike*, but Milton attaches his scathing denunciation of this theft to his comments on the king's first chapter, seeking thereby to undermine all subsequent claims to truthful reporting by an author–king who plagiarizes, and all claims to sanctity by a Christian king who prays pagan prayers:

> [Other Christian kings] have still pray'd thir own, or at least borrow'd from fitt Authors. But this King, not content . . . to attribute to his own making other mens whole Prayers, hath as it were unhallow'd, and unchrist'nd the very duty of prayer it self, by borrowing to a Christian use Prayers offer'd to a Heathen God . . . a Prayer stol'n word for word from the mouth of a Heathen fiction praying to a heathen God; & that in no serious Book, but the vain amatorious Poem of Sr *Philip Sidneys Arcadia*; a Book in that kind full of worth and witt, but among religious thoughts, and duties not worthy to be nam'd . . . much less in time of trouble and affliction to be a Christians Prayer-Book. (362–3)

In the second edition Milton expanded this point, insisting that the plagiarism brings disgrace to the king's entire "Idoliz'd Book, and the whole rosarie of his Prayers."[174] Also, more firmly than in *Areopagitica*, Milton defends authors' property rights, linking the affront to God from this plagiarized prayer first offered to idols with the wrong done to Sidney, the human author, who has a right to his intellectual property, and the wrong done to all Englishmen by Shipmoney and other illegal taxes imposed by the king:

> [He] thought no better of the living God then of a buzzard Idol, fit to be so servd and worshipt in reversion with the polluted orts and refuse of Arcadia's and Romances, without being able to discern the affront rather then the worship of such an ethnic Prayer. But leaving what might justly be offensive to God, it was a trespass also more then usual against human right, which commands that every Author should have the property of his own work reservd to him after death as well as living. Many Princes have bin rigorous in laying taxes on thir Subjects by the head, but of any King heertofore that made a levy upon thir witt, and seisd it as his own legitimat, I have not whom beside to instance. (364–5)

When *Eikonoklastes* concludes, Milton's iconoclastic hammer has attacked not only the idol–king and his book, but also rote prayers, liturgical forms, the Solemn League and Covenant, kings, bishops, and the church of Rome – all idols, in that they are material forms invested with divinity or sanctity, which demand to be taken on implicit faith. In the final pages Milton constructs an allegory of Truth and

Justice with prophetic, apocalyptic resonance.[175] Linking the justice realized in the regicide with the honor accorded the saints in Psalm 149:8, "To bind thir Kings in Chaines, and thir Nobles with links of Iron," he intimates that the English republic may have begun to realize "in these latter days" the millennial "doom" (Revelation 19) to be visited on kings by the King of Kings (598–9). But his concern is still with how to sustain republican government in the meantime. He makes a sharp division among three categories of Englishmen: the wise, whose "constancie and solid firmness" the king cannot hope to unsettle; the "inconstant, irrational, and Image-doting rabble" who are incorrigible idolators, mesmerized by the king's Circean cup of servitude;[176] and the rest, whom his guidance might reclaim. He elaborates that Circe allusion in the second edition:

> [They] like a credulous and hapless herd, begott'n to servility, and inchanted with these popular institutes of Tyranny, subscrib'd with a new device of the Kings Picture at his praiers, hold out both thir eares with such delight and ravishment to be stigmatiz'd and board through in witness of thir own voluntary and beloved baseness. The rest, whom perhaps ignorance without malice, or some error, less then fatal, hath for the time misledd, on this side Sorcery or obduration, may find the grace and good guidance to bethink themselves, and recover. (601)

These lines reveal Milton's profound chagrin and frustration that, after the first edition, so many of his idolatrous countrymen remain "a hapless herd," unresponsive to the best efforts of Milton Ikonoklastes to break the Circean spell.

Salmasius's *Defensio Regia* posed a very different challenge. That ponderous Latin treatise, combining serious argument with fierce denunciation, was the work of a reformed Protestant with a distinguished international reputation as Latinist and scholar. Exuding shock and horror over the regicide and the crimes of the "illegal" Commonwealth government and the army, Salmasius marshals scripture texts supporting the divine right of kings and even of tyrants, analyzes ancient and modern political theory and history to argue the superiority and continuity of monarchical government, and draws the same conclusion from English laws and English history. Milton gladly took up the challenge to match and overpass Salmasius in sound Latinity as well as in political philosophy and historical scholarship, eager to demonstrate that the infant English republic was not the cultural wasteland its enemies claimed, but had reclaimed the noblest traditions of humanist learning. Though the organization of Milton's long treatise is dictated by the need to answer Salmasius point by point, he also expands upon his conception of republican polity and culture.

This work is a prime example of what David Norbrook terms the republic's developing aesthetics of sublimity, set over against the more limited courtly aesthetics of elegance and beauty.[177] In his preface Milton presents the *Defensio* as a prose epic whose theme is the heroic action of his countrymen in defeating, judging, and executing their tyrant king, with God "as our leader:"

> My discourse, indeed, will be of matters neither small nor mean: a king in all his power, ruling according to his lust after he had overthrown our laws and oppressed our religion, at length overcome in battle by his own people which had served a long term of slavery; . . . [and] condemned to capital punishment by the highest court of the realm and beheaded before the very gates of the palace. . . . For what majesty of an high-enthroned king ever shone with brilliance such as that which flashed forth from the people of England when they had shaken off this ancient and enduring superstition. (*CPW* IV.1, 302–3)

An epic-like invocation seeks comparable divine aid for the prose-poet who has been chosen for, and has fully prepared himself for, the writing of this epic:

> Even though the leaders of our state have authorized me to undertake this task . . . a duty second in importance to theirs alone . . . and, although I take great pride in their decision that by their wishes I before all others should be the one to take on this enviable task for the noble liberators of my country (because indeed from early youth I eagerly pursued studies which impelled me to celebrate, if not to perform, the loftiest actions) . . . I lose heart and turn to aid from on high. I call on almighty God, giver of all gifts, to grant that just as success and righteousness attended those famous men who led us to liberty, who crushed in line of battle the insolence of the king and the passion of the tyrant . . . so I may now with good success and in very truth refute and bring to naught the ill-tempered lies of this barbarous rhetorician [Salmasius]. (305–6)

If circumstances preclude the writing of his long-projected epic poem, he wants, it seems, to regard this work as some kind of substitute.

But his purposes here – to win over his chief audience, the learned of Europe – require a mix of genres and styles. Personal invective is prominent among them. He assails the mighty reputation of Salmasius with a barrage of epithets branding him a fool, a pedant, a slavish toady, a meer grammarian, and a bad scholar. "You," he taunts, are a "tricky turncoat," a "merchant of hot air," "a homeless, houseless, worthless man of straw," a "prattling orator," "an unpractised ignoramus," a "dull, stupid, ranting, wrangling advocate," an "empty windbag," a "truant cockeral," a "boring little weevil," a "wretched false prophet," a "luckless wretch" whose brain is befogged, a "slave on horseback," a "black rogue," a "cheap French mountebank," a "crackbrained, moneygrabbing Frenchman."[178] He supports those labels with a mix of questionable rumor and textual evidence, catching the grammarian out in several instances of bad Latin, and repeating the unproved but widely circulated story that Salmasius wrote for hire, taking a hundred sovereigns from the penniless Charles II.[179] Convicting Salmasius of lifting misunderstood tidbits of Roman history and historians (notably Tacitus) out of context, he draws a sharp contrast between Salmasius as a meer commonplacer and himself as a true scholar, deeply versed in the original texts.[180] Salmasius "has spent his time thumbing anthologies and dictionaries and glossaries, instead of reading through good authors with judgment and profit," and has "never tasted a drop of honest scholarship" (338). He is also given to self-contradictions and illogic. He claims that government by one, by a few, or by many is equally "natural," but then states that monarchy is the "most natural" of the three (427).[181] He reads the Pauline text requiring obedience to the powers that be (Romans 13:1) as obligating Christians to submit even to the ruling tyrant Nero, not recognizing that this argument also requires English Christians to submit to the present government (382–5, 395). Also, he locates the claims of English kings to absolute power in the right of ancient conquest, not recognizing that this argument also sanctions the English government that conquered Charles (461).

Drawing on the widespread gossip that Salmasius was dominated by his wife, Milton makes game of him as a "hen-pecked" husband (471). But he is quite serious in linking Salmasius's slavery to an inferior with his readiness to defend a royal absolutism that enslaves others: "You have at home a barking bitch who . . . contradicts you shrilly; so naturally you want to force royal tyranny on others after being used to suffer so slavishly a woman's tyranny at home" (380); you are a "foul Circean beast . . . well used to serving a woman in the lowest sort of slavery where you never had the slightest taste of manly virtue or the freedom which springs from it."[182] Here (as to a lesser extent with King Charles in *Eikon Basilike*) Milton finds a natural connection between a "slavish" personal life and a disposition to practice, or submit to, political tyranny. It is an acute psychological observation, though based on regrettable assumptions about gender hierarchy and couched in gender stereotypes.

At the level of argument, Milton insists that biblical and historical law and example support a republican rather than a monarchical polity, and he cites several examples of tyrannicide approved by God or sanctioned by history. He turns against Salmasius the biblical texts that he (like many others) had cited to support absolute monarchy: Deuteronomy 17 and 1 Samuel 8. In a more detailed exegesis than in *Tenure*, Milton finds in those texts evidence that God first gave the Israelites a republican government, that he recognized their right to change forms of government by granting their request for a king, but that he indicated his antipathy to monarchy by warning them of the evils a king would do:

> God himself bears witness to the right possessed by almost all peoples and nations of enjoying whatever form of government they wish, or of changing from one to another; this God asserts specifically of the Hebrews and does not deny of other nations. A republican form of government, moreover, as being better adapted to our human circumstances than monarchy, seemed to God more advantageous for his chosen people; he set up a republic for them and granted their request for a monarchy only after long reluctance. . . . God indeed gives evidence throughout of his great displeasure at their request for a king – thus in [1 Samuel 8] verse 7: "They have not rejected thee, but they have rejected me, that I should not reign over them." . . . This evidence all proves that the Israelites were given a king by God in his wrath. (344, 369–70).

Also, Milton now finds much more evidence in the gospels of the divine preferance for republicanism. He describes Christ as a "Liberator" propounding a version of liberation theology as he urges his followers to win political freedom and live by republican principles. He reads 1 Corinthians 7:21–5 ("If you can become free, then use your freedom. You are bought for a price; be not the slaves of men") as encouraging "our worthy struggle for freedom" both religious and political, and as placing "our political freedom on a firm foundation" (374–5). He cites to the same purpose Christ's reprimand to the sons of Zebedee when they sought high rank in his kingdom (Matthew 20:20–1): "the princes of the Gentiles exercise dominion over them; and they that are great exercise authority upon them. But it shall not be so among you . . . whosoever will be chief among you, let him be your servant." That text proves that "Amongst Christians . . . there will either be no king at all, or else one who is the servant of all; for clearly one cannot wish to dominate and remain a Christian" (378–9). And in place of the royalist analogy Salmasius so often invokes between divine and human kingship, Milton asserts a flat disjunction, claiming that earthly kingship belongs to Christ alone, at the Millennium: "who, in fact, is worthy of holding on earth power like that of God but some person who far surpasses all others and even resembles God in goodness and wisdom? The only such person, as I believe, is the son of God whose coming we look for" (427–8).

Reiterating his long-standing belief that "the law of God does most closely agree with the law of nature" (422), Milton insists that the law of nature holds forth these same principles of popular sovereignty and republicanism. Like Filmer, Salmasius reads the law of nature as mandating absolute power in the king and forbidding rebellion against him on the ground that the king has the powers of the father of a family.[183] But Milton proclaims this analogy also to be entirely false: "Our fathers begot us, but our kings did not, and it is we, rather, who created kings." Moreover, even paternal power is not absolute: "we do not endure even a father who is tyrannical" (327). Reprising the arguments of *Tenure*, he insists, against both Salmasius and Hobbes,[184] that the people's grant of power to any king or magistrate is always on trust and revocable, since "To grant to any mortal power over one's self on stronger terms than a trust would be the height of madness" (459) and would amount to enslaving oneself. The regicide was justified by the law of nature that subjects the king to law and justice like any other person, and by *Salus Populi*, "that law of Nature and of God which holds that whatever is for the safety of the state is right and just" (317–18). Also, nature, like Aristotle, dictates that forms of government should be suited to the character of the people. A king could conceivably be the "natural" choice if he is "far superior" to all others in wisdom and virtue: Milton speculates that Julius Caesar may have been such a man (449) and he will later conclude that Cromwell probably is. But England should look rather to nature's norm: "where there are many equals, and in most states there are very many, I hold they should rule alike and in turn" (366–7).

In the category of secular history, Milton counters Salmasius's assertion that monarchy has been nearly universal by pointing to the United Provinces as a flourishing contemporary republic and by recounting stories of nations – Greeks, Romans, Italians, Carthaginians, and many more – who in their best days chose republican forms: "surely these nations were more important than all the rest" (432). He meets Salmasius's citations from political philosophers and classical poets by offering countertexts from Aristotle, Plato, Cicero, Sallust, Polybius, Homer, Aeschylus, Euripides, Buchanan, and Hotman to indicate that in fact they denounce tyranny and absolute monarchy, place rulers under the law, and allow to the people the right to overthrow despots and share political power. In Aristotle's *Politics* he finds precepts that equate monarchy itself with tyranny: "It is neither expedient nor just that one be master of all when men are similar or equal. . . . One whom the people does not wish becomes immediately not king but a tyrant" (438). As he does in *Eikonoklastes*, Milton marshals evidence that English kings were always limited by contract, that parliaments or councils superior to kings always existed in fact, and that by English law the Commons alone are supreme "and have power to judge the king" (494). Persuading himself of the English state's republican essence throughout its history, he exults: "I cannot fail to voice my pride in our fathers who, in establishing this state, displayed a wisdom and a sense of freedom equal to that of the ancient Romans or the most illustrious Greeks" (495).

Nonetheless, Salmasius's taunts about the "unrepresentative" English government – the "forty tyrants" of the Council of State, the parliament purged of bishops, lords, and many commoners, the power of the army over the legislature – forced Milton to work through how such a government can sort with the republican ideal preferred by God, nature, and history. Challenged to define who the "people" are that have political rights in the new republic, Milton claims that "all citizens of every degree" are represented in the supremacy of the Commons, in which all, including the nobles, are comprehended. But he accepts limitations on actual representation. He probably approved of the existing property qualification for citizens allowed to vote and hold office, and he argues that, in the present circumstances, the exercise of citizenship must be further restricted:

> Our form of government is such as our circumstances and schisms permit: it is not the most desirable, but only as good as the stubborn struggles of the wicked citizens allow it to be. If, however, a country harassed by faction and protecting herself by arms regards only the sound and upright side, passing over or shutting out the others, whether commons or nobles, she maintains justice well enough. (316–17)

He does not equate the "sound and upright" with religion, nor yet with class: some are nobles and "others are self-made men who follow the course of true nobility through toil and rectitude" (319). But nor are they strictly "of every degree": most are not from the "dregs of the populace" who because of poverty or because they are in service to others cannot fulfill citizenship responsibilties, nor from the nobility whose excessive wealth and luxury often leads them to abnegate those duties, but from "the middle class, which produces the greatest number of men of good sense and knowledge of affairs" (471). The scrivener's son quite approves of the English bourgeois republic.

In justifying the restrictions his government is imposing on citizenship, Milton appeals beyond pragmatism to the classical ideal of government by the best and worthiest who are, by his further definition, the men who love, support, and defend religious liberty and republican freedoms. On the authority of Aristotle and Cicero Milton admits, reluctantly, that "those who long for liberty or can enjoy it are but few – only the wise, that is, and the brave; while most men prefer just masters so long as they are in fact just" (343). On the authority of nature's law he concludes that government exists for the good of all but especially to promote "the well-being of the better citizens" (533), those liberty-lovers who may, when necessary, act for the good of all. On this understanding he can defend the lords' expulsion from parliament and Pride's Purge as actions of and for "the people":

> The soldiers to whom you ascribe the act were themselves not foreigners but citizens, forming a great part of the people, and they acted with the consent and by the will of most of the rest, supported by Parliament. . . . I say it was the people; for why should I not say that the act of the better, the sound part of the Parliament, in which resides the real power of the people, was the act of the people? If a majority in Parliament prefer enslavement and putting the commonwealth up for sale, is it not right for a minority to prevent it if they can and preserve their freedom? (457)

Though he is hesitant about justifying military force used against the legislature, he concludes that the citizen army "which was ever brave and loyal to the state" acted at the behest of the "uncorrupted" part of the Commons and even temporarily replaced that body as the people's representative: "In this affair my belief is, though I hesitate to express it, that our troops were wiser than our legislators, and saved the commonwealth by arms when the others had nearly destroyed it by their votes" (332–3). Similarly, the Independents of the truncated Rump, by seizing power and bringing the king to trial, "stood by their trust in protecting the state, which . . . had been particularly entrusted to their loyalty, wisdom, and courage by the whole people" even though they were deserted by "a great part of the people [who] . . . desired peace and slavery with inaction and comfort upon any terms."[185] He still hopes, however, that living in a republic will teach this populace better values:

> I can still say that their sins were taught them under the monarchy, like the Israelites in Egypt, and have not been immediately unlearned in the desert, even under the guidance of God. But there is much hope for most of them, not to enter on the praises of our good and reverent men who follow eagerly after truth, of whom we have as many as you can imagine anywhere. (386–7)

Milton's peroration is addressed, not to Europe, but to "all Englishmen." It offers "my fellow citizens" the education he thinks they need. He challenges them to refute Salmasius by their deeds as he has done by words, and thereby to prove worthy of God's great blessing in setting them free "from the two greatest evils in human life, the most fatal to virtue, namely tyranny and superstition" (535). Specifically, he challenges his own party in government not to prove "as weak in peace as you have been strong in war" (the characteristic flaw of the British according to his *History of Britain*), but to continue to merit the praise due their famous acts, as the first men to conquer, judge by legal process, and then execute their king. They must now eschew "self-seeking, greed, luxury, and the seductions of success" as well as "the desire to curtail the rights of others," and must preserve freedom by "justice, restraint, and moderation" (535). This sounds like innocuous advice to be good, but Milton means it profoundly: only such a government, he thinks, can overcome divisive religious conflicts and promote republican virtue in the citizenry, thereby moving the country closer to the republican ideal.

9

"Tireless . . . for the Sake of Liberty" 1652–1654

Milton was at least somewhat prepared for the onset of total blindness in February or March, 1652. With his left eye already useless, he had been relying more and more on readers and amanuenses during the past three years as he gradually lost sight in the right eye. Despite periods of despondency he refused to give way to self-pity or to resign his secretarial office with its duties and opportunities for action in the world. By training his prodigious memory he found a way to fulfill those duties, digesting material read to him and dictating translations to council scribes. For his own writings he called on various assistants – sometimes paid secretaries but often friends and former pupils, including his two nephews.[1] John Phillips was probably part of his household during much of this period. But if blindness could be anticipated, other calamities that spring could not. Mary Powell died in May at age twenty-seven, three days after giving birth to a daughter, Deborah. And about six weeks later Milton's only son John died. Milton kept working, but the impact of such losses in such short order must have been devastating.

Political and personal anxieties led Milton to find his poetic voice again in 1652, after (apparently) a four-year hiatus. He turned to the small form of the sonnet, using it as he had in the Fairfax sonnet for panegyric linked to political exhortation; and in the famous sonnet on his blindness he forced that genre to new heights of emotional poignancy and formal complexity. He also came to England's defense again – and his own – against another formidable Latin attack published on the Continent as a continuation of Salmasius's project. Now, however, the government Milton defended was Cromwell's Protectorate, so he had to reformulate some core political principles: now it is not parliament but the Protector who is worthiest to govern and whose government offers the best hope of preserving religious and civil liberties. Characteristically, both in this *Defensio Secunda* (1654) and in sonnets to Cromwell and his friend Henry Vane, Milton took up again the role of adviser to the state and its leaders, urging his own radical program of toleration and church disestablishment. Because the *Defensio Secunda* includes extensive passages of autobiography, albeit shaped by Milton's rhetorical purposes, it provides the most revealing window we have into Milton's sense of himself and his life up to this moment.

"I Do Not Complain About My Own Role"

On March 29, 1652 a long eclipse of the sun cast the nation into temporary darkness, prompting an outpouring of preaching and praying. But Milton's darkness was by this time total and permanent. Though his government duties increased exponentially, now he usually waited at home for council messengers to bring state documents to him (*LR* III, 213, 214); scribes would read to him letters or documents drafted in English which he had to digest, revise as needed, and translate into Latin by dictation. His attendance at the council and its Committee on Foreign Affairs was now infrequent; and, as he admitted a year later, he was no longer "fit" to attend "at Conferences with Ambassadors."[2] This shrinking of his public world surely intensified Milton's sense of loss: no longer did he have regular casual contacts with men of power, affording an opportunity to lobby discreetly for his own views. No longer could he discern men's motives and meanings from facial expressions and body language. Moreover, this proud man, somewhat vain about his appearance, had to endure the humiliation of being led by his nephew or a messenger whenever he came to Whitehall. He took great satisfaction, however, in his continued usefulness to the government and in the signs of their continued value for him:

> [S]ince the loss of my eyesight has not left me sluggish from inactivity but tireless and ready among the first to risk the greatest dangers for the sake of liberty, the chief men in the state do not desert me either but, considering within themselves what human life is like, they gladly favor and indulge me, and grant to me rest and leisure, as to one who well deserves it. If I have any distinction, they do not remove it, if any public office, they do not take it away, if any advantage from that office, they do not diminish it, and although I am no longer as useful as I was, they think that they should reward me no less graciously. (*Defensio Secunda*, *CPW* IV.1, 591)

The council was no doubt relieved to find Milton able to cope with many of his official duties, but he needed help. On February 2, 1652 Lewis Rosin was officially appointed to provide translations from French, and others were occasionally called on for other languages, as needed.[3] On March 11 the council called out of retirement Milton's predecessor as Latin Secretary, Georg Weckherlin, appointing him assistant secretary to the Committee for Foreign Affairs, but Weckherlin was 68 and in poor health. Later that month the council's very able general secretary, Gualter Frost, died, but they replaced him with the even more talented John Thurloe, who by stages also took over some of Weckherlin's responsibilities in regard to foreign affairs and diplomatic conferences.[4] These arrangements were evidently satisfactory, and Milton was reappointed on December 1, 1652, to "bee continued in the Employment hee had the last Yeare & have the same allowance for it" (*LR* III, 283).

In the spring of 1652 Milton received another severe blow. His family Bible carries this cryptic record: "My daughter Deborah was born the 2d of May, being Sunday somwhat before 3 of the clock in the morning 1652. my wife hir mother dyed about 3. days after."[5] Though this marriage was not the ideal union of minds Milton had hoped for, the loss of Mary following so soon upon the total loss of his vision surely made his daily life more lonely and more difficult. He was left with four very young children: Anne (nearly six), Mary (four), John (fifteen months), and the new infant Deborah. He would have had to make arrangements immediately for the older children; Deborah would have been with a wet nurse, and so, probably, was John. Milton's Bible entry continues with notice of another tragedy: "And my son [died] about 6. weeks after his mother" (*LR* III, 228) – that is, on or around June 16.[6] The vague dating suggests that Milton did not know or did not remember when the entry was made some years later, the exact time and circumstances of his son's death, perhaps because John was still with his nurse. Edward Phillips speculated that the child's death might have been due to "the ill-usage, or bad Constitution of an ill-chosen Nurse" (*EL* 71). There are no records of Deborah's baptism or of Mary's and young John's death and burial either in Milton's local parish, St Margaret, Westminster, or in his former parish, St Giles, Cripplegate. Milton, a fierce opponent of the parish system, may have been associated with a congregation whose theology and services were more to his liking but whose records, like those of many City of London churches, were destroyed in the Great Fire. Milton surely felt keenly the loss of his only son. He alludes briefly but revealingly in the *Pro Se Defensio* (1655) to the difficulties of these months: "At that time especially, infirm health, distress over two deaths in my family, and the complete failure of my sight beset me with troubles" (*CPW* IV.2, 703).

From early 1652 until Cromwell dissolved the Rump Parliament on April 20, 1653, Milton worked on diplomatic correspondence and treaty negotiations with several nations. His first important duties involved negotiations between England and the United Provinces. On February 11 the Dutch ambassadors to London submitted a treaty of 36 articles based on the "Intercursus Magnus" that Milton had translated for negotiations in the Hague the previous year.[7] The council produced a "rebuttal" version of all these articles, sending it to Milton on March 8 and 9 to render into Latin; it refused the Dutch request to void the Navigation Act or to concede certain rights concerning fishing and trading in the New World.[8] On March 15 that document was sent to the ambassadors along with a "Paper of Demands," which required that the Dutch pay over £1.5 million as reparations for incidents stretching back to 1618: English ships captured or sunk, and English sailors and merchants killed or abused. Milton was apparently responsible for translating these

15 demands, with some collaboration from Lewis Rosin.[9] To a letter from the Dutch ambassadors seeking some adjustments, Milton translated the council's answer (April 16), insisting that these "Demands" must be met before a treaty could be agreed.[10] England's hard line was prompted by a mix of nationalism, maritime rivalry over sovereignty in the Channel, and commercial self-interest. The trajectory toward war was accelerated by a sea-fight on May 19 in English waters, evidently precipitated by a misunderstanding but seen by the English as flagrant aggression begun while the Dutch were engaged in duplicitous diplomacy. Two new Dutch ambassadors – Willem Nieupoort and Adrian Pauw – were sent to negotiate, and Milton was asked to translate Nieupoort's private instructions, obtained in advance of his arrival (about May 10) by Thurloe's spy network in the Netherlands. Edward Phillips notes that Milton passed that task on to "his kinsman" – either himself or his brother John[11] – no doubt because the papers arrived during those desperate days in early May when Mary Milton was dying or had just died in childbirth. In the *Defensio Secunda* Milton named Pauw among the distinguished foreigners who had paid him special honor; they did not meet but Pauw sent "many messages" to assure Milton of his "great and singular good will towards me" (*CPW* IV.1, 655). Such attentions meant a great deal to Milton at this juncture, reassuring him that he was still highly regarded by the learned of Europe. Apparently, Milton was not involved in those last negotiations (protracted, some thought, so the Dutch might gather useful information about English war preparations); they ended June 30.

In mid-July Milton was dealing with his personal tragedies by continuing to do the work assigned him. Parliament's official *Declaration* of the causes of war with the United Provinces was published July 9 in English,[12] and Milton's Latin version, the *Scriptum Parlamenti,* was probably ready by late July; translations in other languages appeared within a few weeks.[13] Milton had to translate or revise existing translations of a 70-page collection of documents: the official papers, speeches, and responses leading up to the conflict, and narrative of the course of events. Like many Englishmen, Milton admired the Dutch republic which had recently won independence from Spain and regretted these hostilities, which threatened hopes for a Protestant coalition against Rome. He supported his government but, he insists in 1655, with little enthusiasm:

> You are indeed greatly mistaken if you think that there is any Englishman more friendly to the United Provinces than I am, or more willingly united with them; who esteems more honorably that state; who makes more of its industry, arts, genius, and liberty, or more often applauds them; who would less desire a war begun with them, would wage one which had begun more pacifically, or rejoice more seriously when it was concluded; who, finally, ever gave less credit to their detractors. (*CPW* IV.2, 742)

The Anglo-Dutch war was the major event impacting English foreign relations for its duration (summer, 1652–April, 1654), with the English gaining greater international clout as, despite some serious losses, they won most of the sea-battles.[14]

Milton also translated several letters for the council to Ferdinand II, Grand Duke of Tuscany, who had proclaimed neutrality in the Anglo-Dutch war and opened the port of Livorno (Leghorn) to both fleets on condition that they refrain from hostilities within sight of Livorno's lighthouse. On July 29, 1652 the council thanked the duke profusely in Milton's Latin for allowing English ships that refuge against Dutch warships and sent him a copy of the *Scriptum Parlamenti*; on September 16 they again expressed profound gratitude for the safe harbor.[15] On January 14, 1653, however, Milton had to render the council's profound apology for two egregious English violations of Livorno's neutrality: seizing within sight of the lighthouse a captured English warship, and offering violence to Tuscan sentinels while pursuing an escaping prisoner onto shore.[16] Milton produced several other letters to various states for various purposes, among them letters to Hamburg and the Hanseatic towns to protest violence against English merchants (March 12), to decline their requests for relaxation of the Navigation Act (April 8), to welcome officially their envoy Lieuwe van Aitzema, and to express England's desire for continued friendship and trade (April 13).[17]

Milton also had major responsibility for correspondence between the council and the Spanish Ambassador Cardenas, much of it concerning his tentative proposals for a treaty. Milton produced Latin versions of two council letters to him, complaining of his failure to propose articles for a treaty (March 31, 1652), or to specify the changes he would make in a former treaty (August 10); the August letter complains again about Ascham's still unpunished murderers.[18] Milton probably translated some of Cardenas's proposals and replies into English, including the draft treaty of 24 articles Cardenas offered on September 2; and he probably turned into Latin the council's substitute draft (dated November 12) of 35 articles, one of which would protect English Protestants in Spain from the Inquisition when they practiced their religion in private places.[19] As treaty negotiations dragged on without result,[20] a council letter of January 14, 1653 warned the ambassador not to allow English citizens to attend mass at the houses of his ambassadorial staff (649–50). Milton seems to have had little connection with the renewed negotiations over the stalled treaty with Portugal, save for one instance on October 7, 1652, when the council ordered that a paper from the newly arrived Portuguese ambassador be "translated by Mr Milton into English and brought in to the Council to morrow in the afternoon" (*LR* III, 258).

Milton was centrally involved with the complex and ultimately fruitless negotiations for a commercial treaty with Denmark proposed by King Frederick III. He translated parliament's gracious response (April 13, 1652), affirming England's desire to preserve the ancient friendship and trade and inviting ambassadors to London.[21] They arrived in May and Milton likely translated some of the documents exchanged: Denmark's treaty proposals (June 14), the council's reply to these articles and proposal of others (July 8), and the ambassadors' response (July 28).[22] He almost certainly translated the council's letter (July 8) acknowledging Denmark's "friendly desires concerning Peace" between England and Holland and asking the ambassadors to transmit to King Frederick parliament's *Declaration* of the causes of war (Milton's *Scriptum Parlamenti*).[23] The sticking point in the treaty negotiations was England's insistence that Denmark accord it commercial privileges, customs, and tariffs as favorable as those already granted to the United Provinces. In September Milton wrote two letters about the articles under dispute, in one of which the council affects to disbelieve the ambassadors' claim that they have no authority to alter existing customs and tariff arrangments.[24] Negotiations broke down as the English, buoyed with their sea-victory over the United Provinces at Kentish Knock (September 28), decided they could not conclude a treaty with the Danes who were traditional allies of the Dutch.[25] Milton evidently translated the council's curt letter of October 19, protesting that parliament's *Declaration* must have removed "the least Dissatisfaction concerning the Justice and Candor" of England's proceedings in the Dutch war, and insisting that its treaty proposals are entirely "cleare, & moderate."[26] After the Danes impounded English merchant ships in the harbor of Copenhagen and the English responded by impounding all Danish ships in English harbors, Milton wrote a final letter for parliament to King Frederick (November 9, 1652) refusing his explanation of the affair and appointing Richard Bradshaw, the envoy to Hamburg, to negotiate (*CPW* V.2, 634–5). But before the year was out the Danes joined the Dutch in the war, closing the Baltic to English shipping.

Though Milton's official duties concerned foreign affairs, he was surely aware of intensifying domestic conflicts in the months after the Battle of Worcester. Cromwell seemed torn between his conservative impulse to promote stability by restoring some traditional institutions, and his reformist impulse to support radical soldiers and sectaries who were calling for wholesale restructuring of the legal system, broad toleration, abolition of tithes, and poor relief. Bulstrode Whitelocke reports a conference involving a few parliament members and officers in December, 1651, at which some, including Cromwell, were willing to consider a settlement with "something of monarchical power."[27] But for millenarian-minded sectaries any such settlement would be a flagrant repudiation of King Jesus, and for committed republicans any "single person" was deeply repugnant. The Rump Parliament was subject to such conservative–radical conflicts as it debated law reform, poor relief, and church matters, while outside its chambers Lilburne and the Levellers produced new pamphlets and Winstanley presented his blueprint of a communist Digger Utopia to Cromwell.[28] Parliament, urged from all sides to set a terminus to its sitting, fixed that date as November 3, 1654, but could not settle on how to exclude the disaffected from the new elections, and who would judge the qualifications of those elected.[29]

During the spring and summer of 1652 Milton viewed with alarm the growing threat to his cherished goals of religious liberty and church disestablishment. The ascendency of Cromwell and the army halted the establishment of a national Presbyterian system, but many in government and out of it found the upsurge of radical religious activity alarming: Quakers interrupting preachers, John Reeve and Lodowick Muggleton proclaiming themselves the witnesses prophesied in Revelation, Ranters and other Antinomians claiming freedom from the Decalogue and the moral law. Cromwell and his associates determined that a loosely structured state church including Presbyterians, Independents, Baptists, and other moderate sectaries must be established to promote centrist Protestantism – though with broad toleration outside that establishment. They also concluded that tithes or another kind of state maintenance would be necessary to support some nine thousand parish ministers, whose wholesale disaffection or impoverishment would be catastrophic. But Cromwell's precise intentions were difficult to read – even, perhaps, by the man himself. On February 10, 1652 Cromwell's friend and former chaplain John Owen, along with several other Independent clergymen, offered to parliament 15 *Proposals for the Furtherance and Propagation of the Gospel* along with a petition to suppress notorious heresies, submitting as evidence of such heresies the just-published *Racovian Catechism*.[30] Milton, back in August, 1650, had evidently approved publication of that Socinian document.[31] On February 18 parliament established a Committee for the Propagation of the Gospel to consider Owen's proposals and invite others, and another committee to deal with the *Catechism* and the heresy issue. Cromwell was a member of both. The *Proposals* called for a complex system of local ministers and parliamentary committees to approve new ministers and schoolmasters and to eject the "unfit," with tithes or some other settled maintenance assumed. Worship outside the established church was allowed in approved meeting places, but none might preach or write against the fundamentals of the Christian religion. They enumerated 15 such fundamentals, including the orthodox doctrines of the Trinity, Incarnation, Justification by grace, and the Last Judgment; also, the necessity of forsaking sin, the duty of public worship, and recognition that God's will is to be sought in scripture (not from the inner light). By the end of March the *Proposals* had been published, the fundamentals were being much discussed, and orthodox voices were pressuring parliament for a state church, tithes, and repression of heresy.[32]

On April 2 the larger committee made its report on the *Racovian Catechism* to parliament, listing its horrible blasphemies (chiefly, denial of the Trinity, Christ's divinity, and original sin) and indicating that the committee had examined Milton and the publisher Dugard about it; parliament, proclaiming the work "Blasphemous, Erronious and Scandalous," ordered it seized and burned.[33] There is no official summary of the examination of Milton or the contents of his 1650 note approving the catechism; apparently no one wanted to make trouble for the republic's most famous defender.[34] On February 24/March 5, 1652, Lieuwe van Aitzema, the envoy representing the Hanseatic towns, reported what he had learned about that inquiry and Milton's bold response. That he could do so only three days after the committee's investigation ended and a month before it reported to parliament suggests either that he had an inside source or else that the episode was much talked of in government circles:

> There was recently printed here the Socinian *Racovian Catechism*. This was frowned upon by the Parliament; the printer says that Mr. Milton had licensed it; Milton, when asked, said Yes, and that he had published a tract on that subject, that men should refrain from forbidding books; that in approving of that book he had done no more than what his opinion was. (*LR* III, 206)

On April 29, responding to vigorous agitation for and against tithes, parliament began to investigate some alternative form of maintenance, but ordered the continuation of tithes until such alternative was in place.[35]

Opponents of these measures pinned their hopes on Cromwell's long record of supporting broad toleration. In the vanguard of the opposition were Milton's friends Roger Williams and Henry Vane. Roger Williams, a proponent of complete toleration, even of Catholics, Turks, and Jews, and complete separation of church and state, had returned from America about December, 1651 to press some issues relating to his Narragansett Bay Settlements and remained until spring, 1654.[36] Vane's tolerationist principles led him to defend Anne Hutchinson in America and the Socinian John Biddle in England.[37] Williams, Vane, and Milton probably had some personal association in the spring of 1652. Williams directed his correspondents to write him in care of Vane at Whitehall and probably began about this time to exchange language lessons with Milton: he wrote to a friend that "It pleased the Lo: to call me for Sometime and with some persons, to practice the Hebrew, the Greek, Latine French and Dutch. The Secretarie of the Councell, (Mr. Milton) for my Dutch I read [taught] him, read me many more languages."[38] Milton's interest in learning Dutch was probably keenest while he was involved in the Anglo-Dutch negotiations. The two men also discussed methods of learning language, a matter that Milton had addressed in *Of Education*.[39] Milton had been associated with Vane in the Council of State for three years, and probably referred chiefly to him when he later praised some members of this council for "so well joining religion with civil prudence, and yet so well distinguishing the different power of either, and this not only voting, but frequently reasoning why it should be so" (*CPW* VII, 240). It is easy to imagine these three discussing their common repugnance for the proposals under debate and how to oppose them. Williams set forth several pamphlets in rapid succession: in *The Fourth Paper Presented by Major Butler* (*c*. March 30), he quoted Cromwell's famous declaration in the committee, "That he had rather that Mahumetanism were permitted amongst us than that one of God's children should be persecuted," and argued for "a true and absolute *Soul-freedom* to all the people of the Land impartially; so that no person be forced to *pray* nor *pay*, otherwise then as his Soul believeth and consenteth."[40] In April, in *The Bloody Tenet Yet More Bloody*, he restated his radical tolerationist and separatist principles, analyzing the 15 *Propos-*

als with trenchant clarity as nothing more than "*Winding Staires* and *back dores*" to persecution.[41] Vane, a member of every Council of State during the republic, continued his defense of toleration and church disestablishment there and in parliament.[42]

For his part, Milton had recourse to poetry again, addressing sonnets to Cromwell and Vane. Like the Fairfax poem, these are heroic sonnets owing something to Tasso. But in Milton's revision of that kind, the high praises culminate in appeals to these two great men to help defeat the Independent ministers' *Proposals*. While several of Milton's sonnets dealt with dangers or evils in church and state,[43] here for the first and last time he uses that form to urge a particular course of action on a political issue under debate. In these two sonnets Milton assumes as poet the role he so often adopted in prose: that of judicious adviser to magistrates and people.[44] Both are Petrarchan sonnets, but the poem to Cromwell, uniquely among Milton's sonnets, ends with a rhyming couplet.

The sonnet initially titled "To the Lord Generall Cromwell May 1652 On the proposalls of certaine ministers at ye Commtee for Propagation of the Gospell," was no doubt sent to its addressee sometime that month.[45] It appeals to that longtime supporter of toleration before he has taken a formal position on the *Proposals*. Apostrophizing Cromwell as "our cheif of men," Milton casts the octave in the panegyric mode, celebrating Cromwell's victories in battle and the virtues he has exhibited. But the stately, end-stopped lines relegate all that to the past, and the allusions prepare for the sestet's exhortation. The first quatrain portrays Cromwell on an allegorical pilgrimage where, guided by faith and "matchless Fortitude," he has plowed through "a cloud" of war and detractions to gain "peace & truth." That last phrase was often used to define the goals of the revolution, as when the signatories of the *Solemn League and Covenant* promised to "establish these Churches and kingdoms in truth and peace." Allusion to the Covenant recalls the Presbyterian understanding of that phrase as requiring religious uniformity, and the next quatrain points to the battlefields "imbru'd" with blood caused by that understanding, as it praises Cromwell's notable victories over the Scots at Preston, Dunbar, and Worcester.[46] In 1651 parliament struck a coin to celebrate those victories bearing the allegorical figures of Truth and Peace. The octave suggests that Cromwell achieved those goods not by acceeding to but by defeating the Scots and their view of the Covenant.

The *volta* or turn from octave to sestet in the middle of line nine and the run-on lines in the third quatrain mark the movement from past to present, from the recent wars to the peacetime struggles yet to come. Mid-line *voltas* are increasingly common in Milton's sonnets, and serve a variety of purposes. With the line, "peace hath her victories / No less renownd then warr" – an echo of Cicero[47] – Milton points to the "new foes" to be overcome: not now the Presbyterians but the conservative Independent hirelings who seek "to bind our soules with secular chaines." By withholding the principal verb until the final couplet Milton puts intense pressure on the plea he at last voices: "Helpe us." That couplet identifies the new foes with biblical false prophets who are outwardly sheep but inwardly "ravening wolves" (Matthew 7:15). And the contemptuous end rhyme underscores their animality, pointing to the danger they pose by their persecutions (paw) and by their ravenous appetite for public funds (maw): "Helpe us to save free Conscience from the paw / Of hireling wolves whose Gospell is their maw."

Milton's sonnet "To Sir Henry Vane the younger," presented to his statesman friend on July 3, 1652,[48] is almost wholly in the panegyric mode, but its plea, while left implicit, is as powerful. Paralleling the structure of the Cromwell sonnet, the octave focuses on Vane's valuable services in matters of war and the sestet on his even more valuable service in peace to the cause of religious liberty. The sonnet turns on the paradox set forth in its opening apostrophe, "Vane, young in yeares but in sage counsell old."[49] The first quatrain praises Vane's parliamentary role as a "Senatour" (Latin, *senex*, old), equal to those famous Roman senators whose firmness counted for more than the Roman legions in withstanding invaders: "when gownes not armes repelld" Pyrrus and Hannibal. The second quatrain treats Vane's war service: in diplomatic negotiations he could penetrate "the drifts of hollow states hard to be spelld" (the pun on hollow/Holland credits him with recognizing the supposed bad faith of the Dutch ambassadors before the war).[50] He also supplied the military with Machiavelli's crucial requirements for war, "Iron & Gold," by taking the lead in building the strong navy so vital in the Dutch war. The *volta* again comes in the middle of line nine, marking the turn from war to peace but not yet from past to present. The third quatrain compliments Vane for having already learned "which few have don" the proper bounds of the two swords, "spirituall powre & civill, what each meanes / What severs each." That past knowledge is the basis for the implicit plea in the last two lines, which function like a couplet but are not so rhymed:

> Therefore on thy firme hand religion leanes
> In peace, & reck'ns thee her eldest son.

The "young" Vane is, paradoxically, religion's eldest son, and therefore bears primary responsibility for protecting her in the present crisis. Vane knows, and should show others, that the 15 *Proposals* have it wrong, that religion can only be protected if the magistrates leave it strictly alone.

Sometime in June Milton received and answered an admiring letter from the Athenian scholar Leonard Philaras, then ambassador from Parma to the King of France.[51] Praising Philaras for his scholarship and a liberal education worthy of the ancient Athenians, he responds to Philaras's quixotic suggestion that England help free Greece from the Turks with a restatement of his core belief that, like any people desiring freedom, the Greeks must first rekindle the spirit of liberty within themselves. Philaras, he gracefully suggests, might inspire them to do so:

> [It is] most important, that someone should stir and ignite the ancient courage, diligence, and endurance in the souls of the Greeks by singing of that byegone zeal. If anyone could accomplish this – which we should expect from none more than you, because of your eminent patriotism . . . [and] powerful passion for recovering former political liberty – I am confident that neither would the Greeks fail themselves, nor any nation fail the Greeks. (*CPW* IV.2, 853)

That July Milton supported the royalist cleric Brian Walton, former chaplain to the king and also former curate to Richard Stock at Milton's boyhood parish of Allhallows, Bread Street, in his petition for government assistance in preparing a polyglot Bible. A year later he wrote to support Walton's request to import paper for that purpose free of excise taxes.[52] Milton could usually set politics aside when scholarship, family ties, and friendship were involved. At some point in 1651 or 1652 he helped obtain the release of the poet Sir William Davenant, who was awaiting execution in the Tower as a royalist conspirator.[53]

In August, 1652 the *Regia Sanguinis Clamor ad Coelum Adversus Parricidas Anglicanos* (The Cry of the Royal Blood to Heaven Against the English Parricides) was published anonymously in the Hague.[54] In an earlier response to Milton's *Defensio* (*c.* February 18), Robert Filmer attacked that work as well as Hobbes's *Leviathan* and Grotius's *De Juri Belli*, scoffing that Milton's contract theory defends "a miserable liberty, which is only to choose to whom we will give our liberty, which we may not keep."[55] But it was the *Clamor* that prodded Milton to answer. That very effective polemic was generally attributed to Alexander More, pastor of the Walloon church and professor of church history in Amsterdam; he was a friend of Salmasius and his houseguest at Leyden in 1652, where he saw this work through the press and contributed the prefatory epistle addressed to Charles II. The true author was an English royalist, Pierre Du Moulin, who remained unknown until after the Restoration, when he gave his own account of the publication, registering a sadistic pleasure in Milton's bafflement:

> I had sent my manuscript sheets to the great Salmasius, who entrusted them to the care of that most learned man, Alexander Morus. This Morus delivered them to the printer, and prefixed to them an Epistle to the King, in the Printer's name, exceedingly eloquent and full of good matter. When that care of Morus over the business of printing the book had become known to Milton through the spies of the Regicides in Holland, Milton held it as an ascertained fact that Morus was the author of the *Clamor*, . . . meanwhile I looked on in silence, and not without a soft chuckle, at seeing my bantling laid at another man's door, and the blind and furious Milton fighting and slashing the air, like the hoodwinked horse-combatants in the old circus, not knowing by whom he was struck and whom he struck in return.[56]

The printer Adrian Vlacq, eager to promote a profitable controversy, sent the unbound sheets to Samuel Hartlib as they came off the press in July or early August, to pass along to Milton together with an offer to publish his reply.[57] Milton later reported that he was given the unbound sheets in the council and was expected to reply: "Scarce was this book complete in the sheets before it was handed to me in the Council; soon after that session another copy was sent me by the court of inquisitions [parliament's Committeee on Examinations]. It was also intimated that I was expected to serve the state and stop up the mouth of this troublesome crier."[58] Vlacq claimed that he wrote Hartlib as early as October, 1652 denying More's authorship, but if Hartlib passed along this news Milton evidently thought it just a deceptive ploy by More and Vlacq.[59]

The *Clamor* mounts a vigorous attack on the English "parricides," laced with virulent invective against Milton and his *Defensio* as well as fulsome praises of the "great prince of letters, Claudius Salmasius" (*CPW* IV.2, 1,049). It presents a dramatic account ("spectaculum") of the events leading up to the regicide, describing that drama as a savage or monstrous "tragedy," and drawing out resemblances to Christ's crucifixion. It also denounces the crimes of the bloodthirsty English "parricides" against, in turn, the king, the English people, the English church, all kings and peoples, the reformed churches of Europe, and God himself. Indeed, the author argues that this deed was worse than the crucifixion, for the Jews did not recognize Christ whereas the sacrilegious English knew very well that they were murdering a divinely anointed king (1,049, 1,058). It also mounts a vicious attack defaming and degrading Milton's person, character, and life, often portraying his body as disfigured and monstrous.[60] We can imagine his pain and fury as someone read these insults aloud to him, probably over and over as he prepared his response to them; as Michael Lieb points out, the experience of listening to such lacerating assaults would be much more distressing than simply reading them, because a reader confronts the text in private and can control his encounter with it.[61]

More's epistle to Charles II, signed by Vlacq, excoriates Milton as a Cyclops manqué:

> "A monster horrible, deformed, huge, and sightless." Though to be sure, he is not huge; nothing is more weak, more bloodless, more shrivelled than little animals such as he, who the harder they fight, the less harmful they are. It will please you to see your man tearing to pieces this disgrace to the human race. (*CPW* IV.2, 1,045)

The book proclaims Milton a "famished grammicaster," a "hellish gallows-bird," and an "insignificant piece of mud" that the English threw against Salmasius only because Selden refused the task. It describes Milton as a force for disintegration in every sphere of human society: he was "expelled from his college at Cambridge because of some disgrace" and then "fled shame and his country and migrated to Italy"; he sought to destroy the bonds of marriage and the family with his infamous divorce tracts; and then he severed the political bond between king and subject. Indeed this "parracide" was the very executioner of Charles since he admits to having urged on the crime in books that revile the sacred spirit of the king (1,050–1). The *Clamor* concludes with an ode eulogizing Salmasius and a 245-line poem "Against that Foul Rascal John Milton, the Advocate of Parricide and Parricides" that abuses Milton in scurrilous iambics and derogatory epithets: "an ignoble, commonplace little fellow," "a great stinking pestilence," a "swindler, so insignificant, so puny," a "foolish shrew-mouse" twitching the mane of the lion Salmasius, a "dung-heap," "a dark pettifogger, pure corruption and poison," "an unnameable buffoon," a fool who dares to teach the great Salmasius Latin as "a pig teaches Minerva, [or] an evil Thersites teaches a Nestor" (1,078–80).

As summer gave way to autumn and winter, Milton must have found the political situation worrying. Tensions were rapidly mounting between the army and the parliament, whose members were blamed for procrastinating about needed reforms and enriching themselves at public expense. The Dutch war was unpopular with much of the army and the populace. Financially it imposed a heavy burden, as the need to build new ships, maintain the fleet, and pay sailors was met by confiscations of royalist property, increased taxation, and reductions in the size of the army. London merchants suffered serious losses from seizures of English merchantmen, and Denmark's closure of the Sound cut off the Baltic trade in pitch, tar, hemp, and masts, all necessary to the fleet. Everyone suffered from depleted supplies of coal. In August, 1652 the council of army officers had "divers meetings," resulting in a petition to parliament for successive parliaments, broad toleration for Protestants, an alternative to tithes, law reform, poor relief, and other reforms.[62] But parliament, council, and officers came to no agreement;[63] a pamphlet war raged over tithes, Owen's *Proposals*, and the excise tax; and radical congregations urged on by sectarian and Fifth Monarchist preachers demanded a new representative comprised of men of truth, fearing God and hating covetousness. In November, Whitelocke reported a meeting between Cromwell and himself during which Cromwell reportedly speculated, "What if a man should take it upon him to be King."[64] If true, the remark may reveal Cromwell's keen ambition, or simply that he was thinking aloud about a governmental structure consonant with English tradition and affording some balance to the single-house parliament. Along with all this, Milton heard persistent rumors that Salmasius's reply to him was imminent.[65] More's preface predicted that the Dutch will conquer the English "as easily and happily as Salmasius will finish off Milton" (*CPW* IV.2, 1,045). On January 21, 1653 Vossius wrote that some parts of Salmasius's reply were in press and would be devastating: he "sometimes calls Milton a catamite, and says that he was the vilest prostitute in Italy." Heinsius answered that that particular charge is "pure calumny," that in fact Milton made enemies in Italy for his "over-strict morals" and disputes over religion.[66]

I believe that Milton's sonnet beginning "When I consider how my light is spent, / Ere half my days, in this dark world and wide," was prompted by these personal and public anxieties and probably written late in 1652.[67] Various dates from late 1651 to 1655 have been proposed, but in the absence of facts we can only turn to internal evidence and external circumstances.[68] The difficulty with any date in the 1650s arises from the sonnet's second line: what lifespan can Milton be projecting for himself if, at age 43 in 1652, he supposes he has more than half his days before him? Not, obviously, the biblical three score and ten. Probably, as Parker suggests, he has in mind his father's lifespan of at least 84 years.[69] As we have seen, Milton is often inexact about chronology and tends to perceive and represent himself as younger than he is: he predated some of his youthful poems in the 1645 *Poems*, and in the *Defensio Secunda* takes pride in a youthful appearance that belies his actual age by ten years.[70] The time frame of this sonnet is set by thematic and emotional concerns, not the calendar, as Milton seeks to come to terms with the fact that he has been blinded in the prime of life with his major work yet undone. His perception of himself as still youthful, here and elsewhere, offers subconscius support for the hope that there is still time to write his great poem. The title "On His Blindness" has no authority, but most readers agree that the poem is about a spiritual crisis prompted by blindness: how in this darkness to understand and fulfill the responsibilities of vocation, the duties arising both from God's general election and his particular call to each individual?[71] The opening words, "When I consider," imply, not a response to a new condition of blindness, but some passage of time allowing for recurrent questions and answers. Milton thought himself obliged to answer the *Regia Sanguinis Clamor* and the imminent new attack from Salmasius; he had proved that he could carry on with his quotidian tasks of translation and Latin correspondence, but could he produce another major prose epic in defense of his countrymen and himself, to say nothing of his long-planned epic poem? He could write small sonnets in the service of religious liberty, but could he any longer undertake his cherished role as classical orator and humanist counsellor in crises present and future? That those larger challenges seemed all but insurmountable in these months is implied in Milton's *Pro Se Defensio,* when he explained his long delay in answering the *Clamor* by instancing his "infirm health," his distress over the two family deaths, and "the complete failure of my sight" (*CPW* IV.2, 703). As that other vocation sonnet ("How Soon Hath Time") marked the approach of Milton's twenty-fourth birthday,[72] this one may have been prompted by the approach of his forty-fourth birthday on December 9. It is discussed on pages 305–7.

In the months following the publication of *Clamor,* Milton surely collected tidbits of international gossip about More. Most of the reports ascribed the *Clamor* to him and repeated with salacious glee the (mostly accurate) stories about his break with Salmasius over his seduction and refusal to marry an English gentlewoman servant of Madame Salmasius, sometimes adding the false rumor that she was pregnant by him.[73] The earliest report was a letter from Leyden in *Mercurius Politicus* (September 17/27, 1652), observing that More's *Clamor* "hath been much cryed up and down, till the Author decryed himself and his reputation by violating the Chastity of

Monsieur *Salmasius* his Wives Gentlewoman, and getting her with Child."[74] That newsletter also printed a witty though untranslatable Latin epigram that was making the rounds:

> Galli e Concubitu Gravidam, Te, Pontia, Mori
> Quis bene moratam, moriger amque neget?

The distich transposes her nickname Bontia to Pontia (with scandalous allusion to a Roman woman notorious for infanticide), and also plays naughtily on Latin stems: *morus* (black, Gallican, a cock, a mulberry tree, bearing black fruit, a French fool; and *gerere* (well behaved, obedient, accommodating, be-moored, be-fooled, More-bearing, fool-bearing, etc.).[75] Milton also seems to have received information from foreign contacts regarding charges of heresy and licentious behavior against More at Geneva and about the legal and ecclesiastical inquiries into these matters.[76] Some offshoots of the Salmasius controversy were reprinted in 1652: John Phillips's *Responsio* three times and the *Pro Rege . . . Apologia* twice.

As the year turned, Milton heard from two college acquaintances who had sought his influence in furthering their careers. Richard Heath, who had entered Christ's College in 1631 and whom Milton had recommended the previous year for his post as Vicar of St Alkmund's, Shrewsbury, wrote a courteous and admiring letter (now lost) expressing gratitude for Milton's assistance with his studies.[77] Milton's reply (December 13, 1652) commends Heath as an upright pastor and worthy citizen with right-minded views on church and state, and welcomes his expressed desire to live "somewhere near me, so that we might have more frequent and more pleasant intercourse of life and studies" (*CPW* IV.2, 855). After graciously complimenting Heath's "considerable progress" in Latin, he agrees to his request to correspond in English; Heath's specialty was oriental languages, and he evidently felt at some disadvantage with a master Latinist. No further letters or reports of visits survive, but the relationship may have continued; the men shared an interest in Brian Walton's polyglot Bible, which Heath later helped with and Milton supported in the council.[78] The other letter, dated January 15, 1653, was from Andrew Sandelands, a fellow of Christ's during part of Milton's residency. A former adherent of the Scots royalist General Montrose, he sought Milton's support for his elaborate scheme to supply the English navy with timber, masts, and tar from the fir trees of Scotland.[79] He also made the somewhat bizarre request that Milton would "procure to mee the gift of that weatherbeaten scull of my Noble and truly honoble patron." Montrose's skull had for three years been mounted on a spike over Edinburgh prison (*CPW* IV.2, 856–8). Milton's reply is lost. No doubt he turned Sandeland's several papers over to the committees already looking into his proposal and he probably found some polite way to avoid meddling with Montrose's skull.[80] On March 29 Sandelands wrote to Milton again, complaining that government delays in implementing his project had left him short of funds and offering some useful military information about the Marquis of Argyle's hidden cannon, which Milton passed on to the proper authorities.[81]

On February 13, 1653 Milton's assistant Georg Weckherlin died. Though age and ill health had limited his usefulness, someone was needed in his place. In a letter of February 21 to his friend John Bradshaw, president of the council, Milton recommended Andrew Marvell, whose career and qualifications he had learned a good deal about "by report, & [in] the converse I have had with him" (*CPW* IV.2, 859). Marvell was fresh from two years at Nunappleton tutoring Mary Fairfax, daughter of the famous retired general. If his personal acquaintance with Milton was recent, he knew Milton's poetry and prose well, having echoed some of it in his own poems of the early 1650s;[82] probably he also read the sonnet Milton sent to his patron, Fairfax. Shortly before his February 22 interview with Bradshaw he evidently called on Milton to display his abilities and ask his support: besides demonstrating his Latinity did he also read or give Milton some of his poetry? Milton's recommendation is wholehearted; clearly he wanted to be associated with this bright young linguist and poet, though he insists that he can still perform most of his duties and admits, with genial frankness, to a pang of jealousy that such an able assistant might show him up, disadvantaged as he now is:

> [T]here will be with you tomorrow upon some occasion of busines a Gentleman whose name is Mr: Marvile, a man whom both by report, & the converse I have had with him, of singular desert for the state to make use of; who alsoe offers himselfe, if there be any imployment for him . . . he hath spent foure yeares abroad in Holland, ffrance, Italy, & Spaine, to very good purpose, as I beleeve, & the gaineing of those 4 languages; besides he is a scholler & well read in the latin & Greeke authors. . . . .If upon the death of Mr. Wakerley the Councell shall thinke that I shall need any assistant in the performance of my place (though for my part I find noe encumberances of that which belongs to me, except it be in point of attendance at Conferences with Ambassadors, which I much confesse, in my Condition I am not fit for) it would be hard for them to find a Man soe fit every way for the purpose as this Gentleman. . . . I write sinceerely without any other end then to performe my dutey to the Publick in helping them to an able servant; laying aside those Jealosies & that aemulation which mine owne condition might suggest to me by bringing in such a coadjutor. (*CPW* IV.2, 859–60)

Despite this warm endorsement the council chose another young and able linguist, 27-year-old Philip Meadows.[83] Perhaps they already saw in him the potential he later displayed in diplomatic missions to Portugal and Denmark.

Sometime in 1653, most likely, Milton took on as pupil Richard Jones, the son of his good friend Lady Katherine Jones, Viscountess Ranelagh,[84] whose nephew Richard Barry had been his student at the Barbican (1645–7?). Jones was then twelve, and she no doubt thought the arrangement would be mutually beneficial; the boy would learn much by reading to and writing for such a teacher and Milton would have more scribal help – all the more necessary because John Phillips probably left the household sometime in 1652, when he became 21. Jones had only to walk across St James's Park from his home in Pall Mall to be at Milton's garden gate. That was also true for his mother, who came from the distinguished literary and scientific Boyle family.[85] She was one of the best educated women of her time, very knowledgeable in literary and philosophical matters, a student of Hebrew, closely associated with the Hartlib circle, a Cromwellian in politics, and a friend of Milton's from the mid-1640s at least. This is another example of Milton's capacity to value and enjoy the society of able women – others were Margaret Ley and Miss Davis, whoever she was – despite his concept of gender hierarchy. Milton could always qualify ideology by personal experience in particular cases, though such experience did not lead him (as it did with divorce) to call into question received assumptions about gender hierarchy itself.

In the new year the army and parliament clashed head-on over religious questions and over how to regulate parliamentary elections so as to exclude persons perceived by one or another group to be dangerous (royalists, "neuters," disaffected Presbyterians, fanatic sectaries). On February 25 the Rump voted to affirm the principle Milton so vigorously opposed – that the magistrate has power in matters of religion – and then proceeded to take up Owen's 15 *Proposals*, one by one. Many in the army, locating their own and the nation's chief interest in toleration, abolition of tithes, and social reforms, thought that the large citizen army which had shed blood for the Commonwealth had as good a claim to represent it and help settle its government as that poor remnant of parliament, the Rump. Many in the parliament were determined to preserve the principle of parliamentary supremacy over the army and also to establish a state church and rein in the sects. One army faction led by Major-General Thomas Harrison, who was now closely associated with Fifth Monarchists, called insistently for a government by well-affected persons of "known integrity, fearing God, and not scandalous in their conversation" – meaning government by regenerate Saints. Another faction led by Major-General John Lambert promoted government by a select council of officers and civilian leaders, at least for a time. The bad feeling escalated to a crisis on April 19–20, 1653.

Milton surely heard vivid accounts from friends in parliament about the dramatic events of those days. On April 19, at an informal meeting of parliament leaders and army officers, Cromwell proposed that the Rump dissolve itself forthwith and that a council of some forty drawn from both groups govern for a time to put in place speedily the desired reforms and guarantees of toleration. That done, he optimistically explained in the Army Declaration of April 22, "the People might forget Monarchy and understanding their true Interest in the Election of Successive Parliaments, may have the Government setled upon a true Basis."[86] He thought he had an agreement, but on April 20 the Rump acted quickly on a Bill that would retain the principle of parliamentary supremacy and the power of present members, either by recruiting new members to the existing parliament (as Cromwell insisted they planned to do) or by making themselves judges of new members' qualifications in any election.[87] In Ludlow's colorful account, just as the measure was to be voted Cromwell began to denounce the Rump in scathing terms, charging that they had done nothing for the public good, and that they had

> espoused the corrupt interest of Presbytery and the lawyers, who were the supporters of tyranny and oppression, accusing them of an intention to perpetuate themselves in power . . . and thereupon told them, that the Lord had done with them, and had chosen other instruments for carrying on his work that were more worthy . . . then walking up and down the House like a mad-man, and kicking the ground with his feet, he cried out, "You are no Parliament, I say you are no Parliament; I will put an end to your sitting."[88]

Berating the protesting Peter Wentworth and Henry Marten as whoremasters and others as drunkards, he then called in the soldiers and had the speaker removed from the chair.[89] When Vane protested, "This is not honest, yea it is against morality and common honesty," Cromwell railed at him, "O Sir Henry Vane, Sir Henry Vane, the Lord deliver me from Sir Henry Vane." He had clearly counted on Vane's support for the compromise Council of Forty, underestimating the strength of his republican convictions. Cromwell then had the speaker's mace carried off, saying, "What shall we do with this bauble? here, take it away."[90] Milton would also have heard from friends in the Council of State how Cromwell dismissed that body over the strong protests of republicans, including Milton's friend Bradshaw. According to Ludlow, Cromwell

> told them at his entrance, "Gentlemen, if you are met here as private persons, you shall not be disturbed, but if as a Council of State, there is no place for you; and since you can't but know what was done at the House in the morning, so take notice, that the Parliament is dissolved." To this Serjeant Bradshaw answered; "Sir, we have heard what you did at the House in the morning, and before many hours all England will hear it: but, Sir, you are mistaken to think that the Parliament is dissolved; for no power under heaven can dissolve them but themselves; therefore take you notice of that." Something more was said to the same purpose by Sir Arthur Haslerig, Mr. Love, and Mr. Scot; and then the Council of State perceiving themselves to be under the same violence, departed.[91]

What Milton thought of all this at the time is not known. He was probably shocked at first over the affront to the republican principle of parliamentary supremacy that he had so forcefully defended in the *Defensio*. But, as the Digression to the *History of Britain* shows, he shared the army's view of the corruption, reactionary politics, and power-plays of the Long Parliament and he would soon, in the *Second Defense,* charge the Rump Parliament with the same faults and justify Cromwell's dismissal of them:

> When you [Cromwell] saw delays being contrived and every man more attentive to his private interest than to that of the State, when you saw the people complaining that they had been deluded of their hopes and circumvented by the power of the few, you put an end to the domination of these few men, since they, although so often warned, had refused to do so. (*CPW* IV.1, 671)

That phrasing casts the dissolution of parliament as an act reclaiming government from a venal and power-hungry "few."

Cromwell's dismissal of the Rump met with the approval of many, though Vane, Bradshaw, Fairfax, and some others refused to have anything to do with the new government.[92] Cromwell, eager to avoid the appearance and indeed the fact of exercising absolute power, moved quickly to set up governing bodies with some appearance of legality. A new Council of State comprised of army officers and some previous members of the Council of State was in place by the end of April, and by the first week in May the new Nominated Parliament was planned along the lines desired by Harrison, but not as the Sanhedrin of 70 godly men called for by his Fifth Monarchist and millenarian followers. It had twice that number: five from Scotland and six from Ireland nominated by civil and military authorities, and the rest nominated by gathered church congregations in the cities and counties of England and Wales. Cromwell and the Council of State were to make final choices among the nominees. This produced a legislature dedicated to the revolution, with a core of religious radicals though also a sprinkling of nobility, gentry, local officials, and army officers. Practicing lawyers were excluded. Members assembled on July 4 to hear Cromwell review God's providences to the revolutionary cause and charge them to be "faithful with the Saints," to protect the liberties of the most mistaken Christians, and to answer God's call to govern during the hopefully brief interim while the people are not fit to exercise their suffrage: "Who can tell how soon God may fit the people for such a thing, and none can desire it more than I! Would all the Lord's people were prophets. I would all were fit to be called, and fit to call."[93] He presented a document entrusting them with "the Supreme Authority and Government of this Commonwealth" until November 3, 1654, after which they were to arrange for their successors. This "Barebones" Parliament, nicknamed pejoratively for Praisegod Barebone, an Anabaptist leather merchant from London who was one of its prominent members, set up a 31-member Council of State with a six-month term. Milton was informally continued in office by that council and on November 3 formally reappointed by its successor, to serve "in the same Capacity he was in to the last Councell," and at the same salary (*LR* III, 347).

Milton was only minimally involved with the chief diplomatic business of the new government: negotiations with a Dutch embassy that arrived June 17 to try to make peace.[94] Eight papers were exchanged, two of them probably by Milton.[95] One (July 13) restated the English position: it sharply denied the Dutch assertion that the war began through misunderstanding and chance, insisted on harsh reparations for war damages, and urged a close political union amounting almost to annexation of the United Provinces; the other (August 1) responded to a Dutch complaint about the treatment of prisoners of war with the claim that the English were much more humane in such matters than the Dutch. Talks broke off in August. The few other letters Milton produced for this government commonly begin with a review of God's providences in establishing the republic and an affirmation of England's desire for peace with her ancient friends.[96] Among them was the parliament's response (dated November 28) to several letters and a personal envoy from the Swiss cantons urging peace with the Dutch; it praises the Swiss as "the first of mankind throughout all Europe . . . to have acquired liberty for yourselves," thanks them warmly for their "surpassing affection for us and our Commonwealth" and for their good offices in attempting to make peace between Protestant powers, but insists on England's right to demand a "very binding alliance" with the Dutch as the price of peace.[97]

Like many Independents, Milton probably hoped for good things from the Nominated Parliament as regards the causes nearest his heart, religious liberty and church disestablishment. His laconic comment in the *Defensio Secunda* that the electorate had been restricted "only to those who deserved it" (*CPW* IV.1, 671) implies that he accepted, without much enthusiasm, the basis of selection. Some insight into his state of mind can be gleaned from his versions of Psalms 1–8 composed in the week of August 8–15 or thereabouts.[98] As he had in 1648, Milton again found in the Psalms a means of expressing his personal and political anxieties and hopes. These translations register his perception of the widening divide between the virtuous lovers of liberty who can be entrusted with government and the disaffected masses. A major theme of these psalms, set forth in Psalm 1, is God's vindication and protection of the just and his wrath toward the unrighteous.[99] It may reflect his hopes, however qualified, for the Nominated Parliament, whose composition might seem to be indicated in one Miltonic line – "Nor sinners [abide] in th'assembly of just men."[100] Another theme, the suffering, beleaguered psalmist's cry for God's protection against slandering enemies, resonates with Milton's sense of his own situation, grieving, weak, under attack by enemies but confident of God's deliverance: "Lord how many are my foes" (Psalm 3, line 1). Besides the *Clamor*, other recent works had attacked Milton's *Eikonoklastes*, the *Defensio*, and the divorce tracts.[101] Also, John Rowland's *Polemica* responded to John Phillips's *Responsio* to his anonymous *Apologia* – which he now claimed as his, denouncing Phillips – or Milton – for maliciously ascribing it to Bishop Bramhall.[102] Bramhall later claimed that he wrote "roundly" to Milton about that error and about some unspecified scandals that would make Milton "go near to hang himself."[103] That mistake should have prompted

Milton to exercise more caution in attributing the *Clamor* to More, but it did not. Milton of course heard about Salmasius's death on September 3, but he still expected that his attack – long reported as nearly finished – would soon be published posthumously.

These psalm translations are more faithful to the Hebrew than Milton's psalms of 1648, so his additions are striking, though he does not italicize them as before.[104] To the psalmist's description of his grief in Psalm 6:7 Milton adds the word "dark" – "mine Eie / Through grief consumes, is waxen old and dark" – as well as the fact that his enemies "mark" his condition.[105] In these psalms Milton finds comfort in millenarian expectation, but he refocuses the contemporary millenarian fervor attending the Barebones Parliament. To Psalm 2, God begetting his Son and setting him above the Kings of the Earth, Milton adds language assuring those rebel kings and princes of ultimate defeat: "but I, saith hee / anointed have my King (though ye rebell)"; in Psalm 5 he adds a phrase to the speaker's prayers, "and watch till thou appear."[106] To Psalm 4:3, "the Lord hath set apart him that is godly for himself" (AV), Milton makes a significant substitution (ll. 13–16), identifying God's chosen not as the "godly" predestinated elect but as the virtuous foreknown by God as such: "Yet know the Lord hath chose / Chose to himelf a part / The good and meek of heart / (For whom to chuse he knows)." By this insistence on God's foreknowledge rather than predestination, Milton distinguishes himself, in terms he will elaborate in *De Doctrina Christiana*, from most of his Calvinist contemporaries and from the millenarian Saints of the Barebones Parliament ready now to rule for and with Christ. Some formulations seem to speak of Milton's own hopes and fears: "The Lord will own, and have me in his keeping. / Mine enemies shall all be blank and dash't / With much confusion; then grow red with shame."[107]

In these psalm versions Milton undertook a series of metrical experiments. His 1648 psalms were in common meter, the standard verse form for psalms used in congregational prayer or song;[108] these eight psalms are in eight different metrical forms, inspired perhaps by the metrical variety in Calvin's *Geneva Psalter* or by the astonishing experiments with metrical and stanzaic forms in the versions by Sir Philip Sidney and the Countess of Pembroke.[109] Milton's verse forms range from rhymed iambic pentameter couplets to *terza rima*, to elaborate stanzaic patterns,[110] but all of them are characterized by run-on lines and stanzas, pauses within rather than at the ends of lines, and reversed feet. In them Milton continues to experiment with techniques he often used in sonnets, leading toward the flowing verse paragraph of the epics.

The Barebones Parliament self-destructed over the issues of law reform and tithes. The radicals in that body proposed to abolish the Court of Chancery, to reduce the whole structure of English law into a single volume, and to abolish the rights of patrons to present clergymen to livings; on December 10 they carried – by two votes – an act to abolish tithes and all state maintenance for the church. Moderates, believing that chaos threatened if the legal and church establishments were dismantled so entirely and abruptly, contrived a strategy with Cromwell whereby a majority of the House proclaimed their inability to rule and surrendered authority back to Cromwell – thereby avoiding another military coup. Milton's clear-sighted judgment of this body's political ineptitude is evident in the *Defensio Secunda* as he echoes the Cromwellians' rationale for their dissolution:

> The elected members came together. They did nothing. When they in turn had at length exhausted themselves with disputes and quarrels, most of them considering themselves inadequate and unfit for executing such great tasks, they of their own accord dissolved the Parliament. (*CPW* IV.1, 671)

The structure of the new government was already outlined in the *Instrument of Government*, England's first written constitution, drafted by Lambert and a cabal of officers. On December 16 Cromwell was sworn in as Protector; the office was for life, but elective, not hereditary. Reportedly, Lambert offered Cromwell the crown and he refused. Parliaments were to be triennial, and much more representative than Barebones or the Rump. The first parliament of 460 – 30 from Scotland, 30 from Ireland, and the rest from the counties and cities of England and Wales – was to assemble on September 3, 1654 and sit at least five months. All men over 21 "of known integrity, fearing God, and of good conversation," and with an estate worth £200, were eligible to vote or be chosen, except for Roman Catholics, those involved in the Irish uprising, and those who fought for the king and remained "malignant."[111] Bills passed would become law upon the Protector's signature but would do so after 20 days without it. In parliament's intersessions Cromwell was to govern with a permanent Council of State, 15 of whose members were named in the *Instrument* – officers and civilians chosen for their past service and supposed fitness – and laws passed by them required assent of a majority.[112] In theory the *Instrument* created a chief executive with carefully limited powers, but Cromwell's personal, political, and military power weighed against that balance. The *Instrument* also provided for an established church with state maintenance for ministers, but with protection for Christian religious practice outside it, except for popery, prelacy, and disturbers of the peace (Ranters and Quakers). On February 3 the Protectorate Council of State, on Thurloe's recommendation, reappointed Milton without specifying his title or salary, suggesting some initial uncertainty as to just how he would be employed; Philip Meadows was reappointed with the title of Latin Secretary. Later entries make clear, however, that Milton continued as Secretary for Foreign Tongues at his previous salary of about £288 a year.[113]

The transition was comparatively smooth, save for outraged republicans like Ludlow, Overton, and Vane who saw any "single person" as a repudiation of the Good Old Cause, Fifth Monarchists and some sectaries like Harrison and Christopher Feake who saw Cromwell usurping the place of King Jesus soon to appear, and royalists in London and Scotland who mounted plots and insurrections in the interests of Charles II. About February 8 Marchamont Nedham published a strong defense of the Rump's expulsion and the dissolution of Barebones, arguing that the revolution was not about forms of government but about liberties, which the new government would better secure because it separated the legislative and executive powers.[114] For nine months the Protector and council governed without parliament, passing some eighty-two ordinances, among them provisions for the reform of Chancery and for commissions to approve preachers presented to benefices and to eject scandalous or insufficient ministers and schoolmasters. For the first six months of the Protectorate Milton wrote no state letters, or at least none we know of.[115] Nor was Milton involved in the flurry of treaty-making – with the United Provinces, Sweden, Portugal, and Denmark – that quickly settled disputes long mired in negotiations and on terms very favorable to England.[116] But he was no doubt pleased to see several negotiations he had worked on concluded at last, and an end to the war with the Dutch. He was perhaps given a respite from diplomatic duties to complete his answer to the *Regia Sanguinis Clamor*.[117]

The change of government meant that Milton had to revamp whatever part of his answer to the *Clamor* was already drafted, to suit the circumstances of the Protectorate. As he worked on it he had to give some attention to two personal legal cases that began in early 1654 and continued in the courts for years: one, a suit he initiated to recover a long-standing debt of £150 from the heirs of Sir John Cope, now deceased; the other an action brought against him by Mrs Elizabeth Ashworth who had a claim on the Wheatley property, alleging that he had held on to that property after recovering all that was owed him by the Powells.[118] Milton's lawyer brother, Christopher, now practicing in London, handled these legal matters for him; their fraternal bond evidently withstood their political differences.[119]

Just as Milton's manuscript was ready for press or actually in press, several testimonials were presented to him denying More's authorship of *Clamor*. Earlier, Milton had heard one or two denials of or queries about More's authorship, but found it easy to believe the preponderance of testimony on the other side. On April 14/24, however, John Dury wrote Hartlib from the Hague, for transmission to Milton, that he had heard testimony denying More's authorship of the *Clamor* and the pregnancy of Salmasius's servant, and that a court decision had dismissed charges against More in that affair:

> I have understood from one of the Ministers of Middelburg of my acquaintance who is very familiar with Mr Moore that hee is not the author of that booke, but that it is a French minister who lives in France whom Mr Moore did name to him under a promise of secrecy, so that I could not learne his name; and as for the other rumors concerning Bontia who is an English woman; it is false that shee is with childe to him only shee did claime a promise of mariage of him, which he denyes hee ever made to hir and the business hath been agitated before the Court of Justice here, and hee freed from her, and declared innocent of all that is blameworthy in that matter . . . now I would not that Mr. Milton should mistake in all this and spread false reports against a man that is blameles.[120]

On April 19/29 Dury wrote Hartlib again, citing another witness – "Mr. Hotton who is a fierce Royalist" – who also denied More's authorship and reported that More "hath been absolved by the Synod of the French Churches from the vexation that Salmasius Kinswoman put him to; and that Salmasius and hee fell out about the matter before hee died." Dury added, "You may let Mr. Milton know of this lest hee should wrong the innocent and wrong his own Credit by spreading false reports."[121] Hartlib surely did so. But Milton could discount the source – not the respected Dury but the "fierce Royalist" who he wrongly assumed to have been Dury's informant on both occasions. He could also discount the report of the court and synod decisions, having heard from other sources that those matters remained murky.[122] In mid-May, at More's behest, the Dutch ambassador Willem Nieupoort sent emissaries to assure Milton that More did not write the *Clamor*, but Milton could put that down simply to an effort by More to prevent publication of Milton's attack on him. Nieupoort wrote More on June 23/July 3 that Milton would do nothing, being firmly convinced the author was "no other than you," and that his appeal to Thurloe to stop the publication in the interests of the fragile new peace between England and the United Provinces came to nothing because a just-uncovered plot (May 20) on Cromwell's life was just then engaging the entire attention of the officials (*LR* III, 399–402). Milton might have done well to heed Dury's advice in the earlier letter – "truly there would bee more strenth in all these writings, if the personall reproaches were left out" – but he felt that he had to respond in kind to the *ad hominem* attacks in the *Clamor*, and that More was the likeliest, as well as the only available, target.

About May 30, 1654 Milton's long-awaited and already controversial treatise was published by Thomas Newcomb: *Joannis Miltoni Angli Pro Populo Anglicano Defensio Secunda contra infamem libellum anonymum cui titulus, Regii sanguinis clamor ad coelum adversus parricidas Anglicanos*.[123] Breaking free of the chapter-by-chapter formula, it develops an often powerful argument, mixing diatribe, autobiography, panegyric, implicit and explicit advice, and admonition. The diatribe is directed at More's supposed book and scandalous life, as well as Salmasius, Charles I, and the English royalists. Extensive autobiographical passages seek to repair any damage More's attacks may have done to Milton's now considerable reputation abroad; they also provide information about Milton's earlier life and insight into his sense of himself in the early 1650s. Some panegyric passages also function as implicit argument. The fulsome praise of Cromwell legitimates the Protectorate by demonstrating that he alone is worthiest to rule. But Milton's praise of 14 other men by name[124] and his omnibus recognition of "a great many other citizens of pre-eminent merits" as deserving to share power with Cromwell, refashions the Protectorate from a quasi-monarchy to an aristocracy of worthies who have proven their devotion to liberty.

At times Milton uses panegyric to offer implicit but very specific political advice, as when he includes among the named worthies two very visible opponents of the

Protectorate. Colonel Robert Overton had openly declared his opposition and was suspected of plotting an insurrection against Cromwell with his troops in Scotland; when Milton's tract appeared he was in London being examined about the matter, and surely visited his friend Milton. John Bradshaw, president of the Regicide Court, had bitterly denounced the expulsion of the Rump and had remained disaffected from the Protectorate.[125] Masson suggests – rightly I think – that Milton is discreetly advising Cromwell to conciliate and share power with men like Bradshaw and Overton, and also advising them to make their peace with this worthy Protector and help to shape his government by participating in it.[126] Milton claims both men as long-time personal friends: Bradshaw is "the most faithful of friends and the most worthy of trust," as well as the most generous and fearless of patrons; Overton was "for many years . . . linked to me with a more than fraternal harmony, by reason of the likeness of our tastes and the sweetness of your disposition" (*CPW* IV.1, 638–9, 676). Milton does not mention his friend Vane whose rift with Cromwell seemed beyond repair. He handles the requisite praise of Fairfax very differently, as a digression within his panegyric on Cromwell and in terms that relegate Fairfax's splendid service as commander-in-chief of parliament's armies firmly to the past, avoiding any suggestion that this conservative Presbyterian should be restored to the government.[127] Milton concludes with overt political advice in his familiar role as adviser to the state, exhorting Cromwell to safeguard and enlarge liberty by adopting policies he has now repudiated or retrenched: abolition of public maintenance for ministers, removal of all coercive power over religion, and removal of pre-publication licensing laws that restrain press freedom. And he admonishes his fellow citizens most earnestly to make themselves worthy, by virtue, love of liberty, and self-rule, to share in government and exercise their up-coming vote wisely. Clearly, this work is not only directed to a European audience but also to Milton's countrymen at this climactic moment of settling the government anew. Its argument and rhetoric are discussed on pages 307–18.

Milton sent presentation copies to several friends and acquaintances, surely including Cromwell, selected members of the Council of State, and some of those he had singled out for praise, though these copies have not been found.[128] Three went to Andrew Marvell at Eton, one for Marvell himself, one for John Oxenbridge, a fellow of Eton College with whom Marvell was then living in the capacity of tutor to Cromwell's protégé William Dutton, and a third to be passed along, with a letter, to Bradshaw, who was living in the vicinity. In terms indicating his warm admiration for Milton, Marvell's letter of June 2 reports on his visit to Bradshaw to fulfill that charge. Bradshaw did not open Milton's letter in Marvell's presence because, Marvell speculates, he may have thought it contained another recommendation for Marvell like the one Milton had addressed to him before.[129] But Bradshaw displayed "all Respect" to Milton and showed as much satisfaction in the book as a cursory examination and Marvell's account of it would allow for. Expressing great gratitude for his own copy, Marvell promises to "studie it even to the getting of it by Heart," commenting that it scales "the Height of the Roman Eloquence" with its many figures, and that Milton's conquest of Salmasius and More amounts to as great a triumph as Trajan's double triumph over Decebalus. He also inquires with "affectionate Curiosity . . . what becomes of Colonell Overtons businesse." Marvell, also from Hull, evidently knew Overton during his long tenure as governor of Hull Castle, and evidently also knew that Milton was concerning himself about the investigation of Overton. Marvell ends by expressing pleasure "that Mr. Skyner is got near you, the Happiness which I at the same Time congratulate to him and envie" (*CPW* IV.2, 864–5). The letter offers an indication of the warm regard Milton offered to and received from friends of various ages and stations and politics. The comment that Cyriack Skinner now lives near Milton probably indicates that he is now a regular visitor and occasional amanuensis.

Milton also sent a copy of the *Defensio Secunda* to Henry Oldenburg, who had been Breman's envoy to London since the summer of 1653, and followed it by a letter (dated July 6) that begins with a review of their recent exchanges. They had discussed the *Clamor* and Milton's response "several times shortly after you came here from Holland"; then Milton, who was kept by "unexpected business" from answering a letter from Oldenburg at once, sent him the *Defensio Secunda*; and Oldenburg replied with a letter mixing thanks and praise with criticism and advice.[130] That letter agrees, Milton notes, with his harsh judgment of the *Clamor*, but expresses doubts about More's authorship and about the fierceness of Milton's polemics; he also urged Milton to give over such quarrels for more worthy writing. Responding to this "sincere judgement and praise free from flattery," Milton defends his work with candid forthrightness.[131] He reminds Oldenburg that in their earlier discussions "you seemed to have no doubt that the author was Morus, since that was certainly the opinion there and since no one else was named," and asks him to provide any "more certain knowledge" if he has it. As for his writing, Milton expresses pride in his past defenses of liberty as well as some ambivalence as to whether any work could be "nobler," or whether he could accomplish it, given his illness and blindness and his country's needs:

> To prepare myself for other labors, whether nobler or more useful I do not really know (for what among human endeavors can be nobler or more useful than the protection of liberty), I can be easily persuaded, if illness allow and this blindness, which is more oppressive than the whole of old age, and finally the cries of such brawlers. For an idle leisure [*sic*] has never pleased me, and this unexpected contest with the enemies of liberty snatched me unwilling from studies far different and altogether delightful. Not that I regret the contest by any means, since it was necessary, for I am far from believing that I have spent my labor on vain things, as you seem to suggest. (*CPW* IV.2, 866–7)

He ends by seeking a closer relationship with Oldenburg, inviting him, despite this disagreement, to "count me among your friends." Milton can with considerable grace accept criticism from his friends. As for poetry, Milton may have noted that unsold copies of his *Poems* of 1645 were again being advertised in July.[132]

Milton knew he was not finished with More. In July, Thurloe's intelligence network passed along information from the Continent about More's efforts to suppress Milton's book by buying up some five hundred imported copies and attempting, unsuccessfully, to keep Vlacq from publishing it.[133] There were also reports that More was working on an answer to Milton. Milton, however, was called back to his usual duties, producing over the summer of 1654 several Latin letters for the Protector, most of them responding elegantly to congratulations on Cromwell's new position as they deal with various matters of diplomatic protocol: Oldenburg's new Safeguard, letters pertaining to the Spanish and Portuguese ambassadors, congratulations to the new Swedish King Charles X.[134] Milton was not involved in the now intensifying diplomatic negotiations with France and Spain as they competed for an alliance with England.

He was no doubt dismayed when he heard about the conflicts that erupted as soon as Cromwell's first parliament convened on September 3, 1654, with its mix of gentry, a few nobles and knights, longtime parliamentarians, army officers, lawyers, and other men of some property. Though all were at least nominally committed to the Protectorate, they represented many colliding interests: Presbyterians still insistent on a largely Presbyterian establishment and repression of dissent; hardcore republicans for whom Cromwell's new office was a repudiation of their struggle for parliamentary supremacy; Cromwellians who supported toleration, an inclusive church establishment, and other provisions of the *Instrument*; and sectaries intent on much more radical reform in church, law, and state. Some of the disaffected returned to parliament, still uneasy: Fairfax, the Fifth Monarchist Harrison, and the republican Bradshaw, but not Vane or the scholarly John Selden. Immediately after assembling they began to debate whether to recognize the *Instrument of Government*; incensed, Cromwell locked them out of parliament on September 12 and lectured them in the Painted Chamber to the effect that they might revise the *Instrument* in some things but must accept its fundamentals as a core constitution. Before allowing them into parliament he required their signatures to an Engagement to support the government as "settled in a single Person and a Parliament." By September 15 about three hundred had signed and returned, but they set themselves immediately to rewrite the *Instrument* so as to make it parliament's document. Sides were quickly drawn up for the big fights ahead over parliamentary supremacy, toleration, church establishment, and control of the military.

Toward the end of September Milton had a visit from his admired Athenian friend Philaras, then staying in London.[135] He offered to consult, when he returned to Paris, with the famed occulist François Thévenin about Milton's blindness, if Milton would give him an account of his symptoms. Hardly daring to hope that a cure might yet be possible, Milton did so in a poignant letter dated September 28, "that I may not seem to refuse aid whencesoever offered, perhaps divinely" (*CPW*

IV.2, 869). He sets out in exact detail the symptoms that appeared ten years before, three years before, and a few months before his sight was completely destroyed (quoted above at the appropriate places).[136] Now, he says, the mists, swimming images, vapors, and bursts of light are gone, replaced by "pure black, marked as if with extinguished or ashy light, and as if interwoven with it. . . . Yet the mist which always hovers before my eyes both night and day seems always to be approaching white rather than black; and upon the eyes turning, it admits a minute quantity of light as if through a crack" (*CPW* IV.2, 869–70). After offering this account Milton assures Philaras that he has no false hopes, that he is facing his blindness with a "stout and bold" spirit, and that he finds comfort and joy in study, good friends, and God's protection:

> Although some glimmer of hope too may radiate from that physician, I prepare and resign myself as if the case were quite incurable, and I often reflect that since many days of darkness are destined to everyone, as the wise man warns, mine thus far, by the signal kindness of Providence, between leisure and study, and the voices and visits of friends, are much more mild than those lethal ones . . . why should one not . . . find comfort in believing that he cannot see by the eyes alone, but by the guidance and wisdom of God. Indeed while He himself looks out for me and provides for me, which He does . . . surely, since it has pleased Him, I shall be pleased to grant my eyes a holiday. (870)

No other letters from Philaras have been found. Obviously he had no good news to report.

"There Was . . . One Who Could Rightly Counsel, Encourage, and Inspire"

Among Milton's poetic productions of these years, the sonnet traditionally titled "On his Blindness" is a masterpiece, fusing emotional intensity and high art. The octave presents an anxious, even bitter response to total blindness and the vocational crisis it has produced: Milton's light is completely "spent" and his "one Talent" – writing, which includes noble prose defenses of liberty as well as lofty poetry – is now "Lodg'd with me useless." The sestet offers some resolution to that near-rebellion but the hard questions keep recurring: "When I consider" – not once but whenever; "patience to prevent / That murmur, soon replies" – not once, but each time, and not soon enough to forestall the murmur. Milton cannot yet, if indeed he or anyone ever can, entirely repress such complaints:

> When I consider how my light is spent,
>   E're half my days, in this dark world and wide,
>   And that one Talent which is death to hide,

Lodg'd with me useless, though my Soul more bent
To serve therewith my Maker, and present
My true account, least he returning chide,
Doth God exact day-labour, light deny'd,
I fondly ask; but patience to prevent
That murmur, soon replies, God doth not need
Either man's work or his own gifts, who best
Bear his milde yoak, they serve him best, his State
Is Kingly. Thousands at his bidding speed
And post o'er Land and Ocean without rest:
They also serve who only stand and waite.

Milton represents himself first as a helpless wanderer groping over vast spaces in utter darkness with an extinguished lantern. Then, harking back to Sonnet VII,[137] he sees himself as servant to a harsh Divine Taskmaster, characterized through a cluster of biblical allusions pertaining to issues of vocation. He imagines God as the pitiless divine moneylender suggested by the parable of the talents (Matthew 25: 14–30), ready to cast into outer darkness an unprofitable servant who fails to use and increase the single talent given him. Or, as a much harsher master than the vineyard keeper of Matthew 20:1–7, since he seems to demand that his laborers work even by night – despite Christ's statement (John 9:4) that at night "no man can work." Tension builds throughout the octave as Milton describes his painful dilemma: he has been given one talent (the ability to write in the noblest forms of prose and poetry) and unlike the slothful servant in the parable of the talents is eager to use that talent for God and the public good. But he is blind. Even so, it seems that he may be held accountable for using the talent and performing day labor in darkness. In the sestet Patience, emanating from another dimension of himself, offers a very different and more gracious paradigm for the God–man relationship. God is not a master who requires servants to work in counting houses or vineyards but a king of royal state, with myriads of servants who serve him in various ways, in their several stations. So the blind author can place himself, not with those sent on active missions around the world, but with those who (obeying a cluster of biblical directives) "wait on the Lord."[138] This is not a posture of passive resignation in the face of affliction but rather – a persistant theme in Milton – of attentive waiting upon God's time, upon ripeness, upon the clarification of vocation; it implies an ability to abide in hermeneutic uncertainties and to postpone closure.[139] The courtly metaphor even implies that this may be the most worthy role, standing nearest the throne and waiting upon the only true King in his glory.[140]

This sonnet displays the consummate skill Milton has attained in setting speech rhythms against the formal metrical pattern of the Petrarchan sonnet. Throughout, the pauses dictated by meaning and syntax come in the middle of lines, as does the *volta* or turn in the argument. Also, Milton varies the tempo of the lines in sharp counterpoint to the metrics: by his use of short, discrete monosyllables and alliteration on the plosive consonant "d" we are forced to read slowly and with great emphasis, indeed almost to spit out, his bitter question to the universe: "Doth God exact day-labour, light deny'd?" Then, after a short pause to take the emotional force of that question, it is qualified and brought under judgment by the run-on to the next line, "I fondly ask." The changes in tempo in the final lines are also striking: the pseudo-onomatopoeia of "Thousands at his bidding speed" force the voice to mimic that haste. Then the last line achieves a stately dignity as its perfect iambics beat out a solemn drumbeat: "They also serve who only stand and waite." Milton has created here a sonnet whose form is emblematic of its matter: an agonized rebellion that challenges providential order but is yet contained within it is mirrored by disruptions in rhythm and tempo that are yet contained within the metrical pattern of a Petrarchan sonnet. He must have found considerable reassurance in using his talent to create this small masterpiece.

In the *Defensio Secunda* Milton has moved from attentive standing and waiting to vigorous political action. In no other work of his are the representations of self and nation so thoroughly and complexly intertwined, and in no other prose work is there such a range of tones – from high heroic and panegyric, to earnest argument and self-defense, to urgent exhortation and admonition, to witty wordplay, to fierce invective. The body of the work follows the main divisions of the *Clamor*, but Milton offers only brief summaries of his earlier justifications for the regicide, which are almost lost alongside the panegyric, satiric, and admonitory passages. Like the *Areopagitica*, this work is imagined as a classical oration with exordium, narrative, proofs, and peroration; Milton refers to it as "my speech" and calls attention to the perhaps too lofty "exordium" and the very long "proem" or preface (*CPW* IV.1, 548, 554, 557). But the *Defensio Secunda* is much more closely related to oral composition and performance than was *Areopagitica* with its celebration of the book and the liberty of printing. By the same token Milton's most recent polemics – *Eikonoklastes* and the *Defensio* – are texts which engage directly with other written texts and attempt to disable them through textual analysis and response. To the contrary, the *Defensio Secunda* engages with a work imagined as oral, a *Cry* which also incorporates a scathing *ad hominem* assault on Milton. He responds with an answer in kind, a prosecution of More citing evidence and witnesses. That response frames their encounter as an agonistic debate concerned less with argument than with ethical proof, the character of the authors: on the one hand the lecherous, treacherous, priapic More, and on the other, a Milton who is not as he has been described but the precise opposite: attractive, virile, chaste, honorable, a heroic defender of the state at the cost of his eyes, and a blameless servant of God.[141] Milton is not concerned here to interpret events but to establish the character of the several actors: on the one hand the debased Salmasius, More, and Charles, and by contrast, the noble Cromwell, Bradshaw, Queen Christina, Fairfax, and Milton.

Milton consciously models himself on the classical rhetor, expecially those noble defenders of liberty, Cicero and Demosthenes. But, typically, he expects to outdo them. They surpass him in style and eloquence as he is writing in a foreign tongue, but "I [shall] outstrip all the orators of every age in the grandeur of my subject and my theme."[142] That subject is liberty and the heroic English liberators of their country. And his audience is not a few Romans in the Forum but "the entire assembly and council of all the most influential men, cities, and nations everywhere." As orator–teacher, Milton sees himself "leading home again everywhere in the world . . . Liberty herself, so long expelled and exiled" and, like a better trader, introducing to all nations the most excellent of English products, "the renewed cultivation of freedom and civic life" (554–6). But in addition to that conscious self-characterization as rhetor, Milton's new situation as a blind man surely contributes to his choice of the oral mode, cut off as he now is from the direct assessment of an opponent's written text or from direct control of his own written text. Now more than ever he insists that the author's life and character must be the guarantor of the truth and value of his text.

Milton attacks Alexander More with witty scorn and fierce invective, taking him to be the author of the entire *Clamor*, not only (as he was) of the epistle to Charles II, signed by Vlacq.[143] Milton's core assumption about the relation of writing to life helps explain his attitude: as the good orator must be a good man who loves liberty (a Cicero), so the defender of tyranny must be a bad man and a slave to his passions, as More patently is. He therefore deserves every insult, and Milton sees no need to be scrupulous about confirming all the information in the narrative he strings together about More's various misdeeds. More was, Milton reports, condemned by the Church Elders at Geneva "for many deviations from the orthodox faith . . . which he basely recanted and yet impiously retained after recanting" (564–5), and then for adultery with a former maidservant, this one named Nicolarde Pelet.[144] Through Salmasius's influence he received a call from the Walloon church at Middleburgh, Holland, and with difficulty obtained "rather cool" letters of recommendation, which Geneva supplied only to get rid of him. Milton's information here is mostly accurate and he cites his authoritative source, records in the public library at Geneva which someone evidently consulted for him.[145] Milton's other information about More is based on rumor not records, but he gleefully makes the worst of what he has heard, presenting More as a satyr, always into and out of some servant's bed. He reports that More visited Salmasius when he first arrived in Holland and cast lustful eyes on Pontia (Elizabeth Guerret), maidservant to Salmasius's wife, "for this creature's desires always light on servant girls" (568). Frequenting Salmasius's house to collaborate on an answer to Milton's *Defensio* he carried on a liaison with Pontia, seduced her under the promise of marriage, impregnated her, and then abandoned her – violating not only God's law and his ministry but also the obligations of guest to host. The seduction and desertion were true, and also More's falling out with Salmasius and especially with Mrs Salmasius over this business. But the time sequence is confused, the girl was a gentlewoman-attendant, there was no pregnancy, and the civil court held that the breach of promise was not proved.[146] The last installment of More's story is the most inaccurate, and admittedly based on rumor. "I have recently heard," Milton claims, that the church at Middleburgh expelled More, and that the magistrates at Amsterdam barred him from the pulpit.[147] By contrast, Milton takes pains to prove himself a careful investigator when challenging *Clamor's* version of some recent English events. He found out from the officer in charge of the guards at Charles's execution that the story about a man being murdered there for begging God's mercy on the king was "absolutely false" (644–5). Similarly, he sought out the facts about the king's escape to the Isle of Wight "from those who had the best possible opportunity to become acquainted with the whole story," and on that basis denies Cromwell's complicity in it (663–4). But he felt no need to expend such diligence on the rascal More.

Milton peppers his narrative about More with harsh epithets: More is "faithless, treacherous, ungrateful, foulmouthed, a consistent slanderer of men and of women," a "gallows-bird," "the rankest goat of all," the creator, not of a royal tragedy as he thinks, but a satyr play about himself (564, 660). Gleefully transcribing the much-cited epigram from Leyden,[148] Milton continues with such witty wordplay throughout, much of it lost in English translation: on More's name (fool), on the bawdy suggestions prompted by his first adultery in Geneva garden (grafting, treading, fig), on associations invited by changing Guerret's nickname Bontia to Pontia (Pontia Pilata, Pontia the Roman infanticide, Pontifex Maximus). The rumors of pregnancy unleash an outpouring of salacious wit constructing More as bisexual, a hermaphrodite who both begets and conceives. Pontia conceived a little More while More and Salmasius (in a homosexual coupling) conceived an "empty wind-egg," the swollen *Clamor*; also, Salmasius was the midwife who brought forth praises of himself out of a (now female) More.[149] Milton also includes a witty ten-line Latin epigram he probably wrote in 1652 in preparation for Salmasius's long-expected reply; its point is the use of Salmasius's worthless writings as wrappings for fish (580). By contrast Milton invites sympathy for the despised and deceived Pontia whose complaints to synod and magistrate were denied: "the *Cry of the Royal Blood* has easily drowned out the cry of violated honor" and the cries of "the tiny baby whom you [More] begot in shame and then abandoned" (570, 575).

Alongside the invective, much of the *Defensio Secunda* is in the high heroic mode. Milton links it with the *Defensio* as the second part of a prose epic, and sees both these works as fulfilling in some measure his long-planned national epic celebrating the noblest deeds of his countrymen. Like the illustrious Greeks and Romans, the English "Liberators" expelled a tyrant in a "fair and glorious trial of virtue" (550), and Milton's role is to praise and extol those "heroes victorious in battle" (553). In his peroration Milton makes the genre claim explicit, describing his work as an eternizing monument to glorious deeds, and pointing to its epic analogues and structure:

> I have borne witness, I might almost say I have erected a monument that will not soon pass away, to those deeds that were illustrious, that were glorious, that were almost beyond any praise. . . . Moreover, just as the epic poet . . . undertakes to extole, not the whole life of the hero . . . but usually one event of his life (the exploits of Achilles at Troy, let us say, or the return of Ulysses, or the arrival of Aeneas in Italy) and passes over the rest, so let it suffice me too . . . to have celebrated at least one heroic achievement of my countrymen. (685)

In form and tone, the *Defensio Secunda* is more heroic than the first, joining, as David Loewenstein notes, "epic vision to revolutionary polemics" to create a mythopoeic vision of an imagined social order.[150] The vignettes of Cromwell, Fairfax, Bradshaw, Queen Christina, Overton, John Lambert, Charles Fleetwood, and the other officers and statesmen singled out for praise are like a catalogue of epic heroes with distinctly epic virtues: martial prowess often, but more importantly, wisdom, courage, magnanimity, prudence, justice, and *pietas*. They also exhibit the higher virtues demanded of Christians: temperance, self-control, forgiveness of enemies, and conquest over ambition, fears, desires, and passions. The moral qualities necessary for political leadership are emphasized, since in the *History of Britain* Milton had found his countrymen fearless and strong in war but inept at governance. Christina is a peaceful Penthesilea or Camilla: she is a "heroine" of "exalted virtue and magnanimity," "fairness and justice," and "vigorous mind"; and she even surpasses her father Gustavus Adolphus, a martial hero, "as wisdom excels strength, and the arts of peace the craft of war" (604–6). Bradshaw is "an alert defender of liberty and the people," an "incorruptible judge" who presided over the king's trial with "loyalty, sobriety, dignity," an "affable and serene . . . hospitable and generous" friend, and an "able and fearless" patron (638–9). Among the thirteen other named worthies six are army officers, all "brave and fearless" and two (Lambert and Overton) are praised for specific battlefield exploits. But their other qualities are more important: Fairfax joined "supreme courage" with "supreme modesty and supreme holiness," Fleetwood has exhibited "civility, gentleness, and courtesy" from his earliest days, Overton is remarkable for the "sweetness" of his disposition and his mercy to the conquered (669, 675, 76). The other seven are "men famous in private life and the arts of peace," of whom two (Edward Montague and Henry Lawrence) Milton knows to be "men of supreme genius, cultivated in the liberal arts" (676–7). Milton's lengthy tribute to these men alongside Cromwell reconfigures the Protectorate as an aristocratic republic with power shared among good men.

A long encomium of Cromwell identifies him as a superlative epic and Christian hero, "supremely excellent" in prowess on the battlefield and skill in governance as well as in personal virtue. He came "of renowned and illustrious stock," and was long known for "devotion to the Puritan religion and his upright life" (666–7). As captain of an army troop his victories soon surpassed those of the greatest generals because he had already won those victories over the self which Milton always makes the fundamental condition for any public leadership role:

> He was a soldier well-versed in self-knowledge, and whatever enemy lay within – vain hopes, fears, desires – he had either previously destroyed within himself or had long since reduced to subjection. Commander first over himself, victor over himself . . . he entered camp a veteran and past-master in all that concerned the soldier's life. (667–8)

Declining to describe his many victories in the civil wars, Milton praises especially the leadership qualities he first displayed in the army, inviting comparison with the model Persian general and ruler, Cyrus the Great. He attracted men "who were already good and brave, or else he made them such, chiefly by his own example"; no one ever raised a "larger or better-disciplined army in a shorter space of time . . . cherished by their fellow-citizens," formidable to the enemy but merciful when they surrendered, and "an inspiration to all virtue and piety" (668–9). His later accomplishments are seen to flow from this preparation: Ireland was all but lost until Cromwell broke the rebels' power in a single battle; Scotland was subdued in a year, adding "to the wealth of England that realm which all our kings for eight hundred years had been unable to master." After this, Cromwell showed himself "as mighty in deliberation as in the arts of war:" he toiled in parliament to pass needed laws, then dismissed the "few men" of the Rump Parliament when they contrived delays and pursued their private interest, and finally accepted the Protectorate when it was thrust upon him at the Nominated Parliament's collapse (670–1). Proclaiming him "the man most fit to rule" (672), Milton emphasizes his magnanimity – for Spenser the supreme epic virtue – in refusing the title of King. Terming him *pater patriae*, Milton associates him with Cicero, who was first granted that title, and also with Rome's founder Aeneas, implicitly contrasting him with that unworthy claimant to patriarchal kingship, Charles I.

But the epic hero celebrated at greatest length is Milton himself. His self-portrait, developed in several places and over many pages, is rich in self-revelation as autobiography fuses with art and Milton judges his life against heroic models. More's spiteful depiction of Milton in his Epistle to Charles as "a monster, dreadful, ugly, huge" or rather "feeble, bloodless, and pinched" stung him to provide a striking verbal picture of himself whose accuracy, he claims with amusing exaggeration, can be attested by "many thousands of my fellow citizens, who know me by sight, and . . . not a few foreigners" (584). That description accords him the physical grace, spirit, strength, and even chivalric accomplishments proper to epic heroes:

> Ugly I have never been thought by anyone, to my knowledge . . . I admit that I am not tall, but my stature is closer to the medium than to the small. Yet what if it were small, as is the case with so many men of the greatest worth in both peace and war? . . . I was not ignorant of how to handle or unsheathe a sword, nor unpractised in using it each day. Girded with my sword, as I generally was, I thought myself equal to anyone, though he was far more sturdy, and I was fearless of any injury that one man could inflict on another. Today I possess the same spirit, the same strength, but not

> the same eyes. And yet they have as much the appearance of being uninjured, and are as clear and bright, without a cloud, as the eyes of men who see most keenly. . . . In my face . . . still lingers a color exactly opposite to the bloodless and pale, so that although I am past forty, there is scarcely anyone to whom I do not seem younger by about ten years. (582–3)

He decided not to take on the "toils and dangers" of military service in order to serve in a role better suited to his talents but "no less perilous" (552). While he "admire[s] the heroes victorious in battle," he rejoices in his own role of "defending the very defenders" and he represents that as an epic encounter: when Salmasius "was attacking us and our battle array . . . I met him in single combat and plunged into his reviling throat this pen, the weapon of his own choice."[151]

At one point (612–28) Milton offers a sequential autobiographical narrative, parts of which I have treated earlier in relation to the relevant stages of his life. Considered as a whole, this passage functions as an *apologia*, to show foreigners and Englishmen alike "that I am incapable of ever disgracing honorable speech by dishonorable conduct, or free utterances by slavish deeds" (611). It serves also as ethical proof to establish Milton's character as the good orator, with worthy parents, good breeding, eminently respectable friends, unselfish motives, and illustrious deeds. And it helps to assimilate him to his own pantheon of English epic heroes by displaying his unstained virtue and his vigorous defense of liberty in all arenas. He came "of an honorable family," had a rigorous and extensive education and self-education, left the university with an MA and the respect of all, and then studied for five years in retirement at home, traveled abroad where he met famous men of the stature of Galileo and Grotius and was befriended by many "eminent in rank and learning" (612–15). He defended Protestantism boldly in the very teeth of the Roman Jesuits, lived in the sinks of iniquity in Europe "free and untouched by the slightest sin or reproach," and then cut his voyage short to join his fellow-citizens "fighting for liberty" at home (619–20). In several tracts opposing the bishops he took part with those "exposing themselves to danger for the sake of the Gospel"; in several tracts on divorce he sought "to advance the cause of true and substantial liberty" which is from within; and in a tractate on education and another on freedom of the press he undertook to promote that virtue and inner liberty which are requisite for citizens in a free commonwealth (622–4). He wrote *Tenure* not to make specific recommendations about Charles but to advise what may be done against tyrants; he was engaged in writing the history of his country when the Council of State sought his services; he wrote *Eikonoklastes* not to insult the king but to serve "Queen Truth" (628). A few pages earlier he cast the council's charge to him to write against Salmasius as an epic mission given to a worthy knight: "It was I and no other who was deemed equal to a foe of such repute . . . and who received from the very liberators of my country this role, which was offered spontaneously with universal consent, the task of publicly defending (if anyone ever did) the cause of the English people and thus of Liberty herself" (549). He makes his blindness part of his character as epic bard and epic hero, placing himself with blind classical and biblical seers (Tiresias, Phineus, Isaac, and Jacob), as well as with blind generals and statesmen (Timoleon of Corinth, Appius Claudius, Caecillius Metellus, and Dandolo the Doge of Venice). Also, drawing a parallel between Achilles' choice of glorious victory over Troy at the cost of early death and his own choice of service to country in conquering Salmasius at the cost of his remaining vision, he finds his choice more noble, "as duty is of itself more substantial than glory (587–8).

More's sneers about Milton's blindness also prompt Milton to recognize and represent himself as a Christian hero. He has painfully considered – as what Puritan would not – that his blindness might be a divine punishment for heinous sin, but a rigorous self-examination has affirmed the essential goodness of his life and motives. The statement sounds self-righteous, but I think we need not doubt the self-examination that produced it:

> I call upon Thee, my God, who knowest my inmost mind and all my thoughts, to witness that (although I have repeatedly examined myself on this point as earnestly as I could, and have searched all the corners of my life) I am conscious of nothing, or of no deed, either recent or remote, whose wickedness could justly occasion or invite upon me this supreme misfortune. . . . I have written nothing . . . that I was not then and am not now convinced that it was right and true and pleasing to God. And I swear that my conduct was not influenced by ambition, gain, or glory, but solely by considerations of duty, honor, and devotion to my country. I did my utmost not only to free my country, but also to free the church. (587)

Accordingly, he takes his blindness as an occasion for practicing Christian patience in affliction: "I stand unmoved and steady." He draws consolation from his many friendships, from the continued honor and employment offered by his government, and especially from the evidences of God's "fatherly mercy and kindness towards me," and so he is able to "bow to his divine will" (589–91). Moreover, he anticipates that physical blindness may lead him (as it has others) to heightened spiritual insight, the inner light of prophecy:

> There is a certain road which leads through weakness, as the apostle teaches, to the greatest strength. . . . To be sure, we blind men are not the least of God's concerns. . . . Divine law and divine favor have rendered us not only safe from the injuries of men, but almost sacred. . . . And divine favor not infrequently is wont to lighten these shadows again, once made, by an inner and far more enduring light.[152]

In this treatise Milton bases his political theory more firmly than before on two Platonic/Aristotelian principles which he equates with natural law: that the best and most worthy, whatever their numbers, should govern; and that particular forms of government will necessarily conform to the nature of the citizens:

> [N]othing is more natural, nothing more just, nothing more useful or more advantageous to the human race than that the lesser obey the greater, not the lesser number the greater number but the lesser virtue the greater virtue, the lesser wisdom the greater wisdom. Those whose power lies in wisdom, experience, industry, and virtue will, in my opinion, however small their number, be a majority and prove more powerful . . . than any mere number, however great. (636)

He still regards England as a republic (561, 673), but his view of the English populace is far darker than in the *Defensio*, and he makes a still sharper divide between the virtuous citizens who "freed the state from grievous tyranny and the church from unworthy servitude," and the mob that "venomously attacked" their heroic achievements (549). The true "people" are that multitude of liberators, not "this mob of ours" that still idolizes tyrants (551–2). Accordingly, the worthy, liberty-loving minority has the right and duty to act for the whole people, and the majority – if it has become a mob – does not have the right Milton accorded the people in *Tenure*, of reclaiming their inherent sovereign power from their delegates:

> If, after receiving supreme power to decide on the gravest matters, they were forced once more to refer those questions, which especially exceed the comprehension of the masses, I do not say to the people (for with this power they are themselves now the people) but to the mob, which, conscious of its own inexperience, had originally referred all things to them, what would be the end of this referring back and forth? . . . Who denies that times may often come when a majority of the citizens are wanton, preferring to follow Cataline or Antony rather than the sounder party of the Senate? Nor for that reason ought the upright citizens to fail in striving against the disaffected and acting bravely, having regard rather for their duty than for their small number. (634–5, 648)

On these terms England is an aristocratic republic whose true citizens are dedicated to the noblest ends of government, "the restoration of liberty both to civil life and to divine worship" (550). If the Protector and his government will set policies that assure such liberty they will have achieved the best form of a republic possible at this time, albeit a form Milton thinks imperfect and hopes will be temporary: "a people torn by so many factions (as after a storm, when the waves have not yet subsided) does not permit that condition in public affairs which is ideal and perfect" (680).

He still equates absolute monarchy with tyranny (561–2), but in this tract he does not repeat (though he still believes) his earlier arguments for the inherent superiority of an aristocratic republic. Rather, since he is addressing the nations of Europe, most of them monarchies, he insists that his tracts distinguish sharply between kings and tyrants and that Queen Christina's praises of his *Defensio* prove "that I had uttered no word against kings, but only against tyrants – the pests and plagues of kings." His long digression on Christina makes her illustrate the principle that monarchy is justified when the ruler surpasses all others by, as in her case, "a well-nigh divine virtue and wisdom" (604). But the excessive hyperbole of this portrait suggests that it represents an ideal, not an actual monarch. Christina is not only wise but her mind bears the very image of the goddess of wisdom; that wisdom is innate, not gained simply from books; her mind is "of heavenly origin, that purest particle of the divine air which has fallen . . . into these remote regions"; she equals the Queen of Sheba in presenting "the most brilliant exemplar of royal virtues." Also, her exalted magnanimity is evident not only in her rule but in something "far more august and sublime" – the renunciation of kingship.[153] Milton has heard about Christina's projected abdication, but not, obviously, that she intended to become a Catholic. Given his harsh view of female rule in the *History of Britain* it seems ironic that he makes a queen his ideal monarch, even though rhetorical utility dictates that choice. He can of course regard Christina as one of those exceptional women allowed for in *Tetrachordon*, for whom gender norms are superseded by the "higher and more natural law" that the most worthy should rule.[154] More to the point, however, the excessive hyperbole precludes a literal reading of this panegyric, allowing it to register Milton's conviction that only such superlative qualities – in the realm of the divine rather than the human – could justify monarchical rule. Moreover, if this ideal queen is about to give up her throne, on what basis can lesser monarchs retain theirs?

Cromwell's Protectorate is also justified by the natural law of rule by the worthiest: "there is nothing in human society more pleasing to God, or more agreeable to reason, nothing in the state more just, nothing more expedient, than the rule of the man most fit to rule. All know you to be that man, Cromwell" (671–2). But Milton's portrait of Cromwell points to his actual achievements in war and peace and to virtues which, however exalted, are still on the human scale. Milton describes Cromwell not as a king manqué but as the temporary guardian of the republic's liberties. He did not take over the government but merely picked up the reins when all others dropped them: "Cromwell, we are deserted! You alone remain. On you has fallen the whole burden of our affairs" (671). The titles Milton accords him square with that conception: "the greatest and most illustrious citizen, the director of public counsels, the commander of the bravest armies, the father of your country . . . the liberator of your country, the author of its liberty, and likewise its guardian and savior" (672). He also shows a keen awareness of the dangers that might lie ahead, as he implores Cromwell, most earnestly, not to violate or infringe the liberties he is charged to defend and enlarge:

> Consider again and again how precious a thing is this liberty which you hold, committed to your care, entrusted and commended to you by how dear a mother, your native land. That which she once sought from the most distinguished men of the entire nation, she now seeks from you alone and through you alone hopes to achieve. Honor

> this great confidence reposed in you. . . . Honor too what foreign nations think and say of us, the high hopes which they have for themselves as a result of our liberty, so bravely won, and our republic, so gloriously born. . . . Finally, honor yourself, so that, having achieved that liberty in pursuit of which you endured so many hardships and encountered so many perils, you may not permit it to be violated by yourself or in any degree diminished by others. Certainly you yourself cannot be free without us, for it has been so arranged by nature that he who attacks the liberty of others is himself the first of all to lose his own liberty and learns that he is the first of all to become a slave. And he deserves this fate . . . if that man than whom no one has been considered more just, more holy, more excellent, shall afterwards attack that liberty which he himself has defended, such an act must necessarily be dangerous and well-nigh fatal not only to liberty itself but also to the cause of all virtue and piety. (673)

He lays out in the clearest terms the temptations and pitfalls, moral and political, that beset one who exercises such large powers. If Cromwell were to be "captivated" by the title of king, he would become that worst of evils, an idolator, worshipping "the gods that you had conquered" (672). Cromwell should also fear that he may not be up to the almost superhuman challenge:

> You have taken upon yourself by far the heaviest burden, one that will put to the test your inmost capacities, that will search you out wholly and intimately, and reveal what spirit, what strength, what authority are in you, whether there truly live in you that piety, faith, justice, and moderation of soul which convince us that you have been raised by the power of God beyond all other men to this most exalted rank. To rule with wisdom three powerful nations, to desire to lead their peoples from base customs to a better standard of morality and discipline than before . . . to refuse no toil, to yield to no allurements of pleasure, to flee from the pomp of wealth and power, these are arduous tasks compared to which war is a mere game. These trials will buffet you and shake you, they require a man supported by divine help and instructed by all-but-divine inspiration. (673–4)

Milton then takes upon himself to instruct Cromwell how to avoid these dangers, so that he can "restore to us our liberty, unharmed and even enhanced" (674) – presumably when a more representative government is possible. His first recommendation refigures the government from a quasi-monarchy to an aristocratic republic: Cromwell should share power with "a great many other citizens of pre-eminent merits" (677–8) on the basis of virtue and devotion to liberty's cause, not social rank. Most of these worthies are "citizens of the better stamp" with "ample or moderate means," but some are to be "more highly valued because of their very poverty" (674). His chief proposition – again – is separation of church and state, assuring toleration and the abolition of public maintenance for the clergy. Milton hopes to persuade Cromwell to rethink his compromises on these matters and to adopt Milton's impolitic but hardly unreasonable proposal for a nation torn by religious strife:

> I would have you leave the church to the church . . . and not permit two powers, utterly diverse, the civil and the ecclesiastical . . . to undermine and at length destroy each other. I would have you remove all power from the church (but power will never be absent so long as money, the poison of the church, the quinsy of truth, extorted by force even from those who are unwilling, remains the price of preaching the Gospel). (678)

On the vital matter of religious liberty he urges Cromwell to resist those (the proponents of doctrinal fundamentals) who "do not believe themselves free unless they deny freedom to others" (679), and to side instead with those (like Williams and Vane) who believe that "all citizens equally have an equal right to freedom in the state" (679).

Reprising *Areopagitica*, Milton also urges Cromwell to enlarge personal liberty and thereby promote republican virtue in the citizenry. He should reform the laws, not by overturning the legal system itself or the Court of Chancery as some Barebones radicals proposed, but by repealing laws that unnecessarily restrict freedom, that forbid "actions of themselves licit, merely because of the guilt of those who abuse them." Laws, he insists, only curb wickedness, "but nothing can so effectively mould and create virtue as liberty" (679). Cromwell should also abolish the licensing ordinances that still hamper free inquiry and publication, those laws that Milton contravened in allowing publication of the *Racovian Catechism*: "May you permit those who wish to engage in free inquiry to publish their findings at their own peril without the private inspection of any petty magistrate, for so will truth especially flourish" (679). And, harking back to *Of Education*, he asks Cromwell to "take more thought" for the education of the young, suggesting (without any details) a merit system whereby access to public education is reserved for those who have demonstrated their talent and commitment – "who have already acquired learning." Whatever he has in mind, he does not want "the teachable and the unteachable, the diligent and the slothful instructed side by side at public expense" (679).

In the peroration, Milton admonishes his fellow citizens to acquire the virtues that alone can make them free within and thereby able to value and sustain a free republic. Those in government must acquire, as Englishmen in the past did not, the moral and political virtues necessary for the "arts of peace." They must cast out superstition, practice "true and sincere devotion to God and men," expel avarice, ambition, luxury, and all extravagance, "help those cruelly harrassed and oppressed," and "render to every man promptly his own deserts" (680–1). If they instead fall into royalist excesses and follies God will abandon them and others will rule them. He urges citizens to exercise their vote worthily if they hope to retain it. Neither "Cromwell himself, nor a whole tribe of liberating Brutuses" (682) could win liberty a second time for a people that throw it over. Let them not send to parliament delegates who buy votes with feasts, drink, and appeals to faction, or who are given to violence, corruption, bribery, or embezzlement of state funds, or whose inner servitude precludes devotion to liberty and the nation's liberators. Finally, in an eloquent *cri de coeur*, Milton adjures the English to become the virtuous and liberty-loving citizens they must be if they are to exercise political power, laying out in clear terms that natural law whereby virtue goes hand in hand with liberty, vice with slavery:

> [T]o be free is precisely the same as to be pious, wise, just, and temperate, careful of one's property, aloof from another's, and thus finally to be magnanimous and brave, so to be the opposite to these qualities is the same as to be a slave. And by the customary judgment and, so to speak, just retaliation of God, it happens that a nation which cannot rule and govern itself, but has delivered itself into slavery to its own lusts, is enslaved also to other masters whom it does not choose. . . . You, therefore, who wish to remain free, either be wise at the outset or recover your senses as soon as possible. If to be a slave is hard, and you do not wish it, learn to obey right reason, to master yourselves. Lastly, refrain from factions, hatreds, superstitions, injustices, lusts, and rapine against one another. Unless you do this with all your strength you cannot seem either to God or to men, or even to your recent liberators, fit to be entrusted with the liberty and guidance of the state and the power of commanding others, which you arrogate to yourselves so greedily. (684)

Milton asserts as strongly as ever the religious and civil liberties he most values, but he now must rely on Cromwell to achieve them. He still wants a more representative government, but unless citizens rise to the challenge of living in a free republic they will need a Protector: "Then indeed, like a nation in wardship, you would rather be in need of some tutor, some brave and faithful guardian of your affairs" (684). That, however, represents a falling off from their past glory: "If the most recent deeds of my fellow countrymen should not correspond sufficiently to their earliest, let them look to it themselves" (685). Milton's political theory as articulated in this tract assumes that the ancient republican virtues and the emerging personal liberties he so cherishes are inextricably linked, that virtue in the citizenry is at once the ground for, and the product of, liberty. There is no easy escape from this vicious – or rather virtuous – circle, since Milton cannot allow the majority to follow its very different notion of virtue and liberty by recalling the king (thereby threatening religious liberty and curtailing personal freedom); nor will he, with the Barebones "Saints," equate political virtue with regeneracy. He can only hope that Cromwell will heed his call for expanded liberties, and that the resulting change in the political culture will, with the grace of God, produce the citizens the republic needs.

10

"I . . . Still Bear Up and Steer Right Onward" 1654–1658

During the remaining years of Oliver Cromwell's Protectorate, Milton's diplomatic correspondence comprised around ninety known letters, translations, and treaty documents (and probably more). He wrote several protests about commercial matters, but his Latin was especially in demand for the Protector's impassioned appeals for Protestant unity in the face of the Catholic menace, in response to the massacre of the Waldensians and Sweden's conflicts with other Protestant powers. During periods of relative leisure Milton pressed ahead with several projects: bringing his *History of Britain* up to the Norman Conquest, working on a Latin *Thesaurus* and on the theological compendium that was to become *De Doctrina Christiana*, and perhaps beginning *Paradise Lost*. He also delivered his final round in the Salmasius–More controversy, responding to More's answer to his *Defensio Secunda* with a scathing and very personal treatise, the *Pro Se Defensio*.

Milton made no explicit comment on the direction taken by the Protectorate government during these years, constrained by having chosen to continue his appointment in the Secretariat. But he had few close associates in government after his republican friends, Vane and Bradshaw, had broken with Cromwell. He was surely disappointed by some of the Protector's policies that went directly counter to his advice in the *Defensio Secunda* about church disestablishment and the enlargement of personal liberty. He shows no sympathy for the "court party" seeking to settle a new dynasty in Cromwell and he still believes that a republic is the best form of government for free men. But he is less disposed than his republican friends to make a sovereign and representative parliament the *sine qua non* of a republic, since religious freedom had proved to be safer with Cromwell than with any of his parliaments. Also, as Milton prepared state letters for Cromwell, he no doubt came to admire his leadership in foreign affairs and especially in promoting European Protestant solidarity against Rome. He was also pragmatist enough to recognize that Cromwell's government was the only viable immediate option. As he continued to work for Cromwell, he could blame the policies he disliked chiefly on the unstable political circumstances and the disaffected masses, and hope for better times. But his ambivalence is indicated in some passages of the *History of Britain*, in his edition of *The Cabinet Council*, a collection of Machiavellian political maxims attributed to Sir Walter Raleigh, and perhaps most strongly by the fact that he offered no word of praise or advice to the Proector during these years, and no verses for his death.

Milton seems to have enjoyed these relatively quiet years. European travelers regularly called on the famous author of the *Defensio*. He took a special interest in several promising young scholars, reaching out to them almost as surrogate sons. Longtime friends and former pupils visited often and some of them served as occasional amanuenses. He corresponded about scholarly matters with a widening circle of learned acquaintances and exchanged warm and affectionate letters with absent friends. He also married again after four years as a widower and apparently enjoyed this time the love and domestic society whose lack he so bitterly lamented in the divorce tracts, as well as the comfort of a well-ordered household. But his wife died within two years and their infant daughter died also, at less than five months old. Milton's muse sang of the pleasures and the tragedies of these years in five sonnets: a ringing prophetic denunciation of the slaughter of the Waldensians; two "invitation" sonnets in the Jonsonian mode celebrating the delights of recreation with friends; a poem revisiting the trauma of his blindness in more optimistic terms; and a poignant lament exposing his grief and agonizing sense of loss at the death of his wife. The first and last of these are, along with the first sonnet on his blindness, his grandest achievements in the genre.

"I Have Discharged an Office . . . Not Unuseful to the State"

The first Protectorate parliament, which got underway on September 3, 1654, contained many Presbyterians and other religious conservatives and also republican irreconcilables. They immediately set about to rework all the provisions of the *Instrument of Government*, seeking to limit Cromwell's powers and to deny him the veto he demanded over matters relating to "fundamentals." They also threatened the cause nearest to Milton's heart, religious liberty, by excluding from toleration several ill-defined categories – Atheism, Blasphemy, Popery, Prelacy, Licentiousness, and Profaneness – and by requiring profession of some 20 articles of faith (expanding Owen's 15) from clergy on public stipend. Cromwell also met with continued opposition from republicans and religious radicals, especially Fifth Monarchists. Milton's friend Overton, who had reconciled with Cromwell as Milton had implicitly urged in the *Defensio Secunda* and had returned to Scotland as General Monk's second-in-command, was soon implicated in an army plot against Cromwell. He was arrested in December and committed to the Tower on January 16, 1655.[1]

During the autumn and winter of 1654–5 Milton set about to answer More's defense of himself, called *Fides Publica*. Sometime in October, 1654 Adriaan Vlacq published in the Hague a new edition of Milton's *Defensio Secunda* along with that incomplete answer; More had gone to Paris before finishing it and Vlacq was unwilling to delay publication.[2] *Fides Publica* begins with a prefatory epistle by George Crantz, a theologian friend of More's, which characterizes Milton as "a fabulist and a meer poet" and defends More as a scholar, a skillful preacher, and a noble genius whose temper invites hostilities but who is innocent of Milton's charges.[3] A preface by Vlacq, "Typographus Pro Se-Ipso," reviews the publication history of *Clamor*: the manuscript came from an unknown author to Salmasius; Vlacq agreed to publish it and invited Milton (through Hartlib) to reply; when Milton's reply at last appeared – Vlacq wonders why so tardily – it castigated Vlacq for signing the dedication to Charles. Taking a leaf out of the *Defensio Secunda*, Vlacq defends himself by reviewing his life in London, Paris, and the Hague, and emphasizing his scholarly contributions in mathematics. He published both works, he explains, because printers often publish on both sides of an issue, and he signed the dedicatory letter to Charles because he was asked to and because such practices are common. Quoting his exchange with Hartlib two years earlier denying More's authorship of *Clamor*, he concludes that Milton knowingly defamed More "with calumnies and the blackest lies" (*CPW* IV.2, 1,093).

In the *Fides Publica* itself, More categorically denies writing any part of the *Clamor*, but equivocates about the Epistle to Charles, which he did write. He declares that he knows the author and looks forward to the day he will reveal himself. Milton, he insists, had learned from Dury and Nieupoort that More was not the author but he was unwilling to lose so much witty wordplay on More's name.[4] This is perceptive: the difficulty involved in rewriting the *Defensio Secunda* (already two years overdue) no doubt helped Milton convince himself that he need not credit those few contrary reports. With witty irony More denies reproaching Milton for blindness or deformity even as he renews the insult; he had supposed Milton mentally, not physically, blind, or else as suffering from "blind self-love"; and he had even thought Milton handsome on the strength of "that elegant picture prefixed to your Poems" (1,103) – the Marshall engraving Milton so despised.[5] Some other shafts also came close enough to the mark to arouse Milton's fury: that Milton pursued private injuries implacably; that his scholarly claims are undermined by his wanton and abusive language; and that he supposes his pen a sword to kill the living and the dead. He calls attention also to Milton's admonitory stance toward Cromwell in the *Defensio Secunda* – a stance Milton proudly assumed but might not care to have quite so clearly spelled out:

> Sometimes you would even appear more lofty than the very exalted Cromwell, whom you address familiarly, without any preface of honor, whom you advise under the guise of praising, for whom you dictate laws, set aside titles, and prescribe duties, and

> to whom you suggest counsels and even present threats if he should act in any other fashion. To him you grant arms and empire, for yourself you lay claim to genius and the toga. (1,109)

As for the morals and heresy charges against him, More vigorously denies all the scandals Milton laid to his charge, accusing Milton of deliberate lies, libel, and calumny. He uses the effective strategy of reprinting testimonials from civil and ecclesiastical councils that seem to clear him of all charges. The eight from Geneva included in this first part (dated January–March, 1648) are followed by two testimonial letters (May 9, 1649) from the respected theologian John Diodati whom Milton had mentioned visiting in Geneva.[6]

Sometime in April 1655 Vlacq published More's *Supplementum Fidei Publicae.*[7] In it More gives his own version of his affair with Elizabeth Guerret (Pontia): the trouble arose because Madame Salmasius sought to trap him in an unpropitious marriage with Guerret, and both the Synod at Utrecht and the secular high court decided the cases in his favor. The 13 additional testimonial letters from Geneva, Middleburg, and Amsterdam comprise more than half of the volume; they are meant to portray a man widely admired as a scholar and a minister and publically cleared of every charge against him. Though formally exculpatory, the letters themselves reveal that More attracted controversy and charges of licentious conduct wherever he went, and that the Walloon churches of the United Provinces were a hotbed of intense infighting and partisanship.

Milton claims that he began work on his answer to *Fides Publica* in October 1654, finished it in February, 1655, and dealt with the *Supplementum* as soon as it appeared.[8] He made no effort to conflate the two parts, but simply provided a new heading for the second section, "The Answer of John Milton Englishman to The Supplement of Alexander More." Milton's *Pro Se Defensio* may have been substantially finished by mid-May, but it was not published until around August 8, 1655,[9] as Milton's work on it was interrupted by his extensive diplomatic correspondence relating to the Waldensian crisis. For this tract, Milton assiduously gathered additional information about More from the ever-active Hartlib circle, from foreign news reports in *Mercurius Politicus*, from Thurloe's spies, and from his own contacts in various cities; most of it confirmed his earlier portrait of More as a womanizing scoundrel.

Some of Milton's most damaging information dealt with More's career in Geneva. On March 24, 1655, Milton wrote to thank Ezekiel Spanheim for a letter sent to him six months earlier.[10] Ever a dilatory correspondent, Milton wrote now, with due apologies, to inform Spanheim that he was using part of his letter without his name in the *Pro Se Defensio.*[11] As quoted there and dated October 14, 1654, Spanheim's letter assures Milton that his charges against Salmasius are those "commonly repeated in the mouths of all his greatest friends even, charges which can be clearly corroborated by the authority and assent of the whole assembly"(*CPW* IV.2,

781). From some source Milton received additional information from records in the Geneva archives and library documenting More's doctrinal aberrations and subsequent recantation, and his adultery with the serving woman Nicolarde Pelet.[12] Those records display the conflict between the church authorities (the Company) who were probing the several charges against More and the civil authorities (the Council) who were eager to hush them up to avoid scandal. The certification letters More needed for Middleburg, which he quotes proudly, also caused conflicts and long delay, providing solid ground for Milton's suspicions about them.[13] Dury's letters to Hartlib sometimes included information to be passed on to Milton: while Dury's sources had led him to doubt More's authorship of *Clamor*, he found much evidence supporting Milton's unflattering description of More's character. In a letter from Basel (October 3) Dury notes that More "is very evill spoken off, & . . . most of the French Synod [at Middleburg] labour to have him silenced."[14] Another, from Zurich (November 18), observes that "many here are well pleased that hee [Milton] hath handled Morus roughly, but some think that Morus is wronged . . . truly I believe, where there is so much smoke there must bee some fire." He also passes along news of a man cured of blindness after twenty years as an encouragement that Milton might someday recover his sight.[15]

Milton also collected new information on the More–Pontia affair. A principal informant was probably Lieuwe van Aitzema, the envoy to the Hague from the Hanseatic towns and for several years a paid informant for Thurloe; he had visited Milton during his mission to England in 1652 and they no doubt spoke of More.[16] On January 29, 1655 Aitzema wrote Milton that, partly because of More's attacks, he was planning a Dutch translation of Milton's divorce tract and wondered if Milton cared to add or correct anything.[17] Milton's answer (February 5) recalls how much he enjoyed Aitzema's two visits and offers to send him all three divorce tracts. He assures Aitzema that he does not want to make any changes, but indicates that if Aitzema uses *Doctrine and Discipline* it should be the revised edition. He also indicates his preference for a Latin rather than a Dutch translation, since he knows "by experience" how the "common herd is wont to receive uncommon opinions" (*CPW* IV.2, 871–2).

Milton now had the story, circulated by Heinsius and Vossius, of Elizabeth Guerret's physical attack on More when he repudiated her (*LR* III, 277–8). Also, Thurloe probably passed on information from an unidentified correspondent (November 23, 1654) about the ambiguities surrounding More's secular trial at the Hof van Holland. The case dealt only with breach of promise of marriage and the decision went against Guerret because she could not meet the difficult standard of proof for that plea. But court charges were assessed against More "for reasons" – evidently because the court credited the lechery and fornication to which servants and numerous witnesses testified. Thurloe's informant drew that conclusion from More's failure to include the final court decision among the documents in his *Supplementum*, and adds that More may have left Amsterdam permanently, since "they love well his renowne & learning, but not his conversation; for they doe not desire that he should come to visit the daughters of condition, as he was used to do."[18] Also, Milton probably had reports of the politicing at the Utrecht synod: More's friends first tried to stop the reading of the charges the Leyden consistory brought on Guerret's behalf and then defeated the motion to have More barred from Walloon pulpits. More makes a point of that, but, as Milton observes, their bare failure to bar him was hardly a rousing confirmation of innocence and Leyden (though not Amsterdam as Milton had erroneously stated) did refuse More its pulpits.[19]

Milton used this information in his *Pro Se Defensio,* sometimes as general background, sometimes by quoting letters from Dury, Spanheim, Oldenburg, and others. This treatise is Milton's least attractive work: it is a tissue of vituperation and a strained defense of a serious error. But Milton's identification of his country's cause with his own self-defense gives it a public dimension, and his struggle with the issues posed by his mistake – proper standards of evidence, the uses of defamation, the meaning of authorship – holds considerable biographical interest. He also describes some scenes as literary comedy: More desporting with Pelletta in a debased Garden of Eden, and the mock-epic battle of More and Guerret, fought with slashing fingernails. *Pro Se Defensio* follows More's structure, answering first his unfinished *Fides Publica* and then his *Supplementum*, taking up his several arguments and pieces of evidence in turn. In the first part Milton deals summarily with the prefaces by Crantz and Vlacq, then with More's denial of authorship of the *Clamor*, then with More's licentious behavior with Pontia in the Hague and with Pelletta in Geneva; and finally with More's testimonial letters from Geneva. In the second part he analyzes the letters More supplies in the *Supplementum* that purport to clear him of wrongdoing.

In his exordium to the first part, Milton represents his polemic battle with More as a continuation of his compatriots' war. Theirs is now over but he must fight on in his familiar role of epic hero engaged in single combat: "for me alone it remains to fight the rest of this war . . . against me they direct their venom and their darts" (*CPW* IV.2, 698–9). Like Scipio Africanus who had to turn from noble warfare against Hannibal to far less worthy battles, yet remained true to himself, Milton expects that "I who have not heretofore failed the people or the state shall not here fail myself" (700). He recurs often to the twinned issues of praise and blame, here, self-praise and the poetics of satire. He has not praised himself, he insists, but only offered "a plain and simple narration of my affairs" to clear the good name of the people's defender (735). And, as in the anti-prelatical tracts and *Colasterion*,[20] he justifies his use of foul language in attacking More by the practice of Erasmus, Thomas More, the Fathers of the church, and the biblical writers, in whom "words unchaste and plain thrust out with indignation signify not obscenity, but the vehemence of gravest censure."[21] Also, classical rhetoricians like Cicero, Plato, and the Socratics approve "pleasantries intermixed and interspersed sometimes in the gravest matters" (771). In the peroration to the first part – a passage that might more properly serve as peroration to the whole if Milton had had time or inclination to rework it – he argues that the judicious assignment of both praise and blame is vital to a commonwealth, and that the learned who practiced such rhetoric in school on classical subjects should apply it appropriately to their own contemporaries:

> To defame the villainous and to praise the good . . . constitute almost the sum of justice; and truly we see that for the right management of life they are of almost equal moment . . . no one but the upright alone has the power and the courage to accuse freely and intrepidly. We who as youths under so many masters are accustomed to toil at imaginary eloquence, and think that its rhetorical force lies in invective no less than in praise, do at the desk bravely strike down, to be sure, the names of ancient tyrants. If chance allows, we kill Mezentius over and over again in stale antitheta. . . . [I]t were proper . . . when the Commonwealth requires it, casting exercise-shafts aside, now to venture into the sun, and dust, and field of battle, now to exert real brawn, brandish real arms, seek a real enemy. (794–5)

When such as More are revealed as "inwardly vile, nay, openly and patently criminal," the use of learning in private reproof is a public service:

> If I have now, impelled by all possible reasons, prosecuted in a most just vituperation not merely my personal adversary but the common enemy of almost all mankind, an execrable man, a disgrace to the reformed religion and especially to the sacred order, a dishonor to learning, a most pernicious preceptor of youth, a preacher impure in sacred matters . . . I do indeed hope (for why should I distrust?) that herein I have discharged an office neither displeasing to God, unsalutary to the church, nor unuseful to the state. (796)

Milton takes up first the weakest part of his case, his mistaken claim that More wrote the *Clamor*. Milton flatly denies bad faith, appealing to the "common report, unanimous, invariable" (704) of More's authorship and quoting a few examples, mostly without attribution. The few countervailing reports he not unreasonably dismissed, he claims, since they originated either from More himself or from suspect royalists.[22] But at last, reluctantly, he has to withdraw his claim that More wrote the tract itself. He deals with that uncomfortable fact by applying to More a conception of authorship very different from the individualistic model he has been forging for himself throughout his polemic, involving originality of thought, denial of substantive influence from others, transformation of borrowings and conventions so as to make them his own, and emulation of models with the intention of surpassing them.[23] The *Clamor* he now deals with as an example of an older mode of collaborative authorship, allowing that More, Vlacq, Crantz, Salmasius, and various other unknowns may be involved with it and thereby responsible for it. Throwing down the gauntlet to More, he declares he will admit himself vanquished if he does not prove either that More is the actual author of *Clamor* or has given "sufficient cause" to be considered the author.[24] But to do that he has to define authorial responsibility very broadly indeed:

> If I find that you wrote or contributed one page of this book, or even one versicle, if I find that you published it, or procured or persuaded anyone to publish it, or that you were in charge of its publication, or even lent yourself to the smallest part of the work, seeing that no one else comes forth, for me you alone will be the author of the work.[25]

He can, he is almost sure, lay Vlacq's preface to More's account (More never denied that). He also invokes the legal definition whereby, in Roman and English law, a publisher or printer is held responsible with the author, or even in his place if he is unknown; on that ground, "he who published that *Cry* must be considered its author" (701). Since More was the "proven overseer and editor of that book," Milton can proclaim him the author by "the justice and laws of all nations" (735–6). So he asserts boldly, to hide his discomfort, that identifying the primary author is irrelevant: "what now becomes of the author, or where on earth he lives, I do not linger over" (746).

Milton is much more effective as he embellishes his narrative of More's licentious behavior. Employing intensive textual analysis, he refutes More's arguments and subjects his testimonial letters to a rigorous deconstruction that reveals their inadequacies when weighed by customary canons of evidence. He also draws on information from his own sources. Many of the Geneva letters predate the writers' full knowledge of the scandals about More. Diodati's letters were written after he retired and was no longer in close touch with affairs. Other Geneva letters are "cold," suggesting that they were produced to help dispatch More to Middleburg before the scandals broke open. More's failure to produce the final letter from Geneva to Middleburg suggests that it was far from exculpatory. Most of the letters More cited in the *Supplementum* do not address the relevant charges against him. Also, More's report of the decisions of the civil court and the Utrecht synod are suspect, and the documents cited do not clear him of the morals charges.

Milton declines to name the witnesses he quotes against More. This weakens his case, but he probably needed to protect Thurloe's sources and he was scrupulous about not involving correspondents like Spanheim in his quarrels without their express permission.[26] So he proclaims loftily that "in affairs well known in themselves, I do not hold it necessary" to give names (716), and he also insists that the testimony of others is unnecessary for a virtuous man like himself, who "surrounds himself with his own integrity" (791). Questioning the probative value of testimony is a common theme with Milton, whether it be from living witnesses or (in the antiprelatical tracts) ancient authorities, since the witnesses, like those who seek their support, "are alike the good and the bad" (791). They are especially suspect in this case, and Milton has a sharp warning for those who, out of partiality, timidity, mistaken charity, a spirit of forgiveness, or a desire to avoid scandal have written for

More. They allow the contagion to creep "from the pastor into the flock, from the doctor into the school." As for scandal, it can only be removed by demonstrating "that there is no place for pests of this kind to abide in the reformed church" (793).

To defend himself against More's attacks, Milton revisits some episodes in his past life. He again asserts his moral probity during his travels, underscoring the contrast to More: "in all those places where so much license is allowed I lived upright and undefiled by any flagitious or immodest conduct" (772). He objects to More's statement that he represented himself as "a candidate for martyrdom" at Rome for defending the Protestant religion (More did exaggerate, though Milton certainly suggested that he might be in some danger).[27] He gives both a public and a private reason for answering the *Clamor*: "because I was so ordered, I say, publicly by those whose authority ought to have weight with me. . . . Then because I was expressly injured" (767). And to More's query as to why he did not also answer other attacks on the regicide he responds with asperity, betraying his weariness with these polemics: "because I go not to public business uncalled . . . because I was not injured. . . . Because I am my own master; because I had not leisure; in fine, because I am a man, possessed of a human nature, not an iron one" (767–8). To More's description of him as an upstart "mushroom," he asserts, revealingly, "To me it was always preferable to grow slowly, and as if by the silent lapse of time" (819). And, answering More's charge that he disparaged Greek letters in disparaging More as a professor of Greek, he proudly asserts his knowledge of and love of that literature: "Since I am not unlearned in Greek, and since, if anyone does, I value it highly, you were able to fabricate nothing more foolish. . . . For I had said, not that they were a disgrace to you, but that you were a disgrace to them" (822–3).

Milton was irate over More's ironic reference to the Marshall engraving, insisting that he acceded to the bookseller's arrangement only "because there was no other [engraver] in the city at that time" (751).[28] And he responds with special fury to More's jibes about his blindness even as he denied knowing about it: "You reproach me with Cyclopean blindness, and, what is more impudent, in the very act of denying that you did this, you do it again," by alluding to his eyes as "removable" like those of witches (750). Milton here reveals a keen sensitivity about his physical appearance, though perhaps not the deep-seated psychic need for self-purification through violent destruction of enemies that Michael Lieb discerns at the core of Milton's last two Defences.[29] Milton takes a fierce but yet comic revenge in his portrait of More and Pontia engaged in a mock-epic battle that leaves More as a grotesque figure with face "engraved" by Pontia. They meet at Salmasius's house, Pontia to make wedding plans, More to renege on his promise; she flies furiously at his face and eyes with "nails unpared"; he defends himself in womanish combat with his own "dreadful nails"; but she triumphs, leaving More "with face in tatters," forced "to hide from the world" (747–50).

Milton found little occasion for direct political comment in this work, but he emphasized his admiration and affection for the two Protestant republics with which

More was associated, praising the United Provinces[30] and especially Geneva. Extolling Geneva's liberty and peace and the civic virtues that sustain it as a republic, he implicitly offers it as a model for England which has not yet managed to settle a republic and which is badly in need of those civic virtues:

> I admire first her zeal and her worship of a purer religion; then I honor almost as much the prudence, fairness, moderation, and constancy in that republic, by which, though hemmed in by narrow boundaries and by threatening and powerful neighbors on both sides, she has for so many years preserved and defended herself in the height of liberty and peace . . . which is the beginning and end of all civil life. (785)

While Milton was concerned with More, parliament, in a forthright assertion of parliamentary sovereignty, sent Cromwell their revised *Instrument of Government*, requiring him to accept all 60 articles. They had done nothing else, deferring Bills for funding the army and navy and the government so as to force Cromwell to continue their sitting beyond the mandated five months. But Cromwell determined to rid himself of their obstruction and, by creative calculation of months on the basis of 28-day lunar months, dismissed parliament on January 22. Their revised constitution died with them, along with any hope of raising the much-needed funds by parliamentary authority, and Cromwell and his council continued to govern by the terms of the original *Instrument*.

If Milton regretted the demise of yet another parliament he probably accepted Cromwell's action as necessary to assure stability and protect religious toleration. Thurloe's spies uncovered a planned Leveller revolt in February and a much more dangerous royalist uprising scheduled for early March. Shortly before their dismissal parliament had unleashed its persecuting zeal on John Biddle, a Socinian who had been arrested on earlier occasions for preaching and publishing anti-Trinitarian doctrine. Parliament arrested him, convicted him, burned his books, and on January 15, 1655 set about to determine a dire punishment for him.[31] Milton, himself on the way to becoming an anti-Trinitarian if not already one, was no doubt glad to see that threat deflected by parliament's dismissal. Released in March, Biddle was soon arrested again for preaching anti-Trinitarianism to a small Socinian congregation in London, but in October Cromwell saved him from the grave danger of a trial by exiling him to the Isle of Scilly with an annual pension. Cromwell's mounting concern for public order prompted an ordinance against Quakers and Ranters (February 15) which affirmed their liberty of conscience but held them liable to arrest as disturbers of the peace if they disrupted church services. Yet Cromwell intervened to release George Fox and some of his followers from a particularly harsh imprisonment, and in private conversation seemed, Fox thought, quite sympathetic to Quaker views.[32] In December, 1655 Cromwell called a conference to consider the readmission of Jews to England; nothing was decided but Cromwell quietly allowed some Jewish immigration and the continuation of Jewish worship in an existing London synagogue. Milton found in Cromwell's tolerationist inclinations his chief reason to continue supporting the Protector, despite his failure to follow *Defensio Secunda*'s proposals for church disestablishment and expanding personal liberty. But Milton was not moved, as his friend Marvell was, to write a lengthy panegyric poem on the first anniversary of Cromwell's reign as Protector, or to celebrate any event in his life and reign.[33]

From October 1654 to May 1655 Milton had little diplomatic correspondence. He may have been given a respite to work on the *Pro Se Defensio*. The letters he did write concerned the promotion of a Protestant League, a matter close to Milton's heart. Cromwell sent parallel letters (October 27) to the King of Sweden and to the consuls and senators of Bremen lamenting the outbreak of hostilities between them that threatened the interests of all Protestants, and urging them to peace (*CPW* V.2, 678–81). In the second letter Cromwell voices, in Milton's Latin, his wish "that the entire name of Protestants should finally by brotherly consent and harmony unite into one" (680). Writing (April 4, 1655) to the French Prince of Tarente who had sought his friendship but was also reconciling with the French court, Cromwell urges him to confess his ancestral Protestant faith openly and to protect it in his homeland, stating that his own primary goal is "to serve either the enlargement, or the preservation, or, most important, the peace of the Reformed church" (682–3). Milton was paid his usual quarter-salary on February 13, 1655, but on April 17, in an economy measure that reduced or eliminated several salaries in the Secretariat, Milton's was reduced from £288 to £150 and made payable for life. This order designates Philip Meadows Secretary for the Latin Tongue and gives Milton no formal title, perhaps reflecting the council's initial intention to pension Milton off to deserved retirement.[34] But they soon reconsidered, or perhaps responded to Milton's unwillingness to accept that status. Like several others for whom the April 17 order was revised or rescinded, Milton's salary was soon increased to £200, placing him on a par with Meadows.[35] As Robert Fallon shows, Milton did a great deal of work throughout Cromwell's Protectorate for Secretary of State Thurloe, who now managed foreign affairs under Cromwell's direction.

The Protector had occasion to realize almost immediately that he needed Milton to produce the impassioned denunciations and stirring calls for Protestant unity occasioned by the slaughter of the Waldensians, a notorious event in the annals of Protestant martyrology. In April, 1655 Carlo Immanuel II, Duke of Savoy, for reasons not fully understood, ordered his army to root out and destroy the Waldensians, or Vaudois, who for centuries had lived in the mountainous regions of the Piedmont practicing what contemporary Protestants saw as a survival of primitive Christianity uncontaminated by Rome. Historically they descended from a late twelfth-century sect led by Pierre Valdes, which was at length excommunicated but guaranteed toleration in certain regions of the Savoy by an edict of 1561. On April 17 troops were sent purportedly to force those living outside the designated regions to withdraw to them or else convert, but on August 24 a massacre began through all the supposedly protected villages. Letters and documents recorded in graphic detail the fighting, burning, pillaging, and savage butchery: women ripped open or impaled on spikes; men nailed upside down to trees; many hacked, tortured, and roasted alive; children ripped apart and their brains eaten; fugitives huddled high in the mountains freezing and starving; men, women, and children flung from precipices; some "tyed Neck and Heels together, and rowled down some Precipices"; "fearful scriechings, made yet more pitiful by the multitude of those Eccho's, which are in those Mountains and Rocks"; scattered bones, "here a Head, and there a Body; here a Leg, and there an Arm."[36] According to a contemporary historian of the affair, Samuel Morland, reports arrived in England, "Letters upon letters, just like *Job's* Messengers . . . with the sad and doleful Tidings," spurring Cromwell to make himself spokesman for the shocked Protestant nations, sending out nine "pathetical and quickening Letters" in May and June, and raising money at home and abroad for the Waldensians' relief.[37] Milton's high rhetoric was called upon for all these letters as well as, probably, for the draft of the bold speech which Cromwell's ambassador extraordinary to Savoy, Samuel Morland, delivered before the Duke on June 24.[38] It allows the duke deniability but describes graphically the horrors done in his name:

> [Cromwell] hath been informed . . . that part of those most miserable people, have been cruelly massacred by your forces, part driven out by violence and forced to leave their native habitations, and so without house or shelter, poor and destitute of all relief, do wander up and down with their wives and children, in craggy and uninhabited places, and Mountains covered with snow. . . . Oh the fired houses which are yet smoking, the torn limbs, and ground defiled with bloud! Virgins being ravished, have afterwards had their wombs stuffed up with gravel and Rubbish, and in that miserable manner breathed out their last. Some men an hundred years old, decrepit with age, and bed-rid, have been burnt in their beds. Some infants have been dashed against the Rocks, others their throats cut, whose brains have with more than Cyclopean cruelty, being boiled and eaten by the Murtherers. . . . Heaven it self seems to be astonied with the cries of dying men. . . . Do not, O thou most high God, do not thou take that revenge which is due to so great wickednesses and horrible villanies! Let thy blood, O Christ, wash away this blood! (*CM* XIII, 485–7)

Six letters prepared by Milton are dated May 25, though they were drafted somewhat earlier. That to the Duke of Savoy[39] was to be delivered by Morland at the time of his speech: it avoids describing the horrors, which Morland would recount verbally, and instead appeals to the duke to rescind his edict and restore the Waldensians to their rights, property, and religious liberty, reminding him "that the inviolable right and power of conscience are in His [God's] possession alone"(*CPW* V, 684–7). Parallel letters to Louis XIV of France and to Cardinal Mazarin – Cromwell's customary practice during the king's minority – were to be delivered by Morland en route to Savoy, to bespeak their influence with the duke (698–701).

The letter to the young king mentions but affects to disbelieve a report that French troops participated in the massacre, and urges him to a policy of toleration as the means to civic peace and to strengthen bonds with Protestant nations. The letter to Mazarin suggests that French toleration of Protestants and aid in the Waldensian enterprise will advance the negotiations then in hand for a treaty between France and England. Letters to the Protestant powers – Charles Gustavus of Sweden, the States General of the United Provinces, the Evangelic Cities of Switzerland, and Frederick III, King of Denmark – sound common themes in much the same language: a review of the barbarities, a report on Cromwell's efforts, a plea to send their protests to Savoy and their aid to the Waldensians, and an invitation to join in some common action if the evil is not redressed. The terms are, however, carefully tailored to the country addressed.[40] Responding imaginatively to these horrors, Milton wrote at about this time (May–June, 1655) his great sonnet, "Avenge O Lord thy slaughter'd Saints," which conflates details and graphic images from the reports Milton was hearing and writing about with echoes of biblical prophetic denunciation.[41] It is discussed on pages 352–4.

Over the next several weeks Milton's state letters continued to deal with this issue. In June Cromwell sent £2,000 from his treasury for the refugees' relief, with a letter (June 7) asking the Senate of Geneva to manage the distribution "in the fairest manner to those who are most needy."[42] The next month Cromwell dispatched an envoy to France, Geneva, and Savoy, with a letter (July 31) to Louis XIV and a brief cover to Mazarin urging the king to redouble his pressure on Savoy and to protect the refugees and all Protestants in areas under French control (708–10). Cromwell's appeals, his threats of invasion, and the Waldensians' own fierce counterattacks bore fruit: Mazarin and the Swiss brokered a treaty (August 18) by which Savoy restored the Waldensians to their liberties and property.

Apparently Milton was not involved in the complex negotiations with Spain which culminated in a war mostly centered in the New World; this so called "Western Design" – an expedition to attack Spanish colonies in the West Indies – was spectacularly unsuccessful save for the capture of Jamaica in May, 1655. Nor was Milton involved in negotiating the alliance with France, formalized in a treaty of peace and commerce signed on October 24. For whatever reason, he had a few months' respite from diplomatic duties after the Waldensian crisis and so had little direct contact with officialdom as Cromwell put in place his scheme for oversight and control of local government by the soon-to-be-infamous major-generals. Proclaimed on October 11, the plan called for dividing the counties of England into ten (later eleven) districts, with the appointment of a major-general to command the militia in each. Their major function was to suppress any royalist insurrections and to destroy the culture that nurtured them by prohibiting cock fights, bear baitings, stage plays, horse races and the like, by ejecting royalist clergy from churches and from positions as private tutors or chaplains, and by inflicting harsh sentences of imprisonment or banishment on known or suspected "malignants." They were also to put down drunkenness, vagrancy, swearing, cursing, blasphemy, and Sabbath breaking, to report on scandalous or unfit ministers and magistrates, and to raise funds for their own maintenance and for the depleted government coffers by collecting a 10 percent levy on royalist property. The laws against royalists were sometimes harshly, sometimes erratically, enforced. And while the major-generals' charge mostly involved seeing that the often lax local magistrates and justices of the peace enforced existing laws, the perception was of a new moral police repressing local pastimes and habits. Cromwell also put forth a new ordinance (August 18) to suppress scandalous books and pamphlets and to regulate printing, and another (September 5) to abolish the few remaining independent newsletters, leaving only two government organs run by Nedham and Thurloe.[43] Milton probably accepted the need to keep close watch on plotters and former malignants and to collect new taxes from royalists. But the orders to regulate morals, censor the press, and settle the church establishment more firmly go directly against his recommendations to Cromwell and the paean to personal liberty in the *Defensio Secunda*. Milton was still willing to work for Cromwell's government, recognizing that he would do more than most to protect religious liberty. But he could not have approved the direction the Protectorate was taking.

In his recurring periods of leisure or lessened activity, Milton worked on some ongoing projects: the early biographers mention a Latin *Thesaurus*, the *History of Britain*, a "*Body of Divinity*" out of the Bible, a *Greek Thesaurus*, and (perhaps) the beginnings of *Paradise Lost*.[44] Edward Phillips states that shortly after More "quitted the field" Milton turned first to his never-completed Latin *Thesaurus* and to the *History*:

> He [then] had leisure again for his own Studies and private Designs; which were his foresaid *History of England*, and a *New Thesaurus Linguae Latinae*, according to the manner of *Stephanus*; a work he had been long Collecting from his own Reading, and still went on with it at times, even very near to his dying day; but the Papers after his death were so discomposed and deficient, that it could not be made fit for the Press; However, what there was of it, was made use of for another Dictionary.[45]

The early biographers also record details of Milton's daily life during such times of leisure, emphasizing his delight in all kinds of music, his temperance in diet and drinking, his affable conversation, and the visits of many friends. He enjoyed company. Aubrey claims that he was much visited by learned foreigners who "importuned [him] to goe into Fr[ance] & Italie"; and that many came to England chiefly "to see O[liver] Protector & Mr. J. Milton" (*EL* 7). His student Richard Jones, the son of his friend Lady Ranelagh, came to read to and write for him on some regular basis. According to Edward Phillips, Lady Ranelagh visited frequently throughout these years, as did "above all" his former student Cyriack Skinner; both lived nearby.[46] In the spring of 1656 Jones left to study at Oxford with a private tutor, Milton's friend Henry Oldenburg, the erstwhile agent for Bremen and a student of science; Milton may have recommended him to Lady Ranelagh. There were also visits from other "particular Friends that had a high esteem for him:" Phillips specifies Andrew Marvell, Marchamont Nedham (presumably not so often as when Milton was nominal licenser for *Politicus*), and Edward Lawrence, elder son of the powerful president of Cromwell's Council of State and perhaps also a former student at the Barbican house. Young Lawrence was a virtuous and studious young man with bright prospects and literary interests, according to Oldenburg and the poet William Davenant.[47] Oldenburg was probably an occasional visitor while he was in London, as were Hartlib (who now lived at Charing Cross), Theodore Haak, John Dury when he was home from his travels, and others of the learned circle that formed around Hartlib and Lady Ranelagh's brother, the scientist Robert Boyle.[48]

Edward Lawrence was the recipient of one sonnet and Cyriack Skinner of two sonnets written by Milton in the winter of 1655–6. All three exhibit and express Milton's delight in warm friendships and the companionship of intelligent young men; Lawrence was about 28 and Skinner 22. Skinner copied part of his into the Trinity manuscript, an indication that he sometimes served as amanuensis for Milton in this period.[49] That sonnet and the one to Lawrence, in the Horatian vein, describe the delights and the value of recreation in pleasant society – a persistent theme of Milton's – and also afford a glimpse of his recreations with these young friends. The other sonnet to Skinner, "Cyriack, this three years day," is occasioned by the three years' anniversary of Milton's total blindness in 1652 – not the precise day, but the year.[50] The sonnet proudly proclaims Milton's capacity to sustain his spirits because he takes pride in having sacrificed his eyes in the service of liberty, a theme Milton sounds with some frequency in these years. At this juncture he wants to assure friends and enemies alike that his terrible affliction has not defeated him; and no doubt he has derived strength from finding ways to continue his studies and his writing. If the cheerfulness seems a bit strained, it gives evidence of Milton's remarkably sanguine temperament. These three sonnets are discussed on pages 352–6.

Milton's nephew John Phillips was no longer a member of his household. Milton probably helped him find some employment in Scotland with his acquaintance from Christ's, Arthur Sandelands.[51] On August 17, 1655, nine days after the publication of Milton's *Pro Se Defensio*, John Phillips burst upon the literary scene with an anonymous poem in rhyming couplets, *A Satyr against Hypocrites*.[52] Sometimes witty and often grossly indecent with its language of stinks and the lechery of "Fat Wives," the poem's ridicule of hypocritical Puritans and their practices recalls Jonson's *Bartholomew Fayre*. It debunks Puritan church services and fast-day sermons for social posturing, canting biblical language, and out-of-tune psalmody, and describes clergy and laity turning immediately after church to gluttony, drunkenness, and fornication. London (Presbyterian) parish clergy preach meekness but are avaricious, ambitious of political power, and eager to control others; ignorant mechanics claim they are called by the Spirit to preach; and Fifth Monarchists cry for war against Antichrist in an orgy of violence: "Fall on, fall on, kill, kill."[53] Milton's reaction to his nephew–pupil's first poetic publication (if he knew it) was probably mixed. Phillips could have picked up some of these views from Milton, who was no friend of establishment clerics of any stripe, and he had had ample opportunity to gain from Milton himself both models of and practice in writing coarse and indecent satire.[54] But Phillips's blanket condemnation of Puritanism is in the vein of royalist satire and at times implies that the old religion was closer to true Christianity.[55] The poem ends with a Milton-like distinction between hypocrites who dwell on the "husk and shell" of religion and those who "By a true knowledge, doe obtaine the fruit."[56] Milton was probably happier with John's translation a few months later (*c.* January 9, 1656) of Bartolomé de las Casas' exposé of Spanish maltreatment of the Indians, dedicated to Cromwell and offered as support for his war against Spain.[57]

From December, 1655 Milton's correspondence for the Protector greatly increased, in part because the other Latin Secretary, Philip Meadows, was appointed on February 19, 1656 as special envoy to Portugal; he left around March 11 and returned in July, but he was then recovering from an attempt on his life. During the several months before the second Protectorate parliament met on September 17, 1656 Milton translated fourteen or so letters about captured ships or goods to be restored, merchants' property seized for debt, or English merchants' claims against foreign parties.[58] Three letters to Portugal in August had larger import. One agrees to renogotiate the clauses Portugal wanted to modify in a treaty just agreed to; the others strongly protest the assault on Meadows and demand that the perpetrators of this "cruel and wicked crime" be punished lest peace between the two countries be endangered.[59]

Milton probably contributed some memorable language to several letters dealing with Cromwell's efforts to promote a Protestant League against Rome and Spain. In January, 1656 Cromwell wrote to the Evangelic Cantons of Switzerland recalling the Waldensian massacre and offering them encouragement and monetary relief in their struggle with the Roman Catholic canton of Schwyz: "Do not allow your laws and confederations – nay your liberty of conscience and your very religion – to be trampled down by the worshippers of idols" (717–18). Several letters address or concern King Charles X of Sweden as the pivot of such an alliance. Cromwell congratulated him (February 7, 1656) on the birth of a son who will be an Alexander to his Philip of Macedon, and also on his conquest of Poland: "we do not doubt that the tearing away by your arms of the Kingdom of Poland from the command of the Pope, as if from the horned beast, and the making of peace with the Duke of Brandenburg, will have great importance for the peace and advantage of the church" (721–2). Even letters for departing or traveling diplomats are placed in the context of Charles X's importance to the Protestant struggle.[60] In August Cromwell sent parallel letters to the United Provinces and to Sweden offering to mediate a dispute

Plate 1 Milton, age ten. Artist unknown.

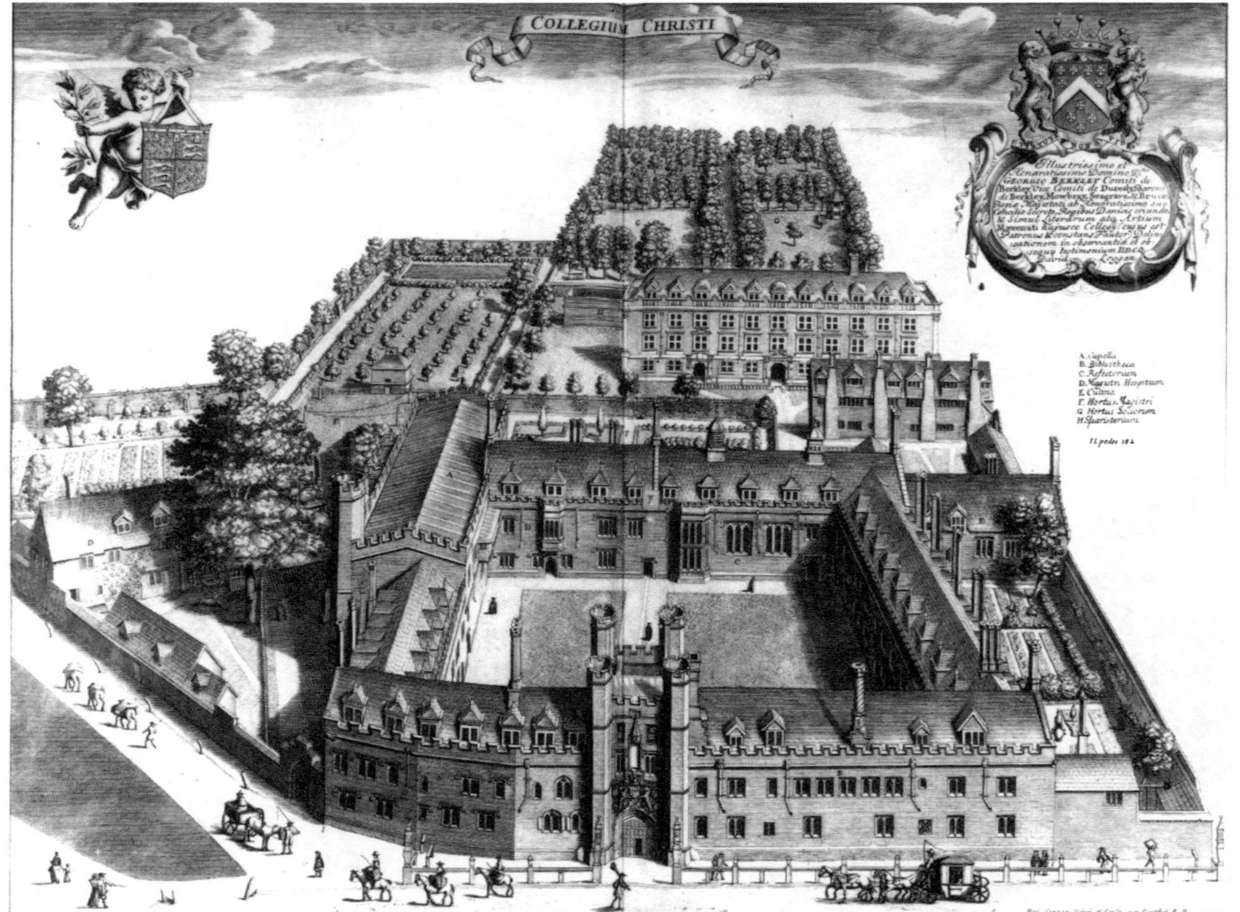

Plate 2 Christ's College in about 1688, from David Loggan, *Cantabrigia Illustrata*, Cambridge, 1690.

Plate 3 The "Oslow" portrait of Milton, by an unknown artist.

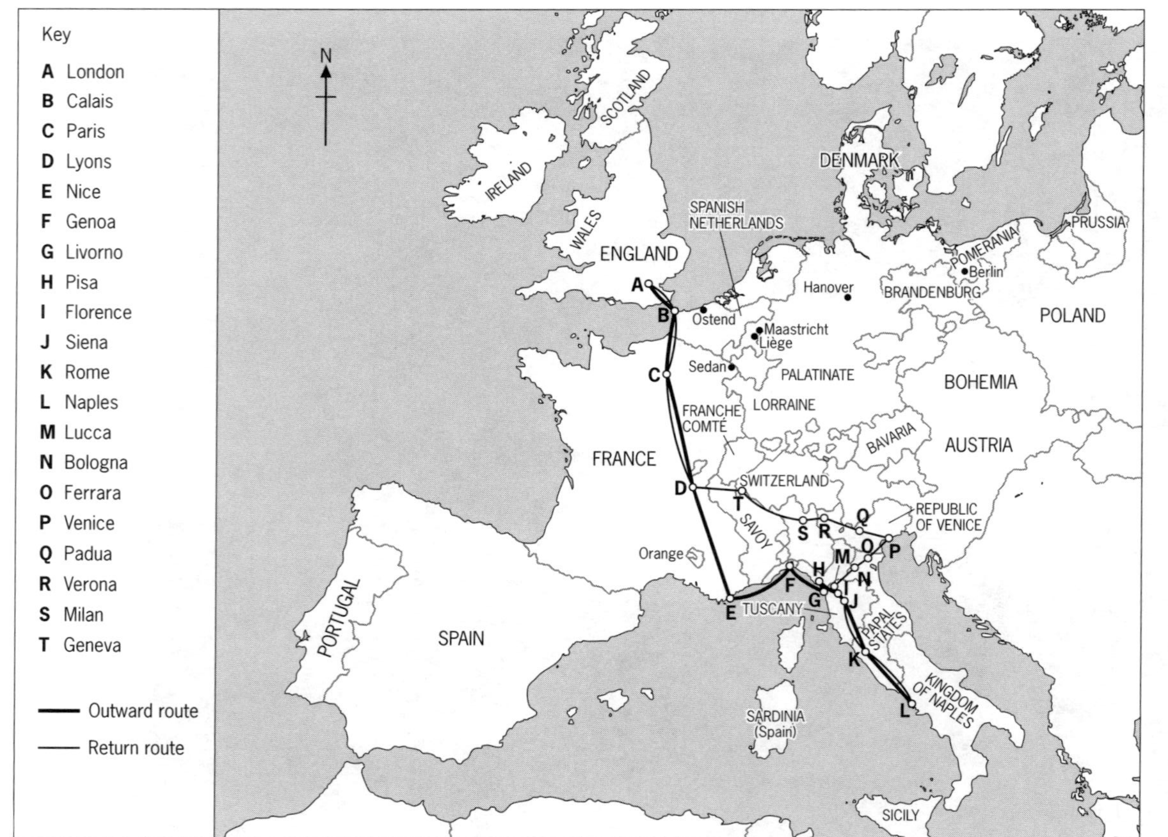

Plate 4 Milton's Italian journey plotted on a map of Europe in 1601.

Plate 5 Cityscape of Florence, *Veduta dell'Arno con Ponte Vecchio disegno* by Israel Silvestre, *c.* 1640.

Plate 6 Milton's house in the Barbican, as it looked in 1864, from the *Illustrated London News*, July 16, 1864.

Plate 7 Engraving of a "Divorcer" from *A Catalogue of the Severall Sects and Opinions*, London, 1646, Broadside.

Plate 8 Engraving by William Marshall, frontispiece to Milton's *Poems*, 1645.

Plate 9 Frontispiece to *Eikon Alethine*.

Plate 10 Milton's house in Petty France, Westminster, in a nineteenth-century engraving published in the *Illustrated London News*, January 9, 1874.

Plate 11 William Marshall's frontispiece to *Eikon Basilike*, 1649.

ΕΙΚΟΝΟΚΛΑ΄ΣΤΗΣ

IN

Anſwer

To a Book Intitl'd

ΕἸΚΩ΄Ν ΒΑΣΙΛΙΚΗ΄,

THE

PORTRATURE of his Sacred MAJESTY
in his *Solitudes* and *Sufferings*.

The Author I. M.

PROV. 28. 15, 16, 17.

15. *As a roaring Lyon, and a ranging Beare, ſo is a wicked Ru-*
ler over the poor people.
16. *The Prince that wanteth underſtanding, is alſo a great op-*
preſſor; but he that hateth covetouſneſſe ſhall prolong his dayes.
17. *A man that doth violence to the blood of any perſon, ſhall fly*
to the pit, let no man ſtay him.

Saluſt. Conjurat. Catilin.

Regium imperium, quod initio, conſervandæ libertatis, atque augendæ reipub. causâ fuerat, in ſuperbiam, dominationemque ſe convertit.

Regibus boni, quam mali, ſuſpectiores ſunt; ſemperque his aliena virtus formidoloſa eſt.

Quidlibet impunè facere, hoc ſcilicet regium eſt.

Publiſhed by Authority.

London, Printed by *Matthew Simmons*, next dore to the gilded Lyon in Alderſgate ſtreet. 1649.

Plate 12 Title page to Milton's *Eikonoklastes*.

Plate 13 William Faithorne's 1658 map of London, showing the general area of Milton's house in Artillery Walk and Bunhill Fields.

Plate 14 Milton's Cottage, Chalfont St Giles.

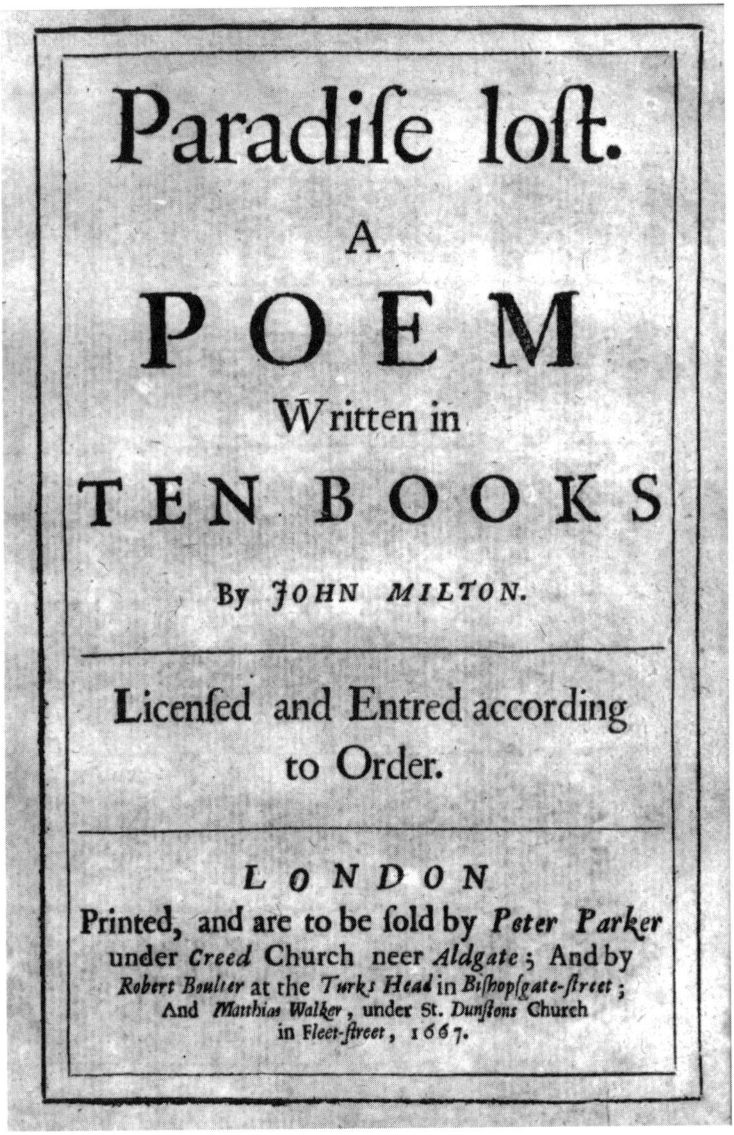

Paradiſe loſt.

A

POEM

Written in

TEN BOOKS

By *JOHN MILTON*.

Licenſed and Entred according to Order.

LONDON

Printed, and are to be ſold by *Peter Parker* under *Creed* Church neer *Aldgate*; And by *Robert Boulter* at the *Turks Head* in *Biſhopſgate-ſtreet*; And *Matthias Walker*, under St. *Dunſtons* Church in *Fleet-ſtreet*, 1667.

Plate 15 Title page, *Paradise Lost*, 1667.

Plate 16 William Faithorne's engraving of Milton, from the frontispiece to the *History of Britain*.

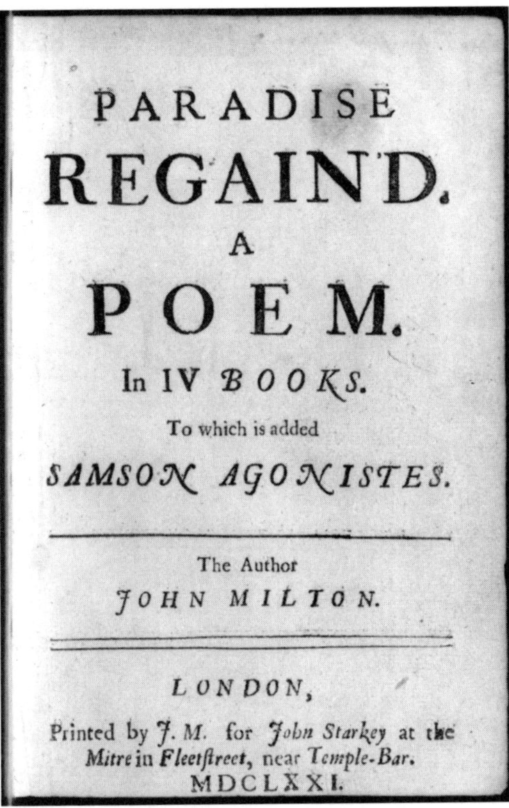

PARADISE
REGAIN'D.
A
POEM.
In IV *BOOKS*.
To which is added
SAMSON AGONISTES.

The Author
JOHN MILTON.

LONDON,
Printed by *J. M.* for *John Starkey* at the *Mitre* in *Fleetstreet*, near *Temple-Bar*.
MDCLXXI.

Plate 17 Title page, *Paradise Regained* and *Samson Agonistes*, 1671.

Plate 18 The engraved stone near the place of Milton's burial, in St Giles Cripplegate.

over Danzig, then under seige by Sweden and defended by Dutch and Danish fleets. To the States General (August 21) Cromwell warns of the great danger to the reformed churches if the United Provinces fall out with Sweden and the Swedish king, "whom God, as we trust, has raised up to be a very brave champion of the orthodox religion," and who is waging a savage war against the "most potent" enemies of the reformed religion.[61] The briefer letter to Charles X rejoices in his victories against the papists but warns him against conflicts with the Dutch and the Danes in the Baltic. The eloquent phrases sound Miltonic:

> Enough and more than enough are the enemies of Protestants everywhere; never have they seemed inflamed with more consuming hate or to have conspired our ruin so utterly. Witness the Alpine valleys flowing not long ago with the blood and carnage of wretches; witness Austria recently shaken with the edicts and proscriptions of its emperor; witness Switzerland. . . . If there should be added to all these evils the dissension of Protestant brethren among themselves . . . the reformed religion itself must be placed in jeopardy and must face the most serious crisis. On the contrary, if all who call themselves Protestants would in fraternal harmony cherish perpetual peace among themselves . . . there would be no reason at all for us to fear what the cunning and the might of the enemy could do to trouble us.[62]

Milton was also involved with the protracted negotiations leading to a military and economic agreement with Sweden that was intended to supplement the 1654 treaty. One sticking point was Charles's desire for a military alliance to aid him in the Baltic and Cromwell's desire that any military action be directed against the Catholic Hapsburgs and Spain. Another was England's effort to interdict the sale of Swedish masts, hemp, and other naval commodities to Spain. The Swedish ambassador, Christiern Bonde, took umbrage at the slow pace of negotiations, which on one occasion he laid to Milton's charge. Bonde complained that on April 21 he delivered to the English commissioners a draft of the treaty provisions he desired and had to wait two weeks for an answer: "it is a scandal that now that Mr Meadowe has gone to Portugal they have no one who can write a decent line of Latin, but the blind Miltonius must translate anything they want done from English to Latin, and one can easily imagine how it goes."[63] Whitelocke's account of the incident (dated May 6, 1656) takes note of Bonde's complaint, which extended to the possible security leaks from the amanuensis, and recorded the commissioners' response: "the Employment of Mr. *Milton* was excused to him, because several other servants of the council fit for that employment, were then absent.[64] This suggests that the government was not above using Milton's blindness as an excuse for their own delaying purposes. Obviously there were other competent Latinists around and Milton probably could have worked more quickly had that been desired. The episode suggests, however, that Milton was sometimes hard pressed to fulfill his duties during the months he was alone in the Latin secretary's role. If he heard about Bonde's slighting comment, it surely rankled.

During the spring and summer of 1656 Milton probably had his attention drawn again to the activities of his younger nephew. In March or April John Phillips edited and published a collection of ribald and scurrilous poems and lampoons in the Cavalier mode: bawdy verses, suggestive songs of lovemaking and dalliance, drinking songs, praises of tobacco, poems to Stuart royalty and court ladies, and a few anti-Puritan pieces.[65] The Council of State judged it to contain "much scandalous, lascivious, scurrilous, and profane matter" and on April 25 condemned it to the fire; the Press Act of August 18, 1655 was directed primarily against this kind of book, though it was only occasionally invoked. John Phillips and his printer Nathanial Brooke were fined and ordered to appear before the council, but there is no record that they did so; conceivably Milton intervened or the council excused Phillips as a favor to Milton. On April 30 copies of the book were burnt in front of the Old Exchange.[66] Milton may, or may not, have seen this publication as a rebellion against the values inculcated by his educational program and, he would have supposed, by Phillips's residence in his household as pupil and sometime assistant. This is the kind of book Milton denounced in *The Reason of Church-Government* as the product of "libidinous and ignorant Poetasters" who bring "corruption and bane" to youth,[67] and it was further subversive in evoking the ethos and personages of the Stuart court. But classicist Milton, steeped in Martial and Ovid and Petronius, would not be shocked by the contents, nor did he ever suppose that the way to improve public morality is to suppress or burn ribald books. Whatever the psychological dynamics, Milton and his younger nephew seem to have had little personal association after this episode.

Edward Phillips's first fruits would have been more acceptable: quite competent translations (February, 1656) of two small Spanish novels by Juan Pérez de Montalbán and an edition later that year of Drummond of Hawthornden's *Poems*.[68] Edward returned to London from Shrewsbury sometime after July 4, 1655 and was evidently in frequent contact with his uncle, sometimes acting as scribe or assistant. He presented copies of Milton's *Eikonoklastes* and *Tenure of Kings and Magistrates* along with his own Spanish novels to the Bodleian Library on June 11, 1656.[69] Interestingly, his *Mysteries of Love & Eloquence* (1658), a conduct book for wits and courtiers on "the Arts of Wooing and Complementing," also contains a "new Invented Art of Logick" whose organization and definitions are largely cribbed from Milton's as yet unpublished *Artis Logicae*, here simplified and presented as an English dialogue.[70] Later, both brothers took on other assignments for Brooke in the vein of Cavalier licentiousness.[71]

In May or June, 1656 Milton wrote to his erstwhile pupil Richard Jones and to his friend Henry Oldenburg, now settled in Oxford as tutor to Jones, who was not enrolled in any college but meant to read in the library and attend some lectures. Oldenburg was eager to associate with the so called "Invisible College" of Baconian natural philosophers and experimental scientists around Oxford. Milton's letters suggest that he was dubious about the benefits of the Oxford sojourn for either of them, and that he retained his strong distaste for the university ethos. His letter to Jones was a response to a letter from him (now lost), which Lady Ranelagh carried but did not deliver for some fifteen days. After noting with pleasure and reciprocating the young man's expressions of affection, Milton, in the role of teacher, corrects his values and attitudes. He warns Jones that the beauty of Oxford he so praises will not be truly felicitous unless Oxford contributes "as much to the character of the inhabitants as it does to their delight" (*CPW* VII, 489). And the Bodleian Library might more properly be called "a storeroom of books than a library" unless students come from it "furnished with the best education." He urges Jones to display "zeal and industry," to obey Oldenburg's "firm and friendly precepts," and to take as an example of virtue and piety "that most excellent woman your mother." Jones visited Milton on June 25, carrying a letter from Oldenburg and taking back Milton's reply. Oldenburg also waxed eloquent about Oxford's natural beauty and proclaimed his desire to study nature "really closely," to eschew controversy and pursue truth. Oxford, he assures Milton, has men devoted to the study of both nature and the liberal arts, though many "still tread the customary path, and never stop brawling over both divine and natural subjects." He ends by commenting on new evidence from an ancient Chinese calendar telling against the theory that humans existed on earth before Adam (490–1). Milton excuses his brief reply (he was "quite busy" when Jones brought Oldenburg's letter), but he again voices skepticism about Oxford's value for them: "what that retreat contributes except plenty of books, I do not know, and I should think the companions of your studies whom you have found there would be such because of the very nature of the place rather than because of its instruction" (492). He agrees about the "empty quibbling" so many engage in, "lest they seem to be doing absolutely nothing worthy of the many taxes by which they are supported at grievous public expense." But he does not think the ancient Chinese calendar can add any authority to the Mosaic books. He passes along greetings from Cyriack Skinner, reciprocating Oldenburg's – a further indication that Skinner was often in Milton's company during these years.

About three months later (September 21) Milton answered another letter from Jones, now lost, sending it by Lady Ranelagh, who was about to leave for Ireland where she was to remain for several years tending to family business. Her departure, Milton wrote, "must grieve us both extremely," since "to me also she has stood in the place of all relations."[72] That Milton parallels his relationship with her to that of mother and son indicates how much he will miss this dear friend. In his mentor role, Milton assures Jones that his fondness for him will increase "the more you show me of your sincere disposition and worthwhile accomplishments" (*CPW* VII, 493–4). He approves Jones's confidence about success in his studies, but not his continued pleasure in Oxford: "Your saying that Oxford does not displease you does not lead me to believe that you have become any more proficient or wiser there: *that* you will have to show me by far different proofs." Moreover, Jones seems to admire overmuch the victories of princes "and similar matters in which force prevails" and he should learn rather to admire exemplars of "justice and moderation." Milton closes with "my fondest greetings to your companion, the distinguished Henry Oldenburg." Five days later the Swiss minister John Zollikofer called on Milton and asked for his autograph. Milton had an amanuensis write in Greek the motto he had used before, from 2 Corinthians 12:9, "I am made perfect in weakness." He attempted a signature but his last name ran off the end of the page and he completed it on the next line. Zollikofer wrote on this page, "The famous blind Milton put this here."[73]

That summer Cromwell sent out writs for a new parliament. Elections and the sitting of a new parliament gave rise to new republican treatises – necessarily somewhat covert – rising to a new opportunity to conform the state more closely to republican principles. Milton might well have been given a copy of *The Healing Question*, written by his old friend Henry Vane but published anonymously; it was intended to reconcile parliamentary republicans and those in and out of the army who were committed to a government of army patriots and sectarian saints.[74] Of necessity, Vane makes some place for a "single person" and allows that for the present, elections must be restricted to the "honest party," but he holds firmly to the sovereignty of parliament as the people's representative and the right to elect successive parliaments as the "proper root" of all civil liberty. He called for the voluntary subordination of the army and Cromwell to parliament and implicitly repudiates the *Instrument of Government*, proposing something like a constitutional convention in which carefully chosen representatives would establish fundamentals, including guarantees of religious and civil liberty.[75] It was not covert enough. Vane was arrested, refused to put up £5,000 as security that he would do nothing "to prejudice the present government," and was remanded to house arrest at Carisbrooke Castle in the Isle of Wight (where King Charles had been kept) from August 21 until December 11.

Milton was likely given a copy of *The Excellencie of a Free-State* which his friend Marchamont Nedham published in June without his name though hardly anonymously, since it contained a series of essays, somewhat revised, from 1651–2 issues of *Mercurius Politicus* that Milton had licensed.[76] The work was registered with the Stationers in November, 1655, then hurried into print when elections were called. Ostensibly a defense of the Protectorate from royalists' subversive advice to bypass parliament and govern by force of arms – thereby making a Stuart restoration more attractive – it in fact cleverly attacks Cromwell for doing just that. Nedham's constantly repeated thesis is that parliament as the people's representative must exercise sovereign power in the state: "the right, liberty, welfare, and safety of a people consists in a due succession of their supreme Assemblies."[77] He extrapolates from Machiavelli and from the example of republics in Athens, Sparta, Rome, the United Provinces, Venice, and Switzerland a long list of the advantages of a republic, and he urges Cromwell to imitate those famous leaders who declined power for themselves and secured the people's liberty in a free state.[78] While the conquered part after a civil war cannot immediately share in government, he insists that the well-affected must be allowed their right to elect and be elected to the representative assembly: "however they may abuse it, it is their right to have it."[79] Nedham got away with this bold gesture and remained editor of *Politicus*. No doubt the government saw the wisdom of keeping this keenly intelligent polemicist, with his serviceable pen and very flexible principles, from moving into overt opposition.

Through Cyriack Skinner Milton probably obtained a copy of the important republican manifesto, *The Common-Wealth of Oceana,* which James Harrington rushed into print in October, 1656 and dedicated to the Lord Protector.[80] If it had not been temporarily confiscated, it would have been out by the opening of parliament.[81] Under the guise of a utopia, Harrington represents Cromwell as the Archon Olphaeus Megaletor (Oliver the great-hearted) who, like a Moses or a Lycurgus, founded a state on "scientific" principles that ensure its permanence: an agrarian law to ensure widespread distribution of property, and a two-house legislature, comprised of a senate to discuss and propose laws, and a 1,050-man assembly to vote on them as the people's representative. The Archon also established complex institutions modeled in some respects on Venice: elaborate systems of elections and voting to produce ever more refined choices of representatives; legislatures, national and local, balanced between permanence and rotation; and annually elected magistrates. Central to Harrington's republicanism is the principle that good institutions will automatically produce good men. Most Puritans, including Cromwell and Milton, held the opposite principle: that only good men, variously defined, could produce a good government. Cromwell, ostensibly cast as the hero of this work, was in fact its antihero.[82] He could hardly miss the lesson at the end of the tale, when Olphaeus Megaletor solemnly resigns his power to parliament and retires to private life, after which he is called back by a grateful government to head the army and accepts that office from the legislature as one subordinate to it.[83]

In the weeks just before and after parliament convened on September 17, 1656, several noted republicans and royalists were incarcerated or forced to give security for loyalty to the Protectorate. Among those elected, about ninety-three republicans and other known opponents of the Protectorate were excluded, though some were later admitted. This parliament voted money for the war with Spain and mostly supported Cromwell's policies on the church, though they were less disposed than he to tolerate the more extreme sects. The *cause célèbre* of that autumn was an act of apparent blasphemy by the Quaker James Nayler, that forced the constitutional issue of parliament's right to determine religious matters without the Protector's assent. On October 24, Nayler enacted a symbolic performance at Bristol of Christ's entry into Jerusalem on Palm Sunday, accompanied by a few women singing "Hosanna in the Highest."[84] He was arrested and sent to London; a ten-day debate by the entire parliament ended in his conviction for the "horrid blasphemy" of claiming, so his accusers maintained, to be the divine Christ. The Blasphemy Act of August 9, 1650 called for six months' imprisonment for a first offense of "atheistic, blasphemous and execrable opinions," but parliament thought that much too mild for Nayler. He barely escaped the death penalty and was punished savagely: on December 18 he was given more than three hundred lashes; on December 27 his forehead was branded with the letter B, his tongue was bored through with a red-hot iron, and he was remanded to Bridewell at parliament's pleasure. Cromwell, through various spokesmen, attempted to influence parliament toward moderation and on December 26 questioned their legal right to proceed without his consent, but he did not countermand their order.[85] In a speech to some army officers on February 27, 1657 he used this case to argue the need for a second house of parliament: "they [this parliament] stand in need of a check or balancing power for the Case of James Nayler might happen to be your own case. By their judicial power they fall upon life and member, and doth the Instrument enable me to control it?"[86]

For Milton the great event of autumn, 1656 was his new marriage after more than four years as a widower. As required by law, the intention of marriage was published three times, between Milton and Katherine Woodcock of the parish of St Mary the Virgin, Aldermanbury. Milton's early biographers say nothing about how and when they met, or how long they had known each other, Edward Phillips reporting only that Katherine was the daughter of one "Captain Woodcock of Hackney" (*EL* 77). What claim Katherine's father, William Woodcock, had to that rank is unclear; he was apparently a spendthrift who at his death in 1642 or 1643 left his wife and four daughters very badly off. Her cousin, Sir Thomas Vyner, a goldsmith, banker, and alderman of London, who was also a treasurer for funds to relieve the Waldensians, may have known Milton and promoted the marriage to secure Katherine's future.[87] She was then twenty-eight and living in London; Milton was within a month of his forty-eighth birthday. They were married on November 12, probably at the Guildhall, by Sir John Dethicke, an alderman and justice of the peace.[88] The Marriage Act, with which Milton was in entire accord, called for a civil ceremony. If Katherine was, as I think, the subject of Milton's sonnet, "Mee thought I saw my late espoused saint,"[89] then this marriage, though brief, was blessed: Milton found in Katherine "love, sweetness, goodness," and delight. As mistress of the house in Petty France she evidently made Milton's life and that of his three daughters easier, more comfortable, and more pleasant; John Ward noted, on the authority of Milton's daughter Deborah, that she was "Very indulgent to her children in law."[90] Anne was then ten, Mary eight, and Deborah four-and-a-half.

In January, 1657 a plot to assassinate Cromwell and burn Whitehall in preparation for a royalist invasion from Europe gave additional impetus to parliament's disposition to settle the government in more traditional, monarchical forms, to make Cromwell king, and to secure the succession. They put an end on January 29 to the thoroughly unpopular major-generals, and the policing of the counties reverted to the ordinary magistracy. From February to May they were at work on a new constitution with Cromwell's monarchy as its capstone, but after much vacillation he refused that title on May 8, moved especially by the continuing fierce opposition from all levels of the army.[91] As enacted, the new constitution, *The Humble Petition and Advice* and its *Supplement,* confirmed Cromwell as Protector and empowered him to choose his successor, making the office quasi-hereditary; a second legislative body known officially as the "Other House" but familiarly as the House of Lords was to contain some forty to seventy persons with life tenure, nominated by the Protector and approved by the Commons; and the Council of State was redefined as a privy council with permanent membership. It determined strict qualifications for voting and eligibility for office, but left parliament as judge of members' qualifications,[92] and required that the Protector's council and great officers be approved by both houses. It also mandated an established church and required all ministers on public maintenance to subscribe to a Confession of Faith – to be agreed by the Protector and the parliament. Toleration was accorded most Protestants, but with more exclusions than in the *Instrument*: Catholics, Laudian Anglicans, anti-Trinitarians, blasphemers, and those who practice profaneness (Ranters) or revile ministers (Quakers).[93]

Milton left no record of his opinion about the change of government but some constants in his thought afford a basis for judgment. He believed, with Aristotle and Machiavelli, that forms of government must respond to historical circumstances and correspond to the nature of the people; and he had seen no reason to revise his conclusion in the *Defensio Secunda* that the English people are as yet wanting in republican civic virtue, making some kind of Protectorate necessary. But he could not have approved of the *Petition and Advice*, whose provisions depart much farther than the *Instrument* from republican forms and from his own primary desiderata: broad religious liberty, church disestablishment, and an uncensored press. He would have been pleased that Cromwell refused the crown, having warned him in the *Defensio Secunda* that to become a king would be a species of idolatry. And he was perhaps reassured by the fact that Cromwell's personal style remained plain and non-regal.[94] But he surely found idolatry enough in the trappings of monarchy associated with Cromwell's elaborate inauguration: the purple velvet robe with ermine, the richly gilt Bible, the sword of state, the massy gold scepter, the trumpet blasts, the cries of "God save the Lord Protector." Yet Milton did not align himself with the Protectorate's hardcore republican enemies and would have been dismayed if he learned that his *Tenure of Kings and Magistrates* was cited by Edward Sexby in *Killing no Murder* to support a call for Cromwell's assassination as a tyrant.[95] But he would have enjoyed the trenchant irony in the series of witty articles by his friend Nedham in *Mercurius Politicus.* Playing off Harrington's fiction, Nedham constructs a story of visitors from Oceana, along with their Archon and "that wondrous wise Republican called *Mercurius Politicus*" landing in Utopia, "where the world has run madding here in disputations about Government" and the wits are afflicted with much scribbling about its forms. The senators have decided that they were wrong about liberty and the principles of natural right and freedom; recognizing now that forms of government are indifferently good, they are turning from a failed republic back to a monarchy with three estates. The narrator claims that he also has given over belief in the superiority of republics to monarchies, having now learned that dissent is faction.[96] The last letter reports that he now repudiates Harrington's schemes "and all the Builders of Castles in the air."[97]

During these agitations and changes in the autumn, winter, and spring of 1656–7 Milton's diplomatic correspondence chiefly involved protests on behalf of wronged shipmasters or merchants.[98] A few other letters concerned Protestant unity. In November Milton translated a letter to Cromwell from Frederick III of Denmark voicing the king's concern that Sweden's war with Poland would eventuate in wider hostilities and damage to trade.[99] Cromwell's answer (December 4) recalls the Alpine valleys "recently overflowing with blood and gore," and warns that "Protestants will . . . suffer the utmost hazard and destruction" unless Denmark and Sweden and all other Protestant powers maintain fraternal harmony (*CPW* V.2, 777–9). A March letter to the Landgrave of Hesse commends him for efforts to make peace between Lutherans and Calvinists and compares his own similar projects promoted "through our friend Dury," setting forth an ideal of brotherly dissent that eschews force or bitterness (782–3). In April Milton prepared the credentialling letter for Richard Bradshaw as envoy to the Great Duke of Moscovy, as well as secret instructions directing him to try to detach Russia from the coalition against Sweden.[100]

Milton's personal correspondence during these months indicates that he was giving time and thought to books and scholarly projects, and that his circle of friends and scholarly acquaintances had enlarged. Four days before his marriage he answered a letter (now lost) from Peter Heimbach, a young man[101] who had visited London – and Milton – before and who now wrote, at Milton's request, to report on the price of atlases published in Amsterdam. The affection and bantering tone of Milton's response and his expressed eagerness for Heimbach's return suggest that he had become a friend. Complaining of the price quoted, 130 Dutch florins, Milton observes ruefully that the "furnishing of a library seems to have become no less costly than that of a villa," and that, since a blind man cannot enjoy maps, "I fear that the more I paid for the book, the more I should mourn my loss" (*CPW* VII, 496). But he wants Heimbach to bring back more information: how many volumes are in the work and which edition is "fuller and more adequate."[102] December 28 brought a letter from Oldenburg commenting on the historical inaccuracy of celebrating Christmas on December 25 and linking the "Bacchanalian orgies" of Christians on that day to Roman Saturnalia. He complains that Oxford is "barren of new ideas" (Milton obviously approved that sentiment), and sends greetings to the "excellent Lawrence" who now does "active service for the state" (495–6). He knows that Milton is close to Edward Lawrence, now 23 and just elected to parliament. In March, 1657 Milton had some part in helping the grandson of Edmund Spenser recover lands confiscated from him in Ireland; Cyriack Skinner cites this as an example of Milton's readiness to help persons of "Wit or Learning" of whatever party.[103]

On March 24, 1657 Milton answered a letter (now lost) from a French scholar and book collector, Emery Bigot, who had called on Milton during a recent visit to England and now wrote for help on a scholarly project. He wanted some doubtful passages checked in his copy of the *Modus Tenendi Parliamentum*, a late medieval treatise about Saxon laws and customs, and asked if the original was in the Tower. Milton had cited that work in the *Defensio* and it was a staple in republican arguments for the sovereignty of parliament.[104] Milton attended to the commission with exemplary thoroughness, calling on his network of scholar friends. He wrote that he had the passages checked against manuscripts owned by John Bradshaw and John Cotton, and that William Ryley, "with whom I am on familiar terms," confirms that there is no copy among the Tower documents in his charge (*CPW* VII, 497–8). Milton also rose quickly to Bigot's offer to obtain books for him. He asks for six histories: three volumes just published in an ongoing edition of the Byzantine historians, one of them a metrical chronicle of the world from the Creation to AD 1081.[105] These requests suggest that Milton was giving serious thought to history and to his epic. Amusingly, frugal Milton managed to indicate his hope to have the books "as cheaply as you can" even as he declined to make that request directly, since the books would have had a fixed price. To Bigot's expressions of admiration for his wise conversation and his courage in bearing his affliction, he responds by restating his belief in the interconnection of life and art, relating it here to issues of authorial originality and inner vision as well as to his continued study of books:

> If I can succeed so that I seem in mind and manners as I seem in my best writings, I shall myself both have added weight to the writings and received greater fame, no matter how small, from them in return, since I shall seem less to have taken what is honest and laudable from the most distinguished authors than to have brought it forth, pure and unalloyed, from the depths of my minds and spirit. I am glad therefore that you are convinced of my peace of mind in this severe loss of sight and in my willingness and eagerness to receive foreign guests. Why should I not quietly bear a loss of light which I expect is not so much lost and recalled as drawn inward to sharpen rather than dull the eye of the mind? For that reason I am not angry at written words nor do I entirely cease studying them, severely though they have punished me. (*CPW* VII, 497)

In the interval between parliament's adjournment on June 26, 1657, the day after Cromwell's investiture, and its return on September 29, Cromwell set about remodeling the council and creating the Other House. Milton prepared only a few letters for him: five concerning the usual private cases – captured ships, goods, and prisoners[106] – and a few others arising from Denmark's declaration of war on Sweden in May, 1657. Milton prepared a credentialling letter (August 20, 1657) for William Jephson, sent by Cromwell as envoy to Sweden to express his dismay and offer his services as mediator, "to avert those calamities, which will necessarily be inflicted out of this war upon the common cause of religion" (*CPW* V.2, 793–4).[107]

A letter to the rulers of Hamburg introduces and seeks protection for Philip Meadows, en route to Denmark as Cromwell's envoy on the same peacemaking mission (793–800). A letter in September to Frederick William, Elector of Brandenburg praises his "shining faith and constancy" in retaining an alliance with Sweden despite surrounding enemies (803–4); ironically, the Elector made peace with Poland on September 19 and agreed to join the coalition against Sweden. In December Milton also produced credentialling letters for George Downing, sent as envoy to the United Provinces to deal with the worsening Anglo-Dutch relations.[108]

These few duties left Milton ample time for his own writing and personal affairs.[109] Also, in early September he was given more help, including the assistant he had earlier asked for, Andrew Marvell.[110] Anthony á Wood notes that Marvell became "very intimate and conversant" with Milton while he served as his assistant,[111] and Milton surely took pleasure in their close association. At about this time, perhaps, the young poet John Dryden was also employed in Thurloe's office for occasional duties.[112] A remarkable happenstance, that the three best poets of the age should be together at the same time in Cromwell's bureaucracy! On October 19 a daughter was born to Milton and Katherine, "between 5 and 6 in the morning," according to the record in his Bible.[113] She was named for her mother. Sometime that year Milton was visited by another of those young European students on their grand tour, 21-year-old Johan Lassenius who was to become a well-known Lutheran theologian.[114] Milton's treatise *Of Education* continued to interest the Hartlib circle: Hartlib sent a copy to the noted mathematician and astronomer Nicolaus Mercator, then resident tutor at Petworth, who termed it "most reasonable," and wished that "our method of teaching was so well designed as that writing advises."[115] Throughout the year Milton could have heard that several of his books, both tracts and poems, had been quoted or advertised for sale.[116]

Milton continued to exchange letters with Oldenburg and Richard Jones, who had left Oxford (to Milton's evident satisfaction) and were residing at Saumur in France. Oldenburg's letter of June 27/July 7 reports on their pleasant journey and safe arrival, expresses affectionate eagerness for a letter from Milton, and passes on the unwelcome news that Alexander More had been elected to the pastorate at Charenton. Somewhat awkwardly he explains his decision not to distribute copies of Milton's *Pro Se Defensio* as Milton had requested because the people there generally approve More's preaching and are paying scant attention to his unsavory life. Oldenburg was clearly unwilling to court unpopularity by associating himself with Milton's quarrel (*CPW* VII, 499–500). Milton's response (August 1) accepts Oldenburg's excuse, but with a not-so-gentle reproach: let him cast away the books if they are burdensome, though Milton thinks they might help to block More's appointment. Rubbing it in, he observes that "a certain learned friend of mine" who was at Saumur last winter (probably Marvell, who was there with his pupil William Dutton in 1656) wrote that Milton's book, which he had passed around to learned men, was much in demand (502–3). Milton's letter to Jones on the same day offers genial teacherly advice: Jones did well to spurn the temptations of Paris for Saumur, but he must not thirst overmuch for Saumur wine unless he dilutes it "with more than a fifth part of the more liberal drink of the Muses"; he should listen to Oldenburg and thereby please his excellent mother; and he must strive to "return to us upright and as accomplished as you can." Milton says he will find that "the most joyful thing of all" (503–4). Oldenburg's reply (October 4/14) reports gossip: Queen Christina is to visit, but people think three queens on the ground – Christina, the French Queen Maria Theresa and the exiled English Queen Henrietta Maria – are rather too many. Jones and he will not go to Italy because of the plague. More is to be presented at Charenton and thinks that Milton's answer has only wounded Milton himself. Oldenburg assures Milton, with some embarrassment, that he would never cast away his writings, "which speak things worthy of immortality" (504–5), and closes with greetings to "your excellent wife" and to Lawrence.

In two letters to Henry de Brass, whom Milton addresses as a young person of distinction and promise, he expatiates on the writing of history. At some visit, de Brass and Milton had discussed the relative merits of Tacitus and Sallust and the young man wrote Milton (in letters now lost) with further observations and questions. Replying (July 15, 1657) with his usual courtesy to intelligent young men who seek him out as an internationally renowned scholar, Milton praises him for traveling to gain "richer learning from every source," though he is already able "to impart knowledge to others" and will soon be equal to anyone in learning. Then he responds to the questions, "lest I seem wholly unresponsive to your great need for my authority." He reaffirms "that I prefer Sallust to any other Latin historian whatever," and that he finds Tacitus worthy chiefly because "he imitated Sallust with all his might" (*CPW* VII, 500–1). That comment registers a moral as well as a stylistic preference. His own analyses in the *History of Britain* found a model in Sallust's interpretative narrative of the Roman republic: the expulsion of kings gave rise to the virtues of industry and justice that called a republic into being; it flourished in adversity but declined in prosperity as avarice and ambition took root. Milton might also see Sallust's eloquent denunciations of corruption and the dangers of military rule as a lesson for the Cromwellian court.[117] To the young man's query as to how a historian can acquire a style equal to the deeds he reports, as Sallust dictates, Milton repeats his familiar equation of writer and subject:

> He who would write worthily of worthy deeds ought to write with no less largeness of spirit and experience of the world than he who did them, so that he can comprehend and judge as an equal even the greatest, and having comprehended, can narrate them gravely and clearly in plain and temperate language. (501)

Milton sets down other principles for writing history: not to use the ornate language of an orator, not to break up the narrative by injecting frequent maxims or judgments, not to invent or conjecture but tell the truth, and to join brevity of words with abundance of matter. De Brass evidently wrote back to question Milton's prohibition of maxims, citing Aristotle's *Rhetoric* on the uses of aphorism. On December 16, after his usual apologies for tardiness, Milton replied a little brusquely that Aristotle was talking about rhetoric, not history, and refers the young man to a reading list – Polybius, Dionysius of Halicarnassus, Diodorus, Cicero, Lucian, and others – whose precepts will help him understand what is suitable to a historian (506–7). Milton's own practice makes clear that he is objecting to the the interposition of *sententiae*, though obviously not to the pointing of moral lessons implicit in the narrative itself.

Milton clearly has been thinking about writing history. He had laid his *History of Britain* aside in 1649 when called to government service, turned back to it after completing the *Pro Se Defensio* in 1655, and before or during 1657 likely completed a draft of the remaining segment – the end of Book IV, and Books V and VI – dealing with the internal wars of the Saxon kingdoms and the recurring Danish invasions, from about 731 to the Norman Conquest in 1066.[118] His grand plan was to bring his history down to his own day, but these last books reveal that he was tiring of the project and the Norman Conquest made a suitable place to pause; they also suggest that he meant to make the work available soon. He wants to piece together a smooth, orderly account of his nation from the best sources available to him, revealing moral and political lessons and providential patterns that may profit the English in their present political crises.

Milton finds this new subject matter and the "monkish" historians that report it wearisome – "so many bare and reasonless actions, so many names of Kings one after another, acting little more then mute persons in a Scene." To make it less so he has "studiously omitted" ecclesiastical history – "the long Bead-roll of Archbishops, Bishops, Abbots, Abesses, and thir doeings" – as well as the local history "better harp'd at in *Camden* and other Chorographers." In part this is an effort to separate civic history from some allied kinds, but it also reflects Milton's concern with narrative style: he declines to "wrincle the smoothness of History with rugged names of places unknown" (*CPW* V.1, 239). It registers as well his perspective as a radical Independent. Saxon church history was a topic of considerable interest for Church of England polemicists, who found precedents before the Conquest for a national church largely free of Roman control.[119] But Milton found little to choose between the English church before and after the Conquest. His history traces the steadily increasing subordination of the Saxon church to Rome, as well as the subjection of Saxon kings to monks and priests, who led them to build and enter monasteries to indulge "religious Idleness" and "mistaken Chastitie," or else to go on pilgrimage when they should be defending England.[120]

For his Saxon history Milton uses, among others, William of Malmesbury and Abraham Wheloc's translations of Bede's *Church History* and the *Anglo-Saxon Chronicle*.[121] And, as in the earlier books, he often invites the reader to share his intense skepticism about such "monkish" sources. The story about a miraculous revelation of the murder of Kenelm he will leave "to be sought by such as are more credulous than I wish my readers to be"; the story of King Edgar as victim of a bed-trick is "fitter for a Novel then a History; but as I find it in *Malmsbury*, so I relate it"; and the story of William the Conqueror ordering his men to spare the countryside he thinks borrowed by the Monks from similar stories about Alexander and Caesar.[122] Milton regrets that in Latin translation he could make little sense of the "extravagant fansies and metaphors" in poems from the *Anglo-Saxon Chronicle* celebrating the Battle of Brunanburh (308–9). Had he wished to use those sources, Milton would have been hard pressed to find Anglo-Saxon scholars to read them to him; in any case, his purpose is not original scholarship but producing an educative humanist narrative.

Some patterns and lessons are repeated from the first segment of the *History*. Again, Milton finds several wicked queens driven by ambition and passion, though also a few worthy ones whose qualities surpass what is usual in women: the martial Elfled was possessed of "vertues more then female" (313); Godiva was "a woman of great praise" (386); and Edith was "commended much for beauty, modesty, and, beyond what is requisite in a woman, learning" (374). And again he finds that the English overvalue war and martial bravery.[123] Treating the Saxon period, Milton can now emphasize some elements of the so called "Saxon myth" invoked by many defenders of the revolution, according to which Englishmen's liberties are embedded in Saxon laws and institutions, and the Norman Conquest brought in its wake feudal oppression and royalist absolutism. Milton's *History* finds that some Saxon kings were rightful targets of tyrannicide; that several kings were chosen by some electorate and bound themselves to observe the ancient Saxon laws; and that Edward the Confessor codified the immemorial common law guaranteeing Englishmen's liberties.[124] He also points to several formal compacts testifying that sovereignty was seen to be vested in the people and only delegated to monarchs upon conditions. Ethelred in exile was restored by "the Nobility and States of *England*" upon his promise "to govern them better then he had done . . . [and] to consent in all things to thir will" (348–9). And William the Conqueror at his coronation gave "his Oath at the Altar in the presence of all the people, to defend the Church, well govern the people, maintain right Law, prohibit rapine and unjust judgment" (402). But Milton elides one element of the Saxon myth that he had emphasized in the *Defensio*: that the ancient constitution vested sovereign power in parliament with the king subordinate to it.[125] This concept of the ancient constitution would provide support for traditional institutions and Milton was not eager to encourage the Protector's moves toward a quasi-royal "single person" and a two-house parliament. Also, Milton's recent experience with parliaments bent on religious repression no doubt gave him pause, highlighting the problem of the tyranny of the majority in a sovereign representative. He did not, like Harrington, Nedham, and Vane, develop a new republican paradigm in the mid-1650s, but like them he found the best models for a free commonwealth in ancient Greece and Rome, and in modern Venice, Geneva, and the United Provinces, not in Saxon England.

Milton treats at some length two superlative rulers, implicitly inviting some comparison with Cromwell. Egbert was "one of the worthiest:" his martial exploits united most of England, giving reason to expect "peace and plenty, greatness, and the flourishing of all Estates and Degrees." But then came the Danes, bringing "Invasion, Spoil, Desolation, slaughter of many, slavery of the rest" (257). King Alfred in fierce wars drove out the Danes and then enjoyed three years of peace, which he spent "in all vertuous enploiments both of mind and body" – thirsting after learning, building schools, translating books out of Latin, providing good laws, enacting stern justice, erecting elegant buildings, relieving foreign churches, and frugally managing his revenues (276–92). Milton had earlier thought of him as a possible epic hero.[126] But his achievements give way to internal strife, degeneration in the populace, and new Danish invasions. Milton concludes that the greatest political achievements of these best kings may in fact have been counterproductive, since local sovereignty (as in the United Provinces or the Swiss cantons) might better have preserved English liberty: had the heptarchy continued and the nation not been united, the invaders might have been better resisted, "while each Prince and people, excited by thir neerest concernments, had more industriously defended thir own bounds" (258). That lesson no doubt underlies his focus on federalism in *The Readie & Easie Way* (1660). He also reports, wryly, the story of King Canute commanding the sea to recede before him and when it would not, recognizing the folly of human beings claiming kingly power:

> Whereat the King quickly riseing, wish'd all about him to behold and consider the weak and frivolous power of a King, and that none indeed deserv'd the name of a King, but he whose Eternal Laws both Heav'n, Earth, and Sea obey. A truth so evident of it self, as I said before, that unless to shame his Court Flatterers who would not else be convinc't, *Canute* needed not to have gone wet-shod home. The best is, from that time forth he never would wear a Crown, esteeming Earthly Royalty contemptible and vain. (366)

Milton's history argues, subtly, against Cromwell's movement toward centralization of power and quasi-monarchical forms.

Milton intended this segment of his history to help rekindle the civic virtue upon which any republican government must rest, by underscoring again the disturbing continuities throughout English history and in the English character.[127] The overarching cause is always the same: the degeneration of the people into vice and its inevitable concomitant, servility of mind: "when God hath decreed servitude on a sinful Nation, fitted by thir own vices for no condition but servile, all Estates of Government are alike unable to avoid it" (259). The Danish invasions were God's punishment on the Saxons who, though now Christian, become fully as wicked and slothful as the Britons were at their arrival, especially in their debased religion – "Ceremonies, Reliques, Monasteries, Masses, Idols, add to these ostentation of

Alms, got ofttimes by rapine and oppression." Later, Edward the Confessor laid the groundwork for the Norman Conquest by the cultural subjugation that began when he gave his Norman allies high office in England: "Then began the English to lay aside thir own antient Customes, and in many things to imitate French manners, the great Peers to speak French in thir Houses . . . a presage of thir subjection shortly to that people, whose fashions and language they affected so slavishly" (377). The Norman Conquest occurred partly because the English could not agree about the choice of their native king, but chiefly because their vices had again made them slavish.[128] If this segment of the *History* was, as I think, mostly written as the Protector was adopting quasi-monarchical forms, it carries political implications. The implicit analogues imply that such institutions will only reinforce slavishness in the populace, and invite conquest by another monarch from France, Charles II.

On December 18, 1657 Milton received a request (now lost) from Peter Heimbach in the Hague, asking his influence with Henry Lawrence, father to his young friend Edward and permanent chairman of Cromwell's council, to secure Heimbach a position as secretary to the newly appointed envoy to the United Provinces, George Downing. Milton answered the same day, "since it concerns your business affairs," stating that he cannot help (*CPW* VII, 507) because Downing has already sailed and has taken a secretary with him. Milton adds a further explanation, hardly necessary if the job is filled: "my influential friends are very few (since I stay nearly always at home – and willingly)." This may be an effort to discourage Heimbach from further solicitations, but "willingly" suggests that Milton is distancing himself deliberately from those now in power – probably in part for ideological reasons as well as to concentrate on more important projects.

When Cromwell's last Protectorate parliament met on January 20, 1658, hopes for settlement under the *Humble Petition and Advice* were quickly dashed. It immediately began unmaking the new constitution, balking especially at the "Other House" as a new House of Lords. The disaffected in parliament, the army, the churches, and elsewhere presented a massive petition with thousands of signatures calling for restoration of the old republic and the Rump. Without warning, Cromwell dissolved parliament on February 4. His harsh rebuke called attention to real dangers: sheer confusion from unmaking a constitution devised with such labor by the last parliament, and the dire threat of royalist insurrections from within and attacks by Charles II from abroad. After cashiering some disgruntled officers, Lambert among them, Cromwell managed to dispel much of the opposition and by July his government seemed stronger than ever. He had thwarted a large-scale royalist conspiracy meant to prepare for Charles II's invasion; he had settled the government in Scotland under General Monk and in Ireland under his second son Henry Cromwell; he had brokered the Treaty of Roeskilde ending the war between Sweden and Denmark (February 27); and he had obtained Dunkirk after the French and English won a notable military victory over Spanish forces there on June 6. However, his grand vision of a Protestant League collapsed as Sweden again invaded Denmark in

August. Also, his treasury was empty and with every passing month the need for money escalated.

In 1658 Milton had a good deal of diplomatic correspondence. As usual, a few letters concerned the losses of merchants and ships,[129] but his pen was chiefly engaged with more important matters. He wrote an enthusiastic letter for Cromwell (March 30/April 2) congratulating Charles X of Sweden on the Treaty of Roeskilde and celebrating his "moderation, equanimity, and prudence" (*CPW* V.2, 819–20). A long letter (May 14) to the Grand Duke of Tuscany protests the denial of harbor and supplies to English ships at Livorno (the duke did not want to offend Spain), and ends by warning that the English will not accept protestations of friendship in the face of overt injuries (*CPW* V.2, 823–5). One pair of letters, to Louis XIV and to Mazarin (*c.* May 20), introduce Thomas, Viscount Fauconberg, the Protector's son-in-law, who was sent to congratulate Louis on the happy prospects for the siege of Dunkirk (826–32); another pair (June 19) congratulates the king and Mazarin on a notable victory there by the combined English and French forces;[130] and a final pair (July 1) thanks both men for promptly fulfilling their promise to turn over Dunkirk to England (844–7). Two letters on May 26 address in urgent terms the renewed threat to the Waldensians from the Duke of Savoy, who is breaking the 1655 treaty. That to the King of France recounts new persecutions – many Waldensians are cast out of their homes, forbidden to practice their religion, ravaged and slain by soldiers – and urges Louis to make them his subjects either by an exchange of territory or by offering them asylum (833–5). That to the Protestant Swiss cantons urges them to offer assistance to their near neighbors and prevent "the tearing away of that most ancient root of a purer religion in these remnants of primitive believers." His hope, he says, is that the English and Swiss will turn "all our resources and strength, all our zeal, to the defense of His church against the fury and madness of her enemies" (836–7). In a letter to Charles X of Sweden (June 4) Cromwell excuses his failure to offer military support in Sweden's wars with the comment that he has been "occupied with warding off our own dangers."[131]

Milton's financial affairs were in pretty good order. On January 14, 1658 he was able to lend £500 to Thomas Maundy, taking a mortgage on a property in Kensington as security.[132] But his marital happiness with Katherine Woodcock was cut short by her death on February 3. Edward Phillips reports that Katherine died in childbed, though in fact she died more than three months after the birth of her daughter (*EL* 71, 77); much later Milton's granddaughter stated that she died from consumption.[133] Phillips may have been out of touch and misinformed, or, more likely, Katherine may have remained weak and ill after the birth so that the family attributed her death to a "consumption" then contracted. The fact that Katherine's mother, Elizabeth Woodcock of Hackney, witnessed Milton's January 14 transaction with Maundy suggests that she may have been living with the Miltons during her daughter's illness. Katherine was buried on February 10 in St Margaret's Church, Westminster.[134] On March 17 the infant daughter died and was buried three days later. Milton's family Bible records these events together: "Katherin my daughter, by Katherin my second wife, was borne the 19th of October, between 5 and 6 in the morning, and dyed the 17th of March following, 6 weeks after hir mother, who dyed the 3rd. of Feb. 1657 [1658]."[135] I think it a near certainty that Milton wrote his poignant sonnet, "Mee thought I saw my late espoused saint," sometime during the difficult weeks following Katherine's death,[136] recording his love and grief for the wife whose face he had never seen and whose loss plunged him again into darkness and loneliness. It is discussed on pages 355–6.

Milton was reading widely and boldly during these months as he worked on, or at least collected more materials for, *De Doctrina Christiana*. A note by Hartlib to Robert Boyle on February 2, 1658 indicates that Milton had obtained a copy of the *Heptaplomeres* by Jean Bodin, which circulated only in manuscript and was risky to own.[137] Conceived in the tradition of the symposium, it is an interchange among seven learned men who represent a wide spectrum of religious opinion – a Catholic, a Jew, a philosophic naturalist, a Lutheran, a Moslem, a Calvinist, and a Skeptic. All their positions are given informed and sophisticated presentation; despite their differences these men exemplify how to live together in charity and toleration, defending their beliefs ultimately by the integrity and sanctity of their lives. Of particular interest and force are arguments for anti-Trinitarianism and divorce by the Jew and the natural philosopher, which parallel some that Milton develops in *De Doctrina*. Milton may also have been working periodically on *Paradise Lost*: John Aubrey reports from Edward Phillips that he began to do so "about 2 yeares before the K. came-in, and finished about 3 yeares after the K's Restauracion" (*EL* 13).

In May Milton published an edition of *The Cabinet Council*, a book of political maxims derived from Bodin, Guicciardini, Lipsius, and especially Machiavelli, that was generally though erroneously attributed to Sir Walter Raleigh.[138] Milton's brief preface claims that some "Learned Man at his Death" gave the work to him, and that he, "finding it lately by chance among other Books and Papers," determined that the work of this notable author should be published. His decision to do so at just this moment is more than happenstance. As Martin Dzelzainis argues, this work invites some comparison with the ironic writings of Nedham, Harrington, and Vane during this period, as it also offers a covert critique of the Protectorate in the form of political advice offered as by Raleigh, not Milton himself.[139] That this is Milton's purpose is suggested by the fact that his tracts had often heaped scorn upon the 'aphorisming pedantry" of all the tribe of "*Aphorismers, and Polticasters*," and had emphasized the dangers of "Cabinet Councels," which in the reign of Charles I invaded the rights of parliament.[140] The implication is, that this is the mode of political discoure appropriate to the times. Some maxims set forth worthy principles. One defines an ideal for the counsellors of rulers – "liberty of speech and magnanimous uttering of what is good and fit" – that Milton long sought to fulfill but seems to think no longer possible. Political maxims in the name of another man are a far cry from *Areopagitica*. Another, about the dangers of vesting power for long in one man, seems to sound a warning from a republican perspective: "In every Republick, an excessive Authority given to one or two persons for a long time, proveth dangerous, chiefly when the same is not restrained. Example, the Dictatorship given to *Caesar* for life, was an occasion to oppress the Liberties of the *Romans*."[141] Milton does not suggest that this is yet Cromwell's case or that there is now any other viable option for England. But he registers his uneasiness about the Protectorate in the fact that from 1654 on he has avoided any direct address to or comment about Cromwell, and in the subtext of what he does write or publish. That subtext is: if the people were only the lovers of liberty they should be, they would have better political discourse and a better republic.

Before Cromwell could call a new parliament, and perhaps this time accept the offer of the crown, nature intervened. An epidemic of influenza swept the country, killing Cromwell's favorite daughter Elizabeth Claypole on August 6, and attacking Cromwell himself. He rallied for a time but then grew steadily worse. Pressed on his deathbed to settle the succession, he reportedly confirmed the choice of his eldest son, Richard – though many refused to credit that story.[142] Milton's reaction to the death of Cromwell on September 3, the anniversary of his great battles of Worcester and Dunbar, is not on record. He was allotted 9s.6d to buy mourning attire for the funeral, as were Marvell, Philip Meadows, and Nathaniel Sterry; John Dryden was allotted 9s. But something might be inferred from what Milton did not do. Both Marvell and Dryden produced lengthy, laudatory funeral elegies for the death and funeral of the Lord Protector. Milton's muse did not even rise to an epitaph.

"Immortal Notes": Milton's Last Five Sonnets

The five sonnets Milton wrote during these years are all occasional poems that deal with specific personal or historical events. They extend the sonnet's range to take in a very wide spectrum of subjects and a stunning range of tone and style; and two of them – the Piedmont sonnet and the sonnet on his deceased wife – bring that genre to new heights of formal complexity and emotional intensity. They do so in part by incorporating other generic elements into the small confines of the Petrarchan sonnet form. No major poet would attempt to follow Milton's achievement in that kind for well over a century.

Both in form and subject "On the late Massacher in Piemont" is unique among Milton's sonnets and in the entire repertoire of the genre. Incorporating many details of the massacre from news reports and his own state letters of protest, this sonnet forces that lyric kind to deal with a historical event of tragic or epic proportions, transforming it into a species of jeremiad. Echoing prophetic language from Lamentations, Psalms, Isaiah and the Book of Revelation, a denunciatory voice calls down God's vengeance for the slaughtered Waldensians, and over the course of the sonnet defines with ever greater complexity what that vengeance might be and when it might come:

Avenge O Lord thy slaughter'd Saints, whose bones
  Lie scatter'd on the Alpine mountains cold,
  Ev'n them who kept thy truth so pure of old
  When all our Fathers worship't Stocks and Stones,
Forget not: in thy book record their groanes
  Who were thy Sheep and in their antient Fold
  Slayn by the bloody *Piemontese* that roll'd
  Mother with Infant down the Rocks. Their moans
The Vales redoubl'd to the Hills, and they
  To Heav'n. Their martyr'd blood and ashes so[w]
  O're all th'*Italian* fields where still doth sway
The triple Tyrant: that from these may grow
  A hunder'd-fold, who having learnt thy way
  Early may fly the *Babylonian* wo.[143]

The first four lines seem to call for immediate divine retribution, pointing to the special claim these martyrs have on God's vengeance, since they retained their gospel purity of worship while the rest of Europe was sunk in pagan or Roman Catholic idolatry – "worship't Stocks and Stones." These lines play off against biblical passages, e.g. Revelation 6:9–10: "the souls of them that were slain for the word of God, and for the testimony which they held . . . cried out with a loud voice, saying, How long, O Lord, holy and true, dost thou not judge and avenge our blood on them that dwell on the earth?"[144] The second segment (lines 5–10) modulates from the immediacy of "Avenge" to "Forget not," as the Miltonic speaker calls on God to record the martyrs' "groanes" and the redoubled "moans" in the book by which humankind will be judged on the Last Day. The graphic image, "roll'd/ Mother with Infant down the Rocks" is set against biblical references to God's exact record of all such sufferings, e.g. Psalm 56:8: "Put thou my tears in thy bottle: are they not in thy book." That book portends inexorable final retribution.[145]

Yet by the enjambment of lines four and five, the two modes of divine vengeance are linked rather than separated. And after the *volta* or turn within line 10, the resolution alludes to other kinds of immediate retribution in all the regions ruled by the papal "triple Tyrant." These lines refer to the parable of the sower (Matthew 13:3), in which the seed of God's Word "brought forth fruit, some an hunder'd-fold," and to Tertullian's aphorism that "the blood of the martyrs is the seed of the Church." Against those reference points, the Waldensians' slaughter may be expected to result in widespread conversions to Protestantism, repudiating the Roman religion and the pope who could perpetrate such horrors. Also, allusion to the classical myth of Cadmus who sowed dragons' teeth and saw them spring up armed warriors intimates that the Protestant military coalition Cromwell called for might rise up against those persecutors now. In the final line, the echo of Jeremiah 51:6 in "Babylonian wo" – "Flee out of the midst of Babylon, and deliver every man his soul: be not cut off in her iniquity; for this is the time of the Lord's vengeance" – predicts violent divine retribution in what may be an imminent apocalypse. In this complex resolution divine vengeance is certain, and the human responsibility is to learn God's ways and flee the Roman Babylon – though perhaps as well, to help inflict some foretaste of the prophesied "wo" now.

In this sonnet, in more striking ways even than in the first sonnet on his blindness, Milton uses run-on lines and strong syntactic breaks within the lines to set the rhetorical and emotional structure against the formal units of octave and sestet and end rhyme. That effect is enhanced by the long "o" sounds that resound throughout – "bones," "cold," "old," "Stones," "groanes," "Fold," "roll'd," "moans," "sow," "grow," "wo" – as if to echo the martyrs' cries.

The sonnet to Lawrence and the first sonnets to Cyriack Skinner make a pair, but on parallel rather than contrasting themes, as was the case with Elegies V and VI or *L'Allegro* and *Il Penseroso*.[146] Both retain the formal divisions of the Petrarchan sonnet but reconceive the genre in the epigrammatic mode of Martial and the Horatian short ode of invitation, with perhaps some recollection of Ben Jonson's "On Inviting a Friend to Dinner."[147] Both explore a familiar Miltonic theme: the need to seek respite from arduous intellectual labor with interludes of relaxation and the delights of refined and temperate pleasure.[148] Both extend invitations of gracious hospitality and urbane companionship: they begin by praising the young men in terms of their distinguished ancestors, then invite them to share various innocent delights, and end by repudiating rigorous asceticism. These celebrations of good pleasure at just this time (1655–6) challenge the mindset prompting the repression of recreations by some of Cromwell's major-generals. Milton's attitude is reminiscent of his claims for good pleasures in *A Masque* and *The Reason of Church-Government*.[149]

"*Lawrence* of vertuous Father vertuous Son" refers in this opening line to Henry Lawrence, the distinguished president of the council and keeper of the library at St James House; it then proffers to his son Edward an open-ended invitation to "Help wast a sullen day" by the fire in dank winter. The octave concludes with a biblical allusion to "The Lillie and Rose, that neither sow'd nor spun," suggesting the folly of an over-rigorous approach to work.[150] The sestet proposes specific pleasures: a "neat repast" with "light and choice" fare, wine, and after dinner a lute warbling Tuscan airs. The invitation is couched tactfully in the form of questions, leaving Lawrence the option of setting places and days and even the specifics of the repast. But the final two lines are declarative, defining the attitude that should govern his acceptance: "He who of those delights can judge, And spare [time] / To interpose them oft, is not unwise."[151]

The sonnet to Skinner gives the first quatrain to a praise of his "Grandsire," Sir Edward Coke, Chief Justice of Common Pleas and Kings Bench and the greatest legal authority of his day: he "taught our Lawes" though other judges often wrench them. The second quatrain offers Cyriack an invitation couched in imperative and immediate terms, to spend a "cheerful hour" of lightsome conversation: "To day deep thoughts resolve with me to drench / In mirth, that after no repenting drawes." "Drench" implies, without saying as much, that wine will accompany and help produce the mirth. Milton urges that they give over deep subjects like mathematics and politics that presumably often concern them ("What the *Swede* intend, and what the *French*"). The first quatrain holds Coke forth as a model for the proper interpretation of laws; Skinner by analogy must learn "To measure life" and its laws correctly, not wrench them. The sestet offers teacherly advice. Cyriack should give primary attention to what will produce "solid good," and keep other duties in perspective, recognizing that Heaven disapproves "that care, though wise in show, / That with superfluous burden loads the day, / And when God sends a cheerful hour, refrains."

In his second sonnet to Skinner, "Cyriack, this three years day," Milton revisits the subject of his blindness three years after it became total,[152] explicitly pairing and contrasting this with his earlier sonnet on that topic. The two sonnets trace the Miltonic speaker's progress from an early struggle to cope with despondency, through patient waiting on God's time, to the attainment of a new confidence and optimism. The poem's cheerful, even triumphant mood seems somewhat forced, revealing, perhaps, Milton's desire to give good example to his student and friend but also his need to cheer himself up periodically by recalling what he has accomplished and what he means still to do. Like the first blindness sonnet this one sets rhetorical speech over against Petrarchan metrics. The first five-and-a-half lines state the painful loss: the eyes (orbs), though clear to outward view, no longer have sight of those other orbs, "Sun or Moon or Starre," or "man or woman." The next segment, with the octave completed in the middle of line nine, insists that he does not argue against Heaven (as before), but can now "bear up & steer / Right onward." The image of a pilot boldly steering a ship with helm "up" into the wind constrasts sharply with the speaker's earlier position among those who "only stand and waite." As if in answer to a question from Cyriack, the rest of the sestet states the grounds of his confidence: pride that he has willingly sacrificed his vision "in libertyes defence," and assurance that God will prove a "better guide" for his journey than those celestial orbs he can no longer steer by. While his supposition that "all Europe talks from side to side" about his *Defensio* is an exaggeration, that work did prompt many letters and visits from the learned of Europe. His concluding epithet terming the world a "vain mask" suggests both the follies of that debased genre and also the world's manifold deceptions, which the blind man's keen spiritual vision may penetrate.

The poignant sonnet, "Mee thought I saw my late espoused saint," makes a contrasting pair with this last poem on blindness, as, after that almost too confident affirmation, Milton portrays himself brought low by the death of his wife, overwhelmed by the sense of loss and darkness. This poem merges the sonnet with the dream–vision: there are precedents for that in the Petrarchan tradition,[153] but none that strike so intense a note of personal love, grief, pain, and loss. It is one of the great love poems in the language, displaying what is not elsewhere evident: Milton's capacity to love a woman deeply and respond to her love.

In this Petrarchan sonnet the first twelve lines present the dream–vision, and the quasi-Shakespearean sonnet structure intensifies the emotion when the turn finally comes in the last two lines:

> Mee thought I saw my late espoused saint
> brought to me like Alcestis from the grave
> whom Joves great son to her glad husband gave
> rescu'd from death by force though pale and faint.
> Mine as whom washt from spot of childe-bed taint
> purification in the old law did save,
> and such, as yet once more I trust to have
> full sight of her in heaven without restraint,
> came vested all in white, pure as her minde:
> her face was vaild, yet to my fancied sight,
> love, sweetness, goodness, in her person shin'd
> soe clear, as in no face with more delight.
> But o as to imbrace me she enclin'd,
> I wak'd, she fled, and day brought back my night.[154]

The opening line introduces ambiguities around "late" – recently wed, recently deceased. "Saint" identifies the visionary lady with the saved in heaven and prepares for the emphasis on her goodness. The first quatrain presents a classical analogue from Euripides' *Alcestis*: she comes, like Alcestis brought back to her husband Admetus from the possession of Death in the underworld, veiled, pale, and faint, and in need of purification because of her consecration to the nether gods.[155] The second segment (five lines) presents an Old Testament analogue: the vision appears like one who has fulfilled the law in Leviticus 12:2–5 for purifying the uncleanness associated with childbirth: 40 days for a male child, 80 for a female. But in her case the white garments symbolize, not bodily purification, classical or Judaic, but the purity of mind that marks her as one saved by grace under the New Law.[156] That purity allows the Miltonic speaker to expect the "full sight" of her in heaven that his blind eyes never enjoyed on earth. The emphasis on purity gains etymological force from Katherine's name in Greek, *katharos*, pure. The next three lines project the mental picture, the "fancied sight" the dream allowed, in which Katherine's essential qualities of "love, sweetness, goodness" shone "soe clear" through the veil. The final two lines, arguably the most poignant in all Milton's poetry, underscore profound ironies: night and sleep allowed a partial escape in vision from the sightlessness and agony of lost love; the new day brings back the dark night of absence, blindness, grief, and desolation.

11

"The Last Words of Our Expiring Libertie" 1658–1660

In the twenty months from Oliver Cromwell's death on September 3, 1658 to the restoration of Charles II in May 1660, the government of England changed six times, economic conditions steadily worsened, the English people showed increasing dissatisfaction with Puritan rule, and the royalists gained strength. The uneasy peace Cromwell had imposed on the Puritan coalition rapidly collapsed, as Cromwellians, army officers, republicans of various stripes, sectaries, rank and file soldiers, conservative Presbyterians, moderate Independents, Fifth Monarchists, and others urged their various principles and models of church and state. For the first several months Milton continued to write state letters for the new Protector Richard Cromwell and then for the restored Rump Parliament, and found some time to work on *De Doctrina Christiana* and *Paradise Lost*. But after Oliver Cromwell's death he urged a return to the more radical ideals of the Commonwealth: he published a new edition of his *Defensio* with its republican theory, and two treatises that argued, respectively, for religious liberty for all Protestants and for church disestablishment. These writings of 1658–9 restate his idea of the Good Old Cause.

For Milton, the value to be preserved above all else – the primary good for government to promote – is religious liberty; reprising *Areopagitica*, he again insists that only an environment of religious freedom can allow good men to serve God conscientiously and develop in virtue. He sees the strict separation of church and state as a corollary to that liberty: like many radical sectaries he would have no church establishment, no tithes, and no government involvement in the choice or support of ministers. Milton did not break with Cromwell over the issue of disestablishment (toleration was always more important), but he urged it again, strongly, when he thought he might find a more receptive audience in the restored Rump Parliament. His treatises, *Of Civil Power* and *The Likeliest Means to Remove Hirelings*, respond to immediate political circumstances but are conceived as a two-part argument outlining his deepest convictions about church–state relations, set forth largely in a plain style that differs markedly from his earlier polemic modes. These proposals move so far beyond mainstream seventeenth-century assumptions as to seem a wildly impractical retreat from the political sphere. But he could reasonably suppose that religious liberty and church disestablishment would help nurture a republican ethos, and might resolve the fierce disputes about doctrine and church order that had been flashpoints of controversy and unrest for twenty years. More than a century later, the constitution of the fledgling United States republic would establish both principles as the basis for civil peace. On these matters, as on divorce, companionate marriage, and a free press, Milton was ahead of his time, as he seems to realize in the final sentence of *The Likeliest Means*: "If I be not heard nor beleevd, the event will bear me witnes to have spoken truth: and I in the mean while have borne my witnes not out of season to the church and to my countrey (*CPW* VII, 321).

After May, 1659 Milton was no longer part of the Secretariat, but he remained well informed about the shifts of power and personnel and on five different occasions offered his advice about settling the government to whoever might listen. These proposals were not ideal models but expedients geared to the rapidly changing circumstances, addressed rhetorically to specific audiences, and concerned above all else to stave off a Stuart Restoration. Milton's certainty that the Stuarts would deny religious liberty to dissenters of all stripes, together with his visceral disgust for Stuart court culture, prompted his relentless opposition to the restoration of Charles II. His several tracts also register his profound belief that papal and Stuart absolutism, as well as the idolatry invited by Roman Catholic and Laudian worship and by the icons of monarchy, promote servility and intellectual bondage in the citizens.

In these last tracts Milton again insists that a republic is the best government for a virtuous and liberty-loving people, but he found himself having to provide models for a republic without large numbers of such citizens. So, more insistently than before, he justifies restricting suffrage and participation in government to the worthy, who are still defined, as in *Tenure* and *Eikonoklastes*, as those who love and support liberty, especially religious liberty. He welcomed the return of the Rump Parliament, imperfect as he thought it to be, as an opportunity to reinstate the republican model put in place in 1649, "without King, Single Person, or House of Lords" and with sovereignty vested in a legislature having at least some claim to be the people's elected representative. During the final months of the Interregnum, in a series of short tracts and two versions of *The Readie & Easie Way*, Milton proposed to perpetuate whatever legislature or council was in place, however faulty he thought them, as an effort to prevent the Restoration and its threat to Puritan religious liberty. He read the English people's desire to recall the king as clear evidence of their degeneracy: they were displaying again the national defects of servility and political ineptitude he had traced in the *History of Britain*, and were reprising the backsliding Israelites in the wilderness who wanted to turn back to Egypt. Milton's models of government in these months are makeshift, provisional, temporary, and anything but utopian, though he shows increasing interest in devising a federal system in which, through participation in local governmental and educational institutions, citizens could be exercised in and fitted for the responsibilities of republican government. In retrospect, after Cromwell's death the Restoration seems inevitable and these proposals seem desperate. But that was not obvious at the time: until the very end Milton could hope that some holding operation might stabilize the situation until a "free commonwealth" could be more securely settled.

On the very eve of the Restoration, when most of his party had run to ground, Milton continued to urge his version of the Good Old Cause. Blind, vulnerable, and already a hated target for royalist revenge because of *Eikonoklastes* and the *Defensio*, he continued with reckless courage to call attention to himself by his writings, placing himself in danger of prison or even execution. This was the more remarkable, since he ran the serious risk of not being able to finish the great epic he had begun. He clearly felt a profound need to make a last desperate effort to recall his countrymen to their better selves, or, failing that, to denounce their degeneracy and bear witness to God's ways with England in the resounding prophetic voice of a new Jeremiah.

"Evills & Discords Incurable"

On September 4 Oliver's elder son Richard Cromwell was proclaimed in Westminster and the City of London, in a progress filled with pomp and pageantry. To the relief of many, his succession met with general acceptance from men of substance who expected his regime to continue the conservative trajectory of the final Oliverian years: gentry and lawyers who were pleased with the establishment of hereditary succession, many royalists who had by now recovered their sequestered estates, and senior army officers. But there was ferment beneath the surface: republicans and commonwealthsmen believed the Protector and the new House of Lords had usurped the rights of the sovereign people; millenarian sectaries still dreamed of a rule of the saints; many in the army thought the Cromwellians had betrayed the religious and social ideals of the revolution. A power struggle soon developed between the Cromwellian "Court Party" and the army officers meeting regularly at Wallingford House, even as the slogan, the "Good Old Cause," was increasingly invoked by the army rank and file and by republicans meeting regularly at the home of Milton's friend, Vane. One worrying manifestation was a flood of petitions and proclamations seeking the appointment of Charles Fleetwood as commander-in-chief of the army, independent of Richard. The mounting debt and the long-standing arrears of army pay led the Council of State to call a parliament for January 27, 1659.

Milton continued his work as Latin Secretary. He provided a pair of letters (dated September 6, 1658) from Richard to Louis XIV and Mazarin informing them of

Oliver's death and promising to maintain the friendships, alliances, and treaty obligations then in place (*CPW* V.2, 850–1). He probably wrote similar letters at about the same time to several other states, though he did not retain copies.[1] In October, Richard protests himself unable "in this beginning of my office and dignity" to act immediately on the request of Charles X of Sweden for military assistance against Denmark, but assures him that he will continue England's alliance with Sweden and will pray for his preservation "as a safeguard and defense for the orthodox church" (852). On November 13, he acknowledges Charles X's condolences for Oliver's death, informs him that he is sending a fleet to the Baltic to supply the requested aid, and refers him for details to the newly appointed ambassador Philip Meadows (855–6).[2] On November 23 Milton probably marched in the magnificent funeral procession from Somerset House to Westminster to deposit the effigies of Oliver in the chapel of Henry VII, where his body had earlier been interred. Milton, Marvell, and Dryden from the Secretariat were among the government officials and household staff who were allotted money to buy mourning for that occasion.[3] Their names appear in the order of march, with the direction that they were to wait in the Privy Chamber with some other clerks, chaplains, and ministers until time to move out; the list pairs Milton with Marvell, who would have had to lead him.[4] If he took part, Milton was no doubt dismayed as Marvell and others described the cost and vanity of that occasion: the magnificently caparisoned and plumed horses and splendid chariot, the elaborate procession through the streets, and especially the regal emblems – purple and ermine robes, crown, sword, scepter, and orb – which decked Cromwell's effigy.[5]

Though he accepted Richard's Protectorate, Milton seems to have felt that the time was auspicious to remind his countrymen of their, and his, notable deeds in support of a different political ideal. Even before Oliver's death he had begun revising his *Defensio*, that proud manifesto for the regicide, popular sovereignty, and a commonwealth government without King, Protector, or House of Lords. He wanted, no doubt, to perfect the work he considered his greatest accomplishment to date, and also to correct any textual errors that Salmasius might point out in his long-expected posthumous answer. Working with an amanuensis it would have taken Milton some time to hear the text read and to make over 250 small changes and corrections that sometimes involve adding or deleting whole lines.[6] He published it in early October,[7] adding a lengthy postscript set apart from the earlier text under a line. It offers the *Defensio* as still useful to teach Englishmen to value the "civil freedom" so nobly won a decade ago, and to cast off the chains forged by ignorance and pretended religion, "unless they themselves prefer and deserve to be slaves" (*CPW* IV.1, 536). He also promises a comparable but greater work that will benefit "men of every land and, particularly, all Christian men," probably a reference to the Latin theological treatise *De Doctrina Christiana*, which he had been working on for many years. Its scope, its use of Latin, and its address to the learned throughout Europe would seem to Milton to complement and indeed surpass the *Defensio*.[8]

As he observed the course of events over the next few months, Milton had reason to fear an imminent, severe retrenchment of religious liberty, now that Oliver's personal commitment to broad toleration could no longer serve as counterweight. Richard was thought to support moderate Presbyterianism, and from September through March he was deluged with petitions – including a letter from General Monk in Scotland – urging him to settle a national Presbyterian church, protect the universities and ministers' tithes, and suppress idolatry, blasphemy, profaneness, "damnable Heresies," and "seducing spirits," i.e. popery, Independency, and the sects.[9] Many conservative Independents were actively seeking accommodation with the Presbyterians in a national church and dissociating themselves from the broader tolerationist ideal of the "heretical" or "erroneous" sects. Their Savoy *Declaration*, published on October 12, 1658, set forth doctrinal norms closely paralleling the Westminster Assembly's Articles of Faith,[10] and recommended toleration only for those "holding the foundation" though differing in church organization. Many of those doctrinal foundations – the Trinity, predestination, the soul's immediate passage to heaven or hell after death, and the magistrate's duty to defend orthodoxy so that "men of corrupt mindes and conversations do not licentiously publish and divulge Blasphemy and Errors"[11] – were contested by Milton in *De Doctrina Christiana*, his ongoing theological project.

During December and January Milton had little diplomatic correspondence,[12] and could give his attention to developing a forceful argument for religious liberty, *Of Civil Power in Ecclesiastical Causes*. It was registered with the Stationers on February 16 and probably published soon after.[13] Ignoring Richard Cromwell, who was still in office, he addressed his treatise "To the Parliament of the Commonwealth of England" and stated in his preface that he had prepared it "against the much expected time of your sitting"(*CPW* VII, 239). By this gesture Milton pointedly looks to the parliament – which he terms "supream Councel" – as the sole locus of government power. He offers this tract as the first installment of a projected two-part treatment of church–state relations, dealing with, respectively, two forces "working much mischief to the church of God, and the advancement of truth; force on the one side restraining, and hire on the other side corrupting the teachers thereof" (241). The argument and rhetoric of both treatises are discussed on pages 382–9.

There was little tolerationist polemic during Richard's reign before *Of Civil Power*, but the major positions and arguments had been worked out over several years. Tolerationist Independents like Cromwell accepted that the magistrate had some responsibility toward religion but held that Christ's lordship over the individual Christian conscience requires toleration of almost all Christians except Catholics, Laudians, Ranters, Quakers, and antinomians – groups variously seen as blasphemers, idolators, or threats to the government or to public order. A few Levellers, Baptists, and Quakers held that the magistrate has jurisdiction only over civil affairs and can have nothing to do with enforcing religious laws against blasphemy, idolatry, and heresy, or with supporting ministers.[14] But very few drew the logical conclusion from this, that toleration should also extend to Jews, Moslems, and Roman Catholics.

Milton's treatise presses a conservative formula – that Christian liberty pertains only to practitioners of true religion – to radical conclusions by redefining what true religion is: not fundamental doctrines but acceptance of scripture alone as the rule of faith, interpreted by the private conscience as informed by the Spirit's illumination. By that definition, the magistrate's defense of true religion can only be the defense of every Christian's right to his own conscientious belief and practice. With the radicals Milton would restrict the magistrate to civil affairs only, on theological and also on pragmatic grounds: to do so would save the parliament "much labor and interruption" (let them recall past dissolutions of parliaments), and it offers the only hope to settle England's troubles. Moreover, since they themselves may be soon in the power of others they should realize that "any law against conscience is alike in force against any conscience" (240). Milton does not, however, suppose that this argument must lead to universal toleration: like certain other radical Independents he finds a basis in natural reason and civic danger to allow some restrictions on Roman Catholics, idolators, and blasphemers.[15] He appeals directly to those MPs (especially Vane) who led the fight for religious liberty before to take up this good cause again:

> One advantage I make no doubt of, that I shall write to many eminent persons of your number, alreadie perfet and resolvd in this important article of Christianitie. Some of whom I remember to have heard often for several years, at a councel next in autoritie to your own, so well joining religion with civil prudence, and yet so well distinguishing the different power of either, and this not only voting, but frequently reasoning why it should be so, that . . . [anyone might see] that then both commonwealth and religion will at length, if ever, flourish in Christendom, when either they who govern discern between civil and religious, or they only who so discern shall be admitted to govern. Till then nothing but troubles, persecutions, commotions can be expected; the inward decay of true religion among our selves, and the utter overthrow at last by a common enemy. (240)

By this address to parliament alone and this direct appeal to those who served so ably in the Commonwealth Council of State, Milton shows his sympathy for, if not yet overt identification with, a loose coalition of republicans, army officers, sectaries, millenarians, and rank and file soldiers who were orchestrating calls throughout February and March for a return to the ideals of the "Good Old Cause."[16] Commonly, they invoked the typology of England as Israel in the wilderness, urging the army to repent its backsliding into the "Apostate" ways of the Protectorate when they chose "a Captain back for Egypt" (Oliver Cromwell), and to return to the original purity of the Commonwealth, en route to the promised land.[17] Though the Protectorate party won enough votes in parliament to establish Richard and the Other House, the extended battles over those issues delayed other necessary business, including supplies and pay to the discontented soldiers. Milton was no doubt pleased when parliament took up the cause of Oliver's political prisoners, among them his friend Major-General Robert Overton, whom he had so warmly praised to Cromwell in the *Defensio Secunda*.[18] Brought back on March 9 from his confinement in Jersey, Overton was welcomed with laurel branches by some fifteen hundred people, and escorted in a triumphal procession to Westminster. He was released a few days later despite efforts by the government to justify his imprisonment and bring him to trial.

At the end of March Moses Wall, a member of the Hartlib circle, answered a letter from Milton (now lost), evidently accompanied by *Of Civil Power*. Wall's letter offers a revealing insight into how a contemporary who knew Milton's work well understood the politics of his tolerationist treatise.[19] Wall thinks of Milton, he says, "with much Respect, for your Friendliness to Truth in your early Years and in bad Times," but he has wondered about Milton's association with the Protectorate: "I was uncerten whether your Relation to the Court, (though I think a Commonwealth was more friendly to you than a Court) had not clouded your former Light, but your last Book resolved that Doubt" (*CPW* VII, 510–11). The parenthetical clause may mean that Milton fared better under a Commonwealth than under the Protectorate court, or that Milton himself was more "friendly" to the Commonwealth. Wall agrees with Milton about the nation's "retrograde Motion of late, in Liberty and Spiritual Truths," but advises pity to the people's human frailty, since their trusted leaders "betray this good Thing committed to them, and lead us back to egypt" (511). He also invites Milton to consider something he usually ignores, the economic grounds for the people's servility: feudal tenures of lands, lack of an assured comfortable subsistence, and "that cursed yoak of Tythes," which he is happy to see Milton proposing to treat (511). Milton may have been chagrined that his associations with the Protectorate had raised doubts about his principles, but he was surely pleased to receive this encouragement from a kindred spirit and to find that the republican politics implicit in *Of Civil Power* had been rightly read.

April produced a crisis. A General Council of Army Officers called for freedom of worship, provision for the army's material needs and arrears, and its own independent commander-in-chief (Charles Fleetwood). Exacerbating the army's anxieties, parliament called for a fast day to repent the "many Blasphemies and damnable Heresies" rife in the land, ordered that the Westminster Assembly's confession of faith be "held forth as the public profession of the nation," and moved to put the armed forces under the joint control of the Protector and parliament.[20] On April 22 the officers forced Richard to dissolve parliament and a Council of Officers assumed *de facto* authority. Some sought rather to control Richard than to depose him but could not stem the anti-Protectorate tide, swelled by the quasi-monarchical trappings of the Protectorate court, the diminution of the army's role, fears that Richard was under the control of crypto-royalists, and perceived threats to liberty of conscience. An avalanche of pamphlets mixing the language of republicanism with the language of the saints advised the army that the only way to redeem its "backsliding" in supporting the Protector and his adherents – "those Canaanites, those Court-Parasites and Apostates" – was to restore the Rump Parliament.[21] The Republicans managed, as Austin Woolrych observes, to identify the Good Old Cause with the Good Old Parliament, though much of the army had condemned the Rump in 1653 for its efforts to rein in the sects and the army (*CPW* VII, 67). A few pamphlets urged Leveller or Harringtonian programs,[22] but most called for the old model: a commonwealth without Single Person or House of Lords, and restoration of the Rump.

Whatever Milton may have expected or hoped from the revived republican sentiment, he continued his diplomatic correspondence for Richard, most of it dealing with vessels or cargo seized or citizens requiring assistance.[23] He addressed a deft rhetorical appeal to the King of France (February 18) in support of the Piedmontese Protestants – this time exiles settled in Provence whose meetings for worship were being obstructed – urging the king not to forbid these Protestants to offer prayers for his safety and prosperity (*CPW* V.2, 860–1). Milton's last letter for Richard was to Charles X of Sweden, dated April 25.[24] About the same time Milton answered a letter (now lost) from Jean de Labadie, a former French Jesuit turned Calvinist who founded a sect dedicated to simple living and communal property, and who had expressed a desire to settle in England. The letter was sent, probably with a copy of his book recounting the difficulties occasioned by his conversion, through Giles Dury, an elder of the French church in London.[25] Milton was clearly pleased by the praises of his *Defensio* that Labadie passed along,[26] and he in turn praised Labadie highly for following the gospel despite persecution. Milton and Dury found a post for Labadie and Milton's letter made him an offer of appointment as minister to a French community in London.[27] Milton often tried to help such petitioners, especially writers or scholars; probably he had not heard the rumors of sexual laxity that Labadie, much like Milton's despised Alexander More, attracted wherever he went, or else he attributed those rumors to Catholic harassment.

On May 6 the Council of Officers invited the Rump Parliament back and published a Declaration all but admitting that they had made a grave mistake in expelling that body in 1653. They acknowledge that they have wandered "divers ways from rightous and equal paths," that the apparent withdrawal of the Lord's presence from them has hitherto frustrated all attempts at settlement, and that the expelled MPs were "eminent Asserters of that Cause, and had a special Presence of God with them."[28] On May 7 a procession of some forty MPs marched into parliament, and soon others returned.[29] Almost immediately the issue was joined that was to bedevil this new attempt to settle a republic: a conflict between parliamentary supremacy and the army's sense of itself as the best protector of the Good Old Cause and virtually an estate of government. On May 13 the officers presented a "Humble Petition and Address" to parliament outlining certain "fundamentals" to be preserved: a commonwealth form without Single Person, King, or House of Lords;

liberty of conscience for most Protestants who profess faith in the Trinity and the Holy Scriptures (exempting only popery, prelacy, and licentious practices); and a two-chamber legislature with an elected representative body and "a select senate, co-ordinate in power, of able and faithful persons, eminent for godliness, and such as continue adhering to this cause."[30] In subsequent months the senior officers (the so called Wallingford House group) remained wedded to some kind of Select Senate, and assumed that much of its membership would be drawn from their number. Milton's friend Henry Vane had proposed a variant of that scheme in *The Healing Question* (1656) as a way to bring parliament and the army together by securing both the principle of representative government and the protection of minority liberties; he now reiterated that proposal in the form of a letter to Harrington, incorporating some Harringtonian as well as millenarian elements.[31] But that idea was anathema to committed republicans who would not brook any infringement on the supremacy of the elected legislature or its control over the military.

On May 15 Milton wrote what seem to be his last letters of state, announcing the Rump Parliament's return to power. The formula in the letter to Charles X of Sweden is closely replicated in that to Frederick III of Denmark: "Since Almighty God . . . in whose power alone are all the revolutions of kingdoms and commonwealths, has seen fit to restore us to our original authority and to the position of supreme power in governing English affairs, we have thought first . . . to inform Your Majesty of this fact."[32] The letters assure both monarchs of parliament's continued friendship, its earnest desire to help reconcile the two warring Protestant powers, and its commission to Philip Meadows, ambassador extraordinary to Sweden, to help negotiate a settlement. Richard did not abdicate formally until May 25, but these letters ignore him completely. In mid-May also, pamphlets by the irrepressible Prynne blamed the restoration of the Rump on the principles of Milton, John Goodwin, and Marchamont Nedham, among others.[33]

Although he did not publish it until August, Milton probably began work sometime in June on the second part of his analysis of church–state relations, *The Likeliest Means to Remove Hirelings out of the church*.[34] No doubt he took some comfort from the Rump's prompt acceptance of the toleration formula in the army's "Humble Petition and Address," though he would not have approved the Trinitarian doctrinal test. Soon, however, fierce debates erupted in parliament and in the press over tithes; supporters and abolitionists deluged the parliament with petitions, prompting Milton to address that issue immediately.[35] On June 27 the abolitionists presented a petition with fifteen hundred signatures, urging legislators not to force maintenance for ministers on those "that for conscience sake cannot hear them, nor own them."[36] Parliament responded on the same day with a resolution to continue tithes "unless this Parliament shall find out some other more equal and Comfortable Maintenance" – strongly suggesting that it did not expect to make a change any time soon.[37] But neither side took the matter as settled.

The most rigid tithe supporters, Presbyterians and some Independents, argued that the clergy's right to them was *jure divino*, citing Mosaic law that awarded the tenth to Old Testament Levites, Abraham paying tithes to the high priest Melchizedek, and New Testament texts proclaiming ministers' right to support.[38] Many also advanced legal and pragmatic arguments: that English law gives ministers as good right to their tithes as landowners to their rents; that opponents of tithes seek to level all property; that without some settled maintenance, religion and learning cannot be spread throughout the land; and that ministers have a right to be compensated for their necessary and expensive university education.[39] Many Independents were willing to consider a substitute for tithes, but they could not agree on one.[40] Sectaries and other radicals often drew on the scholarship of John Selden to argue that tithes pertained only to the Mosaic Law, now abrogated for Christians; many also emphasized the sufferings inflicted on the poor by hard-hearted tithe collectors. They rejected any kind of public maintenance on the grounds that it compells Christians against conscience to support ministers whose teaching they reject; that under the gospel, ministers' support should be voluntary; and that the magistrate has neither right nor responsibility to confirm ministers or order any matters pertaining to the church.[41] The issue of ministers' learning and how it was to be acquired and paid for was inextricably linked to the tithe question. Presbyterians and other conservatives insisted that the established university program of grammar, languages, rhetoric, and divinity studies was essential for the proper interpretation of scripture, since the direct revelation of the Spirit had ceased in apostolic times, and even secular subjects could serve as a handmaid to religion.[42] Many moderates held that scripture alone is sufficient to convey spiritual knowledge, that there is danger in mixing secular learning with divine revelation, and that the Spirit continues to reveal truth to the elect, but accepted that the original languages and some other university subjects could be useful for ministers, and to that end often proposed reforms in the university curriculum.[43] More radical Independents and sectaries insisted that all human learning is entirely useless for the attainment of spiritual knowledge, which must come only from scripture and the Spirit, but they expected ministers would profit from certain subjects – languages and the arts of the trivium – studied elsewhere. William Dell, master of Gonville and Caius College, Cambridge, proposed to secularize the universities, disperse colleges throughout the land, and (anticipating Milton's plan in *The Likeliest Means*) would have students taught languages and arts and a lawful trade in reformed grammar schools, from which God would call some to serve as ministers, "whilst yet they live in an *honest Calling* and *Imployment*, as the *Apostles* did."[44] Some extreme sectaries thought all learning, even the original scriptural languages, to be positively detrimental to spiritual knowledge, since God works best through weak children and unlettered apostles.[45]

Milton's preface challenges the Rump – which he addresses as "supream Senat" – to abolish public maintenance for ministers, commending them for being "in all things els authors, assertors, and now recovers of our libertie" (*CPW* VII, 274–5).

He completed and published the tract after their July 27 vote to continue tithes,[46] formally aligning himself with those determined to regard that vote merely as an interim decision. He urged the Rump to emulate commonwealths that invite public comment on laws before they "pass to a full establishment" (278). His radical case for separation of church and state marshals all the usual sectarian arguments for abolishing not only tithes but any public maintenance for the clergy, and for denying ministers' need for university education, or ordination, or state approval. This tract carries to its logical conclusion Milton's disposition from the time of the antiprelatical tracts to deny any essential distinction between clergy and laity: he now asserts categorically that anyone called by the Spirit can perform any church office. But his proposed separation of church and state was unacceptable to many dedicated republicans: James Harrington challenged Milton's tract directly, insisting that a commonwealth must have a national religion and an endowed ministry, with wide toleration guaranteed, since otherwise the major part of the nation are deprived of their liberty of conscience and will then, inevitably, deprive the minor part of theirs.[47]

Milton's enthusiastic welcome to the Rump contrasts sharply with his denunciation and rejection of that body in 1653. He also seems to repudiate Oliver Cromwell, whom he had hailed as a saviour in 1654, as well as the Protectorate regime which he had served for more than five years. He calls the Rump,

> next under God, the authors and best patrons of religious and civil libertie, that ever these Ilands brought forth. The care and tuition of whose peace and safety, after a short but scandalous night of interruption, is now again by a new dawning of Gods miraculous providence among us, revolvd upon your shoulders. (274)

Along with others who had also repudiated the Rump and supported Cromwell, Milton has persuaded himself that a return to the Commonwealth's first form is a providential act making possible a hopeful new beginning. As the author of *A Short Discourse concerning the work of God in this Nation* put it, the return of the Rump is a sure sign of God again owning the Cause and this parliament.[48] Despite the apparent difficulty of reading Milton's term "short" as a reference to the entire Protectorate era, similar usages with that meaning are common: Woolrych points to a pamphlet of May, 1659, rejoicing in "this morning of Freedom, after a short, but a sharp night of Tyranny and oppression," during which Oliver, the "Grand Backslider," led the army astray.[49] I think this is Milton's meaning, but I doubt that he thinks he was wrong about the Rump's grave failings in 1653, or about Oliver's great promise at the beginning of the Protectorate: unlike many others, he does not describe his support of the Protectorate as backsliding. Rather, his phrase implies that Cromwell had disappointed the high hopes once fairly vested in him: in the *Second Defense* Milton had solemnly warned him that the wrong would be grievous if he did not promote liberty. Milton could conscientiously continue working in the Secretariat, since he found Cromwell a better friend to toleration than most, and since he admired the Protector's foreign policy, especially his support for the Waldensians and for an international Protestant alliance. No doubt he saw himself providing under all the regimes useful service to the nation in the crucial area of foreign relations.

When he advised the Rump that religious liberty and disestablishment must be secured before models of government can be properly considered, Milton underscored his priorities. But he could not long ignore the escalating political instability. Restoration of the Rump was unpopular with many of the gentry who had supported the Protectorate as it turned more conservative, and many radical sectaries feared that the Rump would again attempt to perpetuate its power. A few Levellers revived the notion of an Agreement of the People with subscription restricted to the well-affected; and a few sectaries and millenarians, among them Milton's friend Robert Overton, vigorously denounced the backsliding to a single person and urged the rule of the elect.[50] In August the Presbyterian George Booth began an uprising in support of Charles II (easily put down by Lambert). Several tracts set forth simplified versions of Harrington's *Oceana* as the best solution to the present crisis: his provisions for a bicameral legislature – one house to debate and the other to vote – and his designs to refine elections and to provide for both permanence and rotation influenced many other government models, including Milton's.[51] Sometime during October the so called Rota Club began to meet nightly at the Turk's Head Coffee House to debate Harrington's proposals and principles. Milton kept in close touch with those deliberations through Cyriack Skinner, who was a member. John Aubrey described the discussions as

> the most ingeniose, and smart, that ever I heard, or expect to heare. . . . The room was every evening full as it could be cramm'd. . . . The Doctrine was very taking, and the more because, as to human foresight, there was no possibility of the King's returne. . . . Well: this Meeting continued Novemb., Dec., Jan., till Generall Monke's comeing-in, all these aierie modells vanished.[52]

Week by week tensions mounted between parliament and the army, as the parliament undertook to bring the army and its officers firmly under its civilian control and the army responded with petitions asserting its special status and its ongoing demands.[53] When the Rump foolishly revoked the commissions of nine high officers, including Fleetwood, Lambert called out his troops and on October 13 turned the Rump out of doors yet once more. In its apologia, the army justified its action on the ground that the parliament had sought to perpetuate itself and to ruin the army and thereby the Good Old Cause.[54] During the next two weeks it was not clear whether the army had dissolved or merely suspended the parliament. The Council of Officers held the reins of power, but some members of the Council of State continued to sit; among their last acts was an order for payment to the council's servants, including Milton who was to receive £86.12 of his annual salary of £200.[55] General Monk in Scotland repudiated the *coup* as a military usurpation of the legal civilian government and threatened to march on England in parliament's defense. The Rump's republican defenders claimed that it was the only relic of civil authority remaining and insisted that the sword remain subject to the civil power.[56] The army's defenders invoked *salus populi* again and claimed that the army had a right to represent and act for the people, as a more adequate embodiment of popular sovereignty than the Rump.[57] Vane and Henry Stubbe tried again to unite parliament and army around proposals for a representative parliament and some sort of select senate to guarantee fundamentals.[58]

During the six weeks of the Rump's dissolution (October 13 to December 26) Milton sketched out in two unpublished papers some proposals about government that he was to promote over the next several months as he tried to deal with one crisis after another. Both embody his core republican principles, but modified by the political reality of army power and the royalist threat during "this distracted anarchy" (*CPW* VII, 336). He would have the Rump Parliament (filled up by some process guaranteeing election of the well-affected) become the permanent Grand Council, recognizing that it is the only remaining vestige of an elected legislature, and more important, that it is committed to a republic. He eschews any version of the army's Select Senate plan and also Harrington's very complex model, preferring the simple structure of 1649–53: a unicameral legislature and an executive Council of State.

A conversation on the evening of the army *coup* with some unidentified friend close to the Council of Officers evidently galvanized Milton to dictate a letter to that friend the next day (October 20), with recommendations for a settlement which he directed the friend to pass along to the officers, or not, as he thought best.[59] While the "Letter to a Friend" is a common polemic genre, some such encounter probably did occur much as Milton reports it; indeed, this may have been the start of Milton's association with a loose republican–radical coalition that attempted to deal with the ongoing crises and stave off the restoration of the monarchy. Such a group would find Milton's pen a welcome asset, and his several treatises of these months are closely related to others of similar intent. The designated friend may have been Vane. His proposals show considerable sympathy for Lambert and the army, while Milton was harshly critical of them, but both men recognized that any settlement would have to address the basic desires and fears of both factions.[60] Milton was furious with the army for dissolving the parliament yet once more and he denounced their actions, past and present, echoing contemporary jeremiad language. Their dissolution of the Rump in 1653 was "without just autority"; happily they confessed their "backsliding from the good old cause" and restored it; but now they are again "relapsing & . . . backsliding" into the same fault (324–5). Though not blameless, the Rump has "deserved much more of these nations, then they have undeserved," and God indicated his pleasure in their restitution with the signal victory over Booth's royalist uprising (325). The self-described army of God behaved reprehensibly in renouncing the obedience and fidelity that they owe "to their supreme Magistrates," according to "the light of Nature, the lawes of Humane society, covenant & contract" (327). He allows that the Rump's failure to enact the principles he argued for in his last two tracts might have justified their dissolution as "not complyeing fully to grant liberty of conscience & the necessary consequence thereof, The Removall of a forc't maintenance from Ministers" (330). He does not, however, believe the officers acted from such motives, but rather from "close ambition:" "that Archan" (Lambert), Milton hints, wants to be Protector (328–9). The best resolution would be the restoration of the Rump, with MPs and army officers sworn to mutual protection, which should prove possible, he comments ironically, "if there be that Saintship among us which is talked of" (330). But he recognizes that the army "only now have the power" (329), and so offers a pragmatic compromise based on the temporary settlement under discussion which the friend probably reported to him and which the officers put in place a week later: a 23-member Committee of Safety composed both of officers and MPs. Milton suggests that a much larger body, also composed of army officers and as many MPs as the army would allow, become a permanent, single-chamber legislature, whose members as well as all army personnel would hold place for life, in order to prevent ambition and suspicion between those groups (329–31). All council members must swear to protect "Liberty of conscience to all professing Scripture the rule of their faith & worship," and to abjure any "single person" (330). Just how pragmatic and temporary this and Milton's other proposals for a permanent legislative council may be is indicated by his dismissive comment that "whether the civill government be an annuall democracy or a perpetuall Aristocracy, is too nice a consideracion for the extremities wherein wee are & the hazard of our safety from a common enemie, gapeing at present to devour us" (331). He proposes, as some security against "Oligarchy or the faction of a few," that the permanent legislature might appoint committees "of their faithfullest adherents in every county," which would "give this government the resemblance & effects of a perfect democracie" (331). Those terms, "resemblance & effects," reveal Milton's clear understanding that this proposal would not realize the essence of representative government. Reforms to the law and the courts, long-sought by various radical groups, he also puts off to consider "in due time," after the crisis is past. (332)

In late November or early December, as riots and military maneuvers threatened civil war and it became increasingly evident that the return of the Rump Parliament was the only feasible immediate settlement, Milton dictated the heads of another scheme, adjusted to the changed circumstances: *Proposalls of Certaine Expedients for the Preventing of a Civill War now Feard, & the Setling of a Firme Government.*[61] But he abandoned his intention to work up these notes into a treatise when events made this plan moot. Most republican stalwarts held out for the return of the ousted Rump Parliament; Londoners refused to pay taxes not lawfully voted in parliament;

a flood of petitions denounced the army and called for the return of the Rump or for a new "full and free parliament"; rumors of royalist uprisings abounded; apprentices rioted in London; some old Protectoreans called for the return of Richard;[62] and in early December republican troops took over Portsmouth and attacked several other strongholds. General Monk began marching toward England with the sole intention, he insisted publically and often, of supporting the Rump's claims and settling a Commonwealth government: "I do call GOD to witness, That the Asserting of a Commonwealth is the onely intent of my heart."[63] At this stage he probably meant it, though his action set in motion the trajectory toward a Stuart restoration. A treaty on November 15 prevented open conflict with Lambert's army, but Monk insisted on renegotiating its terms at great length as civil disruptions continued.

The heads of Milton's *Proposalls* revamp some notions from the *Letter to a Friend*, and form the nucleus of the model he would soon flesh out in *The Readie & Easie Way*. Here he calls unequivocally for the Committee of Safety to restore the Rump and make it the perpetual legislature, filling it up with "as many as shal be judged sufficient to carry on the great affairs committed to them" – either nominated by the council and elected by the well-affected people, or vice versa. Again, legislators must swear to the two "fundamentals," religious liberty and abrogation of a single person; and again, legislators, army officers, and soldiers should remain in place for life, so as "to remove ambition the comon cause of disturbance" (336–8).[64] He points to models of a permanent senate in "Rome, Venice, & elsewhere," and also argues through metaphor: the foundation of government "cannot be moveable without great danger to the whole building" (336). To deflect the insistent calls for a full and free parliament, he terms that institution a remnant of Norman slavery and gives his proposed legislature a name he thinks more appropriate to a republic:

> Because the name of parlament is a Norman or French word, a monument of our Ancient Servitude, commonly held to consist necessarily of 3. Estates, King, Lords, & commons; & the two latter to be called by the King to parlie with him about the great affairs of his realme, it might be very agreeable with our freedome to chang the name of parliament (especially now having outlived its honour by soe many dissolucions) into the name of a Grand or Supreme Counsell. (337)

With an appointed Council of State, this Grand Council would make lawes, determine peace and war, manage foreign affairs, raise taxes, and coin money, but would have nothing to do with the church "furder then to defend religion from outward violence" (338). To mitigate the danger of arbitrariness and as a means to attract supporters to his plan, he begins to develop a notion of federalism, diffusing authority to the regions. Many of the radicals' desired reforms he describes as projects to be achieved at the local level, centered in the chief city or town of every county: the administration of civil justice, election of judges and other officers by the (well-affected) people, law reform, schools to teach "all arts & sciences" and thereby make all the land "much more civilized." Also, the just division of the waste Commons (the chief plank in the Diggers platform), will make the nation "much more industrious, rich & populous" (338). Milton seems to be developing an interest in power-sharing between the national government and the regions, but he makes clear that all of this is "of a second consideracion," to be dealt with only after the "absolutely necessary" proposals regarding the Grand Council are in place, without which "wee are like to fall into evills & discord incurable" (339).

During these momentous weeks Milton was also occupied with private matters.[65] On November 22 his long-time friend John Bradshaw died, leaving him a testimonial gift of £10. A satiric funeral elegy linked the notorious president of the regicide council with Milton: "His Justice was a blind as his friend *Milton* / Who slandered the *Kings Book* with an ill tongue."[66] On November 29 Milton signed in a sprawling hand the discharge of Richard Powell's bond of 1627, acknowledging that the family had now paid in full the £500 loan and interest (*LR* IV, 282–3). The next month he received a newsy letter (dated December 2/12) from Henry Oldenburg in Paris, along with one, now lost, from his erstwhile pupil Richard Jones. Oldenburg suggests that Milton might write a history of the English revolution, speculates that the new peace between France and Spain might threaten English Protestants, informs Milton that charges against his adversary More, now a pastor in Paris, are to be taken up by a synod at Loudon, and passes on the rumor that Salmasius's posthumous reply is in press (*CPW* VII, 513–14). On December 20, a few days after his fifty-fifth birthday, Milton wrote back to both men. He reported to Oldenburg that he is "as well as usual," but he firmly rejects the notion of writing about the English conflicts: "What we need is not one who can compile a history of our troubles but one who can happily end them" (515). He agrees that the union of those "enemies of religion and liberty," France and Spain, increases England's vulnerability "in the midst of civil dissensions, or rather insanities," but insists that the chief danger comes from "our crimes" (515). He hopes the forthcoming synod may expel More and asks to be informed when Salmasius's posthumus reply appears. To Jones he writes as teacher and adviser, intimating some concern – warranted as it turned out – about Jones's application and his character. He expects from Jones, he states, not frequent letters but report of "your laudable progress and praiseworthy achievement in the most valuable studies." He sees Jones reprising the story of Hercules' choice, in that he also must choose between the pleasant and flowery ways of vice and the "steep and dangerous slope which is virtue's alone," which he must climb by his own effort and with the aid of his trusty guide, Oldenburg (516).

At length, the officers bowed to necessity and on December 26, 42 MPs marched back into parliament to try one more time to settle a republican government. During January Milton was probably cautiously hopeful that the Rump would manage a settlement and that Monk would continue to support it; as David Norbrook argues, Milton's stop-gap proposal for its continuation "looks more unrealistic with hindsight than it did at the time."[67] Milton was at work on the first version of the *Readie & Easie Way*, in which he casts the Rump as a perpetual legislative council, despite its disappointing resolution on January 13 to retain tithes. As Monk marched toward London he reiterated his support for the parliament in every venue, though his true intentions invited intense speculation. The Rump had become a lightning rod for royalist satire, its nickname ridiculed constantly in broadsides and doggerel verse:

> I have sometimes fed on a Rump in sowce,
> And a man may imagine the Rump of a Lowse;
> But till now was nere heard of the Rump of a House,
> *Which no body can deny.*[68]

On all sides royalists and Presbyterians deluged Monk with petitions appealing for the traditional rights of Englishmen to representative parliaments, and calling for the return of the secluded members, those expelled in Pride's Purge, or for a new "full and free" parliament, either of which was expected to restore the king.[69] Recognizing that not-so-hidden agenda, many increasingly desperate commonwealth supporters urged the Rump Parliament to fill itself up and get its house in order. Praisegod Barebone presented a petition of many thousands against the return of the secluded members.[70] Others urged Monk to become Protector or King.[71] Some sectaries threatened force if they were denied liberty of conscience.[72] Ordered by the Council of State to put down a tax revolt in the City by destroying the City gates and fortifications, Monk began that action but then drew back. On February 11 he gave the Rump an ultimatum: they must issue writs for elections to fill up their numbers within six days, and then quickly disband after arranging for successive parliaments.[73] Londoners, reading the signs aright, engaged in a frenzied celebration marked by the roasting of rumps throughout the city. From Strand Bridge, Pepys describes seeing 31 fires blazing,

> and all along burning, and roasting, and drinking for rumps – there being rumps tied upon sticks and carried up and down. The butchers at the maypole in the Strand rang a peal with their knifes when they were going to sacrifice their rump. . . . Indeed, it was past imagination, both the greatness and the suddenness of it.[74]

Even in Petty France Milton could have heard the uproar and had someone describe the scene to him; he may also have had someone read to him the gleeful reports of that scene in pamphlets and broadsides. On February 18 the Rump at last passed an Election Act to fill up the vacant seats to the number of 400, with suffrage limited to persons "well-affected" to the Commonwealth.

While things were at this pass Milton finished the first draft of his *Readie & Easie*

Way, joining his voice with those who, recognizing the agitation for a free parliament as a Cavalier Trojan horse, were imploring Monk to continue the Rump in power.[75] His title suggests that he also wanted to engage Harrington's tract of February 6, *The Wayes and Meanes Wherby an Equal & Lasting Commonwealth May be suddenly Introduced and Perfectly founded*, which calls for a free parliament structured according to his model; the right institutions, Harrington firmly believed, would preserve a commonwealth in England even if royalists were elected.[76] Milton again urges, as in the *Letter to a Friend* and the *Proposalls,* the simple expedient of preserving the status quo, which at this juncture means filling up and then perpetuating the Rump. He blames the failure to establish a commonwealth earlier on the "disturbances, interruptions and dissolutions which the Parlament hath had, partly from the impatient or disaffected people, partly from some ambitious leaders in the armie" – Lambert's faction most recently (*CPW* VII, 365). He also warns against the "fond conceit of somthing like a duke of *Venice*," giving some credence to the widespread suspicion that Monk,[77] or more likely Lambert, might be "suttly driving on under that prettie notion his own ambitious ends to a crown" (374–5). The tract expatiates at great length on the evils of monarchy, argues the superiority of commonwealth government and God's own preference for it, and expands the judiciary and educational functions the *Proposalls* had vested in local committees. He now imagines councils comprised of the local "nobilitie and chief gentry" (383), thereby offering some species of self-government to those vociferously demanding representation in a free parliament, and also exploring further the concept of federal–regional power-sharing.

He cannot, however, forbear warning the members of the legislature he would perpetuate who are unsound on toleration, that he who seeks "violently to impose what he will have to be the only religon, upon other men's consciences . . . bears a minde not only unchristian and irreligious, but inhuman also and barbarous" (380). Separation of church and state is, he again insists, the only route to peace: parliamentary elections could then be free of factional strife, as "every one strives to chuse him whom he takes to be of his religion; and everie faction hath the plea of Gods cause." Also, "[a]mbitious leaders of armies would then have no hypocritical pretences so ready at hand to contest with Parlaments, yea to dissolve them and make way to their own tyrannical designs: [and] . . . I verily suppose ther would be then no more pretending to a fifth monarchie of the saints" (380). This caustic judgment may encompass Cromwell and the Barebones Parliament, but it targets most obviously the recent machinations of Lambert and Fleetwood. As worthy models he points to the United Provinces, which enjoyed concord and prosperity when they left off persecuting the Arminians, and to Poland, which enjoyed most peace "when religion was most at libertie among them" (382).

But before the treatise in this form could be published events overtook Milton's plan, so he added a preface sometime after February 21 to adapt it to the new conditions (353–5). The enigmatic Monk, still proclaiming publically his commitment to a commonwealth and to toleration so as to keep the army under control, had the members secluded in Pride's Purge returned to parliament on February 21, an action he surely knew would lead to the king's restoration.[78] Again the City of London, reading the signs aright, lit bonfires and rang bells all night in celebration. At this juncture some republican pamphleteers buried their animosity toward the secluded members and urged that the Long Parliament remain in power, one declaring that "it can by no means be accounted either honorable, or just, or safe, or prudent for the present Parliament to dissolve themselves, till first they have fully asserted and vindicated their own just undertaking and the faithful adherents to it and them."[79] Milton's preface and revised plan are devised to persuade the restored Long Parliament to make itself into his perpetual Grand Council: with evident strain he declares that his plan might succeed better now that the parliament is sitting "more full and frequent." He refers hopefully to the resolutions "of all those who are now in power" calling for a free Commonwealth, and studiously omits any reference to the already-voted resolution calling a new parliament for April 25, implicitly inviting them to rescind that order (354–5).

Clearly there is nothing of utopia in this tract, but equally clearly it runs counter to political reality, given the vociferous demand of the English people to be rid of the all-too-permanent Long Parliament and its Rump. Milton of course knew this: in calling his tract *The Readie & Easie Way* he means to point to the simplicity of his plan: just attend to "main matters" and hold to the status quo in place at the national level. He still has some hope that all is not lost, basing that hope on the fact that "God hath yet his remnant, and hath not yet quenchd the spirit of libertie among us" (363–4). He speaks of his sense of duty "with all hazard . . . to forwarn my country in time," and his confidence that there are "many wise men in all places and degrees" who might put "a few main matters . . . speedily into execution" (387). Applying to Charles II Jeremiah's prophecy about God casting out "Coniah and his seed forever" (Jeremiah 22:24–9), he finds some slim basis for supposing that God might yet enable English lovers of liberty somehow to counter "this general defection of the misguided and abus'd multitude" (388). The tract appeared on or shortly before March 3, printed for the Fifth Monarchist bookseller Livewell Chapman, the most active publisher of repulican and radical tracts in 1659–60.[80]

Now that the Presbyterians were in a position of nominal leadership for the first time since Pride's Purge, they tried to impose their own settlement on the nation. Milton surely found most of this dismaying: they reinstituted the Solemn League and Covenant and the Westminster Confession, moved forward in settling Presbyterian ministers and organization in the church, confirmed the right of the clergy to tithes, and annulled the Engagement of 1650 promising fidelity to the Commonwealth "as now established, without a King or House of Lords."[81] They set March 15 as a date to dissolve, but some made a last-ditch effort to continue their session and set their own conditions for a Restoration: Prynne urged that "if the King must come in, it was safest for them that he should come in by their Votes" rather than trusting to a new parliament.[82] Under pressure from Monk, however, they left on March 16, after enacting writs for new elections that imposed no conditions on the traditional electorate and barred from office only Roman Catholics, persons who had abetted the Irish rebellion, or persons who had taken active part against parliament since 1641.[83] In theory this would disqualify Cavaliers, though in practice it did not, despite an order that this proviso be recited at all places of election. Voting began on March 24.

In an effort to secure the selection only of "well-affected" men who would oppose the monarchy, Milton wrote *The Present Means, and Brief Delineation of a Free Commonwealth*, couched as a letter to Monk. Though we have it only in draft form,[84] Milton almost certainly sent a finished version to the general: his Latin epigraph in the second edition of the *Readie & Easie Way* claims to have given advice to Monk.[85] If he published the work, no copies survive. It cannot be precisely dated, but was perhaps drafted in early March before parliament sent out its writs for new elections on the 16th, since it urges an alternative process for those elections to a new parliament as a matter to be acted on "without delay." But it could have been written later, since it urges Monk to impose that alternative process by force if necessary – implying that he should cancel the writs if they have gone forth.[86] Comparable addresses were being published toward the end of March by republicans and radicals, urging Monk to settle a commonwealth government by force if need be.[87] A published letter to Monk, *Plaine English*, reviews all the reasons why the king cannot be trusted, justifies the army's 1648 assault upon parliament as an act of "supreme necessity" to save the Commonwealth, and insinuates that Monk and his army should now in a comparable case oppose the clamor for the king's return, "vigorously asserting the good Cause of these Nations."[88] Roger L'Estrange thought, wrongly, that Milton wrote at least some part of it; he was, it seems, readily identified with such appeals to Monk.[89]

Milton surely knew that all former acts defining qualifications for electors and candidates had been voided on February 21, but he affects to believe that the Rump's February 18 qualifications are still in place; this rhetorical ploy invites Monk to enforce restrictions that would secure the selection of well-affected men opposed to a Stuart restoration and sympathetic to a commonwealth (*CPW* VII, 392–3). Milton now urges Monk to call "the chief Gentlemen out of every County" to manage an election of local councils by the well-affected people in every city or great town; those councils should then elect "the usual number of ablest Knights and Burgesses, engag'd for a Commonwealth" to make up a permanent Grand Council.[90] That Grand Council would have charge of the military "under the conduct of your Excellency," manage public revenues, make general laws, and administer foreign affairs – diplomacy, treaties, peace and war. The local standing councils would, as in Milton's earlier models, manage judicial laws, courts, and local magistracies, as well as all "Ornaments of publick Civility, Academies, and such like" (393). To make common cause with the Harringtonians, Milton now incorporates some elements from their system into his: partial rotation in the permanent Grand Council, a process for refining electors and electees to that Grand Council, and a plan for subjecting laws passed in the Grand Council to the votes of a more popular body – in Milton's scheme, the local councils would substitute for Harrington's 1,000-man popular assembly. But Milton was not suddenly converted to Harringtonian republicanism. Harrington's popular assembly would only give its aye or nay to what the senate proposes without debate, but Milton would have his local assemblies vote only after they "deliberate on all things fully" (394): he cannot imagine any meaningful vote without full and free discussion. If the local officials Monk convenes refuse this plan, Milton urges him to seek out others, or impose the settlement by force, "having a faithful Veteran Army, so ready, and glad to assist you in the prosecution therof" (395). But what is fundamental in all this is that Monk – by force if necessary – impose a process to restrict elections to the new parliament to those "firm" for a free commonwealth, and that that legislature be made perpetual.

Milton's *Readie & Easie Way* was often attacked during March, bringing home to him, if he was not fully aware of it already, how vulnerable he was making himself to royalist revenge and punishment in the ever-more-likely Restoration. By again becoming such a visible participant in the public discourse, he kept reminding his enemies of his status as the most illustrious defender of the regicide and the Commonwealth. A tract by Roger L'Estrange (published anonymously) mocks Milton's project for perpetuating the Rump. Those MPs are, notoriously, not the men of "Abilities and Honesty" called for by his argument, and in any case Monk has now scuttled his scheme:

> I could only wish his *Excellency* [Monk] had been a little civiler to Mr. *Milton*, for just as he had finished his *Model of a Commonwealth,* directing in these very terms the *choyce* of men not addicted to a Single Person, or House of Lords . . . *In come the Secluded Members and spoyl his Project.*[91]

Another witty invective places Milton alongside Nedham and the most notorious regicide traitors who may expect death at Tyburn – Milton because his writing spawned the Commonwealth:

> *John Milton* is their [the Rump's] goos-quil Champion . . . an old Heretick both in Religion and Manners, that by his will would shake off his Governours as he does his Wives, four in a Fourt night, the Sun beams of his scandalous papers against the late Kings book, is the Parent that begot the late Commonwealth. . . . He is so much an enemy to usual practices that I believe when he is condemned to travel to *Tyburn* in a Cart, he will petition for the favor to be the first man that ever was driven thither in a *Wheel-borrow.*[92]

In his 248-page volume *The Dignity of Kingship Asserted*, George Starkey takes violent issue with Milton's concept of liberty of conscience, his scurrilous attacks on

Charles the martyr, and his proposed commonwealth. But, in an effort to exalt his own service to the royalist cause, he pays high tribute to the rhetorical power of Milton's *Readie & Easie Way* to "move the affections," declaring that Milton is "universally owned a learned man" with a command of "ready invention," "expressions pathetical," "smooth and tempting" language, and "a fluent, elegant style."[93]

Much the cleverest of these royalist tracts, *The Censure of the Rota*, satirizes both Harrington and Milton. Written as if by Harrington, it describes the Rota Club discussing and voting on Milton's model, using the complex apparatus of Harrington's ballotting procedures. One member comments that Milton has "achieved the honour to be Styld the Founder of a Sect" for his theory of divorce and practice of it in his life, and that this is the liberty of conscience his Commonwealth would protect.[94] Another member offered Milton meanspirited advice to give over writing, "since you have always done it to little or no purpose . . . though you have scribbled your eyes out." Another pointed perceptively to Milton's "stiff formall Eloquence" and his disposition to deal in universals. Still another ridiculed his assertion that Christ favored a commonwealth, "notwithstanding the Scripture everywhere calls his Government the Kingdom of Heaven, it ought to be Corrected, and Rendered, the Common-wealth of Heaven, or rather, the Common-wealth of this world."[95]

Probably soon after March 16, when the Long Parliament dissolved and election writs went forth, Milton began revising his *Readie & Easie Way*, almost doubling its size. But before finishing it, I think, he rose to a polemic target that allowed for a quick and effective strike against the royalists.[96] On March 25 Matthew Griffith, former chaplain to Charles I and then minister to several clandestine royalist congregations, preached a highly inflammatory sermon in the Mercers' Chapel on the text, "My son, feare God and the King, and meddle not with them that be seditious, or desirous of change." Royalist sermons thundered forth from numerous pulpits during March and April, but Griffith's vengeful tone was especially embarrassing to the court in exile and to many royalists at home who were wooing Presbyterian cooperation in a Restoration with hollow promises of forgiveness and a liberal settlement of religious differences.[97] Griffith portrayed Charles II as an avenging Samson about to wreak sudden destruction on everyone – Presbyterians as well as Independents and sectarian radicals – who had been guilty of sedition against the Lord's anointed. Blatantly asserting regal absolutism and divine right, Griffith virtually made the king a lesser deity by such phrases as "God is an heavenly King, and eternal . . . but the King is an earthly, and dying God. . . . And yet in a qualified sence, they are both *Gods*, and both *Kings*."[98] He published the sermon almost immediately,[99] prefacing it with a fulsome dedication to Monk that urged him to carry on "what you have already so happily begun in the name and cause of God and his Anointed, till you have finish'd this great, and good work." Monk, still declaring for a commonwealth in order to keep the suspicious army and sectaries quiet, was outraged, and on April 5 Griffith was committed to Newgate prison.[100]

Milton probably published his *Brief Notes* on Griffith's sermon during the second week in April.[101] He refers to Griffith's imprisonment, and by April 20 Roger L'Estrange had published an answer to *Brief Notes*, titled with cruel wit, *No Blinde Guides*, and carrying the epigraph, "If the Blinde lead the Blinde, Both shall fall into the Ditch."[102] Neither printer nor bookseller was willing to put his name to Milton's tract, intimidated no doubt by the warrant issued on March 28 for the arrest of the bookseller Livewell Chapman, the principal conduit for republican and radical treatises. *Brief Notes* addresses Monk as one audience, affecting still to believe his "public promises and declarations" in support of a commonwealth and vehemently denouncing Griffith for supposing "most audaciously and falsely" that he would renounce them. But then he challenges Monk to follow through on them quickly, to "deterr such insinuating slanderers" (*CPW* VII, 471). He also addresses the Presbyterians, instancing Griffith's sermon as evidence that the royalists intend to subject all Puritans alike to ruin, perpetual bondage, and vengeance. Milton offers a trenchant and scornful analysis of Griffith's scripture exegesis and logic, and reprises his own often-repeated arguments justifying the regicide and the Commonwealth: all magistrates are equally the Lord's anointed; God himself showed preference for a commonwealth; the English had a right to abolish kingship since all forms of government are always in the choice of a free people; free commonwealths are best for "civil, vertuous and industrious Nations, abounding with prudent men worthie to govern" (481). But now, very reluctantly, he backs away from his earlier fierce repudiation of any Single Person and offers support to those who, during March, were urging Monk to become Protector or King.[103] If the degenerate English people, despairing "of our own vertue, industrie, and the number of our able men," seek "thralldom" under a king, Milton grudgingly allows that they might choose one – Monk – who has stood with the people against tyranny:

> [W]e may then, conscious of our own unworthiness to be governd better, sadly betake us to our befitting thraldom: yet chusing out of our own number one who hath best aided the people, and best merited against tyrannie, the space of a raign or two we may chance to live happily anough, or tolerably. (482)

Significantly, he specifies a temporal limit for such a "raign," refusing to give up hope that the people in time will learn better republican values.

In denying Griffith's claim that monarchy is the "fundamental law" of England, Milton invokes the principle of *Tenure*, that a free people have always the right to change their government: "how could our forefathers binde us to any certain form of Government, more then we can binde our posteritie?" (481). In his point-by-point answer to Milton, L'Estrange picks up on the very evident inconsistency: "If no certain form of Goverment can bind our Posterity," he demands, "what will become of your Standing Council?" He notes also that Milton would allow the people at any time to "Assemble, and *Tumult*, under the colour of a new *Choyce*."[104]

L'Estrange's insight points to what is probably Milton's unspoken assumption, that his Grand Council would be "permanent" only until a free people determine to change it. We can well imagine that Milton himself would demand representative and successive Grand Councils to replace the far from worthy legislatures he has proposed at various times to make permanent, once the threat of a Stuart restoration had passed. L'Estrange also invites a horrified response to Milton's previous treatises: in his divorce tracts Milton proved that devils may take human shapes, showing himself an Incubus "even to your own *Wife*"; in his answer to Salmasius he disgraced the English nation abroad, giving every man "a Horrour for *Mankind*, when he Considers, *You are of the Race*"; and his wickedness in *Eikonoklastes* exceeded even those examples.[105]

As elections went forward in late March and April, there was widespread suspicion that Monk was in negotiation with Charles; the votes were tending, as expected, to a Cavalier interest; royalist pamphleteers were heaping ridicule on all the Puritan leaders, placing Milton prominently among them; and the royalists were winning Presbyterian cooperation in plans to restore Charles II.[106] Some royalist pamphlets advised the electorate to ignore the "new pretended Qualifications" and choose knights and burgesses according to the old ways.[107] Many commonwealthsmen gave over the polemic struggle and went into hiding – Harrington was one – or else stood for election to the new parliament. But a small, now-desperate republican–radical coalition sought to provoke an army uprising by publishing inflammatory tracts predicting loss of pay, corporal punishment, and loss of religious liberty for the soldiers if Charles returned. *An Alarum to the Officers and Souldiers* appeals, as from one soldier to his brothers, for the army again to save themselves and the Commonwealth from extreme peril, since Monk's recent actions show that he cannot be trusted: "there is no other Bulwork of defense against the return of Monarchy but the Army . . . Men armed are seldom harmed."[108] L'Estrange erroneously thought that Milton wrote part or all of that tract as well as *Plaine English* and *Eye-Salve for the English Army*, the last of which he termed "a medicine of the same Composition, which (by general report) strook *Milton* Blind."[109] L'Estrange's readiness to father all of them on Milton shows his continued notoriety as the Commonwealth's premier polemicist, but also that Milton's tactics in his last tracts offer some basis for the assumption that he was associating himself with a radical coalition launching a last-ditch polemic effort.[110] The calls for the army to act bore fruit in a short-lived uprising led by Major-General Lambert, who escaped from the Tower on April 10 and marshaled a small contingent of sectarian and Fifth Monarchist soldiers at Edgehill; they were defeated and dispersed on April 22.

Milton's revised edition of the *Readie & Easie Way* was virtually the last piece of Commonwealth polemic to appear. The fact that L'Estrange, who answered virtually every tract by or supposedly by Milton as soon as it appeared, referred only to the first edition in his April 20 answer to *Brief Notes* may suggest publication sometime after mid-April.[111] Milton had to find a clandestine printer and bear all the costs of publication himself. All the other radical tracts published in the final weeks before the Restoration were anonymous, but Milton boldly inscribed his title page with that very familiar phrase "The author J. M." and took entire responsibility for the work, "Printed for the author."[112] It was a last brave, defiant gesture, taken in full awareness that he might have been signing his death warrant. The revised edition is very rare; only a few copies survive.[113] Milton's explanation for the new edition – that he wanted to correct some faults due to hasty publication and took the occasion to enlarge his argument – is a familiar rhetorical *topos*. He wanted in fact to address some other audiences: his degenerate countrymen crying out for the king, the remaining staunch supporters of a Commonwealth, possibly Lambert's army in the field, and the Convention Parliament which, he tries to believe, may listen to sound "counsel from any in a time of public deliberation" (408). He feels bound to do what he can, up to the last possible moment of decision, hoping that God may open enough minds to the force of his argument and stir up a remnant of lovers of liberty to resist a Stuart restoration. Milton now proposes that the Convention Parliament cast itself as the permanent Supreme Council. The deletions and the extensive additions in the new version[114] are often rhetorically motivated, to appeal to the several groups he would persuade, although many passages restate forcefully his core beliefs. Most references to the Rump Parliament are, naturally, deleted. Several changes address the Presbyterians in and out of parliament, inviting their moral revulsion for the vices of the court they seek to restore; others incorporate some Harringtonian features; still others justify a minority in using force to preserve their freedom – in an effort, perhaps, to marshal support for Lambert's uprising. Milton also expands upon his earlier provisions for local autonomy in education, justice, law, legislation, and control of the militia, describing such a federal system as a hedge against tyranny and as a means to shape a republican culture. Most important, now as always, is that "a few main matters" be put speedily in execution, and that the new parliament become a perpetual Grand Council. It was, of course, hopeless: in the latest additions to the opening and concluding paragraphs Milton voiced his fear that these would be "the last words of our expiring liberty." The complex rhetoric and politics of this tract are discussed on pages 389–97.

Milton probably sent copies to a few sympathetic members of parliament: only 16 Rump Parliament members were reelected amid a sea of Presbyterians and royalists. On May 1 parliament heard the King's Declaration at Breda read, with its promises of toleration and general amnesty except for those designated for punishment by parliament. They immediately voted that England's government is and ought to be by King, Lords, and Commons, sparking a night of revelry which Milton surely heard with dread and dismay. About this time he realized that his money might be lost; he had invested most of his savings from his salary as secretary (about £2,000) in excise bonds, but it was already too late to convert these into cash. On May 5 he transferred at least one of these bonds, and perhaps all of them, to his lawyer friend Cyriack Skinner, who probably suggested that strategy, but he lost the money anyway.[115]

Milton stood in danger of losing not only his money but his life, as parliament set about eagerly to determine the men to be excluded from the amnesty list. Throughout the month of May, he followed the depressing course of events: the king proclaimed with full pageantry and fanfare on May 8, touching off a night of revelling; the selection of seven regicides for immediate execution and continuing debates over others to be punished; the king landing at Dover on May 25 and his triumphal entry into London four days later. According to Phillips, Milton's friends "that wisht him well, and had a concern for his preservation," urged him to give up the Petty France residence and go into hiding until parliament decided whom it would punish, after which he could determine "what farther course to take" (*EL* 74). Grateful no doubt, but also dismayed that blindness forced him to depend entirely upon others in this crisis, he accepted the invitation of an unidentified friend who, at considerable risk, took the rebel polemicist into his home in Bartholomew Close just off West Smithfield – perhaps at the end of May.[116] There, Milton could only stand and wait.

"The Language of . . . the Good Old Cause"

Milton wrote his treatises of this period in close connection with the course of events, adapting his proposals and arguments to changing circumstances and specific audiences. But he strives in them to define and promote what he sees as the great goals of the Good Old Cause and the primary ends of government, religious and civil liberty, with religious liberty the ultimate value. In *Of Civil Power* and its companion discourse on church disestablishment, *The Likeliest Means,* Milton sets forth, without compromise, his own radical vision of the Christian church and of separation of church and state. In both treatises he takes up again the stance of adviser to magistrates, claiming their attention on the basis of his former good service. He wrote of civil liberty before, he reminds Richard's parliament in *Of Civil Power*, "by the appointment, and not without the approbation of civil power"; now his "natural dutie and affection" have led him to offer this treatise on religious liberty to them, though it pertains to all Christian magistrates and might have been written in Latin (*CPW* VII, 239–40). In *The Likeliest Means* he reminds the Rump Parliament of his notable defense of them and the English commonwealth against Salmasius: they should not suppose his "reason and abilitie . . . grown less by more maturitie and longer studie," now that he writes what "may be of moment to the freedom and better constituting of the church" (275).

These two treatises, and especially the first, are unusual among Milton's pamphlets for succinctness, emotional restraint, relatively unadorned diction, and comparatively straightforward syntax. Critics have noted that Milton's English tracts in

1659 and after are couched in a plain style markedly different from his earlier more imagistic and elaborate prose, and exhibit what has been seen as his turn to a new aesthetics of plainness.[117] But some distinctions are in order: the amount of, the kind of, and the reasons for the plainer style differ in the several tracts, as do the rhetorical and aesthetic effects produced by it. In these two treatises, offered as a thoughtful, balanced examination of church order and of the Christian magistrate's proper stance *vis-à-vis* religion, Milton's model is biblical plainness, a style that embodies what the tracts argue, the accessibility of spiritual knowledge to any and all. He ends *Of Civil Power* with a defense of such plainness as especially suited to discourse on religious issues:

> Pomp and ostentation of reading is admir'd among the vulgar: but doubtless in matters of religion he is learnedest who is planest. The brevitie I use, not exceeding a small manual, will not therfore, I suppose, be thought the less considerable, unless with them perhaps who think that great books only can determin great matters. I rather chose the common rule, not to make much ado where less may serve. Which in controversies and those especially of religion, would make them less tedious, and by consequence read ofter, by many more, and with more benefit. (272)

As Susanne Woods notes, one remarkable stylistic feature of these two tracts is the repetition of certain key words: in the first tract "free" appears alone or in variation 28 times, "liberty" 24 times; in the second, versions of "free" appear 49 times, "liberty" 10 times.[118] These repetitions insinuate the overwhelming value and importance of the named qualities, as well as the impact of religious and ecclesiastical freedom on producing a political culture that values liberty.

Of Civil Power (February, 1659) is Milton's most thorough exposition and defense of religious liberty and its concomitant, the almost complete exclusion of the Christian magistrate from any responsibility toward religion. That position is based on a radical extension of the concept of Christian liberty. Most Protestants accepted that Christian consciences must not be forced, but normally that protection was restricted to those practicing "true" religion as defined by certain doctrinal fundamentals. Milton begins by accepting the restriction to "true religion," but he proceeds to define it not by doctrines but by method. Citing the accepted principle that for Protestants the only ground of true religion is scripture interpreted by the private conscience according to the Spirit's illumination, he concludes that the Spirit's invisible action makes anyone's judgment of another's religion wholly impossible:

> These [scriptures] being not possible to be understood without this divine illumination, which no man can know at all times to be in himself, much less to be at any time for certain in any other, it follows cleerly, that no man or body of men in these times can be the infallible judges or determiners in matters of religion to any other mens consciences but thir own. (242–3)

The only external mark of true religion is the acceptance of scripture as the rule of faith, so any conscientious belief or practice based on such reading – that is, any Protestant religion, even Socinianism – must be true religion and not heresy.

From that radical redefinition Milton develops the four basic arguments of his tract with evidence from scripture alone. The tone, the positions taken, and the plethora of scripture texts indicate this tract's affinity with *De Doctrina Christiana*, which Milton has been working on as opportunity allowed. He argues first that the magistrate is not able to judge in matters of religion, since he cannot know whom the Spirit illumines: if he then assumes "infallibility over both the conscience and the scripture" he becomes as much Antichrist as the Roman pope. Second, he has no right to judge or act in religious matters, since Christ has reserved these to his own jurisdiction, which works by inward persuasion and if necessary by church discipline or excommunication, but never by corporal punishment or monetary fines: religion under the gospel is "our free, elective and rational worship" (260). Third, the use of force in religion violates Christian liberty, which sets the believer free from ceremonies and "the forcible imposition of those circumstances, place and time in the worship of God": a basic proof text is Galatians 5:13–14, "you are calld to libertie . . . stand fast therfore in the libertie wherwith Christ hath made us free" (262–4). Fourth, force can do no good, promoting neither the glory of God nor true piety but only implicit faith, conformity, and hypocrisy.

Milton also redefines heresy in terms that render it entirely innocuous, confining it to its original Greek meaning: "the choice or following of any opinion good or bad in religion or any other learning" (247). Accordingly, no Protestant can be a heretic, however far his opinion departs from an orthodox consensus, and he ought to be allowed – as *Areopagitica* had argued – the free expression and publication of his beliefs:

> If by the Protestant doctrine we beleeve the scripture not for the churches saying, but for its own as the word of God, then ought we to beleeve what in our conscience we apprehend the scripture to say, though the visible church with all her doctors gainsay; and being taught to beleeve them only for the scripture, they who do so are not heretics, but the best protestants. . . . [N]othing can with more conscience, more equitie, nothing more protestantly can be permitted then a free and lawful debate at all times by writing, conference or disputation of what opinion soever, disputable by scripture. (248–49)

The only heretic is the Roman Catholic, since he maintains some traditions and beliefs not drawn from scripture, and accepts the authority of the pope as well as scripture and the Spirit, but under the gospel heretics "are punishd by excommunication only" (249). From all this, Milton draws precisely the opposite meaning from the Presbyterian and centrist Independent description of the Christian magistrate's role as defender of true religion: it can only mean defending every Christian's right to his own conscientious belief and practice against any would-be persecutors (256). He flatly denies that the magistrate is, in the usual phrase, *custos utriusque tabulae*, keeper of both tablets of the Decalogue, or even of the second tablet that deals with sins against others. Whatever power magistrates have in relation to any of the commandments, "they had from the beginning, long before *Moses* or the two tables were in being" – that is, by the natural law.[119]

Milton relegates magistrates firmly to the natural order, but yet allows them some limited power to deal with certain loudly decried evils – blasphemy, idolatry, and Roman Catholicism – on the ground that these, properly understood, can be recognized as evils by the light of nature itself:

> Let them cease then to inportune and interupt the magistrate from attending to his own charge in civil and moral things, the settling of things just, things honest, the defence of things religious settled by the churches within themselves; and the repressing of thir contraries determinable by the common light of nature; which is not to constrain or repress religion, probable by scripture, but the violaters and persecuters therof. (258)

This position seems strained, but Milton along with some of his contemporaries had a rationale for it. Blasphemy Milton defines according to its Greek meaning as "any slander, any malitious or evil speaking, whether against God or man or any thing to good belonging" (246) – a definition that joins evil speaking against God with the civil laws on slander and thereby brings it, as Thomas Collier also did, within the purview of the magistrate as a matter of natural law.[120] Milton points to parliament's 1650 blasphemy law – chiefly targetting the Ranters – as defining blasphemy against God "in plane English more warily, more judiciously, more orthodoxally" than most divines (the Westminster Assembly of divines had dictated the sweeping blasphemy ordinance of 1648). Yet he recognizes the danger of invoking the term at all, as neither divines nor parliament members are "unnerring always or infallible" (246–7). Roman Catholicism is a harder case. It cannot claim toleration on the same grounds as Protestantism, since the Catholic conscience, by "voluntarie servitude to mans law [the pope's definition of doctrine], forfets her Christian libertie." It is the only true heresy, but the magistrate cannot refuse to tolerate Catholics on that religious ground: "if they ought not to be tolerated, it is for just reason of state more then of religion." However, that reason of state is not far to seek: Catholicism is less a religion than a Roman political state seeking to exercise universal dominion, and so is "justly therfore to be suspected, not tolerated by the magistrate of another countrey" (254).

The strain is more pronounced in regard to idolatry, which encompasses not only the Roman Catholic mass and icons but also Laudian liturgy and ceremony, and links both to pagan idol-worship. Milton defines idolatry here as "an impietie" against all scripture and quite foreign to any right conscience, whose works are "so manifest, that a magistrate can hardly err in prohibiting and quite removing at least the publick and scandalous use therof" (254–5). This seems to mean that the magistrate may prohibit Roman Catholic and Laudian public worship, though not gatherings in private. That prohibition seems to contravene Milton's principle restricting the magistrate to the natural order but, like some of his contemporaries, he assumed that idolatry, like blasphemy, can be recognized as evil by the natural law. In *De Doctrina Christiana,* though not here, he spells out the basis for that assumption: by God's general call partially renewing the natural faculties of intellect and will, all humans can come to "a knowledge of the way in which he [God] is to be propitiated and worshipped."[121] Since Milton finds idolatry in all its forms so reprehensible and enslaving to the human spirit, he easily assumes that it can be recognized as evil by the light of reason.

The Likeliest Means (August, 1659) is partly written in the plain, unadorned language of exegesis and argument, but with a much more liberal sprinkling of satire and invective against hirelings. In it Milton undertakes to answer the arguments of the tithe supporters and also of those who would substitute some other public maintenance. He begins by agreeing with them that a due maintenance of ministers is a precept of moral law – "the laborer is worthy of his hire." But he then critiques their biblical proof texts and marshals all the evidence – biblical and historical – used by the radical Independents and sects to argue that in gospel times such maintenance must be wholly voluntary. As part of the ceremonial or judicial law, tithes are abolished for Christians, so Old Testament precedents from Abraham and Melchizedek, Jacob, or the Levites mean nothing; Christ, the apostles, ministers in the early church, and "those *Waldenses*, our first reformers" (*CPW* VII, 308) subsisted by wholly voluntary contributions; the history of the church in England proves tithes to be a popish invention; and no other reformed church has retained them.[122] Nor may some other form of public maintenance be substituted, because "it concerns every mans conscience to what religion he contributes" and also because the magistrate is restricted to the civil sphere (308). Characteristically, Milton assumes that scripture and reason teach alike on this point: that it is against justice and equity to require a man "to pay for what he never learnd, or approves not; whereby, besides the wound of his conscience, he becoms the less able to recompence his true teacher" (309).

The rhetoric of Milton's tract is unusual among tithe opponents for focusing less on the wound to conscience than on "hirelings" and the evils they import into the church: hire, he claims, is more damaging than persecution because it corrupts the teachers. This is an effective rejoinder to those who argue that public maintenance is needed to uphold and spread the gospel, but beyond that, Milton's scathing terms reveal the depths of his disdain for the clerical estate as such. The "Simonious decimating clergie" make "unjust claim to other mens goods" (275). Judas was the first hireling, and papists brought this corruption to England. The Presbyterian divines, blinded by "covetousnes and rapine," seize tithes by force and "make the name of Christ accessory to violence" (296–7). Exacting fees for sacraments, marriages, burials, and interment is "wicked, accursed, Simoniacal and abominable" (299). Milton's bourgeois sense of property rights is evident in his tirades against the monopolist, tithe-collecting clergy with their hands in his pockets: they are "a numerous faction of indigent persons, crept for the most part out of extream want and bad nurture, claiming by divine right and freehold the tenth of our estates, to monopolize the ministry as their peculiar" (320). With scornful wit he plays on incumbent–incubus–incumbrance (305), and ridicules the ponderous margins and the politics of Prynne, "a late hot Quaerist for tithes, whom ye may know by his wits lying ever beside him in the margent, to be ever beside his wits in the text, a fierce reformer once, now ranckl'd with a contrary heat" (294). In sum, the clerical estate is thoroughly corrupt:

> When once they affected to be calld a clergie, and became as it were a peculiar tribe of levites, a partie, a distinct order in the commonwealth, bred up for divines in babling schooles and fed at the publick cost, good for nothing els but what was good for nothing, they soone grew idle: that idlenes with fulnes of bread begat pride and perpetual contention with thir feeders the despis'd laitie, through all ages ever since; to the perverting of religion, and the disturbance of all Christendom. (319)

The claim that tithes are a proper recompense for the expenses of a minister's education reawakens all Milton's scorn for those ill-educated students he knew at Christ's College, and for university divinity studies which "perplex and leaven pure doctrin with scholastical trash." It would be far better, he rages, if there were "not one divine in the universitie; no schoole-divinitie known, the idle sophistrie of monks, the canker of religion" (317). The establishment clergy elicits his fierce disdain, as a horde of lower class, ignorant fellows who seek to rise by the ministerial profession:

> [I]t is well known that the better half of them, and oft times poor and pittiful boyes of no merit or promising hopes that might intitle them to the publick provision but thir povertie and the unjust favor of friends, have had the most of thir breeding both at schoole and universitie by schollarships, exhibitions and fellowships at the publick cost; which might ingage them the rather to give freely, as they have freely receivd. Or if they have missd of these helps at the latter place, they have after two or three years left the cours of thir studies there, if they ever well began them, and undertaken, though furnishd with little els but ignorance, boldnes, and ambition, if with no worse vices, a chaplainship in som gentlemans house, to the frequent imbasing of his sons with illiterate and narrow principles. . . . If they had then means of breeding from thir parents, 'tis likely they have more now; and if they have, it needs must be mechanique and uningenuous in them to bring a bill of charges for the learning of those liberal arts and sciences. . . . But they will say, we had betaken us to som other trade or profession, had we not expected to finde a better livelihood by the ministerie. That is that which I lookd for, to discover them openly neither true lovers of learning, and so very seldom guilty of it, nor true ministers of the gospel. (314–5)

Now as then Milton has little understanding of and less sympathy for poor boys without family resources who seek to become ministers, and thereby gentlemen, but who are unable or unwilling to fit themselves for it by arduous intellectual labor.

Yet Milton defines the ministry in terms as egalitarian as those of any radical sectary: since the minister's only necessary knowledge and calling is from above, ministers may be elected by their congregations "out of all sorts and orders of men, for the Gospel makes no difference from the magistrate himself to the meanest artificer, if God evidently favor him with spiritual gifts, as he can easily and oft hath don" (319). For ministers and flock alike the means of attaining to spiritual knowledge is exactly the same: the study of scripture and the Spirit's illumination. The apostles were unlearned men; the first reformers (the Waldensians) were known as the poor men of Lyons; the scriptures are now translated into the vulgar tongue "as being held in main matters of belief and salvation, plane and easie to the poorest."[123] He even defends the artisan and tradesmen tub-preachers. Though our ministers think them "the reproach of this age. . . . It were to be wishd they were all tradesmen; they would not then . . . make a trade of thir preaching" (306). His proposals for the support of the clergy flow from these attitudes. Ministers should be supported by the voluntary contribution of the churches they serve; if those churches cannot provide an adequate subsistence, ministers should live on their own resources (as sons of the gentry might be able to do) or else support themselves by a trade as the apostles did. To plant new churches in neglected areas he proposes (again on the model of the apostles) that itinerant preachers teach for a time in a given area, then appoint elders to carry on "all ministerial offices" in the fledgling church. They might meet in church or chapel or (like the Quakers) in a house or barn: "he who disdaind not to be laid in a manger, disdains not to be preachd in a barn" (304). This missionary activity would be best funded by the charity of established churches, but the magistrate might also contribute, using revenues anciently given to the (then popish) church for superstitious purposes. This blurs somewhat Milton's divide between the civil and religious spheres, but he specifies that the magistrate may only dispense revenues to these purposes that had belonged to the church, applying them to such purposes as the churches themselves "or solid reason from whomsoever shall convince him to think best" (305).

Milton's own "solid reason" leads him to propose that the magistrate fund "schooles and competent libraries to those schooles, where languages and arts may be taught free together, without the needles, unprofitable and inconvenient removing to another place" (305). He probably assumes that such schools would teach lower-class boys generally, though only some of them would receive God's call to the ministry.[124] But for the rhetorical purposes of this tract he focuses on how such schools might produce ministers with a competence of learning and an honest trade, expecting that they then would not "gadd for preferment out of thir own countrey, but continue there thankful for what they receivd freely . . . without soaring above the meannes wherin they were born" (305). This proposal indicates Milton's assumption, shared with some other radical Independents, that while human learning is in no way necessary for ministers, they will find some of it useful. He seems to distinguish between the subject matter – ideas, concepts, insights, and information – which is irrelevant to a minister's function, and the methods or tools which are helpful in explicating scripture. None of the learning that strictly pertains to the minister's role requires university training: they might better be "traind up in the church only, by the scripture and in the original languages [and presumably in the arts of textual analysis] therof at school" (317). Such helps as sermons, notes, commentaries on the Bible, marrows of divinity, and the like can be had in English translations and studied "in any private house" and a minister's "needful library" of such works would cost only about £60. Whatever else might be helpful in other arts and sciences "they can well learn at secondary leisure and at home"(316–18). Anything beyond this is for the minister's own "curiositie or delight" as an educated man, not for his training or function as a minister. As for controversialists, the state might meet their needs by erecting "in publick good store of libraries" where men "of their own inclinations will become able in this kinde against Papist or any other adversarie" (317). Milton implies by this that serious scholars can and should, as he did, pursue their studies at home or in libraries, and employ them voluntarily in the service of the church.

In *Of Education* Milton denounced an "ignorantly zealous divinity" defrauded by the universities of knowledge useful to their calling (II, 375); now he firmly believes that a minister can do God's work in a good and sufficient manner without any reliance on human learning, though (unlike the extreme radicals) he assumes the utility of some tools of learning and suggests means for their acquisition. What drives his analysis is not empathy for the tub-preachers but a desire to collapse entirely all distinctions between clergy and laity, to claim for himself and all the faithful of every class their gospel right as "*a holy and a royal priesthood*"(319), who ought to take full responsibility for their own religious knowledge and practice:

> Christendom might soone . . . be happie, if Christians would but know thir own dignitie, thir libertie, thir adoption, and let it not be wonderd if I say, thir spiritual priesthood, whereby they have all equally access to any ministerial function whenever calld by thir own abilities and the church, though they never came neer commencement or universitie. (320)

Milton the erstwhile aspiring minister, who almost two decades before declared himself "church-outed" by the prelates, is now ready to appropriate any and all ministerial functions to all worthy Christians like himself.

The second edition of *The Readie & Easie Way*, almost twice the length of the first edition and published only days before the Restoration, was Milton's last opportunity to marshal support for the republic. In the body of the tract he makes carefully calculated appeals to various audiences, but the opening and closing passages, probably written last, constitute an impassioned prophetic jeremiad denouncing the depraved electorate bent on "chusing them a captain back for *Egypt*,"[125] as well as a deeply felt personal testimony: "If thir absolute determination be to enthrall us, before so long a Lent of Servitude, they may permitt us a little Shroving-time first, wherin to speak freely, and take our leaves of Libertie" (*CPW* VII, 408–9). As he stares into the abyss, Milton reminds himself and his compatriots of his good service to the Good Old Cause:

> Nor was the heroic cause unsuccessfully defended to all Christendom against the tongue of a famous and thought invincible adversarie; nor . . . our victory at once against two the most prevailing usurpers over mankinde, superstition and tyrannie unpraisd or uncelebrated in a written monument, likely to outlive detraction, as it hath hitherto convinc'd or silenc'd not a few of our detractors, especially in parts abroad. (420–1)

In this work rhetorical appeals and personal testimony intertwine so closely as to be well-nigh inextricable. The prose style is sometimes deliberately plain, to reinforce the simplicity of republican government by contrast with the extravagancies of monarchy and the intricacies of the Harringtonian model. But passages in the satiric or prophetic mode are characterized by dense imagery and striking metaphors.[126]

Like the related models Milton set forth over the past several months, the plan of government he elaborates here is pragmatic, not utopian. The fundamental elements are security for religious liberty; abjuration of a king or Single Person; a single-chamber Grand Council with members sitting for life unless removed for cause; and devolution of certain judicial, educational, and legislative functions to the counties. His political theory again justifies the rule of a worthy minority and the perpetuation of a "Councel of ablest men," but the application is, in the first edition of this tract, first to the Rump (unsound on matters of church disestablishment), and then to the largely Presbyterian Long Parliament that he had already denounced as corrupt, intolerant, and dangerous.[127] Now he substitutes the new parliament about to convene, which will be much worse by his standards. At this point any of them will be "worthy" and "able" if they stave off the Restoration.

One lengthy addition in the opening section reviews the great deeds of that minority who carried through the revolution, to rekindle their determination to hold their course. The Rump contained "a sufficient number to act in Parliament" as representers of the free people of England, but number is not the point: their adherents, "the best affected also and best principl'd of the people, stood not numbring or computing on which side were most voices in Parlament, but on which side appeerd to them most reason, most safetie" (412, 414). They judged the Rump Parliament not by their intentions, which cannot be known, or by their personal goodness (some were manifestly faulty), but by their counsels and actions in support of liberty:

> Neither did they measure votes and counsels by the intentions of them that voted; knowing that intentions either are but guessd at, or not soon anough known. . . . Safer they therefor judgd what they thought the better counsels, though carried on by some perhaps to bad ends, then the wors, by others, though endevord with best intentions . . . judging that most voices ought not alwaies to prevail where main matters are in question. (414–15)

This passsage indicates how Milton could support parliaments, army officers, and leaders – including Cromwell – that he and others criticized severely. It also shows that he did not equate "worthy" citizens with the Saints or the Elect as Vane and many sectaries did. And it prepares for his later argument that an even smaller minority might properly defy an even larger majority.

Much of the treatise addresses Presbyterians in and out of parliament. Milton omits a lengthy section on separation of church and state that would inflame them and adds passages to whip up their moral revulsion for the vices and corruptions of the court they seek to restore, in language that also reveals his visceral disgust for monarchy and for the servility, effeminacy, and civic idolatry it promotes.[128] Monarchy cheats and debases the populace by its dissolute practices, its vast expense, and its invitation to idolatry:

> A king must be ador'd like a Demigod, with a dissolute and haughtie court about him, of vast expence and luxurie, masks and revels, to the debaushing of our prime gentry both male and female; . . . to the multiplying of a servile crew, not of servants only, but of nobility and gentry, bred up then to the hopes not of public, but of court offices, to be stewards, chamberlains, ushers, grooms, even of the close-stool. . . . a single person . . . will have little els to do, but to bestow the eating and drinking of excessive dainties, to set a pompous face upon the superficial actings of State, to pageant himself up and down in progress among the perpetual bowings and cringings of an abject people, on either side deifying and adoring him. (425–6)

Monarchs aim "to make the people, wealthie indeed perhaps and well-fleec't, for thir own shearing . . . but otherwise softest, basest, vitiousest, servilest, easiest to be kept under" (460). It renders servile and unmanly men who ought to practice vigorous republican virtue and claim their freedom:

> And what madness is it, for them who might manage nobly their own affairs themselves, sluggishly and we[a]kly to devolve all on a single person; and more like boyes under age then men, to committ all to his patronage and disposal . . . how unmanly must it needs be, to count such a one the breath of our nostrils, to hang all our felicitie on him, all our safetie, our well-being, for which if we were aught els but sluggards or babies, we need depend on none but God and our own counsels, our own active vertue and industrie. (427)

Good kings, Milton claims, seldom happen except in an elective monarchy. He also reiterates his settled conviction that no man can rightfully hold royal dominion over other men, except for Christ, "our true and rightfull and only to be expected King . . . the only by him [God] anointed and ordaind since the work of our redemption finisht, Universal Lord of all mankinde" (445). All other monarchy is a species of idolatry.

Several passages review for the Presbyterians and other Puritans all the old abuses charged to Charles I and insist that they will escalate in the new court: subjugation of parliaments, the royal prerogative, the negative voice, the militia, a council filled with the king's vicious favorites and courtiers, a new royal revenue, appointment of judges beholden to the crown, idolatry, and mortal danger to liberty of conscience from a Popish queen and queen mother, as well as a royal issue "from the cradle, traind up and governd by *Popish* and *Spanish* counsels" (457). Other additions spell out the punishments – loss of estates, imprisonment, banishment – that all Puritans, including "the new royaliz'd presbyterians," may expect from the king's party. Let them take note of "the insolencies, the menaces, the insultings" of the anonymous royalist pamphleteers, "not daring to name themselves, while they traduce others by name"(451–2) – as they have Milton. In graphic metaphors, Milton evokes for the Presbyterians the assaults to their moral sensibilities and the harsh persecutions in store for them:

> Let our zealous backsliders forethink now with themselves, how thir necks yok'd with these tigers of Bacchus, these new fanatics of not the preaching but the sweating-tub, inspir'd with nothing holier then the Venereal pox, can draw one way under monarchie to the establishing of church discipline with these new-disgorg'd atheismes: yet shall they not have the honor to yoke with these, but shall be yok'd under them; these shall plow on their backs. (452–3)

Other passages, addressed to Puritans generally, extol the superiority of a republic over all other forms. In a characteristic gesture Milton assumes the agreement of all wise and worthy men with his position: "I doubt not but all ingenuous and knowing men will easily agree with me, that a free Commonwealth without single person or house of lords, is by far the best government, if it can be had" (429). Now, as from the time of the *Defensio*, Milton's free commonwealth is not a representative but an aristocratic republic ruled by those whose worthiness is demonstrated by their love of liberty and adherence to a republic. More than any other form of government a free commonwealth aims "to make the people flourishing, vertuous, noble and high spirited" (460). The wisest political theorists in all ages have proclaimed it "the noblest, the manliest, the equallest, the justest government, the most agreeable to all due libertie and proportiond equalitie, both human, civil, and Christian, most cherishing to vertue and true religion" (424). Also, more definitively than before, he makes the case for divine favor to republics. God himself "in much displeasure gave a king to the *Israelites*, and imputed it a sin to them that they sought one" (1 Samuel 8). Christ contrasted the kings of the gentiles who exerercise lordship over others with his own disciples who are rather to serve their brethren (Luke 22:25–6) – with reference, Milton insists, to civil government (424). A free commonwealth best follows Christ's precept, "wherin they who are greatest, are perpetual servants and drudges to the publick at their own cost and charges . . . yet are not elevated above thir brethren; live soberly in thir families, walk the streets as other men, may be spoken to freely, familiarly, friendly, without adoration" (425).

Most important, a free commonwealth is best able to protect liberty of conscience, which, Milton insists, "ought to be to all men dearest and most precious" and clearly was to Milton: "who can be at rest, who can enjoy any thing in this world with contentment, who hath not libertie to serve God and to save his own soul, according to the best light which God hath planted in him to that purpose, by the reading of his reveal'd will and the guidance of his holy spirit?"[129] The other main goal of the Good Old Cause, civil liberty, is not now defined in the expansive terms of popular sovereignty, as in *Tenure*, but as the securing of rights, linked to merit: "the civil rights and advancements of every person according to his merit: the enjoyment of those never more certain, and the access to these never more open, then in a free Commonwealth" (458).

Some appeals are addressed to other republicans, especially those associated with Harringon's Rota Club. Milton answers their criticisms of his first edition and those of the pseudo-Harringtonian *Censure of the Rota*,[130] by defending and expanding upon his idea of a permanent Grand Council. From the first edition he repeats his arguments for permanence: this council is the foundation of the state and it is dangerous to move foundations; political theorists (he summarizes Bodin) argue that making the whole senate successive endangers the Commonwealth; other sovereign councils were or are permanent: the Jewish Sanhedrin, the Areopagus in Athens, the Ancients in Sparta, the Senate in Rome, the Senate in Venice, and the City Councils in the United Provinces "in whom the soverantie hath been plac'd time out of minde" (436–7). Milton surely knew that these various senates and councils differ widely from each other and from his own projected legislature; he cites them as examples of permanence, not as close models. The English outcry for successive parliaments he attributes in part to the "fickl'ness" arising from our "watry situation" – he still believes in climatic influence – but he trusts that "good education and acquisit wisdom" may correct that "fluxible fault" (437). He meets the argument that perpetual senates have historically been balanced by some popular institution (Ephori, Tribunes, etc.) by claiming that such arrangements have been and would again be a source of continuous power struggles.

But he now admits that the Grand Council might be susceptible to corruption or arbitrariness, and so spells out more safeguards against those potential dangers.[131] In accordance with the political theory of *Tenure*, he clarifies that the sovereign power the supreme council holds is "not transferrd, but delegated only" (432). It must control the armed forces and the public revenue, but most of its business, he now specifies, will be in foreign rather than domestic affairs (433, 443). He also incorporates more Harringtonian features into his model: it was no time for commonwealth supporters to quibble over details. To satisfy the "ambition" of those who will not wait their turn to participate in government he grudgingly allows, as he did in the *Letter to Monk*, a Harringtonian "partial rotation" – here, a third of the members, at annual or longer intervals. He will not forejudge "any probable expedient," though he thinks such rotation has "too much affinitie with the wheel of fortune" (435–6), and though he still thinks it safest "to deferr the changing or circumscribing of our Senat, more then may be done with ease, till the Commonwealth be throughly setl'd in peace and safetie, and they themselves give us the occasion" (441–2). That phrase suggests, however, that he foresees future "occasion" for such changes. He knows that the army sectaries – and he himself – would not long endure what will at best be a heavily Presbyterian parliament, and so hints broadly that the people's army could expel this parliament if they prove intolerant and repressive: "Neither do I think a perpetual Senat . . . much in this land to be feard, where the well-affected either in a standing armie, or in a setled militia have thir arms in thir own hands" (435). He also works out in more detail his Harringtonian proposal in the *Letter* to Monk for the progressive refinement of nominators and electors to the Grand Council.[132]

He flatly refuses, however, to accommodate other aspects of the Harringtonian model, which he thinks unwieldy, exotic, and mechanistic, offering to "manacle the native liberty of mankinde; turning all vertue into prescription, servitude, and necessitie, to the great impairing of Christian libertie" (445). Harrington's Agrarian Law will not be needed to control threats to liberty from the acquisition of great wealth if prelates and lords are removed (445–6). Harrington's 1,000-member popular assembly, designed to vote without debate, is not only "troublesom and chargeable" and "unweildie with thir own bulk" but also an insult to reasonable men, allowed "only now and then to hold up a forrest of fingers, or to convey each man his bean or ballot into the box, without reason shewn or common deliberation" (441). Harrington's republic rests on the theory that good government structures will create good citizens and secure the republic; Milton's on the theory that only good (that is, liberty-loving) citizens can sustain a free commonwealth.

In the second edition Milton elaborates upon and reserves still more powers to the counties[133] as an alternative to successive parliaments or to Harrington's rotation. He hopes by this plan to deflect criticisms of permanent council and to satisfy the county elites accustomed to exercise political power. But more than that, he has also come to believe in the division of powers in a federal structure as a hedge against tyranny, as a means to promote educational and judicial reform and make government more representative, and as a means to shape a republican culture. Milton claims that his is a sounder federal model than that of the United Provinces:

not having "many Sovranties united in one Commonwealth, but many Commonwealths under one united and entrusted Sovrantie" (461). He discusses his federal scheme chiefly under the topic of civil rights, as a means to assure the "advancements of every person according to his merit" (458), expanding upon his earlier provisions for local autonomy in education, justice, law, legislation, and control of the militia. Every county will function as a little commonwealth, in which "the nobilitie and chief gentry . . . may bear part in the government:" they would make judicial laws, administer justice through local courts, and elect judges, exercising themselves in such matters "till thir lot fall to be chosen into the Grand Councel, according as thir worth and merit shall be taken notice of by the people" (458–60). Also, as in the *Letter* to Monk, general assemblies in each county would meet on various occasions to "declare and publish thir assent or dissent" on all general laws and taxes proposed by the Grand Council, and he now gives them the added duty of inspecting the public accounts (459, 61). In addition, he projects local schools and academies like those discussed in *Of Education*, wherein the sons of the county elites "may be bred up in thir own sight to all learning and noble education not in grammar only, but in all liberal arts and exercises" (460). This is quite a different education from the one he designed in *The Likeliest Means* for prospective ministers from the lower classes. He now makes explicit his expectation that such education and such experience in local government will prepare citizens for service at the national level, and will spread "much more knowledge and civility, yea religion, through all parts of the land" (460), thereby creating the kind of citizens a republic needs:

> To make the people fittest to chuse, and the chosen fittest to govern, will be to mend our corrupt and faulty education, to teach the people faith not without vertue, temperance, modestie, sobriety, parsimonie, justice; not to admire wealth or honour; to hate turbulence and ambition; to place every one his privat welfare and happiness in the public peace, libertie and safety. (443)

But in the present crisis all such reforms must be "referrd to time" (444).

In several heartfelt passages Milton denounces the besotted multitude who seem ready to creep back to the "detested thraldom of Kingship," displaying the innate political weakness Milton deplored in his countrymen in the *History of Britain* as well as a moral depravity that is proving infectious: a "strange degenerate contagion" or "epidemic madness."[134] In this situation, Milton justifies the liberty-loving minority – a large number he still insists – to act as and for the whole. He divides the nation into two entities, insisting that the rights of liberty-lovers should be preserved by the plan he proposes despite or against the political will of the slavish multitude:

> That a nation should be so valorous and courageous to winn thir liberty in the field, and when they have wonn it, should be so heartless and unwise in thir counsels, as . . .

> basely and besottedly to run their necks again into the yoke which they have broken, and prostrate all the fruits of thir victorie for naught at the feet of the vanquished, besides our loss of glorie . . . will be an ignomine if it befall us, that never yet befell any nation possessd of thir libertie; worthie indeed themselves, whatsoever they be, to be for ever slaves: but that part of the nation which consents not with them, as I perswade me of a great number, far worthier then by their means to be brought into the same bondage. (428)

He also adds a passage explicitly justifying a minority in using force to preserve their freedom, claiming first, that as victors in the war, only the Puritan parties retain full political rights, and then straining to deny the massive support for a Restoration from the Presbyterian majority. But at length he asserts in the baldest terms that a freedom-loving minority has the right to defend its liberty by force, when threatened, even though that means denying the majority the government it desires. The fact that Milton omits the disparaging references to the Fifth Monarchists from the first edition suggests that this appeal specifically targets Lambert's largely Fifth Monarchist battalion in the field and any other diehards who might be persuaded to join them:

> They who past reason and recoverie are devoted to kingship, perhaps will answer, that a greater part by far of the Nation will have it so; the rest therefor must yield. Not so much to convince these, which I little hope, as to confirm them who yield not, I reply; that this greatest part have both in reason and the trial of just battel, lost the right of their election what the government shall be: of them who have not lost that right, whether they for kingship be the greater number, who can certainly determin? Suppose they be; yet of freedom they partake all alike, one main end of government: which if the greater part value not, but will degeneratly forgoe, is it just or reasonable, that most voices against the main end of government should enslave the less number that would be free? More just it is doubtless, if it com to force, that a less number compell a greater to retain, which can be no wrong to them, thir libertie, then that a greater number for the pleasure of thir baseness, compell a less most injuriously to be thir fellow slaves. They who seek nothing but thir own just libertie, have alwaies right to winn it and to keep it, when ever they have power, be the voices never so numerous that oppose it. (455)

The royalist majority certainly thought Milton's version of liberty was some harm to them, and in our time this kind of argument has been used by totalitarian regimes to horrific purposes that would have appalled Milton. But it is worth noting the differences. Milton does not invoke it to support a leader, or a regime, or an ideology, but to justify the defense of religious and intellectual liberty certain to be denied to all the Puritan parties after the Restoration. The issue Milton struggles with here still bedevils even advanced democracies: the clash of majority rule and minority rights. Milton unhesitatingly puts rights first, though he does not extend them universally. He also hoped that the degenerate populace could learn in a republican culture to reject the idolatry and servility he saw as endemic to monarchy.

In the sections apparently added last, the preface and the much-expanded peroration, Milton's strained effort to sustain some hope in a miracle is all but overwhelmed by his anguished recognition that the depraved multitude, like the Israelites in the wilderness, meant to return to their Egyptian captivity. Milton's fundamental political insight is that only those who have attained to a personal experience of freedom and who continually exercise a morally responsible independence of thought and action can properly value or long maintain political freedom. The fierce invective and tragic vision that inform these passages mix with lamentation and a bitter, prophetic jeremiad as, absent enough such lovers of liberty, he foresees the certain collapse of all his political hopes and projects. In the peroration the Miltonic phrases tumble over each other and the metaphors jumble together in a passionate mimesis of the popular torrent sweeping all before it toward the precipice of Restoration:

> Thus much I should perhaps have said though I were sure I should have spoken only to trees and stones; and had none to cry to, but with the Prophet, *O earth, earth, earth!* to tell the very soil it self, what her perverse inhabitants are deaf to. Nay though what I have spoke, should happ'n (which Thou suffer not, who didst create mankinde free; nor Thou next, who didst redeem us from being servants of men!) to be the last words of our expiring libertie. But I trust I shall have spoken perswasion to abundance of sensible and ingenuous men: to som perhaps whom God may raise of these stones to become children of reviving libertie; and may reclaim, though they seem now chusing them a captain back for *Egypt*, to bethink themselves a little and consider whether they are rushing; to exhort this torrent also of the people, not to be so impetuos, but to keep their due channell; and at length recovering and uniting thir better resolutions, now that they see alreadie how open and unbounded the insolence and rage is of our common enemies, to stay these ruinous proceedings; justly and timely fearing to what a precipice of destruction the deluge of this epidemic madness would hurrie us through the general defection of a misguided and abus'd multitude. (462–3)

12

"In Darknes, and with Dangers Compast Round" 1660–1665

In the years after the Restoration, Milton's worst political fears were realized. Several of his closest associates were brutally executed and others imprisoned. Anglicanism triumphed and religious dissent of all sorts was harshly repressed. The press was rigorously censored. The court of Charles II was awash in licentiousness, scandal, and Catholic influence. Happily, however, his worst personal fears were not realized: though he lived in fear of his life for months, to the surprise of many he escaped a traitor's death or any formal sentence. But his case was bad enough: he was imprisoned for some weeks in 1660; his *Eikonoklastes* and *Defensio* were publically burned by the hangman; he lost Vane, Fleetwood, and other close friends to the executioner; and the plague returned in virulent force in 1665. Also, his domestic life was rife with tension and difficulty: he had to move house often, his finances were strained, his daughters resented the circumstances of their life with him, and he could neither understand nor cope with their defiance.

He had, however, his consolations. His friends remained staunchly loyal, managing by various strategies to win his reprieve, hiding him in time of danger, and providing the assistance a blind man needs in managing his affairs. He had friends, students, and amanuenses to read to him and write for him, though not with the regularity he wanted and needed. A third marriage brought order and domestic comfort to his life, though his daughters complained bitterly about their new stepmother. The muse continued to visit nightly and *Paradise Lost* was taking final shape, though reportedly Milton's poetic vein flowed only for six months of the year. The rest of his time was most likely spent bringing *De Doctrina Christiana* close to completion. The primary amanuensis for that treatise, Jeremy Picard, was associated with Milton in 1658–60, but Milton would have had little time for it in the frantic months when he was writing against the Restoration; no doubt he took it up again when he could, probably giving something like final form to his doctrinal positions and arguments by the mid-1660s, with a view to seeking publication abroad if occasion should offer. In Restoration England publication would have been impossible.

There are numerous stories and anecdotes about Milton during this period, some of questionable reliability, some containing a kernel of truth. Many were recounted long after the fact by persons whose memories might be faulty, who may not have heard or understood Milton properly, or who, like Milton's daughter and granddaughter, wanted to make themselves interesting to later biographers and scholars seeking personal tidbits about the great Milton. The most reliable witnesses are Milton's widow, Elizabeth Minshull, his nephew Edward Phillips, and his student and friend, Cyriack Skinner.

"Fall'n On Evil Days . . . and Evil Tongues"

Milton's fate, like that of the regicides and other prominent supporters of the revolution, depended on whether he would be excepted by name from the general pardon the king promised at Breda, at which time he left it to parliament to decide upon the exceptions. From May 9 onward parliament debated about who should be punished and how. Milton thought himself in imminent danger as he hid for more than three months at an unidentified friend's house in Bartholomew Close.[1] He had reason to worry: he was closely associated in royalists' minds with Cromwell's government and Nedham's notorious news magazines; he had been the first to justify the regicide in *Tenure*; to the very end he had fiercely opposed the king's return; and his *Eikonoklastes* and *Defensio* were still primary targets of royalist outrage. Throughout the summer his emotions were surely on a roller-coaster as every few days friends brought news of debates and decisions about particular persons to be punished. He would also have been dismayed to hear about the deluge of poems, letters, broadsides, petitions, sermons, and tracts celebrating the king's return, and perhaps especially, if he encountered it, the fulsome panegyric, *Astraea Redux*, by his erstwhile colleague in Cromwell's Secretariat, John Dryden, who would soon become the laureate of the new age.[2]

The week of June 11–18 was a period of particular danger for Milton. By then the Commons had voted to exclude a large number of persons from the Indemnity Bill. The most notorious regicides – Cromwell, Bradshaw, Ireton, and Pride – were posthumously attainted of treason on May 14. All the living regicides – not only the signers of the king's death warrant but others instrumental in his trial and execution – were made subject to punishment, ten of them capitally – including Milton's erstwhile associates Major-General Thomas Harrison, Thomas Scott, and Edward Dendy the council's sergeant-at-arms. Cromwell's adviser Hugh Peters was also made subject to death as a regicide because he had promoted the regicide before the fact – a dangerous precedent for Milton who also did so in *Tenure*, largely written before though published only after the king's execution.[3] Milton knew, as everyone did, the horrific details of those public executions for treason and he must have recalled them often as he lay hidden in self-imposed imprisonment, imagining his friends enduring that fate and fearing it for himself. The sentence soon to be imposed on Harrison is typical:

> The Judgment of this Court is . . . That you be led back to the place from whence you came, and from thence to be drawn upon an hurdle to the place of execution; and there you shall be hanged by the neck, and being alive shall be cut down, and your privy members to be cut off, your entrails to be taken out of your body, and, you living, the same to be burnt before your eyes, and your head to be cut off, your body to be divided into four quarters, and head and quarters to be disposed of at the pleasure of the king's majesty, and the Lord have mercy upon your soul.[4]

As Michael Lieb observes, it is a sentence that forces the victim to witness his own emasculation and evisceration, to experience the annihilation of his identity in a public spectacle.[5] Milton, who so often identified with the archetypal poet Orpheus, no doubt imagined himself liable to reenact the dismemberment of Orpheus all too literally. And the polemicist who had so often before constructed himself as a species of epic hero in his combat with the King's book and with Salmasius, now had to wonder whether he could display the physical courage that ordeal would demand. During those anxious months in hiding, his thin-spun life at the mercy of the blind Fury with the abhorred shears, he had to wonder whether he would ever finish the great epic he had begun. There must have been days when the confidence he had sustained through many years of public duties and private troubles in his God-given vocation as poet was badly shaken, and when, like Samson, he must have wondered whether God had abandoned him.

On June 8 the Commons decided to select twenty notable non-regicides for rigorous punishment short of death – a category into which Milton might well fall; the fierce debates over which persons to choose were fueled by Milton's old enemy, William Prynne. The twenty agreed upon included several of Milton's friends and erstwhile associates: Sir Henry Vane, John Goodwin of Coleman Street, Speaker of the Commons William Lenthall, Major-Generals John Lambert, John Desborough, and Charles Fleetwood. Milton's name was floated briefly on June 18 as the possible twentieth man, but it was not seconded.[6] His early biographers attribute his remarkable escape to the maneuvers of friends and supporters in parliament and behind the scenes. Marvell, member of parliament for Hull, was one who, according to Edward Phillips, "acted vigorously in his behalf, and made a considerable party for him" (*EL* 74). Jonathan Richardson heard at third hand that Secretary of State William Morrice and the erstwhile Cromwellian statesman Sir Thomas Clarges "were his friends, and manag'd Matters Artfully in his Favour," prompted by William Davenant whose life Milton had helped save in 1651.[7] These men and perhaps also Sir Arthur Annesley, later a close friend of Milton's,[8] may have acted in part from regard for his learning and talents, and also from a sense that to punish this internationally famous blind scholar would seem meanspirited and prove counterproductive.

Milton's supporters did not protest, and perhaps even encouraged, a resolution on June 16 urging Charles to call in Milton's *Eikonoklastes* and *Defensio* and John Goodwin's *Obstructors of Justice*, to have those books burned by the hangman, and to order the authors arrested by the Commons sergeant-at-arms.[9] That resolution might serve to assure Milton's enemies that he would be separately apprehended and punished and so need not be listed among the twenty, though Goodwin was still included. Milton could then remain in hiding until the Act of Oblivion were signed, after which the resolution against him would presumably be moot. That some such plan was in play is suggested by the timing: on June 27 the king in council ordered that the proclamation against Milton and Goodwin be issued, but that was not done until August 13, after the House of Lords had debated for a month about imposing fiercer penalties on still more persons. They did not name Milton, but he was not home free until a compromise Act of Oblivion was finalized by the two houses.

The king's August 13 proclamation vents outrage against Milton's and Goodwin's books, and seems to propose punishing the books in lieu of the persons. Milton's two books are said to contain "sundry Treasonable Passages against Us and our Government, and most Impious Endeavors to justifie the horrid and unmatchable Murther of Our late Dear Father, of Glorious Memory," while Goodwin's is described in less inflammatory language, as written "in defence of the Traiterous Sentence." But then, instead of the expected directive to apprehend these men, the proclamation states that they "are both fled, or so obscure themselves, that no endeavors used for their apprehension can take effect, whereby they might be brought to Legal Tryal, and deservedly receive condigne punishment for their Treasons and Offences."[10] It provides instead that sheriffs, magistrates, justices of the peace, and university officials confiscate all copies of these books and cause them to be "publickly burnt by the hand of the Common Hangman." The proclamation, reprinted in full in *Mercurius Publicus*,[11] was executed promptly: on August 27 several copies of Milton's and Goodwin's books were solemnly burned at the Sessions House in the Old Bailey, and perhaps also in subsequent weeks and in other venues, though apparently not at Oxford.[12]

The Act of Free and General Pardon, Indemnity, and Oblivion was passed by both houses on August 28 and signed by the king the next day. It excepted 102 persons by name, but not Milton. Oliver Cromwell, Henry Ireton, John Bradshaw, and Thomas Pride and twenty other dead regicides were attainted of treason, their estates were confiscated, and they were made subject to whatever penalties parliament might impose. Forty-nine living regicides were condemned to death: twenty had escaped abroad and the other nineteen had their executions suspended because they had surrendered in expectation of the mercy the King's Proclamation at Breda seemed to promise. Six other regicides were to be punished by all means except death. The non-regicides Vane and Lambert were condemned to execution, but on the understanding that parliament would petition that their lives be spared. The stalwart republican Arthur Hasilrigg was to be imprisoned for life, and twenty others were incapacitated for life from holding any civil, military, or ecclesiastical office.[13] The disposition of many cases, including Milton's, depended more on their connections and their friends than on their records.

When Milton was not excepted from the Act of Pardon, he had reason to suppose himself fully comprehended in it – "pardoned, released, indempnified, discharged, and put in utter Oblivion" for all offenses during the civil wars and Interregnum.[14] Bishop Burnet, like many others, was surprised by his escape:

> *Milton* had appeared so boldly, tho' with much wit and great purity and elegancy of style, against *Salmasius* and others, upon that Argument of the putting the King to death, and had discovered such violence against the late King and all the Royal family, and against Monarchy, that it was thought a strange omission if he was forgot, and an odd strain of clemency, if it was intended he should be forgotten. He was not excepted out of the act of indemnity.[15]

His escape is the more surprising given the barrage of polemic denunciations that linked him with the worst of the offenders. A satiric poem, *Britain's Triumph* (*c.* May 14) denounced Milton the "Image-breaker" along with Bradshaw, Nedham, Harrington, and other Commonwealthsmen, claiming that Milton's best "divorce" would be to commit suicide: "stabb'd, hang'd, or drown'd" he would "rail no more against his *King*."[16] A satiric dialogue between Cromwell and Hugh Peters (*c.* May 17) portrays the indignities and disgraces imposed on the king's family and the nobility and gentry of three nations as the invention of "*Milton,* and *Nedham*, with the help of *Jack Hall*, and the Devill to boot."[17] David Lloyd (*c.* July 26) described him as "a blind Beetle that durst affront the *Royal Eagle.*"[18] A satiric poem (*c.* August 17) places Milton in Pluto's court along with Goodwin and Hugh Peters, all of them fit to write for the devil as they did for Cromwell.[19]

Rejoicing in his happy escape, Milton came out of hiding, ready to reclaim his life and his independence, and to walk about in the sunshine. In early September, probably, his friends arranged a temporary lodging near the bustling Red Lion Inn in what is now Red Lion Square in Holborn, near Bloomsbury. Almost immediately he was confronted with a pseudo-Salmasius publication, Joseph Jane's answer to *Eikonoklastes*, *Eikon Aklastos* (1651), republished as if it were a long-suppressed response by Salmasius. It was dedicated to Charles II by one John Garfeild, who refers to Milton as "one of your Majesties grand enemies," against whom God had evidenced "his particular judgment by striking him with blindness."[20] On September 5/15 the real Salmasius posthumous appeared: Salmasius's son published in Dijon, and soon after in London, Salmasius's partial response to

Milton's *Defensio* – more than three hundred pages of tiny print, in Latin, which dealt only with Milton's first three chapters.[21] No doubt Milton obtained an early copy and had it read to him, chafing at insults he could not now answer. He heard himself traduced as "a teacher in an insignificant London school, [with] . . . a dishonest mind, an evil tongue, an atrocious style," and as "a libeler, a sycophant, an imposter," "a dwarf in stature, a giant in malice" who is "blind with rage, not less in mind than in body." Especially galling, no doubt, were Salmasius's jibes that many who know Milton "earnestly deny that Milton himself knows Latin or can write it," that the faults in Milton's early Latin poetry show him to be a bad Latinist, and that the true author of the *Defensio* is a "French teacher from the lower school."[22]

While living in Holborn, Milton would have learned the fates of several friends and associates. Vane was in the Tower under threat of execution but with some possibility of reprieve. Charles Fleetwood and John Goodwin were incapacitated from holding office. Overton evidently escaped punishment. Nedham fled to Amsterdam but returned soon after the Act of Oblivion secured his safety and took up the practice of medicine; his escape from all punishment occasioned much wonder and protest.[23] Soon Milton had news of the trials of twenty-nine regicides (October 11–16), and of the first ten grisly executions by hanging, disembowelling, drawing, and quartering (October 13–19).[24] The details of the executions were fully reported in the newsbooks, and Milton could hardly help hearing the mobs in the streets as they returned from these bloody occasions.

One autumn day during the parliamentary recess (September 13–November 6), Milton was greatly surprised to find himself arrested and imprisoned by James Norfolke, sergeant-at-arms of the Commons.[25] Apparently, Norfolke did not think that the August 13 proclamation against Milton had been canceled by the Act of Oblivion. We can imagine Milton's anxiety and the difficulties he endured as a vulnerable blind man, wholly dependent on his jailors for every necessity of life, and unsure whether he would soon – or ever – be freed. Unfortunately, those who could tell us when, where, how long, and under what conditions he was incarcerated, and how he reacted to that situation, avoid that topic, being eager in the Restoration milieu to play down Milton's "treasonable" politics. Edward Phillips avoids all reference to Milton's imprisonment and Cyriack Skinner alludes to it obliquely, emphasizing, perhaps misleadingly, its short duration: "For hee early sued out his Pardon; and by means of that, when the Serjeant of the house of Commons had officiously seisd him, was quickly set at liberty" (*EL* 32). We do not know when Milton made formal application for a pardon under the Act of Oblivion or whether a delay occurred in processing it – likely enough, since such applications were very numerous. The pardon was probably granted a day or two before December 15, when the Commons gave order "That Mr. *Milton*, now in Custody of the Serjeant at Arms attending this House, be forthwith released, paying his Fees."[26] A dispute about fees may have delayed his release: two days later Marvell protested that they were exorbitant. The incident is recorded by a parliamentary diarist:

> Dec. 17. The celebrated Mr. John Milton having now laid long in custody of the serjeant at arms, was released by order of the house. Soon after, Mr. Andrew Marvel complained that the serjeant had exacted £150 fees of Mr. Milton; which was seconded by col. King and col. Shapcot. On the contrary, Sir Heneage Finch observed, That Milton was Latin Secretary to Cromwell, and deserved hanging. However, this matter was referred to the committee of privileges to examine and decide the difference.[27]

There is no record of the committee's decision. The £150 charges may point to a rather long stay, as this diarist thought – perhaps eight or ten weeks. Some years later Colonel John Hutchinson waxed indignant at being charged £50 for 24 weeks' imprisonment in the Tower.[28] But it also may be that the sergeant, supported by Solicitor-General Finch who had prosecuted the condemned regicides, wanted to see that Milton was punished severely in his pocketbook, at least. In any case, having spent his fifty-second birthday in prison, Milton was able to spend the holiday season at home. What arrangements were made for his daughters during the months he was in hiding and in prison is not known: they were perhaps with relatives, or some friend or friends, or a servant. These were surely anxious and disruptive times for them, with a father disgraced, economically distressed, and in danger of prison or worse, and without much claim on anyone's care or affection.

Soon after Milton was set at liberty the Convention Parliament was dissolved (December 20), having gone far to re-establish the monarchy and the church on the old lines. In an effort to diffuse the discontent mounting among the Presbyterians in parliament and in the City of London, Charles had issued a proclamation on October 25 offering, on a temporary basis, to accommodate Presbyterians and most incumbent ministers in a national church with a circumscribed episcopacy and flexibility in worship, until an inclusive synod could settle matters of doctrine and liturgy.[29] But parliament pointedly declined such a settlement: instead, high-church bishops were appointed, large numbers of Presbyterian clergy were removed from livings so as to restore sequestered Anglicans and appoint new men, and local magistrates enforced the use of the Prayer Book. Milton could take no joy in the accuracy of his predictions in *The Readie & Easie Way* about the folly of Presbyterian hopes for accommodation. More dismaying still were the repressive measures enacted in response to the uprising on January 6, 1661 led by the Fifth Monarchist Thomas Venner, whose little party of thirty-five or forty men was taken to be the vanguard of widespread sectarian conspiracies. All religious meetings of Anabaptists, Quakers, and other radical Independents and sects were forbidden, local militias enthusiastically searched out suspected sectaries, especially Quakers, and more than 4,500 Friends were put in prison within six weeks.[30] Even before Venner's uprising John Bunyan had been jailed for preaching.

Milton moved to a new house in Jewin Street soon after his release, probably as soon as friends found one suitable for him.[31] This move took him back to a familiar neighborhood: Jewin Street goes off from Aldersgate Street where he had lived in a "pretty garden house" between 1640 and 1645 and, like his next house in the Barbican, it was in the parish of St Giles Cripplegate. But he may still have been in Holborn for the gruesome events of January 30, 1661, marking the anniversary of Charles I's execution. The newsbooks describe how the "odious carcasses" of Cromwell, Ireton, and Milton's friend Bradshaw, who had presided at the king's trial, were disinterred from their burial places in Westminster Abbey:

> On Munday night *Cromwell* and *Ireton*, on two several Carts were drawn to *Holborn* from *Westminster*, after they were digged up on Saturday last, and the next morning Bradshaw; Today [Wednesday] they were drawn upon Sledges to Tyburn, all the way (as before from *Westminster*) the universal outcry of the people went along with them. When these their Carcases were at *Tyburn*, they were pulled out of their Coffines, and hang'd at the several angles of that Triple Tree, where they hung till the Sun was set; after which they were taken down, their heads cut off, and their loathsome Trunks thrown into a deep hole under the Gallows.[32]

Afterwards, the three heads were placed by the hangman on poles on the top of Westminster Hall, where they were to remain until 1684. If Milton were still in Holborn, he had some cause to fear for his safety as he heard the mob raging for two days around the Red Lion Inn, where the bodies were deposited on hurdles to await the January 30 degradations. If he had already moved, he surely heard about and lamented the violations visited upon his former associates.

He had further cause to reflect on his vulnerability as polemic attacks on him continued in 1661: a reprint of Ephraim Pagitt's denunciation of him as a divorcer; a reprint of Starkey's *Dignity of Kingship* answering his *Readie & Easie Way*; a new edition of the *Regia Sanguinis Clamor* which Pierre Du Moulin now owned to, and for which he received the reward of some choice ecclesiastical appointments; and a polemic by George Bate castigating Milton as "a musty pedant" whose tongue was "dipt in the blackest and basest venom" in his *Eikonoklastes* and *Defensio*."[33] Twice in January, 1662, his polemic antagonist Alexander More preached before the king and court at St James's Chapel and there was talk of attaching this eloquent preacher to the English court, though he was soon back in Paris and again in trouble.[34] Richardson heard that Milton in these first Restoration years "was in Perpetual Terror of being Assassinated" by some irate royalist enemy, and that "He then kept Himself as Private as he could" (*EL* 276). He had been released from prison but felt he had to keep himself shut up. No doubt he hated his special vulnerability: a blind man could not even recognize the approach of an assassin, let alone ward off an attack.

In Jewin Street Milton began to feel more secure. He may have put his theological tract and his great poem away during the first year or so after the Restoration when he felt himself in greatest danger, and as time passed began to work on them again. The near brush with death and his continuing if gradually diminishing sense of danger in the years immediately following the Restoration would naturally enough prompt Milton to try to give final formulation to his own statement of religious faith, which he also saw as his most important educational project, *De Doctrina Christiana.* It would also prompt him to try to finish *Paradise Lost* as soon as he could. Both of these works look beyond Milton's immediate compatriots to address all Christendom, present and future. Sometime during or before 1662 he sent to a friend in Germany, probably Lieuwe van Aitzema, a copy of Jean Bodin's *Colloquium Heptaplomeres,* a rare, boldly speculative, heretical dialogue containing forceful arguments for anti-Trinitarianism and divorce by some of the participants. Several letters exchanged between Baron Joannes Christianus de Boineburg and Hermann Conring in 1662 recount their efforts to find and copy for their prince's library Bodin's "horrible book" of "impious ravings"; they lament that the man who had it from Milton will not lend it, and they are also interested in Milton's "book about divorce in English" which the same man has.[35] Milton kept up his continental connections, exchanging his suspect books and theological speculations with European friends as he worked on *De Doctrina Christiana.*

He surely followed events in England with mounting distress. On St George's Day, April 23, 1661, Charles II was crowned with elaborate pageantry and ritual anointing, which Milton would have thought idolatrous. The Cavalier Parliament, which convened on May 8, 1661 and which contained only about fifty Presbyterians, pressed on vigorously to eradicate Puritanism and settle church and state as Charles II and his first minister Clarendon desired. On May 27, 1661 the Solemn League and Covenant was burned by the common hangman; on May 26 all members of parliament were required to receive the sacrament by Anglican rites or be disqualified; on June 18 bishops were restored to the House of Lords. In September twenty notables associated with the Puritan regime were dug up from their burial places in Westminster and thrown into a common pit: among those well known to Milton were the parliamentarian John Pym, the historian and diplomat Dr Isaac Dorislaus, Stephen Marshall the Smectymnuuan, and the wife of Milton's friend John Bradshaw, president of the regicide court.[36] Before the first session of the Cavalier Parliament ended on May 19, 1662, it passed several laws to repress dissent: an Act targetting Quakers imposed fines, imprisonment, and banishment on any who refuse to take oaths or who hold private meetings for worship; a Press Act required all publications to be licensed by a designated official; and an Act of Uniformity required clergy to give formal assent to everything in the *Book of Common Prayer,* to receive ordination from a bishop if not already so ordained, to renounce the Solemn League and Covenant, and (like all civil officials and military personnel) to swear oaths of allegiance, supremacy, and passive obedience to the monarchy. Clergy who refused were to be ejected and made subject to fines and imprisonment if they continued to preach or to serve as schoolmasters or tutors. The terminal date for all this, St Bartholomew's Day (August 24, 1662), produced another massacre, though unbloody: some 2,000 clergy were added to the 500 or so who had already been ejected from their livings. Most of them had no means of support.

Other revenges continued. On April 19 three more regicides were captured abroad, brought back to England, and executed in the usual grisly manner. Most affecting for Milton were the trials of Lambert and Vane: on June 11 both were convicted of treason with the expectation that the king would keep his promise to the Convention Parliament to reprieve them from the death sentence. He did so for Lambert, who behaved with submissiveness and circumspection throughout the trial. Vane, however, defended himself and the Good Old Cause with boldness and indignation, and the king reportedly decided he was too dangerous to let live; at the intercession of his relatives his execution was commuted from the customary horror to simple beheading on Tower Hill. Milton no doubt heard about his courage and his eloquent speech before death, and was pleased to have his sonnet to Vane made the centerpiece of George Sikes's biography, *The Life and Death of Sir Henry Vane*, published almost immediately. Of course, neither the biography nor Milton's sonnet could bear the authors' signatures.[37] Polemicists recounting the punishments of various regicides often associated Milton with them, pointing to his blindness as his direct punishment from God.[38]

Milton's new household in Jewin Street would have included his three daughters, a maidservant, and a mistress to teach the girls; there may have been other servants who lived in or out. In 1661 Anne, the lame one, was 15, Mary was 13, and Deborah 9. Except for the brief period of Milton's second marriage, they had been motherless for ten years. We know almost nothing about their education save for Deborah's later report that they were taught at home by a mistress kept for that purpose.[39] Such arrangements were probably disrupted while Milton was in hiding and in prison. Edward Phillips implies that all of them could read, and states that the two younger were taught (evidently by Milton, for who else could do so?) to read to him in several languages – Hebrew, Greek, Latin, Italian, Spanish, Dutch, and French – with exact pronunciation though without understanding what they read, except in English (*EL* 76–8). Deborah told later interviewers that they did not learn those languages because Milton believed and often repeated in their hearing that "one tongue was enough for a woman." She also astonished those visitors by reciting from memory the opening verses of Homer, Isaiah, Ovid's *Metamorphoses*, and Euripides – which suggests that the girls were taught pronunciation by often repeating those verses.[40] Phillips states that Anne was excused from reading to her father because of her defective speech;[41] she did not learn to write and signed documents with her mark. Mary could sign her name and may have been able to write. Deborah was evidently a competent writer: there were reports that she served at times as Milton's amanuensis – perhaps exaggerated, but quite incredible if it were known she could not write. In later life she kept a school for young children.[42]

Deborah's apparent ability to write puts into question her own daughter's report that Milton did not have his daughters taught to write because he thought it "unnecessary for a woman."[43] Several stories about Milton's relations with his daughters may invite skepticism, as they are reported long after the fact by variously interested witnesses.[44] It seems unlikely that Milton would simply refuse to have his daughters taught to write, if for no other reason than that the presence of able scribes in his own household would have been a godsend to him, given his reduced finances and the departure of some earlier pupil–assistants to other occupations. But if his elder daughters could not or would not learn readily, Milton perhaps excused them with this old canard, which Deborah repeated to her daughter to explain why her aunts could not write, or at least not well. Milton did not educate his daughters as gentlewomen of some fortune might be educated – in music, dancing, drawing, writing, and modern languages – since his circumstances gave them no access to such a station. Yet it seems unlikely that he refused on principle to teach them languages, if for no other reason, again, than that some grasp of the matter in some of the languages they read would have made them much more useful to him. He had valued such learned women as Lady Ranelagh and Lady Margaret Ley, and had any of his daughters seemed keenly interested in books it is hard to believe he would not have responded. I suspect he made some effort to teach Mary and Deborah some elements of Latin at least, using those literary texts Deborah could still recite so many years later, but found them recalcitrant – Mary especially, who as the elder would have been called on first for the reading sessions.

Why they resisted can be readily imagined: they could see no benefit to themselves (only to him) in such learning; they probably resented keenly the loss of station, financial security, dowry, and marriage opportunities that his disgrace brought upon them; they perhaps felt put upon in having to perform the constant personal services a blind man would require; and they did not understand his genius or his ideals. He on the other hand probably did not persist in efforts to teach them more than pronunciation or to awaken a love of learning in them, being always too busy to pay much attention to them or show them much affection; nowhere in his writings or reported statements does he refer to them with love or tenderness. Elizabeth Foster's comment that he "kept his Daughters at a great distance" seems plausible enough.[45] Phillips is carefully nonjudgmental in explaining their deficiencies, leaving it an open question whether they arose from defects in their natures or in their education: "It had been happy indeed if the Daughters of such a Person had been made in some measure Inheritrixes of their Father's Learning; but . . . Fate otherwise decreed" (*EL* 78).

Milton required his daughters' services as rote readers when better help was not at hand. Edward Phillips observed their growing restiveness over the years, understood the reasons for it, and sympathized with them:

> [They] were Condemn'd to the performance of Reading, and exactly pronouncing of all the Languages of whatever Book he should at one time or other think fit to peruse . . . All which sorts of Books to be confined to Read, without understanding one word, must needs be a Tryal of Patience, almost beyond endurance. (*EL* 77)

Their resentments apparently broke out in open rebellion in 1662, as they tried to get money from their blind father by stealing from the household expenses and by the despicable act of selling his books. During the probate hearings on Milton's oral will, Milton's last maidservant, Elizabeth Fisher, recounted a story she had heard Milton tell about his daughter Mary's response to gossip about Milton's intent to remarry:

> The said Mary replyed to the said Maidservant that that was noe News to heare of his wedding but if shee could heare of his death that was something, – and [Milton] further told this Respondent that all his said Children did combine together and counsell his Maidservant to cheat him the decedent in hir Markettings, and that his said children had made away some of his bookes and would have solde the rest of his bookes to the Dunghill women.[46]

The comment suggests that Milton saw himself in 1662 as a vulnerable Lear-figure, persecuted by his daughters where it hurt most. Edward Phillips's comment and the selling of the books suggest that money was a flashpoint. Phillips points to Milton's "constant Frugality; which enabl'd him . . . to bear with patience, and no discomposure of his way of living, the great losses which befell him in his Fortunes" (*EL* 31). With the loss of his savings and no prospect of future employment, Milton doubtless felt that he had to husband his resources very carefully so as to be able to live and pay for the services a blind man and blind author must have. But his daughters, understandably enough, felt themselves deprived of youthful pleasures, comforts, and prospects for marriage. Milton did not admit, or perhaps realize, his share of responsibility for his domestic situation: even with all his troubles he could have done more to show affection and care for his daughters. But he believed himself, and may have been, more sinned against than sinning.

We can assume, though records are scanty, that old friends and associates continued to visit: Edward Phillips, Cyriack Skinner, Andrew Marvell, Lady Ranelagh, and Dr Nathan Paget of Coleman Street, who was both friend and personal physician (*EL* 75). Jeremie Picard probably still served sometimes as a trusted amanuensis. Milton likely had some contact with his former pupil Richard Jones, now back in England and a member of the Royal Society, as well as with his fellow republican polemicist, Marchamont Nedham. Twenty-year-old Samuel Parker was often with him: he had been educated as a Puritan but subsequently conformed and later became Bishop of Oxford. In 1673 Parker included a gratuitous attack on Milton in a satire directed at Marvell, who responded by remarking that he had often observed Parker at Jewin Street, where he "frequented *J. M.* incessently and haunted his house day by day." Marvell's point is that Parker assiduously sought out Milton's acquaintance and advice (apparently about what course to take after the Restoration) but now, Judas-like, has turned on him.[47] From one of his visitors Milton probably heard that Gauden's authorship of the *Eikon Basilike* had become a very open secret; Gauden used it to pressure the king and Clarendon for a wealthy bishopric, receiving as reward the see of Worcester.[48]

Edward Phillips, though he now wrote in the royalist interest,[49] remained close to his uncle and sometimes read to and wrote for him. So did others: Phillips states that many men "greedily catch'd at the opportunity of being his Readers, that they might as well reap the benefit of what they Read to him," and that several boys were "sent by their Parents to the same end" (*EL* 77). One who came was the young Quaker Thomas Ellwood, then 22. He had had a defective early education and despaired of improving his knowledge of Latin without guidance. Ellwood's friend Isaac Pennington and Pennington's friend Dr Paget, both of them friends of Milton, brought Milton and Ellwood together, probably in March or April, 1662. Ellwood took lodgings near Milton's house and began to read to him whatever books he desired every afternoon except Sunday, giving the mornings to his own studies; Milton in turn corrected his pronunciation and explained passages he did not understand. After six weeks Ellwood felt he had made great progress, but then a serious illness forced him to stop; when he recovered, he was pleased to be again "very kindly received by my Master," who had, he thought, conceived a good opinion of him.[50] On October 26, however, Ellwood was arrested at a Quaker meeting-house and spent several months in prison. Upon his release in early 1663 he began to work with Milton again, but gave over when the Penningtons pressed him to stay with them in Buckinghamshire as tutor to their three children.

Toward the end of 1662 Dr Paget produced a resolution for Milton's domestic difficulties: a third marriage. He introduced Milton to Elizabeth Minshull, a young woman of 24 who was Paget's first cousin once removed. Born and bred in Cheshire, she was then living and perhaps working in London. Milton applied for a marriage license on February 11, 1663, listing his intended's London parish as St Andrew, Holborn and describing her as a maiden "att her owne disposing" (*LR* IV, 381). Amusingly, 54-year-old Milton gives his own age as "about 50"; as often before he wants to appear, and seems to think of himself, as younger than he is.[51] His bride he describes as "about 25 years." He made the effort to sign the application himself, a large slanting blotted signature, evidently made with a scratchy pen.[52] They were married on February 24 at St Mary Aldermary, whose rector, Dr Robert Gell, had been a fellow of Christ's College during Milton's residence there.[53] The fact that he held that living through the Protectorate and was reputed to be a preacher of mystical lights suggests that Milton may have chosen a minister with whom he felt some theological affinity. John Aubrey, who knew Elizabeth after the marriage, described her as "a gent[le] person" of a "peacefull & agreable humour" (*EL* 3); reportedly, she could read and write well and had red hair.[54] Though their union began as a marriage of convenience on both sides, Milton and Elizabeth seem to have developed considerable affection and tenderness for each other. But Milton's daughters keenly resented his marriage, both because the new stepmother sought to control them and because they feared (as indeed happened) that she would displace them as heir to Milton's depleted estate.

Soon after the marriage, Edward Phillips notes, Milton moved his family "to a House in the *Artillery*-walk leading to *Bunhill Fields*" (*EL* 75), which was to be his London residence for the rest of his life. It was only a few streets north of the Jewin Street house and still in St Giles Cripplegate parish. It was comparatively small, having only four rooms with fireplaces and some smaller rooms not so provided, but it had a large garden.[55] William Faithorne's 1658 map shows a row of houses along Artillery Walk (one of them would be Milton's) facing the wall that encloses the ground where the London Artillery Company exercised; Bunhill Fields is a large open area nearby with a picturesque row of windmills along one ridge (plate 13).[56] Milton could not enjoy that view, but he could take pleasure, as he always had, in his own garden and in long walks with some attendant. Family members reported that "in warm sunny weather he used to sit at the door of his house" to receive visits from persons of distinction.[57]

After his marriage and move to Bunhill, Milton's life settled into the orderly pattern his early biographers describe. Cyriack Skinner comments that Milton "rendred his Studies and various Works more easy & pleasant by allotting them thir several portions of the day:" he rose early and dictated verses to an amanuensis; he spent evenings reading "choice Poets," and read the Bible and the best commentators often, especially on Sundays (*EL* 33). John Aubrey learned from family members and visitors that Milton usually rose at four or five in the morning; that he liked first to have the Hebrew Bible read to him and then to contemplate; that he would have "his man" return at seven to read to and write for him until dinner; that after dinner he liked to walk three or four hours at a time; and that he went to bed about nine (*EL* 6). However, Phillips claimed, and Milton's widow confirmed, that he worked on *Paradise Lost* chiefly during the winter months: "his Vein never happily flow'd, but from the *Autumnal Equinoctial* to the *Vernal*," and that his efforts to write poetry at other times were "never to his satisfaction" (*EL* 73). Given Milton's lifelong fear that a cold climate might hamper high poetic accomplishment the muse's behavior in this regard probably surprised him.[58] This left half of every year for other projects, including *De Doctrina Christiana*, which is discussed on pages 415–41.

Aubrey also heard that Milton took pleasure in conversation and repartee, at meals and at other times – sometimes, he hints, at others' expense: "Extreme pleasant in his conversation, & at dinner, supper &c: but Satyricall." He learned from Dryden that Milton "pronounced the letter R very hard," which he took to be "a certaine signe of a Satyricall Witt." From Milton's former students, probably, he learned that Milton readily adjusted his manner as he changed roles, from schoolmaster to friend: "he was most familiar and free in his conversation to those to whome most severe in his way of education."[59] Toland heard that, besides walking for exercise, he had a kind of swing: "a Pully to swing and keep him in motion" (*EL* 194). Music remained a special pleasure. Early biographers report that he had "a delicate tunable voice, an excellent ear, could play on the Organ, and bear a part in vocal and instrumental Musick," and that he "play'd much upon an Organ he kept in the House" as well as (perhaps) the bass-viol (*EL* 48, 194, 204). Cyriak Skinner noted two exceptions to his habitual frugality: "he was not sparing to buy good Books; of which he left a fair Collection; and was generous in relieving the wants of his Friends" (*EL* 31). He was said to be very temperate: Aubrey heard that he "rarely dranke between meales," Toland, that he liked food "most in season, or the easiest to be procured," Newton, that he was very temperate but also very discerning and that "what he had he always loved to have of the best."[60] From such details Newton produces what sounds like an eyewitness account of Milton's evenings:

> [Milton] after dinner played on the organ, and either sung himself or made his wife sing, who (he said) had a good voice but no ear; and then he went up to study again till six, when his friends came to visit him and sat with him perhaps till eight; then he went down to supper, which was usually olives or some light thing; and after supper he smoked his pipe, and drank a glass of water, and went to bed. . . . After his severer studies, and after dinner as we observed before, he used to divert and unbend his mind with playing upon the organ or bass-viol, which was a great relief to him after he had lost his sight.[61]

While Milton engaged in most of these activities during his later life, this reconstruction of comfortable regularity, with olives and homey pipe and slippers, is altogether too cosy. His program of reading and writing must have been far less orderly. He often had to depend on the chance visits of friends with the requisite skills, but their occasions often kept them away. In July, 1663 Marvell went abroad as secretary to the Earl of Carlisle, the newly appointed ambassador to Muscovy, Sweden, and Denmark, and did not return until January, 1665. Edward Phillips came less often after October, 1663, when he moved to John Evelyn's country house in Essex to tutor his son.[62] Milton's arrangements with student readers were subject, as in the case of Ellwood, to various disruptions. At times his wife, at other times his unwilling daughters, had to fill in but could not really meet his scholarly needs.[63] Milton's prodigious achievements during these years took place in the face of obstacles, practical and psychological, that can hardly be imagined.

Cyriack Skinner reports that Milton "was visited at his house on Bun-hill by a Chief Officer of State, and desir'd to imploy his Pen on thir behalfe" (*EL* 32). Some such overture was probably made: it would have been quite a *coup* to win over the notorious Milton, and would go far to discredit all his previous polemics. Of course he refused. Newton claimed that his widow "was wont . . . to say, that her husband was applied to by message from the King, and invited to write for the Court, but his answer was, that such a behaviour would be very inconsistent with his former conduct, for he had never yet employed his pen against his conscience."[64]

Life at Bunhill was peaceful, but Milton's anxiety and dismay over the political scene no doubt intensified in 1663–5 as, from his perspective, the Restoration settlement went from bad to worse. During the parliamentary recess Charles II set forth on December 26, 1662 a royal Declaration proposing to dispense with some provisions of the Act of Uniformity, allowing peaceable Nonconformists to worship in their own way. Like many dissenters, Milton would have taken no pleasure in that move, believing that Charles designed it to open the door to Roman Catholics. On May 21, 1662 Charles had married the Portuguese Infanta, Catherine of Braganza, whom he had compared at first sight to a bat; her Roman Catholic entourage and that of Queen Mother Henrietta Maria exacerbated anxieties about widespread Catholic influence at court and encouraged rumors that Charles himself was a secret Catholic. During the next session of parliament (February 18–July 27, 1663) Charles's tolerationist gesture was fiercely opposed and defeated. On July 1, 1664 parliament, alarmed by petitions and letters from "Fanatics, Sectaries, and Non-conformists," passed the notorious Conventicles Act prohibiting any meeting of more than five non-family members for religious services not conforming to the liturgy of the Church of England. Punishments escalated from fines to imprisonment to transportation to the colonies for seven years or, for peers, payment of £100.[65] On October 31, 1665, in the midst of a new Dutch war and in response to the discovery of a planned uprising by a few former republican soldiers, parliament passed the Five-Mile Act. It forbade all Nonconformist ex-ministers or teachers from settling within five miles of any city or corporate town or place where they had formerly preached or taught, effectively banishing them to obscure villages where they would have no contacts or means of livelihood. The Act also mandated that ministers and all teachers of either sex attend Church of England services and take an oath not to seek any alteration in church or state.[66] This completed the so called Clarendon Code, which had been vigorously promoted in parliament by Anglican gentry. Enforcement, though, was spotty, so dissent managed to survive and in some places to thrive.

Milton's enemies did not forget him, and that fact must have caused him continuing frustration, since he dared not answer attacks. At the same time, he probably felt some relief in being freed from the necessity of answering such polemical challenges, and thereby able to concentrate wholly on worthier projects. On the anniversary of the regicide (January 30, 1663), in a sermon preached before Charles II, Robert South denounced Milton as a "blind Adder [who] has spit so much Poison on the King's Person and Cause."[67] That year also James Heath denounced Milton, "since stricken with blindness," for his writings against Salmasius and especially his "impudent and blasphemous Libel, called *Iconoklastes*."[68] In February, 1663 his old enemy Roger L'Estrange attacked the *Tenure* again, and in June of that year, in an argument urging more rigorous and comprehensive regulation of the press, he cited that work as a conspicuous instance of the continuing traffic in reprints or copies of treasonous republican and regicide tracts.[69] In August L'Estrange was appointed one of the licensers of books, granted sole right to publish newsbooks, and given oversight over all publications.[70] He brought to trial several members of the book trade, among them the printer John Twyn for producing a book that draws on Milton's *Tenure* to argue the people's right to execute a monarch, and to urge the assassination of Charles II and members of the royal family in retaliation for the execution of the regicides.[71] When Twyn was convicted of high treason and hanged, drawn, and quartered in February, 1664, Milton must again have been acutely sensible of his danger and his lucky escape.

In the summer of 1665 a threat far greater than royalist polemics forced Milton to move to the country. Around the turn of that year the Great Plague, so termed because of its virulence and terrible mortality rates, began to show itself in scattered parishes in Holborn, Westminster, and the City. No doubt Milton, like Samuel Pepys and many others, soon started to keep careful track of the escalating plague bills and the route of the disease. Overall, about one fifth of the population of London and its Liberties and surrounding parishes died, with Milton's parish, St Giles Cripplegate, one of the hardest hit.[72] By mid-July it was taking a harsh toll in Cripplegate: 421 in the third week of July and 554 the next week.[73] On June 21 Pepys reported a mass exodus: "I find all the town almost going out of town, the coaches and waggons being all full of people going into the country" – leaving in place mostly magistrates and servants.[74] Social ties and duties collapsed: only a few doctors remained in London and only a few pastors, despite pleas to them from the Bishop of London.[75] Milton could not, as Pepys did, observe the fearful signs in the streets as the infection spread like wildfire with the extraordinarily hot weather of June and July, but his friends surely described them to him: neighbors shunning each other, the court removed to Oxford and the Inns of Court shut up, trade all but stopped, houses boarded up with red crosses painted on them and plague victims with their entire households quarantined inside, cemetaries filled to overflowing, plague pits for the reception of corpses that could not be buried individually. Milton's own area, Bunhill, echoed with alarming sounds: dead carts moving through the streets at night to the cry "bring out your dead," church bells tolling steadily and unable to keep up with the numbers of the dying, women and children shrieking as loved ones died, the cries of victims in intolerable pain from the characteristic black buboes or swellings.[76] Defoe writes that the single pest-house in London, to which the first victims were taken, lay just beyond Bunhill Fields and that one of the massive common burial pits for victims was in Bunhill Fields, into which also some "that were infected and near their end, and delirious also, would run . . . and throw themselves."[77]

As a student, Milton had lived through less serious plagues, when Cambridge University was closed and he retreated with his family to the country. He now made plans to take that course again. On June 7 he assigned the statute staple he had from Thomas Maundy in 1658 to Giles and Baldwin Hamey for the sum he paid for it, £500 – probably to raise ready money for the move. His erstwhile student, the young Quaker Thomas Ellwood, writes that Milton asked him to find him a suitable residence in Ellwood's own area of Buckinghamshire, some 23 miles or so out of the city:

> Some little time before I went to *Aylesbury* Prison, I was desired by my quondam Master *Milton* to take an House for him, in the Neighbourhood where I dwelt, that he might get out of the City, for the Safety of himself and his Family, the *Pestilence* then growing hot in *London*. I took a pretty Box for him in *Giles-Chalfont*, a Mile from me; of which I gave him notice: and intended to have waited on him, and seen him well settled in it; but was prevented by that Imprisonment.[78]

As Ellwood was arrested July 1 with several other Quakers and imprisoned for a month, he evidently arranged for Milton's retreat sometime in June. The cottage he found was owned by the eldest daughter of the regicide George Fleetwood: Milton claimed a friendship "from boyhood" with George's brother, Charles.[79] Loading on a cart what belongings he could take with him, Milton brought his family to Chalfont sometime in July, before the very worst of the plague struck London in August and September. While the move caused obvious disruptions in his life and work, he may have welcomed it for reasons other than sheer relief in escaping that dire peril. As a young man he had delighted in occasional rural retreats, and he could now again enjoy salubrious air and pastoral calm in the pretty village of Chalfont St Giles.

"My Best and Most Precious Possession": *De Doctrina Christiana* (1658?–1674)

Though not prepared finally for publication, Milton's *De Doctrina Christiana* is a document of the first importance in tracing the evolution of his fundamental ideas about God, man, the church, and the good life. It formulates and argues his final positions on issues that had concerned him in his prose tracts. And it supplies valuable insights into the assumptions and ideas he dramatized on the stage of his imagination in his late great poems.[80]

It is reasonable, though somewhat arbitrary, to consider *De Doctrina* here; though it was composed and revised over many years, Milton likely undertook during these trying years to formulate more completely and thereby strengthen his religious faith. A fair copy of the whole, from a still earlier draft, was produced by Jeremie Picard, who served as Milton's amanuensis in 1658–60 and perhaps also in the early 1660s.[81] Picard entered many additions and revisions, as did an undetermined number of other amanuenses, between the lines, in large margins evidently left for that purpose, and in substituted leaves. Probably before Milton's death a young acquaintance, Daniel Skinner, began the preparation of another fair copy; he recopied the first 196 pages comprising chapters 1–14, and also pages 571–4. These sections contain the most heterodox arguments and were no doubt heavily revised.[82] Milton's Epistle, perhaps written to accompany Picard's draft or else after Milton completed further revisions, presents the work as substantially complete and ready for publication. While Milton may have dictated minor revisions up to the time of his death, I suspect that the treatise was finished in all essential respects in 1658–65, in tandem with *Paradise Lost*.

Though a few scholars have called into question Milton's authorship of *De Doctrina Christiana* – some of them seeking to distance Milton's poetry from its radical heterodoxies – their arguments have not been widely accepted.[83] Milton's authorship is manifest from the way he here reprises, often in very similar terms, the specific heterodox doctrines, the several extreme positions, and the basic principles – reason, liberty, charity – that inform his earlier prose works and his epic poetry. How the work was composed is becoming clearer from renewed scholarly attention to the 745-page, much-revised manuscript.[84] Its loss and recovery makes a scholarly adventure story. After Milton's death, Daniel Skinner sent this treatise along with a manuscript of Milton's state papers to a Dutch publisher, Daniel Elzevier. Skinner's claim that Milton left "certain works behind him to me," casting him as something like a literary executor, may be greatly exaggerated, but apparently he had had sufficient recent contact with Milton (probably as amanuensis and perhaps also as student) to be allowed access to his papers by his widow.[85] Elzevier, advised by a Dutch theologian that the treatise contained "the strongest Arianism" and pressured by the English Secretary of State Sir Joseph Williamson not to publish Milton's "treasonous" letters, at length returned both manuscripts to Skinner's father early in 1677.[86] Skinner senior promptly turned them over to Williamson, who deposited them in the State Paper Office where they lay forgotten until 1823. They were then rediscovered, still in the original wrappings, and *De Doctrina Christiana* was published two years later.[87]

Addressing *De Doctrina Christiana* "To all the Churches of Christ and to All in any part of the world who profess the Christian Faith," Milton presents it as the great work benefiting all Christendom that he had promised in the revised edition of the *Defensio* (1658).[88] This Epistle describes the stages through which the text evolved. Its first origins were in Milton's boyhood when he undertook, as we know, an "earnest study of the Old and New Testaments in their original languages." At some point, convinced that God demands such an exercise of every believer, he determined "to explore and think out my religious beliefs for myself by my own exertions," and began by going "diligently through some of the shorter systems of theologians," listing "under general headings whatever passages from the scriptures suggested themselves for quotation, to be used hereafter as occasion might require."[89] At this stage he was making a kind of Commonplace Book ("locos communes digerere"), taking over formulations from standard Calvinist theologians and adding relevant scripture citations. Edward Phillips writes that when Milton was keeping his school in the 1640s he dictated to his students on Sundays some part of a "Tractate which he thought fit to collect from the ablest of Divines, who had written of that subject; *Amesius, Wollebius, &c. viz.* A perfect System of Divinity, of which more hereafter" (*EL* 61). Despite that promise Phillips does not say anything more about this work, probably thinking it unwise to call attention to the transformation of an early, largely orthodox manual into the heterodox *De Doctrina Christiana.* As Maurice Kelley shows, elements of that earlier treatise are still present in the existing one, as a first layer: its debts to John Wolleb's *Compendium Theologiae Christianae* and William Ames's *Medulla SS Theologia* are evident in the general organization of books and chapters and in the closely parallel wording of some passages.[90] As Milton gained confidence, the Epistle reports, he examined many larger volumes of divinity and many disputes over doctrines, becoming increasingly dissatisfied with mainstream theologians and their methods of argument. So he set out to devise his own systematic theology based wholly on scripture: "I deemed it therefore safest and most advisable to compile for myself, by my own labor and study, some original treatise which should be always at hand, derived solely from the word of God itself" (*CM* XIV, 7). This reworking produced the second layer of the manuscript we have.

Milton did not, of course, suppose that he needed to revise and develop an original argument about every precept of Christian doctrine. Where he substantially agreed with orthodox definitions and explanations in Wolleb (Wollebius), Ames, Perkins, and others he set them down in very similar terms. Such formulations, repeated with slight variations again and again by theologians in the reformed tradition, Milton would not think of as anyone's property: they belonged to him and to every Protestant. In such cases, he usually adds scripture citations and sometimes inserts a phrase or two that align the doctrine in question with his own heterodoxies: e.g. where other treatises assign humankind's regeneration to the Trinity Milton assigns it to "God the Father, for no one generates except a father."[91] In other cases, when treating doctrines about which he holds heterodox or highly unconventional views, he produces elaborate polemic arguments and scripture citations contesting the orthodox formulations and justifying his own positions. These sections vary in length according to the perceived difficulty of the case: not surprisingly, book I, chapter 5, which challenges the core beliefs of almost all Christendom about the Trinity, receives the longest treatment and its own preface. The manuscript is, then, a multi-layered accretion of materials and arguments gathered and formulated at various times. But Milton claims entire responsibility for all that is here, insisting that he has arrived at these doctrinal positions after long study and now presents them to the world at large as his "best and most precious possession."[92] In further testimony to the substantial completeness of the treatise and its controlling design, he supplies connectives at the beginnings of several chapters to point up the rationale of his organization.[93]

In his Epistle, Milton seeks to forestall resistance to his heterodox or extreme opinions by a rhetoric that lays open the profound personal convictions upon which they rest. For one thing, the belief that God's revelations (like poetic inspiration) come to those who do all they can for themselves by way of study and preparation: "In religion as in other things, I discerned, God offers all his rewards not to those who are thoughtless and credulous, but to those who labor constantly and seek tirelessly after truth."[94] For another, the belief (so vigorously argued in *Areopagitica*) in ongoing divine revelation and the good of free discussion: "I implore all friends of truth not to start shouting that the church is being thrown into confusion by free discussion and inquiry . . . the daily increase of the light of truth fills the church much rather with brightness and strength than with confusion."[95] For yet another, the claim of original scholarship, familiar from the divorce tracts, coupled with the assertion, also urged in *Of Civil Power*, that no doctrine, however far removed from "certain conventional opinions," can be heresy, if it is argued from scripture:

> I devote my attention to the Holy Scriptures alone. I follow no other heresy or sect. I had not even studied any of the so-called heretical writers, when the blunders of those who are styled orthodox, and their unthinking distortions of the sense of scripture, first taught me to agree with their opponents whenever these agreed with the Bible. If this be heresy, I confess, as does Paul in Acts xxiv.14, that *following the way which is called heresy I worship the God of my fathers, believing all things that are written in the law and the prophets* and, I add, whatever is written in the New Testament as well.[96]

This last assumption, he explains, dictates his method in this treatise: while most theological manuals relegate biblical proof texts to the margins, he has sought "to cram my pages even to overflowing, with quotations drawn from all parts of the Bible," leaving "as little space as possible for my own words" (122). While that last claim is not strictly true, Milton does urge his readers to follow, not his opinions as such, but his example in weighing the biblical evidence:

> I do not urge or enforce anything upon my own authority. On the contrary, I advise every reader, and set him an example by doing the same thing myself, to withhold his consent from those opinions about which he does not feel fully convinced, until the evidence of the Bible convinces him and induces his reason to assent and to believe. (121–2)

He still hopes, though without the soaring confidence of *Areopagitica,* that reason and truth, given a fair hearing, will prevail.

Milton follows Wolleb, Ames, and several others in organizing the two books of his treatise after the two parts of Christian doctrine they identify. In chapter 1 he defines Christian doctrine as the doctrine Christ taught for God's glory and man's salvation, and its two parts as "FAITH, or KNOWLEDGE OF GOD, and LOVE, or THE WORSHIP OF GOD."[97] But he adjusts his account of it to his anti-Trinitarianism: Christ taught not of himself but "by divine communication" from the Father, and did so "in all ages," since the name Christ incorporates "the prophets who foretold his coming, and the apostles whom he sent" (126–7).

In his next three chapters Milton treats God's nature and internal decrees as pertaining to the Father alone, pointedly eschewing the customary discussion of the Trinity in this place. Chapter 2, "Of God," repeats conventional ideas about the evidences of God's existence, the impossibility of forming right ideas about God outside of scripture, and the attributes usually ascribed to him: true, simple, immense and infinite, eternal, immutable, incorruptible, omnipresent, omnipotent, one, omniscient, supremely pure and holy, just, most gracious.[98] But he gives special emphasis to God's oneness, citing many confirming biblical texts and explaining them, characteristically, by an appeal to reason:

> What could be more plain and straightforward? What could be better adapted to the average intelligence, what more in keeping with everyday speech, so that God's people should understand that there is numerically one God and one spirit, just as they understand that there is numerically one of anything else. . . . Certainly the Israelites under the law and the prophets always understood that God was without question numerically one, and that there was no other besides him, let alone any equal to him. (147)

Milton's ongoing concern with issues of self-definition and individual authorship at a cultural moment of emergent individualism in the mid-seventeenth century finds an analogue in his emphasis here and throughout *De Doctrina* on God's unitary rather than triune nature, and on the individual essences of God and the Son.

Milton treats the concept of Accommodation in terms that provide an instructive insight into his way of reading biblical texts, and that also have important ramifications for the representation of God in his epic. Like everyone else, he asserts that God "as he really is" is incomprehensible to humans, far beyond "man's imagination, let alone his understanding" (133). In later chapters he specifies that God is invisible and inaudible, manifested to humans only through the Son or through some angel or prophet or other sign, and to the angels and saints in heaven more fully though still partially.[99] Like most Protestants he insists that our idea of God should correspond to the biblical representations of him, since that is how he has accommodated himself to human understanding, but he avoids biblical literalism by emphasizing that all such representations of God are necessarily metaphorical:

> It is safest for us to form an image of God in our minds which corresponds to his representation and description of himself in the sacred writings. Admittedly, God is always described or outlined not as he really is but in such a way as will make him conceivable to us. Nevertheless, we ought to form just such a mental image of him as

> he, in bringing himself within the limits of our understanding, wishes us to form. . . . In short, God either is or is not really like he says he is. If he really is like this, why should we think otherwise? If he is not really like this, on what authority do we contradict God? If, at any rate, he wants us to imagine him in this way, why does our imagination go off on some other tack? (133, 136)

He entirely repudiates all attempts to explain what seems unworthy of God by anthropopathy (the figurative ascription of human feelings to God), making the radical claim that every aspect of God's portrayal of himself in the Bible – including his expression of humanlike emotions and his manifestation in something like human form – should form part of our conception of him:

> We ought not to imagine that God would have said anything or caused anything to be written about himself unless he intended that it should be a part of our conception of him. On the question of what is or what is not suitable for God, let us ask for no more dependable authority than God himself. If *Jehovah repented that he had created man,* Gen. vi.6, *and repented because of their groanings,* Judges ii.18, let us believe that he did repent. . . . If *he grieved in his heart* Gen. vi.6, and if, similarly, *his soul was grieved*, Judges x.16, let us believe that he did feel grief. . . . If it is said that God, after working for six days, *rested and was refreshed*, Exod. xxxi.17, and if he *feared his enemy's displeasure,* Deut. xxxii.27, let us believe that it is not beneath God to feel what grief he does feel, to be refreshed by what refreshes him, and to fear what he does fear. . . . After all, if *God is said to have created man in his own image, after his own likeness,* Gen. i.26, and not only his mind but also his external appearance (unless the same words mean something different when they are used again in Gen. v.3, *Adam begot his son after his own likeness, in his own image*), and if God attributes to himself again and again a human shape and form, why should we be afraid of assigning to him something he assigns to himself, provided we believe that what is imperfect and weak in us is, when ascribed to God, utterly perfect and utterly beautiful? (134–6)

On such principles, the poet Milton can find biblical warrant for portraying God as an epic character who expresses a range of emotions (fear, wrath, scorn, dismay, love), who makes himself visible and audible to his creatures by various means, and who engages in dialogue with his Son and with Adam.

No aspect of *De Doctrina Christiana* is more central to Milton's mature thought than the arguments he develops in chapters 3 and 4, opposing orthodox Calvinist determinism and predestination and insisting that God's eternal decrees provide for genuine freedom of choice to angels and humankind, both before and after their falls. These arguments, often paralleling the beliefs of the Dutch theologian Jacobus Arminius and his Remonstrant followers,[100] provide the theological underpinning for the commitment to liberty and human responsibility, founded upon reason and free will, which had been a constant of Milton's political polemic almost from the outset. Supralapsarian Calvinism insisted that an omnipotent, immutable God whose will is wholly unconstrained must have predestinated certain individuals to salvation (election) and others to damnation (reprobation) from all eternity, with regard only to his will and good pleasure rather than to any quality in them; then he decreed the Creation, and also the Fall with all its consequences, as the necessary means to execute that eternal predestination. As Calvin put it,

> No one can deny that God foreknew what end man was to have before he created him, and consequently foreknew because he so ordained by his decree. . . . And it ought not to seem absurd for me to say that God not only foresaw the fall of the first man, and in him the ruin of his descendents, but also meted it out in accordance with his own decision. For as it pertains to his wisdom to foreknow everything that is to happen, so it pertains to his might to rule and control everything by his hand.[101]

Calvin insists that God's justice and goodness are not hereby compromised because God's will is simply unfathomable to humans. But in practice this position comes close to that of utter voluntarists like Hobbes, for whom God's will itself, as the manifestation of his omnipotence and sovereignty, is what makes a thing just or good, even as the sovereign's will does in human affairs.[102] Infralapsarian Calvinists sought to rescue God's justice and goodness by placing his decrees of election and reprobation after the decree of Creation and the foreseen though not decreed Fall of the human race in Adam. They could then conclude that God showed superlative mercy by his entirely arbitrary gift of grace to elect individuals, while he justly assigned the rest to their deserved reprobate condition. Both groups held to the five principles of Calvinist orthodoxy affirmed at the Synod of Dort (1619) and restated in England in the Westminster Confession (1647): unconditional election (God's eternal decrees of Election and Reprobation have no reference whatever to human merit, desires, or acts); limited atonement (Christ won grace for the elect only); total depravity (fallen humans, with intellects blinded and wills in bondage, cannot intend or perform any good act leading to or meritorious for salvation); irresistible grace (the elect are saved by God's grace, which they can neither resist nor cooperate with); and final perseverance of the saints (whatever their sins and backslidings, the elect cannot finally be lost).[103] The Dort manifesto was directed against the Remonstrant followers of Arminius, whose doctrines made a place for human freedom and moral responsibility. Those doctrines were: conditional election and reprobation (God's predestinating decrees are based on his certain foresight of the faith and virtue, or lack thereof, of particular individuals); general atonement (Christ atoned for all humankind, not a predetermined elect); sufficient grace given to all to renew the fallen understanding and will (all humans are thereby able to accept salvation); resistable grace (humans can reject God's call and grace); and no assurance of final perseverance (even the regenerate may fall from grace).[104]

In the early 1640s Milton ranged himself with orthodox Calvinists against Arminius: like many Puritans, he then associated Arminian doctrine with Roman Catholic and Laudian belief in grace gained through sacraments and good works.[105]

His comment in *Areopagitica* that "the acute and distinct *Arminius*" was perverted by a book he had undertaken to refute (II, 519–20) disavows Arminius but registers a good deal of admiration for him. Milton apparently did not fully realize that *Areopagitica*'s core arguments – purification by trial and the development of virtue through the constant, reasoned choice between good and evil – assume free will, but writing that treatise may have prompted him to reexamine the issue.[106] In *De Doctrina Christiana* Milton asserts, with the Remonstrants, God's general call to all humankind in Christ, God's provision of grace sufficient for salvation to all, and conditional rather than absolute election. But he develops his own version of Arminianism.

In chapter 3 he ascribes to God's "internal efficiency" both his General Decree ordaining from all eternity everything that he meant to do, and his Special Decree of Predestination electing to salvation all humans who believe and persevere, insisting passionately that God formulated these decrees in ways that secure the freedom of his intelligent creatures. God's General Decree established his eternal "idea of every thing," and that idea incorporates radical contingency, leaving many things to the free choices of free creatures, men and angels. Citing a plethora of scripture passages in which God made his actions contingent upon the faith, or obedience, or repentance, or sinfulness of humans, and appealing also to "the standards of mortal reason," Milton concludes that "God has not decreed all things absolutely" and specifically, that he has "decreed nothing absolutely, that he left in the power of free agents."[107] He means by this to set aside all versions of Calvinist determinism grounded upon God's omnipotence, omniscience, and immutability, since human freedom, real and not simply nominal, was part of God's plan from all eternity:

> Nor do we imagine anything unworthy of God, when we assert that those events, those conditions which God himself has chosen to place within the free power of men depend on the will of men; since God purposely framed his own decrees with reference to such conditions, in order that he might permit free causes to act in accordance with that liberty which he himself gave them. It would be much more unworthy of God, to grant man a merely nominal liberty, and deprive him of the reality . . . under the pretext of some sophistical necessity resulting from immutability or infallibility. . . . God is not mutable so long as he determines nothing absolutely which could happen otherwise through the liberty decreed for man.[108]

Appealing, again, to reason, he counters the infralapsarian position by insisting, with an analogy to human foresight, that God's certain foreknowledge does not amount to determination, and that it in no way limits the liberty of choice secured to angels and humans from all eternity by his General Decree:

> The sum of this argument may be thus stated in strict conformity with reason. God of his wisdom determined to create men and angels reasonable beings, and therefore with free will; he foresaw at the same time which way the bias of their will would

> incline, in the exercise of their own uncontrolled liberty. What then? shall we say that this foresight or foreknowledge on the part of God imposed on them the necessity of acting in any definite way? No more, certainly, than if the future event had been foreseen by any human being. For what any human being has foreseen as certain to happen, will not less certainly happen than what God himself has predicted. . . . Nothing happens of necessity because God has foreseen it; but he foresees the event of every action, because he is thoroughly familiar with their natural causes, which, by his own decree, are left to act freely. . . . Thus he knew that Adam would fall of his own free will; his fall was therefore certain, but not necessary.[109]

Milton's deep investment in this argument is founded in its implications for human freedom and moral responsibility. On any Calvinist determinist theory, "we shall have to jettison entirely all man's freedom of action and all attempt or desire on his part to do right . . . liberty will be an empty word, and will have to be banished utterly not only from religion but also from morality and even from indifferent matters" (*CPW* VI, 157, 164).

Chapter 4 describes Predestination as a Special Decree pertaining to humans alone, whereby God, "before the foundation of the world" and foreknowing the Fall, predestined to salvation the general category of "those who should believe and continue in the faith" (*CM* XIV, 91). But he separates himself from Arminius in treating some aspects of predestination. First, he restricts it only to election: denying the reprobation of particular individuals for foreknown sins, he marshals a plethora of scripture passages that make salvation conditional upon faith and proclaim the death of sinners to be wholly contrary to God's express wish. Moreover, while for Arminius God predestines to election particular individuals whose faith and virtue he foresees, Milton refers that term to the general category of believers.[110] It becomes applicable to individuals only as they live out their voluntary choices to believe and to continue:

> It seems then that predestination and election are not particular but only general – that is, they belong to all who believe heartily and continue to believe. Peter is not predestinated or elected as Peter, or John as John, but each only insofar as he believes and perseveres in his faith. In this way the general decree of election is made personally applicable to each particular believer and made sure to those who persevere.[111]

Milton avoids the Pelagian concept that good works may help to merit salvation by stipulating that it is only God's grace, won through Christ's sacrifice and offered at all stages, that makes salvation possible to any. To accommodate scripture texts asserting the potter's right to deal with his pots as he chooses (Romans 9:20–1), he allows that God may give more grace to some than to others. Yet he insists that all are offered grace sufficient for salvation: "he undoubtedly gives grace to all, if not in equal measure, at least sufficient for attaining knowledge of the truth and salvation"; it belongs to God's supreme will "that an equal portion of grace should not be extended to all, but it belongs to his justice that all receive grace sufficient for salvation."[112] Milton's concern for human freedom is further evident in his insistence that God's grace is resistable and that human response to grace is both possible and necessary. It is possible because even after the Fall "some traces of the divine image remain in man" which God's grace further restores; it is necessary, because God willed that "in their own salvation, men should always use their free will" (*CPW* VI, 185–9). The reprobate are not damned by divine decree but because of their own obstinacy and pride: "God . . . excludes no man from the way of penitence and eternal salvation, unless that man has continued to reject and despise the offer of grace, and of grace sufficient for salvation, until it is too late" (194). Even when God punishes especially heinous crimes by hardening the sinner's heart he does so only after "a great deal of forebearance" (199). These positions lie at the heart of the theodicy Milton sets forth in *Paradise Lost* as his justification of God's ways, and they are articulated formally by God in the Council in Heaven (*PL* 3.173–97).

In chapters 5 and 6 Milton explains and argues for his most serious heresy, Arianism, his own and his seventeenth-century contemporaries' preferred term to describe anti-Trinitarian heresy.[113] But the term has specific appropriateness for Milton, as his position on the Godhead comes closest to the Arian heresy denounced at the fourth-century Council of Nicaea. The orthodox Trinitarian position elaborated by Athanasius and Augustine and accepted overwhelmingly by seventeenth-century Christians of all denominations, identified three persons or *hypostases* in the Godhead, one in nature (essence, substance) but distinct in existence (subsistence). The Nicene Creed described the Son as equal to and consubstantial with the Father and his generation from the Father as eternal and natural: he is "only-begotten, *that is, of the substance of the Father,* God of God, Light of Light, *true God of true God, begotten not made, of one substance* [*homoousian*] *with the* Father."[114] We cannot be sure when Milton abandoned that position: he wrote the Nativity ode as an orthodox Trinitarian, though his inability to complete a poem on Christ's Passion or to produce a very effective poem on the circumcision suggests that even in the 1630s the redemptive sacrifice of the incarnate Son was not at the center of his religious imagination.[115] His careful study of the Hebrew Bible as he worked on the divorce tracts may have prompted his attention to the issue of God's oneness; by 1650, when he licensed the *Racovian Catechism,* he showed some sympathy for the Socinians, though in *De Doctrina Christiana* he rejects their belief that the Son came into existence only at Christ's birth and subsequently attained his divine excellence by the Father's gift and his own merit.[116] Arius held that the Son is a subordinate divine person though not generated out of the Father's substance and not a sharer in the divine essence (which cannot be communicated); that he was created by God's will and then made God's agent for the rest of creation; that he is "neither eternal nor co-eternal nor co-unbegotten with the Father, nor does he have his being together with the Father"; and that he holds all that he has by God's gift, "life and being and glories."[117] Since he is a creature – albeit unique and by God's gift divine – he cannot know God save by revelation; he is also mutable and "remains good by His own free will, while he chooseth" as all other creatures do.[118]

Milton introduces his very long chapter 5, on the Son of God, with a new preface urging his readers to weigh his arguments not by orthodox opinion but solely in terms of his scripture evidence. In almost every respect Milton's anti-Trinitarianism is couched in Arian terms: the Son was not generated by any natural necessity or process but produced by God's "free will . . . as a result of his own decree"; he is not eternal but was begotten "within the bounds of time, for the decree itself must have preceded its execution" (*CPW* VI, 208–9); his generation was the first external act of God, as is indicated in texts terming him "the first born of every creature" (Colossians 1:15) and "the beginning of God's creation" (Revelation 3:14). He cannot be co-equal to the Father, since "a supreme God is self-existent, but a God who is not self-existent, who did not beget but was begotten, is not a first cause but an effect, and is therefore not a supreme God" (263–4). The Son's metaphorical begetting – his elevation to kingship celebrated in Psalm 2 – was also by God's will; that mutability and the *kenosis* by which he "emptied himself" of the form of God to become man (Philippians 2:6–8) also shows that he cannot be the supreme God, since "a God who is infinite can no more empty himself than contradict himself, for infinity and emptiness are mutually exclusive terms."[119] Milton marshals many proof texts indicating that the Son ascribes the attributes of divinity – omniscience, omnipresence, divine honor, omnipotence, divine glory – to the Father alone, and ascribes his own participation in them entirely to the Father's gift:

> The Son himself reports that he received from the Father not only the name of God and Jehovah, but also whatever else he has . . . his individuality, his life itself, his attributes, his works, and, lastly, his divine honor. . . . He receives everything from the Father: everything – not only what belongs to him as mediator, but also what belongs to him as Son. (259–60)

Denying the customary application of such texts only to Christ's human nature, Milton insists that once the two natures have coalesced into one person, Christ speaks "as a whole person speaking about a whole person" unless he himself makes a distinction; to suppose otherwise would "rob Christ's speeches and replies of all their sincerity" (218). The Son, he specifies, was appointed Savior and Judge by the Father; he cried out for and obtained the Father's aid during his passion; his resurrection was accomplished by the Father's power; and his place at the right hand of God "implies a glory not primarily or supremely divine, but only approaching that of God" (272).

Milton departs from Arian doctrine on one point only, that while the Son shares, by gift, some part of God's substance and nature, he is not "consubstantial" in the orthodox sense of sharing in the Father's divine essence:

> God imparted to the Son as much as he wished of the divine nature, and indeed of the divine substance also [.] But do not take *substance* to mean total essence. If it did, it would mean that the Father gave his essence to the Son, and at the same time retained it, numerically unaltered, himself. That is not a means of generation but a contradiction of terms. (211–12)

Milton equates *essence* with *hypostasis* (individual being or existence) rather than with *substance* (141–2).[120] Moreover, as he will soon emphasize in discussing Creation, by his monist ontology all beings were created from God's substance, so the Son is not unique in that regard.[121]

The fundamental principle grounding the anti-Trinitarianism of *De Doctrina Christiana* – that God's revelation, though above reason, will accord with reason and the law of nature – reiterates a principle that sounds like a leitmotif throughout Milton's prose. He often appeals to reason to illuminate scripture texts pertaining to the Godhead, and insists that God himself cannot defy the canons of logic:

> The numerical significance of "one" and of "two" must be unalterable and the same for God as for man. . . . Two distinct things cannot be of the same essence. God is one being, not two. One being has one essence, and also one subsistence – by which is meant simply a substantial essence. If you were to ascribe two subsistences or two persons to one essence it would be a contradiction in terms. . . . No one will deny that the Son is numerically different from the Father. And the fact that things numerically different are also different in their proper essences, as logicians call it, is so obvious that no reasonable being could contradict it. Therefore the Father and Son differ from each other in essence. This is certainly the reasonable conclusion.[122]

His orthodox opponents "fly in the face of reason" (213); they wrench both reason and scripture to maintain "an extremely absurd paradox" (218); and their proof texts which seem to infer a Trinity or which apply the term God to the Son, must be held up to the standard of reason:

> Reason is loud in its denunciation of the doctrine in question. . . . Can reason maintain an unreasonable opinion? The product of reason must be reason, not absurd notions which are utterly alien to all human ways of thinking. The conclusion must be, then, that this opinion is consonant neither with reason nor scripture. . . . If God is one God, and the Father, and yet the Son is also called God, then he must have received the divine name and nature from God the Father, in accordance with the Father's decree and will, as I said before. This is in no way opposed to reason, and is supported by innumerable texts from scripture. (222)

This position, Milton insists, is the faith everywhere expressed in scripture and codified in the Apostles' Creed.

In chapter 6 Milton describes the Holy Spirit as

> a minister of God, and therefore a creature, [who] was created or produced of the substance of God, not by a natural necessity but by the free will of the agent, probably before the foundations of the world were laid, but later than the Son, and far inferior to him. . . . The brightness of God's glory and the image of his divine subsistence are said to have been impressed on the Son but not on the Holy Spirit.[123]

Milton explicates most of the biblical texts about the Spirit as references to something other than this "far inferior" divine person. Since the Spirit was not given until the coming of Christ, all uses of that term in the Old Testament refer to some manifestation of "the virtue and power of God the Father" (*CPW* VI, 283). At the Creation, when "the Spirit of God brooded" (Genesis 1:2), the reference is to "God's divine power, not any particular person."[124] At other times "spirit" means an angel, or "the force or voice of God" breathed into the prophets, or the light of truth with which God illumines his people (282–3). In the New Testament it sometimes means the Father himself, or his power and might (as the agent of Mary's conception), or "a divine impulse, light, voice or word sent from above," or sometimes "the actual person of the Holy Spirit or its symbol" or its gifts. Yet even when the Spirit descended in the form of a dove at Christ's baptism it came "not so much in its own right as sent by the Father to be a symbol and minister of divine power . . . [and] a representation of the Father's supreme love and affection for the Son."[125] Biblical texts declare the Spirit to be "subservient and obedient in all things; to have been promised, and sent, and given" by God and the Son; to be numerically distinct from the Father; to share in the divine attributes only by God's commission; to speak and act and move others by God's power; and to be sought as a gift from God, not invoked directly (288–95).

This conception of the Son and the Holy Spirit has important implications for the epic Milton is writing. If the Son is mutable, subject to change, and lacks omniscience, then he has the free will and capacity for moral growth that all intelligent creatures enjoy, and Milton can present his offer in the Council in Heaven to suffer and die for man's redemption as a free and meritorious choice. Later, he can present Christ in *Paradise Regained* as undergoing a genuine temptation. And the Bard's invocations to the Spirit in both poems may be glossed as petitions for illumination from the light of God.

In his treatment of the Creation (chapter 7) Milton again identifies the Father as sole God and Creator and the Son as his agent. Appealing to the maxim in logic that no agent can act unless there is something such as matter to be acted upon, he repudiates the orthodox formula that God created all things *ex nihilo*; he also concludes that there must be "some bodily power in God's own substance, for no one can give what he does not have."[126] Since it is inconceivable that matter existed eternally and independent of God, it must have "originated from God at some particular point of time." Creation is therefore *ex Deo*, and matter is not evil or worthless but "intrinsically good, and the productive seedplot of all subsequent good."[127] Nevertheless, created beings remain free and evil remains possible because, after matter went forth from God, it was detached from him and became mutable and corruptible, subject to the mind and will of the devil or of humans.[128] Milton repudiates the Neoplatonic dualism common to most seventeenth-century Christians – and to Milton himself in his early poems – which posits two distinct substances, matter and spirit, and the immortal soul as pure spirit, trapped in a gross, material body. He urges the soul of the dead bishop of Ely to escape the "sordid prison" ("foedum . . . carcerem," l. 46) of the body and in the Nativity ode terms the body a "darksome house of mortal Clay" (l. 14).[129] By the early 1640s he moves, albeit incompletely and inconsistently, toward monism as he insists that a married couple can only become one flesh if their minds and spirits are united.[130] *De Doctrina Christiana* sets forth a fully developed monist ontology in which spirit and matter differ only in degree of refinement of the one corporeal substance derived from God, of which everything is created.

Milton no doubt felt constrained to work out this issue by the powerful impact of Hobbes's materialism and rigid determinism, which explained everything in the universe in terms of matter in motion, and the choices of the human will as simply "the last Appetite in Deliberation."[131] Milton would have been aware of efforts by the Cambridge Platonists – some of them based in his own college, Christ's – to work out an alternative system in which spirit as incorporeal substance organizes or interacts with bodies.[132] But he worked out an original synthesis, an "animist materialism" or vitalism close to that of his contemporary, Ann (Finch) Conway, whom he probably did not know but who argued, as he did, that "a Body is nothing but a fixed and condensed Spirit, and a Spirit nothing but a subtile and volatile Body."[133] The monism of *De Doctrina Christiana* became the ontological ground of *Paradise Lost*, evident in the descriptions of Chaos and in Raphael's lecture (*PL* 5.469–500) in which he describes matter as produced originally from God's own substance and then, by the will and choice of other beings, able to be disposed toward greater "spiritous" refinement or toward grosser corporeality.

Other elements of Milton's discussion of Creation also find their way into *Paradise Lost*: that God before creating the visible universe produced the highest heaven where he "dwells in unapproachable light" and "reveals himself to the sight of angels and saints (insofar as they are capable of seeing him)";[134] that the creation of the angels and their apostacy took place before the first beginnings of the world; and that time – understood as the measure of motion and as involving the concepts of before and after – existed (contrary to common belief) before the Creation. In describing angels as spirits, Milton means that they are of ethereal substance ("Sunt natura aetherea"); man, he explains, is of a denser but still single substance, "intrinsically and properly one and individual, not compound or separable, not, according to the common opinion, made up and framed of two distinct and different natures, as of soul and body" (*CM* XV, 34, 40–1). Milton denies any form of pre-existence of the soul and gestures toward mortalism – the death of the soul with the body until the final resurrection – a doctrine he will explain further in chapter 13: "The idea that the spirit of man is separate from his body, so that it may exist somewhere in isolation, complete and intelligent, is nowhere to be found in scripture, and is plainly at odds with nature and reason" (*CPW* VI, 318–19). The breath of life God infused into Adam, Milton explains, was not the soul but the vital power that sustains life and faculties; his creation in the image of God refers not to his soul but to his whole being, endowed "with natural wisdom, holiness and righteousness" (324). In all humans, he supposes, the more ethereal soul as well as the denser body must be "generated by the parents in the course of nature," since this is the only way original sin could have been transmitted to Adam's progeny.[135]

The next three chapters deal with God's government of all things, in terms that provide a further basis for the theodicy of *Paradise Lost.* God's ordinary providence Milton equates with nature, whose order and laws God established in the beginning; his extraordinary providence produces effects outside nature, by miracle. God does not cause natural or moral evils, but simply allows them to happen by the operation of natural causes and the choices of free agents. When God chastises evildoers and hardens those who chose evil he is entirely just; but more than that, he "always produces something good and just" out of a sinner's evil.[136] As for temptations, Milton accepts the traditional distinction between evil temptations, by which God provides evil persons opportunities for sin and withdraws his grace from them, and good temptations, by which God tempts the righteous (like Job) so as to exercise their faith or patience, or lessen their self-confidence (388).

Treating God's government of the angels (chapter 9), Milton emphasizes their free will and the limitations on their knowledge, as he does also in *Paradise Lost.* Against the opinion of many Calvinists, he insists that the evil angels revolted from God "of their own free will" and that the good angels remained faithful not by God's predestinating election but by their own will and power: "they are called 'elect' only in the sense that they are beloved or choice."[137] He also contests the view that angels see into God's thoughts, insisting that "they know by revelation only those things which God sees fit to show them, and they know other things by virtue of their very high intelligence, but there are many things of which they are ignorant."[138] In *Paradise Lost* Milton works out the full implications of his monist ontology for angels, portraying them as eating food and enjoying sex; but in the treatise he holds himself to his chosen method and enumerates only those activities for which he can find biblical citations: their obedience, their ministry to believers, their patrol of the earth, their frequent appearance as soldiers, and the leadership of Michael.

Milton treats the conditions of prelapsarian human life (chapter 10) in terms directly relevant to his epic. He asserts that Adam and Eve were bound only by the natural moral law and a single positive law, the divine prohibition against eating the Tree of Knowledge of Good and Evil:

> It was necessary that one thing at least should be either forbidden or commanded, and above all something which was in itself neither good nor evil, so that man's obedience might in this way be made evident. For man . . . would not have shown obedience at all by performing good works, since he was in fact drawn to these by his own natural impulses. . . . Man was made in the image of God, and the whole law of nature was so implanted and innate in him that he was in need of no command. . . . Positive right comes into play when God, or anyone else invested with lawful power, commands or forbids things which, if he had not commanded or forbidden them, would in themselves have been neither good nor bad.[139]

Laying the groundwork for the qualified antinomianism he will assert as a concomitant of Christian liberty in chapter 27, Milton insists that Adam and Eve did not live by a covenant of works containing the substance of the Decalogue, as Wollebius, Ames, and many others claimed. They were not held to Sabbath worship, which is not part of the natural law, so Eden offers no precedent for requiring Sunday observance of Christians.[140] Echoing *Areopagitica*, Milton explains the tree's name and significance not from its nature but from its effects: after the Fall, "not only do we know evil, but also we do not even know good except through evil. For where does virtue shine, where is it usually exercised, if not in evil?"[141]

As marriage was instituted by God in Eden, Milton reprises here his views on marriage and divorce. Like everyone else, he declares that the validity of marriage depends on the mutual consent of the parties, that its fruit is the procreation of children, and that the husband's greater authority was increased after the Fall. But his definition of marriage as "a very intimate relationship between man and woman" alters the usual formula, "between one man and one woman,"[142] allowing him to defend polygamy as a legitimate form of marriage – legitimate because God who could not sanction sin allowed it for the Old Testament patriarchs. Milton argues this point at much greater length than in the divorce tracts, not because he is urging the practice of polygamy but to strengthen the case for divorce: if plural marriage was and is allowable, remarriage after divorce must surely be. Using familiar terms, arguments, and even rhetoric from the divorce tracts, Milton repeats his description of marriage as a contract that can be dissolved when its primary end is not met, and also his definition of that primary end from God's language instituting marriage in Eden:

> Everyone admits that marriage may be dissolved if the prime end and form of marriage is violated; and most people say that this is the reason why Christ permitted divorce only on grounds of adultery. But the prime end and form of marriage is not the bed, but conjugal love and mutual assistance in life. . . . For the prime end and form of marriage can only be what is mentioned in the original institution, and mention is there made of pleasant companionship. . . . No mention is made of the bed or of procreation. . . . It follows that wedded love is older and more important than the mere marriage bed, and far more worthy to be considered as the prime end and form of marriage. Who is so base and swinish [tam prono tamque porcino] as to deny that this is so?[143]

He also reprises familiar exegeses of difficult texts. Christ's apparent prohibition and reference to "hardness of heart" (Matthew 19) pertained only to the Philistines who would divorce for any cause, though in a broader sense "almost all the civil law was given on account of . . . hard-heartedness." Under the Law divorce was always sanctioned for "some uncleaness in the woman that might turn love into hatred."[144] Citing Selden's *Uxor Hebraica*, Milton glosses the term "fornication" (Deuteronomy 24:1) as meaning in the Hebrew either "'any unclean thing' or a defect in some particular which might justly be required in a wife"; more emphatically, he defines it as "anything found to be persistently at variance with love, fidelity, help, and society," referring that definition (as he did also in the *Second Defense*), both to his own exegesis in *Tetrachordon* and to Selden: "as I showed in another work out of other places of scripture, and Selden also demonstrated."[145] As before, and in similar terms, he concludes that marriage must give way "to that natural aversion which anyone may feel for a disgusting object, and also to any really irresistible antipathy," since to be held in a marriage without love is "a crushing slavery."[146]

Milton discusses the Fall, Original Sin and its effects, and the punishment for sin (chapters 11–13) in terms that are largely conventional but often suggestive for *Paradise Lost*. Original Sin was instigated first by the devil and then by man's inconstant nature; like all sins it has two parts, "the will to do evil, and the evil deed itself"; and it contains all sins: Adam was "faithless, ungrateful, disobedient, greedy, [and] uxorious"; Eve was "negligent of her husband's welfare"; both trusted Satan rather than God, committed robbery and murder against their children (the whole human race), and were sacrilegious, proud, and deceitful in aspiring to divinity (*CPW* VI, 383–4). Chapter 12 treats two of the four degrees of death resulting from Original Sin: guiltiness and spiritual death. The latter involves the loss of divine grace and innate righteousness, making for "the extensive darkening" of right reason and the "slavish subjection to sin and the devil which is, as it were, the death of the will."[147] But Milton qualifies that loss, allowing that fallen human faculties can yet produce civil and moral good – "the holiness and wisdom in both word and deed of many of the heathens" – and can respond to God's general call:

> It cannot be denied that some traces of the divine image still remain in us, which are not wholly extinguished by this spiritual death. . . . The freedom of the will is not entirely extinct: first of all, in indifferent matters, whether natural or civil . . . [and] even where good works are concerned, or at least good attempts, at any rate after God has called us and given us grace. (396–7)

In discussing the death of the body (chapter 13), Milton espouses mortalism or Thnetopsychism, the logical concomitant of his monist ontology. In *Lycidas* (1637) he still accepted the orthodox notion that the soul or spirit goes immediately to heaven or hell after death, but he may have been led to rethink this issue in the mid-1640s by Richard Overton's mortalist treatise, *Mans Mortalitie* (1643),[148] which was constantly linked with his *Doctrine and Discipline of Divorce* as examples of dastardly heresy. Milton now argues (as had Overton) that the soul or spirit as well as the body suffers physical death and that the whole person is then resurrected at the last day. More boldly, he insists that "even Christ's soul succumbed to death for a short time when he died for our sins" (405).

Chapters 14–16 analyse Christ's role in humankind's restoration, in terms consonant with Milton's version of Arianism and Arminianism, and also with his portrayal of Jesus in *Paradise Regained*. Restoration is the act of the Father accomplished through Christ, who satisfied for the sins of all humankind by voluntarily fulfilling the law and enduring his Passion and death (415–16, 444–7). As defined by the Council of Chalcedon, the hypostatic union of two natures in the one person of Christ meant that each nature retained its own characteristics and functions, understanding and wills; and that the Logos in his incarnate state emptied out (*kenosis*) the glory and form, though not the essence and power of the Godhead.[149] Appealing both to scripture texts and to reason, Milton pronounces such definitions "sheer vacuity"; Zanchius, he scoffs, defends the orthodox view that the Word assumed human nature rather than the person of a particular man "as confidently as if he had been present in Mary's womb."[150] Milton's christology does not exactly conform to any of the recognized christological heresies;[151] he is led to his conception by his sense of what must pertain to Christ as an individual entity. Reiterating his anti-Trinitarian argument that the terms "nature," "subsistence," and "person" are interchangeable, and insisting that the Logos must unite with a particular human being since human nature cannot exist in the abstract, he concludes that "one Christ, one ens, and one person" is formed (he thinks it presumptuous to say just how) by "a mutual hypostatic union of two natures, or, in other words, of two essences, of two substances, and consequently of two persons" (423–4). He allows the orthodox formula of the communication of properties, whereby what belongs to one nature is sometimes attributed to the other, but assumes that the hypostatic union has produced a single person with a single understanding and will, all of whose sayings and actions refer to this new self. He supposes that the *kenosis* or emptying out means that the Son literally divests himself of whatever divine attributes and powers he enjoyed in heaven, leaving the incarnate Son with a substantially human intellect and will, which can then gain back divine understanding and "*know everything*, John xxi.17, that is, after the Father had instructed him, as he himself acknowledges" (425–6). This christology allowed Milton to present Jesus in *Paradise Regained* as beginning from a condition of limited human understanding of himself and his role.

Milton's discussion of Christ's mediatorial office and its threefold function (chapter 15) largely conforms to orthodox formulas. His prophetic office, exercised from the beginning to the end of the world, involves teaching the whole will of his Father by revealing divine truth and illuminating the mind. His priestly function is that by which he once sacrificed himself for sinners and continues to intercede for humankind. The kingly office, devolved upon him by the Father, involves ruling and preserving his church "by internal law and spiritual power" and conquering his enemies. As he did in *Of Civil Power*, Milton draws a sharp distinction between Christ's rule over conscience and the magistrate's use of physical force in civil matters, insisting that "external force should never be used in Christ's kingdom, the Church."[152] Chapter 16 treats Christ's exercise of his mediatorial office as a function of both his natures. Contesting the orthodox view that Christ's divine nature was not subject to suffering and death and that he rose from the dead by his own divine power, Milton asserts that he endured all the aspects of his humiliation – birth, circumcision, baptism, temptation, and even his Passion and death – in his whole person: "If his divine nature was not suffering too, why was it not there to help him when he cried out?" Also, since the whole of a sacrifice must be killed, "it follows that Christ, the sacrificial lamb, was totally killed."[153]

Milton's analysis of the renovation of humankind by grace (chapters 17–21) is influenced by his version of Arminianism. Whereas Ames and many other Protestants began with Justification, the action of grace by which Christ's merits are substituted for man's sins, Milton takes up first the actual or internal renovation of believers. The first stage, Vocation, he defines as God's general call offered to all humankind, accompanied by sufficient grace to enlighten the mind and renew the will, at least partly (457). All are called and empowered to respond, though some may be called "more clearly and more insistently" than others, or to special missions (455). If answered, this call elicits penitence and faith, which may be temporary and natural or may lead on to Regeneration (chapter 18), which Milton like most Protestants describes as the restoration of the inner man to the image of God, marked by "righteousness and true holiness" and by an enlightened intellect and liberated will, "as if he were a new creature." But he adjusts these formulas to his own beliefs: Regeneration (also called Sanctification) is through Christ but is "by God the Father"; most references to the Spirit in this connection are to "the *divine virtue of the Father*"; and even the new creature can fall from grace (461–4). In chapter 19 Milton describes the several degrees and stages of repentance – recognition of sin, contrition, confession, abandonment of evil, and conversion to good – affirming against many theologians that it precedes saving faith rather than follows it.[154] Contrasting saving faith to historical or implicit or temporary faith, he defines it as a firm persuasion "implanted in us by the gift of God . . . that all those things which God has promised us in Christ are ours, and especially the grace of eternal life" (471). Insisting against many of the orthodox that the object of faith is "not Christ, the Mediator, but God the Father," Milton concludes that "there are a lot of Jews, and Gentiles too, who are saved although they believed or believe in God alone" (475). A further stage, Ingrafting in Christ (chapter 21), brings about the restoration of the intellect "to a very large extent . . . to its former state of enlightenment" and of the will "to its former freedom," producing a larger understanding of spiritual things and a profound love of God, which brings forth good works freely (478–9). God's grace is essential to produce these effects, but "our own effort is always required" (480). Perfection, however, is not possible in this life.

Chapters 22–5 treat humankind's "relative or external growth" by Justification and Adoption, processes he ascribes to the Father alone. With Protestants generally he describes Justification as the imputing of our sins to Christ and of his merits to us, and insists on Christ's "absolutely full satisfaction," leaving no place for human merit. But unlike many of them, he intimates that Justification follows and depends upon actual regeneration: the Father absolves from sin and death "those who are regenerate and ingrafted in Christ" and accounts them righteous, "not by the works of the Law, but through Faith" (485). Also, he disputes the usual view that faith is merely infused, defining it rather as "a habit acquired by frequent actions" (489, 492). Adoption is briefly described as the Father's acceptance as his sons and heirs those who are justified through faith; its first fruit is Christian liberty, to be discussed later. In chapter 25 Milton describes the final stage of regenerate growth on earth, Incomplete Glorification, whereby those justified and adopted experience "a certain awareness both of present grace and dignity and of future glory" (502), and attain through the testimony of the Spirit to an assurance of salvation. However, he flatly denies the Calvinist doctrine of final perseverance, insisting that the "overall tendency" of many scripture texts indicates that this assurance always presupposes the condition, "so long as they cling to faith and charity with all their might" (505). Citing Remonstrant arguments that even a regenerate person may fall irrecoverably (though not easily), Milton now explicitly associates himself with their doctrine.[155]

He turns next to the Covenant of Grace, having at some point added six new chapters to treat aspects of this important topic.[156] That covenant is delivered first through the Law (chapter 26), in two modes. The law of nature was given to Adam and still remains as a "glimmering" in humans after the Fall; it is daily brought nearer to its original perfection in the regenerate (516). The Mosaic Law was given to the Jews alone and was intended to lead them, through a recognition of human depravity, to faith in the promised Messiah; it serves also to lead God's people "from this elementary, childish, and servile discipline to the adult stature of a new creature, and to a manly freedom under the gospel" (517). In chapter 27 Milton treats the Covenant of Grace under the gospel, "written in the hearts of believers through the Holy Spirit," and its concomitant, Christian liberty, which was "not unknown during the time of the law" but has largest scope under the gospel. Fulfilling his promise in *Of Civil Power* to treat this matter further, he now asserts definitively that Christian liberty involves the abolition of the entire Mosaic Law.[157] Characteristically, he claims to have proved this point against "pretty well all the theologians" who suppose that only the Jewish ceremonial and judicial laws are abrogated but that the Decalogue, as an embodiment of enduring moral principles, still binds Christians.[158] As the Decalogue is described as a law of works that cannot justify sinners but instead stimulates sin and leads to slavish fear and death, Milton insists that "we are therefore freed also from the decalogue [decalogo igitur ipso quoque liberamur]."[159] Applying this conclusion to Sabbath observance and marriage, he concludes as he did in the divorce tracts that charity – love of God and one's neighbor – often permits transgression of the written law since it fulfills in spirit all the Law and the Prophets.[160] Milton develops an antinomian position carefully distinguished from the antinomianism of the Ranters by his continual appeal to the law of reason and by his insistence that charity in fact dictates a higher moral standard than the Law:

> The substance of the law, love of God and of our neighbor, should not, I repeat, be thought of as destroyed . . . [but] is now inscribed on believers' hearts by the spirit. . . . It is not a less perfect life that is required from Christians but, in fact, a more perfect life than was required of those who were under the law. The whole tenor of Christ's teaching shows this.[161]

Echoing *Areopagitica* and *Of Civil Power*, Milton also draws out the political implications of the freedom won by "Christ our Liberator" from "coercion and legislation in religious matters."[162]

Turning to the role of the visible church (chapters 28–32), Milton expands upon the radical sectarian ecclesiology of *The Likeliest Means*. Discussing the sealing of the covenant in the two recognized Protestant sacraments, baptism and the Lord's Supper, Milton describes them in conventional Calvinist terms: baptism is a symbol of our death and resurrection with Christ, and the Lord's Supper commemorates and seals the benefits of Christ's death to believers. Quite untypically, however, he sees them as unnecessary if they cannot conveniently take place (557). On the issue of infant baptism he stands with the Anabaptists: infants cannot profess their faith, or undertake a covenant obligation, or pledge themselves to purity of life, so it is "infantile reasoning" to suppose them fit for baptism, which initiates us into the "rational, manly and utterly free service" of the gospel (547–8). He castigates Lutheran consubstantiation and especially Roman Catholic "transubstantiation . . . or cannibalism" as "utterly alien to reason, common sense, and human behavior," and he ascribes continuing errors about the sacraments to faulty textual analysis, such as a failure to recognize such words as "This is my Body" as figures of speech (554–5). Defining the visible church (chapter 29) as the whole multitude of believers whose only head is Christ, Milton judges that believers should join themselves "to a correctly instituted church," but may refrain if they cannot "do so conveniently, or with a good conscience" (568). After the Restoration many dissenters would find that "inconvenient" if not impossible, and the difficulties would escalate for a blind man. But Milton's devaluation of public rites is more than pragmatic: not only after the Restoration but also during the Interregnum, there is no record of Milton's formal membership in any parish or congregation.

Milton's discussion of ministers breaks down all distinctions between clergy and laity, as he insists that all believers may perform all offices relating to Christian worship and practice. In the category of extraordinary ministers he places prophets, apostles, evangelists, and others sent and inspired by God to establish or reform the church "by preaching and by writing" – a definition that makes place for a Milton (570). Ordinary ministers can be any (male) believers with the requisite gifts which, as in *The Likeliest Means*, he sees emanating not from the universities but from God.[163] Any believer can preach the gospel and so can certainly administer the less important rite of baptism. As for the Lord's Supper, it clearly "belongs to all believers, and . . . is not the particular right of any man or order of men" (573, 558).

Chapter 30, "Of the Holy Scripture," might seem to be out of place,[164] but in fact follows from the previous treatment of laity's rights in the visible church. Reiterating the common Protestant principles that the scriptures are "both in themselves, and through God's illumination, absolutely clear" in matters essential to salvation, and that all sorts and conditions of men should read the scriptures, Milton also claims that the gift of prophecy (or public teaching) is "promised to each individual believer" (577–80). He expects that ministers will normally be men of learning, possessed of the usual requisites for public interpretation of scripture: "linguistic ability, knowledge of the original sources, consideration of the overall intent, distinction between literal and figurative language, . . . comparison of one text with another," comparison with the so called analogy of faith, consideration of anomalies of syntax, and knowledge of when the single sense of scripture also incorporates typology (582–3). But such learning is not essential to believers or even to ministers. As in *Of Civil Power*, the individual Christian's right to interpret scripture for himself remains absolute: "Every believer is entitled to interpret the scriptures . . . for himself. He has the spirit, who guides truth, and he has the mind of Christ."[165] Milton's careful attention to scripture passages in *De Doctrina* evidently reinforced his awareness of the corruptions of the New Testament text, transmitted by "untrustworthy authorities" and set down in "a medley of transcripts and editions" (588). He invokes this textual slippage to assert even more strongly than before that the spirit of scripture (charity, liberty, reason) and not the mere letter is to be followed: God, he speculates, may have allowed the written text to be corrupted to convince us that "all things are eventually to be referred to the Spirit and the unwritten word" engraved upon the hearts of believers, which cannot be corrupted (587–90). Citing 1 Timothy 3:15, he locates the church of the living God not in the visible community but in the "hearts of believers."

Chapters 31–2 describe particular churches as independent congregations, and in terms that equate clergy and laity. A church is established by covenant of its members (608); the election of ministers "is in the power of the people" who are to test and judge their teachers (594); and a few members meeting in a private house (as dissenters had to do after the Restoration) constitute a "self-contained and complete church," not subject in religious matters to any other authority (601). After identifying the usual church officers (ministers, deacons, widows), Milton reprises his antitithe arguments from *The Likeliest Means*: to "exact tithes or gospel-taxes" by force or the power of the magistrate is the action of wolves and it does not take place "in any reformed church except ours."[166] Ideally, ministers should serve without pay, living off their own resources or working at "some trade or some respectable profession" (599); otherwise, they should rely on voluntary contributions from their own churches. Chapter 32 describes church discipline – counselling the weak, composing differences among members, and sometimes ejecting sinners – as a spiritual power to be exercised only by a particular church over its own members' inner faculties; it stands in direct contrast to the magistrate's civil power over the bodies of all citizens.[167] Milton's description of church meetings suggests something like Quaker practice; he may have attended some Quaker meetings at Chalfont with his friend Ellwood, or at least liked what he was told about them:

> One man, and he with motives of gain, should not be struck up in a pulpit and have the sole right of addressing the congregation. Instead each believer, according to his personal talents, should have a chance to address his fellows, or to prophesy, teach, or exhort. Even the weakest of the brethren should have an opportunity to interrogate or to ask advice from the older and more learned of those present. (608)

Unlike the Quakers, however, Milton retains the Pauline prohibition against women speaking in church (609).

Book 1 concludes with a largely conventional account of last things and the glorification of those who believe and persevere. In the early 1640s Milton had been at times caught up in the widespread millenarian fervor, but he no longer expects apocalypse soon: Christ, he now says, "will be slow to come" (618). That second coming will inaugurate a scenario like that extracted by Joseph Mede and many others from the Book of Revelation, in which Christ's judgment of the world is coextensive with his thousand-year reign on earth with his saints.[168] That concept allowed Milton in his political tracts to project the Millennium as a reference point for the contemporary political order, which ought to be in preparation for that moment however near or far distant, not by Fifth Monarchist uprisings or theocratic government, but by rejecting idolatry and kingship, disestablishing the church, and promoting religious and intellectual liberty. After that thousand-year reign Satan will mount a last battle against the church, Christ will finally defeat Satan, and then will come the Last Judgment of the rebel angels and all humankind, each "according to the light which he has received" (623–5). The damned will be sent to hell to endure the "second death" of eternal punishment graduated according to their sins; and the saved will enjoy, also in unequal measure, an "eternal and utterly happy life, arising chiefly from the sight of God" and enhanced by the possession of heaven and earth and "all those creatures in both which may be useful or delightful" (630–2).

Book 2, 'Of Good Works," is often close in language, though not in overall conception, to the treatises Milton began from in the 1640s.[169] Like other Protestants, Milton denies that good works are in any way meritorious for salvation, defining them as the works of faith made acceptable to God only through Christ's merits. Milton follows Wollebius in defining virtues as good habits and as the secondary causes of good works, as well as in treating first the general virtues pertaining to the understanding (Wisdom and Prudence), then those pertaining to the will (Sincerity, Promptitude, and Constancy). However, Wollebius, Ames, and most others discuss good works and virtues under the two tables of the Law containing the Ten Commandments, while Milton, believing the Decalogue to be abrogated for Christians, treats them as manifestations of charity, "the love of God and of our neighbor, which is the sum of the law" (640). He categorizes good works and virtues under three general heads: love of and duty toward God, toward ourselves, and toward our neighbor. In treating the first and third of these categories he draws heavily on Wollebius, but for the second, treated only casually in the Calvinist manuals, he looks often to classical moral philosophy. Several manuscript pages of Book 2 bear evidence of revision: biblical texts added, words and phrases inserted or deleted. Also, pages dealing with issues Milton felt strongly about – idolatry, the invocation of angels and saints, and the Sabbath – were copied over, suggesting that they had been heavily revised.[170]

Treating the virtues pertaining to worship of God, Milton first discusses internal qualities – Love, Confidence, Hope, Gratitude, and Obedience and their opposites – and then turns to external worship or religion (chapters 3–7). Taking up invocation and prayer, he insists, as always, on the spirit rather than the letter: sincere internal worship is acceptable without external rites; and no special forms, times, places, dress, or bodily positions are required.[171] Unlike severer Puritans, Milton welcomes hymns and songs in honor of the divine name (683). Unlike the Quakers he thinks that oath-taking in serious matters is lawful, but that wrongful vows and sinful oaths should not be kept and that Catholic vows of chastity, abstinence, or poverty are superstitious renunciations of goods God meant for human use (680–1). His long discussion of idolatry has Catholic practice as its direct target: they err in calling their images layman's books and employ worthless subterfuges to defend "their adoration of saints and angels" (695). He also takes up an issue vital to dissenting parliament members or office-holders who are now required to attend Anglican services (the issue will be revisited in *Samson Agonistes*): whether it is allowable to take part in idol-worship in the performance of some civic duty. He cites 2 Kings 5:17–19 as apparently permitting that practice, but thinks it "safer" to decline such gestures and to relinquish the duties that demand them (694). The prohibition for him is not an absolute, as throughout his prose and poetry he has redefined idolatry to pertain chiefly to internal servility in worshipping anything that is not God. In discussing Zeal for sanctifying the Divine Name he also treats its opposite, blasphemy, defining it here as he did in *Of Civil Power* from the Greek etymology: "any kind of evil speaking, directed against any person," including

God.[172] Convicting of bad faith those who have misused and mystified the term so as to comprehend within it "pretty well any opinion about God or religious matters which did not tally with their own," he carefully excludes from that category all doctrines argued from scripture (such as his own Arianism): "Those who, in all sincerity, and with no desire to stir up controversy, teach or discuss some doctrine concerning the deity which they have quite apparently, as they see it, learned from the Holy Scriptures, are in no sense guilty of the sin of blasphemy" (699–700). As to the circumstances of divine worship, time and place, he challenges the assertion of "our countryman, Ames" that the reasons for keeping the Sabbath are "moral and immutable," referring back to his earlier discussions of prelapsarian Eden and Christian liberty: "we who live under the gospel and are, as I proved in my first book, quite freed from the law, must be emancipated above all from this law about Sabbath-observance," which pertained to the Israelites alone.[173] The church may designate a day for voluntary public observance but it must not be enforced by civil or ecclesiastical authority (714).

Identifying charity and justice as the comprehensive virtues determining our duties toward ourselves and others, Milton focuses first (chapters 8–10) on the self, often drawing on Aristotle's *Ethics*, though he cites only scripture texts. Charity seeks our own temporal and eternal good, and justice mandates self-government and control of the affections: love, hate, joy, sadness, hope, fear, and anger. Temperance, which involves sobriety, chastity, modesty, and decency, regulates desire for the pleasures of the flesh; he describes sins against chastity – "voluptuousness, sodomy, bestiality and so on" – as he has from the time of Prolusion VI as degradations of oneself (726–7). In discussing the virtues regulating appetites for material possessions – contentment, frugality, industry – Milton revealingly includes elegance ("lautitia"), defined as "the discriminating enjoyment of food, clothing and all the civilized refinements of life, purchased with our honest earnings"; his early biographers reported that he ate and drank sparingly but liked what he had to be of the best.[174] Among the virtues regulating attitudes toward honors or distinctions, Milton includes humility, defining it – with a characteristic and revealing exception – as the virtue which "gives a man a modest opinion of himself and prevents him from blowing his own trumpet, except when it is really called-for" (733). He also includes high-mindedness ("Magnanimitas"), manifested when, in seeking, accepting, or avoiding riches, advantages, or honors, "a man behaves himself as befits his own dignity, rightly understood" (735); the definition looks back to Aristotle (*Ethics* IV, ii) and forward to *Paradise Regained* (2.463–83). The virtues needed for repelling evils Milton identifies, as he did in *Of Education*, as fortitude and patience, opposing the latter to the apathy of the Stoics, as he will again in *Paradise Regained*.[175]

Milton's treatment of the virtues and vices relating to one's neighbor (chapters 11–14) remains close to Wollebius. He defines neighbor as "anyone to whom our kindness or help is opportune," but recognizes the special claims of fellow Christians and family members (741–2). The virtues required are humanity, which involves "the common courtesies of life in our dealings with our fellow men"; kindness, which involves wishing all men well and avoiding envy or jealousy; pitifulness, which is sympathy for the misfortunes of others; brotherly or Christian charity, whereby fellow Christians love and help one another; and friendship, defined as "the intimate conjunction of two or more people who perform every virtuous or at least every courteous service for one another."[176] However, Milton looks to his own valued friendships and to the Renaissance cult of friendship more than to scripture texts when he claims that friendship "takes precedent over all blood-relationships" (750). Virtues pertaining to the neighbor's life and honor include doing him no harm, gentleness, forgiving injuries, and respecting his chastity, that last of which dictates refraining from "homosexuality, fornication, violation, adultery, incest, rape, prostitution, and offenses of a similar kind" (756). Among the virtues respecting the neighbor's reputation is veracity; its opposites include deliberate lies, falsehood, and giving false evidence, but not falsehoods intended to save or help others. Milton the poet and rhetorician also excludes from the category of lies "parables, hyperboles, fables and the various uses of irony," since those are intended to instruct, not to deceive (761). Milton's delight in learned conversation is reflected in his definition of urbanity, an aspect of the virtue of candor, as "not only elegance and wit (of a decent kind) in conversation, but also the ability to discourse and to reply in an acute and apposite way" (769–70).[177] The primary virtue pertaining to the neighbor's fortune is honesty, which involves commutative justice in buying and selling, hiring, lending, and borrowing. In this context Milton the scrivener's son, who himself lent money at interest, defends usury on the same basis as every kind of profit-making transaction: it is wrong only if practiced "at the expense of the poor, or solely out of avarice, or to an uncharitable and unjust extent."[178]

Chapters 15–16 deal with reciprocal duties arising from various special relationships. Turning first to the household, Milton adduces the expected biblical texts to define, in conventional terms, the reciprocal duties of husband and wife, parent and child, brothers or other kinsfolk toward each other, tutor and pupil, superior and inferior, master and servant, and master and slave. We hear Milton the erstwhile aggrieved husband in the gratuitous comment as to what woman's creation from a rib implies about her subjection: "it is wrong for one single part of the body – and not one of the most important parts – to disobey the rest of the body, and even the head."[179] We also hear Milton the proud bourgeois in the comment that "nobility of birth and exalted rank are not things to be proud of" (786). He treats the master–slave relation simply by citing biblical texts: he evidently accepted that institution as a given, but made no reference whatever to contemporary practice. Duties to those outside the household include almsgiving according to or even beyond our means to widows, orphans, the weak and helpless, as well as hospitality to travelers and the homeless. But Milton does not condone idleness or social leveling: alms should not be given to "vagrants or beggers by choice," and they should be proportioned to the rank, way of life, and level of education of recipients, so as to "avoid the absurdity of equalizing the unequal" (790).

The final chapter (17) treats the reciprocal duties of magistrate and people and of ministers and church members in distinctly Miltonic terms. The only topic treating kings is headed "The immorality of royal courts" (796). Reprising his argument in *Of Civil Power* and in Book 1, Milton restricts the duties of magistrates toward religion to fostering and protecting it; if they exercise force over conscience or supervision over the church they are as much Antichrist as the pope:

> We may be sure that, since Christ's kingdom is not of this world, it does not stand by force and constraint . . . the gospel should not be made a matter of compulsion, and faith, liberty and conscience cannot be. These are the concerns of ecclesiastical discipline, and are quite outside the province of civil jurisdiction.[180]

Treating the magistrate's duties abroad, Milton argues the legitimacy of war, if undertaken with careful consideration, citing Old Testament precedent and the absence of New Testament prohibition (803). Treating the duties of ministers and church members he chiefly cites scripture texts and points back to his discussions in Book 1.[181] Discussing the obedience subjects are said to owe tyrants, Milton does not reprise his argument in *Tenure*, but he does deny any scriptural authority to the absolutist position by refuting the texts usually cited to support it. 1 Peter 2:13 pertains only to obeying lawful ordinances and verse 18 "is addressed to slaves, and has nothing to do with the duties of free people" (800). The Israelites obeyed Pharaoh but they were nowhere commanded to do so or praised for it; and Daniel's example of obedience in captivity is irrelevant. However, he concedes that "in lawful matters it may be prudent to obey even a tyrant, or at any rate to be a time-server, in the interest of public peace and personal safety" (801). That qualification may mean to sanction his own and other Puritans' prudential behavior in the Restoration regime.

13

"Higher Argument:" Completing and Publishing *Paradise Lost* 1665–1669

The years 1665–9 brought Milton much satisfaction as he finished and published *Paradise Lost*, which he probably began writing in earnest around 1658 with the sporadic and often unsatisfactory help of students, friends, and amanuenses. But these years also brought anxiety and brushes with catastrophe. The Great Plague kept Milton in Chalfont St Giles through the summer and autumn of 1665, and soon after he returned to London he lived through the terror occasioned by the Great Fire (1666). And soon after that, the Dutch sailed up the Medway and destroyed much of the English fleet. On the domestic front, Milton's daughters became increasingly resentful about their lives and prospects, and arrangements were made for them to leave home. They carried their resentments with them.

Into *Paradise Lost* Milton poured all that he had learned, experienced, desired, and imagined about life, love, artistic creativity, theology, work, history, and politics. His political disappointments did not lead him, as is sometimes supposed, to retreat to a spiritual realm, a "paradise within." His epic is in fact a more daring political gesture than we often realize, even as it is also a poem for the ages by a prophet–poet who placed himself with, or above, Homer, Virgil, Ariosto, Tasso, and the rest. It undertakes a strenuous project of educating readers in the virtues, values, and attitudes that make a people worthy of liberty. In the moral realm the Miltonic Bard exercises his readers in discernment, rigorous judgment, imaginative apprehension, and choice by setting his poem in relation to other great epics and works in other genres, prompting a critique of the values associated with those other heroes and genres. In the political realm he encourages them to think again, and think rightly, about the ideological and polemic controversies of the recent war and its aftermath – about monarchy and tyranny, religious and civil liberty, and revolution. The reception history of *Paradise Lost* demonstrates that it was quite possible to ignore, or to misread, the poem's politics and theology – but not, I think, because Milton obscured them out of confusion or misjudgment or to give himself cover from the censors.[1] Rather, when Milton challenges stereotypes he inevitably risks activating them. He engages his readers to work through complex issues and situations to right understandings, and thereby learn to be virtuous and liberty-loving citizens. Milton's fit readers may have been few, but he wanted his poem to produce as many more of them as possible.

He could take pleasure in the fact that *Paradise Lost* sold reasonably well, and in the praises of a few judicious critics. The later issues were supplemented by preliminary matter requested by the printer, including a statement in which Milton defended his use of blank verse against the contemporary norm of rhyme for heroic poetry and drama – an aesthetic debate that had political implications. Soon after he finished his great epic Milton began work on its complement, the brief epic *Paradise Regained*.

"This Subject for Heroic Song Pleas'd Me Long Choosing and Beginning Late"

Sometime in June, 1665, Milton and his family settled into a small, irregular cottage of brick and wooden beams at the edge of the peaceful village of Chalfont, and remained there for eight or nine months. In Milton's time it seems to have had three sitting rooms and a kitchen downstairs, as well as five quite small bedrooms, two of them up a small staircase or ladder (plate 14).[2] There was and is a pleasant garden in which Milton sat to take the air. He could take agreeable walks in the village past an old church and churchyard, inns, timber-joisted houses, and a duck pond, and longer strolls to the market-town of Beaconsfield, about four miles away. Milton had connections in the area, among them the Fleetwoods, the family who held the manor house of the Vache for a century until it was forfeited by the regicide George Fleetwood in 1661.[3] Milton's Quaker friend Isaac Pennington who lived in the next village, Chalfont St Peter, would have introduced him to the rather extensive Quaker community in the area and welcomed him at his mansion, the Grange.[4] But there may have been little socializing at first, since the plague had also reached several Buckinghamshire towns and there were cases in Chalfont St Giles itself.[5] Thomas Ellwood, Milton's Quaker student and friend who had arranged his occupancy of the cottage, was in prison when he arrived and could not visit him until after August 1, "to welcome him into the Country." Ellwood was then given the manuscript of *Paradise Lost* to read, did so, and and returned it to Milton while he was still at Chalfont:

> After some common Discourses had passed between us, he called for a Manuscript of his; which being brought he delivered to me, bidding me take it home with me, and read it at my Leisure, and when I had so done, return it to him, with my Judgment thereupon.

> When I came home, and had set myself to read it, I found it was that Excellent POEM which he entituled *PARADISE LOST*. After I had, with the best Attention, read it through, I made him another Visit, and returned him his Book, with due Acknowledgement of the Favour he had done me, in Communicating it to me. He asked me how I liked it, and what I thought of it; which I modestly, but freely told him: and after some further discourse about it, I pleasantly said to him, Thou hast said much here of *Paradise lost,* but what hast thou to say of *Paradise found?* He made me no Answer, but sate some time in a Muse: then brake of that discourse, and fell upon another Subject.[6]

Apparently, Milton had a draft of *Paradise Lost* in hand by August, 1665, though he probably continued working on it at Chalfont and in London until he gave it to the printer 18 months later. He had been thinking about writing epic for decades – as far back as his collegiate *Vacation Exercise*. In 1642, when he wrote *The Reason of Church-Government*, he was thinking about an epic on the model of Virgil and Tasso with a great national hero, and as he had come to doubt King Arthur's historicity, he considered King Alfred.[7] The Virgilian model, celebrating the founding of the empire of the Caesars which brought with it the ruin of the Roman republic, would be a problematic model for this republican poet. So would Tasso's celebration, within the story of the first crusade, of the restoration of Counter-Reformation hegemony over all kinds of rebellion and dissent.[8] Tasso had decreed that the heroic poem should concern Christian personages, that the plot should take place in an age far enough distant to allow taking poetic liberties with history, and that the supernatural realm should be Christian.[9] We cannot be sure just when Milton decided that the great epic subject for his own times had to be the Fall and its consequences, "all our woe:" not the founding of a great empire or nation, but the loss of an earthly paradise and with it any possibility of founding an enduring version of the City of God on earth. Edward Phillips reports that "several Years before the Poem was begun" he saw the lines that now form the opening of Satan's address to the Sun (*PL* 4.32–41), at which time the speech was designed for the beginning of a tragedy on the Fall along the lines sketched out in the Trinity manuscript.[10]

Milton probably settled on his subject in the later 1650s, as he was losing faith that the English people might become the nation of prophets he had imagined in *Areopagitica*, or that its government might become the aristocratic republic he projected in *Tenure* and the *Defensio*. John Aubrey heard from Edward Phillips that Milton began the poem "about 2 yeares before the K. came-in, and finished about 3 yeares after the K's Restauracion," working on it only during the winter months and spending four or five years on it (*EL* 13). Phillips's own account suggests a somewhat longer period of composition and revision, referring to "all the years he was about this Poem" (*EL* 72–3). The first half may have been substantially completed before 1660, but the Proem to Book VII suggests that much or most of the final six books postdate the Restoration. Declaring that "Half yet remaines unsung," the Bard points to his own perilous position in the Restoration milieu: he is fallen "On evil dayes . . . / In darkness, and with dangers compast round."[11] For a time at least Milton had ample reason to fear, not only that his song might be drowned out by the "barbarous dissonance" of the Restoration court's Bacchic revelers, but also that those revelers might kill and dismember him as the Bacchantes did the archetypal bard, Orpheus.

As he planned his heroic subject in the later 1650s Milton set himself in competition with the great classical and vernacular epic poets of the past – Homer, Virgil, Dante, Ariosto, Tasso, DuBartas, Spenser. He had also to take account of efforts by his English royalist contemporaries to claim and redefine the heroic mode for their own time. William Davenant's *Gondibert*, with a prefatory address to and laudatory response by Hobbes, held forth that work as the ideal modern heroic poem, modeled both on Tasso and on the continental heroic drama.[12] Imitating five-act tragedies, Davenant projected a five-book epic divided into cantos, though he completed and published only half the work, explaining that he was then in prison expecting execution (for attempting a mission for Charles II). If, as report has it, Milton helped accomplish his release,[13] the likelihood increases that Milton came to know Davenant's experiment in epic. Davenant devised a plot with wholly fictional Christian personages, located in a foreign country, Italy, where wonderful deeds and situations might seem more credible. But he avoids one major source of epic wonder, the supernatural, asserting that the classical supernatural is incredible, that representations of the true God and his angels are profane or even blasphemous, and that bardic claims of poetic inspiration are dangerous. Both he and Hobbes link such claims with the "enthusiastic" Puritan sects. He also defends his use of four-line stanzas in alternate rhyme as "more pleasant to the reader in a work of length."[14] The plot explores love and ambition, with the hero, Duke Gondibert, torn between the duties of the active life – courts, warfare, stag hunts, uprisings, knightly activities, and the responsibilities of an heir to the throne – and the attractions of retirement: true love and the joys of learning in the House of Astragon. The work has affinities with the royalist literature of pastoralism and retirement in the late 1640s and 1650s, by Herrick, Vaughan, Fanshawe, and Walton among many others.[15] But the fact that Davenant did not complete his poem after his release suggests that he could not imagine the ending: if Gondibert is at times a figure for the royalists (or Charles II) it was not clear in 1651 whether they would continue in retirement or might again rule.[16] Also, the absence of supernatural personages means that the reader is given no reassurance of an ultimate purpose behind events. The Davenant–Hobbes manifesto and the example of *Gondibert* set Milton a challenge to produce a more worthy modern heroic poem on quite different principles. That challenge was reinforced as Dryden's heroic plays began to be produced and published, defining as norms for the heroic genres royalist politics, the pentameter couplet, and exotic subjects dealing with the conflict of love and honor. In 1667 Dryden observed that heroic plays are flourishing "from the countenance and approbation they have received at Court."[17]

Milton might also contemplate another version of the modern epic modeled on Tasso, Camõens's *Os Lusiadas* in Richard Fanshawe's English translation (1655); it celebrates Portuguese exploration and empire-building, accompanied by the triumph of Christianity, as the major heroic enterprise of Europe in the early-modern period.[18] By its opening echo, "Armes, and the Men," the poem proclaims its place in the Virgilian tradition, and then asserts the superiority of the Portuguese heroes over Aeneas, Odysseus, Alexander, or any others celebrated by the ancient bards. Both the original and the translation are in ten cantos, with eight-line stanzas of alternating rhymes and a concluding couplet. Milton's poem alludes to Camõens in some episodes, and calls at times on the language of exploration and colonization. Also, Milton probably knew or at least heard about Samuel Butler's wildly popular burlesque epic, *Hudibras* (1663? and 1664).[19] The three cantos of each part, written in rollicking octosyllabic couplets, satirize the Presbyterian knight Hudibras (a Don Quixote figure, though with no trace of his idealism) and his Sancho-Panza-like squire Ralpho, who stands for the Independents. Both are supremely incompetent, undertaking mayhem in the name of religion but always coming a cropper; they are buffoons, dishonest, corrupt, unchivalrous, and contemptible. Butler's burlesque epic degrades epic martial heroism, epic heroes, and the epic form itself, as well as the recent English conflict, setting Milton the task of demonstrating that epic is still possible, and that epic heroism is to be found not in battle glory but in a "better fortitude."

Abraham Cowley's incomplete *Davideis* (1656) and its critical preface may have seemed to pose Milton a direct challenge. Milton's widow Elizabeth mentioned Cowley with Spenser and Shakespeare as the English poets Milton "approved most;"[20] that approval was most likely for Cowley's pindaric odes and lyrics, but Milton would have encountered Cowley's attempt at a modern biblical epic published along with them in 1656. Cowley presents himself in the preface as a defeated royalist who has resigned himself to the new order, abandoning an earlier epic on the civil war, since it is "*ridiculous*, to make *Lawrels* for the *Conquered*."[21] He designed his "*Heroical Poem* of the *Troubles of David*" as an epic in twelve books, "not for the *Tribes* sake, but after the *Patern* of our Master *Virgil*." He had intended, and in the four completed books undertakes, to weave in "most of the illustrious *Stories* of the *Old Testament*" and "the most remarkable *Antiquities* of the *Jews*, and of other Nations before or at that *Age*."[22] The poem initially suggests a parallel between Saul and Cromwell, and between David and Prince Charles who, like David, endured trials and dangers in exile; David's residence at the court of King Moab alludes to Charles at the court of Louis XIV. If the projected conclusion, David's anointing at Hebron, was intended to allude to Charles's restoration, Cowley may have stopped writing when he lost confidence in that ending. Milton would have approved Cowley's strong recommendation of biblical subjects for epic, though not his emphasis on martial and regal stories and his use of heroic couplets: "What worthier subject could have been chosen among all the *Treasures* of past times, then the *Life* of this young *Prince*; . . . There is not so great a *Lye* to be found in any *Poet*, as the vulgar conceit of men, that *Lying* is *Essential* to good *Poetry*."[23] Milton might also have taken as a personal challenge Cowley's gesture of handing on the difficult task he could not complete to some better poet:

> He who can write a *prophane Poem well,* may write a *Divine one better*; but he who can do that but ill, will do this much worse. The same fertility of *invention,* the same wisdom of *Disposition*; the same *Judgement* in observation of *Decencies*, the same lustre and vigor of *Elocution*; the same modesty and majestie of *number*, briefly the same kind of *habit* is required to both; only this latter allows better *stuff*, and therefore would look more deformedly, if *ill drest* in it. I am farre from assuming to my self to have fulfilled the duty of this weighty undertaking. But sure I am, that there is nothing yet in our *Language* (or perhaps in *any*) that is in any degree answerable to the *Idea* that I conceive of it. And I shall be ambitious of no other fruit from this weak and imperfect attempt of mine, but the opening of a way to the courage and industry of some other persons, who may be better able to perform it thoroughly and successfully.[24]

At some point while he was writing and revising his epic, Milton decided on a ten-book format, thereby distinguishing his poem from the twelve-book Virgilian model consciously followed by Tasso and Cowley. There is some reason to think that Milton originally planned a twelve-book structure, turned away from it for the first edition (1667), and returned to it for the second (1674). The Proem to Milton's Book VII, which recalls Virgil's invocation to the second half of his poem near the beginning of his Book VII, contains Milton's line "Half yet remaines unsung" (21); this is strictly true for an epic in twelve books but not for a ten-book poem.[25] Milton may have rejected the Virgilian format to emphasize that his is not an epic of conquest and empire, but another reason was surely that royalists had appropriated the Virgilian heroic mode both before and after the Restoration. John Denham translated Book II of the *Aeneid* as a poem in heroic couplets entitled *The Destruction of Troy* (1656), making Aeneas's narrative of and lament for the loss of the Trojan kingdom resonate with the royalist defeat and the loss of Charles I's English kingdom. Denham's poem ends with Priam's death (well before the end of Virgil's Book II), associating it with the beheading of Charles: "On the cold earth lies this neglected King, / A headless Carkass, and a nameless Thing."[26] In what Laura Knoppers terms the "politics of joy" following the Restoration, poets hailed the new era in Virgilian terms as a Golden Age restored, and celebrated Charles II as a new Augustus.[27] His coronation procession was designed as a magnificent Roman Triumph through four elaborate Roman arches that identified him with Augustus, Aeneas, and Neptune. Dryden's *Astraea Redux* rings explicit changes on those motifs: "Oh Happy Age! Oh times like those alone / By Fate reserv'd for Great *Augustus* Throne."[28] Reason enough for republican Milton to find a formal means to withhold his poem from such Virgilian appropriations. His opening lines indicate that the true Restoration will not be effected by an English Augustus but must await a divine hero: "Till one greater Man / Restore us, and regain the blissful Seat."

By his ten-book format, Milton associates his poem explicitly with Lucan's unfinished epic, *Pharsalia*, or *The Civil War*, which was the font of a counter-tradition to Virgil's celebration of an Augustan empire predestined by the gods. Lucan treats the resistance of the Roman republic and its heroes, Pompey and Cato, who were defeated by the victorious tyrant Caesar in a bloody civil war; by ascribing Caesar's victory to contingency and chance rather than the gods, and by having the spirit of the butchered Pompey enter into the future tyrannicide, Brutus (9.1–17), Lucan suggests an ongoing struggle against Caesarism.[29] Lucan's own career was readily assimilated to his epic, since he was forced to commit suicide at age 26 for involvement in a botched conspiracy against Caesar's infamous successor, Nero. By Milton's time Lucan's epic tradition was firmly associated with antimonarchical or republican politics through several editions and translations,[30] especially the 1627 English translation by the Long Parliament's historian-to-be, Thomas May. May's preface designates Pompey the "true servant of the publike State" for his opposition to Caesar in defense of the Senate and the Roman republic, and he adds a couplet at the end terming the future assassins of Caesar, Brutus, and Cassius "more just then Jove" who has seemed to favor Caesar.[31] Milton alludes to and echoes Lucan especially in the treatment of contingency in Satan's flight through chaos, in the portrayal of the War in Heaven as a civil war, and in linking Satan's use of opportunistic republican rhetoric with Caesar's. Milton also found in Lucan a model for the tragic epic: Lucan treats the loss of the Roman republic, Milton the loss of the earthly paradise.[32]

In the Proem to Book IX Milton indicates that verses of his great poem came readily to him – as if inspired and chiefly at night. Yet the difficulties under which Milton labored were clearly phenomenal, dependant as he was upon friends and amanuenses to record his lines when he had them ready.[33] The report of Cyriack Skinner, who sometimes served Milton as an amanuensis, corroborates in more prosaic terms the story of his Muse's "nightly visitations," indicating Milton's habit of composing poetry upon first waking and his urgent need to get his verses set down:

> The time friendly to the Muses fell to his Poetry; And hee waking early (as is the use of temperate men) had commonly a good Stock of Verses ready against his Amanuensis came; which if it happend to bee later than ordinary, hee would complain, Saying, *hee wanted to bee milkd*. (*EL* 33)

Richardson reports that Milton was "perpetually Asking One Friend or Another who Visited him to Write a Quantity of Verses he had ready in his Mind, or what should Then occur"; he also heard that Milton would dictate "perhaps 40 Lines as it were in a Breath, and then reduce them to half the Number" (*EL* 289, 291). Edward Phillips corroborates these accounts of Milton's compositional habits, adding the curious fact that he found himself able to write poetry – or at least epic poetry – only during the winter months:

> There is another very remarkable Passage in the Composure of this Poem, which I have a particular occasion to remember; for whereas I had the perusal of it from the very beginning; for some years, as I went from time to time, to Visit him, in a Parcel of Ten, Twenty, or Thirty Verses at a Time, which being Written by whatever hand came next, might possibly want Correction as to the Orthography and Pointing; having as the Summer came on, not been shewed any for a considerable while, and desiring the reason thereof, was answered, That his Vein never happily flow'd, but from the *Autumnal Equinoctial* to the *Vernal*, and that whatever he attempted [at other times] was never to his satisfaction, though he courted his fancy never so much; so that in all the years he was about this Poem, he may be said to have spent but half his time therein. (*EL* 73)

Phillips here claims to have had primary responsibility for the correction and oversight of a manuscript transcribed over several years by several hands. That account is born out by the manuscript of Book I, the only surviving portion of the fair copy delivered to the printer.[34]

According to Ellwood, Milton returned to his London house in Artillery Walk "after the Sickness was over, and the City well cleansed, and become safely habitable again,"[35] probably in February or early March, 1666. Pepys's diary entry for January 31 notes that people "begin to bustle up and down" around Whitehall, that people living near churchyards were having them covered with lime, and that the king and Duke of York were to return the next day.[36] As Bunhill Fields was the largest plague cemetary in all London, Milton no doubt wanted to be sure it was cleansed before he returned.[37] After he settled again in London Milton evidently began work on *Paradise Regained*, while continuing to make final revisions and corrections on the text of *Paradise Lost*. Edward Phillips was available for such service only during occasional visits, since he had left Evelyn's household in February, 1665 to become tutor to Phillip Herbert at Wilton.[38] Other family members and friends who lived in some proximity to Milton may have given some help: his nephew John Phillips may have been the "schoolmaster" who was taxed on six hearths in Aldersgate Street, and his brother Christopher was regularly reappointed every term from May, 1664 as attendant or reader in the Inner Temple.[39] Some longtime friends were likely visitors: his personal physician Dr Nathan Paget and the bookseller George Thomason, until his death in 1666. Marvell probably came also: some echoes in his "Last Instructions to a Painter" suggest that he saw *Paradise Lost* before publication.[40]

Visitors would have reported to Milton about the second Anglo-Dutch war, which was formally declared on February 22, 1665. Like the first Dutch war (1652–4) this one was sparked by commercial rivalry, trading rights, and the carrying trade with Africa, North America, and the West and East Indies. The battles took place at sea, with the fleet on the English side commanded by Charles II's brother the Duke of York (the future James II), Prince Rupert, and Albermarle (formerly General Monk). Despite the war's popularity and unprecedented grants of money by parliament, the first year brought naval disasters, bungled forays, diplomatic isolation, and near financial collapse for the government.[41] In January, 1666 France and Denmark entered the war on the Dutch side, and that summer a four-day naval battle was fought in the English Channel (June 1–4) with enormous losses on both sides. On August 8–10 the English set fire to about 160 Dutch merchantmen in harbor as well as the chief town on the island of Schelling, a strike celebrated, Pepys reports, by bonfires and celebrations throughout London.[42]

Sometime that summer Milton received a letter, dated May 27/June 6, from his acquaintance Peter Heimbach, who had sought his recommendation in 1657 for an appointment as secretary to the diplomatic envoy to the Hague.[43] Heimbach, now state councillor to the Elector of Brandenburg, had heard rumors of Milton's death and wrote to express his pleasure that the news was false. As in his earlier letter, Heimbach's Latin is awkward and often incorrect and his style is even more fulsome and fawning. Also, his sentiments are inept: among the potpourri of virtues for which he praises Milton he emphasizes "policy" as well as piety and immeasurable erudition, and suggests that Milton, like old Simeon who was ready to die upon seeing the infant Messiah (Luke 2:29), now desires nothing more than to be taken to his heavenly *patria.*[44] Milton's response, dated August 15, is his last known letter to any correspondent. He graciously attributes Heimbach's remarks about his rumored death to concern for his welfare, recalls that he knew Heimbach "as a youth of exceptional promise," and congratulates him on the honor and favor he has earned. But he also pokes witty fun at Heimbach's bad Latin and bad taste.[45] Wryly commenting on how Heimbach "embellishes" his compliments, he underscores the inappropriateness of the Simeon allusion: "I am both alive and well. Let me not be useless, whatever remains for me in this life." He also takes playful issue with the term "*Policy*"; he would prefer "*Patriotism,*" which, he puns, "having allured me by her lovely name, has almost *expatriated* me." And he makes clear that he is not ready yet for the heavenly *patria*: "One's *Patria* is wherever it is well with him."[46] The letter also provides a revealing insight into Milton's difficulties with amanuenses, this one unschooled in the classics:

> If you should find here anything badly written or not punctuated, blame it on the boy who wrote this down while utterly ignorant of Latin, for I was forced while dictating – and not without some difficulty – to completely spell out every single letter. (*CPW* VIII, 4)

Heimbach might, but probably did not, read this as a rebuke to his own awkward Latin diction and style, laboring under no such difficulties. Milton must often have had such anxieties about having to trust his words and thoughts to anyone available.

Sometime after his second stint in prison ended on June 25, 1666, Thomas Ellwood visited Milton again and was shown *Paradise Regained*:

> And when afterwards [after Milton's return] I went to wait on him there (which I seldom failed of doing, whenever my Occasions drew me to *London*), he shewed me his Second Poem, called *PARADISE REGAINED*; and in a pleasant Tone said to me, *This is owing to you; for you put it into my Head by the Question you put to me at* Chalfont; *which before I had not thought of.*[47]

Honest Ellwood surely reported what happened but his story presents some problems. The passage does not make clear when the visit occurred – probably that summer, but possibly at some later time. Also, Ellwood does not, as he did with *Paradise Lost*, claim to have read the new poem, so it is not clear whether he saw it when it was just begun or nearly finished. Finally, though Ellwood obviously believed he had served as a surrogate for Milton's muse in prompting this poem, Milton may have been making a "pleasant" – that is, half-joking – compliment.

We can imagine the anxiety verging on terror that Milton experienced in early September as fire raged for four days throughout London, devastating some 435 acres – two thirds of the entire City – from the Tower to Temple Bar and from the river nearly to Smithfield and London Wall. It broke out early in the morning of Sunday, September 2, in the house of a baker in Pudding Lane, and, thanks to a high wind and drought conditions, spread uncontrollably, destroying 13,200 houses, 89 churches, and goods valued at £3.5 million.[48] The only City church saved was St Giles Cripplegate, the parish that included Milton's residence in Artillery Lane. The toll of public buildings included St Paul's Cathedral, Paul's School that Milton had attended as a boy, the City gates, the Exchange, Guildhall, and Sion College. Blind Milton must have waited through those awful days and nights with a mounting sense of helplessness, smelling the scorching smoke and hearing the roaring fire, the commotion of families fleeing the flames and moaning their losses, and terrified reports by friends and family about the wildly spreading, unpredictable course of the flames. Pepys writes of streets filled with people and loaded carts "ready to run over one another and removing goods from one burned house to another," of showers of firedrops and blinding smoke, of the "horrid, malicious, bloody flame" making an arch of fire a mile long, and of the terror and commotion caused by often unavailing efforts to stop the fire by blowing up buildings.[49] He also reports the widely believed rumors that the French or the Jesuits had set the blaze.[50] Richard Baxter deplores the loss of books from the libraries of ministers, booksellers, and colleges, commenting that he found half-burned leaves of books everywhere.[51] Did members of the Milton household also begin to pack up their goods, including the manuscript of *Paradise Lost* and other unpublished works, for a quick removal if need be? By September 5 or 6 Milton would have learned that the fire had been stopped by the City wall and ditch at Aldergate, Cripplegate, and Moorgate. It had come within a quarter-mile of his house in Artillery Walk, and also spared his former residences in the Barbican and Jewin Street. But the Cheapside neighborhood of his youth, including Bread Street and his property there, as well as his birthplace the Spread Eagle – sometimes visited by admiring foreigners – was entirely destroyed.[52]

Milton did not comment in writing, though others did, about the causes of all these disasters. To many they seemed an augury of an imminent Apocalypse, and to many more they provided a focus for widespread disappointment with the restored Stuarts. Charles's marriage was still barren though his sexual profligacy and royal mistresses had become notorious. Rumors of sexual debauchery also circulated around his brother and heir apparent, James Duke of York and his unpopular Duchess, Clarendon's daughter Anne Hyde. The court was decried as dissolute and a site of open lewdness.[53] Many cavaliers complained that they had not been fully restored to their places and goods, dissenters lamented their persecution under the harshly restrictive Clarendon Code, and City merchants protested the loss of trade due to the war. An outpouring of jeremiad-like sermons and tracts read the events of 1665–6 as God's punishment for sins general and national, and called for repentance:

> The great and famous City of London, once the glory of the world, now lies in ashes, being in four days time by a dreadful and lamentable Fire made a ruinous heap, and a doleful spectacle . . . so that we may all truly take up that lamentation of the Prophet Jer. 1.1. How doth the City remain solitary that was full of people. . . . Surely, every good Christian should humble himself under this heavy Judgement . . . for we have sinned and rebelled, and therefore it is that he hath not spared; let us labour to bear the punishment of our iniquities patiently . . . and turn again unto the Lord: who knows but that he may have a blessing in store for us; and by sanctifying these great afflictions to us, may make us Spiritual gainers by our Temporal Losses.[54]

But as a contemporary letter writer observed, many seized the opportunity to lay the disasters to some particular enemy's charge:

> All see the same desolation, yet, by looking on it with different opinions and interest, they make different constructions as if the object were so. Some thinking it a natural and bare accident, while others imagine it a judgment of God, and are as confident of it as if they saw the hand on the wall. The Quakers say, it is for their persecution. The Fanaticks say, it is for banishing and silencing their ministers. Others say, it is for the murder of the king and the rebellion of the city. The Clergy lay the blame on schism and licentiousness, while the Sectaries lay it on imposition and their pride.[55]

Milton probably had someone read to him Dryden's *Annus Mirabilis*, which appeared in January, 1667[56] and was designed to recoup the king's reputation in the face of all the criticism. Patriarchal imagery covers over his barrenness and profligacy, representing him as a pious and tender father of his people: rebuilding the destroyed navy, directing rescue efforts in the fire, and giving shape to a vision of a reborn and far grander "Augustan" city.[57] With his own epic ready to be published, Milton would have been especially interested in Dryden's preface defending this new kind of heroic poem based on contemporary events and serving royalist interests. Terming his poem "Historical, not Epick," Dryden nonetheless claims the historical kind as a branch of epic, insisting that his poem's "Actions and Actors are as much Heroick, as any Poem can contain." He also lays explicit claim to the Virgilian legacy, proclaiming that Virgil is his master and that he has "followed him every where."[58] Though he admits that the classical poets have an advantage over the moderns in not being tied "to the slavery of any Rhyme," he insists that his four-line stanzas in alternating rhyme are "more noble, and of greater dignity, both for the sound and number, then any other verse in use amongst us," referring to Davenant's preface to *Gondibert* for a better defense.[59] This new claimant to the modern heroic poem would surely goad Milton to publish his own epic as soon as possible – one that would break the bondage of modern rhyme and recover the ancient poets' liberty. And one that would celebrate, not a debauched king, but the only true King and kingdom in heaven, not the heroism of war but the "better fortitude / Of Patience and heroic martyrdom," not a Virgilian earthly empire but an earthly paradise tragically lost. Milton may have been prompted to publish his poem at this juncture by the disarray in the government and the disruption in censorship practices occasioned by all the disasters.[60] But his opportunities for publishing were severely limited because of the enormous losses suffered by printers and booksellers in the fire. Richard Baxter reports that almost all the booksellers in St Paul's Churchyard – the major venue for them – lost their stock.[61] Pepys heard on October 5, 1666 that the lost books – stored in St Faith's crypt beneath Paul's and in some other warehouses – were worth more than £150,000, and that "all the great booksellers [were] almost undone."[62] Among the few located outside the destroyed area were Henry Herringman in the Strand, the fashionable publisher of Dryden, Davenant, and other court poets, and also the press Milton chose – probably for reasons of proximity as well as earlier associations – the Simmons press in nearby Aldergate Street. It was now managed by Samuel Simmons, who was more a printer than a bookseller; his father Matthew Simmons had published Milton's *Bucer, Tenure of Kings and Magistrates*, and *Observations* on the Irish peace.[63] Humphrey Moseley, we recall, claimed to have solicited Milton for his 1645 *Poems* and sought by his format and apparatus to assimilate Milton's lyric volume to his own "series" of courtly poets writing within a patronage model, though Milton's self-presentation within the volume militated against that effort.[64] Now, some twenty years later, Milton probably made the overture to the publisher. With *Paradise Lost* Milton presents himself as he had in his prose tracts, as a new kind of author in a market-oriented system which Peter Lindenbaum aptly terms a "Republican Mode of Literary Production."[65] The legal contract Milton signed with Simmons – the first such formal contract between author and publisher on record – shows Milton exercising an author's right to his intellectual property at a time when copyright was granted only to stationers through entry in the Stationers Register. Milton signed the contract by proxy on April 27, 1667, his signature attested by his seal of the spread eagle and witnessed by one "Benjamin Greene servant to Mr. Milton." Milton assigned rights to the work to Simmons for sums that seem roughly consistent with contemporary levels of payment to writers:[66] £5 to be paid immediately and additional £5 payments when each of the first three editions were sold. These editions were to be capped at 1,500 copies, and Milton was to receive his payment when 1,300 copies were sold from each edition; he could ask for an accounting of sales at reasonable intervals. For any editions beyond the third, Simmons would not owe Milton any further compensation.[67]

As required by the Press Act of May, 1662,[68] the manuscript of *Paradise Lost* had to be licensed as well as registered with the Stationers. Milton's old enemy, Roger L'Estrange, was still very active as licenser in 1667, but Milton by chance or design avoided him. P*aradise Lost* came into the hands of 28-year-old Thomas Tomkyns, rector of St Mary Aldermary and domestic chaplain to the Archbishop of Canterbury, Gilbert Sheldon. Tomkyns's publications mark him as a zealous royalist and high churchman: shortly after he dealt with Milton's poem he published a tractate urging enforced uniformity in religion and strict control of dissenters, to obviate the dangers toleration would pose to political stability.[69] While Milton's manuscript evidently bore only the initials J. M.,[70] the author was surely known to be the notorious Milton, whose regicide and divorce treatises were still being cited and denounced in the press in the mid-1660s.[71] Toland reports that Tomkyns at first denied a license, objecting especially to a passage in Book I:

> I must not forget that we had like to be eternally depriv'd of this Treasure by the Ignorance or Malice of the Licenser; who, among other frivolous Exceptions, would needs suppress the whole Poem for imaginary Treason in the following lines.
>
> —— As, when the Sun new risen
> Looks thro the Horizontal misty Air
> Shorn of his Beams, or from behind the Moon
> In dim Eclipse disastrous Twilight sheds
> On half the Nations, and with fear of change
> Perplexes Monarchs. (*PL* I.594–9; *EL* 180)

At first blush it seems odd that Tomkyns singled out these lines rather than, say, the overt republicanism of the Nimrod passage in Michael's prophecy (12.24–71). But the recent English calamities were being read as God's punishment for the nation's sins, and they had given rise to a spate of dire predictions and forebodings attaching to comets and to the recent solar eclipse (June 22, 1666) which church and government were eager to suppress. As one tract put it, eclipses are always attended by astounding effects such as "the death of Kings and Great persons, alterations of Governments, change of Laws."[72] However, Tomkyns probably thought this complex poem posed little danger to the masses by comparison with more overt subversion in dissenters' sermons and treatises, and so was prevailed upon to give it his (undated) Imprimatur, probably shortly before Milton signed his contract with Simmons at the end of April, 1667.[73]

During the spring and summer months, as printing got underway, Milton may have had some continuing involvement through the agency of some scholarly friend or friends. That summer also he surely shared the amazement, alarm, and indignation of all London when a fleet of 70 Dutch ships, intent on vengeance for the firing of their fleet and the ravaging of Schelling the previous year, sailed up the Medway, June 10–13, 1667. Everyone wondered whether they intended to pillage the towns along the river or perhaps invade and sack London. Since peace overtures were underway, a good part of the English navy had been laid up in dock to save expense, so there was little effective resistance. The Dutch set fire to all the English ships in dock, leveled unfinished fortifications, and sailed away with the half-burnt *Royal Charles* in tow – the ship that had brought the king back to England at the Restoration. They also blockaded the Thames, depriving Londoners of coal and other goods for several weeks. Popular indignation rose to fever pitch, targetting the king, the court, and especially Clarendon, who was forced from office at the end of August and in November fled to France to escape a treason trial. Milton was surely pleased to hear about the downfall of the man associated with the harsh laws repressing dissenters, the Clarendon Code. On June 24 Pepys recorded a friend's conviction that England would be undone, "there being nothing in our power to do that is necessary for the saving us – a lazy prince – no council – no money; no reputation at home or abroad . . . the King doth fallow the women as much as ever he did."[74] Milton may have heard, as Pepys did, unflattering comparisons of Charles to Cromwell, and savored the irony:

> Everybody doth nowadays reflect upon Oliver and commend him, so brave things he did and made all the neighbour princes fear him; while here a prince, come in with all the love and prayers and good liking of his people, and have given greater signs of loyalty and willingness to serve him with their estates than ever was done by any people, hath lost all so soon.[75]

A peace treaty with the Dutch was signed at Breda on July 21, freeing people to think about other things – including an epic poem that would soon appear.

Paradise lost, a Poem in tenne Bookes was registered with the Stationers by Simmons on August 20, 1667: the entry names Tomkyns as licenser and the royalist Richard Royston, publisher of *Eikon Basilike*, as attesting warden, but names the author only by his initials, J. M.[76] Those initials would have identified Milton to many, but do not flaunt his famous name; also, the designation "Poem," here and on the title pages, avoids claiming the work as epic. Milton, or Simmons, evidently decided that an unassuming presentation would be wisest. The poem may have been published and available at the booksellers a month or so after it was registered, though the first documented notice of it is in a letter of November 18 from John Beale to

John Evelyn.[77] Richardson heard that Sir John Denham came into the House of Commons one day with a sheet of the poem wet from the press, and proclaimed it "Part of the Noblest Poem that ever was Wrote in Any Language or Any Age" (*EL* 295), but that story has an apocryphal ring to it. The text of the first edition, a quarto, was well printed, in an attractive format and on good paper – gilt edged in some copies. Readers were probably surprised, however, by the stark presentation of the 1667 issues of the poem: no dedicatory or commendatory verses, no epistle from author or bookseller, no prefatory matter at all to engage the reader's interest or sympathy – not even Simmons's name as printer and publisher (plate 15). That Milton's poem was sent forth into the world bare and unaccommodated suggests that likely presenters and commenders had qualms about associating themselves with the rebel Milton's return to print. Yet he may have been quite willing to see his poem presented without the usual apparatus and authorizing voices, redolent of the patronage system, to make its own way by its own merits. It sold for 3s a copy.

Over the next three years the first edition appeared with six different title pages and was distributed to as many as six different booksellers – a strategy to make it more widely available, spread the risk, and promote sales.[78] The changing title pages indicate continued anxiety on Simmons's part that a poem by the notorious Commonwealth polemicist might be shunned by prospective readers as treasonous or heretical. The first three title pages include, in large type, a message intended to reassure them: "Licenced, and Entred according to order." Two title pages dated 1667 bear Milton's name but the second reduces that name to very small type, as if to avoid calling attention to it; a third (1668) – which may in fact have been the first one used – identifies the author only as J. M.[79] With the fourth title page (1668) Simmons had gained confidence: Milton's name appears in full, as does, for the first time, Simmons's own, and the "Licenced, and Entred" line is omitted. Also, in this issue Simmons includes a brief note taking credit for soliciting from Milton 14 pages of prefatory matter to help readers better understand the content and form of the work: "*Courteous Reader,* There was no Argument at first intended to this Book, but for the satisfaction of many that have desired it, I have procur'd it, and withall a reason of that which stumbled many others, why the Poem Rimes not" (Sig. A 2).[80] Milton provided a fairly detailed prose argument for each of the ten books, all published together at the front, as well as a vigorous defense of his use of blank verse and an errata sheet. The two 1669 issues retain Milton's and Simmons's names and the prefatory matter.[81]

By remarkable coincidence Dryden's essay *Of Dramatick Poesie* was also registered with the Stationers in August, 1667 and was probably available soon after, so this important argument claiming rhyme as the norm for modern poetry of all sorts greeted the reading public at about the same time as Milton's blank verse epic.[82] It is staged as a conversation among four friends who, on June 3, 1665, took a barge on the Thames to follow the noise of the Dutch and English battleships. After Crites and Eugenius argue the excellencies, respectively, of the ancient and the modern poets, and then Lisideius and Neander argue the virtues, respectively, of the French and the English poets, Neander/Dryden makes a case for rhyme.[83] He is answering the case against rhyme in drama urged by Crites, the dramatist Sir Robert Howard, who was described by Toland as a "particular Acquaintance" and "a great admirer of *Milton* to his dying day," as well as "a hearty Friend to the Liberty of his Country" and a vigorous critic of the "Heathen and Popish" Anglican clergy.[84] Howard reportedly told "many pleasant Stories" about Milton, including one in which Milton jested that he had supported the republicans for their frugality, since "the Trappings of a Monarchy might set up an ordinary Commonwealth" (*EL* 186). Their friendship probably began about this time, with the two men drawn together by shared poetic and political views. In Dryden's *Essay* all the debaters acknowledge the stylistic excellence of modern poets in lyric and agree that "the sweetness of English Verse was never understood or practised by our fathers."[85] Neander/Dryden insists that rhyme is also the distinguishing excellence of modern writers of tragedy and heroic drama, who cannot match the great English dramatists of the previous age on other counts; he also affirms, categorically, that "Blank Verse is acknowledg'd to be too low for a Poem, nay more, for a paper of verses; but if too low for an ordinary Sonnet, how much more for Tragedy" – or for epic, he implies, since drama and epic are of the same genus.[86] In his preface, Dryden states that rhyme enjoys the favor of the court, "the last and surest judge of writing."[87]

If Simmons recognized that in this cultural milieu readers expected rhyme and needed an explanation for its absence, Milton was happy to take up the gauntlet thrown down by his erstwhile colleague, now the rising star on the poetic and critical horizon. His note on "The Verse," added in 1668, aggressively challenges not only the new poetic norms but also, by implication, the debased court culture and royalist politics that underpin them:

> The measure in *English* Heroic Verse without Rime, as that of *Homer* in *Greek*, and of *Virgil* in Latin; Rime being no necessary Adjunct or true Ornament of Poem or good Verse, in longer Works especially, but the Invention of a barbarious Age, to set off wretched matter and lame Meeter; grac't indeed since by the use of some famous modern Poets, carried away by Custom, but much to thir own vexation, hindrance, and constraint to express many things otherwise, and for the most part worse then else they would have exprest them. Not without cause therefore some both *Italian* and *Spanish* Poets of prime note have rejected Rime both in longer and shorter Works, as have also long since our best *English* Tragedies, as a thing of it self, to all judicious eares, trivial and of no true musical delight; which consists only in apt Numbers, fit quantity of Syllables, and the sense variously drawn out from one Verse into another, not in the jingling sound of like endings. . . . This neglect then of Rime so little is to be taken for a defect, though it may seem so perhaps to vulgar Readers, that it rather is to be esteem'd an example set, the first in *English*, of ancient liberty restored to Heroic Poem from the troublesome and modern bondage of Riming. (sigs. a 3v–a 4)

This language vindicates Milton's blank verse against the barbarous gothic age and the vulgar taste of the present, associating it with ancient poetic liberty and also with the restoration of English liberty from the bondage of Stuart tyranny.[88] The resonances of this language make Milton's choice of blank verse a liberating act and an aesthetic complement to republican politics and culture.

Milton must have offered presentation copies of *Paradise Lost* to friends, including Edward Phillips, Thomas Ellwood, Andrew Marvell, Cyriack Skinner, and Dr Nathan Paget (whose library contained two copies of the first edition), but none with dedicatory inscriptions have been found.[89] There are a few early responses to the poem in private letters, among them several to John Evelyn from John Beale, a cleric, a former member of the Hartlib circle, and a passionate supporter of the Royal Society who wanted to persuade Milton to write on subjects like optics or atmospheric pressure. On November 11, 1667 he commented on the controversy about rhyme: like Howard and Milton, he describes it as a "Gothish charm" of a barbarous age, but did not mention *Paradise Lost*.[90] On November 18, apologizing for failing to do so sooner, he offers his opinion of *Paradise Lost*: it is "excellent," though less so than the "purer and brighter" inspirations of Milton's youth – the decline resulting from the "decay of age."[91] He cannot, however, forget Milton's polemics: "he writes so good verse, that tis pitty he ever wrote in prose." At some point he sought an introduction to Milton through Evelyn so as to approach him about writing scientific poems, but evidently found no encouragement.[92] Over the next two years, Beale's letters object to various aspects of Milton's epic: the republicanism of the Nimrod passage reveals that "Milton holds to his old Principle," Milton's "Plea for our Original right" is he thinks one of the "great faults in his *Paradise Lost*," the "long blasphemies" of the Devils he finds disturbing, and he mistakenly supposes that the elaborate demonology of the poem shows Milton's harsh Calvinism.[93] Another early reader, the Presbyterian John Hobart, thought many of Milton's prose works "criminall" but praised the epic for its "extraordinary" matter and its likely moral benefit to a wicked age. In letters dated January 22 and 30, 1668, he comments that the verse is "not very common" but has classical precedents, that Milton's epic bears some resemblance to Spenser's, and that Milton can be paralleled with Homer in his blindness, his use of archaic words, and "his raptures & fancy." He declares categorically that *Paradise Lost* is "in the opinion of the impartiall learned, not only above all moderne attempts in verse, but equall to any of the Ancient Poets," and that he himself "never read a thing so august."[94] Clearly, Milton's poem was read and discussed by some number of readers, fit and unfit, from early on.[95]

On April 26, 1669, about eighteen months after its appearance, Simmons paid Milton the second £5, due upon the sale of 1,300 copies; the receipt was signed on his behalf by a friend or scribe.[96] Simmons did not, however, print a second edition then. Perhaps Milton promised a revision soon, in the twelve-book format. Perhaps he heard that Milton was at work on *Paradise Regained* and hoped to print the two together. Or perhaps he was relieved that the press run he contracted for had sold out, and thought Milton's poem would not have much more life in it.[97]

In 1669 or 1670 Milton's daughters left home. His brother Christopher testified in December 1674, at the proving of Milton's will, that his daughters had lived apart from their father "fowr or five yeares last past," and that Milton on his deathbed claimed they were "undutifull and unkind to him" (*LR* V, 3–4). The domestic tensions had apparently reached a breaking point. Edward Phillips hints that the daughters' duty of reading to Milton in languages they did not understand led them by degrees to open rebellion:

> The irksomeness of this imployment could not always be concealed, but broke out more and more into expressions of uneasiness; so that at length they were all (even the Eldest also) sent out to learn some Curious and Ingenious sorts of Manufacture, that are proper for Women to learn, particularly Imbroideries in Gold or Silver. (*EL* 77–8)

Much later, Thomas Birch heard from Milton's granddaughter, Elizabeth Foster, that their departure was due to the "severities" of Milton's third wife, Elizabeth Minshull, toward her stepdaughters,

> the two eldest of whom she bound prentices to Workers in Gold-Lace, without his knowledge, & forc'd the younger to leave his Family. Mrs. Foster confess'd to me, that he was no fond Father, but assur'd me that his Wife's ill Treatment of his Children gave him great Uneasiness; tho' in his State of Health & Blindness he could not prevent it.[98]

This account as reported is dubious. Elizabeth Minshull could not make apprenticeship arrangements, which would require an outlay of funds, without Milton's knowledge and consent, though the idea of settling the daughters elsewhere to relieve the domestic discord may well have originated with her. Milton alludes to such an outlay – "what I have beside don for them" – while explaining that he intended to leave his entire estate to his wife. His maidservant heard him say, more explicitly, that "hee had made provision for his Children in his life time and had spent the greatest part of his estate in provideing for them" (*LR* V, 82, 91). The apprenticeship seems intended to assure them a livelihood outside the family. Elizabeth Foster also told Birch that about this time her mother, Milton's youngest daughter Deborah, became a companion to an Irish aristocrat, one Lady Merian:

> Her mother . . . meeting with very ill treatment from *Milton's* last Wife, left her Father, and went to live with a lady, whom she called lady Merian. This lady going over to Ireland, and resolving to take *Milton's* daughter with her, if he would give his Consent, wrote a Letter to him of her Dessign, and assured him, that as *Chance had throwne his Daughter under her care, she would treat her no otherwise than as his Daughter and her own Companion*. She lived with that Lady, till her Marriage.[99]

How this contact was made and whether Milton provided funds to settle Deborah is not known; Milton's good friend Lady Ranelagh, with her Irish connections, may have helped arrange the matter. Milton probably thought he was doing the best he could for his daughters given his circumstances, the domestic turmoil, and a promise which he seems to have regarded as a contract, to leave his estate to the wife who was taking good care of him. But the daughters thought otherwise and deeply resented Elizabeth Minshull who, as they saw it, had cut them out of the estate they would otherwise have inherited.

"Things Unattempted Yet in Prose or Rhime"

Milton's epic is preeminantly a poem about knowing and choosing – for the Miltonic Bard, for his characters, and for the reader. It foregrounds education, a life-long concern of Milton's, and of special importance to him after the Restoration as a means to help produce discerning, virtuous, liberty-loving human beings and citizens. Almost half the poem is given over to the formal education of Adam and Eve, by Raphael before and by Michael after the Fall.[100] God himself takes on the role of educator as he engages in Socratic dialogue with his Son about humankind's fall and redemption (3.80–343) and with Adam over his request for a mate (8.357–451). Adam and Eve's dialogues with each other involve them in an ongoing process of self-education about themselves and their world. The Miltonic Bard educates his readers by exercising them in rigorous judgment, imaginative apprehension, and choice. By setting his poem in relation to other great epics and works in other genres, he involves readers in a critique of the values associated with those other heroes and genres, as well as with issues of contemporary politics and theology.

The poem's form makes its first overt political statement as, in the 1667 version, Milton eschewed Virgil's twelve-book epic format with its Roman imperialist and royalist associations for the ten-book model of the republican Lucan.[101] But he included the full range of topics and conventions common to the Homeric and Virgilian epic tradition.[102] His poem has invocations to the muse; a beginning *in medias res*; an Achilles-like hero in Satan; a Homeric catalogue of Satan's generals; councils in Hell and in Heaven; epic pageants and games; supernatural powers – God, the Son, and good and evil angels. It also has a fierce battle in Heaven pitting army against army, replete with chariot clashes, taunts and vaunts, and hill-hurlings; single combats of heroes, most notably the Son of God as a lone warrior overcoming the entire Satanic force; narratives of past actions in Raphael's narratives of the War in Heaven and the Creation; and prophecies of the hero's descendants in Michael's biblical history of humankind. Yet at a more fundamental level, Milton's epic defines itself against the traditional epic subject – wars and empire – and the traditional epic hero as the epitome of courage and battle prowess. His protagonists are a domestic pair; the scene of their action is a pastoral garden; and their primary challenge is, "under long obedience tried," to make themselves, their marital relationship, and their garden – the nucleus of the human world – ever more perfect.[103] Into this radically new kind of epic, Milton incorporates many particular genres in many modes: romance, pastoral, georgic, comedic, tragic, rhetorical, lyric.[104] And into his sublime epic high style he incorporated a wide range of other styles: colloquial, dialogic, lyric, hymnic, elegiac, mock-heroic, denunciatory, ironic, oratorical, ornate, plain.

In the Proems to Books I, III, VII, and IX, Milton explores, more profoundly than ever before, the problematics of authorship,[105] an issue that had concerned him almost from the beginning of his career. In no other epic does the poet insert himself so directly and extensively into his work, making his own experience in writing the poem a part of and an analogue to his story.[106] In these proems the Miltonic Bard, with "his garland and singing robes about him,"[107] dramatizes his struggle to understand how prophetic inspiration, literary tradition, and authorial originality combine in the writing of his poem. By his choice of subject, genre, and blank verse, he distances himself from Dryden, Davenant, Cowley, and other contemporary aspirants to epic, but his allusions continually acknowlege debts to the great ancients – Homer, Virgil, Ovid, Lucan, and Lucretius – and to such moderns as Ariosto, Tasso, Du Bartas, Camõens, and Spenser.[108] Yet he hopes and expects to surpass them, since his subject is both truer and more heroic than theirs, and since he looks for illumination and collaboration to the divine source of both truth and creativity. Milton makes his bold claims to originality not as autonomous author but as prophetic Bard.

In the first Proem (I.1–26) Milton's epic proposition and invocation acknowledge derivation from the classical and Renaissance epic tradition through a dense texture of formal and verbal echoes. He highlights the problematics of derivation and originality by claiming originality in Ariosto's very words: "*Cosa non detta in prosa mai ne in rima*," "Things unattempted yet in Prose or Rhime."[109] Also, by referring to Moses and the first words of Genesis – "That Shepherd, who first taught the chosen Seed, / In the Beginning how the Heav'ns and Earth / Rose out of *Chaos*" – he places himself in the line of the prophet–poet who "first taught" the matter his poem now teaches.[110] The invocation points to two divine sources of Milton's poetic power: the Heavenly Muse who formerly inspired the sacred poetry of Moses, David, and the Prophets; and the Spirit of God who must act to illumine this Bard's darkness, raise his fallenness, and instruct him with the Spirit's own knowledge, creating in him a new nature able to produce the universe of his poem. The Bard endeavors to practice the Christian heroism his poem explores as he daringly attempts to soar "Above the *Aonian* Mount" despite his fallenness, and willingly embraces the paradoxical challenge of creating a poem that both is not, and is, his own.

The Proem to Book III, "Hail holy Light" (1–55), a literary hymn to light as a primary manifestation of God, carries on the Miltonic Bard's identification with his story. He associates himself with, but also departs from, the experience of Orpheus, Dante, and Satan as he recounts his poetic journey through Chaos and Hell and back to the regions of light: "Taught by the heav'nly Muse to venture down / The dark descent, and up to reascend, / Though hard and rare." Then he describes a psychological journey through changing emotional states. His moving complaint that the light of God "Revisit'st not these eyes" is followed by a hauntingly evocative pastoral description of classical and biblical sites of poetic and prophetic inspiration where he hears the nightingale sing "darkling" and imagines himself among the great blind bards and prophets of Greece: "Blind *Thamyris* and blind *Maeonides*, / And *Tiresias* and *Phineas* Prophets old." Then follows a poignant lament for Milton's own paradise lost – the light and beauty of the natural world and the access to wisdom and human companionship it provides:

> Thus with the Year
> Seasons return, but not to me returns
> Day, or the sweet approach of Ev'n or Morn,
> Or sight of vernal bloom, or Summers Rose,
> Or flocks, or heards, or human face divine;
> But cloud in stead, and ever-during dark
> Surrounds me, from the chearful wayes of men
> Cut off, and for the Book of knowledg fair
> Presented with a Universal blanc
> Of Natures works to mee expung'd and ras'd,
> And wisdome at one entrance quite shut out. (3.40–50)

The hymn's peroration begs for Celestial Light, the divine illumination even sighted authors must have to treat the subjects he now turns to – Heaven, unfallen Eden, and the Godhead – "things invisible to mortal sight." He does not expect the extraordinary visions of a John of Patmos, but he hopes for the illumination needed to imagine and represent worthily these ineffable places and things.

In the Proem to Book VII (1–39), a hymn to his heavenly muse, he apostrophizes her by the name Urania, but then qualifies, "The meaning, not the Name I call." To suggest that meaning he devises a myth in which she, along with her "sister" the Eternal Wisdom described in Proverbs 8, plays continually before the almighty Father who delights in her "Celestial Song." Identifying her thus as a figure for inspiration in sacred poetry both in heaven and on earth, the Bard implores her to "govern" his song and "fit audience find, though few." Her nightly visits to the Bard's slumbers represent the inexplicable and subconscious element in poetic creation, as well as Milton's nocturnal habits of composition. Continuing his identification of his authorial labors with his poem's heroic action, he presents himself as a successful Bellerophon, favored by God in his ascent to the heavens on the winged horse Pegasus, symbolizing inspired poetry, but now in danger of Bellerophon's ultimate fate: falling to earth and wandering blinded. Contrasting his

Urania with Calliope, the muse of epic poetry who could not save her son, the archetypal poet Orpheus, from the Maenads, Milton reads in Orpheus's fate the dangers to himself and his poem from the contemporary Maenads, the Restoration worshippers of Bacchus:

> But drive farr off the barbarous dissonance
> Of *Bacchus* and his revellers, the Race
> Of that wilde Rout that tore the *Thracian* Bard
> In *Rhodope*, where Woods and Rocks had Eares
> To rapture, till the savage clamor dround
> Both Harp and Voice; nor could the Muse defend
> Her Son. So fail not thou, who thee implores:
> For thou art Heav'nlie, shee an empty dreame. (7. 32–9)

The Miltonic Bard's fourth Proem (9.1–47) is formally a verse epistle on the poetics of the Christian epic. Its placement continues the parallel betweeen the poem's action and the poet's creative act, as Milton assesses various faulty critical positions regarding heroism and the heroic poem just as his protagonists, Adam and Eve, are about to make their fatal wrong choices. The Bard's choices, however, are judicious, reasoned, well-considered, "Since first this Subject for Heroic Song / Pleas'd me long choosing, and beginning late." His tragic argument, the Fall, and the new heroism exemplified in the Son is, he insists, "not less but more Heroic" than the subjects of the great classical epics and is also far nobler than the romance matter characteristic of most modern heroic poems:

> Not sedulous by Nature to indite
> Warrs, hitherto the onely Argument
> Heroic deem'd, chief maistrie to dissect
> With long and tedious havoc fabl'd Knights
> In Battels feign'd; the better fortitude
> Of Patience and Heroic Martyrdom
> Unsung; or to describe Races and Games,
> Or tilting Furniture, emblazon'd Shields,
> Impreses quaint, Caparisons and Steeds. (9.27–37)

The Miltonic Bard is now confirmed in his role as prophet–poet: he need not invoke his muse here since she comes nightly "unimplor'd," and "dictates to me slumbring, or inspires / Easie my unpremeditated Verse." This does not mean that Milton sees himself as the secretary of the Spirit, taking down divine dictation; that simple version of inspiration is belied by his insistence that he has long considered and evaluated various epic subjects, topics, and styles, making complex literary judgments and decisions about his art. Rather, his subject is a given of sacred history whose true meaning must be revealed to him (as to any Christian) by divine illumination. Also, by recognizing Urania's collaboration he avoids making Satan's monomaniacal claim to self-authorship. He recognizes no earthly patron, but expects that his "Celestial Patroness" will help him overcome obstacles: "an age too late" (the Restoration era unfriendly to high poetry), or the cold English climate that he long thought unsuited to poetry, or the burden of his advanced years. These might overwhelm him "if all be mine, / Not Hers who brings it nightly to my Ear." With divine illumination and Urania's collaboration informing his poetic dreams, Milton experiences his magnificent lines cascading forth as a divine gift.

With the striking portrait of Satan in Books I and II, Milton prompts his readers to begin a poem-long exploration and redefinition of heroes and heroism, the fundamental concern of epic. Often he highlights discrepancies between Satan's noble rhetoric and his motives and actions; also, by associating Satan with the heroic genres and the great heroes of literary tradition, he invites the reader to discover how he in some ways exemplifies but in essence perverts those models.[111] Satan at the outset is a heroic warrior indomitable in the face of defeat and staggering obstacles, manifesting fortitude, determination, endurance, and leadership. He prides himself on an Achilles-like obduracy, a "fixt mind / And high disdain, from sense of injur'd merit" (1.97–8), and he commits himself, like Turnus, to revenge, hate, and "eternal Warr / Irreconcilable (1.121–2) – though he has not been wronged like them. He makes martial prowess the test of worth: "our own right hand / Shall teach us highest deeds, by proof to try / Who is our equal" (5.864–6). But instead of winning Achilles-like victories on the battlefield, he is defeated by the Son who wields God's omnipotence and displays it first and chiefly in acts of restoration and new creation. Like Aeneas, Satan departs from a burning city (Hell) to conquer and lead his followers to a new kingdom (earth), but he finds that Hell is his proper kingdom, that he carries it with him wherever he goes. Like Odysseus he makes a perilous journey requiring the use of wit and craft, but not to return home to wife and son; rather, before venturing into Chaos Satan meets but does not recognize his daughter–wife Sin and the offspring of their incestuous union, Death.

Satan casts himself in the mold of the tragic hero Prometheus, enduring with constancy, indomitable will, and "courage never to submit or yield" the punishment meted out by an implacable divine tyrant (1.108) – though Prometheus angered Zeus by bringing the gift of fire to humans, whereas Satan brings them misery and death.[112] Satan claims that his mind will remain unchanged and will transform his surroundings: "The mind is its own place, and in it self / Can make a Heav'n of Hell, a Hell of Heav'n" (1.254–5). But he finds the reverse: "Which way I flie is Hell; my self am Hell" (4.75). Also, like many Romance heroes Satan enters a Garden of Love and courts its lady with exaggerated Petrarchan compliments,[113] but he cannot win love, or find sensual delight, or enjoy sensuous refreshment or ease there. Instead, he sees "undelighted all delight" and feels more intensely than before the agony of his own loneliness, lovelessness, and unsatisfied desire:

> Sight hateful, sight tormenting! thus these two
> Imparadis't in one anothers arms
> The happier *Eden*, shall enjoy thir fill
> Of bliss on bliss, while I to Hell am thrust,
> Where neither joy nor love, but fierce desire,
> Among our other torments not the least,
> Still unfulfill'd with pain of longing pines. (4.505–11)

These Satanic perversions of the heroic find their climax in Book X when Satan returns to Hell intending a Roman triumph that recalls the triumphal celebrations at the Restoration of Charles II.[114] But he is greeted instead with a universal hiss from his followers turned into snakes, as all of them are forced to enact a grotesque black comedy of God's devising. Milton does not use these comparisons to condemn classical epic or romance or tragedy and their heroes, nor yet to exalt Satan as hero. They serve to make primordial evil comprehensible in all its attractiveness, multiplicity, and local manifestations and also, by letting readers discover how Satan has perverted the noblest qualities of literature's greatest heroes, to reveal how susceptible they are to perversion. Finally, he invites readers to measure all other versions of the heroic against the poem's heroic standard: the self-sacrificing love of the Son, the moral courage of Abdiel, and the "better fortitude" of Christ in life and death, with which Adam and Eve are able at last to identify.

Milton's representations of Hell, Heaven, and Eden challenge readers' stereotypes, then and now. All are in process: the physical conditions of these places are fitted to the beings that inhabit them, but the inhabitants interact with and shape their environments, creating societies in their own images. Hell is first presented in traditional terms with Satan and his crew chained on a lake of fire, but they soon rise up and begin to mine gold and gems, build a government center (Pandemonium), hold a parliament, send Satan on a mission of exploration and conquest, investigate their spacious and varied though sterile landscape, engage in martial games and parades, perform music, compose epic poems, and argue hard philosophical questions. Milton portrays Hell as a damned society in the making, with royalist politics, perverted language, perverse rhetoric, political manipulation, and demagoguery. By contrast, he portrays Heaven as a unique place, a celestial city combining courtly magnificence and the pleasures of pastoral nature. In its ethos, though not in its government, it offers some model for human society. The mixture of heroic, georgic, and pastoral activities and modes – elegant hymns suited to various occasions, martial parades, warfare, pageantry, masque dancing, feasting, lovemaking, political debate, the protection of Eden – provides an ideal of wholeness. But, surprisingly, Milton's Heaven is also a place of process, not stasis, complexity not simplicity, and the continuous and active choice of good rather than the absence of evil. Eden is a lush and lovely enclosed garden with a superabundance of natural delights and a wide range of pastoral and georgic activities, and it is preeminently a place of growth and change. Adam and Eve are expected to cultivate and control their burgeoning garden and their own sometimes wayward impulses and passions; to work out their relationship to God and to each other; and to deal with ever-new challenges relating to work, education, love and sex, intellectual curiosity, the duties pertaining to their places in a hierarchical universe, and temptations from Satan. All of these challenges are presented in Milton's poem as components of an ideal human life in innocence, and as preparation for a more exalted state. Milton does not conceive of ideality as static perfection but always associates it with challenge, choice, and growth.

In his representation of Hell and Heaven Milton dramatizes issues long important to him – monarchy, tyranny, idolatry, rebellion, liberty, republicanism – and forcefully reiterates the antimonarchical politics of his treatises.[115] However, by representing both Satan and God as monarchs, and portraying Satan as a self-styled grand rebel marshaling Milton's own republican rhetoric against what he calls the "tyranny of heaven," Milton's poem has seemed to some acute critics to carry ambiguous and seriously unsettling political messages. For Blair Worden, Satan's rhetoric of republicanism signals Milton's profound disillusion with his own party and with political discourse generally, as he "withdraws from politics into faith."[116] For David Norbrook, the representation of heaven as an absolute monarchy remains disconcerting, as does the absence of a heavenly public sphere; Milton's denial of analogy between heavenly and earthly kingship does not, he thinks, entirely disrupt that analogy.[117] For Sharon Achinstein, Milton deliberately confronts readers with images and tropes – notably the Parliament of Hell – that are susceptible of multiple and misleading interpretations, to force them to eschew easy allegories and thereby become "fit readers," able to negotiate political rhetoric and propaganda.[118] He surely offers such a challenge with Satan's rhetoric, but I think Milton makes quite clear his evaluation of monarchy. By demonstrating that there can be no possible parallel between earthly kings and divine kingship he flatly denies the familiar royalist analogies: God and King Charles, Satan and the Puritan rebels. And by associating the imagery and accoutrements of absolute kingship with God, as proper to him alone, he would have readers recognize that the appropriation of them by any earthly monarch is idolatrous.

When the Son is proclamed king over the angels Satan tempts his followers to revolt by using the rhetoric of republican virtue and the rights of a free citizenry that Milton himself used in the *Tenure of Kings and Magistrates*:

> Will ye submit your necks, and chuse to bend
> The supple knee? ye will not, if I trust
> To know ye right, or if ye know your selves
> Natives and Sons of Heav'n . . .
>
> Who can in reason then or right assume
> Monarchie over such as live by right
> His equals, if in power and splendor less,
> In freedome equal? or can introduce

Law and Edict on us, who without law
Erre not, much less for this to be our Lord,
And look for adoration to th'abuse
Of those Imperial Titles which assert
Our being ordain'd to govern, not to serve? (5.787–802)[119]

Abdiel challenges Satan's republican argument by emphasizing the absurdity of the royalist analogy between God and earthly monarchs, explaining that God is absolute monarch of Heaven because he created all other beings, and that the Son rightly enjoys regal status by God's "just Decree" and as God's agent in Creation. So in this instance, though not otherwise, Satan's republican argument from equality is beside the point:

But to grant it thee unjust
That equal over equals Monarch Reigne:
Thy self though great and glorious dost thou count,
Or all Angelic Nature joind in one,
Equal to him begotten Son, by whom
As by his Word the mighty Father made
All things, ev'n thee, and all the Spirits of Heav'n
By him created in thir bright degrees. (5.831–6)

Abdiel and Satan continue this political debate on the battlefield, as Satan derides the loyal angels for exhibiting the servile and slothful spirit Milton so often ascribed to royal courts and courtiers: "traind up in Feast and Song" they will come off badly if they try to match their "Servilitie" with the rebels' "freedom" (6.167–9). Abdiel counters with the natural law argument Milton made in the *Second Defense* to support Cromwell's Protectorate: monarchy is proper and consonant with liberty "When he who rules is worthiest, and excells / Them whom he governs" (6.177–8) – patently true of God if almost never of other rulers. Abdiel also makes the familiar Miltonic and Platonic distinction that relates liberty and tyranny in the first instance to states of soul, which are then replicated in the state:

This is servitude,
To serve th'unwise, or him who hath rebelld
Against his worthier, as thine now serve thee,
Thy self not free, but to thy self enthrall'd. (6.178–81)

The Son is God's viceregent by delegation of power based on merit: after his offer to die for fallen man God proclaims him "universal King," declaring that he has been "Found worthiest to be so by being Good, / Farr more then Great or High" (3.310–11).

In Heaven's monarchy the angels are citizens whose diverse pleasures and responsibilities give the lie to Satan's disparagement of their life as courtly servility. As messengers, Raphael and Michael have large liberty to decide how to carry out their educative and admonitory missions to Adam and Eve. Angels guard the Garden of Eden and its inhabitants against violent attack, though they cannot secure Adam and Eve against temptation. At God's command the loyal angels fight courageously against the rebels threatening their society, though they find they cannot extirpate that evil by their own military might. That fact, as well as the grotesque scenes of cannon shot and hill-hurling, the near-destruction of Heaven's lovely landscape, and Michael's denunciation (12.688–99) of the Giants who sought glory in battle and conquest, has suggested to some that Milton has turned pacifist or that he now repudiates the recent English revolution. But that conclusion is not warranted.[120] These scenes serve rather to demonstrate war's limitations and its costs: however good the cause, however noble the warriors, however divinely authorized and necessary as a response to blatant evil (as Milton always thought the English revolution had been), it cannot finally eradicate evil. These scenes also undermine epic *aristeia*, battle glory, by portraying warfare in its essence and its effects as tragic, not glorious.

Hell is also a monarchy and its king, Satan, has some claim to that status by natural law: he is "by merit rais'd / To that bad eminence" (2.5–6), and he readily assumes "as great a share / Of hazard as of honour" (2.452–3) when, in parody of the Son's offer, he volunteers to go as Hell's emissary to subvert Adam and Eve. But his superiority over his fellows bears no comparison to that of God over his creatures, and his assumption of kingly, indeed divine, honors and status directly contradicts his republican rhetoric opposing the monarchy of God and the Son. "Affecting all equality with God" he delivers his temptation of the angels in Heaven from a splendid "Royal seat" high on a Mount like the one from which Messiah was pronounced King (5.756–66). He opens the Council in Hell as an oriental sultan, a figure for the most extreme absolutism, luxury, and tyranny: "High on a Throne of Royal State, which far / Outshon the wealth of *Ormus* and of *Ind,* / Or where the gorgeous East with richest hand / Showrs on her Kings *Barbaric* Pearl and Gold / Satan exalted sat" (2.1–5). In the uneasy position of defeated military leader and *de facto* king, he opens his Council in Hell by summarizing the grounds upon which his leadership was founded: "just right, and the fixt Laws of Heav'n" (i.e. God's appointment); next, their own "free choice" after his debate with Abdiel; and finally, his proven merit in counsel and in battle (2.18–21). But he concludes with a piece of rhetorical legerdemain, assuming that these legitimate claims to leadership also sanction his assumption of kingship. In fact, his claim now to enjoy a "safe unenvied Throne / Yielded with full consent" (2.23–4) relies on the Hobbesian principle that a society's passive acceptance of a sovereign's power and protection establishes a binding social contract. In this speech he is a Machiavellian prince seeking to secure a new throne by manipulating his followers and pursuing his own goals through force and fraud, "open Warr or covert guile" (2.41).

In Satan's usurpation of a kingship properly belonging only to Christ, Milton alludes to monarchs generally and to any others who, like Cromwell in the final years of the Protectorate, assume quasi-monarchical status. Some aspects of Satan invite association with Cromwell – his use of republican rhetoric and his promotion of rebellion as a cloak for ambition – but the more fundamental associations are with the Stuart monarchs, especially Charles I.[121] Pandemonium is "the high Capital / Of Satan and his Peers" (1.756–7), and within it the "great Seraphic Lords and Cherubim" sit in secret conclave while the common angels, reduced to pygmy size, swarm without (1.777–95). The council held there does not suggest a republican House of Commons, but a House of Lords controlled by a monarch.[122] The powerful peers, as Satan always terms them, debate their own agendas: Moloch urges eternal war at any cost; Belial counsels peace through ignominious inaction; Mammon would build up a rival empire in Hell founded on riches and magnificence, but, ironically, describes that course of action in the language of republican virtue, as a choice of "Hard liberty before the easie yoke / Of servile Pomp" (2.256–7). Then Satan sways the council to his will through the agency of his chief minister, Beelzebub. The scene closes with Satan accorded divine honors: "Towards him they bend / With awful reverence prone; and as a God / Extoll him equal to the highest in Heav'n" (2.477–9). This is an exaggerated version of the idolatry Milton had long associated with the Stuart ideology of divine kingship: in *Eikonoklastes* he denounced Charles I for making himself such an idol, and in *The Readie & Easie Way* predicted that Charles II would do the same.

The association of monarchy with idolatry is also underscored in Milton's long catalogue of fallen angel leaders, described in terms of the idols they are to become in human history (1.392–405). The first in order is "*Moloch*, horrid King besmear'd with blood / Of human sacrifice, and parents tears"; special emphasis is given to "*Astarte*, Queen of Heav'n," to whom the "uxorious King" Solomon, "beguil'd by fair Idolatresses" built a Temple; and the passage ends with Belial, who dwells where priests turn atheist, and "Reigns" in "Courts and Palaces." As is usual in Milton's treatment of idolatry, his emphasis in this account is less on the affront offered to God than on the craven servility and debased vices that idolatry produces in those who worship anything other than the transcendent God. Next to Moloch "homicide," whose worshippers burned their infants alive, was the altar of Chemos, inspiring "wanton rites" and "lustful Orgies" – "lust hard by hate" (406–17). Worshipping Baalim and Ashtaroth, Israel bowed "lowly down / To bestial Gods; for which thir heads as low / Bow'd down in Battel, sunk before the Spear / Of despicable foes" (1.432–7). The love story of Adonis "infected *Sions* daughters" with "wanton passions," and Belial inspired all manner of "injury and outrage" – both homo- and heterosexual rape – in his "Sons . . . flown with insolence and wine" (1.500–5). In fallen Eve also, idolatrous worship of what is not God produces debasing servility, as she offers hymnic praise and "low Reverence" to the Tree of Knowledge of Good and Evil, "as to the power / That dwelt within" (9.795–837).

Milton stages the Nimrod episode as an overt statement of republican principles, with absolute monarchy on earth equated with tyranny, since it involves a man usurping over his equals dominion belonging only to God. In his prophecy of the biblical history to come, Michael reports that Nimrod subjected men to his empire by force, and explains the epithet accorded him, "mightie Hunter," in terms associating him with Charles I's claims of divine-right kingship and denunciation of Puritan rebels: "from Heav'n claiming second Sovrantie; / And from Rebellion shall derive his name, / Though of Rebellion others he accuse" (12.35–7). Adam's fierce castigation reiterates the republican theory of *Tenure*:

> O execrable Son so to aspire
> Above his Brethren, to himself assuming
> Authoritie usurpt, from God not giv'n:
> He gave us onely over Beast, Fish, Fowl
> Dominion absolute; that right we hold
> By his donation; but Man over men
> He made not Lord; such title to himself
> Reserving, human left from human free. (12.64–71)

That natural republicanism is reinforced in Michael's account of the Israelites using their sojourn in the wilderness to found a republic: "there they shall found / Thir government, and thir great Senate choose / Through the twelve Tribes, to rule by Laws ordaind." By contrast, Michael offers a hasty and dismissive summary of the Israelite kings from David to Christ: "Part good, part bad, of bad the longer scrowle, / Whose foul Idolatries, and other faults / Heapt to the popular summe, will so incense / God, as to leave them."[123]

Michael commends Adam for "justly" abhorring Nimrod the first king, but reminds him – in terms reminiscent of many Milton tracts – that outward liberty depends on inner liberty, the product of reason and virtue, and that the Fall allows "upstart Passions" to "catch the Government / From Reason, and to servitude reduce / Man till then free" (12.83–90). That analysis can explain the Stuart Restoration, England's colonial rule in Ireland, and absolute monarchy wherever it exists: inner servitude, either of itself or as a punishment from God, leads to deprivation of outward freedom by "violent Lords." Michael concludes that "Tyrannie must be, / Though to the Tyrant thereby no excuse" (12.95–6), not as a justification for the status quo, but as a natural consequence of human failure.

Milton's epic also probes the politics of empire and colonization. Language relating to those enterprises came readily to Milton, given its contemporary currency.[124] Eden is described in terms often used of the New World: lush, beautiful, prodigiously prolific, needing to be cultivated and tamed; and regarded as a satellite colony by both God and Satan.[125] However, God's relation to Eden is not that of an imperialist to his colony. The epithet "sovran Planter" might associate him with the plantation of settlements, but in context it identifies him as the gardener who planted the delightful Edenic garden. God created the garden and its inhabitants, he does not discover it and conquer them. The angelic military guard in Eden is not to control the inhabitants but to ward off external force. God forbids Adam and Eve one tree but allows them free use of all else. He does not need or want any of Eden's products, nor does he require the inhabitants to labor for him; they need to do so to control the garden's prolific growth and to take responsibility for their world. God does not intend to settle any of the heavenly host in Eden, but wants the inhabitants to increase, multiply, and spread through all the earth, cultivating it for their own uses. And at length he intends to bring Adam and Eve and their descendants to a still better place, Heaven.[126]

By contrast, Satan is represented as an explorer bent on conquest and colonization. He sets out courageously, like the sailors in the *Lusiads*, to sail through an uncharted sea (Chaos), enduring as yet unknown dangers and difficulties. He discovers the site of a future colony, the Paradise of Fools, to be peopled chiefly by Catholics. He discovers the paradise of Eden and intends, after conquering Adam and Eve and Eden, to settle the fallen angels there. He practices fraud on Eve and causes her to lose her rightful domain. Upon first seeing Adam and Eve, he makes clear in soliloquy that he means to use Eden and its inhabitants for his own purposes, that his excursion is about empire-building as well as revenge. He also plans to transport these "natives" and their offspring back to his own country, Hell:

> League with you I seek,
> And mutual amitie so strait, so close,
> That I with you must dwell, or you with me
> Henceforth; . . .
> Hell shall unfold
> To entertain you two, her widest Gates,
> And send forth all her Kings. (4.375–88)

He justifies his enterprise by "public reason just, / Honour and Empire with revenge enlarg'd" – characterized by the narrator as "necessitie, /The Tyrants plea" (4.389–94). After the Fall, Satan's followers eagerly await the return of "their great adventurer from the search / Of Forrein Worlds" (10.440–1). Such associations do not mean that Milton thought exploration and colonization in the Americas necessarily Satanic, though he does make Satan the ancestor of Spaniards who will lay waste the New World.[127] And, as with Satan's degradation of various versions of heroism, his explorations illustrate how susceptible the imperial enterprise is to evil purposes.

Milton's treatment of this theme is also complicated by language and assumptions that bode ill for the future. As Balaçhandra Rajan points out, some similes and descriptive passages in the poem associate Satan with India, imaging it as a place of barbaric luxuries and despotism ripe for colonization.[128] As for the English conquest and colonization of Ireland, nothing in *Paradise Lost* suggests that Milton has changed his mind about his defense of that enterprise in *Observations (*1649).[129] Milton's central political insight, that inner slavery to passions and vices leads to political subjection by tyrannous lords, he applies quite generally, to English, Irish, Israelites, Asians, and any others it may describe. But it holds worrisome potential for imperialists to make selective application, arguing that subject peoples for their barbarism or vices deserve their enslavement.

Following the Genesis text, Milton's God gave Adam and Eve absolute dominion over the earth – a gift often cited to justify exploitation and subjugation of other races, other creatures, and the natural world. But Milton does not allow that gloss: the Nimrod passage explicitly excludes dominion of humans, and in Eden dominion over the creatures means that they are the objects of Adam and Eve's loving care and pleasure.[130] The animals' wonderful variety and their antics delight Adam and Eve, as when the elephant "wreathd / His Lithe Proboscis" to make them mirth (4.346–7); and Eve joyously fosters her flowers and plants. Also, the Creation account in Book VII describes in graphic detail the appearance and activities of all the forms of life God caused the earth to bring forth, indicating that the blind Milton had spent his earlier life closely observing and delighting in nature.

Milton also incorporates into Michael's prophecy the issues closest to his heart for many years: the corruption of the Christian church by "wolves" and the misuse of civil power to force consciences. Beginning with popes and Roman emperors in the early Christian ages and then generalizing to subsequent ages, Michael restates principles urged by Milton in *Areopagitica*, *Of Civil Power*, *The Likeliest Means*, *De Doctrina Christiana*, and elsewhere: Christian liberty, the separation of spiritual and civil powers, the inviolability of conscience and individual faith, and the gift of the Spirit to all believers. A long passage invites direct application to post-Restoration repression of dissent by prelates and magistrates who appropriate to themselves the "Spirit of God, promisd alike and giv'n / To all Beleevers" and who seek to force "Spiritual Lawes by carnal power" (12.519–21). Milton's voice echoes behind Michael's stern judgments:

> What will they then
> But force the Spirit of Grace it self, and binde
> His consort Libertie; what, but unbuild
> His living Temples, built by Faith to stand,
> Thir own Faith not anothers: for on Earth
> Who against Faith and Conscience can be heard
> Infallible? yet many will presume:
> Whence heavie persecution shall arise
> On all who in the worship persevere
> Of Spirit and Truth; the rest, farr greater part,
> Will deem in outward Rites and specious formes
> Religion satisfi'd; Truth shall retire
> Bestruck with slandrous darts, and works of Faith
> Rarely be found. (12.524–37)

Earlier, in the exchange on the battlefield between Abdiel and Satan, Abdiel's language identifies his lone resistance to and departure from Satan's multitudes with the stance of sectarians and dissenters from the established church who will at last, like Abdiel now, be assimilated into God's vast legions:

> there be who Faith
> Prefer, and Pietie to God, though then
> To thee not visible, when I alone
> Seemd in thy World erroneous to dissent
> From all: my Sect thou seest, now learn too late
> How few somtimes may know, when thousands err. (6.143–8)

Certain elements of Milton's theology, set forth in *De Doctrina Christiana* at about the time he was writing his epic, worked greatly to his literary advantage in enhancing the poem's drama. Tasso and most other Christian epic poets and theorists thought it would be impossible and probably sacrilegious to undertake a literary representation of the Christian God, but Milton's principles allow the presention of God as an epic character – though not as a unified, fully realized one or (by human standards) always an attractive one. Since Milton believes that all ideas or images of the incomprehensible God are necessarily metaphoric, but that they should correspond to the way God has presented himself in the Bible,[131] the God of *Paradise Lost* is sometimes anthropomorphic. He displays a range of emotions (fear, wrath, scorn, dismay, love) as he comments on Satan, on humankind's fall, and on the actions of the Son. He engages in dialogue with his Son, with the angels, and with man and woman. In some of his aspects he invites comparison with Jehovah in various Old Testament theophanies, and also with Zeus in Homer and Hesiod and Jove in Ovid. But in Milton's understanding these are all partial reflections: God cannot be seen whole.

Also, Milton's Arianism allows him to portray the Son as a genuinely dramatic and heroic character, whose choices are made and whose actions are taken freely, in a state of imperfect knowledge. Since Milton holds that the Son is not omnipotent or omniscient or eternal, or immutable, but was generated at some point in time by an act of God's will, and that he enjoys whatever Godlike powers he has by God's gift,[132] he can show the Son in Book III engaging in a genuine dialogue with the Father. God's stern words seem to proclaim the Fall as an irreversible event until the Son's questioning appeal elicits a partial statement of God's plan for redemptive grace. Then God seems to pose an insoluble dilemma – "Dye hee or Justice must" (3.210) – after which he calls throughout heaven for a volunteer to substitute for man. The Son then understands and freely takes on his sacrificial role, and God commends him for the love that shows him to be "By Merit more then Birthright Son of God" (3.309). During the War in Heaven the Son accepts the charge from God to conquer the rebel angels, and God infuses into him some part of his own omnipotence: "Into thee such Vertue and Grace / Immense I have transfus'd . . . /

To manifest thee worthiest to be Heir / Of all things, to be Heir and to be King" (6.703–8). In the Creation he is again God's willing instrument and agent: "by thee / This I perform, speak thou, and be it don" (7.163–4). After the Fall, the Son takes the initiative in acting as advocate for sinful humankind, but the Father still proclaims himself as the ultimate source of Adam and Eve's regeneration and of the Son's mediation for them: "All thy request was my Decree" (11.47).

Milton's Arminianism lies at the heart of the theodicy which is the stated intent of *Paradise Lost*: To "justifie the wayes of God to men." As a poet Milton undertakes to accomplish this less by theological argument than by the imaginative vision the entire poem presents of human life and the human condition as good, despite the tragedy of the Fall and "all our woe." That seems a quixotic, though rather wonderful, affirmation from a poet who endured the agony of total blindness throughout his most creative years and experienced the utter defeat of the political cause to which he gave twenty years of his life. That affirmation is inextricably linked with Milton's idea of human freedom, moral responsibility, and capacity for growth and change, grounded upon the version of Arminianism he argues for in *De Doctrina Christiana* and dramatizes in *Paradise Lost*.[133] In the Dialogue in Heaven (3.80–128) God explains and defends his "high Decree" that from all eternity mandates contingency and freedom for both angels and humans and thereby secures to both orders a genuine freedom of choice, whose results he foresees but does not determine. Humans were made "just and right, / Sufficient to have stood, though free to fall," and the same is true of "all th' Ethereal Powers / And Spirits, both them who stood and them who faild." If it were not so, God declares, the noblest acts of faith, love, and true allegiance by angels and humans would be meaningless, and "Will and Reason (Reason also is choice) / Useless and vain" (3.98–109). He concludes:

> So without least impulse or shadow of Fate,
> Or aught by me immutablie foreseen,
> They trespass, Authors to themselves in all
> Both what they judge and what they choose; for so
> I formd them free, and free they must remain,
> Till they enthrall themselves: I else must change
> Thir nature, and revoke the high Decree
> Unchangeable, Eternal, which ordain'd
> Thir freedom: they themselves ordain'd thir fall. (3.120–8)

Most exegetes held that the loyal angels always were unable to swerve from grace, or at least became so after withstanding Satan's temptation, but Milton's angels, as Raphael explains to Adam, are exactly like prelapsarian humans in that they must continually and freely choose to act from obedience and love:

> My self and all th'Angelic Host that stand
> In sight of God enthron'd, our happie state

> Hold, as you yours, while our obedience holds;
> On other surety none; freely we serve,
> Because wee freely love, as in our will
> To love or not; in this we stand or fall. (5.535–40)

God proceeds in the Dialogue in Heaven (3.166–216) to explain his decree of predestination to salvation, which pertains only to humans and not to reprobate angels whose guilt is greater. By that decree, also eternal, God offers grace to all humankind, renewing their "lapsed powers," clearing their "senses dark," softening "stonie hearts," and providing conscience as their guide, so that all who respond, believe, and persist to the end will be saved: "Light after light well us'd they shall attain, / And to the end persisting, safe arrive" (3.196–7). While God offers "peculiar grace" to some who are "elect above the rest," he offers sufficient grace to all, so that only those who neglect and scorn "my long sufferance and my day of grace" will be lost: "none but such from mercy I exclude" (3.198–202). Satan's soliloquy (4.32–113) exposes the mental torment of that reprobate angel who, driven to admit guilt and to lament his grievous loss and misery, is both unwilling and unable to repent, but instead commits himself to ever greater evil: "Evil be thou my Good" (4.110). After the Fall, Adam in soliloquy (10.720–845) voices a comparable mental torment, guilt, misery, and despair, culminating in a wrathful denunciation of Eve which bids fair to leave him utterly alone, cut off from God and human society. But God's grace removes the "stonie" from the hearts of Adam and Eve (11.3–5), and they respond with repentance and reconciliation.

Milton's epic universe is monist, exhibiting the "animist materialism" that Milton sketched out in *De Doctrina Christiana* as a response to Hobbesian mechanistic and deterministic materialism.[134] In the poem as in the treatise, Milton describes spirit and matter as manifestations, differing only in degree, of the one corporeal substance of which all things are created.[135] Raphael's first lecture to Adam and Eve, prompted by Adam's question as to whether angels, being spirits, can eat earthly food, lays out for Adam and Eve the nature of the universe they inhabit:

> O *Adam*, one Almightie is, from whom
> All things proceed, and up to him return,
> If not deprav'd from good, created all
> Such to perfection, one first matter all,
> Indu'd with various forms, various degrees
> Of substance, and in things that live, of life;
> But more refin'd, more spiritous, and pure,
> As neerer to him plac't or neerer tending
> Each in thir several active Sphears assignd,
> Till body up to spirit work, in bounds
> Proportiond to each kind. (5.469–79)

This first matter, emanating from God, is organized in a chain of being which is not fixed but mobile, and which intelligent creatures can by their choices ascend to become "more spiritous and pure" or, alternatively, descend to become more material and gross, as is the case with the fallen angels. Raphael also explains that angels and humans share the same defining quality, reason: "Discursive or Intuitive; discourse / Is oftest yours, the latter most is ours, / Differing but in degree, of kind the same" (5.488–90). Milton's angels eat real food "with keen dispatch / Of real hunger" (5.436–7), fight a real war with real arms, have sex which involves total interpenetration, and can change genders at will. By eating Edenic food, Raphael demonstrates that the same food can nourish both humans and angels, and he suggests that Adam and Eve's own diet can promote their gradual change to angelic state:

> And from these corporal nutriments perhaps
> Your bodies may at last turn all to Spirit,
> Improv'd by tract of time, and wingd ascend
> Ethereal, as wee, or may at choice
> Here or in Heav'nly Paradises dwell;
> If ye be found obedient. (5.496–501)

That lesson might have kept Eve from believing Satan's claim that she would require the special food of the forbidden tree to ascend from human to higher state, and that such transformation would be instantaneous.

Milton could escape the constraints of biblical literalism in treating his subject because from the time of his divorce tracts he gave the indwelling spirit of God priority over the letter of scripture, insisting that the meaning of any scripture text must accord with the dictates of reason and the overarching precept of charity. These interpretative principles emerge from his assumption that a good God intends the good of humankind, and from the antinomian doctrine, spelled out in *De Doctrina Christiana*, that for Christians the Law as law (even the Decalogue) is abrogated, to be replaced by a "more perfect" morality inscribed in the heart. That antinomianism in Milton's humanist version[136] is also central to the educative issues of the poem, as Milton foregrounds for his characters and his readers the problematics of interpreting God's decrees and his works, and the validity of appeals to reason and experience in probing their implications and responding to them. Not blind obedience to law, but thoughtful discrimination is all.

For the angels, the decree requiring interpretation is God's proclamation of his Son as their king. It is staged as a suddden, awe-inspiring declaration, whose literal terms are clear: "your Head I him appoint, / And by my Self have sworn to him shall bow / All knees in Heav'n, and shall confess him Lord: / Under his great Vice-regent Reign abide / United." So is the promised eternal punishment in "utter darkness" for the disobedient (5.600–15). But the ramifications are not clear:

the angels do not yet know why the Son is thus elevated and what his elevation may mean for themselves and their society. That question is at the heart of the tense debate between Satan and Abdiel before Satan's assembled cohort, who have not yet formally committed themselves to rebellion. Milton stages this scene, without precedent in any other treatment of the War in Heaven, so that the issues are spelled out and the angels' choice can be made knowledgeably and freely. Behind Satan's republican language is his envy-driven assumption that glory in heaven is a zero-sum game, that the Son's elevation must bring with it the angels' demotion, and most notably his own. Abdiel counters by appealing to the angels' historical experience of God's goodness to them:

> Yet by experience taught we know how good,
> And of our good, and of our dignitie
> How provident he is, how farr from thought
> To make us less, bent rather to exalt
> Our happie state under one Head more neer
> United . . .
>   nor by his Reign obscur'd,
> But more illustrious made, since he the Head
> One of our number thus reduc't becomes. (5.826–43)

Responding to Abdiel's description of the Son's unique status as God's agent in creating the angels and all else, Satan makes his own appeal to experience: "who saw / When this creation was? remember'st thou / Thy making." He concludes that since they don't remember they must be "self-begot, self-rais'd / By our own quick'ning power" (5.856–61). Abdiel then gives over the argument, recognizing that empiricism in an area to which experience cannot possibly speak – recollection of one's own moment of origin – has led Satan to illogic and monomania.

In prelapsarian Eden the divine decree requiring interpretation is God's prohibition on the Tree of Knowledge of Good and Evil. Again Milton stages a scene setting up the conditions for free choice: Eve precisely recapitulates the terms and meaning of the prohibition when Satan first leads her to the tree, demonstrating that she need not be deceived, that she is "sufficient to have stood." She knows the decree is a direct command of God – "Sole Daughter of his voice" – and as such, distinct from the Law of Reason that governs all other prelapsarian behavior: "the rest, we live, / Law to ourselves, our Reason is our Law" (9.651–4). Milton's version of the Genesis story is unique in having Satan ground his temptation on a false narrative in which the serpent he inhabits supposedly explains that he gained reason and speech by eating apples from the forbidden tree, and concludes that, by analogy, Eve might expect from the same act a proportional rise in the scale of being. He invites her to interpret the prohibition on the tree as injury, a withholding from humans of the knowledge signified by the tree's name. If God is just and means Eve well he will not punish her desire for advancement, as he has not punished the serpent; if he would keep her from such elevation he is not just, "Not just, not God, not feard then, nor obeyd" (9.701). Eve is not required to match Satan in slippery argument: she need only hold on to her initial clear understanding that this command is outside the purview of nature and reason and that it was given to humans, not serpents. But Milton's antinomianism requires that Eve's obedience not be merely legalistic: while she cannot know that Satan has fabricated the serpent's experience, she could (as Abdiel did) construe the implications of the divine law in the light of her own previous experience of God's ways, notably the joy and sweetness of her life in Eden and with Adam.

Milton has Adam and Eve face another interpretative problem in their attempts to read the Book of Nature, foregrounding the challenge the new astronomy was offering to the supposed divine revelation of the Ptolemaic system in the Book of Genesis (4.657–88, 8.13–38). Adam's faulty reasoning about the workings of the cosmos throws up intellectual difficulties which, he declares to Raphael, "onely thy solution can resolve" (8.14). Relying on sense impressions, Adam supposes that the universe is designed on Ptolemaic principles and wonders why God and Nature arranged it so wastefully, with "such disproportions" and superfluous motions. Raphael, however, refuses to resolve this matter on his angelic authority, but instead invents a genre for scientific discourse: he offers a prototype of Galileo's *Dialogue of the Two Chief World Systems – Ptolemaic & Copernican*,[137] setting forth what is ostensibly an even-handed argument on both sides. Raphael thereby removes scientific inquiry from the province of divine revelation and places it squarely in the realm of human speculation. The cosmos of Milton's poem also leaves the cosmology ambiguous, with descriptions that defy precise categorization.

The angel's "benevolent and facil" opening words to Adam – "To ask or search I blame thee not, for Heav'n / Is as the Book of God before thee set, / Wherein to read his wondrous Works" (8.65–8) – explicitly sanction scientific speculation about the cosmos. But he sets aside certain other questions as beyond the ken of man or angel – presumably, God's ways with other worlds and other creatures in the universe (8.167–70). As Raphael shifts from a Ptolemaic to a Copernican argument, he suggests that the cosmic system one credits depends on one's vantage point. To Adam on earth the universe seems Ptolemaic and irrational; to angels who move among the planets it evidently seems Copernican, for Raphael offers a series of provocative suggestions that introduce Adam to advanced scientific speculations beyond his wildest imaginings: that the sun might be the stationary center to the world, that the seemingly steadfast earth might move "Insensibly three different Motions"; that the spots on the moon might be atmospheric clouds producing food for possible moondwellers; that the universe may hold unnumbered galaxies of unimagined immensity (8.122–58). Raphael's method is calculated to help Adam and his descendants discover the attitudes which should govern interpretations of the Book of Nature: distrust of naive sense impressions, awareness that human concerns need not be the focus and end of the entire cosmos, and recognition that the scientific orthodoxy of the moment cannot explain the ways of God and the order of things for all time. As he makes Adam aware of his inevitable limitations in astronomical science, Raphael emphasizes that Adam's primary attention and care should be given to human life and the human world: "thy being," "this Paradise / And thy faire *Eve*" (8.170–4).

At the center of his epic, Milton set a richly imagined representation of prelapsarian love, marriage, and domestic society.[138] It is a brilliant though sometimes conflicted representation, in which Milton's internalization of contemporary assumptions about gender hierarchy, his idealistic view of companionate marriage, his own life experiences, and his deeply felt emotional needs sometimes strain against each other. Most profoundly, he explores through Adam and Eve the fundamental challenge of any love relationship: the uneasy, inevitable, and ultimately creative tension between autonomy and interdependence.

In a sublime epithalamion, Milton celebrates marriage as the foundation of human society, and also gives his representation of Edenic marriage political resonance as he contrasts Adam and Eve's joyous and fulfilled marital love with the sterility and licentious indulgence of "Court Amours" – Charles I's cavaliers and the Bacchic "revelers" of Charles II's Restoration court:

> Haile wedded Love, mysterious Law, true source
> Of human ofspring, sole proprietie
> In Paradise of all things common else.
> By thee adulterous lust was driv'n from men
> Among the bestial herds to raunge, by thee
> Founded in Reason, Loyal, Just, and Pure,
> Relations dear, and all the Charities
> Of Father, Son, and Brother first were known . . .
>
> Here Love his golden shafts imploies, here lights
> His constant Lamp, and waves his purple wings,
> Reigns here and revels; not in the bought smile
> Of Harlots, loveless, joyless, unindeard,
> Casual fruition, nor in Court Amours
> Mixt Dance, or wanton Mask, or Midnight Bal. (4.750–68)

This paean elides female relationships: no mention is made of mothers and sisters, though the Bard implies, with modern anthropologists, that these social bonds are forged through women. He also imagines Adam and Eve's archetypal marriage according to the forms of the Early Modern institution, as an arrangement betweeen the father and the husband which the woman is to accept or (in rare cases) decline.[139] After brief resistance Eve accepts the husband offered by God the Father and the role prescribed for her: to produce "multitudes like thy self," and to be for Adam "an individual solace dear" (4.449–91).

Milton's epic inscribes gender hierarchy, though in a complex and nuanced version. Adam and Eve are described first in terms of their shared nobility, majesty, and authority over all other creatures; their moral and spiritual equality is based on their creation as God's images, exhibiting "Truth, wisdome, Sanctitude severe and pure" (4.287–95). Then their different physical qualities are interpreted as emblems of their unequal natures and roles: "For contemplation hee and valour formd, / For softness shee and sweet attractive Grace, / Hee for God only, shee for God in him" (4.297–9). Later Adam, after admitting to Raphael his unsettling passion for Eve, says that he knows she is inferior to himself in qualities both of mind and body:

> For well I understand in the prime end
> Of Nature her th'inferiour, in the mind
> And inward Faculties, which most excell,
> In outward also her resembling less
> His image who made both, and less expressing
> The character of that Dominion giv'n
> O'er other Creatures. (8.540–6)

Raphael confirms this judgment, urging Adam not to attribute "overmuch to things / Less excellent," to cultivate proper self-esteem so that Eve will "acknowledge thee her Head," to eschew passion, and to love Eve's higher qualities as a means to make a Neoplatonic ascent to heavenly love (8.565–75). More authoritative still, the Son, judging Adam after the Fall, confirms that Adam's proper role is to act as Eve's head and governor, not make an idol of her to set in place of God:

> Was shee thy God, that her thou didst obey
> Before his voice, or was shee made thy guide,
> Superior, or but equal, that to her
> Thou did'st resigne thy Manhood, and the Place
> Wherein God set thee above her made of thee,
> And for thee, whose perfection far excell'd
> Hers in all real dignitie: Adornd
> Shee was indeed, and lovely to attract
> Thy Love, not thy Subjection, and her Gifts
> Were such as under Government well seem'd,
> Unseemly to beare rule, which was thy part
> And person, had'st thou known thy self aright. (10.145–56)

Yet this conventional view of gender is destabilized by elements of Milton's imaginative vision that invite a more egalitarian conception: if Milton could not fully work through such conflicts, he did provide liberalizing perspectives upon which some later feminists could and did build.[140] One such is the poem's unusually fluid concept of hierarchy, the concomitant of Milton's monist ontology: if humans and angels differ only in degree and humans can expect the gradual refinement of their natures to angelic status, the distance between male and female on the hierarchical scale must be minimal. Moreover, Raphael's comment that creatures hold their place on that scale "as neerer to him [God] plac't or neerer tending" (5.476) allows that if Adam is at first "plac't" marginally higher than Eve, their final places will depend on how they develop, whither they "tend." In line with this, in Milton's unique representation of the state of innocence, Adam and Eve are both expected to grow, change, and develop in virtue by properly pruning and directing their erroneous apprehensions and perilous impulses, as well as their burgeoning garden.

Another complicating element is Milton's concept of companionate marriage, an advanced notion as he developed it in the divorce tracts, and he imagined it in much more gracious and idealized terms in the poem. Pleading with God for a mate, Adam points to the great disparity between humans and beasts and to the infinite distance between humans and God, then asks for an equal life partner:

> Among unequals what societie
> Can sort, what harmonie or true delight?
> Which must be mutual, in proportion due
> Giv'n and receiv'd; . . .
>   Of fellowship I speak
> Such as I seek, fit to participate
> All rational delight. (8.383–91)

God states that he always intended exactly such a mate for Adam: "Thy likeness, thy fit help, thy other self, / Thy wish exactly to thy hearts desire" (8.450–1). Consonant with this vision of marriage, Adam and Eve's roles and talents are not sharply segregated by gender, as convention would dictate. Eve performs certain domestic tasks – ornamenting the couple's bedroom bower and preparing and serving the noonday meal when Raphael visits – but otherwise the couple share the physical and intellectual activities of Edenic life. They take equal responsibility for their world, laboring together to maintain its eco-system: in Milton's unique version of Eden their pruning, cutting, and cultivating activities are absolutely necessary to keep the garden from returning to wild. Unique to Milton's Eden also is the fact that Eve names the plants and thereby shares in the authority over nature, the intuitive knowledge, and the power of symbolization that Adam's naming of the animals signifies, albeit in lesser degree.[141] She also receives the same education as Adam, though not in the same manner. As decorum dictated, Adam asked Raphael questions (often framing them faultily) while Eve listened in silence as the angel explained the nature of being, rendered an account of the War in Heaven as a brief epic, and recounted his story of Creation as a hexaemeron. For both, the Edenic curriculum included ontology, metaphysics, moral philosophy, history, epic poetry, and divine revelation. Eve missed the astronomy lesson when she left to tend her flowers, but the

Miltonic Bard insists that she both delighted in and was fully capable of that knowledge and would obtain it later in discussion with Adam – thereby gaining the educational benefit of dialogic interaction that Adam enjoyed with Raphael (8.48–50). Milton portrays Eve as an accomplished reasoner and debater in the marital dispute in Book IX and underscores her intellectual "sufficiency" in the temptation scene by her wry response to Satan's fulsome flattery and her precise statement of the terms of the prohibition as a divine command outside the law of nature.

Milton also accords Eve important areas of initiative and autonomy that further qualify patriarchal assumptions. Both before and after the Fall Eve often proposes issues for discussion, initiates action, and leads in some new direction. She first raises questions about the order of the cosmos; she proposes the proto-capitalist idea of the division of labor to help meet the problem of the garden's burgeoning growth; she first responds to "prevenient grace" and makes the first motion to repentance; she proposes suicide or sexual abstinence to prevent visitation of the Fall's effects on all humankind. When their dialogic interchanges are working properly, Adam responds to, develops, and where necessary corrects Eve's initiatives, as Raphael does Adam's, to advance their common understanding. In the realm of literary creativity, Eve constructs the first autobiographical narrative as she recounts her earliest recollections – with the implications autobiography carries of coming to self-awareness, probing one's own subjectivity, interpreting one's own experience, and so becoming an author (4.449–91). She is as much a lyric poet as Adam, perhaps more so. Their hymns and prayers are joint expressions, but Eve creates the first love lyric in Eden – the delicate, rhetorically artful, sonnet-like pastoral that begins "Sweet is the breath of Morn" (4.641–56). And if Adam brought this lyric form to higher perfection in his *aubade* echoing the Song of Songs (5.17–25), Eve after the Fall perfects the tragic lyric. Adam's agonized complaint, "O miserable of happy" (10.720–862), ends in despair, while Eve's moving lament, "Forsake me not thus, *Adam*" (10.914–36), opens the way to repentance, forgiveness, and reconciliation.

Also, Milton brings the ideology of gender hierarchy up against the characters' different experiences and psychology. Eve and Adam offer very different autobiographical accounts of their creation, first encounter, and marriage, accounts that evidently reflect Milton's reading of female and male psychology. Eve tells of constructing herself first through pleasurable self-contemplation, which she mistakes as a response to another female "shape," and then by freely accepting a marriage relationship; but she does not express any need for completion by another. She recounts as an episode "oft remembered" (4.449–91) how she woke on a flowery bank in some wonderment about herself, and how she then followed a murmur of waters to a pool that reflected a female image bending toward her as she to it "with answering looks / Of sympathie and love" (4.464–5). As a version of the Narcissus myth, Eve's story suggests her potential for self-love, but in most respects she is defined against the Narcissus story. She did not remain fixed forever, enamoured of her watery image, but after listening to the arguments of God and Adam, freely agreed ("I yielded") to reject narcissism, to share love and companionship with Adam in marriage, and to create human society – living images, not watery reflections. Eve's story also presents a classic Lacanian mirror scene: initial symbiosis with maternal earth and water in a place of pleasure before language, then a rupture when God's voice (the Law of the Father) intervenes, leading her to a husband and thereby into language and culture.[142] She at first turns away, finding masculine Adam "Less winning soft, less amiablie milde, / Then that smooth watry image" (4.479–80), but he wins her as his mate by urging his "paternal" claim to her as well as his ardent love. Eve, however, complicates the reading of her story as a simple submission to patriarchy.[143] As she recounts the words spoken to her by God, she almost concludes that God made Adam for her, not vice versa, and that he instituted matriarchy, not patriarchy:

> hee,
> Whose image thou art, him thou shalt enjoy
> Inseparablie thine, to him shalt beare
> Multitudes like thy self [not, like himself], and thence be call'd
> Mother of human Race. (4.471–6)

Moralizing her story, Eve claims to have learned from the first events of her life "How beauty is excelld by manly grace / And wisdom, which alone is truly fair" (490–1). On one reading this seems to be a forthright testimony to male superiority in mind and body. But on another, Eve hereby proclaims (after a brief homoerotic hesitation) her heterosexual attraction to Adam's "manly grace" over female beauty, and then distinguishes wisdom from both physical qualities, implying that it may pertain both to Adam's and her own self-knowledge and wise choices.

Adam's narrative (8.355–99), by contrast, testifies to a psychological and emotional neediness that in some ways undercuts gender hierarchy and recalls Milton's similar testimony in the divorce tracts.[144] Adam reports his initial attempts to discover who he is by contemplating nature and his immediate inference that "some great Maker" created both it and him. Then he recounts his eloquent pleas with God for a mate, emphasizing his keen sense of incompleteness and loneliness without an "equal" companion. Recounting the courtship event he explains Eve's hesitation not as she herself did but by projecting onto her a serene consciousness of self-worth, "That would be woo'd, and not unsought be won," and a demeanor of "obsequious Majestie" in accepting his suit (8.500–10). He underscores the conflict between ideology and experience by emphasizing the disconnect between what he "knows" of Eve's inferiority to him and what he experiences when he is with her:

> when I approach
> Her loveliness, so absolute she seems
> And in herself compleat, so well to know
> Her own, that what she wills to do or say,

Seems wisest, vertuousest, discreetest, best, . . .

Authority and Reason on her waite,
As one intended first, not after made
Occasionally, and to consummate all,
Greatness of mind, and nobleness thir seat
Build in her loveliest, and create an awe
About her, as a guard Angelic plac't. (8.546–59)

Though Raphael rightly rebukes Adam for such potentially dangerous sentiments, Milton allows Adam to qualify the angel's apparently rigid Neoplatonism from the perspective of his (and our) experience of something beyond Raphael's ken, the "mysterious reverence" due the marriage bed and marriage itself, an institution angels do not have (8.598–9). Adam also scores a point, and shows that he understands the implications of monism, as he leads Raphael to acknowledge that happiness for angels as for humans involves some version of sexual love. After Eve's Fall, Adam's instant decision to fall with her arises from his desperate fear of returning to his lonely life before her creation:

How can I live without thee, how forgoe
Thy sweet Converse and Love so dearly joyn'd,
To live again in these wilde Woods forlorn?
Should God create another *Eve*, and I
Another Rib afford, yet loss of thee
Would never from my heart. (9.908–13)

Milton's most brilliant analysis of human psychology occurs in a scene without precedent in other literary versions of the Genesis story: the dispute which occasioned Adam and Eve's separation (9.205–386). In that dialogue, as Adam and Eve enmesh themselves in ever greater misunderstandings, the reader feels on his or her pulses the truth of this archetypal version of all those familiar scenes in which lovers or friends, by no one's design, exacerbate slight disagreements into great divides, leading to unwise decisions and dire results. Eve advances her well-meaning but misguided proposal for temporary separation to meet a genuine problem: the tendency of the garden to "wanton growth." Adam reminds her of the enemy who, if they met him together, "each / To other speedie aid might lend at need" (9.259–60). He might have won his point had he stopped there, but he talks on, unintentionally affronting Eve with a pompous platitude emphasizing the wife's need of her husband's guardianship. Eve, hurt by the implication that she would easily be seduced, responds "as one who loves, and some unkindness meets" (9.271), throwing Adam off balance. Logic deserts him, leading him to assert that the temptation itself would bring dishonor, and Eve picks up on his error. She enjoys having the better of the argument for the moment as she insists, quite rightly, that both must have been created "sufficient" to stand alone against temptation and that temptation itself can be no dishonor. But she goes on to cast herself as a Romance heroine eager to exhibit heroic self-sufficiency and to gain honor in victorious single combat with the enemy: "And what is Faith, Love, Vertue unassaid / Alone, without exterior help sustaind?" (9.335–6). She here goes beyond *Areopagitica's* warfaring Christian who "sallies out and sees her adversary," and echoes, faintly, the Satanic claim to absolute autonomy. She is right to insist that both are sufficient to stand, but quite wrong to infer that "exterior help," divine or human, should therefore be shunned, or that reasonable precautions in the presence of danger violate Edenic happiness. She thinks the goods of autonomy and interdependence are in conflict, but it is precisely the challenge of this first couple to hold them in balance.

Adam's fervent reply speaks both to the logical and the psychological issues involved: explaining how reason may be deceived and lead the will to sin, he ends with an eloquent testimony to the mutual aid the couple continually give each other, and a reminder that temptation will inevitably come unsought, affording Eve an opportunity to win the praise she seeks. Had he stopped here, with this strong argument offering Eve a clear choice, she would almost certainly have given way (if a bit reluctantly), announcing herself convinced by his arguments and comforted by his loving sentiments. But Adam, still off balance and still attributing overmuch wisdom to Eve, talks on and gives away his case:

> But if thou think, trial unsought may finde
> Us both securer then thus warnd thou seemst,
> Go; for thy stay, not free, absents thee more;
> Go in thy native innocence, relie
> On what thou hast of vertue, summon all,
> For God towards thee hath done his part, do thine. (9.370–5)

Besides offering Eve a better rationale for going than any she has thought of, Adam unwittingly intensifies the psychological pressure on her by his repeated imperatives – "Go . . . go . . . rely . . . do" – making it much more difficult for her to stay without seeming to back down ignominiously. It was not Adam's place in prelapsarian Eden to command Eve to stay and thereby control her free choice in the moral sphere; but neither was it his place to help her choose such a dangerous course of action by giving over his proper leadership role. Neither has sinned in this debate because there has been no deliberate choice of evil. Eve has not disobeyed and Adam has tried to act for the best, so the theological imperatives of the biblical story and of Milton's Arminianism are preserved: Adam and Eve remain innocent until they consciously decide to eat the fruit. But as their imperfectly controlled emotions sabotage their dialogic exchange and their misunderstandings result in physical separation, we experience the mounting sense of inevitability proper to tragedy.

In the Fall sequence and its aftermath, it is hardly an exaggeration to say that

Milton's epic turns into an Eviad, casting Eve rather than Adam in the role of central protagonist.[145] The biblical story of course requires that she be the object of the serpent's temptation, but Milton's poem goes much further. Eve initiates the marital dispute, she engages in a lengthy and highly dramatic dialogue with Satan embodied in the serpent, and she analyzes her motives and emotions in probing soliloquies before eating the fruit and before offering it to Adam. After the Fall she accepts God's judgment humbly, while Adam, dismayed to find his grand gesture of falling with Eve unappreciated by her, blames both Eve and the God who gave her to him. Eve responds first to "prevenient grace," and so first breaks out of the seemingly endless cycle of accusations and recriminations, becoming the human means to lead Adam back from the paralysis of despair to love, repentance, and reconciliation, first with his wife and then with God. In her lament/petition to Adam, Eve echoes the Son's offer in the Council in Heaven to take on himself God's wrath for Adam's sin – "Behold mee then, mee for him . . . / On mee let thine anger fall" (3.236–7) – as she proposes to invite God to wreak all his anger on her: "On me, sole cause to thee of all this woe, / Mee mee onely just object of his ire" (10.932–6). While she cannot play the Son's redemptive role, she does become the first human to reach toward the new standard of epic heroism (9.31–2).

Milton designed the last segment of his poem around the issue of postlapsarian education, for Adam, Eve, and the reader. At this juncture Adam and Eve have to learn how to read biblical history (which to them is prophecy), and specifically, how to interpret the *protoevangelium* or messianic promise of redemption signified by the metaphorical curse on the serpent: that the seed of the woman will bruise his head. For Adam, its meaning is progressively clarified by a revelation of future times from his own age to the Apocalypse, presented by the archangel Michael in a series of visionary pageants (Book XI) and narratives (Book XII). Adam has to learn to interpret what he sees and hears by a process, much more strenuous than with Raphael, of faulty formulation, improper response, and correction. He also learns by vicarious experience, identifying so closely with his progeny that he seems almost to live their history with them: he is enraged by the wickedness of Cain, laments the terrors of pestilence and death in a lazar house, weeps for the destruction of the world by the flood, rejoices in the steadfast faith of Abraham, Moses, and the other righteous, and waxes ecstatic over the eventual triumph of Christ with his saints. Under Michael's correction he learns to read history emblematically, as a series of episodes displaying again and again the proliferation of evils his sin has unleashed upon the world. He also learns to read it typologically, as a movement "From shadowie Types to Truth" (12.303) in which the meaning of the messianic promises becomes ever clearer, so that at last, despite sin and death and all our woe, he can proclaim the goodness of God's ways to man: "O goodness infinite, goodness immense! / That all this good of evil shall produce, / And evil turn to good" (12.469–71). Michael then offers him further consolation in the far-off prospect of the Last Judgment and the Millennium, placing less emphasis on heavenly bliss than on the restoration of the fallen earth to its paradisal beauty, so that "the Earth / Shall all be Paradise, far happier place / Than this of *Eden*, and far happier daies" (12.463–5). Michael also points to the apocalyptic climax of this period, the Son's final epic victory against Satan, Sin, and Death, followed by the dissolution in flames of "*Satan* with his perverted World," and the emergence of a new, purged, and refined creation: "New Heav'ns, new Earth, Ages of endless date / Founded in righteousness and peace and love / To bring forth fruits Joy and eternal Bliss" (12.547–51). Then Adam can apply the messianic promise to himself, acknowledging Christ as "my Redeemer ever blest" and as a model for the new heroism (12.560–73).

Adam and the reader are also to take a political lesson from history, as they see how, over and over again, one or a few righteous humans stand out against, but are at length overwhelmed by, the many wicked, resulting in the collapse of all attempts to found a permanent version of the Kingdom of God on earth. Michael sums up that pattern as he comments on the way of the world after Christ's ascension: "so shall the World goe on, / To good malignant, to bad men benigne, / Under her own waight groaning" until Christ's second coming (12.537–51). That tragic vision of an external paradise irretrievably lost, along with the promise of "A paradise within thee, happier far" might seem a recipe for quietism, indicating Milton's retreat from the political arena. But the entire thrust of Michael's prophecy is against any kind of passivity, spiritual, moral, or even political. He shows that in every age the few just have the responsibility to oppose, if God calls them to do so, the Nimrods, or the Pharaohs, or the royalist persecutors of Puritans, even though – like the loyal angels in the War in Heaven – they can win no decisive victories and can effect no lasting reforms until the Son appears. Michael offers Adam and his progeny examples of both kinds of heroism: heroic martyrdom and heroic action. And Adam understands. He has learned that "suffering for Truths sake / Is fortitude to highest victorie," and also that God often uses weak humans to accomplish great things: "by things deemd weak / Subverting worldly strong" (12.565–70).

Eve also learns something of this history by a mode of prophecy that validates her distinct order of experience. She claims to have received in dreams directly from God some understanding of the "great good" to come. Dreams were a recognized vehicle of prophecy, though inferior to vision.[146] How much history Eve's dreams conveyed is left unclear, but they lead her to recognize her own divinely appointed agency in bringing the messianic promise into history. As she speaks the last words we hear in Eden, she voices her own version of the new heroism and claims her central role in God's plan and Milton's poem, as primary protagonist of the Fall but also primary human agent in redemption:

> This further consolation yet secure
> I carry hence, though all by mee is lost,
> Such favour I unworthie am voutsaft,
> By mee the Promis'd Seed shall all restore. (12.620–3)

Milton's poignant, quiet, marvelously evocative final lines are elegiac in substance and tone, conjoining loss and consolation. Prophecy and Providence provide part of that consolation, but so does Adam and Eve's loving union: its continuing comforts and challenges are underscored by the paradoxical description of the pair going forth "hand-in-hand" and "solitarie." The final lines also effect a sharp adjustment of the perspective glass, as we are suddenly translated from the end of time back to the beginning, and watch Adam and Eve go forth to live out all our woe and to enact all that has been foreseen.

> Som natural tears they drop'd, but wip'd them soon;
> The World was all before them, where to choose
> Thir place of rest, and Providence thir guide:
> They hand in hand, with wandring steps and slow,
> Through *Eden* took thir solitarie way.

14

"To Try, and Teach the Erring Soul" 1669–1674

The final years of Milton's life were busy and productive. The comforts of home and garden gave him pleasure, as did the attentive care of his wife Elizabeth, but he continued to resent his "undutiful" daughters. He enjoyed the visits of friends old and new, and taught an occasional student in return for their services in reading and writing for him. He also suffered, by all accounts cheerfully, painful attacks of the gout which increased in frequency and duration. During these years, in part to realize additional income, he revised and prepared for the press several unpublished works begun during his days as a private scholar and schoolmaster in the 1640s: a grammar, an art of logic, and a *History of Britain*. All of these apparently innocuous works allowed him to testify covertly against some norms of Restoration culture. They also allowed him to continue an educative role, endeavoring to help the English people develop the moral virtues and love of liberty that alone could enable them – in God's good time – to gain and sustain freedom in church and state. He was cleaning out his desk drawers and turning that housekeeping to good account.

He also wrote two remarkable new poems that might be seen to complete the program he projected for himself three decades earlier in the *Reason of Church-Government* (1642) and that also seek to advance the moral and political education of his countrymen: a brief epic, *Paradise Regained*, as a counterpart to his "diffuse epic"; and a biblical tragedy, *Samson Agonistes*. He entered the polemic arena again with *Of True Religion*, which again addressed his primary concern for many years, religious toleration for Protestants, but now under the severely constraining conditions of Restoration repression and censorship. He translated a document on the election of a new King of Poland as a covert contribution to the escalating crisis over the Roman Catholic heir apparent, James II. And in the year of his death he published the second edition of *Paradise Lost*, slightly revised and now in a twelve-book format. This was not a time of standing and waiting but of continued political engagement and magnificent poetic accomplishment.

"I Was to Do My Part from Heav'n Assign'd"

On June 28, 1669, publication of Milton's *Accedence Commenc't Grammar*, mostly written in the mid-1640s, was announced.[1] During the 1660s Lily's grammar was reissued in several editions and revised versions, still bearing the royal authorization as the only prescribed grammar for schools, though several Ramist grammars were also available, organized on different principles. Milton's preface, evidently added at this juncture, declares that his new departures and his intent will be clear to the discerning reader:

> Account might be now givn what addition or alteration from other Grammars hath been here made, and for what reason. But he who would be short in teaching, must not be long in Prefacing: The Book it self follows, and will declare sufficiently to them who can discern. (*CPW* VIII, 86)

In this ambiguous challenge Milton hints at subversive elements in his grammar. When he first prepared the text for his own students, he deleted from Lily many items that reinforce structures of royal and ecclesiastical authority and added many new examples from Cicero, from texts dealing with the struggle for justice, social reform, liberty, and civil rights against oppressive power.[2] He now directs his published text to "the elder sort especially" who wish to learn Latin with little teaching and their own industry. As they do so, Milton can hope that the voice of the republican Cicero might have some effect on them, countering the royalist ideology Lily's grammar insinuates.

In late December, 1669 Milton would have learned of the death of his nephew, Christopher's son John.[3] Others well known to him also died that year: Luke Robinson, his acquaintance at Christ's and in the Council of State; Richard Pory, his school and college acquaintance; his old enemy William Prynne; and the diplomat Lieuwe van Aitzema, his friend and correspondent from his days as Latin Secretary. Such news, and his worsening gout, likely prompted thoughts of his own mortality, leading him to dispose of some books. His enemies jeered that he was reduced to that course by poverty, a charge his biographer John Toland countered with a more genteel explanation: "he contracted his Library, both because his Heirs he left could not make a right use of it, and that he thought he might sell it more to their advantage than they could be able to do themselves" (*EL* 192–3). Milton probably did want to realize some money from such books as he would no longer need, since he could no longer engage in controversy. The sale evidently occurred sometime in 1670, at which time Milton resided temporarily with one Millington, an antique bookseller in Little Britain (*EL* 203, 275), probably to select and help price items from his very considerable library. Jonathan Richardson heard that Milton sometimes took walks with Millington leading him by the hand, that he dressed in cold weather in a grey camblet coat rather like those worn by Quakers, and that he customarily wore a sword with a small silver hilt (*EL* 203). Despite the uselessness of a sword to a blind man, Milton clearly wished to hold on to that perquisite of a gentleman. Richardson also comments on his appearance and his life at Bunhill during his last years:

> I have heard . . . that he Us'd to Sit in a Grey Coarse Cloath Coat at the Door of his House, near *Bun-hill* Fields Without *Moor-gate,* in Warm Sunny Weather to Enjoy the Fresh Air, and So, as well as in his Room, received the Visits of People of Distinguish'd Parts, as well as Quality. and very Lately I had the Good Fortune to have Another Picture of him from an Ancient Clergy-man in *Dorsetshire*, Dr. *Wright;* He found him in a Small House, he thinks but One Room on a Floor; in That, up One pair of Stairs, which was hung with a Rusty Green, he found *John Milton*, Sitting in an Elbow Chair, Black Cloaths, and Neat enough, Pale, but not Cadaverous, his Hands and Fingers Gouty, and with Chalk Stones. among Other Discourse He exprest Himself to This Purpose; that was he Free from the Pain This gave him, his Blindness would be Tolerable. (*EL* 203–4)

Never, Edward Phillips states, was the parade of foreign visitors "more frequent than in this place, almost to his dying day" (*EL* 76).[4]

In March or early April, 1670 an eminent member of the House of Lords and "a chief Officer of State" reportedly came to consult with him on the subject of divorce.[5] At issue was a private Bill to enable John Manners, Lord Roos, to remarry after divorcing a wife accused of infidelity. But that case was a stalking horse for efforts to find a way for Charles II to divorce his childless queen and remarry, thereby perhaps producing an heir and preventing the succession of his Roman Catholic brother James. Supported by a phalanx of archbishops, bishops, and crypto-Catholic peers, James strongly opposed the Roos Bill, but many Protestant peers supported it. Charles signed it on April 11, though he made no use of it. Milton would certainly have tried to help. The peer who came to him was probably Arthur Annesley, Earl of Anglesey who, according to Edward Phillips, "came often here to visit him as very much coveting his society and converse; as likewise others of the Nobility, and many persons of eminent quality" (*EL* 76). Milton and Annesley had much in common. Anthony à Wood describes Annesley as "a man of superior tastes and abilities," "much conversant in books," and having "the command of a very smooth, sharp, and keen pen." He was a "great Calvinist" and favored "the dissenting party," but was so free in his sympathies with those of very different persuasions as to leave in doubt where he stood on religious questions.[6] By others, though, Milton was still being ridiculed for his views on divorce and, curiously enough, education. John Eachard remarked snidely: "I am not I'll assure you, any of those occasional Writers, that missing preferment in the University can presently write you their new ways of Education; or being a little tormented with an ill chosen Wife, set forth the Doctrine of Divorce to be truly Evangelical."[7]

No doubt Milton took special pleasure that spring in a glowing tribute to *Paradise*

Lost that his nephew Edward Phillips included in his Latin essay on the major poets from Dante to the present, appended to John Buchler's *Thesaurus* of poetical phrases:

> John Milton, in addition to other most elegant books which he has written, both in English and in Latin, has lately presented to public opinion *Paradise Lost*, a poem which, whether we regard the sublimity of the subject, or the combined pleasantness and majesty of the style, or the majesty of the invention, or the supremely natural images and descriptions, will, if I am not mistaken, be received as truly heroic; for by the votes of the many who are not ignorant how to judge, it is deemed to have achieved perfection in this kind of poetry.[8]

On July 2, 1670 the volume containing *Paradise Regained* and *Samson Agonistes* was licensed for publication, indicating these two poems were then complete, or substantially so; the volume was registered with the Stationers on September 10.[9] Edward Phillips thought that *Paradise Regained* "doubtless was begun and finisht and Printed after the other was publisht, and that in a wonderful short space considering the sublimeness of it" (*EL* 75), but the writing must have begun earlier; Milton's Quaker friend Thomas Ellwood saw at least a partial and perhaps a complete draft of *Paradise Regained* in 1666.[10] But Phillips's comment that Milton "could not hear with patience" the general opinion that it was "much inferiour" to *Paradise Lost* (*EL* 75–6) has the ring of truth.

Phillips also states, accurately, that "it cannot certainly be concluded" when he wrote *Samson Agonistes*. The traditional dating, after *Paradise Regained* and during the years 1667–70, is generally accepted; efforts to place it in the 1640s or 1650s on metrical and biographical grounds, have not proved persuasive.[11] As Blair Worden demonstrates, the language used by and about the imprisoned Samson often echoes that used by and about republicans and regicides in exile and in prison after the Restoration, especially Edmund Ludlow, Algernon Sidney, and Milton's friend Henry Vane.[12] Also, the political and religious issues faced by and debated by Samson, a defeated warrior in God's cause who is enslaved by his enemies and commanded to participate in idolatrous ceremonies, resonate so strongly with the situation of the defeated Puritans that it is almost impossible to imagine its composition at any other time. The severe repressions of the Clarendon Code forbade Nonconformist "conventicles" and required all office holders, parliament members, teachers, university students, and others to attend Anglican services as a public gesture of uniformity; ministers had to use and declare their full acceptance of the *Book of Common Prayer*.[13] But some polemicists were urging limited toleration for dissenters in terms suggestive for Milton's dramatic poem, around the time the first Conventicles Act expired (March, 1668). Nicholas Lockyer compared them to the Israelites enslaved by Pharaoh and John Owen insisted that they were obedient subjects of the king in civil matters though they refused to conform in religion; he also highlighted the folly of expecting to persuade minds by using compulsion and penalties to impose an outward conformity.[14] The vociferous counterarguments by, among others, Thomas Tomkyns, urge enforced attendance at Anglican services to produce unity:

> Uniformity if it were carefully maintained, and diligently looked after, would in a few years recall our Ancient Unity; The People would quickly forget all these fantasies. . . . We should quickly see, that the People would come to the Churches, if there were not so many Conventicles to keep them thence; and if they were but used for a little while to come thither, they would not find the Liturgy to be such a fearful idol as they have been often told of.[15]

Efforts to secure some toleration for dissenters were supported by Charles and the Catholic and crypto-Catholic peers, in the interest, ultimately, of relieving Catholics.[16] But the fiercely Anglican parliament, whenever it convened, quashed all such gestures and forced Charles II to sign an even more stringent Conventicles Act just a few months before Milton's volume was licensed.

Milton's two poems offer two models of political response in conditions of severe trial and oppression. Both poems are fundamentally concerned with education: moral, political, and spiritual. Both contain adumbrations of the Apocalypse, foreshadowed as some thought by the Great Plague and Great Fire; but Milton's poems place that event far off, and are concerned with how to live now and prepare rightly for it. *Paradise Regained* offers in Jesus a model of unflinching resistance to and forthright denunciation of all versions of the sinful or disordered life, and all faulty and false models of church and state. Jesus takes as his immediate kingly role "to guide Nations in the way of truth" (*PR* 2.473), insisting that it would be futile to free the "unrepentant, unreform'd" Israelites (or Englishmen) who worship idols along with God. But he holds out the Millennial hope that God "by some wond'rous call / May bring them back repentant and sincere, / . . . to their native land" (3.426–37). And he prophesies that in that apocalypse his monarchy, like a stone, "shall to pieces dash / All Monarchies besides throughout the world" (4.149–50). As one analogue for that model of resistance David Loewenstein points to contemporary Quakers, the Nonconformist group who were most severely persecuted by the establishment and who denounced it insistently in testimony and tracts.[17] Milton's Quaker friends, notably the Isaac Pennington family and Thomas Ellwood, were often subjected to inquisition and imprisonment.[18] Alternatively, *Samson Agonistes* presents a warrior hero through whose catastrophic act God offered his people a second chance to free themselves from ignominious defeat and slavery, though only after Samson undergoes a searching and painful process of self-analysis, repentance, and new understanding. Israel's freedom, however, depends on whether the community, this time, can seize the Machiavellian *occasione*. Both works dramatize, in different ways, Milton's characteristic stance in the prose tracts: that the attainment of liberty, the exercise of governance, and indeed any worthy action in the service of God and country are predicated on virtue, sound moral and political understanding, and openness to divine illumination.

As well, these poems carry forward Milton's effort to redefine the heroic for the modern age. Even more directly than *Paradise Lost*, these poems challenge the aesthetics and cultural politics of the contemporary heroic drama: its pentameter couplets and what Steven Zwicker terms "its bombast and cant, its aristocratic code of virtue and honor, its spectacle and rhetoric . . . its warring heroes and virgin queens, its exaltation of passion and elevation of empire."[19] Milton's largely dialogic brief epic celebrates in blank verse the heroism of intellectual and moral struggle, and entirely redefines the nature of empire and glory. And his severe classical tragedy, written in a species of free verse with varying line lengths and some irregular rhyme, eschews every vestige of exotic spectacle, links erotic passion with idolatry, and constructs a tragic hero whose intense psychic suffering leads to spiritual growth. Milton's preface to *Samson Agonistes* explicitly sets his practice against that of his contemporaries, describing his tragedy as "coming forth after the antient manner, much different from what among us passes for best."[20] The two-part volume did not appear for some months, until late in 1670 with George Starkey as publisher.[21] The delay may have occurred because Milton, working with inadequate scribes, took some time to see this octavo volume through the press; also, Milton's printer (John Macock) was at the same time producing Milton's *History of Britain* for yet another bookseller, James Allestry.[22] At some point during the printing process, and too late to be inserted at the proper place, Milton added or retrieved ten non-consecutive lines (now numbered as lines 1,527–35, and line 1,537), evidence of his ongoing revision or oversight of the work in progress.[23] *Paradise Regained* and *Samson Agonistes* are discussed on pages 510–36.

Milton's *History of Britain* from the beginnings to the Norman Conquest had been written much earlier, in two stages: the first three and most of the fourth books, including (probably) the famous Digression denouncing the Long Parliament and the Westminster Assembly, in 1648–9; and the rest sometime after 1654.[24] It seems likely, however, that some passages were added in 1670 as Milton prepared his text for publication: probably the final passage of the Digression and the last paragraph of the *History*, with their long, melancholy perspective on past English events and their emphasis on what became Milton's leitmotif in these final years, that only through virtue and sound education can liberty be gained or preserved. At the end of the Digression are these words:

> Hence did thir victories prove as fruitless as thir losses dangerous, and left them still conquering under the same grievances that men suffer conquerd, which was indeed unlikely to goe otherwise unless, men more then vulgar, bred up, as few of them were, in the knowledge of Antient and illustrious deeds, invincible against money, and vaine titles, impartial to friendships and relations had conducted thir affaires. But then from the chapman to the retaler many, whose ignorance was more audacious then the rest, were admitted with all thir sordid rudiments to beare no mean sway among them both in church and state. From the confluence of all these errors, mi[s]chiefs, & misdemeanors, what in the eyes of man cou[ld] be expected but what befel those antient inhabit[ants] whom they so much resembl'd, confusion in the end. (*CPW* V.1, 451)

The final sentences of the *History* apply the moral lessons of the Norman Conquest and the entire work to the present time of apparent "security:"

> *And as the long suffering of God permits bad men to enjoy prosperous daies with the good, so his severity oft times exempts not good men from thir share in evil times with the bad.*
>
> If these were the Causes of such misery and thraldom to those our Ancestors, with what better close can be concluded, then here in fit season to remember this Age in the midst of her security, to fear from like Vices without amendment the Revolution of like Calamities. (*CPW* V.1, 403)

Before publication the *History* met with problems from the censor. Edward Phillips claims that it was "all compleat so far as he went, some Passages only excepted, which, being thought too sharp against the Clergy, could not pass the Hand of the Licencer" (*EL* 75). Toland identifies the passages excised, either from inside information or by an inspired guess:

> We have it not as it came out of his hands; for the Licensers, those sworn Officers to destroy Learning, Liberty and good Sense, expung'd several passages of it wherin he expos'd the Superstition, Pride, and Cunning of the Popish Monks in the *Saxon* Times, but apply'd by the sagacious Licensers to *Charles* the Second's Bishops. (*EL* 185)

This seems plausible: as early as *Of Reformation* Milton related contemporary ecclesiastical evils to a long history of "neere twelve hundred yeares" of rule by blind and ignorant English bishops.[25] The autumn of 1670 saw a tightening of press supervision and licensing after the temporary laxity that followed upon the disasters and political upheavals of the mid-1660s. L'Estrange was probably the censor who made trouble for Milton's *History*, as he took a special interest in books on law and history and was very sensitive to real or imagined slights against bishops.[26] Milton's friend the Earl of Anglesey reportedly kept the suppressed pages "while he lived," which suggests that it was he who negotiated with L'Estrange over the final text of the *History*, as he was later to do for Marvell's *Rehearsal Transprosed*.[27] The suppressed pages were never found. Milton had evidently planned to include the Digression denouncing the Long Parliament and the Westminster Assembly but decided to omit it also, perhaps because the removal of the Saxon bishops' passage destroyed the symmetry of castigating both the new presbyters and the old priests. Or, Anglesey may have persuaded Milton that the Digression could harm the dissenters' cause.[28]

By November 1, 1670 the *History of Britain* had been published and priced at 6 shillings.[29] The 1670 edition was nicely printed in a small quarto of 308 pages, with an elaborate index of 52 pages carefully prepared by some knowledgeable person. It has as frontispiece an engraved portrait of Milton by William Faithorne, probably commissioned by Allestry, which notes Milton's age as 62 over the date, 1670 (plate 16).[30] Faithorne was a well-known engraver and print-seller whose repertoire of portrait engravings includes Queen Henrietta Maria, Cromwell in armor, Fairfax, Gabriel Harvey, Hobbes, Lady Castlemaine, Prince Rupert, and other notables.[31] He claimed that the etching was made from life, that is, from a drawing he made of Milton sometime that year.[32] Milton's wife Elizabeth Minshull was as dissatisfied with the Faithorne engraving as she was with the other frontispiece portraits, telling Aubrey that "the Pictures before his bookes are not *at all* like him" (*EL* 3); she may have thought the sober, unsmiling countenance too severe for a man generally described to be of "a very cheerfull humour" and "Extreme pleasant in his conversation, & at dinner" (*EL* 5–6). But Milton's daughter Deborah (Clarke), many years later, confirmed to the engraver George Virtue that copies made from the Faithorne engraving did resemble Milton as she remembered him.[33] Milton evidently sat for Faithorne sometime in 1670, and his engraving is the best record we have of his appearance in the last years of his life.

Milton's *History* attracted some immediate attention from the learned. In a letter to Anthony à Wood (November 10, 1670), Thomas Blount commented that it had the reputation of stringing old authors together, and "not abstainyng from som lashes at the ignorance or I know not what of those times."[34] In late December, John Beale had learned of the *History* but not seen it.[35] Two weeks later he was immersed in it, writing to Evelyn (January 9, 1671) that he greatly approved of its moral lessons:

> Since I wrote, I have read much of Miltons History. Tis Elegant, chosen with judgment out of best Authors; And wee needed all, & more than all that I have yet seen of his sharpe checks & sowre Instructions. For wee must be a lost People, if wee be not speedily reclaim'd.[36]

There is some evidence that Milton began revisions for a new edition, probably hoping to include the censored material and the Digression, but that edition did not materialize.[37] For reasons that are not clear, within two years rights to reissue the work passed to as many as five booksellers.[38]

As Milton was taking satisfaction from the publication of two splendid new poems and the *History,* he may have learned of Pierre Du Moulin's collection of poems, *Parerga* (probably published in November, 1670), which made public his authorship of *Clamor* and also reprinted his satiric poem from that treatise, "To the beastly blackguard John Milton, Parricide and Advocate of Parricides," in which he declines a duel with the "foul and loathsome" Milton but hands him over to an executioner to be lashed and cudgeled until his body is a mosaic of stripes.[39] In a Latin epistle he takes pride in his virulence: "I had not spared the goads, and had not considered any vehemence too strong, by which so criminal and horrible madness might be reviled." He also sneers at Milton with telling effect for reviling Alexander More in his *Defensio Secunda* when he should have known More was not the author:

> More . . . brought two witnesses . . . who might well have known the author, and who might, if asked, have been able to reveal him. Thus there truly hung over me and my head most certain ruin. But that great Vindicator of justice . . . saved my life through Milton's pride . . . [who] could never be brought to confess himself to be so grossly deceived. . . . And since Milton preferred to have me safe rather than himself ridiculous, I got this reward for my work, that I had Milton, whom I had treated pretty roughly, as my patron and solicitous shield-bearer for my head.[40]

Milton must have hated to have Du Moulin's ridicule resurface, again reviling him and calling attention to the error he had clung to so stubbornly and given over so reluctantly.[41]

In the early months of 1672 Milton prepared his *Artis Logicae Plenior Institutio* for the press and by May 13 it had been published.[42] Some copies, but not all, include an engraved portrait of Milton by William Dolle, taken from the Faithorne engraving and noting Milton's age as 63.[43] Milton probably had at hand a virtually complete manuscript of this text, derived from Ramus and Downame, and prepared during his schoolmastering days in the 1640s.[44] But some changes date from this later period, notably references to the heterodox doctrinal positions he had by now worked out fully in the *De Doctrina Christiana* but apparently did not hold in the 1640s. The most obvious of these is the application of a logical principle, also invoked in *De Doctrina*, as an oblique argument against Trinitarian doctrine: "things which differ in number also differ in essence; and never do they differ in number if not in essence. – *Here let the Theologians awake*."[45] The italicized comment, not in Ramus, is Milton's effort to make the reader attend to the anti-Trinitarian implications of the principle cited, which he cannot state openly. A later instance is Milton's insistence that the text of John 17:3, "The Father alone is true God," be interpreted by the clear logical principle governing exclusives, not explained away by a ridiculous quibble.[46] Another such addition occurs in the chapter on "The Efficient Cause" where, as in *De Doctrina* and *Paradise Lost*, angels and men are identified as free agents, since "the divine will . . . in the beginning gave them the power of acting freely."[47] Such *obiter dicta* suggest that the educational purposes of this work reach beyond supplying a still useful logic textbook for students: Milton would also help the discerning reader understand the implications for theology of generally accepted logical principles. His preface, probably written or revised shortly before publication, underscores his intent to make manifest how orthodox theologians misuse the rules of logic:

> I have even more decidedly made up my mind not to stuff in random rules which come from theologians rather than from logic; for theologians produce rules about God, about divine substances, and about sacraments right out of the middle of logic as though these rules had been provided simply for their own use, although nothing is more foreign to logic, or indeed to reason itself, than the grounds for these rules as formulated by them. (*CPW* VIII, 211)

Milton occasionally cites scripture himself and makes a few theological comments, but he does indeed omit "random rules" contrived to suit theologians.

In his preface, Milton designates Ramus as the most worthy logician, characteristically citing himself as an authoritative judge of that matter, along with "our good Sidney." He also explains that he has interwoven into his text explanatory materials from Ramus's *Lectures on Dialectic* and from the commentaries of others, "except where I disagree with what these commentaries say" (208–10). At this time also, to make his text more saleable, he likely prepared and appended to it his abridgement of Freige's "Life of Ramus," which cuts away five-sixths of Freige's diffuse narrative, producing a spare, unornamented account.[48] Conceived as an exemplary Plutarchian "Life," Milton presents Ramus in several roles: as an intellectual rebel who was unafraid to make bold claims such as "Whatever has been said by Aristotle is fabrication" (399), and in consequence was constantly harassed by his philosophical critics; as a Protestant scholar who was forced into hiding and exile by his Roman Catholic enemies but was highly honored and courted by foreign intelligentsia; and as a Protestant martyr murdered in the massacre on St Bartholomew's Day. The analogies in this story with Milton himself are left unstated, but the fit reader might recognize them.

As he worked over these early treatises for publication, Milton may have heard rumors about secret agreements between Charles II and Louis XIV of France that boded ill for English Protestantism, and speculated with friends about the ultimate purpose of the king's tolerationist gestures. Few knew of the Secret Treaty of Dover, signed on May 22, 1670, in which Charles agreed to join Louis in an invasion of the United Provinces in consideration of a substantial annual monetary subsidy, and also agreed to declare himself a Catholic at some auspicious time, as a first step toward reconciling England with Rome. On December 21, 1671 a bogus treaty was signed, making public the war terms of the secret treaty but not Charles's promise to convert, which would have caused an uproar and possibly open rebellion. On March 17, 1672 Charles joined France in a war against the Dutch – a not unpopular move in a nation still smarting from the shame of the Medway and resentful of Dutch prosperity.

Two days earlier Charles made a gesture toward the other commitment by issuing, as a matter of royal prerogative, a Declaration of Indulgence suspending the penal laws against both Roman Catholics and dissenters and allowing both groups freedom of worship – Roman Catholics in private homes only, dissenters in licensed public meeting houses. He hoped by this to win the support of dissenters and that of moderate Anglicans and Latitudinarians who were prepared to accommodate vast doctrinal differences within the established church if their adherents would give outward acknowledgment to the common ritual and the Thirty-nine Articles. John Hales, for example, had declared his willingness to worship even with Arians.[49] But Charles's gesture stirred up widespread opposition: from parliamentarians who saw the suspension of parliamentary acts as a move toward royal absolutism; from Cavaliers and High Churchmen who saw toleration as treason against the church; and from dissenters who refused to buy their own ease at the cost of unleashing the papal Antichrist in England. "No Popery" agitation was rife in Anglican pulpits and in the press as all sides joined to denounce Roman Catholic "idolatry" and treachery.[50] Dissenters were in some confusion as to whether to take advantage of the Declaration since, as Bishop Gilbert Burnet wryly observed, "Few were so blind as not to see what was aimed at by it."[51] John Salkeld, noting that thousands "shy quite away from it, and dare not own it, nor come near it," sought to reassure his brethren that it was a new manifestation of God's providence to his people and a cause for rejoicing.[52] On the other side, Francis Fullwood, writing as an Anglican to a Presbyterian audience, raised the specter of Independency run riot and the return of popery.[53] Fueling the opposition were the old rumors that papists had been responsible for the Great Fire, fears of a papist takeover when the Roman Catholic Duke of York should ascend the throne, and speculations about the secret Treaty of Dover. Parliament reconvened on February 4, 1673, and on March 8 forced Charles to withdraw his Declaration of Indulgence. On March 19 the Commons passed a Bill "for Ease" of dissenters who were willing to subscribe the doctrinal part of the Thirty-nine Articles and take oaths of Allegiance and Supremacy; it exempted them from penalties and allowed them freedom of public worship in licensed meeting houses. But the Lords scuttled that bill, leaving the issue of dissenters unresolved. Just before its session ended on March 29, parliament passed and the king reluctantly signed the Test Act targetting Roman Catholics: it required all holders of public office, civil or military, to take oaths of Allegiance and Supremacy, to receive the sacrament according to the rites of the Church of England, and formally to renounce transubstantiation.

Milton soon found that his notorious name and works had become an issue in the controversy, in a polemic exchange between his erstwhile acquaintance Samuel Parker – now a major Anlican apologist – and his friend Andrew Marvell. Parker had already published two vigorous defenses of the established church, asserting in Hobbesian terms the absolute authority of the magistrate over religious affairs and denouncing dissenters' arguments for toleration or the rights of conscience;[54] in the summer of 1672 he joined the Anglican clergy's concerted attack on the king's Declaration. In *A Preface Shewing what Grounds there are of Fears and Jealousies of Popery* he ascribes the dangers from popery primarily to the "fanatick party" of Nonconformists whose schisms, dissentions, and blasphemies undermine both church and state, since they are "generally fermented with a Republican leven, and are faln out with Monarchy it self."[55] Marvell replied anonymously to all three treatises in *The Rehearsal Transpros'd,* which takes its name and its witty and scurrilous characterization of Parker as a second Bayes from Buckingham's farce, *The Rehearsal* (1672), in which Dryden was satirized under the name Bayes.[56] Marvell's treatise supports liberty of conscience and the king's policy of indulgence for dissenters, justifying their schism and laying responsibility for it on persecuting bishops. He makes no case for Catholics, save to dismiss the brouhaha about the popish danger as a red herring created by the Anglican establishment. His famous statement that the Good Old Cause "was too good to have been fought for" is preceded by a long passage assigning responsibility for the revolution to Charles I's Laudian advisers who led him to claim absolute prerogative and to exercise power without parliament.[57] His treatise is calculated to separate the king from the Anglican clerics who bid fair to mislead him as they did his father. Answers to Marvell by Parker and his supporters charged that Milton was his source or collaborator. One treatise claims that Marvell plagiarized Milton's *Defensio*: "Come, you had all this out of the Answerer of *Salmasius*."[58] Parker links his satirical treatment of press censorship with the "fustian bumbast" of Milton's *Areopagitica*, and also points out, shrewdly, that the thrust of Marvell's central argument is akin to that of Milton's political tracts:

> If we take away some simpering phrases, and timorous introductions, your Collection will afford as good Precedents for Rebellion and King-killing, as any we meet with in the writings of *J. M.*, in defence of the Rebellion and Murther of the King.[59]

The author of *The Transproser Rehears'd,* perhaps Samuel Butler, links Milton's works with Marvell's satire both in form and matter: "the odds betwixt a *Transproser* and a *Blank Verse Poet,* is not great."[60] His witty barbs are couched in terms that seem intended to draw Milton himself into the quarrel. He attacks *Paradise Lost* for defying the boundaries of rhyme and relying on literary inspiration – analogues, he suggests, of the political rebellion and religious "enthusiasm" of the dissenters. Emphasizing the political–religious–aesthetic linkage, he denounces Milton as a "Leveller," both as a dispenser of political poison and "a *Schismatick* in *Poetry* . . . *nonconformable* in point of Rhyme."[61] Ridiculing the "*blind* Author . . . groping for a beam of *Light*" in his apostrophe to light in Book III, he links that appeal for inspiration to religious enthusiasm – "No doubt but the thought of this *Vital Lamp* lighted a *Christmas* Candle in his brain" – and to Milton's "inventive Divinity, in making *Light* contemporary with its Creator."[62] Marvell, he claims, owes his reprehensible political and ecclesiastical ideas to Milton: "This Doctrine of *killing Kings* . . . if I understand not amiss, is nothing but *Iconoclastes* drawn in Little, and *Defensio Populi Anglicania* in Miniature." Marvell's discourse "of the Liberty of Unlicens'd Printing, p. 6 . . . is little else but Milton's *Areopagitica* in short hand." Marvell concurs "with your *Dear Friend* Mr. *Milton*: who says, that the only true Religion if commanded by the Civil Magistrate, becomes Unchristian, Inhumain, and Barbarous." And Marvell's "Malicious and Disloyal Reflections on the late Kings Raign" indicate that he "clubb'd with" Milton, "made use of *Miltons* pen," and sucked poison from Milton's "most virulent Pamphlets."[63] The author obviously knows the entire corpus of Milton's work; if it is Butler, he may have felt a special animosity for the poet whose sublime, "inspired" epic is the polar opposite of his mock-epic *Hudibras*, which thoroughly debunks all varieties of "enthusiasm" – religious, political, and literary. There is some evidence that Milton penned an answer, but thought better of publishing it.[64]

Sometime before May 6 Marvell published under his own name the second part of the *Rehearsal Transpros'd,* answering Parker's *Reproof.*[65] It reprises his defense of toleration for dissenters, expands his harsh critique of the high Anglican faction in the church, continues the scoffing ridicule of Parker, and includes, in the final pages, a remarkable defense of Milton along with a sharp denial of Milton's influence on or collaboration in his *Rehearsal.* Besides wanting his own authorship acknowledged, Marvell would lose credibility by being associated with Milton's notorious views, so probably we need not take at face value his assertion that he had not been in contact with Milton for over two years. The passage is a rhetorical *tour de force* as well as a testimonial of friendship:

> You resolved to suspect that he had an hand in my former book, wherein, whether you deceive your self or no, you deceive others extreamly. For by chance I had not seen him of two years before; but after I undertook writing, I did more carefully avoid either visiting or sending to him, least I should any way involve him in my consequences. . . . But I take it moreover very ill that you should have so mean an opinion of me, as not to think me competent to write such a simple book as that without any assistance. . . . *J. M.* was, and is, a man of great Learning and Sharpness of wit as any man. It was his misfortune, living in a tumultuous time, to be toss'd on the wrong side, and he writ *Flagrante bello* certain dangerous Treatises. . . . At his Majesties happy Return, *J. M.* did partake, even as you your self did for all your huffing, of his Regal Clemency, and has ever since expiated himself in a retired silence. . . . But he never having in the least provoked you, for you to insult thus over his old age, to traduce him by your *Scaramuccios*, and in your own person, as a School-Master, who was born and hath lived much more ingenuously and Liberally then your self; to have done all this, and lay at last my simple book to his charge, without ever taking care to inform your self better . . . it is inhumanely and inhospitably done.[66]

Milton did however leave his "retired silence" to step forward again as adviser to the nation in regard to toleration, the issue always closest to his heart. His last polemical tract is a small quarto titled *Of True Religion, Haeresie, Schism, Toleration, and What best means may be us'd against the growth of Popery*; he owned it on the title page by that familiar indicator, "The Author *J. M.*"[67] Opposing the "Papal Antichristian Church" to "Our [Protestant] Church," Milton undertakes with consummate rhetorical skill to couch his argument in terms acceptable to the audience he now needs to persuade: moderate Anglicans, latitudinarians, and parliament men. Most likely he began writing sometime after the king's withdrawal of the Declaration of Indulgence (March 8), but did not finish before parliament passed its Test Act and adjourned (March 29), leaving unresolved what might be done about tolerating dissenters. He published it sometime before May 6.[68] No doubt Milton learned from friends and the popular press about the Bills in parliament and the various issues and proposals. But his treatise makes no direct reference to the king's Declaration of Indulgence, nor to the constitutional issue posed by the use of royal prerogative, nor to the Test Act, nor to the Commons Bill for ease to dissenters, nor to the Parker–Marvell controversy and the references to himself. This is reminiscent of his strategy in *Tenure*, when he claimed to be considering the king's trial and execution abstractly, after the fact and without specific reference to it, though he wrote much of the tract while those events were occurring. Here, Milton means his discussion to deal specifically, but covertly, with these various proposals. Unlike Marvell, who welcomed the provision for dissenters in the king's Declaration of Indulgence and ignored the Catholic problem, Milton opposes the terms of that Declaration, treating Catholicism as a clear and present danger for political and religious reasons. He also opposes parliament's approach, offering his own analysis of what should (and should not) be done with Catholics and dissenters.

He urges a far more inclusive toleration of dissenters than the Commons Bill would have allowed, arguing as if from the position of a Protestant Englishman unidentified with any party but drawing support from an (often strained) interpretation of some of the Thirty-nine Articles and from moderate Anglican or latitudinarian voices.[69] As he did in *Of Civil Power*, he again purports to speak for all Protestants in defining true religion as belief and worship founded on scripture, and in rejecting implicit faith, defined as belief "though as the Church believes, against or without express authority of Scripture."[70] Also, as he did in *Of Civil Power*, he adopts a polemic and aesthetic strategy of plainness and brevity, proposing to avoid the "Labyrinth of Councels and Fathers" and cut through the thickets of controversy, focusing on "what is plainer to Common apprehension."[71] But he omits his former arguments based on Christian liberty and the Spirit's illumination as superior to the letter of scripture, to avoid being classed with sectarian "enthusiasts." For the same reason he does not mention the Quakers among the sects and opinions deserving of toleration.

As in *Of Civil Power*, Milton defines heresy as religion that relies on extra-scriptural sources of authority, restricting it thereby to Roman Catholicism. Any errors the several Protestant sects hold are not heresies and do not involve matters essential to salvation. In a neat rhetorical ploy he co-opts the Anglican argument about accepting "things indifferent" and applies it to doctrinal differences most would think far from indifferent, including several of his own heterodoxies – Arianism, Arminianism, and Anabaptism. He does not impute any error to these, as he does to some mainstream doctrines, and he makes a special point of defending Arians:

> The Lutheran holds Consubstantiation; an error indeed, but not mortal. The Calvinist is taxt with Predestination, and to make God the Author of sin; not with any dishonourable thought of God, but it may be over zealously asserting his absolute power, not without plea of Scripture. The Anabaptist is accus'd of Denying Infants their right to Baptism; again they say, they deny nothing but what the Scripture

> denies them. The Arian and Socinian are charg'd to dispute against the Trinity: they affirm to believe the Father, Son, and Holy Ghost, according to Scripture, and the Apostolic Creed; as for terms of Trinity, Triunity, Coessentiality, Tripersonality, and the like, they reject them as Scholastic Notions, not to be found in Scripture, which by a general Protestant Maxim is plain and perspicuous abundantly to explain its own meaning in the properest words. . . . The *Arminian* lastly is condemn'd for setting up free will against free grace; but that Imputation he disclaims in all his writings, and grounds himself largly upon Scripture only.[72]

He agrees that the latitudinarian program of comprehending various sects and doctrines within the established church is possible "if they can agree in the right administration of that wherin they Communicate, keeping their other Opinions to themselves." But he rejects their proposals enjoining obedience to the church in "things indifferent," reiterating the classic Puritan argument that "in Religion nothing is indifferent," and that nothing must be added to the word of God (*CPW* VIII, 422, 428). He insists instead on full and equal toleration of all Protestants either within or alongside any establishment, allowing them "on all occasions to give account of their Faith, either by Arguing, Preaching in their several Assemblies, Publick writing, and the freedom of Printing" (426).

The second half of the treatise treats Roman Catholicism in terms generally accordant with Milton's longstanding views: Catholics fall outside the toleration claimed for true religion grounded upon scripture; Catholics may be suppressed when politically dangerous though not for specifically religious reasons; and Catholic idolatry may be suppressed as palpably evil by the light of nature and therefore within the magistrate's domain.[73] The important difference here is Milton's extensive treatment of the dangers, political and religious, from Roman Catholicism, which, with a crypto-Catholic king on the throne and a professedly Catholic king in the offing, he sees as a growing peril. In *Of Civil Power*, addressed to a securely Protestant magistracy, Milton did not formally object to Catholic worship in private, demanding only that the "furniture" of idolatry – the mass, religious images used in worship, priests – be removed from public places. Now he argues for removing private idolatry also, citing scripture texts indicating God's abhorrence of it, though he does not urge invasive and general searches for idolatrous practice.[74] His specific target here is the king's Declaration, which by allowing private Catholic worship would legitimize the Catholic presence at court and in other high places.

Milton does not resurrect popish plots and bloody treasons, the scare tactics common in the "No Popery" literature.[75] Nor does he mention parliament's punative Test Act. While he saw Catholics as a political danger and wanted them out of places of power, he surely thought it abhorrent to God to require taking communion as a gesture of outward conformity. In *Of Civil Power* he had insisted that "the outward performance . . . of religious and holy duties especialy by prophane and licentious persons, is a dishonoring rather then a worshiping of God" (*CPW* VII,

267–8). He also declares that fines and corporal punishment of Catholics do not accord with "the Clemency of the Gospel more then what appertains to the security of the State" (*CPW* VIII, 431) – thereby distancing himself from vengeful Anglican clerics and parliamentarians who imposed such penalties on those who refuse the Test. Those who act against "the security of the state" can of course be punished. In place of penal laws, Milton proposes free inquiry and amendment of life. Echoing *Areopagitica*, he urges his countrymen to defend against popery by diligent study of scripture and by allowing the free circulation and reading (at least by the learned) of books from all manner of men – "Anabaptists, Arians, Arminians, & Socinians" – so as to stimulate active rather than implicit faith. And echoing the *Defensio*, he urges them to turn away from "Pride, Luxury, Drunkenness, Whoredom, Cursing, Swearing, bold and open Atheism," vices which "oft times bring the slight professors of true Religion, to gross Idolatry" (437–40). This analysis invites the conclusion that it is not the toleration of dissenters, but the vices notoriously associated with the Restoration court that will subject the nation to the "worst of superstitions, and the heaviest of all Gods Judgements, Popery" (440). This emphasis on moral and cultural transformation reprises Milton's familiar linkage of inner slavery and national slavery, idolatry and servility. *Of True Religion* did not elicit much response, though an anonymous letter two years later stated that "J. Milton has said more for it [toleration] in two elegant sheets of true religion, heresy and schism, than all the pre[lates] can refute in 7 years."[76]

Soon after this, Milton prepared a new edition of his shorter poems; the small octavo, identifying the author as "Mr John Milton," was published sometime before November 24.[77] He kept the same format as the 1645 edition – a two-part book that retained all the poems published in 1645 in the same general order and even the satiric Greek epigram on William Marshall, though not his despised engraving. He added 22 new English poems and two in Latin, supplied a Table of Contents for both parts, and ended the volume with the treatise *Of Education*. Hitherto unpublished early poems include the elegy "On the Death of a fair Infant" for his young niece, "At a Vacation Exercise," the translation of Horace's "Pyrra Ode" (published with its Latin original so as to display the excellence of the translation), and, at the end of the Latin Book of Elegies, "Apologus de Rustico & Hero" (A Fable of a Peasant and his Landlord) which points a moral against greed.[78] New post-1645 poems include several sonnets, the psalm sequences he translated in 1648 and 1653, and the Latin verse epistle to Rouse.[79] He could not of course publish his sonnets to Fairfax, Cromwell, and Vane, or his second sonnet to Cyriack Skinner, voicing pride in the service for liberty that cost his eyesight.[80]

This volume registers Milton's very different status and authorial self-presentation in 1673, by contrast with the 1645 *Poems*.[81] There is now no prefatory matter in the English section: the poet of *Paradise Lost* needs and wants no introduction from a bookseller, no reference to his close association with the royalist musician Lawes, no reference in *A Maske* to the Egerton family (the Elder Brother had become a staunch royalist), and no letter from Wotton addressing Milton as an unknown, novice poet. Also, *Comus* is not now set off as a separate section but follows immediately after *Lycidas*. With a few exceptions such as the tribute to Lawes which needs the name to make sense of the praise, Milton excises titles that had linked poems to particular individuals or situations that will not mean much, or will be offputting, to a 1670s audience. He retains a few dates, including the sometimes erroneous indicators of his age to mark his juvenilia, but, as before, his organization owes more to genre, desired self-presentation, and politics than to chronology. The English part now ends with Milton's translation of Psalm 88, whose final lines make an appropriate envoy for Milton, almost 65 years old and witness to many deaths of family and friends:

> Lover and friend thou hast remov'd
>   And sever'd from me far.
> They fly me now whom I have lov'd,
>   And as in darkness are.

The Latin section ends, not with the Diodati elegy as before, but with the elegant ode to Rouse, with its structure of three strophes, antistrophes, and epodes clearly designated. It retains the date, January 23, 1646, when this poem presented the first edition of Milton's *Poems* to the Bodleian, to be enjoyed by future readers; now it can offer this second edition to those readers directly.

When this edition was in preparation, the Catholic crisis was escalating. Charles II's Roman Catholic brother James, heir apparent to the throne, had resigned his post as Lord High Admiral in June, 1673 rather than comply with the Test Act, and on September 30 had married the Italian Catholic princess, Mary of Modena, opening up the prospect of Catholic sons and a settled Catholic succession.[82] Milton's new volume offers some covert testimony in these circumstances. As before, the first poem in the English section is the ode "On the Morning of Christ's Nativity," with its forthright claim to prophetic voice; and it is followed by the two schoolboy psalms calling for God's vengeance on tyrants. *Lycidas* retains its headnote referring to the poet's prophecy of "the ruine of our corrupted Clergie then in their height," inviting comparisons with the post-Restoration Anglican clergy who "shove away the worthy bidden guest" even more fiercely, and with the greatly increased danger from the papist "grim Woolf." Only two sonnets retain titles that point to specific occasions: "On the late Massacre in Piemont" recalls that notorious example of Roman Catholic treachery and persecution; and the sonetto cauduto, "On the new forcers of Conscience under the Long Parliament," tacitly invites comparison with the present parliament's forcing of conscience. The English segment concludes with Milton's two psalm sequences but reverses their chronological order. The more meditative group from 1653, Psalms 1–8, is placed first; Psalms 80–8, written during the anxious months of the Second Civil War (1648), are given the climactic position. They call down God's vengeance on the prideful wicked and the furious foes that – now as then – threaten the Lord's "dear Saints" on every side.[83] Milton published *Of Education* as the final item in this volume, calling attention to its addressee – "To Master *Samuel Hartlib* – and its composition "above twenty Yeares since." This was his only interregnum prose work apparently innocuous enough to republish, but it also accords with his intense focus on education in these last years.

During the final two years of his life failing health from attacks of gout led Milton to make further arrangements about his unpublished papers. At about the time of Richard's succession, he had obtained a collection of personal and diplomatic letters and addresses to Oliver Cromwell, which he now turned over to Thomas Ellwood for safekeeping and publication at some future time.[84] At the suggestion of the Danish diplomatic resident, Milton had copies made of the letters of state he himself wrote as Latin Secretary and offered them to the bookseller Brabazon Aylmer, probably early in 1674.[85] He added 31 of his private letters written from 1625 to 1656. Aylmer's preface to the small octavo he subsequently published sometime before May 26, 1674 explains that he was refused permission to publish the state letters and thought that the private letters would make too slim a volume, so he negotiated with the author through a mutual friend, to see if he had "any little work perhaps laid aside" to fill out the volume.[86] That friend, whoever he was, elicited the seven college orations known as *Prolusions*; Milton perhaps kept – or chose to publish – these particular orations because many of them engage issues of education.[87] Aylmer hoped that "however youthful they are . . . they will be no less salable for me than they were not unpleasing formerly to their hearers when they were recited";[88] evidently Milton's reputation was now such that Aylmer could expect his private letters and youthful orations to be "salable." At about the same time, probably, Milton turned over to Aylmer his *Brief History of Moscovia*, but it was not published until 1682. Aylmer's preface to that work claims that Milton wrote it in his own hand "before he lost his sight" and offered it to Aylmer "sometime before his death," but that he postponed publication in the hope of finding "some other suitable Piece of the same Authour's to have join'd with it."[89] Aylmer seems to have thought there might be a cache of Milton writings yet to surface.

Daniel Skinner's association with Milton may have begun during 1673 or 1674. In a letter to Pepys written after his efforts to publish Milton's state papers and *De Doctrina Christiana* landed him in trouble, Skinner sharply dissociates himself from Milton's views but seems to suggest that he enjoyed for a time the kind of relationship Milton had with some other young men – some tutoring in exchange for services as an amanuensis:

> I happen'd to be acquainted with Milton in his lifetime, (which out of mere love to learning I procur'd, and noe other concerns ever pass'd betwixt us but a great desire and ambition of some of his learning,) I am and ever was . . . farr from being in the least tainted with any of his principles.[90]

Since Milton's state papers came into his hands, he may have been the amanuensis who prepared them first for Aylmer and then, when Aylmer was refused permission to publish them, Milton may have asked Skinner to prepare them, along with *De Doctrina Christiana*, to send to Elzivir in Holland.[91] I think it likely that Skinner began copying *De Doctrina Christiana* in the several months before Milton's death, completing by that time the 194 consecutive pages that are in his hand.[92] Given Milton's efforts in these years to arrange for the publication of all his manuscripts that were or could be soon finished, he surely made similar plans regarding "his best and most precious possession." Evidently he could not bring to completion the Latin *Thesaurus* which he had been compiling for decades; that manuscript is lost, but it formed a substantial component of a Latin dictionary published in 1693.[93]

In the summer of 1674 Milton was given, probably by some Whiggish or republican friend, a copy of an official Latin document announcing the election of a new King of Poland, Jan Sobieski. He translated it and Aylmer published it, most likely in July.[94] Milton omitted the long lists of names and titles of the Polish electors so as to highlight issues of great interest to him and to England at that moment: an elective monarchy, the choice of a superlatively worthy hero replete with all military and civic virtues, the conduct of free elections in accordance with the country's laws, the happy avoidance thereby of the "chances of an Interreign," and the new king's election "without his own Ambition, or the envy of corrupted Liberty." Of major importance is the guarantee of the people's liberties by the king's special oath:

> We will anoint and inaugurate him; Yet so as he shall hold fast and observe first of all the Rights, Immunities both Ecclesiastical and Secular, granted and given to us by his Ancestor of Blessed memory; as also these Law's which we our Selves, in the time of this present and former interriegn, according to the Right of our liberty, and better preservation of the Commonwealth have established. (*CPW* VIII, 451, *Declaration*, 11)

While Milton had some continuing interest in Poland as a bastion of Socinianism, he surely undertook this translation because the prospect of a Roman Catholic succession to the English throne was prompting some to think seriously about breaking the hereditary succession.[95] Under cover of this Polish document Milton resurrects, by implication, something of the theory of *Tenure* regarding the people's right to choose and change their government as they see fit, and also the idea of a covenant binding the king to respect the people's liberties. But Milton did not think it prudent to sign his name to the translation, which might do its work better if not identified with a notorious republican.

Sometime in 1673 or early 1674, Milton began preparing a new edition of *Paradise Lost* in twelve books, by dividing Books VII and X. He added little new material: three lines of transition to the new Book VIII, five lines to the new Book XII, and one added line in three other places. Also, the Arguments were revised to suit the new arrangement, several words and phrases throughout were altered or changed, and most of the errata from the first edition were corrected. Of the nearly nine hundred other changes in typography, spelling, and punctuation, it is hard to know whether most are by Milton or by the compositor, and therefore hard to judge how much revising he actually did.[96] By the change to twelve books he placed his epic securely in the central Virgilian epic tradition, having decided, it seems, to reclaim that tradition and contest its appropriation by the likes of Davenant and Dryden and the courtly heroic. That decision may have been prompted by Dryden's visit sometime in this period. As reported by a contemporary,

> Mr *Dryden* . . . went with Mr. *Waller* in Company to make a visit to Mr. *Milton*, and desire his Leave for putting his *Paradise lost* into Rhime for the Stage. Well, Mr. *Dryden*, says *Milton*, it seems you have a mind to *Tagg* my Points, and you have my Leave to *Tagg 'em*, but some of 'em are so Awkward and Old Fashion'd that I think you had as good leave 'em as you found 'em.[97]

The anecdote displays Milton's wry humor as he alludes to the rhyme/blank verse controversy in terms of fashion, rhyme being like the foppish fad of wearing ribbons "tagged" with bits of metal at the end. Why did Milton agree to Dryden's request? Perhaps because he hoped that those who saw the stage version might be led back to his original, much as we might be led by a film to read the better book. Also, Milton valued old friends and acquaintances: Dryden had been his associate in Cromwell's Secretariat and at least an occasional visitor according to Milton's widow who added the comment that Milton thought him "no poet, but a good rimist."[98] Dryden also indicates that the two authors had some literary discussions: "*Milton* has acknowledg'd to me, that *Spencer* was his Original."[99]

Dryden seems to have intended his rhymed drama or "opera" to serve as part of the festivities for the Duke of York's bride Mary of Modena, but the unpopularity of that match made grand festivities unwise and it was never produced. In his preface Dryden claimed that it had been written in a month – it was registered on April 17, 1674 but published only in 1677[100] – and that "many hundred Copies" were dispersed in manuscript. He probably gave one of them to Milton as a courtesy. Milton would not have liked it. Not only were his soaring lines "tamed" and bounded by rhyme, not only do the angelic and the human characters lack psychological depth, but the politics are very different: Dryden divides Satan's speeches among the fallen angels, so that the entire community (called a "senate" or the "States-General of Hell") plots the continuing rebellion against heaven and the seduction of Adam and Eve. In Milton, rebellion is the act of a would-be usurping monarch, Satan; in Dryden it is the act of a diabolic Long Parliament rising against a Divine King.

Milton's new edition of *Paradise Lost*, published around July 6 by Simmons, offered a potent rejoinder.[101] The book is a nicely printed octavo, though not so handsome as the first edition; it contains an engraving made by William Dolle from the Faithorne engraving, as well as two highly laudatory commendatory poems. The first, in Latin, titled "Paradisum Amissam Summi Poetae" (On the Paradise Lost of John Milton Consummate Poet) and signed S. B. M. D., is generally attributed to the court physician Samuel Barrow, who was evidently Milton's friend. Barrow praises especially the sublimity and scope of Milton's poem – "the story of all things," all places, and all times.[102] He was especially impressed by the episode closest to classical epic, the War in Heaven, which he thought awe-inspiring for its magnificent warriors, grand battles, and especially Messiah's wondrous chariot. He did not recognize, or at any rate did not discuss, Milton's radical revision of the classical epic, but he ends by proclaiming Milton's resounding victory over all ancient and modern epic poets: "Yield, ye writers of Rome, yield, ye writers of Greece . . . Whoso shall read this poem will think that Homer sang only of frogs, Virgil only of gnats."

The second poetic commendation, signed A. M. and titled "On Paradise Lost," is a brilliant rhetorical performance by Milton's good friend Marvell, who casts himself as a skeptic won by degrees to recognize the sublimity of Milton's achievement. Amazed, like Barrow, at the "vast Design," the intent to treat "Heav'n, Hell, Earth, Chaos, All," he first thought Milton might, like a spiteful Samson, pull down the whole edifice of religion: "That he would ruine (for I saw him strong) / The sacred Truths to Fable and old Song" (2–8). Then, thinking better of the project, he feared Milton could not bring it off, that he would perplex or trivialize these matters of faith. Then, with snide reference to Dryden's project, he predicts that "some less skilful hand" would seek fame by "ill imitating" Milton, presuming, "the whole Creations day / To change in Scenes, and show it in a Play" (18–22). But that, he concludes, would be folly, for Milton's perfection is such "that no room is here for Writers left, / But to detect their Ignorance or Theft" (29–30). Indeed, Milton's art and sublimity prove him to be inspired. He is not a blind Samson wrecking the Temple to revenge his eyes, but a blind prophet like Tiresias:

Thou singst with so much gravity and ease;
And above humane flight dost soar aloft
With Plume so strong, so equal, and so soft,
The Bird nam'd from that Paradise you sing
So never flaggs, but always keeps on Wing.
   Where couldst thou words of such a compass find?
Where furnish such a vast expence of mind?
Just Heav'n thee like *Tiresias* to requite
Rewards with Prophesie thy loss of sight. (36–44)

Marvell claims for Milton the religious inspiration that the Anglican establishment so abhorred in the dissenters and the poetic exaltation that Dryden and court culture sought to contain by rhyme. He brings the issue home to Dryden (Bayes) in the concluding lines, making him exemplify the folly of trying to contain genius and inspiration within conventional norms. Then, wryly, he includes his own tribute among the fashionable poems "tagged" with rhyming points[103] that Milton so far surpasses. Marvell offers a fitting tribute to Milton, and in doing so defends individuality and inspiration wherever found:[104]

Well mightst thou scorn thy Readers to allure
With tinkling Rhime, of thy own sense secure;
While the *Town-Bayes* writes all the while and spells,
And like a Pack-horse tires without his Bells:
Their Fancies like our Bushy-pointes appear,
The Poets tag them, we for fashion wear.
I too transported by the Mode offend,
And where I meant to Praise thee must Commend.
Thy Verse created like thy Theme sublime,
In Number, Weight, and Measure, needs not Rhime. (45–54)

"With New Acquist Of True Experience:" *Paradise Regained and Samson Agonistes*

Milton's last major poems, published together as a diptych, continue the educational project of *Paradise Lost*: to create imaginative experiences that will help readers gain moral and political knowledge, virtue, and inner freedom – the "paradise within" that is also the necessary precondition for gaining liberty in the public sphere (plate 17). These poems enact the two forms of heroism pointed to in *Paradise Lost*: "Patience and Heroic Martyrdom" by Jesus tempted in the desert, and the defeat of "worldly strong" by one "deemd weak," the blinded Samson (*PL* 9.32; 12.567–8). Both the brief epic and the classical tragedy portray an isolated hero's hard intellectual struggle in dialogues and debates with a tempter or series of tempters. And for both heroes, the right understanding of themselves, of their different callings, and of a large spectrum of moral and political issues, must precede the fulfillment of those roles. *Paradise Regained* is concerned primarily with the realm of attitudes and choices, *Samson Agonistes* with the realm of public duties and political action. Like *Paradise Lost*, both poems are deeply engaged with contemporary issues as well as with enduring human passions, desires, and fears.

Paradise Regained is a complement, not a sequel to *Paradise Lost*. Milton's only major sources are the few short verses in Matthew 4:1–11, Mark 1:12–13, and Luke 4:1–13 and the exegetical tradition pertaining to them; partly for dramatic effect Milton followed the Luke sequence (stones, kingdoms, tower) rather than the more often cited Matthew sequence. From this slender basis, he produced a narrative in four books, 2,070 blank-verse lines. Contemporary readers were no doubt surprised, as some modern critics have been, by Milton's choice of the temptation in the wilderness as subject rather than the Passion–Crucifixion narrative, and with his portrait of an austere, naysaying Jesus who discounts and refuses all worldly pleasures and goods.[105] But this choice of subject follows naturally from Milton's belief that self-knowledge and self-rule are preconditions for any worthy public action in the world. The temptation episode allows Milton to present Jesus's moral and intellectual trials as a higher epic heroism, as a model for right knowing and choosing, and as a creative and liberating force in history. As a political gesture, it allowed him to develop a model of nonviolent yet active and forceful resistance to the Restoration church and state.[106] Also, this choice contests royalist representations of Charles I's trial and execution as a martyrdom imitative of Christ's Passion and death by presenting Jesus enacting the essential meaning of the term martyr – a witness to the truth.[107] The unmoved Jesus standing firm against every temptation and trial invites association, not with Charles the royal martyr, but with Puritan dissidents subjected to harassment and persecution. The Jesus–Satan debates can also lead readers to think rightly about kingship, prophecy, idolatry, millenarian zeal, the proper uses of civil power, the place of secular learning, and the abuses of pleasure, glory, and power. Significantly, the poem's structure gives primary attention to the Messiah's kingdom and its relation to secular monarchies and their values, giving over Books Two and Three, and much of Book Four, to that issue. Milton's Jesus is the projection of his author in a teaching role, as he undertakes,

> By winning words to conquer willing hearts,
> And make perswasion do the work of fear;
> At least to try, and teach the erring Soul
> Not wilfully mis-doing, but unware
> Misled. (1.222–6)

In the epic proposition and invocation the Miltonic Bard, who in *Paradise Lost* had explored in four extended Proems his authorial anxieties, difficulties, and choices, now adopts a curiously recessive and objective stance throughout. The opening lines, the only time in the poem when he speaks of himself or invokes the inspiring Spirit, are marked by an easy, confident tone:

> I who e're while the happy Garden sung,
> By one mans disobedience lost, now sing
> Recover'd Paradise to all mankind,
> By one mans firm obedience fully tri'd
> Through all temptation, and the Tempter foil'd
> In all his wiles, defeated and repuls't,
> And *Eden* rais'd in the wast Wilderness.
> Thou spirit who ledst this glorious Eremite

Into the Desert, his Victorious Field
Against the Spiritual Foe, and broughtst him thence
By proof the undoubted Son of God, inspire,
As thou art wont, my prompted Song else mute,
And bear through highth or depth of natures bounds
With prosperous wing full summ'd to tell of deeds
Above Heroic, though in secret done,
And unrecorded left through many an Age,
Worthy t'have not remain'd so long unsung. (1.1–17)

The line "inspire, / As thou art wont" suggests that his new confidence stems from his experience of the Spirit's aid in his long epic and his sense of that aid continuing in this "prompted" song, which would be "else mute." It may owe something as well to the greater familiarity of the new locale – the fallen world of history, not the eternal places. Here the Miltonic Bard records what happens, what is said, what seems to be the case, but he does not often comment on speeches and scenes as he did in *Paradise Lost*, having given over the role of authoritative critic and judge to his hero, Jesus.

The epic proposition makes the rather startling claim that this poem treats a vastly more noble and heroic subject than *Paradise Lost*, whose hero conquers his enemy, regains the regions lost to Satan, and establishes his own realm – in this, more like Aeneas than like Adam. These opening lines allude to the verses, then widely accepted as genuine, that introduce the *Aeneid* in most Renaissance editions, supposedly announcing Virgil's movement from pastoral and georgic to an epic subject.[108] That echo and the reference to *Paradise Lost* as a poem about a happy garden suggest, with witty audacity, that Milton has now, like Virgil, graduated from pastoral apprentice-work to the true epic subject, the spiritual warfare and victory of Jesus. Also, several allusions to the Book of Job suggest that Milton is now carrying out a poetic project he imagined a quarter of a century earlier in the *Reason of Church-Government*, when he proposed Virgil and Tasso as models for a long epic and the Book of Job as a "brief model" (*CPW* I, 813). This poem is in part shaped by the exegetical tradition that interpreted Job as epic, and also by the long tradition of biblical "brief epics" in three or four books, in Latin and in the vernacular literatures.[109]

Milton reworked and adapted epic conventions and topics to his unusual subject. He transformed the central epic episode, the single combat of hero and antagonist, into a three-day verbal battle, a poem-long intellectual and moral struggle. The poem begins *in medias res* with Christ's baptism. There are two Infernal Councils (held in mid-air rather than Hell because Satan has now gained that region), and a Council in Heaven in which God prophesies his Son's immediate and ultimate victory over Satan. Also, there are two transformed epic recitals – Christ's meditation about his youthful experiences and aspirations, and Mary's reminiscenses about the prophecies and promises attending the hero's early life – as well as a transformed prophetic vision in which the hero, instead of viewing his *own* destined kingdom as Aeneas does, sees and rejects all the kingdoms that are not his. There is an epic catalogue of the kingdoms of the World displayed to Jesus; a martial pageant of the Parthian warriors; and a few striking epic similes in Book Four, in which Jesus assaulted by Satan is compared to a winepress vainly attacked by buzzing bees, to a solid rock against which waves ineffectually beat, to Hercules conquering Antaeus, and to Oedipus overthrowing the Sphinx. Milton sets up the Jobean "brief epic" frame at the outset, as Satan in the character of "Adversary" wandering to and fro upon the earth comes upon another assembly, Christ's baptism, at which a superlative hero is exalted by God as his champion.[110] Like *Paradise Lost* this poem also incorporates other genres into the epic frame: continuous dialogue in which Satan's inflated epic rhetoric is met by Jesus's spare answers; a pastoral grove where Satan presents a sensuous banquet and also the more refined and enchanting "Olive Groves of Academe"; a romance topos in which Jesus reprises the conventional situation of a young knight who meets his first tests in the wilderness before being recognized as champion or king; and angelic hymns at the beginning and end of the temptation sequence. But this poem eschews the soaring, eloquent style of *Paradise Lost* for one appropriate to this subject: more restrained, dialogic, and tense with the parry and thrust of intellectual exchange.

Milton's Arianism is central to this poem, allowing for some drama in the debate–duel between Jesus and Satan even though the reader knows that Jesus will not fall. In *Paradise Lost* Milton portrayed the Son in heaven as mutable and as sharing only such part of the divine knowledge and power as God devolved upon him at certain times. Here he portrays the incarnate Christ in accordance with *De Doctrina Christiana's* treatment of *kenosis* as a real emptying out of the divine knowledge and power the Son exercised in heaven, so that he is "liable to sin" and subject to death in both natures (*CPW* VI, 438–40). The poem opens with Jesus in that situation: God describes him to the angels in almost Socinian terms: they now and men hereafter are to learn from the temptation episode "From what consummate vertue I have chose / This perfect Man, by merit call'd my Son, / To earn Salvation for the Sons of men" (1.165–7). Then, as Jesus withstands the several temptations, he gains, apparently by divine illumination, an ever more complete understanding of who he is and what he is to do.

The question of identity is the primary focus for the poem's tension, centering on the title "Son of God" bestowed in a special way upon Jesus at his baptism. As Satan later remarks, that title "bears no single sence." Revealing some feelings of sibling rivalry with Jesus, Satan declares, "The Son of God I also am, or was, / And if I was, I am; relation stands; / All men are Sons of God," and then indicates that one purpose of his temptations is to discover "In what degree or meaning thou art call'd / The Son of God" (4.514–20). In his first council a puzzled Satan recognizes that Jesus shows some glimpses of his Father's glory, but he cannot imagine that this humble man is one with the Son in Heaven: "His first-begot we know, and sore have felt, /

When his fierce thunder drove us to the deep; / Who this is we must learn" (1.89–91). Jesus's meditation as he enters the desert shows that he also has no recollection of his former state. He has learned what he knows of himself as the promised Messiah from his mother's testimony and from reading the Prophets: that his birth was miraculous, that he is "King of *Israel* born" and will sit on David's throne; and that he is to work redemption for humankind through "many a hard assay even to the death" (1.254–66). But he does not yet understand the full meaning of the prophetic metaphors, or of the divine Sonship proclaimed at his baptism, or just what his "God-like office now mature" will entail (1.188). He is conscious of his limited human knowledge, being led "to what intent / I learn not yet, perhaps I need not know," but also of the guidance and ongoing illumination of the Spirit: "For what concerns my knowledge God reveals" (1.291–3). These uncertainties sometimes make for moments of emotional distress, as when the hungry Jesus experiences a hunger dream in the desert and questions, "Where will this end" (2.245). Or when Satan "inly rack't" voices his psychic desperation to have it over with, even though it means his destruction: "I would be at the worst; worst is my Port, / My harbour and my ultimate repose, / The end I would attain, my final good" (3.209–11).

In this poem Milton portrays a Satan who has degenerated from what he was in *Paradise Lost*; evil has further coarsened his nature, though he is still cunning, even brilliant. His advantage in the temptations is his direct observation of human motives and human weakness throughout history, which Jesus knows only through wide reading. But more than compensating for that is the divine illumination Jesus merits, leading him to understand the spiritual meaning of the scriptural metaphors and prophecies which the literal-minded Satan cannot fathom. The poem's action turns on a central paradox: Satan appears to do all the acting, dancing around Jesus in a fever of motion, trying one approach and one argument after another, while Jesus remains impassive and unmoved. Yet it is in Jesus's consciousness that real change takes place, as he progresses by somewhat uneven stages to full understanding, whereas Satan cannot resolve the puzzle about Jesus's Sonship and mission until his utter defeat and fall from the tower force realization upon him.

Milton creates epic scope in his brief epic by making the temptation episode encapsulate past and future history through typological reference and allusion. God sets these terms, describing Jesus to the angels as an "abler" Job and a second Adam who will win "by Conquest what the first man lost / By fallacy surpriz'd," and build a new Eden (1.151–5). God also declares that he is to lay down in the wilderness the "rudiments" (157) of his great warfare, epitomizing there the exercise of his office throughout history. The debates between Jesus and Satan make continual reference to commonly accepted Old Testament and classical figures of Jesus and the functions of his office – Moses, Elijah, Gideon, David, Job, Socrates. To these, Satan proposes counter-models – Balaam, Antipater, Caesar, Alexander, the schools of Greek philosophy – or else insists that Jesus must conform himself exactly to his types and thereby limit himself by the mandate of the past. Satan's temptations presume the classical notion of history as cyclical repetition – what has been must be again – whereas Jesus must learn to fulfill and subsume the types so as to redefine history as process and re-creation.[111]

The poem's complex structure develops several interrelated paradigms. At one level Jesus is the "second Adam" withstanding the temptations to which Adam and Eve succumbed, which were linked in the exegetical tradition of the "Triple Equation" to the root sins of humankind enumerated in 1 John 2:16: sensuality (in Protestant versions, distrust), avarice or ambition, and vainglory.[112] That paradigm is explored especially in the first temptation (distrust), and in the first three segments of the second: the sensual banquet, wealth and kingship, and glory. Related to this are the three kinds of lives Plato defines in *The Republic*: the sensual life, the active life, and (in the Athens temptation) the contemplative life. Also, temptations are addressed to the three functions of Christ's office: prophet or teacher (the first temptation); king, i.e. ruler and defender of his church and people (the offers of Israel, Parthia, Rome, and Athens); and priest, i.e. redemptive sacrifice and mediator (the storm and tower temptations).[113] Into all the temptations Milton inserts bold commentary on fraught contemporary issues.

Satan offers the first temptation – to turn stones into bread – in the guise of a shepherd "Following, as seem'd, the quest of some stray Ewe" (1.315), a parody of Jesus's role as good shepherd. The issues involve distrust – accepting the guidance of Satan – and also Jesus's role as prophet or teacher. Satan asks Jesus to accept him formally as a prophet (he gives oracles to the gentiles) and to grant him continued access, as God allowed the reprobate Balaam to prophesy and allows hypocrites and atheists to conduct religious rites at his altars. If Jesus were to accept him on these terms he would sanction that Puritan *bete noir*, the association of holy and profane together in the established church and the abuses it gave rise to both in the Laudian church and in the Restoration:

> Thy Father, who is holy, wise, and pure,
> Suffers the Hypocrite or Atheous Priest
> To tread his Sacred Courts, and minister
> About his Altar, handling holy things,
> Praying or vowing, and vouchsaf'd his voice
> To *Balaam* Reprobate, a Prophet yet
> Inspir'd; disdain not such access to me. (1.486–92)

But Jesus pointedly refuses to sanction the parish principle and those abuses – merely observing that God, for the time being, permits them: "I bid not nor forbid; do as thou find'st / Permission from above; thou canst not more" (1.495–6). Claiming his own role as prophet, Jesus asserts the Miltonic – and radical sectarian – principle of the entire sufficiency of the internal Spirit's teaching, which makes authorized ministers superfluous:[114]

God hath now sent his living Oracle
Into the World, to teach his final will,
And sends his Spirit of Truth henceforth to dwell
In pious Hearts, an inward Oracle
To all truth requisite for men to know. (1.460–4)

The issues in the long kingdoms temptation are focused by the expectation on all sides that Jesus will soon become an earthly king. Satan expects God to advance him in "the head of Nations . . . / Their King, their Leader, and Supream on Earth" (1.98–9). Jesus at first thought himself called "To rescue *Israel* from the *Roman* yoke, / Then to subdue and quell o're all the earth / Brute violence and proud Tyrannick pow'r, / Till truth were freed, and equity restor'd" (1.217–20). And the apostles, anticipating millenarian Puritans, imagine the moment at hand for the Messiah's kingly reign in Israel:

Now, now, for sure, deliverance is at hand,
The Kingdom shall to *Israel* be restor'd: . . .
  God of *Israel,*
Send thy Messiah forth, the time is come;
Behold the Kings of the Earth how they oppress
Thy chosen, to what highth thir pow'r unjust
They have exalted, and behind them cast
All fear of thee, arise and vindicate
Thy Glory, free thy people from thir yoke. (2.35–48)

Countering these expectations, Jesus clarifies what his kingship is to be in history. First, it is the kingdom within "Which every wise and vertuous man attains" (2.468): by his temperance and ethical knowledge Jesus defines that kingdom and offers a trenchent critique of the values and practices of secular monarchies. Second, it is his own spiritual kingdom, the invisible church, which he comes by stages to understand and explain. Finally, it is the millennial rule he will exercise in the distant future, over all realms and monarchs.

Satan offers the kingdoms temptations in the guise of a courtier bred "in City, or Court, or Palace" dispensing needful worldly advice to the rustic Jesus. First, a lavish and deceptive banquet invites the now-hungry Jesus to intemperance by its abundance of sensuous pleasures: "Alas how simple, to these Cates compar'd, / Was that crude Apple that diverted *Eve* (2.348–9). The scene evokes extravagant banquets at the Stuart courts: a table "richly spred, in regal mode"; dishes piled high with the noblest "Beasts of chase, or Fowl of game"; strings and woodwinds playing "Harmonious Airs" (2.340–62), and sexual objects suited to every preference – ladies fairer than those who tempted Romance knights and "tall stripling youths" fairer than Ganymede. Despite Satan's disclaimer, this banquet contains foods forbidden under the Law, to force Jesus either to accept those dietary prohibitions or dispense with them before the appointed time. Also, though presented as nature's free offering, it is quite literally the Devil's table, the very symbol of idolatry. Side-stepping all these intellectual traps, Jesus refuses the banquet as the gift of an evil giver, and lays claim himself, as nature's Lord, to all nature's goods.

To Satan's offer of riches as a necessary means to accomplish great deeds and gain a kingdom, Jesus responds with an extended critique of monarchy based in part on Plato and Aristotle. To Satan's examples of wealthy kings he opposes several Hebrew judges and Roman republican leaders who rose from poverty to greatness,[115] as well as "the shepherd lad" David (439) who became Israel's king. Rejecting "with like aversion" both riches and realms (457), he restates Milton's core political principle, that rule over the self is a better kingship and that without it a ruler is unfit to govern others: "Subject himself to Anarchy within, / Or lawless passions in him which he serves" (2.471–2). Like Aristotle, Jesus claims that it is more magnanimous to give or relinquish a kingdom than to assume one,[116] and then asserts the greater worthiness of his own spiritual kingship:

> But to guide Nations in the way of truth
> By saving Doctrine, and from errour lead
> To know, and knowing worship God aright,
> Is yet more Kingly, this attracts the Soul,
> Governs the inner man, the nobler part,
> That other o're the body only reigns,
> And oft by force, which to a generous mind
> So reigning can be no sincere delight. (2.473–80)

Next, Satan urges Jesus to seek glory and empire by emulating great warriors and world conquerors – Alexander the Great, Julius Caesar, Scipio Africanus, Pompey – and Jesus responds by redefining true fame and the acts that merit it. As in *Lycidas*, true fame is bestowed by God; it cannot emanate from the people at large, "a herd confus'd, / A miscellaneous rabble" (3.49–50). Nor does it rightly belong to conventional epic heroes, military conquerors, and empire-builders, who "rob and spoil, burn, slaughter, and enslave / Peaceable Nations" (3.75–7).[117] It pertains rather to "deeds of peace, by wisdom eminent," to Job who bore Satan's wrongs "with Saintly patience," and the wise teacher Socrates, "For truths sake suffering death unjust" (3.91–8). Emphasizing that Alexander and Caesar "must be titl'd Gods" and idolatrously worshipped (3.81–3), Milton has his hero castigate as "sacrilegious" all those – including by implication divine-right kings – who seek such glory, which to God "alone of right belongs" (3.140–1).[118]

With the line "But to a Kingdom thou art born, ordain'd / To sit upon thy Father *David's* Throne" (3.152–3), Satan turns the discourse from Jesus's own desires and values to the kingly role prescribed by his office. Typically, Satan takes literally the prophecy that Jesus is to reign as king of Israel, while Jesus redefines Israel to refer to the invisible church his spiritual kingdom, and his millennial kingdom to come.

Holding up Judas Maccabaeus as a model of zeal and duty, Satan goads Jesus to seize his kingdom at once, and so free his country from "her Heathen servitude" (3.165–76) to Roman rulers who have violated God's Temple and God's Law. Jesus's answer applies to his historical situation and also to that of Milton's defeated Puritans. Its terms reprove radical millenarian expectation of Christ's imminent return as king, and repudiate Fifth Monarchist uprisings, such as Venner's 1661 rebellion.[119] But they also urge continued expectation of and right preparation for that ultimate Millennial Kingdom by waiting on God's time and learning from present trials:

> What if he hath decreed that I shall first
> Be try'd in humble state, and things adverse,
> By tribulations, injuries, insults,
> Contempts, and scorns, and snares, and violence,
> Suffering, abstaining, quietly expecting
> Without distrust or doubt, that he may know
> What I can suffer, how obey? (3.188–94)

Then Satan from a high mountain shows Jesus a massive parade of Parthian armaments and troops, insisting that he can only gain and maintain the throne of Israel and deliver the ten lost tribes enslaved in Parthian territory by conquest of or league with Parthia and its military might (3.357–70). This offer of the wrong means to establish Christ's kingdom alludes to that constant target of Milton's polemic, the use of civil power by Protestant magistrates to establish, defend, or maintain the church. Jesus insists that his spiritual kingdom, the invisible church, has no need whatever of "fleshly arm, / And fragile arms . . . / Plausible to the world, to me worth naught" (3.387–93). Nor will he need or want such arms to begin his Millennial reign, which was thought to follow soon after the return of the ten lost tribes to Jerusalem and their conversion. Jesus refuses this invitation because he cannot liberate those who enslave themselves by deliberate participation in idolatry: the terms also apply to the English who, as Milton put it in *The Readie & Easie Way*, chose them a Captain back for Egypt when they supported the Restoration of the monarchy and the Anglican church.[120] But he holds out hope that God may – in his good time – call them back in repentance and freedom, the true precondition for the Millennial Kingdom:

> Should I of these the liberty regard,
> Who freed, as to their antient Patrimony,
> Unhumbl'd, unrepentant, unreform'd,
> Headlong would follow; and to thir Gods perhaps
> Of *Bethel* and of *Dan*? no, let them serve
> Thir enemies, who serve Idols with God.
> Yet he at length, time to himself best known,
> Remembring *Abraham* by some wond'rous call

May bring them back repentant and sincere,
And at their passing cleave the *Assyrian* flood,
When to their native land with joy they hast. (3.427–37)

At the end of Book Three Jesus is termed "*Israel's* true King" (3.441), having understood that his Millennial Kingdom cannot be precipitously installed, that his spiritual kingdom, the invisible church, can make no use of civil power, and that political liberation cannot be won for inner slaves. Yet by teaching people how to free themselves from religious and monarchical idolatry Christ's kingship has profound implications for political liberty.

Imperial Rome, with its splendid architecture, sumptuous banquets, and every manifestation of dominion and glory, incorporates all the previous attractions: "ample Territory, wealth and power, / Civility of Manners, Arts, and Arms, / And long Renown" (4.82–4). It is the great kingdom of "all the world" (4.105), described in terms appropriate to the reign of the degenerate and lascivious emperor Tiberius, but also inviting the usual Protestant associations of Rome with the Roman Catholic church, and that church with the great Antichrist in the Book of Revelation.[121] Rome's imperial palace evokes St Peter's basilica, with its "compass huge, and high / The Structure, skill of noblest Architects, / With gilded battlements, conspicuous far" (4.51–3), and its banquets with rare wines quaffed in rich vessels suggest the Mass. Satan's observation that "All Nations now to *Rome* obedience pay" (4.80) points to the danger to Protestant England from Charles II's suspected adherence to, or at least sympathy with, Roman Catholicism and the openly professed Catholicism of his brother and heir. Satan urges Jesus to expel the "monster" Tiberius from his throne and take the empire over, thereby freeing the Roman populace (and Israel as part of the empire) from their "servile yoke:" the defeat of the Roman papal Antichrist was commonly expected to inaugurate the Millennium. But Jesus refuses to free Romans who degenerately abandoned republican virtue and so are "Deservedly made vassel" (4.100), a refusal which extends to Roman Catholics enslaved to the pope and to English Anglicans and Puritans who have invited that danger by restoring the Stuarts. But he then prophesies, in metaphor, that his Millennial Kingdom will at last subdue all others:

What wise and valiant man would seek to free
These thus degenerate, by themselves enslav'd,
Or could of inward slaves make outward free?
Know therefore when my season comes to sit
On *David's* Throne, it shall be like a tree
Spreading and over-shadowing all the Earth,
Or as a stone that shall to pieces dash
All Monarchies besides throughout the world,
And of my Kingdom there shall be no end:
Means there shall be to this, but what the means,
Is not for thee to know, nor me to tell. (4.143–53)

The tree seems to refer to the power of his spiritual kingdom to transform all the earth; the stone refers to his Millennial Kingdom which will crush all earthly monarchies and their evils, according to the usual exegesis of the prophecy in Daniel 2:44. But Jesus refuses to say when or how his Millennial Kingdom will come, intimating that it will come when people are prepared for it, by internalizing and enacting in history the virtue and love of liberty his gospel promotes. At this point a sharp exchange between Jesus and Satan uncovers the unstated condition of these offers: worship of Satan, which is involved whenever any of these worldly goods are made into idols. In some ways this near-last poem reprises Milton's first major poem, the Nativity ode: in both the casting out of idols is the necessary precondition for the establishment of Christ's kingdom in this world.

Milton then contrives a still more striking climax. Satan presents Athens, the zenith of classical learning, poetry, and oratory, as the fount of the nonmaterial goods Jesus needs to achieve his own defined goals, though, significantly, he does not claim that learning is in his gift. The evocative description of pastoral delights in the "Olive Grove of *Academe*" recalls those delightful scenes of retired study in idyllic pastoral surroundings that the young Milton praised in *Il Penseroso,* Prolusion VII, and *Lycidas*:[122]

> See there the Olive Grove of *Academe,*
> *Plato's* retirement, where the *Attic* Bird
> Trills her thick-warbl'd notes the summer long,
> There flowrie hill *Hymettus* with the sound
> Of Bees industrious murmur oft invites
> To studious musing; there *Ilissus* rouls
> His whispering stream. (4.244–50)

The beauty of the passage indicates the continued atttraction of retired study for Milton, but his hero (like Milton himself) resists that lure to continue his active work in the world. The harshness of Jesus's responses seems to reveal Milton's deep-seated anxieties around the issue of learning, for they apparently repudiate the classical learning that has been so important to Milton throughout his life. Classical philosophy is "false, or little else but dreams, / Conjectures, fancies, built on nothing firm" (4.291–2). The Hebrew poets are far superior to classical poets, who sing "The vices of thir Deities, and thir own" (4.340) and, once their "swelling Epithetes" are removed, are "Thin sown with aught of profit or delight" (4.343–5). And the Greek orators are far inferior to the Hebrew prophets in teaching "The solid rules of Civil Government" (4.358).

But Jesus recognizes that Satan's version of learning is tainted, and Milton challenges his readers to make similar discriminations. Satan is here an arch-Sophist, proposing universal knowledge not as a way to truth but as a means to power, glory, and pleasure: "As thy Empire must extend, / So let extend thy mind o'er all the world"; "Be famous . . . / By wisdom" (4.22–3). Satan praises Plato chiefly for the highly refined sensory delights of his pastoral retirement, Aristotle as the teacher of a world conqueror, Socrates for his great influence on later schools, Homer for the envy Apollo showed for his poem, Demosthenes for his ability to promote war – degrading the learning Athens represents even judged by its own humanist lights. Satan also seeks to undermine Jesus's unique role as spiritual teacher by insisting on the *necessity* of classical learning for the contemplative life he seems to favor, the attainment of the inner kingship: "These rules will render thee a King compleat / Within thy self" (4.283–4). He also insists that Christ's prophetic and kingly offices of teaching and ruling by persuasion require him to converse with and confute the gentiles in their own terms. Jesus, however, denies that the classical writers are sources of true wisdom. Having no knowledge of the Creation, Fall, and redemption by grace, they are "Ignorant of themselves, of God much more" (4.310), though he acknowledges and he has himself quoted their moral teachings, informed by the light of nature. Since Jesus's mission is to bring true wisdom into history he will not accept their lower knowledge as in any way necessary, though he may possess it: "Think not but that I know these things, or think / I know them not; not therefore am I short / Of knowing what I aught: he who receives / Light from above, from the fountain of light, / No other doctrine needs" (4.286–90). In this repudiation, Milton's Jesus reinforces for his church the position Milton defended in *The Likeliest Means to Remove Hirelings*, that learning is not necessary to ministers, who require only knowledge of scripture and the Spirit's illumination. Jesus's answer (and Milton's) does not repudiate learning as such, but flatly denies that it is *necessary* to virtue, salvation, or the accomplishment of God's work in the world. Also, in Jesus's refusal to value books above their users, we hear some echo of Milton's frequent disparagement of scholarly authorities, as he insisted on his own originality and authorial parity with other writers and teachers:

> However many books
> Wise men have said are wearisom; who reads
> Incessantly, and to his reading brings not
> A spirit and judgment equal or superior,
> (And what he brings, what needs he elsewhere seek)
> Uncertain and unsettl'd still remains,
> Deep verst in books and shallow in himself,
> Crude or intoxicate, collecting toys,
> And trifles for choice matters, worth a spunge;
> As Children gathering pibles on the shore. (4.321–30)

In the storm–tower sequence Jesus endures with patience the final test of the kingdom within – violence – which foreshadows his Passion and death, the fulfillment of his priestly office. The tower episode is contrived as the ultimate identity test: Satan supposes that by placing Jesus on the pinnacle of the Temple he will save himself by miracle if he is divine, while if he is merely human he will fall or else sin by presumption if he casts himself down expecting divine rescue. But as he calmly maintains the posture into which Satan has thrust him, his passion becomes an active conquest over Satan: he is preserved by God and at the same time, it seems, is granted a full awareness of his divine Sonship: "Tempt not the Lord thy God, he said and stood. / But Satan smitten with amazement fell" (4.561–2). As Milton presents it, these episodes have relevance for Puritan dissidents subjected to the storms and tempests of royalist oppression and invited, like Jesus, to read their plight as a portent of God's displeasure and their coming destruction. But the bright day that follows the storm and Satan's fall from the tower invite a different reading: as Christ's resurrection followed his Passion and his victory on the tower foreshadows his victory over Satan at the Last Day, so may those dissidents expect a better day – and in due time a victory – if they endure their trials patiently, avoid precipitous action, and develop their spiritual strength.

Jesus's victory is celebrated with an angelic banquet and a long hymn of praise that make explicit his identity with the Son in Heaven as the "True Image of the Father" (2.596), and also foreshadow the Millennium. The hymn, like the Father's speech at the outset of the temptation, indicates by shifts in tense and perspective that Jesus's victory is now complete, but that it is also just beginning. He has "now . . . aveng'd / Supplanted Adam" and "regain'd lost Paradise," but he is about to "begin to save mankind" (4.606–8, 634–5). Because Jesus now understands himself and has been exercised in all the "rudiments" or root concerns of his great warfare, he has already won the essential victory. But that victory must now be worked out in history, as others respond to his teaching and are thereby enabled to become virtuous and free. Only then will Christ's Millennial Kingdom come.

Milton ends the poem quietly. Like Adam and Eve wandering forth to begin the human history whose end Adam has foreseen, Jesus returns from the angelic celebration of the prophesied end to his human beginnings, to live out the history the temptation episode foreshadowed: "hee unobserv'd / Home to his Mothers house private return'd" (4.638–9).

The title page of *Samson Agonistes* terms it "A Dramatic Poem," not a drama: Milton did not suppose that it might be presented on the Restoration stage alongside Dryden's exotic tragedies. But as a written text it might still prove "doctrinal and exemplary to a Nation," the effect he had projected in the *Reason of Church-Government* (1642) for a tragedy modeled on Sophocles, Euripides, and the Apocalypse of St John (*CPW* I, 815). In a better society, he might imagine it serving as one of the "wise and artfull recitations" in theaters which he proposed in that tract as a means to entice citizens to virtue (819–20). Milton made large alterations in the biblical story from Judges 13–16: stories of Samson the trickster who tied fiery brands to foxes' tails and set riddles for wedding guests are all but eliminated, as are references to Samson's marriage to the woman of Timna. Also, by changing Dalila from a harlot to Samson's wife, Milton grounds their relationship in marital love and duty. Most important, Milton conflates the biblical strong man with Job and the Psalmist, as, like them, Samson seeks to understand God's ways to him.[123] By such changes Milton creates a hero capable of self-analysis, intellectual struggle, tragic suffering, and bitter self-castigation as he confronts his guilt. Samson is not Milton Agonistes, but Milton put much of himself into Samson's lamentations about blindness and captivity among enemies.

This drama has elicited a cacophony of interpretations. Some see Samson enacting a paradigm of fall and regeneration; others think he remains tragically flawed in his vindictiveness, despair, self-concern, and suicidal revenge.[124] Some find Samson's character undecidable, given the contradictory contemporary uses of the Samson story and the absence of any authoritative vantage point.[125] Read in political terms, the drama has been construed as a near-allegory of the English revolution and its aftermath; as a covert call to English Puritans to rise again; as a repudiation of the English revolution and of all military action; as figuring the situation of the Puritan dissenters in the Restoration; or as projecting the Puritan radicals' expectation of God's destruction of the wicked though his Saints.[126] Milton indeed emphasizes the ambiguous signs and events of the Samson story: the wonders surrounding his birth; the extraordinary strength in his unshorn hair; his awesome deeds; his catastrophic fall; his sense of repudiation by God; his claims to "inner impulses" and "rousing motions"; and his final, violent destruction of the Philistines and himself. Such ambiguous signs, along with such prominent stylistic features as antitheses and either–or constructions, force readers to weigh and choose, but Milton's literary strategies provide some guide among the interpretative possibilities.[127] Milton's Samson does not trace a straightforward trajectory from sin to regeneration, but takes a more realistic, uneven course, often manifesting prideful self-regard, a disposition to blame others, and even despair. But his final, miraculous destruction of the Philistine theater indicates that God has accepted his repentance and has restored his role as judge, that is, as God's agent for the deliverance of his people.

The preface, "Of that sort of Dramatic Poem which is call'd Tragedy," is Milton's only extended commentary on a poem of his own. The title page epigraph quotes the first few words in Greek and the first sentence in Latin of Aristotle's famous definition of Tragedy,[128] and Milton begins by paraphrasing that definition in terms tailored to this work:

> Tragedy, as it was antiently compos'd, hath been ever held the gravest, moralest, and most profitable of all other Poems: therefore said by *Aristotle* to be of power by raising pity and fear, or terror, to purge the mind of those and such like passions, that is to temper and reduce them to just measure with a kind of delight, stirr'd up by reading or seeing those passions well imitated. (3)

Unlike Aristotle, Milton emphasizes the moral profit of tragedy, and also glosses catharsis as a purging or tempering of the passions by aesthetic delight – a concept encapsulated in the drama's final line: "Calm of mind, all passion spent." He also changes the object of imitation: for Aristotle it is "an action," the plot or mythos; for Milton, it is the tragic passions, pity or fear and terror, that are to be "well imitated" – a definition that locates the essence of tragedy in the scene of suffering, here, the agonies and passions of Samson. In Aristotle's paradigmatic tragedy, Sophocles's *Oedipus Rex*, the hero falls from prosperity into abject misery through an error or fault (*hamartia*) that enmeshes him in the toils of Fate; but Milton's tragedy begins with Samson already fallen into misery, like the heroes of Aeschylus's *Prometheus Bound* or Sophocles's *Oedipus at Colonnus*. A still more important model is the biblical tragedy that Milton points to here as he did in *The Reason of Church-Government,* the Book of Revelation, referring here as he did before to the formal characteristics cited by David Pareus: division into acts with a chorus of "heavenly Harpings and Song between."[129] But he seems also to accept Pareus's description of the work's tragic subject: the "sufferings and agons" of the saints throughout history, culminating in the "destruction of the ungodly, with the glorious deliverance of the Church."[130] Milton locates the essence of his tragedy in Samson's pain-wracked struggles and violent death, experiences not negated by the evidence of providential design and the foreshadowing in Samson's final act of the apocalyptic destruction of the wicked.

Pointing to Aeschylus, Sophocles, and Euripides as "the best rule to all who endevour to write Tragedy" in regard to the disposition of the plot, Milton follows the structure of Greek tragedy closely. There is a Prologue spoken by Samson that sets the situation; a Parados or entry song of the chorus; five agons or dialogic struggles with visitors, separated by choral odes; an Exode containing the report of and responses to Samson's death; and a Kommos, containing a funeral dirge and consolations.[131] Like Oedipus in *Oedipus Rex*, Samson gains self-knowledge through the dialogic agons, in Samson's case partly by encountering and overcoming versions of his former self: as a Danite circumscribed by his tribe and family, as a sensualist enslaved by passion, and as a swaggering strong man. Milton states that the chorus is designed "after the Greek manner," but his chorus of Danites is more than the voice of community mores. Especially in the long segment after Samson leaves the scene it falls to them to try to understand what Samson's life and death mean for Israel and what they themselves are called to do. Also, the preface properly indicates the drama's adherence to the neoclassical unities of time and place: the action takes only a few hours with no intervals of time, and the single locale is a shady bank in front of Samson's prison, with all action elsewhere and all violence reported by a messenger. Milton also claimed to exclude "comic stuff" and vulgar personages, evidently considering that his Giant Harapha was distanced sufficiently by his political discourse from origins in the classical comic type, the *miles gloriosus* or braggart soldier.

The preface cites the Greek tragedians as a stylistic model, especially for the choral odes. But Milton's style is boldly experimental: on a ground of blank verse he overlays passages often akin to free verse, marked by irregular line lengths, broken rhythms, a striking use of imagery and sound effects, and intricate rhyming patterns (among the 1,758 lines there are about 150 that rhyme). In Samson's bitter opening lament, the blind Milton's identification with the emotional states of his hero and his consummate metrical art produce lines of great poignancy and power:

> O dark, dark, dark, amid the blaze of noon,
> Irrecoverably dark, total Eclipse
> Without all hope of day!
> O first created Beam, and thou great Word,
> Let there be light, and light was over all;
> Why am I thus bereav'd thy prime decree?
> The Sun to me is dark
> And silent as the Moon,
> When she deserts the night
> Hid in her vacant interlunar cave.
> Since light so necessary is to life,
> And almost life it self, if it be true
> That light is in the Soul,
> She all in every part; why was the sight
> To such a tender ball as th'eye confin'd?
> So obvious and so easie to be quench't,
> And not as feeling through all parts diffus'd,
> That she might look at will through every pore?
> Then had I not been thus exil'd from light;
> As in the land of darkness yet in light,
> To live a life half dead, a living death,
> And buried; but O yet more miserable!
> My self, my Sepulcher, a moving Grave,
> Buried, yet not exempt
> By priviledge of death and burial
> From worst of other evils, pains and wrongs,
> But made hereby obnoxious more
> To all the miseries of life,
> Life in captivity
> Among inhuman foes. (80–109)

This style challenges the heroic couplets that have become normative for Restoration tragedy, and it also marks the culmination of Milton's lifelong experimentation with verse forms. There is nothing like this in Milton's earlier poetry, nor in any previous English verse.

Samson Agonistes is not a point-by-point political allegory, but it invites application to the post-Restoration ethos and the situation of the Puritan dissenters. In *Areopagitica* Milton made Samson a figure for England in the throes of vibrant Puritan reform, "a noble and puissant Nation rousing herself like a strong man after sleep, and shaking her invincible locks" (*CPW* II, 558); he now takes the blinded and defeated Samson, "Eyeless in *Gaza* at the Mill with slaves"(41) and engaged in a painful process of self-scrutiny, as a figure for the defeated Puritans and especially their leaders. The poem achieves a brilliant mimesis of the confusions attending moments of political crisis and choice, requiring readers – and especially the Puritan dissenters – to think through the hard questions raised by the revolution and its failure, so as to prepare themselves should God offer them a new chance at liberty. Some questions raised by Samson's experience – and that of Milton's Englishmen – are these: How is a nation to know the liberators raised up by God to promote change? What signs are reliable indexes of God's favor to or God's rejection of leaders or nations? How can would-be liberators know themselves to be chosen or repudiated? Or know when they are led by God and when by their own desires? Can flawed humans be divine instruments? Does God ever inspire to action outside the law and outside his own law? What imperatives for political action follow from apparent signs of God's special interventions? How far can we take the past as guide to the present? Or guard against leaders' deception or delusion? How does human political action relate to the course of providential history?

Samson's anguished opening soliloquy reveals his physical and psychological pain, misery, bitterness, and despondency. But the first lines – "A little onward lend thy guiding hand / To these dark steps, a little further on; / For yonder bank hath choice of Sun or shade" – intimate that he is being guided by some unseen power to a place affording "choice" of salvation or eternal darkness, a place where he feels "amends, / The breath of Heav'n fresh-blowing" (9–10). Soon, however, his miseries again overwhelm him and restless thoughts rush upon him "like a deadly swarm / Of Hornets arm'd" (19–20). He reinterprets the signs that once seemed clear evidence of his vocation as Nazarite and liberator as a perverse mockery: "God, when he gave me strength, to shew withal / How slight the gift was, hung it in my Hair" (58–9). But, like Adam and Satan at comparable moments in *Paradise Lost*, he has to admit that the fault is his own. In their Parados or entry ode the chorus of Danites, Samson's friends and tribesmen, are shocked and baffled by the contrast between his former great exploits and his present bondage and blindness, sentiments relevant to the oppressed Puritans who have seen their former leaders denounced, reviled, imprisoned, broken, executed, and their very corpses made a spectacle of degradation.[132] The chorus customarily interprets what has happened and is happening in terms of maxims, proverbs, and exemplary histories; they resist coming to terms with the extraordinary. In their entry ode they can only account for Samson's fall by the familiar tragic formula of the wheel of fortune: he was high and now is low, a "mirror of our fickle state" (164).

The Danites shift to a dialogic role for the first agon, in which the question at issue is whether Samson ever had a divine mission to liberate his people – clearly relevant to retrospectives on the English revolution. Full of bitterness at having become an object of ridicule, Samson blames God (as Adam did) for making him too weak in wisdom to cope with his woman. The Danites seek answers in a moralizing formula – "Tax not divine disposal, wisest Men / Have err'd, and by bad Women been deceiv'd; / And shall again" (210–12) – and also in legalisms, throwing up to Samson his marriage out of the tribe. But in doing so they prod Samson to think his way beyond the Hebrew marriage law and Dalila's fault, and admit his own guilt in revealing God's secret: "She was not the prime cause, but I my self, / Who vanquisht with a peal of words (O weakness!) / Gave up my fort of silence to a Woman" (234–6). The Danites then imply that Samson's supposed political mission is discredited by the sad result, that "*Israel* still serves with all his Sons" (240). They never refer to his wonderful past deeds as God-given signs of his calling, and they resist his claim that his first marriage was prompted by an intimate impulse from God as an occasion to begin Israel's deliverance, and his second by a reasonable analogy to that case. Their challenge goads Samson to reclaim his past. Insisting that his extraordinary deeds were an unmistakable sign of his vocation as liberator, he disclaims responsibility for Israel's continued servitude: that is due to the blindness and political cowardice of her governers, "Who seeing those great acts which God had done / Singly by me against their Conquerours / Acknowledg'd not" (243–5) and betrayed him. That judgment also convicts the English parliament who repudiated the deliverance God offered them, and gave over the Commonwealth's defenders to the vengeance of their royalist enemies. It also corrects those dissenters who might judge simplistically by results, accepting royalist interpretations of their defeat and oppression as God's punishment for their rebellion. The Israel–England parallel is reinforced as Samson voices the Miltonic principle that inner servitude leads to political bondage in whatever country:

> But what more oft in Nations grown corrupt,
> And by thir vices brought to servitude,
> Then to love Bondage more then Liberty,
> Bondage with ease then strenuous liberty;
> And to despise, or envy, or suspect
> Whom God hath of his special favour rais'd
> As thir Deliverer; if he aught begin,
> How frequent to desert him, and at last
> To heap ingratitude on worthiest deeds? (268–76)

In the ode that follows – "Just are the ways of God, / And justifiable to Men" (294–5) – the chorus shows some advance in their understanding, as they now acknowledge Samson's deeds and even his inner promptings as divinely inspired and allow that God could dispense with his own laws in regard to Samson's gentile marriages. But they cannot move beyond pat formulas in accounting for Samson's predicament, and soon revert to the un-Miltonic notion that humans cannot begin to understand God's justice or reason about it.[133]

The second agon, between Samson and his father Manoa, centers on what a divinely appointed liberator and his party should do in defeat. In a brilliant characterization, Milton portrays Manoa as an old man whose concerns center on family and family honor. He is dismayed by Samson's suffering, but almost more distressed by the evil of God's ways to him in degrading the son who had elicited such paternal pride: "Who would be now a Father in my stead?" (355). He does not doubt that Samson's former deeds were signs of his divine mission, but he also judges by the Judaic Law and by results, ascribing Samson's fall to his gentile marriages:

> I cannot praise thy Marriage choises, Son,
> Rather approv'd them not; but thou didst plead
> Divine impulsion prompting how thou might'st
> Find some occasion to infest our Foes.
> I state not that; this I am sure; our Foes
> Found soon occasion thereby to make thee
> Thir Captive, and thir triumph. (420–6)

Manoa cannot resist the chiding father's "I told you so." Nor can he resist throwing up to Samson his terrible responsibility for disgracing God, who at the festival for Dagon will be "Disglorifi'd, blasphem'd, and had in scorn / By th' Idolatrous rout amidst thir wine" (442–3). Samson advances in self-knowledge as he refuses to explain his fault in terms of the marriage laws, locating it rather in a slavery to passion worse than his present physical bondage: "Unmanly, ignominious, infamous, / True slavery, and that blindness worse then this, / That saw not how degeneratly I serv'd" (417–19). He takes full responsibility for his sin and its terrible effects: bringing dishonor to God and prompting among the Israelites "diffidence of God, and doubt / In feeble hearts, propense anough before / To waver, or fall off and joyn with Idols" (454–6) – dangers to which the defeated Puritans were also susceptible. He finds some comfort in recognizing that God can defend himself without Samson's help, but that perception also reinforces his sense of uselessness and deepens his dismay.

Manoa's proposal to ransom Samson recalls similar efforts made for some of the English regicides, among them Edmund Ludlow and Colonel John Hutchinson. Others, like Thomas Harrison and Milton's good friend Henry Vane, took Samson's line and refused to escape or allow friends to offer money in their behalf.[134] Manoa sees Samson's decision to remain at the mill as suicidal, observing that his refusals sometimes sound "over-just and self-displeas'd / For self-offence, more then for God offended," and insisting, plausibly enough, that God is better pleased with "Him who imploring mercy sues for life, / Then who self-rigorous chooses death as due" (512–15). Samson's motives for refusing ransom are mixed and not entirely clear even to himself: he senses that he should continue at the mill to expiate his sin and that this debasement befits his former hubris; he recoils viscerally from the prospect of becoming a fixture by the domestic hearth and a mere idol of his past glory; and he sees himself making a self-respecting choice of work over idleness – to "drudge and earn my bread" (573). Also at issue is how to interpret Samson's new growth of hair. Samson reads these "redundant locks / Robustious to no purpose" (568–9) as a public talisman of his failure and uselessness to God and his people. Manoa reads them as a sign that God has further use for Samson, but he indulges a facile optimism in supposing that God will simply obliterate the consequences of Samson's sin and restore his sight so he can again take up his mission. This exchange brings Samson to his nadir, plunging him into despair. His inner experience of sin's terrible effects – "faintings, swounings of despair, / And sense of Heav'ns desertion" (631–2) – leads him to find an absolute disjunction between past and present, election and reprobation: "I was his nursling once and choice delight, / His destin'd from the womb, / . . . But now [he] hath cast me off as never known, / . . . Nor am I in the list of them that hope" (633–47). But Samson can still resist a belief in easy miracles and sense that he should wait where he is, not retreat into privateness and passivity, giving over all engagement with the public sphere. That decision leaves him (and a comparable decision would leave the dissenters) poised to respond when inner reformation is complete, when opportunity comes, and when God might prompt a rousing motion.

In their ode beginning "Many are the sayings of the wise / . . . Extolling Patience as the truest fortitude," the chorus now admits that such proverbial wisdom offers little help to the afflicted, "Unless he feel within / Some sourse of consolation from above" (652–64). They have learned something about inward spiritual experience. But as they echo Job and the Psalmist – "God of our Fathers, what is man!" – they are only able to conclude that an arbitrary God often brings just and unjust alike to a miserable end.

Samson's agon with Dalila, the longest of the five, brings Samson right out of his despair as he resists the temptation to which he earlier succumbed. Here the interpretative focus shifts from the signs associated with Samson to Dalila's self-presentation, which Milton treats as an enigma. Dalila's real nature, her reasons for coming to Samson, her reasons for betraying him, and her claims to repentance, are all open to and are given multiple interpretations, challenging Samson, the chorus, and the reader to penetrate to the truth of character beneath rhetoric and stereotypes. Samson's fierce denunciations – "Out, out *Hyaena*; these are thy wonted arts / And arts of every woman false like thee" (748–9) – and his implacable rebuffs to her pleas for forgiveness, unlike Adam with Eve, have been seen as evidence of Milton's misogyny, or his psychic anxiety about the feminine, or his painful remembrance of his own marital troubles with Mary Powell, or his direct reflection of contemporary gender and societal stereotypes.[135] But while Samson's rage and bitterness against Dalila wells up at times from the depths of Milton's psyche, Milton is not Samson, nor is this scene an endorsement of gender stereotypes.

Like Samson, Dalila speaks constantly of herself and her motives, but she seems to have no inner life; she seems rather to have internalized all the contemporary stereotypes of the feminine. She takes great care about her appearance, sailing in like a ship "bedeckt, ornate, and gay" with perfume and damsel train (712–21) to visit the blind Samson; she weeps delicately, "like a fair flower surcharg'd with dew (728); and she excuses her treachery to Samson by supposed female traits: women's curiosity to know and tell secrets, woman's frailty, and domestic love which seeks to keep her husband safe at home. This portrait of Dalila gives some recognition to the cultural pressures on women in a patriarchal society, but Milton will not excuse woman or man on grounds of gender stereotypes or cultural constraints from the responsibility of developing and following a personal conscience. This harsh standard is egalitarian in insisting that women as well as men can and must act as free moral agents: Samson refuses the claims of female weakness, holding Dalila and himself to the same moral standard – "All wickedness is weakness" (834). And he evidently measures her claims of repentance, conjugal affection, and desire to make amends against his own painful struggles for self-knowledge and true repentance. The reader can also make this comparison and recognize some contrasts. Unlike Manoa and the chorus, Dalila says nothing at all about Samson's pitiful condition and poses no metaphysical questions to the universe. And, unlike Eve, she engages in a constant rhetoric of self-exculpation and shifting excuses. In *Paradise Lost* Milton portrays a marriage knit back together as Adam reconciles with a truly repentant wife. Here he portrays a moral chasm that necessitates divorce: "Thou and I long since are twain" (929).

Dalila's final excuse is an appeal to the authority of state and church: the Philistine magistrates and priests urged her to betray her husband as a civic and religious duty, reinforcing it with authoritative maxims "that to the public good / Private respects must yield" (867–8). This excuse might suggest that there is little to choose between Dalila's motives and Samson's, since he intended his marriage to advance Israel's cause against the Philistines. But Samson denies this implied cultural relativism, declaring that if she had loved him as he loved her she could not have betrayed him (he did not harm her by his actions against Philistia), and that the ungodly deeds of her gods prove that they are no gods. He also denies final authority to civil and religious leaders or to *raison d'état*, appealing to the higher law of nature and nations which privileges the marriage bond above the claims of the state. The issue of cultural relativism is joined again when Samson predicts that Dalila's story will become an exemplum of marital treachery and she offers a counter-interpretation from the Philistine perspective:

> I shall be nam'd among the famousest
> Of Women, sung at solemn festivals,
> Living and dead recorded, who to save
> Her countrey from a fierce destroyer, chose
> Above the faith of wedlock-bands, my tomb
> With odours visited and annual flowers.
> Not less renown'd then in Mount *Ephraim,*
> *Jael* who with inhospitable guile
> Smote *Sisera* sleeping through the Temples nail'd. (982–90)

Readers are expected to supply the appropriate distinctions: Jael violated, for religious and national purposes, the classical code of hospitality protecting a guest, while Dalila violated the intimate claims of love and the high duty of marital fidelity thought to be grounded in natural law.

The Dalila episode asks readers to reaffirm the principle that justified the Revolution – that natural law takes precedence over civil and ecclesiastical authority. Also, Samson's descriptions of Dalila in terms evoking Circe or the Whore of Babylon – "thy ginns, and toyls; / Thy fair enchanted cup, and warbling charms" (933–4) – associate her sexual power with the sensuous attractions of Roman Catholic and high Anglican religious practices. Samson's adamant refusal to allow Dalila to bring him back to her house and bed, projecting the misery of a future life "in perfet thraldom" to her (946), asks to be read at the personal level of the marital relationship and also at the political level of the defeated Puritans' need to resist seduction, subversion, and betrayal.

The chorus has learned something about illusion, deception, and hypocrisy from this episode, but they remain baffled by women, and only manage to voice a masculine counterpart to Dalila's feminine stereotypes, proclaiming man's "despotic power / Over his female" as God's universal law (1,053–5). The political and cultural issues elude them, and they seek refuge from their confusion in a simplistic and general misogyny.

In the agon with the Philistine strong man Harapha, Samson experiences an inward sense of God's pardon that enables him again to take up his vocation as divinely appointed liberator, offering it to the trial of battle and defending it by reasoned political argument. Harapha's insults, pointing to Samson's sorry state as evidence of God's abandonment, echo those the triumphant royalists cast at the defeated Puritans and at blind Milton: "Thee he regards not, owns not, hath cut off / Quite from his people, and delivered up / Into thy Enemies hand" (1,157–9). Despite his apparent disadvantage, Samson offers to fight Harapha in terms that evoke David's victory over Goliath, identified here as one of Harapha's five sons.[136] Samson now interprets his restored hair and strength as a sign of God's continued favor. His heartfelt admission of guilt, affirmation that God was and is the source of his strength, recognition of God's hand in his deserved chastisement, and confidence of God's pardon, provide a model for the oppressed Puritans, echoing the lessons of numerous jeremiads on the occasions of the Great Plague and the Great Fire.[137] This scene implies that from such attitudes, leading to a renewed relationship with God, might come readiness to reclaim political agency and resist oppression:

> In confidence whereof I once again
> Defie thee to the trial of mortal fight,
> By combat to decide whose god is God,
> Thine or whom I with *Israel's* Sons adore. (1,174–7)

Any such readiness must involve recognizing the legitimacy of Samson's earlier appeal to arms – and that of the English revolutionaries. Harapha declares Samson a rebel covenant-breaker and murderer, echoing royalist denunciations of the Puritans before and after the Restoration for rebellion, breaking the Solemn League and Covenant, and regicide. Samson echoes the Miltonic justifications for those actions: natural law which always allows armed resistance to those enslaved – "force with force / Is well ejected when the Conquer'd can" (1,206–7) – and a vocation confirmed by divine mandate and evidenced by superior strength, recalling Milton's defenses of the Rump and the army in *Tenure*, the *Defensio*, and especially the *Readie & Easie Way*.[138]

> I was no private but a person rais'd
> With strength sufficient and command from Heav'n
> To free my Countrey; if their servile minds
> Me their Deliverer sent would not receive,
> But to thir Masters gave me up for nought,
> Th'unworthier they; whence to this day they serve.
> I was to do my part from Heav'n assign'd,
> And had perform'd it if my known offence
> Had not disabl'd me, not all your force. (1,211–19)

As Harapha retreats, revealed to be a "baffl'd coward" (1,237), the chorus's ode shows them sharing so intimately in Samson's psychological recovery that – for a moment – they imagine him charging forth to liberate them, and rejoice that God "into the hands of thir deliverer / Puts invincible might / To quell the mighty of the Earth" (1,270–2). But then, recalling Samson's blindness and captivity, they suppose that his must needs be the more usual form of heroism, the conquest over self upon which he has been engaged, "Labouring thy mind / More then the working day thy hands" (1,298–9). Typically, they pose an either–or alternative, not realizing that conquest over self must precede and can lead to the active heroism of striking a blow for freedom.

The final agon between Samson, the Philistine officer, and the chorus explores the claims and conflict of several kinds of authority: civil power, religious law, conscience, and inward illumination. The officer, as a representative of civil power, requires Samson to perform feats of strength at an idolatrous feast honoring Dagon (1,311–15), analogous to the post-Restoration laws requiring dissenters to participate in the liturgy of an "idolatrous" Anglican church.[139] Samson provides a model for life and action in such circumstances. While the fearful Danite chorus is disposed to yield to civil power in everything, Samson refuses to prostitute holy things to idols – in this case his divinely restored strength – on the basis of religious law: "Our law forbids at thir Religious Rites / My presence" (1,320–1). He appeals as well to the inner testimony of "my conscience" (1,334), and also to a proper self-respect as he scorns to perform as their fool or jester or as a wild beast. Speaking with the Danites after the officer departs, he distinguishes between religious acts and the duties of citizenship: he will not participate in their "Idol-worship," but he will perform "Honest and lawful" labor at the mill, "to deserve my food / Of those who have me in thir civil power" (1,365–7) – a distinction that denies the Anglican construction of dissent as in itself seditious. The chorus suggests outward conformity, a position accepted by some erstwhile Puritans as a way to accommodate to the new regime: "Where the heart joins not, outward acts defile not" (1,368). But Samson rejects that rationalization, as did John Owen, who insisted that conscience involves not only inward opinions but also an obligation "to act accordingly," especially in regard to the worship of God.[140] Samson distinguishes between submitting to actual overwhelming force and obeying commands, claiming that the latter amounts to acceptance of and complicity in one's own slavery: "Commands are no constraints. If I obey them, / I do it freely; venturing to displease / God for the fear of Man" (1,372–4).

Finally, Samson locates the highest authority in divine illumination, affirming God's power to dispense from religious laws "for some important cause," and claiming a sudden, inward experience of "rouzing motions" that disposes "To something extraordinary my thoughts" (1,377–83). These words indicate to the Danite chorus why he has decided to go voluntarily to the feast of Dagon, though his words to the officer imply acceptance of the ideology of civil absolutism: "Masters commands come with a power resistless / To such as owe them absolute subjection; / And for a life who will not change his purpose?" (1,404-6). But that statement is dense with ironies and deliberate ambiguities: in Samson's, and Milton's, view only the divine master is owed absolute subjection, and it is the life of the spirit that must be saved. Samson now acts as an antinomian, but he is no Ranter: his version of antinomianism parallels Milton's in *De Doctrina Christiana*.[141] Samson insists that in moving beyond the Judaic Law he will yet fulfill its spirit, and will be seen to do so by his countrymen, in the public arena: "Nothing to do, be sure, that may dishonour / Our Law, or stain my vow of *Nazarite*" (1,385–6); "in nothing to comply / Scandalous or forbidden in our Law" (1,408–9); "of me expect to hear / Nothing dishonourable, impure, unworthy / Our God, our Law, my Nation, or myself" (1,423–5).[142] Like Jesus going out to the desert, Samson senses that he is under God's direction, and he is open to those further insights that come to Milton's heroes when they are prepared for them by their own moral and intellectual struggles.

The chorus's ode is a simple prayer that God may be with Samson at need. They now credit his inner illumination, they sense that God is leading him, and they hope he will again enjoy divine protection. The poetic language of this prayer is a far cry from their earlier formulas and maxims, suggesting that their vicarious experience of Samson's struggle has worked some change in them, though perhaps only temporary (1,427–37).

In the Exode the focus shifts to Samson's cataclysmic act of pulling down the theater, destroying the Philistines as well as himself. The episode has apocalyptic overtones, evoking the final destruction of Antichrist's forces as well as stories in the Book of Judges of a wrathful God taking revenge on his enemies through Gideon and Jeptha and Samson – analogues that radical Puritans readily applied to their own times.[143] The violence and wholesale destruction Samson here wreaks on God's and Israel's enemies have been read as evidence of his unregenerate wrath, or Milton's wish-fulfillment of obliterating his enemies, or Samson's or Milton's concept of an implacable, irrational, and terrifying God.[144] Wrath is an aspect of Milton's God as it is also of the biblical deity, and Samson here is its human agent. But this violence is not a matter of arbitrary, inexplicable divine fury: it is based on reasoned moral and political principles which Samson, Milton, and Milton's God share. Yet for all that, Samson cannot stand in for Christ at the apocalypse, and his victory in death is very partial.

The chorus, Manoa, and the reader have no direct access to Samson's final act, but must make what they can of it from signs and stories. Heightening the dramatic tension and irony, Manoa's hopeful plans to rescue Samson are interrupted by deafening shouts and screams, leading him to conclude that "they have slain my Son," and leading the chorus to imagine that Samson's eyesight has been restored and that he is destroying his enemies. Then, from a distraught messenger they extract, piecemeal, what he saw and heard: Samson patiently performing feats of "incredible, stupendious force" (1,627); Samson resting between the pillars of the theater; Samson's last ironic words to his captors – "Now of my own accord such other tryal / I mean to shew you of my strength, yet greater; / As with amaze shall strike all who behold" (1,643–5); and then his destruction of the theater and the Philistine nobility within – though not the less guilty "vulgar" outside its walls (1,650–9). Significantly, the messenger did not hear Samson pray for private vengence as did the Samson of Judges 16:28 – "O God, that I may be at once avenged of the Philistines, for my two eyes" – and that change affords some clue to the spiritual state of Milton's hero. But neither messenger nor reader can read the soul from the external signs: Samson's head inclined and eyes fast fixed may indicate "one who prayd, / Or some great matter in his mind revolv'd" (1,636–8) – or both. Milton's much mediated presentation of this scene forces characters and readers to distinguish between what is necessarily opaque – Samson's motives, his spiritual condition, his regeneration – and what they can know clearly: that God has again enabled Samson to strike a blow for Israel's liberation. That is consonant with the way Milton judges leaders in his political tracts: not whether they are or seem to be regenerate, but whether they advance liberty.

Milton portrays the complexity and opacity of human motives as Manoa and the chorus try to explain Samson's cataclysmic act by appealing to all the usual interpretations. Manoa construes it first as simple revenge and suicide (1,590–1). The chorus speaks of a glorious revenge "dearly-bought," but denies suicide: Samson was "self-kill'd / Not willingly, but tangl'd in the fold / Of dire necessity" (1,660–6). Manoa decides at length that "*Samson* hath quit himself / Like *Samson*," and made a heroic end to a heroic life (1,709–11); and the chorus concludes, "Living or dying thou hast fulfill'd / The work for which thou wast foretold / To *Israel*" (1,662–3). Recognizing God's hand in Samson's deed, Manoa intuits that God was "not parted from him, as was fear'd" (1,719), and the chorus rejoices that God at last gave glorious witness to his "faithful Champion" (1,751).

But their responses to Samson's mission and to the changed political situation remain confused. Manoa still blames Samson's blindness and captivity chiefly on "his lot unfortunate in nuptial choice" (1,743) and is too ready to dismiss the tragedy occasioned by the guilt of Samson and Israel. Given Samson's terrible suffering and violent death it is hardly the case that "Nothing is here for tears" (1,721). Also, as Manoa earlier thought to make Samson an icon on the family hearth, so he now plans a glorious shrine for him, with cultic celebrations that comes perilously close to those Dalila imagined for herself. But Manoa can also imagine a new future in which Samson figures as exemplum and challenge: his story might inspire other valiant youth to "matchless valour and adventures high" (1,440), and his deed has already provided Israel with a political *occasione* in Machiavelli's sense: "To *Israel* / Honour hath left, and freedom, let but them / Find courage to lay hold on this occasion" (1,714–16). The Danite chorus gives some indication of a new openness to illumination in their final ode, with its richly evocative imagery of eagle and phoenix representing Samson's restored vision in blindness:

> But he though blind of sight,
> Despis'd and thought extinguish't quite,
> With inward eyes illuminated
> His fierie vertue rouz'd
> From under ashes into sudden flame. (1,687–91)

But they fall back on sententious maxims again in the rhymed sonnet that ends the work, observing that "All is best" and that "in the close" we can best know the champions to whom God and history bear witness. Their statement ignores the drama's demonstration that choices must be made and actions taken *in medias res*, in circumstances always characterized by imperfect knowledge and conflicting testimony. They have learned something but probably not enough: at the end we are led to contemplate the further tragedy that (like Milton's Englishmen) Samson's countrymen may not grasp the new chance for liberty he has won for them. Nor did they. The biblical record shows that Israel did not lay hold on this occasion but continued in corruption and servitude, and that the Danites became open idolators and murderers.[145]

As published, the poem has another coda, ten added lines designed for insertion as lines 1,527–35 and 1,537 but appearing under a bar at the end, labeled "Omissa."[146] We cannot know whether Milton hoped the printer could add them in their right place or wanted this presentation, which allows a glimpse of an alternative, apocalyptic ending. The chorus, in terms that seem out of character for them, imagine Samson with his vision miraculously restored, "dealing dole among his foes" and walking over "heaps of slaughter'd." God, they argue, had done as much for Israel of old and to him "nothing is hard." The final added line, "Of good or bad so great, of bad the sooner," suggests in its proper place that bad news travels faster than good, but may suggest here that great evil will precede great good. This coda allows Milton to have it both ways. Within his text these lines describe a false hope for Samson's physical restoration; here they project a future possibility of liberation and also foreshadow Christ's final victory over the forces of Antichrist.

Milton's tragedy does not offer an optimistic assessment of the possibilities for political liberation. The Samson paradigm shows that all human heroes are flawed, that the signs of God's action in history are inordinately hard to read, that Israelites and Englishmen are more disposed to choose "Bondage with ease than strenuous liberty" (271). Therefore, when God raises up his Samsons, or Gideons, or Cromwells, their political gains soon collapse under the weight of human sin and weakness in themselves and the people. Yet in the drama's historical moment that future is not yet fixed and choices are still possible. If the Israelites, or the English, could truly value liberty, could reform themselves, could read the signs and events with penetration, could benefit from the "new acquist / Of true experience" (1,755–6), moral and political, that Samson's story offers to the Danites and that Milton's dramatization of it offers his countrymen, liberation might be possible: the chance is there. Milton's tragedy implies that liberators must continue to respond to the call of God if it comes to them, and may always, as Milton argued in *The Readie & Easie Way*, reclaim their freedom when they are oppressed, if they have power to do so. But that can only happen when a virtuous citizenry understands the political stakes and values liberty. *Samson Agonistes* is a fit poetic climax to Milton's lifelong effort to help create such citizens.

"My Appointed Day Of Rendering Up"

During his last years Milton suffered increasingly from gout, especially, Aubrey reports, during the spring and autumn, but "he would be chearfull even in his Gowte-fitts; & sing" (*EL* 5). Cyriack Skinner describes, it seems from personal observation, the ravages of his illness: "hee had bin long troubl'd with that disease, insomuch that his Knuckles were all callous, yet was hee not ever observ'd to be very impatient" (*EL* 33). Such patience and cheerfulness suggests an inner strength observers found remarkable. Milton's eldest daughter Anne (the lame one) apparently visited him at least once during 1674.[147] But Milton probably did not hear about his daughter Deborah's marriage to Abraham Clarke, a weaver in Ireland, on June 1 of that year.[148] Milton was happy with his wife Elizabeth and grateful for the efforts she made to care for him and give him pleasure – gratitude that led him to leave his entire estate to her. His maidservant, Elizabeth Fisher, reported an episode in July when he was having a bad fit of the gout: after Elizabeth had cooked something for dinner that he especially enjoyed he commented, "God have mercy Betty, I see thou wilt p[er]forme according to thy promise in providing mee such Dyshes as I think fitt whilst I live, and when I dye thou knowest that I have left thee all."[149] He was still resolved to do nothing further for his daughters beyond the provisions he had already made. About July 20, Milton's lawyer brother Christopher paid his customary visit at the end of the court term before going down to the country for his vacation. Milton was "not well" and, Christopher later deposed, he "spoke what should be his will" if he should die before his brother returned at the next law term:

> Brother the porcion due to me from mr. Powell, my former wives father, I leave to the unkind children I had by her but I have receaved noe part of it and my will and meaning is they shall have noe other benefit of my estate then the said porcion and what I have beside don for them, they haveing ben very undutiful to me. and all the residue of my estate I leave to the disposall of Elizabeth my loveing wife.[150]

Christopher testified further that Milton was at that time "ill of the goute," and that he had declared "in a very calme manner . . . without passion, that his children had been unkind to him, but that his wife had been very kind and careful of him . . . [and that] in former tymes he hath herd him complaine, that they were careless of him being blind, and made nothing of deserteing him."[151]

It seems strange that Christopher, a lawyer, did not draw the will up in form for his brother to sign, but his testimony suggests that Milton expected him to return with it next term; Milton's death intervened and threw the matter into the courts.[152] Like many people, Milton thought he would have more time than he did have to put his affairs in order. Leaving his daughters the Powell debt seems like an empty gesture or even, as Christopher reports it, a calculated slight, but it may not have been so intended. The Powells had regained their property, the debt was a good one, and Milton and his brother may have thought that this was a way to force its payment. The maidservant Elizabeth Fisher gained that impression, testifying that she often heard Milton say,

> that he had made provision for his Children in his life time and had spent the greatest part of his estate in provideing for them and that hee was resolved hee would doe noe more for them liveing or dyeing, for that little p[ar]te which hee had left hee had given it to his wife . . . And likewise told this Deponent [Elizabeth Fisher] that there was a thousand pounds left in Mr. Powells hands to be disposed amongst his Children hereafter . . . hee was at that time very merry and not in any passion or angry humor neither at that time spoke any thing against any of his children. . . . [She] believeth that what is left the deceased's children in the will nuncupative . . . is a good debt; for that the said Mr. Powell is reputed a rich man.[153]

Milton's daughters challenged Milton's will, and the court determined that the conditions for a nuncupative will were not fully met, since Milton was not on his deathbed when he spoke it. Accordingly, instead of leaving the whole of Milton's estate to Elizabeth (about £1,000) they gave her one-third as widow and one-third as administrator, with the other third to be shared among the daughters, £100 each.

Edward Phillips writes that he paid his uncle "frequent visits to the last." On one late visit he may have given Milton great pleasure by reading to him the entries pertaining to him in *Theatrum Poetarum*, Phillips's brief catalogue of ancient and modern poets licensed for printing on September 14, 1674. In the preface he alludes, without the title, to a recently published English heroic poem proving that "the use of Measure alone without any Rime at all, would give far more ample Scope and liberty, both in Style and fancy then can possibly be observ'd in Rime."[154] His entry for "Milton" reads,

> *John Milton,* the Author (not to mention his other Works, both in Latin and English, both in strict and solute Oration, by which his Fame is sufficiently known to all the learned of Europe), of two Heroic Poems and a Tragedy, namely *Paradice lost, Paradice Regain'd*, and *Sampson Agonistes*, in which how far he both reviv'd the Majesty and true Decorum of Heroic Poesy and Tragedy, it will better become a person less related then my self, to deliver his judgement.[155]

Cyriack Skinner describes Milton's peaceful death as if he had been in attendance or at any rate had a detailed account from some who were: "Hee dy'd in a fitt of the Gout, but with so little pain or Emotion, that the time of his expiring was not perceiv'd by those in the room" (*EL* 33). The death was probably from renal failure associated with his gout; the records leave unclear whether he died on November 9 or November 10, 1674. He was buried in St Giles Cripplegate on November 12. Skinner thought it especially fitting that, like the patriarchs and kings of Israel, "he was gather'd to his people; for hee happen'd to bee bury'd in Cripplegate where about thirty yeer before hee had by chance also interrd his Father" (*EL* 34).[156] Phillips, who surely attended the funeral, writes that "He . . . had a very decent interment according to his Quality, in the Church of *St Giles Cripplegate*, being attended from His House to the Church by several Gentlemen then in Town, his principal wellwishers and admirers" (*EL* 76). His place of rest is now marked by a small stone near the altar rail, engraved simply, "Near this spot was buried John Milton. Author of *Paradise Lost*. Born 1608. Died 1674" (plate 18).

Epilogue
"Something . . . Written to Aftertimes"

Milton has probably had a greater influence on major poets and writers over a longer period of time than any other English literary figure except Shakespeare. Later readers and writers looked to him for a powerful formulation of the great biblical myths of Western civilization: the garden state of innocence, Satan or the embodiment of evil, the Fall of humankind, and, assimilated to them, the classical myths of the Golden Age, Pandora, Flora, Prosperine, Scylla and Charybdis, Prometheus, and Creation out of Chaos. Indeed, many readers virtually conflated Milton's portrayal of Eden and the Fall with the Genesis account. Also, Milton was seen to have established literary norms and styles: Harold Bloom claims that English poets from Dryden to T. S. Eliot looked upon Milton as a daunting father figure, who set them a standard of imaginative force and eloquent expression which they felt compelled to imitate or adapt or rebel against.[1] Moreover, subsequent writers sought in Milton their own theological, political and cultural ideals, prompting conflict from the outset between orthodox and reformist versions of Milton's legacy.

His influence soon spread beyond anglophone countries through translations of *Paradise Lost* and some other poems and treatises into Dutch, French, Italian, German, Russian, and Polish, and more recently, Chinese and Japanese. Also, his poems influenced artists in other media. From 1688 onward *Paradise Lost* and sometimes other Milton poems provided a stimulus for distinguished illustrations, of which Blake's are masterpieces. Handel composed an oratorio on texts from *Samson Agonistes*. He also composed a three-part secular oratorio with texts from *L'Allegro* and *Il Penseroso* and a characteristically eighteenth-century conclusion, *Il Moderato*; in the late twentieth century Mark Morris added a ballet to that Handel work. Milton's epic also supplied inspiration, and the libretto, for an impressive opera entitled *Paradise Lost* by the twentieth-century Polish composer Penderecki.

Milton's younger contemporary, Dryden, acknowledged his impact by imitation, praise, appropriation, and ideological revision. Into *The State of Innocence*, his dramatic version of *Paradise Lost*, Dryden imported couplet rhyme and royalist politics, and his satiric brief epic, *Absolom and Achitopel* (1681), written during the exclusion crisis, models the Whig Shaftesbury on Milton's crafty Satan. The temptation scenes of Dryden's *Hind and the Panther* bear Milton's impress and verbal allusions abound in his translations of Virgil. In a laudatory epigram to the 1688 edition of *Paradise Lost*, Dryden proposed Milton as England's poet, surpassing Homer and Virgil – though by locating all of them in a distant epic past he sought to neutralize Milton's politics and literary influence:

> Three poets, in three distant ages born,
> Greece, Italy, and England did adorn.
> The first in loftiness of thought surpassed;
> The next in majesty; in both the last.
> The force of nature could no further go;
> To make a third, she joined the former two.

That handsome 1688 Folio with its commendations, striking illustrations by John Baptist Medina, and subscription by over 500 Englishmen was a major factor in returning Milton to the mainstream, repressing his radical politics and theology, and presenting his epic as the pride of the English nation. While several early readers – among them Defoe, John Toland, John Dennis, and Isaac Newton – recognized and sometimes complained of the Arianism and republicanism in *Paradise Lost*, Addison's influential series of essays for *The Spectator* (1728) sidestepped such issues, emphasizing the poem's classical dimension, evaluating its literary excellence by neoclassical standards, and proclaiming it as the national epic.

A few eighteen-century poets like Richard Blackmore tried to follow Milton in epic, but better poets recognized that he had exhausted that genre, at least for a time, and engaged with the Miltonic legacy in other ways. Pope's brilliant mock epic, *The Rape of the Lock*, parodies passages and supernatural machinery from *Paradise Lost* in recounting a rake's theft of a coquette's lock of hair; and in his satiric epic *The Dunciad* Pope rises to a Miltonic high style in evoking the image of Chaos and Night returned again to uncreate the world. Also, Pope appropriated Miltonic language in his translations of Homer and recast Milton's epic purpose, "To justify the ways of God to man," in defining the intent of his *Essay on Man:* "To vindicate the ways of God to man." Many lesser poets – among them Thomas Gray, James Thomson, Edward Young, William Collins, and William Cowper – attempted to imitate the blank verse and "sublimity" of *Paradise Lost*, or wrote in "Miltonicks," the tetrameter couplets of the very popular companion poems, *L'Allegro* and *Il Penseroso*; their poems were filled with Miltonic allusions, poetic diction, and syntax. Milton came to be regarded as the very type of the great poet, and a chorus of voices agreed with Edmund Burke and Samuel Johnson that his characteristic quality was sublimity. Dr Johnson underscored Milton's greatness but, prompted by his antipathy for Milton's politics and by the neoclassical standards of his age, he also found much to object to in Milton's poetry: the use of pastoral and the mix of Christian and classical supernatural elements in *Lycidas*, the "faults" of language and versification and the want of human interest in *Paradise Lost*, and the lack of a "middle" in *Samson Agonistes*.

Colonial and post-revolutionary Americans embraced Milton as a model of sublime thought and expression, a major source of imitation and quotation, and a valuable support for orthodoxy in several areas. Schoolmasters illustrated points of grammar and rhetoric out of his poems, moralists pointed to his Eve and his Garden of Eden for ideals of womanly virtue and wedded love, ministers cited him to support their own positions and appropriated his images to tell the Christian story. Milton's companion poems prompted a rash of mostly pedestrian mood poems, and New England poets celebrated the Puritan errand into the Wilderness and the New World experience in an epic style derived from Milton and Pope. Philip Freneau's *The Rising Glory of America* in blank verse (1772), Timothy Dwight's *The Conquest of Canaan* (1785) and Joel Barlow's *The Vision of Columbus* (1787) in heroic couplets reworked images, passages, and episodes from *Paradise Lost* – the Infernal Council, Michael's prophecy, Adam and Eve in Eden and their Morning Hymn – often appropriating Milton's words. Both Milton and Pope influenced the first African-American poet, the educated eighteenth-century slave woman Phillis Wheatley. She often imitated Milton's syntax, cadences, themes, and verse forms. In *Phillis' Reply* she terms Milton the "British Homer" and "Europa's Bard," affirming at once her debt to him, her own insufficiencies in high poetry, and the end of his epic tradition: "in him Britania's prophet dies."

But if Milton's example was of little use to poets who made him into a literary icon, reformist and radical statesmen in America, England, and France found much to their various purposes in both his prose and his poetry. In the buildup to the Glorious Revolution (1688) English Whigs – John Locke, Algernon Sidney, John Toland, and Anthony Cooper, Third Earl of Shaftesbury – drew often unacknowledged support from Milton's attacks on sacerdotal kingship and press censorship, and from his arguments for Protestant religious toleration and the contract theory of government in *Areopagitica*, *Tenure*, the *Defensio*, *Of Civil Power*, and *Hirelings*. In 1774 the English Republican historian Catherine Macauley reprised the arguments of *Areopagitica* in *A Modest Plea for the Property of Copy Right*, and her eight-volume *History of England* (1763–83) defended the English revolution, the regicide, and the Commonwealth by marshaling the contract theory arguments of Sidney, Locke, the Levellers, and Milton's *Tenure* and *Defensio*. Often reprinted in England, *Areopagitica* was the first Milton book published in America (1774), and its arguments have continued to echo down the centuries in defense of liberal ideas of toleration and intellectual freedom. Milton's other tracts also served revolutionaries in America, and his poetic imagery and rhetoric was even more important for them. His agonizing pleas to his countrymen in *The Readie and Easie Eay* was used in 1770 to denounce American backsliders; Benjamin Franklin damned British taxation policy as reminiscent of Milton's description of Chaos; and John Adams described British colonial rule in the imagery of Satanic pomp and foolish resistance, citing Milton as one who helped convince him that a republic is the only good government. Jefferson excerpted some 48 passages from *Paradise Lost* and *Samson Agonistes* in his Commonplace book (many of them dealing with Satan's revolt), and in 1776 he called on the antiprelatical tracts in an argument for disestablishing the Church of England in Virginia. In France, Mirabeau's *Sur La Liberté de la Presse,* which paraphrases or translates much of *Areopagitica,* was published four times between 1788 and 1792, and an anonymous treatise on which he collaborated, the *Théorie de la Royauté d'auprès la doctrine de Milton* (1789), undertook to justify the French Revolution and its aftermath with arguments and extracts from the *Defensio* and other Milton tracts. It was republished in 1792 with a preface calling for the trial and execution of Louis XVI.

The English Romantics celebrated Milton as a prophet and a revolutionary in his life and in his art; because they set themselves to take up his prophetic mantle, they were able to respond creatively to his example. Blake's engagement with Milton was both pervasive and profound: Blake and his wife sat nude in their garden reading aloud Book IV of *Paradise Lost*; Blake engaged in visionary conversations with Milton; and Blake's striking illustrations of *Comus, Paradise Lost* and *Paradise Regained* provide brilliant commentaries on those poems. *The Marriage of Heaven and Hell* famously claims Milton for the Devil's party, understanding Milton's Satan as a figure of energy and rebellion; and Blake's several long, epic-like prophetic poems bear the impress of *Paradise Lost* and especially *Paradise Regained.* His poem *Milton* makes that poet an epic hero, one of the angels of the Apocalypse who fell into errors of selfhood by wronging his wives and daughters, his "emanations," and who returns to earth to redeem those errors; entering the foot of his successor poet–prophet Blake, Milton is joined with him in the work of building the new Jerusalem "in England's green & pleasant Land." For Wordsworth, Milton was also a powerful inspiration. In his efforts to revive the sonnet genre he looked to the lofty Miltonic model – "in his hand / The Thing became a trumpet." He invoked Milton in his sonnet *London 1802* as an exemplar of steadfast freedom of mind, noble ideals, virtue, and duty: "Milton! thou shouldst be living at this hour: / England hath need of three." Wordsworth commented astutely and admiringly on many Milton passages, read his poems aloud with his sister Dorothy, often invoked his example in discussing issues of poetics, and in *The Excursion* expressed his epic aspirations in Miltonic blank verse. In defining "the Mind of Man" as its theme Wordsworth's blank verse epic, *The Prelude,* takes off from the promise of a "paradise within" at the end of *Paradise Lost.* It also finds precedent in Milton's Proems to Books I, III, VII, and IX of *Paradise Lost,* which treat the Bard's heroic trials in writing his epic, for a new heroic subject: Wordsworth's development as man and poet. *The Prelude* is dense with verbal and structural echoes and transformations of *Paradise Lost*: Helvellyn recalls Eden, the ascent of Snowdon recalls Adam's ascent of the highest hill of Paradise, the French Revolution reprises the Fall.

The second generation of Romantic poets were also aided in realizing their poetic visions through engagement with Milton. Byron's notorious "Byronic" heroes – Manfred, Cain – are descendents of Milton's Satan in their dark passions, enormous nameless guilt, total alienation, and titanic self-assertion. A defiant critic of all sorts of orthodoxy who died fighting to liberate Greece, Byron praised Milton's intellectual courage in facing down tyrants, and in *Don Juan* wished him back "to freeze once more / The blood of monarchs with his prohecies" and to convict time-serving poets of the present. Strongly influenced by Byron, the revolutionary Russian poet Pushkin also looked to Milton as an embodiment of genius, integrity, and amazing courage. Shelley honored Milton as a republican and a bold inquirer into morals and religion who made his Satan far superior to his God in moral virtue, giving him the best arguments and a character of unsurpassed energy and magnificence. Milton's impress on Shelley's poetry is everywhere: in *Milton's Spirit* he imagines that Milton might again sound his "Uranian lute" to make "sanguine thrones and impious altars" quake; his elegy for Keats, *Adonais*, invites comparison with *Lycidas*; and *Prometheus Unbound*, a poem in four books about the regaining of Paradise, owes large debts to *Paradise Regained* and Jesus's evolving definition of the kingdom within. Keats also admired Milton's zealous liberalism, waxed enthusiastic about several passages of sublimity, beauty, and pathos in *Paradise Lost*, and responded to seeing a lock of Milton's hair with a poem promising to follow his example and rise to nobler philosophic harmonies. His epic fragment *Hyperion* portrays the fall of Saturn and the Titans sympathetically, but treats the rise of the new gods and especially Apollo, god of the sun and of high poetry, as necessary for progress. Miltonic elements range from the sinuous blank verse to the debate of the baffled Titans, to many particulars of image and idiom, but Keats came to believe the Miltonic mode to be antitherical to his own genius, and began the poem over again in other terms. Mary Shelley's novel *Frankenstein*, written at a period when Shelley was reading *Paradise Lost* aloud in the evenings, is a strikingly original recreation of Milton's central myth; its epigram from *Paradise Lost* – "Did I request thee, Maker, from my clay / To mould me man? Did I solicit thee / From darkness to promote me" – invites association of Dr Frankenstein with Milton's God, the creature with Adam, and both with aspects of Satan.

Romantic critics commented at length and often astutely about Milton's poetry, and, like the poets, found his Satan powerfully attractive. Coleridge honored Milton's republicanism and role in the English revolution, characterized him as a "sublimer poet than Homer or Virgil," and ranked him with Shakespeare. He admired the Miltonic Satan's "dark and savage grandeur," but also observed that he displayed the egotism characteristic of "liberticides" from Nimrod to Bonaparte.[2] Hazlitt described Milton's Satan as the most heroic epic subject ever chosen for a poem, and praised Milton for portraying his nature and his rhetoric without any recourse to cheap deformities, while also showing him to embody love of power, pride, self-will, and ambition. And when Walter Savage Landor and the poet laureate Robert

Southey elaborated on and added to Dr Johnson's criticisms of Milton, Thomas De Quincey offered a spirited defense of his poems and prose works.

Victorian poets and critics were usually more restrained and more selective than the Romantics in their responses to Milton. Some honored him as a republican and a lover of liberty. Extracts from *Tenure*, *Eikonoklastes*, and *The Readie and Easie Way* appeared in several Chartist tracts, new editions of his prose praised his heroic patriotism, and David Masson's six-volume biography provided a richly detailed and sympathetic account of his life and times. In 1825 Thomas Macauley produced a long panegyric essay on Milton and his works, prompted by the shocked reactions of some Victorians to the Arianism and other heterodoxies in the newly discovered *De Doctrina Christiana*. Those, he declared, should not surprise any careful reader of *Paradise Lost*. Macauley terms Milton "the glory of English literature, the champion and the martyr of English liberty," praising him especially for recognizing, in *Areopagitica*, the horrors of intellectual slavery and the benefits of a free press in promoting "the unfettered exercise of private judgment."[3] He honored Milton's personal triumph over the greatest difficulties and saw the same qualities in his "wonderful" Satan, whom he thought superior even to Prometheus in energy and noble endurance. Ranking Milton's two epics above all subsequent poems, he valued especially Milton's ability, despite age, anxiety, and disappointment, to adorn *Paradise Lost* with "all that is most lovely and delightful in the physical and in the moral world." By contrast, Matthew Arnold deprecated Milton's character, most of his prose works, and the subject matter of his epic as products of the Hebraic spirit nurtured by Puritanism. But he thought that spirit often countered in Milton's poetry by the Hellenistic influence, making for a patchwork of dazzling lines, splendid passages, and an unfailingly sublime poetic style. He includes several short passages from *Paradise Lost* among his touchstones of highest poetic quality, by which he would have readers form their taste and critical judgment.

Among the Victorian poets, both Arnold and Tennyson at times imitated Milton's blank verse and his diction. In an elegantly crafted poem in alcaics entitled *Milton*, Tennyson paid tribute to Milton's sublime style – "O mighty-mouthed inventor of harmonies, / . . . God-gifted organ voice of England." Gerard Manley Hopkins valued Milton's art, and especially the rhythm and metrics of *Paradise Regained* and *Samson*, above that of any other poetry in any language: terming Milton "the great standard in the use of counterpoint," he pointed to the choruses of *Samson Agonistes* as a forerunner of his own sprung rhythm.[4] Among the Victorian novelists, George Eliot felt his impress strongly. She thought his tractate on education and his divorce tracts especially relevant for her own era, and her novels often refer to or allude to Milton in treating issues of experience and moral choice. In *Middlemarch* Dorothea Brooke compares herself to Milton's daughters when she decides to marry Casaubon so as to assist him with a great intellectual project, though unlike them she expects by doing so to gain wisdom herself; the novel explores the disastrous consequences of her inexperience and naiveté in mistaking the pedant Casaubon for a Milton surrogate. In *Great Expectations* Dickens presents Pip's fall as a bourgeois parody of Adam's, both of them "fondly overcome with Female charm"; the novel ends with Pip and Estella reprising Adam and Eve as they leave a wrecked garden with hands joined.

Nineteenth-century Americans related readily to Milton's theology and politics as well as his poetry, sensing, as R. W. Griswold declared in 1846, that "Milton is more emphatically *American* than any other author who has lived in the United States."[5] New England Unitarians were pleased to find Arianism and Arminianism in Milton's newly recovered *De Doctrina Christiana*, William Ellery Channing proclaiming him a great saint and an inspired master spirit. New England Transcendentalists encountered him through Coleridge and other English Romantics, but also directly. Emerson cited and paraphrased Milton's comments on poetic inspiration in *The Reason of Church-government*, and proclaimed Milton "the sublimest bard of all,"[6] a judgment based on his belief that all of Milton's poetry is a version of his own heroic life of bravery, purity, temperance, toil, self-reliance, and devotion. Honoring especially his defense of the individual conscience in *Areopagitica*, Emerson termed him an "apostle of freedom" in the house, in the state, in the church, and in the press, asserting categorically that "no man can be named whose mind still acts on the cultivated intellect of England and America with an energy comparable to that of Milton."[7] Emerson identified with Milton the prophet, and took the title of his poem *Uriel* from Milton's angel of the sun, conjoining in that figure Satan's rebelliousness and Uriel's devotion to truth. Margaret Fuller, who read Milton at fourteen and identified her own ambition with his, thought Milton's prose works deserve to be studied beyond any other English prose for the exemplar figure they reveal: "If Milton be not absolutely the greatest of human beings, it is hard to name one who combines so many features of God's own image, ideal goodness, a life of spotless nature, heroic endeavor and constancy, with such richness of gifts." Like Griswold she thought him a peculiarly American spirit, who "understood the nature of liberty, of justice – what is required for the unimpeded action of conscience, what constitutes true marriage, and the scope of manly education."[8] During the buildup to the American Civil War *Paradise Lost* supplied rhetorical force to denunciations of the Southern revolt, which Edward Everett in an oration at Gettysburg likened to "that first foul revolt of 'the Infernal Serpent.' "[9] And Lincoln, reading the first books of *Paradise Lost*, was reportedly struck "by the coincidences between the utterances of Satan and those of Jefferson Davis."[10]

In his short story *Rappacini's Daughter* Hawthorne presents a dark version of Milton's Eden, in which a father creates a beautiful garden whose fruit poisons his daughter and her poisoned body infects her lover. In his epic novel *Moby Dick* Melville invests in Captain Ahab the indomitable will and obsession with revenge of Milton's Satan, and embodies in his white whale Satan's (or God's) titanic strength and seeming cosmic malevolence. Throughout the novel the issues foregrounded are those at the core of Milton's epic, debated fruitlessly by his fallen angels, and embodying, Melville thinks, Milton's own profound questioning of theodicy: "Providence, Foreknowledge, Will, and Fate, / Fixt Fate, Free Will, Foreknowledge absolute."[11]. And Walt Whitman took on the mantle of the poet–seer from Milton and Wordsworth as he sang a new, democratic epic celebrating himself as the embodiment of everything in the universe.

In the earlier twentieth century, and especially in England, Milton the poet was seen as an icon of the cultural and literary establishment, to be embraced as such or vigorously rejected, whereas Milton the man was repudiated as a dour Puritan, republican, and regicide. C. S. Lewis praised *Paradise Lost* as a brilliantly realized epic of orthodox Christianity, while William Empson carried on his battle against the God of that same orthodox Christianity who disfigured, as he thought, the text of Milton's epic. T. S. Eliot admitted his antipathy toward Milton the man, arising, as he shrewdly recognized, from the fact that the Civil War has never really ended in England. In several essays beginning in 1922 Eliot launched the modernist attack on Milton's poetry, warning his poet–contemporaries against imitating the poet who had helped produce a "dissociation of sensibility" in English poetry and whose convoluted poetic language violates English norms. He recanted some of this in 1947, acknowledging that Milton had invented a great though inimitable poetic language marked by musicality, long periods, and imagery evoking vast size and limitless space, and that modern poets might learn from him about freedom within form. While American New Critics were echoing Eliot's disparagement of Milton's poetry, American scholars were producing painstaking editions of his entire oeuvre; in the crisis years before and during World War II, that oeuvre was often held forth as an embodiment of Christian humanism and American liberal values of toleration, individualism, and personal freedom. Virginia Woolf's reference to "Milton's bogey" – his ideas of woman's inferiority as a major obstacle to women writers' creativity – in the final chapter of *A Room of One's Own* (1929) shaped the response to Milton of many twentieth-century feminist readers. A similar notion of Milton's repressive effect on women informs Robert Graves' novel imagining Milton's domestic life, *The Story of Mary Powell Wife to Mr Milton* (1943). Some contemporary feminists, however, have been led by Milton, as Catherine Macauley, Margaret Fuller, and George Eliot had been, to write themselves into his programs of reform and intellectual liberty. In that appropriative spirit Malcolm X enlisted Milton for black liberation, identifying his Satan with the popes and kings and other evil forces of Europe, and so concluding that "Milton and Mr. Elijah Muhammad were actually saying the same thing."[12]

Milton's impress on twentieth-century literary texts is often a matter of allusions that evoke his works to supply context or ironic contrast. A few examples must suffice. Eliot's *Four Quartets* contain allusions that incorporate Milton among the many voices commenting on memory and history; Eliot's verse dramas, especially *Murder in the Cathedral*, owe a good deal to *Samson Agonistes*; and Eliot played off Milton's title for his *Sweeney Agonistes*. James Joyce's epic novel *Ulysses* looks to

Milton as well as Homer and Dante for some elements of theme and style. Aldous Huxley evoked the poignant description of Milton's Samson to set the tone for his novel, *Eyeless in Gaza*. Clifford Odets used the title *Paradise Lost* for a 1934 play in which a family is dispossessed from their little Eden – their home – by the forces of capitalism and the Depression; it contains a very minor character called Milton, who lisps and whose chief business is to define the nature of man as 80 per cent alkaline and 20 percent acid. In his poem *Skunk Hour* Robert Lowell imports Satan's line to characterize the mood of his speaker: "I myself am hell." In his poem *Adam and Eve* Karl Shapiro alludes to Milton's scenes of Adam's longing and Eve's creation to rewrite the story of their union. And in the mode of tribute, Jorge Luis Borges' poem entitled *A Rose and Milton* voices a poignant wish that some rose Milton once "held before his face, but could / Not see" might, for that association, be spared oblivion.

In the later twentieth century critics and theorists of every stripe – Marxists, feminists, deconstructionists, new historicists, psychological critics, and more – have made Milton grist for their several mills. And as the new millennium begins, he is still a battleground for our culture wars. On the one hand, so strong is the impulse to reclaim him for orthodoxy that some scholars are casting doubt on his authorship of much or all of his heterodox theological treatise, *De Doctrina Christiana.* On the other hand, critics writing from a Marxist, cultural materialist, or historicist perspective are interrogating all his poetry and prose to situate his complex texts more precisely in their political and cultural milieu, and to examine how they relate to some of the fraught issues of our time: gender roles, marriage and divorce, imperialism, individualism, the artist in society. Postmodernist critics value the dividedness and ambiguities of his texts, the fact that for him truth is not a monolithic closed system but the dismembered body so graphically described in *Areopagitica.* Ideological concerns and critical fashions have changed over three centuries, but what endures is the response of generation after generation of readers to Milton's superlative poetry and to his large vision of the human condition.

Notes

Chapter 1 "The Childhood Shews the Man" 1608–1625

1 British Library Add Ms. 32310. Milton made this entry much later, on the occasion of the birth of his first child Anne (1646). At that same time he also recorded the birth of his brother Christopher (1615) but not of his older sister Anne, who may have died *c.* 1640. He also recorded the ages of her sons, then living and studying with him.

2 *Registers of All Hallows, Bread Street*, Harleian Society, XLIII (London, 1913), 16; in *LR* I, 2.

3 John Stow, *A Survey of London* (London, 1603), 348, 346–53. The building was owned by Eton College and leased to a prominent merchant and alderman of the City of London, Sir Baptist Hicks. By 1632 and perhaps much earlier Milton senior also held a lease on a house called The Red Rose, on the opposite side of Bread Street.

4 *Registers of All Hallows*, 18; *LR* I, 11.

5 *LR* I, 4–5, 7–9, and *Chronology*, 9–10.

6 *EL* 1. His affiliation with Christchurch is not confirmed by college records, but his subsequent musical activities indicate that he had substantial musical training in youth.

7 The story is reported by Aubrey and in more detail by Milton's nephew, Edward Phillips (*EL* 50–1). Parker II, 675–87, 693–6 analyses the records pertaining to Milton's paternal and maternal ancestors.

8 *EL* 51–2. For Milton senior's business affairs and musical activities in these years see *LR* I, 3–102; Parker II, 687–93, and J. Milton French, *Milton in Chancery* (New York, 1939). He had several apprentices, among them Richard Milton (probably a relative) and Thomas Bower, who became his partner in 1625.

9 *EL* 6. Another early biographer, Jonathan Richardson (1734), heard that "he did well on the Organ and Bas-Viol" (*EL* 204).

10 *EL* 51. Aubrey states that Milton senior presented the *In Nomine* to a Polish Prince – probably a mistake for the the Landgrave of Hesse who visited England in 1611 – and that he was rewarded with a gold medal and chain. The *In Nomine* is in a set of partbooks at Oxford, Christ Church, Mus. 423–8.

11 These four songs and six new ones appeared in a manuscript collection (1616) by Thomas Myriell called *Tristitiae Remedium* (BL Add MS 29,372-29-377), and some of them in another anonymous collection of the same year. On Milton's early musical associations and experience see John Harper, "'One equal music': The Music of Milton's Youth," *MQ* 31 (1997), 1–10.

12 Thomas Ravenscroft, *The Whole Book of Psalmes*, London, 1621, 1633.

13 *Chronology,* 18.

14 Milton senior's sonnet is affixed to Lane's unpublished poem "Sir Guy Earle of Warwick." The manuscript, BL Harleian Ms 5243, is dated 1617.

15 *Register of All Hallows,* 169. There may have been other undocumented stillbirths or infant deaths before the poet's birth.

16 Skinner has been persuasively identified as author of this early biography of Milton by Parker (*Milton* I, xiv) and by Peter Beal in *Index of Literary Manuscripts,* Vol II.2 (London, 1993), 85–6. Edward Phillips had little direct knowledge of his grandmother: he was only 6 years old when she died, and got her family name wrong (*EL* 18, 52).

17 William Kerrigan, *The Sacred Complex* (Cambridge, Mass. and London, 1983), 177–80 argues that this association of blindness with his maternal (female) inheritance had a strong impact on Milton's relations with women.

18 Stock's funeral sermon preached by Thomas Gataker, *Abraham's Decease* (London, 1626) affords a basis for this characterization, as do many of his writings, e.g. *A Sermon Preached at Paules Crosse* (London, 1609) and *The Doctrine and Use of Repentance* (London, 1610).

19 James I was censured severely for failing to support his daughter, Elizabeth, and her husband Frederick, the Elector Palatine, after they lost Bohemia and much of the Palatinate in 1620 to the forces of Spain and the Holy Roman Emperor.

20 For an analysis of the annotations and underlinings, and speculations about provenance, see Cedric R. Brown, "A King James Bible, Protestant Nationalism, and Boy Milton," in *Form and Reform in Renaissance England: Essays in Honor of Barbara Kiefer Lewalski*, eds. Amy Boesky and Mary Thomas Crane (Newark, NJ, 2000), 271–87.

21 Cited by Arthur Barker, "Milton's Schoolmasters," *Modern Language Review* 32 (1937), 520. Another teacher may have been Patrick Young, at the time Prebendary and Treasurer of St Paul's; Franciscus Junius later referred to Milton as his "disciple."

22 Milton was 10 years old in 1618, so Aubrey's date is also inconsistent. Young came to London sometime before 1612. Exactly when he became pastor at Ware is not known; he may have combined his pastoral and tutorial duties for a time, before taking up an appointment in Hamburg in 1620. His sabbatarian tract *Dies Dominica* was published pseudonymously in 1639, and in 1640–2 he was primary author of several "Smectymnuan" tracts against Bishop Joseph Hall and prelacy (see chapter 5, pp. 128–31). He was master of Jesus College, Cambridge from 1644 to 1650, at which point he was ejected for refusing to take the Engagement to the new Commonwealth. Conceivably, the reference to a schoolmaster in Essex indicates that Milton had another tutor from Essex, or was tutored in Essex for a time.

23 Though the subject and painter cannot be identified with absolute certainty, tradition and the preponderance of evidence points to Milton as subject. See Leo Miller, "Milton's Portraits," *Milton Quarterly* (special issue, 1976), 3–9.

24 *CPW* I, 311; Elegy IV, ll. 29–32: "Primus ego Aonios illo praeunte recessus / Lustrabam, & bifidi sacra vireta jugi, / Pieriosque hausi latices, Clioque favente / Castalio sparsi

laeta ter ora mero" (*Poems*, 1645; Hughes's translation). Unless otherwise indicated, Milton poems quoted in text and notes are taken from the 1645 *Poems*.

25 The relevant records of St Paul's were destroyed in the Great Fire (1666), but registration records at Christ's College, Cambridge (April 9, 1625) state that Milton was prepared at Paul's.

26 Donald L. Clark, *John Milton at St Paul's School* (New York, 1948), 27–32 thinks he entered in 1615 at age 7, the usual time of entry to grammar school, but most biographers think he entered in 1620. Edward Phillips's statement that he "was enter'd into the first Rudiments of Learning" at Paul's might seem to support Clark, but against that is Phillips's comment that he was sent to school "together with his brother Christopher," who was born in 1615 (*EL* 53). The evidence is not conclusive.

27 *EL* 10. Edward Phillips also reports Milton's "insuperable Industry" in these nocturnal studies, which included both voluntary studies and "the exact perfecting of his School-Exercises" (*EL* 54).

28 John Stow, *A Survey of the Cities of London and Westminster . . . Corrected, improved, and very much Enlarged . . . By John Strype,* 2 vols (London, 1720), I, Bk 1, 163–4.

29 The statutes and rules are set out in Clark, *Milton at St Paul's School*, 38–44, 49–52.

30 John Aubrey, *Lives of Eminent Men*, ed. A. Clark, 2 vols (Oxford, 1898), I, 263.

31 Alexander Gil, Jr., *PARERGA, Sive Poetici Conatus* (London, 1632). See Wood, *Athenae Oxonienses*, 4 vols (London, 1813–20), III, 42–3; Clark, *Milton at St Paul's School*, 83–99; and Barker, "Milton's Schoolmasters," 526–36. Among Gil's early poems are funeral tributes to members of the royal family and several panegyrics.

32 That poem, *In ruinam camerae Papisticae Londoni Octob. 26,"* was published in *PARERGA*. The poem finds providential the fact that the date was November 5 (Guy Fawkes Day) by the Gregorian Calendar. There is an English version in Bodleian MS Ashmole 36, 37.

33 See Parker II, 712–14.

34 "Thyrsis & Damon, eiusdem viciniae Pastores, eadem studia sequuti a pueritia amici erant, ut qui plurimum" (*Poems,* 1673).

35 Donald C. Dorian, *The English Diodatis* (New Brunswick, NJ 1950), 3–96.

36 Charles Diodati, "Sic furua conjux tartarei Jovis," *Camdeni Insignia* (Oxford, 1624), sig. E 4.

37 The curriculum has been reconstructed from contemporary records by Clark, *Milton at St Paul's School*, 100–249.

38 This famous grammar was composed by Lily and Colet between 1510 and 1515; the revision of 1540, with additions by Thomas Robertson, was made mandatory in the schools by Henry VIII. Milton used a text with further revisions that was issued first in 1574 and often thereafter, *A Shorte Introduction of Grammar generallye to be used*, bound with *Brevissima Institutio seu Ratio Grammatices cognoscendae ad omnium puerorum utilitatem per scripta.* See Clark, *Milton at St Paul's School*, 132–3.

39 Harris Francis Fletcher, *The Intellectual Development of John Milton*, 2 vols (Urbana, Ill. 1956–61), I, surveys the texts Milton most likely used for Greek and Hebrew grammar, mathematics, and astronomy.

40 Clark, *Milton at St Paul's School*, 48–50.

41 A loose sheet containing these texts, found in Milton's Commonplace Book in 1874, is the only conjectural example we have of Milton's very neat, schoolboy hand. It is now

in Austin Texas, at the Humanities Research Center (Pre-1700 Manuscript 127); there is an autotype in the Public Record Office, and a photograph in the British Library (Add MS 41,063. I, ff. 84–5.) See *Chronology*, 24.

42 Milton's edition of Aphthonius's *Progymnasmata* was the one that became standard for 150 years, translated and augmented by Reinhard Lorich (1546; 1596); it was often reissued. See Walter MacKellar, ed. *Latin Poems of John Milton* (New Haven, Conn. 1930), 365; and Clark, *Milton at St Paul's School*, 206, 233, 235–7.

43 Stella Revard, *Milton and the Tangles of Neaera's Hair* (Columbia, NY and London, 1997), 11–12, points also to the Greek epigrammatist Meleager and the Renaissance poet Hieronymus Baldi as exemplars for this theme.

44 Mantuan, *Sylvarum*, Bk 4, *Opera*, 3 vols (Paris, 1513), II, f. 1904v.

45 Besides Hebrew, Milton could read the other oriental languages important for the Bible: Aramaic (which he called Chaldee) and Syriac. He proposed teaching those "dialects" in the curriculum he designed in *Of Education*, and taught them to his nephews, according to Edward Phillips (*EL* 61). So it seems likely that his own Hebrew studies made a beginning in Aramaic and Syriac. See Gordon Campbell and Sebastian Brock, "Milton's Syriac," *MQ* 27 (1993), 74–7.

46 *Registers of St Stephen Walbrook, and of St Benet Sherehog, London*, ed. W. Bruce Bannerman, Harleian Society XLIX (1919), 60.

47 The document is in the Pierpont Morgan Library (MA 953). Edward Phillips (*EL* 53) comments on the generous settlement.

48 Christopher Hill, *Milton and the English Revolution* (London, 1977), 27.

49 Joshua Sylvester, *Bartas His Divine Weekes and Workes* (London, 1605, 1621, etc.).

50 Variorum, II.1, 111–18.

Chapter 2 "To Cambridge . . . For Seven Years" 1625–1632

1 See chapter 1, pp. 11–13

2 Samuel Johnson, *Lives of the English Poets*, ed. G. B. Hill, 3 vols (Oxford, 1905), I, 87.

3 See Stella P. Revard, *Milton and the Tangles of Neaera's Hair: The Making of the 1645 Poems* (Columbia, MO., 1997).

4 See *Variorum* I, 3–24; R. W. Condee, "The Latin Poetry of John Milton," in *The Latin Poetry of the English Poets*, ed. J. W. Binns (London, 1974), 58–92; and John K. Hale, "Milton Playing with Ovid," *MS* 25 (1989), 3–20.

5 *LR* I, 90–1. According to the (Latin) record of admission to Christ's, "John Milton of London, son of John, instituted in the elements of letters under Master Gill, prefect of St Paul's School, was admitted as a minor pensioner on February 12, 1624/5, under Master Chappell. He paid for entrance ten shillings." After he matriculated on April 9 he may have returned to London again, since the university was in vacation until the beginning of Easter term (April 28).

6 James Bass Mullinger, *The University of Cambridge*, 3 vols (Cambridge, 1873–1911), I, 398–9.

7 Henry Peacham, *The Compleat Gentleman* (London, 1627), 33.

8 Their residence at Cambridge overlaps with Milton's, at least briefly. See Mullinger, *University of Cambridge*, II, 370–439; Masson, I, 111–45; and John Peile, *Biographical*

Register of Christ's College, 1505–1905, 2 vols (Cambridge, 1910–13), I, 387, 414–16. Other poets of Christ's before Milton's time were Barnabe Googe and the emblematist Francis Quarles (Peile, *Biographical Register*, I, 56, 387, 254).

9 John Peile, *Christ's College* (London, 1900), 121–59, and Peile, *Biographical Register,* I, 211–12, 141–42, 89–90, 94, 295–96, 143–44, 185–6.

10 Mullinger, *University of Cambridge*, II, 567; III, 15–63; John Twigg, *The University of Cambridge and the English Revolution, 1625–1688* (Cambridge, 1990), 11–41. The master of Christ's from 1609 to 1622, Valentine Cary, had been a fervant anti-Calvinist. In Milton's years the university's chief governing officers, the annually elected vice-chancellors, were John Mansell, John Gostlin, Henry Smyth, Thomas Bainbridge, Matthew Wren, and Henry Butts.

11 Donald L. Clark, "John Milton and William Chappell," *Huntington Library Quarterly* 18 (1955), 329–50. Masson (I, 129) quotes a contemporary who claimed that Chappell "Arminianized" many of his students; that doctrinal bent is likely enough, since Archbishop Laud later supported his appointment as Provost of Trinity College, Dublin, and Bishop of Cork. Later also he wrote an art of preaching, *Methodus Concionandi* (London, 1648) and a tract on *The Use of Holy Scripture* (London, 1653).

12 The work was published in Latin in 1627 but not in English translation until after the revolution began (*The Key of the Revelation*, London, 1643), rpt. in *Works*, 1648, 1664. As Christopher Hill points out in *The World Turned Upside Down* (New York, 1972, 95–6), no vernacular translations of seminal works on Revelation and Daniel were published in England until the early 1640s, since prophetic application of the apocalyptic signs to the present historical moment had radical political implications troubling to the establishment (the casting down of kings, the rule of the saints). See John Rumrich, "Mead and Milton," *MQ* 20 (1986), 136–41.

13 Letters to and from Mede and a variety of correspondents are published in Thomas Birch, ed., *The Court and Times of Charles I,* 2 vols (London, 1848). Vol. 1 contains letters written during the 1620s to and from Mede and Sir Martin Stuteville (a kinsman), Dr James Maddus (a Londoner with connections in German universities and the court), Sir William Boswell (Charles I's resident at the Hague), John Pory (writing from Venice, Amsterdam, and Virginia), and others.

14 The curriculum prescribed by the Elizabethan statutes of 1561 – rhetoric in the first year, logic in the second and third, metaphysics in the fourth – had been much modified in practice.

15 *Directions for a Student in the Universitie* by Richard Holdsworth, a tutor at Emmanuel in Milton's time, outlines a course of study in which Latin and Greek literature and the Bible (in Latin, Greek, Hebrew, and English) are studied throughout; first-year tutorials focus on logic and ethics; and students in subsequent years take up politics, rhetoric, physics (natural science), astronomy, geography, metaphysics, and theology. Holdsworth's *Directions* is reprinted in Fletcher (II, 623–64). At Trinity, contemporary records indicate that lectors read and expounded Aristotle to the students, progressing from logic to ethics, physics, and metaphysics; their other major texts were Isocrates, Demosthenes, Plato, Homer, Hesiod, and Cicero. See Fletcher, II, 53–350 and Masson, I, 259–272.

16 According to his records, Bibles, catechisms, Calvinist theology texts, Latin and Greek Grammars, the major classical poets, rhetoricians, and historians as well as English translations of such texts were often purchased, as were some English texts, including Bacon,

Sidney's *Arcadia*, Quarles, and *Purchas his Pilgrimage*. Also, a few books of (chiefly ancient) cosmography, science, and travel and a very few mathematical texts. Mede's account books are reprinted in Fletcher, II, 553–622.

17 Milton's copy of Aratus, *Phaenomena & Diosemia* (Paris, 1559), is now in the British Library. Milton's autograph notes are on the title page (his name, 1631, the price, 2s 6d., and the motto "cum sole et luna semper Aratus erit") and several other pages. The annotations are chiefly corrections of grammar and metrical irregularities (he has checked his edition against others and the scholia) so as to obtain a correct text. See Maurice Kelley and Samuel Atkins, "Milton's Annotations of Aratus," *PMLA* 70 (1955), 1,090–106. An annotated copy of Pindar (now at Harvard) was long thought to be Milton's but probably is not: see Kelley and Atkins, "Milton and the Harvard Pindar," *Studies in Bibliography* 17 (1964), 77–82.

18 They had also to pass an oral examination before the proctors, to propose and answer some question out of Aristotle's *Prior Analytics*, and to have their degrees voted by the graduates and fellows.

19 Purchas died five months later, in September, 1626. See chapter 7, p. 212.

20 Records indicate that the family resided at Hammersmith in Middlesex from 1631 (see note 77), but Milton's father may have obtained a country place there or in the Horton/Colnbrook area (where relatives held property) at about this time, for occasional use in summer and in plague seasons.

21 Most scholars accept this period for the incident with Chappell and for Milton's Elegy I. For another speculative reconstruction of these events see Leo Miller, "Milton's Clash with Chappell," *MQ* 14 (1980), 77–86. Miller dates the rustication and Elegy I, the poem he wrote about that event, to 1627, speculating that Chappell was responding to Milton's public denigration of scholastic disputation in Prolusion IV.

22 The right of whipping belonged to the Praelector and Dean, offices not then held by Chappell (Peile, *Christ's College*, 147–8).

23 *LR* III, 374–5. The letter is from Bramhall to his son (May 9/19, 1654); see chapter 9, n. 103. The evidence would seem to counter the view of some scholars, among them A. N. Wilson, *The Life of Milton* (Oxford, 1983), 18–19, who deny both the whipping and the rustication, suggesting that Milton's "exile" may simply refer to the spring vacation, given his tone of playful exaggeration in describing that event in Elegy I.

24 Translation, Carey. "Nec dudum vetiti me laris angit amor. / Nuda nec arva placent, umbrasque negantia molles, / Quam male Phoebicolis convenit ille locus! / Nec duri libet usque minas perferre magistri / Caeteraque ingenio non subeunda meo." Unless otherwise indicated, all of Milton's poems in this chapter are quoted from *Poems*, 1645. Latin translations are credited when they are not my own.

25 See R. W. Condee, "Ovid's Exile and Milton's Rustication," *Philological Quarterly* 37 (1958), 498–502.

26 One reference might point to a contemporary production of *Romeo and Juliet* or a work with similar plot: "some poor lad [who] leaves joys untasted and dies, his love snuffed out, a fit subject for tears."

27 See Revard, *Tangles of Neaera's Hair*, 8–13, for Milton's use of elegiac topoi stemming from Propertius, Ovid, and the neo-Latin poet Joannes Secundus.

28 Tovey was raised in the household of the Haringtons of Exton and sent to the university by Lucy Harington Russell, Countess of Bedford, which links him with a reformist

Protestant circle. His father was chaplain in the Harington household and he and Charles Diodati's father served as tutors to the hopeful reformist Protestant scion, John Harington, close friend of Prince Henry. Tovey's father was said to have been poisoned by the Jesuits in Rome – a story that may have led Milton when on his travels in Rome to credit warnings of such danger to himself (see chapter 4, pp. 98–99). Tovey later identified himself with the royalist and Laudian position, but at this stage his reformist affiliations were most in evidence. See Donald C. Dorian, *The English Diodatis* (New York, 1939), 43–6; Peile, *Biographical Register*, I, 289; and Gordon Campbell, "Milton's Second Tutor," *MQ* 21 (1987), 81–90.

29 Richard Montagu, *Appello Caesarem* (London, 1625), 71–2.

30 See Mullinger, *University of Cambridge,* III, 25–64; Masson, I, 157–9; and Twigg, *University of Cambridge*, 19–24.

31 Joseph Mede reported only a three-vote majority in a letter to Stuteville, Harleian Ms 390, fol 68v.

32 Leo Miller, "Dating Milton's 1626 Obituaries," *Notes and Queries* 27 (225), 323–4, supplies the date of Ridding's death from an unpublished letter from Mede to Stuteville.

33 Ibid. For Diodati's poem, see chapter 1, n. 36. Dorian, *English Diodatis*, 108–9, points to resemblances between the two works: similar stanzaic form, similar opening theme, similar reference to Proserpine and the thread of life.

34 Ll. 9–12, trans. Hughes. Besides Brunswick and Mansfield, the lines allude to such lost Protestant leaders as Prince Maurice of Orange and several noble English volunteers killed in the fighting around Breda (spring, 1625), e.g. Henry de Vere, Earl of Oxford and Sir Walter Devereaux. See *Variorum*, I, 65–9.

35 See Richard F. Hardin, "The Early Poetry of the Gunpowder Plot," *English Literary Renaissance* 21 (1992), 62–79, for the tradition of poems on this topic. The best known of them, Phineas Fletcher's Latin *Locustae*, a mini-epic of over 800 lines, was written in 1611 when Fletcher was a fellow of King's College, Cambridge, but published only in 1627, in Latin and English. The few parallels are readily explained by the well-established conventions of subject and genre.

36 See Macon Cheek, "Milton's 'In Quintum Novembris': An Epic Foreshadowing," *Studies in Philology* 54 (1957), 172–84. Other likely influences include George Buchanan's anti-Catholic satires and Alexander Gil's *In ruinam Camerae Papisticae,* written in 1623. See chapter 1, pp. 8–9 and notes 31 and 32.

37 "Te tamen interea belli circumsonat horror, / Vivis & ignoto solus inopsque solo; / Et, tibi quam patrii non exhibuere penates / Sede peregrina quaeris egenus opem. / Patria dura parens, & saxis savior albis / Spumea quae pulsat littoris unda tui, / Siccine te decet innocuos exponere faetus." Ll. 83–9 (translation, Carey).

38 "Et tu (quod superest miseris) sperare memento, / Et tua magnanimo pectore vince mala. / Nec dubites quandoque frui melioribus annis, / Atque iterum patrios posse videre lares." (Translation, Carey.)

39 *CPW* I, 311. The letter is misdated in the 1674 *Epistolarum Familiarium* as March 26, 1625, but it almost certainly accompanied the 1627 Elegy IV. See William Riley Parker, "Milton and Thomas Young, 1620–1628," *Modern Language Notes* 53 (1938), 399–407. A later letter (July 21, 1628) accepting Young's invitation to visit praises him as another Zeno or Cicero.

40 The loan was for £500; Powell paid the interest regularly until June 12, 1644, when he defaulted. See *Chronology*, 31–2.

41 Milton's unique use of the Latin ordinal "*undevigesimo*" in dating this poem suggests that it means "in his nineteenth year," i.e. 1627; his usual form, *anno aetatis* 19, would have meant "at the age of 19," i.e. 1628. Parker's date, May, 1630, rests on the dubious assumption that the arrangement of the Elegies in the 1645 edition must be chronological, and the also dubious presumption that a compositor misread Milton's "*uno et vigesimo*" as "*undevigesimo*."

42 "Nec mora, nunc ciliis haesit, nunc virginis ori, / Insilit hinc labiis, insidet inde genis: / Et quascunque agilis partes jaculator oberrat, / Hei mihi, mille locis pectus inerme ferit. / Protinus insoliti subierunt corda furores, / Uror amans intus, flammaque totus eram." (Translation, Carey.)

43 Revard, *Tangles of Neaera's Hair*, 29–30, suggests that the elegy's focus on one girl who appears and disappears recalls Joannes Secundus's *Odes* 1.xi.5. Also see Anthony Low, "Elegia Septima: The Poet and the Poem," in *Urbane Milton,* ed. James Freeman and Anthony Low, *MS* 19 (1984), 105–26.

44 The poem was not published in 1645, but was included in the 1673 volume, with Horace's Latin ode on the facing page. Donald Clark in *John Milton at St Paul's School: A Study of Ancient Rhetoric in English Renaissance Education* (New York, 1948), 178, argues that the poem may have been a school exercise, later revised. He points out, plausibly, that the claim of verbal exactness in translation is meritorious in a school exercise, but that the mature Milton did not value that practice, or ever again attempt it. Most critics, however, assign a later date, assuming that the poem's artfulness would be beyond Milton's schoolboy capacities; a later date also gains force from Milton's failure to date it to an early age, as was his wont with his juvenilia. Shawcross, exceptionally, dates the poem very late, in 1645–6. See *Variorum* II.2, 502–5.

45 Mullinger, *University of Cambridge*, III, 87, 83–9.

46 No other deaths of Phillips's children are recorded at Milton's date. Their first child, John, was baptized January 16, 1625 and buried March 15, 1629 (the John Phillips who was Milton's pupil was born about 1631). Anne was baptized on January 12, 1626 (*LR* I, 103).

47 Revard (*Tangles of Neaera's Hair*, 56–61) points to epigrams by Giovanni Pontano and Marc-Antonio Flaminio, and the mythic transformations in Pindar's *Olympian* I and II.

48 *CPW* I, 314. In Prolusion VI (July or August, 1628) he mentions that he has just returned from London and intends to spend the summer at Cambridge (*CPW* I, 266).

49 In 1642 he explained that some of the studious gentry support the prelates because the "monkish and miserable sophistry" of their university education has incapacitated them for "all true and generous philosophy" (*Reason of Church Government, CPW* I, 854). In *Of Education* (1644) he forcefully charged the universities with bringing students to a "hatred and contempt of learning," producing "an ambitious and mercenary, or ignorantly zealous Divinity," lawyers who know nothing of justice and equity,"and statesmen "unprincipl'd in vertue, and true generous breeding," who are thereby susceptible to tyranny (*CPW* II, 374–6).

50 The poem may have been prompted by George Hakewell's recent, much discussed modernist treatise, *An Apologie of the Power and Providence of God* (London, 1627), which contrasts sharply with the poetic vision in Donne's *First Anniversary,* describing the world as moribund and decaying.

51 Conceivably, both these poems were written for other occasions, and the poem for this

occasion is lost. I see no convincing reason, however, to accept John Shawcross's alternative dating – June, 1631 for the poem and July 2, 1631 for the letter to Gil ("The Dating of Certain Poems, Letters, and Prolusions Written by Milton," *English Language Notes* 2 (1965), 261–2.

52 Edward Phillips thought Milton had for King "a particular Friendship and Intimacy" (*EL* 54). Norman Postlethwaite and Gordon Campbell in "Edward King, Milton's 'Lycidas': Poems and Documents," MQ 28 (1944), 79–80, argue that they were close friends, chiefly on the strength of the headnote, Phillips's testimony, and the emphasis on King's learning in most of the tributes to him in *Juxta Eduardo King Naufrago*. But Milton's "a learned friend" seems formulaic and Phillips's comment obviously derives from it.

53 See Cedric C. Brown, *John Milton: A Literary Life* (New York, 1995), 2–8, 18, for a reconstruction of the festival and a perceptive analysis of Milton's self-presentation in the several parts of that exercise. Thomas R. Hartman argues ("Prolusions," *ME*, VII, 37–9) that Prolusion VI in its various parts precisely parodies a specific event, the University Commencement Exercises, but the parallels he adduces seem somewhat strained.

54 The poem was first printed in *Poems,* 1673, and is quoted from that edition.

55 His address to the eldest, Substance, as "King" may indicate that Edward King played that role; and the address to Relation beginning "Rivers arise" probably identifies that personification with a student named Rivers, either George or his brother Nigel.

56 See Clark, *Milton at St Paul's School,* 83–99; Barker, "Milton's Schoolmasters," 526–36; Parker II, 712–14.

57 This is in part a precis of a very long treatise by the Jesuit philosopher Francis Suarez, in *Disputationes Metaphysicae* (Mainz, 1605).

58 Cambridge University Archives, Supplicats 1627, 1628, 1629, fol. 331; the supplication is in Milton's hand. He also signed the three Articles of Religion in the University Subscription Book (Subs I, 286). *Chronology*, 37.

59 This portrait, now at the National Portrait Gallery, London, is generally believed to be one of two (the other is the schoolboy portrait) that remained in the possession of Milton's widow, according to Aubrey's report and that of Milton's daughter, Deborah Clarke. It later came into the possession of Arthur Onslow, Speaker of the House of Commons. Some doubt surrounds the attribution, based on the discrepancy between the youthful appearance of the subject and the inscribed age, the discrepancy between the brown eyes of the portrait and the usual representation of Milton with gray eyes, and the somewhat unclear provenance of this portrait. But none of this seems decisive enough to discredit the chain of attribution over three centuries. For a skeptical argument underscoring the dubiety of the attribution, see Leo Miller, "Milton's Portraits."

60 In *Poems,* 1645 he dates it "*anno aetatis 20.*"

61 For discussion of some sources – Callimachus, Ovid, Horace, George Buchanan's "Maiae Calendae" among others – see A. S. P. Woodhouse, "Notes on Milton's Early Development," *University of Toronto Quarterly* 13 (1943–4), 66–101; and D. C. Allen, "Milton as a Latin Poet," in *Neo-Latin Poetry of the Sixteenth and Seventeenth Centuries*, eds. James E. Phillips and D. C. Allen (Los Angeles, 1965), 30–52.

62 Revard, *Tangles of Neaera's Hair*, 17–27.

63 Ll. 55–60, 95–6. "Exuit invisam Tellus rediviva senectam, / Et cupit amplexus Phoebe subire tuos; / Et cupit, & digna est, quid enim formosius illa, / Pandit ut omniferos

luxuriosa sinus, / Atque Arabum spirat messes, & ab ore venusto / . . . Sic Tellus lasciva suos suspirat amores; / Matris in exemplum caetera turba ruunt." (Translation, Hughes.)

64 This was a pro forma honor granted by one university to those who earned a degree from the other; Diodati had earned his Masters' degree at Oxford the previous year.

65 Diodati's letters are now in the British Library, Add Ms 5016*, fols. 5, 71.

66 John T. Shawcross, "Milton and Diodati," *MS* 7 (1975), 141, 156–7, argues for some overt homosexual experience, probably in 1628–9, followed by some rupture in the relationship; more cautiously, in *John Milton: The Self and the World* (Lexington, 1993), 43–59, he suggests that Diodati was clearly homosexual, but that Milton probably repressed such urges, except, perhaps, with Diodati. These speculations seems to me to rest on a strained overreading of the poems and letters exchanged between them. I agree with William Kerrigan in *The Sacred Complex* (Cambridge, Mass., 1983, 49) that had Milton recognized or acted upon a sexual attraction to men, he would not have idealized youthful virginity (his own and that of the Lady in *A Maske*), nor would he have routinely listed sodomy among the acts "opposed to chastity" in the *Christian Doctrine* (*CPW* VI, 726–57). Milton's consistent habit is rather to justify his own impulses and experiences, sexual or otherwise – a disposition that prompted him to write defenses of chastity and arguments for polygamy and divorce.

67 He bought della Casa's *Rime & Prose* (Venice, 1563) for tenpence and inscribed his name and date on the title page. This work, bound with Dante's *L'Amoroso Convivio* (Venice, 1529) and Benedetto Varchi's *Sonetti* (Venice, 1555) is now in the New York Public Library (*KB 1529). Maurice Kelley, "Milton's Dante–Della Casa–Varchi Volume," *New York Public Library Bulletin* 66 (1962), 499–504, argues that marginalia in the della Casa and Varchi volumes, and probably in the Dante as well, are Milton's.

68 Translation, Hughes, as are subsequent translations from Elegy VI.

69 "Mitto tibi sanam non pleno ventre salutem, / Qua tu distento forte carere potes. / At tua quid nostram prolectat Musa camoenam, / Nec sinit optatas posse sequi tenebras? / Carmine scire velis quàm te redamémque colámque, / Crede mihi vix hoc carmine scire queas. / Nec neque noster amor modulis includitur arctis, / Nec venit ad claudos integer ipse pedes.

70 "Namque Elegia levis multorum cura deorum est, / Et vocat ad numeros quemlibet illa suos; / Liber adest elegis, Eratoque, Ceresque, Venusque, / Et cum purpurea matre tenellus Amor. / Talibus inde licent convivia larga poetis, / Saepius &veteri commaduisse mero. / Ad qui bella refert, & adulto sub Jove caelum, / Heroasque pios, semideosque duces, / Et nunc sancta canit superum consulta deorum, / Nunc latrata fero regna profunda cane, / Ille quidem parcè Samii pro more magistri / Vivat, & innocuos praebeat herba cibos; / . . . Additur huic scelerisque vacans, & casta juventus, / Et rigidi mores, & sine labe manus. / Qualis veste nitens sacra, & lustralibus undis / Surgis ad infensos augur iture Deos. / . . . Diis etenim sacer est vates, divumque sacerdos, / Spirat & occultum pectus, & ora Jovem."

71 "At tu siquid agam, scitabere (si modo saltem / Esse putas tanti noscere siquid agam) / Paciferum canimus caelesti semine regem, / Faustaque sacratis sacula pacta libris, / Vagitumque Dei, & stabulantem paupere tecto / Qui suprema suo cum patre regna colit; / Stelliparumque polum, modulantesque aethere turmas, / Et subitò elisos ad sua fana Deos."

72 Like many critics I believe that Milton refers to the Nativity ode in his rather ambigu-

ous Latin lines, "Te quoque pressa manent patriis meditata cicutis; / Tu mihi, cui recitem, judicis instar eris," usually translated something like this: "For you also these simple strains that have been meditated on my native pipes are waiting; and when I recite them to you, you shall be my judge." Some see this as a reference to the companion poems *L'Allegro* and *Il Penseroso* on the ground that "cicutis" must refer to pastoral poems; Carey thinks the reference is to the Italian sonnets as poems played on Diodati's native pipes – readings which involve dating those works before the Nativity ode; against that is the fact that they show the influence of della Casa's sonnets, which Milton purchased in December, 1629. The Nativity ode itself claims the pastoral generic register and "patriis . . . cicutis" may refer to Milton's native pipes – a poem in English rather than as so often before, in Latin. For Charles Diodati's period of study at the Academy (now University) of Geneva, see Dorian, *English Diodatis*, 130–1.

73 R. Paul Yoder, "Milton's *The Passion*," *MS* 17 (1991), 3–21, argues, I think unconvincingly, that the failure is deliberately staged to make the poetic persona's humiliation and the death of his poem an *imitatio Christi*.

74 J. H. Hanford believes this crisis had serious psychological consequences for Milton's epic aspirations; see "The Youth of Milton," in *John Milton Poet and Humanist* (Cleveland, 1966), 38–40.

75 The date of the capture of Hertogenbosch proves that Milton's letter to Gil is wrongly dated 1628 in the 1674 edition of Milton's *Letters*. See Eugenia Chifos, "Milton's Letter to Gil," *Modern Language Notes* 62 (1947), 37–9. Gil's poem was later published in *Parerga* (1632), pp. 36–40.

76 On April 24, 1630 Joseph Mede wrote to his friend Stuteville that "our University is in a manner wholly dissolved, all meetings & exercise ceasing; in many colleges almost none left. In ours, of 27 messe [fellows] we have not five (BL Harleian MS 390, f. 513v).

77 Milton senior was assessed for poor relief in Hammersmith beginning from Easter (April 10, 1631); he paid his quarterly assessments that year and the next (i.e. through March, 1633). He did not pay the assessments before that date (*Chronology,* 43). In 1633 he was evidently serving as churchwarden in the Hammersmith Chapel of Ease. Chancery Town Depositions (*LR*, I, 276–7, 284–7, 292–3) document his residence in Hammersmith from 1632 to 1635.

78 The opening lines of this sonnet are a close translation of lines 25–6 of Elegy V.

79 Parker argues for spring, 1629 for the "May Morning" song and the sonnet sequence on the basis of similarity in theme to Elegy V. With many critics, I lean to 1630 because Milton was newly attentive to Jonsonian lyric at this point and because his recent purchase of della Casa's sonnets suggests a new interest in that form. The name Emilia is identified by J. M. Smart, ed. *The Sonnets of Milton* (Glasgow, 1921) through references in Sonnet 2, ll. 1–2 to the river Reno and the Rubicon in the region Emilia in northern Italy.

80 The address to Diodati might suggest that the sequence was written before his departure for Geneva (by the end of March, 1630 at the latest). But the sequence might have been sent to him in Geneva or presented to him in England at his return.

81 These sonnets show some adumbrations of Milton's later sonnet manner, in which the thematic development often does not conform to the formal divisions into octave and sestet, quatrains and tercets, and the *volta*, or turn in the argument, often is not placed,

as expected, after the eighth line. See Smart, *Sonnets of Milton*; F. T. Prince, *The Italian Element in Milton's Verse* (Oxford, 1954); and *Variorum* I, 365–74.

82 "Quanto d'ingegno, e d'alto valor vago, / E di cetra sonora, e delle muse."

83 See Mede's letter to Stuteville, October 20, 1630 (BL Harleian MS 390, f. 518).

84 The title is that used in the 1632 Shakespeare Folio; in *Poems,* 1645 the title is simply "On Shakespear. 1630." I quote from the 1645 version, which incorporates a few verbal changes.

85 This might also have been the publisher's decision, as both anonymous poems are new to the second edition and appear on a single added leaf. The discrepancy between Milton's date and the publication date of the Folio is smaller than appears, since he could have written a poem dated 1630 as late as March 1631, according to the old calendar.

86 The pseudo-Shakespearean epitaph begins, "Not monumentall stones preserves our Fame; / Nor sky-aspiring Piramides our name." The circulating version conflates epitaphs for Sir Edward Standly (Stanley) and Sir Thomas Standly (Stanley) that appeared on the Stanley tomb in Shropshire, without attribution. They are reprinted in *Variorum* II.1, 208. Gordon Campbell reported on the tomb and the manuscripts, including a late attribution to Shakespeare by William Dugdale (1663), at the Sixth International Milton Symposium, York, England, July 18–23, 1999.

87 Hanford, "Youth of Milton," 37, cites William Browne's elegy for the Countess of Pembroke for the conceit of the reader turned to marble.

88 Some of Hobson's considerable wealth and property he willed to the town to build a handsome conduit for sanitation. See J. T. Shawcross, "A Note on Milton's Hobson Poems," *RES* n.s. 18 (1967), 433–7.

89 John T. Shawcross, *A Bibliography for the Years 1624–1700* (Binghamton, NY, 1984), 3–5, lists some 25 manuscript versions of one or both of Milton's Hobson poems, which were also printed, anonymously, in contemporary anthologies of humorous verse. *A Banquet of Jests* (1640) contains Milton's second poem, entitled, "Upon old Hobson the Carrier of Cambridge" (pp. 129–31); *Wit Restor'd* (1658) contains Milton's first poem complete, a shorter version of the second comprising lines 1–12, 27–8, and also a third unidentified Hobson poem (pp. 84–5).

90 John Pory describes her death and rumors about her impending conversion in a letter to Sir Thomas Puckering (April 21, 1631), *Court and Times of Charles the First,* II, 106. In a verse miscellany compiled by Francis Baskerville – chiefly panegyrics to the Stuarts and assorted nobility, Cavalier love songs and other social and courtly poems – the Paulet epitaph is ascribed to "John Milton of Chr: Coll Cambr:" (BL Sloane 1446, ff. 37v–38v).

91 An example is Jonson's epitaph for Vincent Corbet (1619).

92 See Dante, *Paradiso*, 32, ll 7–9, James Holly Hanford, "Youth of Milton," 37, noted the apparent echo in the opening lines of Browne's Elegy for the Countess of Pembroke: "Under this marble hearse / Lies the subject of all verse: / Sidney's sister, Pembroke's mother."

93 See note 77. Though Prolusion VII cannot be dated with certainty, most critics place it in 1631–2.

94 These poems have been dated as late as 1633–4 and as early as 1629, but many scholars think the long vacation of 1631 most likely.

95 *LR* I, 227, 243, 257; V, 381; Parker, II, 807.

96 Masson, I, 254–7; Mullinger, *University of Cambridge,* III, 114–17. Another factor was thought to be the recent furor over the conferring of the Doctorate in Divinity on the Laudian Edward Martin and several others, by royal mandate.

97 See chapter 1, pp. 12–13.

98 For a discussion of Milton's self-construction as a solitary scholar, see B. Douglas Trevor, "Learned Appearances: Writing Scholarly and Literary Selves in Early Modern England" (dissertation, Harvard University, 1999), 298–344.

99 Cambridge University Archives, Supplicats 1630, 1631, 1632, fol. 270, No. 124. On July 3 he signed the Subscription Book, graduating as Master of Arts (Cambridge University Archives, Subscription I, p. 377); *Chronology,* 46–7.

100 The term "humble" points to the poem's pastoral elements, since pastoral traditionally belongs to the *genus humilis.*

101 Cf. Isaiah 6:6–7.

102 For Milton's originality, see Robert Shafer, *The English Ode to 1660* (Princeton, NJ, 1918).

103 See Phillip Rollinson, "Milton's Nativity Ode and the Decorum of Genre," *MS* 7 (1975), 165–84; *Variorum* 2.1, 34–8; and Revard, *Tangles of Neaera's Hair,* 64–90. In *Reason of Church Government* Milton listed among the kinds of poems he considered writing, "those magnific odes and hymns wherein Pindarus and Callimachus are in most things worthy" (*CPW* I, 815).

104 Milton draws upon the centuries-old Christian tradition identifying Virgil's Fourth or "Messianic" Eclogue as an unconscious prophecy of the birth of Christ.

105 Some important studies of the poem include Rosemund Tuve, *Images and Themes in Five Poems by Milton* (Cambridge, Mass., 1957), 37–72; Arthur Barker, "The Pattern of Milton's Nativity Ode," *University of Toronto Quarterly* 10 (1941), 167–81; and Revard, *Tangles of Nearea's Hair,* 64–96.

106 Michael Wilding, *Dragon's Teeth* (Oxford, 1987, 14), points to the political resonances such apocalyptic references had in 1629, when vernacular commentaries on the Book of Revelation were suppressed. Puritan commentary on that book typically read signs of the last days in the present times, with alarming implications for the casting down of kings and the rule of the Saints.

107 See Revard, *Tangles of Neaera's Hair,* 66–87.

108 Wilding, *Dragon's Teeth,* 15–16.

109 Revard, *Tangles of Neaera's Hair,* 81.

110 See, for example, Tuve, *Images,* 15–36; Stanley Fish, "What it's like to Read *L'Allegro* and *Il Penseroso,*" *MS* 7 (1975), 77–99; and *Variorum,* I, 224–69.

111 In seventeenth-century anthologies Milton might have seen poems on contrasting themes paired together, though they were not written as companion poems: e.g. John Fletcher's "Hence all you vain Delights" spoken by a personification of Melancholy was often paired with a poem by William Strode called "Against Melancholy." The French poet Saint-Amant published his "La Solitude" in 1624, but its companion, "La Jouissance," postdates Milton's poem by several years.

112 The incest of Aurora and her son Zephyr that produced Mirth, like that of Saturn and his daughter Vesta that produces Melancholy in *Il Penseroso,* carries no guilt in the myths, only allegorical significance.

113 For Renaissance melancholy, see Raymond Klibansky, Erwin Panofsky, and Fritz Saxl, *Saturn and Melancholy* (London, 1964); also Robert Burton's *Anatomy of Melancholy* (London, 1621).

114 See Annabel Patterson, "'Forc'd fingers': Milton's Early Poems and Ideological Constraint," in *The Muses Common-Weale*, ed. Claude Summers and Ted-Larry Pebworth (Columbia, Mo., 1988), 9–22.

Chapter 3 "Studious Retirement:" Hammersmith and Horton, 1632–1638

1 One biographical scenario suggests that Milton rejected the ministry before or upon leaving Cambridge: Masson, I, 333–9; A. S. P. Woodhouse, "Notes on Milton's Early Development," *University of Toronto Quarterly*, 13 (1943–4), 66–101; Douglas Bush, "The Date of Milton's *Ad Patrem*," *Modern Philology* 61 (1963–4), 204–8; and *Variorum* I, 232–40. A contrary scenario proposes that Milton was still expecting to combine poetry and the ministry as late as 1640: John Spencer Hill, *John Milton: Poet, Priest and Prophet* (London, 1979), 27–49. John T. Shawcross, *John Milton: The Self and the World* (Lexington, 1993), 61–70, takes 1637 to be the year of decision.

2 Two Chancery depositions in September, 1631 give Milton senior's legal address as Bread Street, London (*LR* I, 149–50); on September 14, 1632 and again on January 8, 1635 his legal address is noted in Chancery depositions as "Hammersmith in the County of Middlesex." See chapter 2, note 77. In 1634 he declined the honor of serving as Master of the Scriveners' Company, presumably because he had retired to a residence outside London (*LR* I, 284).

3 Writs in a lawsuit against Milton senior from January to March, 1637 designate his residence as Horton. A writ dated March 22, 1637 refers to an earlier writ of May 23, 1636 (now lost) locating him "within 17 myles of London" (Horton's distance). See J. Milton French, *Milton in Chancery: New Chapters in the Lives of the Poet and his Father* (New York and London, 1939), 55–6, 262–4. Also in May, 1636, Milton petitioned to resign from his office as assistant to the Scriveners' Company, on account of his "removal to inhabit in the country."

4 *Survey of London, Hammersmith*, vol. 6 (London, 1915). No record has been found identifying the house the Miltons occupied. After June, 1632, the hamlet had its own place of worship, the chapel of St Paul's, with John Dent as curate.

5 See chapter 2, n. 20.

6 John Harper, in "'One Equal Music': The Music of Milton's Youth," *MQ* 31 (1997), 1–9, argues that Milton senior's musical associates were rather conservative than progressive in their musical taste and practice.

7 Gresham College was established by Sir Thomas Gresham, founder of the Royal Exchange, for the presentation of public lectures – some in Latin, some in English – in Astronomy, Music, Divinity, Geometry, Physick, Civil Law, and Rhetoric. Masson (I, 566) points out that the most famous mathematical teachers of the day, John Greaves, professor of geometry, and Henry Gellibrand, professor of astronomy, were associated with the college.

8 For the documents and an account of the suits, see French, *Milton in Chancery*, 35–67, 236–90. Bower failed to return the widow Downer's £50 upon request, and loaned it

out against her wishes to a defaulting debtor. He also made a large profit by buying back at a large discount bonds held by Cotton, after (perhaps) persuading him they were likely to default. As partner, Milton senior was held liable for half the repayment of £50 adjudged for Rose Downer, and ultimately for all of it when Bower refused to pay his part. Judgments in the Downer–Milton case were delivered in June, 1632, but Milton's efforts to collect from Bower and others continued to June, 1640. The Cotton suit began in May, 1636 but was dismissed on February 1, 1638, with the plaintiff Cotton made to pay costs.

9 French, *Milton in Chancery*, 264.

10 On Euripides' *Tragoediae* (Geneva, 1602), now in the Bodleian (Don.d.27, 28), Milton's inscription on a flyleaf reads: "Jo. Milton pre: [12]s [6]d 1634." Lycophron, *Alexandra. With Commentary of Tzetzes* (Geneva, 1601), now in the University of Illinois library, bears Milton's flyleaf inscription: "Sum ex libris Jo: Miltoni pre: 13s. 1634." Milton made several marginal annotations in both, relating to grammar, metrics, and meaning: see Maurice Kelley and Samuel D. Atkins, "Milton's Annotations of Euripides," *Journal of English and Germanic Philology* 60 (1961), 680–7. The inscription "Jo. Milton" is on the title page of *Pub. Terentii Comoediae Sex* (Leyden, 1635), now at Harvard; numbers indicating the date of purchase are illegible but he probably purchased it close to the year of publication. John Creccelius, *Collectanea ex Historiis* (Frankfurt, 1614), now at the Huntington Library, bears the inscription, "pr. 3s. John Milton 1633 21st October," but the hand seems not to be his. None of these books are excerpted in his Commonplace Book – some evidence that it was begun after 1635.

11 Gil's *Epinikion* (London, 1631) was likely to have pleased Milton especially, being in the tradition of Gil's *In ruinam Camerae Papisticae* and *In Sylvam-Ducis*. In the *Parerga* those poems are surrounded by royal panegyrics and other courtly poems, but Gil opened that volume with his funeral tribute to Prince Henry, the much-lamented hope of the reformists, perhaps as a gesture to recall Charles to Henry's more militant Protestant ideals.

12 See Graham Parry, *The Golden Age Restored* (Manchester, 1981) and Stephen Orgel, *Illusion of Power* (Berkeley, 1975). The principal masques, most of them mounted by Inigo Jones, were: Ben Jonson, *Love's Triumph through Callipolis* (Jan. 9, 1631); Jonson, *Chloridia* (Feb. 22, 1631); Aurelian Townshend, *Tempe Restored* (Feb. 14, 1632); James Shirley, *The Triumph of Peace* (Feb. 3, 13, 1634); Thomas Carew, *Coelum Britannicum* (Feb. 18, 1634); William Davenant, *The Temple of Love* (Feb. 10, 11, 12, 1635); Davenant, *Brittania Triumphans* (Jan. 17, 1638); and Davenant, *Salmacida Spolia* (Jan. 21, 1640).

13 Pastoral provided an important symbolic register for Jacobean masques as well: *Pan's Anniversary* (1620) is set in Arcadia, with James figured as Pan. See Lewalski, "Milton's *Comus* and the Politics of Masquing," in *The Politics of the Stuart Court Masque*, eds. David Bevington and Peter Holbrook (Cambridge, 1998), 296–320.

14 Charles I, *The King's Majesty's Declaration to his subjects concerning lawful sports to be used* (London, 1633).

15 Lucy Hutchinson, *Memoirs of the Life of Colonel Hutchinson,* ed. Julius Hutchinson (London, 1968), 42. Written shortly after the death of her husband in 1664 and certainly before 1671, it was first published in 1806, with many deletions and changes, by a descendent of Colonel Hutchinson in the collateral line.

16 The book carries no publication data, to protect publisher and bookseller.

17 Prynne, *Histrio-Mastix* (London, 1633 [1634]), sig. *** ; Walter Montague, *The Shepheard's Paradise* (London, 1659). Published as a royalist testimonial in 1659, the preface indicates that the play remained long "concealed."

18 Prynne, *Histrio-Mastix*, 225. He cites a myriad of authorities, classical and Christian, to support his claims about the scandal of dancing, pointing directly at "Queenes themselves, and the very greatest persons, who are commonly most devoted to it" (p. 236).

19 *Documents relating to . . . William Prynne*, ed. S. R. Gardiner (Westminster, 1877), 16.

20 The title in the 1645 *Poems* is "*Arcades*. Part of an Entertainment presented to the Countess Dowager of *Derby* at *Harefield*, by some Noble persons of her Family, who appear on the Scene in pastoral habit, moving toward the seat of State." The title suggests that this brief work served as prologue to an evening of festivities and dances.

21 The Miltons' musical associates at this time probably included Lawes, who taught singing to Lady Alice Egerton and her sister, Lady Mary. See Cedric C. Brown, *Milton's Aristocratic Entertainments* (Cambridge, 1985), 181, n. 1.

22 Shawcross, in "Speculations on the Dating of the Trinity MS of Milton's Poems," *Modern Language Notes* 75 (1960), 11–17, argues that the changes in *Arcades* (and *A Maske*) in the Trinity manuscript were all post-performance changes, and that *Arcades* was copied into the manuscript in 1637, the date he assigns to that document. His argument depends on an implausibly rigid application of Helen Darbishire's conclusion that Milton began to change from a Greek "e" to an italic "e" around 1637. While generally true, that date is not a watershed, given that Milton used the italic "e" occasionally before 1637, and as early as 1629 in his signature in the university graduation book for his Bachelors degree. Shawcross's argument is answered by Cedric C. Brown, "Milton's *Arcades* in the Trinity Manuscript," *Review of English Studies*, n.s. 37 (1986), 542–9; and by S. E. Sprott, *John Milton: A Maske. The Earlier Versions* (Toronto, 1973), 5, 9–10.

23 Brown, *Aristocratic Entertainments*, 7–26, 47, and "Milton's *Arcades*: Context, Form, and Function," *Renaissance Drama* 8 (1977), 245–74. Parker, II, 755–8, dates the work 1630, based on his dubious assumption that chronology is the chief determinant of Milton's arrangement in the 1645 *Poems*. The 1632 date is supported by the fact that the third item in the Trinity manuscript is a heavily corrected autograph letter composed directly in that notebook early in 1633.

24 See Brown, "*Arcades* in the Trinity Manuscript." The subtitle, "Part of a Masque," is corrected to "Part of an Entertainment," suggesting that Milton was at first uncertain as to the scope of the festivities planned and the place of dancing in them. The opening lines are crossed-out and verses more suited to song are substituted. Several other changes in stage directions and text indicate that Milton's conception evolved as he learned more about what was wanted for the occasion. The title, *Arcades,* may have been added before publication in 1645.

25 For the countess's household and familial responsibilities, see Brown, *Aristocratic Entertainments*, 16–26.

26 For the charges and depositions in the trial of Mervin Touchet, Earl of Castlehaven, see *A Complete Collection of State Trials and Proceedings for High Treason*, eds. William Cobbett and T. S. Howell, 33 vols (London, 1809), III, cols 401–18. Barbara Breasted, "Comus and the Castlehaven Scandal," *MS* 3 (1971), 201–24, argues the strong impact of that affair on Milton's choice and management of the theme of chastity in *Comus*. Cedric

Brown (*Aristocratic Entertainments*, 20) doubts, reasonably, that Milton would allude directly to the scandal in either work, though these circumstances form the immediate context for *Arcades* and would be well known to its audience.

27 Ll. 2, 17, 15, 36, 25, 94–5. Citations are from the final version in the 1645 *Poems*. The countess surpasses in her merits and her noble progeny wise Latona (mother of Apollo and Diana), Cebele (mother of a hundred gods), and even Juno.

28 In the Trinity manuscript these lines are added twice – to the second song and the third – as they are also in 1645, for maximum effect. It is possible that the lines were added for the publication rather than the performance itself.

29 The dowager countess had danced in Daniel's *Vision of 12. Goddesses* and Jonson's *Masque of Beauty*. Lady Alice's older sisters danced in several later masques: Mary in *The Temple of Love* (1635), and Elizabeth in *Luminalia* (1638). Her brothers John and Thomas, along with their young cousin George, Lord Chandos, danced as torchbearers in *Coelum Britannicum* (1634).

30 Courtly masque dances probably preceded this song, though none are indicated in the text.

31 Citations from this sonnet and Milton's other lyrics of the period are from the versions in the 1645 *Poems*.

32 In "Some problems in the Chronology of Milton's Early Poems," *Review of English Studies* 11 (1935), 276–9, William Riley Parker argues cogently for 1632. Milton's use of the Latin phrase *Anno aetatis* in dating nine early poems would almost certainly extend to his usage in English, meaning not his 23rd year (the year before his 23rd birthday) but the year when he was 23, before his 24th birthday. Parker's argument has been challenged, but not to my mind persuasively, by Ernest Sirluck in "Milton's Idle Right Hand," *Journal of English and Germanic Philology* 60 (1961), 781–4.

33 The final line – "All is, if I have grace to use it so / As ever in my great task-Master's eye" – is enigmatic. The "Taskmaster" reference seems to fuse the conception of God as Lord of the vineyard with that of God as Master of a household demanding an account of his servants' stewardship of the talents (money) given them. Milton refers to both parables in his letter enclosing this sonnet. The line also invites the associations of harshness and injustice often conveyed by the word "taskmaster" in scripture (e.g. Exodus l:11; 3:7; 5:6), as well as many references to God's all-seeing eye (e.g. Psalms 33:18; 34:15).

34 Milton alludes to a text (Isaiah 21:11–12) usually applied to ministers, in terming his friend "a good watch man to admonish that the howres of the night passe on."

35 See F. T. Prince, *The Italian Element in Milton's Verse* (Oxford, 1954), 61–3.

36 For analysis of the careful revisions in the three and a half drafts of this poem in the Trinity manuscript see P. L. Heyworth, "The Composition of Milton's 'At a Solemn Musick,'" *Bulletin of the New York Public Library* 70 (1966), 450–8.

37 The (surely correct) reading in the Trinity manuscript is "concent"; the 1645 *Poems* reads "content."

38 A manuscript of Lawes's music (BL Add. 53723) contains in Lawes's autograph the music and lyrics for five songs: "From ye Heav'ns now I fly," "Sweet Echo," "Sabrina Fayre," "Back Shepherds back," and "Now my task is smoothly done." Other music, including Sabrina's song and the dance music, may have been written by Lawes but not

included in this manuscript, or else supplied by some other musician attached to the household.

39 Parker (II, 792, n. 42) supplies evidence of Bridgewater's moderation in the controversies relating to royal absolutism and especially Laudianism. Leah Marcus, *The Politics of Mirth* (Chicago and London, 1986), 172–9, reviews the conflicting interpretation of his politics in the 1630s and after. Cf. Maryann Cale McGuire, *Milton's Puritan Masque* (Athens, Ga., 1983), 171–2. Marcus in "The Milieu of Milton's *Comus*," *Criticism* 25 (1983), 293–327, discusses Bridgewater's judicial probity, especially in relation to a rape case involving an aristocrat and a country girl. J[ohn] C[ollinges], a dissenting clergyman, published a biographical account of two of Lady Alice's older sisters, *Par Nobile. Two Treatises* (London, 1669), in one of which Frances Egerton credits her father with "seasoning her against Arminian principles" and providing her a Huguenot governess who taught her "to be a *Calvinist* in point of *Doctrine*, and a *Presbyterian* as to Discipline." *The Excellent Woman*, 4.

40 The best account of these revisions is Sprott's introduction to *A Maske: The Earlier Versions* (Toronto, 1973), 3–33. That edition presents the Trinity manuscript, the acting version represented in the Bridgewater manuscript, and the 1637 published version side by side, to highlight changes.

41 Brown, *Aristocratic Entertainments* (26–40) discusses Bridgewater's activities, the circumstances of his two visits to Ludlow in July and September, and the route of his travels in the region between those visits. Several entertainments were presented to him en route, including one at Chirk Castle. See Cedric C. Brown, "The Chirk Castle Entertainment of 1634," *MQ* 11 (1977), 76–86. The family, including Lawes, also made a three-week visit to Lyme Park in Cheshire, where the children and Lawes may have rehearsed their rather demanding parts in *A Maske.*

42 This fair copy is not in Milton's hand nor Lawes's.

43 Omissions include ll. 195–225, 350–65, 735–55 (all line numbers in text and notes are from Hughes).

44 For Gil's witty verses of this period see Leo Miller, "On some Verses by Alexander Gil which John Milton Read," *MQ* 24 (1990), 22–5.

45 Stella P. Revard's translation in *Milton and the Tangles of Neaera's Hair: The Making of the 1645 Poems* (Columbia, 1997), 85. The Greek is "En de theos laoisi mega kreion Basileuen." She notes that the word "king" is not found in the English translation of the Geneva Bible, or in the 1611 AV, or in the Latin Vulgate, or in the Greek of the polyglot Bible, or in the original Hebrew, which uses the word for "dominion."

46 See p. 56 and note 11.

47 This is the suggestion of Arthur and Alberta Turner, *CPW* I, 322.

48 Donald C. Dorian, *The English Diodatis* (New York, 1939), 155, 274.

49 Anthony á Wood, *Athenae Oxonienses . . . to which are added the Fasti, or Annals, of the said University* (1500–1690), 4 vols (London, 1813–20), I, col. 513.

50 In the 1630s the county divisions placed Horton in Buckinghamshire.

51 Christopher Hill, *Milton and the English Revolution* (London, 1977), 38–9, points to several trials of heretics in the region and to the unpopularity of the papermill, due to the low wages paid and fears that the rags carried the plague.

52 *Victoria History of the Counties of England: Buckinghamshire* (London, 1925). British Library Add MS. 37017 contains obviously romanticized watercolor sketches of the house

occupied by the Miltons (pulled down at the end of the eighteenth century) as well as the church and the dovecote, placing them at Colnbrook, not Horton.

53 Wood, *Fasti Oxoniensis*, I, 880. The official register does not mention this incorporation, but Wood cites Milton's report of it to "my friend" (probably Aubrey), and points out (*Fasti*, I, 865) that the then Registrar, John French, regularly omitted to note the incorporation of Cambridge graduates.

54 Bernardo Giustiniani, *De Origine Urbis Venetiarum* (Venice, 1492); there were Italian translations in 1545 and 1608.

55 *LR* I, 292, 296, 304. The copy of Ames, *De Conscientia et eius jure, vel casibus* (Amsterdam, 1635) in the Princeton Library is inscribed *Ex libriis Johannis Miltonii;* it may or may not be his, but Edward Phillips mentions reading Ames with Milton. The Chrysostom, *Orationes LXXX* (Paris, 1604), is in the library of Ely Cathedral, and the Heraclides, *Allegoriae in Homeri fabulas de diis* (Basel, 1544), is in the University of Illinois Library. See Jackson C. Boswell, *Milton's Library* (New York, 1975).

56 The date Milton began the Commonplace Book (BL Add MS 36,354) cannot be certainly determined.

57 For Shawcross's dating and argument see *John Milton: The Self and the World*, 76–7 and 279–80.

58 For the order of Milton's reading see Ruth Mohl's edition of the Commonplace Book in *CPW* I, 362–513, and Mohl, "*John Milton and His Commonplace Book* (New York, 1969); also James Holly Hanford, "The Chronology of Milton's Private Studies," *John Milton Poet and Humanist* (Cleveland, 1966), 75–125; and Harris Francis Fletcher, *The Intellectual Development of John Milton* [1608–32], 2 vols (Urbana, Ill., 1956–61), vol. 2. All point to Milton's change from a Greek "e" to an italic "e" around 1637. But that change was gradual rather than sudden, and while we can assume that texts using the Greek "e" exclusively are early, we cannot assume that the presence of the italic "e" means a text necessarily written after 1637.

59 The Commonplace Book contains 12 references to what Milton calls in one of them an "Index Theologicus," but they were all inserted after 1639.

60 Milton evidently read Eusebius (*Historia Ecclesiastica* and *Vita Constantini*), Socrates Scholasticus (*Historia Ecclesiastica*), and Evagrius Scholasticus (*Historia Ecclesiastica*) in *Ecclesiasticae Historiae Autores* (Paris, 1544).

61 For a full list, see Hanford, "Chronology of Milton's Private Studies," 85–6. He read Sulpicius Severus, *Sacrae Historiae Libri Duo* and George Cedren's *Compendium Historiarum*. From Tertullian he read *De Spectaculis, De Jejuniis,* and *Apologeticus*; from Clement, "Paedagogus" and "Stromata," and from Justin Martyr, *Tryphon* and *Apologia pro Christianis*. He cited Byzantine history out of Nicophorus Gregoras (*Byzantinae Historiae libri XI*) and John Cantacuzenus (*Historiarum libri IV*), and Western history out of Paulus Diaconus (*Historia Miscella*), Sigonius (*De Occidentali Imperio* and *De Regno Italiae*), and Procopius, *De Bello Persico* (i.e. the first two books of his *History of the Wars of Justinian*). For the editions Milton used or may have used, see the bibliography.

62 His edition of Dante, with commentary, was *Dante con L'Expositione di M. Bernardino Daniello* (Venice, 1568). His extract from the *Convivio* was from Canzone IV, on Nobility.

63 The Horton Parish Registers record the burial date "Sara uxor Johannis Milton generosi

Aprilis 6° . . . obiit. 3°" (*LR* I, 321).

64 *A Maske Presented at Ludlow Castle, 1634: On Michaelmasse night, before the Right Honorable, John Earle of Bridgewater, Vicount Brackly, Lord President of Wales, AND one of His Majesties most honorable Privie Counsell* (London: Humphrey Robinson, 1637). It was not entered into the Stationer's Register, and may have appeared January or February, 1638 if the new year was counted from March. Henry Wotton claimed on April 6, 1638 to have seen it "some good while before," along with a copy of Thomas Randolph's *Poems* dated 1638.

65 *A Maske* (1637), sigs A 2-A 2v.

66 The Bridgewater manuscript, which remained at Bridgewater House until this century, has inscribed on the title page the names of the three children and their roles.

67 Shawcross, *John Milton: The Self and the World,* 55, imports the context of Virgil's Second Eclogue, the shepherd Corydon's love for the beautiful and aloof Alexis, to suggest that the epigraph is "consciously reflective of Milton's firm farewell to his former liaison with Diodati." But even if there were evidence to support the scenario Shawcross suggests, there is no reason to suppose Milton would make such a private gesture in this public arena.

68 Ll. 779–806. Here and subsequently I quote from the 1637 (unlineated) text; line numbers are supplied from Hughes.

69 From internal evidence, the Yale editors argue that this letter, dated September 2 in the 1674 edition, should be reassigned to November, as should the subsequent letter dated September 23 (*CPW* I, 325); for the latter, the November date is reinforced by several parallels with *Lycidas*. Gordon Campbell, in *Chronology*, 57, supplies a plausible explanation: Milton probably dated the letters 2.ix.1637 and 23.x.1637, and the printer of the 1674 edition took the Roman numerals to refer to the ninth month of the year beginning in January (i.e. September), rather than the ninth month beginning in March (i.e. November).

70 How long the friends were out of touch is unclear. Diodati's apprenticeship in medicine, probably under his father, and his practice in the North took him effectively out of Milton's orbit, and the hint of family troubles suggests that his mind was taken up with such concerns.

71 Milton's second letter refers to "stepmotherly warfare," evidently a topic of Diodati's letter. His father had recently remarried, and soon after fell out with his sons, disinheriting them all.

72 One trial sheet of the Trinity manuscript (the verso of the last page of *A Maske*) contains drafts of three passages with a fourth crossed out. The "Orpheus" passage (ll. 58–63) and the long flower passage (ll. 134–51) are much worked over. For the stages of composition of *Lycidas* in the manuscript and in the printed version see John Shawcross, "Establishment of a Text of Milton's Poems through a Study of *Lycidas*," *Papers of the Bibliographical Society of America* 56 (1962), 317–31.

73 *Justa Edouardo King Naufrago* (Cambridge, 1638). The title page carries an epigraph from Petronius, "Si recte calculum ponas, ubique naufragium est" (If you rightly cast the reckoning, there is shipwreck everywhere). Part II has a separate title page and pagination, *Obsequies to the memorie of Mr. Edward King;* it was sometimes printed and bound separately. *Lycidas* appears on pp. 20–5 of Part II.

74 There are five autograph corrections in the British Library copy (C 21. c. 42) and

fourteen in the Cambridge University Library copy (Add Ms 154). In addition to misprints, the printer failed to follow Milton's paragraphing, and entirely omitted line 177, "In the blest Kingdoms meek of joy and love." A descriptive heading crowded in at the top of the poem in the Trinity manuscript – "In this Monody the Author bewails a learned Friend, unfortunately drowned in his passage from Chester on the Irish Seas, 1637" – is not in the memorial volume; it was added to indicate genre and circumstance, in preparation for publication in 1645.

75 Of his ten extant Latin poems, seven were written to celebrate the birth of royal children: four for Prince Charles and Princess Mary (1631), and one each for Prince James (1633), Princess Elizabeth (1635), and Princess Anne (1637). Another poem celebrates the king's recovery from smallpox in 1632, one gives thanks for his safe return from Scotland in 1633; and one commends the publication of Hausted's play (1633). The 1637 poem for Princess Anne also includes a supportive reference to the royal fleet in the year when John Hampden was tried for refusing to pay shipmoney. Still more revealing, in 1636 he writes of the Roman church in terms anathema to much of the nation: "sancta maiestas Cathedrae / Dat placidam Italiae quietem" (the holy sovereignty of the Church grants Italy its calm serenity). See Norman Postlethwaite and Gordon Campbell, "Edward King, Milton's 'Lycidas': Poems and Documents," *MQ* 28 (1944), 81–2; and Masson I, 648–9.

76 An example is J. H.'s elegy which includes a descant on cathedrals and their rituals, terming them "quires of angels in epitome / Maugre the blatant beast who cries them down / As savoring of superstition," *Justa Edouardo King*, p. 17. The author is John Haywood, Chancellor of Lichfield Cathedral, who also wrote one of the Latin poems.

77 Many of the English elegies show Donne's influence; R. Brown's employs some pastoral topoi, but not as a controlling conception. Several Latin elegies have mythological personages and sea deities as mourners, but not pastoral topoi.

78 C. Hill, *Milton and the English Revolution*, 49–52.

79 Masson (I, 324), Bush, ("The Date of Milton's *Ad Patrem*," 204–8), and Woodhouse ("Notes on Milton's Early Development," 89–91) argue for 1631–2, before or just after Milton left Cambridge. Parker in "Notes on the Chronology of Milton's Latin Poems," *A Tribute to George Coffin Taylor* (Chapel Hill, NC, 1952), 125–8, and *Milton*, I, 125–8; II, 788–9, argues for 1634. Shawcross in "The Date of *Ad Patrem*," *Notes and Queries* 204 (1959), 358–60, and Sirluck, "Milton's Idle Right Hand," 784–5, argue for 1637 or early 1638. H. A. Barnett, "A Time of the Year for Milton's 'Ad Patrem,'" *Modern Language Notes* 73 (1958), 82–3, argues for spring, 1638. Harris Francis Fletcher, ed., *John Milton's Complete Poetical Works, reproduced in Photographic Facsimile*, 4 vols (Urbana, Ill., 1943–8), 524, thought the poem could be as late as 1645.

80 Ll. 17, 56, 67–8: "Nec tu vatis opus divinum despice carmen"; "Nec tu perge precor sacras contemnere Musas"; "Tu tamen ut simules teneras odisse camoenas, / Non odisse reor, neque enim, pater, ire jubebas." All citations from "Ad Patrem" are from the 1645 *Poems;* translations and line numbers are from Hughes.

81 Ll. 24–34: "Carmine sepositi retegunt arcana futuri / Phoebades, & tremulae pallentes ora Sibyllae; / Carmina sacrificus sollennes pangit ad aras / . . . Nos etiam patrium tunc cum repetemus Olympum, / Aeternaeque morae stabunt immobilis aevi, / Ibimus auratis per caeli templa coronis, / Dulcia suaviloquo sociantes carmina plectro, / Astra quibus, geminique poli convexa sonabunt."

82 R. W. Condee, "The Latin Poetry of John Milton," in *The Latin Poetry of the English Poets*, ed. J. W. Binns (London, 1974), 71–6.

83 Ll. 62–3: "Contigerit, charo si tam propè sanguine juncti / Cognatas artes, studiumque affine sequamur."

84 Ll. 73–6: "Sed magis excultam cupiens ditescere mentem, / Me procul urbano strepitu, secessibus altis / Abductum, Aoniae jucunda per otia ripae, / Phoebaeo lateri comitem sinis ire beatum."

85 Ll. 101–9: "Jamque nec obscurus populo miscebor inerti, / Vitabuntque oculos vestigia nostra profanos. / Este procul vigiles curae, procul este querelae, / Invidiaeque acies transverso tortilis hirquo, / Saeva nec anguiferos extende Calumnia rictus; / In me triste nihil saedissima turba potestis / Nec vestri sum juris ego."

86 Parker, "Chronology of Milton's Latin Poems," 125–8; Parker, I, 125–8, 166–7; II, 788–9, 809.

87 Sirluck, "Milton's Idle Right Hand," 784–5.

88 William Kerrigan, *The Sacred Complex: On the Psychogenesis of Paradise Lost* (Cambridge Mass., and London, 1983), 22–60.

89 Shawcross, "Milton's Decision to Become a Poet," *Modern Language Quarterly* 24 (1963), 21–30; "Milton and Diodati," *MS* 7 (1975), 127–63; *John Milton: The Self and the World*, 56–70.

90 Christopher was "restored into commons" by the Inner Temple on November 26, 1637 (*LR* I, 351) – meaning he was eating there (and not at home) during term time. An infant son was buried at Horton on March 26, 1639, and a daughter baptized there on August 11, 1640 (*LR* I, 409; II, 25).

91 Masson's estimate (I, 736). Milton senior had provided his son with some independence by putting in his name in 1627 an interest-bearing bond from Richard Powell. In April, 1638 he sold a valuable piece of property in Covent Garden, held both in his name and his son's, possibly to help finance Milton's travels.

92 Lawes obtained the letters of passage from Theophilus Howard, Earl of Suffolk, Lord Warden of the Cinque Ports, and sent them to Milton with a brief note, apparently just before Milton's departure in April (Parker, I, 339).

93 The friend, identified by Wotton only as "Mr. H. . . . your said learned Friend" (*CPW* I, 340), was probably John Hales, also a fellow of Eton. How Milton met him is uncertain, but he became known later for liberal religious views – toleration and Socinianism (Masson, I, 537). Horton is only a few miles from Eton.

94 There may be some debt to the prose dream narrative (with interspersed passages of dialogue and song) by Henrik van der Put (Erycius Puteanus), *Comus, sive Phagesiposia Cimmeria, Somnium* (Louvain, 1610; Oxford, 1634). This work makes Comus, who is an androgyne and has a palace, a figure for contemporary depraved manners and customs.

95 Aurelian Townshend and Inigo Jones, *Tempe Restored: A Masque Presented by the Queen and Fourteen Ladies to the King's Majesty at Whitehall on Shrove Tuesday, 1632* (London, 1631 [1632]); Thomas Carew, *Coelum Britannicum. A Masque at Whitehall in the Banqueting House on Shrove Tuesday Night, the 18th of February, 1633* [1634] (London, 1633 [1634]). See Lewalski, "Milton's *Comus* and the Politics of Masquing," in *Politics of the Stuart Court Masque*, 296–320.

96 Neither the Trinity manuscript nor the printed text have stage directions for Revels

dances. Milton could hardly take it upon himself to dictate on this point, but his text invites and makes place for Revels between the masque dances and the Spirit's epilogue.

97 See John Creaser, "The Present Aid of This Occasion: The Setting of *Comus*," in *The Court Masque,* ed. David Lindley (Manchester, 1984), 111–34.

98 See McGuire, *Milton's Puritan Masque.* Citations of *A Maske* are from the 1637 version; customary line numbers are supplied from Hughes.

99 Brown, *Milton's Aristocratic Entertainments*, 57–77.

100 Some earlier critics, themselves mesmerized by the power of Comus's rhetoric, have failed to recognize the force of the Lady's response. See *Variorum* II.3, 784–852.

101 Revard, *Tangles of Neaera's Hair,* 131–56.

102 In the Trinity manuscript the first epilogue is crossed out, and the expanded version added there.

103 Citations are from *Poems,* 1645.

104 Hebrews 12:26–7 reads, "Yet once more I shake not the earth only, but also heaven. And this word, Yet once more, signifieth the removing of those things that are shaken, as of things that are made, that those things which cannot be shaken may remain." See Joseph A. Wittreich, Jr., *Visionary Poetics* (San Marino, 1979), 137–53.

105 [George] Puttenham, *The Arte of English Poesie* (London, 1589), 39, identifies two classical varieties of funeral song: "funerall songs were called *Epicedia* if they were sung by many, and *Monodia* if they were uttered by one alone."

106 Revard, *Tangles of Neaera's Hair,* 165–79.

107 The traditional funeral elegy and its parts are discussed in O. B. Hardison, *The Enduring Monument* (Chapel Hill, NC, 1962); Ellen Lambert, *Placing Sorrow* (Chapel Hill, NC, 1975), and G. W. Pigman, *Grief and English Renaissance Elegy* (Cambridge, 1957).

108 See *Variorum* II.2, 544–65, for allusions and a resumé of criticism; also Revard, T*angles of Nearea's Hair,* 179–90. Some principal sources include Theocritus, *Idyl I,* for Daphnis; Mochus's *Lament for Bion*; Bion's *Lament for Adonis* (Idyl I); Virgil's Eclogue V for Daphnis (Julius Caesar) and Eclogue X for Gallus; Petrarch, Eclogues II, VI, VII; Mantuan, Eclogue IX; Sannazaro, *Piscatory Eclogue I*; Castiglione, *Alcon*; Joannes Secundus, *Orpheus, ecloga,* and Spenser, *Shepheardes Calender*, especially "November" (Lament for Dido), "July," and "September."

109 Revard, *Tangles of Neaera's Hair,* 190–3, calls attention to an anonymous elegy for Sir Philip Sidney, in which a university community (Damoetas among them), along with the nature deities and the whole realm of Arcady mourn the loss of a good shepherd and champion of Protestantism named Lycidas. The two-part volume was published in Oxford in 1587; the *Lycidas* elegy is from the second part, entitled *Peplus Illustrissimi Viri D. Philippi Sidnaei Supremis Honoribus Dicatus.*

110 Along with the flower passage, the Orpheus passage (ll. 58–63) is the most heavily revised in the poem – on a separate page preceeding the poem in the Trinity manuscript, and in the margins.

111 L. 77. In Virgil's Eclogue VI, 3–5, Apollo plucked the ears of the pastoral poet Virgil, warning him against attempting epic subjects. The final line of the Orpheus passage also hints at some consolation in its reference to another aspect of the myth: Apollo guarded the head of Orpheus on its journey to Lesbos, where it brought that island the gift of song.

112 As Cedric Brown notes in "Milton and the Idolatrous Consort," *Criticism* 35 (1993), 429–30, the grim wolf's devouring points to Catholic worship in the chapel at Somerset House and the string of notorious converts in the queen's circle – most recently the Countess of Newport in October, 1637. Milton first wrote in the Trinity manuscript, "And nothing said," modified it in the manuscript and the university volume to "And little said" (recognizing a tame royal proclamation on the matter in December), then reverted to "nothing" in 1645 – since nothing sufficient to stem the abuse had been said.

113 Cf. Isaiah 56:10 – 57:1: "His watchmen are blind: they are all dumb dogs, they cannot bark; sleeping lying down, loving to slumber. Yea, they are greedy dogs which can never have enough, and they are shepherds that cannot understand: they all look to their own way, every one for his gain, from his quarter. . . . The righteous perisheth, and no man layeth it to heart: and merciful men are taken away, none considering that the righteous is taken away from the evil to come."

114 See *Variorum* II.2, 686–704 for a survey of interpretations of this image, the poem's most debated crux.

115 See Lawrence Lipking, "The Genius of the Shore," *PMLA* 111 (1995), 205–21.

116 Wittreich, *Visionary Poetics*, 142–3. Cf. 2 Kings 2:14–15: "And he took from him the mantle of Elijah that fell from him, and smote the waters. . . . And when the sons of the prophets which were to view at Jericho saw him, they said, The spirit of Elijah doth rest on Elisha."

Chapter 4 "I Became Desirous . . . of Seeing Foreign Parts, Especially Italy" 1638–1639

1 He was in Florence by August 20/30. Because the Continent had adopted the Gregorian or new-style calendar and England had not, he immediately lost ten days upon arrival: i.e. May 10 in London was May 20 in Paris. Dates are given in both styles, in text and notes.

2 *CPW* IV.1, 614–20. The early biographies – Skinner, Phillips and Aubrey – all paraphrase this account.

3 *CPW* I, 614–15. Wotton provided a personal introduction to Michael Braithwaite, who had served with Wotton when he was ambassador to Venice and who was at this time tutor to Scudamore's son. Sir John Scudamore, whose name Milton mistakenly records as Thomas, was Baron Dromore and Viscount Sligo in the Irish Peerage, and joint-ambassador to France along with Sir Robert Sidney, Earl of Leicester. Milton refers to other letters of introduction but does not specify the writers.

4 *EL* 19. As Milton's student and friend, Skinner had many opportunities to hear Milton express his feelings about the French.

5 See Richard Tuck, *Philosophy and Government, 1572–1651* (Cambridge, 1993), 154–201.

6 Hugo Grotius, *De jure belli ac pacis* (Paris, 1625), I.3.12.

7 *Adamus Exul* (The Hague, 1601) may have contributed something to *Paradise Lost*; *Christus Patiens,* in *Poemata Collecta* (Leyden, 1617), to *Paradise Regained* and *Samson*. George Sandys produced an English translation of *Christus Patiens* (London, 1640).

8 John Evelyn, *The Diary*, ed. E. S. DeBeer, 5 vols (Oxford, 1955), II, 180.

9 On September 16 he read a Latin poem in the Svogliati Academy (*LR* I, 389). Academy records for July may refer to visits by Milton, though he is not mentioned by name (*LR* V, 385–6).

10 The impact of Italian art on Milton is much disputed. Roland M. Frye, *Milton's Imagery and the Visual Arts* (Princeton, NJ, 1978), collects many visual parallels, arguing that these visual traditions inform Milton's conceptions of characters, events, and places in his great epics. Michael O'Connell, "Milton and the Art of Italy," in Mario Di Cesare, *Milton in Italy* (Binghamton, NY, 1991), 215–36, argues that Milton was likely unimpressed or actively repelled by much Italian art, owing to England's backwardness in the visual arts, to the iconoclasm that rendered religious art suspect, and to the absolutist politics and Counter-Reformation ethos informing the Baroque art everywhere on view. But it is also the case that Milton describes his journey as part of polemic treatises addressed to Puritan audiences, in which discourses on Italian art would be counterproductive. See Diane McColley, *A Gust for Paradise* (Chicago, 1993) for a sensitive appraisal of the way such arts might inform Milton's poems, not as influence but as visual environment. John Evelyn's *Diary* reports what was available to be seen throughout Italy, if the traveler wished.

11 See John Arthos, *Milton and the Italian Cities* (London, 1968), 16–20; A. Field, *The Origins of the Platonic Academy of Florence* (Princeton, NJ, 1988); D. S. Chambers and F. Quiviger, eds, *Italian Academies of the Sixteenth Century* (London, 1995); and Estelle Haan, *From Academia to Amicitia: Milton's Latin Writings and the Italian Academies* (Philadelphia, 1998), 3–4.

12 See, for example, Haan, *From Academia to Amicitia*, 8–9; Eric Cochrane, *Tradition and Enlightenment: Florence in the Forgotten Centuries* (Chicago, 1973), 4–27.

13 Salvino Salvini, *Fasti consolari dell'accademia Fiorentina* (Florence, 1717), 488–50.

14 There are no records of his attendance at the Apatisti but he mentions six of its members as friends, most of them also members of the Svogliati (Parker, II, 824); see Haan, *From Academia to Amicitia*, 10–37.

15 Arthos, *Italian Cities*, 12.

16 His only other hexameter poems were "Ad Patrem" and the mini-epic on Guy Fawkes Day; the former might be too personal and the latter would hardly do for this audience. He might, of course, have composed something new for this occasion, now lost, but this is less likely given his penchant for saving all his verse. See pp. 102–4 for his later visits to the Svogliati.

17 Minutes (Biblioteca Nazionale, Florence, Magliabechiana MS, Cl.IX. cod. 60, fol. 47) quoted in Haan, *From Academia to Amicitia*, 13–14. See Neil Harris, "Galileo as Symbol: The 'Tuscan artist' in *Paradise Lost*," *Annali dell'Istituto e Museo di Storia della Scienza di Fierenze* 10 (1985), 3–29.

18 The manuscript is by Anton Francesco Gori, a member of the Apastasti writing a century later but evidently with access to records now lost (Manoscritto Marucelliano A. 36.f. 53r, Florence, Biblioteca Marucelliana); cited in Haan, *From Academia to Amicitia*, 36.

19 His works include *Poematum Libri Duo* (Padua, 1628), *Elogia Historica* (Florence, 1937), *Corollarium Poeticum, scil. Poemata* (Florence, 1636), and *Adlocutiones et Elogia, Exemplaria,*

Cabalistica, Oratoria, Mixta Sepulcralia (Florence, 1636) – the last containing historical essays and occasional poems in Latin and Italian.

20 *Chronology* 61–2; Masson, I, 773–4; Arthos, *Italian Cities*, 6, 19–20. Evelyn observed among his collections "one bust of marble as much esteemed as the most antique in Italy, and many curious manuscripts; his best paintings are, a Virgin of del Sarto, mentioned by Vasari, a St. John, by Raphael, and an *Ecce Homo*, by Titian" (*Diary*, II, 186–7).

21 Benedetto Buonmattei, *Della Lingua Toscana* (Florence, 1643).

22 Carlo Dati, *Vite de Pittori Antichi* (Florence, 1667). Other works include an edition of Tuscan prose writers, *Prose Fiorentine raccolte dallo Smarrito Academico della Crusca* (Florence, 1661), and *Discorso Dell'Obbligo di ben parlare la propria lingua* (Florence, 1657).

23 Coltellini was about 25 years old in 1638, a lawyer of repute, and devoted to the study of ancient languages and the purity of Tuscan. Later he published *Endecasillabi*, 2 parts (Florence, 1641, 1652), and was four times president or consul of Florence. Chimentelli studied law, was a member of several academies, and was later appointed professor of Greek at Pisa. He was ordained to the priesthood in 1662 and associated with the Della Crusca's Italian dictionary project. Fioretti was a grammarian and student of poetry. Frescobaldi belonged to an old Florentine family and was an original member of the Apatisti (Masson, I, 776–9). Francini was a young Italian poet who left many poems in manuscript.

24 *CPW* II, 765. He may have excluded Malatesti from the list of Italian friends mentioned in the *Defensio Secunda*, because this writer of risque verse would not help the rhetorical defense of himself that he there undertakes.

25 The manuscript entitled *La Tina: Equivoci Rusticali di Antonio Malatesti, compositi nella sua Villa di Taiano il Settembre dell anno 1637: Sonetti Cinquanta: Dedicati all' Ill*[mo]. *Signore et Padrone Oss*[mo] *Signor Giovanni Milton, nobile Inghlese*, was discovered on a bookstall in London in 1757 and copied. It has since disappeared, but it was published in London that year by one Thomas Brand with the title *La Tina. Equivoci Rustici*. The title page records the dedication "al Grande Poeta Inghilesi Giovanni Milton." Cf. *LR* I, 375–6.

26 Harris, "Galileo as Symbol," 3–29.

27 *CPW* II, 715. See Marjorie Hope Nicholson, "Milton and the Telescope," *ELH* 11 (1935), 8–10.

28 See chapter 13, pp. 478–9, for discussion of Milton's uses of Galileo and of this text in *Paradise Lost*. He may also have purchased Bernardo Davanzati's just-published *Scisma d'Inghilterra* (Florence, 1638), a history of the English Schism whose "ducking imprimaturs" he holds up to scorn in *Areopagitica* (*CPW* II, 503–4, 518). See William Shullenberger, "'Imprimatur': The Fate of Davanzati," *Milton in Italy*, ed. Di Cesare, 173–96. Other books perhaps purchased in Florence include Giovanni Villani's *Croniche . . . nelle quali si tratta dell' origine di Firenze* (Venice, 1637), which he later used in teaching Italian to his nephews, and Guicciardini's *Historia d'Italia* (Florence, 1636). See *Chronology*, 61.

29 See articles by Neil Harris, Charles Huttar, and Edward Chaney in *Milton in Italy*, ed. Di Cesare, 71–146. Given the time-frame of Milton's departure for Rome, if this visit occurred at all it could not have been when the leaves were falling.

30 Arthos, *Italian Cities*, 67.

31 Urban VIII (Maffeo Barberini), *Poesie Toscane* (Rome, 1637) and *Poemata* (Paris, 1620).

32 Masson, I, 795.

33 Salzilli contributed eleven Italian sonnets, three *canzoni*, and one *ottava* to Lodovico Grignani, ed., *Poesie de' Signori Accademici Fantastici di Roma* (Rome, 1637). See James Freeman, "Milton's Roman Connection" in *Urbane Milton*, ed. Freeman and Anthony Low (Pittsburgh, 1984), 90–1.

34 Estelle Haan's translation in "Written Encomiums," *Milton in Italy*, ed. Di Cesare, 526–7.

35 The title in the 1645 *Poems* is *Ad Salsillum poetam Romanum agrotantem. Scanzontes, Poemata*, 70.

36 A letter of April 4, 1644 from Salzilli indicates that he survived at least until that date. See Freeman, "Milton's Roman Connection," 97.

37 Milton does not follow the requirement that the penultimate foot be iambic; in 19 out of 41 lines he has a spondee in that fifth foot. He seems to have allowed himself, in Latin, the greater license of Greek Scazons.

38 See Freeman, "Milton's Roman Connection," 96–100; Haan, "Written Encomiums," 526–31; and Haan, *From Academia to Amicitia*, 81–98.

39 Ll. 31–2, "Sic ille charis redditus rursum Musis / Vicina dulci prata mulcebit cantu." Translation, Haan, *From Academia to Amicitia,* Appendix, 187.

40 See Edward Chaney, *The Grand Tour and the Great Rebellion* (Geneva, 1985), 245–51, 282–5. "N" was the customary designation when the given name was not known to the scribe.

41 Evelyn, *Diary*, II, 282–3. Evelyn met there the mathematician Athanasius Kircher and also the historian and poet Famianus Strada.

42 Chaney, *The Grand Tour*, 244–51.

43 *Poemata* p. 4, in *Poems*, 1645, "Ad Joannem Miltonum. Graecia Maeonidem, jactet sibi Roma Maronem, / Anglia Miltonum jactat utrique parem."

44 Wood, col. 130. But Wood's source, a letter from William Joyner, suggests merely that their time overlapped, not that they met. Gawan had "been at Rome with the antimonarchical Mr. Milton, though as he told me, unacquainted with him." See Parker, II, rev. Campbell, p. 1,229; Chaney, *The Grand Tour*, 389–92; and Allan Pritchard, "Milton in Rome," *MQ* 14 (1980), 92–7.

45 See Margaret Byard, "'Adventrous Song': Milton and the Music of Rome," *Milton in Italy*, ed. Di Cesare, 305–28, and Lacy Collinson-Morley, *Italy after the Renaissance* (London, 1930), 84–8. Early examples of opera were Monteverdi's *Arianna* (1607) and *Orfeo* (1608).

46 Bernardino Telesio (1509–88) attacked medieval Aristotelianism and abstract reason, laying some groundwork for the scientific method and empiricism; his *De natura rerum iuxta propria principia* (Naples, 1565, 1586) was placed on the Index. Giordano Bruno (1548–1600) was forced to leave Italy in 1563 due to his views on transubstantiation and the Immaculate Conception; after several years he returned, and was burned at the stake in Rome, chiefly for his belief in multiple worlds and his Pantheistic tendencies.

47 See Luigi Salvatorelli, *A Concise History of Italy*, trans. Bernard Miall (New York, 1940), 415–50; Collinson-Morley, *Italy After the Renaissance*, 31–54. Campanella is best known for his utopian *Cittá del sole* (City of the Sun) (1623), guided by experimental science and based on collectivism; it may have been meant as a sketch for the constitution of Naples, should it become a free city. He composed most of his philosophical works and some sonnets in prison.

48 Evelyn, *Diary*, II, 146.

49 Tasso (1544–95) wrote his pastoral drama *L'Aminta* (Ferrara, 1581, first performed 1573) and his great epic *Gerusalemme Liberata* (Rome, 1581) under the patronage of the Duke of Ferrara. Then melancholy and religious torments of conscience, the Inquisition, and his frantic passion for the duke's sister, Leonora d'Este, led the duke to imprison him as a lunatic. After his release he remained subject to bouts of mental illness for the rest of his life. From 1588 till his death in 1595 he lived from time to time with Manso. His later publications include *Di Gerusalemme Conquistata* (Rome, 1593), *Il Manso, overe Dell' Amicitia* (Naples, 1596), and *Le Sette Gionate del Mondo Creato* (Viterbo, 1607).

50 *L'Adone* (Paris, 1623); *La strage degl'innocenti* (Naples [1632]). Marino was also Tasso's successor in lyric and pastoral; his other volumes include *L'Epitalami* (Paris, 1616), *La Galaria* (Milan, 1620), and *La Sampogna* (Paris, 1620).

51 Manso's *Vita di Torquato Tasso* (Naples, 1619) was reprinted twice at Venice and in 1634 at Rome. Milton refers to a life of Marino by Manso but there is no record of it. Manso also wrote five dialogues on love, *Paradossi, ovvero dell'Amore Dialoghi* (Milan, 1608), in each of which Tasso is a speaker; and another set of dialogues on Love and Beauty, *L'Erocallia dell' Amore e della Bellezza* (Venice, 1618). His sonnets and canzoni, *Poesie Nomiche . . . divise in Rime Amorose, Sacre, e Morali* (Venice, 1635) are chiefly in the affected style of Marino.

52 Masson, I, 811–12.

53 In *Epitaphium Damonis*, 181, Milton refers to these gifts as "pocula" – cups – employing the pastoral convention of rewards in shepherds' singing contests and the Renaissance convention of referring to poems as imaginary cups. See Michele De Filippis, "Milton and Manso: Cups or Books," *PMLA* 51 (1936), 745–56; and *Variorum*, I, 318; Haan, *From Academia to Amicitia*, 119, suggests that the books were likely the *Erocallia* and the *Poesie Nomiche*.

54 *Poemata*, p. 4, in *Poems*, 1645: "Ut mens, forma, decor, facies, mos, si pietas sie, / Non Anglus, verum herclè Angelus ipse fores." See Haan, *From Academia to Amicitia*, 130–6.

55 *Poemata*, p. 72, in *Poems*, 1645: Joannes Baptista Mansus Marchio Villensis vir ingenii laude, tum literarum studio, nec non & bellica virtute apud Italos clarus in primis est. Ad quem Torquati Tassi dialogus extat de Amicitia scriptus . . . In authorem Neapoli commorantem summa benevolentia prosecutus est, multaque ei detulit humanitatis officia. Ad hunc itaque hospes ille antequam ab ea urbi discederet, ut ne ingratum se ostenderet, hoc carmen misit." Trans. Haan, *From Academia to Amicitia*, 190–1.

56 Wotton had promised to send along news "in any part where I shall understand you fixed" (*CPW* I, 343).

57 We cannot be sure when and where Milton had this news – perhaps as late as Venice or, less likely, not until he visited Diodati's uncle in Switzerland. Parker (I, 174–5; II, 826–7) speculates that he heard the news in Naples and that it helped him decide to revise his travel plans. See also Parker's "Milton and the News of Charles Diodati's Death," *Modern Language Notes* 71 (1957), 486–8.

58 Among them Fynes Moryson, William Lithgow, and Edward Herbert, whose reports on their "escape from Rome" took on the character of an identifiable genre. Milton couches his story in these same terms, wishing, perhaps, to defuse criticism that his long sojourn among the Italian Catholics might invite. See Diana Benet, "The Escape from Rome," in *Milton in Italy*, ed. Di Cesare, 42–4, and Collinson-Morley, *Italy After the*

Renaissance, 7–9. There were also reports that Jesuits had poisoned John Tovey, the father of Milton's tutor, for immoderate zeal (*Nugae Antiquae* [1792], III, 158–9). And Wotton's letter had warned Milton about speaking out too freely (*CPW* I, 342–3).

59 *LR* III, 322. The statement appears in a private letter to his friend Vossius (February 19, 1653), commenting on the Salmasius–Milton controversy. Anthony à Wood also heard this rumor, probably from the circles of English Roman Catholics who traveled in Rome: "I have heard it confidently related, that for his said Resolutions . . . the English Priests at *Rome* were highly disgusted, and it was question'd whether the Jesuits his Countrymen there, did not design to do him mischief" (*EL* 38). See Pritchard, "Milton in Rome," 95.

60 In the *Pro Se Defensio* (1655) Milton calls Alexander More a liar for claiming "that I wrote 'I was a candidate for martyrdom at Rome; that plots on my life were laid by the Jesuits'" (*CPW* IV.2, 774). His general remarks about Jesuit plots implied some danger, but he was not willing to see them read as a claim of threatened martyrdom.

61 Masson, I, 801. The details of this visit are set out in Milton's letter to Holste (*CPW* I, 333–6), dated March 29, 1639 in the holograph original in the Vatican library, but one day later (March 30) in Milton's *Epistolarum Familiarium* (1674). See Joseph McG. Bonkel, "The Holograph of Milton's Letter to Holstenius," *PMLA* 68 (1953), 617–27.

62 Evelyn, *Diary*, II, 300. Evelyn remarks also on the striking prospect from the library into the Belvedere Garden.

63 Leo Miller, in "Milton and Holstenius Reconsidered," *Milton in Italy*, ed. Di Cesare, 573–87 has identified the gift book as Holste's *Demophili Democratis et Secundi Veterum Philosophorum Sententiae Morales* (Rome, 1638). It has, on facing pages, the Greek text and Holste's Latin text of the ancient authors. This explains Milton's often misunderstood description of the gift as "quorum et unius duplici," which refers to one book bipartite in language and format. The date of the dedication to Carolus and Maphaeus Barberini (December 5, 1638) makes clear that Milton met Holste and the cardinal on his second visit to Rome. Holste also edited Athanasius (Paris, 1627), Porphyry (Rome, 1639), and some axioms of the later Pythagoreans (Rome, 1638).

64 It is not a certainty that Milton saw this performance, but comments about it from several travelers square with his, and the dates fit. For other possibilities see Arthos, *Italian Cities*, 81–6.

65 See Arthos, *Italian Cities*, 68–70. One Thomas Windebank wrote on September 10, 1636: "I have been to visit the Cardinal Barberino . . . who, having notice of my arrival here, sent to visit me first. He is so obliging and courteous to all our nation that I have less wonder at the honour he doth me" (Masson, I, 799).

66 See Byard, "Milton and the Music of Rome," in *Milton in Italy*, 321–4.

67 *Applausi Poetici alle glorie della Signora Leonora Baroni*, ed. Vincenzo Costanzuli (Rome, 1639).

68 See Frederick Hammond, *Music and Spectacle in Baroque Rome* (London, 1994), 86.

69 André Maugars, *Response . . . de la Musique d'Italie*, ed. Ernest Thoinan (Paris, 1865), 37–8. He dated this note October 1, 1639.

70 The first epigram, ll. 4, 9–10, "Nam tua praesentem vox sonat ipsa Deum. / . . . Quod si cuncta quidem deus est, per cunctaque fusus, / In te una loquitur, caetera mutus habet," *Poemata*, p. 42, in *Poems*, 1645; translations of the Leonora epigrams are from Hughes. Critics have been puzzled by references to a personal guardian angel, to the

"Third Mind," and to what seems like vague pantheism in the final lines. But Milton is simply using the vocabulary of fashionable Italian Neoplatonism as a vehicle for compliment and as a means to figure the divine power of music and poetry. See Diane McColley, "Tongues of Men and Angels," in *Urbane Milton*, 127–48.

71 *LR* I, 408. The main business of this meeting was the reading and explication of the seventh chapter of Aristotle's *Ethics* by G. Bartolommei; Antinori and Girolami also read verse (Masson, I, 823–4).

72 *CPW* I, 335. He was told that nothing could be copied without previous permission, and that no one could even bring a pen to the table when examining the manuscripts. He passed along to Holste the suggestion made to him, that the manuscript could be copied by Giovanni Battista Doni, a brilliant scholar then at Rome but expected soon at Florence.

73 They were most likely offered to Milton on his second visit, since he apparently made no response to them (as he did to Salzilli in Rome and Manso in Naples) until he wrote *Epitaphium Damonis,* after returning to England.

74 For the Latin text see *Poemata*, p. 16, in *Poems,* 1645. My translation.

75 For Italian text see *Poemata*, p. 5–9, in *Poems,* 1645. My translation.

76 "Ad Salsillum," ll. 9–16: "Haec ergo alumnus ille Londini Milto; / Diebus hisce qui suum linquens nidum / Polique tractum, (pessimus ubi ventorum, / Insanientis impotensque pulmonis / Pernix anhela sub Jove exercet flabra) / Venit seraces itali soli ad glebas, / Visum superba cognitas urbes fama / Virosque doctaeque indolem juventutis." Translation, Hughes.

77 Susanne Woods, "'That Freedom of Discussion Which I Loved,'" *Milton in Italy,* ed. Di Cesare, 9–18.

78 It was ruled by a *gonfoliere*, nine ancients, and self-perpetuating councils, and was under the protection of the Grand Duke of Florence. Salvatorelli, *Concise History of Italy*, 425.

79 Collinson-Morley, *Italy after the Renaissance*, 22; Evelyn, *Diary*, II, 192–3.

80 Cf. *CPW* IV.1, 619. Gordon Campbell speculates plausibly (*Chronology*, 66) that many of the Italian books later cited in Milton's Commonplace Book were probably included in this shipment. See note 28 for some possible purchases in Florence. In Rome Milton may have picked up George Conn's *De Duplici Statu Religionis Apud Scotis* (Rome, 1628), which he later cited in *Areopagitica*. Books published in Venice (though perhaps bought elsewhere) include Francesco Berni's revision of the *Orlando Innamorato,* Boccalini's *De' Ragguagli*, Dante's *Divina Commedia* with Daniello's exposition, Savonarola's *Oracolo della Rinovazione*, Tassoni's *Pensieri*, Tasso's *Goffredo* (the pirated 1580 version of the *Gerusalemme Liberata*), and a five-volume collected *Works* of Chrysostom. For the editions Milton used, or may have used, see bibliography.

81 Arthos, *Milton and the Italian Cities*, 109.

82 Thomas Coryat, *Coryats Crudities*, 2 vols (London, 1611), I, 326; cf. Evelyn, *Diary*, II, 446–50.

83 Diane McColley, *Poetry and Music in Seventeenth-Century England* (Cambridge, 1999), 200–1, 271, summarizes the kinds of music they produced, much of it traditional and choral. Luca Marenzio (1553–99) wrote 18 books of madrigals setting texts by Sannazaro, Petrarch, Tasso, and Guarini, as well as motets for the church year. Orazio Vecchi (1550–1605) directed the choirs at the cathedrals of Reggio and Modena and at the court of Modena, producing entertainments such as the comedy *L'Amfiparnaso* (1594);

he published books of motets as well as *Dialoghi da Cantarsi et Concertarsi* (Venice, 1608). Carlo Gesualdo (1560–1613) wrote penitential music, the *Responsoria* (1611), as well as *Sacra Cantiones* for five, six, and seven voices (1603). Antonio Cifra (1584–1629) was a prolific composer of monadies; his *Sacra Cantiones* (Venice, 1638) was published the year before Milton's visit. That same year Monteverdi (1567–1643) published his eighth book of madrigals, *Madrigali Guerrieri, et Amorosi* (Venice, 1638), some with solo, virtuoso parts.

84 In *Of Education* Milton recommends that the students in his ideal academy learn directly from various practitioners, including anatomists (*CPW* II, 394).

85 See especially *Ready and Easie Way* (*CPW* VII, 371–4).

86 Evelyn, *Diary*, II, 431–2. For the widespread view of Venice as the embodiment of the ancient republican ideal articulated especially by Polybius, Cicero, and Machiavelli, see Zera S. Fink, *The Classical Republicans* (Evanston, Ill., 1962), 28–51; for the political theory articulated to defend its government, especially by Paolo Sarpi, see Tuck, *Philosophy and Government*, 94–102

87 Salvatorelli, *Concise History of Italy*, 420–3.

88 See *Of Reformation*, *CPW* I, 581, 585; *Areopagitica*, *CPW* II, 501–13.

89 *Diary*, II, 488–9. Speaking of Verona he also declared that "here, of all places I have seen in Italy, would I fix a residence."

90 Evelyn, *Diary*, II, 491. The usual route to Milan from Verona led by the towns of Castel Nuovo, San Marco, Brescia, Ponte di San Pietro, and Cologno Monzese; it was plagued with highwaymen and gypsy predators. See A. M. Cinquemani, "Through Milan and the Pennine Alps," *Milton in Italy*, ed. Di Cesare, 51.

91 Cinquemani, "Through Milan and the Pennine Alps," 51–60.

92 Evelyn, *Diary*, II, 501.

93 Ibid., II, 508–11.

94 Masson, I, 832.

95 The Diodatis did not then own the house now known as the Villa Diodati, which Byron later occupied. The cause of Charles's death was perhaps plague or smallpox, since he and his sister Philadelphia, lodging in the same London house, died within days of each other. Philadelphia was buried on August 10 and Charles on August 27. See Donald C. Dorian, *The English Diodatis* (New York, 1939), 174.

96 "Coelum non animam muto dum trans mare curro," p. 110. Cerdogni's album is in the Houghton Library, Harvard (XI.3.43).

97 His purchases may have included the five-volume edition of Jacques-August de Thou's *Historia sui Temporis* (Geneva, 1620).

98 If he bought books in France, either going or coming, they might have included the collected works of Basil and Gregory of Nyssa, Phillipe de Commines' *Memoires*, Bernard di Girard's *Histoire de France*, and André de Chesne's *Histoire Génerale d'Angleterre, d'Escosse, et d'Irland*. See Campbell, *Chronology*, 67. For editions Milton used, or may have used, see bibliography.

99 Milton states that he was away about 15 months, and that he arrived home "at almost the same time as Charles broke the peace and renewed the war with the Scots" (*CPW* IV.1, 620). In fact, the actual outbreak of that war (the Second Bishops' War) was almost a year later, on August 20, 1640. This may be a simple mistake in dating, or, more likely, it indicates Milton's sense that almost from the outset Charles was sabotag-

ing the accord signed with the Scots on June 24, 1639 that ended the First Bishops' War. Rhetorically, this move telescopes the intervening months and makes a smooth segue to Milton's account of his response to the national crisis.

100 *Poemata*, p. 77, in *Poems,* 1645: "Thyrsis & Damon eiusdem viciniae Pastores, eadem studia sequuti a pueritia amici erant, ut qui plurimum . . . Damonis autem sub persona hic intelligitur Carolus Deodatus ex urbe Hetruriae Luca paterno genere oriundus, caetera Anglus; ingenio, doctrina, clarissimisque caeteris virtutibus, dum viveret, juvenis egregius."

101 "Quod tibi purpureus pudor, & sine labe juventus / Grata fuit, quod nulla tori libata voluptas, / En etiam tibi virginei servantur honores; / Ipse caput nitidum cinctus rutilante corona, / Letaque frondentis gestans umbracula palmae / Aeternum perages immortales hymenaeos; / Cantus ubi, choreisque furit lyra mista beatis, / Festa Sionaeo bacchantur & Orgia Thyrso." Translation, Carey.

102 The relevant verses are Revelation 7:4: "Lo, a great multitude, which no man could number, of all nations, and kindreds, and people, and tongues, stood before the throne, and before the Lamb, clothed in white robes, and palms in their hands." Revelation 14:3: "And they sung as it were a new song before the throne. . . . These are they which were not defiled with women; for they are virgins. These are they which follow the Lamb whithersoever he goeth." Revelation 19:7–8: "The marriage of the Lamb is come, and his wife hath made herself ready. And to her was granted that she should be arrayed in fine linen, clean and white: for the fine linen is the righteousness of saints."

103 Lines 9–13 of the poem suggest that two harvests have passed since Diodati's death, August, 1638. An apparently unique copy of the private printing is in the British Library (C 57.d.48). It is in four leaves, undated, without author's or printer's names.

104 There is a one-day discrepancy between the manuscript (the letter sent to Dati) dated April 20, and the printed letter in the *Epistolarum Familiarium* (1674), dated April 21. As with his letter to Holste (see note 61) it seems that Milton made a copy of the letter for himself the day after he wrote the original, and so dated it.

105 See chapter 3, p. 69.

106 Dati's reply of November 1, 1647 includes, in the spirit of the academy exchanges, a long excursus on the usage of "rapidus," taking off from a tercet of Petrarch. See *CPW* II, 766–73.

107 Anthony Low, "Mansus: In Its Context," *Urbane Milton*, eds. Freeman and Low, 108. For Mansus's distich, see above, p. 98.

108 Giovanni Battista Manso, *Poesie Nomiche* (Venice, 1635). Encomia from Manso's fellow academicians and others were appended under the title *Poesie Diversi a Gio. Battista Manso, Marchese di Villa,* 225–326. See Haan, *From Academia to Amicitia*, 137–48, and Stella P. Revard, *Milton and the Tangles of Neaera's Hair: The Making of the 1645 Poems* (Columbia, Mo., 1997), 215–24.

109 Ll. 7–10, 25. All translations of *Mansus* are from Hughes.

110 Ll. 25–35, 38. "Manse pater, jubeo longum salvere per aevum / Missus Hyperboreo juvenis peregrinus ab axe. / Nec tu longinquam bonus aspernabere Musam, / Quae nuper gelida vix enutrita sub Arcto / Imprudens Italas ausa est volitare per urbes. / Nos etiam in nostro modulantes flumine cygnos / Credimus obscuras noctis sensisse per umbras, / Qua Thamesis late puris argenteus urnis / Oceani glaucos perfundit gurgite crines. / Quin & in has quondam pervenit Tityrus oras. / . . . Nos etiam

colimus Phoebum, nos munera Phoebo."

111 Revard, *Tangles of Neaera's Hair*, 217–18.

112 Ll. 78–84: "O mihi si mea sors salem concedat amicum / Phoebaeos decorasse viros qui tam bene norit, / Si quando indigenas revocabo in carmina reges, / Arturumque etiam sub terris bella moventem; / Aut dicam invictae sociali foedere mensae, Magnanimos Heroas, & (O modo spiritus ad sit) / Frangam Saxonicas Britonum sub Marte phalanges." Milton's choice of subject sets his projected poem in the tradition of Spenser's *Faerie Queene*.

113 Ll. 49–55: "Fortunate senex, ergo quacunque per orbem / Torquati decus & nomen, celebrabitur ingens, / Claraque perpetui succrescet fama Marini, / Tu quoque in ora frequens venies plausumque virorum, / Et parili carpes iter immortale volatu."

114 R. W. Condee, "The Latin Poetry of John Milton," in *The Latin Poetry of the English Poets*, ed. J. W. Binns (London, 1974), 78–9, points to the pun on Manso's name, linking him to Chiron: "Nobile mansueti cessit Chironis in antrum," l. 60. Cf. Revard, *Tangles of Neaera's Hair*, 219–24.

115 Ll. 94–100: "Tum quoque, si qua fides, si praemia certa bonorum, / Ipse ego caelicolum semotus in aethera divum, / Quo labor & mens pura vehunt, atque ignea virtus / Secreti haec aliqua mundi de parte videbo / (Quantum fata sinunt), & tota mente serenum / Ridens purpureo suffundar lumine vultus / Et simul aethereo plaudam mihi laetus Olympo."

116 Cf. Horace, Satires, I.l. 64–7. See Low, "Mansus: In its Context," 123.

117 The term carries that sense in the titles of funeral poems by Bion and Moschus. For the generic distinctions between *elegos*, *epikedion*, and *epitaphios* in the Hellenistic period, see Gordon Campbell, "Imitation in *Epitaphium Damonis*," *Urbane Milton*, ed. Freeman and Low, 165–8.

118 The *Variorum* records some 70 citations of Virgil's Eclogues (especially nos. 5 and 10), 35 to the Georgics, and 40 to the *Aeneid*. The words of the refrain echo Eclogue 7.4; the carved cups recalls Eclogue 3. The name of the mourner Thyrsis points to Theocritus, as does the device of the recurrent refrain. The theme of the mourner absent from the deathbed of the friend recalls Castiglione's *Alcon*.

119 See Dorian, *English Diodatis*, 177–8.

120 Ll. 12–17: "Dulcis amor Musae Thusca reinebat in urbe. / Ast ubi mens expleta domum, pecorisque relicti / Cura vocat, simul assueta seditque sub ulmo, / Tum vero amissum tum denique sentie amicum, / Coepit & immensum sic exonerare dolorem." Translations of *Epitaphium Damonis* are by Hughes.

121 In a still closer verbal echo – "Ite domum pasti" – Thyrsis in Virgil's Elegy 7, line 44 sends his well-fed steers home "for shame" for intruding on their master's song (and perhaps on his lovemaking). In both cases the pastoral animals are well cared for.

122 See Janet Knedlick, "High Pastoral Art in *Epitaphium Damonis,*" *Urbane Milton,* ed. Freeman and Low, 152–4.

123 See Condee, "Latin Poetry of John Milton," 82–8.

124 Ll. 37–58, 109–11: "At mihi quid tandem fiet modo? quis mihi fidus / Haerebit lateri comes, ut tu saepe solebas / Frigoribus duris, & per loca foeta pruinis. / . . . Quis fando sopire diem, cantuque solebit? / Ite domum impasti, domino jam non vacat agni. / Pectora cui credam? quis me lenire docebit / Mordaces curas, quis longam fallere noctem / Dulcibus alloquiis . . . / Quis mihi blanditiasque tuas, quis tum mihi risus, / Cecropiosque sales referet, cultosque lepores? / . . . At jam solus agros, jam pascua

solus oberro, / . . . Aut si sors dederit tandem non aspera votis, / Illum inopina dies qua non speraveris hora / Surripit, aeternum linquens in saecula damnum."

125 Ll. 125–38: "Quamquam etiam vestri nunquam meminisse pigebit / Pastores Thusci, Musis operata juventus, / Hic Charis, atque Lepos; & Thuseus tu quoque Damon. / Antiqua genus unde petis Lucumonis ab urbe. / O ego quantus eram, gelidi cum stratus ad Arni / Murmura, populcumque nemus, qua mellior herba, / Carpere nunc violas, nunc summas carpere myrtos, / Et potui Lycidae certantem audire Menalcam. / Ipse etiam tentare ausus sum, nec puto multum / Displicui, nam sunt & apud me munera vestra / Fiscellae, calathique, & cerea vincia cicutae. / Quin & nostra suas docuerunt nomina fagos / Et Datis, & Francinus, erant & vocibus ambo / Et studiis noti, Lydorum sanguinis ambo."

126 "Silvae" were poetic sketches or minor poems; in his 1645 *Poems* Milton titled his poems in non-elegiac meter, *Sylvarum Liber*. Milton echoes Virgil's farewell to the forests, "concedite silvae," in Eclogue 10, 63, and also Virgil's renunciation of pastoral verse in Eclogue 7, 24, "pendebit fistula pinu."

127 Ll. 155–72: "Ipse etiam – nam nescio quid mihi grande sonabat / Fistula, ab undecima jam lux est altera nocte, / Et tum forte novis admoram labra cicutis, / Dissiluere tamen, rupta compage, nec ultra / Ferre graves potuere sonos; dubito quoque ne sim / Turgidulus, tamen & referam; vos cedite, silvae. / Ite domum impasti, domino jam non vacat, agni. / Ipse ego Dardanias Rutupina per aequora puppes / Dicam, et Pandrasidos regnum vetus Inogeniae, / Brennumque Arviragumque duces, priscumque Belinum, / Et tandem Armoricos Britonum sub lege colonos; / Tum gravidam Arturo fatali fraude Jögernen, / Mendaces vultus, assumptaque Görlois arma, / Merlini dolus. O mihi tum si vita supersit, / Tu procul annosa pendebis fistula pinu / Multum oblita mihi, aut patriis mutata camoenis / Brittonicum strides, quid enim? omnia non licet uni / Non sperasse uni licet omnia."

128 Ll. 180–3: "Haec tibi servabam lenta sub cortici lauri, / Haec, & plura simul, tum quae mihi pocula Mansus, / Mansus Chalcidicae non ultima gloria ripae / Bina dedit, misum artis opus, mirandus & ipse."

129 Manso's *Poesie Nomiche* concludes with the poem "La Fenice" (The Phoenix) and his *Erocallia* concerns theories of love. See note 53.

Chapter 5 "All Mouths Were Opened Against . . . the Bishops" 1639–1642

1 Legislation to this purpose was passed in the Glasgow Assembly, November 21 to December 20, 1638.

2 For example, Max Weber, *The Protestant Ethic and the Spirit of Capitalism*, trans. Talcott Parsons (New York, 1958); R. H. Tawney, *Religion and the Rise of Capitalism* (New York, 1926); Samuel R. Gardiner, *History of the Great Civil War, 1642–1649* (London, 1886–91); Lawrence Stone, *The Causes of the English Revolution, 1629–1642* (London, 1972); Christopher Hill, *The Century of Revolution, 1603–1714* (New York, 1966), *Puritanism and Revolution* (London, 1958), *The World Turned Upside Down: Radical Ideas During the English Revolution* (London, 1972).

3 For example, Conrad Russell, *The Origins of the English Civil War* (New York and London, 1973), *Parliaments and English Politics, 1621–1629* (Oxford, 1979), and *The*

Causes of the English Civil War (Oxford, 1990); J. S. Morrill, *The Revolt of the Provinces* (New York, 1976); Kevin Sharpe, *Faction and Parliament* (Oxford, 1978); Mark Kishlansky, *Parliamentary Selection* (New York, 1986).

4 For example, in Richard Cust and Ann Hughes, eds, *Conflict in Early Stuart England, 1603–1642* (London and New York, 1989); Thomas Cogswell, *The Blessed Revolution* (Cambridge, 1989); Geoff Eley and William Hunt, eds, *Reviving the English Revolution* (London, 1988).

5 See, for example, *CPW* I, 533–4, 555, 557, 917.

6 See Janel Mueller, "Embodying Glory: The Apocalyptic Strain in Milton's *Of Reformation*," in David Loewenstein and James G. Turner, eds, *Politics, Poetics, and Hermeneutics in Milton's Prose* (Cambridge, 1990), 9–40.

7 The bookseller George Thomason, Milton's friend, collected some 22,000 pamphlets and other publications in the period 1640–60, indicating the month and day he acquired each. His collection is now in the British Library. I record Thomason's dates of acquisition in parenthesis, as an indication of approximate dates of publication. See George Thomason, *Catalogue of the Pamphlets, Books, Newspapers, and Manuscripts relating to the Civil War, the Commonwealth, and Restoration*, 2 vols (London, 1908). For the Marprelate controversy see Raymond Anselment, "*Betwixt Jest and Ernest:" Marprelate, Milton, Marvell, Swift and the Decorum of Religous Ridicule* (Toronto, 1979). For the print revolution, see Sharon Achinstein, *Milton and the Revolutionary Reader* (Princeton, NJ, 1994).

8 For this Christian rhetorical tradition, see Peter Auski, "Milton's 'Sanctifi'd Bitternesse': Polemical Technique in the Early Prose," *Texas Studies in Literature and Language* 19 (1977), 363–76.

9 The margins of William Prynne's massive tomes were laden with citations of biblical chapter and verse, and other authorities, but this practice of "marginal Prynne" was only an exaggeration of contemporary habits, especially among Puritans. See B. Douglas Trevor, *Learned Appearances: Writing Scholarly and Literary Selves in Early Modern England* (Dissertation, Harvard University, 1999), 323–40.

10 Douglas Stewart, "Speaking to the World: The *Ad Hominem* Logic of Milton's Polemics," *The Seventeenth Century* 11 (1996), 35–60.

11 Until June, 1644 he received annual interest of £24 on a loan to Richard Powell (*LR* II, 103) and until May, 1642 he received £12 annually on a loan to Sir John Cope (*LR* I, 357–8). There may have been other investments (Parker, II, 840).

12 See chapter 4, p. 109, 117.

13 Just when Milton worked on the list of topics is not known, but probably during the first several months after his return, and before June, 1641 when he began to be caught up in pamphlet controversy. His comments in the *Reason of Church-Government* (1641) about weighing literary possibilities (*CPW* I, 812–15) seem related to this exercise. The Trinity manuscript is cited in the text and notes as *TM*.

14 Under the heading "other Tragedies," the first page lists "Adam *ex* in Banishment," "The flood," and "Abram in Aegypt." The remaining Genesis topics are on the second page: "The Deluge," "Sodom," "Dinah" (with a cast of characters), and "Thamar" (with a brief sketch). Exodus topics begin at the top of the second column on page two, and the Old Testament list continues in the remaining space in column one. The Samson topics are: "Samson pursophorus [the Fire-brand-bringer] or Hybristes, or Samson

marriing [marrying] or in Ramath Lechi Jud. 15. Dagonalia. Jud. 16."

15 The subjects given brief elaboration are "Dinah," "Thamar pregnant," "The Moabites" (on a later page), "The Eliade," "Abias Thersaeus," "Ahab," "Achabaei Cunoborumani" (Ahab devoured by dogs), "Hesekiah Besieged," and "The Taking of Jerusalem." Milton may have thought them promising, or wanted to clarify his ideas about them.

16 The sources cited are Bede, Geoffrey of Monmouth, William of Malmesbury, John Speed, and Raphael Holinshed.

17 Some of these topics were included earlier on the Old Testament list, but not there developed.

18 The fourth version does not supersede the third, but contains the directive, "compare this with the former draught."

19 Phillips states that he saw these ten lines "several Years before the Poem was begun" along with some others designed for the beginning of that tragedy (*EL* 72). This points to a further stage in Milton's plan for such a tragedy, with Satan acting as prologue rather than Moses or Gabriel as in the *TM* sketches. Some elements from the sketches reappear in Milton's epic: a masque of the evils of the world is one generic element in Books 11 and 12 and a debate of Justice and Mercy lies behind the dialogue of the Father and the Son in Book 3. See Lewalski, *Paradise Lost and the Rhetoric of Literary Forms* (Princeton, NJ, 1985), 118–22, 259–62.

20 Milton's note on *Christus patiens* projects a classical structure like that he would later use for *Samson Agonistes:* "The Scene in the garden beginning from the comming thither till Judas betraies & the officers lead him away the rest by message & chorus. his agony may receav noble expressions" (*TM*, 41).

21 *TM* 40. These lines are crowded in, as an afterthought. Also, Milton's note on Egfride, king of the Northumbrians, states, with allusion to the contemporary Scots war, that Egfride "made warre for no reason on men [the Scots] that ever lov'd the English" (*TM* 37).

22 *EL* 62. Milton probably made the move, and acquired the household furnishings mentioned, when his father gave up his house at Horton. Christopher Milton and his wife were still at Horton with Milton senior on August 11, 1640, when Christopher's daughter Sara was baptized there, but soon after they all moved to Reading. Edward Phillips places Milton's anti-episcopal tracts (May, 1641–April, 1642) "in the one or two first" years of Milton's residence in Aldersgate. Milton paid taxes in his new house on April 29, 1641.

23 Phillips identifies them as "Mr. *Alphry* and Mr. *Miller,*" i.e. Thomas Alfray of Catsfield, Sussex, and John Miller of Litton, Middlesex, admitted to Gray's Inn in 1633 and 1628 respectively (Masson, II, 209). Nothing more is known of them or of Milton's association with them. Gaudy Days were regular festival times at the Inns of Court; Milton either participated in those festivities with his friends, or enjoyed feasts and entertainments with them in the City.

24 See chapter 2, pp. 31, 45. Phillips's statement gives some support to Christopher Hill's portrait of Milton as "more sociable and clubbable than is often thought" (*Milton and the English Revolution*, London, 1977, 9), though Hill stretches the point to portray him as a jovial frequenter of taverns, consorting there with the radical fringe (ibid., 97–9).

25 See chapter 6, pp. 173–5.

26 *EL* 60. Phillips lists Cato, Varro, Pliny's *Natural History*, Cornelius Celsis, Vitruvius's *Architecture*, Lucretius, Hesiod, Homer, Aratus's *Phaenomena*, Apollonius Rhodius's *Argonautica*, Plutarch, Xenophon's *Institutes of Cyrus*, and several others. For the quadrivial studies he specifies Urstisius's Arithmetic, Riff's Geometry, Petiscus's Trigonometry, and John de Sacro Bosco's *De Sphaera*.

27 Giovanni Villani, *Chroniche . . . nelle quali si tratta dell'origine di Firenze* (Venice, 1537); Pierre Avity, *Les Empires, royaumes, estats . . . et principautez du monde* (St Omer, 1614), trans. E. Grimstone, *The Estates, Empires, and Principalities of the World* (London, 1615).

28 Historical MSS Commission, Third Report (1872), 3.

29 Bede, *Historia Ecclesiastica Gentis Anglorum*; William of Malmesbury, *De Gestis Regum Anglicorum*; John Hardyng, *Chronicle*; John Stow, *Annales, or General Chronicle of England*; Raphael Holinshed, *Chronicles of England, Scotland, and Ireland*; John Speed, *The Historie of Great Britaine*; Sir Thomas Smith, *De Republica Anglicorum*; William Camden, *Annales Rerum Anglicarum et Hibernicarum, Regnante Elizabetha ad Annum Salutis 1589*; John Hayward, *The Life and Raigne of King Edward the Sixt*; William Lambard, *Archeion, or a Commentary upon the High Courts of Justice in England*; André du Chesne, *Histoire générale d'Angleterre, d'Ecosse, et d'Irlande*; George Buchanan, *Rerum Scoticarum Historia*; Edmund Campion, *The History of Ireland*; Edmund Spenser, *A View of the Present State of Ireland*. See James Holly Hanford, "The Chronology of Milton's Private Studies," *John Milton: Poet and Humanist* (Cleveland, 1966), 88–96; *CPW* I, 362–513; Jackson C. Boswell, *Milton's Library* (New York and London, 1975); and my bibliography for the editions Milton used or may have used for these works and those listed in notes 30 and 31.

30 Joannes Sleidan, *Commentarii de Statu Religionis et Reipublicae, Carolo Quinto, Caesare*; Paulus Jovius, *Historia Sui Temporis*; Nicolo Machiavelli, *Dell' Arte della Guerra* and *Discorsi*; Girolamo Savonarola, *Oracolo della Renovatione della Chiesa*; Paolo Sarpi, *Historia Del Concilio Tridentino*; and Bernard de Girard, *L'Histoire de France*. Others include Philippe de Commines, *Les Memoires*; Sesellius (Claude de Seissel), *De Monarchia Franciae*; and Jacques Auguste du Thou, *Historia sui temporis*.

31 Chaucer, *Canterbury Tales* and *Romaunt of the Rose*, in *Workes*, ed. Speght; Gower, *Confessio Amantis*; Aristotle, *Ethics*; Caesar, *Commentaries*; Lactantius, *De Ira* and *Divinae Institutiones*; Cyprian, *De Singularitate Clericorum*; Johannes Cuspinian (Hans Spiesshaymer), *Historia Caesarum et Imperatorum Romanorum*; Joannes Sinibaldus, *Geneanthropeia*; Sozomen, *Historia Ecclesiastica*; Roger Ascham, *Toxophilus: The Schoole of Shootinge*.

32 From the topic "Of Poetry" (*CPW* I, 381). Other such extracts deal with the punishment of magistrates for bribery and corruption, the evil of forbidding marriage to the clergy, and King Alfred as promoter of learning, under the topics "Of Justice," "Marriage," "Of the Knowledge of Literature," "Of Poetry," and "Of Lust" (*CPW* I, 378, 388, 381, 369). For dating, see Hanford, "Milton's Private Studies," 88–96.

33 *CPW* I, 424. He also cites examples of lawyers bending the laws to princes' wishes (426).

34 *CPW* I, 502–3; Ascham, *Toxophilus*.

35 *CPW* I, 442. Cf. Smith, *De republica Anglorum*, 10. Lambard, *Archeion*, is cited to the effect that by ancient English custom the lord chancellor, the chief justice, and the treasurer were elected or deposed by parliament (449).

36 Smith (supplemented by Aristotle) supplies terms for Milton's distinction between a king and a tyrant: "'A K. is who by succession or election commeth with good will of

the people to his goverment, and doth administer the com-welth by the laws of the same and by equity, and doth seeke the profit of the people as his owne.' and on the contrarie, 'he that coms by force, breaks laws at his pleasure, maks other without consent of the people, and regardeth not the wealth of the commons, but the advancement of himselfe, his faction, and his kindred' he defines for a tyrant" (*CPW* I, 443).

37 Also, from Stow's examples, Milton concludes that kings "scarcely recognize themselves as mortals" save at their coronation when they are soliciting popular support, and on their deathbeds when they confess "that they are wretched mortals" (*CPW* I, 431–2).

38 See pp. 138–9.

39 The petition denied bishops' *jure divino* claims; it allowed for compromise, but it also prepared the way for further retrenchment of their powers.

40 [J]oseph [H]all, *Episcopacie by Divine Right Asserted* (London, 1640). The chief biblical texts Hall and others cite to support the *jure divino* argument are directives for the Old Testament high priests and Levites, and references in Paul's epistles and the Book of Revelation (chapters 2 and 3) to Titus, Timothy, and the "Angels' of the Asian churches, all taken to be bishops.

41 [J]oseph [H]all, *A Humble Remonstrance to the High Court of Parliament* (London, 1640 [1641]), 6; Thomason dates it January (1641). As concessions to his opponents, Hall makes some place for "conceived" or individual prayer and preaching in the church service and allows that continental reformed churches without bishops are true churches.

42 The Smectymnuans hint that they recognize Hall as author of the *Humble Remonstrance* (pp. 71–2) from the similarity of the arguments here to those in the earlier tract. The primary scripture texts cited for the Presbyterian system are 1 Timothy 5:17, 1 Corinthians 12:28, 1 Peter 5:1, and Romans 12:7–8.

43 *CPW* I, 966. The evidence for Milton's authorship, summarized in *CPW* I, 961–5, involves identical page references to editions of Holinshed, Speed, and Stow in the Postscript and in Milton's Commonplace Book, as well as parallels in phrasing and diction, and what seems like an acknowledgment of authorship in Milton's *Animadversions* (*CPW* I, 730).

44 [Joseph Hall], *A Defence of the Humble Remonstrance* (London, 1641). He appended to it, and translated from the Latin, two short pamphlets by Dr Abraham Scultetus of the University of Heidelberg on the divine right of episcopacy. While preserving his anonymity here, he virtually admits his authorship of the *Remonstrance* (p. 136).

45 It is, Hall says, "borrowed (for a great part) out of [Alexander Leighton's] *Sion's Plea* and [Prynne's] *Breviate* consisting of a rhapsodye of Histories" (159). In his *Animadversions* Milton threw that charge back on Hall: "How wittily you tell us what your wonted course is upon the like occasion" (*CPW* I, 730).

46 In April or May, 1641 Hall urged Ussher to "bestow one sheet of paper upon these distracted times, showing the Apostolical origin of it [episcopacy], and the grounds of it from Scriptures and the immediately succeeding antiquity. Every line of it, coming from your Grace's hand, would be . . . worth more than volumes to us."

47 The treatise setting forth this proposal, *The Reduction of Episcopacy unto the form of Synodical Government received in the Ancient Church,* was not printed until 1656. See Thomas Corns, *Uncloistered Virtue: English Political Literature, 1640–1660* (Oxford, 1992), 16–17.

48 Ussher, *The Judgment of Doctor Rainoldes* (London, 1641). The title alludes to a recently

reprinted *Letter* of John Rainolds, an Elizabethan Calvinist divine who had refused a bishopric; it argued that bishops and presbyters originally held the same powers in the primitive church and that bishops were simply the elected presidents of councils or synods of elders. Early in 1641 the antiprelatical faction had reprinted that letter as *The Judgement of Doctor Reignolds Concerning Episcopacy,* but Ussher builds his case from an earlier Rainolds text emphasizing the bishops' primacy, *The Summe of the Conference Betweene John Rainoldes and John Hart* (London, 1584), 535–6.

49 See Thomas Corns, "The Freedom of Reader-response": Milton's *Of Reformation* and Lilburne's *The Christian Mans Triall,"* in *Freedom and the English Revolution,* eds. R. O. Richardson and G. M. Ridden (Manchester, 1986), 93–103. At some point Milton presented a copy of this work to one J. H. (probably John Hales, the "learned Friend" Wotton mentions; see chapter 3, n. 93). The Bodleian copy is inscribed "Ex dono authoris accepi J.H. (D. 12. 6 Linc)." Conceivably, the tract addresses Hales as the "Friend."

50 See chapter 3, pp. 65–6.

51 See Janel Mueller, "Contextualizing Milton's Nascent Republicanism," in Paul G. Stanwood, ed., *Of Poetry and Politics* (Binghamton, NY, 1995), 261–82.

52 Hall had praised the English bishops Latimer, Ridley, and Grindel as highly honored Marian martyrs, as had John Foxe in his enormously popular *Acts and Monuments* (Book of Martyrs).

53 Peloni Almoni, *A Compendious Discourse* (London, 1641). While discussing the testimony of Irenaeus (AD 184) about bishops, Almoni observes that "the late unworthy authour of a Booke intituled, *Of Reformation* hath found some quarrel against him [Irenaeus]: but Fevordentius . . . hath well answered such exceptions" (sig. A 4).

54 *Of Prelatical Episcopacy* (London, 1641); *CPW* I, 625–6, 652.

55 Stanley Fish, "Wanting a Supplement": The Question of Interpretation in Milton's Early Prose," in David Loewenstein and James G. Turner, eds, *Politics, Poetics, and Hermeneutics in Milton's Prose* (Cambridge, 1990), 41–68, claims that Milton's failure to argue from scripture despite these statements indicates his uncomfortable sense that, in fact, scripture does need the supplement of commentary. Milton's point, however, is that his opponents have already conceded the Presbyterian interpretation of these scripture verses.

56 As Thomas Kranidas points out in "Words, Words, Words, and the Word: Milton's *Of Prelatical Episcopacy,*" *MS* 16 (1982), 154–5.

57 Corns, *Uncloistered Virtue,* 19–26.

58 Smectymnuus, *A Vindication* (London, 1641). Hall published a 103-page answer to this tract on July 28, misleadingly entitled *A Short Answer to the Tedious Vindication of Smectymnuus* (London, 1641), but thereafter he gave over the contest.

59 *Animadversions* (London, 1641); *CPW* I, 664.

60 One model for this is the Cynic–Stoic Diatribe. See Maureen Thum, "Milton's Diatribal Voice: The Integration and Transformation of a Generic Paradigm in *Animadversions,*" *MS* 30 (1993), 3–25. Hall himself had made earlier use of this common polemic method.

61 The allusion is to Hall's verse satires, *Virgidemiarum* (London, 1597–8) containing *Toothlesse Satyrs* and *Byting Satyrs.* Milton targets as well the imaginary voyage or dystopia that Hall published under the name Mercurius Britannicus, *Mundus alter & idem* (London, 1605). See Richard McCabe, "The Forms and Methods of Milton's *Animadver-*

sions," *ELN* 18 (1981), 266–82; Thomas Kranidas, "Style and Rectitude in Seventeenth-century Prose: Hall, Smectymnuus, and Milton," *Huntington Library Quarterly* 46 (1983), 237–48; James Egan, "Creator–Critic: Aesthetic Subtexts in Milton's Antiprelatical and Regicide Polemics," *MS* 30 (1993),49; and Anselment, *Betwixt Jest and Ernest*, 61–93.

62 Page 676. On the basis of this passage, the anonymous author who answered Milton's tract inferred Milton's own licentious character and lifestyle, to which Milton takes furious umbrage in the *Apology*. See p. 139.

63 Pages 727–8. Continuing the metaphor, he claims the freedom of sons to be obedient only to their true mother, the reformed catholic church as a whole.

64 A minister is not made by ordination but by "the calling of God . . . and his own painfull study and diligence." The laity is well able to judge the fitness of ministers (*CPW* I, 715). A "plaine unlearned man that lives well by the light which he has" is a better pastor than "a hireling Clergy though never so learned" (720). A "true Pastor of Christs sending . . . requires either nothing, if he could so subsist, or a very common and reasonable supply of humane necessaries" (721).

65 *A Grand Remonstrance Presented to the King at Hampton Court, Dec. 1, 1641 in the Name of the Commons of England,* in John Rushworth, *Historical Collections of Private Papers of State,* 8 vols (London, 1721–2), IV, 438–51.

66 Rushworth, *Historical Collections* IV, 425, 428.

67 *Reason of Church-Government* (London, 1641 [1642]). The date of writing is indicated by references to the Irish uprising and the imprisonment of the twelve bishops, and the absence of reference to the episode of the five members. The publication date indicates publication sometime before March 25, 1642, when the year changed according to the Julian Calendar.

68 *Certain Briefe Treatises* (Oxford, 1641). Extracts from the nine authors – Richard Hooker, Launcelot Andrewes, James Ussher, Martin Bucer, John Rainolds, Edward Brerewood, Francis Mason, and John Dury – are presented in three separate tracts within this collection, each with its own title page: *A Summarie View of the Government Both of the Old and New Testament* (Andrewes and Hooker)*; The Originall of Bishops and Metropolitans; briefly laid downe* (Bucer, Rainolds, Ussher, Brerewood)*; The Validity of the Ordination of the Minis[t]ers of the Reformed Churches Beyond the Seas* (Mason and Dury). The collection was most likely published by Ussher.

69 See *CPW* I, 748. Thomason obtained some 90 tracts in December, 1641, 200 in January, 1642, and 160 in February. In *The Humble Petition of Many thousand Poor People* "of the meanest rank and quality" (January 31, 1642) the signatories lament their economic woes and blame them on the bishops and the Catholic lords of the Privy Council. On the same day *The Humble Petition of 15000 Poore Labouring Men, Known by the Name of Porters, and the Lowest Members of the Citie of London* decry the decline of trade and warn that they would soon be forced to extremities if not relieved. February 4, 1642, brought two petitions from women: one of them, *The Humble Petition of Many Hundreds of Distressed Women, Trades-mens Wives, and Widdowes,* complained mainly of the bishops, the Catholic lords, and the abuses of religion.

70 Stephen Marshall, *Meroz Cursed or, A Sermon preached to the honourable Houses of Commons . . .* February 23, 1641 (London, 1641 [1642]). The text is Judges 5:23, "'Curse ye Meroz,' said the angel of the Lord, 'curse ye bitterly the inhabitants thereof; because

they came not to the help of the Lord, to the help of the Lord against the mighty.'" Marshall's sermon is less militant than the text allows for, chiefly urging prayer, repentance, and moral support as the "helps" presently required of English Puritans. But the biblical text, repeated over and over again in the sermon, reverberates with a militancy implied if not quite explicit.

71 Joseph Hall, et al.(?), *A Modest Confutation* (London, 1642).

72 Ibid., 36.

73 Ibid., A 3–A 3v.

74 *An Apology* (London, 1642). Its reference to the "miraculous and losseless victories" in Ireland (*CPW* I, 927) seems to allude to parliament's April 8 petition asserting that recent English victories against the rebels obviated the need for the invasion the king proposed to mount.

75 This tract and *Reason of Church-Government* were both published by John Rothwell; Thomas Underhill published Milton's first three pamphlets.

76 See Egan, "Creator–Critic," 45–54, and Kranidas, "Style and Rectitude," 237–48. He judges Hall merely a "drawling versifier" in his poetic satires, according to the standards he imbibed from his good education, "inur'd and season'd betimes with the best and elegantest authors of the learned tongues, and thereto brought an eare that could measure a just cadence, and scan without articulating" (*CPW* I, 914–16).

77 Page 939. See Anselment, *Betwixt Jest and Ernest,* 85–93.

78 Pages 948–9. Cf. Augustine, *De Doctrina Christiana,* IV.vi.9–10.

79 Page 920, italics mine. Though Milton also urges the king to prove "a true defender of the Faith" in this matter, his hopes clearly rest with the parliament.

80 He cites as their accomplishments: laying tyranny "groveling upon the fatall block" (Strafford's execution), freeing us from the doctrine of tyranny (the king's absolutist and *jure divino* claims), releasing "the elect Martyrs" from prison, and abolishing the required liturgy (924).

81 The Confuter apparently inferred this character from *Animadversions;* see above, pp. 132, 136. Milton asserts that the Confuter described him from "odde ends which from some penurious Book of Characters he had been culling out and would faine apply" (*CPW* I, 882–3). See Egan, "Creator–Critic," 53.

82 Pages 883–4. He continues: "I could not . . . think I had that regard from them for other cause then that I might be still encourag'd to proceed in the honest and laudable courses, of which they apprehended I had given good proofe. And to those ingenuous and friendly men who were evere the countnancers of vertuous and hopefull wits, I wish the best, and happiest things, that friends in absence wish one to another." This seems a surprisingly positive comment on his university experiences (see chapter 2, pp. 28–30), but Milton quickly proceeds to separate the fellows he here praises as friends (Tovey? Mede?) from the "sicknesse" that now plagues both universities – their despised curriculum and especially their increasingly Laudian politics.

83 Pages 885–6. The reference is to the Protestation of May 3, 1641, to defend Protestantism against the encroachments of popery.

84 Masson (II, 402, 481) thought so, but Hanford rejects that reading in "Milton and the Art of War," in *John Milton, Poet and Humanist* (Cleveland, OH, 1966), 244. For Milton's contacts with military affairs, see Robert Fallon, *Captain or Colonel: The Soldier in Milton's Life and Art* (Columbia, Mo., 1984).

85 See chapter 2, p. 43.

86 See chapter 1, pp. 12–13; chapter 3, p. 68. His biblical allusions are to 1 Corinthians 6:13; 13:7; 2 Corinthians 11.2; Revelation 14:1–5.

87 Pages 890–2. *Reason of Church-Government* also includes a long passage on due self-esteem that offers a revealing insight into the basis of the rigorous self-discipline Milton here describes: "He that holds himself in reverence and due esteem, both for the dignity of Gods image upon him, and for the price of his redemption . . . accounts himselfe both a fit person to do the noblest and godliest deeds . . . and would blush at the reflection of his own severe and modest eye upon himselfe, if it should see him doing or imagining that which is sinfull though in the deepest secrecy . . . this honourable duty of estimation and respect towards his own soul and body . . . will leade him best to this hill top of sanctity and goodnesse above which there is no higher ascent but to the love of God" (*CPW* I, 842). See Richard Strier, "Milton against Humility," *Religion and Culture in Renaissance England,* eds. Claire McEachern and Debora Shuger (Cambridge, 1997), 258–86.

88 See Thomas Kranidas, *The Fierce Equation: A Study of Milton's Decorum* (The Hague, 1965), 13–71; and Thomas Corns, *The Development of Milton's Prose Style* (Oxford, 1982).

89 Keith Stavely, *The Politics of Milton's Prose Style* (New Haven, Conn., and London, 1975), 1–53, argues that Milton's tracts had little political effect, chiefly because of their exalted poetic texture; for a counterargument, see David Loewenstein, *Milton and the Drama of History* (Cambridge, 1990), 1–34.

90 *CPW* I, 561. The axiom, somewhat altered, is from Cyprian's 74th Epistle.

91 Pages 599–600. This comparison is reinforced later as Milton compares Presbyterian assemblies of ministers to parliament: in both, the king is denominated the Head, but in parliament "he can do nothing alone [or] against the common Law," and in assemblies "neither alone, nor with consent against the Scriptures" (606). Mueller, "Contextualizing Milton's Nascent Republicanism," 267, underscores Milton's daring in employing language of the three estates, which had been banned as treasonous since 1606, and had all but vanished from English political discourse until 1640. Mueller compares Milton's language to that of Scottish and English republican theorists, especially Henry Parker in *The Case of Shipmoney* (London, 1640), who pointed to the movement throughout Europe toward "republists, or to conditionate and restrained forms of government" (pp. 7–8).

92 Page 590. For the pervasive pattern of monstrous generation and birth, commonly invoked by royalists against Puritans but here turned against the prelates' claims of legitimate patriarchal descent, see Kristen Poole, *Reforming Reformation: The Grotesque Puritan and Social Transformation in Early Modern England* (Dissertation, Harvard University, 1996), 232–76.

93 *CPW* I, 583. Milton terms it a revision of Menenius Agrippa's tale (reported in Livy, *Historia,* III, 20v) of the revolt of the other members of the body against the belly. Henry Parker, *Case of Shipmoney,* revises the import of the fable to argue that, since the king as the belly receives heat from all, he should distribute nourishment to all (p. 20).

94 Page 614. He images England's troubles in the trials of the Israelites in the desert and the terrors of Apocalypse: her enemies "stand now at the entrance of the bottomlesse pit expecting the Watch-word to open and let out those dreadfull *Locusts* and *Scorpions,* to *re-involve* us in that pitchy *Cloud* of infernall darknes" (614).

95 Chapters 3, 4, and 5 in Book I.

96 *CPW* I, 827. Stanley Fish, "*The Reason of Church Government*:" *Self-consuming Artifacts* (Berkeley, Calif., 1972), 265–362, argues that Milton promises and then intentionally subverts rational discourse in this tract in order to throw the reader back on the sole authority of scripture.

97 Extending this family metaphor he also insists that Christ as the church's husband must have prescribed "his own ways" to improve her health and beauty, since "of any age or sex, most unfitly may a virgin be left to an uncertaine and arbitrary education . . . expecially if bethroth'd" (755).

98 Egan, "Creator–Critic," 49, notes that this portrait makes a deliberate contrast to the pithy, sententious sketches Hall produced in his *Characters of Vertues and Vices* (London, 1608). See also John F. Huntley, "The Images of Poet and Poetry in Milton's *The Reason of Church-Government*," in Michael Lieb and John T. Shawcross, eds, *Achievements of the Left Hand* (Amherst, Mass., 1974), 83–120.

99 See chapter 3, pp. 60–1.

100 Pages 802–3. The first words of Isaiah in chapters 13, 15, 17, 19, 21, 22, and 23 refer to the prophet's "burden." See Reuben Sanchez, "From Polemic to Prophecy: Milton's Uses of Jeremiah in *The Reason of Church-Government* and *The Readie and Easie Way*," *MS* 30 (1993), 27–40.

101 "Time servs not now, and perhaps I might seem too profuse to give any certain account of what the mind at home in the spacious circuits of her musing hath liberty to propose to her self, though of highest hope, and hardest attempting" (812–13).

102 Pages 813–15. He cites Origen as authority for the Song of Songs as pastoral drama, "consisting of two persons and a double *Chorus*," and David Pareus as authority for the Book of Revelation as tragedy, "with a sevenfold *Chorus* of halleluja's and harping symphonies." Pareus and others describe Revelation as tragedy, not only for its form but also its subject matter. See Lewalski, "*Samson Agonistes* and the 'Tragedy' of the Apocalypse," *PMLA* 85 (1970), 1,050–62.

103 Pages 816–17.

104 See chapter 3, p. 56–8.

105 See p. 124.

106 See Joseph A. Wittreich, Jr., "The Crown of Eloquence: The Figure of the Orator in Milton's Prose Works," in Lieb and Shawcross, *Achievements of the Left Hand*, 3–54.

107 Pages 560, 570, 579–80. Two of his three Chaucer references are to *The Plowman's Tale*, an anonymous work of Wycliffite tendencies which was commonly attached to the *Canterbury Tales* in the sixteenth century. It redefines Chaucer's idealized Plowman character in the mold of Langland's *Piers Plowman*, making him a proto-Protestant. The third reference is to the description of the Friar in the "General Prologue."

108 See Anselment, *Betwixt Jest and Ernest*, 61–93.

Chapter 6 "Domestic or Personal Liberty" 1642–1645

1 Ernest Sirluck, "Milton's Idle Right Hand," *Journal of English and Germanic Philology* 60 (1961), 749–85.

2 *CPW* II, 581, from *Tetrachordon*. Citations of the first edition of the *Doctrine and Discipline of Divorce* are designated *DDD* 1 in text and notes, and refer to the edition in

J. Max Patrick, ed., *The Prose of John Milton* (Garden City, NY, 1967). The second edition (*DDD* 2) and all other tracts of this period are cited from *CPW* II.

3 He also refuses to demonize the sectaries that the Presbyterians most abominated: Anabaptists, Familists, and Antinomians. He terms their views "fanatick dreams" but finds most of them zealous and "not debausht," simply led to extremes by "the restraint of some lawfull liberty" (*DDD* 1, 163).

4 He allows that Arminius was "perverted" from Calvinist orthodoxy by reading a book he undertook to confute, but describes him in admiring terms: "the acute and distinct *Arminius*" (*CPW* II, 519).

5 Stephen Fallon, "The Metaphysics of Milton's Divorce Tracts," in David Loewenstein and James Grantham Turner, eds, *Politics, Poetics, and Hermeneutics in Milton's Prose* (Cambridge, 1990), 69–83.

6 Powell's financial affairs were in some disarray in 1642, due to his improvident and somewhat shady dealings, and he was in some danger of losing his Forest Hill estate. In 1627 Milton's father had placed in Milton's name a loan of £300 with Powell, bringing interest of £12 semi-annually. Powell had hitherto paid faithfully, but may have asked for an extension of the interest due June 12 and Milton's visit may have been to discuss the matter. See J. Milton French, *Milton in Chancery: New Chapters in the Lives of the Poet and his Father* (New York and London, 1939), 71–99 and 167–83; and Parker, II, 866–70.

7 See Parker, II, 865, for the evidence fixing the date as summer, 1642.

8 See chapter 5, p. 140.

9 Cyriack Skinner's biography has a similar take on the situation: "Shee, that was very Yong, & had bin bred in a family of plenty and freedom, being not well pleas'd with his reserv'd manner of life," left shortly to return to her mother (*EL* 22). Aubrey reports that she was used to much company and merriment and adds (offering no evidence or authority) that she hated to hear Milton's nephews cry when beaten (*EL* 14).

10 "An Ordinance of the Lords and Commons Concerning Stage-Plays," September 2, 1642, John Rushworth, *Historical Collections of Private Papers of State*, 8 vols (London, 1721–2), V, 1.

11 "I did not avoid the toils and dangers of military service without rendering to my fellow citizens another kind of service that was much more useful and no less perilous. . . . Having from early youth been especially devoted to the liberal arts, with greater strength of mind than of body, I exchanged the toils of war, in which any stout trooper might outdo me, for those labors which I better understood, that with such wisdom as I owned I might add as much weight as possible to the counsels of my country and to this excellent cause, using not my lower but my higher and stronger powers." *Defensio Secunda*, 1654 (*CPW* IV.1, 552–3). See Robert Fallon, *Captain or Colonel* (Columbia, Mo., 1984), 47–56.

12 The sonnet in *TM* is in the hand of a copiest, as is this heading. It is crossed out, and a second title appears below it in Milton's hand, "When the assault was intended to ye City." Preparatory to circulation or publication Milton perhaps wished to remove the possible suggestion that he was hiding behind his own door, pleading for his safety. In the editions of 1645 and 1673 the poem simply bears the number VIII. Milton's poems of this period are cited from *Poems, 1645*.

13 See Janel Mueller, "On Genesis in Genre: Milton's Politicizing of the Sonnet in 'Cap-

tain and Colonel,'" in *Renaissance Genres*, ed. Barbara K. Lewalski (Cambridge, Mass., 1986), 213–40. Also see F. T. Prince, *The Italian Element in Milton's Verse* (Oxford, 1954).

14 See David Norbrook, *Writing the English Revolution* (Cambridge, 1999), 127–9.

15 Some poems to women by Jonson and Daniel, as well as some dedicatory sonnets, provide analogues for Sonnets IX and X.

16 None of the tentative identifications are persuasive. Parker suggests the "Lady" of *Comus*, Alice Egerton, aged 23 in 1642 and still unmarried, or else (even less plausibly given the poem's terms) that this sonnet is a courtship poem to Mary Powell (II, 875).

17 Holbein's illustrations of the *Table of Cebes* shows young people trifling at the foot of the rugged mountain of Truth, while others struggle up a steep path. Cf., Hesiod, *Works and Days*, ll, 287–92 and Plato, *Republic* 2. 364C. (Unless otherwise noted, citations from classical authors are from the Loeb Classics editions.) Mary chose to sit at Christ's feet rather than join in Martha's busy housewifery (Luke 10:42); Ruth, following her Hebrew mother-in-law into exile, chose the path of religious truth and duty (Ruth 1:14).

18 Sonnet X was not composed in *TM*, but copied there in Milton's hand, as was the title. It is untitled in both editions of the *Poems*, presumably to remove the personal reference. Phillips (*EL* 64) claims the relationship began soon after Mary's departure.

19 Margaret was over thirty when she married Hobson on December 30, 1641. Parker (II, 876) argues that the poem predates that marriage because her married name is not used, but ladies of high rank often retained their titles of birth if they married into a lower rank. The couple lived in Aldersgate Street at least two or three years; in March 1644 Hobson was assessed for property there. See Fallon, *Captain and Colonel*, 55–6.

20 James Ley, Earl of Marlborough, had as chief justice presided at Bacon's trial for corruption. For an analysis of the conflicting and sometimes disparaging reports on Ley and his career see Annabel Patterson, "That Old Man Eloquent," in *Literary Milton: Text, Pretext, Context,* eds. Diana Trevino Benet and Michael Lieb (Pittsburgh, 1994), 36–44, and *Variorum* II.2, 383–6.

21 Isocrates was 98 years old in 338 BC, and probably died soon after that conquest from natural causes. But Milton evidently believed his source, Dionysius of Halicarnassus, who wrote that Isocrates saw the battle of Chaeronéa as a great betrayal – a military conquest of Athens and Thebes rather than the Panhellenic League headed by Phillip which he had long sought. Milton could thereby see Ley as responding to a comparable betrayal by Charles. See John Leonard, ed., *John Milton: The Complete Poems* (London, 1998), 647.

22 That title, naming him a collector of revenues for the king, is used in a letter of November 7, 1644 (*LR* II, 110–11). He was often fined as a delinquent by the parliament.

23 Skinner states in his biography that Milton taught his nephews from the time "of his first settling" and "as it happen'd, the Sonn of some friend" (*EL* 24). Skinner, known to have been Milton's pupil, must have come to him at the latest by 1643 when he was 16; four years later he entered Lincoln's Inn.

24 The dates of many entries are uncertain, but J. H. Hanford's informed speculations in "The Chronology of Milton's Private Studies," John Milton: Poet and Humanist (Cleveland, OH, 1966), 88–103, invite this conclusion. A few items postdate 1650 and are in the hands of various amanuenses. I cite entries from *CPW* I, 362–508.

25 See chapter 3, pp. 65–6 and chapter 5, pp. 126–7.

26 Among the histories are Gildas, *De Excidio et Conquestu Britanniae*; Giovanni Villani, *Chroniche . . . nelle quali si tratta dell'origine di Firenze* (a book Edward Phillips studied with Milton); Guicciardini, *Storia d'Italia*; Sesellius (Claude de Seissel), *De Monarchia Franciae*, trans. Johannes Sleidan; Pierre Gilles, *Histoire ecclesiastique des Eglises reformées . . . apelées eglises Vaudoises* (on the Waldensians); and Pietro Sarpi, *Istoria del Concilio Tridentino*. His reading in Roman and early church history included Theodoret, *Historia Ecclesiastica*; Socrates Scholasticus, *Historia Ecclesiastica*; and Codinus (Georgius Curopalata), *De Officiis Magnae Ecclesiae et Aulae Constantinopolitanae*. For editions he used or may have used of works cited here and in the following notes, see Hanford, "Milton's Private Studies," 87–98; Jackson C. Boswell, *Milton's Library* (New York and London, 1975); and my bibliography.

27 De Thou (Thuanus), *Historia sui Temporis*; Girard, *L'Histoire de France*. See chapter 5, note 30

28 The biblical commentaries include Peter Martyr, *In Librum Judicum*; Basil, *Homiliae*; *In Psalmum I, In Hexameron VIII, In Principium Proverbium*; Chrysostom, *In Genesim Homiliae*; Rivetus (André Rivet), *Praelectiones in Caput XX Exodi*; Peter Martyr (Vermigli), *In Librum Judicum*. For Hebraica, besides Selden's *De Jure Naturali* and *Uxor Hebraica,* he cites William Schickhard, *Jus Regium Hebraeorum*.

29 Justinian, *Institutiones Juris Civilis*; Leunclavius, *Juris Graeco-Romani*; Henry Spelman, *Concilia, Decreta . . . in Re Ecclesiastica Orbis Britanniae*; and Jean Bodin, *De Republica*; on warfare, he took notes from Robert Ward, *Animadversions of Warre*, and Sextus Frontinus, *Strategematicon*. On noble titles he cites John Guillim, *A Display of Heraldrie*.

30 Francisco Berni, *Orlando Innamorato Nuovamenta Composto*; Sir Philip Sidney, *The Countesse of Pembroke's Arcadia*; Trajano Boccalini, *De' Ragguagli di Parnasso*; Tasso, *Gerusalemme Liberata*; Alessandro Tassoni, *Deici Libri di Pensieri Diversi*; Jacob Phillipp Tomasini, *Petrarcha Redivivus*.

31 Sir Walter Raleigh, *The History of the World*; Samuel Purchas, *Hakluytus Posthumus or Purchas His Pilgrimes*.

32 "Moral" entries include the founding of the most ancient universities of Europe, Paris, and Pavia (*CPW* I, 378), the invention of the organ and the musical scale (383), the "exquisite reasoning" in the argument for suicide in Sidney's *Arcadia* (371), and the cures for gluttonous indulgence used by Indians in Sumatra (368).

33 He instances a married clergy in the ancient church, and in medieval France the fact that Charlemagne kept concubines and that bastards inherited equally with legitimate children. Also, that polygamy was allowed to the ancient Jews and practiced by the early Christian Germans and Britons (*CPW* I, 413). His examples of divorce include Charlemagne, William of Orange, René, Duke of Lorraine, and Henry IV, King of France.

34 Sinibaldus, *Geneanthropeia*. He also cites Raleigh's story, in *History of the World,* 293, that prohibiting polygamy lost the Congo to Christianity, adding his own conclusion that this prohibition has "more obstinat rigor in it then wisdom" (*CPW* I, 411).

35 He cites de Thou (Thuanus) on the legality of the Scots deposing Mary, on the Dutch Estates General disclaiming obedience to Phillip (*CPW* I, 445, 455), and on justifications by ministers and lawyers allowing French Protestants and Scots reformers to renounce loyalty to Catholic monarchs. From Girard he gathers that the kings of France

were elected and could be freely deposed until the time of Hugh Capet (461). From Guicciardini, Sesellius, Peter Martyr, and Sleiden, he concludes that the German and Greek emperors swear to abide by conditions (436); that the king of France submits to decrees of parliament, which is called "the 'bridle' of the king" (458); and that the Holy Roman Emperor may be forced to abide by his agreements "by arms if it cannot be done otherwise" (456).

36 Known as the Treaty of Oxford.

37 See Fredrick S. Siebert, *Freedom of the Press in England, 1476–1776* (Urbana, Ill., 1952), 165–201. An order of January 29, 1642 provided simply that all publications carry the name of the author or printer. Two subsequent orders attempted more control, but were largely ineffectual: that of August 26, 1642 provided that no book or pamphlet publish anything "false or scandalous, to the proceedings of the Houses of parliament," and that of March 9, 1643 extended the scope of the previous Act to all "scandalous and lying Pamphlets." In April, 1643 the Stationers had petitioned parliament to reinstate and strengthen their traditional powers to control publication.

38 The 1637 decree forbade anyone to print, import, or sell "any seditious, schismaticall, or offensive Bookes or Pamphlets" or any publication not first licensed and entered in the Stationers Register; the names of author and printer had to be affixed to all texts; the number of master printers was limited to twenty and the number of presses, journeymen and apprentices was also fixed; unlicensed presses were forbidden. The Stationers Company was given powers of search and seizure.

39 Of the 149 members 119 were divines: the rest were parliament members – 10 from the Lords, 20 from the Commons, among them the Erastian John Selden.

40 Thomas Goodwin, Phillip Nye, William Bridges, Jeremiah Burroughs, and Sidrach Simpson; all had recently returned from exile in Holland. In *An Apologeticall Narration*, published in early January, 1644, addressed to parliament, and signed by the five, they distinguished their "non-separating" position sharply from that of the separatist sects.

41 Milton declared in *Tetrachordon* that he "saw, and was partaker, of your Vows and solemne Cov'nants" (*CPW* II, 578).

42 *A Solemn League and Covenant for Reformation and Defense of Religion, the honour and happiness of the king, and the Peace and Safety of England, Scotland, and Ireland* (London, 1643, September 21), 2–3.

43 Phillips indicates (*EL* 66) that Milton "often visited" Blackborough, who lived in the nearby lane of St Martins Le Grand. Milton's sonnet on the death of Catherine Thomason (1646) suggests a personal and probably long-standing relationship. Alexander Gil, Jr., had died in 1642.

44 Patterson, "No Meer Amatorious Novel?" in David Loewenstein and James Grantham Turner, eds, *Politics, Poetics, and Hermeneutics in Milton's Prose* (Cambridge, 1990), 92.

45 *The Doctrine and Discipline of Divorce* (London: T. P. and M. S. in Goldsmiths Alley, 1643). T. P. was Thomas Payne; M. S. was Matthew Simmons.

46 The epigraph to the first edition justifies Milton's engagement with this issue and claims the status of public benefactor: "Matth. 13.52. Every Scribe instructed to the Kingdome of Heav'n, is like the Maister of a house which bringeth out of his treasurie things old and new."

47 One such myth is a revision of Plato's allegory on the birth of Love from (male) Plenty and (female) Penury. Milton turns the gendered couple into abstractions so as to associ-

ate Edenic loneliness with the man, Adam. Love is the son of "sinles *Penury* or *Lonelines* of the soul" begotten in Paradise of the sociable aptitude intended in marriage. When Penury "cannot lay it self down by the side of such a meet and acceptable union" Hate is engendered – not sinful Hate, but "naturall dissatisfaction and the turning aside from a mistaken object" (152).

48 Charles Hatten, "The Politics of Marital Reform and the Rationalization of Romance in *The Doctrine and Discipline of Divorce*," *Milton Studies* 27 (1991), 109–11.

49 Cf. 1 Corinthians 7:10–16. And see Cedric C. Brown, "Milton and the Idolatrous Consort," *Criticism* 35 (1993), 419–39.

50 For one thing, he cites Malachi 2:16 which he renders, "he who hates, let him divorce" on the authority of "Calvin and the best translations," though Calvin did not read that corrupted text as warranting divorce. The AV renders it, "For the Lord . . . saith that he hateth putting away."

51 Jason Rosenblatt, *Torah and Law in Paradise Lost* (Princeton, NJ, 1993), 82–97, claims that Milton could read the Hebrew Bible and the comparatively easy and widely available commentary of Rashi, but drew much of his knowledge of the tradition of rabbinical commentary from the profound Hebraic scholarship of John Selden.

52 Milton cited Hugo Grotius's *Annotationes in libros Evangeliorum* (Amsterdam, 1641) on the meaning of "uncleanness" in Judges 19:2, on the laws of the first Christian emperors allowing for civil divorce for many causes (145, 180), on Christ's specification of "adultery" as only one example of other like cases, on marriage as ordained for mutual help and comfort as well as for copulation, and on charity as the beginning and end of Christ's commands (178–9).

53 Rosenblatt (*Torah and Law*, 103) notes that the term "Charity" is used some 92 times in the divorce tracts. This compares with 122 occurrences in all Milton's prose.

54 See chapter 5, pp. 144–6.

55 Appeals to Charity as a basis for revising the abhorrent literal meaning of certain biblical texts is an exegetical tradition reaching back to Augustine. But Augustine usually resorted in such cases to allegorical interpretation, a mode of exegesis generally decried by Protestants and avoided by Milton.

56 Milton also alludes to Romans 13:10, 1 Corinthians 13:1–13, and 1 Timothy 1:5, which identify love or charity as essence of the gospel and the fulfillment of the Law.

57 The first edition has 48 small quarto pages; the second, 88. The additions sometimes expand a single paragraph or passage into several pages, especially in the first seven chapters of Book II. A copy at the Bodleian (Wood B 29) bears the name "Je. [or Jo.] Hales" as owner – probably Milton's learned friend John Hales of Eton. A third and fourth edition appeared in 1645; neither shows evidence of Milton's attention, and neither was licensed or registered.

58 *The Doctrine and Discipline of Divorce Restor'd to the Good of Both Sexes, From the bondage of Canon Law, and other mistakes, to the true meaning of Scripture in the Law and Gospel compar'd. Wherin also are set down the bad consequences of abolishing or condemning of Sin, that which the Law of God allowes, and Christ abolisht not. Now the second time revis'd and much augmented, in Two Books* (London, n.p., 1644). The revised edition reprints the epigraph from Matthew 13:52 and adds a new epigraph from Proverbs 18:1, striking at detractors who judge without reading: "He that answereth a matter before he heareth it, it is folly and shame unto him."

59 In a postscript to *Bucer* he comments that his divorce argument did "not find a permission to the Presse" (479) Since *Bucer* was licensed, this suggests that he attempted to obtain a license for *DDD* 2 at the outset or (as Parker, I, 163, supposes) when he wanted to reprint it. The print run was exhausted before *Bucer* appeared and *DDD* 2 was not reprinted for more than five months – still without license.

60 In *Bucer* he again expresses gratitude to parliament but declines to specify just what he is grateful for – presumably because they did not act on the numerous calls to suppress his divorce tract and prosecute him (*CPW* II, 435).

61 Page 224. Rosenblatt, *Torah and Law*, 98.

62 In 1654 he expressed the wish "that I had not written it in the vernacular, for then I would not have met with vernacular readers, who are usually ignorant of their own good, and laugh at the misfortunes of others" (*CPW* IV.1, 610).

63 Page 331. He also adds several passages on the nature of the Law and the meaning of hardness of heart, especially Book II, chapters 3–7.

64 He cites the *Guide to the Perplexed* by Moses ben Maimon or Maimonides (1135–1204), to the effect that the Jews were permitted divorce to preserve peace in the family. He cited Grotius and others to the effect that the magistrate may permit divorce to promote civil peace (344); Fagius "so eminent in *England* once," he cites on several occasions to the effect that the Deuteronomaic law allows magistrates to permit divorce to Christians (239, 243, 344). Fagius (1504–49) was a German Protestant reformer and a noted Hebraist who briefly held a lectureship in Hebrew at Cambridge University. Milton refers to his *Thargum, Hoc Est, Paraphrasis Onkeli Chaldaica in Sacra Biblia* (Strassburg, 1546). He also finds support in "*Fagius, Calvin, Pareus, Rivetus*" for his assertion that a meet and happy conversation is the chief end of marriage, but he stretches a point to claim that they "as willingly and largely assent as can be wisht" (246). For Grotius, see chapter 4, p. 89.

65 Page 350. John Selden (1584–1654) was a jurist, legal scholar, Hebraist, member of parliament for Oxford, and delegate to the Westminster Assembly. Milton praises his *De Jure Naturali et Gentium juxta Disciplinam Hebraeorum* (London, 1640) as more useful than all the canon lawyers to "whoever studies to be a great man in wisdom, equity, and justice" (*CPW* II, 350). Also, Milton may have consulted in manuscript Selden's *Uxor Ebraica* [The Hebrew Wife] *seu de Nuptiis & Divortis ex Jure Civili, Id Est, Divino & Talmudico* (London, 1646); in 1654, in the *Defensio Secunda* (*CPW* IV. 1, 625), Milton claims to have found support for his divorce argument from "our distinguished countryman Selden . . . in his *Hebrew Wife*, published about two years later." See Elvion Owen, "Milton and Selden on Divorce," *Studies in Philology* 43 (1946), 233–57.

66 Page 292. Another remarkable sequence reads God's Creation and Judgement as divorcing actions, separating enmities and contrarieties in nature: "by his divorcing command the world first rose out of Chaos, nor can be renew'd again out of confusion but by the separating of unmeet consorts" (272–3).

67 Page 225. See Patterson, "No Meer Amatorious Novel," 95–6.

68 Yet another allegory rewrites the story of Eros and Anteros, as if told by another Diotima to another Socrates: "Thus mine author sung it to me" (255–6). Eros (Love), not blind but with only one eye, loses all his "fierie virtue" when he mistakes disguised imposters for his twin brother Anteros (reciprocal Love); he is restored upon finding Anteros, "showing us that Love in mariage cannot live nor subsist, unless it be mutual" (255–6).

The application to marriage strains both the literal and cultural terms of this Platonic myth, as Milton again accommodates a myth to himself by figuring as male both the initiation of (married) love and the need for reciprocity.

69 James Turner, *One Flesh: Paradisal Marriage and Sexual Relations in the Age of Milton* (Oxford, 1987), 229.

70 See chapter 2, p. 31.

71 See G. H. Turnbull, *Hartlib, Dury, and Comenius: Gleanings from Hartlib's Papers* (London, 1947), and Michael Leslie's description of the retrieval and publication of materials by and relating to the circle, "The Hartlib Papers Project: Text Retrieval with Large Datasets," *Literary and Linguistic Computing* 5 (1990), 58–69. Charles Webster edited several tracts by Hartlib and Dury in *Samuel Hartlib and the Advancement of Learning* (Cambridge, 1970).

72 Turnbull, *Hartlib, Dury, and Comenius,* 40.

73 Timothy Raylor, "New Light on Milton and Hartlib," *MQ* 27 (1993), 19–30. The lists containing the name of "Mr Milton" are among the Hartlib Papers, 72 bundles, at the Sheffield University Library (8/40/9r–10v and 8/40/8v). Raylor argues, plausibly, that this is not the "Major John Milton" who was also known to be living in London, since the military title is customarily used for officer contributors.

74 There is, however, no reason to assume with Ernest Sirluck (*CPW* II, 184–216) that Hartlib refused to publish Milton's tract because of disagreements about educational theory. It is more likely that Milton did not want to be closely identified with that circle.

75 Hartlib, *Ephemerides* (Hartlib Papers, 30/4/91a); Turnbull, *Hartlib, Dury, and Comenius,* 39. Culpepper's letter was dated November 12, 1645. For Dury, see note 82. Later, Theodore Haak heard and passed on the news that Milton was at work on a history of Britain and an epitome of Purchas, i.e. the *History of Moscovia* (see chapter 7, p. 212).

76 Milton could have met Comenius sometime during his visit to England from September, 1641 to June, 1642, but there is no evidence that he did so.

77 Jan Amos Comenius, *Janua linguarum reserata* (Leszno, 1631); a Latin–English–French edition was published by John Anchoran (1631) and by Thomas Horne (1636). By 1644 it had reached its sixth English edition. His *Didactica Magna* was not published until 1657, in Amsterdam, but the scheme was summarized in several earlier tracts, including Hartlib's *Reformation of Schools* (London, 1642).

78 Edward Phillips alludes to "some of his Adversaries calling him Paedagogue and Schoolmaster" (*EL* 57) as a term of reproach.

79 See Lewalski, "Milton and the Hartlib Circle: Educational Projects and Epic Paedeia," in Diana Benet and Michael Leib, eds, *Literary Milton* (Pittsburgh, 1994), 202–19; and Sirluck, *CPW* II, 184–216.

80 Milton probably alludes to the Act of June 15, 1641 that calls for use of the confiscated property of bishops, deans and chapters for the advancement of learning.

81 At St Paul's School Milton used a revised edition of William Lily's required *Shorte Introduction of Grammar* with the *Brevissima Institutio* (London, 1574; many editions). See chapter 1, note 38. "Or any better" may suggest that Milton had already drafted or was planning his own Latin grammar, *Accidence Commenc't Grammar,* published in 1669 (see chapter 7, pp. 207–8 and chapter 14, p. 490).

82 For his "noble" schools, the Hartlib circle member John Dury proposed a similar progression of subjects and books. His treatise *The Reformed School* (London, 1650) seems to have adopted several features from Milton's treatise in a gesture of accommodation, especially the study of poetics.

83 Martin Bucer, *De Regno Christi ad Edw. VI* (Basle, 1577).

84 *The Judgement of Martin Bucer, concerning Divorce, Writt'n to Edward the sixt, in his second Book of the Kingdom of Christ. And now Englist. Wherin a late Book restoring the Doctrine and Discipline of Divorce, is heer confirm'd and justify'd by the authoritie of Martin Bucer* (London: Matthew Simmons, 1644). Milton translates chapters 15–47 of the second book, and argues from Bucer's dedication that he meant his treatise especially for England.

85 Page 479. He rather overstates Erasmus's freedom to publish; his *Institution of Christian Marriage* was placed on the Index in 1559 and later expurgated.

86 He also translated sections describing early Christian emperors who recognized several causes for divorce, and on Roman law which allowed divorce by mutual consent without stated cause.

87 Classic statements of the secularist position are Henry Robinson, *Liberty of Conscience: or the Sole Means to Obtaine Peace and Truth* (London, 1644) published around March 24, and William Walwyn's *Compassionate Samaritane* (London, 1644), published anonymously in June or July. Both also argue briefly for a free press.

88 John Goodwin's *Theomachia* (London, 1644, *c.* October 4) argues for very broad toleration, but excludes things "certainly known" to be not from God. Henry Burton's *A Vindication of Churches, Commonly Called Independent* (London, 1644, *c.* November 14) denies the magistrate any power over conscience but gives him the duty of protecting and defending religion, so that he need not tolerate the open practice of popery or extreme heterodoxy.

89 Williams published anonymously his *Queries of Highest Consideration* (London, 1644, *c.* February 9) which defends absolute religious liberty as the only means to safeguard the true spiritual church from the world. That argument is developed at greater length in his most famous tolerationist plea, *The Bloudy Tenent, of Persecution, for the Cause of Conscience Discussed* (London, 1644, *c.* July 15).

90 *Mans Mortalitie* was published anonymously in London, *c.* January 19, 1644, but with false publication data (Amsterdam, 1643) to deflect the censors. The second edition appeared a few months later. Milton was probably not yet a Mortalist but would become one.

91 Palmer, *Glasse of Gods Providence* (London, 1644), title page and page 57. On August 14 the Commons thanked Palmer for his sermon and ordered it printed.

92 *Journal of the House of Commons,* III, 606. The Westminster Assembly also urged parliament to suppress several offenders: Anabaptists, Antinomians, Seekers, the Independent tolerationist John Goodwin, the Mortalist Overton and the Divorcer Milton.

93 Oliver Cromwell, *Writings and Speeches,* 4 vols, ed. W. C. Abbott (Cambridge, 1937), I, 294. The reputation of parliament's top generals was in decline. Essex's defeat in Cornwall by the king's armies freed the king to march back to Oxford, threatening a new attack on London. In the very fierce Battle of Newbury (October 27) the king probably had the worst of it, but many thought that Generals Waller and Manchester had not pressed their advantage.

94 William Prynne, *Twelve Considerable Serious Questions, Touching Church Government* (London, 1644, *c.* September 16).

95 *An Answer . . . A Plea for Ladies and Gentlewomen, and all other Maried Women against Divorce. Wherein, Both Sexes are vindicated from all bondage of Common Law, and other mistakes whatsoever: And the unsound Principles of the Author are examined and fully confuted by the authority of Holy Scripture, the Laws of this Land, and sound Reason* (London, 1644).

96 The author instances a property transaction concerning Milton's property at Aldersgate as an example of binding contract (33). Also, denying Milton's argument that social conventions prevent adequate trial of a virgin's capacity for conversation before marriage, he claims that everyone save kings and princes has opportunity for that, "if you have so much time" (*Answer,* 15).

97 Caryl wrote: "To preserve the strength of the mariage bond and the Honour of that estate, against those sad breaches and dangerous abuses of it, which common discontents (on this side Adultery) are likely to make in unstaied mindes and men given to change, by taking in or grounding themselves upon the opinion answered, and with good reason confuted in this Treatise, I have approved the printing and publishing of it" (*CPW* II, 727).

98 *Answer,* 17.

99 He repeats the Augustinian canard that had conversation been a primary need God would have given Adam a male companion, since "man ordinarilie exceeds woman in naturall gifts of minde and in delectableness of converse" (*Answer,* 12).

100 Ibid., 8–9: "Who sees not, how many thousands of lustful and libidinous men would be parted from their Wives every week and marrying others; and upon this, who should keep the children of these divorcers which sometimes they would leave in their Wives bellies? how shall they come by their Portions, of whom, or where? and how shall the Wife be endowed of her Husband's estate? Nay, commonly, to what Reproach would the woman be left to, as being one left who was not fit for any ones company? and so who would venture upon her again?"

101 *Areopagitica* (London, n.p., 1644). There were no further editions in Milton's lifetime, nor (except in collected editions in 1697 and 1698) in the seventeenth century. However, several extensive, though unacknowledged, adaptations were published at moments when censorship was again feared. See Sirluck, *CPW* II, 480.

102 Milton proposed substituting for this new ordinance the one "next before this," choosing to overlook two intervening and more restrictive measures of August 26, 1642 and March 9, 1643. See note 37.

103 Page 570. See above, p. 161 and note 38. Milton supports those who labor in the production of books – authors and printers – against the idle would-be monopolists, the Stationers who held legal copyright. See Elizabeth Magnus, "Originality and Plagiarism in *Areopagitica* and *Eikonoklastes,*" *English Literary Renaissance* 21 (1991), 87–101.

104 In this letter to Leonard Philaris, dated September 28, 1654 (*CPW* IV.2, 869) Milton reports that "It is ten years, I think, more or less" since he began to notice these symptoms.

105 These were the possibilities most often suggested by 50 leading neuro-opthalmologists who were given the circumstances of the case, in a survey conducted by Shannon Murray and reported at the International Milton Symposium, Bangor, Wales, July,

1995. As Milton always insisted that his eyes remained clear, he cannot have had cataracts. His own diagnosis was *gutta serena*, a "drop serene." For his association of blindness with food and digestive difficulties, see William Kerrigan, *The Sacred Complex: On the Psychogenesis of Paradise Lost* (Cambridge, Mass., and London, 1983), passim.

106 Under this Ordinance parliament members (from whose numbers these generals came) pledged to give over any other office, military or civil, during the war. The Commons passed it on December 19, the Lords the following April. Cromwell, both MP and lieutenant-general, fell within the scope of the Ordinance, but parliament voted an exception for him.

107 Known as the Treaty of Uxbridge.

108 *Journal of the House of Lords*, VII, 116, 118: Justices Reeve and Bacon were charged on December 28 "to examine the said *Woodward* and *Milton*, and such others as the Master and Wardens of the Stationers Company shall give Information of."

109 Like Milton, Woodward was a schoolmaster, a friend of Hartlib's, and author of several pamphlets. The "Papers" he confessed to may have been *As You Were*, written in defense of the radical Independent John Goodwin of Coleman Street and published, also anonymously and without a license, about November 13, 11 days before *Areopagitica*.

110 Daniel Featley, *The Dippers Dipt* (London, 1645, *c.* February 7); the dedicatory epistle was dated January 10, when Featley was in prison as a malignant. Three editions appeared in 1645, and others in 1646, 1647, 1651, and 1660.

111 Both bear the identification "By the former Author J. M" on the title page, and the preface to *Tetrachordon* is signed "John Milton." Some, and perhaps most, of *Tetrachordon* was written first, since *Colasterion* contains two references to that work.

112 Palmer was a principal author of the anonymous *Scripture and Reason Pleaded for Defensive Armes* (London, 1643, *c.* April 14). Milton offers to deduce his conclusions regarding divorce from Palmer's own arguments, "which I shall pardon him, if he can deny, without shaking his own composition to peeces" (582).

113 *Colasterion: A Reply to a Nameles Answer Against The Doctrine and Discipline of Divorce. Wherein the trivial Author of that Answer is discover'd, the Licencer conferr'd with, and the Opinion which they traduce defended* (London, n.p., 1645).

114 Phillips indicates that the scheme fell through when the new modeling of the army forced Waller's resignation. Milton's comment in the *Second Defense* (see note 11) may suggest that the choice of military service was once offered to him. See Parker, II, 894–5, and Fallon, *Captain and Colonel,* 60.

115 The timing is indicated by Phillips's report that their first child was born "within a year" of Mary's return; that child's birthdate is July 29, 1646.

116 Euripides, *Medea*, ll. 298–301. Trans. Arthur S. Way (London and New York: Loeb, 1912–19).

117 *Tetrachordon: Expositions upon the foure chief places in Scripture which treat of Mariage, or nullities in Mariage . . . Wherin the Doctrine and Discipline of Divorce, as was lately publish'd, is confirm'd by explanation of Scripture, by testimony of ancient Fathers, of civill lawes in the Primitive Church, of famousest Reformed divines, And lastly, by an intended ACT of the Parlament and Church of England in the last yeare of Edward the sixth* (London, n.p., 1645).

118 Page 605. See note 5. Milton also suggests that the phrase "one flesh" intends at the simplest level to remove any suspicion of pollution in the marriage act (613). After

critiquing various definitions of marriage, he defines it as "a divine institution joyning man and woman in a love fitly dispos'd to the helps and comforts of domestic life 612."

119 Pages 661–2. See Sirluck, introduction, *CPW* II, 156–8.

120 In the Song of Songs he points to the singing "of a thousand raptures between those two lovely ones [Christ and the Church] farre on the hither side of carnal enjoyment."

121 See Ann Baynes Coiro, "Milton and Class Identity: The Publication of *Areopagitica* and the 1645 *Poems*," *Journal of Medieval and Renaissance Studies* 22 (1992), 261–89.

122 Muslim and pagan cults would seem to fall under Milton's exclusion but that issue would hardly arise in seventeenth-century England. Jews would not be targetted if they were to return to England, given Milton's recognition of the Hebraic Covenant and Law as divinely given and perpetual. Milton would have encountered the view that natural law is embodied in the Noachide laws in Selden's *De Jure Naturali et Gentium juxta Disciplinam Hebraeorum* (Of the Law of Nature and Nations According to the Rule of the Hebrews) which he cites in the divorce tracts and again in this work.

123 The Seventh Oration of Isocrates, the *Areopagiticus*, written *c.* 355 BCE, proposes that the Areopagus, the Court of the Wise, which had become a criminal court of limited jurisdiction, again exercise control over education and the censorship of manners. Isocrates also composed his orations to be read. Milton's title may allude as well to Paul's address to the Athenians on the hill called Areopagus, identifying the God he declares to them with the "unknown god" to whom they have erected a shrine (Acts 17:18–34).

124 See Sharon Achinstein, *Milton and the Revolutionary Reader* (Princeton, NJ, 1994), 3–70.

125 Norbrook, *Writing the English Republic,* 125–39.

126 Milton quotes lines 438–41, in Greek and then in English. See Annabel Patterson, *Censorship and Interpretation: The Conditions of Writing and Reading in Early Modern England* (Madison, Wis., 1984), 115–16.

127 Milton's tract especially addresses the Erastian MPs, led by Selden, who were concerned to prevent further Presbyterian encroachment on parliament's control over the church.

128 Achinstein, *Milton and the Revolutionary Reader,* 58–67.

129 Pages 514–16. As Sirluck notes (*CPW* II, 516) the Palmer did not accompany Guyon to Mammon's cave (as he did to the Bower of Bliss); Milton's mistake stems from his belief that reason must always dictate virtuous choice.

130 See Nigel Smith, "*Areopagitica*: Voicing Contexts, 1643–45," in David Loewenstein and James Grantham Turner, eds, *Politics, Poetics, and Hermeneutics in Milton's Prose* (Cambridge, 1990), 103–22.

131 Page 563. See *Faerie Queene* III, passim, and for Proteus, Book III, canto viii.

132 Pages 553–4. The next sentence sounds like a prediction of imminent apocalypse: "We reck'n more then five months yet to harvest; there need not be five weeks, had we but eyes to lift up, the fields are white already" (554). But the allusion (John 4:35) is to preaching and gathering a harvest of prepared souls: "Say not ye, there are yet four months, and then cometh harvest? behold, I say unto you, Lift up your eyes, and look on the fields; for they are white already to harvest." Why Milton changed four months to five is unclear.

Chapter 7 "Service . . . Between Private Walls" 1645–1649

1 See chapter 5, pp. 150–2.

2 Thomas Hobbes, *The History of the Civil Wars of England* (London, 1679), 4. As early as 1640 Henry Parker could toss off the comment, "wee know that of all kindes of government Monarchiale is the worst:" *The Case of Shipmoney briefly discoursed* (London, 1640), 22.

3 This illustration of the Barbican house, with whatever alterations over the centuries, is from the *Illustrated London News* (July 16, 1864), 45. The house was demolished in 1864 or 1865.

4 The exact date of the move is uncertain: see Masson, III, 442–3 and Parker, I, 299. For Cyriak Skinner, see chapter 6, note 23.

5 Viscountess Ranelagh was a learned woman from the distinguished Boyle family; her brother was the scientist Robert Boyle. After the Irish rebellion (1641) she fled Ireland and remained in London during most of the 1640s and 1650s. She was apparently estranged from her husband, Arthur Jones, second viscount in the Irish peerage. Just when Milton came to know her is not clear; for their further contacts see chapter 9, p. 309, and n. 85).

6 *EL* 24–5, 67. Aubrey mentions one "Mr Packer who was his Scholar" (*EL* 8), but no likely person of that name has been identified; Aubrey may have misheard Packer for Picard, the Jeremy Picard who later became one of Milton's amanuenses (Parker, II, 925). Edward Lawrence, son of the parliamentarian Henry Lawrence and the addressee of Sonnet XX, may also have been Milton's pupil at some time.

7 The register entry reads, "Master Mozeley. Entred . . . under the hand of Sr NATH: BRENT and both the wardens a booke called *Poems in English & Latyn*, by Mr John Milton" (*SR 1640–1708*, I, 196).

8 Milton, *Poems*, 1645, sigs a3–a4. The book evidently appeared late in 1645; George Thomason dated his copy January 2, 1646.

9 He had already published James Howell's *Dodona's Grove* (London, 1640, 1645). But his editions of Suckling, *Fragmenta Aurea* (London, 1646), Crashaw, *Steps to the Temple* (London, 1646), Shirley, *Poems* (London, 1646), and Cowley, *The Mistress* (London, 1647) all postdate Milton's *Poems*. Moseley subsequently acquired copyrights for Sir John Denham's *Coopers Hill* (London, 1642) and Carew's *Poems* (London, 1640), as well as for works by other poets and dramatists past and present.

10 Waller's *Poems* (London, 1645) was entered in the Stationers Register on December 14, 1644. Moseley added some of Waller's speeches in parliament to the volume: his stand with parliament against shipmoney and Laud, and also his abject apology and plea for his life after being caught in the plot. Waller was in exile in France when the volume was first published by Thomas Walkley, who then sold his rights to Moseley.

11 *CPW* IV.2, 750–1. For the epigram and picture, see below, and plate 8.

12 In *TM* the first draft is followed by a fair copy, both in Milton's hand; the fair copy is titled (in the hand of an amanuensis) "To Mr Hen: Laws on the publishing of his Aires." Another copy in *TM*, in a scribal hand, used this title and then modified it to "To Mr. H. Lawes, on his Aires." That last title must postdate 1653, when Lawes's *Ayres and Dialogues* was first published; it is used in Milton's *Poems* (1673). For Milton's six sonnets of 1646–8, I cite the versions in the Trinity manuscript.

13 In *Choice Psalmes put into Musick, for Three Voices*, which contained settings by Henry and his brother William who had recently died fighting for the king, Milton's sonnet bore the title, "To My Friend Mr. *Henry Lawes*." The sonnet was not reprinted in the Lawes volumes of 1653 or 1655, suggesting that the political divide was then too great: the lyrics and commendatory poems in those volumes are mostly by royalists.

14 Cf. Waller's commendation of Lawes in *Ayres and Dialogues* (London, 1653):

> So others with Division hide
> The Light of Sense, the Poets Pride,
> But you alone may truly boast
> That not a syllable is lost;
> The Writer's and the Setter's skill
> At once the ravish't Eare do fill. (sig. b v)

In his *Second Book of Ayres and Dialogues* (London, 1655) Lawes defines himself as a self-conscious reformer of English song: "Yet the way of *composition* I chiefly profess (which is to shape *Notes* to the *Words* and *Sense*) is not hit by too many: and I have been often sad to observe some (otherwise able) Musitians guilty of such lapses and mistakes in this way" (sig. a 2v).

15 Other song writers who allowed the melodic line to follow the pace of the verse were William Lawes, John Wilson, Simon Ives, Charles Coleman, John Gamble, and earlier, Thomas Campion. In this they followed a style of monody begun in Italy about twenty-five years earlier: see Willa M. Evans, *Henry Lawes* (New York, 1941). For an argument questioning the influence of the new Italian *secunda practica* on Lawes's music and Milton's musical aesthetic, see John Harper, "'One equal music:' The Music of Milton's Youth," *MQ* 31 (1997), 1–10. See chapter 1, p. 3 and note 11; also chapter 4, pp. 101–2, 106.

16 Casella sang the first *canzone* from Dante's *Convivio,* "Amor che ne la mente ni ragiona" (Love that discourses in my mind). See Charles S. Singleton, trans., *The Divine Comedy: Purgatorio*, I, 20 and II, 35 (Princeton, NJ, 1973).

17 Many Presbyterians in the Westminster Assembly, prompted by the Scots Commissioners (Samuel Rutherford, Alexander Henderson, Robert Baillie, and George Gillespie), pressed for independent ecclesiastical commissions to try the orthodoxy and probity of ministers and elders, as well as admission to the sacrament and excommunication. The Erastians in parliament, led by the formidable scholar John Selden, held out for parliament's oversight and final jurisdiction over such commissions.

18 Letter to William Lenthall, Speaker of the House of Commons, June 14, 1645, in W. C. Abbott, ed., *Writings and Speeches of Oliver Cromwell*, 4 vols (Cambridge, 1937), I, 360.

19 See Kristen Poole, "Deforming Reformation: The Grotesque Puritan and Social Transformation in Early Modern England" (dissertation, Harvard University, 1996), 153–278.

20 For example, William Prynne, *Foure Serious Questions of Grand Importance* (London, 1645, *c.* August 25); and Samuel Rutherford, *The Divine Right of Church-Government and Excommunication* (London, 1646, *c.* March 3).

21 *A Letter of the Ministers of the City of London . . . Against Toleration,* 6; *Certain Additionall*

Reasons . . . by the Ministers of London (London, 1646).

22 *The Humble Petition of the Lord Mayor, Aldermen, and Commons of . . . London,* 2.

23 *A Confession of Faith of . . . Anabaptists* (London, 1646, *c.* January 28).

24 E[phraim] P[agitt], *Heresiography* (London, 1645), sig. A4.

25 *A Catalogue of the Severall Sects and Opinions* (London, 1646, *c.* January 19) carries engravings of several heretics, among them the "Divorcer."

26 P[agitt], *Heresiography,* 2nd edn (London, 1645), 142. In the third and fourth editions (London, 1647) this sentence is repeated (145–6) and Milton is also discussed under the heading of "Independents" – "*Mr. Milton* permits a man to put away his wife upon his meere pleasure, without any fault in her, but for any dislike, or disparity of Nature" (86–7).

27 Robert Baillie, *A Dissuasive from the Errours of the Time* (London, 1645, *c.* November 24). This formula appears in a table of contents, and is repeated as a marginal note on page 116, along with this comment: "Concerning Divorces, some of them goe farre beyond any of the *Brownists,* not to speak of Mr. *Milton,* who in a large Treatise hath pleaded for a full liberty for any man to put away his wife, When ever he pleaseth, without any fault in her at all, but for any dislike or dysempathy of humour."

28 Thomas Edwards, *Gangraena: Or a Catalogue and Discovery of many of the Errours, Heresies, Blasphemies, and pernicious Practices of the Sectaries of this Time* (London, 1646), 34.

29 Edwards, *The Second Part of Gangraena* (London, 1646), 10–11.

30 Selden's *Uxor Ebraica* (London, 1646) was entered into the Stationers Register on September 2, 1645, though the publication date is 1646. Milton cites and praises the work in his Commonplace Book (*CPW* I, 402), in the *Defensio Secunda* (IV.1, 625), in *The Likeliest Means* (VII, 299), and in the *De Doctrina* (VI, 378). He may have seen it in manuscript while writing his divorce tracts: see chapter 6, note 65.

31 Scholars date these two sonnets variously, from late 1645 to mid 1647. The priority of "I did but prompt" is suggested by its composition, in Milton's hand, on the bottom of the page in *TM* that carries the first draft and fair copy of the Lawes sonnet. Two versions of Sonnet XIV on Catherine Thomason (dated December, 1646) appear on the verso of that leaf, in Milton's hand. "I did but prompt" is numbered 11 in TM, although in the edition of 1673 Milton numbered this poem 12 and the sonnet on *Tetrachordon* 11. For that volume he may have wanted to place the more general defense of his several divorce treatises after the poem pertaining only to one of them. The *Tetrachordon* sonnet (also in Milton's hand) appears on the recto in *TM* following that bearing the Lawes sonnet and "I did but prompt." Between these two leaves another leaf has been pasted in with scribal copies of these sonnets ordered as in 1673: 11 (changed to 12) "I did but prompt"; 12, "A booke was writt"; 13, "To Mr. Hen. Lawes"; and 14, "When Faith & Love," on Catherine Thomason.

32 See Janel Mueller, "The Mastery of Decorum: Politics as Poetry in Milton's Sonnets," *Critical Inquiry* 15 (1987), 475–508. Milton may intend Latona's twin-born progeny to allude to his twinned publication (March 4, 1645) of *Tetrachordon* and *Colasterion.*

33 See, for example, *Tenure*: "none can love freedom heartilie, but good men; the rest love not freedom, but licence" (*CPW* III, 190); "libertie hath a sharp and double edge fitt onelie to be handl'd by just and vertuous men" (*Hist. Brit., CPW* V.1, 449); "If we consider that just and naturall privileges men neither can rightly seek, nor dare fully claime, unlesse they be ally'd to inward goodnesse, and stedfast knowledge, and that the

want of this quells them to a servile sense of their own conscious unworthinesse, it may save the wondring why in this age many are so opposite both to human and to Christian liberty" (*Tetrachordon*, *CPW* II, 587).

34 Lines 5–9. These references – to James Gordon, Lord Aboyne, and Alexander MacDonnell (also known as MacColkitto and MacGillespie) – argue for a date in the earlier months of 1646, when these references would still be fresh. Their royalist forces in Scotland suffered a crushing defeat in mid-September, 1645.

35 "Thy age, like ours, O soul of Sir John Cheek / hated not learning wors then toad or Asp, / when thou taught'st Cambridge & King Edward Greek." The lines have received various interpretations. I follow J. M. Smart, *The Sonnets of Milton* (Glasgow, 1921), 73–4, who cites evidence from Cheke himself of his age's hatred of and resistance to Greek.

36 There is no draft in Milton's hand in *TM*, only a copy (with several corrections) in the hand of an amanuensis, on the same page and just after the sonnet to Vane. Milton evidently wrote it on a loose sheet and had it copied in later. For the 1673 edition a handwritten note indicates that it is to be inserted just after the *Tetrachordon* sonnet. Some critics date this sonnet in 1648, when parliament had taken further steps to settle Presbyterian government and had (on May 2) passed its Blasphemy Act. But the references to Edwards and Baillie point, I think, to 1646, when they were especially active and when Milton had more hope of influencing parliament.

37 From March 5–14 ordinances were passed settling details of the Presbyterian organization, but on April 17 parliament proclaimed that it reserved to itself the amount of toleration to be granted to "tender consciences that differ not in fundamentals of Religion." The June compromise provided a list of specified offenses upon which the elders could act alone, but a parliamentary commission was to judge other offences and to serve as an appeals court.

38 A. S. is the Scots Presbyterian divine and polemicist Adam Stewart (who signed his pamphlets A. S.); he was one of the first to answer the *Apologetical Narration* by the Westminster Assembly Congregationalists with his *Observations and Annotations upon the Apologeticall Narration* (London, 1644). Samuel Rutherford was one of the four Scots divines in the assembly; his pamphlets include *The Due Right of Presbyteries* (London, 1644) and *The Divine Right of Church-Government and Excommunication* (London, 1646, *c.* March 3).

39 See note 27.

40 See Smart, *Milton's Sonnets*, 126–7.

41 The Roman Catholic Council of Trent, that spearheaded the Counter-Reformation. See Mueller, "The Mastery of Decorum," 496–7.

42 Milton crossed out his first version of line 17 – "Cropp yee as close as marginall P —— 's eares" – probably recognizing that such a reference to Prynne's punishment was meanspirited and that the line might be read as proposing physical punishment of the Presbyterians.

43 *EL* 52. Christopher's fines were set at £80 and £200; he paid the first fine but not the second, perhaps forgiven it through Milton's intervention (Parker, II, 929).

44 The book of tracts in the Bodleian (4o F.56 Th, kept at Arch.G.e.44) contains eleven works, the five antiprelatical tracts, *DDD* 2 and the three later divorce tracts, *Areopagitica*, and *Of Education*. The inscription to Rouse is in Milton's hand and he supplied as well

an autograph list of contents. *Of Reformation* and *DDD* 2 contain a few verbal corrections, probably in Milton's hand. The 1645 *Poems* did not arrive, and Milton sent a second copy a few months later: see p. 209.

45 Rouse may have had parliamentary sympathies, but in any case he was interested in the pamphlet materials. In 1645, while Oxford was still in the king's hands, he obtained copies of Milton's *DDD* 1 and *Areopagitica*, and asked for the rest. He also acquired "a great fraught" of books from the bookseller George Thomason in 1650. See Edmund Craster, "John Rouse," *Bodleian Library Record* 5 (1955), 130–46.

46 See J. Milton French, *Milton in Chancery: New Chapters in the Lives of the Poet and his Father* (New York and London, 1939), passim., and Parker, II, 932–4. Forest Hill was mortgaged to Sir Robert Pye for 31 years in 1640, and taken over by Laurence Farre, a servant of Pye, in May or June, 1646. This may have been a stratagem to secure the property; Powell named "his loving friend" Pye as an overseer to aid the executor of his will. Powell's household goods had been sold and the town of Banbury seized the timber on his estate. He was allowed to compound for and regain possession of his property at Wheatley, but it had been mortaged to Edward Ashworth for £400 in 1632, with £300 and some accrued interest yet owed. Powell reported to the Committee on Composition that his losses and debts amounted to some £3,000; they set his fine at £180, which he could not pay.

47 Milton's bond from 1627 was for £300; the overdue interest amounted to about £1,372. Powell also owed Milton £1,000 for Mary's marriage portion. Skinner's *Life* cites Mary's comment (*EL* 22), which may of course have been a convenient excuse.

48 The first several entries in the Bible were made at this time. The birth of his first child evidently prompted Milton to set up his immediate (male) family tree. Those first entries record his birth and that of Christopher "about a month after Christmass at 5 in the morning 1615," and note the ages of Edward and John Phillips, then members of his household: "Edward Phillips was 16 year old August 1645"; "John Phillips is a year younger about Octob."

49 *EL* 67. She is described as "lame and almost helpless" in the court proceedings incident to Milton's oral will (*LR* V, 212–15). Edward Phillips notes that she was excused from reading to her blind father "by reason of her bodily infirmity, and difficult utterance of Speech" (*EL* 77).

50 The Phillips nephews, Skinner, and a few other pupils seem to have remained. Thomas Gardiner was admitted to Emanuel College, Cambridge on July 11, 1646.

51 Edward Phillips claims that this *Thesaurus Linguae Latinae* was planned "according to the manner of *Stephanus*," and that it was "a work he had been long since Collecting from his own Reading, and still went on with it at times, even very near to his dying day" (*EL* 72). See Leo Miller, "Lexicographer Milton Leads Us to Recover His Unknown Works," *MQ* 24 (1990), 58–62. See chapter 14, p. 507 and n. 93.

52 *Accidence Commenc't Grammar* (London, 1669). Anthony à Wood claimed that Milton's *Grammar* was first published in 1661, but no such edition has been found (*LR* IV, 359). With the exception of James Shirley's *Via ad Linguam Latinam Complanata* (London, 1649), all the grammarians from whom he draws illustrative examples were published before 1647. The preface, which redirects the work to mature students, was probably added just before publication. See chapter 14, p. 490.

53 For Lily's Grammar, see chapter 1, note 38.

54 For Milton's relation to Lily and other grammar texts, see J. Milton French, "Introduction," *CPW* VIII, 32–83; and French, "Some Notes on Milton's *Accedence Commenc't Grammar*," *Journal of English and Germanic Philology* 60 (1961), 641–50. For Milton's relation to the Ramist grammars see Gordon Campbell, "Milton's *Accidence Commenc't Grammar*," *MQ* 10 (1976), 39–48.

55 See, for example, Petrus Ramus, *Grammatica* (Paris, 1559), and the English Ramist grammars that preceded Milton's: Paul Greaves, *Grammatica Anglicana* (Cambridge, 1594); Thomas Granger, *Syntagma Grammaticum* (London, 1616); and Ben Jonson, *The English Grammar,* in *Works,* 2 vols (London, 1640).

56 While Ramus and the Ramist grammarians claimed these were not properly parts of a grammar book they did discuss them; Milton excluded the topics of letters, syllables, spelling, pronunciation, and versification.

57 See Wyman Herendeen, "Milton's *Accidence Commenc't Grammar* and the Deconstruction of 'Grammatical Tyranny'," in Paul Stanwood, ed., *Of Poetry and Politics* (Binghamton, NY, 1995), 295–312.

58 Some theological comments, the preface, and an appended "Life" of Ramus were most likely added just before publication. See chapter 14, pp. 497–8.

59 Milton used the *Dialecticae libri duo* (Basel, 1572) of Ramus (Pierre de la Ramée) along with Downame's *Commentarii in P. Rami . . . Dialecticam* (Frankfurt, 1601). He cites definitions from Ramus, often in italics; he abridges Downame's very lengthy commentary, and draws about half of his sample logical exercise almost verbatim from Downame (Bk 1, ch. 3, 111–13). But he adds his own third example. See Walter J. Ong, "Introduction," *CPW* VIII, 144–205; and Ong, *Ramus, Method, and the Decay of Dialogue* (Cambridge, Mass., 1958).

60 Aristotelian rhetoric involved five parts: invention, disposition, ornament, pronunciation, and memory; the first two overlap in some ways with logic, but propose somewhat different ways of inventing and organizing arguments. Ramus assigned these first two parts to logic, giving only ornament to rhetoric, on the assumption that the same logical processes underpin all forms of knowledge.

61 Either Milton was wrong about the date of her death (it was December 6) or his date indicates when he composed the sonnet.

62 The reference to George Thomason occurs in Milton's 1647 letter to Carlo Dati (*CPW* II, 765). The inscribed tracts are *Of Reformation*, *The Reason of Church-Government*, *An Apology*, and *Areopagitica.*

63 R. L. Ramsay, "Morality Themes in Milton's Poetry," *Studies in Philology* 15 (1918), 142. The *Everyman* analogue is closest in the first draft of the poem in *TM.*

64 *LR* II, 164. The date of the will is wrongly transcribed as the "thirtieth of December." On February 27, 1651 Powell's widow took oath that her husband "died near the first day of January [1647] . . . at the house of Mr. John Milton, situate in Barbican, London" (see Parker, II, 931).

65 The will stipulated that his wife was to be executor if his son refused, as in fact he did, evidently to clear the way for Anne Powell to claim Wheatley. It also asked the son to pay from the estate the jointure to his wife, for which he had given a bond of £2,000 but had never been able and still was not able to pay, and also to satisfy his debts and provide portions for his other unmarried children. See notes 46 and 47.

66 A jury in Oxfordshire was charged to determine what properties might be seized to

discharge this debt. Pye, in possession of the manor at Forest Hill, brought a suit in Chancery in February to make Milton disclose his claim; his answer described his bond and noted that it antedated Pye's mortgage. See note 46.

67 See discussion in Parker, I, 306–11 and II, 932–4; French, *Milton in Chancery*, 294–315; *LR* III, 10. That Milton allowed her to live there rent free is suggested (though not proved) by the fact that subsequent records document the rental of the other cottages and lands, but not of the house and messuage.

68 The Oxfordshire court noted on that date that she "exists in full life at Wheatley" (*LR* II, 198).

69 The poem was first published in 1673. The manuscript copy, in a fine scribal hand, is at the Bodleian (Ms.Lat. Misc. d.77, kept at Arch F.d.38), as is the presentation volume (8o M.168. Art, kept at Arch G.f.17).

70 The inscription is undated, but the contents indicate that it was bound sometime after March 4, 1645. Young did not deposit the collection in the King's Library as Milton no doubt hoped, and it eventually came to Trinity College, Dublin (Shelf mark R.dd.39). It contained the same tracts as the Rouse volume except for *Of Education*.

71 G. H. Turnbull, *Hartlib, Dury, and Comenius: Gleanings from Hartlib's Papers* (London, 1947), 39. Hall wrote first on December 17, indicating that he has had "a loving and modest express from worthy Mr. Milton" and asking if Hartlib thinks Milton would entertain "a constant correspondence." On December 21 he wrote again indicating that he was "ambitious of the acquaintance of Mr Milton," the author of the Education treatise. On January 4 he informs Hartlib that he plans to "address" himself to Milton next week, and on January 8 asks Hartlib for an introduction. In letters to Hartlib of February 7 and March 22 Hall refers ambiguously to some denial on Milton's part: "I am sorry Mr. Milton dos [is] abundare suo sensu" ["fully persuaded in his own mind"] (Hartlib 60/14/3a–6b; 9a–12b, 18a–19b, 39a–40b).

72 *EL* 4,10 (Aubrey). The exact day of his death is not recorded.

73 Milton senior's will has not been found, but Skinner's *Life* makes several references to an inheritance (*EL* 31–3): "The moderate Patrimony his Father left him"; "His moderate Estate left him by his Father"; "By the great fire in 1666 he had a house in Bread street burnt: which was all the Real Estate hee had." That house was not Milton's boyhood home but a large house called The Red Rose on the west side of Bread Street. Milton held a 21-year lease to this property, arranged by his father; it began in March, 1632 and was renewed in 1649 for another 24 years. See chapter 8, n. 37.

74 *CPW* II, 759–65. Milton states that he gave the letter to "Bookseller James [Allestree], or to his master, my very familiar acquaintance." A holograph manuscript – evidently the copy sent to Dati – is in the New York Public Library. Milton's letter is dated "Pascatis feriâ tertiâ MDCXLVII," that is, on the third day of Easter week 1647, i.e. April 20. In his *Letters* (1674) he dated it "Londino, Aprilis 21, 1647," probably because he transcribed his own copy the following day and dated it accordingly. For Dati, see chapter 4, pp. 93, 102–3.

75 See chapter 4, p. 105.

76 Milton's divorce tracts were denounced, for example, in a draft of the Westminster Assembly's proposed Confession of Faith, *The Humble Advice*, 41 (London, 1646, *c.* December 7); a broadside, *These Trades-men are Preachers in and about the City of London.*

or, A Discovery of the Most Dangerous and Damnable Tenets (London, 1647, *c.* April 26); *A True and Perfect Picture of our present Reformation* (London, 1648, *c.* March 16); and [John Warner], *The Devilish Conspiracy* (London, 1649, *c.* February 4), 18–19. In all these the author is not named, but is assumed to be well known. Milton is castigated by name in *A Testimony to the Truth of Jesus Christ* (*c.* December 14, 1647), 19, signed by 50 Presbyterians of the Sion College group.

77 A series of pamphlets and petitions to parliament in 1645–7 by John Lilburne, William Walwyn, Richard Overton, and John Wildman – often written from prison – persistently called on the Commons for sweeping reforms. For example, [William Walwyn?], *Englands Lamentable Slaverie* (London, 1645, *c.* October 11); and [Overton], *A Remonstrance of Many Thousand Citizens, and other Free-born People of England, to their owne House of Commons* (London, 1646, *c.* July 7). The so-called "Large Petition" to the Commons summarizing those demands and denying any veto to king or House of Lords was ordered burned on May 20, 1947.

78 See, for example, Richard Overton, *An Appeale From the Degenerate Representative Body the Commons of England Assembled at Westminster: To the Body Represented. The Free People in General . . . And in Especiall, To his Excellency, Sir Thomas Fairfax* (London, 1647, *c.* July).

79 Among them, "The Humble Petition of the Officers and Souldiers" (London, 1647, *c.* March 21); many petitions presented in May, 1647 were published together in September, with the title *A Declaration of the Engagements, Remonstrances, Representations, Proposals, Desires, and Resolutions from His Excellency Sir Tho: Fairfax, and the generall Councel of the Army* (London, 1647).

80 Edward Phillips did not enroll at Magdalen Hall, Oxford until March, 1649; John did not attend any university. Cyriack Skinner was admitted to Lincoln's Inn on July 31, 1647. Two cryptic notes by Samuel Hartlib, probably in 1647, contain references (crossed out) to "Mr Miltons Academie" and "Removing of Mr. Milton," supporting the supposition that Milton's move marked the end of his school (*Hartlib Papers, Ephemerides,* 47/9/33A–34A, cited in Turnbull, *Hartlib, Dury, Comenius,* 40). Hartlib listed Milton as one of ten potential "Commissioners" in relation to an Act setting up a Council for Schooling, possibly in 1647, though more likely in 1650 (47/13/3A–4B).

81 In *CPW* II, 766–73. Dati's letter is dated November 1 (October 22, English style). The holograph is in the New York Public Library.

82 See chapter 3, p. 69.

83 Turnbull, *Hartlib, Dury, Comenius,*40–1. Hartlib attributes that news to Theodore Haak.

84 *CPW* VIII, 474–5. The title indicates the scope: *A Brief History of Moscovia and of other less-known Countries lying eastward of Russia as far as Cathay* (London, 1682). See chapter 14, p. 506.

85 Richard Hakluyt, *The Principal Navigations, Voiages, Traffiques, and Discoveries of the English Nation,* 3 vols (London, 1598–1600), I, 221–514; Samuel Purchas, *Hakluytus Postumus, or Purchas His Pilgrimes,* 4 vols (London, 1625), III, 415–60, reprints the best previous work on Russia, Giles Fletcher the Elder's *Of the Russe Common Wealth* (London, 1591). Milton does not cite it directly, but says that Fletcher's "Relations, being judicious and exact, are best read entirely by themselves" (*CPW* VIII, 534–5). There is other material on Russia in Purchas, III, 522–51, 738–806.

86 *CPW* VIII, 493–4, 523.

87 *The Case of the Armie Truly Stated . . . Humbly proposed by the Agents of five Regiments of Horse . . . October 15, 1647* (London, 1647), 4–5. For the June 14 *Declaration* and copies of army petitions to and responses from parliament in 1647, see *A Declaration of the Engagements, Remonstrances, etc.* (London, 1647).

88 *Case of the Army*, 15; *An Agreement of the People . . . As it was proposed by . . . the Generall Approbation of the Army, Offered to the joynt Concurrence of all the Free Commons of England* (London, 1647, *c.* November 3).

89 For the text of the Putney Debates, see A. S. P. Woodhouse, ed., *Puritanism and Liberty* (Chicago, 1951), pp. 1–124.

90 The psalms are dated April, 1648 in Milton's 1673 *Poems*, the only early text and the one I quote from.

91 See William B. Hunter, "Milton Translates the Psalms," *PQ* 40 (1961), 485–94, for the first suggestion; John K. Hale, "Why Did Milton Translate Psalms 80–88 in April 1648?" *Literature and History* III (1994), 55–62, emphasizes the formal considerations as well as Milton's broad paralleling of England with Israel at this time.

92 See Margaret Boddy, "Milton's Translation of Psalms 80–88," *Modern Philology* 64 (1966), 1–9.

93 Psalm 82, ll. 1–8. Cf. 82:1–2 in the AV: "GOD standeth in the congregations of the mighty; he judgeth among the gods. / How long will ye judge unjustly, and accept the persons of the wicked?"

94 Psalm 85, 33–40, 53–6. In the AV, verse 13 (which the last four lines paraphrase and expand) is rendered simply: "Righteousness shall go before him; and shall set us in the way of his steps."

95 Death is ordained for those who "by Preaching, Teaching, Printing or Writing, maintain and publish that there is no God, or that God is not present in all Places, doth not know and foreknow all Things . . . or that the FATHER is not GOD, the SON is not GOD, or that the HOLY GHOST is not GOD, or that They Three are not One Eternal GOD; or that shall in like manner maintain and publish that CHRIST is not GOD equal with the FATHER, or shall deny the Manhood of CHRIST . . . or that . . . CHRIST is not the SON of GOD . . . or that the Bodies of Men shall not rise again after they are dead; or that there is no Day of Judgment after Death." Those who maintain or publish, and refuse to renounce, such Errors as "that Man by Nature hath Free-Will to turn to GOD," that there is a Purgatory, that "the Baptizing of Infants is unlawful," that observation of the Lord's day is not obligatory, or that "the Church-Government by Presbytery is Anti-Christian or unlawful" are to be imprisoned. *Journal of the House of Lords*, X, 240–1.

96 This date is confirmed by Milton's present-tense reference to the "fals North" and their "broken League." By their July 8 invasion Scotland broke the Solemn League and Covenant binding them to support parliament; their defeat on August 17 had not yet occurred. The sonnet is in Milton's hand in the Trinity manuscript, from which I quote.

97 Known as the Treaty of Newport.

98 BL Add MS 32.320.

99 The parish records of St Giles in the Fields note the baptism of "Mary, daughter of John Milton, Esq., and Mary, his wife" (*LR* II, 220).

100 *A Remonstrance of His Excellency Thomas Lord Fairfax, Lord General of the Parliaments*

Forces, and of the General Council of Officers (London, 1649) demanded that crown lands and revenues be sequestered for public uses, that the army's arrears be met, that successive annual or biennial parliaments be guaranteed, that parliament be supreme in all things with no negative voice from a king or any other, that fundamental liberties – religious freedom, freedom from impressment in the army, and amnesty – be guaranteed as irrevocable, and that such a constitution be established by an "Agreement of the People."

101 See David Underdown, *Pride's Purge* (Oxford, 1971), 143–72, 211–12.

102 "When these works [*The Tenure* and his previous polemics] were completed and I thought that I could look forward to an abundance of leisure, I turned to the task of tracing in unbroken sequence, if I could, the history of my country, from the earliest origins even to the present day. I had already finished four books [Quatuor iam libros absolveram] when . . . the Council of State . . . desired to employ my services, especially in connection with foreign affairs" (*CPW* IV.1, 627–8).

103 For Hartlib, see p. 212, and note 83. The book Milton used for the last part of Book IV is Simeon of Durham's *De Gestis Regum Anglorum*, which only became available to him with the publication of Roger Twysden's edition, in *Historiae Anglicanae Scriptores* X (London, 1652). Milton's statement in the preface to *Moscovia* that he intended, after the example of Paulus Jovius's account of Muscovy and Britain, to "assay something in the description of one or two Countreys . . . and I began with Muscovy" (*CPW* VIII, 474–5) also suggests that he conceived these two projects at about the same time.

104 Milton's comment on antiquarian history is in *Of Reformation* (*CPW* I, 541–2). See William Camden, *Britannia* (London, 1590); trans. Philamon Holland, *Britain: or a chorographicall description* (London, 1618); Thomas May, *History of the parliament of England* (London, 1647). For May's significance to the revolution see David Norbrook, "Lucan, Thomas May, and the Creation of a Republican Literary Culture," in Kevin Sharpe and Peter Lake, eds, *Culture and Politics in Early Stuart England* (Stanford, Calif., 1993), 45–66; and Nigel Smith, *Literature and Revolution in England, 1640–1660* (New Haven, Conn., 1994), 342–5.

105 "Digression," *CPW* V.1, 451.

106 See Cedric Brown, "Milton and the Idolatrous Consort," *Criticism* 35 (1993), 419–39.

107 Page 80. Milton reports the abuse of Boadicea and her daughters by the Romans, but does not allow that to be an excuse for her to lead a military action.

108 Page 85. Milton also treats the introduction of Christianity to Britain, the disruptions caused by the heresies of Arius and Pelagius (a Briton), and the continuing incursions of the Picts from the north and the Scots from Ireland.

109 French Fogle (*CPW* V.1, xxxix–xl) supposes that the first two books were written in late 1647, the third (with the Digression) during the chaotic months of January–April, 1648. Nicholas Von Maltzhan, in *Milton's History of Britain* (Oxford, 1991), 22–48, takes Milton at his literal word that he wrote the first four books (the fourth then ending as he concluded his summary of Bede's account) after the king's execution and after he completed *Tenure*. He argues (rightly I think) that the general thrust of the Digression is consonant with that of the *History* as a whole and must have been written along with Book III. But I agree with Austin Woolrych in "Debate: Dating Milton's *History of Britain*," *The Historical Journal* 35 (1993), 929–43, that the Digression could

hardly have been written during the hopeful weeks after the king's execution, which Milton so vigorously defended in *Tenure.* I do not, however, accept Woolrych's argument that the Digression dates from February or March, 1660. The specific evils it castigates pertain to the 1640s, there were other things to complain of in 1660, and at that point Milton's energy was directed to preventing the king's return, by whatever means.

110 See Von Maltzhan, *Milton's History of Britain,* 118–40. Milton read Gildas in Jerome Commelin's *Rerum Britannicarum* (Heidelburg, 1587). See Commelin, pp. 115–16; *CPW* V.1, 132–3.

111 From 1642 onwards parliament solicited voluntary loans of money, plate, and horse on the surety of the "public faith" and promise of repayment at 8 percent interest; assessments on both individuals and political groups promised similar terms. The term "public faith" was often spoken with contempt, and it was freely said that parliament men helped themselves from such levies. See C. V. Wedgwood, *The King's War, 1641–1647* (London, 1655), 196–7.

112 Page 445. The nation was not legally bankrupt, but substantially so, Milton suggests, by reason of the constant need for new assessments.

113 Since the *History* was likely revised before and after publication, it is probable that the final despairing summary sentences of the Digression were added when Milton was readying that segment for possible publication in a reissue of the work in 1671. C. H. Firth, "Milton as a Historian," *Essays Historical and Literary* (Oxford, 1938), 102, supposed that at least the final sentence must have been added in 1670. See chapter 14, pp. 494–5 and n. 37.

114 See John Goodman, *Right and Might Well Met* (London, 1649, *c.* January 2).

115 See the Whitehall Debates in Woodhouse, *Puritanism and Liberty,* 125–78.

116 The Levellers published their own unadulterated Agreement of the People on December 15: *Foundations of Freedom or An Agreement of the People* (London, 1648).

117 *CPW* II, 774–5. The letter is dated December 4 (November 24, English style); the holograph is BL Add MS 5016*, fols 9–10v. Dati had been appointed to the chair and lectureship of the Florentine Academy, and had recently given the funeral oration for the uncle of the grand duke. He also reports that Chimentelli had been chosen as Professor of Greek Literature at Pisa.

118 *A Complete Collection of State Trials,* eds. William Cobbett and T. S. Howell, 33 vols (London, 1809–26), IV, cols 1,070–1.

119 Ibid., col. 1,121.

120 *CPW* III, 242. Though Prynne published several speeches and pamphlets during these weeks, his *Briefe Memento to the Present Unparliamentary Junto* (London, 1649, January 4) is the specific target of Milton's reference to "new apostolic scarecrows who, under show of giving counsel, send out their barking monitories and mementos" (194). Milton also scoffs at royalist petitions and letters such as John Gauden's *Religious and Loyal Protestation* (London, 1649, January 5) and Henry Hammond's *To the Lord Fairfax and his Councell of Warre* (London, 1649, January 15), terming them "the unmaskuline Rhetorick of any puling Priest or Chaplain, sent as a friendly Letter of advice . . . and forthwith publisht by the Sender himself" (195). The tracts subscribed by lists of ministers are: *A Serious and Faithful Representation of the Judgements of Ministers of the Gospel within the Province of London* (London, 1649) and *A Vindicaiton of the Ministers of the*

Gospel in . . . London (London, 1649).

121 *State Trials* IV, cols 1,141–2.

122 Andrew Marvell, "An Horatian Ode upon Cromwel's Return from Ireland," ll. 53–64, in *The Poems and Letters of Andrew Marvell*, ed. H. M. Margoliouth, et al., 2 vols (Oxford, 1971), I, 91–4.

123 *Journal of the House of Commons*, VI, 133, 138–9, 149, 166. The resolutions formally abolishing the king and Lords were passed March 17. See Samuel R. Gardiner, *History of the Commonwealth and Protectorate, 1649–1660*, 4 vols (London, 1894–1901), I, 196–7, 215–16.

124 For the Levellers, see especially John Lilburne, *Englands New Chains Discovered* (London, 1649, *c.* February 26). The officers had presented their compromise Agreement of the People to parliament on January 20 – *A Petition . . . Concerning the Draught of an Agreement of the People* (London, 1649) – but the king's trial focused attention elsewhere.

125 *The Tenure of Kings and Magistrates* (London, 1649). The tract is signed with Milton's initials only – "The Author J. M." – but those initials would have identified him to many readers. It was unlicensed but bore the publisher's name, Matthew Simmonds; he had also published *Bucer* and probably other Milton divorce tracts.

126 *Reason of Church-Government, CPW* I, 816. See chapter 5, pp. 151–2.

127 See Louis L. Martz, *Poet of Exile* (New Haven, Conn., 1980), 31–59; Thomas Corns, "Milton's Quest for Respectability," *Modern Language Review* 77 (1982), 769–79; and Annabel Patterson, "Forc'd Fingers," in *The Muses Common-Weale,* ed. Claude J. Summers and Ted-Larry Pebworth (Columbia, Mo., 1988), 9–22.

128 For Lawes, see pp. 200–1. Edmund Waller's title page a few months earlier used the same formula: "All the Lyrick Poems in this Booke were set by Mr. Henry Lawes Gent. of the Kings Chappell, and one of his Majesties Private Musick."

129 He was right about reader preferences: Milton's volume took nearly 15 years to sell out its first printing. See C. W. Moseley, *The Poetic Birth: Milton's Poems of 1645* (Aldershot, 1991).

130 Richard Johnson, "The Politics of Publication: Misrepresentation in Milton's 1645 *Poems*," *Criticism* 36 (1991), 45–71. He suggests, plausibly, that royalist Moseley was complicit in the design of this portrait.

131 The Greek is:

'Αμαθεῖ γεγράφθαι χειρὶ τήνδε μεν εἰκόνα
Φαίης τάχ' ἄν, πρὸς εἶδος αὐτοφυὲς βλέπων
Τὸν δ' ἐκτυπωτιὸν οὐκ ἐπιγνόντες φίγοι
Γεγᾶτε φαύλοχυ δυσμίμημα ζωγράφου.

Masson's (III, 459) translation. The verses must have been added late in 1645, after the engraving was finished and before the book's publication.

132 Lines 27–8, in which Thyrsis first introduces himself as budding singer: "Baccare frontem / Cingite, ne vati noceat mala lingua futuro" (Wreathe my brow with fragrant plants, lest an evil tongue harm your bard to be). See C. W. Moseley, *Poetic Birth*, 82. See also Leah Marcus, "John Milton's Voice," *Unediting the Renaissance* (London, 1996), 204–24.

133 See David Norbrook, "Levelling Poetry: George Wither and the English Revolution, 1642–1649," *English Literary Renaissance* 21 (1991), 217–56.

134 See chapter 3, p. 75. He prefaces the Latin and Greek poems with the eulogies offered him on his Italian travels by Manso, Giovanni Salsilli, Carlo Dati, Antonio Francini, and Selvaggi (see chapter 4, pp. 95–8, 102–4).

135 See chapter 2, pp. 23–4, 42.

136 Lines 3–6: "Harmful error led me wrong, and my unruly youth was an immoral teacher – until the shady Academy offered me the Socratic waters, and taught me to put off the yoke to which I had submitted." Trans. C. Moseley, *Poetic Birth,* 231.

137 "To my Lady," in *Poems, &. Written by Mr. Ed. Waller* (London, 1645), sig. A 2r–v. Waller insists that poetry is the business of youth, not sober maturity: "These Nightingales sung only in the spring, it was the diversion of their youth . . . So that not so much to have made verses, as not to give over in time, leaves a man without excuse."

138 Stella P. Revard, "Ad Joannem Rousium," *MS* 19 (1984), 205–26; also *Milton and the Tangles of Neaera's Hair: The Making of the 1645 Poems* (Columbia, Mo., 1997), 237–66. The poem was published last in the 1673 volume, serving there as a kind of envoy.

139 Translations are from Hughes.

140 See, for example, *Variorum* I, 324–7; E. M. W. Tillyard, *Milton* (London, 1930), 169–72; Walter MacKellar, *The Latin Poems of John Milton* (New Haven, Conn., 1930), 358–60; and Revard, "Ad Joannem Rousium."

141 See page 223.

142 See, for example, Milton's commentary on Machiavelli from the 1640s in the Commonplace Book, *CPW* I, 421, 443; also see Van Maltzhan, *Milton's History of Britain*, on the impact of Sallust and Tacitus on Milton's *History*.

143 See Martin Dzelzainis, "Milton's Classical Republicanism," and Thomas Corns, "Milton and the Characteristics of a Free Commonwealth," in David Armitage, Armand Himy, and Quentin Skinner, eds, *Milton and Republicanism* (Cambridge, 1995), 3–42. Also, Quentin Skinner, "Milton and the Politics of Slavery," Lecture, Sixth International Milton Symposium, York, England, July 18–23, 1999.

144 That theory was fully developed in Filmer's *Patriarcha* (London, 1680), but was intimated in *The Necessity of the Absolute Power of all Kings* (London, 1648), and asserted throughout his *Observations Concerning the Original of Government* (London, 1652).

145 See Victoria Kahn, "The Metaphorical Covenant," in Armitage, et al, *Milton and Republicanism*, 82–105.

146 See Blair Worden, "English Republicanism," *The Cambridge History of Political Thought, 1450–1700,* ed. J. H. Burns (Cambridge, 1991), 443–57.

Chapter 8 "The So-called Council of State . . . Desired to Employ My Services" 1649–1652

1 The principal modern editions of Milton's State Papers are *CPW* V.2 (introduced by J. Max Patrick) and the Columbia edition (vol. 13). The primary manuscript collections are: the Columbia manuscript (Columbia University X823M64/S52) compiled not earlier than 1659 by an unknown scribe who had access to one of Milton's files, and the Skinner manuscript (PRO SP 9/194) prepared in 1674 from another file. From a third manuscript collection which has not survived, two printed editions appeared in 1676 from different continental publishers but with the same title, *Literae Pseudo-Senatus*

Anglicani, Cromwellii. Another collection, with some differences among the letters, four unpublished sonnets, a *Life* of Milton, and a catalogue of his works, was published by Milton's nephew Edward Phillips as *Letters of State* (London, 1694). These have been supplemented by letters found in foreign chancelleries and English government deposits, and reported in various studies by Leo Miller. The best study is Robert T. Fallon, *Milton in Government* (University Park, Pa., 1993), which analyzes the letters by country and circumstance, and supplies a list, with provenance.

2 See chapter 7, p. 209.

3 See chapter 4, p. 89 for earlier expressions of Milton's anti-French prejudice. Both Latin and French were much used in diplomatic exchanges.

4 A Council Order of March 13 appointed a committee to offfer the position to him, consisting of "Mr Whitlocke, Sr. Henry Vane, Lo. Lisle Earle of Denbigh, Mr. Martyn, Mr. Lisle, or any two of them" (*LR* II, 234).

5 Georg Weckherlin had served in that post since 1644.

6 See chapter 6, pp. 172–3. The Shadow Secretariat also included René Augier and Lewis Rosin; see Fallon, *Milton in Government*, 247–50.

7 Blair Worden, *The Rump Parliament, 1648–1653* (Cambridge, 1974), passim.

8 Samuel R. Gardiner, *History of the Commonwealth and Protectorate, 1649–1660*, 4 vols (London and New York, 1894–1901), I, 6–7.

9 Moreover, the sale of confiscated property (dean and chapter lands, crown property, and some estates of royalists who failed to compound) made it more difficult to reconcile former enemies to the new regime.

10 On February 19, 1651 the council ordered "That after ye Councell is set noe Minister of the Councell shall be present at any debates but onely the Secretary [Gualter Frost] and his Assistant [Gualter Frost, Jr.] without special order of the Councell" (PRO SP 25/66, p. 11). On February 10, 1651 the council ordered "That Mr. Milton the Secr for forreigne languages be appointed to attend this committee [Foreign Affairs] at their meetings" (PRO SP 25/17, p. 59). The order referred to the current meetings with the Portuguese ambassador, but probably set the terms for many such sessions.

11 Fallon argues persuasively that Milton would likely have handled most or all of the correspondence relating to a particular issue or problem and so was probably responsible for many more papers than are formally credited to him, some not now available; they would include translations of many letters from foreign states into English for the council. He was the only secretary engaged in the Hamburg correspondence (*Milton in Government*, viii, 37, 42).

12 See Fallon, *Milton in Government*, 1–22, and J. Max Patrick, *CPW* V.2, 477. It is hard to know how much leeway Milton was given, and when, but where several drafts exist it is sometimes possible to trace contributions that add rhetorical force or precision, not merely stylistic felicity. Edward Phillips in the introduction to *Letters of State* states that he "is not thought to have written his own Selfe, but what was dictated to him by his Superiors" (sig. A 3). But in 1694 Phillips was concerned to play down Milton's responsibility for the then discreditable substance of the letters and offer them simply as examples of elegant Latin style.

13 *CPW* V.2, 479–84. Milton presumably dictated both Latin drafts; both have corrections in his hand. The letters were approved by the council on March 26, reported to parliament which ordered a few changes, and sent out on April 2.

14 *CPW* V.2, 479. This letter, which also designated the Deputy of the Merchant's Company, Mr Isaac Lee, to serve also as parliament's diplomatic agent in Hamburg, was never delivered, since Lee declined to take on that function in such a dangerous situation.

15 See chapter 2, p. 27. For the attacks on other envoys – Charles Vane in Lisbon and Anthony Ascham in Madrid, see pp. 252–3.

16 *CPW* V.2, 488. On May 18 Milton was ordered to translate from French to English several letters expressing dismay over this murder and indicating the measures being taken to apprehend the culprits and protect the new emissary, Walter Strickland; but his versions of those letters have not been found. Milton also translated from German (or at least corrected the translation of) an intercepted, largely personal letter dated April 13 from Princess Sophie (cousin to Charles II and resident in the Hague) to her brother Prince Maurice (*CPW* V.2, 485–87). He probably also dictated the translation from French of Sophie's letter of the same date to her brother Prince Rupert, the legendary Cavalier general. The former but not the latter has corrections in Milton's hand.

17 That earlier tract, unsigned, was by John Lilburne, *Englands New Chains Discovered* (London, 1649, *c.* February 26). This one, also unsigned, was by Lilburne, Thomas Prince, and Richard Overton, *The Second Part of England's New Chains Discovered* (London, 1649, *c.* March 24).

18 John Lilburne, Thomas Prince, and Richard Overton, *The Picture of the Council of State* (London, 1649, *c.* April 11).

19 The Levellers were answered in several tracts, notably *A Declaration of the Commons Against a Scandalous Book* (London, 1649, *c.* March 27), and [John Hall], *The Discoverer* (London, 1649, *c.* July 13).

20 See chapter 6, pp. 178–9.

21 They ordered "That Mr. Milton be appointed to make some observations upon the Complication of interests which is now amongst the several designers against the peace of the Commonwealth. And that it be made ready to be printed with the papers out of Ireland which the House hath ordered to be printed." PRO SP 25/62, p. 125.

22 *Articles of Peace, Made and Concluded with the Irish Rebels, and Papists, by James Earle of Ormond, For and in behalfe of the late King, and by vertue of his Autoritie. Also a Letter sent by Ormond to Col. Jones, Governour of Dublin, with his Answer thereunto. And a Representation of the Scotch Presbytery at Belfast in Ireland. Upon all which are added Observations* (London, 1649). Though not mentioned in this lengthy title, Milton also included Ormond's proclamation (February 26, 1649) of Charles II as "King of *England, Scotland, France* and *Ireland,* Defender of the Faith, etc." just after Jones's letter.

23 Joad Raymond, paper for the Sixth International Milton Symposium, 18–23 July, 1999.

24 Thomas Corns, "Milton's *Observations upon the Articles of Peace,*" in Loewenstein and Turner, eds, *Politics, Poetics, and Hermeneutics,* 127–8.

25 *CPW* III, 308. For the 1641 massacre, see chapter 5, p. 134.

26 He cites an example from Jacques August de Thou, in which the French *parlament* denied the king's right to alienate the patrimony of the crown, of which he is only usufructuary, even in cases of extreme necessity; he also cites Holinshed's example of King John deposed by his barons for giving his crown to the pope (*CPW* III, 306; I, 441).

27 See chapter 7, p. 219.

28 Article 22 of the treaty rescinds prohibitions on some of those practices: plowing by holding on to the horse's tail, and threshing by burning oats in their husks.

29 He offers a challenge to the Rump and the council with a prayer "that all thir ensuing actions may correspond and prove worthy that Impartiall and noble peece of Justice" (311).

30 *CPW* III, 310–11. Clement Walker in *Anarchia Anglicana* (London, 1649), had labeled the regicides "declar'd atheists."

31 Gardiner, *Commonwealth and Protectorate*, II, 30. John Owen was a principal proponent and Cromwell later lent his support. The Pauline reference is to the Jews as the root of a cultivated olive tree, and the gentiles the branches grafted upon it.

32 At Drogheda the garrison of 2,600 was given no quarter, and at Wexford, in almost indiscriminate slaughter, about 2,000 were killed by the victors. By 1653 the last resistance had been overcome. See Corns, "Milton's *Observations*," 123.

33 *LR* II, 245, 255, 256. Both were arrested for suspected dealings with enemies of the state. The first commission was given either to Frost or Milton; the second both to the sergeant at arms, Edward Dendy, and Milton.

34 The council ordered Mr Randolph to be retained as clerk of the papers of state at Whitehall and that "Mr. Milton is to have an inspection into that Office" (PRO SP 25/62. p. 533).

35 *Eikon Basilike: the Portraiture of his Sacred Majestie in his Solitudes and Sufferings* (London, 1648 [1649]). There is no formal record in the council's Order Book, but in the preface to *Eikonoklastes* Milton claims he took on this task "as a work assign'd rather, then by me chos'n or affected. Which was the cause both of beginning it so late, and finishing it so leisurely, in the midst of other imployments and diversions" (*CPW* III, 339).

36 *LR* II, 250. Hall was appointed on May 14 "to make answer to such pamphletts as shall come out to the prejudice of this Commonwealth," and was paid £100 a year for his labors. Hall's *An Humble Motion to the Parliament* (London, 1649) echoes Milton's harsh critique of licensing in *Areopagitica* (pp 28–30) and also his critique of university education in *Of Education* (25–6).

37 Phillips's account of Milton's residences and writing in 1649–51 is confusing (*EL* 69–71). But since he states that Milton lived there only "until his designed apartment in Scotland Yard was prepared for him" – in November, 1649 or soon after (*LR* II, 273, 314) – the "book" he describes as written and published during Milton's residence in Charing Cross must refer back several paragraphs to *Eikonoklastes* (October or November, 1649). Milton also petitioned for, and in November was awarded, a renewal of his lease on the Red Rose in Bread Street.

38 Joseph Hall, *Resolutions . . . of Divers Practicall Cases of Conscience* (London, 1649, *c.* April 9), 389–91. Also, the epilogue addressed to Elizabeth of Bohemia in Christopher Wase's translation, *Electra of Sophocles* (London, 1649, *c.* April 5) refers scornfully to "the froward Miltonist" untwisting the nuptial knot and signing a "Bill of plain Divorce."

39 John Goodwin, *The Obstructours of Justice* (London, 1649), 78–80.

40 See Nigel Smith, *Literature and Revolution in England, 1640–1660* (New Haven, Conn., and London, 1994), 32–5, 54–70, and especially Joad Raymond, *The Invention of the Newspaper* (Oxford, 1996), 1–79.

41 *Mercurius Britanicus* began publishing in August, 1643; this quasi-official parliamentary newsbook engaged more or less directly with the royalist publication *Mercurius Aulicus*.

42 From mid-April through June, 1649 the newsbook bore the title *Mercurius Pragmaticus (for King Charles II)*.

43 The council's order of November 14 specified that he was to be released from Newgate after taking the Engagement to support the Commonwealth. He wrote to a friend that Bradshaw's favor "hath once more turned the wheel of my fortune; who upon my single letter hath been pleased to indulge me my liberty." Blair Worden, "Milton and Marchamont Nedham" in David Armitage, Armand Himy and Quentin Skinner, eds, *Milton and Republicanism* (Cambridge, 1995), 162.

44 Nedham's tract, *Certain Considerations* (London, 1649, *c.* August 1) may have pleased Milton by supporting *Areopagitica*'s case, though on different grounds. Nedham, with obvious reference to his own case, argued that for reasons of civil peace and as a safety valve for discontent the new government ought to allow publication of diverse views, mutinous or disaffected opinion, satires and pasquils, and the like. (For the Milton–Nedham friendship, see note 101.)

45 "Act Against Unlicensed and Scandalous Books," *Journal of the House of Commons*, VI, 298. Such tracts were circulating, the Act declared, "to the intolerable dishonour of the Parliament and the whole Government of this Commonwealth." Cf. Raymond, *Invention of the Newspaper*, 73–9, and Fredrick S. Siebert, *Freedom of the Press in England, 1476–1776: The Rise and Decline of Government Controls* (Urbana, Ill., 1952), 221–5.

46 Responsibility for oversight was shared among the clerk of the parliament (Henry Scobell), the council's secretary (Frost, and in a few cases, Milton), and the army secretary (John Rushworth).

47 The previous licenser of newsbooks, Gilbert Mabbott, was removed from his post May 22 as too lenient; one news sheet reported that he wanted to resign because he now believed (summarizing arguments from *Areopagitica*) that "it is lawfull . . . To print any Booke, Sheete, &c. without Licenceing, so as the Authors and Printers do subscribe their true Names thereunto, that so they may be lyable to answer the contents thereof;" *Perfect Diurnall*, no. 304 (May 21–8, 1649), 2,531. Cf. *The Kingdom's Faithful and Impartiall Scout*, no. 18 (May 25–June 1), 143.

48 Hartlib, *Ephemerides* for 1650, in G. H. Turnbull, *Hartlib, Dury, and Comenius: Gleanings from Hartlib's Papers* (London, 1947), 41.

49 The first issue of the second edition almost certainly appeared before October, since the publisher's address on the title page is given in the form used before October, but not after, *Chronology*, 102. The second and third issues appeared *c.* February 15, 1650.

50 Milton and the sergeant at arms, Edward Dendy, were authorized "both or either one" to search his books and papers, and report on whatever they find "that may be prejuditiall to the Commonwealth" (*LR* II, 268–9). Walker's books were *The History of Independency* (London, 1648) and *Anarchia Anglicana* (London, 1649, August or September). On November 13 he was committed to the Tower to await trial for high treason.

51 Walker, *Anarchia Anglicana*, 199–200.

52 The Stationers Register has this entry for the bookseller John Grismond: "Entered for his copy under the hand of Master Milton, Secretary to the Council of State, a booke called *Histoire entiere et veritable du Proces de Charles Stuart Roy d'Anglitere, &c.*" The title page carries the publication data "London: J. g., 1650" (*c.* March 3).

53 The first edition appeared *c.* February 4, 1649; a few copies may have circulated on the day of the king's death. Thomason dated his copy February 9. For the text's compli-

cated history see Francis F. Madan, *A New Bibliography of the 'Eikon Basilike'* (London, 1950). The first edition did not contain the four prayers printed at the end in most later editions.

54 He claimed entire responsibility for authorship in a letter to Clarendon after the Restoration (*LR* IV, 369), but his authorship was suspected soon after publication. See chapter 12, p. 410, n. 48. Charles may have provided some notes or papers to him.

55 On February 23, 1649 James Cranford licensed to John Playford the printing of these prayers, which were apparently in a separate manuscript; around April 16 Playford published *His Majesties Prayers which he used in the time of his sufferings, delivered to Dr. Juxon immediately before his death* (London, 1649). William Dugard published a different manuscript with these prayers around March 15, 1649; he was arrested the following day but soon released. That same day Matthew Simmons, printer to the Council of State, entered the work (evidently as a blocking action) in his own name, under the license of Joseph Caryl. For an account of the now discredited charge that Milton and Bradshaw connived in the inclusion of Pamela's prayer from Sidney's *Arcadia* as the first of the king's prayers, to provide a basis for Milton's subsequent denunciations, see Parker, II, 963–6; CPW III, 152–9; and Madan, *Bibliography of the 'Eikon Basilike,'* passim. Also see Lois Potter, *Secret Rites and Secret Writing: Royalist Literature, 1641–1660* (Cambridge, 1989), 177.

56 *CPW* III, 150. The first editions were in quarto, but there were also other formats, from handsome folio to duodecimo.

57 Walker, *Anarchia Anglicana*, 12.; *The Princely Pellican* (London, 1649, *c.* June 2).

58 *Eikon Alethine* (London, 1649, *c.* August 26). A copy of this tract in the NYPL has "Jo:s Milton" on the title page as owner, but the signature is probably not in Milton's hand. The tract was likely produced with the council's sanction and is addressed both to them and to "the Seduced People of England."

59 Ibid., sig. A 3.

60 See, for example, sig. A 1v, p. 1. Sirluck, "*Eikon Basilike, Eikon Alethine*, and *Eikonoklastes*", *Modern Language Notes* 69 (1954), 479–501, calls attention to allusions to Gauden's name and previous writing.

61 *Eikon Alethine*, sig. A 3v.

62 *Eikon Episte* (London, 1649, *c.* September 11).

63 J. M., *Eikonoklastes* (London, 1649). Thomason dates the quarto October 6, but that may be an error. The semi-official newsletter *A Briefe Relation of Some Affairs*, no. 9 (November 13–20, 1649), published, as *Eikonoklastes* was, by Matthew Simmonds, claims that it was "published the last weeke."

64 The council order reads: "That Mr. Milton shall have the lodgings that were in the hands of Sr John Hippesley in Whitehall for his accommodation as being Secretary to this Councell for forreigne Languages" (*LR* II, 273).

65 In the *Defensio Secunda* Milton denies that several worthier men (rumor specified John Selden) were first asked and refused this commission. He implies that he was present in the council when it was, by unanimous consent, given to him: "It was I and no other who was deemed equal to a foe of such repute and to the task of speaking on so great a theme, and who received from the very liberators of my country this role, which was offered spontaneously with universal consent" (*CPW* IV.1, 549).

66 Claude Saumaise, i.e. Salmasius, *Defensio Regia, Pro Carolo I. Ad Serenissimum Magnae*

Britanniae Regem Carolum II. Filium natu majorem, Heredem & Successorem legitimum. Sumptibus Regiis (Leyden: Elzivir, 1649). On November 29, 1649 the council ordered careful searches of ships from Holland to confiscate the book.

67 Richelieu's other two greats were Grotius and Bigonius. The Italian Bonifacius termed Salmasius, "by the common consent of Scholars, the most learned of all who are now living" (Masson, IV, 164).

68 *Journal of the House of Commons,* VI, 306–7. The wording provoked intense controversy. A similar engagement had been required of members of the Council of State in February, 1649

69 *Commons Journal,* VI, 306–7, 317, 324, 342.

70 Gardiner, *Commonwealth and Protectorate,* I, 5

71 Dury argued in *Considerations Concerning the Present Engagement* (London, 1649, *c.* December 4) that "he to whom God hath committed the plenary administration of public affairs with unconfrontable power, is God's viceregent . . . either by vertue of a contract, which makes a law, or by vertue of a conquest, which is bound to no law but the will of the Conqueror" (p. 15). He was answered by *The Humble Proposals of Sundry Learned Divines* (London, 1649, *c.* December 19), and replied on January 15, 1650 with *Just Re-proposals.* Other tracts pro and con followed throughout the next several months.

72 Nedham, *The Case of the Commonwealth of England, Stated* (London, 1650, *c.* May 8), 15, 19. On May 24 Nedham was voted a gift of £50 for services rendered and an annual pension of £100 for future services, limited first to "[one] yeare by way of probation" (*LR* II, 309) – a reasonable caution, given his penchant for changing sides. For the complex appeals to Machiavellian force and persuasion in this debate, see Victoria Kahn, *Machiavellian Rhetoric from the Counter-Reformation to Milton* (Princeton, NJ, 1994), 156–65.

73 For example, Lilburne, Overton, and Prince, *Picture of the Councel of State* (*c.* April 11, 1649, reprinted October, 1649); William Walwyn, *The Fountaine of Slaunder* (London, 1649, *c.* May 30); Lilburne, Walwyn, Overton, and Prince, *An Agreement of the Free People of England* (London, 1649, *c.* May 1); and Lilburne, *Legall Fundamentall Liberties* (London, 1649, *c.* June 8).

74 Important Digger tracts of 1650 include: *Fire in the Bush, An Appeal to all Englishmen,* and *A New Years Gift to the Parliament and the Army.* See Winstanley's *Works,* ed. George Sabine (Ithaca, NY, 1941), and Thomas Corns, *Uncloistered Virtue: English Political Literature, 1640–1660* (Oxford, 1992), 150–74.

75 For example, Abiezer Coppe, *A Fiery Flying Roll* and *A Second Fiery Flying Roule* (London, 1649, *c.* January 4, 1650), and Lawrence Clarkson, *A Single Eye All Light, No Darkness* (London, 1650, *c.* October 4). Also see Nigel Smith, *Perfection Proclaimed* (Oxford, 1989).

76 Lines 81–2, 119–20, Andrew Marvell, *Poems and Letters,* ed. H. M. Margoliouth, revd Pierre Legouis and E. E. Duncan Jones, 2 vols (Oxford, 1971), 91–4.

77 See chapter 7, p. 214 and n. 95.

78 *Of Civil Power in Ecclesiastical Causes* (1659), *CPW* VII, 246.

79 *CPW* I, 477, 505. The entries from 1650 and after, all in the hands of amanuenses, include Machiavelli's *Discorsi sopra la Prima Deca de Tito Livio,* in *Opera;* Berni, *Orlando Inamorato Rifatto*; Boiardo, *Orlando Inamorato*; Rivetus, *Praelectiones in Caput XX Exodi*; Augustine, *De Civitate Dei*; Dante, *Purgatorio,* in *Dante con L'Expositione di M. Bernardino Daniello*; Nicetas Acominate, *Imperii Graeci Historia*; James Buchanan, *Rerum Scoticarum*

Historia; Signonius, *De Occidentali Imperio*; Angelo di Costanzo, *Historio del Regno di Napoli*. For editions used, or probably used, see Hanford, "Chronology of Milton's Private Studies," 75–92, *CPW* I, 362–513, and my bibliography.

80 There was no English version: Milton's eyesight and health could not stand up to the task of translation, and the work was, in any case, intended for a learned audience.

81 PRO SP 25/65, p. 11.

82 *CPW* V.2, 496–8. The council order refers to the letter "prepared" by Milton, which may indicate that its skillful rhetoric owes something to him.

83 *CPW* V.2., 514–15 and 519–22. This letter used the title "internuntius" rather than the higher title of "resident" or "orator." Hamburg accorded Bradshaw full honors at his arrival, but then exploited the new government's initial awkwardness with these diplomatic niceties as a ground for failing to pursue serious negotiations with him. A follow-up letter (May 31) uses the appropriate term for the higher rank and insists on attention to the Merchant Adventurers' troubles. See Fallon, *Milton in Government*, 34–43.

84 See Fallon, *Milton in Government*, 43–53 and 88–95.

85 A letter of the same date to be carried by Admiral Popham asks Phillip to allow Popham's fleet to enter Spanish ports for resupply, as needed. Later letters (November 7, 1650) expressed gratitude for the use of harbors in Andalusia and Galicia and asked that this continue (*CPW* V.1, 527–8).

86 *CPW* V.2, 505–10. Milton's letter to Portugal defends the change of government, urges the king to rely on the published writings and declarations of the Commonwealth rather than "the utterly shameless and false accusations of incorrigible men," and again protests that the renegades find harbors and sell their plunder in Lisbon.

87 King John continued to give the royalist fleet under Prince Rupert safe harbor; he also imprisoned English merchants in Portugal and destroyed some English merchant ships.

88 The Spanish authorities at first ignored sanctuary, and seized, convicted, and prepared to execute the prisoners. But threatened with excommunication they returned them to the church. All subsequently escaped, but the one Protestant among them was recaptured and executed. See p. 262, and Fallon, *Milton in Government*, 88–95.

89 Two were from the Council of State to the governor of Tetuan in North Africa over a dispute with an English merchant company in which hostages were taken (*c.* January 30 and August 25); another was from the council to the Regent of Flanders seeking help in recovering an English heiress abducted and forced into a marriage contract there (March 28, 1650). *CPW* V.2, 503, 525–6, 511–13.

90 *LR* II, 295, 315, 321. The last charge was given either to Milton or Gualter Frost, allowing them to decide which one should join the committee of five ministers who were to make the inventory.

91 *LR* II, 327–8. Prynne was arrested June 30 and imprisoned without trial until February, 1653. Milton was also charged the previous month (May 15) to search the trunks and report on the contents of some unnamed person (*LR* II, 307–8).

92 *Catechesis Ecclesiarum* (Racovia [London], 1651). A false place of publication was supplied to disguise the English publisher, and the name of the licenser is not indicated in the Register entry. The *Commons Journal* for April 2, 1652 refers to but does not quote Milton's note. See chapter 9, pp. 284–5 and n. 30 for the later developments.

93 *LR* II, 291–2. A committee of the council was ordered to supply the council member Luke Robinson (who was abroad or about to go) with such of parliament's Acts and

"Mr Miltons bookes as they shall judge necessary to be spread in those parts." George Wither also made use of *Tenure* in G. W., *Respublicana Anglicana* (London, 1650, *c.* October 28), 38–41.

94 An allusion on p. 208 to Anthony Ascham's murder in Madrid, news of which reached England on June 19, proves its publication after that date. A presentation copy, now at the British Library, is inscribed (not in Milton's hand) "Ex dono authoris G. Dury." This is Giles Dury, elder of the French church and associated with St Martin in the Fields. A copy now in Trinity College, Cambridge belonged to Richard Vaughan, Earl of Carbery and (from 1652) husband of Alice Egerton, the Lady of *Comus*. Another copy, now in the Beinecke Library, Yale, is inscribed in Latin as the gift of John Phillips to John Barker.

95 [Joseph Jane] *Eikon Aklastos* (London, 1651, *c.* April), 4, 28, 267. A later answer to Milton, in Latin, was *Carolus I, Britannarum Rex* (Dublin, 1652), attributed to Claude Morisot, who took some material from the court physician George Bate's anonymous defense of the king in *Elenchus Motuum Nuperorum in Anglia* (Paris, 1650). Bate's 1650 edition does not mention Milton, though the second and successive editions in 1661 do.

96 *LR* III, 31, 279. The work was published in London, *c.* November 20, 1652, for distribution in France: *Eikonoklastes, ou réponse au Livre intitulé Eikon Basilike* (*LR* III, 159–60).

97 An official journal, *A Brief Relation of Some Affaires and Transactions*, was begun in September, 1649 by the council's direction, and edited by its secretary, Gualter Frost.

98 The *Stationers Register, 1640–1708* indicates the journal's irregular registration: numbers 1–10 (June 13–August 15) and numbers 19–32 (October 17–January 16, 1651) were not registered at all; numbers 11–12 (22–29 August), numbers 13–15 (September 5–19), and numbers 16–18 (September 16–October 10) were registered "by permission of authority" at irregular intervals. Milton may have been the "authority" that registered the newsletter from its inception, but probably not, since he was then hard at work on the *Defensio*.

99 Milton's name appears once only as licenser for *The Perfect Diurnall* (October 6, 1651).

100 Mylius, agent for the Count of Oldenburg, arrived in London in late August. An entry in his *Tagebuch* indicates that Christopher Arnold told him on August 30 that Milton was out of town; he mentions Milton's return on October 15 and in a letter to Milton the next day writes that he has "long wished your return" (*CPW* IV.2, 828). See below, pp. 260–64, and Leo Miller, *John Milton and the Oldenburg Safeguard* (New York, 1985), 26, 310.

101 Phillips mentions Nedham as one of the "particular Friends that had a high esteem" for Milton and often visited him during the period – mid-December, 1651 to 1660 – when he lived in Petty France (*EL* 78). Anthony à Wood (*EL* 44) dates the friendship to before September, 1651, when, he reports, "it was the usual practice of *Marchm. Nedham* a great crony of *Milton*, to abuse *Salmasius* in his publick Mercury called *Politicus* (as Milton had done before in his *Defensio*)." See Worden, "Milton and Marchamont Nedham," in Armitage, et. al, *Milton and Republicanism*, 156–80.

102 *CPW* V.2, 529–31. For the council's order, see n. 10. On April 23 the council ordered that a letter to Guimarães be translated into Latin – probably by Milton, though he is not explicitly named. Patrick argues persuasively (*CPW* V.2, 546–50) for Milton's

extensive participation in these sessions. Milton's summary of the English versions of these documents survive, but not his Latin versions. Fallon (*Milton in Government* 51–3) suggests that the working papers, correspondence, and documents pertaining to this and other treaties, as well as the treaties themselves, were probably in Milton's possession but withheld from publication as being impolitic and probably illegal.

103 *LR* III, 13–14. With the death of the Statholder William II on November 6, 1650, the Dutch set aside the House of Orange, whose strong ties to the Stuarts were cemented by the marriage of William to the eldest daughter of Charles I, Mary, and established a republic. The English Commonwealth, eager to establish close ties with that Protestant republic, sent a distinguished embassy to the Hague in March, 1651, but they met cold and even hostile opposition, and returned empty-handed after three months.

104 On March 27, 1651 Milton was directed to send to the Spanish ambassador a protest regarding seizures, arrests, and imprisoment of English merchants at Malaga, and it is likely though not certain that he composed that letter (*CSPD* 1651, 134). Other complaints were written in April, to no avail. On May 30 he was ordered to put into Latin a petition from Alderman John Dethick, one of the owners of the ship *May Flower*, whose goods and those of other owners were seized in Flanders in 1649 for debts allegedly owed; and also a letter from the council to the Spanish ambassador, Don Alonso de Cardenas, seeking his "effectuall" intervention and strongly protesting slanders being laid on the parliament. Petitions and counter-petitions had already been exchanged and an admiralty court found Dethick's complaint justified, but more than a year had passed with no action. On June 26 Milton was ordered to carry Dethick's new petition and the council's letter to Cardenas (*CPW* V.2, 551–2).

105 *CPW* V.2., 535–56. This letter of July 14 from parliament to the king of Spain assumes, diplomatically, that the king had not been informed (or had been misinformed) about the many previous protests concerning injuries to the English merchants in the Canary Islands. It reminds the king of the mutual benefits of trade and warns that without redress and future security they "cannot do business any longer in those places."

106 *Pro Populo Anglicano Defensio* (London, 1651). The date of publication is noted in the *Nouvelles Ordinaires de Londres,* no. 34 (February 27–March 9, 1651) published by Dugard, who had also published Milton's *Defensio*: "The reply made to the injurious book of M. de Saumaise by Mr. John Milton . . . came out on Monday last, to the great pleasure and approval of everybody" (136). Dugard had been imprisoned in February, 1650, for attempting to publish Salmasius's *Defensio Regia*, but in April his press and his headmastership of the Merchant Taylors' School were restored to him and thereafter (like Nedham) he worked for the republic. See Parker, II, 973, and *LR* II, 301–2.

107 For bibliographical details see Parker, II, 973–5, 979–83, and (revd) 1,128. In 1651, besides the reissues there was at least one other quarto edition printed at Gouda, and at least six duodecimo editions, published in Utrecht, Leyden (by Elzevir), Amsterdam, and the Hague. In one Paris edition, Salmasius and Milton were bound together, with a joint title page.

108 One presentation copy (now at the Pierpont Morgan Library) is dated August, 1651, another (at Harvard) is dated February 24, 1651; recipients are unknown. Other copies are undated. One (now at the University of Texas) is inscribed in Milton's hand to the council secretary Gualter Frost. Others are inscribed from Milton but by other

hands: one to the Bodleian (though not personally to Rouse), one (at Harvard) to Charles Vane the erstwhile Portuguese ambassador and Henry Vane's brother, one to Hartlib. The printer Dugard presented one (now at Durham University) to Sir Henry Vane with a lengthy inscription. One copy was inscribed "*ex dono authoris*" (not in Milton's hand) to a collector, John Morris (Parker II, revd, I, 237). A copy owned by the Elder Brother in *A Maske* (now Earl of Bridgewater) is at the Huntington Library; on the title page he wrote "*Liber igni, Author furcâ, dignissimi*" (This book is most deserving of burning, the author of the gallows). Parker, II, 979–80.

109 BL Add MS 32,310.

110 In his *Defensio Secunda* (*CPW* IV.1, 596) Milton vehemently denied receiving a reward for this work. For his accusation of Salmasius, see p. 272.

111 In January, February, and March, 1651, *Mercurius Politicus* nos. 33, 37, and 39 carried references to Milton's forthcoming answer to Salmasius. In no. 37 (February 13–20), p. 604, a letter dated from Leyden (February 6/16) reads, "I am thankfully glad of the promise *Politicus* gives us of *Salmasius* Answer, which we greedily expect, and *Salmasius* himself seems to desire it; *Goliah*-like, despiting all his adversaries as so many *Pigmies*.

112 See Leo Miller, "Milton's *Defensio* Ordered Wholesale for the States of Holland," *N&Q* 231 (1986), 33.

113 *Mercurius Politicus*, no. 43 (March 27–April 3, 1651), 697

114 *Mercurius Politicus*, no. 57 (July 3–10, 1651), 914–15. This is probably from Nicholaas Heinsius, then at Leyden. See *LR* III, 46–50 for other reports of the book burning in Toulouse in late June and in Paris on July 6.

115 *Mercurius Politicus*, no. 58 (July 10–17, 1651), last page.

116 On September 8 a correspondent reported from Delft in *Mercurius Politicus* no. 66 (September 4–11, 1651), 1,056: "The reason why Salmasius left Sweden was because Milton's book having laid him open so notoriously, he became thereby very much neglected, the Queen not having sent for him, nor seen him for the space of two months, so that perceiving a decay of her favor, he came himself and desired leave of departure, which was very readily granted, the Queen having at length understood, how impolitick it is for any Prince, to harbor so pernitious a Parasite, and Promoter of Tyranny."

117 Both men were in the queen's service, Heinsius traveling in Europe and Vossius at Stockholm. Heinsius had long been at enmity with Salmasius and Vossius fell out with him in political struggles at court. Edward Phillips repeats the Christina story (*EL* 70), no doubt on Milton's authority. For a refutation, marshaling evidence of the queen's continued favor to Salmasius until his death in 1653, see Kathryn A. McEuen, *CPW* IV.2, 962–82.

118 Letters of Vossius to Heinsius (April 12 and 19, 1651), *LR* III, 15–16, 19. Despite their bias, the Heinsius–Vossius letters contain a core of credible information about the reception of Milton's *Defensio*; they themselves describe it as "clear, concise, witty" and speculate about who this Milton might be (see *LR* III, 14–16, 24–5, 29–31, 33, 59–60, 65). On May 29 Vossius reported that he had learned from his uncle, Francis Junius, that Milton was a gentleman, "skilled in many languages . . . courteous, affable, and endowed with many other virtues," and also that he was a "disciple of Patrick Young." Milton had sent a volume of his writings to Patrick Young (see chapter 7, p. 210), so they evidently had had some association.

119 *Defensio Secunda* (*CPW* IV.1, 655). The claim is repeated by Edward Phillips and John Aubrey (*EL* 7, 74).

120 *LR* III, 53–64. From a letter to Georg Richter, vice-chancellor of the University of Altorf. Leo Miller dates it October 7, 1651 in "The Date of Christopher Arnold's Letter," *N&Q* 229 (1984), 323–4. Another visitor was the Dutch ambassador James Ulitius, who reported in December that he had made a point of arranging "beforehand for intimacy with Milton" through mutual friends (*LR* III, 108, 142–3).

121 The Latin address reads: "Doctissimo Viro, meoque fautori humanissimo, D. Chrisophoro Arnoldo dedi hoc, in memoriam cum suae virtutis, tum mei erga se studii. Londoni. An:D. 1651 Novem: 19." Arnold's autograph book is in the British Library (Egerton MS 1324. fol. 85v).

122 See chapter 7, p. 209. He also had other financial dealings. He purchased an excise bond on May 13, 1651 for £400 from a George Foxcroft, at 8 percent interest. During 1649–51 he was also making, but sometimes failing to make on time, payments on the lease of the Red Rose in Bread Street, which no doubt provided him some rents. He made the final payment on December 20, 1651 (*LR* II, 298–9; III, 26–9; and Parker, II, 996–7).

123 See *LR* II, 312–13, 322–5, 331–2.

124 *LR* III, 10–12, 20–2. Her rights were also at issue in parallel suits involving the new owners of Forest Hill.

125 Public Record Office Composition Papers, SP 23/110, 595–7. The petition proper is first dated July 11, then July 16; this note, with a copy of Milton's note below it, appears on a cover page, dated July 16. She stipulates that she brought £3,000 to her late husband, but now has only an estate (Wheatley) worth £80, which is attached by Milton for his debt, and from which she has only her thirds of £26.13.4 "to maintaine her selfe and 8 children." While she is clearly in some straits, she then had only four children under 20; presumably the others were not dependent on her.

126 For three more years Anne Powell continued her suits for reimbursement for the illegal seizures at Forest Hill, and on May 4, 1654 finally obtained a judgment ordering a rebate of £192.4.1 to be paid to her or to her son Richard, once John Pye paid his fine to compound for the Forest Hill property (*LR* III, 374).

127 [John Rowland], *Pro Rege* [Apology for the king and people of England, against the Defence, destructive of king and people of England, by John the multifarious, alias Milton the Englishman] (Antwerp, 1651). The work was often wrongly ascribed to John Bramhall, former Bishop of Derry.

128 *Pro Rege*, sig. ⋆.⋆ 4v.

129 *CPW* IV.2, 890–91. There is no real contradiction between John's claim that he volunteered for the task and Edward's statement that Milton "committed this task to the youngest of his Nephews."

130 See Robert Ayers's introduction to Phillips's *Responsio, CPW* IV.2, 875–85, and Parker, II, revd, 1,219. There are no references to any event later than September and the mention of Charles vanishing "into a loud fart" alludes to his disappearance after the Battle of Worcester (September 3).

131 John Phillips, *Responsio* [*The response of John Phillips, Englishman, to the most puerile Apology for the King and People of England by some anonymous sneak*] (London, 1652 [1651]). It was published by Dugard, who dated it to the next year as was usual with

late-year publications. The text is translated in *CPW* IV.2, 889–961; the copy in BL (599.a.22) identifies John Phillips as "Milton's Amanuensis."

132 Mylius recorded Christopher Arnold's remark to him at the Old Exchange in Westminster, that Milton was some "vier meilen von hinnen"; since the German *meile* is approximately four kilometers this would be approximately the distance of Hammersmith. See Miller, *John Milton and the Oldenburg Safeguard,* 310.

133 Parker, II, 992, quotes a leading opthalamist of the seventeenth century, François Thévenin, on these cures. See also J. Holly Hanford, "John Milton Forswears Physic," *Bulletin of the Medical Library Association* 32 (1944), 23–34.

134 *CPW* IV.2, 835. Edward Phillips (*EL* 71) speculates about reasons for the move: "whether he thought [the Whitehall apartment] not healthy, or otherwise convenient for his use, or whatever else was the reason."

135 *EL* 71. Plate 10 is a nineteenth-century engraving of the house published in *Illustrated London News* (January 9, 1874), 21, shortly before the house was demolished in 1877. In the nineteenth century the house was owned by Jeremy Bentham, whose tenant from 1811 was William Hazlitt. John Stuart Mill also lived there.

136 Among them: Georg Weckherlin (the former Secretary for Foreign Languages), Samuel Hartlib, Theodore Haak, Sir Oliver Fleming, Christopher Arnold, Gualter Frost, and Henry Neville.

137 Miller in *Oldenburg Safeguard* translates relevant sections of the *Tagebuch* and analyzes the Milton–Mylius relationship.

138 Oliver Fleming explained this to Mylius on October 20; the rule was meant to prevent bribery, undue influence, or revelation of secret matters (Miller, *Oldenburg Safeguard,* 62).

139 It was headed by Bulstrode Whitelocke, keeper of the Great Seal, and included Henry Vane, Henry Mildmay, and John Trevor.

140 Miller, *Oldenburg Safeguard,* 62–7. On the same day Mylius wrote to Weckherlin that he had at last heard in council the "great Milton." Weckherlin had praised Milton to Mylius in a letter of October 6: "When they discharged me, they replaced me with a man of the highest esteem, Mr. Milton, who has already often edited state papers, also writing against Salmasius and against the King. . . . He is a sound man, learned in Latin and Greek and especially Italian" (Miller, *Oldenburg Safeguard,* 69, 53–4).

141 On October 25 Milton was summoned to the council meeting, presumably to hear Whitelocke's scheduled report on the Oldenburg negotiations. On the 27th Milton was asked to find out what "Mr White" intended in proposing a second impression with "some additionalls" to his book, for which Frost was ordered to pay White £50. This is almost certainly *The Life and Reigne of King Charles* (London, 1652, *c.* January 29), in part also an answer to the king's book; this second edition notes (179) that *Eikon Basilike* has already been sufficiently handled in *Eikonoklastes* "without mittens by a Gentleman of such abilities as gives place to none for his integrity, learning, and judgment."

142 *CPW* IV.2, 831–2. Mylius promptly sent the drafts back to Milton for future reference, along with an effusive letter of thanks. He noted in his *Tagebuch* his worry that Milton is not dealing directly with his affair – "it is not to my liking." Progress was slowed by reports that the Count of Oldenburg was negotiating with Scottish royalists in the Hague, which Mylius had to refute with elaborate documentation. Mylius had

a visit from John Dury on November 18 "in a really bad storm, so as to be so much the more secret and unrecognized," who brought a report from Milton that Whitelocke was perturbed about those reports, but Dury later told him (December 6) that Whitelocke was disregarding those unproved assertions (Miller, *Oldenburg Safeguard,* 82, 86, 91, 102).

143 Miller, *Oldenburg Safeguard*, 93. The affair did not move: on November 26 Whitelocke reported to parliament, which referred the matter back to the Council of State, which referred it again to committee.

144 Ibid., 97.

145 *CPW* IV.2, 835–6. Mylius's answer (January 1) effusively expresses his gratitude, his distress at hearing "that you suffer from headache and inflammation of the eyes," and his prayer to God to restore and preserve Milton "for the good of your country" (837).

146 Mylius alludes to earlier meetings in a letter to a friend on January 2: "Milton . . . is among the friends whom I see from time to time, but not as much as I wish because he does not always come by and because of bad health is often away" (Miller, *Oldenburg Safeguard*, 126–7). This may be Mylius claiming more than he has in fact accomplished, or he may be referring to casual encounters rather than private visits. Still, Milton's use of Mylius's first name suggests some growth in intimacy.

147 Miller, *Oldenburg Safeguard*, 128.

148 *CPW* V.2, 558. Milton had in fact produced a version of this letter by May 22, but it was only signed in January. He also produced another letter to the grand duke, signed January 20, which exists only in drafts. See Miller, "Another Milton State Paper Recovered," *English Language Notes* 25 (1987), 30–1.

149 *CPW* V.2, 570–1. See p. 253.

150 *CPW* V.2, 560–9; Leo Miller, *John Milton's Writings in the Anglo-Dutch Negotiations, 1651–1654* (Pittsburgh, 1992), 94–111. On January 23, 1652 the council ordered Milton to supply an English translation of the ambassadors' protest over the seizures. He also wrote the council's reply (January 29), claiming to be dealing expeditiously with the various claims and to have suspended the seizures. Milton probably translated all the correspondence relating to these matters, and evidently dealt directly with at least one member of the Dutch embassy; Mylius reported on January 20 that as he was leaving "one of the Dutch came to him" (Miller, *Oldenburg Safeguard*, 146).

151 Miller, *Oldenburg Safeguard*, 130–1.

152 Ibid., 134–5.

153 The dispute concerned the right to collect tolls on the Weser river, which Oldenburg claimed and Breman challenged; the right was guaranteed to Oldenburg in the Treaty of Westphalia. Milton thought the matter could be quickly resolved if Mylius would appeal directly to friendly council members. He did so, but protested bitterly to Milton in a letter of January 21 about all the "sandbanks and rocks" in his path (*CPW* V.2, 841–3).

154 Miller, *Oldenburg Safeguard*, 171–2.

155 Ibid., 179–80.

156 *CPW* IV.2, 846–7. His explanation to Whitelocke downplays the extent of his association and collaboration with Mylius: "The Agent himself was with me this morning and desird earnestly to see the Copy, which because it was a thing granted to him by the Councell at his request, I thought it could be no tresspass to lett him see, and it

pleas'd him well anough when he had read it; onely he desir'd that where the two marks be on the margent of the English copy this clause [about successors] might be inserted."

157 *CPW* IV.2, 848. On February 20 Mylius recorded in his *Tagebuch* that two days before he had sent his kinsman – probably again Edward Phillips, though possibly John – to assure him that there had been some progress on his affair in the parliament, despite opposition.

158 Miller, *Oldenburg Safeguard*, 199.

159 Ibid., 214–15. Milton was in fact 43.

160 This Marshall frontispiece to *Eikon Basilike* is from a 1649 edition in the Houghton Library. Marshall had earlier transposed the face of King Charles onto a frontispiece image of David with his harp, for a translation of Virgilio Malvezzi's *Il Davide Perseguitato*, making that translation by Robert Ashley, *David Persecuted* (London, 1647), into a royalist commentary.

161 See chapter 7, pp. 226–7.

162 Owen Felltham's epigraph also makes this equation: "Here Charles the First and Christ the Second lies." See Lana Cable, "Milton's Iconoclastic Truth," in Loewenstein and Turner, eds. *Politics, Poetics, Hermeneutics,"* 135.

163 See Richard Helgerson, "Milton Reads the King's Book: Print, Performance, and the Making of a Bougeois Idol," *Criticism* 29 (1987), 12–14; Corns, *Uncloistered Virtue*, 213; and Sharon Achinstein, *Milton and the Revolutionary Reader* (Princeton, NJ, 1994), 162–8.

164 Steven N. Zwicker, *Lines of Authority* (Ithaca, NY, and London, 1993), 37–59, and Norbrook, *Writing the English Republic*, 204–12.

165 *CPW* III, 341. This language recalls *Areopagitica's* statement about the power of books to distill the living spirit of their authors. See chapter 6, p. 193.

166 *CPW* III, 340–1. Cf. PL VI, 119–26.

167 *CPW* III, 343. In the second edition, with more evidence in hand about the relative popularity of the king's book and his own, he specifies his audience yet more precisely: "few, perhaps, but those few, such of value and substantial worth, as truth and wisdom, not respecting numbers and bigg names, have bin ever wont in all ages to be contented with" (*CPW* III, 339–40).

168 Pages 473, 481. Another example: the king repents for shedding the traitor Strafford's blood but not for the bloodshed his wars caused, "a million of his Subjects lives not valu'd in comparison of one *Strafford*" (376).

169 These arguments reprise some developed in *Tenure*. See chapter 7, pp. 230–1.

170 Achinstein, *Milton and the Revolutionary Reader*, 155–68.

171 See David Loewenstein, *Milton and the Drama of History: Historical Vision, Iconoclasm, and the Literary Imagination* (Cambridge, 1990), 62–73.

172 Milton might have heard of E. R.'s verse renderings of the king's *Divine Penitential Meditations and Vows* (*c.* June 21, 1649).

173 From the Anglican liturgical perspective, of course, Charles has every right to adapt to his own purposes prayers like the Psalms which belong to the church and all its members. Also, he might well recognize in David's Psalms, as all the devout may, an anatomy of his own soul. See Lewalski, *Protestant Poetics and the Seventeenth Century Religious Lyric* (Princeton, NJ, 1979), 39–53.

174 Pages 363–4. The second edition also informs the incredulous just where to find Pamela's prayer in the *Arcadia* and which of the king's prayers plagiarizes it: his "Prayer in time of Captivity." For the controversy surrounding these prayers, see note 55.

175 Likening himself to Zorobabel whose praise of Truth freed the Israelites from the Babylonian captivity, he hopes his praise of Justice might "set free the minds of English men from longing to returne poorly under that Captivity of Kings, from which the strength and supreme Sword of Justice hath deliverd them" (583–5).

176 *CPW* III, 488, 601. See Loewenstein, *Milton and the Drama of History*, 71.

177 Norbrook, *Writing the English Republic*, 208–9.

178 *CPW* IV.1, 316, 319, 323, 324, 325, 335, 339, 406, 426, 450, 514, 527.

179 *CPW* IV.1, 308–10, 313–14, 449. Salmasius's title page bore the phrase *Sumptibus Regia,* "at the king's expense," which may simply have been an effort to protect it by linking with the king's name. Salmasius denied receiving a reward, but the rumor (and the supposed amount) was often repeated.

180 For example, if Salmasius "had chosen to read Tacitus himself, instead of copying so carelessly extracts from any source," he would know Tacitus to be "a noble writer most opposed to Tyranny" (443).

181 Milton would also have the Presbyterians take note that Salmasius urged the abolition of bishops in an earlier treatise but in this work argues that they are necessary (314–15).

182 Page 518. Other examples: "you go abroad seeking to burden others with tyranny, so at home you labor under the most shameful and unmanly form of slavery" (471); "You bear in your belly . . . another papacy, for, as your wife's wife, a wolf impregnated by a bitch, what else could you bring forth but a monstrosity or some new papacy" (483); you are not a Balaam but a "talkative ass sat upon by a woman" (534).

183 For Filmer see chapter 7, n. 145.

184 Hobbes's *Humane Nature* and *De Corpore Politico* were published in London in February and May, 1650; their central ideas were crystallized in *Leviathan*, published in Paris in 1651.

185 Page 518. Or again, "Only those called Independents knew how to be true to themselves until the end and how to use their victory" (511).

Chapter 9 "Tireless . . . for the Sake of Liberty" 1652–1654

1 Cyriack Skinner states in his *Life* of Milton, "The Youths that hee instructed from time to time served him often as Amanuenses, & some elderly persons were glad, for the benefit of his learned conversation, to perform that Office" (*EL* 33). The comment seems to pertain especially to the period after the Restoration, but was probably true long before. Only a few of Milton's amanuenses from 1652–4 have been identified: see Peter Beal, *Index of English Literary Manuscripts*, vol. 2, part 2 (London, 1993), 83–6. Edward Phillips transcribed the letters to Bulstrode Whitelocke and Mylius (February 12 and 13, 1652; see chapter 8, pp. 263–4), and two citations from Machiavelli in the Commonplace Book, p. 197 (*CPW* I, 475–7). Cyriack Skinner came to live near Milton sometime in 1654 and probably began to help him then (see p. 303); later, he transcribed sonnets XXI and XXII in the Trinity manuscript (*TM*). Shawcross in *ME* 41–2 attributes to John Phillips several of Milton's letters to Mylius, the "Ode to

Rous," and some entries in the Commonplace Book; very likely he did a good deal of transcribing for Milton in 1652 and before, but Peter Beal finds the single known sample of his hand insufficient to make comparisons and finds several hands in the texts Shawcross ascribes to him. Unknown amanuenses transcribed other Commonplace Book entries, personal letters, and some sonnets in *TM*, including those to Cromwell and Vane.

2 In the *Pro Se Defensio* (*CPW* IV.2, 860). However, he indicates in the *Defensio Secunda* that he attended some meetings with the various European ambassadors who descended on England after Worcester: "Certainly other men in Parliament, and I myself in the Council, have often heard their ambassadors and legates . . . asking of their own free will for our friendship and alliance" (*CPW* IV.1, 652).

3 PRO, SP 25/66, p. 287. For example, Theodore Haak for Dutch and Weckherlin for German.

4 Beginning in July, 1652, Thurloe was attending and preparing correspondence for the Committee on Foreign Affairs; on December 1 the council appointed him "Clerk to the Council and the Committee for Foreign Affairs."

5 *LR* III, 220–1. Milton managed somehow to write the first two, possibly three, words of the entry regarding Deborah's birth himself; it was completed by another hand. The lines about the deaths of Milton's wife and his son John are in the hand of Jeremie Picard; he began this entry with "Hir," crossed it out and wrote "my wife hir mother."

6 Picard seems to have added the note about the death of Mary and John in February, 1658, at the time he recorded the birth and death of Milton's daughter Katherine and the death of his second wife, Katherine Woodcock.

7 See chapter 8, p. 255.

8 Miller, *Anglo-Dutch Negotiations*, 31.

9 Miller, *Anglo-Dutch Negotiations*, 22–30, and pp. 112–53 for the documents. An earlier version of the demands, drafted by Milton for the Hague negotiations the previous year, was published in the 1676 *Literae Pseudo-Senatus Anglicani*, 70–4.

10 Miller, *Anglo-Dutch Negotiations*, 37–40 and (for the document) 180–4.

11 *EL* 79: "The *Dutch* sent away a *Plenipotentiary*, to offer Peace upon much milder terms, or at least to gain more time. But . . . the Parliament had procured a Copy of their Instructions in *Holland*, which were delivered by our Author to his Kinsman that was then with him, to Translate for the Council to view, before the said *Plenipotentiary* had taken Shipping for *England*; an Answer to all he had in Charge lay ready for him, before he made his publick entry into *London*."

12 *A Declaration of the Parliament . . . Relating to the Affairs and Proceedings between this Commonwealth and the States General of the United Provinces* (London, 1652).

13 A council order of July 13 directed "That Mr. Thurloe doe appoint fitt persons to translate ye Parliaments Declaration into Latine ffrench and Dutch." The Hanse ambassador, Lieuwe van Aitzema, notes in his journal sometime after July 9/19, "The Declaration enactment was set into French by Rosin, and into Latin by Milton:" Miller, *Anglo-Dutch Negotiations*, 45. A council order of July 20 (*LR* III, 233) directing the printer Dugard to "speake with Mr Milton Concerning the printing the Declaration" indicates that Milton had primary responsibility for the Latin document, *Scriptum Parlamenti Reipublicae Angliae* (London, 1652). Thomason's date is August, but it was probably ready by July 28, since it was included with a letter to the Grand Duke of

Tuscany the following day. Miller, *Anglo-Dutch Negotiations,* 196–269 reprints the English *Declaration* and the Latin *Scriptum*.

14 There was no land action. The sole Dutch victory was at Dungeness on November 28, 1652. The definitive victory for the English was at the Texel (July 31, 1653).

15 *CPW* V.2, 625–7. On November 23, to show their gratitude for the duke's "good will and amity," they agreed to his request for the release of a Tuscan merchant ship, despite a contrary judgment by the Admiralty Court (641–2).

16 *CPW* V.2, 651–5. On this occasion parliament made a special point of seeing that the changes they made in the document were exactly rendered in Milton's Latin version: *Journal of the House of Commons* VII, 246. For these incidents and their long aftermath see Robert T. Fallon, *Milton in Government* (University Park, Penn., 1993), 112–20.

17 *CPW* V.2, 584–7; 608–12; Leo Miller, "New Milton Texts and Data from the Aitzema Mission, 1652," *Notes and Queries* 37 (1990), 285–6. Letters from parliament in Milton's Latin include one to Queen Christina (March 11, 1652) that desires increased amity and trade and invites a replacement for the Swedish envoy who had died suddenly (*CPW* V.2, 582–3); and another (January 8, 1653) to the Doge of Venice responding to his cordial greetings with assurances of reciprocal favor and good will (647–8). The council (February 2) wrote to ask the Doge's assistance in a mercantile dispute involving a Venetian citizen (656–7).

18 *CPW* V.2, 601–3, 622–4. See chapter 8, p. 253.

19 See Fallon, *Milton in Government*, 94–8, for evidence of Milton's involvement with these treaties. Daniel Skinner's 1676 prospectus for a volume of Milton's state papers included among the contents these Spanish treaties, which he could only have had from Milton's files. On other matters, Milton wrote for the council to Cardenas (November 11), thanking the Spanish warmly for opening Porto Longone to an English fleet damaged in a Dutch attack, but another letter carrying the same date firmly defends the seizure of two Spanish ships carrying Dutch goods, softening the tone somewhat by the promise of an inquiry in Admiralty Court (*CPW* V.2, 636–40). An undated letter of 1653 complains of the seizure in Flanders of an English merchant ship, insisting that the Spanish see to its return; a similar letter was sent directly to the governor involved, the Marquis of Leida (*CPW* V.2, 643–6).

20 In February, 1653 Cardenas was still seeking to negotiate on the basis of the old treaty; on September 9 he returned a copiously annotated version of the 35 articles, accepting only 12 without change.

21 The council assigned this letter to Weckherlin, but it was evidently passed on to Milton, since he retained two Latin versions among his papers (*CPW* V.2, 604–7).

22 Fallon (*Milton in Government*, 100–11) argues for Milton's extensive involvement in the Danish negotiations, on the ground that Thurloe was short-staffed and would have seen the efficiency of having one secretary carry through a complex set of negotiations.

23 Miller, *Anglo-Dutch Negotiations*, 270–2, 68–9. This letter, discovered by Miller, may have been withheld until Milton's translation was ready.

24 *CPW* V.2, 628–33. These letters are undated. *CPW* dates them October 14 and 22 but Fallon (*Anglo-Dutch Negotiations*, 104, n. 74) argues persuasively for September 13, two days before they were presented to the ambassadors; the later dates would place them after negotiations had broken off.

25 The ambassadors reaffirmed their position on September 21, and the council responded curtly (October 5) that they had better return home to secure authority to treat. They had already asked permission to depart.

26 This is a new letter discovered by Miller, *Anglo-Dutch Negotiations*, 276–7.

27 Bulstrode Whitelocke, *Memorials of the English Affairs*, 4 vols (Oxford, 1853), vol. 3, 372–4, dates the meeting December 10; present from parliament were Speaker William Lenthall, Whitelocke, Thomas Widdrington, and Chief Justice St John; the army officers were Cromwell, Thomas Harrison, Charles Fleetwood, Edward Whalley, and John Desborough. One suggestion was to bring back Charles I's third son as king.

28 In January, 1652 Lilburne was brought to trial and exiled on charges of promoting a false, malicious, and scandalous petition against Arthur Hasilrigg; see *Declaration of the Army concerning . . . Lilburne* (London, 1652). Winstanley's *Law of Freedom in a Platform* appeared early in 1652. See chapter 8, pp. 249–50.

29 See Blair Worden, *The Rump Parliament, 1648–1653* (Cambridge, 1974), 265–98.

30 Owen, dean of Christ Church, had been Cromwell's chaplain in Ireland. The 29 signers included four of the original five Independents of the Westminster Assembly, as well as John Dury. See *Journal of the House of Commons* VII, 86 (February 10). The *Racovian Catechism* was entered in the Stationers Register by Dugard on November 13, 1651 (with no mention of the licenser's name). Thomason dates his copy *c.* March, 1651 (i.e. 1652), but it was available by January 27, 1652, when Dugard was arrested for the publication; two days later the Stationers Register entry was cancelled at Dugard's request.

31 See chapter 8, p. 253 and note 92.

32 *The Humble Proposals of Mr. Owen, etc.* (London, 1652, *c.* March 31). When they were republished on December 2 as *Proposals for the furtherance and propagation of the Gospell in this Nation* the 15 doctrinal fundamentals were appended (p. 12). Also see the news sheets *Several Proceedings in Parliament*, no. 130 (March 18–25), p. 2,025, and no. 131 (March 25–April 1), pp. 2,037–9. Tracts supporting the proposals include Giles Firmin, *Separatism Examined* (London, 1652, *c.* March 15) and Stephen Marshall, *A Sermon preached to the Lord Mayor* (London, 1652, *c.* April 5). See Samuel R. Gardiner, *History of the Commonwealth and Protectorate, 1649–1660*, 4 vols (London and New York, 1894–1901), II, 31.

33 *Journal of the House of Commons* VII, 113–14. A broadside dated April 2 published the resolutions and the order for burning. An English translation, *The Racovian Catechisme*, was published in Amsterdam (*c.* June 8, 1652) and imported to England.

34 The *Commons Journal* entry for April 2, 1652 (VII, 114) simply refers to the examination of Mr John Milton and a note under his hand.

35 *Commons Journal* VII, 128 (April 29).

36 For Williams see chapter 6, pp. 178–9.

37 See *CPW* IV.1, 174–6 and *DNB*. Vane (1613–62) emigrated to New England in 1635, was elected Governor of Massachusetts Bay Colony in 1636, and ousted from office in 1637. He returned to England, became in the 1640s a leading member of parliament and a leading member of the Council of State under the republic. He devoted himself for many years to the build-up of the navy and was also constantly called upon as a skillful negotiator – with Charles after the civil wars, and with the Dutch ambassadors in 1652. For Biddle, see chapter 10, p. 328.

38 For Williams's association with Vane see Masson, IV, 395. In a letter to the City of Providence Williams spoke of Vane as "my kinde freind and ancient acquaintance" and in a letter of July 12, 1654 to John Winthrop referred to the language lessons with Milton: *The Correspondence of Roger Williams,* ed. Glenn La Fantasie, 2 vols (Hanover and London, 1988), II, 389, 393. Williams wrote a letter to Mrs Anne Sadleir, daughter of his old patron Sir Edward Coke and aunt of Milton's pupil Cyriack Skinner (undated but perhaps sometime in 1652), in which he recommended Milton's *Eikonoklastes* to that ardent royalist. She replied: "If I be not mistaken, that is he that has wrot a book of the lawfulnes of devorce, and if report sais true he had at that time two or thre wives living. This perhaps were good Doctrine in new England, but it is most abominable in old, England. For his book that he wrot against the late King that you would have me read, you should have taken notice of gods judgment upon him who stroke him with blindnes" (*Correspondence,* I, 378–9).

39 Williams's letter continues: "Grammar rules begin to be esteem'd a Tyrannie. I taught a young Gentlemen, a Parliamt mans Sons (as we teach our children English) by words, phrazes, and constant talk" (*Correspondence*, II, 393).

40 *The Fourth Paper Presented by Major Butler* (London, 1652), preface and p. 17. A marginal note referring to "that great Controversie of the *Bloody Tenet*, between Mr. *Cotton* and my self" proves that this anonymous work is by Williams. The tract is offered as a defense of four principles by Major William Butler; one of the signers was Henry Vane's brother Charles. Williams included a copy of the 15 *Proposals* but said he had not yet seen a copy of the doctrinal fundamentals.

41 Williams, *The Bloody Tenant yet More Bloody* (London, 1652, *c.* April 28), 319. Williams also published that month *The Hireling Ministry None of Christs* (London, 1652).

42 Vane's speeches are not on record, but his principles were well known. Robert Baillie, the Scots representative to the Westminster Assembly, reported that "Cromwell and Vane [would] . . . have a libertie for all religions, without any exceptions" and that Vane argued "prolixlie, earnestlie, and passionatelie . . . for a full libertie of conscience to all religions," Baillie, *Letters and Journals . . . 1637–1662,* 3 vols (Edinburgh, 1841), II, 230, 235. Vane's brother Charles, briefly envoy to Portugal, was one of the petitioners against Owen's scheme for an established church. Milton gave Charles Vane an elegant folio presentation copy of his *Defensio* with a title page inscription. See chapter 8, n. 108.

43 "Captain or Colonel," "I did but prompt the age," "A book was writ of late," "On the New Forcers of Conscience," and the Fairfax sonnet.

44 In the same month (May, 1652) John Lilburne from his exile abroad, in his own interest paid tribute to that Miltonic stance, urging Cromwell and the army officers to take the "excellent and faithfull advice" of their "valiant and learned Champion" who, after routing Salmasius "turnes his speech [in the peroration to the *Defensio*] to his Masters that had set him on worke," addressing them "with much *faithfullness* and Freedom." Lilburne, *As You Were* (Amsterdam, 1652); *LR* III, 219–20.

45 It was first printed with some variations by Edward Phillips in *Letters of State* (1694); this title in *TM* is crossed out and Phillips omits it as too occasional. The Fairfax, Cromwell, and Vane sonnets (and that to Cyriack Skinner on Milton's blindness) could not be included in the revised edition of *Poems* (1673) in the Restoration milieu. My citations are based on the version in *TM.*

46 See E. A. J. Honigmann, ed., *Milton's Sonnets* (London, 1966), 147. The phrase is biblical in origin: "For there shall be peace and truth in my days" (Isaiah 39:8). Significantly, Milton refers only to the battles in Scotland (against the Presbyterians), not to those in England or Ireland. Roger Williams's *Bloody Tenet* and *Bloody Tenet yet More Bloody* were also set forth as dialogues between Truth and Peace.

47 Cicero, *De Officiis* I, xxii, 74: "Vere autem si volumus judicare, multae res exstiterunt urbanae maiores clarioresque quam bellicae." *Cicero*, vol. 21, trans. Walter Miller (Cambridge, Mass., 1918), 76.

48 The sonnet bears this title in *TM*. Since Vane's father (also in parliament) was named Henry, the son's usual style was "The Younger." The sonnet was first printed anonymously in [George Sikes], *The Life and Death of Sir Henry Vane* (London, 1662), 93–4, just after Vane's execution. Sikes introduces the sonnet with the comment, "the Character of this deceased Statesman . . . I shall exhibite to you in a paper of Verses, composed by a learned Gentleman, and sent him [Vane], July 3, 1652." Sikes's brief description of Vane's character and accomplishments simply expands upon the terms supplied by Milton's sonnet. The sonnet was reprinted in *Letters of State* (1694). My citations follow the version in *TM*.

49 His style, "The Younger," is the basis for the paradox. In 1652 he was about 40 but he had a long string of accomplishments to his credit at a very young age.

50 Edmund Ludlow also commended Vane's discernment in the matter of proposed treaties with Charles I, when he "so evidently discovered the design and deceit of the King's answer" (*Memoirs*, I, 208).

51 *CPW* IV.2, 851–3. Philaras, known in France as Villeré, had first sent greetings to Milton through René Augier, a naturalized English citizen sometimes employed by the council to do French translations. Milton's letter is dated by the month only, from London, not his house in Petty France (Westminster). He may have been staying with family or friends during his time of troubles.

52 Walton had the encouragement of Ussher and Selden for his grand project, and it would naturally interest Milton. The council praised it but referred his request to parliament, and on July 20 sent a copy of that order to Milton, as one who had supported or perhaps presented Walton's petition. On July 9, 1653 the council decided "upon the reading of the Letter written from Mr. Milton to Sir Gilbert Pickering" to discover how much paper Walton needed, and on July 15 issued the permit (*LR* III, 231–2, 335–6; Masson, IV, 447, 524).

53 Davenant had been apprehended at sea transporting weavers from France to Virginia, and in 1651 was under sentence in the Tower. On October 9, 1652 he wrote to Bulstrode Whitelocke thanking him for his release. Jonathan Richardson reports information from Davenant's son that Milton was instrumental in working his rescue. See chapter 12, n. 7, and *EL* 272.

54 The date is indicated by a reference in the preface to the outbreak of the Dutch war. Adriaan Vlacq published three editions in the Hague in 1652, two duodecimos and a quarto. In his preface Vlacq claims that the unknown author sent Salmasius a manuscript of the work several months before it was published. English quotations are from the sections translated by Paul M. Blackford (*CPW* IV.2, 1,042–81).

55 Filmer, *Observations concerning the Originall of Government* (London, 1652), 17, 23.

56 Du Moulin, *Parerga, Poematum libelli tres* (Cambridge, 1670), III, 141. English trans.

French (*LR* III, 242–3). Du Moulin also admitted authorship in his *Replie to a Person of Honour* (Cambridge, 1673), 40. See chapter 14, pp. 496–7.

57 Vlacq's preface, "Typographus pro se-ipso," prefixed to his pirated edition of the *Defensio Secunda*, sig. x 3v declares: "He [Hartlib] asked me to send him every week the single sheets thus far fresh from the press. I did so, and only asked that if Milton wished to reply to it, he would arrange to have a copy sent to me to be printed, if he could persuade Milton to do so. But he never once wrote to me. . . . I have often wondered why Milton did not reply at once to the aforesaid book" (*LR* III, 245).

58 *Pro Se Defensio* (*c.* August 8, 1655), *CPW* IV.2, 703.

59 Vlacq's preface states: "I wrote to Hartlib once . . . who answered me on October 29, 1652, in these words translated from the English: "I am glad that you have written to me that More is not the author of that most vile and scandalous book" (*LR* III, 270).

60 Michael Lieb, *Milton and the Culture of Violence* (Ithaca, NY, 1994), 159–75.

61 Ibid., 175–80.

62 *To the Supreame Authoritie the Parliament . . . The Humble Petiition of the Officers of the Army* (London, 1652, August 12). Other demands included dismissal of disaffected and scandalous magistrates, an end to tax abuses, sinecures, and monopolies, payment of soldiers' arrears and of the Commonwealth's debts. See Worden, *The Rump Parliament*, 307–8.

63 Cromwell claimed that some ten or twelve informal meetings between officers and selected parliament members were held after October 1 (Cromwell, *Writings and Speeches of Oliver Cromwell*, ed. W. C. Abbott, 4 vols. (Cambridge, 1937) III, 55).

64 Whitelocke, *Memorials*, III, 548–51. Whitelocke's rejoinder was a proposal for the recall of Charles II, upon conditions.

65 Reports came regularly from the Continent reporting it almost finished or in press. See *LR* III, 34, 40–1, 44–7, 173, 248–51. The irrepressible Heinsius and Vossius circulated other rumors about Milton: that his blindness was a judgment of God, that he was dead. (*LR* III, 252, 248).

66 *LR* III, 316, 321–2. See chapter 4, p. 99.

67 My citations are from the only early version, the 1673 *Poems*.

68 See *Variorum* II.2, 442–52. The 1655 date, proposed by Hanford, Woodhouse, Parker (II, 1,042–3), Shawcross, and others assumes that the sonnets in the 1673 edition are in chronological order, so that placement of this sonnet after the Piedmont sonnet (no. XVIII), April–May, 1655, argues for a date later that year. But there is no reason to assume strict chronology. As C. J. Morse suggested in "The Dating of Milton's Sonnet XIX" (*TLS*, September 15, 1961), 620, when Milton omitted the Fairfax, Cromwell, and Vane sonnets from the 1673 *Poems*, he likely placed the Piedmont sonnet where it would round off a group of public sonnets, following them with a group on private themes. Honigmann (*Sonnets*, 173) argues, implausibly, that "When I consider" is really about loss of inspiration, not blindness, and dates it from 1644, when "half my days" would make better literal sense.

69 Parker, II, 1,043. Milton senior's birthdate is uncertain: he himself referred to several approximate birthdates between 1562 and 1569 (Parker, II, 684–5). Since John Aubrey reported that he read without spectacles at age 84 (*EL* 4–5) he was thought to be at least 84 at the time of death.

70 See chapter 7, p. 228, and below, pp. 311–12.

71 See Dayton Haskin, *Milton's Burden of Interpretation* (Philadelphia, 1994), for a nuanced argument locating the sonnet in a complex discourse in which the parable of the talents was seen to figure issues of election, hermeneutics, and social duty. To recognize that context does not, however, require denying (as Haskin almost does) the significance of blindness and autobiographical reference.

72 See chapter 3, p. 60.

73 About November 9, 1652 John Frederick Gronovius declared to Heinsius: "I easily understand [the author of *Clamor*] to be Morus"; on January 21, 1653 he reiterated that ascription: "That More was the author of that tirade I recognized immediately from the style." On January 17 the Swiss agent Jean Baptiste Stouppe wrote to a friend in Zurich attributing the *Clamor* to More and recounting the scandal about More and the maid "whom he had promised to marry as he has not done" (*LR* III, 274, 314–15). For other reports see *LR* III, 292–3, 315–17. The gentlewoman's name was Elizabeth Guerret.

74 *Mercurius Politicus*, no. 121, 1,910 (September 23–30, 1652).

75 Pontia is satirized in Juvenal, *Saturae*, VI, 637–42, and Martial, *Epigrammaton*, II, 34–6. For the Latin wordplay and archival evidence proving that the rumored pregnancy was indeed false, see Paul Sellin, "Alexander Morus and John Milton (II)," in *Contemporary Explorations in the Culture of the Low Countries*, ed. W. Shetter and I. Van der Cruysse (Lanham, 1996), 277–86; and also Sellin, "Alexander Morus Before the Hof van Holland," in *Studies in Netherlandic Culture and Literature*, ed. M. Bakker and B. Morrison (Lanham, 1994), 1–11.

76 His informants were probably Frederick Spanheim (Geneva), Lieuwe van Aitzema (the Hague), and Phillippe Diodati (son of the Geneva theologian John Diodati and cousin to Milton's dear friend Charles) who was pastor at Leyden from 1651. See Kester Svendsen in *CPW* IV.2, 687–93, and Paul Sellin, "Alexander More Before the Synod of Utrecht,' *Huntington Library Quarterly* 38 (1996), 239–49. See pp. 308–9 and chapter 10, pp. 322–24.

77 The register of presentations to benefices from 1649–54 (BL Add MS 36792, fol. 28) records on July 23, 1651 Milton's recommendation of Heath, which Heath had presumably requested of him. He may have been one of Milton's pupils at some point. See Austin Woolrych, "Milton and Richard Heath," *Philological Quarterly* 53 (1974), 132–5.

78 See above, p. 288.

79 Sandelands enclosed in the letter his correspondence with Colonel Lilburne in Scotland and an elaborate outline of the scheme (*LR* III, 312–14).

80 See Parker, II, 1,024 for the discussions of Sandeland's project in the Committees on Trade and the Admiralty, from July, 1652 through June, 1653.

81 *CPW* IV.2, 861; *CSPD* 1652–3, 241, 266. On April 8, 1653 the council considered the Argyle business – presumably the deception revealed in Sandeland's letter.

82 There are echoes of *Lycidas* in Marvell's Cromwell poems, e.g. "beaked promontory," *Lycidas*, l. 94, *The First Anniversary*, l. 358; also *Lycidas*, l. 71, "That last infirmity of Noble mind," *A Poem upon the Death of O. C.*," l. 22, "Those nobler weaknesses of humane Mind."

83 There is no record of Meadows' first appointment; on October 17, 1653 the council ordered that Meadows "now employed by the Council in Latin translations, do also assist Mr. Thurloe in the dispatch of Foreign Affairs," granting him an additional £100 "to be added to the £100 per annum he now receives of the Council" (*LR* III, 345–6). For three years he worked as Milton's assistant for Latin correspondence.

84 See chapter 7, p. 199, and note 5.

85 Masson, V, 230–5. Robert Boyle, the experimental chemist, was an active member of the Hartlib circle and of the so called "Invisible College" of scholars and scientists, especially those interested in scientific experiments. Another brother was Roger Boyle, Lord Broghill, president of Cromwell's Council in Ireland and soon to be author of several poems and plays.

86 *Declaration of the Lord General . . . Shewing the Grounds and Reasons for the dissolution of the late Parliament* (London, 1653, *c.* April 22), 6.

87 The exact provisions of the Bill are not known as Cromwell carried it away with him when he dissolved the House. See Worden, *Rump Parliament*, 332–4.

88 Edmund Ludlow, *Memoirs,* ed. C. H. Firth, 2 vols (Oxford, 1894), I, 351–3. Ludlow drew on varioue eye-witness accounts.

89 Whitelocke, *Memorials*, IV, 5.

90 Ludlow, *Memoirs*, I, 353

91 Ibid., 357.

92 The army issued its first explanatory *Declaration* of the reasons for the dissolution on April 22; a second and third *Declaration* were published on May 3. See Cromwell, *Writings and Speeches*, ed. Abbott, III, 5–8, 21.

93 Ibid., 64.

94 Secret exchanges of letters, initiated by the Dutch before the Rump Parliament dissolved, culminated in arrangements for the new embassy to England. None of these letters are Milton's. See Miller, *Anglo-Dutch Negotiations*, 70–2.

95 Ibid., 72–3, 278–93.

96 A letter for the council to Frederick, Duke of Holstein (July 26) dealt with the Safeguard being negotiated for that state, modeled on the one Milton had prepared for Oldenburg. It was approved by parliament on December 1. Milton may or may not have been involved with the revisions tailoring the Safeguard to Holstein, but the document was substantially his. See Miller, *Oldenburg Safeguard*, 274–6. At some point during these months Milton translated letters, nearly identical, from the council to the Marquis of Leida and to the Spanish ambassador Cardenas complaining that an English ship was seized at Ostend and its sailors treated barbarously (*LR* III, 304–5).

97 Milton's translation was completed October 8, but held to be given to the envoy at his return. The text and the complicated history of the Swiss letters (December 13, 1652 and February 13, 1653) and this much-delayed English reply are in *CPW* V.2, 660–6.

98 Psalm 2 is dated August 8, 1653 and the following psalms on succeeding days, ending with August 15. Milton gave only the year date, 1653, to Psalm 1, but it was almost certainly translated at about this time. They were first printed in *Poems* 1673, from which all quotations are taken.

99 Mary Ann Radzinowicz, *Toward Samson Agonistes* (Princeton, NJ, 1978), 198–208, points to the strong ethical thrust in Milton's choice of psalms and use of psalmic materials.

100 The relevant verse (5) in the AV is: "Therefore the ungodly shall not stand in the judgment, nor sinners in the congregation of the righteous."

101 Late in 1652 two German dissertations attacking the *Defensio* were published: James Schaller (with response by Erhard Kieffer), *Dissertationis ad quaedam loca Miltoni* (Strasbourg) and Caspar Ziegler, *Circa Regicidium Anglorum Exercitationes* (Leipzig). *LR* III,

123, 276–7. The arguments of *Doctrine and Discipline* were attacked by Henry Hammond in *A Letter of Resolution* (London, 1653 [1652], *c.* November 1).

102 John Rowland, *Polemica* (London, 1653). See chapter 8, pp. 258–9.

103 *LR* III, 374–5. The letter from Bramhall to his son (May 9/19, 1654) asserts that John Phillips's "lying abusive book was written by Milton himself. . . . If Salmasius his friends knew as much of him as I, they would make him go near to hang himself. But I desire not to wound the nation through his sides, yet I have written to him long since about it roundly. It seems he desires not to touch upon that subject."

104 At times his formulations recall other English psalm versions, especially the AV, the *Book of Common Prayer*, and the verse translations of George Buchanan, George Sandys, and Sir Philip Sidney.

105 The AV reads: "Mine eye is consumed because of grief: it waxeth old because of all mine enemies."

106 In the AV, Psalm 2:6 reads: "Yet have I set my king upon my holy hill of Zion"; Psalm 5:3 reads: "O Lord in the morning will I direct my prayer unto thee, and will look up." Other Miltonic augmentations include a generalization added to Psalm 7: "God is a just Judge and severe" (l. 43), and to Psalm 8 a description of God's enemy as one "That bends his rage thy providence to oppose" (l. 8).

107 Cf. AV, Psalm 6:10: "Let all mine enemies be ashamed and sore vexed: let them return and be ashamed suddenly."

108 See chapter 7, pp. 213–14.

109 For Calvin's psalter see William Hunter, "The Sources of Milton's Prosody," *Philological Quarterly* 28 (1949), 142. The Sidney–Pembroke psalms, though not published until the twentieth century, circulated widely in manuscript and were well known.

110 For Psalm 1 Milton (like Sidney) used rhymed iambic pentameter couplets but with the sense running on from line to line; for Psalm 2, *terza rima*, the verse form of Dante's *Divine Comedy* and Sidney's Psalm 7; for Psalm 3 a stanza of six iambic lines of varying length rhyming aabccb; for Psalm 4 a stanza of five iambic trimeter lines and one pentameter rhyming abbacc; for Psalm 5 eight quatrains of alternating trimeter and pentameter couplets rhyming abab; for Psalm 6, iambic pentameter quatrains rhyming abba; for Psalm 7, ten stanzas of iambic tetrameter rhyming ababba and a final quatrain rhyming aabb; and for Psalm 8, six quatrains of iambic pentameter rhyming abab, with run-on stanzas as well as lines.

111 Roman Catholics and Irish rebels were excluded forever; royalist malignants for the first four parliaments, unless they demonstrated a change of heart.

112 Cromwell could add up to six others with the council's consent, and could make replacements when needed from nominees proposed by parliament and the council.

113 *LR* III, 355–6. On the same day Cromwell signed a warrant for payment to the staff, including Milton, of their back salary from July 4, 1653 to January 1, 1654.

114 [Marchamont Nedham], *A True State of the Case of the Commonwealth* (London, 1654). Nedham claims that the principle of the people's sovereignty is preserved in the new parliamentary structure and the provision (hereafter) for an elective Protector. Nedham did not sign his name, probably because the work might have more effect if not identified with a known government propagandist.

115 Fallon points out (*Milton in Government*, 121–39) that the Council Record Books no longer provide a good record of Milton's activities, since Cromwell took foreign af-

fairs directly into his own hands and Thurloe, who acted as a foreign minister, tended not to record which secretary performed what tasks.

116 In April, 1654 a treaty with the United Provinces ended that war, awarding damages to England and a close alliance, though not the near-annexation England had at first demanded. In April also, a treaty with Sweden established free commerce and a political alliance between those two countries. In July a treaty with Portugal conceded everything England demanded, including a large indemnity for damages inflicted by royalist fleets in Portuguese ports. And on September 14 a treaty with Denmark opened the Sound to English commerce on the same terms as the Dutch.

117 Milton's writings continued to be valued as a weapon in the English cause: on April 1, 1653 the council ordered that John Dury's French translation of *Eikonoklastes* be sent to France without duty (*LR* III, 327). Booksellers also sought to cash in on his enhanced reputation: in 1654 unsold copies of the *Reason of Church-Government* and *Apology for Smectymnuus* were reprinted together.

118 Milton's initial claim against the Copes has not been found; on June 16 he refers to it as initiated "longe since" and "lately" contested by them; he began a suit in Chancery June 16, 1654 which dragged on at least till 1659, its resolution unknown. See J. Milton French, *Milton in Chancery: New Chapters in the Lives of the Poet and his Father* (New York and London, 1939), 124–45, 189–205, 325–95. Elizabeth Ashworth probably began her suit in February, 1654; it was answered by Christopher for his brother on February 22, and also dragged on for many years.

119 Milton may have taken note periodically of his mother-in-law's petitions and suits over her illegally seized property at Forest Hill, but he was not directly involved. See chapter 8, pp. 257–8 and notes 125–6. Her claims were periodically reviewed and investigated throughout 1652 and 1653, until they were at last settled and she was ordered a rebate of £192.4.1 on May 4, 1652 (*LR* III, 119–20, 260–8, 280–1, 293–5, 308–10, 325, 328–33, 335–9, 341–3, 345- 7, 352–3, 357–66, 374, 412–13). Christopher Milton acted as counsel for Mrs Powell and her son Richard in some of her suits.

120 G. H. Turnbull, *Hartlib, Dury, and Comenius: Gleanings from Hartlib's Papers* (London, 1947), 42. A mark in the margin indicates that this portion is to be communicated to Milton.

121 Ibid., 42–3. In this letter also a line in the margin marks the passage pertaining to Milton. The source named is Godofred Hotton, a minister in Amsterdam.

122 See chapter 10, pp. 323–4 and Sellin, "Alexander More Before the Synod of Utrecht."

123 *Defensio Secunda* (London, 1654).

124 Nine are members of the Council of State: Major-General John Desborough, Lieutenant-General Charles Fleetwood, Major-General John Lambert, Henry Lawrence, Edward Mountague, Sir Gilbert Pickering, Walter Strickland, William Sydenham, and Philip Sidney, Lord Lisle.

125 Bulstrode Whitelocke is a less obvious case. He had opposed the dissolution of the Rump and was attacked by Cromwell on that occasion, but Cromwell had recently appointed him ambassador to Sweden (September 14, 1653), largely, Whitelocke thought, to get him out of the way. See Cromwell, *Writings and Speeches* ed. Abbott, II, 638, 642; III, 98–102.

126 Masson, IV, 607.

127 Fairfax is enjoying a "most delightful and glorious retirment, which is the end of all

labors and human action, even the greatest." Milton also revises Fairfax's motives for retirement, which stemmed, as he knew, from Fairfax's strong objection to the execution of Charles and the invasion of Scotland. Milton suggests rather that he retired for ill health and only because he had firm confidence in his successor, Cromwell, as a "strong and faithful" defender of liberty and English interests (669–70).

128 Anthony à Wood reports that Milton presented a copy (now lost) to the Bodleian on June 11, 1654 (Bodleian Wood Ms F.47, fol. 626).

129 *CPW* IV.2, 863–5. Marvell also refers to other letters now lost: Milton's initial letter to Marvell giving him these commissions, Milton's letter to Bradshaw, and Marvell's first letter to Milton to which this is a follow-up, offering a more complete account. If Milton answered this letter, it also is lost. With the comment about the recommendation, Marvell may be hinting that he would still like to have a post in the government secretariat.

130 *CPW* IV.2, 865–7. These Oldenburg letters have not been found. The two men became closer friends and exchanged several later letters. See chapter 10, pp. 000–00.

131 He begins graciously by apologizing for not writing before, and by inviting Oldenburg to write in English if he wants to hone his skills, since he uses it "more accurately and successfully than any other foreigner I know" (*CPW* IV.2, 866).

132 In Thomas Washbourne's *Divine Poems* (London, 1654), *c.* July 28.

133 *LR* III, 407, 411–12. Vlacq's editions have a somewhat altered title: Joannis Miltoni Angli *Defensio Secunda Pro Populo Anglicano*. The first carries a false imprint (London: Newcomb, 1654), the second his own imprint (The Hague: Vlacq, 1652) as well as a exculpatory preface defending himself as one who acted even-handedly in the More/Milton quarrel, motivated only by commercial profit.

134 Two letters (June 29) are to the Count of Oldenberg: the first assures him that his Safeguard will be confirmed by the Protector's authority; the second thanks him for a gift of horses delivered by his son (*CPW* V.2, 667–70). A letter of July 25 to the King of Portugal is the usual *recreditif* praising the departing Portuguese ambassador with whom a treaty has just been concluded (673–4). Another (September 4) to the Spanish prime minister acknowledges the appointment of a new ambassador to replace Cardenas and offers polite expressions of friendship (677). A letter of August 29 congratulates Charles Gustavus, who has just ascended the Swedish throne at Queen Christina's abdication, and assures him that the recently signed treaty will remain in force (675–6). A letter, *c.* July 18 to the governor of the Spanish Netherlands is about a private matter: property seized from an Englishman there by another Englishman as satisfaction for a debt claimed (671–2).

135 Masson, IV, 639.

136 See chapter 6, p. 181, and chapter 8, pp. 251, 259–60.

137 See chapter 3, p. 60.

138 For example, Psalm 27:14: "Wait on the Lord; be of good courage, and he shall strengthen thine heart." Also Psalm 37:7; Isaiah 33:2; Luke 12:36–7.

139 See Haskin, *Milton's Burden of Interpretation*, 113.

140 Cf. Spenser's "Hymne of Heavenly Love" (ll. 64–8) for a parallel with the angels' service: "There they . . . / About him wait, and on his will depend, Wither with nimble wings to cut the skies, / When he them on his messages doth send, Or on his owne dread presence to attend" (*Variorum* II.2, 466–7).

141 See Douglas Stewart, "Speaking to the World: The *Ad Hominem* Logic of Milton's Polemics," *The Seventeenth Century* 11 (1996), 47–57; and Lieb, *Milton and the Culture of Violence*, 181–225.
142 Page 554. See chapter 5, p. 150 for his similar statement in *Reason of Church-Government.*
143 See p. 289 and note 54.
144 Milton calls her Claudia Pelletta in his *Pro Se Defensio*.
145 The documents are still there. See Kester Svendson, "Milton and Alexander More: New Documents," *Journal of English and Germanic Philology* 60 (1961), 799–806, and *CPW* IV.2, 687–93.
146 See pp. 294–5 and note 75. Milton claimed that More undertook to defend Salmasius who in return promised him the chair of theology at Middleburg but, as Paul Sellin shows in "Alexander Morus Before the Hof van Holland," 1–11, More received that call in 1649. Since Milton's *Defensio* only appeared in 1651, the Salmasius–More collaboration on the response to it, and therefore the More–Pontia affair, had to occur in 1652. Sellin also shows that the court case turned entirely on the issue of breach of promise, not the facts of the case. See chapter 10.
147 Page 660. There were questions raised about More's orthodoxy and licentiousness at Middleburgh, but as Paul Sellin notes, "Alexander Morus before the Synod of Utrecht," 239–49, More left Middleburgh at his own volition, to accept the post at Amsterdam. See chapter 10, pp. 322–4.
148 See p. 292.
149 Pages 569–71. At times the language hints at sodomy (579, 630). Milton also visits on More versions of charges leveled against himself: More has procured "the most brutal of all divorces" in seducing Pontia under cover of an engagement; she was the "royal property" of Salmasius and he has turned her into a republic (610).
150 Loewenstein, "Defense," in Loewenstein and Turner, eds, *Politics, Poetics, and Hermeneutics,* 187–8.
151 *CPW* IV.1, 553–6. He responds to charges that he is a mere unknown by insisting that he has not rushed into print and that at one point in their lives Homer and Demosthenes were also unknown. He makes an ambiguous reference to a work long withheld from publication (the long-considered epic?), which would have brought fame; and he comments even more ambiguously that he would not have published "even this, unless a fitting opportunity presented itself" (607–8).
152 Pages 589–90. The first sentence quotes Hebrews 11:34, the text Milton has used as his motto for some time; see chapter 8, p. 257.
153 Pages 605–6. The assertion that wisdom is not gained through books, and that the highest magnanimity is the renunciation of kingship, are later articulated by Christ in *Paradise Regained* IV, 321–30; II, 481–3 – further evidence of the ideality of this portrait.
154 See chapter 6, p. 190.

Chapter 10 "I . . . Still Bear Up and Steer Right Onward" 1654–1658

1 A satirical poem found in his possession though perhaps not by him denounced Cromwell as the "ape of a King / A tragical Caesar acted by a clown." Overton denied the

conspiracy charges and claimed he had not written but merely copied the poem (Masson, V, 163–4).

2 For Vlacq's pirated editions see chapter 9, note 133. This combined (duodecimo) edition has the title *Joannis Miltoni Defensio Secunda Pro Populo Anglicano; . . . Accessit Alexandri Mori Ecclesiastae, Sacrarumque litterarum Professoris Fides Publica, Contra calumnias Joannis Miltoni Scurrae* (The Hague, 1654). A note to the reader at the end of the book explains why it is incomplete and promises to publish the rest when available. I quote from the selections, including the prefaces by George Crantz and Vlacq, included in *CPW* IV.2, 1,086–128, trans. Paul Blackford.

3 He also quotes Salmasius on the Bontia affair in terms that invite an unintended meaning, as Milton gleefully pointed out: "If More erred at all in this respect [had an affair with Bontia] I am a pander and my wife is a bawd" (*CPW* IV.2, 1,087, 803).

4 See chapter 9, p. 292. More quotes in their entirety Nieupoort's two letters to him reporting his unsuccessful efforts to persuade Milton that, since he erred in naming More the author of *Clamor*, he should stop publication of the *Defensio Secunda*.

5 Page 1,103. See chapter 7, pp. 226–7.

6 See chapter 4, p. 108.

7 *Alexandri Mori . . . Supplementum Fidei Publicae, Contra Calumniae Joannis Miltoni* (The Hague, 1655).

8 The translation of this passage in *CM* IX, 229 makes better sense of the Latin than that in *CPW*: "That More may not unbraid me with having taken another two years to put him to the rout, I have had by me this my defence, now two months; and such was the longing desire with which I expected this supplement to the *Public Faith*, that the time seemed an age to me."

9 *Joannis Miltoni Angli Pro Se Defensio Contra Alexandrum Morum Ecclesiasten, Libelli famosi, cui titulus, Regii sanguinis clamor ad coelum adversus Parricidas Anglicanos, authorem recté dictum* (London, 1655).

10 He was the son of a noted theologian in Geneva, Frederick Spanheim, who had long been an enemy to More and Salmasius.

11 *CPW* IV.2, 873–4. Milton's excuse is that he received the letter, inexplicably, almost three months late, and then delayed almost another three months in answering it. Spanheim's letter is lost but is quoted in the *Pro Se Defensio*. Milton also refers to other Genevans – Jean Louis Calandrin and the Turretini brothers – who may have provided some information; he proposes that subsequent correspondence between himself and Spanheim be sent through the Turretinis, one of whom is in England.

12 Introduction, *CPW* IV.2, 689–90, 722, n. 55. Milton Latinizes the woman's name as Claudia Pelletta.

13 *CPW* IV.2, 757, n. 140.

14 *LR* III, 426. Dury denies that he informed More that Milton meant to attack him in the *Defensio Secunda* but acknowledges that Hotton might have passed on that news. Several of Dury's letters contain greetings for Milton. For Dury's reports about denials of More's authorship, see chapter 9, pp. 300–1.

15 *LR* III, 442. An unsigned letter to Hartlib from Leyden suggests that Milton write to Geneva and to Salmasius's widow for further information about More.

16 *ME* I, 34–5. See chapter 9, pp. 284–5. Another Leyden correspondent was probably

Phillippe Diodati, nephew of John Diodati and one of the ministers charged to plead the case against More at the April synod.

17 *CPW* IV.2, 871. A Dutch translation of the *Doctrine and Discipline* was published in 1655.

18 LR III, 443–4: "The trueth is Morus durst not add the [court] sentence against Pontia; for the charges are recompensed and where there is payement of charges (that is to say the action of Pontia is good; but that the proofes fayle hir) yea I beleeve that Morus was faine to purge [perjure] himself upon oath." See Sellin, "Morus before the Hof van Holland," 1–11.

19 *CPW* IV.2, 809–10. Paul R. Sellin, "Alexander More before the Synod of Utrecht," *Huntington Library Quarterly* 58 (1996), 239–48, points out that the whole matter was again addressed at the synod of Tergou, April 23–28, 1659, when More's behavior with Guerret was described much as Milton had it from his sources. That synod also charged him with licentious behavior with several other women, in Amsterdam and Middleburg, and with frequenting brothels. Milton had wind of some of those scandals: besides Peletta of Geneva and Guerret of Leyden he alludes to a "heroine" of the "Tibaltiana," a maid whose fate was likened to Pontia's, a strumpet of Amsterdam, and a widow whose chastity More assailed while consoling her for the death of her husband (*CPW* IV.2, 777–8, n. 199; 809–10, n. 277).

20 See chapter 5, pp. 137–8, and chapter 6, pp. 182–4.

21 *CPW* IV.2, 744. In regard to the prophets, he comments that the "rabbins . . . set down their Keri, for that which is written plainly. As for me, I confess I prefer to be plain of speech with the sacred writers then speciously decent with the futile Rabbins" (745).

22 See chapter 9, p. 301. The representations of the Dutch ambassador Nieupoort he traces back to More, and he seems to believe, or wants to believe, that both of Dury's letters identify the royalist Hotton as his informant, thought in fact only one does so.

23 See especially chapter 5, p. 152 and chapter 6, pp. 177–8.

24 Pages 701–2. He repeats the same either/or proposition soon after: "you are he whom I declare either to be the author of that abominable outcry or to be justly regarded as the author" (704).

25 Pages 712–13. To the same point he claims that More's statement to Hotton denying authorship itself argues some involvement: "this ought to be called your manifest confession that you are a party either in composing this libel, or, with a very few others, in procuring its composition; that if you are not the author, yet certainly you are his ally and assistant; that either by your labor or by your counsel this book was published. If this be the case . . . I need not fear . . . to have accused you falsely if either I have affirmed that you are the very author, or have counted you in his company" (710).

26 Of the eight letters Milton excerpts, three are to Hartlib from Dury (identified), two are to Milton (one anonymous, one by Spanheim but not named), and three others are also anonymous but one of them, from Leyden, had been printed in *Mercurius Politicus* (September 27, 1652).

27 *CPW* IV.2, 774. See chapter 4, p. 98–9.

28 See chapter 7, pp. 226–7.

29 Michael Lieb, *Milton and the Culture of Violence* (Ithaca, NY, 1994), 217–25.

30 See chapter 9, p. 281.

31 His offense would not qualify as blasphemy by the Blasphemy Act of 1650 (see chapter

8, p. 251), but by the Blasphemy Act of 1648 it would warrant the death penalty; as a repeat offender he would at least face a long imprisonment or banishment.

32 George Fox, *Journal*, ed. Norman Penney (London, 1924), 105–6.

33 Marvell's unsigned *First Anniversary of the Government under O.C.* (London, 1655) was probably written in late December, 1654; it was advertised in *Mercurius Politicus* (January 1–18, 1655) as "newly printed and published"; Thomason dates it January 17. The work eulogizes Cromwell as another Gideon – a judge mightier than kings – satirizes his opponents, and emphasizes his indispensability. The poem pays tribute to Milton with an allusion to his Nativity ode: "And Stars still fall, and still the Dragons Tail / Swinges the Volumes of its horrid Flail" (ll. 151–2). Marvell also wrote a poem on the marriage of Cromwell's daughter Mary to Lord Fauconberg (November 19, 1657).

34 BL Stowe Ms 142, ff. 60, 61 has Milton's signature (by proxy) for his quarter salary. In the Council Order Books for April 17, 1655 the order for Milton appears in a separate paragraph following the sentence announcing the reduction of Gualter Frost, Jr.'s salary from £400 to £300: "That the former yearly Sallary of Mr. *John Milton* of 288li &. formerly charged to the Councells Contingencies, be reduced to one hundred and fiftie pounds per Ann, and payd to him dureing his life out of his Highnesse Exchequer:" SP 25/76/30; *CSPD* 8:127 (1655). There are no salary entries for Nedham, John Hall, or George Vaux, perhaps indicating some intent to terminate their formal services.

35 The changes occurred but are not formally recorded. Nedham continued to receive his salary, as did George Vaux. Frost's salary was paid at £365, not £300; Milton's salary as of October 25, 1659 is listed as £200 (Masson, V, 177–83). Robet T. Fallon, *Milton in Government* (University Park, Penn., 1993), 130–9, notes that financial records for the considerable expenses of the secretary of state's office have been lost or destroyed, and with them records of Milton's salary and the full range of his services.

36 The letters were printed in June as part of the Protector's effort to marshal support for the cause, in *A Collection of Several Papers . . . Concerning the Bloody and Barbarous Massacres*, ed. Jean Baptiste Stouppe (London, 1655), 34–5. Later in June a Latin translation appeared intended to enlist international support. The quotes are from a letter dated May 8, and from *Weekly Post*, no. 231 (June 12–19, 1655), 1,844.

37 Samuel Morland, *The History of the Evangelical Churches of the Valleys of Piemont* (London, 1658), sigs a v, a 2.

38 See Fallon, *Milton in Government*, 143–51. Attribution to Milton rests on close parallels between the speech and the several letters and Milton's sonnet, and on the fact that the speech and letters were copied in the same hand and deposited as a single bundle in the public archives. Also the youthful Morland, who had but three days to prepare for his mission, would likely not have been entrusted to draft a speech in the Protector's own name, and he does not claim credit for it in his *History*.

39 In the Skinner manuscript a draft of the letter to the Duke of Savoy is dated May 10 (*CPW* V.2, 685–7); four letters to other Protestant powers, also dated May 25, were rough drafted some days earlier, and then some of their contents reshuffled.

40 Pages 688–97. In the letter to the Swedish king, Cromwell's desire to form and lead a Protestant coalition had to give way to a tactful recognition of Charles X's superior claim as leader of international Protestantism. But Cromwell asserts his own leadership forcefully in the letter to the United Provinces, urging that if Savoy persists in seeking to destroy "those men among whom our religion was handed down from the very first

doctors of the Gospels and was preserved uncorrupted, or else restored to its pristine wholeness long before it was among other nations, we swear that we are prepared to seize upon some common plan, along with yourselves and other reformed brethren and allies, which will make it more completely possible for us to look properly to the welfare and relief of so many afflicted men" (692–3).

41 The sonnet is not in the Trinity manuscript (*TM*). It was first published in 1673 with the title, "On the late Massacher in Piemont," and I quote from that edition.

42 Pages 706–7. Responding to an inquiry from the Prince of Transylvania about joining a Protestant League if one existed, Cromwell (May 31) welcomed his cooperation on matters of common concern to Protestants and recycled a passage on the Waldensian matter (702–4).

43 Only *Mercurius Politicus* and *The Public Intelligencer* were to continue after October 3, appearing respectively on Thursdays and Mondays.

44 Cyriack Skinner's *Life* is confusing about dates and sequence, but he seems to suggest that the *Latin Thesaurus* came first: "It was now [i.e. when Milton had a substitute at the office of secretary and had work sent home to him] that hee began that laborious work of amassing out of all the Classic Authors, both in Prose and Verse, a *Latin Thesaurus* to the emendation of that done by Stephanus; Also the composing *Paradise Lost* And the framing a *Body of Divinity* out of the Bible: All which, notwithstanding the several Calamities befalling him in his fortunes, hee finish'd after the Restoration: As also the *Brittish history* down to the Conquest . . . & had begun a *Greek Thesaurus* (*EL* 29). John Aubrey on the strength of Edward Phillips's information says Milton began *Paradise Lost* two years before the king came in, i.e. 1658 (*EL* 13).

45 Two octavo volumes "all or mostly taken from the *Latin Thesaurus* writ by Joh. Milton Uncle to Edw. Phillips" were said by Anthony à Wood (*Athenae Oxoniensis* IV, 763) to have been published by Edward Phillips in 1684 as *Enchiridion Linguae Latinae* and *Speculum Linguae Latinae*, but no copies have been found. Toland reports that "*Milton's Thesaurus Linguae Latinae* . . . has bin of great use to Dr. [Adam] *Littleton* in compiling his Dictionary" (*EL* 192). See chapter 14, p. 507 and n. 93.

46 *EL* 74; see chapter 9, pp. 293–4. The interconnections are interesting: Marvell obviously knew Skinner, as he wrote of his pleasure that Skinner was now "got near" Milton; also, Skinner is the brother of that Anne Sandleir who was a correspondent and friend of Roger Williams; see chapter 9, p. 285 and n. 38.

47 See J. M. Smart, *The Sonnets of Milton* (Glasgow, 1921), 111–14; for Oldenburg's continual friendly greetings to Lawrence, see pp. 342, 345.

48 This "Invisible College" interested in experimental science and Baconian reformations of knowledge formed the nucleus of the Royal Society after the Restoration; Oldenburg was to become its first secretary.

49 These sonnets were first published in 1673; Skinner copied ll. 5–14 of the first sonnet to him into *TM*. The Lawrence sonnet is not in *TM*. My quotations are from *Poems*, 1673.

50 This sonnet, like those to Fairfax, Cromwell, and Vane, was withheld from publication in 1673 because of Milton's reference to losing his vision in the service of liberty; it was published with those poems in 1694, in Phillips's "Life of Milton" prefixed to the *Letters of State*. In that publication, though not in *TM*, it bears the title, "To Mr. CYRIAC SKINNER Upon his Blindness." The phrase, "three years day" almost certainly bears the very usual meaning "space of time"; cf. Shakespeare, 2 Henry VI

2.1.2: "I saw not better sport these seven years' day," and *Variorum* 2.2, 482–3. I quote the text from *TM*.

51 A letter from Sandelands (April 11, 1654) indicates that he had employed "Mr John Phillips (Mr Miltons Kinsman)" in gathering information about crown lands in Scotland (*LR* III, 367), and had received an interim report from him. See chapter 9, p. 292.

52 *A Satyr against Hypocrites* (London, 1655). On March 14, 1655 this work was registered mistakenly with the Stationers in the name of Edward Phillips and the publisher Nathanial Brooke. The second edition (also 1655) was longer and more polished; it omits a particularly obscene passage but adds others. Edward Phillips in *Theatrum Poetarum,* Part II (London, 1675), 115, assigns it to his brother and credits Milton with forming his style.

53 *A Satyr against Hypocrites,* 13.

54 For Phillips's *Responsio* to Alexander More, written under Milton's supervision, see chapter 8, pp. 258–9.

55 For example, "There stood the Font, in times of Christianity, / But now 'tis tak'n down, men call it Vanity" (3); "These are the men that plague and over-run / Like Goths and Vandals all Religion" (21).

56 *Satyr against Hypocrites,* 22

57 J. P., *Tears of the Indians* (London, 1656), a translation of Las Casas's *Destruycion de las Indias.* The dedication is signed J. Phillips.

58 At least five went to France. Three to Louis XIV asked him to honor the treaty of November 3, 1655 and restore merchandise seized from English ships; and a pair to the king and Mazarin introduce William Lockhart as the new ambassador to France (*CPW* V.2, 713- 14, 719–20, 729–30, 735–6). A letter to the Doge of Venice (December, 1655) sought return of an English ship forced to sail in the Turkish fleet and then captured by the Venetians (715–16). Two letters to the rulers of Algiers (April, 1656) promise to help resolve their complaints that English ships and flags are used by the French and Dutch as cover to attack Algerian ports and ships; a third (June, 1656) asks release of an English ship and goods captured by an Algerian fleet (723–6, 740–1). Four letters to the United Provinces (727–8, 737–9, 760–1) concern a ship captured at Flushing and its goods sold (April 1); a follow-up complaint about Englishmen unsuccessful in their efforts to claim an inheritance in Dutch courts (May 30); shipowners carrying Dutch insurance baulked in their efforts to collect when their ship was lost (May 31); and an annual stipend for an invention 33 years in arrears and now owed to the English heir of the inventor (September 10, 1656). A letter to Portugal in July concerned a debt the Brazil company owes English tradesmen for transportation and storage (745).

59 They are dated only by the month. The first two are addressed to King John IV, the third to his chief minister Count Odemira (*CPW* V.2, 748–53).

60 Two letters (April 10 and July 30, 1656) lavishly praise the departing Swedish diplomats who successfully completed an Anglo-Swedish treaty in July, 1656; the second expresses Cromwell's wish that God may keep the king "unharmed to defend His church and to be the support of the Swedish state" (*CPW* V.2, 731–2, 746–7). A special letter to Charles X accompanies a general passport for George Romswickel (June 13), asking protection and safety for him from all Protestant powers. Both commend Romswickel for relinquishing "Popish superstition" and high office to embrace the reformed religion through "his own study and labor" (742–4).

61 He enumerates the dangers: the Swiss cantons are "anxiously expecting new commotions"

stirred up by the pope and Spain; the counsels of the Spanish "are again devising for the Waldensians of the Alps that same slaughter and ruin which they most cruelly brought upon them last year"; the German Protestants under the emperor are under siege; and "we ourselves are occupied with a war against Spain" (*CPW* V.2, 756–9).

62 *CPW* V.2, 755. The letter was perhaps sent with Christiern Bonde when he departed soon after August 21. There is no day date.

63 Cited in Fallon, *Milton in Government*, 173–5. As Fallon argues, Bonde's reports indicate that Milton worked on the entire treaty and its various drafts. It is published in *CM* XIII, 564–91, but not in *CPW*.

64 Bulstrode Whitelocke, *Memorials of the English Affairs, from the Beginning of the Reign of Charles the First to the Happy Restoration of King Charles the Second*, 4 vols (Oxford, 1853), IV, 257.

65 J. P., *Sportive Wit* (London, 1656). This work was said to have been collected by "a Club of sparkling Wits, viz. C. J. B. F. J. M. W. T"; the Epistle Dedicatory is signed J. P. The book was registered March 17, 1656 and published soon after.

66 Reported in *Nouvelles Ordinaires de Londres*, no. 309, p. 1,238 (May 1, 1656).

67 *CPW* I, 818. See chapter 5, p. 151.

68 Edward published the Montalbán novels together under the titles *The Illustrious Shepherdess* and *The Imperious Brother* (London, 1656, *c.* February 12). They were dedicated to aristocratic ladies in a bid for patronage. William Drummond of Hawthornden, *Poems*, ed. E[dward] P[hillips] (London, 1656).

69 The transcription in Milton's presentation copy of *Eikonoklastes* (MS 4o Rawl. 408), "ex dono Authoris. Jun. XI. MMCLVI," seems to be in the hand of Thomas Barlow, who had succeeded Rouse as librarian in 1652. See chapter 8, note 79. For Edward Phillips's changes of residence see Parker, II, 989–90.

70 E. P., *The Mysteries of Love & Eloquence: Or, the Arts of Wooing and Complementing* (London, 1658). This work also draws on Thomas Blount's *Glossographia* (London, 1656). Among the Milton borrowings are some heads of chapters, many particular examples, a much condensed final chapter on Ramist method, and a concluding section insisting that the poet reaches beyond the usual methods for greater effect and power. For Milton's *Artis Logicae* see chapter 7, p. 208, and chapter 14, pp. 497–8.

71 See William Godwin, *Lives of Edward and John Phillips* (London, 1815). John Phillips may have edited *Wit and Drollery* (London, 1656, *c.* January 18); the preface is signed J. P.

72 The Latin is "mihi omnium necessitudinum loco fuit," *CM* XII, 78–83. Her departure and the delivery of this letter were delayed, as her pass for Ireland was not granted until October 7 (*CSPD*, 1656–7, p. 583).

73 *LR* IV, 118–19; the album is in the Bibliothek der Vadiana, Stadtbibliothek, St Gall, Switzerland. "Joannis Milto" is on one line; about half an inch below, "nius."

74 [Henry Vane], *A Healing Question Propounded and resolved upon occasion of the late publique and seasonable Call to Humiliation, in order to love and union among the honest party, and with a desire to apply Balsoms to the wound, before it becomes incurable* (London, 1656). It was registered with the Stationers on May 28.

75 Vane insisted that the right to parliamentary elections is "the natural right which the whole party of Honest men adhering to this Cause, are by successe of their Arms restored unto, and may claim as their undeniable privilege" (4); that sovereignty must be

in the whole body of the people adhering to the cause "and by them derived unto their successive Representatives" (15); and that religious liberty must be secured as a fundamental with which magistrates may not meddle, but rather content themselves with "dealings in the things of this life between man and man" (6).

76 [Nedham] *The Excellencie of a Free-State: Or, The Right Constitution of a Common-Wealth* (London, 1656, *c.* June 29). See Blair Worden, "Marchamont Nedham and the Beginnings of English Republicanism," in David Wootten, ed., *Republicanism, Liberty, and Commercial Society, 1649–1776* (Stanford, Calif., 1994), 45–81. Also, Worden, "Milton and Marchamont Nedham," in David Armitage, Armand Himy, and Quentin Skinner, eds, *Milton and Republicanism* (Cambridge, 1995), 156–80.

77 Nedham, *Excellencie of a Free-State*, 242. He critiques what he sees as present or imminent dangers in the Protectorate: a Council of State not constantly subject to parliament threatens to become a tyranny; an elective monarchy (proposed for Cromwell) will soon turn into a hereditary one; and an army not subject to the people's representatives will impose on liberty.

78 Page 18. Some advantages he lists are: that the people are the best keepers of their own liberties and the best judges of their own interests; that republics nourish virtue, promote liberty, and discourage the vice and luxury that lead to tyranny; and that free states make nations prosperous, as England may see from the commercial success of the United Provinces.

79 Ibid., 245.

80 Harrington, *The Common-Wealth of Oceana* (London, 1656). It was entered in the Stationers Register September 19, and *Mercurius Politicus* for October 29 to November 6, 1656 advertises it as "newly published." Harrington's preface states that he distributed the book among three presses to get it out while parliament was sitting and might revamp the government. We do not know when Skinner became interested in Harrington, but in 1659 he was a member of Harrington's political club, the Rota.

81 See Blair Worden, "Harrington and 'The Commonwealth of Oceana,'" and "Harrington's 'Oceana,'" in David Wootton, ed., *Republicanism, Liberty, and Commercial Society*, 82–138; also James Harrington, *Political Works,* ed. J. G. A. Pocock (Cambridge, 1977), 6 n.

82 Harrington also implied a criticism of Cromwell's blue laws being enforced by the major-generals: "to tell men that they are free, and yet to curb the genious of a people in a lawfull Recreation unto which they are naturally inclined, is to tell a tale of a Tub" (205).

83 Harrington devises a tombstone for Olphaeus Megaletor, implicitly urging Cromwell to seek such titles instead of a royal title: "Lord Archon and sole Legislator of Oceana, Pater Patriae, the Greatest of Captaines, the Best of Princes, the happiest of Legislators, the most Sincere of Christians."

84 For a penetrating analysis of the ambiguities surrounding Nayler's gesture, see Leo Damrosch, *The Sorrows of the Quaker Jesus* (Cambridge, Mass., 1996).

85 He did intervene to lighten Nayler's sufferings in Bridewell.

86 Cromwell, W*ritings and Speeches*, ed. Allen, IV, 417–18.

87 This is the plausible speculation of Smart (*Sonnets,* 121–4), who discovered most of what is known about Katherine Woodcock. The family were supported by wealthy relatives and lived rent-free in Hackney, in Vyner's picturesque Elizabethan mansion.

88 *The Registers of St. Mary Aldermary, London . . . 1558 to 1754*, Publications of the Harleian Society, LXI (London, 1931), 152, record the marriage on November 12, 1656: "The Agreement and Intention of Marriage betwene John Milton Esqr. of the Parish of Margeretts in Westminster: and Mrs Katharine Woodcocke of the Parish of Marys in Aldermanbury: was Published three severall Markett Days in three severall weekes (vizt) on Wensday the 22th and Monday the 27th of October and on Monday the 3d of November and no exceptions being made against their Intentions They were Acording to the Actt of Parlaimentt: Maryed the 12th of November by Sr John Dethicke Knight and Alderman one of the Justices of Peace for this Citty of London."

89 I quote from the version in TM.

90 *LR* IV, 216. Ward was professor of rhetoric at Gresham College. His notes, sent to Milton's editor Thomas Birch, are in BL Add. MS 4,320, p. 232; they are based on a visit to Milton's daughter Deborah Clarke around 1727, and to his granddaughter Mrs Elizabeth Foster on February 10, 1738. On many matters he is an unreliable reporter, as are his informants, but there is no reason to doubt this information.

91 Major-Generals John Lambert, Colonel William Sydenham, John Desborough, and Charles Fleetwood remained strongly opposed, and petitions were sent in from many regiments. Also, Anabaptist ministers and many gathered churches protested vigorously, and the Fifth Monarchists planned an uprising for April. See Charles H. Firth, *The Last Years of the Protectorate, 1656–1658*, 2 vols (New York, 1964), I, 107–66.

92 Excluded were Roman Catholics and all who fought against parliament or plotted against the Protectorate unless reconciled, and also atheists, blasphemers, scoffers against religion, execrable heretics, profaners of the Lord's Day, drunkards, and others not of "good conversation."

93 Firth, *Last Years of the Protectorate*, I, 167–200.

94 See chapter 9, p. 316. For Cromwell's self-presentation, see Laura Lunger Knoppers, *Constructing Cromwell* (Cambridge, 2000), 129–30.

95 [Edward Sexby and Silas Titus], *Killing Noe Murder* (printed in Holland, 1657, *c.* May), sig. B 2. The title page lists a fictitious William Allen as author. Milton is cited (sig. B2) to answer an objection that tyrannicide is permitted in the Bible by God's inspiration but not in contemporary society: "I answer with the learned Milton, that if God commanded these things, tis a signe they were lawfull and are commendable."

96 *Mercurius Politicus*, no. 252, 7,643–44, 7,674–5 (March 19–26); *Mercurius Politicus*, no. 255, 7,675, 7,690–2 (March 26–April 2). In the *Case of the Commonwealth* (see chapter 9, p. 249) Nedham also asserted the Machiavellian principle that forms of government must be suited to the nature of the people, but here, with evident irony, he asserts the cynical view that one form of government is as good as another, monarchy as conducive to liberty as a republic.

97 *Mercurius Politicus*, no. 256, 7,706 (April 2–9).

98 Two parallel letters to Louis XIV and Mazarin (*c.* September 25) call attention to ships and goods seized by a French privateer, and a third to the king concerns a London merchant unable to complete a purchase of hides from a captured ship. Two letters (October 1656) are to the King of Portugal: one introduces Thomas Maynard as consul for trade, the other concerns a ship and goods seized from one Thomas Evans. A letter to the Senate of Hamburg (October 16) threatens retaliation unless justice is obtained in a long-standing litigation over goods willed to but withheld from two English citizens.

A letter (October 22) to the King of Sweden urges payment of the arrears owed a professional soldier who has fought for Sweden. A letter to the King of France (January? 1657) presses an earlier complaint about the seizure in Dunkirk of a ship belonging to the former mayor of London, John Dethicke. A request to the King of Denmark asks restoration of merchants' goods improperly seized with a ship that refused to pay tariffs (*CPW* V.2, 768–74, 780–1, 784–5).

99 This letter's presence in the Columbia manuscript means Milton was the translator; very likely he translated many incoming letters for which evidence is not available (*CPW* V.2, 775–6).

100 The credentialling letter was dated April 10. Bradshaw, then envoy to Hamburg, could not get official permission to enter Russia and so had to return. On April 10 also, Milton prepared a letter to Danzig to seek the release, or more lenient treatment, of a captured Swedish general.

101 Probably he was not yet 21, since Milton addresses him as "adolescens" (*CPW* VII, 495).

102 The atlas Milton originally inquired about is not known: perhaps Jan Blaeu's *Geographia,* 11 vols (Amsterdam, 1662), four volumes of which were advertised in 1650 for 150 guldens or Dutch florins. John Jansen's *Novus Atlas,* 8 vols (Amsterdam, 1658), was not complete until 1658. Individual volumes of both editions were on sale earlier.

103 *LR* IV, 138–9; *EL* 30. The man is William Spenser. He appealed to Cromwell, who wrote on March 27 asking that the lands be restored, noting that William Spenser had renounced the popish religion and referring to Edmund Spenser's tract "touching the reduction of the Irish to civility." It is not clear what Milton's good offices were: perhaps a recommendation to Cromwell, perhaps a draft of Cromwell's letter (the Spenser reference sounds like Milton), perhaps some appeal through Lady Ranelagh (Edmund Spenser's wife was also a Boyle).

104 *CPW* IV.1, 485, 491.

105 The Byzantine histories are: Theophanes, *Chronographia* (a chronicle of events AD 284–813); Codinus, *Excerpta de Antiquitibus Constantinopolitanis* (treating the history, topography and monuments of Constantinople); and Manasses, *Breviarum Historicum* (the 7,000-line metrical history). All were published in sumptuous folios in Paris in 1655. He also asked for the *Liber Pontificalis* (Book of Popes) attributed to a ninth-century anti-pope Anastasius Bibliothecarius. In addition, he wanted, if they had been published (they had not), the *Annales* of Michael Glycas (a history of the world from the Creation to AD 1118), and the twelfth-century history by Johannas Sinnamus, a continuation of the *Alexiad* by Anna Comnena. The books would be paid for and dispatched through Thurloe's agent, Jean Baptiste Stouppe.

106 A letter in August, 1657 to the French ambassador complained of the seizure of the *Speedwell* and the sale of her cargo at Brest, and a second letter to him in October asked for attention to a disputed claim over ownership of goods seized on the *Maria* (*CPW* V.2, 791–2, 805–6). A letter of September 10 asks the Grand Duke of Tuscany to seize the captain of *The Little Lewis* who stole what he contracted to transport for the Turks; a later letter in December asks for the release of the man, ship, and merchandise (801–2, 812–13), since the Turks' claim has been satisfied. A fifth letter (October 22) to the Doge and Senate of Venice asks help in obtaining the release of an English ship captain seized by the Turks while fighting for Venice, and enslaved for five years (808–9).

107 Five brief letters of the same date introduce and bespeak protection for Jephson from the rulers of Brandenburg, Hamburg, Bremen, Lubeck, and Norway whom he would greet en route.

108 One letter (which exists in two versions) went to the United Provinces, and one to Holland, recognizing it as "so great a part" of the confederation (*CPW*, V.2, 814–17). Issues which brought the two nations again to the brink of war involved shipping, trade, and the Dutch war with Portugal which threatened England's use of the harbor of Lisbon for its war against Spain.

109 These included some court cases: on June 5 the court settled the long-standing suit of Elizabeth Ashworth and declared Milton's claim against the Powells satisfied, ordering him to return Wheatley to them (*LR* IV, 149–54).

110 The Order Books on September 8 call for the appointment of "Mr. Sterry" (Nathanial) to substitute for Philip Meadows in his absence, at £200. There is no formal note of Marvell's appointment, but on December 2, 1657 he was paid a quarter's salary, indicating an appointment dating from about September 2 (*LR* IV, 172–3). In *The Rehearsal Transpros'd* (London, 1672), part II, 127, Marvell states that he had no involvement with the Interregnum government until 1657, when he accepted "an imployment, for which I was not altogether improper."

111 Wood, *Athenae Oxonienses*, IV, 231.

112 The fact that Dryden was granted money for funeral garments at Cromwell's death in September, 1658 and wrote a funeral elegy for him suggests that he held an appointment for some period before that time. On October 19, 1659 there was an order to pay him £50.

113 Also, the parish registers, *Memorials of St Margaret's Church Westminster: . . . 1539–1660*, ed. A. M. Burke (London, 1914), 250, under the date October 19, 1657, list the birth of "Katherin Milton d. of John and of Katherin. This is Milton Oliver's secretary." The last sentence seems to have been added later.

114 Biographical entries about him always claim friendship with the celebrated Milton. See Leo Miller, "Milton and Lassenius," *MQ* 6 (1972), 92–5.

115 See Timothy Raylor, "New Light on Milton and Hartlib," *MQ* 27 (1993), 22–3. Mercator's letter to Hartlib was dated September 22; in an earlier letter (July 28) he reports that he had passed along his copy of Milton's treatise to one Mr Bridges, chaplain at Petworth.

116 The 1645 *Poems* were quoted in Joshua Poole, ed., *The English Parnassus* (London, 1657), under such headings as beauty, light, blindness, etc: selections are taken from the Nativity ode, *L'Allegro,* and *Lycidas*. Henry Stubbe praised Milton's Latin and Greek style – "that glory of our English nation" – in his anonymous *Clamor, rixa, joci* (London, 1657, *c.* June 17), 45. The *Reason of Church-Government* and *Apology for Smectymnuus* are advertised in John Rothwell's *Catalogue of the Most Approved Divinity Books* (London, 1657, *c.* June 13), 93. And on September 15 William London's *Catalogue of the Most Vendible Books* (London, 1657) lists *Of Reformation*, *Of Prelatical Episcopacy*, *Reason of Church-Government*, the *Defensio*, *Eikonoklastes*, and the 1645 *Poems*.

117 Sallust, *Bellum Catalinae* (The War with Cataline) and *Bellum Jugurthinum* (The War with Jugurtha], trans. J. C. Rolfe (Cambridge, Mass.,1930). Tacitus was also a favorite of republicans, but he could be used either as a guidebook for absolute monarchy or in

praise of republicanism; Milton had engaged with Salmasius over just this interpretative ambiguity: see chapter 8, p. 272.

118 See chapter 7, n. 109. Just before publication Milton likely revised some parts and added the final sentence or sentences. See chapter 14, pp. 494–5.

119 Nicholas Von Maltzahn, *Milton's History of Britain: Republican Historiography in the English Revolution* (Oxford, 1991), 176–88.

120 *CPW* V.1, 231–2, 265–6, 321.

121 Wheloc published a combined edition of Bede's *Church History* and Alfred's *Anglo-Saxon Chronicle* with Old English and Latin translation in parallel columns, adding to it William Lambarde's *Archaionomia*, a collection of Old English laws: *Historiae Ecclesiastica Gentis Anglorum Libri V . . . Ab augustissimo veterum Anglo-Saxonum Rege Aluredo (sive Alfredo) examinati; . . . Quibus accesserunt Anglo-Saxonicae Leges* (London, 1644). Milton depended as well on Henry of Huntington's *Historia Anglorum*, Matthew of Westminster's *Flores Historiarum*, and William of Malmesbury's *Gesta Regum and Gesta Pontificum*, all of which with some other early historians were edited by Henry Savile, *Rerum Anglicarum Scriptores post Bedam* (London, 1596).

122 Pages 252, 327, 308. Also, a narrative of the Scots being aided by a vision in conquering King Athelstan "seems rather to have been the fancy of some Legend then any warrantable Record" (251).

123 For example, Siward did not properly understand that "true fortitude glories not in the feats of War, as they are such, but as they serve to end War soonest by a victorious Peace" (385).

124 Canute, he points out, "commanded to be observ'd the antient *Saxon* Laws, call'd afterwards the Laws of *Edward* the Confessor, not that He made them, but strictly observ'd them" (364).

125 See Von Maltzahn, *Milton's History of Britain,* 189–23; J. C. A. Pocock, *The Ancient Constitution and the Feudal Law* (Cambridge, 1957).

126 See chapter 5, p. 123.

127 He points out that the various invaders are, by ancient origin, of the same stock: the barbarous Saxons are said to be from a part of Denmark, and the later barbarous Danish invaders were of the same stock as the Normans, so that "*Danes* drove out *Danes,* thir own posterity. And *Normans* afterwards, none but antienter *Normans*" (258).

128 The specific vices he paraphrases out of William of Malmesbury: "The Clergy . . . had lost all good literature and Religion, scarse able to read and understand thir Latin Service: he was a miracle to others who knew his Grammar. The Monks went clad in fine stuffs, and made no difference what they eat; which though in it self no fault, yet to their Consciences was irreligious. The great men giv'n to gluttony and dissolute life, made a prey of the common people, abuseing thir Daughters whom they had in service, then turning them off to the Stews, the meaner sort tipling together night and day, spent all they had in Drunk'ness, attended with other Vices which effeminate mens minds. Whence it came to pass, that carried on with fury and rashness more then any true fortitude or skill of War, they gave to *William* thir Conqueror so easie a Conquest. Not but that some few of all sorts were much better among them; but such were the generality" (402–3).

129 One letter (March, 1658) to the Duke of Curland asked payment of the stipend due a Scots skipper in the duke's service; another (April 7) to the Grand Duke of Tuscany

sought justice for an English captain being defrauded of his ship and goods in a Livorno court; another (August, 1658) to the King of Portugal asks the appointment of a conservator to aid an English merchant captured by pirates whose goods are being unjustly withheld by the Portuguese (*CPW* V.2, 818, 821–2, 848–9).

130 The letter to Mazarin also thanks him for sending his own nephew with the French embassy and praises the "supreme courage and prudence, for which you are so renowned" as a model for all would-be governors of nations (842–3).

131 *CPW* V.2, 838–9. Fallon, *Milton in Government*, 171, argues that Milton may well have written more letters to and about Sweden and the Protestant League in these months, as well as, perhaps, preparing the diplomatic packets for Jephson and Meadows.

132 *LR* IV, 200–11. The documents were signed on Milton's behalf and also witnessed by Jeremie Picard, who was then acting as Milton's amanuensis; another witness was Elizabeth Woodcock, Milton's mother-in-law. See James Holly Hanford, "Rosenbach Milton Documents," *PMLA* 38 (1923), 290–6. Masson calculates that before 1660 Milton had about £4,000 variously invested. He had income from rentals of about £150 a year, from Maundy £30, and his salary of £200 from the secretaryship (Masson, VI, 444–5).

133 *LR* IV, 215. Thomas Birch reports this correction from Mrs Elizabeth Foster, Milton's granddaughter. Cf John Ward (BL Add Ms 4320, 232).

134 *Memorials of St. Margaret's Church, Westminster: The Parish Registers, 1539–1660*, ed. A. M. Burke (London, 1914), 651.

135 Milton's Bible, BL Add Ms 32,360. The entry is in the hand of Jeremie Picard. The Parish Registers of St Margarets, 651, report the burial March 20 of "Mrs Katherin Milton, ch[ild]."

136 The counterargument, put by Parker (II, 1,945) and others, rests on the assumption that lines 5–6 refer to a wife who died in childbirth, as Mary Powell did and Katherine (literally) did not. But in fact the lines are an elaborate comparison, and do not ascribe her death to childbirth: the dream–vision appeared "like" Alcestis, and "as" one purified in the Old Law from childbed taint. If that last comparison has any literal force it could only refer to Katherine, for whom the requisite 66 days for such purification had elapsed; Mary died three days after giving birth. Moreover, the whole sonnet describes an image with veiled face, who will only be seen in "full sight" in heaven, in reference, it seems, to the wife never seen physically. The fact that the sonnet was entered into *TM* by Jeremie Picard, Milton's amanuensis at this time, further reinforces the case for Katherine. Moreover, nothing suggests that Milton thought of Mary Powell in such tender terms as these, and his nuncupative will reinforces that fact (see chapter 14, pp. 537–8). See Anthony Low, "Milton's Last Sonnet," *MQ* 9 (1975), 80–2, for a convincing restatement of the case for Katherine. I cite the version of the sonnet in *TM*.

137 Bodin's *Colloquium Heptoplomeres* was first published in part in 1841 and then in a complete edition (Schwerin, 1857). Hartlib's comment is from a letter to Robert Boyle in Boyle's *Works,* 6 vols (London, 1772), VI, 100. See *LR* IV, 371–4 and Louis Bredvold, "Milton and Bodin's *Heptaplomeres,*" *Studies in Philology* 21 (1924), 399–402. Sometime in 1662 Milton sent his copy to an unidentified friend in Germany. See chapter 12, p. 406.

138 [T. B.], *The Cabinet-Council: Containing the Cheif Arts of Empire, and Mysteries of State;*

Discabineted In Political and Polemical Aphorisms, Grounded on Authority, and Experience; and illustrated with the choicest Examples and Historical Observations. By the Ever-renowned Knight, Sir Walter Raleigh, Published By John Milton Esq. (London, 1658). Martin Dzelzainis, "Milton and the Protectorate in 1658," in Armitage, et al, *Milton and Republicanism,* 191–2, identifies the sources as Bodin's *Les six livres de la République,* Machiavelli's *Il Principe* and *Discorsi*, Lipsius's *Politicorum sive Civilis Doctrinae libri sex,* and Francisco Sansovino's *Concetti politici* (mostly taken from Machiavelli's several works and Guicciardini's *Storia d'Italia*).

139 Dzelzainis, "Milton and the Protectorate in 1658," 181–205.

140 Cited in Dzelzainis, "Milton and the Protectorate in 1658," 194. See *CPW* I, 598; III, 465.

141 *Cabinet Council,* p. 164.

142 There was a good deal of controversy about a paper said to contain his earlier nomination of Richard, which at the time of Cromwell's death could not be found. His verbal statements were attested by Thurloe, Thomas Goodwin, and others of the council. See the summary in Firth, *Last Years of the Protectorate,* 298–307.

143 See note 41.

144 Cf. Luke 18:7: "And shall not God avenge his own elect, which cry day and night unto him . . . ?" Also Psalm 141:7: "Our bones are scattered at the grave's mouth"; and Psalm 44:22: "Yea, for thy sake are we killed all the day long; we are counted as sheep for the slaughter."

145 Cf. Revelation 20:12: "And another book was opened, which is the book of life; and the dead were judged out of those things which were written in the books, according to their works."

146 See note 49, also chapter 2, pp. 35–7, 48–52.

147 There are echoes, among many others, of Horace's *Odes* 1.5, 1.16, 1.9, 2.9, and 2.11. As is usual with Milton, these sonnets do not rework specific classical poems, but evoke the spirit of many.

148 In, for example, *L'Allegro,* Prolusion VII, *Reason of Church-Government* and *Tetrachordon.* See chapter 2, pp. 31, 45, chapter 5, pp. 151–2, and chapter 6, pp. 189–90.

149 See chapter 3, pp. 80–1.

150 Matthew 6:28–9: "Consider the lillies of the field, how they grow; they toil not, neither do they spin; And yet I say unto you, That even Solomon in all his glory was not arrayed like one of these."

151 For the controversy over these lines see *Variorum* II.2, 474–6. The reading sometimes advanced – "spare" in the sense of "refrain from" as a counsel to limit such pleasure – goes against the thrust of this sonnet. Moreover, the specific allusion to the schoolbook *Catonis Disticha,* 3.5, "Interpone tuis interdum guadia curis: / Ut possis animo quemvis sufferre laborem" (Interpose now and then enjoyment amidst your care / that you may be able to bear in your mind whatever toil you find) reinforces the meaning suggested here.

152 See note 50.

153 Cf. Smart, *Sonnets*, 125–6, and Leo Spitzer, "Understanding Milton," *Hopkins Review* 4 (1950–1), 16–27. Cf. Sidney, *Astrophel,* no. 38; Desportes, *Diane*, no. 35; Drayton's "The Vision of Matilda," and also Aeneas's vision of Creusa in *Aeneid* 1.789–95.

154 See note 136.

155 The quatrain echoes lines from Euripides, *Alcestis*, 1,136, 1,117, 1,144–6.

156 The point is not that Katherine has fulfilled the days of supposed uncleanness (though the requisite 80 days have indeed passed), but rather that her salvation does not depend on bodily purification but on her purity of mind, which testifies to Christian election. Cf. Revelation 19.8: "And to her [the Lamb's bride] was granted that she should be arrayed in fine linen, clean and white: for the fine linen is the righteousness of saints."

Chapter 11 "The Last Words of Our Expiring Libertie" 1658–1660

1 A letter of that date was addressed to the States General (SP 84/162/164–5), and another was surely sent promptly to Charles X of Sweden, England's other major ally. See Robet T. Fallon, *Milton in Government* (University Park, Penn., 1993), 169.

2 Another letter (probably not delivered) introduces Sir George Ayscue who was to bring a naval force to Sweden (*CPW* V.2, 853–4); it was written around October 26, but on January 7 his ship was still in port. Disease among the crew had caused delays, so the expedition was probably aborted.

3 See chapter 10, p. 352. Meadows's name is listed but crossed out since he was on his mission to Sweden and could not be present.

4 The order of march, listing categories of marchers and several names in each, together with their places of waiting in Somerset House, is in BL Lansdowne MS 95 (no. 2) ff. 1–15. Listed in pairs as "Secretarys of the French and Latin Toungs" (l. v) are Dryden and Sterry, Marvell and Milton, and Hartlib; "Mr. Pell" and "Mr. Bradshaw" are also listed but crossed out.

5 The broadside and newsbook accounts stressed the costly magnificence of the accoutrements, and list the categories of the marchers, but not their names: *The True Manner of . . . Conveyance of His Highenesse Effigies* (London, 1658); also *Mercurius Politicus* 443 (November 18–25), 23–4; and *The Publick Intelligencer* 152 (November 22–29, 1658), 21–3. That issue of *Mercurius Politicus* also advertises Milton's revised *Defensio* (p. 29). Also see Laura Lunger Knoppers, *Constructing Cromwell: Ceremony, Portrait, and Print 1645–1661* (Cambridge, 2000), 139–45.

6 Besides the verbal changes there were some 700 differences in spelling and punctuation; it is hard to know how many of these were simply incidental (Parker, I, 518).

7 The Thomason copy is dated simply "Octob." but as this is the third of seventeen entries for that month in Thomason's manuscript catalogue, it probably appeared early.

8 *CPW* IV.1, 537. Milton would probably think *Paradise Lost* to be another order of accomplishment, not directly comparable to the *Defensio*. On several occasions during 1658 and at least until June, 1659, Milton was also occupied with a Chancery suit harking back to the loan he had made in 1638 to Sir John Cope which he had been unable to collect. See *LR* IV, 232–4, 236–8, 241–3, 252–3, 257, 271–2.

9 "A Paper sent by General Monk from *Scotland* to the Protector *Richard Cromwell*," dated September 15, called on Richard to convene another Assembly of Divines, to favor "moderate presbiterian divines," and settle the church, so as to put a stop to "that progresse of blasphemy and profanes, that I fear is too frequent in many places by the great extent of toleration," John Thurloe, *A Collection of the State Papers of John Thurloe, Esq*., ed. Thomas Birch, 7 vols (London, 1742), VII, 387. Each week the government-

sponsored newsbooks published several petitions, e.g. from Northampton, Southampton, Cumberland, and Stamford: *The Publick Intelligencer,* no. 154 (London, December 6–13, 1658), 62; no. 157 (December 27, 1658–January 3, 1659), 134; no. 158 (January 3–10, 1659), 134; no. 160 (January 17–24, 1659), 162.

10 [Savoy] *Declaration of the Faith and Order owned and practised in the Congregational Churches in England* (London, 1658). Presenting this document to Richard as proof that Independency is not "the sink of all Heresies and Schisms," Thomas Goodwin claimed that it demonstrated their harmony with the orthodox at home and abroad: *Mercurius Politicus* 438 (October 7–14), 924. The Westminster Assembly's Confession of Faith, together with its Longer and Shorter Catechisms, had been reissued earlier in 1658. See chapter 6, p. 161.

11 Savoy *Declaration*, 42.

12 Two letters in late January, 1659 concerned private matters. One (January 27) to the governors of West Friesland asks their assistance in securing justice for an English widow unable to collect a large debt from a soldier of that state. Another (January 28) to the King of Sweden asks his help in freeing Samuel Piggott's two ships, impounded by the Swedish fleet (*CPW* V.2, 857–9).

13 J. M., *A Treatise of Civil Power in Ecclesiastical Causes: Shewing that it is not lawfull for any power on earth to compell in matters of Religion* (London, 1659). It was advertised in *The Publick Intelligencer* 163 (February 7–14), and in *Mercurius Politicus* 554 (February 10–17). Thomason does not seem to have obtained a copy.

14 See above, chapter 6, pp. 178–9. A Leveller pamphlet of February 16, 1659, *The Leveller: Or the Principles and Maxims Concerning Government and Religion, Which are asserted by those commonly called Levellers* (London, 1659), specifies as examples of the magistrates' sphere, "Injustice, Faith-breaking, Cruelty, Oppression."

15 Cf. Thomas Collier, *The Decision & Clearing of the Great Point Now in Controversie about the Interest of Christ and the Civill Magistrate in the Rule of Government in this World* (London, 1659), sig. A2, published in May though written earlier; and Henry Stubbe, *An Essay in the Defense of the Good Old Cause* (London, 1659), published in September, though the "Premonition to the Reader" is dated July 4. Stubbe was Under-Keeper of the Bodleian and a friend of Vane. Like Milton, both men restrict the magistrate to the natural order but also assume that blasphemy and idolatry can be recognized as evil by the light of reason alone.

16 See, for example, R. Fitz-Brian, *The Good Old Cause Dress'd in Its Primitive Lustre* (London, 1659, *c.* February 16), 5, which recalled nostalgically "those virgin daies" when there was "a mutuall, strict, and lovely harmony and agreement . . . between the Parliament, and the honest unbiass'd people of the Nation."

17 *The Cause of God and of These Nations* (London, 1659, *c.* March 2), 7, 23–8, denounced the backsliding of the Protectorate in reviving the pomp and vanity of a court; and *A Call to the Officers of the Army and all Good Hearts,* signed S.R., H.W. and R. P. (London, 1659, *c.* February 26), 5, exhorted the English in a species of jeremiad, to awake and repent and "to stand in the good old way, and to return into that path, where the Lord met you and owned you." See Laura L. Knoppers, "Milton's Readie and Easie Way and the English Jeremiad," in Loewenstein and Turner, eds. *Politics, Poetics, and Hermeneutics*, 213–17.

18 See chapter 9, pp. 301–2.

19 Wall, an erstwhile student of Emanuel College, Cambridge, wrote from Caversham. The original of his letter is also lost, but a copy made by Revd Josiah Owen of Rochdale is in BL Add MS 4292, ff. 264v–265v. The date, May 26, is almost certainly a mistake for March 26. As Austen Woolrych notes ("Introduction," *CPW* VII, 83), had Wall written after May 7 his Commonwealth sympathies would have led him to refer to the Rump's restoration. His language suggests that the Protectorate "Court" is still in being.

20 Woolrych, "Introduction," *CPW* VII, 62–3.

21 *To the Officers and Soldiers of the Armies of England, Scotland, and Ireland . . . The Humble Petition and Advice of Divers well-Affected to the good Old Cause . . .* [from] *Southwark* (London, 1659, April 27), 7; cf. *The Humble Remonstrance . . . of Major General Goffs Regiment* (London, 1659, April 26), 2; *The Good Old Cause Explained, Revived, and Asserted. And the Long Parliament Vindicated* (London, 1659).

22 The Levellers called for a new, freely elected parliament in *The Honest Design: or The True Commonwealths-man* (London, 1659, *c.* May 2); and *The Humble Desires of a Free Subject* (London, 1659, *c.* May 2). See also [James Harrington], *Pour Enclouer le Canon* (London, 1659, *c.* May 2).

23 A letter to Mazarin (February 19) asks his favor to Lady Richmond, who intended to reside in France with her young son. Another (February 22) to Mazarin follows up a previous letter seeking payment to Peter Pett for his ship seized and sold. A letter to Portugal (February 23) congratulates the king on a recent victory over the Spanish, "our common enemy," and appeals for payment owed to Alexander Bunce for the hire of his ship; another, in April, asks reparations for a shipowner whose vessel was seized (*CPW* V.2, 862–6). In most collections both letters are misaddressed to John IV, who died in November, 1656, but are properly addressed to Alphonso VI in the Lünig collection; see Leo Miller, "Milton's State Letters: The Lünig Version," *N&Q* 215 (1970), 412–14. Two letters to the Grand Duke of Tuscany are dated April 19: the first asks that ship and goods owned by Sir John Dethicke and others be seized, as the ship's captain was thought to be defrauding them; the second letter asks restoration of merchandise seized by Italian creditors from English traders (867–9).

24 It asked that he allow David Fithy to fulfill a contract to export hemp from Riga, normally forbidden (870). In most collections both letters to Portugal are misaddressed.

25 The book was *Lettre à ses Amis de la Communion Romaine* (Montauban, 1651); possibly he also sent his *Declaration de Jean de Labadie . . . Contenant les raisons que l'ont obligé à quitter la Communion de l'Eglise Romaine* (Montauban, 1650). Milton's letter refers to their mutual friend "our Durie" – almost certainly Giles Dury, not John (*CPW* VII, 508–10).

26 Remarkably enough, from Pierre Du Moulin of Nímes, the father of the true author of *Clamor.*

27 The appointment was to the Somerset House Chapel, formerly served by Jean d'Espagne who had died, Milton reports, "a few days ago." The April 21 date on Milton's letter to Labadie is surely wrong, since Jean D'Espagne died on April 25. Probably, as Parker (I, 525) suggests, this is a copyist's mistake for April 27.

28 *A Declaration of the Officers of the Army, inviting the Members of the Long Parliament to return to the Exercise and Discharge of their Trust* (London, 1659, May 6), 2–3. In meetings with republicans at Vane's house some officers tried to preserve a figurehead position for Richard, but were flatly refused.

29 On their first day of business (May 9) William Prynne and a few others secluded in Pride's Purge took seats and refused to leave; only by adjourning for dinner could the Rump get rid of them.

30 *The Parliamentary or Constitutional History of England*, ed. William Cobbett, et al., 2nd edn, 24 vols (London, 1761–73), III, cols 1,552–4; *Commons Journal* VII, 651.

31 [Henry Vane], *A Needful Corrective or Ballance in Popular Government* (London, 1659, May?). A manuscript note on the Bodleian copy ascribes the tract to Vane, or as written with his advice and approbation. The Select Council or Senate would have a negative over the broadly representative popular assembly in matters pertaining to the exclusion of a single person and liberty of conscience; it might also propose legislation and take on the executive duties of a Council of State. For a season at least it would be composed of, and elected by, either Saints renewed by grace or those who had proved in arms their devotion to the Commonwealth. For the first edition of the *Healing Question*, published in March, 1656, see chapter 10, p. 338.

32 *CPW* V.2, 871–3. There is some question whether letters of June 30 to Sweden and Denmark are Milton's; they appear in none of the collections and their similar formulas are likely to be simple repetitions used in several such letters. See J. M. French and Maurice Kelley, "The Columbia Milton," *N&Q* 195 (1952), 244–6.

33 William Prynne, *A True and perfect Narrative of what was done, spoken by and between Mr. Prynne, the old and newly Forcibly late secluded Members, the Army Officers, and those now sitting . . . on . . . the 7. and 9. of this instant May* (London, 1659, May 18), 50. Cf. Prynne, *The Re-Publicans and Others Spurious Good Old Cause, briefly and truly anatomized* (London, 1659, *c.* May 13), 10.

34 J. M., *Considerations Touching the Likeliest Means to remove Hirelings out of the church. Wherein is also discours'd of Tithes, Church-fees, Church-revenues; and whether any maintenance of ministers can be settl'd by law* (London, 1659). Harrington refers to this tract in *Aphorisms Political* (London, 1659, *c.* August 31), 4–5, so it was probably completed, as Woolrych speculates, around August 1 and appeared in mid-August (*CPW* VII, 84–5).

35 *CPW* VII, 278. For tithe supporters see, for example, "The Petition of Divers Justices of the Peace, Gentlemen, Ministers of the Gospel, Freeholders, and Other Considerable Inhabitants in the County of Sussex," in *The Publick Intelligencer* 183 (June 27–July 4, 1659), 553; "The Humble Petition of Divers Well Affected Persons in the Town of *Warminster*," in *The Publick Intelligencer* 177 (May 16–23, 1659), 447. For sectarian abolitionists, see "The Humble Petition of the Baptised Congregations Assembled at Alisbury, in the County of Bucks," *Mercurius Politicus* 569 (May 26–June 2, 1659, dated May 28,) 471; "The Humble Representation and Petition of Many Wel-Affected Persons in the Counties of Somerset, Wilts, and Some Part of Devon, Dorset, and Hampshire," *Mercurius Politicus* 571 (June 9–16, 1659, dated June 14), 487; *The Humble Petition of Divers Freeholders and Other Inhabitants of the County of Hertford* (London, 1659, June 24), broadside; *The Humble Representation of Divers Freeholders and Others . . . Inhabiting within the County of Bedford* (London, 1659, June 17), broadside.

36 *The Copie of a Paper Presented to the Parliament* (London, 1659, June 27), 5.

37 *Proclamation*, Monday, June 27, 1659, broadside; *Commons Journal* VII, 694. In its first form the resolution read "until," not "unless"; on June 14 petitioners had been promised that the parliament would seek an alternative maintenance "with all convenient speed"; *Commons Journal* VII, 683; *Mercurius Politicus* 571 (June 9–16), 510.

38 For example, 1 Timothy 5:18; 1 Corinthians 9:11, 13–14; Galatians 6:6. The transfer of tithes (as God's portion) from Old Testament Levites to Christian ministers was argued by analogy with the Sabbath, still required but transferred to Sunday. Many mined John Selden's *The History of Tithes* (London, 1618) for examples of pagans tithing according to the law of nature, but Selden drew the opposite conclusion: "Some did, and only sometimes, and of some things" (28).

39 See, for example, William Prynne, *Ten Considerable Quaeries Concerning Tithes* (London, 1659, *c.* June 27); Immanuel Bourne, *A Defence and Justification of Ministers Maintenance by Tythes* (London, 1659, *c.* June 30); *A Caution Against Sacriledge: Or Sundry Queries Concerning Tithes* (London, 1659, *c.* July 11), and from the Independent side, Giles Firmin, *Tythes Vindicated from Anti-Christianism and Oppression* (London, 1659, *c.* April 6). Tithe supporters drew on Henry Spelman, *The Larger Treatise Concerning Tithes* (London, 1647), as Milton recognized by a reference to "Thir zealous antiquary, *Sir Hen. Spelman*" (*CPW* VII, 299).

40 William Sprigge in *A Modest Plea for an Equal Common-wealth against Monarchy* (London, 1659, *c.* September 28), argued the special responsibility of the magistrate as teacher of the nation to fund ministers for neglected areas, whereas the established gathered churches should support their own ministers. See also *The Moderate Man's Proposall to the Parliament about Tithes* (London, 1659, *c.* June 29), and *A few Proposals . . . holding forth a Medium or Essay for the Removing of Tithes* (London, 1659, *c.* August 20).

41 See, for example, John Osborne, *An Indictment against Tythes* (London, 1659, *c.* July 18); Anthony Pearson, *The Great Case of Tythes Truely Stated,* 3rd edn (London, 1659); *A Declaration of the Present Sufferings of about 140 Persons of the People of God* [Quakers] (London, 1659, *c.* April 23); [Henry Stubbe], *A Light Shining out of Darkness* (London, 1659, *c.* June 17; 2nd edn November 8).

42 See, for example, Edward Reynolds, *A Sermon Touching the Use of Humane Learning* (London, 1658, September); [Matthew Poole], *A Model for the Maintaining of Students of Choice Abilities at the University, and principally in order to the Ministry* (London, 1658, April). Poole proposed establishing a fund to maintain poor students at the university to complete their divinity studies, after which the most able might take fellowships and others serve the church in needy areas.

43 See, for example, W. G., *The Arraignment of Ignorance. As also the excellency, profit, and benefit of Heavenly Knowledge* (London, 1659, January); John Owen, *Of the Divine Originall, Authority, Self-Evidencing Light and Power of the Scriptures* (London, 1658, November); *Sundry Things from Severall Hands Concerning the University of Oxford* (London, 1659, *c.* June 29).

44 William Dell, "The Right Reformation of Learning, Schools, and Universities" with *The Tryal of Spirits Both in Teachers & Hearers . . . Whereunto is added . . . that Humane learning, is not a Preparation appointed by Christ, either for the Right Understanding, or Right Teaching the Gospel. With a brief Testimony against Divinity-Degrees in the Universities* (London, 1660), 153–8. Cf. [Stubbe], *A Light Shining out of Darknes*; and Sprigge, *A Modest Plea for an Equal Common-wealth* (London, 1659).

45 See, for example, the Fifth Monarchist John Canne, *The Time of Finding* (London, 1659) and George Fox, *A Primer for the Schollers and Doctors of Europe* (London, 1659).

46 That vote might not yet have occurred when Milton wrote sentences referring to "the just petition of many thousands" and "the debate before you" (275).

47 In *Aphorisms Political* (London, 1659), nos. 37 and 38, 4–5, Harrington paraphrases Milton, but does not mention him by name.

48 That sentiment was often repeated. In *A Short Discourse* (London, 1659, *c.* June 15) the author reads the recent interruptions as God's means to purge and purify his people, and urgently warns the restored MPs against corruption and against a "persecuting spirit," since the Kingdom of Christ to come is to embody all his Saints.

49 *A Publick Plea Opposed to a Private Proposal* (London, 1659, *c.* May 18), title page, 3. The referent of Milton's phrase is disputed; some (e.g. Wolfe and Woolrych) think it pertains to the entire period of Cromwell's Protectorate; others (e.g. Masson, Fallon, and Corns) only to the three-week interregnum between the dissolution of Richard's parliament and the return of the Rump. Hunter suggests the eight months of Richard's Protectorate. See the survey in Woolrych, "Introduction," *CPW* VII, 85–7.

50 For the Levellers see, for example, Samuel Duncon, *Several Proposals Offered to the Consideration of the Keepers of the Liberties of the people of England* (London, 1659, *c.* July 6). In *An Essay toward Settlement upon a sure foundation, being a testimony for God in this perilous time by a few who have been bewailing their own abominations* (London, 1659, September 19, broadside), Overton and 19 other signers denounce the "haughty and abusive spirit, found in the late Single Person," and would prohibit all his supporters from places of power unless they were truly repentant. See also Christopher Feake, *The Fifth Monarchy, or Kingdom of Christ, in Opposition to the Beast's, asserted* (London, 1659, *c.* August 23).

51 Harrington's tracts of these weeks include *A Discourse, Shewing that the spirit of parliaments with a Council in the intervals, is not to be trusted for a Settlement* (London, 1659, *c.* July 28); *Politicaster: or, A comical discourse in answer unto Mr. Wren's Monarchy Asserted, against Mr. Harrington's Oceana* (London, 1659, August); and *Aphorisms Political.* Other tracts promoting his program include *A Proposition in Order to the Proposing of a Commonwealth or Democracie* (London, 1659, *c.* June 14); *A Common-Wealth or Nothing; or, Monarchy and Oligarchy prov'd parallel in tyranny* (London, 1659, *c.* June 14); *A Commonwealth, and Commonwealths-men, Asserted and Vindicated* (London, 1659, *c.* June 28); and *A Model of a Democraticall Government* (London, 1659, *c.* August 31).

52 John Aubrey, *Brief Lives*, ed. Oliver Lawson Dick (London, 1949), 125, dates the inception of the Rota Club from the beginning of Michaelmas Term. Other members included the erstwhile Leveller John Wildman, Henry Neville, Samuel Pepys, and William Petty the mathematician.

53 In their Derby Petition of September 22 they declared "God . . . [has] given a Spirit to the Army fixed and faithful to the Interest of his people, and our good Cause" and called for a Select Senate, payment of their arrears, appointment of Fleetwood as permanent commander- in-chief, and a guarantee that no officer or soldier would be dismissed except by court-martial. Reprinted in *The Humble Representation and Petition of the Officers of the Army to the Parliament* (London, 1659, *c.* October 5). See also Edmund Ludlow, *Memoirs,* ed. C. H. Firth, 2 vols (Oxford, 1894), II, 99–148.

54 *Considerations upon the late transactions and proceedings of the Army, in reference to the Dissolution of the Parliament* (London, 1659, *c.* October 20).

55 The figure indicates that the reduction in salary ordered on April 17, 1655 had been mostly reversed. See chapter 10, p. 329.

56 For example, The *Parliaments Plea: Or XX Reasons for the Union of the Parliament and*

Army (London, 1659, *c.* October 25); and *The Grand Concernments of England ensured by a constant Succession of Free Parliaments, with some smart Rebukes to the Army* (London, 1659, *c.* October 25).

57 For example, *The Armys Plea for Their Present Practice* (London, 1659, *c.* October 24); *The Armies Vindication of This Last Change, Wherein, is plainly Demonstrated, the Equity, Power, and Right of the Army to Settle these Nations upon the Foundations of Righteousnesse and Freedome* (London, 1659, *c.* October), 4–7.

58 A new edition of Vane's *Healing Question*, dated in the Harvard copy October 18, 1659, affirms that both parliament and army represent the well-affected people and emphasizes the necessity of their firm union. Henry Stubbe in *A Letter to an Officer of the Army concerning a select Senate* (London, 1659, October 26) calls for a "Select Senate" of nine or thirteen "Conservators of Liberty" to be elected by those who had fought for or adhered to the Commonwealth, with a charge to preserve the fundamentals and control the militia, the ministry, and the universities. The popular legislature, freely chosen by the traditional electorate, would deal with all other matters – war, peace, taxation, and the like.

59 *A Letter to a Friend, Concerning the Ruptures of the Commonwealth*, dated by Milton October 20, was first published in Toland's edition from a manuscript originating with Edward Phillips. A somewhat different and apparently prior version is in the Columbia manuscript.

60 Woolrych, "Introduction," *CPW* VII, 121, thinks Vane and Milton were at this juncture too far apart and suggests the dying John Bradshaw as the friend. Besides Vane and Stubbe, arguments for reconciliation between Rump and army were urged by several Independent ministers, including John Owen, Phillip Nye, and William Bridges. See Ludlow, *Memoirs*, II, 139–70, and Woolrych, *CPW* VII, 114.

61 He made these notes sometime between October 27 when the "present" Committee of Safety was set up, and December 24 when the Rump was again restored. Woolrych believes that Milton's references to a threatened civil war point to the period between November 3 and 15, when Monk and Lambert seemed ready to faceoff (*CPW* VII, 129–40), but that threat was rather quickly dispelled, whereas the danger of widespread civil conflicts escalated steadily. This draft was first published in *CM* XVIII, 3–7; in the Columbia manuscript, pp. 19–21, it is erroneously placed before rather than after the "Letter to a Friend."

62 Royalist letters to Clarendon on October 28 reported the maneuvers for Richard: *Calendar of Clarendon State Papers*, IV, 425; there were similar reports in December and as late as February, 1660.

63 George Monk, "To the Speaker," in A *Declaration of the Commander-in-chief of the Forces in Scotland, Also . . . Three Letters from the Lord General Monck* (London, 1659, *c.* October 20), 7. For Monk's complex moves and motives, see Godfrey Davies, *The Restoration of Charles II, 1658–1660* (San Marino, 1955), ch. 2.

64 He suggests that those judged insufficient might be removed and worthier chosen, but refuses to press that point now, "lest it be misinterpreted."

65 The previous summer Milton evidently decided not to extend his lease of the Red Rose in Bread Street beyond its expiry in 1674, and on June 10 it was granted from that date to Thomas Hussey.

66 *A Guildhall Elegie* (London, 1659). Thomason dates it November 9, but this is obviously a mistake for November 29.

67 David Norbrook, *Writing the English Republic: Poetry, Rhetoric, and Politics, 1627–1660* (Cambridge, 1999), 415.

68 *The Re-Resurrection of the Rump: Or, Rebellion and Tyranny revived* (London, 1660 [1659], December 31), broadside. See also *A New-Years-Gift for the Rump* (Oxford, 1660, January 5); *Fortunate Rising, or the Rump Upward* (London, 1660, *c.* January 20); and *The Breech Wash'd by a Friend to the Rump* (Oxford, 1660, January 19).

69 For example, *A Letter to General Monk expressing the sense of the well-affected people of England, old Parlamenters and Old Puritanes* (London, 1660, January 22), broadside. Lamenting his declarations in support of the Rump, the letter claims that the signers, "The Commons of England," cannot accept the Rump or the "Faerie Commonwealth that has never been seen"; they urge readmission of the secluded members and a return to the old sound foundations of King, Lords, and Commons.

70 *Mr Praise-God Barbone his Petition. As it was presented to Parliament, Thursday the ninth of February, in behalf of himself and many Thousands* (London, 1659 [1660], *c.* February15). Cf. *A Coffin for the Good Old Cause* (London, 1660, *c.* February 2), which appeals to the still-sitting Rump to fill itself up quickly since "as you are, you are not a *Competent Representative*," and then to "Lead the Van" toward a Commonwealth settlement.

71 *The Pedegree and Descent of His Excellency, General George Monck* (London, 1660, *c.* February 3) traced Monk's descent from King Richard III, suggesting a legitimate ground for his assumption of the throne. Several royalist pamphlets warned Monk against that temptation: The *Letter to General Monk* of January 22 (see note 69) observed, "some think there is now lying before you a sore temptation . . . of making your self a Protector, a King, or what you please, and it is verily thought you might do it with a far more universal acceptance then *Oliver* did."

72 For example, [S. T.], *Moderation: Or Arguments and Motives Tending Thereunto, humbly tendred to the Parliament* (*c.* February 3), 25, claimed that "the *least just blame* will fall on them, who, in seeking *simply* for self security, shall be led to impose in any wise on others, and would not otherwise do it, could they but be safe in peace and *equal* liberty."

73 *A Letter from His Excellencie the Lord General Monck and the Officers under his Command to the Parliament.* (London, 1660, February 11).

74 Samuel Pepys, *Diary*, ed. Robert Latham and William Matthews, 11 vols (London, 1970), I, 52.

75 See, for example, *A Declaration of many thousand well-affected Persons, Inhabitants in and about the Cities of London and Westminster, expressing their adherence to this present Parliament; also their sense of a Free Parliament, so much cried up by the cavaliers* (London, 1660, February), broadside.

76 James Harrington, *The Wayes and Meanes Whereby an Equal & Lasting Commonwealth may be suddenly Introduced and Perfectly founded with the Free Consent and Actual Confirmation of the Whole People of England* (London, 1660, *c.* February 8). See also, [Harrington], *The Rota: Or, A Model of a Free-State or Equall Common-Wealth* (London, 1659 [1660], *c.* January 9).

77 A report had it that several members of parliament, "desperate from guilt and fanaticism, promised to invest him [Monk] with the dignity of Supreme Magistrate," but he refused to hear such "wild proposals:" *Parliamentary or Constitutional History of England* III, col. 1,579.

78 In a published letter to the army regiments, *A Letter from the Lord General Monck . . . To the several and respective Regiments and other Forces in England, Scotland, and Ireland,* in *A Collection of Letters and Declarations sent by General Monck* (London, 1660, *c.* February 21), 41–3, he explained that he did so because the perpetual sitting of the Rump is inconsistent with a free state. He promised not to repeal the ordinances for the sale of royal and ecclesiastical property, not to return to the old bondage, not to permit pro-monarchical activity, and to continue spiritual and civil liberty.

79 *No New Parliament: Or some queries or Considerations Humbly offered to the present Parliament-Members* (London, 1660, March 12), 4–5. See also [Marchamont Nedham?], *News from Brussels, in a Letter from a Neer Attendant on his Majesties Person.* (London, 1660, *c.* March 10), a satire emphasizing the eagerness of the court in exile for revenge against Presbyterians as well as sectaries and seeking thereby to move the Long Parliament to retain control and oppose a restoration.

80 J. M., *The Readie & Easie Way to Establish a Free Commonwealth, and The Excellence therof Compar'd with The inconveniences and dangers of readmitting kingship in this nation* (London, 1660). Thomason acquired it on March 3 but Wood (*EL* 46) claims publication in February, as does a contemporary book list (*LR* IV, 301).

81 Their new Council of State excluded Vane, Arthur Haselrigg, and the other prominent republicans. They appointed Monk commander-in-chief and he began purging the officer corps of "the more obnoxious officers:" *Parliamentary or Constitutional History,* III, col. 1,584.

82 Ibid., III, cols 1,591–2. For the various proposals see Thurloe, *State Papers,* VII, 887, and *CSPD* 1659–60, 393–5. Some called for suspension of episcopal government for three years and a synod to settle controversial issues; others proposed forcible imposition of Presbyterianism upon the nation and permanent banishment of the queen, Edward Hyde, and other members of the court.

83 *Commons Journal* VII, 873–5, 880; *CSPD* 1659–60, 395.

84 *The Present Means, and Brief Delineation of a Free Commonwealth, Easy to be Put in Practice, and without Delay, in a Letter to General Monk,* first published in Toland's edition (1698) II, 799–800, where it is said to have been printed "from the Manuscript" (now lost). This draft is undated, unsigned, and lacks a formal address to Monk or the expected compliments to him.

85 "Et nos consilium dedimus Syllae, demus populo nunc" (We have advised Sulla himself, advise we now the people) adapted from Juvenal I, 15–16. Lucius Cornelius Sulla (138–78 BCE) was a dictator who held unlimited powers; the immediate context suggests that the allusion is to Monk rather than to Oliver Cromwell.

86 Woolrych argues (*CPW* VII, 189–90) that Milton's letter must have been written during the first few days of March to have had any chance of implementation, given travel conditions in seventeenth-century England, the announced date (March 15) of the Long Parliament's dissolution, and the date (April 25) set for the assembly of the new parliament. But Milton may not have thought the Long Parliament would actually give over according to schedule: there was some sentiment in that body to manage the settlement of the government itself.

87 N. D. [Marchamont Nedham?], *A Letter Intercepted, in which the two different Forms of Monarchy and Popular Government are briefly controverted* (London, 1660, March 23), 12–13, declares that "the setling of a Government so excellently good [requires] the kind,

and powerful hands of some man, or more, who in that particular must be, more than *Heroes*" – leaving little question that the leader in question is Monk.

88 *Plaine English to his Excellencie the Lord Monk and the Officers of the Army: Or, A Word in season, not onely to them, but to all Impartial Englishmen* (London, 1660, March 23), 1, 7.

89 [Roger L'Estrange], *Treason Arraigned, in Answer to Plain English: Being a Traiterous and Phanatique Pamphlet, which was Condemned by the Council of State* (London, 1660, *c.* April 3), 2–3, ascribed that tract to either Milton or Nedham or both – "a *Blot of the same Pen that wrote ICONOKLASTES*."

90 Page 394. Though the grammar leaves it somewhat unclear whether elections to the Grand Council are to be by the well-affected populace or the local councils, Milton would hardly have called for creation of the local councils first, given the urgency of settling the central government, had he not intended that they be the choosers.

91 [Roger L'Estrange], *Be Merry and Wise, Or, A Seasonable Word to the Nation, shewing the Cause, the Growth, the State, and the Cure of our Present Distemper* (London, 1660, *c.* March 13).

92 [Samuel Butler?], *The Character of the Rump* (London, 1660, March 19), 2–3. For a plausible argument assigning this tract and also *The Censure of the Rota* (see note 94) to Samuel Butler, see Nicholas von Maltzhan, "Samuel Butler's Milton," *Studies in Philology* 92 (1955), 482–95. Cf. William Colline, *The Spirit of the Phanatiques Dissected and the Solemne League and Covenant solemnly discussed in 30 Queries* (London, 1660, *c.* March 24), 7–8, who perceptively suggests that Milton's federalist model is borrowed from the United Provinces and offers to send him, as well as Harrington, to *terra incognita*, or More's *Utopia*, to frame a free state there.

93 [George Starkey], *The Dignity of Kingship Asserted in Answer to Mr. Milton's Ready and Easy Way to Establish a Free Commonwealth* (London, 1660), xx, xix, ix, 5, xi. It was corrected in print by the author on March 29 and registered on March 31 (*SR 1640–1708*, II, 255), so it probably appeared early in April. It was republished as *Monarchy Triumphing over Traiterous Republicans* (London, 1661); see chapter 12, p. 405.

94 [Samuel Butler?], *The Censure of the Rota upon Mr. Milton's Book, Entituled, The Ready and Easie Way to Establish a Free Commonwealth* (London, 1660, March 20), 4, 11–12. See note 92.

95 Ibid., 4–10.

96 Robert Ayers (*CPW* VII, 398–400) argues that the revised *Readie & Easie Way* was completed and published during the first week of April and before *Brief Notes*, since Milton stated his intention to publish "in the midst of our Elections to a free Parlament, or their sitting to consider freely of the Government." I do not find convincing his reading of "or" in this statement as "ere" (indicating publication before the parliament assembled). I also find somewhat strained his attributing to Milton such a careful calculation that the "midst" of the elections would have occurred in the first week of April. The scenario I describe here seems more probable: much of the tract finished during the elections, as Milton's retention of a passage charging the people to return "able men, and according to the just and necessarie qualifications" makes clear (431–2); but the preface and some other additions and revisions added after publication of *Brief Notes*, reflecting Milton's sense (as the "or" indicates) that the revised tract in fact might not appear until after the parliament convenes. That is the body, after all, that would have to put its provisions into practice.

97 A flood of royalist "Declarations" appeared with this message of moderation in April, from the "nobility and gentry" of Essex, Oxford, Hertford, Kent, London, and elsewhere. See Davies, *Restoration of Charles II,* and R. S. Bosher, *The Making of the Restoration Settlement* (New York, 1951), 130–8.

98 Matthew Griffith, *The Feare of God and the King. Pressed in a Sermon, Preach'd at Mercers Chapell, on the 25th of March, 1660* (London, 1660), 1, 53.

99 The sermon was published with another tract reviewing the rebellion from the time of Shipmoney onward: *The Samaritan Revived, And the course he then took to cure the wounded Traveller.* That work has its own title page, and its pagination indicates that it was published or at least printed first, though in this edition it is appended to the sermon. Thomason dates the joint publication March 25 in reference to the sermon's date; it was registered with the Stationers on March 31 (*SR 1640–1706*, II, 255).

100 *CSPD* 1659–60, 572.

101 J. M., *Brief Notes upon a Late Sermon, Titl'd The Fear of God and the King; Preachd, and since Publishd, by Matthew Griffith, D.D. and Chaplain to the late King. Wherin many Notorious Wrestings of Scripture, and other Falsities are observd* (London, 1660).

102 [Roger L'Estrange], *No Blinde Guides. In Answer to a seditious pamphlet of J. Milton's, intituled, Brief Notes upon a late Sermon . . . by Matthew Griffith* (London, 1660, April 20).

103 At a meeting on March 13, described in several tracts and letters, a group of republicans represented to Monk that the people in rejecting a commonwealth are not good judges of what is best for themselves, so, "since a *Single Person* was necessary . . . there could not be one fitter than he for that Office." Monk reportedly declined. See Edward Phillips's continuation of Baker's *Chronicle, A Chronicle of the Kings of England . . . with a Continuation . . . to the Coronation of his Sacred Majesty, King Charles the Second* (London, 1665), 755.

104 *No Blinde Guides,* 11.

105 Ibid., 1–2.

106 For example, *A Remonstrance & Address of the Armies of England, Scotland, and Ireland: To the Lord General Monck* (London, 1660, April 9) promised over the signatures of several largely Presbyterian regiments that they would not meddle in government, having "great expectation of the next Parliament" (7).

107 For example, *Considerations: Being the Legitimate Issue of a True English Heart: Presented to the Freeholders, and to the Free Men of Several Corporations in this Nation; to Regulate their Elections* (London, 1660).

108 *An Alarum to the Officers and Souldiers of the Armies of England, Scotland, and Ireland* (London, 1660), published before April 5, the date of Roger L'Estrange's (anonymous) answer, *Double Your Guards: In Answer to a Seditious Pamphlet, Entituled, An Alarum to the Armies of England, Scotland, and Ireland* (London, 1660).

109 [L'Estrange], *Physician Cure Thy Selfe: Or an Answer to a Seditious Pamphlet, entituled Eye-Salve for the English Army* (*c.* April 23), 2. In *Double Your Guards,* L'Estrange claims that this tract and *Plaine English* are "the *issue of the Same Brayne*" (3). Later, in *L'Estrange His Apology* (London, 1660, *c.* June 6), he admits his error, having learned that both tracts were by a "Renegade Parson" (113).

110 An apparently contemporary note on the copy of Nedham's *Newes from Brussels* in the Bodleian Library ascribes the writing and production of that tract and *An Alarum to the*

Armies to a coalition of republicans and radicals including Sir Henry Vane, Thomas Scot, Major Salloway, Marchamont Nedham, Praisegod Barebone, and the printer, Livewell Chapman.

111 See notes 102, 109.

112 J. M., *The Readie & Easie Way to establish a free Commonwealth; and the excellence therof compar'd with the inconveniences and dangers of readmitting Kingship in this Nation.* The second edition revised and augmented (London, 1660). No printer's or bookseller's name appears.

113 Wing lists three copies.

114 See Stanley Stewart, "Milton Revises *The Readie and Easie Way*," *MS* 20 (1984), 105–24.

115 The transfer was witnessed by his amanuensis Jeremie Picard and by one Elizabeth Wightman, who has not been identified. On May 13 the endorsement to Skinner was recorded in the Registrar's Office (*LR* IV, 291, 317–18). Skinner's *Life* of Milton states that the £2,000 came from his secretary's salary and Edward Phillips reports that he placed it "into the Excise Office, but neglecting to recal it in time, could never after get it out, with all the power and interest he had in the great ones of those times" (*EL* 32, 78). Skinner collected interest on June 5, but that was the last interest ever paid (Parker, I, 562–3; II, 1,075–6).

116 Skinner's *Life* says he retired "at the first return of the Court," which literally would mean the very end of May, 1660; Toland assigns a somewhat earlier date, "The King being ready to land" (*EL* 32, 175). Cf. Godfrey Davies, "Milton in 1660," *Huntington Library Quarterly* 18 (1955), 353.

117 Thomas Corns, *The Development of Milton's Prose Style* (Oxford, 1982), 60–5; and James Egan, "Milton's Aesthetics of Plainness, 1659–1673," *The Seventeenth Century* 12 (1997), 57–80.

118 Susanne Woods, "Elective Poetics and Milton's Prose: *A Treatise of Civil Power* and *Considerations Touching the Likeliest Means to Remove Hirelings out of the Church*," in Loewenstein and Turner, eds, *Politics, Poetics, and Hermeneutics*, 200.

119 Page 271. He promises for "some other time" a full examination of the question whether Christians are bound to the Decalogue at all, considered as "two legal tables" – another reference to his ongoing work on *De Doctrina Christiana*, where he considers this matter at length.

120 For the comparable positions of Thomas Collier and Henry Stubbe articulated a few months later, see note 15. Milton may also rely on John Selden's exposition of the laws given to Adam and Noah (the Noachide laws, including prohibitions of blasphemy and idolatry) as a biblical formulation of natural law in *De Jure Naturali et Gentium*. See Jason P. Rosenblatt, *Torah and Law in Paradise Lost* (Princeton, NJ, 1994), 126–7.

121 *CM* XVII. 345. In *The Ancient Bounds; or, Liberty of Conscience asserted and vindicated* (London, 1645), Joshua Sprigge insisted that idolatry, such as the worship of images and the "breaden-god," were matters "which a *Heathens* light should not tolerate, Nature carrying so far" (7). This notion of the basis in natural reason for some understanding of God and his worship derives from scholastic tradition. Also see note 120.

122 His analysis of British history takes issue with a favorite authority of the tithe supporters, Henry Spelman's *Concilia, Decreta, Leges, Constitutiones . . . in Re Ecclesiarum Orbis Britannici* (London, 1639). See note 39.

123 Page 302. He notes the availability of English Bible translations with plenty of notes, and thinks that "som where" may be found a handbook of divinity without obfuscating metaphysical notions (304). He may refer to his own *De Doctrina Christiana*, then in preparation; it is in Latin, but he may have hoped to produce an English version in some future, more tolerant era.
124 For a similar proposal from William Dell, see p. 366 and note 44.
125 *CPW* VII, 463. Laura L. Knoppers, "Milton's *The Readie and Easie Way* and the English Jeremiad," in Loewenstein and Turner, eds, *Politics, Poetics, and Hermeneutics*, 213–25.
126 Corns, Development of Milton's Prose *Style*, 65.
127 In the Digression to the *History of Britain*; see chapter 7, pp. 220–1.
128 The first edition terms monarchy "burdensom, expensive, useless and dangerous" (355); this one terms it "unnecessarie, burdensom and dangerous" (409), exactly reproducing the language of the Act of March 17, 1649 proclaiming a commonwealth.
129 Page 456. In this edition, with its necessary address to Presbyterians, Milton omits the long passage from the first edition in which he warns the Rump and then the Long Parliament that to impose religious orthodoxy by repression is unchristian, irreligious, inhuman, and also destabilizing to the state. (*CPW* VII, 380–2).
130 See Stanley Stewart, "Milton Revises the *Readie and Easie Way*," 205–24.
131 In these additions he seems to be responding to L'Estrange's *Be Merry and Wise* and to *The Censure of the Rota*. See pp. 377–8.
132 This would be, he insists, a much needed improvement on the common practice of committing all to the "noise and shouting" of the body of freeholders lustily bawling out names of their candidates. See J. E. Neale, *The Elizabethan House of Commons* (New Haven, Conn., 1950), 86–7.
133 He now makes a point of distinguishing such county government sharply from the massively unpopular county committees imposed by the Stuarts and Cromwell. When he began considering local elites in *A Letter to a Friend* he blurred that point.
134 Pages 422, 463. The first edition reads "strange degenerate corruption" (357).

Chapter 12 "In Darknes, and with Dangers Compast Round" 1660–1665

1 Cyriack Skinner says he went into hiding "at the first return of the Court," which in strictly literal terms would mean the very end of May; Edward Phillips implies that Milton's "abscondance" took place soon after the Restoration (*EL* 32, 74). Milton was still trying to make financial arrangements in early May; see chapter 11, pp. 381–2.
2 *Astraea Redux: A Poem on the Happy Restoration and Return of his Sacred Majesty Charles the Second* (London, 1660, *c.* June 19). A year later Dryden wrote *To His Sacred Maiesty, A Panegyrick on his Coronation* (London, 1661).
3 Masson, VI, 170–8, points to Milton's vulnerability for the thesis of *Tenure*.
4 *Complete Collection of State Trials and Proceedings for High Treason*, eds. William Cobbett and T. S. Howell, 33 vols (London, 1809), V, col. 1,034.
5 Michael Lieb, *Milton and the Culture of Violence* (Ithaca, NY, 1994), 76–7.
6 Godfrey Davies, "Milton in 1660," *Huntington Library Quarterly* 18 (1955), 356.
7 *EL* 271–3. A letter now in the Pierpont Morgan Library from Jacob Tonson to an

unknown addressee, reports the story told to him by Davenant's son: "when his father was in the tower he was very much assisted by Mr. Milton in gaining his Liberty, & if I am not very much mistaken he at the same time told me his father in return upon ye restoration was very helpfull to Milton, & Milton was very acknowledging for it & uppon that score offered his assistance in doing any thing that should be grateful to Sr William." For Milton's aid to Davenant, see chapter 9, p. 288, and note 53.

8 Annesley, soon to be Earl of Anglesey, was a leader in the Commons and a prime mover in the Restoration; Edward Phillips writes that he was on intimate terms with Milton later, "as much coveting his society and converse" (*EL* 76). See chapter 14, pp. 491, 495.

9 *Commons Journal* VIII, 66. The resolution was duly reported in the news sheets: *Mercurius Publicus* 25 (June 14–21, 1660), 391, and *The Parliamentary Intelligencer* 26 (June 18–25, 1660), 401–2.

10 *A Proclamation for . . . suppressing of two Books,* SP 45/11, p. 14.

11 *Mercurius Publicus* 33 (August 9–16, 1660), 534–5; the proclamation is summarized in *The Parliamentary Intelligencer* 34 (August 13–20, 1660), 538.

12 *The Parliamentary Intelligencer* (September 3–10), 589, reports the burning "This Week" as does *Mercurius Publicus* (September 6–13), 578. Leo Miller in "The Burning of Milton's Books in 1660: Two Mysteries," *English Literary Renaissance* 18 (1988), 424–37, argues plausibly that the absence of Milton's gift books (see chapter 7, pp. 206, 209–10) from the Bodleian catalogues of 1674 and 1738 and their subsequent reappearance indicates that they were hidden away in 1660 to save them. If there were copies of Milton's books at Cambridge University, as seems likely though there is no record of his sending them, they were perhaps burnt according to this edict, as none presently there date from that time.

13 "An Act of Free and General Pardon, Indemnity, and Oblivion," *Anno Regni Caroli II . . . .XII* (August 29, 1660); *Commons Journal* VIII, 139–40; *Lords Journal* XL, 146–8.

14 Ibid.

15 Gilbert Burnet, *History of My Own Time*, ed. Osmund Airy, 2 vols (Oxford, 1897), vol. 1, 163.

16 [George Starkey], *Britain's Triumph, for her Imparallel'd Deliverance* (London, 1660), broadside. In his signed tract, *Royal and other Innocent Bloud crying . . . for due vengeance* (London, 1660, *c.* June 18), 18, he demanded vengeance for Milton's glorification of traitors and murderers in the *Defensio.*

17 *A Third Conference Between O. Cromwell and Hugh Peters in Saint James's Park* (London, 1660). L'Estrange, *Apology* (*c.* June 6), repeated his earlier attacks (see chapter 11, pp. 377–80).

18 David Lloyd, *Eikon Basilike. Or the True Portraiture of his Sacred Majesty Charls the II in Three Books* (London, 1660), II, 65; it was published with a different title page under the initials R. F. *The Picture of the Good Old Cause* (London, 1660. *c.* July 14) mentions Milton prominently as an example of God's judgments, "struck totally blind, he being not much above 40 years old."

19 Collonel Baker, *The Blazing-Star . . . Or, Nolls Nose. Newly Revived, and taken out of his Tomb* (London, 1660), 5.

20 *Salmasius His Dissection and Confutation of the Diabolical Rebel Milton, in his Impious Doctrines of Falshood, Maxims of Policies . . . [which] by reason of the rigid Inquisition after Persons*

and Presses by the late Merciless Tyrant Oliver Cromwell durst not be sold publickly in this Kingdom (London, 1660), 22 .

21 Salmasius (Claude Saumaise), *Ad Joannem Miltonum responsio, opus posthumum, Claudio Salmasii* (Dijon, 1660). The dedication to Charles II was dated September 1. The English edition, *Claudio Salmasii ad Johannem Miltonum Responsio, Opus Posthumum* (London, 1660), was registered in London on September 19, and advertised as newly published in *Mercurius Publicus* 49 (November 29–December 6, 1660), 785. Thomason acquired it in December.

22 *Ad Johannem Miltonum Responsio*, 2–5, 8, 21, 218; *LR* IV, 344–8.

23 One tract that insisted he not be allowed to escape scot-free given all his malice and wickedness was *A Rope for Pol, or a Hue and Cry after Marchemont Needham, the late scurrilous newswriter; being a Collection of his horrid Blasphemies against the King's Majesty, his person, his cause, and his friends, published in his weekly Politicus* (London, 1660, September 7).

24 Colonel Thomas Harrison, John Carew, John Cook (one of the king's prosecutors), Hugh Peters, Major Thomas Scott, Gregory Clements, Colonel Adrian Scroope, and Colonel John Jones were executed at Charing Cross; Captain Daniel Axtell and Colonel Francis Hacker at Tyburn. The other regicides remained in prison under sentence of execution, though it was not carried out; many died there.

25 Milton was still at large on August 13 since the Proclamation of that date claimed he had absconded and was unreachable. Masson's guess that he was apprehended during the parliamentary recess is plausible, since his friends were not then at hand to protect him.

26 The pardon is entered on page 65 of the 98-page docket for December: PRO Dockets Signet Office, Index 6812: "December 1660. A pardon granted to John Milton of the parish of St. Giles in the field in the county of Middlesex, Gentleman. Signed by Mr. Secr. Nicholas." The pardons were probably listed in the order of granting. See *Commons Journal* VIII, 208; and Davies, "Milton in 1660," 359.

27 *Parliamentary or Constitutional History of England,* IV, col. 162. The Commons ordered the committee to call Milton and the sergeant before them, "to determine what is fit to be given the Serjeant for his Fees." *Commons Journal* VIII, 209.

28 Lucy Hutchinson, *Memoirs of the Life of Colonel Hutchinson*, ed. James Sutherland (Oxford, 1973), 362.

29 See R. S. Bosher, *The Making of the Restoration Settlement: The Influence of the Laudians, 1649–1652* (New York, 1951), 143–218. This plan looks back to proposals of Archbishop James Ussher in the early 1640s (see chapter 5, p. 129), and to similar recent schemes of Richard Baxter.

30 *Commons Journal* VIII, 247. See Ronald Hutton, *The Restoration* (Oxford, 1985), 150–1.

31 Phillips writes that Milton, after receiving his pardon, "stay'd not long" in Holborn Street before he "remov'd to *Jewin Street*" (*EL* 71).

32 *Mercurius Publicus*, 4 (January 24–31, 1661), 64.

33 Translation mine. [George Bate], *Elenchi Motuum Nuperorum in Anglia* (London, 1661, *c.* January), 237–8. In the first edition (1650) this passage does not appear. Starkey's *Dignity of Kingship* was republished as *Monarchy Triumphing over Traiterous Republicans. Or the Transcendent Excellency of that Divine Government fully proved against the utopian Chimeras of our Ridiculous Commonwealthmen* (London, 1661). See chapter 11, pp. 377–8.

34 Masson, VI, 422–3. Evelyn's *Diary* records that the king and "a world of Roman Catholics" at court came to hear "this eloquent Protestant" (III, 311). In June, 1662 he was suspended from his new pastorate at Charenton pending investigation of a complaint against him.

35 *LR* IV, 371–4. See chapter 10, p. 351 and note 137. Richard H. Popkin in "The Dispersion of Bodin's Dialogues in England, Germany, and Holland," *Journal of the History of Ideas* 49 (1988), 157–60, notes that Milton's friend Henry Oldenburg (then in Paris) read Bodin's work in the summer of 1659 and exchanged letters with Samuel Hartlib about it, indicating his intention to have a copy made; it has not been found. Hartlib's letter of January 30, 1660 states that he had a copy but it was not his own.

36 Masson, VI, 221–8.

37 See chapter 9, p. 287 and note 48. Sikes probably consulted Milton about publishing the sonnet but may simply have found it among Vane's papers.

38 For example, in *The Traytors Perspective-glass* (London, 1662) the author "I. T." listed various punishments suffered by the regicides, among them Milton, who was "strucken blind" immediately after he wrote his "seditious Antimonarchical Book against the King" and his answer to "learned *Salmasius*" (21–2).

39 John Ward's notes in BL Add Ms 4,320, fol. 232 report that comment from an interview with Deborah shortly before her death in 1727; he repeated it in a letter to Thomas Birch (February 10, 1738), who printed it in "An Historical and Critical Account of the Life and Writings of Mr. John Milton" prefixed to his edition, *A Complete Collection of the Historical, Political, and Miscellaneous Works of John Milton*, 2 vols (London, 1738), I, lxii.

40 Ward's letter of February 10, 1738 to Thomas Birch. See note 39.

41 *EL* 76–8. He explains that she was excused "by reason of her bodily Infirmity, and difficult utterance of Speech, (which to say truth I doubt was the Principal cause of excusing her)." Phillips's "doubts" (suspects) that she was excused not for her lameness but because her speech was difficult to understand.

42 Their signatures and Anne's mark appear in legal documents settling their claims on Milton's estate (Milton family MSS in New York Public Library); see chapter 14, pp. 536–8. Aubrey heard from some source that "Deborah was his Amanuensis" (*EL* 2), and Deborah reportedly made the same claim when she offered a presentation copy of *Paradise Lost* to her friend Elizabeth Lord, dated June, 1727 (*LR* V, 321), but her title page inscription no longer survives. A public appeal made for her in 1727 notes that the daughter of a man who is the "Boast and Glory of our *English* Poetry" is now reduced to gain part of her slender support by teaching "poor Infants the first Elements of Reading" (*Mist's Weekly Journal*, no. 106, April 29, 1727), 1.

43 Birch, "Life," I, lxii.

44 Stories recounted during the first half of the eighteenth century come from Milton's widow, his daughter Deborah (Clarke), and Deborah's daughter Elizabeth Foster, who were approached by editors and biographers seeking details of Milton's life, and of course wanted to oblige with something interesting. Sometimes those scholars offered them presents of money or sought aid for them as Milton's relicts.

45 Birch, "Life," I, lxii.

46 Prerogative Court of Canterbury, Deposition Book, 1674, ff. 312–313v, cited in *LR* V, 222.

47 Andrew Marvell, *The Rehearsal Transpros'd: The Second Part* (London, 1673), 379. Marvell is answering Parker's treatise, *A Reproof to the Rehearsal Transpros'd* (London, 1671). See chapter 14, pp. 499–501.

48 Gauden's letter to Clarendon of January 21, 1660 (1661) claims that "what goes under the late blessed King's name, the *Eikon* or Portraiture of hys Majesty in hys Solitudes and sufferings . . . was wholy and only my invention . . . which I sent to the King in the Isle of Wight . . . hys Majesty graciously accepted, owned, and adoped it as hys sense and genius:" *Catalogue of the Clarendon State Papers,* ed. O. Ogle et al., 5 vols (Oxford, 1892), III, Supplement, xxvii–xxx. See chapter 8, pp. 247–8.

49 In 1660 he published a new edition and continuation of Baker's *Chronicle* to 1658, *A Continuation of the Chronicle of England to the end of the year 1658 . . . more especially relating unto the transactions of Charles, crowned King of the Scots at Scone on the first day of January, 1650* (London, 1660), which treats Charles I with sympathy throughout, and assumes that Charles II is the rightful ruler of the realm. John Phillips published several works of Restoration buffoonery, among them *Montelion, 1660, or The Prophetical Almanack* (London, 1660), and *Don Juan Lamberto, or a Comical History of the late Times* (London, 1660). There is no indication that John kept up much contact with his uncle.

50 Thomas Ellwood, *The History of the Life of Thomas Ellwood,* ed. J[oseph] W[yeth] (London, 1714), 131–7.

51 See the pre-dating of several poems in the 1645 *Poems,* chapter 7, p. 228.

52 The marriage allegation, dated February 11, reads: "which day personally appeared John Milton, of ye parish of St. Giles, cripplegate, London, Gent., aged about 50 yeares and a Widdower, and alledged that he intendeth to marry with Elizabeth Minshull, of ye parish of St. Andrew, Holborne, in ye county of Midd., Mayden, aged about 25 years and att her owne disposing, and that he knoweth of noe lawfull lett or impediment by reason of any precontract, consanguinity, affinity, or otherwise, to hinder the said intended marriage, and of ye truth hereof he offered to make oath, & prayed Licence to be marryed in ye parish church of St. George in ye Borough of Southwark, or St. Mary Aldermary in London." (*Allegations for Marriage Licenses issued from the Faculty Office of the Archbishop of Canterbury at London, 1543–1869,* Harleian Society XXIV (London, 1886), 68.) Masson (VI, 475) reproduces a facsimile of Milton's signature.

53 *The Registers of St. Mary Aldermary, London . . . 1558 to 1754,* ed. J. L. Chester, Harleian Society, Registers V (London, 1880), 30: "John Milton of the Parish of St. Gyles Crippellgate and Elizabeth Minshall of the parish of St. Andrews Holborne married by licence the 24th of February, 1662 [1663]."

54 This is Thomas Newton's hearsay information "from a gentleman who had seen his widow in Cheshire." See his "Life of Milton," prefixed to his edition of *Paradise Lost: A Poem, in Twelve Books,* 2 vols (London, 1749), I, 252–3, n. 305.

55 This house, in the area known as "Cripplegate Parish without the Freedom," was taxed at "four hearths" in 1674 (Masson, VI, 483–4). The time of the move is put in some question by the fact that in September, 1665 Milton was listed as being 18 months in arrears for taxes on a house having "eight herths" in Cripplegate Ward extra, Redcrosse Street (the Jewin Street house, which stood close to Redcross Street). But the tax collector may not have known of Milton's move when he reported the overdue taxes. Though Edward Phillips's chronology is often vague after 1663, his association of this move with Milton's third marriage is plausible; also, the fact that Cyriack Skinner's

biography mentions only Bunhill as Milton's residence after he left Petty France suggests that he did not stay long in Jewin Street. Parker's speculation that Milton moved after his daughters left home, *c.* 1669, has no evidentiary support and seems implausible.

56 Artillery Walk is indicated by an arrow.

57 Newton, "Life of Milton," I, xlix, had this information from Milton's granddaughter, Elizabeth Foster, who had it from her mother. Newton claims that Elizabeth Foster confirmed several facts which he took from Birch's "Life of Milton." See note 39.

58 Newton reported that visitors to Elizabeth Milton confirmed Milton's seasonal composing habits ("Life of Milton," I, lvi). For Milton's fears about England's cold climate, see *Mansus,* ll. 27–9, 35–8, and *PL* 9.44–6.

59 *EL* 6, 12. Richardson heard from some who visited Milton's daughter Deborah in later life that "He was Delightful Company, the Life of the Conversation, and That on Account of a Flow of Subject, and an Unaffected Chearfulness and Civility" (*EL* 229).

60 *EL* 6, 194; Newton, "Life of Milton," I, lviii; his source was Milton's granddaughter, Elizabeth Foster.

61 Newton, "Life of Milton," I, xlviii, li.

62 Evelyn noted in his *Diary* that "This Gent: was nephew to *Milton,* who writ against *Salmasius's 'Defensio,'* but not at all infected with his principles . . . though brought up by him:" *The Diary*, ed. E. S. de Beer, 5 vols (Oxford, 1955), III, 365. In Evelyn's fine library Phillips was preparing the fourth edition of Richard Baker's *Chronicle*, recasting and rewriting his earlier *Continuation* to include the events of the Restoration to the coronation of Charles II in 1661.

63 Milton's widow claimed to have been his amanuensis at times (Newton, "Life of Milton," I, lvi–lviii).

64 Newton, "Life of Milton," I, lvii. Richardson heard what sounds like an embroidery on this story, in which the post was said to be that of Latin Secretary and an exchange between Milton and his wife is imagined: "*Milton* Withstood the Offer; the Wife press'd his Compliance. *Thou art in the Right* (says he) *You, as Other Women, would ride in your Coach; for Me, My Aim is to Live and Dye an Honest man*" (*EL* 280).

65 "An Act to prevent and suppress Seditious Conventicles," *Anno Regni Caroli II . . . Decimo Sexto* (London, 1664). Any who returned before seven years would be subject to death. Quakers were to be jailed and transported for refusing to take judicial oaths.

66 "An Act for Restraining Non-Conformists from Inhabiting in Corporations," *Anno Regni Caroli II . . . .XVII* (London, 1665).

67 Bodleian, MS Rawlinson E. 69, 21.

68 James Heath, *A Brief Chronicle of the Late Intestine War in the Three Kingdoms* (London, 1660), 435 ; the attack was reprinted in 1664. George Bate's sneering reference (see p. 405) was also reprinted in 1663. Milton's works were also prominently mentioned in *Cabala, or an Impartial Account of the Non-Conformists Private Designs, Actings, and Ways. From August 24, 1662 to December 25 in the same year* (London, 1663), 11–12, a burlesque of several major Nonconformist writers. As "Blind Milton" he was also ridiculed in the almanac *Poor Robin* for the years 1664–70 (see *LR* IV, 397).

69 Roger L'Estrange, *Toleration Discussed* (London, 1663), 34. L'Estrange, *Considerations and Proposals In Order to the Regulation of the Press: Together with Diverse Instances of Treasonous, and Seditious Pamphlets, proving the Necessity thereof* (London, 1663, June 3).

70 Masson, VI, 328.

71 [Anon.], *A Treatise of the Execution of Justice: wherein is clearly proved, that the execution of Judgment and Justice, is as well the Peoples as the Magistrates duty: And that if Magistrates pervert Judgment, the People are bound by the Law of God to execute Judgment without them, and upon them* (London, 1663, October?).

72 See Paul Slack, *The Impact of Plague in Tudor and Stuart England* (London, 1985); for Cripplegate, p. 151.

73 The Cripplegate figures are from Daniel Defoe, *The Journal of the Plague Year,* ed. J. H. Plumb (New York, 1960), 24. Pepys notes that the plague bills listed over 1,700 deaths overall (the official figure was 1,843) in the week ending July 25, and 2,020 the week ending August 1 (*Diary* VI, 173, 180).

74 Pepys, *Diary* VI, 133.

75 Slack, *Impact of Plague*, 246, 286.

76 Pepys, *Diary* VI, 128–208.

77 Defoe, *Journal of the Plague Year*, 66.

78 Ellwood, *Life*, 233.

79 *CPW* IV. 1, 675.

80 The classic account of *De Doctrina Christiana* (*DDC*) is Maurice Kelley's introduction to his edition of that work in *CPW* VI; Kelley's *This Great Argument: A Study of Milton's De Doctrina Christiana as a Gloss upon Paradise Lost* (Princeton, NJ, 1941) may overstate some parallels with *Paradise Lost*, but most instances are persuasive.

81 See chapter 11, note 115.

82 For an analysis of copyists' hands, see Kelley, *This Great Argument*, 40–1. Picard's corrections and additions are of course evident only after page 196, in the part of the manuscript not recopied by Skinner. The amanuensis designated by Kelley as Hand A recopied Picard's pages 549–52, evidently after revision; Kelley thinks one scribe's hand also appears in the Commonplace Book.

83 The challenge was posed by William B. Hunter, "The Provenance of the *Christian Doctrine*," *Studies in English Literature* 33 (1992) 129–42, with responses by Lewalski and John Shawcross, 143–66. Hunter expanded upon his argument in *Visitation Unimplor'd: Milton and the Authorship of De Doctrina Christiana* (Pittsburgh, 1998). Substantial answers include Christopher Hill, "Professor William B. Hunter, Bishop Burgess, and John Milton," *Studies in English Literature* 54 (1994), 165–93; Lewalski, "Milton and *De Doctrina Christiana*: Evidences of Authorship," *MS* 36 (1999), 203–28; and the introduction and several essays in *Milton and Heresy,* ed. Stephen Dobranski and John P. Rumrich (Cambridge, 1998). In 1971, Hunter, C. A. Patrides, and J. B. Adamson accepted Milton's authorship in their joint publication *Bright Essence* (Salt Lake City, 1971), but sought either to downplay its heterodoxy (Hunter) or to disparage its theology as unworthy of Milton and irrelevant to his supposedly orthodox epic poems (Patrides).

84 The manuscript (SP 9/61), now in the Public Record Office, Kew, was mounted onto the stubs of pages in three volumes and rebound in 1934; pages 626–36 were mistakenly renumbered so the manuscript contains ten pages more than the pagination indicates. As Maurice Kelley noted in "Considerations Touching the Right Editing of John Milton's *De Doctrina Christiana*," *Editing Seventeenth-Century Prose*, ed. D. I. B. Smith (Toronto, 1972), 31–51, the somewhat regularized text in *CM* gives a mislead-

ing impression of the manuscript. Recently, the manuscript has been analyzed by a British consortium: Gordon Campbell, Thomas Corns, John K. Hale, David Holmes, and Fiona Tweedie, "The Provenance of *De Doctrina Christiana*," *MQ* 31 (1997), 67–121. They conclude, on the basis of a stylistic comparison with Milton's Latin *Defences*, that some portions of *DDC* (especially the preface) are more "Miltonic" than other parts; but the validity of that exercise is compromised by the generic incomparability between the polemic *Defenses* (which the preface resembles) and the biblical exegesis that comprises much of the treatise. For a critique of their arguments and conclusions, including their suggestion that Milton may have been revising a text by some other author, see Lewalski, "Milton and *De Doctrina Christiana*," 203–28, and the introduction to Dobranski and Rumrich, eds, *Milton and Heresy*.

85 See chapter 14, pp. 506–7; Bodleian, Rawlinson MS A 185, fols 271–4. Skinner sent the manuscripts to Elzevir in Amsterdam late in 1675. In a letter to his sometime patron Samuel Pepys, November 9/19, 1676, he claims that he "happen'd to be acquainted with Milton in his lifetime, (which out of mere love to learning I procur'd . . .)," but he insists that he was not at all "tainted" by Milton's views. This suggests that he was probably one of the young men who at various times exchanged their services in reading and writing for Milton's teaching, and that he was now concerned to downplay the extent of the association. If, as Hunter suggests, he only looked at Milton's papers after his death, it would behoove him to say so and remove himself yet further from the Miltonic taint. An unidentified informant described Skinner to the secretary of state as "a scholar and a bold young man who has cull'd out [from Milton's papers] what he thought fitt" (Campbell, et al., "Provenance of *De Doctrina Christiana*," 71–3). Skinner hoped to profit from publishing Milton's manuscripts, but the attempt seriously derailed his career.

86 See Kelley's narrative in *CPW* VI, 3–10, and the series of letters exchanged between Elzevier, Daniel Skinner, Skinner's father, and Williamson, reprinted in Campbell, et al., "Provenance." Elzevier's letter (February 9/19, 1677) to Skinner senior, who had intervened to try to extricate his son from his difficulties, explains that he has returned the two manuscripts he received: "les deux manuscriptes de Milton à scavoir ses ouvres en Theologie et ses lettres au Principes." Elzevier's earlier letter to Williamson (November 10/20, 1676) admits that he had agreed to publish "the Letters of Milton and another manuscript on Theology," but assures Williamson that he has since found in them things "fitter to be suppressed than published" and has determined to publish neither (Campbell, et al., "Provenance," 69, 84–5, 77–9; SP 84/203 fols 106–7; SP 84/204 fol. 123–4).

87 Milton's name was added in two places: *Joannes Miltonus Anglus* is inscribed before the preface addressed to all the Churches of Christ, added perhaps in 1825 at the time of publication. The first three words added to the volume title before Book 1, *Joannis Miltoni Angli De Doctrina Christiana ex sacris duntaxat libris petita disquisitionum libri duo. Posthumi* may be in Skinner's hand, along with the initials I. M. following the preface. The word "posthumi" seems to have been added to that title after a still legible period – perhaps when Skinner offered the volume to Elzivir for posthumous publication.

88 *CPW* VI, 117. See above, chapter 11, p. 360. Citations in text and notes, and English translations, are from *CPW* VI (trans. John Carey), unless specified as taken from the

Columbia edition (*CM* XIV–XVII, trans. Charles Sumner), or as my own. Citations of the treatise in Latin are from the Columbia edition.

89 My translation. Cf. *CM* XIV, 4. Eleven entries in the surviving Commonplace Book (*CPW* I, 477, 484, 416, 449, 501, 504, 365, 402, 407, 444) seem to refer to a lost "Theological Index" that contained at least 42 pages and probably many more. These references pertain to issues treated in the existing Commonplace Book: *Church, Church Goods, Councils, Idolatry, Pope,* and *Religion not to be Forced*; ten of them are in Milton's hand and seem to have been entered *c.* 1640–3 or a little later; the eleventh, from 1651–2, is in Edward Phillips's hand (*CPW* VI, 16–17). The topics suggested by the shorter systems of theologians would have been entered in this or another lost index.

90 See *CPW* VI, 19–22, and Kelley, "Milton's Debt to Wolleb's *Compendium Theologiae Christianae,*" *PMLA* 50 (1935), 156–65. Both John Wolleb (Wollebius), *Compendium Theologiae Christianae* (Amsterdam, 1633), trans. *The Abridgment of Christian Divinitie* (London, 1650), and William Ames (Amesius), *Medulla S. S. Theologiae* (Amsterdam, 1627), trans. *The Marrow of Sacred Divinity* (London, 1638, 1642), were very popular with Puritans. The conclusion of Campbell, et al., "Provenance," that in places Milton's treatise seems to be a palimpsest of texts conforms to the story Milton's Epistle tells about the work's evolution.

91 "Ex Deo Regeneratur. Patre nimirum: nemo enim gignit, nisi pater" (*CM* XV, 366).

92 My translation. "Haec si omnibus palam facio, si fraterno quod Deum testor atque amico erga omnes mortales animo, haec, quibus melius aut pretiosius nihil habeo, quam possum latissime libentissimeque impertio, tametsi multa in lucem protulisse videbor" (*CM* XIV, 8). Campbell, et al., "Provenance," 110, conclude that the manuscript is unfinished and therefore that its doctrinal positions cannot be taken as final; but the Epistle, which they recognize as Miltonic, offers the tract as Milton's carefully considered and admittedly heterodox theological manifesto. Had Milton seen a way to publish during his lifetime he would have had a fair copy made of the whole and would have tidied up a few misplaced references.

93 For example: "Up to now I have examined God from the point of view of his nature: now we must learn more about him by investigating his efficiency"; or, "We have been discussing GENERAL PROVIDENCE. SPECIAL PROVIDENCE is concerned particularly with angels and men." *CPW* VI, 153, 343. See also, for example, the beginnings of chapters 5, 6, 9, 12, 14, 15, 16, 17, 22, 26, 28, 29, 31, 33 in Book 1, and chapters 7 and 11 in Book 2.

94 *CPW* VI, 120. Compare the passage about the creation of poetry in *Reason of Church-Government* (*CPW* I, 820–1), and see chapter 5, p. 152.

95 Page 121. Cf *Areopagitica, CPW* II, 561–6, and chapter 6, pp. 195–7.

96 Pages 123–4; cf. *Of Civil Power, CPW* VII, 246–7.

97 Page 128. In *Of Civil Power* Milton defines evangelic religion as "faith and charitie, or beleef and practise." Cf. Wollebius, *Abridgment,* 1, 11.

98 Some comments prepare for later arguments: even the omnipotent God cannot do anything that implies a contradiction. And while God's omniscience necessarily involves foreknowledge of men's acts before they are born, men remain "free in their actions" (145–6, 150).

99 Pages 251–6, 297, 312.

100 Paul Sellin, "John Milton's *Paradise Lost* and *De Doctrina Christiana* on Predestination," *Milton Studies* 34 (1996), 45–60, points out that the treatise departs from Arminius in some respects, but it certainly does not, as he claims, "tilt" toward supralapsarianism, or differ substantially on this and other counts from the theodicy in *Paradise Lost.* He has been answered in persuasive detail by Stephen Fallon, "Milton's Arminianism and the Authorship of *De doctrina Christiana*," *Texas Studies in Literature and Language* 41 (1999), 103–27; see also Lewalski, "Milton and *De Doctrina Christiana*, 216–23. Sellin has responded in "*Futher Responses*," *MQ* 33 (1999), 38–51.

101 John Calvin, *Institutes of the Christian Religion,* III, xxiii, 7, ed. John T. McNeill, trans. F. L. Battles, 2 vols (Philadelphia, 1960), II, 955–6.

102 Hobbes, *Leviathan*, 186–93.

103 *The Judgement of the Synode Holden at Dort, Concerning the Five Articles* (London, 1619), 3–5, 24, 31–2, 37–40, 53–8.

104 The Remonstrants took their name from the five articles set forth in *Remonstrances* published by Simon Episcopius and his followers in 1610, reprinted by Philip Schaff, ed., *A History of the Creeds of Christendom*, 3 vols (London, 1877), III, 545–9. Cf. Jacobus Arminius, *Opera Theologica* (Leyden, 1629), 390–1, 636–43, 952–7 and *The Writings of James Arminius,* trans. James Nichols and W. R. Bagnall, 3 vols (London, 1825–89), I, 589–92; II, 392–7. See Stephen Fallon, "Milton's Arminianism."

105 In his *Apology against a Pamphlet* (1642) Milton claims (wrongly) that the Arminians "deny originall sinne." In the *Doctrine and Discipline of Divorce* (1643) he states that "the Jesuits, and that sect among us which is nam'd of *Arminius*, are wont to charge us of making God the author of sinne" (*CPW* I, 917; II, 293).

106 He could turn to Jacobus Arminius and Stephanus Curcellaeus, *Examen Theseum F. Gomare de Praedestinat. cum Curcellanei Vinciis* (Amsterdam, 1645), or his countryman John Goodwin, *Redemption Redeemed* (London, 1651).

107 *CM* XIV, 64, 68: "Nihil itaque Deus decrevisse absolute censendus est, quod in potestate libere agentium reliquit"; "non omnia absolute a summo Deo decerni."

108 My translation. "Neque indignum quicquam affingitur Deo, si quos eventus, quas conditiones in potestate hominis libera sitas esse Deus ipse voluit, eas ab arbitrio hominis pendere affirmemus; quandoquidem addixit Deus iis conditionibus decreta ipse sua, ut causas liberas ex ea libertate agere sineret, quam ipse iis indidit. Illud indignius Deo esset, verbo ostendi, re adimi libertatem homini, quae necessitate quadam sophistica immutabilitatis videlicet aut infallibilitatis non coactionis . . . non est mutabilis Deus, si praecise nihil decernit quod per libertatem homini decretam aliter se habere potest" (*CM* XIV, 72–6).

109 My translation. "Summatim sic se res habet, rationi summe consentanea. decrevit Deus pro sua sapientia, angelos atque homines rationis, adeoque liberae voluntatis compotes creare: praevidet simul quam illi in partem, sua integerrima libertate utentes, suopte arbitrio essent inclinaturi. Quid ergo? nam hac Dei providentia sive praescientia impositam esse iis necessitatem ullam dicemus? profecto non magis, quam si mortalium quisquam hoc idem praevidisset. Quod enim quivis mortalium certo praevidit eventurum, id non minus certo eveniet, quam quod Deus ipse praedixit . . . sic novit Adamum sua sponte lapsurum; certo igitur lapsurus erat; non necessario" (*CM* XIV, 82–6).

110 Pages 180–1, 191–2. Milton explains the classic Calvinist text Romans 8:28–30 as

pertaining to a general, conditional election, not to the election of certain individuals in preference to others.

111 My translation. "Praedestinatio itaque et electio videtur nulla esse singularis, sed duntaxat generalis; id est, eorum omnium qui ex animo credunt et credere persistunt; praedestinari neminem aut eligi qua Petrus est aut Joannes, sed quatenus credit credensque perseverat: atque tum demum generale electionis decretum credenti unicuique singulatim applicari et perseverantibus ratum fieri" (*CM* XIV, 106).

112 My translation. "Quod si Deus neminem nisi non obedientem, non credentem reiicit, certe gratiam etsi non parem attamen sufficientem omnibus impertit, qua possint ad agnitionem veritatis et salutem pervenire. . . . Causa igitur cur Deus non omnes pari gratia dignetur, est suprema ipsius voluntas; quod sufficienti tamen omnes, est iustitia eius" (*CM* XIV, 146–8).

113 John R. Rumrich, "Milton's Arianism: Why it Matters," in *Milton and Heresy,* eds. Dobranski and Rumrich 75–92, demonstrates the ubiquity of the term, and also notes the several early readers of Milton's epic poem who found Arianism in it, among them Defoe, John Toland, John Dennis, Newton, Joseph Warton, and Thomas Macaulay.

114 *Documents of the Christian Church,* ed. Henry Bettenson (New York, 1958), 36. See Henry A. Wolfson, *The Philosophy of the Church Fathers* (Cambridge, Mass., 1956), 332, 359–61; and J. N. D. Kelly, *Early Christian Doctrines* (London, 1958), 223–79.

115 See chapter 2, pp. 38–9, chapter 3, p.62.

116 See chapter 8, p. 253; *CPW* VI, 419. The Socinians held that the Son was simply the human Christ, that he was made Lord and given his divine exellence by gift of the Father and by his own merit, that he was ignorant of the mind and will of the Father until his baptism and temptation, at which time he was rapt up into heaven and instructed by God concerning his mission. See *The Racovian Catechisme* (Amsterdam, 1652), 27–164; [John Biddle], *The Apostolical and True Opinion concerning the Holy Trinity* (London, 1653); and H. John McLachlan, *Socinianism in Seventeenth-Century England* (Oxford, 1951).

117 "The Confession of the Arians," in *Christology of the Later Fathers,* ed. E. R. Hardy and Cyril R. Richardson (Philadelphia, 1954), 333–4.

118 Athanasius, *Four Discourses against the Arians,* ed. A. Robertson (Oxford, 1892), 309.

119 Page 275. A similar argument appears in the *Racovian Catechism,* 119. In the same place, Milton argues that the words "he did not reckon it robbery to be equal with God, Phillip. 2:6" demonstrate that he is not the supreme God, "For 'to consider' means, surely, to have an opinion, but there is no place for 'opinion' in God." Cf. Milton's *Artis Logicae, CM* XI, 308: "opinio tamen in Deum non cadit, quia per causas aeque omnia cognoscit." For a fuller discussion of such parallels with Arianism, see Michael Bauman, *Milton's Arianism* (Frankfurt and New York, 1987), 19–70, and Lewalski, *Milton's Brief Epic* (Providence and London, 1966), 133–63.

120 Milton explicates in his own terms that favorite proof text of the orthodox, John 1:1, "In the beginning was the Word, and the Word was with God, and the Word was God," insisting that to be from the beginning of creation, to be with God, and to be the only begotten and visible divinity, are very different things than to be the one, invisible and eternal God, "so different that they cannot apply to one and the same essence" (273).

121 Pages 307–9. These considerations undermine the claims of Hunter, et al. in *Bright*

Essence that the Son's sharing of the divine substance aligns him with a more nearly "orthodox" subordinationist view of the Trinity than with Arius.

122 Pages 212, 262. In the *Artis Logicae* Milton developed the same logical argument about number, pointing in a gratuitous comment to its anti-Trinitarian implications. See chapter 14, pp. 497–8.

123 My translation. Cf. *CM* XIV, 402.

124 Similarly, the figure speaking in Proverbs 8 "is not the Son of God but a poetical personification of Wisdom" (304).

125 *CPW* VI, 284, 285. In *Paradise Regained* the Spirit's descent is presented as the Father's testimony to and illumination of Christ.

126 My translation. Cf. *CM* XV, 24.

127 My translation. See *CM* XV, 18, 22.

128 See *CM* XV, 24: "sed nec materia nec forma peccat; egressa tamen ex Deo; et alterius facta quid vetat, quin iam mutabilis per rationcinia Diaboli atque hominis ab ipsis prodeuntia contagionem contrahat et polluatur."

129 Also, il Penseroso seeks to learn from Plato about those regions where the "immortal mind" has "forsook / Her mansion in this fleshly nook" (ll. 89–92).

130 See Stephen Fallon, "The Metaphysics of Milton's Divorce Tracts," in Loewenstein and Turner, eds, *Politics, Poetics, and Hermeneutics*, 69–83. See also Jason P. Rosenblatt, *Torah and Law in Paradise Lost* (Princeton, NJ, 1994), 71–137. Christopher Kendrick, *Milton: A Study in Ideology and Form* (London, 1986), 20–35, calls attention to a similar tendency manifested in the metaphors of *Areopagitica,* e.g. the book as "the pretious life-blood of a master spirit" (493).

131 Hobbes, *Leviathan* (London, 1651), 30. See Stephen Fallon, *Milton Among the Philosophers* (Ithaca, NY, and London, 1991). John Aubrey heard from Milton's widow that "Mr Hobbs was not one of his acquaintance: yet her husband did not like him at all: but he would grant him to be a man of great parts, a learned man. Their Interests and tenets did run counter to each other" (*EL* 7).

132 See the discussion of Henry More, Ralph Cudworth, and Benjamin Whichcote in Fallon, *Milton among the Philosophers*, 50–78.

133 Ann (Finch) Conway, *The Principles of the Most Ancient and Modern Philosophy*, ed Peter Lopston (The Hague, 1982), 217. The work was written in English, probably shortly before her death in 1679; a Latin translation was published in 1690. See Fallon, *Milton Among the Philosophers*, 117–36; the term "animist materialism" is from Fallon (98).

134 *CM* XV, 31–3: "Coelum beatorum seu Paradisus . . . ubi etiam Deus angelis et sanctis quantum illi capiunt, se praebet conspiciendum."

135 *CPW* VI, 319, 321. Milton cites Aristotle's statement that the soul is wholly contained in every part of the body as a "very strong" argument that "the human seed, that intimate and most noble part of the body, [is not] destitute and devoid of the soul of the parents, or at least of the father, when communicated to the son in the act of generation" (321–2). Milton's qualification allows the possibility that the father's semen may be the carrier of the soul.

136 Page 333. Cf. *PL* 12.469–73: "O goodness infinite, goodness immense! / That all this good of evil shall produce, / And evil turn to good; more wonderful / Then that by which creation first brought forth / Light out of darkness!"

137 Pages 343–5. Cf. *PL* 5.535–40, Raphael to Adam: "My self and all th' Angelic Host

that stand / In sight of God enthron'd, our happie state / Hold, as you yours, while our obedience holds; / On other surety none; freely we serve, / Because wee freely love, as in our will / To love or not; in this we stand or fall."

138 Pages 347–8. Cf. *PL* 8.224–31, Raphael's explanation to Adam that he does not know of man's creation because he was absent that day; also God's statement to Michael that he will "enlighten" him about the future events that he is to reveal to Adam (*PL* 11.113–16).

139 Pages 351–3. Cf. Eve's careful statement of the distinction between natural and positive law in *PL* 9.651–4.

140 Pages 353–4. A cross-reference points to Book 2, chapter 7, which treats Christian worship. See pp. 438–9, and the discussion of Christian liberty, pp. 434–5.

141 Pages 352–3; cf. Areopag*itica, CPW* II, 514.

142 *CPW* VI, 355, 369–70. Cf. Wollebius, *Abridgment*, 312–13, and Ames, *Marrow of Sacred Divinity*, 323.

143 *CPW* VI, 381. See *CM* XV, 176–7, and chapter 6, this volume. Cf. from *The Doctrine and Discipline of Divorce* and *Tetrachordon:* no "Law or Cov'nant how solemn or strait soever . . . should bind against a prime and principall scope of its own institution." "In Gods intention a meet and happy conversation is the chiefest and the noblest end of marriage." The inbred desire of joining "in conjugall fellowship a fit conversing soul . . . is properly called love." To affirm that the bed is the highest end of marriage "is in truth a grosse and borish opinion." Marriage was not given to remedy "the meer motion of carnall lust . . . God does not principally take care for such cattell" (*CPW* II, 245–6, 251, 269).

144 Pages 372–5. See chapter 6.

145 My translation follows both Sumner and Carey in recognizing a direct reference to Milton's *Tetrachordon*. I find Paul Sellin's challenge to this reading unpersuasive ("The Reference to John Milton's *Tetrachordon* in *De Doctrina Christiana*," *SEL* 37 (1997) 137–49, and his further comments in "Some Responses," *MQ* 33 (1999) 38–43; see my discussion in "Milton and *De Doctrina Christiana*," 208–10. The Latin reads: "Fornicationis autem vox si ad orientalium normam linguarum exigatur, non adulterium solum significabit, sed vel quicquid *res turpis aliqua* dicitur, vel rei defectus quae in uxore merito requiri potuit, Deut. 24.1. (ut cum primis Seldenus in Uxore Hebraea multis Rabbinorum testimoniis demonstravit) vel quicquid amori, fidelitati, auxilio, societati, id est, primae instiutioni pertinaciter contrarium, ut nos alias ex aliquot scripturae locis et Seldenus idem docuit, reperitur" (*CM* XV, 170–2). The parallel exegeses in *De Doctrina* and *Tetrachordon* for the term "fornication" are also quite striking (*Tetrachordon, CPW* II, 672–3). The similar citation of Selden and himself on the meaning of fornication in the *Second Defense* (*CPW* IV, 624–6) occurs in a passage reviewing his past publications: "Concerning also what should be thought about the single exception, fornication, I also delivered my own opinion and that of others; and that most celebrated man our countryman Selden demonstrated it more fully in his *Hebrew Wife*, published about two years later [quid item de excepta solum fornicatione sentiendum sit, & meam aliorumque sententiam exprompsi, & clarissimus vir Seldenus noster, in Uxore Hebraea plus minus biennio post edita, uberius demonstravit]" (*CM* VIII, 132, my translation).

146 "Non amatam nec iniuria neglectam, fastiditam, exosam, servitutis gravissimae sub

iugo (tale enim est coniugium si abest amor) a viro neque amante neque amico acerbissima lege retineri, ea demum durities est omni divortio durior" (*CM* XV, 164). Cf. *Doctrine and Discipline,* "to retain still, and not be able to love, is to heap up more injury . . . not to be belov'd & yet retain'd, is the greatest injury to a gentle spirit" (*CPW* II, 253).

147 Page 395. Cf. *PL* 11.1,125–31; 12.83–90.

148 See chapters 6, pp. 178–9 and chapter 7, pp. 202–3.

149 In *Documents of the Christian Church,* ed. Bettenson, pp. 66–8. Cf. Philippians 2:6–8.

150 Pages 421–3. Hieronymus Zanchius, "De Incarnatione Filii Dei," *Opera Theologicorum,* 8 tom. (Heidelberg, 1613), VII, cols 114–44.

151 For example, Docetism, Apollinarianism, Theopaschitism, Nestorianism, etc. For discussion of these in relation to Milton see Lewalski, *Milton's Brief Epic,* 148–57. For Socinianism, see note 116.

152 Page 436. See chapter 11, pp. 384–5; *PL* 12.566–9.

153 Pages 438, 440. Cf. p. 270.

154 Adam's repentance exhibits some of these stages: see *PL* 10, 829–33, 1,099–105.

155 Page 512. He refers to and summarizes passages from the "Defensio sententiae Remonstrantium circa Articulum V de Perseverantia," *Acta et Scripta Synodalia Dordracena Ministrorum Remonstrantium in Faederato Belgio* (Harderwijk, 1620), 323–4.

156 A cross-reference in chapter 13 points to chapter 27 as containing a discussion of eternal death, but that subject is now treated in chapter 33. Milton evidently intended to follow his chapter on Imperfect Glorification with a brief one on the Covenant of Grace (26), followed by the treatment of Perfect Glorification and the punishment of the damned (27), but then decided that issues pertaining to the Covenant of Grace and Christian liberty required several chapters that should properly come before the treatment of last things. He forgot to change the cross-reference.

157 See Of *Civil Power* (*CPW* VII, 271), and chapter 11, note 119.

158 Pages 533–4. See, for example, Ames, *Morrow,* xxxix, 9, 176, and Wollebius, *Abridgment,* 73. Milton found one theologian who agreed with him, Zanchius, but says that he confused the issue by admitting "a whole host of exceptions" (533). See Zanchius, *Commentarius in Epistolam Sancti Pauli ad Ephesios, Opera Theologicorum* II, Tom vi, 91.

159 *CM* XVI, 124, my translation.

160 As before he cites Matthew 22:37–40. See chapter 6, p. 168, and *Colasterion, CPW* II, 750.

161 Pages 532, 535. Joan Bennett, in *Reviving Liberty: Radical Christian Humanism in Milton's Great Poems* (Cambridge, Mass., 1989), 97–109, distinguishes between "voluntarist" antinomians at whose fringes were the Ranters, and a "humanist antinomianism" founded on an Arminian belief in free will, and an appeal to the law of nature apprehensible by the "strenuous efforts of the regenerate moral reason."

162 Pages 536–8. See chapter 11, pp. 383–5.

163 "It is not the Universities . . . but God who has given us pastors and teachers," 572. Cf. *Likeliest Means CPW* VII, 315–16; and chapter 11, pp. 388–9.

164 It has been so regarded, because it comes between the chapter devoted to the visible church, and that devoted to particular churches.

165 Pages 583–90. Cf. *Of Civil Power, CPW* VII, 242–3.

166 Pages 598–9. Cf *Likeliest Means, CPW* VII, 281: "our English divines, and they only of

all Protestants, demand tithes." See also the repeated formula in *DDC*, "How are we to live then? you may ask?" (599), and in *Likeliest Means,* "But how they shall live when they are thus bred and dismissd, will be still the sluggish objection" (*CPW* VII, 305).

167 Pages 611–13. Cf. *Of Civil Power*, *CPW* VII, 271, and *PR* 2.476–8.

168 See chapter 2, p. 19, and note 13.

169 Wollebius's *Abridgment of Christian Doctrines* treats the worship of God in the Second Book, indicating that it consists "in true holiness, and righteousness, or in the study of good works" (II.i, p. 241).

170 The Picard draft of pages 549–52, dealing with idolatry and the invocation of angels and saints, was recopied, as were pages 571–4, dealing with the Sabbath.

171 He makes the special point that covering or not covering the head is a matter of custom, depending on social symbolism. In Europe it is customary to pray bareheaded (in sign of subjection to God), but to preach or listen to sermons with the head covered "as befitting mature and free-born sons" (673).

172 *CPW* VI, 699. Cf. *CPW* VII, 246; see above, chapter 11, p. 385.

173 Pages 706–8. Milton also briefly reprises the argument of chapter 27 (525–36), making application to the Sabbath. Cf. Ames, *Medulla*, II, xiii, 9, 472.

174 Page 732. See p. 412, and also the invitation Sonnets XX and XXI (chapter 10, pp. 354–5). Cf. Aristotle, *Ethics*, IV.i., trans. H. Rackham (London and New York, 1926) and Richard Strier, "Milton against Humility," *Religion and Culture in Renaissance England*, eds Claire McEachern and Debora Shuger (Cambridge, 1997), 258–86.

175 "Sensibility to pain and complaints or lamentations, are not inconsistent with true patience, as may be seen from the example of Job" (740). Cf. *Of Education*, *CPW* II, 409, and *PR* 3.92–5, and 4.300–8. Milton's discussion of the opposites to this virtue follows Wollebius's discussion of patience toward God in *Abridgment*, II, iii, p. 254.

176 Pages 744, 750. Cf. Wollebius, *Compendium* II, viii, p. 226: "Amicitie est charitas duobus pluribusve intercedens, qua mutua, vera, & singulari benevolentia se complectuntur ad praestanda officia honesta & possibilia."

177 Candor's opposites include evil suspicion, calumny, abuse, insults, litigiousness, and flattery. Its other components are simplicity, trustworthiness, courtesy, and frankness.

178 Pages 776–7. Cf. Milton's notes on Rivetus in Commonplace Book, *CPW* I, 419. Under the second such virtue, generosity, Milton treats liberality, munificence, and gratitude and their opposites.

179 Page 782. Milton would of course be aware that creation from the rib was sometimes made an argument for woman's comparative equality: not from the head to rule her husband, not from the foot to be his slave, but from a rib, to signal fellowship and (near) parity.

180 Page 799. Old Testament precedent, Milton insists, cannot apply. Then, "the law of God was absolutely explicit, so that the magistrate's decision could be unquestionably correct. Nowadays, on the other hand, Christians are often persecuted or punished over things which are controversial, or permitted by Christian liberty, or about which the gospel says nothing explicit" (798). Cf. *Of Civil Power*, *CPW* VII, 260

181 This passage was likely written before the Restoration, since it refers to bishops who "once" imposed ignorant, idle, avaricious, and doctrinally misleading ministers on the church, and to magistrates who often do so now, "thus depriving the people of their right of election" (805).

Chapter 13 "Higher Argument:" Completing and Publishing *Paradise Lost* 1665–1669

1 Aschah Guibbory restates the last position in *Ceremony and Community from Herbert to Milton* (Cambridge, 1998).

2 The house was split into two tenaments in 1683, but was all one in Milton's time. The portion now shown as Milton's cottage, set up as a small museum, contains the kitchen, a parlor fronting the street, and a sitting room abutting the garden, set up as Milton's study.

3 In *Defensio Secunda* (*CPW* IV, 675), Milton described George Fleetwood's brother Charles as his longtime friend. Milton's cottage was owned by George Fleetwood's eldest daughter.

4 See chapter 12, p. 410 for Ellwood's record of that friendship.

5 Masson, VI, 494.

6 Thomas Ellwood, *The History of the Life of Thomas Ellwood.* ed. Joseph Wyeth (London, 1714), 233. See pp. 450–1 for Ellwood's perhaps inflated claim that this conversation gave Milton the idea for Paradise Regain*ed.*

7 See chapter 2, p. 32; chapter 5, p. 123.

8 David Quint, *Epic and Empire* (Princeton, NJ, 1992), 21–31, 50–96, 213–47.

9 Torquato Tasso, *Discorsi del Poema Eroico* (Naples, 1594); *Discorsi dell'Arte Poetica e del Poema Eroico,* ed. Luigi Poma (Bari, 1964).

10 See chapter 5, p. 124. John Aubrey heard from Phillips that he saw these lines "about 15 or 16 yeares before ever his Poem was thought of" (*EL* 13).

11 My quotations and citations of book and line numbers are from the 1674 twelve-book edition, because that is Milton's final version and the one most familiar to readers. The political import of the ten-book structure is discussed below; only a few new lines are added to make the transitions.

12 Hobbes, in a surprisingly blinkered aesthetic judgment, declared: "I never yet saw any poem, that had so much shape of Art, health of Morality, and vigour and beauty of expression as this of yours," predicting that it will live as long as the *Iliad* or the *Aeneid.* William Davenant, *Gondibert: An Heroick Poem* (London, 1651), 86.

13 For the story, see chapter 8, p. 288 and note 53.

14 Davenant, *Gondibert*, 25.

15 See, for example, Robert Herrick, *Hesperides: or the Works both Humane and Divine* (London, 1648); Henry Vaughan, *Olor Iscanus* (London, 1651); Richard Fanshawe, trans. Giovanni Battista Guarini's *Il Pastor Fido* (London, 1647, 1648); and Izaak Walton, *The Compleat Angler, or The Contemplative Man's Recreation* (London, 1653).

16 Davenant's dedication to his father, Charles Cotton, published later, suggests that heroic poetry and its values died with the king's death. It puns on the loss of "Sovereign sence," and declares "Dead to Heroick Song this Isle appears." See Lois Potter, *Secret Rites and Secret Writing* (Cambridge, 1989), pp. 85–112.

17 Dryden, preface to *The Indian Emperour, or The Conquest of Mexico by the Spaniards* (London, 1667), sig. A 2; it was produced in early 1665 and published in 1667. *The Indian-Queen* by Sir Robert Howard and Dryden (January, 1664) treats the conquest of Mexico by Montezuma, and the *Indian Emperour* treats the Spanish conquest of his

kingdom twenty years later. Both explore rightful rule, the danger of rebellion, and the consolidation of monarchical power. In his essay "Of Heroic Plays" prefixed to *The Conquest of Granada by the Spaniards* (London, 1672), Dryden states that "an heroic play ought to be an imitation, in little, of an heroic poem," with love and valor as their subject. These norms, he declared, "Sir William Davenant had begun to shadow" in both genres.

18 Luis de Camões, *Os Lusiadas* (Lisbon, 1572); *The Lusiad, Or, Portugals Historicall Poem: Written in the Portingall language by Luis de Camões, and now newly put into English by Richard Fanshaw* (London, 1655).

19 [Samuel Butler], *Hudibras. The First Part. Written in the time of the late Wars* (London, 1663); it may have appeared in 1662. *Hudibras. The Second Part* (London, 1664). Part III was published in 1678.

20 *Paradise Lost: A Poem, in Twelve Books*, ed. Thomas Newton, 2 vols (London, 1749), I, lvi.

21 Abraham Cowley, *Davideis, Or a Sacred Poem of the Troubles of David,* in *Poems* (London, 1656), sig. a 4.

22 Ibid., sig. b v.

23 Ibid., sigs b 2–b 2v.

24 Ibid., sigs b 4–b 4v.

25 Virgil claims that his second half will treat the grander theme of Aeneas's wars to found what will be the Roman empire of Augustus; Milton reverses that claim as he proposes to turn from the grand affairs of Heaven and Hell to the less exalted, tragic subject of the Fall and the loss of Eden. Also, Books VII and X, divided in the second edition, are somewhat longer in the 1667 edition than the other books: Book VII has 1,290 lines and Book X has 1,540, while the others range from 761 (Book III) to 1,190 lines (Book VIII: in the twelve-book version Book IX).

26 John Denham, *The Destruction of Troy* (London, 1656), printed for the royalist publisher Humphrey Moseley. Denham claims to have written this poem around 1636, but if so he surely revised it after the regicide. In the preface (sig. A3v) Denham explains his theory of translation, an effort to make Virgil speak "not onely as a man of this Nation, but as a man of this age."

27 Laura Lunger Knoppers, *Historicizing Milton* (Athens, Ga., and London, 1994), 67–122.

28 John Dryden, *Astraea Redux* (London, 1660), ll. 320–1. The epigraph is from Virgil's Fourth Eclogue (l. 6): "Iam redit et Virgo, redeunt Saturnia regna" (Now the Virgin [Astraea] returns, and the reign of Saturn [the Golden Age] begins).

29 Quint, *Epic and Empire,* 131–57.

30 See David Norbrook, "Lucan, Thomas May, and the Creation of a Republican Literary Culture," in *Culture and Politics in Early Stuart England,* eds. Kevin Sharpe and Peter Lake (Stanford, Calif., 1993), 45–66. Lucan was associated with anticourt critique and an aristocratic republicanism in an edition of the *Pharsalia* by Hugo Grotius (Leyden, 1614) and English translations by Arthur Gorges (1614) and Thomas Farnaby (1618).

31 Thomas May, *Lucans Pharsalia: or The Civill Warres of Rome* (London, 1627), sig. a 4. May dedicates individual books of the *Aeneid* to noblemen, many of them associated with the Leicester/Essex party of reformist opposition to royal policies. While May's subsequent versions and "continuations" of Lucan in Latin and English (1630, 1640) waver in their ideological thrust and include panegyric dedications to Charles I, in *The*

History of the Parliament of England, which began November the third, MDCXL (London, 1647), May associated the Long Parliament's cause with Lucan's noble republicans (I, 14, 20; III, 30–1). After the Restoration May was disinterred from Westminster Abbey along with other notorious supporters of the republic. See David Norbrook, *Writing the English Republic* (Cambridge, 1999), 23–62.

32 Lucan, *Pharsalia*, trans. J. D. Duff (Cambridge, Mass., 1928). For analysis of the many debts and echoes, see Norbrook, *Writing the English Republic*, 438–67; and Quint, *Epic and Empire*, 255–6, 305, 307.

33 For the challenge offered by these necessary collaborations to the idea of the solitary author, see Stephen B. Dobranski, *Milton, Authorship, and the Book Trade* (Cambridge, 1999), 33–40.

34 The manuscript is in the Pierpont Morgan Library (MA 307), a very legible fair copy. According to Peter Beal, ed., *Index of English Literary Manuscripts* (London, 1993), II, 2, 95, and 103, the amanuensis who copied it also made an entry in Milton's Commonplace Book (p. 249). Corrections in other hands, on 33 quarto pages, are chiefly by Edward Phillips, but also others. The printer evidently preserved the Book I manuscript because it bore the license to publish and notation of entry in the Stationers Register. See note 73.

35 Ellwood, *Life*, 234.

36 Samuel Pepys, *Diary*, ed. Robert Latham and William Matthews, 11 vols (London, 1970; rpt. 1985), VII, 31–2.

37 About the time Milton returned, the authorities were turning that plague pit into a cemetary for dissenters, which was to hold John Bunyan and William Blake, among many others (Masson, VI, 499–500).

38 Parker, revd edn, II, 1,104.

39 *Chronology*, 203–4.

40 See especially Marvell's lines 142–6, which echo *PL* 2.747–802. Marvell's poem is dated September 4, 1667 in Bodleian Mss Eng. poet. d. 49; Milton's poem was probably not available in print until some weeks later (*Chronology*, 206).

41 Pepys, *Diary*, VI, 122–3.

42 Ibid., VII, 247–9.

43 See chapter 10, p. 342.

44 *CM* XII, 316–19; trans. *CPW* VIII, 2–3.

45 For example, Heimbach had used the term *suspicio* as meaning "respect"; Milton puns on its more usual contemporary meaning, "to suspect."

46 *CM* XII, 112–15; trans. *CPW* VIII, 3–4.

47 Ellwood, *Life*, 314. Ellwood discusses that visit immediately after reporting Milton's return from Chalfont, but Ellwood was in prison again from March 13 to June 25, so the visit almost certainly occurred sometime after June.

48 David Ogg, *England in the Reign of Charles II*, 2 vols (Oxford, 1934), I, 305.

49 Pepys, *Diary*, VII, 270–5.

50 Ibid., VII, 271–9.

51 Richard Baxter, *Reliquiae Baxterianae* (London, 1696), Part III, 16.

52 Anthony à Wood reports that foreigners had sometimes "out of pure devotion gone to *Breadstreet* to see the house and chamber where he was born"; and also that "he had a house in *Breadstreet* burnt, which was all the real Estate he had then left" (*EL* 48). The

lease of the Red Rose had been transferred (see chapter 11, note 65), but Milton's tenure did not expire until 1674.

53 The king's affairs with Lady Castlemaine and others were common knowledge, and also his courtship of the reluctant Frances Stewart; the Duke of York was linked with Sir John Denham's wife, and the Duchess of York with Henry Sidney and others.

54 *Londons Sad Calamity by Fire; Being a Warning-piece to England* (London, 1666), 2.

55 Letter dated September, 1666, cited in James P. Malcolm, *Londinium Redivivum; or, An Ancient History and Modern Description of London*, vol. 4 (London, 1807), 80. Among the tracts that interpreted the plague, fire, and Dutch war as a divine testimony against the Clarendon Code was *A Few Sober Queries* (London, 1668), 4.

56 *Annus Mirabilis: The Year of Wonders* (London, 1667), dated November 10, 1666 in Dryden's prefatory letter to Sir Robert Howard.

57 See Stephen N. Zwicker, *Lines of Authority* (Ithaca, NY, and London, 1993), 90–107.

58 "An account of the ensuing Poem, in a Letter to the Honorable, Sir Robert Howard," *Annus Mirabilis,* sig. A 5v.

59 Ibid., sigs A 5v–A 6v.

60 See Von Maltzhan, "The First Reception of *Paradise Lost* (1667)," *Review of English Studies* 47 (1996), 488–9; and Masson, VI, 564–6.

61 Baxter, *Reliquiae Baxterianae,* Part III, 16.

62 Pepys, *Diary*, VII, 309.

63 Matthew died in 1654 and his wife Mary took over the shop; in 1662 Samuel finished his apprenticeship and his name began to appear on imprints, either with his mother or alone. Samuel's name appears only on eleven imprints from 1662 to 1680, including Milton's *Paradise Lost* and *Accidence Commenc't Grammar.* See D. M. McKenzie, "Milton's Printers," *MQ* 14 (1980), 87–91; and Peter Lindenbaum, "The Poet in the Marketplace," in *Of Poetry and Politics,* ed. Paul Stanwood (Binghamton, NY, 1995), 247–62.

64 See chapter 7, pp. 226–8.

65 Peter Lindenbaum, "John Milton and the Republican Mode of Literary Production," in *The Yearbook of Literary Studies: Politics, Patronage, and Literature in England,* ed. Andrew Gurr, et al., 21 (1991), 121–36.

66 Peter Lindenbaum, "The Poet in the Marketplace," 258, provides some comparisons: Dryden, £20 for *Troilus and Cressida;* Baxter, £10 after publication of *Saints Everlasting Rest* in 1649; George Herbert's widow, apparently nothing for *The Temple*; William Prynne, only presentation copies for *Histriomastix* (1633).

67 The contract is BL Add MS 18,861; Cf. *LF* IV, 429–31.

68 See chapter 12, p. 406.

69 [Thomas Tomkyns], *The Inconveniences of Toleration, or, An Answer to a Late Book, Intituled, A Proposition Made to the King and Parliament, for the Safety and Happiness of the King and Kingdom* (London, 1667). Tomkyns is answering [David Jenkins], *A Proposition for the Safety and Happiness of the King and Kingdom . . . By way of Accommodation and Indulgence in Matters of Religion* (London, 1667), which argued that the king should keep the moral and political force of liberty of conscience on his side, and that in the face of calamities and wars sober Protestants should be tolerated as a bulwark against the wild sectaries and Jesuits. It was dated June 18 and available in early August, 1667. See also [Thomas Tomkyns], *The Rebel's Plea Examined: or Mr. Baxter's Judgment concerning the late War*

(London, 1660).

70 Evident from the entry in the Stationers Registers. See note 76.

71 *Eikonoklastes* is cited as a "Villanous Book" in Thomas Sprat's *Observations on Monsieur de Sorbier's Voyage into England* (London, 1665), 58–9; [Pierre Nichole], *The Pernicious Consequence of the New Heresie of the Jesuits against the King and the State* (London, 1666), sig. A 4v, links Milton and other republicans with the Jesuits as advocates of regicide. David Lloyd attacked *Eikonoklastes* in *Memoires of the Lives, Actions, Sufferings, and Deaths of those Noble, Reverend, and Excellent Personages that Suffered . . . in our Late Intestine Wars* (London, 1668), 221. Also, for seven consecutive years beginning in 1664, "Blind Milton" was mentioned as an object of ridicule in *Poor Robin*, a satiric almanac.

72 John Gadbury, *Vox Solis: or, an Astrological Discourse of the Great Eclipse of the Sun* (London, 1667), 2. See Nicholas Von Maltzahn, "The First Reception of *Paradise Lost* (1667)," *Review of English Studies* 47 (1996), 481–7.

73 "IMPRIMATUR: Tho. Tomkyns, RRmo. in Christo Patri ac Domino, Dño Gilberto, Divina Providentia Archiepiscopo Cantuariensi, a sacris domesticis. Richard Royston. Intr. per Geo: Tokefeilde Ck" (Let it be Printed: Thomas Tomkyns, one of the religious servants of the most reverend father and lord in Christ, Lord Gilbert, by divine providence Archbishop of Canterbury. Richard Royston. Entered by George Tokefield, clerk). In *LR* IV, 433–4. The entry is now barely legible in the manuscript. The contract Milton signed with Simmons on April 27, 1667 describes the poem as "lately licensed to be printed."

74 Pepys, *Diary*, VIII, 286

75 Ibid., 333 (July 12, 1667).

76 The entry reads: "Master Sam. Symons. Entred for his copie under the hands of Master Thomas Tomkyns and Master Warden Royston, a booke or copie intituled *Paradise lost A Poem in Tenne bookes* by J. M.," *SR 1640–1708*, II, 381.

77 BL Evelyn Papers JE A 12, fols. 69, 68. See Nicholas Von Maltzahn, "Laureate, Republican, Calvinist: An Early Response to Milton and *Paradise Lost* (1667)," *MS* 29 (1992), 181–98. Hugh Amory, "Things Unattempted Yet: A bibliography of the first edition of *Paradise Lost*," *Book Collector* 32 (1983), 41–66, notes that printing did not normally wait upon registration, and that Simmons likely began soon after signing the contract. Von Maltzahn, "First Reception," 487–8, points out that an average rate of about two sheets a week was usual, and that the next year Simmons registered a work five weeks before its appearance.

78 Hugh Amory, "Things Unattempted Yet," 41–66, identifies four separate issues, with six different title pages (and one variant). See also R. G. Moyles, *The Text of Paradise Lost: A Study in Editorial Procedure* (Toronto, 1985), 21–8.

79 The poem may have been first presented for sale with the 1668 title page bearing just the initials, since that formula corresponds most closely to the entry in the Stationers Register; and the 1667 title pages, though printed earlier, may have been used later. For this argument see Amory, "Things Unattempted Yet," 45–51, and Von Maltzhan, "First Reception," 488. The first 1667 title page reads: "*Paradise lost. A Poem. Written in Ten Books* By John Milton. London: Printed, and are to be sold by Peter Parker under Creed Church near Aldgate; And by Robert Boulter at the Turks Head in Bishopsgate-street; And Matthias Walker, under St. Dunstons Church in Fleet-street, 1667." The

first three title pages list these three booksellers. Dobranski, *Milton, Authorship, and the Book Trade,* 37–9, notes that variation in authors' names on title pages was common and often had more to do with printshop convenience than deliberate intent. Still, these variations go well beyond the norm.

80 One state presents this note in six lines, the other reduces it to three lines, omitting the reference to rhyme.

81 One issue omits the "Printer to the Reader."

82 John Dryden, *Of Dramatic Poesie, An Essay* (London, 1668). The bookseller Herringman registered the work with the Stationers on August 7, 1667; L'Estrange was the licenser. The title page bears the date 1668, as was usual with late-year publications.

83 Crites was Sir Robert Howard, Dryden's brother-in-law; Eugenius was Charles Sackville, Earl of Dorset; Lisideius was Sir Charles Sedley; and Neander, Dryden.

84 *EL* 185–6. Howard's strictures against rhyme in drama first appeared in the preface to his *Four New Plays* (London, 1665), sigs a 4v–b, which includes *The Indian Queen* written with Dryden. It sets the topics for Dryden's defense of rhyme in his *Essay.* Howard excuses his own use of rhyme against his principles with the wry comment that "it was the fashion," and he thought best "as in all indifferent things, not to appear singular."

85 Eugenius specifies that "In the epique or lyrique way it will be hard for them to show us one such amongst them, as we have many now living, or who lately were so. They can produce nothing so courtly writ, or which expresses so much the Conversation of a Gentleman, as Sir *John Suckling*; nothing so even, sweet, and flowing as Mr. *Waller*; nothing so Majestique, so correct, as Sir *John Denham*; nothing so elevated, so copious and full of spirit, as Mr. Cowley," *Dramatick Poesie*, 7.

86 Ibid., 66–7.

87 Ibid., sig. A 3.

88 Stephen Zwicker, "Lines of Authority," in *Politics of Discourse*, ed. Kevin Sharpe and Stephen Zwicker (Berkeley, Calif., 1987), 249.

89 Parker, II, 1,116.

90 BL, MS Evelyn Papers, JE A 12, fol. 69 (Beale to Evelyn, November 11, 1667).

91 BL, MS Evelyn Papers, JE A 12, fol. 68 (Beale to Evelyn, November 18, 1667). See Von Maltzahn, "Laureate, Republican, Calvinist", 181–98.

92 BL, MS Evelyn Papers, JE A 12, fol. 71. Somewhat ambiguously, he expresses his appreciation to Evelyn in a letter of April 2, 1668, noting that he had received "a letter from Mr. Milton by your Friendly conveyance," but that his infirmities have kept him from replying either to Evelyn or Milton. As he wrote readily to others, it seems that either he had second thoughts about engaging Milton after studying his poem more carefully, or that Milton was politely discouraging.

93 Von Maltzahn, "Laureate, Republican, Calvinist," 187–94. BL MS Evelyn Papers, JE A 12, fol. 93.1v (December 18, 1669); JE A 13, fol. 108.2 (December 24, 1670).

94 Bodleian MS Tanner 45, fols 258, 271. Cf. Von Maltzhan, "First Reception of *Paradise Lost*," 490–3.

95 This contradicts the dubious story reported by Richardson, that the poem was unknown until 1669, when Lord Buckhurst discovered it and called it to Dryden's attention, who reportedly exclaimed, "This Man . . . Cuts us All Out, and the Ancients too" (*EL* 295–6). Dryden may have said something like this when he first read *Paradise*

Lost, and he probably read it early on. But Richardson's story, based on hearsay, points to a later date. He refers to the edition "produced" by the Earl of Dorset, which must be the 1688 edition for which he was a prominent subscriber. He also reports a remark by Dryden that he would not have translated his Virgil in rhyme if he had it to do again – but he began that work only in 1693.

96 The receipt is now in the library of Christ's College, Cambridge (MS 8). The witness was Edmund Tipton.

97 He may also have been too much involved in the project of bringing out, in parts and then as a whole, the massive *Exposition with Practical Observations on the Book of Job* by Joseph Caryl. The complete work was published in 1676–7, but early parts began to appear in 1643, from different printers; the Simmons house by stages bought up all the rights.

98 Thomas Birch, letter to P. Yorke, November 17, 1750, BL Add Ms. 35, 397, f. 321v. The visit took place on November 13.

99 Thomas Birch, ed. A *Complete Collection of the Historical, Political, and Miscellaneous Works of John Milton,* 2 vols (London, 1738), I, 61–3. Lady Merian has not been identified.

100 See, for example, Kathleen Swaim, *Before and After the Fall* (Amherst, Mass., 1986); and Mary Ann Radzinowicz, "Man as a Probationer of Immortality," in *Approaches to Paradise Lost,* ed. C. A. Patrides (Toronto, 1968), 31–51.

101 See pp. 447–8.

102 See, for example, C. W. Bowra, *From Virgil to Milton* (London, 1945); Francis Blessington, *Paradise Lost and the Classical Epic* (Boston, Mass., and London, 1979); G. K. Hunter, *Paradise Lost* (Totowa, NJ, 1979); and Martin Mueller, "The Tragic Epic," in *Children of Oedipus* (Toronto, 1980), 213–30.

103 See, for example, Harold Toliver, "Milton's Household Epic," *MS* 9 (1976), 105–20; and T. J. B. Spencer, "*Paradise Lost*": The Anti-Epic," in *Approaches to Paradise Lost,* ed. Patrides, 81–98.

104 See, for example, Richard S. Ide and Joseph A. Wittreich, "Composite Orders: The Tenres of Milton's Last Poems," *MS* 17 (1983); Lewalski, *Paradise Lost and the Rhetoric of Literary Forms* (Princeton, NJ, 1985); John R. Knott, *Milton's Pastoral Vision* (Chicago, 1971); Anthony Low, *The Georgic Revolution* (Princeton, NJ, 1985), 310–22; and Sara Thorne-Thomsen, "Milton's 'Advent'rous Song': Lyric Genres in *Paradise Lost.*" Dissertation, Brown University, 1985.

105 See Joan Webber, *Paradise Lost: Milton and His Epic Tradition* (Seattle and London, 1979), 101–63; Anne Ferry, *Milton's Epic Voice* (Chicago, 1983), 20–43; William Kerrigan, *The Prophetic Milton* (Charlottesville, Va., 1974), 1–16, 125–86; George de F. Lord, "Milton's Dialogue with Omniscience," in *The Author in His Work,* ed. Louis L. Martz and Aubrey Wiliams (New Haven, Conn., and London, 1978), 31–50; and Marshall Grossman, *Authors to Themselves: Milton and the Revelation of History* (Cambridge, 1987).

106 The *Divine Comedy* has Dante the pilgrim as hero, but while its spirit is epic its form is not. See Irene Samuel, *Dante and Milton* (Ithaca, NY, 1966).

107 See the preface to Book II, *Reason of Chuch-Government, CPW* I, 808, where Milton justifies the Bardic poet in speaking more of himself than the "mere" prose writer.

108 For the Homer/Virgil debts see note 102; for Lucan, see p. 448 and notes 30, 31. Also see, for example, Richard DuRocher, *Milton and Ovid* (Ithaca, NY, and London,

1985); John Steadman, *Milton and the Renaissance Hero* (Oxford, 1967); A. Bartlett Giamatti, *The Earthly Paradise and the Renaissance Epic* (Princeton, NJ, 1966); Wayne Shumacher, "*Paradise Lost* and the Italian Epic Tradition," in *Th' Upright Heart and Pure,* ed. Amadeus P. Fiore (Pittsburgh, 1967), 7–24, 87–100; Kathleen Williams, "Milton, Greatest Spenserian," in *Milton and the Line of Vision,* ed. Joseph A. Wittreich (Madison, Wis., 1975), 25–55; and Quint, *Epic and Empire.*

109 Ariosto, *Orlando Furioso*, I.2.2 (Ferrara, 1516), 2.

110 See Jason Rosenblatt, "The Mosaic Voice in *Paradise Lost,*" *MS* 7 (1975), 107–32.

111 See, for example, John Steadman, *Milton and the Renaissance Hero* and Lewalski, *Paradise Lost and the Rhetoric of Literary Forms,* 55–78.

112 Some parallels are explored, to different purpose, in R. J. Zwy Werblowsky, *Lucifer and Prometheus* (London, 1952).

113 Giamatti, *The Earthly Paradise and the Renaissance Epic*, 295–351.

114 Knoppers, *Historicizing Milton,* 96–114.

115 See, for example, Mary Ann Radzinowicz, "The Politics of *Paradise Lost,*" in *Politics of Discourse,* eds. Sharpe and Zwicker, 204–29; Michael Wilding, *Dragon's Teeth: Literature in the English Revolutio* (Oxford, 1987), 204–58; Stevie Davies, *Images of Kingship in Paradise Lost* (Columbia, Mo., 1983)*;* and Joan Bennett, *Reviving Liberty: Radical Christian Humanism in Milton's Great Poems* (Cambridge, Mass., 1989)*,* 33–58.

116 Blair Worden, "Milton's Republicanism and the Tyranny of Heaven," in *Machiavelli and Republicanism,* eds. Gisela Bock, et al. (Cambridge, 1990), 225–41.

117 Norbrook, *Writing the English Republic*, 467–80.

118 Sharon Achinstein, *Milton and the Revolutionary Reader* (Princeton, NJ, 1994), 173–223.

119 See chapter 8, p. 233. Satan's misapplication of this rhetoric is contextualized by Cataline's exhortation to his greedy and dissolute soldiers, as reported by Sallust: "Awake, then! Lo, here, here before your eyes is the freedom for which you have yearned, and with it riches, honor, and glory . . . unless haply I delude myself and you are content to be slaves rather than to rule:" Sallust, *The War with Cataline*, 20.1–17, trans. J. C. Rolfe (Cambridge, Mass., 1965), 35–9. Another is Caesar's speech upon crossing the Rubicon denouncing Pompey as a tyrant, as reported by Lucan: "we are but dislodging a tyrant from a state prepared to bow the knee:" Lucan, *Pharsalia* i.299–351, trans. J. D. Duff (Cambridge, Mass. 1928), 24–9.

120 See on this point Robert Fallon, *Captain or Colonel* (Columbia, Mo., 1984), 202–34.

121 For the Cromwell associations see Worden, "Milton's Republicanism," 242–4; Norbrook, *Writing the English Republic*, 452–5; and Achinstein, *Milton and the Revolutionary Reader,* 177–202. For the associations with Charles I, see Bennett, *Reviving Liberty*, 33–58.

122 See Wilding, *Dragon's Teeth,* 205–31.

123 *PL* 12.224–6, 335–9. See Norbrook, *Writing the English Republic*, 464–5.

124 See Quint, *Epic and Empire,* 992, 253–67; and J. Martin Evans, in *Milton's Imperial Epic* (Ithaca, NY, and London, 1996).

125 Evans, *Milton's Imperialist Epic,* 77–103, assimilates Adam and Eve, unwarrantably in my view, to the condition of indentured servants working for God, or to New World Indians needing to be evangelized and controlled.

126 J. M. Evans suggests that Hell might be seen as God's penal colony, designed from the

beginning as a place of harsh punishments and hard living conditions for the angel rebels against heavenly society (*Milton's Imperial Epic*, 41). But again there are large differences: God chiefly leaves the fallen angels on their own in Hell, to build their cities, to explore, to form military regiments, to write poetry and discuss philosophy, to build a bridge to earth, and even to escape (as Satan does, physically) and discover earth.

127 Michael's reference to "as yet unspoil'd / *Guiana,* whose great Citie *Geryons* Sons / Call *El Dorado*" (11.409–11) makes Satan the progenitor of Spanish conquests and exploitations of New World lands and peoples in their search for gold.

128 For example, *PL* 2.1–6, 636–43. See Balachandra Rajan, *Under Western Eyes: India from Milton to Macaulay* (Durham, NC, and London, 1999), 50–66.

129 See chapter 8, pp. 240–4.

130 I owe this insight to Diane McColley.

131 See chapter 12, pp. 419–20

132 See chapter 12, pp. 424–6.

133 See chapter 12, pp. 420–4 and note 100. Also see Lewalski "Milton and *De Doctrina Christiana,*" *MS* 36 (1998), 203–28.

134 See chapter 12 and notes 130, 133.

135 Stephen Fallon, *Milton Among the Philosophers,* 102.

136 See chapter 12, pp. 434–5 and note 161; also Joan Bennett, *Reviving Liberty*, 94–118.

137 Galileo Galilei, *Dialogo . . . sopra i due massimi sistemi del mondo, tolemaico, e copernicano* (Florence, 1632), trans. Stilman Drake, 2nd edn (Berkeley, Calif., 1967). See Lewalski, *Paradise Lost and the Rhetoric of Literary Forms*, 46–50. Du Bartas's widely read hexaemeral poem, *La Semaine,* trans. Joshua Sylvester, *Bartas his Divine Weekes and Workes* (London, 1605, 1621, etc.) presents a Ptolemaic universe as revealed in Genesis.

138 For a range of views on this representation, see Diane McColley, *Milton's Eve* (Urbana, Ill., 1983); Christine Fruola, "When Eve Reads Milton: Undoing the Canonical Economy," *Criticial Enquiry* 10 (1983), 321–47; and essays in Julia Walker, ed., *Milton and the Idea of Woman* (Urbana, Ill., and Chicago, 1988).

139 See, for example, Marcia Landy, "Kinship and the Role of Women in *Paradise Lost,*" *MS* 4 (1972), 3–18; and Janet Halley, "Female Autonomy in Milton's Sexual Poetics," in Walker, ed., *Milton and the Idea of Women,* 230–53.

140 For such liberalizing uses of Milton, see Joseph A. Wittreich, Jr., *Feminist Milton* (Ithaca, NY, and London, 1987).

141 See Lewalski, "Innocence and Experience in Milton's Eden," in Thomas Kranidas, ed., *New Essays on Paradise Lost* (Berkeley, Calif., 1969), 86–117.

142 See Jacques Lacan, *Ecrits: A Selection*, ed. and trans. Alan Sheridan (New York, 1977), 1–7, 30–113, for discussion of identity formation in terms of movement from a narcissistic "mirror stage" to a symbolic stage in which the self is understood through its various relationships.

143 For the view that it presents such submission see Mary Nyquist, "The Genesis of Gendered Subjectivity," in Nyquist and Margaret Ferguson, eds, *Re-Membering Milton* (New York and London, 1987), 99–127; and Halley, "Female Autonomy in Milton's Sexual Politics," 230–53.

144 See chapter 6, pp. 165–6.

145 I owe the term to Earl Miner.

146 The classic biblical text is Joel 2:28: "I will pour out my spirit upon all flesh; and your sons and your daughters shall prophesy, your old men shall dream dreams, your young men shall see visions." Cf. John Smith, "Of Prophecy," in *Select Discourses* (London, 1660).

Chapter 14 "To Try, and Teach the Erring Soul" 1669–1674

1 J. M., *Accedence Commenc't Grammar, Supply'd with sufficient Rules, For the use of such as, Younger or Elder, are desirous, without more trouble then needs, to attain the Latin Tongue; the elder sort especially, with little teaching, and thir own industry* (London, 1669). It was announced in the *Term Catalogues* I, 14, licensed June 28, 1669. The first issue lists only Milton's initials, the printer, S. Simmons (again), and his shop in Aldersgate Street; the second issue gives the author's full name and lists John Starkey in Fleetstreet as bookseller.

2 See chapter 7, pp. 207–8.

3 Registers of St Nicholas, Ipswich, Suffolk, ed. Edward Cookson (London, 1897), 154; *LR* IV, 450.

4 John Aubrey, at that point a member of the Royal Society, observed that Milton was visited by the learned, "more then he did desire" (*EL* 6).

5 Both Anthony à Wood and Cyriack Skinner report the incident (*EL* 41, 31).

6 Wood, IV, 182–3. Masson, VI, 640, speculates that the officer of state who accompanied Angelsey may have been the Lord Keeper, Sir Orlando Bridgman .

7 John Eachard, *The Grounds & Occasions of the Contempt of the Clergy and Religion* (London, 1670), sigs A 4v–A 5. Also, a much revised second edition of Roger L'Estrange's *Toleration Discuss'd* (London, 1670), 64–5, renews the attack on Milton's *Tenure.*

8 Edward Phillips, "Compendiosa Enumeratio Poetarum," in John Buchler's *Sacrarum Prophanarumque Phrasium Poeticarum Thesaurus*, 17th edn (London, 1669), 399. The *Term Catalogues* (I, 40) include the book with those published in Easter term, 1670.

9 The first edition carried the endorsement "Licensed, July 2, 1670." The registration by John Starkey names Tomkyns as licenser: "Entred . . . under the hands of Master THO. TOMKYNS and Master Warden ROPER a copie or booke intituled *Paradise regayn'd;* A Poem in 4 Bookes. the Author, John Milton. To which is added *Samson Agonistes,* A drammadic Poem, by the same Author" (*SR* II, 415.) The first issue bears the title page "*Paradise Regain'd. A Poem. In IV Books. To which is added Samson Agonistes.* The author, John Milton. London: Printed by J. M. for John Starkey, at the Miter in Fleetstreet, 1671." The printer is probably John Macock. *Samson Agonistes* has its own title page: "*Samson Agonistes, A Dramatic Poem*"; author, printer, bookseller, and date are repeated in the same form. My citations are from this first edition.

10 See chapter 13, pp. 450–1. Phillips also misdated the publication of *Paradise Lost* as 1666, not 1667.

11 Parker, I, 313–22; II, 903–17, argues that the poem was written in 1647, and possibly completed in 1652–3, citing the occasional use of rhyme which Milton rejects in his epics, and some analogues with his prose tracts of the war years. But the argument about rhyme is beside the point in a work whose metrics are unlike anything else Milton wrote. Michael Lieb, *Milton and the Culture of Violence* (Ithaca, NY, 1994), 226–

60, suggests that the Samson–Harapha encounter evokes Milton with Salmasius in the 1650s and may well date from that period. Most recent scholars favor the traditional late date, citing numerous and pervasive post-Restoration allusions and analogous situations. See, for example, Christopher Hill, *Milton and the English Revolution* (London, 1977), 487–91; Mary Ann Radzinowicz, *Toward Samson Agonistes: The Growth of Milton's Mind* (Princeton, NJ, 1978), 387–407; and Laura Lunger Knoppers, *Historicizing Milton: Spectacle, Power, and Poetry in Restoration England* (Athens, Ga., and London, 1994), 142–59.

12 Blair Worden, "Milton, *Samson Agonistes*, and the Restoration," in Gerald Maclean, ed., *Culture and Society in the Stuart Restoration* (Cambridge, 1995), 111–36.

13 See chapter 12, pp. 406–7, 413. Also see Sharon Achinstein, "*Samson Agonistes* and the Drama of Dissent," *MS* 33 (1996), 133–58; and Worden, "Milton, *Samson Agonistes*, and the Restoration."

14 Nicholas Lockyer, *Some Seasonable and Serious Queries Upon the late Act Against Conventicles* (Oxford, 1670), 8; [John Owen], *Indulgence and Toleration Considered: In a Letter to a Person of Honour* (London, 1667), 18–20; Charles Wolseley, *Liberty of Conscience the Magistrates Interest* (London, 1668), 13, 20–2. Owen argues that such liberty will unite all dissenters with the king against the papists.

15 [Tomkyns], *The Inconveniences of Toleration*, 6. See chapter 13, note 69. The ubiquitous Roger L'Estrange in an anonymous tract, *Toleration Discussed, in Two Dialogues. I. Betwixt a Conformist and a Non-Conformist. 2. Betwixt a Presbyterian and an Independent* (London, 1670) argues that toleration undermines law and causes confusion in church and state, and that claims of conscience are a cover for conspiracy to overthrow the king. Another anonymous pamphlet, *Toleration Disapprov'd and Condemn'd by the Authority and Convincing Reasons of King James, Parliament in 1662, etc.* (London, 1670), concludes that those who think Church of England worship is not sinful are schismatics if they do not accept it; those who think it is sinful will strive to overthrow it and so are dangerous to church and state.

16 See Masson, VI, 566–74.

17 David Loewenstein, "The Kingdom Within: Radical Religious Culture and the Politics of *Paradise Regained*," *Literature and History* III (1994), 63–89. See, for example, *The Examination and Tryall of Margaret Fell and George Fox* (London, 1664), 14–15, 7. Fell, on trial in 1664 for holding religious meetings and refusing the Oath of Allegiance, affirmed that "I owe Allegiance to the King as he is King of *England*, but Christ Jesus is King of my Conscience." See also William Dewsbury, *The Word of the Lord to all the Inhabitants of England* (London, 1666), 3–8; and Samuel Crisp, *An Epistle to Friends, Concerning the Present and Succeeding Times* (London, 1666), 14.

18 See chapter 13, pp. 443, 450.

19 Its foremost practitioner, John Dryden, had staked out his position in several dramas (see chapter 13, p. 445 and note 17) and in the essay *On Dramatick Poesie* (1667/8). See Steven N. Zwicker, "Milton, Dryden, and the Politics of Literary Controversy," in Maclean, ed., *Culture and Society*, 139–40, 151.

20 *Samson Agonistes*, p. 4.

21 It was advertised in the *Term Catalogues*, licensed November 22, 1670, I, 56, though the title pages of all copies are dated for the new year, as often happens with late-year publications. Starkey was also named as bookseller for the second issue of Milton's *Grammar*, with Simmons as printer.

22 Or the delay might have been caused by Simmons if he thought the new poem violated the clause in Milton's contract agreeing not to print "any other Booke or Manuscript of the same tenor or subject [as *Paradise Lost*]" without Simmons's consent. Also, if Milton made substantial changes in the work after licensing, it would have to be submitted again.

23 Stephen Dobranski, *Milton, Authorship,and the Book Trade* (Cambridge, 1999), 41–61, persuasively argues that it would be almost impossible for this omission to be a printer's error in setting the original text, though these lines might have been overlooked had they been submitted on a loose page.

24 See chapter 7, pp. 216–22, and notes 103 and 109, and chapter 10, pp. 346–9.

25 *CPW* I, 603. See Nicholas Von Maltzhan, *Milton's History of Britain: Republican Historiography in the English Revolution* (Oxford, 1991), 13.

26 Von Maltzhan, *Milton's History of Britain*, 12–14. The censor's name is not recorded, but his approval must have been gained, after negotiation. There is no record of registration with the Stationers, perhaps because of Allestry's death and a change of publisher. While licensing and registration of all publications was required by law, only about half the works published between 1662 and 1679 were licensed, due to the inefficiency and jealousy of the two agents charged with enforcement, L'Estrange as Surveyer of the Press, and the Stationers Company. See Fredrick S. Siebert, *Freedom of the Press in England, 1476–1776: The Rise and Decline of Government Controls* (Urbana, Ill., 1952), 243.

27 *EL* 75, 186. See Von Maltzhan, *Milton's History of Britain,* 15.

28 L'Estrange published a truncated version of Milton's Digression titled *Mr John Miltons Character of the Long Parliament and Assembly of Divines. In MDCXLI. Omitted in his other Works, and never before Printed, and very seasonable for these times* (London, 1681). He made it into a piece of Tory polemic castigating parliaments and dissenters in the midst of the Exclusion Crisis, which was prompted by Whig efforts preemptively to prevent the succession of the Roman Catholic James II. L'Estrange's preface asserts that this "Character" was part of Milton's *History* "and by him designed to be Printed: But out of tenderness to a Party . . . it was struck out for some harshness" (sig. A2v).

29 John Milton, *The History of Britain, That part especially now call'd England. From the first Traditional Beginning, continu'd to the Norman Conquest.* Collected out of the antientest and best Authours thereof (London, 1670). Its publication is noted in a letter of November 1 from Thomas Blount to Anthony à Wood (Bodleian MS Wood F 40. fol. 80). The first title page lists James Allestry as bookseller; he died on November 3 and a new title page was issued by November 22, naming Spencer Hickman as bookseller, with the date 1671. This version, along with the *Paradise Regained/Samson Agonistes* volume, is listed in the *Term Catalogues*, I, 56, licensed November 22, 1670.

30 Frontispiece from the *History of Britain*, with the notation "Gul. Fairthorne ad Vivum Delin. et sculpsit. Joannis Miltoni Effigies Aetat: 62. 1670." As Milton was not 62 until December 9, 1670, Allestry evidently expected to publish the *History* late in the year.

31 Faithorne fought on the king's side in the civil wars, and was for some time in exile in Paris. He published a treatise, *The Art of Graveing and Etching* (London, 1662).

32 A crayon drawing in pastels that resembles the engraving may possibly be Faithorne's original; it is now in the library of Princeton University. For a review of the evidence pertaining to its authenticity, see Leo Miller, "Milton's Portraits: An *Impartial* Inquiry

into their Authentication," *MQ* (Special Issue, 1976), 3–7, 18. David Piper, compiler of the *Catalogue of Seventeenth Century Portraits in the National Portrait Gallery, 1625–1714* (Cambridge, 1963), 237, thinks it is not convincing stylistically as Faithorne's work and that it was probably derived from the engraving.

33 Virtue recorded his visit to Deborah Clarke in his Notebook for August 10, 1721, and in a letter to Charles Christian, dated August 12 (quoted in Miller, "Milton's Portraits," 4–5). Deborah made a point of stating that Joseph Addison, John Ward, and other visitors had remarked on her close resemblance to portraits they had seen of her father, which would be the engravings and their copies. Some sentimentalized accounts describe her waxing ecstatic over a crayon drawing of Milton. Richardson reports at second-hand that she cried out "in a Transport, – 'tis My Father, 'tis my Dear Father! I see him! 'tis Him! and then She put her Hands to several Parts of Her Face, 'tis the very Man! Here, Here –" (*EL* 229). The story was repeated with other embellishments by Francis Blackburne, in his *Memoirs of Thomas Hollis* (London, 1780), 620. Whatever Deborah felt for Milton, she found it advantageous to present herself to inquirers as a tender and loving daughter.

34 Bodleian Library, Wood MS F 40. f.82. Later, Blount quoted approvingly from Milton's *History* in his *Animadversions upon Sir Richard Baker's Chronicle, and Its Continuation* (London, 1672), 20, 58, 98–9. See Nicholas Von Maltzhan, "Laureate, Republican, Calvinist: An Early Response to Milton and *Paradise Lost* (1667)," *MS* 29 (1992), 191, n. 31.

35 In a letter of December 24, 1670 to John Evelyn, Beale observed, "Milton is abroad againe, in Prose, & in Verse, Epic, & Dramatic:" Evelyn Papers, BL, JE A 13, MS 108. f. 2v. See chapter 13, pp. 455–6, and Von Maltzhan, "Laureate, Republican, Calvinist," 191.

36 Evelyn Papers, BL JE A 13, MS Letters 109 f. 1v. Cf. Von Maltzhan, "Laureate, Republican, Calvinist," 191. In December, Milton's old friend Henry Oldenburg sent a copy to Francis Vernon in Paris. The next year, Milton's sometime correspondent and acquaintance from 1656–7, the French scholar Emery Bigot (see chapter 10, p. 343), took note of it in letters to Heinsius and Lorenzo Panciatichi (*Chronology*, 211–12).

37 The manuscript copy of the Digression at Harvard (Harvard English MS 901) contains a reference to the place in the 1670 printed text where the Digression should be placed (p. 110). Also, a canceled (and not fully worked out) sentence in the manuscript adopts the tone of a settled judgment upon long-past events, qualifying a statement about venal and corrupt clerics: "But all were not such. Whither all were such or were not, many yet living can witness, and the things themselves manifest Yet the more active part of them such were." These and some other changes entered above lines suggest that the Digression was being corrected with a view to publication sometime after the 1670 edition. Toland's text of the *History* in his edition of Milton's *Works* (1698) makes several additions to the original edition which may be authorial; he claims that his version was taken from a copy "corrected by the Author himself" (*LR* V, 27). See *CM* XVIII, 516–17; the additions are in *CM* XVIII, 256–7.

38 On December 29, 1672 the bookseller Sir Thomas Davies registered Milton's *History of England*, indicating that he had rights to it from John Dunmore; in the following entry on that same date, the bookseller John Martin enters the work, indicating that Davies had assigned those rights to him. Dunmore obtained rights to it on August 24, 1671 from Spencer Hickman (*SR 1640–1708*, II, 451–2).

39 Petri Molinaei (Pierre Du Moulin), *Parerga. Poematum Libelli Tres* (Cambridge, 1670), Book II, sigs F8–F8v, 36–42. Lieb, *Milton and the Culture of Violence*, 242, sees the Harapha episode in *Samson* as Milton's riposte to the violent attack on him in the *Regia Sanguinis Clamor*, and especially this poem.

40 *Du Moulin, Parerga*, Book III, 141–2; trans. *LR* V, 22–3.

41 His divorce tracts and other early works were also still circulating. The bookseller John Starkey's *Catalogue* issued on May 29, 1971 listed not only *Paradise Regained* and *Samson* but also *Tetrachordon* and *Accidence Commenc't Grammar* (*Chronology*, 212). Samuel von Pufendorf cites *Doctrine and Discipline of Divorce* in *De Jure Naturae* (Lund, 1672).

42 *Joannis Miltoni Angli, Artis Logicae Plenior Institutio, Ad Petri Rami Methodum Concinnata, Adjecta est Praxis Annalytica & Petri Rami vita* (London, 1672). In the first issue Spencer Hickman, identified as Printer to the Royal Society, serves as both printer and bookseller, but a new title page substituted in many copies of this issue and dated 1673, identifies him as printer (S. H.) and the bookseller as R. Boulter, at a new address. For some reason having to do with Milton's revisions or a major printing error or something else, pages 1–4 were reprinted and substituted for the original pages, and the gatherings were reconstituted, leaving stubs. The *Term Catalogues* licensed May 13, 1672, list the work (I, 115).

43 Dolle's portrait is too big for the book's duodecimo format, suggesting that it may have been intended for another work. It would fit the *Paradise Regained/Samson* volume printed for Starkey, or the 1674 *Paradise Lost* printed for Simmons. Hickman may have been promised Milton's *Artis Logicae . . . Institutio* while he was involved with the *History of Britain* and arranged for Dolle to make a copy of the Faithorne engraving.

44 See chapter 7, p. 208.

45 "Quae igitur numero, essentia quoque differunt; & nequaquam numero, nisi essentia, differrent. *Evigilent hic Theologi*:" *Artis Logicae . . . Institutio,* I.7; *CM* XI, 58–9; cf. *CPW* VI, 212, 262; and chapter 12, p. 426.

46 *Artis Logicae . . . Institutio* II.3; *CM* XI, 314–15; cf. *CPW* VI, 214–15.

47 *Artis Logicae . . . Institutio* I.5; *CM* XI, 42–3; cf. *CPW* VI, 159–60; and chapter 12, p. 429.

48 See Leo Miller, "Milton Edits Freigius' 'Life of Ramus,'" *Renaissance and Reformation* 8 (1972), 112–14. There would be no reason for Milton to condense Freigius's life of Ramus while he was using his *Artis Logicae . . . Institutio* with his own students.

49 See, for example, John Hales, *Golden Remains* (London, 1673) and his earlier classic *A Tract concerning Schisme and Schismatiques* (London, 1642), which became increasingly popular after the Restoration. Cf. Edward Fowler, *The Principles and Practices of Certain Moderate Divines of the Church of England* (London, 1670).

50 See, for example, Edward Stillingfleet, *A Discourse concerning the Idolatry Practised in the Church of Rome* (London, 1671), reissued three times by 1673. Bishop Gilbert Burnet reports that "Popery was every where preached against. . . . The bishops, he of London in particular, charged the clergy to preach against popery, and to inform the people aright in the controversies between us and the church of Rome:" *History of My Own Time*, ed. Osmund Airy, 2 vols (Oxford, 1897), I, 555.

51 Burnet, *History*, I, 554.

52 John Salkeld, *The Resurrection of Lazarus, or, A Sermon Preached upon Occasion of the King's Declaration for Liberty of Conscience* (London, 1673, preached on April 23, 1672), 17. See

also *Indulgence not to be Refused, Comprehension Humbly Desired* (London, 1672); *Short Reflections upon a Pamphlet Entituled Toleration not to be Abused* (London, 1672); and [Richard Baxter], *Sacrilegious Desertion of the Holy Ministry and Rebuked and Tolerated Preaching of the Gospel Vindicated* (London, 1672).

53 [Francis Fullwood], *Toleration not to be Abused, Or, A Serious Question Soberly Debated and Resolved upon Presbyterian Principles* (London, 1672).

54 [Samuel Parker], *A Discourse of Ecclesiastical Politie, wherein the authority of the Civil Magistrate over the Consciences of Subjects in Matters of External Religion is Asserted; the Mischiefs and Inconveniences of Toleration are Represented, and all Pretenses Pleaded in Behalf of Liberty of Conscience are fully answered* (London, 1670 [1669]). He was answered, anonymously, by John Owen in *Truth and Innocence Vindicated: in a Survey of a Discourse Concerning Ecclesiastical Polity* (London, 1669), which argues the supreme claims of conscience. Parker replied with *A Defence and Continuation of the Ecclesiastical Politie* (London, 1671).

55 Sig. c 6. This treatise was prefixed to *Bishop Bramhall's Vindication of Himself* (London, 1672).

56 [Andrew Marvell], *The Rehearsal Transpros'd: Or, Animadversions upon a late Book, Intituled, A Preface Shewing What Grounds there are of Fears and Jealousies of Popery* (London, 1672, September). The book was printed clandestinely without license, and distribution of the first impression was prevented by L'Estrange; the king intervened in its behalf at the behest of Anglesey. Marvell claims (174) to have seen Parker's *Preface* in June or July, 1572.

57 *Rehearsal Transpros'd*, 303–4. This tract, addressed to Charles II, invites him by implication to see more clearly than his father did the dangers in the absolutist rhetoric and the intolerance of the bishops: "Whether it were a War of Religion, or of Liberty, is not worth the labour to enquire. Which-soever was at the top, the other was at the bottom; but upon considering all, I think the Cause was too good to have been fought for. . . . after all the fatal consequences of that Rebellion, which can only serve as Sea-marks unto wise Princes to avoid the Causes, shall this sort of Men still vindicate themselves as the most zealous Assertors of the Rights of Princes?"

58 [Anthony Hodges?], *S'Too him Bayes: Or Some Observations upon the Humour of Writing Rehearsal's Transpros'd* (Oxford, 1673), 130. Another, *A Common-place Book out of The Rehearsal Transpros'd* (London, 1673), 35–6, alludes to Milton's *Accedence*, urging Marvell to consult "blind *M.* who teaches School about *Moor-fields*" about his grammar.

59 [Samuel Parker], *A Reproof to the Rehearsal Transprosed* (London, 1673), 212, 191. The treatise was advertised as published in the *Term Catalogue* licensed May 6, 1673 (I, 134).

60 *The Transproser Rehears'd: Or the Fifth Act of Mr. Bayes's Play* (London, 1673), announced in the *Term Catalogue* licensed on May 6 (I, 135). It has traditionally been ascribed to Richard Leigh, but Nicholas Von Maltzahn, "Samuel Butler's Milton," *Studies in Philology* 92 (1955), 482–95, makes a strong case, from internal and external evidence, for ascribing it to Samuel Butler, along with some witty pre-Restoration royalist satires. See chapter 11, pp. 377–8 and note 92.

61 *Transproser Rehears'd,* 147, 43. He jeers that Milton "is more notoriously ridiculous" in that he produces in the middle of verses the "jingling" rhyme he disparages at their ends (pp. 41–2). See Sharon Achinstein, "Milton's Spectre in the Restoration: Marvell, Dryden, and Literary Enthusiasm," *Huntington Library Quarterly* 59 (1997), 1–29.

62 *Transproser Rehears'd,* 41–2.

63 Ibid., 72, 131, 110, 146–7. Other passages (pp. 9, 30, 32, 55, 98, 113, 126, 126–8, 132, 135–7) attack Milton's antiprelatical and divorce tracts, ridicule the "prodigious Conjunction of a *Latin Secretary* and an *English School-master,*" and condemn Milton and Marvell ("*Nol's Latin Clerks*") for using the sort of Italianate obscenity Milton defends in his *Apology*.

64 Edward Phillips states that shortly before his death he "prepared for the press an answer to . . . a Scurrilous Libel against him" but that it was "never publisht" (*EL* 76).

65 Andrew Marvell, *The Rehearsall Transpros'd: The Second Part. Occasioned by Two Letters: The first Printed, by a nameless Author, Intituled, A Reproof, etc. The Second Letter left for me at a Friends House, Dated Nov. 3, 1673. Subscribed J. G. and concluding with these words, If thou darest to Print or Publish any Lie or Libel against Doctor Parker, By the Eternal God I will cut thy Throat* (London, 1673). The work carries what looks like a mock license, dated May 1, 1673 and thereby in conflict with the date of the second letter.

66 Ibid., 340–2. See chapter 12, pp. 409–10 for Marvell's account in this passage of his first meeting with Parker, an erstwhile Puritan who was a frequent visitor to Milton just after the Restoration.

67 The typeface is reduced in the final eight lines of page 15 and on page 16, in order to fit the text into 16 pages.

68 It was advertised in the *Term Catalogue* for Easter, 1673, licensed on May 6 (I, 135). It has been suggested that Milton wrote after parliament's adjournment, hesitating to introduce himself into an ongoing parliamentary debate but hoping to influence the passage of a toleration Bill in the next parliament. However, I see no reason to suppose he waited so long. Keith Stavely, "Preface," *CPW* VIII, 412–13, 417 n.) dates the tract's composition after March 13 because he thinks the title echoes the King's Proclamation of that date, praising parliament for its concern "for the preservation of True Religion established in this Kingdom." But Milton's title could have been supplied later to a tract already underway, and in any case the term "true religion" and references to the growth of popery were constants in the parliamentary debates throughout the session.

69 Milton's comment that many sects, even anti-Trinitarians, may be incorporated within a church coextensive with Protestantism may owe something to the treatises of John Hales, especially his *Golden Remains*, 47–55; see note 49 and *CPW* VIII, 422–4. Milton appeals especially to Articles 6, 19, 20, and 21 of the Thirty-nine Articles.

70 *CPW* VIII, 420. Cf. chapter 11, pp. 384–5.

71 Pages 3–4; *CPW* VIII, 418–19. Cf. James Egan, "Milton's Aesthetic of Plainness, 1659–1673," *The Seventeenth Century* 12 (1997), 59; and Peter Auksi, *Christian Plain Style: The Evolution of a Spiritual Ideal* (Montreal, 1995), 277–303. As Keith Stavely points out, Milton almost certainly alludes to Edward Stillingfleet, *A Discourse concerning the Idolatry Practiced in the Church of Rome*, as one who has recently defeated the Roman Catholics in the "intangl'd wood" of councils and Fathers. Milton rejects that terrain, though as an irenic gesture he tempers his usual scorn for arguments from antiquity, allowing their usefulness to "Learned Men" (418).

72 *CPW* VIII, 424–6. Cf. *De Doctrina*, *CPW* VI, 554–5, 153–202, 544–50, 203–98 (esp. 214, 218), 189–90, 153–202. And see chapter 12, pp. 422–7.

73 For that argument, see chapter 11, pp. 385–6 and chapter 12, pp. 438–9.

74 Reuben Sanchez in "The Worst of Superstitions: Milton's *Of True Religion* and Religious Tolerance," *Prose Studies* 9 (1986), 21–37, suggests that Milton would have supported full

religious toleration if he could, as evidenced by apparent gestures of encoding and contradiction. In a persuasive rejoinder, Martin Dzelzainis, "Milton's *Of True Religion* and the Earl of Castlemaine," *The Seventeenth Century* 7 (1992), 53–69, denies that claim.

75 Ray Tumbleson makes this point in "Of True Religion and False Politics: Milton and the Uses of Anti-Catholicism," *Prose Studies* 15 (1992), 262.

76 *CSPD*, 1675–6, p. 89. The author may have been a Quaker.

77 *Poems, &. Upon Several Occasions. Both English and Latin, &. Composed at Several Times. With a small Tractate of Education To Mr. Hartlib* (London, 1673). The publisher/bookseller is Thomas Dring. The printer is probably William Rawlins, identified as W. R. on the separate title page of the Latin poems: *Joannis Miltoni Londinensis Poemata. Quorum pleraque intra Annum aetatis Vigesimum Conscripsit* (London, 1673). The work is listed in the *Term Catalogue* licensed November 24, 1673 (I, 151).

78 See chapter 1, pp. 10–11, chapter 2, pp. 26–8, 32.

79 See chapter 7, pp. 209–10, 213–14 and chapter 9, pp. 297–8.

80 See chapter 7, p. 215, chapter 9, pp. 286–7, chapter 10, p. 355.

81 See chapter 7, pp. 226–8.

82 James had two daughters by his first marriage to Anne Hyde, Clarendon's daughter, who were being raised as Protestants.

83 See chapter 7, pp. 213–14.

84 They were not published until 1743, under the title *Original Letters and Papers of State, Addressed to Oliver Cromwell. Concerning the Affairs of Great Britain. From the Year MDCXLIX to MDCLVIII. Found among the Political Collections of Mr. John Milton,* ed. John Nicholls (London, 1743). The preface claims that they "had long been treasured up by the famous *Milton*" who perhaps intended to use them in some "particular or general history of his times," and from him came into the possession of Ellwood and then Ellwood's biographer and editor (p. iv). The collection contains some private documents and letters by and to Cromwell, as well as letters of state from 1649 to 1658. The last one is addressed to Richard Cromwell after his accession.

85 This is Toland's information (*EL* 188).

86 Joannis Miltonii Angli, *Epistolarum Familiarium Liber Unus: Quibus Accesserunt, Ejusdem, jam olim in Collegio Adolescentis, Prolusiones Quaedam Oratoriae* (London, 1674), sigs A 3–A 3v. The volume is listed in the *Term Calalogue,* licensed May 26, 1674 (I, 17); it was registered July 1 (*SR 1640–1708*, II, 181).

87 See chapter 2, pp. 28–34, 43–5.

88 *Epistolarum Familiarium*, sig. A 3v.

89 John Milton, *A Brief History of Moscovia: And Of other less-known Countries lying eastward of Russia as far as Cathay. Gather'd from the Writings of several Eye-Witnesses* (London, 1682), sig. A 4v. See chapter 7, p. 212.

90 See chapter 12, p. 416 and notes 85 and 86.

91 Elzivir's 1674 catalogue listed several of Milton's earlier Latin books: the 1645 *Poemata*, the *Defensio*, the *Defensio Secunda*, and the *Defensio Pro Se* (*LR* V, 69).

92 Milton probably intended to have a clean copy of the entire manuscript, but after Milton's death, Skinner perhaps declined to put himself to the trouble of doing that but did copy a few additional pages that were especially illegible. See chapter 12, p. 416 and note 82.

93 Adam Littleton's *Linguae Latinae liber dictionarius quadripartus. A Latine dictionary, in four*

parts (London, 1678), seems to have made (unacknowledged) use of Milton's work. But his manuscripts are acknowledged as an independent major source in the *Linguae romanae dictionarium luculentum novum. A new dictionary . . . The whole completed and improved from the several works of Stephens, Cooper, Gouldman, Holyoke, Dr. Littleton, a large manuscript, in three volumes, of Mr. John Milton* (London, 1693). The preface acknowledges large use of Littleton, and also states that "we had by us, and made use of, a Manuscript collection in three *Large Folios* digested into Alphabetical order, which the learned Mr. *John Milton* had made, out of *Tully, Livy, Caesar, Sallust, Quintus, Curtius, Justin, Plautus, Terence, Lucretius, Virgil, Horace, Manelius, Celsus, Columella, Varro, Cato, Palladius;* in short out of all the best and purest *Roman* Authors" (sig. A2v).

94 *A Declaration, Or Letters Patents of the Election of this present King of Poland, John the Third, Elected on the 22 of May last past, Anno Dom. 1674. Containing the Reasons of this Election, the great Vertues and Merits of the said Serene Elect . . .* (London, 1674). The Latin original, *Diploma Electionis S. R. M. Poloniae* 1674, was the official announcement of Sobieski's election. Conceivably, Aylmer came by the document first and gave it to Milton to translate, but the political resonance of the work supports the scenario I suggest. It was first identified as Milton's in Edward Phillips's list of his works in his edition of the *Letters of State Written by Mr. John Milton* (London, 1694), liii.

95 See Nicholas Von Maltzhan, "The Whig Milton, 1667–1700," in Armitage, et al., eds, *Milton and Republicanism,* 231.

96 For the statistics, see Harris Francis Fletcher, ed., *John Milton's Complete Poetical Works, reproduced in Photographic Facsimile,* 4 vols (Urbana, Ill., 1943–8), III, 55, 57.

97 *The Monitor,* vol 1, no. 17, April 6–10, 1713. The incident is reported more briefly by Aubrey (*EL* 7) and by Richardson (*EL* 296).

98 *Paradise Lost,* ed. Newton, 1749, I, lvi–lvii.

99 John Dryden, *Fables Ancient and Modern* (London, 1700), preface, sig. *A.

100 John Dryden, *The State of Innocence, and Fall of Man: An Opera Written in Heroique Verse, and Dedicated to her Royal Highness, the Dutchess* (London, 1677). Dryden's prefatory "Apology for Heroique Poetry; and Poetique License" declares that he meant to lay the work "at the feet of so Beautiful and Excellent a Princess," and that, "at a Months warning . . . 'twas wholly Written, and not since Revis'd." Responding to the embarrassing hyperbolic praises of one of his commenders who disparages Milton by contrast, Dryden pointedly disclaims any such judgment, "The Original being undoubtedly, one of the greatest, most noble, and most sublime *POEMS*, which either this Age or Nation has produc'd" (sig. b).

101 Masson, VI, 712–13, speculates that news of the pending Dryden play may have galvanized Simmons to bring out a new edition promptly.

102 Trans. Michael Lieb, "S. B.'s 'In Paradisum Amissam': Sublime Commentary," *MQ* 19 (1988), 72–8.

103 Marvell alludes to Milton's reported rejoinder to Dryden when he requested permission to make an "Opera" of the epic; see p. 508.

104 See Achinstein, "Milton's Spectre in the Restoration," 1–29.

105 See, for example, Stanley Fish, "Inaction and Silence: The Reader in Paradise Regained," in Joseph A. Wittreich, Jr., ed., *Calm of Mind: Tercentenary Essays on Paradise Regained and Samson Agonistes* (Cleveland, Ohio, and London, 1971), 25–47; and Alan

Fisher, "Why is Paradise Regained So Cold?" *MS* 14 (1980), 195–217.

106 See p. 493 and note 17.

107 See Knoppers, *Historicizing Milton*, 13–41.

108 See the Loeb *Virgil*, ed. H. Rushton Fairclough (London and Cambridge, Mass., 1960), I, 240–1: "Ille ego, qui quondam gracili modulatus avena / carmen, et egressus silvis vicina coegi / ut quamvis avido parerent arva colono, / gratum opus agricolis; at nunc horrentia Martis / Arma virumque cano. . . ." (I am he who once tuned my song on a slender reed, then, leaving the woodland, constrained the neighboring fields to serve the husbandmen, however grasping – a work welcome to farmers: but now of Mars' bristling. Arms and the Man I sing.)

109 Among them are Sannazaro's *De Partu Virginis*, Vida's *Christiad*, and Giles Fletcher's *Christ's Victorie and Triumph* (1610), the second book of which treats Christ's temptation in the wilderness as Spenserian allegory. See Barbara K. Lewalski, *Milton's Brief Epic: The Genre, Meaning, and Art of Paradise Regained* (Providence and London, 1996), 3–129.

110 See Job 1:6–12. The character Job is named on six occasions (*PR* 1.147, 369, 425; 3.64, 67, 95); the book is quoted twice (1.33–4, 368). And either the book or the tradition of commentary on it are alluded to on at least ten other occasions.

111 Lewalski, "Time and History in *Paradise Regained*," in *The Prison and the Pinnacle*, ed. Balachandra Rajan (Toronto, 1972), 49–81.

112 See Elizabeth M. Pope, *Paradise Regained: The Tradition and the Poem* (Baltimore, 1947).

113 Here as in *De Doctrina Christiana* (*CPW* VI, 430–7) Milton conceives that office and its three functions as many Protestant exegetes do.

114 See chapter 11, pp. 388–9.

115 Jesus cites the judges Gideon and Jeptha, as well as heroes of the Roman republic, Quintius, Curtius, Fabricius, and Regulus (*PR* 2.445–9).

116 Aristotle, *Nicomachean Ethics* IV.ii.1123b, trans. H. Rackham (Cambridge, Mass., and London, 1926). For Milton's praise of Queen Christina of Sweden for relinquishing a kingdom see Defens*io Secunda*, *CPW* IV.1, 605–6, and see above, chapter 9.

117 This tirade is reminiscent of Michael's denunciation of the Giants who sought fame by slaughter and conquest (*PL* 11.640–99).

118 For the echoes throughout this episode of Cicero, Seneca, and various Stoic–Christian texts denouncing Alexander and Caesar for seeking false renown conferred by the multitude and for the impiety of seeking divine honors, see Lewalski, *Milton's Brief Epic*, 236–41.

119 Knoppers, *Historicizing Milton*, 123–41; see chapter 12, p. 404.

120 *CPW* VII, 463; and see chapter 11, p. 397.

121 Cf. John Lightfoot's exegesis of the kingdoms' temptation: "The object that the Devill presented *Christ* withall in this spectacle, was Rome, her Empire and glory. For 1. That Empire is called by the very name of *all the world, Luke* 2.5. . . . When *Satan* cannot at the entrance of the Gospel perswade Christ by all the pompe at *Rome,* to do like *Antichrist*, he setteth up *Antichrist* at *Rome,* to bee an enemy to the Gospel in all the continuance of it:" *The Harmony of the Foure Evangelists*, 2 vols (London, 1644–7), II, 30–2.

122 See chapters 2, pp. 42–5, 51–2, and chapter 3, p. 82–3. And see B. Douglas Trevor, "Learned Appearances: Writing Scholarly and Literary Selves in Early Modern Eng-

land" (dissertation, Harvard University, 1999), 298–368.

123 For the many psalmic echoes, see Mary Ann Radzinowicz, *Toward Samson Agonistes,* 188–260.

124 Classic accounts of the regenerate Samson are in Arnold Stein, *Heroic Knowledge* (Minneapolis, 1957) and John H. Steadman, "'Faithful Champion': The Theological Basis of Milton's Hero of Faith," *Anglia* 77 (1959), 12–28; for the unregenerate Samson see Irene Samuel "*Samson Agonistes* as Tragedy," in *Calm of Mind: Tercentenary Essays on Paradise Regained and Samson Agonistes,* ed. Joseph A. Wittreich, Jr. (Cleveland, Ohio, 1971), 237–57.

125 See Joseph A. Wittreich, Jr., *Interpreting Samson Agonistes* (Princeton, NJ, 1986), and Stanley Fish, "Spectacle and Evidence in *Samson Agonistes,*" *Critical Inquiry* 15 (1989), 556–86.

126 The positions, respectively, of Jackie DiSalvo, "'The Lords Battels': *Samson Agonistes* and the Puritan Revolution," *MS* 4 (1971), 39–52; Christopher Hill, *Milton and the English Revolution,* 428–48; Samuel "*Samson Agonistes* as Tragedy"; Achinstein, "*Samson Agonistes* and the Drama of Dissent," 133–58; and David Loewenstein, "The Revenge of the Saint: Radical Religion and Politics in *Samson Agonistes,*" *MS* 33 (1996), 159–80.

127 See Lewalski, "Milton's *Samson* and the New Acquist of True [Political] Experience," *MS* 24 (1999), 233–51.

128 The epigraph reads: "Arist. Poet. Cap. 6. Tragodia mimesis, praxeos spondaias, etc. Tragoedia est imitatio actionis seriae, &c. Per misericordiam & metum perficiens talium affectuum lustrationem." Milton of course means the reader to recall the entire definition: "Tragedy is, then, a representation [*mimesis,* imitation] of an action that is heroic and complete, and of a certain magnitude – by means of language embellished with all kinds of ornament, each used separately in the different parts of the play; it represents men in action and does not use narrative; and through pity and fear it effects relief to those and similar emotions." See *The Poetics* 6.1, trans. W. Hamilton Fyfe, *Aristotle,* vol. 23 (Cambridge, Mass., 1973), 24–5.

129 David Pareus, *A Commentary upon the Divine Revelation of the Apostle and Evangelist John,* trans. Elias Arnold (Amsterdam, 1644). See chapter 5, p. 131 and note 102.

130 Ibid., p. 20. See Lewalski, "*Samson Agonistes* and the 'Tragedy' of the Apocalypse," *PMLA* 85 (1970), 1,050–62.

131 W. R. Parker, *Milton's Debt to Greek Tragedy in Samson Agonistes* (Baltimore, 1937); and Anthony Low, *The Blaze of Noon: A Reading of Samson Agonistes* (New York, 1974).

132 See chapter 12, pp. 400–6. Also, Knoppers, *Historicizing Milton,* 42–66, and Worden, "Milton, *Samson Agonistes,* and the Restoration," in Maclean, ed., *Culture and Society in the Stuart Restoration,* 122–6.

133 For the limitations of the chorus, see Joan S. Bennett, "Liberty Under the Law: The Chorus and the Meaning of *Samson Agonistes,*" *MS* 12 (1978), 141–63.

134 Vane reportedly said, when friends spoke of giving thousands of pounds for his life, that "If a thousand farthings would gain it, he would not do it." *The Tryall of Sir Henry Vane, Kt.* (London, 1662); and Worden, "Milton, *Samson Agonistes,* and the Restoration," 119–22.

135 For a range of views, see Susanne Woods, "How Free are Milton's Women," Jackie

DiSalvo, "Intestine Thorne: Samson's Struggle with the Woman Within," and John C. Ulreich, Jr., "Incident to all Our Sex: The Tragedy of Dalila," all in Julia Walker, ed., *Milton and the Idea of Woman* (Champaign, Ill., 1988), 15–31, 185–229; and John Guillory, "Dalila's House: *Samson Agonistes* and the Sexual Division of Labor," in Margaret Ferguson, et al., eds, *Re-Writing the Renaissance: The Discourses of Sexual Difference in Early Modern Europe* (Chicago, 1986), 106–221.

136 Lines 1,247–9. See, for example, John M. Steadman, "Milton's Harapha and Goliath," *Journal of English and Germanic Philology* 60 (1961), 786–95; Lieb, *Milton and the Culture of Violence*, 247–50.

137 See chapter 13, p. 452; also, Knoppers, *Historicizing Milton,* 142–63.

138 For example, "They who seek nothing but thir own just libertie, have alwaies right to winn it and to keep it, when ever they have power, be the voices never so numerous that oppose it" (*CPW* VII, 455).

139 See p. 492; also, Achinstein in "*Samson Agonistes* and the Drama of Dissent," 133–58; and Lewalski, "Milton's *Samson* and the New Acquist of True [Political] Experience," 244–5.

140 [John Owen], *Indulgence and Toleration Considered: In a Letter unto a Person of Honour* (London, 1667), 12–18.

141 See *CPW* VI, 530–6; and chapter 12, pp. 434–5. Also see Joan Bennett, *Reviving Liberty: Radical Christian Humanism in Milton's Great Poems* (Cambridge, Mass., 1989), 133–60; and Norman T. Burns, "'Then Stood Up Phinehas': Milton's Antinomianism, and Samson's," *MS* 33 (1996), 27–46.

142 For an argument focusing on the harmony in this drama between the Judaic Law and the Spirit, Samson and his community, see Jason Rosenblatt, "Samson's Sacrifice," in Amy Boesky and Mary Crane, eds, *Form and Reform in Renaissance England* (Newark, 2000), 321–37.

143 Loewenstein, "The Revenge of the Saint," 159–80.

144 See Michael Lieb, "'Our Living Dread': The God of *Samson Agonistes,*" *Milton Studies* 33 (1996), 3–23; and Loewenstein, "The Revenge of the Saint," 159–80.

145 See Northrop Frye, *Spiritus Mundi: Essays on Literature, Myth, and Society* (Bloomington, 1976), 222.

146 See Dobranski, *Milton, Authorship, and the Book Trade,* 41–61.

147 Marie Fisher, sister of the domestic servant Elizabeth Fisher who was with Milton for about a year before his death, testified at the court hearing on Milton's will that she had seen Anne Milton once, but did not remember whether she was lame and helpless. Other testimony indicates that Marie often visited her sister at Milton's house, so she must have seen Anne there (*LR* V, 218).

148 *Chronology*, 216. When court papers pertaining to Milton's oral will were first drawn up in December, 1674, they referred to Deborah by her maiden name (*LR* V, 216). Later, she and her husband signed the final agreements.

149 From Elizabeth Fisher's deposition of December 15, 1674, *LR* V, 82, 220. On another occasion, about two months before his death, Elizabeth Fisher's sister Marie, who was then visiting, reported hearing a similar remark: "Make much of mee as long as I live for thou knowest I have given thee all when I dye at thy disposal" (*LR* V, 217).

150 From Christopher Milton's deposition about Milton's will on December 5, 1674, in the Prerogative Court of Canterbury (*LR* V, 91, 213).

151 Christopher Milton's deposition, December 5, 1674 (*LR* V, 214). Christopher also reported, as from Elizabeth Milton, that her husband had indicated to her that, if there were any overplus above £1,000, it was to go to Christopher's children. But Christopher honorably admits that he did not himself hear any such thing from his brother (215). If true, this reveals Milton's continuing resentment of his daughters; or, it may more clearly reveal Elizabeth Milton's animus toward them.

152 Copies of the relevant papers are in *LR* V, 226–32.

153 From Elizabeth Fisher's testimony, May 15, in the prerogative Court of Canterbury, *LR* V, 220–3.

154 Edward Phillips, *Theatrum Poetarum, or A Compleat Collection of the Poets, Especially the Most Eminent, of all Ages* (London, 1675), sig. **r–v.

155 Ibid., 123–4. He did, however, deliver his own judgment in the entry for his brother, John Phillips, added after Milton's death. He attributes John's success as a poet chiefly to his education by Milton, "an Author of most deserv'd Fame late deceas't, being the exactest of Heroic Poets, (if the truth were well examin'd, and it is the opinion of many both Learned and Judicious persons) either of the Ancients or Moderns, either of our own or whatever Nation else" (114–15).

156 Milton's choice, if it was his, to be buried in his parish church even though he was not a regular parishioner and was no friend of the Anglican establishment, probably was motivated by the desire to lie beside his father. He would have had no reason to seek burial in the Nonconformist cemetary at Bunhill Fields since he was never formally associated with any such congregation.

Epilogue: "Something . . . Written to Aftertimes"

1 Harold Bloom, *The Anxiety of Influence: A Theory of Poetry* (New York, 1973).

2 Letter 164, to John Thelwell, December 17, 1776; and *The Statesman's Manual*, 1816, cited in Joseph A. Wittreich, Jr., *The Romantics on Milton: Formal Essays and Critical Asides* (Cleveland, Ohio, and London, 2970), 157, 228–9.

3 "Milton," from the *Edinburgh Review*, August, 1825.

4 From a letter of Hopkins to Richard Walter Dixon, October 5, 1878, cited in James Thorpe, ed., *Milton Criticism: Selections from Four Centuries* (London, 1951), 372. In a letter to Robert Bridges, February 15, 1879, Hopkins states that he "hopes in time to have a more balanced and Miltonic style."

5 R. W. Griswold, *Papers on Literature and Art* (New York, 1846), I, 35.

6 *Journals and Miscellaneous Notebooks of Ralph Waldo Emerson*, ed. William Gilman, et al., 16 vols (Cambridge, Mass., 1960), II, 106–7.

7 Milton," *North American Review*, July, 1838.

8 In her review of R. W. Griswold's edition of Milton's Prose, *New York Daily Tribune*, October 7, 1845; Fuller, *Paper on Literature and Art*, 2 vols (New York, 1846), I, 36, 38–9.

9 Cited in Daniel Aaron, *The Unwritten War: American Writers and the Civil War* (New York, 1973), 343.

10 Noted in *The Diary of George Templeton Strong*, ed. Allan Nevins and M. H. Thomas, 4 vols (New York, 1852), III, 368.

11 Robin Grey, *The Complicity of Imagination: The American Renaissance, Contests of Authority, and Seventeenth-Century English Culture* (Cambridge, 1997), 213–27.
12 Malcolm X (with the assistance of Alex Haley), *The Autobiography of Malcolm X* (New York, 1965), 186.

Select Bibliography

Primary Milton Manuscripts

Columbia Manuscript, Columbia University X823M64/S52 (State Papers).

The Commonplace Book, British Library Add. MS. 36,354.

"The Digression" from the *History of Britain*, Houghton Library, Harvard University, English MS 901.

Joannis Miltoni Angli De Doctrina Christiana. Ex Sacris Duntaxat Libris Petita Disquissitionum Libri Duo. Posthumi. Public Record Office, Kew, SP 9/61.

A Letter to a Friend, Concerning the Ruptures of the Commonwealth. Columbia Manuscript; Columbia University Library X823M64/S52. First published in Toland's edition, 1698.

Paradise Lost, Book I, J. Pierpont Morgan Library, New York City.

Proposalls of Certaine Expedients for the Preventing of a Civill War Now Feard, & The Settling of a Firme Government. Columbia Manuscript, Columbia University Library, X823M64/S52; first published in Columbia Milton XVIII, 3–7.

Skinner Manuscript, PRO SP 9/194 (State Papers).

Trinity Manuscript, Trinity College, Cambridge, R. 3.4. Facsimile reproduction, Menston: Scolar Press, 1972.

Milton: First Editions

J. M. *Accidence Commenc't Grammar. Supply'd with sufficient Rules, For the use of such as, Younger or Elder, are desirous, without more trouble then needs, to attain the Latin Tongue; the elder sort especially, with little teaching, and thir own industry.* London: S. Simmons, 1669.

[John Milton] *Animadversions upon the Remonstrants Defence, Against Smectymnuus.* London: Thomas Underhill, 1641.

[John Milton] *An Apology Against a Pamphlet Call'd A Modest Confutation of the Animadversions upon the Remonstrant against Smectymnuus.* London: John Rothwell, 1642.

Areopagitica; A Speech of Mr. John Milton For the Liberty of Unlicenc'd Printing, To the Parliament of England. London, 1644.

[John Milton] *Articles of Peace, Made and Concluded with the Irish Rebels, and Papists, by James Earle of Ormond, For and in behalfe of the late King, and by Vertue of his Autoritie. Also a Letter sent by Ormond to Col. Jones, Governour of Dublin, with his Answer thereunto. And a Representation of the Scotch Presbytery at Belfast in Ireland. Upon all which are added Observations*. London: Matthew Simmons, 1649.

Joannis Miltoni Angli, Artis Logicae Plenior Institutio, Ad Petri Rami Methodum concinnata, Adjecta est Praxis Annalytica & Petri Rami vita. Libris duobus. London: Spencer Hickman, 1672.

John Milton. *A Brief History of Moscovia and of other less-known Countries lying eastward of Russia as far as Cathay. Gather'd from the Writings of Several Eye-witnesses*. London: Brabazon Aylmer, 1682.

Brief Notes upon a Late Sermon, Titl'd The Fear of God and the King: Preachd, and since Publishd, by Matthew Griffith, D. D., and Chaplain to the late King. Wherin many Notorious Wrestings of Scripture, and other Falsities are observd by J. M. London, 1660.

The Cabinet-Council: Containing the Cheif Arts of Empire, and Mysteries of State; Discabineted in Political and Polemical Aphorisms, grounded on Authority, and Experience; and illustrated with the choicest Examples and Historical Observations. By the Ever-renowned Knight, Sir Walter Raleigh. Published by John Milton Esq. London: Thomas Newcomb, 1658.

Mr John Milton's Character of the Long Parliament and Assembly of Divines. In MDCXLI. Omitted in his other Works, and never before Printed, and very seasonable for these times. London, 1681. (Edited in truncated version by Roger L'Estrange.)

Colasterion. A Reply to a Namles Answer Against The Doctrine and Discipline of Divorce. Wherein The trivial Author of that Answer is discover'd, the Licencer conferr'd with, and the Opinion which they traduce defended. By the former Author, J. M. London: Matthew Simmons, 1645.

Considerations Touching the Likeliest Means to remove Hirelings out of the church. Wherein is also discours'd of Tithes, Church-fees, Church-revenues; and whether any maintenance of ministers can be settl'd by law. The author J. M. London: T[homas] N[ewcomb for L. Chapman], 1659.

[John Milton, trans.] *A Declaration, or Letters Patents of the Election of this present King of Poland, John the Third, Elected on the 22 of May last past, Anno Dom. 1674. Containing the Reasons of This Election, the great Vertues and Merits of the said Serene Elect, His eminent Services in War, especially in his last great Victory against the Turks and Tartars, whereof many Particulars are here related, not published before*. London: Brabazon Aylmer, 1674.

[John Milton] The Doctrine and Discipline of Divorce: Restor'd to the Good of Both *Sexes, From the Bondage of Canon Law, and other mistakes, to Christian freedom, guided by the Rule of Charity. Wherein also many places of Scripture have recover'd their long-lost meaning*. London: T. P. and M. S., 1643.

The Doctrine and Discipline of Divorce: Restor'd to the good of both Sexes, from the bondage of Canon Law, and other mistakes, to the true meaning of Scripture in the Law and Gospel compar'd. Wherein also are set down the bad consequences of abolishing or condemning of Sin, that which the Law of God allowes, and Christ abolisht not. Now the second time revis'd and much augmented, In Two Books. The Author J. M. London, 1644.

Eikonoklastes in Answer to a Book Intitl'd Eikon Basilike, The Portrature of his Sacred Majesty in his Solitudes and Sufferings. The Author J. M. London: Matthew Simmons, 1649; 2nd edn, "Publish't now the second time, and much enlarg'd," London: Thomas Newcomb, 1650. Another issue identifies the booksellers: "Printed by T. N. and are to be sold by T[homas] Brewster and G[regory] Moule."

Joannis Miltonii Angli, Epistolarum Familiarum Liber Unus: Quibus Accesserunt, Ejusdem, jam olim in Collegio Adolescentis, Prolusiones Quaedam Oratoriae. London: Brabazon Aylmer, 1674.

The History of Britain, That part especially now call'd England. From the first Traditional Beginning, Continued to the Norman Conquest. Collected out of the Antientest and best Authors thereof by John Milton. London: James Allestry, 1670.

Hobson epitaphs, in *A Banquet of Jests,* London, 1640; *Wit Restor'd*, London, 1658.

[John Milton] *The Judgement of Martin Bucer, Concerning Divorce. Writt'n to Edward the sixt, in his second Book of the Kingdom of Christ. And now Englisht. Wherin a late Book restoring the Doctrine and Discipline of Divorce, is heer confirm'd and justify'd by the authoritie of Martin Bucer.* London: Matthew Simmons, 1644.

Letters of State, written by Mr. John Milton, To most of the Sovereign Princes and Republicks of Europe. From the year 1649. Till the Year 1659. To which is added, An Account of his Life. Together with several of his Poems; And a Catalogue of his Works, never before Printed [ed. Edward Phillips, London], 1694.

Literae Pseudo-Senatus Anglicani Cromwelii, Reliquorumque Perduellium nomine ac jussu conscriptae a Joanne Miltono. Amsterdam: [Peter and John Blaeu], 1676.

J. M. "Lycidas," in *Obsequies to the memorie of Mr. Edward King,* Part II of *Justa Edouardo King naufrago, ab Amicis moerentibus.* Cambridge: Thomas Buck and Roger Daniel, 1638.

[John Milton] *A Maske Presented at Ludlow Castle. 1634: On Michaelmasse night, before the Right Honorable, John Earle of Bridgewater, Vicount Brackly, Lord President of Wales, and one of His Majesties most honorable Privie Counsell.* London: Humphrey Robinson, 1637.

[John Milton, *Of Education. To Master Samuel Hartlib.* London: Thomas Underhill, 1644.] No title page.

[John Milton] *Of Prelatical Episcopacy, and Whether it may be deduc'd from the Apostolical times by vertue of these Testimonies which are alledg'd to that purpose in some late Treatises.* London: Thomas Underhill, 1641.

[John Milton] *Of Reformation Touching Church-Discipline in England: and the Causes that hitherto have hindred it. Two Books. Written to a Freind.* London: Thomas Underhill, 1641.

Of True Religion, Haeresie, Schism, Toleration, And what best means may be us'd against the growth of Popery. The Author J. M. London, 1673.

"On Shakespear," in *Mr William Shakespeares Comedies, Histories, and Tragedies*. London, 1632.

Paradise lost. A Poem Written in Ten Books By John Milton. London: [Printer, Samuel Simmons], to be sold by Peter Parker, Robert Boulter, and Matthias Walker, 1667.

Paradise Lost. A Poem. In Twelve Books. The Author John Milton. The second edition, Revised and Augmented by the same author. London: S. Simmons, 1674.

Paradise Regain'd. A Poem. In IV Books. To which is added Samson Agonistes. The author John Milton. London: J. M. for John Starkey, 1671.

Poems of Mr. John Milton, Both English and Latin, Compos'd at Several Times. London: Humphrey Moseley, 1645.

Poems, &c. Upon Several Occasions. By Mr. John Milton: Both English and Latin, &c. Composed at Several Times. With a small Tractate of Education to Mr. Hartlib. London: Thomas Dring, 1673.

[John Milton] *The Present Means, and Brief Delineation of a Free Commonwealth, Easy to be Put in Practice, and without delay, in a Letter to General Monk* [1660, first published in Toland's edition, 1698].

Joannis Miltoni Angli Pro Populo Anglicano Defensio. Contra Claudii Anonymi, aliàs Salmasii, Defensionem Regiam. London: William Dugard, 1651; "Editio Emendatior" 1651.

Joannis Miltoni Angli Pro Populo Defensio Contra Claudii Anonymi, aliàs Salmasii Defensionem

Regiam. Editio correctior & auctior, ab Autore denue recognita. London: Thomas Newcomb, 1658.

Joannis Miltoni Angli Pro Populo Anglicano Defensio Secunda. Contra infamem libellum anonymum cui titulus, Regii sanguinis clamor ad coelum adversus parricidas Anglicanos. London: Thomas Newcomb, 1654.

Joannis Miltoni Angli Defensio Secunda Pro Populo Anglicano: Contra infamem libellum [etc.]. The Hague: Adriaan Vlacq, 1654.

Joannis Miltoni Angli Pro Se Defensio Contra Alexandrum Morum Ecclesiasten, Libelli famosi, cui titulus, Regii sanguinis clamor ad coelum adversus Parricidas Agnlicanos, arthorem rectè dictum. London: Thomas Newcomb, 1655

The Readie & Easie Way to Establish a Free Commonwealth, and The Excellence therof Compar'd with the inconveniences and dangers of readmitting kingship in this nation. The author J. M. London: Printed by T[homas] N[ewcomb] and are to be sold by Livewell Chapman, 1660.

The readie and easie way to establish a Free Commonwealth, etc. The second edition revis'd and augmented. The author J. M. London, Printed for the Author, 1660.

John Milton. *The Reason of Church-government Urg'd against Prelaty*. London: John Rothwell, 1641.

Miltons Republican-Letters, or A Collection of such as were written by Comand of the Late Commonwealth of England; from the Year 1648–1659 [NP] 1682.

The Tenure of Kings and Magistrates. Proving, that it is Lawfull, and hath been held so through all Ages, for any, who have the Power, to call to account a Tyrant, or wicked King, and after due conviction, to depose, and put him to death, if the ordinary Magistrate have neglected, or deny'd to doe it. And that they, who of late, so much blame deposing, are the Men that did it themselves. The author J. M. London: Matthew Simmons, 1649.

The Tenure of Kings and Magistrates, etc. 2nd edition, "Published now the second time with some additions, and many Testimonies also added out of the best & learnedest among Protestant Divines asserting the position of this book." The Author J. M. London: Matthew Simmons, 1649.

Tetrachordon: Expositions Upon the foure chief places in Scripture, which treat of Mariage, or nullities in Mariage Gen. 1.27.28. compar'd and explain'd by Gen. 2.18. 2.24. Deut. 24.1.2 Matth. 5.31.32. with Matt. 19 from the 3d v. to the 11th. l Cor. 7. from the 10th to the 16th. Wherin the Doctrine and Discipline of Divorce, as was lately publish'd, is confirm'd by explanation of Scripture, by Testimony of ancient Fathers, of civill lawes in the Primitive Church, of famousest Reformed Divines, and lastly, by an intended Act of the Parlament and Church of England in the last yeare of Edward the sicth. By the former author, J. M. London, 1645.

A Treatise of Civil Power in Ecclesiastical Causes. Shewing, That it is not lawfull for any power on earth to compell in matters of Religion. The author J. M. London: Thomas Newcomb, 1659.

Major Modern Editions and Scholarly Aids

Birch, Thomas, ed. *A Complete Collection of the Historical, Political, and Miscellaneous Works of John Milton*, 2 vols. London, 1738.

Carey, John, ed. *John Milton: Complete Shorter Poems*. London: Longman, 1997.

Fletcher, Harris Francis, ed. *John Milton's Complete Poetical Works, reproduced in Photographic*

Facsimile, 4 vols. Urbana: University of Illinois Press, 1943–48.

Fowler, Alastair, ed. *John Milton: Paradise Lost*. London: Longman, 1998.

Honigmann, E. A. J., ed. *Milton's Sonnets*. London: Macmillan, 1966.

Hughes, Merritt Y., ed. *John Milton: Complete Poems and Major Prose*. Indianapolis, Ind.: Odyssey-MacMillan, 1957.

Hunter, William B., et al., eds. *A Milton Encyclopedia,* 9 vols. Lewisburg: Bucknell University Press, 1978–83.

McKellar, Walter, ed. *The Latin Poems of John Milton*. New Haven, Conn.: Yale University Press, 1930.

Newton, Thomas, ed. *Paradise Lost: A Poem, in Twelve Books*, 2 vols. London, 1749.

Patterson, F. A., et al., eds. *The Works of John Milton*, 18 vols in 21. New York: Columbia University Press, 1931–8.

Patrick, J. Max, ed. *The Prose of John Milton*. Garden City, NJ: Doubleday, 1967.

Smart, J. M., ed. *The Sonnets of Milton*. Glasgow: Maclehose, Jackson, 1921.

Sprott, S. E., ed. *John Milton: A Maske. The Earlier Versions*. Toronto: University of Toronto Press, 1973.

Toland, John, ed. *A Collection of the Historical, Political, and Miscellaneous Works of John Milton*, 3 vols. Amsterdam [London], 1698.

A Variorum Commentary on the Poems of John Milton, vol. 1, eds. Douglas Bush, J. E. Shaw, and Bartlett Giamatti; vol. 2, eds. A. S. P. Woodhouse and Douglas Bush; vol. 4, ed. Walter MacKellar. New York: Columbia University Press, 1970–5.

Wolfe, Don M., et al., eds. *Complete Prose Works of John Milton*, 8 vols. New Haven, Conn.: Yale University Press, 1953–82.

Bibliographies, Catalogues, Registers, Public Documents

Allegations for Marriage Licences issued from the Faculty Office of the Archbishop of Canterbury, at London, 1547–1869. Harleian Society 24. London, 1886.

Calendar of the Clarendon State Papers Preserved in the Bodleian Library, 5 vols, ed. O. Ogle, et al. Oxford: Clarendon Press, 1869–1970.

Calendar of the State Papers, Domestic Series, of the reign of Charles I, 1625–49. London: HM Stationery Office, 1858–97; *1649–1660*, 13 vols. London: HM Stationery Office, 1875–86; *of the reign of Charles II*. London: HM Stationery Office, 1860–1947.

Catalogue of the Pamphlets, Books, Newspapers, and Manuscripts relating to the Civil War, the Commonwealth, and Restoration, 2 vols, collected by George Thomason, 1640–60. London: William Clowes & Sons, 1908.

Catalogue of Seventeenth Century Portraits in the National Portrait Gallery, 1625–1714, ed. David Piper. Cambridge: Cambridge University Press, 1963.

Clavell, Robert. *The General Catalogue of Books Printed in England since the Dreadful Fire of London, 1666 to the end of Trinity Term, 1674*. London, 1674.

A Complete Collection of State Trials and Proceedings for High Treason, 33 vols, eds. Willaim Cobbett and T. S. Howell. London, 1809–26.

Cooper, R. W., et al., *Athenae Cantabrigiensis*, 3 vols. Cambridge, 1858–1913.

Index of English Literary Manuscripts, Vol. II, Part 2, 1625–1700, ed. Peter Beal. London: Mansell, 1993, 69–104.

London, William. *Catalogue of the Most Vendible Books in England*. London, 1657.

Memorials of St. Margaret's Church, Westminster: The Parish Registers, 1539–1660, ed. A. M. Burke. London, 1914.

Peile, John. *Biographical Register of Christ's College, 1505–1905*. Cambridge, 1910–13.

Pollard, A. W. and G. R. Redgrave, et al. *A Short-title Catalogue of Books printed in England, Scotland, Ireland, etc.*, 2nd edn, 3 vols. London: Bibliographical Society, 1976–91.

The Registers of All Hallows, Bread Street, and of St. John the Evangelist, Friday Street, London, ed. W. Bruce Bannerman. Harleian Society Registers, XLIII. London, 1913.

The Registers of St. Mary Aldermary, London . . . 1558 to 1754, ed. J. L. Chester. Harleian Society Registers, V. London, 1880.

The Registers of St. Nicholas, Ipswich, Suffolk, ed. Edward Cookson. London, 1897.

Rothwell, John. *Catalogue of the Most Approved Divinity Books . . . Continued down to the Present Year, 1657*. London, 1657.

Shawcross, John T. *Milton: A Bibliography for the Years 1624–1700*. Binghamton, NY: MRTS, 1984.

State Trials, 4 vols, ed. H. L. Stevens. London: Duckworth, 1889.

The Statutes of the Realm, 9 vols in 10. Vol. 5, 1625–80. London: Eyre and Strahan, 1810–22.

The Term Catalogues, 1668–1709, 3 vols, Vol. I, 1668–1682, ed. Edward Arber. London, 1875–94.

A Transcript of the Registers of the Company of Stationers of London, 1554–1640, 5 vols, ed. Edward Arber. London, 1875–94.

A Transcript of the Registers of the Worshippful Company of Stationers from 1640–1708, 3 vols, ed. George E. B. Eyre, et al. London: Roxburghe Club, 1913–14.

Wing, Donald, et al. *Short-Title Catalogue of Books printed in England, Scotland, etc. . . . 1641–1700,* revd edn, 3 vols. New York: MLA, 1982–8, 1994.

Wood, Anthony á. *Athenae Oxonienses . . . to which are added the Fasti, or Annals, of the said University [1500–1690]*, 3rd edn, 4 vols, ed. Philip Bliss. London, 1813–20.

Major Biographies and Biographical Resources

Boswell, Jackson C. *Milton's Library*. New York and London: Garland, 1975.

Brown, Cedric C. *John Milton: A Literary Life*. London: MacMillan, 1995.

Campbell, Gordon. *A Milton Chronology*. London: MacMillan, 1997.

The Early Lives of Milton, ed. Helen Darbishire. London: Constable, 1932. Contains: John Aubrey, *Minutes of the Life of Mr. John Milton*, 1–15; [Cyriack Skinner], *The Life of Mr. John Milton*, 17–34; Anthony á Wood, *Fasti Oxonienses*, 35–48; Edward Phillips, *The Life of Mr. John Milton*, 49–82; John Toland, *The Life of John Milton*, 83–197; Jonathan Richardson, *Explanatory Notes and Remarks on Milton's Paradise Lost . . . With a Life of the Author*, 201–330.

Fletcher, Harris Francis. *The Intellectual Development of John Milton* [1608–32], 2 vols. Urbana: University of Illinois Press, 1956–61.

French, J. Milton, ed. *The Life Records of John Milton*, 5 vols. New Brunswick, NJ: Rutgers University Press, 1949–58.

Hill, Christopher. *Milton and the English Revolution*. London: Faber and Faber, 1977.

Masson, David. *The Life of John Milton: Narrated in Connexion with the Political, Ecclesiastical and*

Literary History of His Time, 7 vols. London, 1881–94; rpt. Gloucester, Mass.: Peter Smith, 1965.

Parker, William Riley. *Milton: A Biography*, 2 vols. Oxford: Clarendon Press, 1968; revd Gordon Campbell, 1996.

Primary Texts and Manuscripts

Acta et Scripta Synodalia Dordracena Ministrorum Remonstrantium in Foederato Belgio. Harderwijk, 1620.

An Act Against Unlicensed and Scandalous Books. London, 1649.

Aeschylus, trans. Herbert W. Smyth. 2 vols. Cambridge, Mass. and London: Harvard University Press and Heinemann, 1956–7.

An Agreement of the People for a Firme and Present Peace, Upon Grounds of Common-Right and Freedome; As it was proposed by the Agents for the Five Regiments of Horse, and since by the Generall Approbation of the Army, Offered to the joynt Concurrence of all the Free Commons of England. London, 1647

An Agreement of the Free People of England, Tendered as a Peace-Offering to this Distressed Nation. By John Lilburne, William Walwyn, Richard Overton, and Thomas Prince. London, 1649.

An Alarum to the Officers and Souldiers of the Armies of England, Scotland, and Ireland. London, 1660.

Almoni, Peloni. *A Compendious Discourse Proving Episcopacy to be of Apostolicall and Consequently of Divine Institution*. London, 1641.

Ames, William. *De Conscientia et eius jure, vel casibus, libri quinque*. Amsterdam, 1635; trans. *Conscience, wth the Power and Cases thereof*. London, 1639.

Ames, William. *Medulla S.S. Theologiae*. Amsterdam 1627; trans. *The Marrow of Sacred Divinity, drawne out of the Holy Scriptures*. London, 1638, 1642.

Angelo di Constanzo, *Historia del Regno di Napoli*. Aquila, 1581.

Anno Regni Caroli II . . . .XII, XVI–XVII. London, 1660, 1664–8.

Anonymous. *An Answer to a Book Intituled, The Doctrine and Discipline of Divorce, or, A Plea for Ladies and Gentlewomen, and all other Maried Women against Divorce. Wherein, Both Sexes are vindicated from all bondage of Common Law, and other mistakes whatsoever: And the unsound Principles of the Author are examined and fully confuted by the authority of Holy Scripture, the Laws of this Land, and sound Reason*. London, 1644.

Aphthonius, Sophista. *Progymnasmata*, trans. and ed. Reinhard Lorich. London, 1546, 1596; often reprinted.

Applausi poetici alle glorie della signora Leonora Baroni, ed. Vincenzo Constazuli. Rome, 1639.

Aratus. *Phaenomena & Diosemeia*. Paris, 1559.

Ariosto, Lodovico. *Orlando Furioso*. Ferrara, 1516; trans. John Harington, London, 1591.

Aristotle, *The Nicomachean Ethics*, trans. H. Rackham. Cambridge, Mass. and London: Harvard University Press and Heinemann, 1926.

Aristotle, *Opera*, 2 vols. Geneva, 1597.

Aristotle, *The Poetics*, trans. W. Hamilton Fyfe. Cambridge, Mass. and London: Harvard University Press and Heinemann, 1973.

Arminius, Jacobus and Stephanus Curcellaeus, *Examen Theseum F. Gomare de Praedestinat.*

cum St. Curcellanei Vinciis, Quibus Suam et Armini Sententiam de Jure Dei Increaturas, Adversus Mosis Amyraldi Criminationes, Defendit. Amsterdam, 1645.

Arminius, Jacobus. *Opera Theologica.* Leyden, 1629; *The Writings of James Arminius*, trans. James Nichols and W. R. Bagnall. 3 vols. London, 1825–78.

Ascham, Roger. *Toxophilus, The Schole of Shootinge.* London, 1545.

Athanasius, *Four Discourses Against the Arians,* ed. A. Robertson. Library of Nicene and Post-Nicene Fathers, 2nd Series, Vol. IV. Oxford, 1892.

Aubrey, John. *Lives of Eminent Men,* ed. A. Clark. 2 vols. Oxford, 1898; *Brief Lives,* ed. Oliver Lawson Dick. London, 1949.

Augustine, *De Civitate Dei.* Venice, 1475.

Augustine, *De Doctrina Christiana,* trans. D. W. Robertson. Indianapolis, Ind.: Bobbs-Merrill, 1958.

d'Avity, Pierre, *Les Empires, royaumes, estats . . . et principautez du monde.* St Omer, 1614; trans. E. Grimstone, etc., *The Estates, Empires, and Principalities of the World.* London, 1615.

Bacon, Francis. *A Wise and Moderate Discourse, Concerning Church-Affaires.* London, 1641.

Baillie, Robert. *A Dissuasive from the Errours of the Time: Wherein the Tenets of the Principall Sects, and especially of the Independents, are drawn together in one Map.* London, 1645.

Baillie, Robert. *The Letters and Journals . . . 1637–1662.* 3 vols. Edinburgh, 1841.

Baker, Collonel. *The Blazing Star . . . Or, Nolls Nose. Newly Revived, and taken out of his Tomb.* London, 1660.

Baker, Richard. *A Chronicle of the Kings of England, from the time of the Romans government unto the raigne of our soveraigne lord king Charles.* London, 1641. See Edward Phillips, *A Continuation of the Chronicle of England.*

Barebone, Praise-God. *Mr Praise-God Barbone his Petition. As it was presented to Parliament, Thursday the ninth of February, in behalf of himself and many Thousands.* London, 1659 [1660].

Baron, Robert. *Erotopaignion, or the Cyprian Academy.* London, 1647.

Basil. *Homiliae,* in *Opera.* 2 vols. Paris, 1618.

[Bate, George] *Elenchus Motuum nuperorum in Anglia.* Paris [1650].

Baxter, Richard. *Reliquiae Baxterianae: or, Mr. Richard Baxter's Narrative of the Most Memorable Passages of his Life and Times.* London, 1696.

[Baxter, Richard] *Sacrilegious Desertion of the Holy Ministry Rebuked and Tolerated Preaching of the Gospel Vindicated.* London, 1672.

Beale, John. "Letters," BL MSS. Evelyn Papers, JE A 12, fols 68, 69, 71, 93.1v; JE A 13, fols 108.2v, 109.1v.

Bede, *Bedae Anglosaxonis Historiae Ecclesiasticae Gentis Anglorum Libri V,* in Commelin, *Rerum Britannicarum.*

Bede, *Historiae Ecclesiastica Gentis Anglorum Libri V. A Venerabili Beda . . . ,* ed. Abraham Wheloc. Cambridge, 1644. q.v.

Berni, Francisco. *Orlando Innamorato Nuovamente Composto.* Venice, 1541.

[Biddle, John] *The Apostolical and True Opinion concerning the Holy Trinity.* London, 1653.

Birch, Sir Thomas, ed. *The Court and Times of Charles I,* 2 vols. London, 1848.

Birch, Sir Thomas. "Letters," BL Add MS. 35,397, f. 321.

Blackburne, Francis. *Memoirs of Thomas Hollis.* London, 1780.

Blaeu, Jan. *Geographia,* 11 vols. Amsterdam, 1662.

Blount, Thomas. *Glossographia, or, A Dictionary interpreting all such hard words . . . as are now used in our refined English Tongue.* London, 1656.

Boccaccio, Giovanni. *Vita di Dante, Poeta Fiorentino*. Florence, 1544, 1576.

Boccalini, Trajano. *De' Ragguagli di Parnasso*. Venice, 1630.

Bodin, Jean. *Colloquium Heptaplomeres de Rerum Sublimium Arcanis Abditis*. Schwerin, 1857; *Colloqium of the Seven about the Secrets of the Sublime*, trans. Marion Leathers Daniels Kuntz. Princeton, NJ: Princeton University Press, 1975.

Bodin, Jean. *De Republica libri sex*. Frankfurt, 1591; *Les Six livres de la république*. Lyon, 1580; *The Six Bookes of a Commonweale*, trans. Richard Knolles. London, 1606.

Bourne, Immanuel. *A Defence and Justification of Ministers Maintenance by Tythes*. London, 1659.

Boyle, Robert. *The Works of the Honourable Robert Boyle*. 6 vols. London, 1772.

The Breech Wash'd by a Friend to the Rump. Oxford, 1660.

Bucer, Martin. *De Regno Christi ad Edw. VI*, in *Scripta Anglicana*, ed. Conradus Hubertus. Basle, 1577.

Buchanan, George. *De Juri Regni apud Scotos, dialogus*. Edinburgh, 1579.

Buchanan, George. *Rerum Scoticarum Historia*. Edinburgh, 1582.

Buonmattei, Benedetto. *Della Lingua Toscana, Libri Due*. Florence, 1643.

Burnet, Thomas. *History of My Own Time*, ed. Osmund Airy. 2 vols. Oxford, 1897.

Burton, Henry. *A Vindication of Churches, Commonly Called Independent*. London, 1644.

Burton, Robert. *The Anatomy of Melancholy*. London, 1621.

[Butler, Samuel?] *The Censure of the Rota upon Mr. Milton's Ready and Easy Way to Establish a Free Commonwealth*. London, 1660.

[Butler, Samuel?] *The Character of the Rump*. London, 1660.

Butler, Samuel, *Hudibras. The First Part. Written in the time of the late Wars*. London, 1663; *Hudibras. The Second Part*. London, 1664; *Hudibras. The Third and last Part*. London, 1678.

[Butler, Samuel?] *The Transproser Rehears'd: Or the Fifth Act of Mr. Bayes's Play*. London, 1673.

Cabala, or an Impartial Account of the Non-Conformists Private Designs, Actings, and Ways. From August 24, 1662 to December 25 in the same year. London, 1663.

C. Julii Caesaris Quae Extant, etc. Leyden, 1635.

Caesar, Julius. *The Gallic Wars*, trans. H. J. Edwards. Cambridge, Mass. and London: Harvard University Press and Heinemann, 1970.

A Call to the Officers of the Army and all Good Hearts, signed W. R., H. W., and R. P. London, 1659.

Calvin, John. *Institutes of the Christian Religion*, ed. John T. McNeill, trans. F. L. Battles. 2 vols. Library of Christian Classics, vols XX–XXI. Philadelphia: Westminster Press, 1960.

Camden, William. *Annales Rerum Anglicarum et Hibernicarum, Regnante Elizabetha ad Annum Salutis 1589*. London, 1615; Part II, 1627.

Camden, William. *Institutio Graecae Grammatices Compendaria in Usum Scholae Westminsteriensis*. London, 1595, 1604, 1608, 1617, etc.

Camõens, Luis de. *Os Lusiadas*. Lisbon, 1572; *The Lusiad, Or, Portugals Historicall Poem: Written in the Portingall language by Luis de Camõens, and now newly put into English by Richard Fanshaw*. London, 1655.

Campanella, Tommaso. *La Cittá del sole* [City of the Sun], ed. N. Bobbio. Turin, 1941.

Campion, Edmund. *The History of Ireland. Collected by Three Learned Authors, viz. Meredith Hammer . . . Edmund Campion and Edmund Spenser*. Dublin, 1633.

Canne, John. *The Time of Finding*. London, 1659.

Cantacuzene, John. *Historiarum libri VI,* trans. Jacobus Ponanus. Ingolstadt, 1603.

Carew, Thomas. *Poems.* London, 1640.

The Case of the Armie Truly Stated, together with the mischiefes and dangers that are imminent, and some suitable remedies, Humbly proposed by the Agents of five Regiments of Horse, to their respective Regiments, and the whole Army . . . October 15, 1647. London, 1647.

Castiglione, Baldessar. *Opere Valgari e Latine,* ed. G. Antonio and G. Valpi, Padua, 1733.

A Catalogue of the Severall Sects and Opinions in England and other Nations. London, 1649.

Cato. *Disticha Moralia.* London, 1628.

The Cause of God and of These Nations. London, 1659.

A Caution against Sacriledge: Or Sundry Queries Concerning Tithes. London, 1659.

Cedren, Georges. *Compendium Historiarum a Mundo Conditio.* Basel, 1516.

Certain additionall Reasons to those presented in a Letter by the Ministers of London to the Assembly of Divines. London, 1646.

Certain Briefe Treatises Written by Diverse Learned Men, Concerning the Ancient and Moderne Government of the Church. Wherein, Both the Primitive Institution of Episcopacie is Maintained, and the Lawfulnesse of the Ordination of the Protestant Ministers beyond the Seas likewise defended [ed. James Usher?]. Oxford, 1641.

[Chappell, William] *Methodus Concionandi.* London, 1648.

[Chappell, William] *The Use of Holy Scripture.* London, 1653.

Charles I. *The King's Majesty's declaration to his subjects concerning lawful sports to be used.* London, 1633.

Charles I [John Gauden]. *Eikon Basilike: The Portraiture of his Sacred Majestie in his Solitudes and Sufferings.* London: Richard Royston, 1649.

Charles I [John Gauden]. *His Majesties Prayers which he used in the time of his sufferings, delivered to Dr. Juxon, immediately before his Death.* [London], 1649.

Chaucer, Geoffrey. *Canterbury Tales, Romaunt of the Rose,* in *The Workes of our Ancient and Learned English Poet Geffrey Chaucer,* ed. Thomas Speght. London, 1602.

Chrysostom, John. *Opera Onmia.* 5 vols. Venice, 1582–3.

Chrysostom, John. *Orationes LXXX.* Paris, 1604.

Cicero, esp. *De Officiis, De Oratore, Verrine Orations,* "Pro Quinctio," 28 vols. Cambridge, Mass. and London: Harvard University Press and Heinemann, 1968–79.

Clarkson, Lawrence. *A Single Eye All Light, No Darkness.* London, 1650.

Clement of Alexandria. *Stromata, Paedagogus,* in *Opera.* Paris, 1629.

Codinus [Georgius Curopalata]. *De Officiis et officialibus magnae ecclesiastiae et aulae Constantinopolitanae.* Paris, 1625.

Codinus [Georgius Curopalata], et al. *Excerpta de Antiquitatibus Constantinopolitanis.* Paris, 1655.

A Coffin for the Good Old Cause: Or, A Sober Word by way of Cuation to the Parliament and Army. [London, 1660].

A Collection of Several Papers Sent to his Highness the Lord Protector . . . Concerning the Bloody and Barbarous Massacres, Murthers, and other Cruelties, committed on many thousands of Reformed, or Protestants dwelling in the Vallies of Piedmont, by the Duke of Savoy's Forces, joyned therin with the French Army, and severall Irish Regiments, ed. Jean Baptiste Stouppe. London, 1655.

Collier, Thomas. *The Decision & Clearing of the great Point now in Controversie about the Interest of Christ and the Civil Magistrate in the Rule of Government in this World.* London, 1659.

Colline, William. *The Spirit of the Phanatiques Dissected and the Solemne League and Covenant solemnly discussed in 30 Queries.* London, 1660.

C[ollinges], J[ohn], *Par Nobile: Two Treatises*. London, 1669.
Coltellini, Agostino. *Endecasillabi,* 2 parts. Florence, 1641, 1652.
Comenius, Jan Amos. *Didactica Magna*. Amsterdam, 1657.
Comenius, Jan Amos. *Janua linguarum reserata*. Leszno, 1631.
Commelin, Jerome, ed. *Rerum Britannicarum, id. est Angliae, Scotiae, Variorumque Insularum ac Regionem Scriptores* (Gildas, Geoffrey of Monmouth, Bede, etc.) Heidelberg, 1587.
Commines, Philippe de. *Les Mémoires*. Paris, 1552.
A Common-place Book out of The Rehearsal Transpros'd. London, 1673.
A Commonwealth, and Commonwealths-men, Asserted and Vindicated. London, 1659.
A Common-Wealth or Nothing; or, Monarchy and Oligarchy prov'd parallel in tyranny. London, 1659.
A Confession of Faith of seven Congregations in London which are commonly called Anabaptists. London, 1646.
The Confession of the Arians, Addressed to Alexander of Alexandria, in E. R. Hardy and Cyril R. Richardson, eds, *Christology of the Later Fathers*. Library of Christian Classics, vol. III. Philadelphia: Westminster Press, 1954.
Conn, George. *De Duplici Statu Religionis Apud Scotis*. Rome, 1628.
Considerations: Being the Legitimate Issue of a True English Heart: Presented to the Freeholders, and to the Free Men of Several Corporations in this Nation; to Regulate their elections of Members to Serve in the next Parliament, to be holden the 25th of April, 1660. London, 1660.
Conway, Anne Finch. *The Principles of the Most Ancient and Modern Philosophy,* ed. Peter Lopston. The Hague: Martinus Nijhoff, 1982.
The Copie of a Paper Presented to the Parliament. London, 1659.
[Coppe, Abiezer] *A Fiery Flying Roll . . . being the last Warning Piece at the dreadfull day of Judgement*. London, 1649.
[Coppe, Abiezer] *A Second Fiery Flying Roule: To all the Inhabitants of the earth, specially the rich ones*. London, 1649.
Coryat, Thomas. *Coryat's Crudities*. 2 vols. London, 1611.
Costanzo, Angelodi, *Historia del Regno di Napoli*. Aguila, 1581.
The Covenant, With a Narrative of the Proceedings and Solemn Manner of Taking it by the Honourable House of Commons, and Reverent Assembly of Divines the 25th of September. London, 1643.
Cowley, Abraham. *Davideis, Or, A Sacred Poem of the Troubles of David,* in *Poems*. London, 1656.
Cowley, Abraham. *The Mistress*. London, 1647.
Crashaw, Richard. *Steps to the Temple*. London, 1646.
Crisp, Samuel. *An Epistle to Friends, Concerning the Present and Succeeding Times*. London, 1666.
Cromwell, Oliver. *Writings and Speeches of Oliver Cromwell,* ed. W. C. Abbott. 4 vols. Cambridge: Cambridge University Press, 1937.
Cuspinian, Joannes [Hans Spiesshayer]. *Historia Caesarum Et Imperatorum Romanorum*. Frankfurt, 1601.
Cyprian. *De Singularitate Clericorum*, in *Opera*, ed. Simon Goulart with commentary by Jacobus Pamelius. Geneva, 1593.
Dante Alighieri. *Dante con L'Expositione Di M. Bernardino Daniello*. Venice, 1568.
Dante Alighieri. *The Divine Comedy*, trans. Charles S. Singleton. 6 vols. Princeton, NJ:

Princeton University Press, 1973.

Dante Alighieri. *L'Amoroso Convivio*. Venice, 1563.

[Dati, Carlo] *Discorso Dell'Obbligo di ben parlare la propria lingua*. Florence, 1657.

Dati, Carlo, ed. *Raccolte dallo Smarrito Academico della Crusca*. Florence, 1661.

Dati, Carlo. *Vite de Pittori Antichi*. Florence, 1667.

Davanzati, Bernardo. *Scisma d'Inghilterra*. Florence, 1638.

Davenant, William. *Gondibert: An Heroick Poem*. London, 1651.

A Declaration of many thousand well-affected Persons, Inhabitants in and about the Cities of London and Westminster, expressing their adherence to this present Parliament; also their sense of a Free Parliament, so much cried up by the cavaliers, and others, that know not what it is. [London, 1660].

A Declaration of the Commander-in-chief of the Forces in Scotland, Also . . . Three Letters from the Lord General Monck. London, 1659.

A Declaration of the Commons Assembled in Parliament, Against a Scandalous Book Entituled, The Second Part of Englands New Chains Discovered. London, 1649.

A Declaration of the Engagements, Remonstrances, Representations, Proposals, Desires, and Resolutions from his Excellency Sir Tho: Fairfax, and the generall Councel of the Army. London, 1647.

Declaration of the Lord General and his Councel of Offficers, Shewing the Grounds and Reasons for the dissolution of the late Parliament. London, 1653.

A Declaration of the Officers of the Army, inviting the Members of the Long Parliament to return to the Exercise and Discharge of their Trust. London, 1659.

A Declaration of the Parliament of the Commonwealth of England, Relating to the Affairs and Proceedings between this Commonwealth and the States General of the United Provinces of the Low Countreys. London, 1652.

A Declaration of the Present Sufferings of about 140 Persons of the People of God [Quakers]. London, 1659.

Defoe, Daniel. *A Journal of the Plague Year*, ed. J. H. Plumb. New York: New American Library, 1960.

Dell, William. "The Right Reformation of Learning, Schools, and Universities," with *The Tryal of Spirits Both in Teachers & Hearers . . . Whereunto is added . . . that Humane learning, is not a Preparation appointed by Christ, either for the Right Understanding, or Right Teaching the Gospel. With a brief Testimony against Divinity Degrees in the Universities*. London, 1660.

Della Casa, Giovanni. *Rime et Prose*. Venice, 1563.

Denham, John. *Cooper's Hill*. London, 1642.

Denham, John. *The Destruction of Troy. An Essay upon the Second Book of Virgil's Aeneis*. London, 1656.

Dewsbury, William. *The Word of the Lord to all the Inhabitants of England*. London, 1666.

Diodati, Charles. "Sic furua conjux tartarei Jovis," *Camdeni Insignia*. Oxford, 1624.

Diodati, Giovanni, *Pious Annotations upon the Holy Bible*. London, 1645.

Documents of the Christian Church, ed. Henry Bettenson. New York: Oxford University Press, 1958.

Documents Relating to the Procedings against William Prynne, ed. S. R. Gardiner. Westminster: Camden Society, 1877.

Downame, George. *Commentarii in P. Rami . . . Dialecticam*. Frankfurt, 1610.

Drummond of Hawthornden, William. *Poems*, ed. E[dward] P[hillips]. London, 1656.

Dryden, John. *Annus Mirabilis: The Year of Wonders*. London, 1667.

Dryden, John. *Astraea Redux: A Poem on the Happy Restoration and Return of his Sacred Majesty*

Charles the Second. London, 1660.

Dryden, John. *Fables Ancient and Modern.* London, 1700.

Dryden, John. *The Indian Emperour, or The Conquest of Mexico by the Spaniards.* London, 1667.

Dryden, John. *Of Dramatic Poesie, An Essay.* London, 1668.

Dryden, John. "Of Heroic Plays," prefixed to *The Conquest of Granda by the Spaniards.* London, 1672.

Dryden, John. *The State of Innocence, and Fall of Man: An Opera Written in Heroique Verse, and Dedicated to her Royal Highness, the Dutchess.* London, 1677.

Dryden, John. *To His Sacred Majesty: A Panegyrick on his Coronation.* London, 1661.

Du Bartas, Guillaume de Saluste. *La Semaine, ou creation du monde.* Paris, 1578; *La Seconde semaine, ou enfance du monde.* Paris, 1584. See Joshua Sylvester, *Bartas his Divine Weekes and Workes.*

Du Chesne, André. *Histoire générale d'Angleterre, d'Escosse, et d'Irelande.* Paris, 1634, 1641.

[Du Moulin, Pierre] Petri Molinaei. *Parerga, Poematum libelli tres.* Cambridge, 1670.

[Du Moulin, Pierre] *Regii sanguinis clamor ad coelum adversus parricidas Anglicanos.* The Hague, 1652.

Du Moulin, Pierre. *A Replie to a Person of Honour.* London, 1675.

Duncon, Samuel. *Several Proposals Offered to the Consideration of the Keepers of the Liberties of the People of England.* London, 1659.

Dury, John, trans. *Eikonoklastes ou réponse au livre intitulé Eikon Basilike, ou Le Pourtrait de sa sacrée majesté durant sa solitude et ses souffrances, par le Sr. Jean Milton.* London, 1652.

D[ury], J[ohn] *Considerations Concerning the Present Engagement: Whether it may lawfully be entered into, Yea or No?* London, 1649.

Dury, John. *Just Re-Proposals to Humble Proposals.* London, 1650.

Dury, John. *The Reformed School.* London, 1650.

Eachard, John. *The Grounds & Occasions of the Contempt of the Clergy and Religion.* London, 1670.

Ecclesiasticae Historiae Autores. Paris, 1544; Basle, 1549.

Edwards, Thomas. *Gangraena: Or a Catalogue and Discovery of many of the Errours, Heresies, Blasphemies, and pernicious Practices of the Sectaries of this time, vented and acted in England in these four last years.* London, 1646.

Edwards, Thomas. *The Second Part of Gangraena: Or a fresh and further Discovery of the Errors, Heresies, Blasphemies, and dangerous Proceedings of the Sectaries of this time.* London, 1646

Eikon Alethine. The Portraiture of Truths most sacred Majesty truly suffering though not solely. Wherein the False colours are washed off, wherewith the Painter-steiner had bedawbed Truth, the late King, and the Parliament, in his counterfeit Piece entitled Eikon Basilike. London, 1649.

Eikon Episte, or, the faithful Portraiture of a Loyall Subject, in Vindication of Eikon Basilike . . . in Answer to an Insolent Book, intituled, Eikon Alethine: Whereby occasion is taken to handle all the controverted points relating to these times. London, 1649.

Ellwood, Thomas. *The History of the Life of Thomas Ellwood.* ed. J[oseph] W[yeth]. London, 1714.

Englands Lamentable Slaverie. Proceeding from the Arbitrarie will, severitie, and Injustices of Kings, Negligence, corruption, and unfaithfulnesse of Parliaments, Covetousness ambition, and variableness of Priests, and simplicitie, carelessnesse, and cowardlinesse of People. [William Walwyn?]. London, 1645.

[Episcopius, Simon] *Confessio, sive Declaratio, Sententiae Pastorum, qui in Foederato Belgio*

Remonstrantes vocantur. Harderwijk, 1622.

An Essay Toward Settlement upon a sure foundation, being a testimony for God in this perilous time by a few who have been bewailing their own abominations. [Signed by John Owen, Robert Overton, Vavasor Powell, and 17 others.] London, 1659.

Euripides. *Tragoedia quae extant*. 2 vols. Geneva, 1602; *Euripides*, trans. David Kovacs. 4 vols. Cambridge, Mass. and London: Harvard University Press and Heinemann, 1994–8.

Eusebius Pamphili, *Historiae Ecclesiasticae lib. X*, in *Ecclesiasticae Historiae Autores* (q.v.).

Evelyn, John. *The Diary*, ed. E. S. DeBeer. 5 vols. Oxford: Clarendon Press, 1955.

The Examination and Tryall of M. Fell and George Fox. London, 1664.

Eye-Salve for the English Army. London, 1660.

Fagius, Paulus. *Thargum, Hoc Est, Paraphrasis Onkeli Chaldaica in Sacra Biblia . . . Additis in Singula Fere Capita Succinctis Annotationibus*. Strassburg, 1546.

Faithorne, William. *The Art of Graveing and Etching, etc*. London, 1662.

Feake, Christopher. *The Fifth Monarchy, or Kingdom of Christ, in Opposition to the Beast's, asserted*. London, 1659.

Featley, Daniel. *The Dippers Dipt, or the Anabaptists Duck'd and Plung'd over Head and Eares*. London, 1644.

A Few Proposals . . . holding forth a Medium or Essay for the Removing of Tithes. London, 1659.

A Few Sober Queries. London, 1668.

F[ilmer], R[obert]. *The Necessity of the Absolute Power of all Kings, and in particular of the King of England*. London, 1648.

[Filmer, Robert] *Observations Concerning the Originall of Government upon Mr Hobs Leviathan, Mr Milton Against Salmasius. H. Grotius De Jure Belli*. London, 1652.

Filmer, Robert. *Political Discourses . . . viz., Patriarcha, or the natural power of Kings, etc*. London, 1680–79.

Firmin, Giles. *Separatism Examined: or, A Treatise wherein the grounds for Separation from the Ministry and Churches of England are weighed and found too light*. London, 1652.

Firmin, Giles. *Tythes Vindicated from Anti-Christianism and Oppression*. London, 1659.

Fitz-Brian, R. *The Good Old Cause Dress'd in Its Primitive Lustre*. London, 1659.

Fletcher, Giles. *Of the Russe Common Wealth*. London, 1591.

Fletcher, Giles (the Younger). *Christs Victorie, and Triumph*. London, 1610.

Fletcher, Phineas. *Locustae: vel pietas Jesuitica*. 2 parts. [Cambridge], 1627. With *The Locusts or Apollyonists*.

Fortunate Rising, or the Rump Upward. London [1660].

Foundations of Freedom or An Agreement of the People Proposed as a Rule for Future Government in the Establishment of a Firm and Lasting Peace. Drawn up by Several Well-Affected Persons, and Tendered to the Consideration of the General Council of the Army. And Now Offered to the Consideration of all Persons. London, 1648.

Fowler, Edward. *The Principles and Practices of Certain Moderate Divines of the Church of England*. London, 1670.

Fox, George. *The Journal of George Fox*, ed. Norman Penney. London, 1924.

Fox, George. *A Primer for the Schollers and Doctors of Europe*. London, 1659.

Freige, Joannus Thomas. *Petri Rami Vita*, in Petrus Ramus, *Praelectiones in Ciceronis Orationes Octo Consulares Una cum Ipsius [P. Rami] Vita per Joannem Thomam Freigium Collecta*. Basle, 1575.

Frontinus, Sextus Julius. *Strategematicon*. Antwerp, 1585.

Frost, Gualter, ed. *A Brief Relation of Some Affaires and Transactions, Civil and Military, Both Forraigne and Domestic.* London, September, 1649–October 1650.

[Fullwood, Francis] *Toleration not to be Abused, Or, A Serious Question Soberly Debated and Resolved upon Presbyterian Principles.* London, 1672.

G., W. *The Arraignment of Ignorance. As also the excellency, profit, and benefit of Heavenly Knowledge.* London, 1659.

Gadbury, John. *Vox Solis: or, an Astrological Discourse of the Great Eclipse of the Sun.* London, 1667.

Gaddi, Jacopo. *Adlocutiones et Elogia, Exemplaria, Cabalistica, Oratoria, Mixta Sepulcralia.* Florence, 1637.

Gaddi, Jacopo. *Corollarium Poeticum. scil. Poemata, Notae, Explicationes Allegoricae Olim Conscriptae.* Florence, 1636.

Gaddi, Jacopo, *Elogia Historica Tum Soluta Cum Vincia Numeris Oratione Perscripta et Notis Illustrata.* Florence, 1637.

Gaddi, Jacopo. *Poematum libri due.* Florence, 1628.

Galileo Galilei, *Dialogo . . . sopra i due massimi sistemi del mondo, tolemaico, e copernicano.* Florence, 1632. Trans. Stillman Blake, Berkeley: University of California Press, 1967.

Gataker, Thomas. *Abraham's Decease. . . . Delivered at the funerall of Mr. R. Stock.* London, 1627.

Gauden, John. *The Religious and Loyal Protestation of John Gauden against the Purposes of the Army and others; about the trying and destroying our Soveraign Lord the King.* London, 1649.

Gil, Alexander (Sr). *Logonomia Anglici.* London, 1619.

Gil, Alexander (Sr). *The Sacred Philosophie of the Holy Scripture.* London, 1635.

Gil, Alexander (Sr). *A Treatise Concerning the Trinitie of Persons in Unity of the Deitie.* London, 1601.

Gil, Alexander, Jr. *Epinikion, de gestis successibus et victoriis Regis Sueciae in Germania.* London, 1631. Published with *The New Star of the North Shining upon the Victorious King of Sweden.* London, 1631, 1632.

Gil, Alexander, Jr. *Gratulatoria dicata Sereniss. ac Potentiss. Carolo Regi, & Caledone ad Trinobantes suos reverso.* London, 1641.

Gil, Alexander, Jr. *Parerga, Sive Poetici Conatus.* London, 1632.

Gildas. *De Excidio et Conquestu Britanniae,* in Commelin, *Rerum Britannicarum* (q.v.).

Gilles, Pierre. *Histoire ecclesiastique des eglises reformés . . . en quelques valées de Piedmont . . . apelées eglises Vaudoises.* Geneva, 1644.

Girard, Bernard de, Sieur de Haillen. *L'Histoire de France.* Paris, 1576.

Giustiani, Bernardo. *De Origine Urbis Venetiarum.* Venice, 1492.

The Good Old Cause Explained, Revived, and Asserted. And the Long Parliament Vindicated. London, 1659.

Goodwin, John. *Hubristodkaia. The Obstructours of Justice; or, a Defence of the Sentence passed upon the late King by the High Court of Justice. Opposed chiefly to the Serious Representation of some of the Ministers of London; as also to the Humble Address of Dr. Henry Hammond.* London, 1649.

Goodwin, John. *Might and Right Well Met, Or a Briefe Enquiry into the Proceedings of the Army.* London, 1649.

Goodwin, John. *Redemption Redeemed.* London, 1651.

Goodwin, John. *Theomachia: Or, the Grand Impudence of Men Running the Hazard of Fighting Against God, in Suppressing any Way, Doctrine, or Practice.* London, 1644.

Goodwin, John. *Twelve Considerable Serious Cautions*. London, 1646.

Goodwin, Thomas, Phillip Nye, et. al. *An Apologeticall Narration, Humbly Submitted to the Honourable Houses of Parliament*. London, 1644.

Gower, John. *Confessio Amantis*. London, 1532.

Granger, Thomas. *Syntagma Grammaticum*. London, 1616.

Greaves, Paul. *Grammatica Anglicana*. Cambridge, 1594.

Gregoras, Nicephorus. *Byzantinae Historiae Libri XI*. Basel, 1562.

Gregory of Nyssa. *Opera*. Paris, 1638.

Griffith, Matthew. *The Feare of God and the King. Pressed in a Sermon, Preach'd at Mercers Chapell, on the 25th of March, 1660. Together with a brief Historical account of the Causes of our unhappy Distractions, and the onely way to Heal them*. London, 1660.

Grignani, Lodovico, ed. *Poesie de Signori Accademici Fantastici di Roma*. Rome, 1637.

Grotius, Hugo. *Adamus Exul*. The Hague, 1601.

Grotius, Hugo. *Annotationes ad Vetus Testamentum*. 3 vols. Paris, 1644.

Grotius, Hugo. *Annotationes in Libros Evangeliorum*. Amsterdam, 1641.

Grotius, Hugo. *De jure belli ac pacis libri tres*. Paris, 1625.

Grotius, Hugo. *Tragoedia, Christus Patiens*, in *Poemata Collecta*. Leyden, 1617; trans. [George Sandys], *Christs Passion: A Tragedie with Annotations*. London, 1640.

Guicciardini, Francesco. *Historia d'Italia*. Florence, 1636.

A Guildhall Elegie. London, 1659.

Guillim, John. *A Display of Heraldrie*. London, 1632.

Hakewell, George. *An Apologie of the Power and Providence of God*. London, 1627.

Hakluyt, Richard. *The Principal Navigations, Voiages, Traffiques, and Discoveries of the English Nation*. 3 vols. London, 1598–1600.

Hales, John. *Golden Remains*. London, 1673.

[Hales, John] *A Tract concerning Schism and Schismatiques*. London, 1642.

[Hall, John] *The Discoverer. Being an Answer to England's New Chains*. London, 1649.

H[all], J[ohn]. *An Humble Motion to the Parliament of England. Concerning the Advancement of Learning: And Reformation of the Universities*. London, 1649.

[Hall, Joseph] *A Defence of the Humble Remonstrance, against the Frivolous and false Exceptions of Smectymnuus*. London, 1641.

H[all], J[oseph]. *Episcopacie by Divine Right Asserted*. London, 1640.

H[all], J[oseph]. *An Humble Remonstrance to the High Court of Parliament*. London, 1641.

[Hall, Joseph?] *A Modest Confutation of a Slanderous and Scurrilous Libell, Entituled, Animadversions upon the Remonstrants Defense Against Smectymnuus*. London, 1642.

[Hall, Joseph] Mercurius Britannicus. *Mundus alter & idem*. Frankfurt [London], 1605.

H[all], J[oseph]. *Resolutions and Decisions of Divers Practicall Cases of Conscience in Continuall Use amongst Men*. London, 1649.

[Hall, Joseph] *A Short Answer to the Tedious Vindication of Smectymnuus*. London, 1641.

[Hall, Joseph] *Virgidemiarum, Sixe Bookes . . . of Satyrs. First three Bookes. Of tooth-lesse satyrs. Virgidemiarum, the three last Bookes. Of byting satyres*. 2 parts. London, 1597–8.

Hammond, Henry. *A Letter of Resolution to six Quaeres, of present use in the Church of England*. London, 1653 [1652].

Hammond, Henry. *To the Lord Fairfax and his Councell of Warre: The Humble Addresse of Henry Hammond*. London, 1649.

Hardyng, John. *Chronicle*. London, 1543.

Harrington, James. *Aphorisms Political.* London, 1659.

Harrington, James. *The Common-Wealth of Oceana.* London, 1656.

Harrington, James. *A Discourse, Shewing that the spirit of parliaments with a Council in the intervals, is not to be trusted for a Settlement.* London, 1659.

Harrington, James. *Political Works,* ed. J. G. A. Pocock. Cambridge: Cambridge University Press, 1977.

Harrington, James. *Politicaster: or, A comical discourse in answer unto Mr. Wren's Monarchy Asserted, against Mr. Harrington's Oceana.* London, 1659.

Harrington, James. *Pour enclouer le canon.* London, 1659.

[Harrington, James] *The Rota: Or, A Model of a Free-State or Equall Common-Wealth.* London, 1659 [1660].

Harrington, James. *The Wayes and Meanes Whereby an Equal & Lasting Commonwealth may be suddenly Introduced and Perfectly Founded with the free consent and Actual Confirmation of the Whole People of England.* London, 1660.

Hartlib Collection. *Ephemeridis, etc.* (MSS). Published on CD-Rom, Sheffield University.

Hartlib, Samuel. *The Reformation of Schools.* London, 1642.

Hayward, John. *The Life and Raigne of King Edward the Sixt.* London, 1630.

Heath, James. *A Brief Chronicle of the late Intestine War in the Three Kingdoms.* London, 1660.

Heraclides of Pontus. *Allegoriae in Homeri fabulas de diis.* Basel, 1544.

Herrick, Robert. *Hesperides: or the Works both Humane and Divine.* London, 1648.

Hesiod. *Works and Days,* in *The Homeric Hymns and Homerica.* Cambridge, Mass. and London: Harvard University Press and Heinemann, 1954.

Histoire entière et véritable du proces de Charles Stuart Roy d'Angleterre. London, 1650.

Historiae Byzantinae Scriptores tres graeco-latini. Geneva, 1615.

Historiae Ecclesiasticae Scriptores Graeci. Paris, 1544; Basel, 1562; Latin trans., Geneva, 1612.

Hobart, John. "Letters," Bodleian MS Tanner 45, fols 258, 271.

Hobbes, Thomas. *De Corpore Politico, or, the elements of law, moral and politick.* London, 1650.

Hobbes, Thomas. *The History of the Civil Wars of England. From the Year 1640 to 1660.* [London], 1679; *Behemoth, or the Long Parliament,* ed. Ferdinand Tönnies. London: Frank Cass, 1969.

Hobbes, Thomas. *Humane Nature, or, the fundamental elements of policie.* London, 1650.

Hobbes, Thomas. *Leviathan: Or the Matter, Forme, & Power of a Common-wealth ecclesiasticall and civill.* London, 1651.

Holinshed, Raphael. *The first and second volumes of Chronicles of England, Scotland, and Ireland.* With *The Third Volume of Chronicles.* London, 1587.

Holste, Lukas [Lucas Holstenius]. *Demophili Democratis et Secundi Veterum Philosophorum Sententiae Morales.* Rome, 1638.

Homer. *The Iliad,* trans. A. T. Murray, revd William F. Wyatt. 2 vols. Cambridge, Mass. and London: Harvard University Press and Heinemann, 1999.

Homer. *The Odyssey,* trans. A. T. Murray, revd George E. Dimock. 2 vols. Cambridge, Mass. and London: Harvard University Press and Heinemann, 1995.

The Honest Design: Or, The True Commonwealths-man. London, 1659.

Horace. *Odes and Epodes,* trans. C. E. Bennett. Cambridge, Mass. and London: Harvard University Press and Heinemann, 1978.

Horace. *Satires, Epistles, and Ars Poetica,* trans. H. Rushton Fairclough. Cambridge, Mass. and London: Harvard University Press and Heinemann, 1977.

Howell, James. *Dodona's Grove.* London, 1640, 1645.

The Humble Desires of a Free Subject. London, 1659.

The Humble Petition of Divers Free-holders and Other Inhabitants in the County of Hertford. London, 1659. Broadside.

The Humble Proposals of Mr. Owen, Mr. Tho. Goodwin, Mr. Nye, Mr. Sympson, and other Ministers . . . under debate by a Committee this 31 of March, 1652. for the furtherance and Propagation of the Gospel in this Nation. London, 1652.

The Humble Proposals of Sundry Learned Divines. London, 1649.

The Humble Remonstrance . . . of Major General Goffs Regiment. London, 1659.

The Humble Representation and Petition of the Officers of the Army to the Parliament. London, 1659.

The Humble Representation of Divers Freeholders and Others . . . Inhabiting within the County of Bedford. London, 1659.

Hutchinson, Lucy. *Memoirs of the Life of Colonel Hutchinson*, ed. Julius Hutchinson. London: Dent, 1968; ed. James Sutherland. Oxford: Oxford University Press, 1973.

Illustrated London News. London, 1847, 1864.

Isocrates. "Areopagiticus," in *Isocrates*, trans. George Norlin, 3 vols. Cambridge, Mass. and London: Harvard University Press and Heinemann, 1954, II, 104–57.

[Jane, Joseph] *Eikon Aklastos. The Image Unbroken. A Perspective of the Impudence, Falsehood, Vanitie, and Prophannes, Published in a Libell entitled Eikonoklastes, against Eikon Basilike, or the Portraiture of his Sacred Majestie in his Solitudes and Sufferings*. [London], 1651.

Jansen, John. *Novus Atlas*. 8 vols. Amsterdam, 1658.

[Jenkins, David] *A Proposition for the Safety & Happiness of the King and Kingdom, both in Church and State, and Prevention of the Common Enemy; By Way of Accommodation and Indulgence in Matters of Religion*. London, 1667.

Johnson, Samuel. *Lives of the English Poets*, ed. G. B. Hill. 3 vols. Oxford: Clarendon Press, 1905.

Jonson, Ben. *The English Grammar*, in *Works*. 2 vols. London, 1640.

Jonson, Ben. *Works*. London, 1616.

Journal of the House of Lords [Lord's Journal]. London: British Library, State Paper Room.

Journal of the House of Commons [Commons Journal]. London: British Library, State Paper Room.

Jovius, Paulus. *Historia Sui Temporis*, in *Opera Quotquot Extant Omnia*. 2 vols. Basel, 1578.

The Judgement of the Synode Holden at Dort, Concerning the Five Articles. London, 1619.

Justin Martyr. *Tryphon, Apologia pro Christianis*, in *Opera*. Paris, 1615

Justinian. *Institutiones Juris Civilis*. Louvain, 1475.

Labadie, Jean de. *Declaration de Jean de Labadie . . . Contenant les raisons que l'ont obligé à quitter la Communion de l'Eglise Romaine*. Montauban, 1650.

Labadie, Jean de. *Lettre à ses amis de la communion romaine*. Montauban, 1651.

Lactantius. *De Ira Dei, Divinae Institutiones*, in *Opera*. Antwerp, 1532.

Lambarde, William. *Archeion, or a Commentary upon the High Courts of Justice in England*. London, 1635.

Lawes, Henry. *Ayres and Dialogues, for One, Two and Three Voyces*. London, 1653.

Lawes, Henry. *The Second Book of Ayres and Dialogues, for One, Two, and Three Voyces*. London, 1655.

Lawes, Henry, and William Lawes. *Choice Psalmes put into Musick, for Three Voices*. London, 1648.

Leighton, Alexander. *An Appeal to the Parliament Or, Sion's Plea against the Prelacie*. London, 1628.

A Letter of the Ministers of the City of London, presented to the Assembly of Divines, against Toleration. London, 1646.

A Letter to General Monk expressing the sense of the well-affected people of England, old Parlamenters and Old Puritanes. London, 1660.

Leunclavius, Joannes. *Juris Graeco-Romani, tam Canonici quam Civilis*. 2 vols. Frankfurt, 1596.

The Leveller: Or the Principles and Maxims Concerning Government and Religion, Which are asserted by those commonly called Levellers. London, 1659.

The Leveller Tracts, 1647–1653, ed. William Haller and Godfrey Davies. New York: Columbia University Press, 1944.

[L'Estrange, Roger] *Be Merry and Wise, Or, A Seasonable Word to the Nation, shewing the Cause, the Growth, the State, and the Cure of our Present Distemper*. London, 1660.

L'Estrange, Roger. *Considerations and Proposals In Order to the Regulation of the Press. Together with Diverse Instances of Treasonous, and Seditious Pamphlets, proving the Necessity thereof*. London, 1663.

[L'Estrange, Roger] *Double Your Guards: In Answer to a Seditious Pamphlet, Entituled, an Alarum to the Armies of England, Scotland, and Ireland*. London, 1660.

L'Estrange, Roger. *L'Estrange His Apology. With a Short View, of some Late and Remarkable Transactions, leading to the happy Settlement of these Nations*. London, 1660.

[L'Estrange, Roger] *No Blinde Guides. In Answer to a seditious pamphlet of J. Milton's, intituled Brief Notes upon a lae Sermon, titl'd, The Fear of God and the King, by Matthew Griffith*. London, 1660.

[L'Estrange, Roger] *Physician Cure Thy Selfe: Or an Answer to a Seditious Pamphlet, entituled Eye-Salve for the English Army*. London, 1660.

[L'Estrange, Roger] *Toleration Discussed, in Two Dialogues, 1. Betwixt a Conformist and a Non-Conformist. 2. Betwixt a Presbyterian and an Independent*. London, 1670.

[L'Estrange, Roger] *Treason Arraigned, in Answer to Plain English: Being a Trayterous and phanatique Pamphlet which was condemned by the Counsel of State*. London, 1660.

The Life and Reigne of King Charls, or, the Pseudo-Martyr Discovered. London, 1651.

Lightfoot, John. *The Harmony of the Foure Evangelists*. 2 vols. London, 1644–7.

Lilburne, John. *As You Were, Or, Lord General Cromwel and the Grand Officers of the Armie their Remembrancer . . . May 1652*. [Amsterdam?], 1652.

Lilburne, John. *A Declaration of the Army concerning Lieut. Col. John Lilburne*. London, 1652.

[Lilburne, John] *Englands New Chains Discovered: Or, the Serious Apprehensions of a Part of the People, in behalf of the Commonwealth*. London, 1649.

Lilburne, John. *The Legall Fundamentall Liberties of the People of England*. London, 1649.

Lilburne, John, Thomas Prince, and Richard Overton. *The Picture of the Councel of State held forth to the Free People of England*. London, 1649.

[Lilburne, John, Thomas Prince, and Robert Overton] *The Second Part of England's New Chaines Discover'd*. London, 1649.

Lily, William. *A Shorte Introduction of Grammar generallye to be used* [with] *Brevissima Institutio seu ratio grammatices cognoscendae ad omnium puerorum utilitatem perscripta*. London, 1574. Many editions.

Linguae Romanae Dictionarium . . . The Whole completed and improved from several Works of Stephens, Cooper, Gouldman, Holyoke, Dr. [Adam] Littleton, a Large Manuscript, in three Volumes, of Mr. John Milton, etc. London, 1693.

Lipsius, Justus. *Politicorum sive Civilis Doctrinae libri sex*. Leyden, 1589; Antwerp, 1599, 1615.

Livy. *Historiarum ab urbe condita Libri qui Extant XXXV.* Venice, 1572.

Livy, trans. H. O. Foster, et al., 14 vols. Cambridge, Mass. and London: Harvard University Press and Heinemann, 1939–59.

Lloyd, David. *Eikon Basilike. Or the True Protraiture of his Sacred Majesty Charls the II in Three Books.* London, 1660.

Lloyd, David. *Memoirs of the Lives, Actions, Sufferings, and Deaths of those Noble, Reverend and Excellent Personages that Suffered . . . in our Late Intestine Wars.* London, 1668.

Lockyer, Nicholas. *Some Seasonable and Serious Queries Upon the late Act Against Conventicles.* Oxford, 1670.

The London Printers Lamentation, or, the Press opprest, and overprest. London, 1660.

Londons Sad Calamity by Fire; Being a Warning-piece to England. London, 1666.

Lucan. *Pharsalia*, trans. J. D. Duff. Cambridge, Mass.: Harvard University Press, 1928.

Lucan. *Pharsalia,* ed. Hugo Grotius, Leyden, 1614; ed. Thomas Farnaby, London, 1618; trans. Arthur Gorges, *Lucan's Pharsalia: containing the Civill Warres between Caesar and Pompey*, London, 1614; trans. Thomas May, *Lucans Pharsalia: or The Civill Warres of Rome*, London, 1627; revd edns 1630, 1640.

Lucretius. *De Rerum Natura,* trans. W. H. D. Rouse. Cambridge, Mass. and London: Harvard University Press and Heinemann, 1975.

Ludlow, Edmund. *Memoirs,* ed. C. H. Firth. 2 vols. Oxford: Clarendon Press, 1894.

Machiavelli, Niccolo. *Dell'Arte della Guerra.* London, 1587; trans. Peter Whitehorne, *The Arte of Warre.* London, 1560 [1562].

Machiavelli, Niccolo. *Discorsi . . . sopra la prima deca di toto Livio.* London, 1584.

Machiavelli, Niccolo. *Tutte le Opere di Nicolo Machiavelli.* 5 parts. Geneva, 1550.

Maimonides [Moses, ben Maimon]. *Rabbi Mosis Maiemonidis Liber Doctor Perplexorum,* trans. J. Buxtorf. Basel, 1629.

Malatesti, Antonio. *La Tina: equivoci rusticali.* London, 1757.

Malcolm, James P., ed. *Londinium Redivivum; or, An Ancient History and Modern Description of London,* vol. 4. London, 1807.

Manasses, Constantinus. *Breviarium Historicum.* Paris, 1655.

Manso, Giovanni Battista. *L'Erocallia ovvero dell' Amore e della Bellezza.* Venice, 1618.

Manso, Giovanni Battista. *Paradossi, ovvero dell'Amore Dialoghi.* Milan, 1608.

Manso, Giovanni Battista. *Poesie Nimiche . . . divise in Rime Amorose, Sacre, e Morali.* Venice, 1635.

Manso, Giovanni Battista. *Vita di Torquato Tasso.* Naples, 1619.

Mantuan, Giovanni Battista Spagnuoli. *Sylvarum,* book 4, in *Opera,* 3 vols. Paris, 1513.

Marino, Giovanni Battista. *L'Adone.* Paris, 1623.

Marino, Giovanni Battista. *La strage degl'innocenti.* Naples, 1632.

Marshall, Stephen. *Meroz Cursed or, A Sermon preached to the honourable House of Commons . . . Feb. 23, 1641.* London, 1641 [1642].

Marshall, Stephen. *A Sermon Preached to the Lord Mayor and Aldermen of the City of London.* London, 1652.

Martyr, Peter. *In Librum Judicum . . . Commentarii.* Zurich, 1571.

Marvell, Andrew. *Poems and Letters,* ed. H. M. Margoliouth, revd Pierre Legouis and E. E. Duncan Jones. 2 vols. Oxford: Clarendon Press, 1971.

[Marvell, Andrew] *The Rehearsal Transpros'd: Or, Animadversions upon a late Book, Intituled, A Preface Shewing What Grounds there are of Fears and Jealousies of Popery.* London, 1672.

[Marvell, Andrew] *The Rehearsall Transpros'd: The Second Part.* London, 1673.

Maugars, André. *Response fait á un curieux sur le sentiment de la musique d'Italie, escrite á Rome le premier octobre 1639.* Avec notes et éclaircisements par Er[nest] Thoinan. Paris, 1865.

May, Thomas. *The History of the Parliament of England, which began November the third, MDCXL.* London, 1647.

[Mede, Joseph] *Clavis Apocalyptica, ex innatis et insitis visionum characteribus eruta et demonstrata,* London, 1627; trans. *The Key of the Revelation,* London, 1643, 1650; rpt. in *Works*, 2 vols, London, 1648, 1664.

Mede, Joseph. "Letters Written by Joseph Meade, Fellow of Christ's College, Cambridge, to Sir Martin Stuteville, at Dalham in Suffolk, Dec. 1620 to April 1631." BL, Harleian MSS, 309, 390.

Mercurius Aulicus. *A Diurnall, communicating the intelligence and affaires of the Court to the rest of the Kingdom* [ed. Sir John Birkenhead]. Jan. 1, 1643–Sept. 7, 1645. Weekly, with interruptions. Revived at various times (Jan. 25–May 18, 1648, Aug. 7–28, 1649, March 13–April 3, 1654) with somewhat different title and auspices.

Mercurius Aulicus, for King Charles II. August 4–Sept. 4, 1649.

Mercurius Publicus, April 5, 1660–Aug. 20, 1663, weekly.

Mist's Weekly Journal no. 106, April 29, 1727.

A Model of a Democraticall Government. London, 1659.

The Moderate Man's Proposall to the Parliament about Tithes. London, 1659.

Monk, George. *A Collection of Letters and Declarations sent by General Monck.* London, 1660.

Monk, George. *A Letter from the Lord General Monck.* London, 1660. Broadside

Monk, George. *A Letter from the Lord General Monck and the Officers under his Command to the Parliament.* London, 1660.

Monk, George. *The Speech and Declaration of his Excellency the Lord General Monck, Delivered at Whitehall the 21. of February, 1659.* London, 1659 [1660].

The Monitor, vol. 1, nos. 1–21, London, 1713, no. 17.

Montagu, Richard. *Appello Caesarem. A Just Appeale from Two Unjust Informers.* London, 1625.

Montague, Walter. *The Shepheard's Paradise. A Comedy Privately acted before the late King Charles by the Queen's Majesty, and Ladies of honour.* London, 1659.

More, Alexander. *Alexandri Mori Ecclesiastae, Sacrarumque litterarum Professoris Fides Publica, Contra calumnias Joannis Miltoni Scurrae* [with *Defensio Secunda*]. The Hague, 1654.

More, Alexander. *Alexandri Mori Ecclesiastae & Sacrarum Litteratum Professoris Supplementum Fidei Publicae, Contra Calumniae Joannis Miltoni.* The Hague, 1655.

[Morisot, Claude Barthelemy] *A Securi et Calamo Miltoni Vindicatus.* Dublin, 1652.

Morland, Samuel. *The History of the Evangelical Churches of the Valleys of Piemont.* London, 1658.

Nedham, Marchamont. *The Case of the Common-wealth of England Stated. Or, The Equity, Utility, and Necessity, of a Submission to the Present Government: . . . With a Discourse of the Excellence of a Free State, above a Kingly-Government.* London, 1650.

Nedham, Marchamont. *Certain Considerations Tendered in all Humility, to an Honourable Member of the Councell of State.* London, 1649.

[Nedham, Marchamont] *The Excellencie of a Free-State: Or, the Right Constitution of a Common-Wealth. . . With some Errors of Government and rules of Policie.* London, 1656.

N. D. [Nedham, Marchamont?] *A Letter Intercepted, in which the two different Forms of Monarchy and Popular Government are briefly controverted.* London, 1660.

[Nedham, Marchamont and Thomas Audley, eds] *Mercurius Britanicus: Communicating the Affaires of Great Britaine: for the Better Information of the People* (Sept. 5, 1643–May 18, 1646, weekly, with interruptions.) Revived at various times with somewhat different title.

[Nedham, Marchamont, ed.] *Mercurius Politicus.* June 6, 1650–April 12, 1660, weekly, with some interruptions.

[Nedham, Marchamont, ed.] *Mercurius Pragmaticus. Communicating Intelligence from all parts, especially from Westminster and the Head Quarters.* Sept. 14 1647–April 17, 1649, weekly, with interruptions; *Mercurius Pragmaticus, for King Charles II.* April 17, 1649–May 28, 1650.

[Nedham, Marchamont] *News from Brussels. In a letter from a neer attendant on his Majesties person.* London, 1660.

[Nedham, Marchamont, ed.] *The Publick Intelligencer, Communicating the Chief Occurrances and Proceedings within the Dominions of England, Scotland, and Ireland.* Oct. 1, 1655–April 9, 1660, weekly.

[Nedham, Marchamont] *A True State of the Case of the Commonwealth of England, Scotland, and Ireland . . . in reference to the late established Government By a Lord Protector and a Parlament.* London, 1654.

A New-Years-Gift for the Rump. Oxford, 1660.

Nicetas Acominate. *Imperii Graeci Historia.* Paris, 1647.

[Nichole, Pierre] *The Pernicious Consequence of The New Heresie of the Jesuits against the King and the State.* London, 1666.

No New Parliament: Or some queries or Considerations Humbly offered to the present Parliament-Members. London, 1660.

Original Letters and Papers of State, Addressed to Oliver Cromwell. Concerning the Affairs of Great Britain. From the Year MDCXLIX to MDCLVIII. Found among the Political Collections of Mr. John Milton, ed. John Nicholls. London, 1674.

Osborne, John. *An Indictment against Tythes.* London, 1659.

Overton, Richard. *An Appeale From the Degenerate Representative Body the Commons of England Assembled at Westminster: To the Body Represented. The Free People in General . . . And in Especiall, To his Excellency, Sir Thomas Fairfax, Captaine Generall, and all the Officers and Soldiers Under his Command.* London, 1647.

O[verton], R[ichard]. *Man's Mortallitie. Or, A Treatise Wherein 'tis proved, both Theologically and Philosophically, that whole Man (as a rationall Creature) is a Compound wholly mortall, contrary to that common distinction of Soule and Body.* Amsterdam [London], 1643 [1644].

Ovid, esp. *Epistulae ex Ponto, Tristia, Heroides, Amores, Metamorphoses,* ed. Grant Showerman, et al. Cambridge, Mass. and London: Harvard University Press and Heinemann, 1977–89.

[Owen, John] *Indulgence and Toleration Considered: In a Letter to a Person of Honour.* London, 1667.

Owen, John. *Of the Divine Originall, Authority, Self-Evidencing Light and Power of the Scriptures.* London, 1658.

[Owen, John] *Truth and Innocence Vindicated: in a Survey of a Discourse Concerning Ecclesiastical Polity.* London, 1669.

P[agitt], E[phraim]. *Heresiography: Or, A Description of the Hereticks and Sectaries of these latter times.* London, 1645.

Palmer, Herbert. *The Glasse of Gods Providence Towards His Faithfull Ones. Held Forth in a Sermon preached to the two Houses of Parliament, at Margarets Westminster, Aug. 13, 1644 . . .*

The Whole is applyed specially to a more carefull observation of our late Covenant, and particularly against the ungodly toleration pleaded for under pretence of Liberty of Conscience. London, 1644.

[Palmer, Henry] *Scripture and Reason Pleaded for Defensive Armes*. London, 1643.

Pareus, David. *A Commentary upon the Divine Revelation of the Apostle and Evangelist John*, trans. Elias Arnold. Amsterdam, 1644.

[Parker, Henry] *The Case of Shipmoney briefly discoursed, according to the grounds of Law, Policy, and Conscience*. London, 1640.

[Parker, Henry] *Jus Populi. or, a discourse as well concerning the Rights of Subjects as of Princes*. London, 1644.

[Parker, Samuel] *A Defence and Continuation of the Ecclesiastical Politie*. London, 1671.

[Parker, Samuel] *A Discourse of Ecclesiastical Politie, wherein the authority of the Civil Magistrate over the Consciences of Subjects in Matters of External Religion is Asserted: the Mischiefs and Inconveniences of Toleration are Represented, and all Pretenses Pleaded in Behalf of Liberty of Conscience are fully answered*. London, 1670 [1669].

[Parker, Samuel] "A Preface Shewing what Grounds there are of Fears and Jealousies of Popery," prefixed to John Bramhall, *Vindication of Himself*. London, 1672.

[Parker, Samuel] *A Reproof to the Rehearsal Transpros'd*. London, 1673.

The Parliamentary Intelligencer [ed. G. Dury]. Dec. 19, 1659–Dec. 31, 1660, weekly.

The Parliamentary or Constitutional History of England [eds. William Cobbett, et al.] 2nd edn, 24 vols. London, 1761–3.

Paulus Diaconus. *Historia Miscella*. Ingolstadt, 1603.

Peacham, Henry. *The Compleat Gentleman*. London, 1627.

Pearson, Anthony. *The Great Case of Tythes Truely Stated, Clearly Opened, and Fully Resolved*. 3rd edn. London, 1659.

The Pedigree and Descent of His Excellency, General George Monck. London, 1660.

Pepys, Samuel. *Diary*, eds. Robert Latham and William Matthews. 11 vols. London: G. Bell, 1970, rpt. 1985.

A Perfect Diurnall of the Passages in Parliament. Sept. 5, 1642–June 19, 1643, weekly.

A Perfect Diurnall of some Passages in Parliament. June 26, 1643–Nov. 12, 1649, weekly.

A Perfect Diurnall of some Passages and Proceedings of and in relation to the Armies of England, Scotland, and Ireland. Dec. 10, 1649–Sept. 5, 1655, weekly.

Petition of the Lord Mayor, Aldermen and Common Council concerning Church-Government. Presented to the House of Peers. London, 1646.

A Petition from . . . Fairfax and the General Council of Officers . . . To . . . The Commons of England in Parliament Assembled, Concerning the Draught of an Agreement of the People. London, 1649.

Phillips, Edward. "Compendiosa Enumeratio Poetarum," in John Buchler, *Sacrarum Prophanarumque Phrasium Poeticarum Thesaurus*. 17th edn. London, 1669.

Phillips, Edward. *A Continuation of the Chronicle of England to the end of the year 1658 . . . more especially relating unto the transactions of Charles, crowned King of the Scots at Scone on the first day of January, 1650* [continuation of Baker], London, 1660; *A Chronicle of the Kings of England . . . with a Continuation . . . to the Coronation of his Sacred Majesty, King Charles the Second*. London, 1665.

P[hillips], E[dward] *The Illustrious Shepherdess: The Imperious Brother* [translations of novels five and three, respectively, of Juan Pérez de Montalbán's *Successos y Prodigos de Amor*]. London, 1656.

P[hillips], E[dward]. *The Mysteries of Love & Eloquence: Or, the Arts of Wooing and Complementing*. London, 1658.

Phillips, Edward. *Theatrum Poetarum, or A Compleat Collection of the Poets, Especially the Most Eminent, of all Ages*. London, 1675.

Phillips, John. *Don Juan Lamberto, or a Comical History of the late Times*. London, 1660.

Phillips, John. *Joannis Philippi Angli Responsio Ad Apologiam Anonymi cujusdam tenebrionis pro Rege & Populo Anglicano infantissimam*. London, 1652.

Phillips, John. *Montelion, 1660, or The Prophetical Almanack*. London, 1660.

[Phillips, John] *A Satyr Against Hypocrites*. London, 1655.

P[hillips], J[ohn]. *Sportive Wit: The Muses' Merriment. A New Spring of Lusty Drollery, Jovial Fancies, and Ála mode Lampoons, On Some Heroick Persons of these Late Times. Collected for the publick good, by a Club of sparkling Wits, viz. C. J. B. F. J. M. W. T.* London, 1656.

P[hillips], J[ohn] *The Tears of the Indians: being An Historical and true Account of the Cruel Massacres and Slaughters . . . Committed by the Spaniards in the Islands of Hispaniola, etc.* [translation of Bartolomé de las Casas, *Brevissima Relación de las Destruyción de las Indias*]. London, 1656.

P[hillips], J[ohn] *Wit and Drollery, Joviall Poems*. London, 1656.

The Picture of the Good Old Cause. London, 1660. Broadside.

Pindar, trans. W. H. Race, 2 vols. Cambridge, Mass. and London: Harvard University Press and Heinemann, 1997.

Plaine English to his Excellencie the Lord Monk and the Officers of the Army: Or, A Word in season, not onely to them, but to all Impartial Englishmen. London, 1660.

Plato. *Dialogues,* trans. H. N. Fowler, et al. 9 vols. Cambridge, Mass. and London: Harvard University Press and Heinemann, 1953–5.

Plato. *The Republic,* trans. Paul Shorey. 2 vols. Cambridge, Mass. and London: Harvard University Press and Heinemann, 1953.

Poole, Joshua, ed. *The English Parnassus*. London, 1657.

[Poole, Matthew] *A Model for the Maintaining of Students of Choice Abilities at the University, and principally in order to the Ministry*. London, 1658.

The Princely Pellican. Royal Resolves Presented in Sundry Choice Observations Extracted from his Majesties Divine Meditations. With Satisfactory Reasons to the kingdom, that His Sacred Person was the only Author of them. London, 1649.

A Proclamation for calling in, and suppresing of two books written by John Milton . . . and also a third Book . . . written by John Goodwin. London, 1660.

Procopius. *De Bello Persico,* in *Historiarum libri VIII*. Augsburg, 1607.

Proposals for the furtherance and propagation of the Gospell in this Nation . . . as also Some Principles of Christian Religion . . . which were also presented in explanation of one of the said proposals. London, 1652.

A Proposition in Order to the Proposing of a Commonwealth or Democracie. London, 1659.

Prynne, William. *A Breviate of the Prelates Intolerable Usurpation, Both upon the Kings Prerogative Royall, and the Subjects Liberties*. London, 1637.

Prynne, William. *A Brief Memento to the Present Unparliamentary Junto Touching their Intentions and Proceedings to Depose and Execute Charles Stuart, Their Lawfull King*. London, 1649.

Prynne, William. *Four Serious Questions of Grand Importance concerning Excommunication and Suspention from the Sacrament*. London, 1645.

Prynne, William. *Histrio-mastix: or, The Players Scourge and Actors Tragedy*. London, 1633 [1632].

Prynne, William. *The Re-Publicans and Others Spurious Good Old Cause, briefly and truly anatomized*. London, 1659.

Prynne, William. *Ten Considerble Quaeries Concerning Tithes*. London, 1659.

Prynne, William. *A True and perfect Narrative of what was done, spoken by and between Mr. Prynne, the old and newly Forcibly late secluded Members, the Army Officers, and those now sitting . . . on . . . the 7. and 9. of this instant May*. London, 1659.

Prynne, William. *Twelve Considerable Serious Questions, Touching Church Government*. London, 1644.

A Public Plea Opposed to a Private Proposal. London, 1659.

Purchas, Samuel. *Hakluytus Posthumus, or Purchas his Pilgrimes*. 4 vols. London, 1625.

Puteanus, Erycius [Henrik van der Put]. *Comus, sive Phagesiposia Cimmeria. Somnium*. Louvain, 1610; Oxford, 1634.

Puttenham, [George]. *The Arte of English Poesie*. London, 1589.

R. E. *The Divine Penitential Meditations and Vows of His Late Majestie in his Solitude at Holmby House, Faithfully turned into Verse*. London, 1649.

[Racovian Catechism] *Catechesis Ecclesiarum. Quae in Regno Poloniae & magno Ducatu Lithuaniae . . . Cui accedit Faustii Socini Senensis Vita*. Racoviae [London], 1651; trans. *The Racovian Catechisme: Wherein you have the Substance of the Confession of those Churches, which in the Kingdom of Poland, and the Great Dukedome of Lithuania . . . do affirm*. Amsterdam, 1652.

Rainoldes, John. *The Judgement of Doctor Reignolds Concerning Episcopacy, Whether it be Gods Ordinance*. London, 1641.

Rainoldes, John. *The Summe of the Conference Betweene John Rainoldes and John Hart: Touching the Head and the Faith of the Church*. London, 1584.

Raleigh, Sir Walter. *History of the World*. London, 1617.

Ramus, Petrus [Pierre de la Ramée] *Dialecticae libri duo*. Basel, 1572.

Ramus, Petrus. *Grammatica*. Paris, 1559.

Ravenscroft, Thomas. *The Whole Booke of Psalmes*. London, 1621, 1633.

A Remonstrance & Address of the Armies of England, Scotland, and Ireland: To the Lord General Monck. London, 1660.

A Remonstrance of His Excellency Thomas Lord Fairfax, Lord General of the Parliaments Forces, and of the General Council of Officers. London, 1649.

A Remonstrance of Many Thousand Citizens, and other Free-born People of England, To their owne House of Commons [by Richard Overton?]. London, 1646.

The Re-Resurrection of the Rump: Or, Rebellion and Tyranny revived. London, 1660. Broadside.

Reynolds, Edward. *A Sermon Touching the Use of Humane Learning*. London, 1658.

Rivet, André [Rivetus] *Praelectiones in Caput XX Exodi*. Leyden, 1637.

Robinson, Henry. *Liberty of Conscience: or the Sole Means to Obtaine Peace and Truth*. London, 1644.

A Rope for Pol, or a Hue and Cry after Marchemont Needham, the late scurrilous newswriter; being a Collection of his horrid Blasphemies against the King's Majesty, his person, his cause, and his friends, published in his weekly Politicus. London, 1660.

Rowland, John. *Polemica, sive Supplementum ad Apologiam Anonymam pro rege & populo Anglicano, adversus Jo: Milton defensionem populi Anglicani. Et Iraenica sive cantus receptui ad Christianos omnes*. London, 1653.

Rowland, John. *Pro Rege et Populo Anglicano Apologia, contra Joannis Polypragmatici (alias Miltoni*

Angli) Defensionem Destructivam Regis et Populi Anglicani. [Apology for the king and people of England, by John the Multifarious, alias Milton the Englishman.] Antwerp, 1651.

Royal and other Innocent Bloud crying aloud to Heaven for due vengeance. London, 1660.

Rushworth, John. *Historical Collections of Private Papers of State.* 8 vols. London, 1721–2.

Rutherford, Samuel. *The Divine Right of Church-Government and Excommunication. To which is added a briefe Tractate of Scandal.* London, 1646.

Rutherford, Samuel. *The Due Right of Presbyteries.* London, 1646.

[Rutherford, Samuel] *Lex, Rex: The Law and the Prince.* London, 1644.

Salkeld, John. *The Resurrection of Lazarus, or, A Sermon Preached upon Occasion of the King's Declaration for Liberty of Conscience.* London, 1673.

Sallust, *The War with Cataline, The Jugurthine War,* trans. J. C. Rolfe. Cambridge, Mass. and London: Harvard University Press and Heinemann, 1965.

Salmasius [Claude Saumaise] *Ad Joannem Miltonum responsio, opus posthumum.* Dijon, 1660; London, 1660.

Salmasius [Claude Saumaise] *Defensio Regia, Pro Carolo I. Ad Serenissimum Magnae Britanniae Regem Carolum II. Filium natu majorem, Heredem & Successorem legitimum. Sumptibus Regiis.* Leyden, 1649.

Salmasius His Dissection and Confutation of the Diobolical Rebel Milton, in his Impious Doctrines of Falshood, Maxims of Pollicies . . . [which] *by reason of the rigid Inquisition after Persons and Presses by the late Merciless Tyrant Oliver Cromwell durst not be sold publickly in this Kingdom.* London, 1660.

Salvini, Salvino. *Fasti consolari dell'Academia Fiorentina.* Florence, 1717.

Sannazaro, Jacopo. *Du Partu Virginis.* Naples, 1526.

Sansovino, Francisco. *Concetti politici, raccolti dagli scritti di diversi authori Greci, Latini, volgari.* Venice, 1603.

Sarpi, Paolo. *Istoria del Concilio Tridentino.* London, 1619.

Saville, Henry, ed. *Rerum Anglicarum Scriptores post Bedam.* London, 1596.

Savonarola, Girolamo. *Oracolo della Rinovatione della Chiesa.* Venice, 1536.

Schaff, Philip. *A History of the Creeds of Christendom.* 3 vols. London: Hodder and Stoughton, 1877.

Schaller, James. *Dissertatio ad loca quaedam Miltoni.* Strasbourg, 1652.

Schickhard, William. *Jus Regium Hebraeorum.* Strassburg, 1625.

Scriptum Parlamenti Reipublicae Angliae De iis quae ab hac Repub. cum Potestatibus Foederatarum Belgii Provinciarum Generalibus, & quibus progressibus acta sunt. London, 1652.

Seissel, Claude de [Sesellius] *De Monarchia Franciae, sive De Republica Galliae et Regum officiis,* trans. Johannes Sleidan. Lyon, 1626.

Selden, John. *De Jure Naturali et Gentium juxta Disciplinam Hebraeorum.* London, 1640.

Selden, John. *The History of Tithes.* London, 1618.

Selden, John. *Uxor Ebraica. seu de Nuptiis & Divortis ex Jure Civili, Id Est, Divino & Talmudico, Veterum Ebraeorum, Libri Tres.* London, 1646.

Seneca. *Moral Epistles,* trans. Richard M. Gummere. 3 vols. Cambridge, Mass. and London: Harvard University Press and Heinemann, 1953.

Seneca. *Moral Essays,* trans. John W. Besore. 3 vols. Cambridge, Mass. and London: Harvard University Press and Heinemann, 1951–8.

A Serious and Faithful Representation of the Judgements of Ministers of the Gospel within the Province of London. London 1649.

[Sexby, Edward and Silas Titus] William Allen [pseud.], *Killing Noe Murder. Briefly discourst in three Quaestions*. Holland, 1657.

Shirley, James. *Poems, &c.* London, 1646.

Shirley, James. *Via ad Linguam Latinam Companata*. London, 1649.

A Short Discourse Concerning the Work of God in This Nation. London, 1659.

Short Reflections upon a Pamphlet Entituled Toleration not to be Abused. London, 1672.

Sidney, Sir Philip. *The Countesse of Pembroke's Arcadia*. London, 1621, 1635, etc.

Sigonius. *De Occidentalali Imperio*. Frankfurt, 1618.

Sigonius. *De Regno Italiae*. Frankfurt, 1575, 1591.

[Sikes, George] *The Life and Death of Sir Henry Vane*. London, 1662.

Simeon of Durham. *De Gestis Regum Anglorum,* in Roger Twysden, ed., *Historiae Anglicanae Scriptores X*. London, 1652.

Sinibaldus, Johann Benedict. *Geneanthropeia, sive de hominis generatione decateuchon*. Rome, 1642.

Sleidan, Joannes. *Commentarii de Statu Religionis et Reipublicae, Carolo Quinto, Cesare*. Strassburg, 1555.

Smectymnuus [Stephen Marshall, Edmund Calamy, Thomas Young, Matthew Newcomen, William Spurstow] *An Answer to a booke entituled, An Humble Remonstrance. In which, the Original of Liturgy and Episcopacy is Discussed*. London, 1641.

Smectymnuus. *A Vindication of the Answer to the Humble Remonstrance, from the Unjust Imputations of Frivolousnesse and Falsehood: Wherein the Cause of Liturgy and Episcopacy is further debated*. London, 1641.

Smith, John. "Of Prophecy," in *Select Discourses*. London, 1660.

Smith, Thomas. *De Republica Anglorum. The Maner of Governement or policie of the Realme of England*. London, 1583.

A Solemn League and Covenant for Reformation and Defense of Religion, the honour and happiness of the King and the Peace and Safety of England, Scotland and Ireland. London, 1643 (Sept. 21).

Socrates Scholasticus. *Historia Ecclesiastica, libri VII,* in *Ecclesiasticae Historiae Autores* (q.v.).

Sophocles, trans. Hugh Lloyd-Jones. 3 vols. Cambridge, Mass. and London: Harvard University Press and Heinemann, 1994–6.

Sozomen, Hermius Salamanes. *Historia Ecclesiastica,* in *Historiae Ecclesiasticae Scriptores Graeci*. Geneva, 1612.

Speed, John. *The Historie of Great Britaine*. London, 1623.

Spelman, Henry. *Concilia, Decreta, Leges, Constitutiones . . . in re Ecclesiastica Orbis Britanniae*. London, 1639.

Spelman, Henry. *The Larger Treatise Concerning Tithes*. London, 1647.

Spenser, Edmund. *The Faerie Queene*. London, 1596.

Spenser, Edmund. *A View of the Present State of Ireland*. See Campion, *The History of Ireland*.

Sprat, Thomas. *Observations on Monsieur de Sorbier's Voyage into England*. London, 1665.

Sprigge, Joshua. *The Ancient Bounds; or, Liberty of Conscience asserted and vindicated*. London, 1645.

Sprigge, William. *A Modest Plea for an Equal Common-wealth against Monarchy*. London, 1659.

[Starkey, George] *Britain's Triumph, for her Imparallel'd Deliverance*. London, 1660. Broadside.

[Starkey, George] *The Dignity of Kingship Asserted in Answer to Mr. Milton's Ready and Easy Way to Establish a Free Commonwealth*. London, 1660; rpt. as *Monarchy Triumphing over Traiterous Republicans. Or the Transcendent Excellency of that Divine Government fully proved*

aginst the utopian Chimeras of our Ridiculous Commonwealthsmen. London, 1661.
Starkey, George. *Royal and other Innocent Blood crying aloud to heaven for due Vengeance*. London, 1660.
S[tewart], A[dam] *Some Observations and Annotations upon the Apologetical Narration*. London, 1644.
Stillingfleet, Edward. *A Discourse concerning the Idolatry Practised in the Church of Rome*. London, 1671.
Stock, Richard. *The Doctrine and Use of Repentance*. London, 1610.
Stock, Richard. *A Sermon Preached at Paules Cross*. London, 1609.
S'Too him Bayes: Or Some Observations upon the Humour of Writing Rehearsal's Transpros'd. Oxford, 1673.
Stow, John. *Annales, or Generall Chronicle of England*. London, 1615.
Stow, John, *A Survey of the Cities of London and Westminster . . . Corrected, Improved, and very much Enlarged . . . by John Strype*. 2 vols. London, 1720.
Stow, John, *A Survey of London. Conteyning the Originall, Antiquity, Increase, Moderne Estate, and description of that City*. London, 1603.
[Stubbe, Henry] *Clamor, Rixa, Joci, Mendacis, Furta, Cachine. or, A Severe Enquiry into the late ONEIROCRITICA*. London, 1657.
Stubbe, Henry. *An Essay in Defense of the Good Old Cause*. London, 1659.
[Stubbe, Henry] *A Light Shining out of Darknes* [revised]. London, 1659.
Suckling, Richard. *Fragmenta Aurea*. London, 1646.
Sundry Things from Severall Hands Concerning the University of Oxford. London, 1659.
Sylvester, Joshua. *Bartas his Divine Weekes and Workes* [with other works]. London, 1605, 1611, 1621, etc.
T., I. *The Traytor's Perspective-glass. Or, Sundry Examples of Gods just judgments executed upon many Eminent Regicides*. London, 1662.
T., S. *Moderation: Or Arguments and Motives Tending thereunto, humbly tendred to the Parliament*. London, 1660
Tacitus. *The Histories*, trans. C. H. Moore; *The Annals*, trans. John Jackson. 4 vols. Cambridge, Mass. and London: Harvard University Press and Heinemann, 1937.
Tasso, Torquato. *Aminta; favola boscareccia*. Ferrara, 1581.
Tasso, Torquato. *Apologia . . . in difesa della sua Gerusalemme Liberata*. Mantua, 1585.
Tasso, Torquato. *Discorsi . . . dell'arte poetica, et, in particolare, del poema heroico*. Venice, 1587; ed. Luigi Poma, Bari, 1964.
Tasso, Torquato. *Di Gerusalemme Conquistata*. Rome, 1593.
Tasso, Torquato. *Discorsi del Poema heroico*. Naples, 1594.
Tasso, Torquato. *Il Goffredo*. Venice, 1580.
Tasso, Torquato. *Il Manso, ovvero Dell' Amicitia, Dialogo del Sig. Torquato Tasso al Molte Illustre Sig. Giovanni Battista Manso*. Naples, 1596.
Tasso, Torquato. *La Gerusalemme Liberata*. Ferrara, 1581.
Tasso, Torquato. *Le Sette Giornate del Mondo Creato*. Viterbo, 1607.
Tassoni, Alessandro. *Dieci Libri di Pensieri Diversi*. Venice, 1636.
Tertullian. *De Spectaculis, De Jejuniis, Apologeticus*, in *Opera*. Paris, 1634.
A Testimony to the Truth of Jesus Christ, and to our Solemn League and Covenant. London, 1647.
These Trades-men are Preachers in and about the City of London, or, a discovery of the most dangerous and damnable tenets. London, 1647.

Theodoret. *Historia Ecclesiastica, lib. II,* in *Ecclesiasticae Historiae Autores* (q.v.).

Theophanes, the Confessor. *Chronographia.* Paris, 1655.

A Third Conference Between O. Cromwell and Hugh Peters in Saint James's Park. London, 1660.

Thou, Jacques-Auguste de [Thuanus]. *Historia sui Temporis.* 5 vols. Geneva, 1620.

Thurloe, John. *A Collection of the State Papers of John Thurloe, Esq.*, ed. Thomas Birch. 7 vols. London, 1742.

Toleration Disapprov'd and Condemn'd by the Authority and Convincing Reasons of King James, Parliament in 1662, etc. London, 1670.

Tomasini, Giacomo. *Petrarcha Redivivus.* Padua, 1635.

[Tomkyns, Thomas] *The Inconveniences of Toleration, or, An Answer to a Late Book, Intituled, A Proposition Made to the King and Parliament, for the Safety and Happiness of the King and Kingdom.* London, 1667.

[Tomkyns, Thomas] *The Rebel's Plea Examined: or Mr. Baxter's Judgment concerning the late War.* London, 1660.

To the Supreame Authoritie of the Common-wealth of England. The Humble Petition of the Officers of the Army. London, 1652.

A Treatise of the Execution of Justice: wherein is clearly proved, that the execution of Judgment and Justice, is as well the peoples as the Magistrates duty; And that if Magistrates pervert Judgment, the People are bound by the Law of God to execute Judgment without them, and upon them. London, 1663.

A True and Perfect Picture of our present Reformation. London, 1648.

The True Manner of the most Magnificent Conveyance of His Highenesse Effigies from Somerset House to Westminster on Tuesday, November 23, 1658. London, 1658. Broadside.

Twysden, Roger, ed. *Historiae Anglicanae Scriptores X.* London, 1652.

Urban VIII (Maffeo Barberini). *Poemata.* Paris, 1620.

Urban VIII (Maffeo Barberini). *Poesie Toscane.* Rome, 1637.

Ussher, James. *The Judgment of Dr. Rainoldes touching the Originall of Episcopacy. More largely confirmed out of Antiquity.* London, 1641.

Ussher, James. *The Reduction of Episcopacie unto the form of Synodical Government received in the antient church.* London, 1656.

[Vane, Henry] *A Healing Question Propounded and resolved upon occasion of the late publique and seasonable Call to Humiliation, in order to love and union among the honest party, and with a desire to apply Balsoms to the wound, before it becomes incurable.* London, 1656; rpt. 1659.

[Vane, Henry] *A Needful Corrective or Ballance in Popular Government.* London, 1659.

Varchi, Benedetto. *I Sonnetti.* Venice, 1565.

Vaughan, Henry. *Olor Iscanus.* London, 1651.

Vida, Marcus Hieronymus. *Christiad.* Cremona, 1535.

Villani, Giovanni. *Chroniche . . . nelle quali si tratta dell'origine di Firenze.* Venice, 1537.

A Vindication of the Ministers of the Gospel in . . . London, from the Unjust Aspersions Cast upon Their Former Actings for the Parliament. London, 1649.

Brutus, *Vindiciae Contra Tyrannos* [by Philippe Du Plessis Mornay or Hugh Languet]. Basle, 1579.

Virgil. *Eclogues, Georgics, Aeneid,* trans. H. Ruston Fairclough, 2 vols. Cambridge, Mass. and London: Harvard University Press and Heinemann, 1960.

Walker, Clement. *The History of Independency.* London, 1648.

[Walker, Clement] *Theodorus Verax, Anarchia Anglicana.* London, 1649.

Walker, Edward. *A Full Answer to . . . William Lilly*. London, 1652.

Waller, Edmund. *Poems, &c.* London, 1645.

Walton, Izaak. *The Compleat Angler, or The Contemplative Man's Recreation*. London, 1653.

[Walwyn, William] *The Compassionate Samaritane*. London, 1644.

Walwyn, William. *The Fountaine of Slaunder*. London, 1649.

Ward, Robert. *Animadversions of Warre, or a Militarie Magazine of the Truest Rules, and Ablest Instructions, for the Managing of Warre*. London, 1639.

[Warner, John] *The Devilish Conspiracy and Damnable Murder committed by the Jewes*. London, 1649.

Wase, Christopher. *Electra of Sophocles*. The Hague, 1649.

[Westminster Assembly] *The Humble Advice of the Assembly of Divines concerning a Confession of Faith*. London, 1646; reissued 1658, with *A Larger Catechism* and *A Shorter Catechism*.

Wheloc, Abraham, ed. *Historiae Ecclesiastica Gentis Anglorum Libri V . . . Ab augustissimo veterum Anglo-Saxonum Rege Aluredo (sive Alfredo) examinati; . . . Quibus accesserunt Anglo-Saxonicae Leges*. London, 1644.

Whitelocke, Bulstrode. *Memorials of the English Affairs, from the Beginning of the Reign of Charles the First to the Happy Restoration of King Charles the Second*. 4 vols. Oxford: Oxford University Press, 1853.

William of Malmesbury. *De Gestis Regum Anglicorum*, in Henry Saville, *Rerum Anglicarum Scriptores post Bedam*. London, 1596.

Williams, Roger. *The Bloudy Tenant, of Persecution, for the Cause of Conscience Discussed*. London, 1644.

Williams, Roger. *The Bloody Tenant yet More Bloody, by Mr. Cottons endeavour to wash it white in the blood of the Lambe*. London, 1652.

Williams, Roger, *The Correspondence of Roger Williams*, ed. Glenn W. La Fantasie. 2 vols. Hanover and London: University Press of New England, 1988.

W[illiams], R[oger] *The Fourth Paper Presented by Major Butler to the Honourable Committee of Parliament, for the Propagating the Gospel of Christ Jesus*. London, 1652.

Williams, Roger. *The Hireling Ministry None of Christs, or, A Discourse touching the Propagating the Gospel of Christ Jesus*. London, 1652.

[Williams, Roger] Queries of Highest Consideration, Proposed to [the five Independent Ministers, the Scots Commissioners, and] *the Houses of the High Court of Parliament*. London, 1644.

Winstanley, Gerrard. *An Appeal to all Englishmen to judge between bondage and freedom*. London, 1650.

Winstanley, Gerrard. *Fire in the Bush*. London, 1650.

Winstanley, Gerrard. *The Law of Freedom in a Platform, or, true Magistracy restored*. London, 1652.

Winstanley, Gerrard. *A new-years Gift for the Parliament and Armie*. London, 1650.

Winstanley, Gerrard. *Works*, ed. George Sabine. Ithaca, NY: Cornell University Press, 1941, 1965.

W[ither], G[eorge] *Respublicana Anglicana*. London, 1650.

Wolleb, John [Wollebius] *Compendium Theologiae Christianae*. Amsterdam 1633; trans. *The Abridgment of Christian Divinitie*, London, 1650.

Wolseley, Charles. *Liberty of Conscience the Magistrates Interest*. London, 1668.

Woodhouse, A. S. P. *Puritanism and Liberty. Being the Army Debates (1647–9) from the Clarke*

Manuscripts, with Supplementary Documents. Chicago: University of Chicago Press, 1951.
[Young, Thomas] *Dies Dominica, sive Succincta Narratio ex S. Scripturarum.* London, 1639.
Zanchius, Hieronymus. *Opera Theologicorum,* 8 tom. Heidelberg, 1613.
Ziegler, Caspar. *Circa Regicidium Anglorum Exercitationes.* Leipzig, 1652.

Biographical, Historical, and Critical Studies

Achinstein, Sharon, *Milton and the Revolutionary Reader.* Princeton, NJ: Princeton University Press, 1994.
Achinstein, Sharon, "Milton's Spectre in the Restoration: Marvell, Dryden, and Literary Enthusiasm," *Huntington Library Quarterly* 59 (1997), 1–29.
Achinstein, Sharon, "*Samson Agonistes* and the Drama of Dissent," *MS* 33 (1996), 133–58.
Allen, D. C., "Milton as a Latin Poet," in James E. Phillips and D. C. Allen, eds, *Neo-Latin Poetry of the Sixteenth and Seventeenth Centuries.* Los Angeles: Clark Memorial Library, 1965, 30–52.
Amory, Hugh, "Things Unattempted Yet," *The Book Collector* 32 (1983), 41–66.
Anselment, Raymond. *"Betwixt Jest and Ernest": Marprelate, Milton, Marvell, Swift and the Decorum of Religious Ridicule.* Toronto: University of Toronto Press, 1979.
Armitage, David, Armand Himy, and Quentin Skinner, eds, *Milton and Republicanism.* Cambridge: Cambridge University Press, 1995.
Arthos, John, *Milton and the Italian Cities.* London: Bowes & Bowes, 1968.
Auksi, Peter, "Milton's 'Sanctifi'd Bitternesse': Polemical Techniques in the Early Prose," *Texas Studies in Literature and Language* 19 (1977), 363–81.
Auksi, Peter, *Christian Plain Style: The Evolution of a Spiritual Ideal.* Montreal: McGill–Queen's University Press, 1995.
Barker, Arthur, "Milton's Schoolmasters," *Modern Language Review* 32 (1937), 517–36.
Barker, Arthur, "The Pattern of Milton's Nativity Ode," *University of Toronto Quarterly* 10 (1941), 167–81.
Barker, Arthur, *Milton and the Puritan Dilemma, 1641–1660.* Toronto and Buffalo: University of Toronto Press, 1942.
Barnett, H. A., "A Time of the Year for Milton's 'Ad Patrem,'" *Modern Language Notes* 73 (1958), 82–3.
Bauman, James, *Milton's Arianism.* Frankfurt and New York: Peter Lang, 1987.
Benet, Diana Treviño, "The Escape from Rome: Milton's *Second Defence* and a Renaissance Genre," in Mario Di Cesare, ed., *Milton in Italy: Contexts, Images, Contradictions.* Binghamton, NY: MRTS, 1991, 29–49.
Benet, Diana Treviño and Michael Lieb, eds, *Literary Milton: Text, Pretext, Context.* Pittsburgh: Duquesne University Press, 1994.
Bennett, Joan S., *Reviving Liberty: Radical Christian Humanism in Milton's Great Poems.* Cambridge, Mass.: Harvard University Press, 1989.
Blessington, Francis C., *Paradise Lost and the Classical Epic.* Boston, Mass. and London: Routledge & Kegan Paul, 1979.
Bloom, Harold, *The Anxiety of Influence: A Theory of Poetry* (New York, 1973).
Boesky, Amy, and Mary Thomas Crane, eds, *Form and Reform in Renaissance England: Essays in Honor of Barbara Kiefer Lewalski.* Newark: University of Delaware Press, 2000.

Bonkel, Joseph M., "The Holograph of Milton's Letter to Holstenius," *PMLA* 68 (1953), 617–27.

Bosher, R. S., *The Making of the Restoration Settlement: The Influence of the Laudians, 1649–1652*. New York: Oxford University Press, 1951.

Bowra, C. M., *From Virgil to Milton*. London: Macmillan, 1945.

Bradner, Leicester, "Milton's 'Epitaphium Damonis.'" *Times Literary Supplement* (August 18, 1932), 581.

Bradner, Leicester, *Musae Anglicanae: A History of Anglo-Latin Poetry, 1500–1925*. New York: Modern Language Association, 1940.

Breasted, Barbara, "*Comus* and the Castlehaven Scandal," *MS* 3 (1971), 201–23.

Bredvold, Louis, "Milton and Bodin's *Heptaplomeres*," *Studies in Philology* 21 (1924), 399–402.

Brown, Cedric C., "The Chirk Castle Entertainment of 1634," *MQ* 11 (1977), 76–86.

Brown, Cedric C., "Milton's *Arcades*: Context, Form, and Function," *Renaissance Drama* 8 (1977), 245–74.

Brown, Cedric C., "Milton's 'Arcades' in the Trinity Manuscript," *Review of English Studies*, n.s. 37 (1986), 542–9.

Brown, Cedric C., *Milton's Aristocratic Entertainments*. Cambridge: Cambridge University Press, 1985.

Brown, Cedric C., "A King James Bible, Protestant Nationalism, and Boy Milton," in Amy Boesky and Mary Thomas Crane, eds, *Form and Reform in Renaissance England: Essays in Honor of Barbara Kiefer Lewalski*. Newark: University of Delaware Press, 2000.

Brown, Cedric C., "Milton and the Idolatrous Consort," *Criticism* 35 (1993), 419–39.

Burns, Norman T., "Then Stood up Phinehas": Milton's Antinomianism, and Samson's," *MS* 33 (1996), 27–46.

Bush, Douglas, "The Date of Milton's *Ad Patrem*," *Modern Philology* 61 (1963–4), 204–8.

Bush, Douglas, *John Milton: A Sketch of his Life and Writings*. New York: Macmillan, 1964.

Byard, Margaret, "'Adventrous Song': Milton and the Music of Rome," in Mario Di Cesare, ed., *Milton in Italy: Contexts, Images, Contradictions*. Binghamton, NY: MRTS, 1991, 305–28.

Cable, Lana, "Milton's Iconoclastic Truth," in David Loewenstein and James Grantham Turner, eds, *Politics, Poetics, and Hermeneutics in Milton's Prose*. Cambridge: Cambridge University Press, 1990, 135–51.

Campbell, Gordon, "Imitation in *Epitaphium Damonis*," in James A. Freeman and Anthony Low, eds, *Urbane Milton: The Latin Poetry*. *MS* 19. Pittsburgh: University of Pittsburgh Press, 1984, 165–77.

Campbell, Gordon, "Milton's Accidence Commenc't Grammar," *MQ* (1976), 39–48.

Campbell, Gordon, "Milton's Second Tutor," *MQ* 21 (1987), 81–90.

Campbell, Gordon, and Sebastian Brock, "Milton's Syriac," *MQ* (1993), 74–7.

Campbell, Gordon, Thomas N. Corns, John K. Hale, David I. Holmes, and Fiona J. Tweedie, "The Provenance of *De Doctrina Christiana*," *MQ* 31 (1997), 67–121.

Carey, John, *Milton*. New York: Arco, 1970.

Chambers, D. C., and Quiviger, F., eds, *Italian Academies of the Sixteenth Century*. London: Warburg Institute, 1995.

Chaney, Edward. *The Grand Tour and the Great Rebellion: Richard Lassels and 'The Voyage of Italy' in the Seventeenth Century*. Geneva: Slatkine, 1985.

Cheek, Macon, "Milton's 'In Quintum Novembris': An Epic Foreshadowing," *Studies in Philology* 54 (1957), 172–84.

Chew, Beverly, "Portraits of Milton," *Bibliographer* 2 (1903), 92–101.

Chifos, Eugenia, "Milton's Letter to Gill, May 20, 1628," *Modern Language Notes* 62 (1947), 37–9.

Cinquemani, A. M., "Through Milan and the Pennine Alps," in Mario Di Cesare, ed., *Milton in Italy: Contexts, Images, Contradictions*. Binghamton, NY: MRTS, 1991, 51–60.

Clark, Donald Lemen, *John Milton at St. Paul's School: A Study of Ancient Rhetoric in English Renaissance Education*. New York: Columbia University Press, 1948.

Clark, Donald Leman, "John Milton and William Chappell," *Huntington Library Quarterly* 18 (1955), 329–50.

Cochrane, Eric, *Tradition and Enlightenment in the Tuscan Academies, 1690–1800*. Chicago: University of Chicago Press, 1961.

Cochrane, Eric, *Florence in the Forgotten Centuries, 1527–1800: A History of Florence and the Florentines in the Age of the Grand Dukes*. Chicago and London: University of Chicago Press, 1973.

Cogswell, Thomas, *The Blessed Revolution: English Politics and the Coming of War, 1621–1624*. Cambridge: Cambridge University Press, 1989.

Coiro, Ann Baynes, "Milton and Class Identity: The Publication of *Areopagitica* and the 1645 *Poems*," *Journal of Medieval and Renaissance Studies* 22 (1992), 261–89.

Collinson-Morley, Lacy, *Italy After the Renaissance: Decadence and Display in the Seventeenth Century*. London: Routledge, 1930.

Condee, R. W., "Ovid's Exile and Milton's Rustication," *Philological Quarterly* 37 (1958), 498–502.

Condee, R. W., "The Latin Poetry of John Milton," in J. W. Binns, ed., *The Latin Poetry of the English Poets*. London: Routledge, 1974, 58–92.

Cooper, Charles Henry, *Annals of Cambridge*. 5 vols. Cambridge, 1842–56.

Corns, Thomas, *The Development of Milton's Prose Style*. Oxford: Clarendon Press, 1982.

Corns, Thomas, "Milton's Quest for Respectability," *Modern Language Review* 77 (1982), 769–79.

Corns, Thomas, "The Freedom of Reader-response: Milton's *Of Reformation* and Lilburne's *The Christian Mans Triall*," in R. O. Richardson and G. M. Ridden, eds, *Freedom and the English Revolution*. Manchester: Manchester University Press, 1986, 93–110.

Corns, Thomas, "Milton and the Characteristics of a Free Commonwealth," in David Armitage, Armand Himy, and Quentin Skinner, eds, *Milton and Republicanism*. Cambridge: Cambridge University Press, 1995, 25–42.

Corns, Thomas, "Milton's *Observations upon the Articles of Peace*: Ireland under English Eyes," in David Loewenstein and James Grantham Turner, eds, *Politics, Poetics, and Hermeneutics in Milton's Prose*. Cambridge: Cambridge University Press, 1990, 123–34.

Corns, Thomas, "'Some Rousing Motions': The Plurality of Miltonic Ideology," in Thomas Healy and Jonathan Sawday, *Literature and the English Civil War*. Cambridge: Cambridge University Press, 1990, 110–26.

Corns, Thomas, *Uncloistered Virtue: English Political Literature, 1640–1660*. Oxford: Clarendon Press, 1992.

Craster, Edmund, "John Rouse," *Bodleian Library Record* 5 (1955), 130–46.

Creaser, John, "The Pesent Aid of This Occasion: The Setting of *Comus*," in David Lindley, ed., *The Court Masque*. Manchester: Manchester University Press, 1984, 111–34.

Cust, Richard, and Ann Hughes, eds, *Conflict in Early Stuart England: Studies in Religion and Politics, 1603–1642*. London and New York: Longman, 1989.

Damrosch, Leo, *The Sorrows of the Quaker Jesus: James Nayler and the Puritan Crackdown on the Free Spirit*. Cambridge, Mass.: Harvard University Press, 1996.

Davies, Godfrey, "Milton in 1660," *Huntington Library Quarterly* 18 (1955), 351–63.

Davies, Godfrey, *The Restoration of Charles II, 1658–1660*. San Marino: Huntington Library, 1955.

Davies, Stevie, *Images of Kingship in Paradise Lost: Milton's Politics and Christian Liberty*. Columbia: University of Missouri Press, 1983.

Davis, J. C., *Fear, Myth, and History: The Ranters and the Historians*. Cambridge: Cambridge University Press, 1986.

De Filippis, Michele, "Milton and Manso: Cups or Books," *PMLA* 51 (1936), 745–56.

Di Cesare, Mario, ed., *Milton in Italy: Contexts, Images, Contradictions*. Binghamton, NY: MRTS, 1991.

Diekhoff, John S., *Milton on Himself: Milton's Utterances upon Himself and his Works*. London: Cohen and West, 1939.

DiSalvo, Jackie, "Intestine Thorne: Samson's Struggle with the Woman Within," in Julia M. Walker, ed., *Milton and the Idea of Woman*. Urbana and Chicago: University of Illinois Press, 1988, 211–29.

DiSalvo, Jackie, "'The Lords Battels': *Samson Agonistes* and the Puritan Revolution," *MS* 4 (1971), 39–52.

Dobranski, Stephen, *Milton, Authorship, and the Book Trade*. Cambridge: Cambridge University Press, 1999.

Dobranski, Stephen B., and John P. Rumrich, eds, *Milton and Heresy*. Cambridge: Cambridge University Press, 1998.

Dorian, Donald C., *The English Diodatis*. New York: Oxford University Press, 1939.

DuRocher, Richard J., *Milton and Ovid*. Ithaca, NY and London: Cornell University Press, 1985.

Dzelzainis, Martin, "Milton's Classical Republicanism," and "Milton and the Protectorate in 1658," in David Armitage, Armand Himy, and Quentin Skinner, eds, *Milton and Republicanism*. Cambridge: Cambridge University Press, 1995, 3–24.

Dzelzainis, Martin, "Milton's *Of True Religion* and the Earl of Castlemaine," *The Seventeenth Century* 7 (1992), 53–69.

Egan, James, "Creator–Critic: Aesthetic Subtexts in Milton's Antiprelatical and Regicide Polemics," *MS* 30 (1993), 45–66.

Egan, James, "Milton's Aesthetics of Plainness, 1659–1673," *The Seventeenth Century* 12 (1997), 57–83.

Eley, Geoff, and William Hunt, eds, *Reviving the English Revolution: Reflections and Elaborations on the Work of Christopher Hill*. London: Verso, 1988.

Emerson, Ralph Waldo, "Milton," *North American Review*, July, 1838.

Evans, J. Martin, *Milton's Imperial Epic: Paradise Lost and the Discourse of Colonialism*. Ithaca, NY and London: Cornell University Press, 1996.

Evans, Willa M., *Henry Lawes: Musician and Friend of Poets*. New York: Modern Language Association, 1941.

Fallon, Robert T., *Captain or Colonel: The Soldier in Milton's Life and Art.* Columbia: University of Missouri Press, 1984.

Fallon, Robert T., *Divided Empire: Milton's Political Imagery*. University Park: Pennsylvania University Press, 1995.

Fallon, Stephen, "The Metaphysics of Milton's Divorce Tracts," in David Loewenstein and James Grantham Turner, eds, *Politics, Poetics, and Hermeneutics in Milton's Prose.* Cambridge: Cambridge University Press, 1990, 609–83.

Fallon, Robet T., *Milton in Government.* University Park: Pennsylvania University Press, 1993.

Fallon, Stephen, "Milton's Arminianism and the Authorship of *De doctrina Christiana,*" *Texas Studies in Literature and Language* 41 (1999), 103–27.

Fallon, Stephen, *Milton Among the Philosophers: Poetry and Materialism in Seventeenth-Century England.* Ithaca, NY and London: Cornell University Press, 1991.

Ferry, Anne D., *Milton's Epic Voice: The Narrator in Paradise Lost.* Chicago: University of Chicago Press, 1983.

Field, A., *The Origins of the Platonic Academy of Florence.* Princeton, NJ: Princeton University Press, 1988.

Fink, Zera S., *The Classical Republicans: An Essay in the Recovery of a Pattern of Thought in Seventeenth-Century England.* Evanston, Ill.: Northwestern University Press, 1962.

Firth, Charles H., "Milton as a Historian," in *Essays Historical and Literary*. Oxford: Oxford University Press, 1938, 61–102.

Firth, Charles H., *The Last Years of the Protectorate, 1656–1658.* 2 vols. New York: Russell & Russell, 1964.

Fish, Stanley, "Inaction and Silence: The Reader in *Paradise Regained*," in Joseph A. Wittreich, Jr., ed., *Calm of Mind: Tercentenary Essays on Paradise Regained and Samson Agonistes.* Cleveland, Ohio and London: Case Western University Press, 1971, 25–47.

Fish, Stanley, "*Reason* in The Reason of Church Government," in *Self-Consuming Artifacts.* Berkeley: University of California Press, 1972, 265–302.

Fish, Stanley, "Spectacle and Evidence in *Samson Agonistes,*" *Critical Inquiry* 15 (1980), 556–86.

Fish, Stanley. *Surprised by Sin.* Cambridge, Mass.: Harvard University Press, 1967, 1997.

Fish, Stanley, "Wanting a Supplement: The Question of Interpretation in Milton's Early Prose," in David Loewenstein and James Grantham Turner, eds, *Politics, Poetics, and Hermeneutics in Milton's Prose*. Cambridge: Cambridge University Press, 1990, 41–68.

Fish, Stanley, "What it's like to Read *L'Allegro* and *Il Penseroso*," *MS* 7 (1975), 77–99.

Fisher, Alan, "Why is *Paradise Regained* So Cold?" *MS* 14 (1980), 195–217.

Freeman, James A., "Milton's Roman Connection: Giovanni Salzilli," in James A. Freeman and Anthony Low, eds, *Urbane Milton: The Latin Poetry. MS* 19. Pittsburgh: University of Pittsburgh Press, 1984, 87–104.

Freeman, James A., and Anthony Low, eds, *Urbane Milton: The Latin Poetry. Milton Studies* 19. Pittsburgh: University of Pittsburgh Press, 1984.

French, J. Milton, "The Autographs of John Milton," *ELH: English Literary History* 4 (1937), 300–30.

French, J. Milton, *Milton in Chancery: New Chapters in the Lives of the Poet and his Father.* New York: Modern Language Association; London: Oxford University Press, 1939.

French, J. Milton, and Maurice Kelley, "The Columbia Milton," *N&Q* 195 (1952), 244–6.

Fruola, Christine, "When Eve Reads Milton: Undoing the Canonical Economy," *Critical Enquiry* 10 (1983), 321–47.

Frye, Northrop, "Agon and Logos," in *Spiritus Mundi: Essays on Literature, Myth, and Society*. Bloomington: Indiana University Press, 1976, 201–27.

Frye, Roland M., *Milton's Imagery and the Visual Arts: Iconographic Tradition in the Epic Poems*. Princeton, NJ: Princeton University Press, 1978.

Fuller, Margaret. *Papers on Literature and Art*, 2 vols (New York, 1846) I, 36–9.

Gardiner, Samuel R., *History of the Great Civil War, 1642–1649*. 3 vols. London & New York: Longmans, 1886–91.

Gardiner, Samuel R., *History of the Commonwealth and Protectorate, 1649–1660*. 4 vols. London and New York: Longmans, 1894–1901.

Giamatti, Bartlett A., *The Earthly Paradise and the Renaissance Epic*. Princeton, NJ: Princeton University Press, 1966.

Gilmartin, Kevin, "History and Reform in Milton's *Readie and Easie Way*," *MS* 24 (1988), 17–41.

Godwin, William, *Lives of Edward and John Phillips: Nephews and Pupils of Milton*. London, 1815.

Grey, Robin, *The Complicity of Imagination: The American Renaissance, Contests of Authority, and Seventeenth-Century English Culture*. Cambridge: Cambridge University Press, 1997.

Grossman, Marshall. *"Authors to Themselves": Milton and the Revelation of History*. Cambridge: Cambridge University Press, 1987.

Guibbory, Aschah, *Ceremony and Community from Herbert to Milton: Literature, Religion, and Cultural Conflict in Seventeenth-Century England*. Cambridge: Cambridge University Press, 1998.

Guillory, John, "Dalila's House: *Samson Agonistes* and the Sexual Division of Labor," in Margaret W. Ferguson, Maureen Quilligan, and Nancy J. Vickers, eds, *Re-writing the Renaissance: The Discourses of Sexual Difference in Early Modern Europe*. Chicago: Chicago University Press, 1986, 106–22.

Haan, Estelle, "'Written Encomiums': Milton's Latin Poetry in its Italian Context," in Mario Di Cesare, ed., *Milton in Italy: Contexts, Images, Contradictions*. Binghamton, NY: MRTS, 1991, 521–47.

Haan, Estelle, *From Academia to Amicitia: Milton's Latin Writings and the Italian Academies*. Philadelphia: American Philosophical Society, 1998.

Hale, John K., "Milton Playing with Ovid," *MS* 25 (1989), 3–20.

Hale, John K., "Milton's Self-representation in *Poems . . . 1645*," *MQ* 25 (1991), 1–48.

Haller, William, *Liberty and Reformation in the Puritan Revolution*. New York: Columbia University Press, 1955.

Halley, Janet E., "Female Autonomy in Milton's Sexual Politics," in Julia M. Walker, ed., *Milton and the Idea of Woman*. Urbana and Chicago: University of Illinois Press, 1988, 230–53.

Hammond, Frederick, *Music and Spectacle in Baroque Rome: Barberini Patronage Under Urban VIII*. New Haven, Conn.: Yale University Press, 1994.

Hanford, James Holly, "The Chronology of Milton's Private Studies," *PMLA* 36 (1921), 251–314. Reprinted in *John Milton Poet and Humanist*. Cleveland, Ohio: Press of Western Reserve University, 1966, 75–125.

Hanford, James Holly, "John Milton Forswears Physic," *Bulletin of the Medical Library Association* 32 (1944), 23–34.

Hanford, James Holly, "Milton in Italy," *Annuale Mediaevale* (1964), 49–63.

Hanford, James Holly, "Rosenbach Milton Documents," *PMLA* 38 (1923), 290–6.

Hanford, James Holly, "The Youth of Milton: An Interpretation of his Early Literary Development," in *Studies in Shakespeare, Milton, and Donne*. New York: Macmillan, 1925, 89–163. Reprinted in *John Milton Poet and Humanist*. Cleveland, Ohio: Press of Western Reserve University, 1966, 1–74.

Hardin, Richard F., "The Early Poetry of the Gunpowder Plot: Myth in the Making," *English Literary Renaissance* 22 (1992), 62–79.

Hardison, O. B., *The Enduring Monument*. Chapel Hill: University of North Carolina Press, 1962.

Harper, John, "'One Equal Music': The Music of Milton's Youth," *MQ* 31 (1997), 1–10.

Harris, Neil, "Galileo as Symbol: The 'Tuscan Artist' in *Paradise Lost*," *Annali dell'Istituto e Museo di Storia della Scienza di Firenze* 10 (1985), 3–29.

Haskin, Dayton, *Milton's Burden of Interpretation*. Philadelphia: University of Pennsylvania Press, 1994.

Hatton, Charles, "The Politics of Marital Reform and the Rationalization of Romance in *The Doctrine and Discipline of Divorce*," *MS* 27 (1991), 95–113.

Healy, Thomas, and Jonathan Sawday, *Literature and the English Civil War*. Cambridge: Cambridge University Press, 1990.

Helgerson, Richard, "Milton Reads the King's Book: Print, Performance, and the Making of a Bourgeois Idol," *Criticism* 29 (1987), 1–25.

Herendeen, Wyman H., "Milton's *Accedence Commenc't Grammar* and the Deconstruction of Grammatical Tyranny," in Paul G. Stanwood, ed., *Of Poetry and Politics: New Essays on Milton and His World*. Binghamton, NY: MRTS, 1995, 295–312.

Heyworth, P. L., "The Composition of Milton's 'At a Solemn Musick,'" *Bulletin of the New York Public Library* 70 (1966), 450–8.

Hill, Christopher, *The Century of Revolution: 1603–1714*. Edinburgh: T. Nelson, 1961.

Hill, Christopher, *The English Bible and the Seventeenth-Century Revolution*. London: Allen Lane, 1993.

Hill, Christopher, "Professor William B. Hunter, Bishop Burgess, and John Milton," *Studies in English Literature* 54 (1994), 165–93.

Hill, Christopher, *Puritanism and Revolution: Studies in Interpretation of the English Revolution of the Seventeenth Century*. London: Secker & Warburg, 1958.

Hill, Christopher, *The World Turned Upside Down: Radical Ideas During the English Revolution*. New York: Viking, 1972.

Hill, John Spencer, *John Milton: Poet, Priest and Prophet: A Study of Divine Vocation in Milton's Poetry and Prose*. London: Macmillan, 1979.

Hunter, G. K., *Paradise Lost*. Totowa, NJ: Rowman and Littlefield, 1979.

Hunter, William B., "A Bibliographical Excursus into Milton's Trinity Manuscript," *MQ* 19 (1985), 61–71.

Hunter, William B., "The Date and Occasion of *Arcades*," *English Language Notes* 11 (September, 1973), 46–7.

Hunter, William B., "Milton Translates the Psalmes," *Philological Quarterly* 40 (1961), 485–94.

Hunter, William B., "The Provenance of the *Christian Doctrine*," *Studies in English Literature* 32 (1992), 129–42. Responses by Lewalski and John Shawcross, 143–66.

Hunter, William B., "The Provenance of the *Christian Doctrine*," *Studies in English Literature* 33 (1993), 191–207.

Hunter, William B., "Responses," *MQ* 33 (1999), 31–7.

Hunter, William B., "Some Problems in Milton's Theological Vocabulary," *Harvard Theological Review* 57 (1964), 353–65.

Hunter, William B., "The Sources of Milton's Prosody," *Philological Quarterly* 28 (1949), 125–44.

Hunter, William B., *Visitation Unimplor'd: Milton and the Authorship of De Doctrina Christiana.* Pittsburgh: Duquesne University Press, 1998.

Hunter, William B., C. A. Patrides, and J. H. Adamson, *Bright Essence: Studies in Milton's Theology.* Salt Lake City: University of Utah Press, 1971.

Huntley, John F., "The Images of Poet and Poetry in Milton's *The Reason of Church-Government,*" in Michael Lieb and John T. Shawcross, eds, *Achievements of the Left Hand: Essays on the Prose of John Milton.* Amherst: University of Massachusetts Press, 1974, 83–120.

Hutton, Ronald, *The Restoration: A Political and Religious History of England and Wales, 1658–1667.* Oxford: Clarendon Press, 1985.

Ide, Richard S., and Joseph A. Wittreich, Jr., eds, *Composite Orders: The Genres of Milton's Last Poems, MS* 17 (1983). Pittsburgh: University of Pittsburgh Press, 1983.

Johnson, Richard M., "The Politics of Publication: Misrepresentation in Milton's 1645 *Poems,*" *Criticism* 36 (1991), 45–71.

Kahn, Victoria, *Machiavellian Rhetoric from the Counter-Reformation to Milton.* Princeton, NJ: Princeton University Press, 1994.

Kahn, Victoria, "The Metaphorical Covenant," in David Armitage, Armand Himy, and Quentin Skinner, eds, *Milton and Republicanism.* Cambridge: Cambridge University Press, 1995, 82–105.

Kelley, Maurice, "Considerations Touching the Right Editing of John Milton's *De Doctrina Christiana,*" in D. I. B. Smith, ed., *Editing Seventeenth-Century Prose.* Toronto: Hakkert, 1972, 31–51.

Kelley, Maurice, "Milton's Dante–Della Casa–Varchi Volume," *New York Public Library Bulletin* 66 (1962), 449–504.

Kelley, Maurice, "Milton's Debt to Wolleb's *Compendium Theologiae Christianae,*" *PMLA* 50 (1935), 156–65.

Kelley, Maurice, *This Great Argument: A Study of Milton's De Doctrina Christiana as a Gloss upon Paradise Lost.* Princeton, NJ: Princeton University Press, 1941.

Kelley, Maurice, and Samuel D. Atkins, "Milton's Annotations of Aratus," *PMLA* 70 (1955), 1,090–106.

Kelley, Maurice, and Samuel D. Atkins, "Milton's Annotations of Euripides," *Journal of English and Germanic Philology,* 60 (1961), 680–7.

Kelley, Maurice, and Samuel D. Atkins, "Milton and the Harvard Pindar," *Studies in Bibliography* 17 (1964), 77–82.

Kelly, J. N. D., *Early Christian Doctrines.* London: A. & C. Black, 1958.

Kendrick, Christopher, *Milton: A Study in Ideology and Form.* London: Methuen, 1986.

Kerrigan, William, *The Prophetic Milton.* Charlottesville: University of Virginia Press, 1974.

Kerrigan, William, *The Sacred Complex: On the Psychogenesis of Paradise Lost.* Cambridge, Mass. and London: Harvard University Press, 1983.

Kishlansky, Mark, *Parliamentary Selection: Social and Poltical Choice in Early Modern England.* New York: Cambridge University Press, 1986.

Klibansky, Raymond, E. Panofsky, and Fritz Saxl, *Saturn and Melancholy.* London: Nelson, 1964.

Knedlik, Janet Leslie, "High Pastoral Art in *Epitaphium Damonis,*" in James A. Freeman and

Anthony Low, eds, *Urbane Milton: The Latin Poetry. MS* 19. Pittsburgh: University of Pittsburgh Press, 1984, 149–75.

Knoppers, Laura Lunger, *Constructing Cromwell: Ceremony, Portrait, and Print 1645–1661.* Cambridge: Cambridge University Press, 2000.

Knoppers, Laura Lunger, *Historicizing Milton: Spectacle, Power, and Poetry in Restoration England.* Athens, Ga. and London: University of Georgia Press, 1994.

Knoppers, Laura Lunger, "Milton's *The Readie and Easie Way* and the English Jeremiad," in David Loewenstein and James Grantham Turner, eds, *Politics, Poetics, and Hermeneutics in Milton's Prose.* Cambridge: Cambridge University Press, 1990, 213–25.

Knott, John R., *Milton's Pastoral Vision: An Approach to Paradise Lost.* Chicago: Chicago University Press, 1971.

Kranidas, Thomas, *The Fierce Equation: A Study of Milton's Decorum.* The Hague: Mouton, 1965.

Kranidas, Thomas, ed., *New Essays on Paradise Lost.* Berkeley: University of California Press, 1969.

Kranidas, Thomas, "Style and Rectitude in Seventeenth-century Prose: Hall, Smectymnuus, and Milton," *Huntington Library Quarterly* 46 (1983), 237–69.

Kranidas, Thomas, "Words, Words, and the Word: Milton's *Of Prelatical Episcopacy*," *MS* 16 (1982), 153–66.

Labriola, Albert C., "Portraits of an Artist: Milton's Changing Self-image," in James A. Freeman and Anthony Low, eds, *Urbane Milton: The Latin Poetry. MS* 19. Pittsburgh: University of Pittsburgh Press, 1984, 179–203.

Lacan, Jacques, *Ecrits: A Selection*, ed. and trans. Alan Sheridan. New York: Norton, 1977.

Lambert, Ellen, *Placing Sorrow: A Study of the Pastoral Elegy Convention from Theocritus to Milton.* Chapel Hill: University of North Carolina Press, 1976.

Landy, Marcia, "Kinship and the Role of Women in *Paradise Lost*," *MS* 4 (1972), 3–18.

Leach, A. F., *Milton as Schoolboy and Schoolmaster.* London: British Academy, 1908.

Le Comte, Edward, *Milton's Unchanging Mind.* Port Washington, NY: Kennikat Press, 1973.

Leishman, James B., *Milton's Minor Poems.* London: Hutchinson, 1969.

Leslie, Michael, "The Hartlib Papers Project: Text Retrieval with Large Datasets," *Literary and Linguistic Computing* 5 (1990), 58–69.

Lewalski, Barbara K., "Innocence and Experience in Milton's Eden," in Thomas Kranidas, ed., *New Essays on Paradise Lost.* Berkeley: University of California Press, 1969, 80–117.

Lewalski, Barbara K., "Milton and *De Doctrina Christiana*: Evidences of Authorship," *MS* 36 (1999), 203–28.

Lewalski, Barbara K., "Milton and the Hartlib Circle: Educational Projects and Epic *Paideia*," in Diana Treviño Benet and Michael Lieb, eds, *Literary Milton: Text, Pretext, Context.* Pittsburgh: Duquesne University Press, 1994, 202–19.

Lewalski, Barbara K., *Milton's Brief Epic: The Genre, Meaning, and Art of Paradise Regained.* London: Methuen, 1966.

Lewalski, Barbara K., "Milton's *Comus* and the Politics of Masquing," in David Bevington and Peter Holbrook, eds, *The Politics of the Stuart Court Masque.* Cambridge: Cambridge University Press, 1998, 296–320.

Lewalski, Barbara K., "Milton's *Samson* and the 'New Acquist of True [Political] Experience,'" *MS* 24 (1999), 233–51.

Lewalski, Barbara K., *Paradise Lost and the Rhetoric of Literary Forms.* Princeton, NJ: Princeton University Press, 1985.

Lewalski, Barbara K., "*Samson Agonistes* and the 'Tragedy' of the Apocalypse," *PMLA* 85 (1970), 1,050–62.

Lewalski, Barbara K., "Time and History in *Paradise Regained*," in Balachandra Rajan, ed., *The Prison and the Pinnacle*. Toronto: Toronto University Press, 1972, 49–81.

Lieb, Michael, *Milton and the Culture of Violence*. Ithaca, NY: Cornell University Press, 1994.

Lieb, Michael, "Milton's *Of Reformation* and the Dynamics of Controversy," in Michael Lieb and John T. Shawcross, eds, *Achievements of the Left Hand: Essays on the Prose of John Milton*. Amherst: University of Massachusetts Press, 1974, 55–82.

Lieb, Michael, "Our Living Dread": The God of *Samson Agonistes*," *Milton Studies* 33 (1996), 3–23.

Lieb, Michael, and John T. Shawcross, eds, *Achievements of the Left Hand: Essays on the Prose of John Milton*. Amherst: University of Massachusetts Press, 1974.

Lindenbaum, Peter, "John Milton and the Republican Mode of Literary Production," in Andrew Gurr, et al., eds, *The Yearbook of Literary Studies: Politics, Patronage, and Literature in England, 1558–1658*, 21 (1991), 121–36.

Lindenbaum, Peter, "The Poet in the Marketplace: Milton and Samuel Simmons," in Paul G. Stanwood, ed., *Of Poetry and Politics: New Essays on Milton and His World*. Binghamton, NY: MRTS, 1995, 249–62.

Lipking, Lawrence, "The Genius of the Shore: Lycidas, Adamastor, and the Poetics of Nationalism," *PMLA* 111 (1996), 205–21.

Loewenstein, David, "An Ambiguous Monster": Representing Rebellion in Milton's Polemics and *Paradise Lost*," *Huntington Library Quarterly* 55 (1992), 295–315.

Loewenstein, David, "The Kingdom Within: Radical Religious Culture and the Politics of *Paradise Regained*," *Literature and History* 3 (1994), 63–89.

Loewenstein, David, *Milton and the Drama of History: Historical Vision, Iconoclasm, and the Literary Imagination*. Cambridge: Cambridge University Press, 1990.

Loewenstein, David, "The Revenge of the Saint: Radical Religion and Politics in *Samson Agonistes*," *MS* 33 (1996), 159–80.

Loewenstein, David, and James Grantham Turner, eds, *Politics, Poetics, and Hermeneutics in Milton's Prose*. Cambridge: Cambridge University Press, 1990.

Lord, George de F., "Milton's Dialogue with Omniscience in *Paradise Lost*," in Louis L. Martz and Aubrey Williams, eds, *The Author in His Work: Essays on a Problem in Criticism*. New Haven, Conn. and London: Yale University Press, 1978, 31–50.

Low, Anthony, *The Blaze of Noon: A Reading of Samson Agonistes*. New York: Columbia University Press, 1974.

Low, Anthony, "*Elegia Septima*, The Poet and the Poem," in James A. Freeman and Anthony Low, eds, *Urbane Milton: The Latin Poetry. Milton Studies* 19. Pittsburgh: University of Pittsburgh Press, 1984, 21–36.

Low, Anthony, "Mansus: In Its Context," in James A. Freeman and Anthony Low, eds, *Urbane Milton: The Latin Poetry. Milton Studies* 19. Pittsburgh: University of Pittsburgh Press, 1984, 105–26.

Low, Anthony, "Milton and the Georgic Ideal," in Low, ed., *The Georgic Revolution*. Princeton, NJ: Princeton University Press, 1985, 310–22.

Low, Anthony, "Milton's Last Sonnet," *MQ* 9 (1975), 80–2.

MacKellar, Walter, ed. and trans., *The Latin Poems of John Milton*. New Haven, Conn.: Yale University Press, 1930.

McCabe, Richard, "The Form and Methods of Milton's *Animadversions Upon the Remonstrants Defence Against Smectymnuus*," *English Language Notes* 18 (1981), 266–72.

McColley, Diane, *A Gust for Paradise: Milton's Eden and the Visual Arts*. Urbana: University of Illinois Press, 1993.

McColley, Diane, *Milton's Eve*. Urbana: University of Illinois Press, 1983.

McColley, Diane, *Poetry and Music in seventeenth-century England*. Cambridge: Cambridge University Press, 1997.

McColley, Diane, "Tongues of Men and Angels: *Ad Leonoram Romae Canentem*," in in James A. Freeman and Anthony Low, eds, *Urbane Milton: The Latin Poetry*. *MS* 19. Pittsburgh: University of Pittsburgh Press, 1984, 127–48.

McGuire, Maryann Cale, *Milton's Puritan Masque*. Athens, Ga.: University of Georgia Press, 1983.

McKenzie, D. F., "Milton's Printers: Matthew, Mary, and Samuel Simmons," *MQ* 14 (1980), 87–91.

McLachlan, H. John, *Socinianism in Seventeenth-Century England*. Oxford: Oxford University Press, 1951.

Maclean, Gerald, ed., *Culture and Society in the Stuart Restoration*. Cambridge: Cambridge University Press, 1995.

Madan, Francis F., *A New Bibliography of the "Eikon Basilike" of Charles the First, with a Note on the Authorship*. London: Quaritch, 1950.

Magnus, Elizabeth M., "Originality and Plagiarism in *Areopagitica* and *Eikonoklastes*," *English Literary Renaissance* 21 (1991), 87–101.

Marcus, Leah S., "The Milieu of Milton's *Comus*: Judicial Reform at Ludlow and the Problem of Sexual Assault," *Criticism* 25 (1983), 293–327.

Marcus, Leah S., "Milton as Historical Subject," *MQ* 25 (1991), 120–7.

Marcus, Leah S., *The Politics of Mirth: Jonson, Herrick, Milton, Marvell, and the Defense of Old Holiday Pastimes*. Chicago and London: University of Chicago Press, 1986.

Marcus, Leah S., *Unediting the Renaissance: Shakespeare, Marlowe, Milton*. London and New York: Routledge, 1996.

Martz, Louis L., *Poet of Exile: A Study of Milton's Poetry*. New Haven. Conn.: Yale University Press, 1980.

Miller, Leo, "Another Milton State Paper Recovered and a Mystery Demystified," *English Language Notes* 25 (1987), 30–1

Miller, Leo, "The Burning of Milton's Books in 1660: Two Mysteries," *English Literary Renaissance* 18 (1988), 424–37.

Miller, Leo, "The Date of Christoph Arnold's Letter," *Notes & Queries* 229 (1984), 323–4.

Miller, Leo, *John Milton and the Oldenburg Safeguard: New Light on Milton and his Friends in the Commonwealth from the Diaries and Letters of Hermann Mylius*. New York: Loewenthal Press, 1985.

Miller, Leo, *John Milton's Writings in the Anglo-Dutch Negotiations, 1651–1654*. Pittsburgh: Duquesne University Press, 1992.

Miller, Leo, "Lexicographer Milton Leads Us To Recover His Unknown Works," *MQ* 24 (1990), 58–62.

Miller, Leo, "Milton and Holstenius Reconsidered: An Exercise in Scholarly Practice," in Mario Di Cesare, ed., *Milton in Italy: Contexts, Images, Contradictions*. Binghamton, NY: MRTS, 1991, 573–87.

Miller, Leo, "Milton and Lassenius," *MQ* 6 (1972), 92–5.

Miller, Leo, "Milton Edits Freigius' 'Life of Ramus,'" *Renaissance & Reformation* 8 (1972), 112–14.

Miller, Leo, "Milton's 1626 Obituaries Dated," *Notes & Queries* 225 (1980), 323–4.

Miller, Leo, "Milton's Clash with Chappell: A Suggested Reconstruction," *MQ* 14 (1980), 77–87.

Miller, Leo, "Milton's *Defensio* Ordered Wholesale for the States of Holland," *Notes & Queries* 231 (1986), 33.

Miller, Leo, "Milton's Portraits: An *Impartial* Inquiry into their Authentication," *MQ* (Special Issue), 1976.

Miller, Leo, "Milton's State Letters: The Lünig Version," *Notes and Queries* 215 (1970), 412–14.

Miller, Leo, "New Milton Texts and Data from the Aitzema Mission, 1652," *Notes and Queries* 235 (1990), 279–88.

Miller, Leo, "On Some Verses by Alexander Gil which John Milton Read," *MQ* 24 (1990), 22–5.

Milner, Andrew, *John Milton and the English Revolution: A Study in the Sociology of Literature.* London: Macmillan, 1981.

Mohl, Ruth, *John Milton and His Commonplace Book.* New York: Ungar, 1969.

Morrill, J. S., *The Revolt of the Provinces: Conservatives and Radicals in the English Civil War, 1630–1650.* New York: Barnes & Noble, 1976.

Morse, C. J., "The Dating of Milton's Sonnet XIX," *Times Literary Supplement* 15 (Sept. 1961).

Moseley, C. W. R. D., *The Poetic Birth: Milton's Poems of 1645.* Aldershot: Scolar Press, 1991.

Moyles, R. G., *The Text of Paradise Lost: A Study in Editorial Procedure.* Toronto: University of Toronto Press, 1985.

Mueller, Janel M., "On Genesis in Genre: Milton's Politicizing of the Sonnet in 'Captain or Colonel,'" in Barbara Kiefer Lewalski, ed., *Renaissance Genres: Essays on Theory, History, and Interpretation.* Cambridge, Mass.: Harvard University Press, 1986, 213–40.

Mueller, Janel M., "The Mastery of Decorum: Politics as Poetry in Milton's Sonnets," *Critical Inquiry* 15 (1987), 475–508.

Mueller, Janel M., "Embodying Glory: The Apocalyptic Strain in Milton's *Of Reformation*," in David Loewenstein and James Grantham Turner, eds, *Politics, Poetics, and Hermeneutics in Milton's Prose.* Cambridge: Cambridge University Press, 1990, 9–40.

Mueller, Janel M., "Contextualizing Milton's Nascent Republicanism," in Paul G. Stanwood, ed., *Of Poetry and Politics: New Essays on Milton and His World.* Binghamton, NY: MRTS, 1995, 263–82.

Mueller, Martin, "The Tragic Epic: *Paradise Lost* and the *Iliad*," in *Children of Oedipus and Other Essays on the Imitation of Greek Tragedy, 1550–1800.* Toronto: University of Toronto Presss, 1980, 213–30.

Mullinger, James Bass, *The University of Cambridge*, 3 vols. Cambridge: Cambridge University Press, 1873–1911.

Neale, J. E., *The Elizabethan House of Commons.* New Haven, Conn.: Yale University Press, 1950.

Nicholson, Marjorie Hope, "Milton and the Telescope," *ELH: English Literary History* II (1935), 1–32.

Norbrook, David, "Levelling Poetry: George Wither and the English Revolution, 1642–1649," *English Literary Renaissance* 21 (1991), 217–56.

Norbrook, David, "Lucan, Thomas May, and the Creation of a Republican Literary Culture," in Kenneth Sharpe and Peter Lake, eds, *Culture and Politics in Early Stuart England*, Stanford, Calif.: Stanford University Press, 1993, 45–66.

Norbrook, David, *Writing the English Republic: Poetry, Rhetoric, and Politics, 1627–1660.* Cambridge: Cambridge University Press, 1999.

Nyquist, Mary, "The Genesis of Gendered Subjectivity in the Divorce Tracts and *Paradise Lost*," in Mary Nyquist and Margaret Ferguson, eds, *Re-membering Milton: Essays on the Texts and the Traditions.* New York and London: Methuen, 1987, 99–127.

O'Connell, Michael, "Milton and the Art of Italy: A Revisionist View," in Mario Di Cesare, ed., *Milton in Italy: Contexts, Images, Contradictions*. Binghamton, NY: MRTS, 1991, 215–36.

Ogg, David, *England in the Reign of Charles II.* 2 vols. Oxford: Clarendon Press, 1934.

Ogg, David, *Europe in the Seventeenth Century*. London: A. & C. Black, 1960.

Ong, Walter J., *Ramus, Method, and the Decay of Dialogue.* Cambridge, Mass.: Harvard University Press, 1958.

Orgel, Stephen, *Illusion of Power: Poltical Theater in the English Renaissance*. Berkeley: University of California Press, 1975.

Owen, Elvion, "Milton and Selden on Divorce," *Studies in Philology* 43 (1946), 233–57.

Parker, William Riley, "Milton and the News of Charles Diodati's Death," *Modern Language Notes* 71 (1957), 486–8.

Parker, William Riley, "Milton and Thomas Young, 1620–1628," *Modern Language Notes* 53 (1938), 399–407

Parker, William Riley, *Milton's Debt to Greek Tragedy in Samson Agonistes*. Baltimore: Johns Hopkins University Press, 1937.

Parker, William Riley, "Notes on the Chronology of Milton's Latin Poems," in Arnold Williams, ed., *Tribute to George Coffin Taylor.* Chapel Hill: University of North Carolina Press, 1952, 113–31.

Parry, Graham, *The Golden Age Restored: The Culture of the Stuart Court, 1603–1642*. Manchester: Manchester University Press, 1981.

Patrides, C. A., ed., *Approaches to Paradise Lost: The York Centenary Lectures*. Toronto: University of Toronto Press, 1968.

Patterson, Annabel, *Censorship and Interpretation: The Conditions of Writing and Reading in Early Modern England*. Madison: University of Wisconsin Press, 1984.

Patterson, Annabel, "'Forc'd Fingers': Milton's Early Poems and Ideological Constraint," in Claude J. Summers and Ted-Larry Pebworth, eds, *The Muses Common-Weale: Poetry and Politics in the Seventeenth Century*. Columbia: University of Missouri Press, 1988, 9–22.

Patterson, Annabel, *Pastoral and Ideology: Virgil to Valéry*. Berkeley: University of California Press, 1987.

Patterson, Annabel, "No Meer Amatorious Novel?" in David Loewenstein and James Grantham Turner, eds, *Politics, Poetics, and Hermeneutics in Milton's Prose*. Cambridge: Cambridge University Press, 1990, 85–101.

Patterson, Annabel, "That Old Man Eloquent," in Diana Treviño Benet and Michael Lieb, eds, *Literary Milton: Text, Pretext, Context*. Pittsburgh: Duquesne University Press, 1994, 22–44.

Peile, John, *Christ's College*. London: F. E. Robinson, 1900.

Pigman, G. W., *Grief and English Renaissance Elegy*. Cambridge: Cambridge University Press, 1985.

Piper, David, *Catalogue of Seventeenth-century Portraits in the National Portrait Gallery, 1625–1714*. Cambridge: Cambridge University Press, 1963.

Pocock, J. C. A., *The Ancient Constitution and the Feudal Law: A Study of English Historical Thought in the Seventeenth Century*. Cambridge: Cambridge University Press, 1957.

Poole, Kristen, "Deforming Reformation: The Grotesque Puritan and Social Transformation in Early Modern England." Dissertation: Harvard University, 1996.

Pope, Elizabeth M., *Paradise Regained: The Tradition and the Poem*. Baltimore: Johns Hopkins University Press, 1947.

Popkin, Richard H., "The Dispersion of Bodin's Dialogues in England, Germany, and Holland," *Journal of the History of Ideas* 49 (1988), 157–60.

Postlethwaite, Norman, and Gordon Campbell, eds, "Edward King, Milton's "Lycidas": Poems and Documents," *MQ* 28 (1944), 77–111.

Potter, Lois, *Secret Rites and Secret Writings: Royalist Literature, 1642–1660*. Cambridge: Cambridge University Press, 1989.

Prince, F. T., *The Italian Element in Milton's Verse*. Oxford: Clarendon Press, 1954.

Pritchard, Allen, "Milton in Rome: According to Wood," *MQ* 14 (1980), 92–7.

Quint, David, *Epic and Empire: Politics and Generic Form from Virgil to Milton*. Princeton, NJ: Princeton University Press, 1992.

Radzinowicz, Mary Ann, "Man as a Probationer of Immortality: *Paradise Lost* XI and XII," in Patrides, ed., *Approaches to Paradise Lost*, 31–51.

Radzinowicz, Mary Ann, *Milton's Epics and the Book of Psalms*. Princeton, NJ: Princeton University Press, 1989.

Radzinowicz, Mary Ann, "The Politics of *Paradise Lost*," in Sharpe and Zwicker, eds, *Politics of Discourse*, 204–29.

Radzinowicz, Mary Ann, *Toward Samson Agonistes: The Growth of Milton's Mind*. Princeton, NJ: Princeton University Press, 1978.

Rajan, Balachandra, ed., *The Prison and the Pinnacle*. Toronto: Toronto University Press, 1972.

Rajan, Balachandra, *Under Western Eyes: India From Milton to Macaulay*. Durham, NC and London: Duke University Press, 1999.

Raylor, Timothy, "New Light on Milton and Hartlib," *MQ* 27 (1993), 19–31.

Raymond, Joad, *The Invention of the Newspaper: English Newsbooks, 1641–1660*. Oxford: Clarendon Press, 1996.

Revard, Stella P., "'Ad Joannem Rousium': Elegiac Wit and Pindaric Mode," *MS* 19 (1984), 205–26.

Revard, Stella P., *Milton and the Tangles of Neaera's Hair: The Making of the 1645 Poems*. Columbia: University of Missouri Press, 1997.

Rollinson, Philip, "Milton's Nativity Ode and the Decorum of Genre," *MS* 7 (1975), 165–84.

Rosenblatt, Jason P., "The Mosaic Voice in *Paradise Lost*," *MS* 7 (1975), 207–32.

Rosenblatt, Jason P., "Samson' Sacrifice," in Amy Boesky and Mary Thomas Crane, eds, *Form and Reform in Renaissance England: Essays in Honor of Barbara Kiefer Lewalski*. Newark: University of Delaware Press, 2000, 321–37.

Rosenblatt, Jason P., *Torah and Law in Paradise Lost*. Princeton, NJ: Princeton University Press, 1994.

Rumrich, John P., "Milton's Arianism, Why it Matters," in Stephen Dobranski and John Rumrich, eds, *Milton and Heresy*, Cambridge: Cambridge University Press, 1998, 75–92.

Rumrich, John P., "Mead and Milton," *MQ* 20 (1986) 136–41.

Russell, Conrad, *The Causes of the English Civil War.* Oxford: Clarendon Press, 1990.

Russell, Conrad, *The Origins of the English Civil War.* London: Macmillan, 1973.

Russell, Conrad, *Parliaments and English Politics, 1621–1629.* Oxford: Clarendon Press, 1979.

Salvatorelli, Luigi, *A Concise History of Italy From Prehistoric Times to our own Day*, trans. Bernard Miall. New York: Oxford University Press, 1940.

Samuel, Irene, *Dante and Milton: The Commedia and Paradise Lost.* Ithaca, NY: Cornell University Press, 1966.

Samuel, Irene, *Plato and Milton.* Ithaca, NY: Cornell University Press, 1947.

Samuel, Irene, "*Samson Agonistes* as Tragedy," in Joseph A. Wittreich, Jr., ed., *Calm of Mind: Tercentenary Essays on Paradise Regained and Samson Agonistes.* Cleveland, Ohio and London: Case Western University Press, 1971, 237–57.

Sanchez, Reuben, "From Polemic to Prophecy: Milton's Uses of Jeremiah in *The Reason of Church Government* and *The Readie and Easie Way*," *MS* 30 (1993), 27–44.

Sanchez, Reuben, "The Worst of Superstitions: Milton's *Of True Religion* and the Issue of Religious Tolerance," *Prose Studies* 9 (1986), 21–38.

Schumacher, Wayne, "*Paradise Lost* and the Italian Epic Tradition," in Amadeus P. Fiore, ed., *Th'Upright Heart and Pure.* Pittsburgh: Duquesne University Press, 1967, 7–24, 87–100.

Sellin, Paul R., "Alexander Morus before the Hof van Holland: Some Insight into Seventeenth Century Polemics with John Milton," in Martinus A. Bakker and Beverly H. Morrison, eds, *Studies in Netherlandic Culture and Literature.* Lanham: University Press of America, 1994, 1–11.

Sellin, Paul R., "Alexander More before the Synod of Utrecht," *Huntington Library Quarterly* 58 (1996), 239–49.

Sellin, Paul R., "Alexander Morus and John Milton (II): Milton, Morus, and Infanticide," in William Z. Shetter and Inge Van der Cruysse, eds, *Contemporary Explorations in the Culture of the Low Countries.* Lanham: University Press of America, 1996, 277–85.

Sellin, Paul R., "Further Responses," *MQ* 33 (1999), 38–51.

Sellin, Paul R., "John Milton's *Paradise Lost* and *De Doctrina Christiana* on Predestination," *MS* 34 (1996), 45–60.

Shafer, Robert, *The English Ode to 1660.* Princeton, NJ: Princeton University Press, 1918.

Sharpe, Kevin, *Faction and Parliament: Essays on Early Stuart History.* Oxford: Clarendon Press, 1978.

Sharpe, Kevin, and Peter Lake, eds, *Culture and Politics in Early Stuart England.* Stanford, Calif.: Stanford University Press, 1993.

Sharpe, Kevin, and Steven N. Zwicker, eds, *Politics of Discourse: The Literature and History of Seventeenth-Century England.* Berkeley: University of California Press, 1987.

Shawcross, John T., "The Date of *Ad Patrem*," *Notes and Queries* 204 (1959), 348–50.

Shawcross, John T., "The Dating of Certain Poems, Letters, and Prolusions Written by Milton," *English Language Notes* 2 (1965), 251–62.

Shawcross, John T., "Establishment of a Text of Milton's Poems through a Study of *Lycidas*," *Papers of the Bibliographical Society of America* 56 (1962), 317–31.

Shawcross, John T., *John Milton: The Self and the World*. Lexington: University Press of Kentucky, 1993.

Shawcross, John T., "Milton and Diodati: An Essay in Psychodynamic Meaning," *MS* 7 (1975), 127–64.

Shawcross, John T., "Milton's Decision to Become a Poet," *Modern Language Quarterly* 24 (1963), 345–58.

Shawcross, John T., "Milton's Sonnet 19: Its date of Authorship and its Interpretation," *N&Q* 202 (1957), 442–6.

Shawcross, John T., "A Note on Milton's Hobson Poems," *Review of English Studies*, n.s. 18 (1967), 433–7.

Shawcross, John T., "Speculations on the Dating of the Trinity MS of Milton's Poems," *Modern Language Notes* 75 (1960) 11–17.

Shuger, Deborah, *Sacred Rhetoric: The Christian Grand Style in the English Renaissance*. Princeton, NJ: Princeton University Press, 1988.

Siebert, Fredrick S., *Freedom of the Press in England, 1476–1776: The Rise and Decline of Government Controls*. Urbana: University of Illinois Press, 1952.

Sirluck, Ernest, "*Eikon Basilike, Eikon Alethine,* and *Eikonoklastes*," *Modern Language Notes* 69 (1954), 479–501.

Sirluck, Ernest, "Milton's Idle Right Hand," *Journal of English and Germanic Philology* 60 (1961) 749–85.

Slack, Paul, *The Impact of Plague in Tudor and Stuart England*. London: Routledge, 1985.

Smith, Nigel, "*Areopagitica:* Voicing Contexts, 1643–5," in David Loewenstein and James Grantham Turner, eds, *Politics, Poetics, and Hermeneutics in Milton's Prose*. Cambridge: Cambridge University Press, 1990, 103–22.

Smith, Nigel, *Literature and Revolution in England, 1640–1660*. New Haven, Conn. and London: Yale University Press, 1994.

Smith, Nigel, *Perfection Proclaimed: Language and Literature in English Radical Religion, 1640–1660*. Oxford: Clarendon Press, 1989.

Spencer, T. J. B., "*Paradise Lost*: The Anti-Epic," in C. A. Patrides, ed., *Approaches to Paradise Lost: The York Centenary Lectures*. Toronto: University of Toronto Press, 1968, 81–98.

Spitzer, Leo, "Understanding Milton," *Hopkins Review* 4 (1950–1), 16–27.

Stanwood, Paul G., ed., *Of Poetry and Politics: New Essays on Milton and His World*. Binghamton, NY: MRTS, 1995.

Stavely, Keith, *The Politics of Milton's Prose Style*. New Haven. Conn. and London: Yale University Press, 1975.

Steadman, John, "Faithful Champion": The Theological Basis of Milton's Hero of Faith," *Anglia* 77 (1959), 12–28.

Steadman, John, *Milton and the Renaissance Hero*. Oxford: Clarendon Press, 1967.

Steadman, John, "Milton's Harapha and Goliath," *Journal of English and Germanic Philology* 60 (1961), 786–95.

Stein, Arnold, *Heroic Knowledge: An Interpretation of Paradise Regained and Samson Agonistes*. Minneapolis: University of Minnesota Press, 1957.

Stewart, Douglas, "Speaking to the World: The *Ad Hominem* Logic of Milton's Polemics," *The Seventeenth Century* 11 (1996), 35–60.

Stewart, Stanley, "Milton Revises *The Readie and Easie Way*," *MS* 20 (1984), 205–24.

Stone, Lawrence, *The Causes of the English Revolution, 1629–1642.* London: Routledge, 1972.

Strier, Richard, "Milton against humility," in *Religion and Culture in Renaissance England*, eds. Claire McEachern and Debora Shuger. Cambridge: Cambridge University Press, 1997, 258–86.

Survey of London, Volume 6: Hammersmith. London: London County Council, 1915.

Svendson, Kester, "Milton and Alexander More: New Documents," *JEGP* 60 (1961), 799–806.

Swaim, Kathleen, *Before and After the Fall: Contrasting Modes in Paradise Lost.* Amherst: University of Massachusetts Press, 1986.

Tawney, R. H., *Religion and the Rise of Capitalism.* New York: Harcourt, 1926; 1952.

Thorne-Thomsen, Sara, "Milton's 'Advent'rous Song': Lyric Genres in *Paradise Lost.*" Dissertation: Brown University, 1985.

Thum, Maureen, "Milton's Diatribal Voice: The Integration and Transformation of a Generic Paradigm in *Animadversions*," *MS* 30 (1993), 3–25.

Tillyard, E. M. W., *Milton.* London: Chatto & Windus, 1930; 1951.

Toliver, Harold E., "Milton's Household Epic," *MS* 9 (1976), 105–20.

Trevor-Roper, Hugh, *Catholics, Anglicans and Puritans: Seventeenth Century Essays.* Chicago: University of Chicago Press, 1987.

Trevor, B. Douglas, "Learned Appearances: Writing Scholarly and Literary Selves in Early Modern England." Dissertation: Harvard University, 1999.

Tuck, Richard. *Philosophy and Government.* Cambridge: Cambridge University Press, 1993.

Tumbleson, Ray, "*Of True Religion* and False Politics: Milton and the Uses of Anti-Catholicism," *Prose Studies* 15 (1992), 253–70.

Turnbull, G. H., *Hartlib, Dury, and Comenius: Gleanings from Hartlib's Papers.* London: University Press of Liverpool, 1947.

Turner, James G., *One Flesh: Paradisal Marriage and Sexual Relations in the Age of Milton.* Oxford: Clarendon Press, 1987.

Turner, James G., "The Poetics of Engagement," in David Loewenstein and James Grantham Turner, eds, *Politics, Poetics, and Hermeneutics in Milton's Prose.* Cambridge: Cambridge University Press, 1990, 257–75.

Tuve, Rosemond, *Images and Themes in Five Poems by Milton.* Cambridge, Mass.: Harvard University Press, 1957.

Twigg, John, *The University of Cambridge and the English Revolution, 1625–1688.* Cambridge: Boydell Press, 1990.

Ulrich, John C., "Incident to all Our Sex: The Tragedy of Dalila," in Julia Walker, ed., *Milton and the Idea of Woman.* Urbana and Chicago: University of Illinois, 1988, 185–210.

Underdown, David, *Pride's Purge: Politics in the Puritan Revolution.* Oxford: Clarendon Press, 1971.

Victoria History of the Counties of England: Buckinghamshire. London: St Catherine's Press, 1925.

Von Maltzhan, Nicholas, "The First Reception of *Paradise Lost* (1667)," *Review of English Studies* 47 (1996), 479–99.

Von Maltzhan, Nicholas, "Laureate, Republican, Calvinist: An Early Response to Milton and *Paradise Lost* (1667)," *MS* 29 (1992), 181–98.

Von Maltzahn, Nicholas, *Milton's History of Britain: Republican Historiography in the English*

Revolution. Oxford: Clarendon Press, 1991.

Von Maltzhan, Nicholas, "Samuel Butler's Milton," *Studies in Philology* 92 (1955), 482–95.

Von Maltzhan, Nicholas, "The Whig Milton, 1667–1700," in David Armitage, Armand Himy, and Quentin Skinner, eds, *Milton and Republicanism*. Cambridge: Cambridge University Press, 1995, 229–53.

Walker, Julia M., ed., *Milton and the Idea of Woman*. Urbana and Chicago: University of Illinois Press, 1988.

Webber, Joan, *The Eloquent I: Style and Self in Seventeenth-century Prose*. Madison: University of Wisconsin Press, 1968.

Webber, Joan, *Milton and His Epic Tradition*. Seattle and London: University of Washington Press, 1979.

Weber, Max, *The Protestant Ethic and the Spirit of Capitalism*, trans. Talcott Parsons. New York: Scribners, 1958.

Webster, Charles, ed., *Samuel Hartlib and the Advancement of Learning*. Cambridge: Cambridge University Press, 1970.

Wedgwood, C. V., *The King's Peace, 1637–1641*. London: Collins, 1955.

Wedgwood, C. V., *The King's War, 1641–1647*. London: Collins, 1958.

Werblowsky, R. J. Zwy, *Lucifer and Prometheus*. London: Routledge, 1952.

Wilding, Michael, *Dragons Teeth: Literature in the English Revolution*. Oxford: Clarendon Press, 1987.

Williamson, George C., *Milton Tercentenary: The Portraits, Prints and Writings of John Milton exhibited at Christ's College, Cambridge, 1908*. Cambridge: Cambridge University Press, 1908.

Williams, Kathleen, "Milton, Greatest Spenserian," in Joseph A. Wittreich, Jr. ed., *Milton and the Line of Vision*. Madison: University of Wisconsin Press, 1975.

Willis, Robert, *Architectural History of the University of Cambridge*, ed. John Willis Clark. Cambridge: Cambridge University Press, 1886.

Wilson, A. N., *The Life of John Milton*. Oxford and New York: Oxford University Press, 1983.

Wittreich, Joseph A., Jr., ed., *Calm of Mind: Tercentenary Essays on Paradise Regained and Samson Agonistes*. Cleveland, Ohio and London: Case Western University Press, 1971.

Wittreich, Joseph A., Jr., "'The Crown of Eloquence': The Figure of the Orator in Milton's Prose Works," in Michael Lieb and John T. Shawcross, eds, *Achievements of the Left Hand: Essays on the Prose of John Milton*. Amherst: University of Massachusetts Press, 1974, 3–54.

Wittreich, Joseph A., Jr., *Feminist Milton*. Ithaca, NY and London: Cornell University Press, 1987.

Wittreich, Joseph A., Jr., *Interpreting Samson Agonistes*. Princeton, NJ: Princeton University Press, 1986.

Wittreich, Joseph A., Jr., *Visionary Poetics: Milton's Tradition and his Legacy*. San Marino: Huntington Library, 1979.

Wolfe, Don M., *Milton in the Puritan Revolution*. New York and London: Nelson, 1941.

Wolfson, Harry A., *The Philosophy of the Church Fathers*. Cambridge, Mass.: Harvard University Press, 1956.

Woodhouse, A. S. P., "Notes on Milton's Early Development," *University of Toronto Quarterly*, 13 (1943–4), 66–101.

Woods, Susanne, "Elective Poetics and Milton's Prose: *A Treatise of Civil Power* and *Consid-*

erations Touching the Likeliest Means to Remove Hirelings Out of the Church," in David Loewenstein and James Grantham Turner, eds, *Politics, Poetics, and Hermeneutics in Milton's Prose.* Cambridge: Cambridge University Press, 1990, 193–211.

Woods, Susanne, "How Free are Milton's Women," in Julia M. Walker, ed., *Milton and the Idea of Woman.* Urbana and Chicago: University of Illinois Press, 1988, 15–31.

Woods, Susanne, "'That Freedom of Discussion which I Loved': Italy and Milton's Cultural Self-definition," in Mario Di Cesare, ed., *Milton in Italy: Contexts, Images, Contradictions.* Binghamton, NY: MRTS, 1991, 9–18.

Woolrych, Austin, "Debate: Dating Milton's *History of Britain,*" *The Historical Journal* 35 (1993), 929–43.

Woolrych, Austin, "Milton and Cromwell: 'A Short but Scandalous Night of Interruption?'" in Michael Lieb and John T. Shawcross, eds, *Achievements of the Left Hand: Essays on the Prose of John Milton.* Amherst: University of Massachusetts Press, 1974, 185–218.

Woolrych, Austin, "Milton and Richard Heath," *Philological Quarterly* 53 (1974), 132–5.

Worden, Blair, "English Republicanism," in J. H. Burns, ed., *The Cambridge History of Political Thought, 1450–1700.* Cambridge: Cambridge University Press, 1991, 443–57.

Worden, Blair, "Milton and Marchamont Nedham," in David Armitage, Armand Himy, and Quentin Skinner, eds, *Milton and Republicanism.* Cambridge: Cambridge University Press, 1995, 156–80.

Worden, Blair, "Marchamont Nedham and the Beginnings of English Republicanism, 1649–1656," "James Harrington and 'The Commonwealth of Oceana,' 1656," and "Harrington's 'Oceana': Origins and Aftermath, 1651–1660," in David Wootton, ed., *Republicanism, Liberty, and Commercial Society 1649–1776.* Stanford, Calif.: Stanford University Press, 1994.

Worden, Blair, "Milton, *Samson Agonistes,* and the Restoration," in Gerald Maclean, ed., *Culture and Society in the Stuart Restoration.* Cambridge: Cambridge University Press, 1995, 111–36.

Worden, Blair, "Milton's Republicanism and the Tyranny of Heaven," in Gisela Bock, Quintin Skinner, and Maurizio Viroli, eds, *Machiavelli and Republicanism.* Cambridge: Cambridge University Press, 1990, 225–41.

Worden, Blair, *The Rump Parliament, 1648–1653.* Cambridge: Cambridge University Press, 1974.

Wootten, David., ed., *Republicanism, Liberty, and Commercial Society, 1649–1776.* Stanford, Calif.: Stanford University Press, 1994.

Yoder, R. Paul, "Milton's *The Passion,*" *MS* 17 (1991), 3–21.

Zwicker, Steven N., *Lines of Authority: Politics and English Literary Culture, 1649–1689.* Ithaca, NY and London: Cornell University Press, 1993.

Zwicker, Steven N., "Lines of Authority: Politics and Literary Culture in the Restoration," in Kevin Sharpe and Steven N. Zwicker, eds, *Politics of Discourse: The Literature and History of Seventeenth-Century England.* Berkeley: University of California Press, 1987, 230–70.

Zwicker, Steven N., "Milton, Dryden, and the Politics of Literary Controversy," in Gerald Maclean, ed., *Culture and Society in the Stuart Restoration.* Cambridge: Cambridge University Press, 1995, 137–58.

Index